DOS
POWER
TOOLS™

2nd Edition,
Revised for DOS 5.0

DOS POWER TOOLS™

2nd Edition, Revised for DOS 5.0

Techniques, Tricks, and Utilities

Paul Somerson

BANTAM BOOKS

TORONTO • NEW YORK • LONDON • SYDNEY • AUCKLAND

DOS Power Tools, 2nd Edition, Revised for DOS 5.0
A Bantam Book / July 1991

Contents

Preface

Many PC users think DOS is simply the few seconds of disk grinding between the time they hit the power switch and the time their favorite software pops onto the screen. They've learned how to format a disk and copy a floppy but are ignorant of the genuine magic it can perform in the right hands. Still, even experienced users often miss important shortcuts and tricks. This book and the programs on the accompanying disk will make mastering any DOS system a breeze.

If you've ever wondered why computers aren't easier to deal with, you're not alone. It's really not your fault — the standard DOS manual is a fat, inscrutable alphabetical reference crammed with useless details on how to use Norwegian characters or hook your computer to a nuclear reactor. It doesn't try very hard to help you. If General Patton were alive today he'd slap it.

Worse, the DOS manual makes even the few things that you have to do every day — like print out files — insanely complex. A typical entry on its PRINT command reads:

Format: [d:][path]PRINT[/D:device][/B:buffsiz]
                 [/U:busytick][/M:maxtick][/S:timeslice]
                 [/Q:quesiz][/C][/T][/P][[d:[path]
                 [filename][.ext] . . .]

Clear? And it follows this madness with six pages of dense, oblique prose that would make Hemingway weep. So what's a busytick? According to the manual it "specifes the number of clock 'ticks' PRINT waits until the PRINT device is available. . . If PRINT waits longer than /U:busyticks, it gives up its time slice." Clock ticks? Print device? Time slice? Give us all a break.

You don't really have to understand what maxticks are, or what a buffsiz is. But knowing about these details can actually save you time and trouble. In this case, they'll let you print one or more documents without tying up your whole system, so you can start working on other documents right away. We'll explain every one of these PRINT terms later in crisp, understandable English. And in any case we'll give you a handful of PRINT shortcuts you can type in to start speeding up your own work, even if you don't want to learn what it all means.

So Who's This Book For?

Glad you asked. It's for every serious user who wants to work faster, smarter, and better.

If you're starting out, or if you want a refresher course in the fundamentals, plunge in at the beginning. If you happen to be a black belt expert, you'll still learn plenty; just skim over the first few chapters (we'll bet that even advanced users will find tricks they didn't know).

But no matter where you start, you'll soon find yourself collecting armloads of powerful tips, shortcuts, and advanced techniques. Trust us. Hundreds of thousands of smart readers do on a regular basis.

But a Whole Book On DOS?

This book starts with DOS. But it shows users at every level how to operate their whole systems better. DOS affects every aspect of operation, from keyboards to screens to printers to modems to disk drives.

You can nibble at it and pick up the few techniques you need to get a specific job done, or devour every word and become a true PC guru. If you want the hex numbers and the undocumented commands and the environment variables it's all here. But if all you want to do is master the basics and make your time at the computer so efficient you won't believe you ever did it the hard way, you can do that too.

Okay, So What Exactly Is DOS?

It's easier to start with what DOS isn't. It isn't very easy, friendly, or forgiving. Several years ago IBM responded to such criticism by publishing a booklet with little dancing birds in the margins. This didn't solve the problem. Users still did things the hard way, or avoided doing anything tricky in the fear they'd damage their files (and they were often right to worry).

Sometimes using DOS is a little like manipulating plutonium in the next room through a thick glass window using remote- control robot hands. It's far too clumsy. And s-l-o-w. What you really want to do is just get in there and grab what you're working on and knead it into shape. But the mechanisms DOS provides are cumbersome and seemingly difficult to master.

Using a PC means creating, changing, displaying, printing, copying, moving, and storing files. DOS does the really dirty work for you — interpreting and processing the commands you type, loading programs into memory, salting away your work in a semipermanent form that can readily be retrieved and altered, or sending data down a cable to a printer or another computer.

DOS has a truly limited vocabulary of a few dozen commands to handle all of this. Many of these commands are primitive, incomplete, even purposely crippled to protect you from yourself. Some are useless. The trick is to master the important ones, supercharge the incomplete ones, learn the effective DOS shortcuts that can automate your daily chores, and get your hands on a few necessary tools that DOS forgot. This book shows you how, with step-by-step instructions — and provides a slate of powerful programs to do all the hard work for you.

Keeping Current

One reason DOS is so thorny is that it has to adapt to a rapidly changing technology while remaining compatible with the older hardware and all the original commands. Even so, it should be a whole lot friendlier and easy to get along with. That's where we come in.

Times really have changed. The reason its creators called it DOS (short for *Disk Operating System*) was that it let users work with floppy disks, which were revolutionary two decades ago, but are commonplace to even kindergarteners now. These days optical disks (laser-based storage systems somewhat similar to audio CDs) and even a few hard disks can put a gigabyte — a billion characters' worth — of storage space at your fingertips in a fraction of a second.

(Some system manufacturers are even starting to talk about terabytes — a trillion characters' worth. Sending a terabyte of data to someone over a 1,200-baud modem would take over two millenia, give or take a century.)

To put this in perspective, when IBM introduced its first PC in 1981 it actually stuck a plug on the back so users could store data on cassette tape recorders — a method so inefficient it's laughable today.

Impatient?

To be a real power user you should understand what makes your system tick, and be familiar with its evolution and internal structure. This is especially important because DOS comes in so many flavors, revisions, and dialects that you have to know how to handle the important differences between versions.

If you see a term in the early chapters of this book that you don't fully grasp, don't worry. It will all be explained in detail a little later. However, if you just can't wait to plunge in and start boning up on specific tips, jump ahead to the following chapters.

How to Use This Book

The shortest distance between two points may be a straight line, but frankly, we prefer the scenic route. It may take you just a bit longer, but it's a lot more fun. When you travel on an expressway you often miss the sights.

This book will turn anyone into a true power user. But don't be scared by its size. You don't have to start at page 1 and follow it all the way through to the end (although if you do, you'll become an absolute DOS wizard). Most readers tend to jump around from place to place, and this book is designed to accommodate them.

You can use this book and disk several different ways:

- If you're still fairly new at this, you can learn the ropes quickly by glancing at the Up to Speed section.
- If you need the best possible tips on a specific area such as organizing your hard disk, harnessing the color abilities of your new monitor, automating complex file management tasks, or taming your keyboard, jump directly to that particular chapter.
- If you're interested in wringing the maximum horsepower out of your system, be sure to investigate the advanced techniques in the DOS Tools pages.
- And if you really want to stomp on your system's accelerator, step through every last trick in the Power User Secrets section.

No matter what your level, be sure to try the programs on the accompanying disks. They'll make it a snap to master every aspect of your system.

Warning!

As with any power tools, be extremely careful when using the programs and tips in this book and on the disks.

Read the appropriate manual entries carefully before running any of the programs. Not all programs will work on all systems (for instance, some are designed for EGAs, ATs, or PS/2 systems only). And just as you wouldn't plug too many power tools into the same outlet, if you want to load lots of different programs into memory at once, experiment with them to see how your hardware configuration handles it before working with any unsaved data.

The final section of this book contains two additional resources — a detailed program manual and a series of handy DOS quick reference charts. The manual is more than just a list of command syntaxes. It's jam-packed with tips, technical explanations, and ingenious customization hints. Both are extremely useful.

No Os

Note that in virtually every example in the text, a 0 is the numeral zero and not a capital o. Similarly, a 1 is a one and not a lowercase L. This book assumes you're using a version of DOS 2.1 or later. If you're not, go out right now and get your hands on the very latest version available.

While virtually all the tricks included here are utterly safe, a few (like those that deal with advanced disk modification techniques) are so powerful that you have to use extreme caution when trying them. The text includes stern warnings about these, but be sure you observe the following rules: read each entire section carefully before attempting the procedures mentioned, don't try modifying any of the procedures, and if you're really nervous, don't execute them. The book contains thousands of other equally useful but less fearsome tips to try.

Finally, the book makes extensive use of a technique called *redirection* to create and modify files. In most cases, this involves creating a small text file that DOS redirects, or feeds, into its DEBUG file-customization program. When creating these small text files or scripts be sure to use a "pure-ASCII" word processor. The DOS 5.0 EDIT, or older versions EDLIN editor will create such files, as will the ASCII/text modules of popular word processors such as Microsoft *Word*, *WordStar*, *XyWrite*, or *WordPerfect*.

As it's used here, a pure-ASCII file is one that, with just a few exceptions, contains nothing other than the letters, numbers, and punctuation that you can type directly from the keyboard. Most word processors throw in other nontext characters to handle formatting commands such as underlining or margin settings. But just about every word processor lets you create files without these formatting characters.

You can test whether your own word processor is capable of producing such files by using the DOS TYPE command to display them. If you create a file called TEST.FIL, for example, just make sure you're at the DOS A> or C> prompt and type:

```
TYPE TEST.FIL
```

If all you see is clear, unadulterated text, you're probably safe. But if you see odd characters, or if the text jumps and beeps its way across the page, look at your word processor's manual under "DOS files" or "Text files" or "ASCII files" and try again.

Whether you're just starting out, or you're an old hand at DOS, the tips and programs included here will make you the master of your system rather than the other way around. Isn't that why you started using a computer in the first place?

This second edition revised for DOS 5.0 includes all the earlier magic — and adds critical new tips, shortcuts, and power-user techniques on DOS 5.0, using extended and expanded memory, advanced video tricks, the shell, and much, much more. And it brings you over 100 new utilities to handle the really tricky parts. Try it; you won't believe how easily it will help you truly master things — or how hard it used to be before you learned its secrets.

Special thanks to all the people who made this revised edition possible: the authors of the the utility programs who were so generous with their creations; John Woram, Tom Sheldon, and Bradley Dyck Kliewer, who provided the technical depth and range for much of the new material; and the Bantam staff and freelancers --Janice Borzendowski, Maureen Drexel, Steve Gambino, Steve Guty, Barbara Hanson, Randall Pink, Jeff Rian, Cheryl Smith, Tom Szalkiewicz, and Raine Young--who pulled it all together.

Kenzi Sugihara
Vice President and Publisher
Bantam Electronic Publishing

Part I

Getting Up to Speed

The Development of DOS

Personal computers began appearing in the mid 1970s, initially as hobbyist toys that didn't even have keyboards or screens. The first real one, named Altair by a magazine editor's 12-year old daughter who liked a Star Trek episode that took place in that star system, was built around a jazzed-up calculator chip, the Intel 8080. (Today Intel supplies the state-of-art CPUs for all of IBM's desktop computers.) Produced as a do-it-yourself kit by a company called MITS (for Micro Instrumentation Telemetry Systems), it originally came with 256 bytes of memory, enough to hold only three or four lines of text. Since it lacked a keyboard, you entered information into it by flipping a series of switches on the front panel in binary on-off sequences. Because it had no screen, you had to decode the binary patterns of blinking lights it produced. And it didn't let you store information permanently. Compared to that, DOS is positively telepathic.

Two teenagers, Bill Gates and Paul Allen, who had gotten their digital feet wet by starting Traf-O-Data, a company that made Intel-based computers to measure how many cars rolled over a rubber hose stretched across a road, happened to see a picture of the Altair on the cover of *Popular Electronics* magazine, and developed a version of the BASIC programming language for it. Gates later upgraded Altair BASIC to give it primitive file-management disk-storage abilities, something that would come in handy later. The pair subsequently changed the company name to Microsoft; by 1976 the industry had progressed to the point where Gates was already railing against software pirates (although back then users were making illegal copies of punched paper tape rather than floppy disks). A few years later Gates became the world's youngest billionaire.

Soon after the Altair introduction, a coterie of hard-driving salespeople and "est" devotees became the market leaders with their IMSAI 8080, another Intel-chip machine, and the first computer aimed squarely at small businesses. To let users store data efficiently, IMSAI developed a floppy disk drive whose motors and circuits were run by a program called CP/M (short for Control Program for Microcomputers), which it had licensed from Intergalactic Digital Research — later shortened to Digital Research. Digital Research's Gary Kildall had created CP/M while working for Intel, to scale down the mainframe PL/I programming language into a version that would fit on a microcomputer. Intel hadn't seen much value in this brand new CP/M operating system and had given Kildall all rights to it.

The early versions of DOS owe quite a bit to CP/M. In fact, things like the COM formats of CP/M and DOS and the basic system calls were so similar that programmers could easily switch up from CP/M. CP/M used a command interpreter called CCP (for Console Command Processor), and two fundamental system files called BDOS and BIOS that handled files and I/O. This arrangement is nearly identical to the DOS COM-MAND.COM, IBMDOS.COM, and IBMBIO.COM system trio. What was especially remarkable about CP/M was that it took up only 4K of space. DOS 1.0 doubled that, and has been mushrooming ever since.

Chain store magnate and leathercrafter Charles Tandy tried unsuccessfully to buy computers from IMSAI, then ended up creating his own system, the TRS-80, which contained a competing Zilog Z-80 chip, boasted slightly more than 4,000 characters of memory (a page or two of text), and came fully assembled rather than in kit form. To shave a few dollars off the price he designed it to work entirely in uppercase letters. Customers snapped them up as fast as Tandy could make them.

What really kicked the microcomputer business into high gear, however, were a handful of visionary renegades from California and Florida.

In 1976 Steves Wozniak and Jobs, whose early careers included a stint peddling "black box" devices to circumvent AT&T long distance billing computers, bought some MOS 6502 chips and built a few hundred copies of a computer that they christened the Apple I. It too worked in uppercase characters only. Their second-generation Apple II offered an optional floppy disk drive, and sold several orders of magnitude more. One reason for its success was a revolutionary program called *VisiCalc*, which was cobbled together by Dan Bricklin, Dan Fylstra, and Bob Frankston. *Visicalc* turned Wozniak and Jobs's little computer into a powerful financial analysis and planning machine.

But not all operating systems work on all chips. The increasingly popular CP/M ran on chips made by Zilog and Intel but not on the Apple's MOS processor.

Microsoft's Gates and Allen moved to Seattle to write programming languages for computers built around Intel and Zilog processor chips and running CP/M. Dismayed that their languages wouldn't work on MOS-based Apples, they considered translating them all to run on Apple's proprietary operating system, an arduous job. Instead, they joined the crowd, licensed CP/M, and sold it along with an add-in board that had a Zilog chip on it. Apple owners could stick the Microsoft board in their systems and run any CP/M programs.

But Apple was an eight-bit machine and Gates and Allen felt Intel's new 16-bit processors were the wave of the future. So did a local board maker named Tim Patterson who worked for Seattle Computer Products. All earlier processor chips managed data in eight-bit chunks. Intel's new 8088/8086 chip family doubled the processing power.

Patterson's board sported an 8086, and he needed a new 16-bit operating system to take advantage of it. Digital Research had announced that it was planning to tweak CP/M into a 16-bit CP/M-86 version, but Patterson couldn't wait. In early 1980 he started work on one of his own design called QDOS (for Quick and Dirty Operating System) that was to become 86-DOS (or SCP-DOS) and eventually just plain DOS. To make it relatively easy for programmers to translate CP/M software to his system, he retained fundamental CP/M file-management structures and mimicked the way it loaded and ran programs. Patterson then added a device called a File Allocation Table (FAT) which Gates had used in Altair disk BASIC , and a few other refinements.

DOS 1.0

In late 1980, IBM approached Microsoft and revealed that it was considering production of its own eight-bit personal computer. Vast helpings of money, ego, pride, and general corporate paranoia have tempered the details of this exchange, but the popular version is that IBM wanted Microsoft to design a version of BASIC for its new machine that would be delivered on a ROM chip inside the IBM chassis. Gates was happy to oblige and wanted to do a whole raft of languages, as the story goes, but argued that IBM should consider a 16-bit computer instead. When IBM asked who made a 16-bit operating system, Gates is said to have suggested that IBM contact Gary Kildall — and supposedly even dialed the phone to Digital Research himself.

Here the tale gets very fuzzy. According to one telling of it, when IBM trooped down to see Digital Research the next day, Kildall's wife and lawyer were hesitant to sign IBM's strict nondisclosure agreements. Other stories had Kildall out flying his plane while IBM executives waited impatiently for him to land. Microsoft's own publications admit that Gates and Allen had heard rumors that Kildall was about to buy a version of BASIC from a Microsoft competitor and give it away free with every copy of CP/M-86, which didn't exactly endear him to them.

In any event, Gates and Allen bought the rights to Patterson's 86-DOS for around $50,000 and proposed to IBM that Microsoft provide BASIC, FORTRAN, Pascal, COBOL, an 8086 Assembly language, and the 86-DOS operating system for the new computer. IBM agreed in November 1980, and on August 12, 1981 introduced the world to its new PC and its main operating system, Microsoft's DOS 1.0 (which IBM called PC-DOS). At the announcement, IBM mentioned that users would someday be able to buy two competing operating systems: CP/M-86 or the UCSD p-System. But IBM priced these much higher than DOS, and since they were late in reaching the market and received little support from other software vendors, they went nowhere.

Computer hardware (the chips and disk drives and other parts inside the cabinet) isn't useful without software (the programs that put the chips through their paces). And IBM didn't initially offer much software — *EasyWriter*, a bug-filled version of a mediocre word processor; *Adventure*, a mainframe text game adapted for smaller computers; a DOS version of *VisiCalc*; some artless business software; a few Microsoft languages; and one or two other packages.

The most popular and powerful programs back then — *dBASE II* and *WordStar* — ran only on CP/M systems. One of IBM's highest priorities was to make it easy for software vendors to translate programs from CP/M to DOS, and it was smart enough to know that making it easy meant making the two operating systems similar.

Many of the DOS features that today's users truly hate — such as overly brief eight-character filenames with three-character extensions, terse prompts like A>, and unfriendly or missing messages (such as stony silence in response to file deletions) were directly swiped from CP/M. So were underlying structures such as File Control Blocks (FCBs), Program Segment Prefixes (PSPs), and reliance on CP/M's memory loading addresses.

DOS did change a few CP/M quirks. File lengths that were rounded off in CP/M were reported precisely in DOS. Some commands were turned around to be more logical. Programmers could treat input and output to peripheral devices such as printers and screens the same way that they handled files. DOS's variable record lengths made disk storage and retrieval far more efficient. DOS could load and run larger EXE-format files in addition to the smaller standard CP/M-style COM-format files which were limited to 64K. And it could keep a program loaded in memory but inactive so that users could pop it onto their screens whenever they needed it. DOS relied on a FAT, first used by Bill Gates and Tom Patterson, to keep track of where all the various pieces of a file were stored, and could read and write more than one piece of data at a time, which speeded up disk activity significantly.

DOS at least theoretically made it easier for programmers to create their own versions of the COMMAND.COM user interface, although none has ever caught on. But the ability to run scripts of commands called batch files did become very popular. When DOS reported inevitable errors, it did so in a slightly friendlier way than CP/M, and it handled severe hardware errors far better. DOS also sniffed out new disks automatically while CP/M forced users to log such changes manually, and it kept track of the date files were created or changed.

It also split the COMMAND.COM user interface into several parts, a mixed blessing. When the PC was new, and IBM offered it with a maximum 65,536 characters of memory (which is usually rounded off to 64K), this feature was welcome since it let other space-hungry software temporarily steal a few thousand characters of memory space from DOS. When the user was finished with the software he'd have to then insert his DOS disk in drive A: so the part of DOS that hadn't been stolen could reload the part that had. Trouble was that a short time later users were buying systems with ten times that much memory, and the amount of space freed up by this technique was relatively insignificant. But floppy disk users still had to contend with keeping a DOS disk handy to reload the "transient" stolen part.

One of the worst things about the first IBM PC and its operating system was that it could store only 163,840 (160K) characters of data on floppy disks that were clearly capable of squirreling away twice that much. A standard floppy disk has two usable sides, but IBM's original drives (and DOS) took advantage of just one.

And the initial DOS release contained several nasty bugs. In mid-1982 IBM began selling PCs with double-sided drives, and released DOS version 1.1 to handle the new storage abilities and fix several of the early bugs. Microsoft then released its own similar generic DOS upgrade, which it called MS-DOS 1.25.

The initial release of DOS was tiny and relatively crude. Version 1.0 TIME and DATE commands were separate short programs rather than part of the main COMMAND.COM user interface. While the DOS 1.0 directory listing noted the date a file was created or changed, it ignored the time. The MODE command couldn't set communications speeds or protocols, or let the PC's parallel printer adapter work with the many serial printers on the market. You weren't able to have the COPY command join (or *concatenate*) smaller files into larger ones. The onscreen prompts and messages were especially ugly and cryptic.

DOS 1.1 fixed all these problems, or at least made them less irritating. The biggest problem of all was that DOS was still constrained by its CP/M heritage and its clanky internal structure. And although IBM doubled the amount of disk storage space from 163,840 (160K) characters to 327,680 (320K), users found this was far from enough. They demanded disks that were faster and more efficient.

DOS 2.0

In March 1983, IBM announced its PC-XT, a beefed up version of the standard PC that came with three additional internal expansion slots (for a total of eight), a ten-megabyte hard disk, a heftier power supply, and a new version of DOS — 2.0.

The new hard disk (which IBM referred to as a *fixed* disk) could hold the equivalent of more than 31 double-sided floppies. But all that storage space introduced a new problem. DOS 1.0 and 1.1 had crammed all the file information for each floppy disk into a single directory. A single-sided floppy directory had room for a maximum of 64 entries, and you could fit only 112 on a double-sided diskette.

Keeping track of all the files on a hard disk meant coming up with a new DOS file management and directory system. CP/M had dealt with large disks by splitting (or *partitioning*) them evenly into smaller ones, an inelegant and inefficient solution. But UNIX, an operating system developed by the phone company, could handle vast volumes of files with relative style and ease. Microsoft had licensed UNIX, and was offering a version of it called XENIX. At the heart of UNIX/XENIX was a *hierarchical* or *tree-structured* directory system that gave users lots of flexibility in dividing up the available storage space.

Microsoft adapted this tree-structured system as the core of a significantly new incarnation of DOS — version 2.0. But it blundered slightly. UNIX used a slash (/) to identify the hierarchical subdirectory levels that acted as branches on the tree structure. But earlier DOS versions used such slashes as *switches*, command suffixes (such as the /S in FORMAT /S) that turned certain optional features on and off. Microsoft substituted a backslash (\ ) to identify subdirectory levels, which ended up confusing a whole generation of DOS and UNIX users, and caused much consternation abroad where foreign keyboards often didn't come with backslash characters.

IBM and Microsoft also had to find a way to deal with an explosion in the number and type of devices that manufacturers were stamping out for the PC. One of DOS's main roles was to manage the communication between the PC and anything you could hook up to it. If DOS had to contain explicit internal tables and instructions for every possible external device it would end up being absurdly large and cumbersome.

Microsoft designed a new version of DOS with *hooks* in it so that manufacturers of peripheral equipment could supply installable *device driver* programs to hook the new hardware effortlessly into the operating system. Users could load these specific additional sets of instructions into DOS as needed, through a special CONFIG.SYS file. This file also let users customize the configuration of their systems by telling DOS such things as how much memory it should devote to disk buffers (areas of memory that hold disk data for speedy access), how many files could be opened simultaneously, and how frequently DOS should check to see whether a user might be hitting the Ctrl-Break panic button. It also made it easy for users to load a replacement command processor if they weren't planning on using the standard COMMAND.COM, or tell DOS if they were storing COMMAND.COM in an unusual place. And it gave users extended screen and keyboard control with ANSI.SYS, a special device driver supplied by Microsoft in an unsuccessful attempt to standardize certain parts of the user interface across different computer systems.

Version 2.0 introduced several commands most users can't live without. It's hard to believe, but versions 1.0 and 1.1 didn't offer any way to clear the screen. CLS now does it, although unless you're one of the few users taking advantage of ANSI, it will reset your screen colors to drab grey on black. This version was the first to offer batch file commands such as ECHO, IF, FOR, SHIFT, and GOTO. If you haven't yet mastered these, you'll be amazed at how they can help automate drudgework. We'll show you how (and point out tricks for retaining colors when you clear your screen) a bit later.

DOS 2.0 also introduced a raft of commands and utilities to give users control of hard disks, although some, like the pathetic TREE command — designed to "display the entire directory structure" — were a bad joke. DOS 4.0 finally fixed this.

Perhaps to compensate, IBM threw in a gem that has become a power user's best friend — the mini-assembler in DEBUG. You can become an absolute computer whiz without ever having to learn a single thing about hex codes or assembly language. But if you want to climb inside your system and stomp on the gas pedal, there's no better way. It's a lot easier than you think.

One of the most significant changes in DOS 2.0 was the way it dealt with files internally. To remain compatible with CP/M, DOS versions 1.0 and 1.1 kept track of critical file information with a device called a File Control Block (FCB). But as programs became more sophisticated they were forced to manipulate the data stored in FCBs directly, which was awkward and potentially dangerous. And FCBs had no provisions for subdirectory names.

DOS 2.0 introduced *file handles* as an optional way to streamline disk management. Once DOS knew about a particular file in a particular subdirectory, it could act on that file simply by using a two-character shorthand code called a handle. In addition, DOS established five special handles that made it a snap to switch inputs and outputs. Normally the keyboard and screen (which DOS collectively refers to as the console or *CON*) act as both the input and output. But DOS 2.0 let users "redirect" input and output to or from printers, files, or other devices. And it allowed users to *pipe* streams of data through filters to do things like turn uppercase files into lowercase ones, strip out extraneous characters, or sort records in alphabetical order.

The sample filters DOS 2.0 provided are actually pretty useful. They'll let you slog through files and skim out the text you want saved or discarded. They'll sort your directories (or any list of names, numbers, or items that have carriage returns at the end of each entry) lightning fast. And they'll pause your displays for you so you'll never again have text scroll off your screen too quickly to read.

To top it off, DOS 2.0 provided rudimentary background processing. DOS was originally designed as a single-tasking operating system that let users do just one thing at a time. But the designers of version 2.0 threw in a PRINT *spooler* command that could print out one file while a user was actively working on another.

While spoolers are nothing new, this one was. Spoolers normally lop off a big chunk of RAM and trick DOS into sending files to memory that were really destined for the printer. Then they wait for a quiet moment and re-route the files onto your printed page. When they're done printing, however, they still hold onto all the memory they hogged — very inefficient. The DOS PRINT command reads files off your disks and uses your precious memory much more sparingly. It watches how you work, and about 18 times each second, if you're not doing something at that precise moment, it sneaks a few characters at a time to the printer. Your computer is so blazingly fast that this "time slicing" technique makes it appear that it's doing two things at once, when what it's really doing is alternating so quickly you don't notice it. And the best part is that if you happen to be working on something that takes more of your computer's constant attention than usual, you can adjust how frequently the spooler tries to intercede.

In addition, DOS increased the number of 512-byte sectors — the wedge-shaped magnetic pie slices on a floppy disk that actually hold your data — from eight to nine. While DOS kept the number of tracks in each sector at 40, this upped the storage capacity of double-sided floppy disks from 320K to 360K. DOS 2.0 also let users add electronic volume *labels* to their disks, gave them access to a part of memory called the *environment* in which critical system settings were maintained, made memory allocation more efficient, and threw in more than two dozen new commands.

With so many changes and new features, you'd think a brand new version of DOS such as 2.0 would be filled with insidious bugs. And you'd be right. In March 1984, a year after the PC-XT introduction, IBM released DOS version 2.1 to excise these software errors — and to handle a hardware error it produced called the PC*jr*.

The less said about the PC*jr* the better. While it provided more colors onscreen in graphics mode than IBM's real microcomputers, and came with three-voice sound that could play chords, it was utterly nonstandard inside and out. In fact, it used such a cheap, flimsy disk drive that DOS 2.1 actually had to slow down the drive performance so the thing wouldn't crash.

What's especially sad about this is that lots of users still rely on DOS 2.1, which means they have to put up with unacceptably slow drive access times even though they're using machines that could handle much higher speeds. A pity. And one of many good reasons to upgrade to a more recent DOS edition.

Microsoft ended up producing versions 2.05, 2.11, 2.2, and 2.25 with an added modicum of international time, date, keyboard, and currency support. These may come in handy if you need to work with Korean Hangeul or Japanese Kanji characters; today Microsoft sells DOS in more than 60 assorted languages.

DOS 3.0

IBM's PC and PC-XT brought microcomputing into the mainstream of American business. But these machines were both relatively slow and small. In fact, they weren't really even true 16-bit computers. While a 16-bit Intel 8088 central processing unit (CPU) ticked away inside each one, their system *bus* — the connecting pathway of wires that ties the CPU to all the other parts of the system — was a bottleneck that worked in eight-bit chunks only.

IBM introduced its first genuine 16-bit system, the PC-AT. Compared to IBM's earlier releases, this was a rocket ship of a computer. Inside was an 80286 CPU with a trick up its sleeve — it could run everything IBM and Microsoft threw at it and could also accommodate Microsoft's next-generation OS/2 operating system. And it needed a new version of DOS — 3.0.

Engineers measure computer performance in many ways. Two prime indicators are the clock speed of the CPU and the average access time of the hard disk. The faster the clock, the faster a computer processes instructions and the faster just about everything runs. The speedier the hard disk average access time, the speedier it can read and write programs and data. The higher the clock speed and the lower the average access time, the nimbler the system.

Both the PC and the PC-XT ran at 4.77 megahertz (MHz). IBM sold many different brands of hard disks for the XT, and the average access time was somewhere between 80 and 115 milliseconds.

The official clock speed of IBM's first AT was 6 MHz, but users quickly found out that by replacing a socketed $4 quartz crystal on the main system board they could boost performance to 8 or even 9 MHz without any ill effects. (IBM is famous for publishing ultraconservative specifications and holding down performance a bit on purpose.) When IBM discovered that users were hot-rodding their systems, they wrote a program that acted as a speed governor and put it onto a system ROM chip to prevent tampering.

All of IBM's AT hard disks ran at speeds of 40 milliseconds or better. Unfortunately, the first big batch of PC-ATs came with CMI-brand drives that crashed in shockingly high numbers. Hard disks — rapidly spinning precision-crafted aluminum platters with magnetic coatings on both sides — need precise feedback on where their magnetic read/write heads are located. If the location mechanism is off by even a tiny bit the heads can write bad data over good or wipe out important tables that tell the computer where files are stored.

Hard disk heads actually "fly" on a cushion of air directly above the surface of the platters themselves. All decent hard disks retract or *park* the magnetic heads when the power goes off so they don't sink down and plow furrows into your data. To save money, CMI disks used what many believe was an unreliable implementation of *wedge servo* technology. Most other hard disks used a dedicated positioning surface, a whole side of a hard disk platter that contained no user data and instead acted as a map to the platters that did. But not CMI's AT drives. And these drives didn't park the heads when you turned the power off. The heads just dropped down onto the data area and scraped against it.

IBM never really admitted doing anything wrong, but tens of thousands of users know differently. If this black episode in microcomputing history had a silver lining, it was that it taught hard disk users how absolutely imperative it is to make frequent and comprehensive backup copies of their work.

In any event, a PC-AT running at 8 MHz was 67 percent speedier than a standard PC or PC-XT. The PC-AT hard disk was twice as fast as the speediest PC-XT drive, which made everything seem a lot more energetic, and ended up turbocharging disk-intensive applications such as database searches. On top of all that, the PC-AT could deal with memory in 16-bit chunks, while the PC and PC-XT had to lumber along with half that amount. Clone makers soon began producing respectable AT imitations that chugged along even faster. To avoid falling behind the competition too much, IBM eventually had to nudge the performance upward slightly each time it refined the AT design.

IBM's newest PS/2 line of hardware and the many high-performance clones on the market make even the fastest IBM PC-AT look like it's standing still. With CPU speeds of 20 and even 24 MHz, hard disk access times in the high teens, and a 32-bit bus that moves information nearly four times as efficiently as the one in the original PC, these hot new microcomputers give refrigerator-sized minicomputers a run for their money.

The PC-AT was originally delivered with a 20-megabyte hard disk, although subsequent versions have enhanced both the AT's speed and the size of its hard disk. Still, 20,480,000 characters' worth of storage meant that backing it all up would take 56 standard 360K *double-density* floppies. The mind reels. Apparently, so did IBM's. It dropped a *quad-density* floppy disk drive, which could hold 1.2 megabytes of data — or the equivalent of nearly four 360K floppies — into each PC-AT. IBM refers to these as *high-capacity* drives. Unhappy users have called them something else, unprintable here.

The PC-AT's new DOS, version 3.0, could handle the increased floppy disk storage. But it also had to understand every other floppy format. In the space of six years IBM had introduced single-sided and double-sided drives, with eight or nine sectors, and in double or quad density, so downward compatibility meant knowing how to deal with:

- 160K single-sided 5-1/4 inch drives
- 180K single-sided 5-1/4 inch drives
- 320K double-sided 5-1/4 inch drives
- 360K double-sided 5-1/4 inch drives
- 1.2M double-sided 5-1/4 inch drives

Well, there's compatibility and there's compatibility. Out of the 25 different possible combinations of using the DISKCOPY command to move information from one to the other, 16 won't work.

What's more, IBM's PS/2 hardware uses 3-1/2 inch diskettes, a whole new ball game. These smaller diskettes are sturdier, easier to transport, and vastly more efficient at storing information. IBM characteristically complicated matters by producing two different and slightly incompatible 3-1/2 inch formats, one that holds 720K and one capable of storing 1.4 megabytes of data. The 5-1/4 inch 320/360K floppy format won't go away very quickly, since so many vendors have made it the standard for program distribution. But the PC-AT's 1.2 megabyte drive and the low-end PS/2 720K diskette are orphans.

All IBM microcomputers gave users a clock and calendar that could stamp DOS directory listings with the time and date files were created or most recently changed. But users had to set the clock each time they started (*booted up*) their systems, unless they had purchased an add-in board with a battery-driven clock on it (and most did). The PC-AT came with its own internal battery-run clock/calendar, although it wasn't until DOS version 3.3 that users could reset it easily.

Figure 1.1 shows the configurations of all of IBM's PCs through the PS/2 80.

Model	ID Byte	CPU	Speed (MHz)	I/O Bus (Bits)	Maximum RAM	Keyboard	DOS Version
PC	FF	8088	4.77	8	640K	old	1.0
XT	FE	8088	4.77	8	640K	old	2.0
PC*jr*	FD	8088	4.77	8	640K	special	2.1
AT	FC	80286	6/8	16	15M	both	3.0
PC/2	FB	8088	4.77	8	640K	both	–
XT/286	FC	80286	6	16	15M	both	–
Convertible	F9	80C88	4.77	8	640K	special	–
Model 25	FA	8086	8	8*	640K	new	–
Model 30	FA	8086	8	8*	640K	new	–
Model 50	FC	80286	10	16	16M	new	3.3+
Model 60	FC	80286	10	16	16M	new	3.3+
Model 70	F8	80386	16/20	32	4G	new	3.3+
Model 80	F8	80386	16/20	32	4G	new	3.3+

*Models 25 & 30 have a 16-bit memory bus. Data on late-model machines courtesy of John Woram's *PC Configuration Handbook*.

Figure 1.1.   Hardware Configurations of IBM's Personal Computers

Program developers live by a rule: "The software is never finished." Each release of DOS or any commercial application is quickly followed by a version with bug fixes, speedups, and forgotten utilities. Market considerations force manufacturers to ship everything at the earliest possible date. Microsoft officially admits that DOS 3.0 "wasn't quite ready" at the introduction of the PC-AT. But it went out the door anyway.

Today, virtually every desk in America has a telephone in one corner. IBM's vision of the future puts a computer terminal next to it, and strings all the terminals together electronically. Networking computers this way does have lots of advantages. It lets users "mail" messages and files to each other, and share centralized data bases of information. Someday when everyone has to send text to everyone else and when it's easier and cheaper to consult a far wider range of databases, this will be attractive.

Networks can also let users share expensive peripherals like plotters or laser printers, but it doesn't make much sense to install three $1,500 network hookups to share one $1,500 printer. Today networks are interesting to a minority of users only — although the number grows as the costs and headaches often associated with using them are reduced. Networks introduce their own special set of problems. Two users may reach for the same data base records at the same time, and something has to mediate the conflict. Worse, giving users access to centralized information means someone has to decide who has the authority to read what files and change which data. And then something has to keep track of the authorization levels and enforce it all, and make sure the right data is routed to the right place.

Microsoft designed DOS version 3.0 to support the official IBM PC network hardware. Unfortunately, the AT was ready before the network features of DOS were, and the Microsoft designers had to deactivate these features in the final product. They finally turned them back on in version 3.1, released in November 1984. But DOS 3.1 was picky; it would handle only certain "well-behaved" networks. ("Misbehaved" products are ones that use undocumented commands, or bypass software safeguards by manipulating hardware directly, or otherwise bend industry rules to enhance performance.)

DOS 3.0 introduced a streamlined method for integrating FCBs and handles. And while it provided a small handful of new features, none was a radical departure from DOS 2.1. In fact, IBM stated in its documentation that "DOS 3.0 does not replace DOS 2.1." But it did fix a nasty 2.1 oversight, by making it harder for users to format their hard disks if they weren't careful. (It wasn't until version 2.0 that DOS asked for confirmation if users tried to delete all the files on their disk with a single ERASE *.* command.) Version 3.0 also let users make files read only to prevent any inadvertent changes or deletions.

Version 3.1 provided better *aliasing* features to combine drives and directories and to trick DOS into treating a subdirectory like a disk drive. DOS 3.2 introduced users to 3-1/2 inch diskettes (although the tools it provided to handle this were downright awful), made it easier for them to upgrade DOS versions, and gave them one of the best, but least-used, new commands, XCOPY.

DOS 3.3, tossed off by IBM pitchmen at the introduction of the PS/2 as an "interim solution" and the operating system for a string of dogs including the PC Convertible, Portable PC, and PC*jr*, deftly excised a heap of user headaches, and added a few sizzling new tricks.

As all seasoned hard disk users are aware, working efficiently on a hard disk machine means pigeonholing related programs and data in electronic file drawers called subdirectories. But users who are currently working in one subdirectory often want to execute a program or look at data stored in another.

Since version 2.0, users had been able to tell the PATH command to check specified subdirectories for executable files (with filenames ending in COM, EXE, or BAT). This let users run programs in other subdirectories, but it didn't let them get at distant data.

Nonexecutable files remained immune to even the most comprehensive search, forcing power users to purchase commercial "path extender" programs such as *FilePath* or *File Facility*, or struggle with the DOS 3.1 SUBST command. The DOS 3.3 APPEND command made the process relatively easy — and a lot cleaner.

Serial ports are your system's main gateway to the outside world. Version 3.3 let MODE work with four serial ports rather than just two (OS/2 can juggle up to eight), and cruise along at up to 19,200 baud, double the previous limit. And IBM finally recognized that at least twice a year users need to reset their internal IBM clocks and provided a way to do this without having to hunt down their Diagnostics disks, figure out which option adjusts the time, and then grind through all the irritating preliminary screens. The 3.3 TIME and DATE commands automatically adjusted IBM CMOS memory to reflect the change.

Another improvement was the newfound ability of the DOS 3.3 ATTRIB command to gang-process all files in a directory and its related subdirectories, which made it easier to create backups and prevent inadvertent file deletions or changes. Unfortunately, the same process used by ATTRIB can also "hide" files from casual snooping, but IBM won't show you how. (We will.)

The original DOS architects preferred working with 512-byte disk sectors, and used a FAT to keep track of what data is in which sector. When they designed the FAT they used 16-bit addresses, which allowed a maximum of 65,536 (64K) table entries. This clamped a firm 32 megabyte limit (512 x 65,536 = 33,554,432 bytes) on the size of any physical hard disk. To get around this limit, manufacturers either had to increase the sector size, which made their hardware nonstandard and relatively wasteful, or come up with a whole new file management scheme, which ended up being even more nonstandard.

IBM tuned DOS 3.3 to divide physical hard disks into smaller *logical* drives, and fixed the FDISK command to create *extended* DOS partitions in addition to the *primary* ones users were able to carve out previously. Each extended partition could be further subdivided into logical drives 32 megabytes or smaller, with their own drive letters. Compaq quickly made it even easier to use enormous hard disks, by introducing a DOS version (3.31) that boasted 32-bit FAT addresses.

To expedite directory searches with the new generation of larger hard disks, DOS 3.3 provided a filename *cache* utility called FASTOPEN. Caches keep track of things in memory rather than on disk, speeding up many processes significantly. FASTOPEN notes the location of files and subdirectories (which are really just special classes of files) the first time you hunt for them, and then directs DOS to the exact spot on the disk the next time you have to deal with them.

The DOS BACKUP command had always been so pathetic that an entire industry of third-party backup software has evolved to fill in the gaps. While the version 3.3 enhancements aren't going to put all those developers out of business, they will bring some users back into the fold. Under previous DOS versions you had to format a tall stack of disks before starting the backup process. If you ran out of formatted disks halfway through you had to abort and either find a way to catch up, or start the whole elaborate, time-consuming procedure over again.

In DOS 3.3 the BACKUP command can summon the FORMAT command and prepare unformatted disks if necessary — with certain irritating restrictions. And you have to limit the disks and drives you use; it still can't mix and match. The DOS 3.3 BACKUP works faster and more efficiently than older versions, by copying all smaller files to a single enormous one, and by creating a guide file that tells DOS how to take the big file apart and restore it properly later. It will also create a log file telling you what it did where.

The DOS 3.3 RESTORE gives you added flexibility in restoring backed-up files by date and time, as well as those deleted or changed since you backed them up, or files that are no longer on the target disk. Better yet, while older versions of RESTORE let you accidently obliterate your current system files (IBMBIO.COM, IBMDOS.COM, and COMMAND.COM or their generic counterparts) with older backed-up versions, DOS 3.3 RESTORE won't. Inadvertently mixing versions of hard disk system files is like replacing a heart surgeon, in the middle of an operation, with a tree surgeon.

Batch files can take much of the anguish out of tricky or repetitive tasks. The first thing most power users do when they create a batch file is turn off the display by issuing an ECHO OFF command. This stops DOS from littering your screen with the frantic prompts, messages, and other electronic graffiti a batch file triggers. But users had no authorized way of preventing this ECHO OFF command from adding to the screen clutter itself. Version 3.3 users can prevent such clutter simply by prefacing any command with a @ symbol.

In addition, DOS 3.3 could CALL one batch file from another, execute it, and then return to the original batch file and continue executing it. Doing this kind of "nesting" under previous editions of DOS meant that each batch file had to load its own separate version of COMMAND.COM, do its work, exit, and drop back to yet another version — which was sort of like restarting a movie each time a latecomer walked into the theatre. DOS 3.3 also documented environment variables for the first time, which let users pass information back and forth from application to application.

DOS 3.0 to 3.2 came in five international flavors. By executing the appropriate KEYBxx command, users could transform the keyboard into British, German, French, Italian, or Spanish modes. With version 3.3, IBM totally revamped the way DOS handled foreign alphabets. IBM's manuals have gotten a bit better over the years, but the three abstruse and seemingly contradictory chunks on this international support virtually defy comprehension. IBM prefaced its long appendix-like treatment of the topic with the caveat "You can use code page switching without fully understanding everything about it." After poring over the text, you'll know why this was included. And if you live in the United States, you'll take one look, put your hand over your heart, and say "Thank God we're Americans."

For the first time, DOS 3.3 set a default number of disk buffers based on your system's configuration. Under previous versions, it assumed every PC and XT user really wanted only two and every AT user only three. DOS will now sniff out what hardware you have available, and allocate from two buffers (minimal RAM and no high density floppies, 3-1/2 inch diskettes, or hard disks) to 15 (any machine with 512K or more of RAM). If you're using a big hard disk you may want more than 15. Better yet, you should try a commercial file cache program.

DOS 4.0

Through seven years of upgrades, IBM and Microsoft still hadn't made it any easier to learn the ropes, or do simple tasks like move groups of files from one place to another. Beginners who thought they could just press a button or two and have their new computers do all the work found themselves staring at a lonely DOS prompt on an otherwise blank screen. Worse, DOS still made it too easy for even experienced users to do dangerous things like wipe out their work by copying older versions of files onto newer ones.

Some users relished the challenge and learned to rattle off thorny strings of DOS commands bristling with backslashes and inscrutable parameters like MAXTICK, TIMESLICE, QUESIZ, and CODEPAGE. Many operated solely by brute force and avoided doing anything the least bit complex. Others bought special menu-based interface programs called DOS shells to step them over the rough spots, or else gave up and bought Macs.

One of the most irksome problems was that DOS couldn't really handle single hard disks bigger than 32 megabytes. It forced users to employ silly schemes like dividing up one large storage device into little pieces, so that a single 200 meg hard disk might end up as drives C:, D:, E:, F:, G:, H:, and I:. While IBM had always been the first hardware manufacturer to solve such problems, this time Compaq became frustrated with such limitations and made a special arrangement with Microsoft to introduce a slightly enhanced version it called 3.31. (Another irritating constraint was that DOS couldn't use more than 640 kilobytes of RAM for most tasks.)

Then on a steamy 1988 summer afternoon in New York City (and with little fanfare) IBM released a new incarnation of DOS called 4.0, which was quickly followed by a bug fix called 4.01. Collectively most users referred to these new versions either as "DOS 4" or "the big, expensive, new version of DOS that nobody uses." As with every other major new version of DOS, this one increased in size, and added some powerful new utilities. But it also came with a DOS shell cleverly named the "DOS Shell" that promised to tame just about every formerly nightmarish system chore. Unfortunately it didn't.

Microsoft and IBM wanted DOS to fade away so they could sell expensive new programs like *Windows* and OS/2 and *Presentation Manager* (PM), and pricey new hardware. Users were demanding huge machines with tons of RAM and hard disk space and friendly features, and it was growing increasingly difficult to graft such things onto what was essentially a tricked-up version of CP/M and Unix, with the worst drawbacks of each.

However, by the end of the '80s, according to Microsoft chairman Bill Gates (who licenses all copies of DOS and knows the real numbers), various hardware manufacturers had sold an astonishing 60 million DOS systems. While vendors were hyping their hot new 80386- and 80486-based machines, tens of millions of users owned systems that lacked the sophisticated chips, expensive color graphics, and whopping amounts of memory required to handle OS/2. And frankly, huge numbers of DOS users really didn't need the fancy multitasking or data exchange abilities of OS/2.

What they *did* want was something easier, smarter, friendlier, and more powerful. DOS 4.0 was a step in the right direction, but a baby step. Microsoft finally realized that some users wanted more power and ease but simply weren't going to need complex OS/2-like operating systems, and it privately announced that a friendlier DOS 5 would be forthcoming.

DOS 5.0—Room to Move

After months of testing, Microsoft finally released MS-DOS 5.00 in June of 1991. Corroborating the rumors that circulated while it was in beta, it features an organized and sanctioned workaround to the worst aspects of the 640K barrier, allowing much of DOS itself to reside in the area above 640K, and providing support for loading device drivers and TSR programs in this memory space. On a typical 386-or-better system with more than 640K of memory, DOS 5.0 will, with a bit of fine-tuning, leave more than 620K free for applications. In addition, an improved Shell, on-line help, a new BASIC interpreter, an enhanced command-line edit capability, and a long-awaited alternative to EDLIN are included, along with some significant improvements to familiar commands like DIR and ATTRIB. It also provides a number of features that users previously had to seek in third-party software, such as the capability to unerase a file, or unformat a disk. And for the first time, DOS directly supports task swapping — if you've got the patience to put up with the DOS shell. A full treatment of these and other topics follows, in the next chapter.

Figure 1.2 shows the relative sizes of the various versions of DOS. You can use the chart provided to look at the size of COMMAND.COM on diskettes formatted with the /S option and determine the DOS version number. Note that while DOS 4.0 was a whopping six times larger than the first DOS version, and 38 percent fatter than its immediate predecessor, DOS 5.0, when loaded into high memory, takes up only as much space as DOS 2.1 did.

Figure 1.3 traces the addition of commands through versions of DOS, up to 5.0. Figure 1.4 shows which commands were modified in which versions.

DOS 1.0 — 13312 bytes used by system files

COMMAND	COM	3231	8-04-81	12:00a
IBMBIO	COM	1920	7-23-81	12:00a
IBMDOS	COM	6400	8-13-81	12:00a

DOS 1.1 — 14336 bytes used by system files

COMMAND	COM	4959	5-07-82	12:00p
IBMBIO	COM	1920	5-07-82	12:00p
IBMDOS	COM	6400	5-07-82	12:00p

DOS 2.0 — 40960 bytes used by system files

COMMAND	COM	17664	3-08-83	12:00p
IBMBIO	COM	4608	3-08-83	12:00p
IBMDOS	COM	17152	3-08-83	12:00p

DOS 2.1 — 40960 bytes used by system files

COMMAND	COM	17792	10-20-83	12:00p
IBMBIO	COM	4736	10-20-83	12:00p
IBMDOS	COM	17024	10-20-83	12:00p

DOS 3.0 — 60416 bytes used by system files

COMMAND	COM	22042	8-14-84	8:00a
IBMBIO	COM	8964	7-05-84	3:00p
IBMDOS	COM	27920	7-05-84	3:00p

DOS 3.1 — 62464 bytes used by system files

COMMAND	COM	23210	3-07-85	1:43p
IBMBIO	COM	9564	3-07-85	1:43p
IBMDOS	COM	27760	3-07-85	1:43p

DOS 3.2 — 69632 bytes used by system files

COMMAND	COM	23791	12-30-85	12:00p
IBMBIO	COM	16369	12-30-85	12:00p
IBMDOS	COM	28477	12-30-85	12:00p

DOS 3.3 — 78848 bytes used by system files

COMMAND	COM	25307	3-17-87	12:00p
IBMBIO	COM	22100	3-18-87	12:00p
IBMDOS	COM	30159	3-17-87	12:00p

DOS 4.0 — 108544 bytes used by system files

COMMAND	COM	37637	6-17-88	12:00p
IBMBIO	COM	32816	8-03-88	12:00p
IBMDOS	COM	36000	8-03-88	12:00p

DOS 5.0 — 118669 bytes used by system files

COMMAND	COM	47845	4-09-91	5:00a
IO	SYS	33430	4-09-91	5:00a
MSDOS	SYS	37394	4-09-91	5:00a

Figure 1.2.   Relative Sizes of All IBM DOS Versions

New External Commands

DOS 1.0	DOS1.1	DOS 2.0/2.1	DOS 3.0	DOS 3.1	DOS 3.2	DOS 3.3	DOS 4.0	DOS 5.0
BASIC.COM	EXE2BIN.EXE	ANSI.SYS	ATTRIB.COM	BASIC.PIF	DRIVER.SYS	4201.CPI	DOSSHELL.BAT	DELOLDOS.EXE
BASICA.COM		ASSIGN.COM	GRAFTABL.COM	BASICA.PIF	REPLACE.EXE	5202.CPI	MEM.EXE	DOSKEY.COM
CHKDSK.COM		BACKUP.COM	KEYBFR.COM	JOIN.EXE	XCOPY.EXE	APPEND.EXE	XMAEM.SYS	DOSSWAP.EXE
COMMAND.COM		FDISK.COM	KEYBGR.COM	SUBST.EXE		COUNTRY.SYS	XMA2EMS.SYS	EDIT.COM
COMP.COM		FIND.EXE	KEYBIT.COM			DISPLAY.SYS		EGA.SYS
DATE.COM		GRAPHICS.COM	KEYBSP.COM			EGA.CPI		EMM386.EXE
DEBUG.COM		MORE.COM	KEYBUK.COM			FASTOPEN.EXE		HELP.EXE
DISKCOMP.COM		PRINT.COM	LABEL.COM			KEYB.COM		HIMEM.SYS
DISKCOPY.COM		RECOVER.COM	SELECT.COM			KEYBOARD.SYS		LOADFIX.COM
EDLIN.COM		RESTORE.COM	SHARE.EXE			LCD.CPI		MIRROR.COM
FORMAT.COM		SORT.EXE	VDISK.LST			NLSFUNC.EXE		QBASIC.EXE
LINK.EXE		TREE.COM	VDISK.SYS			PRINTER.SYS		SETVER.EXE
MODE.COM								UNDELETE.EXE
SYS.COM								UNFORMAT.EXE
TIME.COM								

New Internal Commands

DOS 1.0	DOS 1.1	DOS 2.0/2.1	DOS 3.0	DOS 3.1	DOS 3.2	DOS 3.3	DOS 4.0	DOS 5.0
COPY	DATE	BREAK	COUNTRY	(none)	(none)	CALL	INSTALL	DEVICEHIGH
DIR	DEL	BUFFERS	DEVICE			CHCP	SWITCHES	LOADHIGH
ERASE	REN	CD	FCBS				TRUENAME	LH
PAUSE	TIME	CHDIR	LASTDRIVE				(undocumented)	
REM		CLS						
RENAME		CTTY						
TYPE		ECHO						
		ERRORLEVEL						
		EXIST						
		EXIT						
		FILES						
		FOR						
		GOTO						
		IF						
		MD						
		MKDIR						
		PATH						
		PROMPT						
		RD						
		RMDIR						
		SET						
		SHIFT						
		VER						
		VERIFY						
		VOL						

Note: Files with extensions are predominantly external commands or device drivers. Those without extensions are either internal commands (part of COMMAND.COM) or configuration commands that work specifically with CONFIG.SYS.

Figure 1.3. New DOS Commands and Utilities

Modified External Commands

DOS 1.0	DOS 1.1	DOS 2.0/2.1	DOS 3.0	DOS 3.1	DOS 3.2	DOS 3.3	DOS 4.0	DOS 5.0
(none)	(TIME.COM)	CHKDSK.COM	FORMAT.COM	LABEL.COM	ATTRIB.EXE	ATTRIB.EXE	ANSI.SYS	ATTRIB.EXE
	(DATE.COM)	COMP.COM	BACKUP.COM	TREE.COM	COMMAND.COM	BACKUP.COM	APPEND.EXE	DOSHELL.EXE
	FORMAT.COM	DEBUG.COM	RESTORE.COM	LINK.EXE	DISKCOMP.CM	FDISK.COM	BACKUP.COM	FORMAT.COM
	CHKDSK.COM	DISKCOMP.COM	DISKCOMP.COM		DISKCOPY.COM	GRAFTABL.COM	CHKDSK.COM	MEM.EXE
	ERASE.COM	DISKCOPY.COM	DISKCOPY.COM		FORMAT.COM	MODE.COM	DISPLAY.SYS	RAMDRIVE.SYS
	DISKCOMP.COM	EDLIN.COM	GRAPHICS.COM		SELECT.COM	RESTORE.COM	DISKCOMP.COM	SMARTDRIVE.SYS
	DISKCOPY.COM	FORMAT.COM					DISKCOPY.COM	
	LINK.EXE				* environment size		FASTOPEN.EXE	
	DEBUG.EXE						FDISK.COM	
	MODE.COM						FORMAT.COM	
							GRAFTABL.COM	
							GRAPHICS.COM	
							KEYB.COM	
							MODE.COM	
							PRINTER.SYS	
							REPLACE.EXE	
							SELECT.EXE	
							SHARE.EXE	
							SYS.COM	
							TREE.COM	
							VDISK.SYS	

Modified Internal Commands

DOS 1.0	DOS 1.1	DOS 2.0/2.1	DOS 3.0	DOS 3.1	DOS 3.2	DOS 3.3	DOS 4.0	DOS 5.0
(none)	(none)	DIR	DATE	(none)	SHELL	ECHO	BUFFERS	DIR
		DEL ERASE	(external command paths okay)			DATE	COUNTRY	
						TIME	DEL	
							DIR	
							ERASE	
							LABEL	
							REM	
							TIME	
							VOL	

Figure 1.4.   Modified DOS Commands and Utilities

DOS 5.0: An Overview

The first edition of the IBM Disk Operating System, or DOS, was introduced in 1981 to support the company's entry into the world of personal computers. Right from the start, DOS was perceived to be an IBM product, although it was in fact developed by Microsoft — with a little help from Big Blue of course. "IBM" and "DOS" were printed on the spine of the manual, but inside, "Disk Operating System by Microsoft, Inc.," was printed on the title page. Blurred authorship notwithstanding, DOS version 1.0 was not much more than a grab bag of features "borrowed" from earlier operating systems, with a COMMAND.COM processor that was some 3231 bytes long. Today, the file with the same name eats up almost 50K bytes. Back in version 1.0 days, you had to run separate standalone programs to set the date and time. You couldn't store more than 160Kb on a single diskette. You could rename, copy or erase a file, but if you wanted to do much more than that, you were out of luck. But this wasn't such a big deal way back then. IBM sold its PC-1 with a measly 16Kb of RAM inside, and many users stored data on analog audio cassettes.

In early 1982 IBM acknowledged that the operating system had a few little problems and released what it called the Version 1.1 DOS Upgrade (some others called it the "DOS 1.0 bug fix"). The manual noted: "We've just brushed the surface of the many enhancements." Big Blue was not kidding.

Over the years, subsequent DOS enhancements have brought us hard disk support, the hierarchical file system, networks, all sorts of diskette sizes, and a foreign alphabet — the latter often used to describe much of the former. For good measure, the IBM/Microsoft marriage partners even threw in a collection of tantalizing utility programs; some good, some bad and some just plain awful. To help feed and clothe the ever-expanding clone marketplace, Microsoft began distributing its part of the operating system to other manufacturers, some of whom would add enhancements before bundling it with their own hardware systems.

But almost immediately after the release of each new DOS version, some new hardware would outpace the new operating system, much to the distress of the user in search of "more": more hard disk space, more RAM, more colors, more this and more that. Oh yes, and an interface that would please the normal human, if not the computer nerd.

From time to time the DOS programming wizards would announce new solutions to various longstanding problems. But wait: isn't "DOS programming wizards" one of those oxymorons, like "military intelligence" or "business ethics"? Aren't one of these partners the same wonderful people who brought us *TopView* and *DisplayWrite*? And did not these very same wizards sell (or *try* to sell) a lot of truly wretched accounting software designed for an obsolete minicomputer?"

Well, yes. But every now and then the wizards would get something right and help DOS dig its way out of the software doghouse. For DOS version 3.2, they developed XCOPY — one of the finest DOS utilities ever. And over the years since DOS 1.0, the companies everyone loves to hate have spent much effort burnishing other facets on the surface of the operating system that everyone loves to hate. Today, some shine brightly. Others could use a bit more polish.

Yesterday's History: DOS 4.0

In the long march towards the ultimate operating machine, DOS 4.0 was a giant step. Backwards. Its bug list was long, and over the first two years of its life, IBM released a regular stream of CSDs (Corrective Service Diskettes) to its authorized dealers. By mid-1990 the various updates had fixed many of its quirks, and history may yet celebrate DOS 4.0 as a powerful marketing tool — for OS/2. However, version 4.0 did have its good points, a few of which are listed here. These features were significantly different from, or simply didn't exist in, the earlier DOS editions. Most of the features described here have been retained or improved in DOS 5.0.

Ease of Installation

You didn't have to worry much about installing DOS 4.0; the INSTALL diskette took care of most of the chores for you. It figured out what kind of hardware you had and busied itself creating system subdirectories, copying the proper files into them, and making all the proper configuration settings (well, *almost* all the proper settings).

The DOS Shell

Users who previously needed a dog-eared manual and a bottle of Excedrin to get up and running were jolted by the sight of the new DOS Shell, a friendly full-color screen that offered to load any application or take care of mundane diskette and file chores at the touch of a few keys.

The DOS Shell brings prompt relief to anyone suffering the discomforts of a C> prompt allergy, and it protects both the neophyte and the guru from such esoterica as, say

```
[d:] [path] FORMAT   d: [/S] [/1] [/8] [/V] [/B] [/4] [/N:9] [/T:80] [/F]
```

All that, merely to prepare a diskette for use. The Shell does away with such turgid command-line syntax in favor of the point-and-shoot menu style that has made the (gasp!) Apple Macintosh so popular. For a company's MIS department, it may be ranked as a blessing from above, since it allows the executive computerphobe to get through the business of the day by simply negotiating an onscreen menu, rather than by making endless calls downstairs to Corporate 911.

Yet some users neither want nor need a layer of insulation between themselves and their operating system. In fact, there are those who regard the DOS shell as some kind of infoclam defense against penetration from the outside world. Such folk prefer to navigate the old-fashioned way — by executing their orders at the DOS prompt. It may not look pretty, but it's often faster, especially for those who know their way around the keyboard. For such users, DOS 4.0 made some effort to standardize the way it interpreted instructions. For example, the early DOS rules for switches and other command tail parameters (all that business following the FORMAT command above) were not always consistent. Sometimes you could type in your backslashes and other punctuation in one long, endless chain, and sometimes you couldn't: you'd need to use *delimiters* — symbols (space, comma, etc.) that separate one switch or other parameter from another. And of course you'd have to get all your variables right, or else try to guess which one was wrong. In early versions of DOS, a FORMAT B: /S /Z command would display a terse "Invalid parameter" message. It was up to you to guess which parameter was invalid.

Things are better now. DOS 4.0 helped out by reporting "Invalid switch /Z" so you knew just where the problem lay, if not yet how to fix it. But DOS 5.0 takes care of even that little detail (see below).

Improved Disk and RAM Management

DOS 4.0 finally broke through two nasty barriers — the 32 Mbyte hard disk ceiling and the 640Kb RAM limit. While earlier versions let users slice an enormous hard disk into smaller *logical* drives, each no greater than 32 Mbytes, DOS 4.0 let you treat any size hard disk as a single drive. And, for the first time, DOS acknowledged that the user may need more than minimal RAM. In previous editions, RAM addresses above 640K were all but ignored. You could install an electronic disk up there, but that was about it. DOS 4.0 opened up the higher-memory real estate to other applications by supporting the LIM (Lotus/Intel/Microsoft) Expanded Memory Specification. In the IBM version of DOS 4.0, the required device driver — XMA2EMS.SYS (Big Blue has a way with names) — would work only with IBM-brand EMS memory (surprise!), but Microsoft's generic driver (HIMEM.SYS) works well on most systems.

Other Improvements

All DOS upgrades have provided more and better system tools, and DOS 4.0 was no exception. It introduced several new utilities, and supercharged nearly two dozen existing commands. The new goodies ranged from friendlier formatting to better backups, most of which have been carried forward into DOS 5.0, as described below.

And Now, DOS 5.0

But first, another backward glance. Prior to version 5.0, users might have purchased the operating system directly from IBM, in which case it was — according to the accompanying User's Manual — the "IBM Operating System." For the vast IBM-compatible market, Microsoft supplied an OEM (Original Equipment Manufacturer) DOS directly to the hardware manufacturer, who might make some modifications before delivering it to the end-user. In this case, it was usually bundled with the computer itself, and a retail sale of this brand of DOS was rare.

But effective with DOS 5.0, the Microsoft marketeers have come out of their own DOS marketing shell with two versions of DOS, both described here.

The Upgrade Path

A new MS-DOS 5.0 Upgrade package is available through traditional retail outlets, such as your friendly(?) local computer dealer. This version can only be installed on a system that is already up and running with an earlier version of DOS installed. It will not install itself on a brand new machine.

The OEM Version

This is the new DOS in the old familiar format, as sold to the user by IBM and the other OEMs out there in hardwareland. This is the version to buy for your brand new computer.

Unless otherwise noted, this chapter follows the DOS path described in the Microsoft MS-DOS version 5.0 manual.

New Feature Summary

To help you decide if DOS 5.0 is for you, here's a brief list of some features that are either new or considerably enhanced over previous versions, notably over DOS 4.0. Later on, each of these features will be described in greater detail.

Memory Management

As noted in the first paragraph of this chapter, DOS has not gotten smaller with age. But with that age has come wisdom: DOS is now smart enough to install much of itself above the 640Kb point, thus freeing valuable conventional memory space for running your applications. With an 80386 or better microprocessor, various device drivers and programs can also be moved out of the conventional memory area, again leaving more space below for other programs. And if you're wondering just what is going on inside all that RAM, the MEM command shows where all your loaded programs have landed, and where the free space is. With luck, and good memory management, there should be plenty of it.

Oops Guard

The new UNFORMAT and UNDELETE utilities do just what you think they do.

The Help Screen

Except for DOS, just about every application out there offers the user some sort of onscreen help. Now, so does DOS. Just follow any command with /? and, instead of the command being executed, the screen displays a brief explanation of the command, followed by a list of the various switches and other parameters that are available. It doesn't always eliminate the need for the manual, but it might offer just enough information to jog your own memory.

A New Editor

For years, DOS gurus have lamented the limitations of the EDLIN utility, which was, and is, a cheap-and-dirty little line editor. If not quite all you needed to write the next great American novel, it was, and is, all you need to knock off a quickie batch file, or something no more demanding than that.

EDLIN bashers now have a bigger target to shoot at. Although old EDLIN itself is still around, and still does what it does quite nicely, the new EDIT utility is a full-screen editor with considerably more power and flexibility.

Bigger Partitions

As noted above, the old 32Kb hard disk limit is gone. DOS 5.0 supports disk partitions of up to two gigabytes, which is 1,073,741,824 times two. If that won't do, you're probably too verbose.

Better Directories

Starting now, you can append various switches to the familiar DIR command, to sort your directory list alphabetically, by date/time, by type (i.e., extension) and/or by file size. If you have a favorite sorting style, you can specify it as a default setting in the DOS environment.

The Basic BASIC

It's gone! Good old GWBASIC has given way to QBASIC, a scaled-down version of the Microsoft QuickBASIC language, which is sold separately. According to the manual,

QBASIC "provides a complete environment for programming in the BASIC language." That depends on how one defines "complete." Actually, QuickBASIC is complete. QBASIC leaves out all the compiling options. But it should be enough to convince you that Microsoft's *really* complete version is well worth having around, especially for those times when you need a little something done, but you don't feel quite up to facing the complexities of C or the arcana of assembly.

A Few Steps Beyond F3

Most DOS users know about hitting function key F3 to bring the last command back to the screen. It's quite helpful when that command was one of those dreadful lines with all sorts of parameters, and you only got one of them wrong. But what if you want the *next*-to-last command, or maybe the one before that? With the TSR (Terminate, Stay Resident) DOSKEY program loaded, you can use the arrow and page up/down keys to fetch various command lines that were entered prior to the one that now appears on screen.

Denser Data

The DOS 5.0 manual lists a new switch (/f:2.88) for the familiar FORMAT command. The addition lets you format 2.88Mb 3.5" diskettes, or it will just as soon as the necessary hardware (drives) and software (diskettes) hit the market. There was talk of a 2.88 diskette drive for the IBM models 90 and 95, but both machines made their debut with 1.44Mb drives as standard. But sooner or later the drives will show up, and DOS 5.0 is ready for them.

Easier Installation

Not the least of DOS 5.0's attractions is its hassle-free installation. Upgrading from an earlier DOS is easy; installing DOS 5.0 on a brand new computer is easier still. The DOS 5.0 Installation section below shows how to do both. After that, we'll take a closer look at some of the bells and whistles.

A Few Pre-installation Notes

Until version 4.0, DOS was downward compatible; each new version could handle just about anything created by an older version. For example, insert an old single-sided 160Kb diskette into a 1.2 Mb drive and type DIR — after a few seconds you'll see the directory of diskette files.

For the sake of that downward compatibility, when any command format was changed, the command will usually still operate in the old format as well as the new. For example, here are the new (DOS 4.0 and 5.0) and old ways to set the parameters for a serial communications port:

```
MODE COM1:2400, N, 8, 1
MODE COM1 BAUD=2400 PARITY=NONE DATA=8 STOP=1
```

DOS 4.0 and 5.0 recognize either format, while only the first one will function with pre-DOS 4.0 operating systems.

However, there was one little compatibility problem that IBM introduced in its own version of DOS 4.0. Assuming you had previously formatted your hard disk with an earlier IBM DOS (3.3, for example), there would be no problem in upgrading to the latest DOS. But if you had the temerity to use a non-IBM DOS in the past, then Big Blue would not be pleased with you. During an upgrade to the new IBM DOS, the installation routine would display an "Invalid media type" error message and quit. The problem is due to a special eight-character "OEM identification field" in the boot sector at the beginning of a hard disk partition. This field stores the manufacturer's name and the version of DOS resident on the hard disk. If it was an IBM version, the field contained the letters "IBM " (with a space after the "M"). If not, it contained something like "MSDOS" or "OS2." When IBM's installation routine looks at this spot on the disk, if it sees anything other than "IBM " it grinds to a halt and issues that invalid media error message.

Compaq and some other non-IBM vendors actually put the letters "IBM " in this location just to be sure they remain as compatible as possible with IBM versions. However, if your hard disk does not pass an IBM media inspection, and you know your way around DEBUG, you can modify the OEM ID field so that IBM DOS will install itself without incident. To see what's in the OEM ID field in your system, make sure your DOS DEBUG program is handy, and type the following lines exactly as they appear but make sure to read these notes first.

Note 1: Type carefully. Don't experiment, and heaven forbid, don't enter a W (Write) command unless you're *sure* you know what you're doing. In fact, before trying this, back up your entire hard disk. Typing in the following lines without error won't hurt anything, but it's a good excuse to make sure you're completely backed up.

Note 2: The following DEBUG instructions assume your hard disk is drive C. The DEBUG utility refers to drives by number rather than by letter, and it starts numbering at 0 rather than at 1. So, drive A is 0, drive B is 1, C is 2 and so on. This can be initially confusing, so be incredibly careful when using DEBUG and drive numbers!

For a system with a bootup hard disk C, type DEBUG and press the Enter key. When you see the DEBUG hyphen prompt at the left edge of your screen, type:

```
L 100 2 0 1
```

The terse command instructs DEBUG to load (L) data to memory address 100, from drive C (2). The drive-C data to be loaded begins at disk sector 0, and comprises 1 sector only. The hard drive light will blink on for an instant, and then you'll see another DEBUG hyphen prompt. Then type:

```
D 103 L5
```

which means; display (D) on screen the data bytes beginning at address 103. List (or display) five bytes only (L5).

If your hard disk was formatted with IBM DOS, you'll see the magic letters "IBM" over at the right side of your screen. If the disk was formatted with some other version, you should see something like "MSDOS" over there instead. The whole works should look like this:

```
C> DEBUG
-L 100 2 0 1
-D 103 L5
xxxx:0100        49 42 4D 20 20                    IBM
-
```

If you see something other than the IBM signature, and you want to upgrade to an IBM DOS, you can do it via the DEBUG utility. Just be careful. One little finger slip and you might corrupt your hard disk boot record, which you really don't want to do. If you want to try this, continue reading here. Otherwise, just hit Q key and then press the Enter key to quit DEBUG. Or to continue, type the following lines at the hyphen prompt:

```
-E 103 "IBM "
-W 100 2 0 1
-Q
```

In the first line (-E) above, make sure you insert a blank space after the letters IBM and before the final closing quotation mark. The next line (-W) writes the new information into sector 0 and the final line (-Q) quits DEBUG.

Now reboot and try the installation again. When you're finished, restore all your backed up files to the hard disk.

A DOS Uninstallation

If you're taking the DOS upgrade path, the installation procedure described below will be augmented by an "uninstall" procedure. This requires one or two scratch diskettes, depending on your diskette and hard drive capacity. If necessary, the diskette(s) may be used later on to restore your system's previous DOS version, and might be regarded as an insurance policy for those who have learned the hard way never to trust a DOS version number that ends with a zero.

After DOS 5.0 is installed, you'll discover an OLD_DOS directory on drive C. As the name suggests, OLD_DOS contains nothing more mysterious than your old DOS version, whatever it was. If you decide to return to this version, insert your UNINSTALL 1 diskette in drive A, reboot and follow the onscreen directions. Your old AUTOEXEC.BAT and CONFIG.SYS files will be returned to drive C, as will the old COMMAND.COM and system files. DOS 5.0 will be removed and your previous version will once again be in place. Microsoft does not say why you would ever want to do this, but there it is, just in case you do.

The OLD_DOS directory is of course created on the day you do the upgrading, so its date and time stamps record when that upgrade took place. Next, the new DOS 5.0 files are moved into your original DOS directory to replace the old ones that were just copied into OLD_DOS. But since the old DOS directory (not the files, just the directory) remains intact, its date and time stamps indicate when it was originally created. Thus, the OLD_DOS directory appears to be newer than the new one. You might want to remember this little bit of trivia, just so you don't lose sleep later on wondering why your DOS directory seems to be so much older than the files it contains.

Once you've determined that DOS 5.0 is really where it's at, you'll probably want to free up the space occupied by that new OLD_DOS directory and its contents. To do so, log onto the DOS 5.0 directory, type DELOLDOS and press the Enter key. Follow the onscreen instructions to remove the old DOS. But wait a while just to be safe, for once OLD_DOS is gone, the UNINSTALL diskette(s) won't bring it back.

A Setup: The DOS 5.0 Installation Procedure

Perhaps it's just change for the sake of change, but the former Install procedure is now called Setup, and it comes to you on multiple 3.5″ or 5.25″ diskettes. During the install . . . oops, *Setup* procedure, you will be prompted to insert MS-DOS 5.0 Disk x into drive A and press the Enter key to continue. Depending on the set of diskettes you use, the prompts will of course appear at different points during the complete procedure. The description below applies to a setup made from the 5.25″ diskettes and to a DOS directory on drive C; that is, on your hard disk.

To begin a completely new installation, boot the system with MS-DOS SETUP diskette 1 in drive A. To upgrade, boot with your old DOS and then insert diskette 1 in drive A. Log onto that drive, type SETUP and press the Enter key. In either case, you'll see a brief "Please wait" message as the Setup program inspects your system configuration. This is followed by a "Welcome to Setup" screen which reminds you of the help screens that are available during the Setup procedure. If you are upgrading an earlier DOS, the screen message reminds you to have one or two UNINSTALL diskettes ready.

The next screen prompts you to enter "Y" if you use a network, or "N" if you don't. If you answer in the affirmative, you are prompted to exit Setup and review the documentation for making network files compatible with DOS 5.0. After doing so, resume the Setup procedure.

If you are upgrading an earlier DOS, the next screen prompts you to "Back up hard disk(s)" before continuing. If you elect to do so, follow the onscreen prompts. When the backup procedure is done, reinsert Setup diskette 1 in drive A and press the Enter key. Otherwise, select the "Do not back up hard disk(s)" option.

Press the Enter key to continue your Setup. When you do, the screen displays the following default settings:

```
DATE/TIME   : today's date and time
COUNTRY     : United States
KEYBOARD    : US Default
INSTALL TO  : Hard Disk

The settings are correct.
```

If all the settings are not correct, select the appropriate line by pressing the up arrow key until that line is highlighted. Then press the Enter key to display a list of available options. Again, using the arrow keys, highlight the desired new option (say, some other country). Press the Enter key once more to return to the screen shown above. The new option should now be seen. When you have finished making changes, highlight the "settings are correct" line and press the Enter key to move on to the next screen, which displays

```
Install to              : C:\DOS
Run Shell on startup    : YES


The listed options are correct.
```

As before, change either option if you wish to do so, and then press the Enter key to continue the installation. (The Shell option is described in its own section later on in this chapter.)

If you are upgrading an earlier version of DOS, you will be prompted to insert an UNINSTALL diskette in drive A. Follow the onscreen prompts to format and prepare the UNINSTALL diskette(s). Then reinsert the Setup diskette in drive A and continue the installation as described in the section below entitled, "Your Hard Disk is Formatted."

However, if this is a new installation and your hard disk is not yet formatted, you will instead be prompted to make one of the following choices:

```
Allocate all free hard disk space for MS-DOS.
Allocate some free hard disk space for MS-DOS.
Do not allocate free hard disk space for MS-DOS.
```

This is as good a place as any to learn about the Help (F1) key, for there's more to those first two choices than first meets the eye. For example, you may indeed want to allocate all free hard disk space to MS-DOS, *but* you may also want to divide that space into several partitions. If so, then although the first choice looks like the right choice, it isn't. If you pick it by accident, Setup creates one monster DOS partition on your hard disk. If that's what you really wanted, then fine, you got it. But if you were planning to create two or more partitions, you *should* have picked the second choice in the above list. So before making any "obvious" choice that is not based on previous installation experience, press the F1 key to verify that your choice is the right one. Often enough it's not, and in such cases a quick scan of the help screen will spare you a bit of time and a lot of aggravation.

If you select choice two, you will be prompted to insert disk 2 into drive A. When you do, the first of several FDISK screens is seen, and you can go about the work of setting up a primary and an extended partition, and then divide the latter into several logical drives. If you're not sure how to get through all this, both the FDISK utility and partitions are described in detail later on in this chapter.

When you are finished with FDISK, you will be prompted to (re)insert disk 1 in drive A and press the Enter key. When you do, the system reboots itself and displays the following prompt:

```
Hard disk partition C: is unformatted.
MS-DOS version 5.0 does not recognize
unformatted media.


        Exit Setup
        Format Partition
```

To continue, select the "Format Partition" option and press the Enter key. An onscreen message continuously updates the percentage of the partition that has been formatted. When the partition is completely formatted, the screen display repeats for each remaining unformatted partition.

If you wish to complete the DOS 5.0 installation, you must take the time now to format each partition. In other words, you can't postpone formatting the remaining partitions for another day. If you decide to "Exit Setup," that's just what will happen; you get dumped back to the DOS prompt and have to restart the installation. When you do, you wind up right back here where you left off. So sit tight, finish the formatting and then move on to the next step in the DOS installation, as described immediately below.

Your Hard Disk Is Formatted

Regardless of how you got here, you are now ready to finish the DOS installation and get on to other things. Insert SETUP disk 1 in drive A (if it is not already there) and press the Enter key. You should see the following screen:

```
MS-DOS version 5.0 is now being set up.

Setup installs a basic MS-DOS system.  See the 'Microsoft
MS-DOS User's Guide and Reference' to learn about additional
features.

You may want to read the chapter on optimizing your system
in the manual.  This chapter describes how to fine-tune
MS-DOS to achieve maximum performance.

   x% complete
```

For the moment, forget about seeing that manual for additional features or boning up on system optimization. You'll be too busy inserting diskettes in drive A in response to an onscreen prompt which periodically overlays the screen shown above.

As the contents of each setup diskette are copied to the DOS directory on drive C, the "x% complete" legend updates itself and a horizontal bar gives a graphic progress report.

In addition, the lower right-hand corner of the screen keeps you posted with a "Reading filename" message.

If an error occurs during the setup operation, you'll see a message like this:

```
An error occurred while reading or writing to drive

               A:

          Try the operation again.
          Fail the operation.
```

Note the filename that appears in the lower right-hand corner of the screen. If it's something not absolutely essential to your computer's well-being (say, GORILLA.BAS), you may decide not to try the operation again. However, if the file is potentially important (for example, anything with a COM or EXE extension), retry it a few times before giving up. If the error persists, make a note of the file name, select the "Fail" option and continue the installation. When you're done installing everything else, try the EXPAND command (described below) to copy the troublesome file to the DOS directory.

When all the files have been transferred, remove the last SETUP diskette from drive A and press the Enter key. The system reboots itself, and if all's well, you'll be ready to do whatever it is that made you buy the computer in the first place.

Old Bats and Config Considerations

If your system previously held an earlier DOS version, SETUP either modified the old CONFIG.SYS and AUTOEXEC.BAT files, or it created an entirely new set of these files. In the latter case, your original files are saved with numeric extensions in place of the usual SYS and BAT extensions. It's a good idea to compare the contents of the old files and the new ones, to make sure that nothing important has been left out. If you find that DOS 5.0 has indeed forgotten to include some critical line from your original configuration or batch file, you can edit the new version to restore the missing information. If you can't find your originals, have a look on the UNINSTALL diskette, where they'll appear as CONFIG.DAT and AUTOEXEC.DAT.

With DOS 5.0 installed, watch the onscreen display carefully the first few times the system is booted. If you see any error messages such as "filename not installed," "wrong DOS version," or whatever, there's probably something in your CONFIG.SYS or AUTOEXEC.BAT file that needs to be fixed. For example, an old DOS 4.0 VDISK.SYS driver in your configuration file does not automatically get replaced by DOS 5.0's RAMDRIVE.SYS file. You'll have to edit the CONFIG.SYS file yourself to make the necessary change.

A Closer Look at DOS 5.0

The rest of this chapter reviews many of the DOS 5.0 enhancements in detail. To keep descriptions reasonably short and screen displays reasonably clear, remember that each line typed in by the user must end by pressing the Enter key and, when a screen prompt calls for a user response (usually Y or N), the user will press the appropriate key.

Since memory management and the related commands are such an important — and potentially confusing — aspect of DOS 5.0, this subject is discussed first and then followed by details about the other DOS 5.0 features.

Memory Management

Users of earlier DOS versions complained about two annoying constraints — the 32 Mbyte hard drive barrier, and the 640Kb RAM wall. It was possible to get around the 32 Mb limitation by splitting massive drives into smaller logical ones with their own drive letters. But, until version 4.0, DOS didn't provide any mechanism for using large amounts of memory past 640K. Its only concession to this was the ability to use "extended" memory for large VDISK RAMdisks.

Not all expanded memory hardware will work with the supplied DOS 4.0 drivers. But, since the DOS version doesn't really let users do much with expanded memory, and since boards come with their own expanded memory drivers, this isn't much of a loss.

The DOS 4.0 MEM command reports the amount of expanded memory available. And DEBUG 4.0 lets technically oriented users see the status of expanded memory with the XS command, allocate EMS with XA, map it to a logical page with XM, and deallocate it XD.

While users often confuse extended and expanded memory, these two kinds of memory enhancements are very different. The only similarity is that they don't use the system's main 640Kb of memory.

Of Modes and MEM

As the PC family moves ever farther away from its PC (as in IBM PC) roots, new jargon is coined to increasingly confuse the user. For example, there's now a "real" mode (as opposed to an "unreal" one?) and also a protected mode. Protected against *what*?, one might ask, and get an answer that has little to do with the word "protected." Sometimes it makes you wonder who thinks these terms up, and where they studied English.

With DOS 5.0 offering so much more memory management capability than its predecessors, a quickie look at a few potentially confusing terms may come in handy for negotiating the memory-related features described later in the chapter.

Real Memory

In computer jargon, the term refers specifically to the system memory that lies within the 1Mbyte addressing limit of the 8088 (IBM PC & XT) and 8086 (PS/2 models 25 and 30) microprocessors. Such memory is accessed via the familiar segment:offset address format, in which the segment gives the address of a paragraph (16-byte) boundary, and the offset indicates the number of bytes above that address. Thus, 4000:0100 points to a segment that begins at (decimal) paragraph 16384 (4 x 4096). Multiply that number by

16 to find the absolute address of the segment, which is 262144. Then add the offset (0100 = decimal 256) to find the actual address.

This memory is "real" in the sense that the segment:offset address points directly to a specific physical/logical memory location. So by extension, one might expect that *any* directly addressable memory (say, the 80286's 16Mb, or the 80386's 4Gb) is no less real than that first 1Mb. Yet the term is — as IBM might put it — "reserved" for just that part of the total system memory that can be accessed via the 20 address lines (A0-A19) of an 8088 and 8086 MPU.

Virtual Memory

The ANSI and ISO standards organizations prefer to call it virtual *storage*, but everybody else uses *virtual memory* to refer to data residing on a large storage medium, such as a hard disk. Such memory is accessed by mapping it into real memory addresses.

Real Mode

When any microprocessor addresses the 1Mb real memory area described above, it is said to be operating in the *real mode*. Therefore, this is the only mode in which the 8088 and 8086 can operate. Subsequent MPUs (80 x 86) can of course operate in the real mode for the sake of compatibility, or in the protected mode described next.

Protected Mode

Beginning with the 80286 microprocessor, memory far beyond the 1Mb limit became accessible to any operating system/hardware combo that was up to the challenge of managing all that space. To break the former 1Mb limit, the segment:offset format described earlier is replaced by a Selector:offset addressing scheme. Instead of having a segment point to a paragraph boundary, the selector points to a 64-bit *segment descriptor* stored in a separate local or global descriptor table. In turn, the descriptor points to the segment's starting address. The offset functions as before.

In the 80286 MPU, 24 bits within the segment descriptor define the segment's starting address, which means that 2^{24} = 16Mb is available. If that's not enough, the 80386 MPU picks up an additional eight bits, for 2^{32} = 4G-bytes of memory addressing capability.

Well, this is all very impressive, but what's it got to do with that word "protected?"

Nothing. Unfortunately for readers in search of computer terms that follow the usual laws of common sense, *protected mode* does nothing to describe enhanced memory-addressing prowess. Instead, it merely refers to the memory protection feature that is an added attraction of the latest batch of MPUs. The protected mode makes sure that memory allocated to any application is protected against invasion from other programs running at the same time. Otherwise, there would be regular system crashes as one's word processor ran amok through the spreadsheet, or worse.

As its name suggests, the protected mode does its job without regard to the type of memory — real or virtual — that needs protection. In other words, the real and protected modes are not mutually exclusive. But of course, this feature is not retroactive; if you don't have a '286 or better, you get real (only) but you don't get protected (ever). Just one more reason for upgrading.

Categories of Random Access Memory

Figure 2.1 is a simplified PC memory map, and each memory area seen in the figure is described briefly here. Unfortunately, as already noted, the computer industry is devoted to descriptive terms that convey almost no meaning, and worse, that look pretty much like other terms with quite different meanings. Therefore, it may be necessary to read at least a few of the following descriptions several times to distinguish one from another.

Base Memory

The amount of memory actually installed in the conventional memory area. These days it should be 640Kb, which is the limit of the conventional memory area.

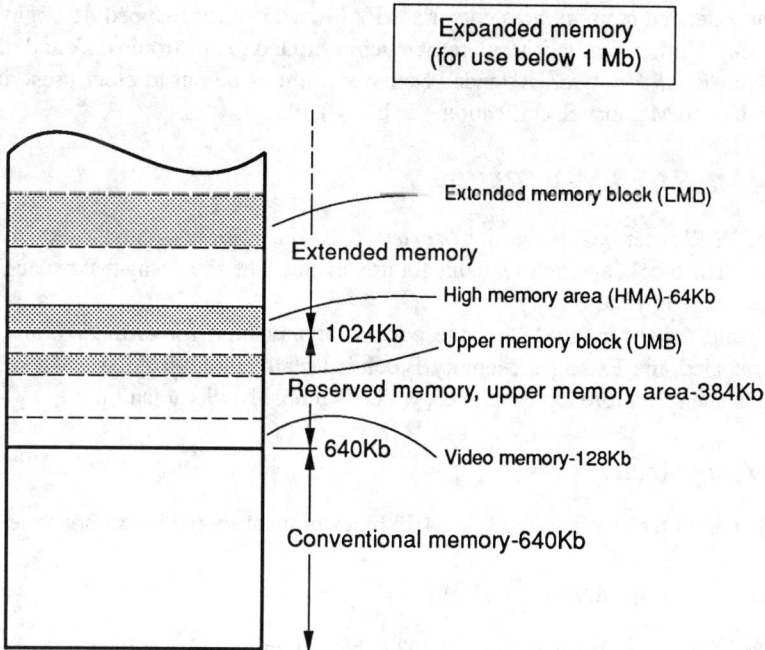

Expanded memory
(for use below 1 Mb)

Extended memory block (EMD)

Extended memory

High memory area (HMA)-64Kb

1024Kb   Upper memory block (UMB)

Reserved memory, upper memory area-384Kb

640Kb   Video memory-128Kb

Conventional memory-640Kb

Figure 2.1.   PC Memory Map

Conventional Memory

Also called User Memory since it is immediately available for user applications, this is the 640Kb area beginning at absolute address zero.

Expanded Memory

This is unassigned random access memory that may be mapped into lower memory addresses. In the real mode, a device driver shuffles 16Kb chunks of expanded memory in and out of page frames located below 1Mb, as described by an EMS (Expanded Memory Specification, described below).

Expansion Memory

A term loosely applied to any random access memory used to expand a personal computer's capacity. Due to the similarity between "expanded" and "expansion," it's important to remember that the latter term applies to *any* additional RAM, and is frequently encountered in describing various memory devices that may be installed within the Conventional (user) or Extended Memory areas.

Extended Memory

The extended memory area comprises RAM installed (or mapped) to begin at 1024Kb (1Mb). Until recently, it was pretty much restricted to electronic disk and disk caching applications. However, Extended Memory can now be put to other uses via the XMS (Extended Memory Specification, see below).

Extended Memory Block (EMB)

The XMS describes the creation of *extended memory blocks* within the Extended Memory area. The blocks are then available for use, in much the same way that expanded memory is managed by the EMS.

Note that although "X" is the popular abbreviation for eXtended, and "E" is for Expanded, the Extended Memory Block is usually abbreviated as EMB. XMB would have been the more logical choice, which is probably why it isn't used.

High Memory Area (HMA)

This XMS term defines the first 64Kb block of memory in the extended memory area.

Reserved or Upper Memory Area

This is the area between 640 and 1024Kb, containing video memory, ROM on various installed adapters, expanded memory RAM, etc. The system ROM BIOS is located at the top of this memory area.

Upper Memory Block (UMB)

This is a block of unused memory within the Reserved Memory Area between 640K and 1024K. DOS 5.0 can load much of itself within this area, thus freeing up conventional memory for user applications.

Video Memory

Also referred to as *graphics memory*, this is the 128Kb area immediately following conventional memory, which is occupied by the RAM on various display adapters.

Better Memory Management Tactics

One of DOS 5.0's noteworthy features is its ability to release much of the conventional memory space formerly taken up by device drivers, TSR programs and by DOS itself. By kicking all this stuff up beyond the 640Kb barrier, DOS 5.0 gives the user considerably more room in which to run applications.

But of course the additional free space doesn't just show up automatically because you're using DOS 5.0. To get it, you must first configure your system with the appropriate memory management drivers and then load DOS, other device drivers and your TSR programs into the upper reaches of RAM. To do all this, you'll need to add a few lines to your configuration file to set up the necessary memory management schemes, and then make further changes to get everything up and running. The following sections show what you need, and where you need it. We begin with a quick look at memory management specifications, then move on to the drivers that take advantage of these specs, and conclude with instructions on how to load whatever you want to load into upper memory.

A Pair of Memory Management Specifications

Assuming you've survived the memory mine field planted above, the next step in the operating system obstacle course is to get your programs safely across the same rocky road. To bring some semblance of order to a potentially chaotic subject, the following two memory specifications have been introduced.

EMS (Expanded Memory Specification)

When the PC was first introduced, users could take advantage only of the bottom 640Kb of RAM — and some of this was needed for DOS functions, BIOS tables, etc. As programs grew in size, and needed more memory space for data, vendors began thinking up schemes for exceeding the 640Kb limit. Not long after Big Blue introduced the PC AT, Lotus and Intel got together to see what could be done to to break through the barrier. Shortly thereafter they were joined by Microsoft, and the trio introduced the

Lotus/Intel/Microsoft Expanded Memory Specification — or LIM EMS for short. Actually, it was properly introduced as LIM EMS version 3.2, to signify its compatibility with a certain operating system then in widespread use. The specification gave users (mostly users of enormous spreadsheets) an additional eight Mb of memory in which to romp with their data.

Next, another set of industry players — AST, Quadram and Ashton-Tate — produced a superset of LIM EMS, which they called EEMS (*Enhanced* EMS). It didn't really go anywhere, although Quarterdeck's DESKview window-oriented multitasking software used it and became something of a success.

Still later, the LIM folks issued their own enhanced EMS version 4.0, and added multitasking abilities of their own. EMS 4.0 also upped the RAM limit from 8 Mb to 32 Mb, and it quickly became the standard. DOS 4.0 supported this version, and so does DOS 5.0.

The Expanded Memory Specification has not repealed the real mode address law, which still stands at that old 1Mb memory limit. Instead, it permits expanded memory to be paged into the addressable memory area. At first, EMS could handle only four page frames within the Reserved Memory area above 640Kb. However, EMS 4.0 can juggle as many as 50 pages within any 1 Mb area, provided they don't conflict with main system RAM, video buffers, ROM BIOS code, etc.

But you can't just pop in an EMS driver and expect your programs to automatically use all that extra memory; each application must be specifically written (or rewritten) to do its own expanded memory management.

Expanded Memory and DEBUG

If you use EMM386.EXE or some other device driver that supports expanded memory, the DOS DEBUG utility will show you the status of that memory. Just type DEBUG and press the Enter key. When you see the DEBUG's hyphen prompt, type XS (eXpanded-memory Status) to display a status report such as:

```
Handle 0000 has 0018 pages allocated

Physical page 04 = Frame segment 4000
Physical page 05 = Frame segment 4400
Physical page 06 = Frame segment 4800
     (additional pages listed here)
Physical page 03 = Frame segment DC00

   18 of a total    28 EMS pages have been allocated
    1 of a total    40 EMS handles have been allocated
```

XMS (Extended Memory Specification)

The Extended Memory Specification is conceptually similar to the Expanded Memory Specification just described, except that it uses extended memory to perform much the same functions.

A Duo of Drivers and a DOS Command

DOS 5.0 provides two memory management device drivers and a new command that loads much of DOS itself into the high memory area. To make use of these features, your configuration file must be modified as described here. Once this is done, you can move most of your device drivers and TSR programs out of conventional memory, also described below.

HIMEM.SYS

This extended memory specification (XMS) driver provides an entry into extended memory to those programs that can take advantage of it. As part of its memory management chores, HIMEM makes sure that programs do not try to load themselves into the same memory addresses.

The following device command line must appear in your CONFIG.SYS file ahead of any other device lines that load programs or drivers into reserved or extended memory (such as EMM386.EXE below).

```
DEVICE=HIMEM.SYS
```

EMM386.EXE

As indicated by the filename, this driver is an expanded memory manager (EMM) which wants to see an 80386 or better MPU. Actually, it's an expanded memory *emulator*, since it uses your system's extended memory to emulate expanded memory. With the appropriate device driver line added to your CONFIG.SYS file, EMM386.EXE provides expanded memory to any application that needs it.

The driver will also supply UMB (Upper Memory Block) management within the reserved memory area, thus allowing programs and other device drivers (but not itself) to be loaded into reserved memory. In this context, it is sometimes referred to as a "UMB provider" without identifying it by name (perhaps just to make sure you're paying attention).

Assuming your computer has extended memory available, and an 80386 or better MPU, first add the extended memory manager HIMEM.SYS line described above to your CONFIG.SYS file. Then insert the following line with the appropriate parameter:

Device line	Memory to be managed is
`DEVICE=EMM386.EXE ram`	expanded and reserved
`DEVICE=EMM386.EXE noems`	reserved only

Running DOS on High

One of the ways in which DOS 5.0 can save conventional memory is to load much of itself into the High Memory Area, that is, into the first 64Kb of extended memory. For example, with DOS loaded in the usual manner, the MEM /c command will show that

MSDOS has chewed a 54144-byte chunk out of conventional memory. DOS 5.0's new DOS command can be used to move a 40Kb chunk of DOS out of conventional memory, thus freeing up that amount of space for other use. The same command is also used to provide the link to reserved memory that is required by EMM and other drivers, as shown here.

Device line	*Purpose*
DOS=high	load part of DOS into HMA
DOS=umb	provide a link between conventional and reserved memory
DOS=high,umb	do both

The umb parameter must be included if you plan to load device drivers into reserved memory, as described later in this section.

Driver/DOS Summary

Assuming you want to sweep out your conventional memory as described above, just add the following lines to your CONFIG.SYS file:

```
DOS=high, umb
DEVICE=HIMEM.SYS
DEVICE=EMM386.EXE ram (or noems)
```

Make sure that the HIMEM line appears before the EMM386 line. The DOS= command line can appear at any location in the file.

Loading Drivers and TSRs in Reserved Memory

Finally, it's time to modify your CONFIG.SYS and AUTOEXEC.BAT files so that your other device drivers and TSR programs will be loaded into reserved memory instead of taking up space in conventional memory. There's almost nothing to it: just change every DEVICE line to DEVICEHIGH in your configuration file. Thus:

Device line	*Purpose*
DEVICE=HIMEM.SYS	load HIMEM into conventional memory (as required — it can't be loaded into reserved memory)
DEVICEHIGH=ANSI.SYS	load ANSI into reserved memory
DEVICEHIGH=filename.ext	load some other driver into reserved memory

Some device drivers expand to take up more space than the size indicated by a directory listing would indicate. If the expanded space exceeds that available in the UMB area, there could be a device error or a system crash. If this happens, the DEVICEHIGH line can be revised to include a size parameter. To find the required size, first load the device driver in the usual manner. Now execute the DOS MEM /PROGRAM command (described below) to display the amount of memory occupied by various installed programs, including the device driver of interest. Finally, modify the DEVICEHIGH line to include this value, as follows:

```
DEVICEHIGH size=xxxx (path and name of device driver)
```

In either of the above examples, the device driver will be loaded into low memory if there is not enough UMB space available for it.

In your AUTOEXEC.BAT file, use the LOADHIGH command to load other programs into reserved memory. In the following examples, a typical path instruction is included for illustration purposes.

Command line	Purpose
`C:\UV\UV on`	load Personics UV (*UltraVision*) utility into conventional memory
`LOADHIGH C:\UV\UV on`	load the UV utility into reserved memory

Not all programs are compatible with the LOADHIGH command, so do a little experimenting to determine if your program runs properly from within the reserved memory area. In case of any unpredictable results, try the same operation with the program loaded in conventional memory. If this cures the problem, then the program is indeed incompatible with UMB. If not, then there is some other problem which should be resolved before trying LOADHIGH again.

As a final caution, note that although the LOADHIGH command can be executed from within a batch file, it cannot itself be used to load a batch file into the UMB area.

A Look at Memory Savings

The original PC architecture was designed way back when full-fledged applications like *WordStar* needed only about 90Kb, and 640Kb seemed like a generous amount. The ancient 8088 chip could work with (or *address*) only one Mbyte of RAM, and it needed to employ the old segment:offset trick just to sneak past the first 64Kb.

These days many applications can barely squeeze into 640K, and serious users often find themselves ramming megs of RAM into their systems. A microprocessor like the 80386 or the awesome i486 can address vast quantities of RAM, and vendors are trying to convince users that they have to run lots of memory-hungry applications at the same time. Today's systems can take advantage of far more RAM than the old and conventional 640Kb of "user memory" by using extended and expanded memory.

Prior to DOS 4.0, the existence of such "high" memory was barely acknowledged, and there were no DOS tools to examine it. But with DOS 4.0 came the powerful MEM command, which provided a report on system memory allocation — including extended and expanded memory. And by appending a /DEBUG or /PROGRAM switch to the command, DOS displayed an incredibly detailed map of what was where in memory.

MEM /PROGRAM, or MEM /P, tells you about all programs currently loaded in memory (you may be surprised how many you see when you first try it). The more powerful MEM /DEBUG, or MEM /D, supplements the /PROGRAM data with valuable information on device drivers and DOS/BIOS low-memory areas. The option isn't for everyone, since much of the information is fairly exotic, and all numbers are in hex notation. However, it can be extremely helpful if you're trying to shoehorn lots of popup programs into memory, since it shows how much RAM each one consumes. It also lets you spot ill-mannered TSRs that lop off wasteful amounts of memory every time you run them. And if you're a programmer or someone with an insatiable curiosity about how your system works, you'll just love the MEM /D command.

DOS 5.0 adds a new switch to the MEM command, and this may be used to get a general idea of how the conventional memory area is affected by all the memory management described above. Here's a brief description, followed by several screens of memory-usage information.

MEM /CLASSIFY (or MEM /C)

When /C is appended to the MEM command, the screen shows a concise report of conventional and upper-memory usage. For example, the listing below is a simple CONFIG.SYS listing, immediately followed by the memory report delivered by typing MEM/C and then pressing the Enter key.

```
DEVICE=C:\DOS\SETVER.EXE
DEVICE=C:\DRIVERS\ANSI-UV.SYS
DEVICE=C:\DRIVERS\RCD.SYS /f


Conventional Memory :


Name                  Size in Decimal        Size in Hex
- - - - - - - - - -    - - - - - - - - - - -   - - - - - - - - -

MSDOS                 54144    ( 52.9K)         D380

SETVER                  400    (  0.4K)          190

ANSI-UV                1664    (  1.6K)          680

RCD                   10912    ( 10.7K)         2AA0

COMMAND                4704    (  4.6K)         1260

SETVID                  720    (  0.7K)          2D0

UV                    19456    ( 19.0K)         4C00

DE                     2256    (  2.2K)          8D0

FREE                     64    (  0.1K)           40

FREE                 559744    (546.6K)         88A80


Total  FREE :        559808    (546.7K)
```

```
Total bytes available to programs :                    559808
(546.7K)
Largest executable program size :                      559600
(546.5K)


    4456448 bytes total contiguous extended memory
    4456448 bytes available contiguous extended memory
```

The last two lines show that all contiguous extended memory is available for use. But for the moment, this use is limited to electronic disks and disk caching.

Note that MS-DOS occupies 52.9Kb of conventional memory and is followed by the three drivers loaded by the CONFIG.SYS file. The SETVID, UV, and DE entries are three utilities loaded by the AUTOEXEC.BAT file (not shown).

To free up some space, the first thing to do is get DOS (most of it, that is) out of conventional memory, and this is done by adding two lines to the configuration file, as shown here:

```
DOS=HIGH
DEVICE=C:\DOS\HIMEM.SYS
DEVICE=C:\DOS\SETVER.EXE
DEVICE=C:\DRIVERS\ANSI-UV.SYS
DEVICE=C:\DRIVERS\RCD.SYS /f
```

Now type MEM/C again to display the following memory report:

```
Conventional Memory :


    Name             Size in Decimal        Size in Hex
 - - - - - - - - - -   - - - - - - - - - - - - - - - - - -   - - - - - - - - - - - -

    MSDOS           13536     ( 13.2K)         34E0
    HIMEM            1184     (  1.2K)          4A0
    SETVER            400     (  0.4K)          190
    ANSI-UV          1664     (  1.6K)          680
    RCD             10912     ( 10.7K)         2AA0
    COMMAND          2624     (  2.6K)          A40
    SETVID            720     (  0.7K)          2D0
    UV              19456     ( 19.0K)         4C00
    DE               2256     (  2.2K)          8D0
    FREE               64     (  0.1K)           40
    FREE           601216     (587.1K)        92C80

Total  FREE :      601280     (587.2K)


Total bytes available to programs :                    601280
```

```
(587.2K)
Largest executable program size :                              601072
(587.0K)

   4456448 bytes total contiguous extended memory
         0 bytes available contiguous extended memory
   4390912 bytes available XMS memory
           MS-DOS resident in High-Memory Area
```

Note that both the MSDOS and COMMAND sizes are smaller and there is therefore more conventional memory available. Also, the lines at the bottom of the listing have changed. The contiguous extended memory is gone, but there are now 4390912 bytes of XMS memory available. This is still extended memory, but it's no longer contiguous because the first 64Kb of it are missing since HIMEM.SYS has picked it up for use by MS-DOS, as reported in the last line above.

But now, back to conventional memory space. The next step is to move the three device drivers (SETVER, ANSI-UV, RCD) into the upper-memory area, which is accomplished by modifying the DOS= command, installing the EMM386 expanded memory emulator/manager, and changing the DEVICE lines to DEVICEHIGH, as shown below. In this example, the ram parameter on the EMM386 line enables expanded memory management, as described earlier.

```
DOS=HIGH,UMB
DEVICE=C:\DOS\HIMEM.SYS
DEVICE=C:\DOS\EMM386.EXE ram
DEVICEHIGH=C:\DOS\SETVER.EXE
DEVICEHIGH=C:\DRIVERS\ANSI-UV.SYS
DEVICEHIGH=C:\DRIVERS\RCD.SYS /f
```

To move the three utilities (SETVID, UV, DE) into upper memory, change each line in the AUTOEXEC.BAT file to begin with LOADHIGH=filename. Having done all that, the SETVER, ANSI-UV and RCD drivers should all be loaded into upper memory, along with the three utilities just mentioned. But one of them, UV, still appears in the conventional memory area, as shown here.

```
Conventional Memory :


    Name                Size in Decimal           Size in Hex
    ------------        ---------------------     -------------

    MSDOS               13552     ( 13.2K)            34F0
    HIMEM                1184     (  1.2K)             4A0
    EMM386               9424     (  9.2K)            24D0
    COMMAND              2624     (  2.6K)             A40
    UV                  19456     ( 19.0K)            4C00
    FREE                   64     (  0.1K)              40
```

```
    FREE                608832        (594.6K)        94A40


Total   FREE :          608896        (594.6K)


Upper Memory :


    Name                Size in Decimal           Size in Hex
    - - - - - - - - - - - -     - - - - - - - - - - - - - - - - - - - - -     - - - - - - - - - - - -
    SYSTEM              163840        (160.0K)        28000
    SETVER                 400        (  0.4K)          190
    ANSI-UV               1664        (  1.6K)          680
    RCD                  10912        ( 10.7K)         2AA0
    SETVID                 720        (  0.7K)          2D0
    DE                    2256        (  2.2K)          8D0
    FREE                 16672        ( 16.3K)         4120


Total   FREE :           16672        ( 16.3K)


Total bytes available to programs (Conventional+Upper) : 625568   (610.9K)
Largest executable program size :                        608688   (594.4K)
Largest available upper-memory block :                    16672   ( 16.3K)


    655360 bytes total EMS memory
    262144 bytes free EMS memory


   4456448 bytes total contiguous extended memory
         0 bytes available contiguous extended memory
   0097090 bytes available XMS memory
          MS-DOS resident in High-Memory Area
```

The reason our UV utility is still parked down there in the conventional memory lot is simple: at the moment, the largest available upper-memory block is only 16.3Kb, as reported above. Since that's not enough room for UV, the LOADHIGH command is ignored and the utility stays put.

The shortage of upper memory is because the ram parameter on the EMM386 line in CONFIG.SYS has enabled expanded memory support, and in so doing, has whittled away at the available memory. (See the EMM386.SYS section earlier in the chapter for more details.) Since we don't need expanded memory, we can fix this by changing ram in line 3 to noems (No Expanded Memory) and try again.

```
DOS=HIGH,UMB
DEVICE=C:\DOS\HIMEM.SYS
DEVICE=C:\DOS\EMM386.EXE noems
DEVICEHIGH=C:\DOS\SETVER.EXE
DEVICEHIGH=C:\DRIVERS\ANSI-UV.SYS
```

```
DEVICEHIGH=C:\DRIVERS\RCD.SYS /f
```

Conventional Memory :

Name	Size in Decimal		Size in Hex
MSDOS	13552	(13.2K)	34F0
HIMEM	1184	(1.2K)	4A0
EMM386	9424	(9.2K)	24D0
COMMAND	2624	(2.6K)	A40
FREE	64	(0.1K)	40
FREE	628304	(613.6K)	99650

Total FREE :   628368   (613.6K)

Upper Memory :

Name	Size in Decimal		Size in Hex
SYSTEM	163840	(160.0K)	28000
SETVER	400	(0.4K)	190
ANSI-UV	1664	(1.6K)	680
RCD	10912	(10.7K)	2AA0
SETVID	720	(0.7K)	2D0
UV	19456	(19.0K)	4C00
DE	2256	(2.2K)	8D0
FREE	62736	(61.3K)	F510

Total FREE :   62736   (61.3K)

```
Total bytes available to programs (Conventional+Upper) : 691104   (674.9K)
Largest executable program size :                        628160   (613.4K)
Largest available upper memory block :                    62736   ( 61.3K)

    4456448 bytes total contiguous extended memory
          0 bytes available contiguous extended memory
    4205568 bytes available XMS memory
            MS-DOS resident in High Memory Area
```

The above exercise is just one example of how DOS 5.0 can be tweaked for optimum memory management. There are many additional memory management parameters for just about every command line shown above.

Other DOS 5.0 Features

In addition to the enhanced memory management facilities described above, DOS 5.0 introduces a lot of other operating system bells and whistles. Some early DOS commands have been souped up with extra parameters or switches, and several entirely new commands and utilities have been added to the repertoire. Three of the latter (MIRROR, UNDELETE and UNFORMAT) are included under license from Central Point Software, and are part of that company's *PC Tools* software. The UNFORMAT utility is equivalent to *PC Tools'* REBUILD utility.

Attribute Command (ATTRIB)

In every file header, the byte following the filename and extension is the *file attribute byte*, in which each bit defines a file parameter. Effective with DOS 5.0, the ATTRIBute command allows all file attribute bits to be changed. Each such attribute is described here.

Attribute bit	Determines if
archive	data has been written to the file since the last backup session
hidden	the filename appears in the directory listing
read-only	the file is write-protected
system	the file is a system file

If the attribute bit is set (1), the file possesses the attribute defined by that bit; if the bit is cleared (0), that attribute is disabled. To set or clear a file attribute, type the ATTRIB command, followed by a plus (set) or minus (clear) sign, and the name of the file, as shown here:

ATTRIB command	Purpose
ATTRIB +p filename	Set the attribute bit defined by p.
ATTRIB -p filename	Clear the attribute bit defined by p.
ATTRIB	Display all file attributes of all files in the current directory.
ATTRIB /S	Display files in this directory and in its subdirectories.
ATTRIB ±p filename /S	Set (+) or clear (-) the attribute bit defined by p for all files with filename in this directory and in its subdirectories.

The last example above may be useful for modifying all files with a common extension, as for example, all *.SYS files.

Replace the p above with one of the following parameters. To change more than one file attribute, simply repeat the p parameter, as required.

Attribute parameter	Purpose
+A	set archive bit
-A	clear archive bit
+H	set hidden-file bit
-H	clear hidden-file bit
+R	set read-only bit
-R	clear read-only bit
+S	set system-file bit
-S	clear system-file bit

The ATTRIB command can also be used to search out all occurrences of a certain filename, or all filenames that contain a common extension. For example, to search all subdirectories for files with an EXE extension, just type

```
ATTRIB \*.EXE /s
```

DEBUG Your Hex Math

The DEBUG utility has been around forever, and there's nothing new to report for DOS 5.0. However, there is an often overlooked feature that may help anyone who can't figure out how the sum of FE and DC is 1DA and the difference is 22 (or can't even figure out what all that means).

With DEBUG loaded, just type an H and follow it with any two hexadecimal numbers. When you press the Enter key, the next line reports the sum and difference of the numbers. Thus:

```
-H FE DC
01DA  0022
-
```

This can come in handy for those quick hex calculations that need to be done every once in awhile. However, there is one little caution. The answers are given only in four digits, thus the sum of say, F000 and 1000 (10000) is reported as 0000. So if any such value appears to be less than the sum of its parts, you need to append a hex 1 to the beginning of the number.

DIRectory Command Enhancements

Even the lowly old DIRectory command has been souped up with several new DOS 5.0 switches. In each case the format is as follows:

```
DIR /X:p
```

where X is the desired switch and p is some modifying parameter. To specify additional switches, simply repeat the /X as appropriate. Note that not all switches are followed by a parameter.

Attributes (/A:p)

This switch displays only those files whose attribute is specified by the letter following the colon. For example, use the following:

Attribute switch	Displays
/A:A	files ready for archiving (for backup)
/A:-A	files that have already been archived
/A:D	directory names only
/A:-D	filenames only (no subdirectories listed)
/A:H	hidden files
/A:-H	files that are not hidden
/A:R	read-only files
/A:-R	files that are not read-only
/A:S	system files
/A:-S	all files except system files
/A	all hidden, system and regular files

Bare (Show File Names only) (/B)

This switch displays a bare directory listing; that is, one in which only the filename and extension is displayed. If the /B switch is used together with /W (wide), the latter switch is ignored.

Search Subdirectories (/S)

The /S switch shows the contents of the current directory and all its subdirectories. Or you can use it to search for one or more files lost in the maze of directories and subdirectories. For example,

Search switch	Displays
/S	all directory and subdirectory listings
/S filename.ext	a specific file
/S WS*.*	all files beginning with WS
/S *.EXE	all files with an EXE extension

The search may be narrowed as required. For example, to search an entire drive, type the command from the root directory. Or, log onto any subdirectory to confine the search to just that directory and its own subdirectories. If the search switch finds the desired file or files, the directory containing the file(s) is displayed, followed by the names of the files. This is followed by the name of the next directory (if any) and its files, and so on until all occurrences of the searched item have been found.

The search switch is helpful for flushing out all the backup files that accumulate over time. Just log onto the root directory and type

```
DIR /S *.BAK
```

Or, type a specific filename to make sure that the same name does not exist in two separate locations.

Combination Bare Name and Search (/B/S)

When these two switches are both appended to the DIRectory command, each line displays the complete path name followed by the name (only) of the appropriate file.

Sort Order (/O:p)

The directory listings may be sorted as specified by a letter following the colon, as indicated here.

Sort switch	Directory is sorted
/O:D	by date and time; earliest first
/O:-D	by date and time; latest first
/O:E	alphabetically by extension
/O:-E	alphabetically by extension, in reverse order
/O:G	with directories grouped before filenames
/O:-G	with directories grouped after filenames
/O:N	alphabetically by filename
/O:-N	alphabetically by filename, in reverse order
/O:S	by size; smallest first
/O:-S	by size; largest first

Preset Directory Display

If you would like to use one or more of the above switches every time you execute the DIRectory command, simply add the *directory command* (DIRCMD) environment variable to your AUTOEXEC.BAT file. For example, to display your directory listings sorted in reverse alphabetical order, include hidden files, and pause when the screen is full, add the following line to the batch file.

```
SET DIRCMD=/O:-N/A/P
```

The next time the system is rebooted, the DIR command will display the directory listing as specified by SET DIRCMD.

Wide Directory Listing (/W)

When the DIR command is followed by the /W (wide) switch, all displayed directories are enclosed in square brackets, as shown in this sample line from a wide directory listing.

```
COMMAND.COM    [DOS]      [MACE]      GENS386.SYS    IBMCDROM.SYS
```

A DIRectory Search and Destroy Mission

The DIR command can be used in conjunction with the FIND command, to locate all filenames that contain a certain string. This can be quite handy for flushing out all those backup files that accumulate on your hard disk over time. For example, the following one-liner searches the root directory and all subdirectories on drive C for files with a BAK extension, and writes the complete path and filename for each such file into a new file named HITLIST.

```
DIR C:\ /S /B | FIND "BAK" > C:\HITLIST
```

The following QuickBASIC program will now erase every backup file whose name is in your HITLIST, after which it destroys the evidence by wiping out the HITLIST itself:

```
OPEN "C:\HITLIST" FOR INPUT AS #1
WHILE NOT EOF(1)
  INPUT #1, FILENAME$
  KILL FILENAME$
WEND
KILL "C:\HITLIST"
CLOSE #1: END
```

If you'd rather be asked if it's OK to kill each file, just replace the KILL FILENAME$ line above with the following two lines:

```
PRINT "OK to kill "; FILENAME$; : INPUT OK$
IF OK$ = "Y" OR OK$ = "y" THEN KILL FILENAME$
```

How Many Bytes?

As a final enhancement, the DOS 5.0 directory listing tallies up the bytes of all files in the current directory and gives that figure to the right of the number of files in the directory. The second line reports — as before — the number of free bytes remaining on the complete disk. Thus:

```
xx file(s)            xxxxx bytes
                    xxxxxxx bytes free
```

DOSKEY

When the DOSKEY utility is loaded, it maintains a record of your recent DOS commands, which may be recalled by pressing the up and down arrow keys or the page up and down keys. To use the utility, type either DOSKEY at the DOS prompt or add the command to your AUTOEXEC.BAT file.

After DOSKEY has been loaded, and several DOS commands have been issued, you can toggle through these commands by pressing one of the following keys:

Press this key	*To go*
Up arrow	to the previous command
Down arrow	to the next command
Page up	to the earliest command
Page down	to the latest command
Left arrow	back one character (nondestructive)
Right arrow	forward one character
Ctrl+Left arrow	back one word (nondestructive)
Ctrl+Right arrow	forward one word
Home	to the beginning of the line
End	to the end of the line
Escape key	clear the present command line

Repetitive presses of an up or down arrow key will toggle forward or backward through the entire list, one command at a time. When the first (or last) command is reached, the next keypress will return to the top (or bottom) of the list, and subsequent keypresses will again toggle through the list.

DOSKEY also lets you define keypress macros for repetitive tasks, or your own custom commands. If, for example, you just can't live without the Unix **ls** command,

```
DOSKEY ls=dir
```

will give you at least the illusion of being able to run part of Unix on your PC.

DRIVPARM

The default operating parameters of a block device can be changed by inserting a DRIVPARM (Drive Parameters) command in your configuration file. A *block device* is any mass storage device, such as a diskette or hard disk drive, or a tape drive, Bernoulli box, etc. The term is used because data is sent to and from such a device in blocks — generally, of 512 bytes.

The DRIVPARM command's /I switch supports a 3.5″ diskette drive in a PC whose ROM BIOS does not recognize this size device. Or, within certain limits, you can change drive capacity. For example, a 5.25″ 1.2Mb drive can be tricked into thinking it's a 360Kb or smaller capacity drive. Or, a 3.5″ 1.44Mb drive can be downgraded to 720Kb. Unfortunately, you can't convince a low-capacity drive to function at some higher capacity though.

The command line syntax is

```
DRIVPARM=/D:d /F:f /I
```

where

```
d     physical drive number (0 = drive A, 1 = drive B, etc.)
f     desired drive type
      0     160-360Kb              5.25"
      1     1.2Mb                  5.25"
      2     720Kb                  3.5"
      5     hard disk
      6     tape drive
      7     1.44Mb                 3.5"
      8     read/write optical disk
      9     2.88Mb                 3.5"


/I    specify a 3.5" drive, if not supported by ROM BIOS
```

Other DRIVPARM switches specify the number of heads (/H), sectors (/S) and tracks (/T).

If you attempt to trick say, a 1.44Mb drive into 2.88Mb capacity (nice try!), and then format a diskette in that drive, the following error message will be seen:

```
Formatting 2.88M
Parameters not supported by drive.
```

However, the DRIVPARM command may be useful if it becomes necessary to do a DISKCOPY operation between drives of the same size but of dissimilar capacities. It may also be used to revise the track and sector configuration of a tape drive.

EDIT

For those who need more editing power than is available in DOS EDLIN, DOS 5.0 offers a new full-screen editor for creating ASCII files. To begin editing, simply type EDIT, optionally followed by the name of the file you wish to edit. The EDIT utility recognizes keystroke combinations used by *Microsoft Word* and *WordStar*.

To use the maximum number of lines possible on your monitor display configuration, type EDIT /H at the DOS prompt. Once the editor is up and running, an extensive set of help screens is available to answer just about any question that might come up.

The EDIT utility requires the presence of the QBASIC.EXE file, which is also resident in the DOS subdirectory. So even if you have no plans to use QBASIC, don't erase it if you expect to use the editor. In any case, the remarks in the QBASIC section below about cursor shape in the insert mode apply to the EDIT utility, as well as to QBASIC.

EXPAND

Most of the files on the DOS 5.0 installation diskettes are in a compressed format. For each such file, the three-letter file name extension ends with an underline character; thus the compressed FORMAT.COM is listed as FORMAT.CO_, DRIVER.SYS is DRIVER.SY_, and so on. A compressed file is not directly executable; in order to run, it must first be expanded to its full size. This takes place automatically as DOS 5.0 installs itself, and in the process each underline is automatically replaced by the appropriate letter.

In the event of subsequent damage to, or loss of, a file, you can return to the DOS installation diskettes and expand just the file for which you need a fresh copy. Assuming the compressed file is on a diskette in drive A, and you want the expanded copy to be written into the DOS subdirectory on drive C, the command line syntax is:

```
EXPAND A:FILENAME.CO_ C:\DOS\FILENAME.COM
```

As just shown, the command expands one file at a time and must be repeated for each compressed program that you wish to expand. This is no big deal if you just want to expand a file or two, but you may prefer to run a batch file if you need to expand more than a few files. If so, create a batch file called X.BAT which contains the following lines:

```
FOR %%X IN (A:\*.EX_) DO EXPAND %%X C:\DOS
CD \DOS
RENAME *.EX_ *.EXE
```

The first line (which just about defies comprehension) really means the following:

1. Find the first file defined by (A:*.EX_). That is, a file on drive A whose extension is EX_.
2. FOR each such file (temporarily called "X") DO the following:
    EXPAND it (i.e., EXPAND %%X).
3. Write the expanded file to the C:\DOS subdirectory.

By comparison, the next two lines are a piece of cake: log onto the DOS subdirectory and change each file named *.EX_ to *.EXE.

To expand all compressed files on drive A, change the batch file expression in parentheses to (A:*.??_) and add a RENAME line for every other file category (RENAME *.CO_ *.COM, and so on).

Friendlier Formatting

The eight different diskette formats encountered in PC applications are listed below. Fortunately, not all are in wide use today: most 5.25" diskettes are now formatted at either 360Kb or 1.2Mb, with the first three configurations (160, 180, 320Kb) phased out in favor of the last two. Nevertheless, it may be necessary to format a 5.25" diskette at one of the lower capacities for use in someone's older machine.

For 3.5" diskettes, both 720Kb and 1.44Mb capacities are in wide use, with the 2.88Mb diskette expected to reach the market momentarily. It doubles the capacity of the 1.44Mb diskette by packing 36 sectors into the track, which probably makes it double-quadruple (octuple?) density. Such diskettes require a new diskette drive.

Capacity	Sides	Tracks /side	Sectors /track	Density	Use format size switch
5.25" diskettes					
160Kb	one	40	8	double	/f:160
180Kb	one	40	9	double	/f:180
320Kb	two	40	8	double	/f:320
360Kb	two	40	9	double	/f:360
1.2Mb	two	80	15	quadruple	/f:1200 or 1.2
3.5" diskettes					
720Kb	two	80	9	double	/f:720
1.44Mb	two	80	18	quadruple	/f:1440 or 1.44
2.88Mb	two	80	36		/f:2880 or 2.88

The Format of FORMAT

The FORMAT command must be followed by a drive letter parameter and optionally by one or more switches to modify the procedure as required for the specific application. In all cases, the command is written as

```
FORMAT A: /x /y /z
```

where x, y, z are replaced by the actual letter(s) required. Switches that are new to DOS 5.0 are described in the following sections.

Sizing Up the Format

The size switch listed above may be ignored for most routine operations, since the diskette is automatically formatted at the default capacity of the drive in use. However, when it becomes necessary to format a diskette at a capacity lower than that of the drive, then the switch must be appended to the format command line, as shown here.

```
FORMAT A: /f:xxxx
```

The /f:xxxx style of specifying the desired diskette capacity was introduced in DOS 4.0. For prior versions, it was necessary to append switches for tracks-per-side (/T:40, for example) and sectors-per-track (N:/8) data. The /f:2880 size is new to DOS 5.0, and requires a 2.88Mb diskette drive.

Some Format Size Cautions

Note that there are 40 tracks per side on all 5.25″ diskettes except the 1.2Mb diskette, which accommodates 80 tracks per side. In order to write 80 tracks in the same space formerly occupied by 40, the read/write head on a 1.2Mb drive is considerably narrower than the head on any other 5.25″ drive, and therefore is the written track on the diskette surface. This of course presents no problem when a 1.2Mb drive is used with a 1.2Mb diskette. But when such a drive formats a diskette to any other capacity, the diskette may not work properly in some non-1.2Mb drives. This is because the narrow diskette track width does not line up properly with the wide read/write head on the lower capacity drive. Therefore, before formatting a lot of 360Kb diskettes in a 1.2Mb drive, do one or two and try them out in the 360Kb drive. To be on the extra-safe side, at the first opportunity copy all critical files to another diskette that actually was formatted in a 360Kb drive.

Many 1.44Mb drives will format any 3.5″ diskette at either 720Kb or 1.44Mb. So it may seem like a bargain to buy 720Kb diskettes and format them at 1.44Mb. You may even get away with it for awhile. But, due to the different magnetic characteristics of the two types of diskette surfaces, there's a very good chance that your "1.44Mb" diskettes will eventually become unreadable. In which case, the bargain will not be such a bargain after all. So find some other way to save money, and buy the kind of diskettes you really need for the job at hand.

Safe Formatting

Effective with DOS 5.0, the default format mode is a "safe format," in which your stored programs, data files, etc. are not erased during the FORMAT operation. Instead, only the FAT (file allocation table) and the root directory are wiped clean. As a consequence, the entire disk surface appears to be (and in fact, is) ready to be reused. However, the "missing" data can be recovered by the UNFORMAT command, should you discover (it happens) that you really didn't mean to do that format in the first place.

The safe format features can be disabled — and formatting speeded up — by appending the /Q and/or /U switches after the FORMAT command, as shown here:

```
FORMAT A: /Q /U
```

If neither the /Q nor the /U switch is used, the disk is safe-formatted. The use of either switch modifies the operation as described below.

The /Q ("quick") Switch

This switch deletes the FAT and root directory, but saves this information elsewhere on the disk surface for subsequent use by the UNFORMAT utility. The data area is left intact, and the disk surface is not scanned for bad sectors. Therefore the /Q switch should be used only on a previously formatted surface that you know is in good shape. In fact, if the disk is brand new (unformatted) then an attempt to do a quick format will display the following error message:

```
Invalid existing format.
This disk cannot be Quickformatted.
Proceed with Unconditional Format (Y/N)?
```

The /Q switch also does not work with 160Kb and 320Kb diskettes that were previously formatted with DOS versions other than than MS-DOS 5.0.

The /U ("unconditional") Switch

This switch also deletes the FAT and root directory, but does not retain this information elsewhere for use by the UNFORMAT utility. The data area is likewise erased, and the disk surface is scanned for bad sectors. With all data deleted, the disk surface cannot be unformatted later on.

The /Q and /U Switches

To save even more formatting time, use both switches to reformat a diskette that is known to be in good shape. The /Q switch prevents the /U switch from erasing the data area, so data can be recovered by the UNFORMAT utility.

Safe Format Summary

The table below summarizes the effect of each switch on the FORMAT command.

Format switch	Saves unformat info	Checks for bad sectors	Wipes out program data
none	yes	yes	no
/Q	yes	no	no
/U	no	yes	yes
/Q /U	no	no	no

Note: These new DOS 5.0 switches make the FORMAT utility a bit more foolproof. Now you must go to the trouble of appending the /U (only) switch if you *really* want to do a thorough sector check and data erasure. Any other switch choice, including no switches at all, leaves you with a recoverable disk. In other words, this is the only option that performs a *complete* format procedure.

Use the /U switch to format a new diskette. With no previous information that needs to be saved, this cuts down on formatting time yet insures that the surface is good.

When a formatted disk is reformatted to a different configuration (size, sectors, tracks), the format is by default unconditional, since the track and sector layout must be rewritten to suit the new configuration. If you wish to do this, but do not use the /U switch, the following warning message will be seen before the format begins:

```
Existing format differs from that specified.
This disk cannot be unformatted.
Proceed with Format (Y/N)?
```

Add a Label

The FORMAT command's /V:label switch has been around since DOS 4.0, and it hasn't changed with DOS 5.0. It lets you enter the desired volume label at the beginning of the FORMAT procedure, and if you use it, you won't be prompted for a label later on. However, don't use the label switch if you're going to format more than one diskette, unless you want all the diskettes to have the same label. Or, if you don't mind "cheating," append the /V: switch to the FORMAT command anyway, then hold down the Alt key and type in 255 at the number keypad area of the keyboard. This gives each formatted diskette a "label" of one blank space, which should at least prevent one diskette from being confused with another later on.

Format Error Messages

If you attempt to format a disk that is almost full, the following error message may show up:

```
Drive B error. Insufficient space for the MIRROR image file.
There was an error creating the format recovery file.
This disk cannot be unformatted.
Proceed with Format (Y/N)?
```

Despite the sinister tone of the warning, you can still unformat the diskette later on by using the UNFORMAT command before writing new data. However, if you see this message in the first place, consider it a warning to stop for a closer look at the directory contents. Are you sure you want to consign everything to oblivion? If so, use the /Q and /U switches described above to provide your files with a quick and painless death.

If you wish to proceed with formatting, but want to maintain the option to unformat later on, answer *no* ("N" or "n") and make room for the UNFORMAT.DAT file by transferring a few files elsewhere. Then repeat the FORMAT instruction.

Help Screens

The DOSHELP.HLP file in the DOS subdirectory contains a brief description of each MS-DOS and batch command. To display this list, simply type HELP at the DOS prompt and press the Enter key.

For a more detailed help screen, type HELP, a space, and then the desired command name. Or for slightly faster assistance, type the command name first and follow it with the /? switch. For example, for help with the DIR command, type either

```
C>HELP DIR
```

or

```
C>DIR /?
```

to display the following help screen.

```
Displays a list of files and subdirectories in a directory.

DIR [drive:] [path] [filename] [/P] [/W] [/A[[:]attributes]]
   [/O[[:]sortorder]] [/S] [/B] [/L]

  [drive:] [path] [filename]
         Specifies drive, directory, and/or files to list.
  /P          Pauses after each screenful of information.
  /W          Uses wide list format.
  /A          Displays files with specified attributes.
  attributes  D  Directories          R  Read-only files
              H  Hidden files         A  Files ready for archiving
              S  System files         -  Prefix meaning "not"
  /O          List by files in sorted order.
  sortorder   N  By name (alphabetic)  S  By size (smallest first)
              E  By extension (alphabetic)  D  By date & time (earliest first)
              G  Group directories first  -  Prefix to reverse order
  /S          Displays files in specified directory and all subdirectories.
  /B          Uses bare format (no heading information or summary).
  /L          Uses lowercase.

Switches may be preset in the DIRCMD environment variable. Override
preset switches by prefixing any switch with - (hyphen) — for example, /-W.
```

When you type HELP plus the command name, DOS searches the DOSHELP.HLP file, and if it finds the name the complete help screen is displayed. For internal commands, the help screen information is read from the COMMAND.COM file. For external commands, the information resides in the external program itself. Thus, the DIR help screen is embedded in COMMAND.COM, while the debug utility's help screen is an integral part of the DEBUG.EXE program.

If the desired command name is not listed in the DOSHELP file, then a "Help not available for this command" message is seen and DOS does not bother looking for a help screen. The message may mean help is indeed not available, or simply that DOS didn't find the command name in DOSHELP.HLP, as is the case with the undocumented TRUENAME command (described below).

To bypass the search through DOSHELP.HLP, simply type the command name first, followed by the /? switch. This sends DOS directly to COMMAND.COM or to the appropriate external file to display the appropriate help screen. In the case of TRUENAME, the help screen ("Reserved command name") still isn't much help though.

MIRROR

The new DOS 5.0 MIRROR.COM utility is a TSR program that saves disk-recovery data for subsequent use by the UNFORMAT and UNDELETE commands that are described below. For example, to keep track of future deletions on a diskette in drive B, simply type MIRROR B: /TB at the DOS prompt (no colon after the drive letter following the /T switch). This creates a read-only MIRROR.FIL file on the diskette and, the next time you delete a file on that diskette, file-recovery data is written to a hidden PCTRACKR.DEL on the diskette. The screen displays are shown here.

```
B:\>MIRROR A: /TA


Creates an image of the system area.
Drive A being processed.
The MIRROR process was successful.
Deletion-tracking software being installed.


The following drives are supported;
Drive A - Default files saved.
Installation complete.
```

With MIRROR in place, recovery from an accidental FORMAT or DELETE (or ERASE) is considerably faster and less susceptible to error. If the MIRROR command line is written into your AUTOEXEC.BAT file, then every time the system is booted, MIRROR saves a copy of the file allocation table and root directory for the specified drive(s). The information is written to a read-only file named MIRORSAV.FIL.

Saving Partition Information

The MIRROR utility can also save hard disk partition information to a diskette for subsequent use by the UNFORMAT utility, should the need arise. To use this feature, type the following command at the DOS prompt:

```
MIRROR /PARTN
```

Now press the Enter key to display the following message:

```
The partition information from your hard disk drive(s) has been read.

Next, the file PARTNSAV.FIL will be written to a floppy disk.  Please
insert a formatted diskette and enter the name of the diskette drive.
What drive? A
```

Assuming drive A is correct, press the Enter key. Or type in some other drive letter. The PARTNSAV.FIL file is written to the diskette in the designated drive, and "Successful" is displayed on screen. It's a good idea to make frequent use of this feature, as a regular part of your disaster insurance program. For further details, refer to "Rebuilding a Partition Table" in the Unformat section below.

Quick! Where's the BASIC?

The old familiar GWBASIC has been replaced by *Microsoft's QuickBASIC Interpreter*. The DOS 5.0 QBASIC program offers many of the features of *Microsoft*'s complete QuickBASIC program, although it is not possible to compile the BASIC programs created with the interpreter. For that, you'll need to buy the complete program, which is sold separately.

To delete line numbers from a program written under the earlier GWBASIC, load QBASIC and then run the included REMLINE.BAS program. Many programs change the cursor shape from its standard blinking underline to a horizontal rectangle as a visual cue that the insert mode is enabled. In this mode text may be inserted into a line without overstriking whatever is already there. Instead, characters to the right of the cursor simply move right to make room for the inserted text. Although QBASIC also offers this facility, it keeps you on your toes by reversing the de facto cursor standard: a blinking underline indicates the (default) insert mode, while a *vertical* rectangle appears when the insert mode is disabled.

Note that the new DOS 5.0 EDIT utility requires the presence of the QBASIC.EXE file. So, even if you have no plans to use QBASIC, don't erase it unless you also don't want the EDIT utility.

SETVER

Once DOS 5.0 is installed, if an application displays a "Wrong DOS version" error message, the SETVER command can be used to modify a DOS version table stored in the MSDOS.SYS hidden file. To view the existing table, type SETVER without any parameters and press the Enter key. This displays a table of existing programs and the DOS version required for each one, as shown by the following table excerpts:

```
EXCEL.EXE        4.10
MSCDEX.EXE       4.00
IBMCACHE.SYS     3.40
NET.COM          3.00
METRO.EXE        3.31
```

If your version of say, WHATEVER.EXE demands DOS 3.10, you can add this information to the table by entering the following command:

```
SETVER WHATEVER.EXE 3.10
```

To make sure you're properly impressed by the gravity of fooling around with version numbers, the following message is displayed:

```
WARNING - The application you are adding to the MS-DOS version table
may not have been verified by Microsoft on this version of MS-DOS.
Please contact your software vendor for information on whether this
application will operate properly under this version of MS-DOS.
If you execute this application by instructing MS-DOS to report a
different MS-DOS version number, you may lose or corrupt data, or
cause system instabilities. In that circumstance, Microsoft is not
responsible for any loss or damage.

Version table successfully updated. The version change will take
effect the next time you restart your system.
```

To verify that the table has indeed been updated, type SETVER again and press the Enter key to display the revised table. Note that although the above warning message indicates that the change has already been written to the version table, you must reboot the system in order for it to take effect. So if you decide you don't want to keep the change in the table, delete it before rebooting by typing

```
SETVER WHATEVER.EXE /DELETE
```

Note: Although SETVER modifies the version table hidden within itself, neither the length of the file nor its file creation date are changed.

SETVER and Virus Detection Utilities

Some some virus detection utilities display a warning message if a file has been recently modified, while others monitor the system files for tampering. Since the SETVER command modifies the SETVER.EXE file, such utilities will either report this file as a as a possible suspect for virus infection, or warn you of impending attack as SETVER is about to revise the version table.

If virus detection is a consideration, you may want to run a routine virus check before using the SETVER command, to make sure no files are corrupted. Then, use the SETVER utility as required and follow it up by immediately running the virus check once again, this time ignoring the warning message; or if an online virus detection utility prevents SETVER from doing its work, temporarily disable it until SETVER is finished.

The SHELL Game

For the DOSaphobic computer user, the big news about DOS 4.0 was the brand-new shell. If you just couldn't handle long, involved, exacting DOS commands, and didn't like the idea of facing a blank screen each time you started up, the shell did away with all that. You'd never again have to stare at a DOS prompt unless you really wanted to.

The Shell can indeed make hours at the keyboard far less intimidating for anyone who refuses to crack the manual. Once you learn which keys control what operations, you'll be amazed at how easy it is to to run, print, move, copy, delete, rename, view or sort just about anything. Yet the Shell isn't for everyone. Yes, it can make life easier for the casual user, the beginner and the confirmed DOS hater. But if you're reading this book, you may not want or need it, although you should know how to configure it and what it can do in case you have to set things up for a DOS novice.

The Shell can do a few things that DOS alone can't do, such as renaming subdirectories. In the pre-Shell era you had to go through a four-step ritual: 1. Create a new subdirectory, 2. Copy the old subdirectory files into it, 3. Delete the files in the old subdirectory, and 4. Remove the now-empty old subdirectory. Five minutes of nuisance work just to rename a subdirectory. And if you made a mistake during the copying process, you could actually wipe out all your files by concatenating them into one big useless file.

Installing the Shell

During the initial DOS 5.0 installation procedure, a DOSSHELL line is inserted into your AUTOEXEC.BAT file, unless you chose not to select this option, as described earlier in this chapter in the DOS 5.0 installation section. If the Shell is not automatically loaded during bootup, you can start it from the DOS prompt at any time simply by typing DOSSHELL and pressing the Enter key.

In either case, the first screen you'll see is the MSDOS Shell screen shown in Figure 2.2. The screen is divided into several sections.

Menu Bar

This is a single line across the top of the screen which lists the available menus. On startup the listed menus are; File, Options, View, Tree and Help. Press the *Actions* function key (F10) to gain access to these menu options. When you do, the File option is highlighted,

```
                    Starting address
              segment    decimal        contents*
              in hex      in Kb      begin extended memory

                         1024
              FC00        100
              F800        992        ■ BIOS      ■ BASIC
              F400        976
              F000        960
              EC00        944
              E800        928
              E400        912
              E000        896
              DC00        880
              D800        864        ■ LIM XMS    ░ token ring
              D400        848
              D000        832
              CC00        816        ■ token ring
              C800        800        ■ XT hard disk  ■ ESDI controller
              C400        784
              C000        768        ■ EGA        ■ VGA
              BC00        752
              B800        736                     ░ C/GA
              B400        720
              B000        704                     _ MDA (4Kb)
              A000        640        ░ VGA, MCGA

              8000        512
              6000        384        ░ Conventional**
              4000        256          memory area
              2000        128
              0000        000

              *   Each line = 16Kb
              **  Each line = 128Kb

              ■ = ROM;  ░ = RAM
```

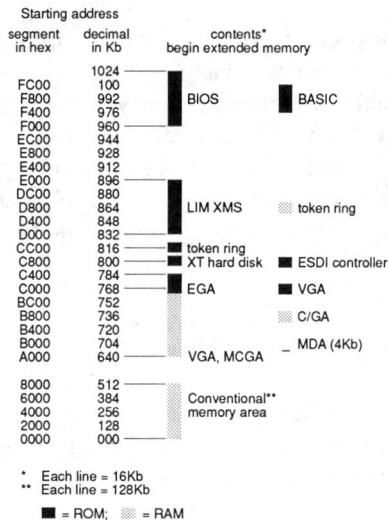

Figure 2.2.   MS DOS Shell Screen

and you can toggle through all the others by pressing the Tab key or using a mouse if one is installed.

As a typical example, wander over to Options, press the Enter key to view the pull-down Options menu, and select *Colors*. You can do this in one of three ways: drag the mouse down to Colors, or type the letter "o" (as in cOlors), or hit the down arrow key a few times to move the highlight bar to Colors and then press the Enter key. In any case, you'll see a menu of screen colors, including those perennial favorites, Hot Pink, Emerald City and Turquoise. If you're leery (you should be) about any of these decorator delights, preview it by toggling over to the Preview bar. Then take two Excedrin and go back to one of the other selections.

Drive Selector

Immediately below the Menu Bar is the name of the current directory, followed by a list of all your active drive letters. The current drive letter is highlighted.

Directory Tree

Just below the Drive Selector area, the left side of the screen shows the directory tree for the current drive. The tree is pruned though: it only shows the first level of subdirectories within the current directory. If any of these contain subdirectories of their own, a plus sign shows up within the brackets to the immediate left of the name. To view the next level of subdirectories, toggle down to one of these plus signs and press the + key. Or press Ctrl-Shift-Asterisk to light up the complete directory tree. As you toggle through the directory tree, the File List to the right of the screen shows the filenames in the selected directory.

File List

The area to the immediate right of the Directory Tree shows the first eight files within the current directory.

Program List Area

On start up, the bottom half of the screen shows a "Main" menu listing of four options: Command prompt, Editor, MS-DOS QBasic and [Disk Utilities]. The brackets around the latter option indicate that it leads to additional options. These are disk copying, backup and restore, quick and regular format and undelete.

Perhaps the biggest attraction of the DOS Shell is that it gives a reasonably clear map of the total system, which is certainly a lot more informative than staring at a DOS prompt and wondering what's really out there. Given a mouse or some hands-on experience navigating the Shell via the keyboard, it's quite easy to get from anywhere to just about anywhere else in the system. On the other hand, you can get there a lot faster from the DOS prompt, provided you know where you want to go in the first place.

If you're still feeling your way around your PC, or around DOS 5.0, stick with the Shell for awhile. You'll know when it's time to seek out the DOS prompt. In the meantime, don't overlook the possibilities of task-swapping.

Task Swapping

If you need multitasking, you'll just have to switch to OS/2. Oh yeah? Before you chuck DOS, select Options and toggle on down to *Enable Task Swapper*. When you enable the option, the Active Task List in the lower right-hand quadrant of the screen lists the programs you want to run simultaneously. Assuming there are not yet any names in the list, just start any program by highlighting its name in the appropriate subdirectory and pressing the Enter key. While the program is running, press Ctrl+Esc to return to the DOS Shell. The name of the program should now be seen in the Active Task List. Now start some other program.

To return to the first program, hold down the Alt key, press the Tab key once but do *not* release the Alt key. The screen clears, and a bar at the top lists a program name or MS-DOS Shell. Press the Tab key a few times to toggle through the available selections (which come from your Active Task List). When you see the desired name at the top of the screen, release the Alt key, and that program starts running. Now use the Alt and Tab keys to switch back and forth between programs. (It takes a bit of practice.)

To remove a program from the active list, simply exit the program in the usual manner. The program name disappears from the Active Task List. Or, you can Tab over to the Active Task List, select the program you want to delete, and press the Delete key. If the program happens to be active, you will be warned about a potential data loss. You can either return to the program and make an orderly exit, or bail out from here anyway.

You can also add a program to your active list by selecting its name and pressing Shift+Enter. The name shows up on the active list and the program can be run as just described.

To disable the Task Swapper, first delete all programs from the Active Task List, then select Options and again move down to *Enable Task Swapper*. When you press the Enter key, the now-empty Active Task List is deleted from your screen.

Undeleting a Deletion

File destruction need not always be wholesale: it's just as easy to accidentally erase just a file or two with the FORMAT command. In this case, the DOS 5.0 UNDELETE command comes in handy. For example, let's say you've just erased COMMAND.COM from drive C, and that the MIRROR utility is in place. Let's see what happens when you simply type UNDELETE. The screen display will look like this:

```
Directory: C:\
File Specifications: *.*

Deletion-tracking file contains    1 deleted files.
Of those,    1 files have all clusters available,
             0 files have some clusters available,
             0 files have no clusters available.

MS-DOS directory contains    1 deleted files.
Of those,    1 files may be recovered.

Using the deletion-tracking file.

    COMMAND  COM    47845  3-22-01  5:10a  ...A  Deleted: (date and time)
All of the clusters for this file are available. Undelete (Y/N)?Y

File successfully undeleted.
```

If the MIRROR utility had not been loaded, then the final lines of the screen display would look like this:

```
    ?OMMAND  COM    47845  3-22-01  5:10a  ...A  Undelete (Y/N)?Y
    Please type the first character for ?OMMAND .COM: C

File successfully undeleted.
```

The /L (list) switch can be used with UNDELETE to simply display a list of all files and subdirectories found by the UNFORMAT utility.

Unformatting a Format

If you've ever lost important files by accidentally formatting a diskette, you'll appreciate DOS 5.0's new UNFORMAT command, which restores such information, provided certain conditions are met. The diskette must have been previously formatted under DOS 5.0's default "safe format" mode, in which information essential to file recovery is preserved for future use. And, you must not have written new files to the disk before attempting the unformat procedure.

Assuming the MIRROR utility is active, you can unformat your diskette by simply typing

```
UNFORMAT A:
```

You'll see a screen display that looks like this:

```
Restores the system area of your disk by using the image file created
by the MIRROR command.

WARNING !!          WARNING !!

This command should be used only to recover from the inadvertent use of
the FORMAT command or the RECOVER command. Any other use of the UNFORMAT
command may cause you to lose data! Files modified since the MIRROR image
file was created may be lost.

Searching disk for MIRROR image.

The last time the MIRROR or FORMAT command was used was at (time) on (date).
The prior time the MIRROR or FORMAT command was used was at (time) on (date).

If you wish to use the last file as indicated
above, press L. If you wish to use the prior
file as indicated above, press P. Press ESC
to cancel UNFORMAT.
L


The MIRROR image file has been validated.
Are you sure you want to update the system area of your drive B (Y/N)? Y

The system area of drive B has been rebuilt.
You may have to restart the system.
```

Type DIR B: to display your directory listings. If all went well, all the files in your root directory and subdirectories are recovered.

A Worst-Case Unformat

Now let's assume that Edsel Murphy has been "helping" you maintain your system. You have a critical diskette that was formatted with the /Q *and* the /U switches, so although the data area is not erased, the FAT and directory listings have not been saved. And of course you forgot to use the MIRROR utility. Well, all is not lost (yet). Retry the UNFORMAT command with the /U switch. Whatever this /U stands for (the manual doesn't say), it permits UNFORMAT to work (slowly, very slowly) in the absence of the MIRROR file. However, only your subdirectories and the files contained therein will be recovered. Files in the root directory remain lost.

The following example shows the various screen displays when the /U switch is used to unformat a diskette in drive B.

```
UNFORMAT B: /U


Insert disk to rebuild in drive B:
and press ENTER when ready.


  CAUTION !!
This attempts to recover all the files lost after a
format, assuming you've not been using the MIRROR command.
This method cannot guarantee complete recovery of your files.


The search-phase is safe: nothing is altered on the disk.
You will be prompted again before changes are written to the disk.


Using drive B:

Are you sure you want to do this?
If so, press Y; anything else cancels.
?Y


Searching disk...
100% searched, 2 subdirectories found.
Files found in the root: 0
Subdirectories found in the root: 2


Walking the directory tree to locate all files...
Path=B:\


Path=B:\SUBDIR.1\
(the recovered subdirectory 1 contents appear here)


Path=B:\SUBDIR.2\
(the recovered subdirectory 2 contents appear here)


Path=B:\
```

```
Files found: xx
Warning!  The next step writes changes to disk.

Are you sure you want to do this?
If so, press Y; anything else cancels.
? Y


Checking for file fragmentation...
Path=B:\
Path=B:\SUBDIR.1\
Path=B:\
Path=B:\SUBDIR.2\
Path=B:\
xx files recovered.


Operation completed.
```

Type DIR B: to see what your unformatted diskette looks like. Since the prior FORMAT did not save the root directory and MIRROR was not in use, no files in your root directory are recovered and your subdirectories have lost their original names and are now labeled SUBDIR.1, SUBDIR.2, and so on. It's not great, but it's better than losing the whole works.

Rebuilding a Partition Table

The UNFORMAT utility may also be employed to restore a corrupted hard disk partition table. To do so, type UNFORMAT /PARTN at the DOS prompt. You will be prompted to insert the diskette containing PARTNSAV.FIL into drive A. (See "Saving Partition Information" in the MIRROR section above for details on the PARTNSAV.FIL file.).

With the PARTNSAV.FIL diskette in place, press the Enter key to display a summary of the partition table that will be rebuilt on your hard drive, such as the one shown here.

```
Partition information was saved by MIRROR 6M, (date and time)
Old partition information for fixed disk # 1 (DL=80h)
```

		Total_size		Start_partition			End_partition			
Type		Bytes	Sectors	Cyl	Head	Sector	Cyl	Head	Sector	Rel#
DOS16	Boot	32M	65504	0	1	1	31	63	32	32
DOS16		30M	61408	32	1	1	61	63	32	32
DOS16		30M	61408	62	1	1	91	63	32	32
DOS16		23M	47072	92	1	1	114	63	32	32

```
Options: Q - quit, take no action.
         1 - restore partition records for fixed disk # 80h.
Which option?
```

To continue, press the 1 key. You will be asked if you're really sure this is what you want to do. If so, type YES and again press the Enter key to actually do the restoration. When the operation is completed, press the Enter key one more time to reboot the system.

DOS Documented and Otherwise, or, When All Else Fails, Read the Manual

Not the least attraction of DOS 5.0 is its entirely new documentation, some of which is actually written in English. Here's a brief overview of what you'll find.

DOS 5.0 User's Guide And Reference.

This 600+ page manual is divided into the following sections:

Part 1 MS-DOS Fundamentals
1   Learning About Your Computer
2   Command-Line Basics
3   MS-DOS Shell Basics
Part 2 Working with MS-DOS
4   Working with Files
5   Working with Directories
6   Managing Disks
7   Advanced Command Techniques
8   Customizing MS-DOS Shell
9   Working with MS-DOS Editor
Part 3 Customizing MS-DOS
10   Working with Batch Programs
11   Customizing Your System
12   Optimizing Your System
13   Customizing for International Use
Part 4 MS-DOS Reference
14   Commands
15   Device Drivers
Appendixes
A   Keyboards and Their Codes
B   Messages
Index

Perhaps the best feature of the *User's Guide and Reference* is its "Commands" chapter (14), which includes just about everything you need to know for daily operations. Listed alphabetically are all the DEBUG and EDLIN parameters, batch commands, FORMAT instructions and, of course, all the routine DOS commands. The layout will come as blessed relief to users upgrading from IBM's DOS 4.0 manual, in which it was almost impossible to find anything without consulting the index first.

For further information about various commands, the cross-referencing to earlier chapters is good but not great. For example, the DOS command in Chapter 14 suggests that, "For an introduction to using the DOS command and reserved memory, see Chapter 12." Needless to say, there are no headings in that chapter for either the DOS command or for reserved memory. No doubt the information is buried in there somewhere (it's a big chapter) but you'll have to do a page-by-page search to ferret it out. Once you do find it, mark the DOS section of Chapter 12 accordingly, in case you need to find it again later.

The front of the book information is extensive, but could be better organized — you'll need to do a lot of skipping around to find all you need to know about any topic. Again, make your own marks as you go, for future reference. At the back of the book many error messages don't show up in the "Messages" appendix (B), and the index still needs some work.

Well, software documentation is *supposed* to be difficult to read, if only to make books like *DOS Power Tools* so valuable. But as such tomes go, the *Microsoft User's Guide and Reference* is a cut or two above much of the competition, if not yet up there with Herman Melville and friends.

Don't forget to README

In addition to the *User's Guide*, don't overlook the README, APPNOTES, UMB and any other text files found in the DOS subdirectory — look for files with a TXT extension. Here you'll find the latest information on changes that didn't make it into the regular documentation, up-to-date notes on various hardware compatibility issues, memory management details, and so on.

The Packing List

Another bit of documentation is the PACKING.LST file found on one of the DOS 5.0 distribution diskettes. This uncompressed file shows the names of all the programs on the entire set of diskettes. For the benefit of users who will install DOS 5.0 on diskettes, PACKING.LST also shows the correct contents for each diskette that will be made during the installation.

Neither list of filenames is in alphabetical order, which is no big deal unless you refer to the list frequently, in which case it's a nuisance. If you want to sort the list for easier access, first make a copy of that part which lists the distribution diskette files. Using your word processor, search for every hard carriage return symbol and replace it with a tab *and* a return symbol. Now move the cursor down to the first filename on the last diskette. Replace every tab return pair with tab-(x)-return, where x is the number of the last diskette. Now move up to the next-to-last diskette and do it again, but this time make x the number of that diskette. Repeat the procedure for each diskette in the list. When you're finished, sort the list. The result should look something like this:

```
5202.cp_        (5)
ansi.sy_        (2)
```

```
append.ex_      (5)
appnotes.txt    (6)
assign.co_      (5)
attrib.ex_      (5)
autoexec.bat    (1)
backup.ex_      (5)
cga.gr_         (3)
```

and so on. The number in parentheses is of course the diskette on which the listed file is found.

The Undocumented Side of DOS

Psst, want to look at something you're not supposed to see? It's easy, if you enjoy a little detective work. It's the kind of snooping every experienced user does if there's even the slightest hint of undocumented goodies lying within the latest version of DOS. The trick is first to find one of them, and then to figure out what to do with it.

The first part is easy. DOS comes with two kinds of commands, external and internal. The external commands are the ones you see in the DOS directory — all those standalone programs with the COM and EXE extensions, such as CHKDSK.COM or XCOPY.EXE. To run any one of these, all you need do is type its name (minus the extension) and hit the Enter key — that is, assuming the program with that name is in the current directory, or that your PATH control knows where to find it.

However, the names of important commands such as DIR, COPY, RENAME, ERASE — as well as batch file commands like GOTO, ERRORLEVEL and IF — don't show up in the DOS directory at all. Instead, the main COMMAND.COM file contains both the name and the instruction code for each of these commands. Hence, they're referred to as internal commands, and DOS stores them in a *dispatch table* at the very end of the COMMAND.COM file.

All internal commands have priority over external commands and batch files with the same name. So unless you know a little trick (add a .\ prefix), you'll never be able to run a batch file called DIR.BAT, since DOS will find its internal DIR command first and never even get to your DIR.BAT file.

If you want to see COMMAND.COM's table of internal commands, just type DEBUG \COMMAND.COM and then type the lines below that start with DEBUG's hyphen prompt. The intervening lines are displayed in response to your instructions.

```
-S 100 fffe "PATH=PROMPT"
xxxx:A7A3
xxxx:E003

-D A7A3
```

What all this means is that you've instructed DEBUG to search for the "PATH=PROMPT" string, which it finds at the two locations beginning with xxxx. In the last (-D) line, you're telling DEBUG to display the first occurrence of that string, which happens to mark the beginning of COMMAND.COM's dispatch table. You should see the string on the right-hand side of the screen, followed by some meaningless (to you, that is) characters and a lot of periods.

Now alternately press D and the Enter key a few times to move through the complete table. Interspersed amongst all the meaningless characters, you'll see NOT, ERRORLEVEL, EXIST, DIR, CALL and all the other internal commands. Keep an eye out for words you don't recall seeing before. Like TRUENAME.

So, now you know there's this new DOS command called TRUENAME, but with no documentation you don't know what it does. Unless you're an absolute DOS DEBUG demon, now's the time to bail out of DEBUG. Press Q and the Enter key to return to the DOS prompt.

Well, go ahead and get it over with: type TRUENAME at the DOS prompt and see what happens.

Nothing. It turns out that the command only does something after you've used SUBST, ASSIGN or JOIN. Taking SUBST as an easy example, it's used to assign a single drive letter to a long subdirectory path, as in SUBST H: C:\LETTERS\FINANCE\MARCH

From now on, whenever you need access to

```
C:\LETTERS\FINANCE\MARCH, simply log onto drive H instead.
```

But what is drive H's true name? Just type TRUENAME H: to find out. As you may suspect by now, you'll see the C:\LETTERS (etc.) line displayed on screen. So, it turns out that TRUENAME can help sort through the confusion generated by SUBST and the other two DOS "alias" commands, ASSIGN and JOIN.

SUBST can fool old *dBASE* or early *WordStar* programs into loading their overlay files from a subdirectory instead of a diskette, and it lets you put a single drive letter instead of a long search path into your PATH and APPEND strings. Besides, it's a lot easier to switch back and forth between \PROGRAMS\NEW\WORDPROC\MSWORD and \DOS\UTILS\DISK\TOOLS by referring to them as drives M and T.

ASSIGN will soothe a cranky application that insists on having certain files on diskettes in drives A or B. And with JOIN, files in different locations can be treated as if they were all in one place.

All this can be useful. But if you're doing too much of it at 3:00 AM and you make backup copies or delete files without thinking about what you're doing, you can really screw things up. In this case, TRUENAME comes to the rescue by reporting the real identity of each drive or subdirectory. For example, if you're logged onto drive T and can't remember what it really is, just type TRUENAME and press the Enter key. You'll be reminded that drive T is your \DOS\UTILS\DISK\TOOLS subdirectory. Or if you're elsewhere at the moment when uncertainty strikes, type TRUENAME followed by the drive letter in question and a colon. Again, TRUENAME gives you the information you need.

Very nice, but why is there no documentation in either DOS 4.0 where TRUENAME was introduced, or in DOS 5.0? Well, there's an old saying that

> *Hardware folks work from dawn 'til setting sun,*
> *But a programmer's job is* never *done.*

There's always some little bit of code that wants tweaking, or an exotic bug that needs to be sprayed. Most of the time the programmers get all the kinks out (well, most of the kinks) before the software is released. If a feature isn't working just right yet, it can be disabled before the production runs, yet the feature's instruction code may remain in place, even though the feature itself is not quite ready to be brought to the public's attention.

It wasn't always like this. In the early days, some software actually went out the door with known bugs crawling around inside. Today, this doesn't usually happen. Or if it does, the manual carries lots of warnings not to do the thing that still has the bug.

TRUENAME *seems* to work well, and if there are bugs they're rather well-behaved (so far). Since it wasn't entirely disabled, maybe it won't cause havoc. But then again, maybe it will. So if you're the overly cautious type, don't tempt the fates by invoking its name. But if your files are all backed up (really), and you like to live dangerously, well . . .

Beyond 5.0

It seems that every time you pick up a computer publication, the guru-de-jour is predicting the imminent demise of DOS. It's possible to make a strong case for a slick multitasking operating system with a friendly front end, but OS/2 isn't it. It's also easy to make a case for something as friendly and intuitive and technologically dazzling as the Mac or the NeXT machine, but the massive body of DOS software offers a tenfold quantity advantage over the software for those two sexy systems put together. And people buy their hardware because of the software. It's even possible to consider an interim step like some of the new and markedly improved *Windows* versions, but if you're interested in a GUI (Graphical User Interface), Apple does it better.

The truth is that the huge base of IBM-compatible systems isn't one market; it's three. At the beginning of the 1990s, according to Microsoft chairman Bill Gates, there were over 40 million DOS machines in use. One market comprises several million high-priced, high-end corporate systems stuffed with expensive peripherals that let their users talk to mainframes all day. There's another market of systems used for education, impressing office visitors, and letting the kids zap aliens. This might include a subset of a few million doddering antiques and closet dwellers. But take all that away from Bill's 40 million DOSers and you're still left with a nice little core market of 20 to 30 million serious average users.

Many of these folks struggle along as best they can, avoiding anything tricky and running batch files set up by someone else a long time ago. These low-current users are intimidated by the hardware and software documentation, and are reluctant to spend whatever time it might take to become power users. Which is unfortunate.

But these millions of users do have a lot of investment tied up in their DOS. They or their companies have spent a bundle of bucks to buy hardware and software. Even more important, they've spent their own time learning how to copy files, format disks, start a program, load data and do all the dozens of chores we all face daily. Is this megagroup suddenly going to chuck it all and run to OS/2? Not likely.

The real tragedy is that DOS *is* extremely powerful and flexible, if you know just the right tricks and have just the right tools. But the DOS manual is no great teaching aid, and DOS sometimes doesn't provide the tools anyway, although DOS 5.0 certainly goes a long way to remedy both ills. But of course there is still much that needs to be done. For example, should one really have to deal with crotchety IF ERRORLEVEL syntax; and shouldn't DOS provide at least one program for returning ERRORLEVEL codes? Why even give this powerful feature an intimidating name like ERRORLEVEL? Even though it can be used to report whether your formatting operation ran into trouble, it's vastly more useful as an interactive tool.

Some programmers hate DOS because it doesn't give them all the memory they need for fat, sloppy code or slapping on tons of flashy features. On the other hand, other programmers like DOS because they can write tight, efficient Assembly Language code (which you really can't do as easily with OS/2), and because their programs can communicate directly to the hardware.

Face it — DOS is never going to be OS/2. But at least for a while, neither is OS/2. Software upgrades have to be vastly better than their predecessors, or users just can't be bothered. Until someone can demonstrate that a hot new operating system is significantly better, the millions of DOS users will remain faithful.

In the future, DOS will get even friendlier and more tractable, but it's never going to be a slick multitasking protected mode system with decent interprocess communications, terrific memory management, and an awesome interface.

Go back and read that last sentence again. It was taken word-for-word from the previous version of *DOS Power Tools, Second Edition.* So if you've read this chapter carefully, you may want to suggest that a writer must never say "never." DOS 5.0 has chipped its way into multitasking, memory management is much improved, and the interface — if not totally awesome — is at least much improved.

But do most users really need even more than this? Only if new applications suddenly arrive that blow today's software into the weeds and don't run under DOS. This hasn't happened, and it probably won't for a few years. Besides, DOS works on just about anything from an old PC-1 to a pocket machine to the newest high-end hardware. OS/2 doesn't want to play on any of the 8088 and 8086 systems.

If you really need to run several huge programs concurrently and swap data from one to the other, and you have a sufficiently new system, try OS/2. But if you're like most users, you'll benefit even more — at least for the next few years — by learning how to tame DOS and add powerful tools to it. This book shows you how.

Disk Organization, Files, Filenames

The first thing most users do when they walk over to a computer equipped with a hard disk is type DIR to see what's there. On a well-organized system you'll probably see something like:

```
Volume in drive C is WORKDISK
Volume Serial Number is 104F-16CD
Directory of C:\

COMMAND  COM    37637   6-17-88  12:00p
CONFIG   SYS       47  10-18-90   7:07a
AUTOEXEC BAT      256  10-18-90  12:01a
DOS        <DIR>       10-18-90   7:09a
WORDSTAR   <DIR>       11-06-90  12:22a
DBASE      <DIR>        2-11-90  12:00a
LOTUS      <DIR>       12-03-90  12:02a

    7 File(s) 28220672 bytes free
```

However, try this on a disorganized floppy disk system and you'll see a real mess:

```
Volume in drive A has no label
Volume Serial Number is 104F-16CD
Directory of A:\
```

```
        TF86_CDY RPT       65387    1-01-80    7:07a
        TF86_CDY BAK       54396    1-01-80   12:01a
        RRXWFEB7 4QS        6754    1-01-80    7:07a
        FIN_54TT RPT       11239    1-01-80   11:01p
        SPELLIT          <DIR>      1-01-80   12:02a
        PROSEWIZ EXE       86456    4-17-87    9:54p
        FIN_54TT BAK        9437    1-01-80    5:07p
        COMMAND  COM       37637    6-17-88   12:00p
        AUTOEXEC BAT         256    1-01-80   12:01a
          .
          .
          .
        etc.
```

When you type DIR and press the Enter key, DOS shows you what's in the directory that you happen to be using. Directories are storage bins, like drawers in a file cabinet. Just as some file cabinets prevent you from opening more than one file drawer at once, you can look at the contents of only one directory at a time. Each line in the main part of a DIR listing represents either a single file stored in that directory, or the name of another related directory on the same disk.

And just as some well-organized workers keep their file cabinets in meticulous shape and can find any document in seconds, while others live in the shadow of chaos and can't find anything without tedious searching, disks can be well-organized or in total disarray. Fortunately, once you know the basic techniques and have a few powerful programs handy, your computer can do all the organizing for you. This book will show you the tricks and provide the programs you need.

The Physical Disk

All diskettes and hard disks use the same basic technology. The surface of each is coated with a material that can store lots of isolated magnetic charges. An electromagnetic coil of wire or special "stepping" motor propels a tiny magnetic *read-write head* over the surface of the disk. When you want to store information, you tell a controller circuit to move the magnetic head to an unused part of the disk, then send signals into the head that alter the magnetic charges on a small adjacent area of the surface. When you want to retrieve information, you have the controller move the head to the appropriate area and tell the head to sniff out the pattern of magnetic charges located there.

It's actually a lot more complicated than this. When you issue a command, something has to interpret your typing and figure out what you're trying to do. If it determines that you want to load a program, it has to decipher the name and location of the file, and look on the appropriate disk to make sure it's there. Files are normally stored in small chunks scattered over the surface of the disk, and something has to thread all the chunks together, then find an unused area in memory and copy the chunks there in the right order. At this point things get even more complex, since something has to rope off the area of memory that holds the program, set up other memory areas for storage, see if you entered any parameters after the name of the program that need processing, and pass control to the program.

Fortunately, DOS handles all the details. All you have to do is type in the filename and press Enter.

Individual floppy disks on IBM's earliest PC could hold a mere 64 files, or 160,256 bytes of programs and data. As users began demanding bigger and more efficient systems, manufacturers first tried cramming additional storage space onto the same 5-1/4 inch floppies. But as space needs skyrocketed, vendors started introducing increasingly large hard disks — as well as 3-1/2 inch diskettes that could store as much as 1,457,664 bytes of information — more than nine times the capacity of the first PC diskettes.

IBM's first hard disk, for the XT, held ten megabytes; the first for the AT could store 20 megs. Users accustomed to floppy disks initially wondered how they could possibly fill so relatively enormous a storage space. But having all their programs and files at their fingertips was so seductive that users quickly clamored for more. Stacks of today's muscular hard disks and optical disks can salt away bytes in the gigabyte range (*giga* means billion and is pronounced "jig-guh" the way gigantic is pronounced "jy-gan-tic" — although most users say "giga" with a hard g as in "gargantuan").

But DOS wasn't designed for such massive storage. It doesn't store data in long, continuous, uninterrupted blocks of space. If it did, making additions and deletions to files would become insanely inefficient, since each time you made a file longer, DOS would have to find a brand new uninterrupted amount of disk area to store the enlarged file. So DOS divides files up into little pieces and stores the pieces in small areas called *clusters*.

Clusters are made up of *sectors*. Each sector — the smallest possible user storage area on any DOS disk — is 512 bytes long. On some disks, like the earliest single-sided 160K and 180K floppies, or the high-density 1.2 megabyte 5-1/4 inch and 1.44 megabyte 3-1/2 inch diskettes, each cluster contains just one sector. At the other end of the scale, the absurdly inefficient ten-megabyte XT hard disk allots eight sectors to each cluster, which means it takes 8 x 512, or 4,096 bytes to store even the smallest file on an original XT. And some mammoth DOS 5.0 hard disks are even worse.

When you store a file on a disk, DOS splits it into cluster-sized chunks and starts looking for vacant parts of your disk to hold these chunks. On a newly formatted hard disk, all these chunks can be continuous and uninterrupted. But on a disk that's seen months or years of heavy use — especially one that's nearly filled with data — DOS has to look long and hard to find empty spaces, and may end up dividing a typical file into dozens of fragmented clusters scattered all over the surface of your disk.

DOS relies on a chart called the File Allocation Table (FAT) to remember which clusters on the disk are temporarily unused, and to keep track of where all the scattered chunks of your files are located. It also uses a special nondisplaying part of the disk's directory to steer itself into each file's very first cluster. But while the directory contains the address of the initial cluster, the FAT maintains the addresses of all the rest of any file's clusters. The FAT is so important that most disks contain two identical copies, and

DOS updates both each time it adds, deletes, or changes a file. This way if one copy of the FAT becomes damaged, DOS can consult the other for the vital mapping information it needs.

A raw disk is sort of like a tract of undeveloped land that someone wants to turn into a housing development crammed with one-acre lots. At first the land is just one large uniform property that may have some random buildings, hills, gulleys, and dirt roads on it. The first thing the developer does is flatten out the property, divide the land into lots, and build a grid of roads that lead to each individual lot. He may find that one or two lots contain jagged rocks or swampy areas that can't easily be converted into homes. Then he constructs a main office and puts a map of the development on the wall, displaying the addresses of each lot and marking off the few that have cliffs or quicksand that prevent them from being sold. As buyers start purchasing homes, the developer crosses off these lots one by one.

Fresh from the factory, a disk is just one large uniform surface that has some random information on it (left over from the manufacturing process). The first thing a user has to do with a disk is *format* it, which divides the disk into uniform sectors, evens out the random magnetic hills and valleys in key places, creates the underlying maps and structures, and reports any "bad" sectors that are magnetically unstable or unfit for holding data.

(Actually, hard disks require two kinds of formatting, *low-level* and *high-level*. To continue our analogy, a low-level format is like drawing a map of the land. A high-level format is like actually putting in roads. Most hard disks come from the factory with the low-level formatting already done. And today many dealers even do the DOS high-level formatting to spare users the grief of having to read the manual.)

When the developer first starts hawking his hundreds of homes, the map of available lots is wide open, except for the few that are too craggy or wet to build on. Likewise, when a disk is first formatted, its map of available sectors is wide open, except for the few that are magnetically unsuited to store information. If one huge clan of families approached the developer just as he started selling, and wanted to buy a long string of homes adjacent to each other, the developer could easily put them all in a row, then cross an entire contiguous block of homes off the map. But if the developer sold most of the building lots to unrelated families, the map would start filling up in somewhat random order. Over the years, many of these unrelated families would sell their individual homes and move out, and the development would always contain some homes that were temporarily vacant. If the clan descended on the development a few years after it was built, they probably wouldn't be able to find a string of homes next to each other, and would have to settle for one here, one there, one way over there, etc.

When a disk is newly formatted and empty, you can store files in relatively contiguous clusters. But as you add new files and erase old ones, and make existing files smaller and larger, you end up with pieces of your files all over the disk. It's far faster to load and write files that aren't scattered in many pieces. Hard disk users should periodically make full file-by-file backup copies of all their files, reformat their disks, and then put all the important files back. This has three good effects:

1. It makes sure everything is backed up.
2. It unfragments files so they load faster. When you back up a file, DOS takes all the scattered pieces from the far-flung reaches of your hard disk and puts them all together in one continuous area on the newly formatted backup floppy or tape. When you go back later and restore your backed up files to the newly formatted hard disk, DOS writes the file in one long, efficient, continuous piece. Of course, as soon as you start editing it again, the efficiency plummets. Because programs don't change much, however, reformatting your disk and then copying programs back to it may speed up loading dramatically.
3. It cleans up unwanted files, giving you lots more free space on your hard disk. You'll be surprised at how many files you'll decide aren't worth copying back to the hard disk once you've backed them up. Having them available on a backup floppy or tape means you can always retrieve them if you need to. But by not copying them back to your hard disk, you'll end up with free space for new files — and you'll prevent the wasteful "churning" DOS is forced to do when it tries to hunt down the few vacant sectors on an overstuffed hard disk.

DOS had a serious design problem when it came to large hard disks. When you asked it to store a file, DOS consulted the FAT to find out where the unused sectors were located. And when you later asked DOS to load a file, it looked up the locations of the bulk of the file's sectors by again examining the FAT.

The engineers who originally designed DOS had to decide how big the FAT should be. Making it too small meant limiting the number of bytes users could store on a single disk. But if they made it too large, they would have ended up with an ungainly FAT that would have taken up too much raw space on each disk. (And remember, this was back in the days when a standard diskette held a trifling 160K, the standard PC came with 16K of RAM, and IBM seriously thought users were going to store their data on cheap tape recorders.) They finally settled on giving the FAT a maximum of 16-bit addresses, which meant that the largest possible table could have 64K worth of entries. Since each entry on the chart was a sector 512 bytes long, the maximum size of any single DOS disk was 64K x 512, or 32 megabytes.

The first IBM hard disk FAT, for the XT, used 12-bit, or 1.5 byte, addresses. Each address was made of three hexadecimal digits (16-bit addresses use four hex digits). But since FAT values are maintained as even pairs of hex digits, and because of the "back-words" storage technique used by the CPU, juggling 12-bit FAT addresses can be a real headache. Fortunately, DOS does all the work.

While 32 megabytes must have seemed enormous in the early 1980s, today it can seem small and cramped. The FDISK command in IBM's PC-DOS 3.3 let users divide one large physical hard disk into several smaller *logical* drives, each 32 megabytes or less, and each with its own drive letter. Compaq DOS version 3.31 extended the idea of logical drives by adding 32-bit FAT addresses, which allow logical drives as large as half a gigabyte. IBM's DOS 4.0 finally smashed through the 32 Mb barrier, allowing single enormous hard drives.

File Types

Files are either executable or nonexecutable. Executable files come in two classes — most are *programs* (with COM or EXE extensions) that your system can run, such as *WordStar*, or CHKDSK, or *1-2-3*. But DOS can also execute *batch* files (with BAT extensions), which are sequential lists of DOS commands and program names. DOS churns through batch files a line at a time, executing any DOS commands on each line and running any programs you've specified there.

Most other files store data, in one of two forms. Some data files are in *text* or *low-bit ASCII* format, which means that they contain nothing but the alphanumeric characters you could produce on a conventional typewriter. You can use the DOS TYPE command to read such ASCII files (although the TYPE command can also handle *high-bit* ASCII characters without missing a beat). But such files waste lots of space, and aren't very secure from prying eyes. Many data files are stored in proprietary nontext formats that compress the data more efficiently than ASCII files, and keep the information safe from snoopers. If you try using the DOS TYPE command on these, you'll either see a meaningless mass of what look like random characters, or a few familiar words interspersed with gibberish.

Some special kinds of nonexecutable files, with extensions like SYS or DRV, contain instructions that your operating system uses to control hardware better. The DOS ANSI.SYS device driver gives you enhanced keyboard and screen control. VDISK.SYS turns some of your memory into a virtual disk (as IBM calls it), or RAMdisk. And DRIVER.SYS lets you use some of IBM's external oddball drives.

You may also see files on recent DOS disks that have PIF extensions, which stands for Program Information File. IBM invented the PIF file for use with its *TopView* operating environment. Although *TopView* is now extinct, Microsoft also used PIF files for its *Windows* operating environment. Some programs are specially written to run under Microsoft *Windows*. But many normal programs that run under DOS can still run under *Windows*. Microsoft refers to these programs as either *standard applications* or *old applications*.

Windows looks for a PIF file whenever you want to run an old application. The PIF file contains information about the program and tells *Windows* things like how much memory the application needs and how "well-behaved" the program is. An "ill-behaved" program generally writes directly to the display memory. Virtually all word processors, spreadsheets, and graphics programs do. *Windows* cannot run these programs in a window and may have trouble multitasking them. It has to give up the entire display because it has no way of knowing when the program will write to the screen. (A program that does not write directly to display memory, but instead goes through DOS or the BIOS to display everything, can be run in a window, share the screen with other applications, and often be multitasked.)

Program Files

Programs all sport either COM or EXE extensions. The COM stands for *command* and the EXE for *executable* files, but they're really both executable. They're also unreadable.

If you manage to peek inside one (using the COPY /B trick mentioned below) all you'll see is beeping, flashing gibberish punctuated by any error messages and English-language prompts or instructions that happen to be imbedded inside the program code.

The gibberish is really just an artifact. Each byte of every program has a value between 0 and 255; your system interprets strings of these values as instructions that put your programs through their paces. But since IBM's version of the ASCII character set contains 256 separate characters with values between 0 and 255, when you display the contents of a program onscreen your system prints the ASCII characters that happen to represent the value of each byte. These characters generally have nothing to do with the actual program instructions. The beeping and flashing is caused when your system tries to display certain very low values that DOS interprets as *control* characters.

COM files are *memory image* files. The pattern of bytes in the file on the disk is exactly the same as the pattern when the file is loaded into memory, which isn't the case with EXE files. They can't be larger than 64K, and are generally more compact than EXE files. DOS always loads COM files at offset 100H (which is why DEBUG starts COM files at address 100H), and squeezes a 256-byte Program Segment Prefix (PSP) beneath it. The bottom half of the PSP contains a lot of important addresses that tell DOS where to find the things it needs, and the top half contains a copy of the *command tail* — the part of the command line that you entered at the DOS prompt after the filename. Any parameters and switches show up here. DOS also uses this upper area as a default Disk Transfer Area (DTA), a file I/O buffer space.

The COM file extension came from the older CP/M operating system, since the first versions of DOS were heavily based on CP/M. In fact, the COM file formats of CP/M and DOS (including the PSP that DOS builds when it loads a COM file) are practically identical. For software developers, this similarity helped ease the early transition to the PC. Programmers could ignore the segmented addressing scheme of the 8086 and work with just 64K of program and data space, the same as under CP/M.

EXE files are gradually replacing COM files. The mix of code and data in the same segment and the calculation of segment addresses outside the code segment are two of the major stumbling blocks that limit PC programs to one megabyte of addressable memory and prevent them from running under the 80286 extended-memory protected mode. Strictly speaking, COM files no longer exist under OS/2, although you can still run these programs in a "DOS Mode" session. For the millions of older systems running DOS, however, COM programs will still work as advertised.

While programmers once prided themselves on what tight, sleek assembly language COM programs they could write, EXE programs today are often pieced together by teams of coders who use higher-level languages like C and end up with enormous, often sloppy programs that are relative memory hogs.

The EXE format started with DOS and can handle programs larger than 64K; in fact, an EXE file can snatch around 600K in a typical maxed-out system. It does this by using multiple segments for program code, data, and a special storage area called the *stack* (see Chapter 7). Each of these segments can be 64K long. DOS looks at a special *header* at the beginning of any EXE file to figure out how and where to load the individual segments. Every EXE header contains information that DOS needs to load the program into memory correctly, juggle the segment assignments, and allocate space for it to run. You can't see this header information if you load the EXE file directly into DEBUG, because DEBUG uses the header to perform all the space allocation and fix-ups and gets the program ready to run. But you can look at the header if you first rename the file to give it an extension other than EXE and then load it into DEBUG. (But then you won't be able to run it in DEBUG, so don't try.)

Use the following commands to examine the first part of the file header on a sample EXE program called SAMPLE.EXE:

```
RENAME SAMPLE.EXE SAMPLE.XXX
DEBUG
N SAMPLE.XXX
L 0
D 0
Q
```

One value in the header specifies the number of 16-byte paragraphs needed after the end of the loaded program. This extra memory space is used for the *heap* and the *stack*. During calculations, the stack is used to store intermediate results. The heap is used by the program mostly for dynamic storage. If a program executes a STRING$ command or DIMensions an array, the result has to be put somewhere, and it goes in the heap. In a program that does a lot of dynamic string and array allocation, the heap can get pretty cluttered up and disorganized. At times, normal execution can grind to a halt while the program cleans up the heap in a process technically referred to as "garbage collection."

You can examine the PSP by loading the EXE file (not the renamed XXX file) or COM file into DEBUG. To look at SAMPLE.EXE, type:

```
DEBUG SAMPLE.EXE
D 0 L 100
Q
```

In all DOS versions before 3.3 users received a utility called EXE2BIN that can translate certain kinds of EXE files into COM (BIN stands for *binary*) files. (In 3.3 IBM moved EXE2BIN to the *DOS Technical Reference Manual*.) Only EXE files that have been specially prepared, generally in assembly language, can be successfully turned into COM files. These programs must not contain a stack segment, must have no references to relocatable segments, and must begin execution at offset 100H in the file. Since an executable EXE file must have a stack segment and generally uses separate code and data segments, the two formats are essentially incompatible.

Nonprogram Files

Programs produce and process data. This data is either in pure-low-bit-ASCII text format or in some compressed proprietary form.

A "pure-low-bit" ASCII file contains only letters, numbers, punctuation, the symbols "#$%&'()*+-/<=>@[\]^_'{|}~, tabs, and variations of the carriage return/line feed combination that tells your system to end one line and start the next one. Such files can't include most characters with ASCII values less than 32 or greater than 127.

Word processors often use special proprietary formats that rely on ASCII characters lower than 32 or greater than 127 to keep track of things like settings (margins, line spacing, etc.) and special printing tricks (underlines, boldfaces, pitch changes, etc.). But most good word processors include a mode that will let you create and edit pure-ASCII files. Or if they don't, they'll usually let you strip out any offending characters from their proprietary formats and leave just the letters, numbers, and punctuation.

Pure-low-bit ASCII files are usually called just ASCII files, text files, or DOS files. You can tell if a file is pure ASCII by using the DOS TYPE command to display its contents onscreen. If it looks like normal everyday text, it's probably pure ASCII or close to it. However, if it's jumbled, or littered with smiling faces, math symbols, crooked lines, and foreign language characters, it's not a pure-ASCII file.

If you have a file punctuated with jumbled characters, you can view the stripped contents by using the DL.EXE program on one of the accompanying disks, and using the F option to toggle the high bits off. Most word processors have the ability to produce a straight ASCII file; those that don't often can be converted to straight ASCII through the conversion routines of one that does. For example, you can use WordPerfect's CONVERT utility to convert WordStar files to WordPerfect format, and then save it in WordPerfect's DOS text format to get an ASCII file.

While powerful word processors — with their abilities to move and copy blocks of text, perform formatting magic, and search for and replace strings of characters — are at one end of the editing spectrum, the DOS COPY CON command is at the other. The DOS EDLIN text editor is somewhere in between, although few users ever bother with EDLIN, since everyone either uses word processors, program editors, or even the character handling features of programs like *1-2-3* to create small text files.

All COPY CON can really do is copy characters from the keyboard to a file. The only "editing" it offers is the ability to erase mistakes on the current line with the backspace or left arrow key. But it's fast and convenient, and it lets you create short files without having to leave DOS or have your word processor handy.

COPY CON creates absolutely pure ASCII text files, without any embedded codes, except to indicate the end of the file. It's simple to create a file such as a batch file using COPY CON. First, just pick a filename that ends with BAT, such as DIRSIZE.BAT, type it in after the command COPY CON at the DOS prompt, and press the Enter key:

```
COPY CON DIRSIZE.BAT
```

DOS will drop the cursor down a line and just sit there waiting for you to do something. Start typing up to 127 characters of text per line (126 if it's the last line). If you make a mistake, you can backspace it away *only* if it's on the same physical line of the screen as the cursor. Lines *wrap* down one row on the screen when they reach 80 characters, so if you're typing the 81st and you notice a goof at character 79, you're out of luck. (To abort the process and start again, press Ctrl-Break.) When you're done typing each line, press Enter key to start the next one.

In this case, type in a command to sort the DIR listing in reverse size order and discard extraneous lines:

```
DIR | FIND "-" | FIND /V "<" | SORT /R /+14 | MORE
```

(To make this work, you'll have to have the DOS FIND.EXE, SORT.EXE, and MORE.COM files on the same disk as the batch file you're creating, unless they're in a subdirectory that your PATH command knows about.) Before pressing the Enter key at the end of the line, press the F6 function key. You'll see a ^Z onscreen. This tells DOS you're done. Then press the Enter key and you should see the message:

```
1 File(s) copied
```

Check the directory and you'll see a new file called DIRSIZE.BAT. If you do have the FIND.EXE, SORT.EXE, and MORE.COM files handy, typing DIRSIZE at the DOS prompt will produce a directory listing sorted by file size, with the biggest files at the top.

If for some reason you have changed the meaning of the F6 key (either with ANSI.SYS or a commercial macro-writing program like *ProKey*), you could instead hold down the Ctrl key and press Z. Or you could even hold down the Alt key, type 26 on the number pad (not the top row keys), and then release the Alt key. All three methods will put an ASCII character 26 end-of-file marker at the end of the file.

Most of the time you can put the ^Z end-of-file marker at the end of the last command rather than on an extra line all by itself at the very end of the file. However, certain commands, such as ECHO, require that you follow the command with a carriage return rather than an end-of-file marker. And if you do put the Ctrl-Z on a line by itself, the batch file will usually end up putting two prompts on the screen after it finishes executing.

Creating Filenames

You can't store any information on any disk unless you give it a filename. Unfortunately, because of its CP/M heritage, DOS limits the length of all filenames to 11 characters, just enough to remind you what's inside the file, but far too few if your file contains chart #2 for the fourth quarter income report on the Airframe Division of Amalgamated Electronics, since you'll end up with some cryptic entry like ADAE4QIN.CH2.

Filenames can contain:

- the letters A through Z
- the numerals 0 through 9
- the characters ' ~ ' ! @ # $ % ^ & ( ) - _ { }
- high-bit characters (with ASCII values over 127)

Filenames can't contain:

- spaces
- characters treated as spaces, such as = ; , tab
- the "wildcard" characters ? and *
- characters with special DOS meanings . : " \ / | < > + [ ]
- control characters (with ASCII values less than 33)
- lowercase letters (DOS automatically uppercases these)

Many of the ASCII characters with values between 128 and 165 are foreign language versions of a, e, i, o, u, and y. When creating filenames, the American version of DOS tends to ignore the wide range of accent marks and treat these as the plain old vowels. And DOS turns all lowercase letters into their uppercase versions, which means that you can't have one file called:

`autoexec.bat`

and a different one called:

`AUTOEXEC.BAT`

(Actually, if you use the brute-force techniques described in Chapter 9 on DEBUG, you can do this, by loading and writing absolute sectors. But while DOS will acknowledge that this lowercase file exists by including it in DIR listings, it won't let you change or delete or examine it — except with DEBUG. This does let you keep the file secure, but fooling around with your directory directly is a bad idea unless you know exactly what you're doing and are sure all your files are backed up. And on a hard disk, where you can really lose big if you make one silly mistake, it's an especially bad idea.)

This capitalized exclusivity also means that upper- and lowercase pairs of special characters such as the ones with values 128/135, 145/146, 148/153, 129, 154, and 164/165 automatically turn into their uppercase versions.

Using some of the more unusual high-bit ASCII characters for filenames can keep prying fingers away, since few users have ASCII charts handy when they snoop inside someone else's system, and even fewer know the Alt-keypad method of generating these odd characters (described in Chapter 6). There's nothing more confounding to a casual snoop than entering a DIR command and seeing an entire screen full of gibberish where the filenames should be.

If you try to create a filename using ASCII 127 (with the Alt-keypad technique), DOS will just backspace the previous character away. But you can use this character in a filename, if you find a way to type it in. BASIC lets you do it. Try typing in the following CHAR127.BAS program:

```
100 'CHAR127.BAS
110 OPEN CHR$(127) FOR OUTPUT AS #1
120 PRINT #1,"It works..."
130 CLOSE:SYSTEM
```

Then, at the DOS prompt, type:

```
BASICA CHAR127.BAS
```

(or GWBASIC CHAR127 if you're using a generic MS-DOS version of BASIC).

The CHAR127.BAS program will create a file with a single ASCII character 127 as the filename. This character will show up in DIR listings as a delta (which looks like a little house).

You can view it by typing:

```
DIR ?
```

because using the single ? wildcard in a DIR command will display all the filenames that are just one character long.

If you try to use an illegal character, such as an asterisk, DOS will discard everything from the asterisk on. So if you type:

```
A>COPY CON NOTE*IT
```

DOS will discard the asterisk and the IT that follows, and create a file called NOTE.

Reserved Filenames

DOS is selfish about its internal names for devices such as printers, communications hardware, the keyboard/screen combination (which is collectively called the console, or CON), and a special dummy device with interesting properties, known as NUL. One reason for this hands-off attitude is that you can use some DOS commands on devices as well as files. For instance, while the COPY command is great for backing up your files to another disk or subdirectory (the more recent XCOPY command is even better), you can also use COPY in conjunction with the CON device to create files:

```
COPY CON FILENAME
```

Using COPY this way tells DOS to take whatever the user is typing at the keyboard and put it in a file called FILENAME (or any other legal filename you specify). And if you type:

```
COPY /B COMMAND.COM CON
```

you'll be able to see the entire contents of COMMAND.COM onscreen, since copying a file to CON reads it from a disk and sends it to your display. You can't do this with a TYPE COMMAND.COM command, since all but the very shortest executable files contain addresses or instructions loaded with ASCII 26 characters. The DOS TYPE command interprets these ASCII 26 characters as end-of-file markers, and grinds to a halt as soon as it stumbles over the first one.

The /B that appears directly after the COPY command in the above example is called a *switch*. Switches turn optional command features on and off (and can also furnish needed values and settings at the same time). In this case, the /B switch tells DOS to look at the directory listing, figure out the exact number of bytes in the file you want copied, and copy them all — including any ASCII 26 characters it sees (which it displays as little arrows). You can slap lots of different switches onto various commands, producing such nightmarish results as:

```
PRINT /D:LPT2 /B:8192 /U:2 /M:4 /S:20 /Q:20 B:\INFO\FIL1 C:\FIL2
```

This particular thorny command would use DOS's *background* printing feature to print two files in a row — one on drive B:, the other on drive C: — using the second of two printers that were attached to your system. And it would let you run another program while the files were printing. (See the next chapter for a full discussion of backslashes and subdirectories.)

DOS refers to the prompt and all the commands, switches, filenames, and miscellaneous parameters following it as the *command line*. Everything after the actual command itself is called the *command tail*. Here's an example:

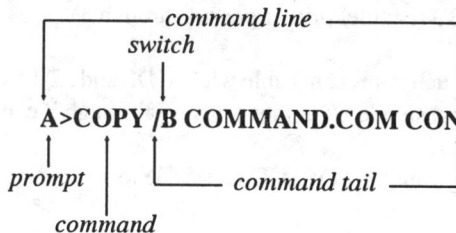

CON isn't the only device that's useful with COPY. You could print out a copy of your AUTOEXEC.BAT file with the command:

```
COPY AUTOEXEC.BAT PRN
```

And COPY isn't the only command that works with devices. If you wanted to send a formfeed command to your printer to advance the paper, you could do it with:

```
ECHO ^L > PRN
```

(You create the ^L by holding down the Ctrl key and typing L. Typing ECHO ^L PRN without the > redirection symbol won't do anything other than printing a ^L PRN onscreen.)

Because DOS has to know when you want it to use PRN or CON as a device, you can't use such *reserved* device names as filenames. Names like:

- CON
- PRN
- PRN.XYZ

are invalid. (PRN.XYZ is no good because DOS interprets the dot after PRN as a space, leaving the filename as just PRN.) However, you could use PRN as the extension, or along with other characters in the filename. These are all legal:

- DRIVER4.PRN
- XYZPRN
- PRN1.CON

But stay away from the following reserved DOS device names:

```
CLOCK$
CON (keyboard/screen)
AUX (first serial port)
PRN (first parallel printer)
NUL (dummy device)
COM1, COM2, COM3, COM4 (serial ports 1 through 4)
LPT1, LPT2, LPT3 (parallel printer ports 1 through 3)
```

COM1 is pretty much interchangeable with AUX, and LPT1 with PRN. NUL is useful for getting rid of most simple DOS messages — although it can't suppress serious error messages.

If you try copying your COMMAND.COM file to something called ABC.COM, with the command:

```
COPY COMMAND.COM ABC.COM
```

DOS will oblige, and print a:

```
1 File(s) copied
```

message. If you then type DIR to see what's on your disk, you'll see two files with identical sizes:

```
COMMAND    COM     47845    3-22-91   12:00p
ABC        COM     47845    3-22-91   12:00p
```

But if you try copying it to a file called NUL.COM, with the command:

```
COPY COMMAND.COM NUL.COM
```

DOS will interpret this command as

```
COPY COMMAND.COM NUL
```

and discard the .COM part. Copying a file to the NUL device makes DOS go through the motions but not actually copy anything. It will still print a:

```
1 File(s) copied
```

message, but when you type DIR you won't see any file called NUL.COM. Similarly, if you try copying your startup AUTOEXEC.BAT file to one called PRN.BAT, with the command:

```
COPY AUTOEXEC.BAT PRN.BAT
```

DOS will toss the .BAT part and interpret this command as:

```
COPY AUTOEXEC.BAT PRN
```

Since copying any file to the PRN device will cause it to be printed on your default LPT1 printer, this command will either print out your AUTOEXEC.BAT file (if your printer happens to be turned on and connected properly) or freeze your system as DOS tries to print a file to a printer that's not responding.

You can also run into trouble if you try to create a file that has the same name as a subdirectory entry. If you're in a directory that has a subdirectory called BIN branching off of it, typing DIR will produce a listing that includes something like:

```
BIN             <DIR>      12-15-90   10:59p
```

If you then try to create a file called BIN, you'll see a message that makes it look as if you just created a file called BIN even though you didn't.

```
COPY CON BIN
This is a test
^Z
This is a test
        1 File(s) copied
```

This happens because subdirectories are really just special kinds of files, and you can't have two files in the same directory with the same name. When you try to create a file called BIN, DOS looks at the directory and sees there's already a file with that name. However, instead of reporting that it can't create the file, it lies. If you think that's unfriendly, you're right. But you have to very careful with filenames in general. If you've been working on a 100,000-byte file called LIFSTORY that's on drive A: and you type:

```
COPY CON LIFSTORY
Oops
```

and press the F6 function key (to tell DOS you're at the end of the file) and then the Enter key, DOS will wipe out the 100,000 byte file and replace it with the new four-byte file you just created.

Similarly, if you want to print out a short file, such as your startup AUTOEXEC.BAT file, you can type:

```
COPY AUTOEXEC.BAT PRN
```

which will copy the file to your default printer. But if you accidentally switch the order and type:

```
COPY PRN AUTOEXEC.BAT
```

DOS will print a:

```
0 File(s) copied
```

message — and then wipe out your AUTOEXEC.BAT file. Gone. So be very careful with filenames. And make sure you have everything backed up.

The Parts of a Filename

Filenames can be as short as one character, or as long as 11. Once they grow past eight, however, they start encroaching on the filename extension. Most users refer to the entire name of the file as the filename, which isn't technically correct. According to IBM, the whole thing is really called a *filespec* (short for file specification), and has three parts:

d:FILENAME.EXT

where:

d:	is the drive the file is on
FILENAME	is the actual filename
EXT	is the optional filename extension

A period separates the filename from its extension, although DOS doesn't display periods in DIR listings. You don't have to use a period when you're dealing with files that don't have extensions, although doing so won't hurt. So you could create a file called TEST by typing either:

```
COPY CON TEST
```

or:

```
COPY CON TEST.
```

Technically you need to include a drive letter in the filespec, since you can have two similarly named files on two drives with utterly different contents — A:DATAFILE can be totally unrelated to B:DATAFILE. However, DOS tries to second-guess you if you omit something it needs. If you're on drive A: and you want to have DOS give you a report on the status of your file and memory use, you can type:

```
A:CHKDSK.COM
```

or simply:

```
CHKDSK
```

In the second version of this command, DOS fills in the missing (A:) drive letter and (COM) extension for you by furnishing *defaults*. Since you were already logged onto drive A: DOS makes drive A: the default. Whenever you issue a command that needs a drive letter, DOS will try using the current drive. And you don't need to supply the COM extension when you're running a command like CHKDSK. The reason for this is a bit complicated:

When DOS sees something on the command line, it tries to figure out, or *parses*, what you typed by first capitalizing it if necessary, then looking for delimiters (spaces, and things like commas and equal signs that act the same as spaces), switches (like /B), drive letters, subdirectory paths, and filenames. It assumes that the very first thing you typed on the command line after the prompt is the main command itself.

This command can be one of four things: an internal command, an external command, the name of the application program, or a typo or missing filename.

Internal commands are the instructions that execute many of the fundamental DOS operations such as DIR and TYPE. They are actually buried inside the main DOS COMMAND.COM command processor. DOS first compares what you typed to the list maintained inside COMMAND.COM. In version 5.0 the list contains these commands:

BREAK	LH
CALL	MD
CD	MKDIR
CHCP	NOT

CHDIR	PATH
CLS	PAUSE
COPY	PROMPT
CTTY	RD
DATE	REM
DEL	REN
DIR	RENAME
ECHO	RMDIR
ERASE	SET
ERRORLEVEL	SHIFT
EXIST	TIME
EXIT	TRUENAME (undocumented)
FOR	TYPE
GOTO	VER
IF	VERIFY
LOADHIGH	VOL

Some of these are just parts of larger commands. EXIST and ERRORLEVEL really only work with IF. FOR and IN DO work together. And NOT doesn't do anything by itself. These few have slightly different properties (which you'll see a bit later) from the others on the list.

If it finds a match, COMMAND.COM then runs the proper instructions, which are also kept inside COMMAND.COM, to execute the command. If it can't find a match, it starts looking in the default directory for an *external* command or applications program with the name you typed. If it can't find the specified filename in the current directory, it will see if you've specified a PATH and start looking in all the directories that this PATH specifies.

External commands are separate programs, outside of COMMAND.COM. DOS version 5.0 contains 50 of these, all of which end in COM or EXE:

APPEND.EXE	HELP.EXE
ASSIGN.COM	JOIN.EXE
ATTRIB.EXE	KEYB.COM
BACKUP.EXE	LABEL.EXE
CHKDSK.EXE	LOADFIX.COM
COMP.EXE	MEM.EXE
DEBUG.EXE	MIRROR.COM
DISKCOMP.COM	MODE.COM
DISKCOPY.COM	MORE.COM
DOSKEY.COM	MSHERC.COM
DOSSHELL.COM	NLSFUNC.EXE
DOSSHELL.EXE	PRINT.EXE
DOSSWAP.EXE	QBASIC.EXE

EDIT.COM	RECOVER.EXE
EDLIN.EXE	REPLACE.EXE
EMM386.EXE	RESTORE.EXE
EXE2BIN.EXE	SETVER.EXE
EXPAND.EXE	SHARE.EXE
FASTOPEN.EXE	SORT.EXE
FC.EXE	SUBST.EXE
FDISK.EXE	SYS.COM
FIND.EXE	TREE.COM
FORMAT.COM	UNDELETE.EXE
GRAFTABL.COM	UNFORMAT.COM
GRAPHICS.COM	XCOPY.EXE

Users sometimes forget that these DOS external commands are actually separate programs, and that they won't work unless the appropriate programs are in the default directory or are in a directory that their PATH command knows about. (And yes, COMMAND.COM, the part of DOS that actually processes the commands you enter, can be an external command itself, and a very useful one as you'll soon see.)

You can also type the name of an application program on the command line. DOS doesn't give its external commands any priority over commercial applications with similar names. It simply tries to run an internal command first and if that doesn't work, it then looks for a file in the current directory that has a matching filename and a COM, EXE, or BAT extension. If it happens to find a DOS program that fits the bill, it runs it. But if you didn't have any external DOS commands handy, and for some reason you renamed your main WS.COM *WordStar* file to CHKDSK.COM, typing CHKDSK would run *WordStar*.

Other commands such as BUFFERS, BREAK, DEVICE, FILES, FCBS, LAST-DRIVE, STACKS, COUNTRY, SHELL, INSTALL, IFS, CPSW, COMMENT, REM, and SWITCHES are installation programs that work with CONFIG.SYS and are part of the IBMBIO.COM or generic IO.SYS file.

Finally, if DOS doesn't understand what you've entered, you've probably mistyped a command or entered the name of a file that DOS cannot locate. This is usually a PATH problem.

The PATH Command

The PATH command specifies a list of the important directories you want DOS to search when it can't find an executable program in the current directory. DOS keeps this list in a special section of memory called the *environment*.

If you weren't able to use PATHs to tell DOS where to search, you'd either have to keep copies of all your important programs in all your subdirectories, or you'd always have to specify each program's precise location each time you ran it. And if you're wondering why DOS can't just search in every single directory, doing so on even a medium-sized hard disk could take a while each time you typed a command. A typical PATH might look something like:

```
PATH D:\;C:\;C:\BIN;C:\DOS;C:\DOS\BAT;C:\SK;C:\DOS\NORTON
```

which tells DOS to look in the following places for the file you specified, if it can't find it in the current directory:

D:\ (the root directory of drive D:)
C:\ (the root directory of drive C:)
C:\BIN
C:\DOS
C:\DOS\BAT
C:\SK
C:\DOS\NORTON

If you wanted to run a program that wasn't in the current directory or in any of the places listed in your PATH statement, DOS wouldn't be able to run it unless you explicitly entered the name of the directory this file happened to be in. So if the CHKDSK.COM command was in a subdirectory called:

```
C:\LIONS\TIGERS\AND\BEARS
```

and your PATH didn't mention this subdirectory, typing just:

```
C>CHKDSK
```

wouldn't run the program. Even though it was on your disk, if DOS couldn't find it, it couldn't run it. You could run it, however, by typing:

```
C:\LIONS\TIGERS\AND\BEARS\CHKDSK
```

or:

```
\LIONS\TIGERS\AND\BEARS\CHKDSK
```

Here's a fine point but an important one: Note the initial backslash character at the very beginning. By putting this backslash character there, you're telling DOS that the specified PATH for the CHKDSK file started at the root directory. If you omitted this initial backslash:

```
LIONS\TIGERS\AND\BEARS\CHKDSK
```

DOS would assume that the first directory in the list — LIONS — was a directory one level below whatever directory you happened to be in at the time. If you were logged into the root directory, this wouldn't matter. But if you were already in a directory called \WIZ\OZ, and you omitted the initial backslash before LIONS, DOS would think you were really telling it to run:

```
\WIZ\OZ\LIONS\TIGERS\AND\BEARS\CHKDSK
```

And if you happened to be in one called \INCOME\REPORT\4Q, DOS would assume you meant:

```
\INCOME\REPORT\4Q\LIONS\TIGERS\AND\BEARS\CHKDSK
```

When you include an initial backslash in a PATH, you are giving DOS an explicit PATH. When you omit the backslash you give DOS a relative path — one that starts a level down from whatever directory you are in at the time.

If you made a typing mistake when you entered the command, or specified a program that DOS couldn't find, all you'd get would be an error message that told you:

```
Bad command or file name
```

Also, remember that DOS can execute only three kinds of files — those that end in COM or EXE or BAT. So if you had just the following files on your disk:

- CHKDSK
- CHKDSK.WKS
- CHKDSK.BAS
- CHKDSK.DBF
- CHKDSK.SYS
- CHKDSK.DRV
- CHKDSK.PIF

and you typed CHKDSK, all you'd get would be the "Bad command or file name" error message, even though DOS uses extensions such as SYS or PIF (but not on executable programs).

By including the name of a subdirectory in your PATH, you tell DOS to look in that directory for executable files (with COM, EXE, or BAT extensions). But PATHs are for executable files only; DOS won't be able to find nonexecutable files, such as your data files, or *overlay* files that help programs work, in subdirectories specified in your PATH. To have DOS search through your directories to find nonexecutable files, use the APPEND command introduced with version 3.3.

DOS will always execute internal commands first, then COM files, then EXE files, and finally BAT files. So if you have these three files on your disk:

- RUNME.COM
- RUNME.EXE
- RUNME.BAT

and you type RUNME, you'll always run RUNME.COM. You'll never get a chance to run either RUNME.EXE or RUNME.BAT, since DOS always tries to run COM files before any other kind of program. If you erased RUNME.COM, you could run RUNME.EXE, but you'd never be able to run RUNME.BAT while either RUNME.COM or RUNME.EXE was in the same directory.

But that's if you try just RUNME without any extension. What if those three RUNME files are on your disk, and you include the extension by typing RUNME.EXE or RUNME.BAT? Sorry, out of luck. DOS will still execute RUNME.COM.

If you have any separate programs on your disk that happen to have the same name as most of the internal DOS commands, you'll never be able to run these at all. This means you can't ever create executable files like BREAK.COM, REM.EXE, DATE.COM, or SET.BAT, since DOS will look inside COMMAND.COM, find a match, and execute the internal command before it has a chance to run the external COM, EXE, or BAT version.

While most of the internal commands will indeed preempt external versions, you can actually use four parts of internal command names in external programs: ERRORLEVEL (which under certain circumstances DOS truncates to ERRORLEV), EXIST, INDO, and NOT.

So don't try creating a batch file that has the same basic filename as a program you're using. If you wanted to set up a batch file that logged into your WP subdirectory, activated underlining on an EGA screen, then ran *WordPerfect* (and you had a program called UNDERLIN.COM handy to handle this) you could do it with something like:

```
CD C:\WP
UNDERLIN ON
WP
```

However, you couldn't name this batch file WP.BAT, since typing WP would simply bypass the WP.BAT file and load the WP.EXE program. Instead, name it something like W.BAT.

Well, okay, if you're a stickler, there actually is a way to run a program that has the same name as an internal command.

All you have to do is prefix the similarly named program with a drive letter or path. For example, if you had a special program on your disk that sorted the directory, and you were using something newer than DOS 2.x and just had to name it DIR.COM, you could run it by typing:

```
.\DIR
```

The .\ is DOS shorthand that specifies a file in the current directory. If you omitted this prefix, all you'd get is the normal DOS DIR listing, since COMMAND.COM always gives internal commands priority over external commands with the same name. However, prefacing a command with a drive letter or path designation tells DOS that you want to execute an external file rather than an internal command.

You won't be able to add a .\ prefix like this in DOS versions 2.x, since version 3.0 was the first that let you specify a drive and path before external commands. But if you're logged into a directory called C:\WORK and the DIR.COM program also happens to be in that directory, you could run it by entering:

```
\WORK\DIR
```

You really shouldn't have to worry about this, however, since you can almost always come up with a name that's slightly different from the actual internal DOS command.

Fooling COMMAND.COM's knee-jerk reflex to give internal commands priority can actually save you grief. Say your office is short of PCs, and you have to share your hard disk system with a less sophisticated user. Your worst fear is that your co-worker will try to format a floppy disk, forget to add the drive letter in the FORMAT command, and end up wiping out the contents of the hard disk.

This was all too easy on older versions of DOS. Newer versions of FORMAT.COM won't do anything unless the user specifies a drive letter. And newer versions can also tell if a user is trying to reformat a hard disk, and won't budge unless the user types in the hard disk's volume label. Still, the message DOS prints:

```
Enter current Volume Label for Drive C:
WARNING, ALL DATA ON NON-REMOVABLE DISK
DRIVE C: WILL BE LOST!
Proceed with Format (Y/N)?
```

is confounding to someone who has no idea what a non-removable disk is, and if a new or clumsy user has a deadline and needs to format a disk, well, that's what backups are for.

Hard-disk-format victims have devised all sorts of solutions to prevent hard disk format. The best is obviously to remove the FORMAT.COM program from your disk, or rename it to something that would throw beginners off track. But a new user could always bring a floppy disk copy of FORMAT.COM over and copy it onto the hard disk.

If you don't mind patching COMMAND.COM, you can prevent most FORMAT heartache by tricking COMMAND.COM into thinking FORMAT is an internal command. DOS maintains a table of internal commands inside COMMAND.COM and always checks there first when you enter something on the command line. FORMAT is six letters long. Three internal commands — PROMPT, RENAME, and VERIFY — also have six letters in their names. If you replace the six letters in one of these entries with the letters "FORMAT" DOS will see FORMAT on the table when it checks to see if you entered an internal command, and won't execute any external program with the same name.

But putting FORMAT in the table means getting rid of one of the existing six-letter table entries. Fortunately, RENAME has a shorter version, REN. So if you replace the letters RENAME in the table with FORMAT you'll still be able to rename files by using REN. But changing the letters R-E-N-A-M-E to F-O-R-M-A-T in the lookup table won't change the actual instructions that DOS uses to rename files. So if a user enters FORMAT, DOS will see it on the table and execute the rename procedure. Since you can't rename files unless you specify an existing name and a new name, all you'll get is an error. Typing:

```
FORMAT OLDNAME.TXT NEWNAME.DOC
```

will rename a file called OLDNAME.TXT to NEWNAME.DOC. And typing:

```
FORMAT C:
```

will just produce an "Invalid number of parameters" message.

But this won't work if a user boots off a diskette and executes the FORMAT command that's on the floppy. And patching COMMAND.COM isn't always such a good idea. If you do it, be sure that all versions of COMMAND.COM on your disk are identical. Otherwise DOS can become confused.

You could use either the *Norton Utilities* or DEBUG to change RENAME to FORMAT. Once you've patched COMMAND.COM, use REN to rename FORMAT.COM to FORMAT[].COM (where [] stands for an ALT+255 null). To do this, type:

```
REN FORMAT.COM FORMAT
```

but don't press the Enter key yet — hold down the Alt key and type 255 on the numeric keypad, then release the Alt key. The cursor will move over one space. Then type:

```
.COM
```

and press the Enter key.

Finally, create a batch file called F.BAT:

```
ECHO OFF
CLS
ECHO Insert disk in drive A: and
PAUSE
FORMAT[] A: /V /S
```

Remember to type in FORMAT[] (where [] represents Alt+255) when creating your batch file, or this won't work.

To patch COMMAND.COM with DEBUG, first make a backup copy of COMMAND.COM called COMMAND.OLD so that if you make a mistake you can start over. Then type:

```
DEBUG COMMAND.COM
```

Find out how long your version is by typing:

```
RCX
```

and pressing the Enter key twice. You'll see something like:

```
CX BAE5
```

Take the four-digit hex number following the CX and type:

```
S 100 LBAE5 "RENAME"
```

(substituting the four-digit hex number if yours is different from BAE5). Press the Enter key and you should see something like:

```
48B8:81DC
```

Ignore the leftmost four digits, preceding the colon. Take the rightmost four digits and type:

```
E 81DC "FORMAT"
```

(substituting the four-digit hex number if yours is different from 81DC). Press the Enter key. Then press W (and Enter) to write the new version back to disk, and Q (and the Enter) to quit DEBUG. Once you've patched COMMAND.COM, reboot.

Another simple way to prevent unwanted formatting is to rename FORMAT.COM to something innocuous like DATA.COM and then insert a simple reboot routine at the beginning of your old FORMAT.COM file. Type in FORMAT and the system will reboot. Type in DATA and you can format disks. Make sure you have DEBUG.COM handy, and type in the following ten lines to create both files.

```
DEBUG
N FORMAT.COM
L
N DATA.COM
W
N FORMAT.COM
E 100 B8 40 00 8E D8 B8 34 12
E 108 A3 72 00 EA 00 00 FF FF
W
Q
```

Be sure to press the Enter key at the end of each line. You could of course create a tiny 16-byte reboot file called FORMAT.COM, but the short length would be a tipoff to an unauthorized user that something was amiss.

If you try this, you can format a floppy in drive A: by typing:

```
DATA A:
```

And if you type FORMAT at the DOS prompt your system will do a warm reboot. If you really want to be safe, change the 34 12 at the end of the line that begins E 100 to 7F 7F, so the line looks like:

```
E 100 B8 40 00 8E D8 B8 7F 7F
```

This will make your system do a long cold boot with all the slow memory diagnostics.

Before DOS 5.0, some users created a file on every disk that contained a sorted DIR listing. You can do this easily if you have the DOS programs MORE.COM, FIND.EXE, and SORT.EXE handy. (It's best to have them on a hard disk in a subdirectory that your PATH knows about.) Just type:

```
DIR | SORT | FIND "-" | FIND /V "<" > DIRFILE
```

The DIR command produces a list of files as well as a report on how many bytes are free, how many files are there, and what the volume label is, if one exists. The | is the *pipe* sign, and the > is a *redirection* sign. The default devices for input and output (*I/O*) are obvious: input usually comes from the keyboard; output usually goes to the screen. But starting with version 2.0, DOS let you mix and match I/O. You can take output that would normally appear on your screen, and instead reroute it to your printer or modem — or capture the characters by turning them into a file on your disk. Similarly, you can take characters in a file on your disk and feed them into a program just as if you were typing them at the keyboard. And you can *filter* files through pipes on the way from one place to another. This lets you do things like search for or screen out certain characters, or sort jumbled lists into orderly ones. Piping and redirection of I/O are extremely powerful tools that you'll use often.

Using the SORT command as shown above will arrange the DIR listing in rough alphabetical order. The first FIND command will screen out most of the miscellaneous DIR information and leave just the filenames, since files all have hyphens in their creation dates but miscellaneous "bytes free" or "Volume in" reports rarely use hyphens. The second FIND will weed out any subdirectory listings, because each contains a <DIR> instead of a size:

```
Volume in drive C is WORKDISK          ◄──────┐   Miscellaneous DIR
Volume serial Number is 104F-16CD             │   information mostly
Directory of C:\                       ◄──────┘   filtered out by first
                                                  FIND command

COMMAND   COM    47845   14-09-91    5:00a
CONFIG    SYS       47   10-18-90    7:07a
AUTOEXEC  BAT      256   10-18-90   12:01a
DOS           <DIR>      10-18-90    7:09a ◄──┐   Subdirectory
WORDSTAR      <DIR>      11-06-90   12:22a     │  listings filtered out
DBASE         <DIR>       2-11-90   12:00a     │  by the second FIND
LOTUS         <DIR>      12-03-90   12:02a ◄──┘  command

        7 File(s)    28220672 bytes free   ◄──┐   Miscellaneous DIR
                                               │  information filtered
                                               │  out by first FIND
                                               │  command
```

The final redirection command sends the output to a file called DIRFILE. You could then view the sorted list of files on your disk by typing:

```
TYPE DIRFILE
```

If your list was longer than 24 files, you could type:

```
MORE < DIRFILE
```

which would show you a screenful at a time (assuming you were using a monitor that displayed the standard 25 lines), then pause and prompt you to press any nonshift key to view another screenful.

If you do this to all your disks, you'll end up with a different version of DIRFILE on each one. The one on drive A: is really A:DIRFILE, the one on B: is B:DIRFILE, etc. And when you do just about anything with these files you have to use the appropriate drive letters, so they really are part of the filespec.

Even though IBM's various manuals don't seem to agree in their definition of the filespec, a file's PATH is just as important as its drive letter, especially on a hard disk, and should be thought of as a fourth filespec component. Just as you can have two similarly named files called A:DIRFILE and B:DIRFILE, you can also create C:\DOS\DIRFILE and C:\WORD\DIRFILE on the same physical disk.

Wildcards

You don't have to specify the PATH if you're referring to files in the current — or default — subdirectory. If you're logged into a subdirectory called \DOS and you want to check out your COMMAND.COM file, all four commands below will produce the same result:

```
DIR COMMAND.COM
DIR C:\DOS\COMMAND.COM
DIR \DOS\COMMAND.COM
DIR .\COMMAND.COM
```

DOS is very flexible, and provides even more ways to ferret out just the COMMAND.COM file entry. In DOS 5.0, you could type:

```
DIR \COMMAND.COM /S
```

to see occurrences of COMMAND.COM. Or you could simply type DIR and use a DOS filter to screen out everything that didn't have the character string "COMMAND COM" in it:

```
DIR | FIND "COMMAND COM"
```

Unfortunately, you'd have to specify "COMMAND COM" rather than "COM-MAND.COM" because that's how the DIR listing displays it. DOS is flexible, but consistently inconsistent.

You could also isolate COMMAND.COM in directory searches by looking for a part of its filename:

```
DIR | FIND "COMMAND"
```

However, if you had a game on your disk called COMMANDO.EXE, and a list of *WordPerfect* commands called WCOMMAND.LST, this filtering technique would find all three files with the characters "COMMAND" in their names.

Finding one file is easy. However, you might want to look at an entire class of related files, such as all the COM files on your disk, at one time. Or you may have several customized versions of COMMAND.COM, such as COMMAND1.COM and COM-MAND2.COM on your disk and want to look at the date you created each version.

DOS makes it easy to list such groups of files, by using one of two special symbols on the command line. IBM calls this pair — an asterisk (*) and a question mark (?) — *global file name characters*. Everyone else calls them *wildcards*.

A question mark can stand for any single character (including a blank, or no characters). An asterisk can represent up to 11 characters. If you apply this rule to the character string:

```
?UN
```

you could substitute ten single characters in place of the ? and end up with English words — BUN, DUN, FUN, GUN, HUN, NUN, PUN, RUN, SUN, TUN (a big barrel).

If you tried this with the character string:

```
SYL*
```

you could substitute all sorts of character combinations of varying lengths in place of the * and end up with words like SYLLABLE, SYLLABUB, SYLLABUS, SYLLOGISM, SYLPH, and SYLVAN. Of course, not all of these could be filenames, because some are longer than eight characters. If you tried to create a file called SYLLOGISM, DOS would end up calling it SYLLOGIS.M since it allows a maximum of eight characters to the left of the extension.

Suppose your disk contained the following files:

- COMMAND.COM
- COMMAND.CO
- COMMAND.EXE
- C.COM
- COMMAND1.COM
- COMMAND.C
- ZOMMAND.COM
- COMMAND.ZOM

- COMMA.COM
- COMMAND
- COMM.AND
- ZZZ.1
- REDLINE.DBF

The broadest possible wildcard directory search would be:

```
DIR *.*
```

which is really the same as:

```
DIR
```

or:

```
DIR *
```

or:

```
DIR ????????.???
```

An asterisk to the left of a period lets DOS substitute from one to eight characters there. An asterisk to the right of a period lets DOS substitute from zero to three characters there. A filename needs at least one character to the left of the period, but can get by just fine with no characters after the period. One asterisk used by itself can stand for all 11 possible characters. When you issue a DIR command without anything after it, DOS internally puts *.* after it. And it then turns all the asterisks into the correct number of question marks. So when you type DIR, DOS first translates it to DIR *.* and then finally to DIR ????????.??? (both of which will show all your files).

Incidentally, you could also see the complete set of files in any directory by typing:

```
DIR .
```

but this technique doesn't have anything to do with wildcards. Used this way, the period following DIR is shorthand for the current subdirectory itself, just as a double period represents the parent directory. You can see these special directory entries by logging into any subdirectory and typing DIR. You'll see, for example,

```
Volume in drive C is WORKDISK
Volume Serial Number is 104F-16CD
Directory of C:\DOS

.              <DIR> 3-15-90 5:15p
..             <DIR> 3-15-90 5:15p
```

Wildcards really come in handy when you use them to isolate certain parts of filenames. For instance, you could limit your search to files that end in COM only with the command:

```
DIR *.COM
```

This tells DOS to accept anything on the left side of the period, but to screen out all files that have something other than a COM to the right of the period. This command would display every file on the above sample list that ended in COM, and no others:

- COMMAND.COM
- C.COM
- COMMAND1.COM
- ZOMMAND.COM
- COMMA.COM

If you put the asterisk on the other side of the period:

```
DIR COMMAND.*
```

DOS wouldn't care what was after the period, but would list only those files with the precise letters "COMMAND" — and only those letters — before the period:

- COMMAND.COM
- COMMAND.CO
- COMMAND.EXE
- COMMAND.C
- COMMAND.ZOM
- COMMAND

This variation would list plain old COMMAND (with no extension) because an asterisk to the right of a period can stand for three, two, one, or no characters. COMMAND with no extension is really the same as:

```
COMMAND.
```

but you rarely see it listed that way.

However, this particular search won't list COMMAND1.COM, since COMMAND1 is not equal to COMMAND, and you told DOS to list only those files with the exact string "COMMAND" to the left of the period. If you wanted to include COMMAND1.COM in the list, you'd have to broaden the previous command either with:

```
DIR COMMAND*.*
```

or:

```
DIR COMMAND*
```

or even with:

```
DIR COMMAND?.*
```

Remember, asterisks can represent from one to 11 letters, but a question mark always represents just one character. All three of the above commands would produce the same result:

- COMMAND.COM
- COMMAND.CO
- COMMAND.EXE
- COMMAND1.COM
- COMMAND.C
- COMMAND.ZOM
- COMMAND

You should always try to limit wildcard searches by making them as explicit as possible. A command like:

```
DIR C*.COM
```

would list any file that started with C and ended with COM:

- COMMAND.COM
- C.COM
- COMMAND1.COM
- COMMA.COM

You could limit the search to list only files that ended in COM and that started with the letter C but had five or fewer characters to the left of the period, with:

```
DIR ?????.COM
```

which would yield:

- C.COM
- COMMA.COM

If you wanted files that started with the letter C and had extensions that started with the letter C, you could try:

```
DIR C*.C*
```

or:

```
DIR C*.C??
```

which would both list:

- COMMAND.COM
- COMMAND.CO
- C.COM
- COMMAND1.COM
- COMMAND.C
- COMMA.COM

To narrow this search to files that started with the letter C and had extensions shorter than two characters long, this would do it:

```
DIR C*.??
```

You'd see just:

- COMMAND.CO
- COMMAND.C

You get the idea. One thing to watch out for is that once DOS sees an asterisk, it ignores everything following the asterisk up to the next period or the end of the filename. So:

```
DIR C*QQQ.COM
```

will list

- COMMAND.COM
- C.COM
- COMMAND1.COM
- COMMA.COM

just as if you had typed:

```
DIR C*.COM
```

And trying:

```
DIR *OMMAND.*OM
```

or even:

```
DIR *HELLOTHERE
```

will list every file on your disk, since DOS ignores what comes after the asterisks and treats these two commands as:

```
DIR *.*
```

and:

```
DIR *
```

What you probably meant to type rather than DIR *OMMAND.*OM was:

```
DIR ?OMMAND.?OM
```

which will yield:

- COMMAND.COM
- ZOMMAND.COM
- COMMAND.ZOM

since all three of these are the same except for the very first letter and the first letter of the extension. The more specific you make the command, the more you'll limit the search.

Wildcards are especially useful in deleting groups of files and in making backups. Many word processors create backup files with BAK extensions, and these can eat up lots of space. Once you've determined that you don't need these files any longer, you can wipe out the whole gang of them with a simple command:

```
DEL *.BAK
```

And wildcards can take the drudgery out of backups. If you spent all day working on the fourth quarter projections, and all the files have 4Q0 extensions (for fourth quarter of 1991), you can copy them all from your hard disk to a floppy with the command:

```
COPY *.4Q9 A:
```

(or the even better DOS 3.2 and later XCOPY *.4Q0)

Of course, many applications use their own extensions, so you may have to put identifying codes at the beginning rather than the end of the filename. If you were working on the Sturm and Drang accounts, you might want to give these files names like:

- 4Q0STURM.WK1
- 4Q0DRANG.WK1

The problem with naming files this way is that you later might want to copy all your Drang accounts to one disk, and they might have names like:

- 4Q0DRANG.WK1
- DRANG.RPT
- 90DRANG.MEM

You could put the DRANG part at the beginning of the filenames:

- DRANG4Q0.WK1
- DRANG.RPT
- DRANG90.MEM

which would let you handle them with a DRANG*.* wildcard. But this way you wouldn't necessarily be able to use wildcards to find all the files with 4Q0 in them. STURM4Q0 and DRANG4Q0 have the same number of letters, which would let you use ?????4Q0, but a filename like GUB4Q0 would throw the process off.

DOS doesn't make it easy to use wildcards when the string of characters you want to isolate is in different places in the filenames. But you can employ a combination of sophisticated DOS tricks to do it, as long as the DOS FIND.EXE program is either in your current directory or is in a directory that your PATH knows about. It gets a little complicated (no one ever said DOS would be easy) so you may want to refer to the chapter on batch files before you tackle this:

Use your pure-ASCII word processor, EDLIN, or the DOS COPY CON command to create two BAT files. (Before you try this, be sure you don't already have a file on your disk called DOIT.BAT, because this process will erase it. If you do, either rename the existing file, or change all the references in COPYSOME.BAT and NEXTFILE.BAT from DOIT.BAT to something else.)

First, COPYSOME.BAT:

```
ECHO OFF
IF %2!==! GOTO OOPS
IF EXIST DOIT.BAT DEL DOIT.BAT
FOR %%A IN (*.*) DO COMMAND /C TESTTHEM %%A %1 %2
COMMAND /C DOIT
DEL DOIT.BAT
GOTO END
:OOPS
ECHO Enter a string to search for, and a drive
ECHO or directory to copy the matching file to
:END
```

Then, TESTTHEM.BAT:

```
ECHO OFF
ECHO COPY %1 %3 | FIND "%2" >> DOIT.BAT
```

Then, to copy any filename with the string DRANG in it to drive A:, just type:

```
COPYSOME DRANG A:
```

Or to copy the files to \WORK\ACCT\1990, type:

```
COPYSOME DRANG \WORK\ACCT\1990
```

The COPYSOME.BAT batch file will first make sure that you entered both a string of characters to search for and a drive or directory to copy the matching files to. If you forget one or the other it will abort the process and print an error message.

Be sure you enter the string first and the drive or directory second. And make certain that you enter the string in all uppercase letters, and that you don't put quotation marks around the string.

COPYSOME will then use a FOR batch command to take all the filenames in your directory one by one and feed them into the second TESTTHEM.BAT batch file. The:

```
%%A %1 %2
```

at the end of the FOR command will pass three parameters to TESTTHEM.BAT. Each time the FOR command cycles through, this will replace %%A with the name of the file, %1 with the character string you're trying to match, and %2 with the drive or directory you want to copy everything to. But by the time these parameters reach TEST-THEM.BAT, the parameters shift slightly:

%%A in COPYSOME becomes %1 in TESTTHEM
%1 in COPYSOME becomes %2 in TESTTHEM
%2 in COPYSOME becomes %3 in TESTTHEM

Each time COPYSOME passes these parameters to TESTTHEM, TESTTHEM translates the:

```
ECHO COPY %1 %3 | FIND "%2" >> DOIT.BAT
```

line to something like:

```
ECHO COPY 90DRANG4.MEM A: | FIND "DRANG" >> DOIT.BAT
```

The command at the beginning of this line would normally use ECHO to display the text following the word ECHO. But this batch file pipes this text through the FIND filter. FIND will look at the text to see if it contain the specified string (in this case "DRANG").

If the text doesn't contain the specified string, nothing else will happen and the process will continue with the next filename. But if FIND does locate the string it passes the string through to the very end of the command. Here, the final:

```
>DOIT.BAT
```

command takes any text that survived the FIND test and adds it to a file called DOIT.BAT. Note that a single > sign creates a new file and redirects data into it. A double >> sign will create a file if none exists, and will append data to the file if it's already there. You have to use a double >> sign here because each time you find a filename with the characters DRANG in it, you're going to add an additional line to DOIT.BAT, and you don't want each new line to wipe out the old one.

So if COPYSOME.BAT passes TESTTHEM.BAT parameters like:

```
%%A = 90DRANG4.MEM
 %1 = DRANG
 %2 = A:
```

TESTTHEM plugs these into its main command and ends up with:

```
ECHO COPY 90DRANG4.MEM A: | FIND "DRANG" >> DOIT.BAT
```

Since the characters "DRANG" are indeed in the string:

```
COPY 90DRANG4.MEM A:
```

the FIND filter passes this string through to the:

```
>DOIT.BAT
```

command, where the string is appended to the DOIT.BAT file.

However, if COPYSOME passes TESTTHEM parameters that don't include the specified characters, such as:

```
%%A = 90STURM4.MEM
 %1 = DRANG
 %2 = A:
```

TESTTHEM will turn this into:

```
ECHO COPY 90STURM4.MEM A: | FIND "DRANG" >> DOIT.BAT
```

The FIND test won't pass anything through, since the characters "DRANG" aren't in the COPY 90STURM4.MEM A: string.

When the FOR command in the COPYSOME.BAT file has worked all the way through the (*.*) set of files, COPYSOME will execute the command in the next line:

```
COMMAND /C DOIT
```

This will run the DOIT.BAT file you just created, and make all the copies. When DOIT has made its last copy, DOS will delete DOIT.BAS and the process ends.

Whew. Okay, it's convoluted, but it shows what you can do by slapping together a few DOS commands. And once you have both the COPYSOME.BAT and TESTTHEM.BAT batch files on your disk, you don't have to worry about how they work. You just use them. It's a whole lot easier than sitting down with (shudder) paper and pen and making a list of all the files you have to copy and then typing in the COPY commands one by one.

Incidentally, if you're using a version of DOS 3.3 or later, replace the:

```
FOR %%A IN (*.*) DO COMMAND /C TESTTHEM %%A %1 %2
```

line in COPYSOME.BAT with:

```
FOR %%A IN (*.*) DO CALL TESTTHEM %%A %1 %2
```

Do the same thing with the COMMAND /C DOIT line that follows. Prefix the initial ECHO OFF with a @ sign (so it looks like @ECHO OFF), which will prevent it from displaying onscreen.

Using CALL will expedite things a bit and get rid of some screen clutter. The COPYSOME.BAT batch file turns ECHO OFF to prevent commands from showing up on the screen as they execute. But when you use COMMAND /C to run another batch file, DOS loads a second copy of COMMAND.COM, which turns ECHO on again for the second batch file. CALL leaves the ECHO state alone. If it's off in the first batch file, CALL leaves it off.

Be careful when you're using a command such as REN (or its longer version RENAME) or DEL (or its longer cousin ERASE) with wildcards, since the wildcard may end up including more files than you intended.

If you tried to delete all your BAK backup files by typing:

```
DEL *.BA*
```

you would erase anything with an extension beginning with BA. Since this includes batch files (which end in BAT) and BASIC program files (which normally end in BAS), you'd delete far more than you wanted. The safe way to delete or rename is to use the DIR command with the wildcard structure first, and then to use the DEL or REN. DOS makes this easy, since it lets you use the F3 key to duplicate any or all of what you typed in the previous command.

So if the only files in your directory that had extensions beginning with BA were indeed backup files, you could type:

```
DIR *.BA*
```

and see something like:

```
Volume in drive C is WORKDISK
Volume Serial Number is 104F-16CD
Directory of C:\ACCOUNT

SCHEDULE BAK      16256   10-17-90   12:01a
4Q0DRANG BAK      21256   10-24-90    6:32a
DRANG    BAK      32932   11-12-90   11:40a
90DRANG  BAK       9674   11-15-90    1:23p


4 File(s) 4122624 bytes free
```

you could then just type DEL and press F3:

```
DEL *.BA*
```

However, if you tried typing DIR *.BA* and you saw:

```
Volume in drive C is WORKDISK
Volume Serial Number is 104F-16CD
Directory of C:\ACCOUNT

AUTOEXEC BAT        256    2-11-90    3:15p
SCHEDULE BAK      16256   10-17-90   12:01a
RUN      BAT        128    2-12-90    7:28a
4Q0DRANG BAK      21256   10-24-90    6:32a
DRANG    BAK      32932   11-12-90   11:40a
CHART    BAS      28932    8-22-90    8:32p
90DRANG  BAK       9674   11-15-90    1:23p


7 File(s) 4122624 bytes free
```

you could see that the DEL *.BA* would have erased too much. If this happens, just narrow the focus of the wildcard by changing the command to DEL *.BAK instead.

DOS is a little protective of your files. If you type just:

```
DIR C*
```

DOS will display everything beginning with the letter C (such as COMMAND.COM). But if you type:

```
DEL C*
```

DOS won't erase COMMAND.COM or anything else that has an extension of any kind. (It will, however, erase files that begin with C but don't have extensions.) It's decent of DOS to make the directory search wildcards broader than the deletion wildcards.

One place that a wildcard can come in very handy is in fixing filenames with spaces in them. DOS won't let you put a space in a filename, but some programs (and even BASIC) will. If you try to create a file called

```
SPACE IT
```

DOS 5.0 will get confused and print an error message that warns:

```
 Too many parameters - IT
```

But you can create such a file with BASIC. Type in the following short BADNAME.BAS program:

```
100 ' BADNAME.BAS
110 OPEN "SPACE IT" FOR OUTPUT AS #1
120 PRINT #1,"Ooops..."
130 CLOSE:SYSTEM
```

Then, at the DOS prompt, type:

```
A>BASICA BADNAME
```

(or GWBASIC BADNAME if you're using a generic MS-DOS version of BASIC). The BADNAME.BAS program will create a file with a space in it called SPACE IT. To see this file, just type:

```
 DIR S*
```

and sure enough you'll see:

```
 SPACE IT 11 11-17-90 5:31p
```

If you try to rename or copy or delete the file, you won't be able to, since DOS will interpret the space as the end of the filename, not a character in the middle. Depending on what you're trying to do all you'll get is error messages like:

- Invalid number of parameters
- Duplicate file name or File not found
- Invalid parameter
- File not found

You could remove the space by loading your disk's directory sectors into DEBUG and changing the name with the DEBUG E command. But why bother, when a simple wildcard operation can do it for you? Just type:

```
REN SPACE?IT SPACEIT
```

and you'll end up with something called **SPACEIT** that will respond to all normal DOS commands.

Filename Extensions

Filenames can contain from one to eight characters. Extensions can have from zero to three characters. You don't have to use extensions, but they help you organize or search for data. However, you can't use an extension without a filename preceding it. These are all valid filenames:

- A
- A.B
- A.BB
- A.BBB
- AAAAAAAA
- AAAAAAAA.B
- AAAAAAAA.BB
- AAAAAAAA.BBB
- {(_)}
- '~'!@#%$.^&-
- $

These aren't:

- AAAAAAAAA   (more than eight characters in the filename)
- .AAA   (no filename)
- AAAAAAAA.AAAA   (more than three characters in the extension)
- AAAAAA A   (space in the filename)
- AA+AA/A   (illegal characters + and / in filename)
- ?   (illegal character)

If you do try creating a file such as:

ABCDEFGHIJKLM.NOPQRSTUVWXYZ

```
|_____|   |__|
 filename     .ext
```

DOS will truncate the filename to the first eight characters before the dot, and the extension to the first three characters after the period, producing:

```
ABCDEFGH.NOP
```

Extensions are important, since they tell DOS which files it can try to execute and which it can't, and how in memory to load the executable ones. You and your programs can use extensions to organize your files. Most applications keep track of their specialized data files by giving them extensions, such as WKS for old-style *1-2-3* worksheets and DBF for old-style dBASE database files.

And by using extensions you can exploit DOS's formidable wildcard abilities. Without this wildcard magic it would be a real headache to do simple everyday chores like copying all your database files from drive C: to drive B:. First you'd have to type DIR to see all the files in your logged subdirectory, and then write down the names of each one that you thought was a database file. Then you'd have to copy them one by one. Instead, assuming you're on drive C: and that all your database files end with a DBF extension, you can simply type:

```
COPY *.DBF B:
```

Normally DOS will print a message when it's done, reporting how many files it copied. If you want to suppress this message, just stick a > NUL on the end of the command. This redirects the output of the command (which in this case is just the "File(s) copied" message) into a special DOS device called NUL that simply discards the characters. Typing:

```
COPY *.DBF B: > NUL
```

will make the copies and avoid screen clutter. Doing this isn't such a good idea when you're making important backup copies, since you want to know the number of files that DOS actually was able to copy. If you have 30 files on your disk that have a DBF extension and DOS reports:

```
2 File(s) copied
```

you can tell something is wrong, and go back and fix the problem before it's too late.

However, most serious users have to issue so many commands to set things up properly when they start working that they put all these commands in a special startup file called AUTOEXEC.BAT. DOS executes this startup file automatically when you power up each day. These users also know that they can improve performance by lopping off a chunk of memory and convincing DOS to treat this memory as a super-fast disk called a RAMdisk. So their AUTOEXEC.BAT files are filled with commands to copy files from floppies or hard disks to RAMdisks. This normally produces a long cascade of "1 File(s) copied" messages. Adding a > NUL to each COPY command in your AUTOEXEC.BAT will do away with these unsightly messages.

(Incidentally, IBM and Microsoft have had more than half a decade to cram sophisticated tricks into DOS and generally refine it. It's hard to believe that they still have DOS printing an idiotic message like "1 File(s) copied." Or refusing to tell you how many files DOS erased when you use a wildcard with the DEL or ERASE commands.)

In this chapter we described the basic principles of data storage and the physical properties of the disk. While the PC will place data in its own convenient locations, it's up to you to impose a structure on that data by organizing it into files and assigning those files unique and descriptive names. DOS has some inflexible rules that define what it will and will not recognize in a filename. We've presented those rules here, as well as some simple tips to help you create workable filenames.

In the next chapter we'll take a closer look at how to manage these files on a hard disk.

Hard Disks Made Easy

The single most important productivity enhancement for most users is a fast hard disk. A hard disk gives you instant access to all your files, speeds up operation dramatically, and makes "disk full" errors a lot less common. Floppies are how new software products are packaged, and how you back up your files — unless you use a tape drive or Bernoulli box. They're also for the birds. Hard disks used to be expensive and unreliable. That's all changed. Today they're inexpensive and unreliable. I've personally replaced seven hard disks over the past three years, and have to perform tedious daily ministrations to keep my current one purring.

Even the most expensive hard disks are frail and transitory. Many users wedge PC-ATs or PS/2s into floor stands beneath their desks, which is fine until they start playing knee-hockey with their systems. Others blithely slide working XTs back and forth across their desks to make room for paperwork, or routinely lift a corner of the chassis to retrieve something that's burrowed beneath it.

You've all probably seen versions of the famous illustration where a human hair, a smoke particle, and even the greasy schmutz of a fingerprint seem enormous compared to the gap between the magnetic head of a hard disk and the rotating disk platter itself. With tolerances slightly above the angstrom level, dropping a chassis a quarter inch, or tapping it with your toe, is the hard disk equivalent of an atom bomb going off directly overhead.

It's true that packages like the *Norton Utilities* and *Mace Utilities*, and even the dangerous DOS RECOVER command, can rescue parts of text files that remain intact after a bounced magnetic head has plowed little oxide furrows into the disk surface. But these programs aren't very good at resurrecting program files, or chunks of data stored in binary format. And when you see a message like:

```
General Failure error reading drive C
Abort, Retry, Ignore, Fail?
```

well, that's what backups are for.

If you set up your hard disk properly, you'll not only take the anguish out of daily backups, but you'll also end up working a whole lot smarter and more efficiently. While you'll have to learn how to handle subdirectories, the tips and utilities provided here should make it a breeze. Once you learn the basics — and install the tools you'll find in this chapter — you'll be able to solo with the best of them.

Formatting the Hard Disk

Hard disks require two kinds of formatting, *low-level* and *high-level*. These days the fundamental low-level formatting is done at the factory. You or your dealer have to do the high DOS-level formatting.

Dealers nowadays test and set up hard disks before shipping them to purchasers. Unfortunately, they also usually follow the questionable advice in the DOS manual and copy all the files from the two DOS floppy disks onto the root directory. For best performance, you should clean things up if you log into a brand new hard disk, type DIR, and see the listing scroll off your screen. But you can't just erase or move all the files there; you'll learn which ones have to stay in a moment.

If your dealer or MIS department didn't set up your system, it's fairly straightforward.

(If you have a hard disk that no one has touched, and all you see when you try to start is a "161 — System Options Not Set" message, hunt for the SETUP program, which on older systems IBM perversely buried on its Diagnostics disk. Put this disk in drive A:, turn the computer on, press F1 when prompted, and answer the questions about date, time, hard disk type, floppy disk type(s), and memory size. If you need to know the drive type, check to see that it's not in the documentation that came with your system. If it's not, take the cover off the computer and look for the number on the label on the front of the drive. If all else fails, call your dealer. DOS 4.0 combed out the wrinkles and made installation a whole lot easier.)

Once the setup program has run, insert your DOS disk in drive A: and turn your system on. Press the Enter key twice when asked for the date and time. Type in:

```
FDISK
```

and press the Enter key, and when you see the "Fixed Disk Setup Program" screen, accept the defaults by pressing the Enter key again to create a DOS partition, and then once more to tell the program you want to devote the entire hard disk to DOS.

You can slice up a standard hard disk into as many as four partitions, and jump from one to the other by using FDISK. Take our word for it, unless you have a penchant for dabbling in other operating systems, you don't want to.

After you've answered the partitioning questions, press any key and your system should reboot. This time, unless you're using an AT or XT-286 or PS/2 with a battery-operated clock, enter the correct date and time when asked. Type:

```
FORMAT C:/S/V
```

and, if necessary, verify that you want to proceed by entering Y.

The /S suffix, or *switch* tells DOS you not only want to format the hard disk, but want to add the three system files — IBMBIO.COM, IBMDOS.COM (or their non-IBM-specific cousins), and COMMAND.COM — to it so you can boot without having to stick a DOS floppy disk in drive A:.

If you forgot to add the /S, or if your system is delivered with a hard disk that's been FDISKed and formatted but without these three system files, turn your system on with your main DOS disk in drive A:, enter the correct date and time, and then type:

```
SYS C:
COPY COMMAND.COM C:
```

The /V switch tells DOS to let you add a volume name. This doesn't really do much except let you personalize your directory listings and CHKDSK reports, and avoid the pesky "Volume in drive C has no label" messages. With recent versions of DOS you can always go back and use the LABEL command to add or revise the volume label.

Subdirectory Structure

Many users who are either lazy or are befuddled by the terse explanation of subdirectories in the DOS manual end up dumping all their files into the main, or *root* directory. It's called a root directory because all other subdirectories branch off of it in a shape vaguely resembling an upside-down tree, or more accurately, a family tree, with the progenitor planted at the top and all the descendants fanning out beneath him. A simple representation looks likes this:

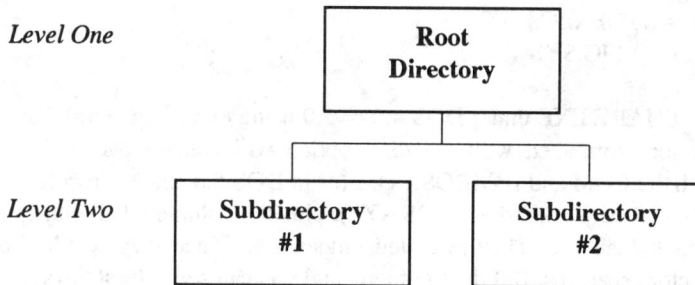

Level One   **Root Directory**

Level Two   **Subdirectory #1**   **Subdirectory #2**

You could make the tree much more complex, with third, fourth and fifth levels dangling below the second, each one bristling with additional subdirectories. Too few subdirectories and you end up with unmanageable numbers of files in each; too many and you can run into PATH problems (more about that later).

Note that the schematic representation of your subdirectory structure doesn't have to be in the form of a symmetric tree. An equally valid way to describe the above setup is:

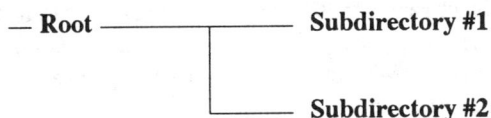

```
— Root ─────────┬───── Subdirectory #1
                │
                └───── Subdirectory #2
```

Note also that the root of the tree is at the top, so it's really an upside-down tree. A lower level is one farther away from the root. As you go higher in the tree you get closer to the root. This sounds confusing, and it is. Just be thankful that IBM didn't choose UNIX instead of DOS.

IBM's XT and AT hard disks (which in its typically contrary way IBM calls *fixed* disks because they're fixed in place and not removable like floppies) can hold between ten and 30 million characters; under DOS 4.0 and 5.0, newer systems can squirrel away as many as half a billion. With storage space so capacious, keeping similar files grouped together is a necessity. Otherwise, you (and DOS) would have to sort through hundreds or thousands of files each time you wanted to find a single program to run.

Just as you can't be at two places at the same time (unless you have a good lawyer), DOS lets you log into only one subdirectory at a time. When you first boot up, DOS logs you into the root directory of either your hard disk or the diskette in drive A:. If you installed the necessary DOS system files on your hard disk, and if you either didn't have a floppy disk in drive A: or had one there but left the drive A: door open, you'll boot off the hard disk. If this doesn't happen it's probably because you either have some bizarre brand-X hard disk or an early PC with an old ROM chip that doesn't understand hard disks.

You really need only three files in your root directory:

- COMMAND.COM
- AUTOEXEC.BAT
- CONFIG.SYS

Plus SHARE.EXE under DOS 4.0 or 5.0 using extra-large hard disks. Actually, a root directory formatted with the /S/V option will contain two additional, *hidden* files, IBMBIO.COM and IBMDOS.COM (or in DOS 5.0 and Microsoft's earlier versions of MS-DOS IO.SYS and MSDOS.SYS), plus the volume label, which is also stored in a small hidden file. They're called hidden files since they won't show up in normal directory searches. But they're there, and you can see at least the system files at the top of the list when you type:

```
CHKDSK C:/V
```

IBMBIO.COM contains additions and corrections to the gut-level device-handling BIOS routines that come with your system on ROM chips. IBMDOS.COM provides other fundamental services for things like copying and deleting files, searching through the directory, or reading the keyboard.

Technically, you can patch these system files and put the COMMAND.COM, AU-TOEXEC.BAT, and CONFIG.SYS files in other places than the root directory. But playing with your hidden files is like playing with fire.

COMMAND.COM is the primary command interpreter, processor, and loader that watches what you type at the DOS prompt. When it sees you trying to execute an *internal* command such as DIR, TYPE, RENAME, COPY, or ERASE, it can dispatch these right away, since the main routines for these are stored inside COMMAND.COM (which is why they're called internal commands). When it can't find an internal command to match what you typed — such as FORMAT, SORT, or 123 — it looks in a set of directories you specify, called a *path*, for files with COM, EXE, or BAT extensions, and tries to load or execute these *external* commands. In addition, a disposable part of COMMAND.COM looks for the startup AUTOEXEC.BAT file to execute immediately after bootup.

Every hard disk system should have an AUTOEXEC.BAT file, if only to set the proper system prompt. But it's also handy for loading resident popup programs like *SideKick* into memory, changing screen colors, setting operating modes (to switch monitors or specify communications protocols, for instance), copying files into RAMdisks, and otherwise automatically configuring your system the way you like it.

The normal DOS hard disk prompt is a cryptic:

```
C>
```

which tells you only that at that moment DOS recognizes drive C: — rather than the other drives in your system — as the active drive. Once you start creating subdirectories and jumping around from one to another, you'll want to know which subdirectory you're currently logged into. By issuing the command:

```
PROMPT $P$G
```

you'll tell DOS to report the name of the subdirectory along with the drive that's active, each time you finish executing a command or program. The root directory prompt will change to:

```
C:\>
```

The solitary backslash is DOS's shorthand for indicating the root directory. If the backslash-greater-than-sign combination is too visually jarring, you could adapt the prompt to:

```
PROMPT $P:
```

which will make the root directory appear as:

```
C:\:
```

Remember, the \ sign all by itself stands for the root directory. You can always see what's in the root directory, for instance, by typing:

```
DIR \
```

Later, when you add other subdirectories, you'll connect subdirectory names and their files with \ characters. So a subdirectory called DOSPT that's one level down from the root directory would actually be called \DOSPT. And if you were to branch an additional subdirectory off of \DOSPT, and called it \UTIL, the actual name of this new subdirectory would be \DOSPT\UTIL. A file called TOOLS.DOC in this new subdirectory would then be called \DOSPT\UTIL\TOOLS.DOC.

One of the handiest, but most confusing, aspects of naming files in subdirectories is that you could pepper your hard disk with other TOOLS.DOC files. So a TOOLS.DOC file on drive C: in the \DOSPT subdirectory would really be C:\DOSPT\TOOLS.DOC, while a different version in the root directory would be C:\TOOLS.DOC. The full name of any file has three parts — drive letter, path, and the actual filename-plus-extension.

A representation of this structure would be:

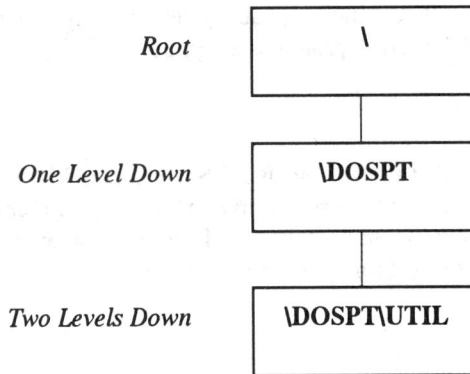

Root	\
One Level Down	**\DOSPT**
Two Levels Down	**\DOSPT\UTIL**

The root directory doesn't have a user-defined name such as DOSPT, so DOS designates it as just \ with nothing following it. The DOS manuals clearly state that the maximum length of any subdirectory path — the list of directory names from the top (root) to the deepest level — may be no longer than 63 bytes, measured from the beginning of the first name to the end of the last name, excluding slashes in front or at the end.

DOS function call 47H (Get Current Directory) requires a 64-byte area in memory to return the current directory path. It is not preceded by a backslash but it is terminated by a hex 0, so this is consistent with the 63-character restriction.

How many nested levels are allowed in a directory structure? Although the manuals never say so, the answer is obviously 32. If each of the subdirectory names is one letter long and they are separated by backslashes, then 32 levels would make the total length 63.

Of course, 32 nested levels of subdirectories would place an enormous drain on DOS as well as on the human user's mental faculties. What happens if you attempt to go beyond

32? Don't even try. You may get away with it but DOS will make life hard after that and you'll have difficulty just removing that snarl of subdirectories.

Directory Limits

You can store up to 64 files in the root directory of a single-sided floppy disk (if you can still find one), and 112 files in the root directory of a more common 360K floppy and 720K 3 1/2″ disk. The root directory on the 1.2 megabyte floppy and 1.44 megabyte high-density 3 1/2″ disk holds 224. And there's space on most hard disk root directories to store 512 files.

But don't test this out on your hard disk. If you do, you'll end up after the 509th with a "File creation error" message (the 510th, 511th, and 512th are the two hidden system files and the hidden volume label). Any subdirectory entries you may have in the root directory are really just special types of files, so they're included in the count too. So you may run out of room well before you actually have a chance to create the 512th file.

The number of directory entries in a subdirectory is limited only by available space on the disk. That's because each subdirectory is really just a special kind of file that keeps track of other files. Because the subdirectory itself is a file, it can grow the same way a data file grows when you add information to it.

Remember — if you really want to organize your hard disk properly, don't put any other files on your root directory than the ones mentioned above. Then, when you type:

```
DIR C:\
```

all you'll see is one screenful of your bootup files and main subdirectory listings. It'll be an index into your hard disk.

Disk Tools

When IBM introduced its hard disk XT, it added several UNIX-like *hierarchical* subdirectory features (as well as a UNIX-like tree structure) to the new release of DOS that accompanied it (version 2.0). Among these powerful new commands were:

- MKDIR (and MD)
- RMDIR (and RD)
- CHDIR (and CD)
- PATH

Nobody anywhere ever uses the command names MKDIR, RMDIR, and CHDIR, since the shorthand versions MD, RD, and CD will do just fine. Of course, since the IBM DOS documentation is not exactly what you'd call friendly, you can't look up these commands by hunting for the shorter versions in the alphabetical reference manual. MD, CD, and RD aren't even in the manual's index. Nice touch, IBM.

The MD command creates a new subdirectory. The first thing you should do after running FDISK and FORMAT is create a DOS subdirectory. To do this, type:

```
MD \DOS
```

If you are sure you are in the root directory, you can also type:

```
MD DOS
```

since both commands will do the same thing — create a subdirectory one level down from where you currently are, in the root directory.

By omitting the backslash (as in MD DOS) you're saying "create a directory called DOS that's one level down in the subdirectory tree from where I currently am." By including the backslash (as in MD \DOS) you're saying "create a directory called DOS that is one level down from the root directory," since the single backslash specifies the root directory.

The method that *omits* the backslash uses relative locations. The technique that *includes* the backslash uses absolute locations. Both have their advantages. We'll discuss this in more detail later. This is a critical distinction, and a point of real confusion among new hard disk users. (Many DOS commands allow alternate phrasings. For instance, you can use several different syntaxes to perform the same COPY command, depending on what you want to do and where you currently are.)

Once you've created the \DOS subdirectory, log into it (or Change Directories) from the root directory by issuing the CD DOS (or CD \DOS) command. Here's a shortcut — once you've typed MD \DOS to create the subdirectory, type the letter C and then press F3. F3 repeats the previous command, so it will fill in the command line with the rest of what you typed at the previous DOS prompt. So at the C> prompt you'd type:

```
MD \DOS
```

then press the Enter key. Then you'd type:

```
C
```

and press F3. As soon as you did you'd see:

```
CD \DOS
```

Press the Enter key and DOS will log you into your new \DOS subdirectory, and you'll see:

```
C>
```

How do you know you're in the \DOS subdirectory? If you type in DIR you'll get something like:

```
Volume in drive C is POWER_TOOLS
Volume Serial Number is 104F-16CD
Directory of C:\DOS

        .            <DIR>        6-10-90  10:48p
        ..           <DIR>        6-10-90  10:48p
            2 File(s)   20840448 bytes free
```

You can see the current directory in the second line of the DIR report. But if you remembered to set your prompt to $P: you could automatically tell which directory you were logged into, since instead of:

```
C>
```

as soon as you typed CD \DOS you'd see:

```
C:\DOS:
```

Typing CD by itself will also display the current subdirectory. But that's an extra step.

Notice that DOS already thinks you have two files in the \DOS subdirectory with the peculiar names . and .. and with <DIR> where the file size usually goes. Dot notation will be covered a bit later. The <DIR> tells you you're dealing with subdirectory entries. Now go back to the root directory. You can do this one of two ways.

You can use the absolute location technique and issue a command that says "move to the root directory":

```
CD \
```

or you can say "move one level up from where I am" with the command:

```
CD ..
```

You could have typed CD\ rather than CD   \, and CD.. rather than CD   .. since in this case DOS isn't picky about extra spaces (unless you're using one of the older DOS versions, in which case the space between the CD and the .. is mandatory). The double dot stands for the *parent* directory of the one you're currently logged into — the directory (or subdirectory) directly one level up toward the root. In this case the only level up is the root.

If you're curious, the single dot stands for the directory you're currently in. This shorthand actually comes in handy when you're prompted for a subdirectory name and you're in one five levels deep and would rather type a single period than a long, elaborate pathname — although just pounding on the Enter key sometimes works in such situations.

If you're deep inside one subdirectory like A\B\C\D\E\F\G and you're using the DOS COMP utility to compare a file there with another file deep within another directory like \1\2\3\4\5\6, you can enter:

```
COMP \1\2\3\4\5\6\PROGRAM
```

COMP will respond with a message to enter the directory the other version of the file is in. Just type a period, which tells DOS to look at the subdirectory you're currently logged into. Or, you could specify the period on the command line, as was done earlier:

```
COMP \1\2\3\4\5\6\PROGRAM  .
```

or:

```
COMP  .  \1\2\3\4\5\6\PROGRAM
```

You can also use the dot to simplify erasing all the files in a subdirectory. Instead of typing:

```
DEL *.*
```

all you really have to type is:

```
DEL  .
```

This technique can be potentially dangerous, however. If you let someone who doesn't understand subdirectories use your system you can run into trouble. If a novice user doesn't have a clue what the . and .. represent in a directory listing but does know about the DIR and ERASE commands, and somehow logs into a directory one level down from the root, he or she may be tempted to erase these mysterious double dot entries and end up deleting all the files in the current and root directories.
    DOS will respond with a:

```
Are you sure (Y/N)?
```

warning when you try to erase an entire subdirectory like this, but that's not a threatening enough message to a novice. You can make this message meaner by patching COM-MAND.COM, but many users feel COMMAND.COM is sacrosanct and shouldn't be touched. If you're not one of these, here's how to avoid potential mass-erasure problems like this by changing the message from:

```
Are you sure (Y/N)?
```

to:

```
Now hit the N key!!
```

First, make sure you have a copy of DEBUG.COM handy, and then make a backup copy of COMMAND.COM called COMMAND.OLD so that if you make a mistake you can start over. Then type:

```
DEBUG COMMAND.COM
```

Find out how long your version is by typing:

```
RCX
```

and pressing the Enter key twice. You'll see something like:

```
CX 9305
```

Take the four-digit hex number following the CX and type:

```
S 100 9305 "Are you sure"
```

(substituting the four-digit hex number if yours is different from 9305). Press the Enter key and you should see something like:

```
4938:7CB2
```

Ignore the first four digits preceding the colon. Take the rightmost four digits and type:

```
E 7CB2 "Now hit the N key!!"
```

(substituting the four-digit hex number if yours is different from 7CB2). Press the Enter key. Then press W (and Enter) to write the new version back to disk, and Q (and Enter) to quit DEBUG. Once you've patched COMMAND.COM, reboot.

If you do this, make sure you don't mix patched and unpatched versions of COM-MAND.COM on the same disk, or you'll confuse DOS.

In any event, once you've used the CD\ or the CD .. command, and you're back in the root directory, type DIR and you'll see a new listing along with:

```
Volume in drive C is POWER_TOOLS
Volume Serial Number is 104F-16CD
Directory of C:\
COMMAND   COM     47845    4-09-91    5:00a
CONFIG    SYS       128    4-09-91    6:30a
AUTOEXEC  BAT       640    4-09-91    8:12p
DOS            <DIR>       4-09-91   10:48p
```

The <DIR> tells you that you now have a subdirectory one level down from the root directory.

Customizing Your Prompt

The PROMPT command can do all sorts of tricky things, such as reporting the time and date, or the DOS version. If you ask it to, it will print the current time whenever you do something that summons another DOS prompt, such as press the Enter key again, or finish executing a program. It will not act as a clock and display the continuously changing time. And it will display time in hundredths of seconds based on a 24-hour clock. If you want it to print just the hours and minutes, you can backspace away everything else, with the command:

```
PROMPT It's now $T$H$H$H$H$H$H
```

Users who discover the PROMPT command's flexibility invariably end up creating strange prompts such as:

```
PROMPT +$Q$Q$Q$Q+$_$B $N$G $B$_+$Q$Q$Q$Q+$_
```

which produces:

```
+ = = = = +
|  C>  |
+ = = = = +
```

or:

```
PROMPT $L$N$G $L$N$G$_    $B$_    $Q$Q$Q$Q$_
```

which yields:

```
<C> <C>
     |
    _|_
```

A less frivolous use of the PROMPT command is in sending escape sequences to the ANSI.SYS extended screen driver, which can give you precise control over the way your monitor looks and works. The real strength of including $P in any PROMPT command is that when you log into a subdirectory, DOS will display the name of that subdirectory. So if your PROMPT setting is $P: and you create a subdirectory called STAR in which you keep all your *WordStar* files, and you move from the root directory into that subdirectory, your prompt will change from:

```
C:\:
```

to:

```
C:\STAR:
```

To see the command that most recently configured your prompt, type SET on a line by itself, which displays the system's environment — the fundamental settings that tell DOS where to look for key files and how to prompt the user. To restore the prompt to its original C> just type PROMPT with nothing following it.

Customizing your prompt isn't all roses. Once you tell DOS to include the subdirectory name in the prompt, it will relentlessly seek one out. So if you have a $P in your PROMPT command and log into a floppy drive, then remove the disk from that floppy drive and do something that generates an "Abort, Retry, Ignore, Fail?" message, DOS won't budge until you stick the diskette back in the floppy slot. Only newer versions of DOS give you the additional option to "Fail" which actually lets you succeed here. If you are offered this option, type F, then enter the drive letter of your hard disk.

A second disadvantage is that if you have tons of multilayered subdirectories with long directory names, and you're logged into one five levels deep, the prompt may be so long that your commands wrap around the right edge of your screen. The best solution is to keep subdirectory names short. In addition to preventing wraparound problems, this makes it far easier to switch between subdirectories. It's a lot simpler to type \WST\UT than \WORDSTAR\UTILITY, especially when you're doing it several times a day. (While you're at it, truncate the names of programs you use every day. Why type EDITOR when you could just key in ED? If you don't like the idea of renaming your files you can always create batch files with short names that can run programs with longer ones.) Also, resist the temptation to use extensions in subdirectory names since they'll just make the whole process more cumbersome and prone to error.

Another solution to wraparound ills is to end all your prompts with a $_ which jumps the cursor down to column 1 of the line below. Unfortunately, doing this will confuse certain DOS utilities like MORE that are designed for single-line prompts and will end up scrolling information off the screen before you can read it.

The CONFIG.SYS File

Apart from AUTOEXEC.BAT, the only other file that normally has to be in the root directory is CONFIG.SYS. Your system will run without a CONFIG.SYS file, but will work better with one. And certain programs demand one. If you're using a database manager, for instance, that handles more than eight open files at once, you have to prepare DOS for juggling the extra ones with a FILES= command in CONFIG.SYS.

But where CONFIG.SYS really shines is in increasing disk-read buffers, loading device drivers, and adding logical drives to your system.

For some odd reason, IBM specified a default of two buffers for the XT, and a paltry three for the AT. Recent DOS versions allocate 15 buffers for any system with more than 512K of RAM. Buffers are simply chunks of memory set aside to store the data your system most recently read from or wrote to your disk, although some buffers don't store written data. If you have to go back and read or write the same data, it's far speedier to do so via these memory buffers than to have to move the magnetic heads again and slurp up or slap down the information on the physical disks one more time.

Buffer needs vary from system to system, and the number of buffers is often a topic of heated discussion when tech types get together. Virtually everyone agrees that three is a joke. Somewhere around ten or 15 seems right for XT users, and 20 or 30 for AT users and other power users. Specifying too many is as detrimental to performance as too few, since your system will end up wasting time as it churns through endless reams of data it will never use.

If you currently have a directory crammed with hundreds of files, it's easy to demonstrate how increasing the number of buffers can help boost performance. First, make sure you don't have a CONFIG.SYS file, or if you do, that it doesn't contain a BUFFERS= command. If yours does, rename it temporarily.

Reboot, and issue a DIR command. The first few dozen files scroll rapidly by, but eventually the buffers fill, and the display suddenly turns balky. If you get tired of watching your files bounce slowly upward, interrupt the directory listing by holding down the Ctrl key and tapping either the C key or the ScrollLock key. Then, when you're back in the root directory at the DOS prompt, create a CONFIG.SYS file by typing:

```
COPY CON CONFIG.SYS
```

and then pressing the Enter key. The cursor will drop down a line. Type:

```
BUFFERS=20
```

and then press Enter, the F6 function key, and then the Enter key again. You'll see the message:

```
1 File(s) copied
```

Reboot and reissue the DIR command. Now virtually all the files will fly by, not just the first few, since your system can load a giant chunk of directory data from your disk into memory at one pass and not have to keep reading the disk in little sips.

CONFIG.SYS is also where you instruct your system to load device drivers such as the DOS VDISK.SYS *virtual disk* (RAMdisk), or drivers to link your basic hardware with mice, nonstandard external storage devices, 3-1/2 inch outboard floppy drives, or giant hard disks. Under DOS 4.0, you can use the INSTALL command to load your TSR programs here.

And it's where you tell DOS how many drives you're going to want to use. When you boot up, DOS assumes a maximum of five (drives A: through E:). But if your system is loaded to the gills with hard disks, half-heights, microfloppies, and other exotica, you might need more. And if you use the SUBST command to fool your system into treating a subdirectory like a disk drive to get around PATH or environment limitations, you'll have to prearrange it with a LASTDRIVE= CONFIG.SYS command.

Apart from the hidden DOS system files, COMMAND.COM, AUTOEXEC.BAT, and CONFIG.SYS, a well-organized disk's root directory should contain no other nonhidden files.

Some users don't mind having their important DOS utilities in their root directory, and cut through the clutter of a messy directory with a DIR/P (paused directory) or DIR/W (wide directory) command. This won't radically degrade performance, and may actually be a hair faster than storing the utilities in a separate \DOS subdirectory, if the files are kept at the very beginning of the hard disk directory. But it's even faster to keep them on a RAMdisk. And clutter gets to be a bad habit. Soon you start dumping files anywhere.

As mentioned earlier, it's a good idea to clean up a root directory cluttered with extraneous files. If all a dealer or corporate systems installer did when setting up your brand new system was copy all the DOS files from their original floppies to your root directory, you can go ahead and erase everything except COMMAND.COM (which is required to reboot the computer).

You can see if all the files in your root directory are also on your DOS disk either by putting the DOS disk in drive A: and then typing:

```
DIR C:/W
```

and then:

```
DIR A:/W
```

for a wide-display filenames-only listing. Or, turn on your printer and either type:

```
DIR C: > PRN
```

and then:

```
DIR A: > PRN
```

or hold down the Ctrl key and press P (or PrtSc) to toggle your printer on so that it echoes everything simultaneously to the printer and the screen, and type DIR C: and then DIR A: for a printed copy of your directory listing. If you used the Ctrl-P (or Ctrl-PrtSc) technique to turn simultaneous printing on, hold down the Ctrl key and type P (or PrtSc) once more to toggle it off.

You can also see what's on your disk by sorting the files in order of their extension. The command:

```
DIR | SORT /+10 | MORE
```

will make it easy. For this to work, the DOS SORT.EXE and MORE.COM files must be on the current directory, or be in directories that you've included in your PATH command.

The DOS COMP utility can also come in handy here. If your DOS disk is in drive A:, type:

```
COMP . A:
```

(The period used in this example is a shorthand way to indicate whatever directory you are currently in.)

Any way you do it, if you see that all you have on your root directory is DOS files, erase all the files except COMMAND.COM (you'll put them back in their proper places later). If you have AUTOEXEC.BAT or CONFIG.SYS files, examine their contents by using the TYPE command. To see what's inside CONFIG.SYS, just type:

```
TYPE CONFIG.SYS
```

If you see other files listed, such as:

```
DEVICE=RAMDRIVE.SYS 360 /E
DEVICE=ANSI.SYS
DEVICE=MOUSE.SYS
```

you'll want to leave VDISK.SYS, ANSI.SYS, and MOUSE.SYS where they are on the root directory. Later you can move them out of the root directory to a subdirectory called \BIN (so named because that's where you store your programs, which are in binary, nontext format), and change the CONFIG.SYS file so that it says:

```
DEVICE=\BIN\RAMDRIVE.SYS 360 /E
DEVICE=\BIN\ANSI.SYS
DEVICE=\BIN\MOUSE.SYS
```

Similarly, if you use the TYPE command to examine AUTOEXEC.BAT and see that it loads *SideKick* with the command SK, leave SK.COM in the root directory for now. Later, if you create a third-level subdirectory below \BIN called \BIN\KICK, and move your *SideKick* files there, you would change the line in your AUTOEXEC.BAT file from:

```
SK
```

to:

```
\BIN\KICK\SK
```

The TYPE command is terrific for peeking into short text files. But if a file is longer than 24 lines, the beginning will scroll off the screen before you can read it. To prevent this, use the MORE.COM utility, which shows you the contents of files a screenful at a time. If your AUTOEXEC.BAT is getting long, type:

```
MORE < AUTOEXEC.BAT
```

You could also enter:

```
TYPE AUTOEXEC.BAT | MORE
```

but the first method is more efficient and easier to type.

Important Files

You should now copy all the important files from your DOS floppy disks into your new DOS subdirectory. You can log onto drive A: and type:

```
COPY *.* C:\DOS
```

or, while in the root directory in drive C:, type:

```
COPY A:*.* \DOS
```

Or you could log into C:\DOS (with the CD DOS or CD \DOS command) and simply type:

```
COPY A:*.*
```

or:

```
COPY A:.
```

Even better is to use the XCOPY command introduced with DOS 3.2. COPY works one file at a time. XCOPY will read in as many commands in one gulp as memory allows, then spit them out in one continuous stream without bouncing back and forth repeatedly the way COPY does. XCOPY is also a terrific backup tool.

If you're logged into C:\DOS and you have XCOPY handy, just type:

```
XCOPY A:
```

Make sure you copy the important files from both the main DOS floppy disk and the supplemental one. Starting with DOS 3.3, these are called "Operating" and "Startup" disks. With DOS 4.0 you get three "Operating" disks, plus an "Install," a "Select," and a "Shell."

However, you can skip some of the files nobody ever uses, such as VDISK.LST (a long assembly language source code file for programmers), anything that ends with a BAS extension (unless you think DONKEY is an exciting and challenging game), and some of the stranger utilities such as KEYBIT.COM and KEYBFR.COM which load in foreign keyboard templates (in this case Italian and French). These foreign utilities were all combined into one file called KEYB in version 3.3.

You can also toss BASIC, since BASICA does everything BASIC does and more. In fact, with version 3.3, BASIC just loads BASICA. It's hard to believe, but some of the programs on some of the more recent versions of DOS will work only on the PC*jr*; try running MUSICA.BAS for instance. Do however copy DEBUG.COM, which, for some bizarre reason is not on the main DOS disk. Incidentally, while IBM removed the documentation for DEBUG from the 3.3 manual, it left the program on the disk.

Now that you've created a subdirectory (called \DOS) one level down from the root directory, go ahead and create another subdirectory on the same level as \DOS, called \BIN. But be careful. Why?

If you're currently logged into either the root directory or the \DOS directory, you could create \BIN with the absolute command:

```
MD \BIN
```

This command in effect says "create a subdirectory one level down from the root directory and call it BIN." The single \ prefix means "one level down from the root directory."

However, if you forget the backslash and try the command:

```
MD BIN
```

two different things will happpen, depending on where you currently are on your hard disk, since omitting the backslash makes this a relative command rather than an absolute one.

Typing MD BIN will create a subdirectory that's one level down from where you currently are. So if you're currently logged into the root directory, MD BIN will create a subdirectory called \BIN that's one level down from the root.

But if you're currently logged into \DOS, which is already one level down from the root, and you type MD BIN, you'll end up creating a subdirectory called \DOS\BIN that's one level down from \DOS and two levels down from the root. That's because leaving out the backslash in the MD command makes it a relative rather than an absolute command .

To recap, if you already have a subdirectory called \DOS, but you're currently logged into the root directory:

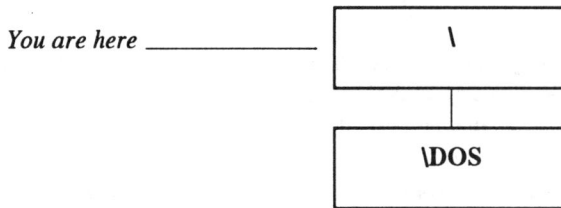

You are here _____

```
            \
```
```
          \DOS
```

and you type MD BIN, you'll end up with:

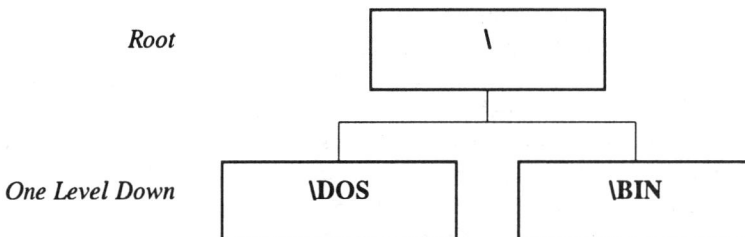

Root

```
            \
```

One Level Down

```
   \DOS            \BIN
```

which is what you want. But if you're already one level down, in \DOS:

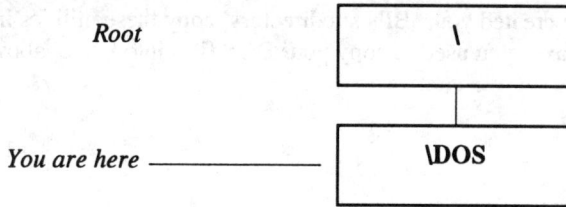

Root

```
┌─────────────────────┐
│          \          │
└─────────────────────┘
           │
```

You are here ─────────────

```
┌─────────────────────┐
│        \DOS         │
└─────────────────────┘
```

and you type MD BIN, you'll get:

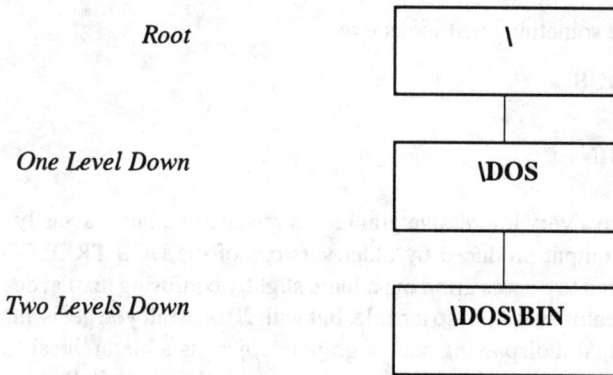

Root

```
┌─────────────────────┐
│          \          │
└─────────────────────┘
           │
```

One Level Down

```
┌─────────────────────┐
│        \DOS         │
└─────────────────────┘
           │
```

Two Levels Down

```
┌─────────────────────┐
│      \DOS\BIN       │
└─────────────────────┘
```

Actually, it really doesn't matter which way you set up your subdirectories. Most users aren't really comfortable creating tree structures any more complex than one or two levels deep. A few prefer intricately filigreed systems. For best results, *keep it simple.* The only real reason to create lots of subdirectories branching off of each other is if your work demands it.

For instance, if you're a CPA with many clients, each one deserves its own subdirectory, and each will require still deeper subdirectory levels of organization. It's good practice to keep records separated by year or quarter or even month, depending on the quantity of files. But while it might make sense to keep expenses in one subdirectory and income in another, it would be ridiculous to have one called:

```
\SMITHCO\1990\JUNE\EXPENSES\OFFICE\PENCILS
```

and another:

```
\SMITHCO\1990\JUNE\EXPENSES\OFFICE\STAPLES
```

If you've followed the earlier instructions properly, you now have two subdirectories called \DOS and \BIN, each one level down from the root directory. \DOS contains all the important files you copied from your two main DOS disks. \BIN should contain all the smaller non-DOS utilities and batch files you use every day.

Once you've created your \BIN subdirectory, copy these utilities into it (by adapting any of the syntaxes you used to copy your DOS files into \DOS, above). Log into \BIN by typing:

```
CD \BIN
```

and run **VTREE** by typing:

```
VTREE
```

You should see something that looks like:

```
┌──── DOS
│
└──── BIN
```

This may not be a very impressive graphic representation, but it's vastly better than the nearly useless output produced by older versions of the DOS TREE.COM utility. All TREE.COM used to do was grind out a long, slightly confusing textual description. With just two subdirectories it's not so terrible, but with 20 or 30 all you get is an unmanageable scrolling mess. And displaying such a graphic object as a hierarchical tree with words alone is like trying to describe colors to someone who's congenitally blind.

You can make TREE slightly more useful by adding an /F switch, which will display all the files in all the subdirectories. But even this use of TREE is overshadowed by the far better CHKDSK /V, which also lists all the files on your disk. CHKDSK /V displays full pathnames; TREE /F doesn't. And TREE pads all its listings with unnecessary spaces, which makes it scroll rapidly off your screen. As a bonus, CHKDSK /V adds the standard CHKDSK report detailing the number of files, bytes free, etc. And it displays the hidden files; TREE /F doesn't. Finally, CHKDSK /V is far faster.

Incidentally, early versions of TREE contain a nasty bug. When the TREE command in PC-DOS 2.0, 2.1, and 3.0 encounters a directory with an extension, such as UTILS.NEW, it stops in its tracks after it has finished listing any directories below the one with the extension. DOS didn't get around to fixing it until version 3.1.

Earlier TREE versions also don't list files in the root directory when you specify the /F parameter after TREE. The upgraded TREE in DOS versions 3.1 and later also fixes this problem.

If you're not using DOS 4.0 or 5.0, copy VTREE.COM into your \BIN subdirectory. Then type:

```
ERASE \DOS\TREE.COM
```

Note that in the above example, the full name of the primitive DOS utility that you just expunged was \DOS\TREE.COM rather than just TREE.COM. That's because you can have different versions of similarly named files in different subdirectories. You can even have similarly named subdirectories; if you wanted to (but trust us, you don't) you could have a subdirectory called \DOS and one called \BIN\DOS on the same disk.

For instance, you could rename VTREE.COM to TREE.COM and put it in \BIN. So if you keep the original DOS version in the \DOS subdirectory, your hard disk would then contain files called \DOS\TREE.COM (which is the original DOS version) and \BIN\TREE.COM (which is the renamed version of VTREE.COM). To run the original DOS version, you'd type:

```
\DOS\TREE
```

To run VTREE.COM, which for this example you renamed to TREE.COM, you'd type:

```
\BIN\TREE
```

If you were in the root directory, and you hadn't yet used the PATH command to tell DOS where to look for executable files, and you typed:

```
TREE
```

you wouldn't run either \DOS\TREE or \BIN\TREE; all you'd get is a "Bad command or file name" message. As discussed above, when you type a command like TREE at the DOS prompt, COMMAND.COM first checks whether it's an internal command, and when it discovers it's not, checks the current directory and then a PATH — a specified set of directories — for a file by that name with a COM, EXE, or BAT extension. If \DOS and \BIN aren't yet included in the path, COMMAND.COM won't check in those subdirectories, and won't run either version of TREE.COM.

You can tell COMMAND.COM to check in both of these subdirectories with the command:

```
PATH C:\DOS;C:\BIN
```

or:

```
PATH C:\BIN;C:\DOS
```

The difference between these two is that if the top path is active, DOS will look in the \DOS subdirectory before it looks in \BIN. In the second example it will examine \BIN before \DOS. If DOS finds a TREE file ending in COM, EXE, or BAT, it will stop looking and execute the file. So if the first path is in use, typing TREE will run the DOS version of TREE. If the second path is in use, DOS will find the renamed version of VTREE and run it. If you had files called TREE.COM, TREE.EXE, and TREE.BAT in either subdirectory, DOS would run TREE.COM. It always looks for COM files first, then EXEs, and finally BATs. But it won't look for filenames with any other extensions, such as data files or program overlays. If you have a version of DOS 3.3 or later, you can use the APPEND command to mimic the PATH command and find any kind of file. If you're using an earlier version, you can purchase a commercial PATH extender like *Filepath* or *File Facility*. But save yourself heartache and upgrade to the most current DOS version available.

It's best to include a PATH command like either of the ones above in your startup AUTOEXEC.BAT file. And if you're using a PATH extender or APPEND, add a separate line in your AUTOEXEC.BAT for it too.

As mentioned above, the SET command can show you the command you entered to customize your prompt. Typing SET on a line by itself will also display the current path setting, as will typing PATH by itself. You can always modify your existing path setting by following the PATH command with the new list of subdirectories, joined together with semicolons.

A smarter technique for adding path settings is to use environment variables. These variables weren't documented until version 3.3, and they don't work at all in version 3.0. And you have to make sure you have enough environment space to accommodate these variables.

The environment is a special area of memory that DOS uses to store important settings like your current PROMPT setting, what directories your path includes, and where to look for your main copy of COMMAND.COM. You can also park variables there by using the SET command, and retrieve them in batch files by wrapping the variable name in percent signs. So if you wrote a small batch file that included just the lines:

```
SET COLOR=BLUE
ECHO %COLOR%
```

the first line of the batch file would insert the string:

```
COLOR=BLUE
```

into the environment, and the second line would look in the environment for the value, replace %COLOR% with BLUE, and display the word:

```
BLUE
```

on screen. If you later typed:

```
SET COLOR=RED
```

and ran a batch file that included the line:

```
ECHO %COLOR%
```

it would print:

```
RED
```

To get rid of the COLOR environment variable, just type:

```
SET COLOR=
```

with nothing after the equals sign. At any point you can see all your environment settings by typing:

```
SET
```

at the DOS prompt.

However, DOS sets up a default environment that's only 160 bytes long, and this space fills up quickly. You can make it bigger, but the method varies with the DOS version you're using. Under DOS 2.0 and 2.1 you can patch COMMAND.COM at address ECF to represent the number of 16-byte memory paragraphs that will make up your new environment. (For DOS 2.11 the address is DF3.) DOS 3.0 and 3.1 lets you put a:

```
SHELL [d:][path]COMMAND.COM /E:n /P
```

command in your CONFIG.SYS file, where n is the number of 16-byte *paragraphs*. For versions 3.2 and later, use the same SHELL command but specify the actual number of bytes rather than paragraphs. You can increase the size from the default of 160 bytes up to 32K in DOS 3.2, 3.3, 4.0, and 5.0, but the maximum size in earlier versions is 62 paragraphs, or 992 bytes.

Once you've made sure you have enough environment space, create a small batch file called ADDPATH.BAT by getting into DOS, typing in the lines below, pressing the Enter key at the end of each one, and then pressing the F6 key and the Enter key one final time when you're all done. Do it right and you'll get a "1 File(s) copied" message afterwards:

```
COPY CON ADDPATH.BAT
ECHO OFF
IF %1!==! GOTO OOPS
PATH=%PATH%;%1
GOTO END
:OOPS
ECHO Enter the new directory after %0
ECHO that you want to add to your PATH
:END
```

To test it out, assuming you don't already have PATH set, create a simple PATH to your C:\DOS directory with the command:

```
PATH=C:\DOS
```

Then type either PATH or SET to make sure you typed it in properly. To extend the path so it included C:\BIN, you'd ordinarily have to type:

```
PATH=C:\DOS;C:\BIN
```

But if you have ADDPATH.BAT handy, all you have to do is type:

```
ADDPATH C:\BIN
```

Then type SET or PATH again and you'll see the path setting has indeed been extended.

When the PATH statement is short, this doesn't save much typing. But when your path goes all the way across the screen, you'll appreciate it. It works by using an environment setting as a variable. The %PATH% is a variable that tells DOS "look inside the current environment setting and substitute, in place of the %PATH% in the batch file, whatever follows the word PATH=." The technique also uses what is called a replaceable parameter — the %1. When DOS sees this in a batch file, it replaces the %1 with the first word or string of characters you typed on the command line immediately following the name of the batch file.

So if the batch file is called ADDPATH, and at the DOS prompt you typed:

```
ADDPATH HELLO
```

it would replace the %1 with HELLO.

The "IF %1!==! GOTO OOPS" (note the double equal sign) tests to see whether you typed anything in after the name of the batch file. If you did type something in, like C:\BIN, DOS replaces the %1 with C:\BIN and turns the test into:

```
IF C:\BIN!==! GOTO OOPS
```

Now C:\BIN! is clearly not equal to !, so the test fails. However, if you entered nothing after the name of the batch file, %1 would be equal to nothing, and DOS would turn the test into:

```
IF !==! GOTO OOPS
```

Sure enough, ! does equal !, so the batch file will jump to the "label" called :OOPS, where it prints a message providing instructions. (Labels are preceded with colons and don't execute.) This effectively jumps around the "PATH=%PATH%;%1" command if you forgot to enter an additional path extension. DOS will replace the %0 in the line that says "ECHO Enter the new directory after %0" with the name of the batch file itself. This way, if you change the name of the batch file from ADDPATH.BAT to something else, DOS will always display the current name in the instructions.

If you did enter a new subdirectory that you wanted tacked onto the end of your path, DOS would *concatenate* it when it came to the "PATH=%PATH%;%1" line. It would replace the %PATH% with the current path and the %1 with the new subdirectory you just typed in. And it would tack on the semicolon DOS uses to separate subdirectories. If the current path was:

```
PATH C:\DOS
```

and you typed in:

```
ADDPATH C:\BIN
```

you'd end up with:

```
PATH C:\DOS;C:\BIN
```

The equal sign sometimes used after PATH is optional; DOS treats it as a space. Typing:

```
PATH C:\DOS
```

or:

```
PATH=C:\DOS
```

will produce identical results. If you do like to experiment with your path settings, you can always make it easy to reset everything by typing:

```
PATH > OLDPATH.BAT
```

at the DOS prompt before you make any changes. This redirects the environment string into a batch file called OLDPATH.BAT. When you're done changing the PATH, just type:

```
OLDPATH
```

at the DOS prompt to put things back to normal. Sometimes you may need to add directories to your PATH setting temporarily, then get rid of the additions when you're done. You can adapt the process described above by modifying ADDPATH slightly:

```
COPY CON ADDPATH.BAT
ECHO OFF
IF %1!==! GOTO OOPS
SET P1=%PATH%
PATH=%PATH%;%1
GOTO END
:OOPS
ECHO Enter the new directory after %0
ECHO that you want to add to your PATH
:END
```

Then create another called PATHOLD.BAT that restores the original PATH:

```
ECHO OFF
PATH=%P1%
SET P1=
```

For instance, if you want to add C:\BIN to your existing PATH temporarily, type:

```
ADDPATH C:\BIN
```

just the way you did before. But when you're done, to restore things the way they were before you made the addition, just type:

```
PATHOLD
```

The new "SET P1=%PATH%" line simply creates a dummy variable called P1 that stores the contents of the old PATH, before you make any PATH changes. PATHOLD.BAT then takes the original PATH — stored under the P1 environment variable — and puts things back the way they were, then gets rid of the dummy P1.

The only problem with this is that you have to single-step your way through. If you add one directory and later want to get rid of it and add another one, you have to run PATHOLD before you add the second one. If you don't, ADDPATH will add the second new one onto the first.

The DOS RAMdisk

As every power user knows, a RAMdisk is a section of memory that some software has tricked DOS into treating like an additional physical disk drive. RAMdisks are far faster than even the fastest hard disks, since they contain no moving parts. The tradeoff, of course, is that RAMdisks are volatile; all data stored on them vanishes when you turn the power off or when the current in your wall socket hiccups.

To install the free RAMdisk that comes with later versions of DOS, make sure the DOS RAMDRIVE.SYS program is in your C:\DOS subdirectory, and include this line in your CONFIG.SYS file:

```
DEVICE=C:\DOS\RAMDRIVE.SYS
```

This command will set up a virtual drive D: with a default 64K of available space. If you want a larger RAMdisk, you can specify the number of bytes at the end of the command, plus, in DOS 5.0, the sector size, maximum number of files or directories, and whether to use extended or expanded memory. For example,

```
DEVICE=C:\DOS\RAMDRIVE.SYS 360
```

would set up a drive D: that's the same size as a standard double-sided floppy. However, IBM won't let you DISKCOPY into it. RAMdisk software from other manufacturers, such as AST's *SUPERDRV*, will let you use the DISKCOPY command. IBM's VDISK and Microsoft DOS 5.0's RAMDRIVE driver will let you create multiple virtual disks, configure the sector size and number of directory entries, and, in the most recent versions of DOS, use extended or expanded memory.

Under DOS 4.0 and 5.0, you can install VDISK.SYS or RAMDRIVE.SYS in extended or expanded memory. Using expanded memory can be a problem on some systems with proprietary caches that conflict with the DOS BUFFER command. (In DOS 4.0 you need to specify /X after your BUFFERS command to use VDISK's /X expanded memory abilities.) A safer way is to put RAMDRIVE into extended memory. To create a 128K RAMdisk in extended memory, include a line in your CONFIG.SYS file that reads:

```
DEVICE=C:\DOS\RAMDRIVE.SYS 128 /E
```

The trick is to figure out which major programs, batch files, and utilities you use frequently and insert a cascade of commands in your AUTOEXEC.BAT file to copy those files to the RAMdisk. Then make sure your path includes this new drive. In the example used above, the path would now look like:

```
PATH=D:\;C:\DOS;C:\BIN
```

Putting D:\ first means that the root directory of the RAMdisk is the first place DOS will look.

It's smart to put all your batch files except the tiniest ones into a RAMdisk, since batch files execute one slow line at a time. Watching even a hard disk grind its way through a medium sized batch file is no fun.

Let's say you use three programs very often — CHKDSK.COM, a color-setting and screen-clearing program called C.COM, and BROWSE.COM. Your AUTOEXEC.BAT file would contain the lines:

```
COPY C:\CHKDSK.COM D: > NUL
COPY C:\C.COM D: > NUL
COPY C:\BROWSE.COM D:Z.COM > NUL
```

The > NUL at the end of each line gets rid of the "1 File(s) copied" messages. Notice that the third line not only copies BROWSE.COM to D: but also renames it to Z.COM. That's because Z is a lot easier to type than BROWSE since Z is one letter long and happens to be at the lower lefthand corner of the keyboard.

Protecting AUTOEXEC.BAT and CONFIG.SYS

Most software packages these days either come with instructions that suggest creating one or more dedicated subdirectories, or have their own installation programs that do it automatically.

However, these automatic installers can be downright dangerous. Some replace your versions of AUTOEXEC.BAT and CONFIG.SYS with their own, when they really ought to modify yours rather than trashing them. Others hide files, which makes it difficult to remove subdirectories.

You can prevent your AUTOEXEC.BAT and CONFIG.SYS files from being written over by using the TYPE or BROWSE commands or your word processor to examine the program's BAT and installation programs. If you see a command that simply copies that program's versions of AUTOEXEC.BAT and CONFIG.SYS to your hard disk, you can use your word processor to adapt your existing files rather than watch them get trashed.

A smart idea is to maintain a small subdirectory called \BAKUP containing nothing but your current versions of COMMAND.COM, AUTOEXEC.BAT, and CONFIG.SYS. Every time you update one of these, copy it to the \BAKUP subdirectory. Then when a program installs itself destructively you can type:

```
COPY \BAKUP \
```

This is shorthand — you could have said:

```
COPY \BAKUP\*.* \
```

Or, you can log into the root directory and just type:

```
COPY BAKUP
```

DOS thinks that when you tell it to perform a task such as copying or deleting and you specify just the name of the subdirectory, you are asking it to do something to all the files in the subdirectory. So if you have a \BIN directory and you type:

```
DEL \BIN
```

DOS assumes you want to wipe out every file in the subdirectory just as if you had typed:

```
DEL \BIN\*.*
```

In both cases it will warn you in its quirky way with the message:

```
Are you sure (Y/N)?
```

(DOS 4.0 and 5.0 make it clearer by adding a message "All files in directory will be deleted!")

Keeping duplicates of your important root directory files in a \BAKUP subdirectory is also a good idea if you try to get too tricky. While DOS usually pauses to warn you if you try to delete all the files in a directory, you can sidestep the protection. Execute either of the commands:

```
FOR %A IN (*.*) DO DEL %A
```

or:

```
ECHO Y | DEL *.*
```

and DOS will merrily wipe out every last nonhidden file. The syntax for the above FOR command is correct if you type it in at the DOS prompt (be careful if you try this). But if you want to use it in a batch file replace both single % signs with double %% signs (and be even more careful).

An easy way to keep your files safe is to use the ATTRIB command to make them all read-only so they can't be deleted, overwritten, or changed. Just type:

```
ATTRIB *.* +R
```

Hidden Files

Hidden files can be a real problem with subdirectories. Few users keep the same subdirectory structure for very long. Most end up cutting and pasting branches of the tree as they get more sophisticated or desperately short of space, or when they replace applications packages with newer ones.

The RD command removes subdirectories, but only when they're empty. If you've left even one file or lower-level subdirectory in them, you won't be able to expunge the subdirectory.

Some programs, in spiteful attempts at copy protection, install hidden files that you can't see in normal directory searches. If you try to remove a subdirectory that you think is empty, and you see this message:

```
Invalid path, not directory,
or directory not empty
```

first check to see if you've left any subdirectories branching off the one you want to get rid of. If so, you have to move or erase the contents of those lower-level subdirectories first, then use the RD command to remove them.

If there aren't any files or lower-level subdirectories, some nasty application has probably planted a hidden file there. You can check on this by executing the CHKDSK /V | MORE command, which will show all the files on your disk a screenful at a time, including the hidden ones. Then use ATTRIB.EXE to unhide the file.

Warning: Some commercial software packages not only hide files but scramble the arrangement of DOS sectors beneath the hidden file. If at all possible, always try to use the deinstallation program that came with the software package before using a utility to reveal the program so you can erase it.

Changing the file attributes to "hidden" or "read-only" will prevent programs from overwriting them. These utilities use function 43H of INT 21 to first check the existing attribute byte, and change only the bits that need modification. ORing the existing value with 1 makes it read-only; ORing it with 2 makes the file hidden. ANDing it with FE takes away the read-only attribute; ANDing it with FD unhides the file. This way it leaves other attributes (system or archive) as they were.

Unfortunately, you can't use function 43 to change the attribute byte of subdirectories or volume labels, so this won't let you meddle with those.

Be careful when hiding files *en masse*. If you issued a command such as:

```
FOR %A in (*.*) DO HIDE %A
```

you'd end up with a whole directory of hidden files. You won't be able to use a similar command to unhide them all at once, since DOS won't see any files to unhide. You'll have to unhide all your files individually. The safest thing to do if you hide lots of files is first create a master file listing all the filenames, and put this master file in another directory or on another disk. If you're on drive C: you could use a command like:

```
DIR > B:C-HIDDEN.LST
```

Of course, with DOS 5.0, you can use the enhanced features of ATTRIB.EXE to unhide files *en masse* rather simply with

```
ATTRIBU -h *.*
```

Making all your root directory files hidden may look interesting, but it can confuse anyone else who tries to work with your system. Making them read-only will prevent other programs from changing (or deleting) them, but you'll still see them in normal DIR searches.

Some awful installation programs change things as they proceed. They may rename a driver file on the original disk or delete files once they've copied them to a hard disk. If the installation process is interrupted, or if it's so dumb that it doesn't know when something's gone wrong, you may have trouble reinstalling things later.

Another clever way to prevent having software packages replace or otherwise modify AUTOEXEC.BAT is to make your AUTOEXEC.BAT tiny and have it run another start-up batch file with a different name that does all the real work. This way if something clobbers the file on your disk named AUTOEXEC.BAT, it won't hurt your real startup file.

To do this, just put the following two lines in your AUTOEXEC.BAT:

```
ECHO OFF
SETPATH STARTUP
```

All this does is execute another batch file called SETPATH.BAT:

```
SET NORMPATH=C:\DOS;C:\UTIL;C:\
PATH %NORMPATH%
%1
```

SETPATH.BAT sets the path, and then executes the STARTUP.BAT file, since its %1 replaceable parameter refers to the word STARTUP in the last line of the AUTOEXEC.BAT file.

The STARTUP.BAT file contains all commands you normally would have placed in an AUTOEXEC.BAT file:

```
PROMPT $P$G
PRINT /D:PRN /Q:32
CARDFILE C:\UTIL\CARDFILE.TXT
DOSKEY
CTYPE /MA
SPEEDUP
```

There are several advantages to this technique:

- The AUTOEXEC.BAT file is simple to recreate if it is destroyed or inadvertently modified.
- The PATH command is in its own separate batch file, making it easy to change if directories are added or removed.
- The SETPATH.BAT file can quickly restore the default path if it has been changed.
- By creating a batch file like ADDPATH.BAT:

    ```
    PATH %NORMPATH%;%1
    ```

    it's easy to add a new directory to the path temporarily, and then restore it later with SETPATH.BAT. Don't try this with buggy DOS 3.0 however.
- If all memory resident programs are removed by utilities such as INSTALL/REMOVE, running STARTUP.BAT restores the memory resident programs as they were at power-on time.

Another ingenious protection solution is to change COMMAND.COM so it looks for a file with a name other than AUTOEXEC.BAT. In fact, the first file COMMAND.COM tries to execute doesn't even have to end in .BAT.

Subdirectory Navigation

It's easy to create new subdirectories and move around inside existing ones if you have the right tools handy and follow a few simple rules.

The first rule is to remember that when you want to move up — toward the root directory — all you have to do is type:

```
CD ..
```

(or CD   ..) to jump to each successive parent directory. However, when you finally land in the root directory, you can't move up any more levels, trying to do so will produce an "Invalid directory" message.

It is especially easy to back out to the root directory by using the F3 key. If you're in a subdirectory five levels deep called:

```
LEV1\LEV2\LEV3\LEV4\LEV5
```

(you can tell this by the C:\LEV1\LEV2\LEV3\LEV4\LEV5: prompt that your PROMPT $P: command displays) and you want to jump back to the root directory, you can do this the easy way, by typing:

```
CD \
```

or, you can jump upward a level at a time by typing:

```
CD ..
```

once and then tapping the F3 key four more times. Each time you do, DOS will repeat the earlier command, and since that command is CD .. it will bounce you rapidly rootward.

To move in the other direction, down from the root directory to LEV5, you could of course simply type:

```
CD \LEV1\LEV2\LEV3\LEV4\LEV5
```

However, you can't type:

```
CD \LEV5
```

because that would tell DOS to jump you into a subdirectory called \LEV5 that was just one level down from the root directory. The real name of the \LEV5 subdirectory above is not just \LEV5; it's \LEV1\LEV2\LEV3\LEV4\LEV5.

Another way to get from the root directory to there is by using the relative version of the CD command to bounce you down one level at a time. Note that since DOS keeps track of each subdirectory by its full pathname rather than by just its particular branch on the tree, you could have a path like:

```
C:\SHARE\AND\SHARE\ALIKE
```

since the subdirectory:

```
C:\SHARE
```

is utterly different from:

```
C:\SHARE\AND\SHARE
```

One is a single level down from the root directory, while the other is three levels down. However, having similar names like this is confusing, and is a bad idea for an important reason you'll see later.

To go from the root to the lowest branch one level at a time, you'd type:

```
CD SHARE
CD AND
CD SHARE
CD ALIKE
```

When you're on one branch of a tree it's easy to bounce around from one subdirectory to another on the same level. If you have a tree that looks like this:

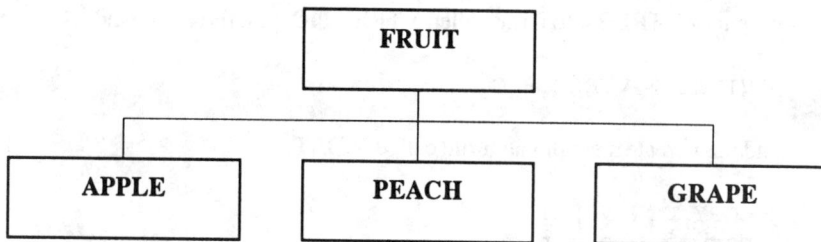

and you're currently in \FRUIT\APPLE and you want to jump to \FRUIT\GRAPE, you can type in:

```
CD ..\GRAPE
```

since the .. is shorthand for the parent directory (\FRUIT). But jumping from one deep branch of your subdirectory structure to a completely different branch can be a bad typist's nightmare.

If you're currently logged into:

```
\FRUIT\PEACH
```

and you want to jump to:

```
\PROGS\STAR\VER3\MEMOS\MERGER
```

you'd normally have to type in:

```
CD \PROGS\STAR\VER3\MEMOS\MERGER
```

Awful. But there's a far easier trick. If your hard disk is set up properly you can simply type:

```
MERGER
```

and DOS will zap you there.

The trick is to create either a slate of small batch files — or one huge batch file — to do all the switching. If you had a batch file called MERGER.BAT on your hard disk, in a subdirectory included in your path, with the contents:

```
CD \PROGS\STAR\VER3\MEMOS\MERGER
```

typing MERGER would execute that batch file, which would in turn execute the proper thorny CD command. This is why it's a good idea to have subdirectories that avoid confusingly similar names. You can create a new batch file every time you issue an MD command to create a new subdirectory.

But how do you know what directories are on your disk? Simple. Just redirect the output of VTREE into a file called VTREE.PIC with the command:

```
VTREE > VTREE.PIC
```

and then create a small batch file called V.BAT:

```
COPY CON V.BAT
BROWSE VTREE.PIC
```

(If you're using DOS 4.0 or 5.0, substitute TREE for VTREE.) Press the Enter key after each line, and when you're finished, press the F6 function key and then the Enter key one more time.

Redirect the output of VTREE into VTREE.PIC every time you create a new subdirectory or remove an existing one. Then, assuming BROWSE.COM and V.BAT are in a subdirectory that you've included in your PATH, each time you type:

```
V
```

you'll see an instant graphic representation of your subdirectory tree structure. You can use the arrow and PgUp/PgDn keys to move around in the tree. Pressing Esc will return you to DOS where you can switch to the target subdirectory by using one of the BATMAKR programs described above.

If you have *SideKick*, an even better adaptation of this method is to use *SideKick*'s notepad as a window that displays the VTREE.PIC file as the default. Store VTREE.PIC in your \BIN subdirectory. Bring up *SideKick*'s main menu, and type F7 or S for the setup menu. Type in \BIN\VTREE.PIC as the new Notefile name and press F2 to save this as the default. Then whenever you pop up *SideKick* and select the notepad, the graphic representation will jump onto the screen. Press QG to turn on the graphics line characters that connect the subdirectories.

Once you've created a lot of individual switcher files, make sure that whenever you create a new subdirectory, you also create a batch file (which goes in \BIN or \BAT) that simply contains the full pathname of the subdirectory with a CD\ prefix. So if you're adding a new directory called 1\2\3\4\5, create a batch file called 5.BAT:

```
CD \1\2\3\4\5
```

and put this batch file into \BIN or \BAT. Then, just type 5 to jump directly into your \1\2\3\4\5 directory.

You'll obviously have a problem with this if your disk contains two subdirectories with similar names, such as \ACCOUNT\1990\TAX and \ACCOUNT\1991\TAX. In this case you'd have to either change one of the names slightly, or forego this technique.

Some users feel this is too wasteful, since each file, no matter how small, can take up from 2K to 8K. However, this is a small price to pay for ease of tree-hopping.

Finding Files

Users have their own favorite ways to find files buried deep inside a long-forgotten subdirectory. The FF and WHEREIS programs on one of the accompanying disks can help. But by executing a simple FINDFILE.BAT batch file you can have DOS do it:

```
ECHO OFF
IF %1!==! GOTO OOPS
ECHO NOW SEARCHING DIRECTORIES FOR "%1"
CHKDSK /V | FIND "%1" | MORE
GOTO END
:OOPS
ECHO Enter a filespec (or part of one) after %0
:END
```

FINDFILE exploits the /V feature of CHKDSK.COM. The /V option lists all files in all subdirectories, but you wouldn't know this from some of the early DOS manuals, which describe it with meaningless remarks like saying it will "display a series of messages indicating its progress, and provide more detailed information about the errors it finds." The more recent editions of the manual are a little clearer.

Adding a /V switch makes it a snap to search for a particular file. FINDFILE pipes the output of CHKDSK /V through the FIND.EXE and MORE.COM filters, so you have to have these DOS utilities on the same subdirectory as FINDFILE.BAT or in a directory your path knows about.

If you wanted to search for BASICA.COM, for instance, you would simply type:

```
FINDFILE BASICA
```

If you typed:

```
FINDFILE BASIC
```

the batch file would locate both BASIC.COM and BASICA.COM, and any other filename with the capital letters BASIC in it. You may also use parts of names. Typing:

```
FINDFILE ASICA
```

would find BASICA.COM. This comes in handy if you want to look for files with the same extensions. Enter:

```
FINDFILE .COM
```

and you'll see all your COM files. Remember to enter capital letters only. And don't put quotes around the filenames or parts of filenames you want to find — the batch file will do this for you automatically. FINDFILE won't display a special message telling you no matches were found if it comes up empty. But this will be obvious when no matches are displayed on your screen. The only real problem with this is that FINDFILE.BAT is slow, especially on a nearly full hard disk, since it has to pipe hundreds or thousands of filenames through a filter, and create temporary files while it does so. You could redirect the output of CHKDSK /V into a file and adapt FINDFILE so it looks at the existing list of filenames instead of having to recreate the list each time. The tradeoff is that such a list has to be updated frequently, and ends up always being at least a bit out of date.

(You can do the same trick with ATTRIB \filename /S.)

Moving Files

When users normally move a file from one subdirectory to another, they first copy the file with the COPY command and then use ERASE to delete the original. Or they write a short batch file to do it:

```
COPY %1 %2
ERASE %1
```

The problem with such a batch file is that if an incorrect destination is specified, it can fail to make the copy but then go ahead and erase the original anyway. You could try the following MOVEIT.BAT batch file:

```
ECHO OFF
IF NOT %2! == ! GOTO TEST
```

```
ECHO You must specify what to move
ECHO and where to move it to, eg:
ECHO %0 CHKDSK.COM \DOS
GOTO END
:TEST
IF NOT EXIST %2\%1 GOTO COPY
ECHO %1 is already in %2
ECHO To prevent overwriting %1, press
ECHO Ctrl-Break right now. Otherwise
PAUSE
:COPY
COPY %1 %2\%1>NUL
IF NOT EXIST %2\%1 GOTO ERROR
ERASE %1
GOTO END
:ERROR
ECHO Error in destination specified, or
ECHO the file to be moved is not in
CD
:END
```

MOVEIT.BAT starts by checking to see if you entered the correct number of parameters, and gives you a help message if you didn't. It then copies the file, using %2\%1 so you don't have to spell out the name of the file in both locations (wildcards will work). However, this limits you a bit, since you have to be in the directory of the file you are trying to copy. (You could modify it to COPY %1 %2 if you like, which would allow you to copy files without having to first log into those files' subdirectory — but you would have to spell out the name of the file in both places.) Finally, it erases the original file only if it finds the new one.

It's smart to confirm that the copy was indeed made before deleting the original. But versions of DOS earlier than 3.0 will have problems with IF EXIST tests and paths.

MOVEIT.BAT checks to make sure the file isn't already at the destination subdirectory before you copy it, which prevents you from accidentally overwriting files. If you see a message warning you that you're about to obliterate an existing file, just press Ctrl-Break and then the Y key to abandon the process. Otherwise, press any key to proceed.

Fine-Tuning Your Hard Disk System

While DOS limits the number of files you can shoehorn into the root directory, and smart users know to keep their root directories small, the number of files in each of your subdirectories is limited only by the amount of space on your disk.

But it's not wise to let your subdirectories get too big, unless you have an easy way to back them up.

The DOS BACKUP and RESTORE commands aren't very slick, but they're free and can split large files up and spread them over several disks. You can back up incrementally, by having BACKUP copy only files created or changed after a certain date, or modified since the last time you backed up. You can tell BACKUP to dig down into your subdirectory structure and overwrite earlier versions or add a new version along with the old.

But, BACKUP should format brand new disks automatically. And it changes backed-up programs slightly so you can't just run them unless you first RESTORE them. You have to be careful (and use the /P switch) when you're restoring files backed up with earlier DOS versions so you don't write the wrong system files onto your hard disk. DOS 3.3 and later versions are careful about this; earlier ones weren't.

Because of all these potential problems, many users keep their subdirectories small enough so each can be copied onto a single floppy disk. And they're starting to discover the terrific DOS 3.2 XCOPY command as a better way to create backups. This obviously won't work with giant files. If you work with large files, you have to either grit your teeth and use BACKUP, or buy a tape drive or Bernoulli box.

Do get into the habit of backing up regularly. The morning you turn your system on and hear a sound like a wrench in a blender, you'll be glad you did.

Backing up just the files you changed or added recently is better than not backing up at all, but when your hard disk goes south, you'll have to spend days putting all the little puzzle pieces back together. It's a good stopgap measure, but nothing beats making complete archive copies of the whole disk.

A real advantage to backing up everything at once is that you'll be able to streamline your file structure and end up working far faster. The routine process of adding to and editing down your files each day ends up sowing little file fragments more or less at random over the surface of your disk.

You should periodically copy all your files to a backup medium (and get rid of the duplicates, BAK versions, and dead data in the process), reformat your hard disk, and then copy everything back. You'll notice an immediate improvement in speed. When you do this, put the subdirectories that you path to at the very beginning of your directory by making sure they're the first ones you copy to the newly formatted disk.

One final pearl is obvious, but bears repeating. Think before you FORMAT. Even though the latest versions of DOS make you type in a Y and then press the Enter key before going ahead and wiping everything out, late at night you may misinterpret the question or press a Y when you meant N, or have some aberrant and lethal combination of JOIN, APPEND, and SUBST bubbling away under the surface that steers an innocent floppy request into a jolt of panic. (And never run RECOVER, unless you're really desperate, since this will bollix up everything and turn your hard disk structure and all the files on it into anonymous mush.)

A few seconds into the formatting process the hard disk FATs and directories get zeroed out, and any attempt at resurrection is only a best guess. It is possible to bring much of your data back to life with a utility like Mace's or Norton's, especially if you let them park a copy of your FAT ahead of time. But don't tempt fate.

If you're working on something time-sensitive and critically important, stop frequently while you're working and make a working copy to a floppy. It is possible to corrupt a hard disk if you're writing to it and the local power company decides that moment would be a good one to switch generators. You can set up a batch file to automate the process.

Otherwise you might end up spending the rest of the evening patching together little shards of your work that you've fished out of the magnetic murk.

If you notice that performance is degrading, or hear the percussive rhythm of repeated read retries, run Norton's disk diagnosis and repair programs. This takes a few minutes, but can ferret out developing problems and zap out bad sectors better than DOS can. And if Norton reports grief, back up everything pronto and hie down to your dealer. When hard disks start whimpering they go downhill real fast. Hard disk problems never just go away.

Caveat Emptor

If you don't yet own a hard disk, remember, no matter what kind of hard drive you're considering, don't buy yourself trouble. Make sure it's (1) safe, and (2) fast. While no hard disk is immune to potential disaster, some are more fragile than others. Since most users back up their data infrequently, a hard disk problem can wipe out weeks of work.

Don't buy a hard disk unless its heads *retract* automatically when you turn the power off. Otherwise, they'll just drop down to the disk and take a bite out of whatever data's there.

And don't get stuck with a low-speed disk in a high-speed system. While you can measure hard disk performance many different ways, the most common single gauge is *average access time* in milliseconds. The lower the number, the faster the drive. IBM's original PC-XT drives crept along at 80 to 115 ms. Today's best performers are in the very low teens. You can make things even faster by using buffers or a disk cache, by setting up your hard disk files and directories properly and keeping things pruned and orderly, reformatting, then restoring only the files you truly need and making sure they're unfragmented.

While other factors can influence speed, average access time is a fairly reliable performance indicator. Take pains *not* to buy a hard drive that's dragging its foot, especially in a computer that runs at a relatively high clock speed.

Hex Class

Ok, this is your chance. If you're fairly new to all this, or if all you want is a thorough mastery of the DOS commands, with a double armload of time-saving tricks and ingenious shortcuts thrown in, turn to the next chapter. Because it's time to talk about binary and hex. You can get by just fine without them. But if you really want to make your system hum, you should know your way around inside. And inside means hex numbers.

It's really not all that difficult; it's just that discussions of 1s and 0s are not inherently absorbing. Still, being a power user means knowing at least a little about all this so that later when we talk about things like binary bit masks (to give you total control over the shift keys on your keyboard) and hexadecimal addresses (to help you recover lost data) you don't just scratch your head and turn on HBO. So here goes. We'll try to make it as painless as possible. And we'll throw in a few surprises you'll like.

There's no such thing as a little bit pregnant, or a little bit dead. You either are or you aren't. Life offers few such absolutes. A hundred people look at a sculpture in an art museum. A third love it. A third hate it. A third look at their watches.

If you watch old Fred Astaire movies you rarely see objects that are all black or all white. Some things are close, but if you look carefully you'll admit that they are 2 percent grey or 98 percent grey. And most things are closer to the middle of the scale.

High-contrast photographic paper, on the other hand, is designed to produce a stark black-on-white image without any greys whatsoever. You put it into a darkroom enlarger and project a normal photographic negative with lots of shadows and grey shades onto it. Anything that's 49.99 percent grey or lighter doesn't trigger the silver salts and remains bright and white; wherever anything is 50 percent grey or darker, however, the paper turns jet black.

The world is analog. A dot of color on a TV screen is produced by a fast-changing wave-shaped signal and can be one of hundreds of thousands of hues and tints. However, the waveform is subject to all kinds of distortion and deterioration; make a copy of a TV show on a VCR and then a copy of the copy, and after a few generations play it back on the same TV set and you'll see the colors and the general sharpness are very different from the original. Each copy chews up the shape of the wave a little; after thousands of copies all you'd have is hissy static and a demonstration of entropy in action.

Computers are digital. A dot on a computer screen is produced by a hard, cold, unchanging numeric value. Create a graphics image on a digital computer and make hundreds of successive copies of it and display the 500th one on the same computer and it will have the exact same colors as the original. When you copy a file containing the data that make up the picture, all the mechanisms involved make sure if the value of the first dot in the file was a 69, it remains a 69. It's easier to pack more information into an analog signal. But if you need precision, you have to sacrifice a little quantity for quality. And when you're dealing with computers, the integrity of your data is sacrosanct.

The fundamental building block of digital information is a *bit* (short for *binary digit*). One bit can't store much information by itself; it has a short menu — on or off, 1 or 0, "high" or "low." But in the right chip at the right time, a single bit can trigger instructions that change or move lots of other bits, and when you start stringing millions of them together incredibly fast, you can get some real work done.

Some people are adept at fudging their way through life, laying down dense fog like a PT boat. But you can't fudge a bit. It's either in one state or the other — one of life's few absolutes. Binary numbering makes a lot of sense on a digital computer, a system made up of hundreds of thousands of interconnected switches that are either on or off. Simple two-position switches can indicate the status of something (like an "occupied" sign on a jet), store data (a W or L is what you really want to know about what your local baseball team did the night before), or execute important decisions (like switching tracks to send Chicago trains either north to Boston or south to Washington). But bits are most useful when arranged in groups of eight called *bytes*. A byte is a convenient way to store eight related pieces of information, such as the condition of eight different status indicators deep in the heart of your main chips. It's also handy for representing a letter, number, or special character such as 1/2 or the symbol for pi. And while chips deal with long binary streams of 1s and 0s, humans prefer friendlier alphabets.

Your system is built to move information in one, two, or four byte chunks — depending on whether you're using an eight-bit, 16-bit, or 32-bit computer — rather than in lots and lots of individual bits. (Actually, some second-level processors, like those used by newer display adapter boards, even work with halves of bytes called *nibbles*, and a base-8 numbering system called *octal*. If you're genuinely interested in such sleight-of-hand, you may want to dabble in octal a little later.)

If you noticed that everything so far seems to be divisible by the number 2, you're right. It all leads back to binary. Display adaptors use one, two, four, or eight bits to specify colors. PCs rely on a mixture of eight and 16. Systems based on Intel's 80286 chip, can handle 16 from stem to stern. And the latest crop of 80386 and 80486 powerhouses devour 32 at a single gulp. Users once added extra computer memory in packages of about 64,000 bytes. Today the number has jumped to roughly sixteen times that.

We all like round numbers. Folks who make it to 100 get on the evening news. The advent of a decade is important enough; we're on the verge of a new century and millenium, and the celebration will undoubtedly be eye-popping, all because of a few well-placed zeros.

The computer industry likes round numbers too. But in this business they should really be called "around" numbers, since the two most common big ones — a K for kilobyte (around a thousand bytes) and M for megabyte (around a million bytes) are actually 1,024 and 1,048,576, respectively.

Inflation is affecting even these numbers. Huge storage devices (optical disks and monstrous hard disks) that can salt away a *gigabyte* (around a billion characters) or two are appearing on the scene. (Incidentally, the word is pronounced JIG-uh-byte, not GIG-uh-byte, since it comes from the same root as giant and gigantic rather than gargantuan.) And chip makers love to see our reaction when they start talking about the 80386/80486's ability to address a terabyte (around a trillion bytes). (The root for this word, which means monster, was last in the news as "teratogenic" when it described the property of the drug thalidomide to deform offspring.)

One kilobyte is 2^{10} (2 x 2 x 2 x 2 x 2 x 2 x 2 x 2 x 2 x 2). One megabyte is 2^{20}. So when you see a memory board that holds 64K, it actually can juggle 64 x 1,024, or 65,536 bytes. And when someone tells you a PC's 8088 chip can directly handle a megabyte of memory, they mean 1,048,576 rather than just a paltry one million memory locations. However, it's far easier to call these amounts Ks and megs, which everyone does anyway.

Working with binary or hex numbers isn't intrinsically harder than dealing with decimals; it's just that we've all had so much practice with decimal calculations that we're pretty handy with them by now. But play with binary and hex for a while and you'll pick it up pretty fast.

Odds are that we use a decimal (base-10) system because human have ten fingers and toes. So let's count toes. In decimal it's easy. But start with 0 instead of 1 to make it a little less dull.

0
1
2
3
4
5
6
7
8
9

Ten toes, ten digits. At this point you run out of both. Any more and you have to go to double-digits.

Counting in binary is easy too. The decimal system has ten digits to play with. When you run out, you have to start using more than one digit, and you do it by putting a 0 in the column where the single digits were, and a 1 in the next column.

The binary system has two digits to play with, 0 and 1. When you run out, you also put a 0 in the column where the single digits were, and a 1 in the next column. Only you run out a lot sooner. So you have to keep putting 0s in the columns where you just ran out and 1s in the next column over to the left. Counting toes in binary looks like this:

0	(the first number, just as with decimal)
1	(ran out of single digits; shift over one column)
10	
11	(ran out of double-digits; shift again)
100	
101	
110	
111	(that's all the triple-digits; shift one more time)
1000	
1001	(last toe)

People often pad binary numbers out with 0s, so the same counting process could just as easily look like:

```
0000
0001
0010
0011
0100
0101
0110
0111
1000
1001
```

How do you translate a decimal number into binary format? The key is to become comfortable with the first nine powers of 2. Remember that 2^0 is equal to 1.

$$2^8 = 256$$
$$2^7 = 128$$
$$2^6 = 64$$
$$2^5 = 32$$
$$2^4 = 16$$
$$2^3 = 8$$
$$2^2 = 4$$
$$2^1 = 2$$
$$2^0 = 1$$

Look at the binary version of this chart and you'll see an interesting pattern that will make sense in a moment:

$$2^8 = 100000000$$
$$2^7 = 010000000$$

```
2^6 = 001000000
2^5 = 000100000
2^4 = 000010000
2^3 = 000001000
2^2 = 000000100
2^1 = 000000010
2^0 = 000000001
```

Now pick a number to translate: 13.

The goal is to see which of the powers of 2 make up this number. Consult the chart and look for the biggest number that's equal to or smaller than the one you've picked (13). Obviously the number that fits this description is 8. Since 8 is the fourth one in the chart, the binary version of 13 will have four binary digits, and the leftmost one will be a 1 (although you could stick 0s on the left, since leading 0s don't mean anything in binary just as they don't in decimal; 00000027 is the same in decimal as just plain 27). Then, since you already considered the 8, get rid of it. Subtract it from 13.

1 _ _ _

After subtracting 8 from 13, you're left with 5. Look at the chart again. The next number under 8 is 4. Since you can safely subtract 4 from 5 without ending up with a negative number, put another 1 in the next position over to the right, and subtract the 4 from 5 to leave a remainder of 1.

1 1 _ _

Consult the chart again. The next lower number after 4 is 2. But you can't subtract the 2 from 1 or you'd end up with a negative number. So you'll put a 0 in the next position over.

1 1 0 _

The last number on the chart is 1. You can subtract 1 from the remainder of 1 and still not have a negative number, so put a final 1 in the rightmost position.

1 1 0 1

Decimal 13 is equal to binary 1101.

Another way to look at what you just did is to say 13 is made up of 1   1   0   1

1	x	2^3	=	8
1	x	2^2	=	4
0	x	2^1	=	0
1	x	2^0	=	1
		Total	=	13

Going from binary to decimal is easier. Pick a number: 00110100. Ignore the 0s on the left side (remember, 00000027 in decimal is equal to plain old 27). This leaves a six-digit binary number, 110100. Turn it on its side and put it next to the lowest six entries on the chart. Mutiply as indicated, then add up the result:

```
1   x   2^5   =   32
1   x   2^4   =   16
0   x   2^3   =   0
1   x   2^2   =   4
0   x   2^1   =   0
0   x   2^0   =   0
          Total   =   52
```

You don't really need the chart. You do need to remember the sequence of 1, 2, 4, 8, 16, 32, 64, 128, 256. Then whenever you see a binary number, just count over from the right, and in your head say "that's no 1s plus no 2s plus a 4 (subtotal=4) plus no 8s plus a 16 (subtotal 20) plus a 32 (total 52)." It's easier than it sounds.

Pattern Recognition

While your system can deal with 256 different characters, all it's really doing is handling 256 different numeric values. In one of the only fairly successful attempts to standardize anything on the PC, IBM adopted (and added to) a character-numbering system called ASCII (pronounced as-kee, and standing for the American Standard Code for Information Interchange). In every ASCII file a capital A has a value of decimal 65, a capital B 66, a lowercase a 97, a lowercase b 98, etc.

Your keyboard lets you type 95 characters directly — 26 uppercase and 26 lowercase letters, ten digits, a space, and 32 punctuation marks:

!"#$%&'()*+,-./:;<=>?@[\]^_'{|}~

In addition, your keyboard and computer have to agree on codes for other important operations such as tabs, backspaces, escapes, carriage returns, line feeds, form feeds (otherwise known as page breaks), and so on. You can generate these codes by holding down the Ctrl key and pressing letter keys; to generate a 3 you'd hold down the Ctrl key and press a C (since C is the third letter in the alphabet). You can use a Ctrl-C, abbreviated as ^C, to stop many DOS operations in their tracks, just as with Ctrl-ScrollLock. (However, in IBM BASIC, a ^C will act as a carriage return.) A few of the important operations (some in DOS; some in BASIC) with ASCII codes below 32 are shown in Figure 5.1.

Ctrl Code	ASCII Value	What it does in DOS and/or BASIC
	0	Nul
^B	2	Jump to previous word
^C	3	Break; carriage return in BASIC
^E	5	Erase to end of line
^F	6	Jump to next word
^G	7	Beep
^H	8	Backspace
^I	9	Tab
^J	10	Line feed
^K	11	Home (sometimes)
^L	12	Form feed
^M	13	Carriage return
^N	14	End of line
^P	16	Toggle echo to printer on and off
^Q	17	Restart scrolling in CP/M type operations
^R	18	Toggle Insert/overtype
^S	19	Toggle scrolling on and off
^Z	26	End of file
^[	27	Esc
^\	28	Cursor right
^]	29	Cursor left
^^	30	Cursor up
^_	31	Cursor down

Figure 5.1.   Control Code Operations

You can fit all the letters of the alphabet, digits, punctuation, and control codes (with ASCII values lower than 32) into 128 characters. Early seven-bit systems could address only 128 characters, since 2^7 is 128. IBM added one bit to this system and doubled the number of characters to 256.

The leftmost side of a number is the *high order* side and the rightmost side the *low order* one. This is obvious; for the decimal number 567, for instance, the 5 stands for how many hundreds and the 7 for how many ones. Hundreds are higher than ones in any system, so the 5 is on the high side and 7 on the low side.

Because adding this additional bit meant slapping it onto the leftmost side, ASCII numbers over 128 — which all have a 1 as the leftmost digit — are sometimes referred to as *high-bit* characters.

IBM's high-bit characters let you use foreign languages, create mathematical formulas, and draw box-character pictures and borders. IBM also added a few printable symbols to the ASCII characters with values under 32 (for instance, decimal ASCII character 11 produces the biological male sign and character 12 the female sign).

BIOS provides many different methods for writing characters. You could use something like BIOS service hex 0E, which treats the screen like a teletype, advancing the cursor automatically each time it prints a character, and wrapping text down to the next line when necessary.

However, this service gives special treatment to four ASCII characters:

- decimal 7 — beep
- decimal 8 — backspace
- decimal 10 — linefeed
- decimal 13 — carriage return

If you use it to print these four, you won't see their character symbols onscreen. Try to write an ASCII 7 with service 0E, for instance, and instead of displaying the small centered dot character that IBM assigned to a character 7, all you'll get is a beep.

BIOS services 09 and 0A will print the characters IBM assigned to all 256 ASCII values, including the troublesome four above. All three services, 09, 0A, and 0E, will display three ASCII characters as blanks:

- decimal 0 — null
- decimal 32 — space
- decimal 255 — blank

The difference between services 09 and 0A is that service 09 can change the attribute as it writes each character, while service 0A can't. But with both of these you have to advance the cursor yourself, since BIOS won't do it for you.

The SHOWCHAR.COM program will first use BIOS service 08 to read the attribute at the current cursor position, and will then use service 06 to clear the screen to that position. Then it will display all 256 characters in rows of 32.

```
MOV    AH,8          ; read attribute at cursor
INT    10            ; do it
MOV    BH,AH         ; move attribute into BH
MOV    AX,0600        ; clear screen
XOR    CX,CX         ; starting wth upper lefthand corner
MOV    DX,1849        ; and using whole 25 x 80 screen
INT    10            ; do it
XOR    DX,DX         ; put cursor in upper left corner
XOR    BH,BH         ; of page 0
MOV    CX,1          ; just print one character at a time
PUSH   AX            ; save value of character
MOV    AH,02          ; set cursor position
INT    10            ; do it
POP    AX            ; restore value of character
```

```
MOV   AH,0A        ; write character to screen
INT   10           ; do it
INC   AL           ; get ready for next character
ADD   DL,2         ; two columns over
CMP   DL,40        ; is cursor at end of row?
JNZ   12F          ; no, so skip next routine
INC   DH           ; otherwise move down a line
XOR   DL,DL        ; and back to beginning of line
CMP   AL,FF        ; is it last character?
JNZ   0117         ; no, go back and print next one
RET                ; yes, bye
```

You can create a script file that will produce the program for you. Create a script file called SHOWCHAR.SCR that contains the following nine lines:

```
E 0100 B4 08 CD 10 88 E7 B8 00 06 31 C9 BA 49
E 010D 18 CD 10 31 D2 30 FF B9 01 00 50 B4 02
E 011A CD 10 58 B4 0A CD 10 FE C0 80 C2 02 80
E 0127 FA 40 75 04 FE C6 30 D2 3C FF 75 E4 C3
N SHOWCHAR.COM
RCX
34
W
Q
```

Be certain you press the Enter key at the end of each line, especially the last one with the Q. Then make sure DEBUG.COM version 2.0 or later is handy at the DOS prompt, type:

```
DEBUG < SHOWCHAR.SCR
```

Displaying the ASCII characters in rows of 32 shows that the lowercase alphabet letters have values that are decimal 32 (hex 20) higher than their uppercase cousins.

You can experiment with this program to change the way it displays characters. For instance, once you've created it, you can type:

```
DEBUG SHOWCHAR.COM
E 115 D0 07
E 123 EB 0A
N SHOWFULL.COM
W
Q
```

The basic SHOWCHAR.COM program displays only one of each character at a time. SHOWFULL.COM will display 2,000 (hex 7D0) characters at a time — a full 25 x 80 screenful. BIOS will flash through all 256 full screens of characters in a few seconds.

Or, to see the difference between services 09 and 0A, first use a pure-ASCII word processor or EDLIN to create the following ADDCOLOR.SCR script file. Be sure to press the Enter key at the end of each line, especially the last one with the Q:

```
E 11D 88 C3 B4 09 CD 10 FE C0 80 C2 01 80 FA
E 12A 40 75 04 FE C6 30 D2 3C FF 75 E2 C3
N SHOWCOLR.COM
RCX
36
W
Q
```

Then, at the DOS prompt, type:

```
DEBUG SHOWCHAR.COM < ADDCOLOR.SCR
```

and you'll end up with a variation of SHOWCHAR.COM called SHOWCOLR.COM that displays each character using the ASCII value of the character as the attribute. If you're using a color monitor, you'll see all 256 possible attributes.

SHOWCOLR.COM will display four rows of characters, rather than the eight produced by SHOWCHAR.COM. All four rows will be in color, and because of the BIOS color numbering system, the foreground colors in the bottom two rows will be blinking. The four rows will be divided into four chunks of background colors that are each 16 characters wide. Within these chunks, each of the 16 characters will have a different foreground color. The leftmost eight will appear in normal colors, while the rightmost eight will appear as high-intensity (bright) colors.

Here's why:

It's easiest to see how this works by using the hex value of each attribute. All attributes can be expressed as two-digit hex numbers. The lefthand and righthand digits can each range from 0 to F, which yields decimal 256 possible values from 00 through FF.

The lefthand digit represents the background color, and the righthand digit the foreground color. So on a color system, a number like 71 will produce blue (1) text on a white (7) background, while 17 will yield white text on a blue background. The hex color assignments are shown in Figure 5.2.

However, a value like 4E will produce bright yellow text (E) on a red (4) background, while E4 will produce bright blinking yellow text on a red background. Any value that has a lefthand digit higher than 7 will blink. So a number like 71 won't blink, while a number like 81 will.

Value	Color	Value	Color
1	Blue	9	Bright blue
2	Green	A	Bright green
3	Cyan (Lt Blue)	B	Bright cyan
4	Red	C	Bright red
5	Magenta	D	Bright magenta
6	Brown	E	Bright yellow
7	White	F	Bright white

—— background only ——

←————————————————— **foreground** —————————————————→

Figure 5.2. Hex Color Assignments

Any value that has a righthand digit higher than 7 will appear as a high-intensity color. So a number like 47 will produce a normal, low-intensity color, while 48 will display something in high-intensity.

When you type something like:

```
DEBUG SHOWCHAR.COM < ADDCOLOR.SCR
```

what you're doing is using the redirection abilities of DOS (versions 2.0 and later) to take characters in a file and treat them as keystrokes that DEBUG uses to create a file. DEBUG doesn't care where its keystrokes are coming from — a live user at the keyboard or a file that contains keystrokes that the user put there long ago.

Redirecting script files like this makes a lot of sense when you're using DEBUG to create files, since it lets you check your typing, and since you can often adapt script files so DEBUG can create customized variations of programs for you.

To create files using this technique, make sure you use a pure-ASCII word processor, the DOS EDLIN line editor, or the DOS COPY CON command. If you're not sure whether your word processor can produce pure ASCII text (a file composed of just letters and numbers and punctuation, and not containing anything else), just load it up and type a paragraph and save it as a short file called TEST. Then exit your word processor and get into DOS and type:

```
TYPE TEST
```

You could also use lowercase letters, by typing:

```
type test
```

since DOS translates all characters into uppercase before trying to do anything serious with them, except in a few rare examples such as the with ANSI.SYS keyboard and screen extender that are discussed later.

Either way, if all you see is the text you typed and nothing else, your word processor should do just fine for creating script files. But if your screen fills with "garbage" characters that jump around and beep and clear the screen, you'll have to use another method. Most word processors have a way to create pure-ASCII files; check your manual under "text files" or "ASCII" or "DOS files" or "program editing."

To create the file directly in DOS, make sure you're at the DOS prompt, and type:

```
COPY CON SHOWCHAR.SCR
```

and press the Enter key. The cursor should do nothing except drop down a line and blink dully at you.

Start typing the script, line by line. Make sure each line is absolutely correct before you press the Enter key at the end of it; if you make any mistakes use the backspace key to erase them and then type in the right characters.

Be sure to press the Enter key at the end of each line, especially the last one (with the lonesome Q).

When you're all done, and you're sure you've pressed the Enter key after the final Q, the cursor should be directly below the Q. Press the grey F6 function key and then press the Enter key one last time. When you press the F6 key you'll see a ^Z appear, and then when you press the final Enter key you'll see a "1 File(s) copied" message. You'll then be back at the DOS prompt again. If you want, type DIR SHOWCHAR.SCR and you should see the file you just created with a number just under a thousand beside it, and a date and time. If you don't, you did something wrong and should start the whole process over again.

The COPY CON FILENAME (where FILENAME stands for the name of the file you want to create and not the word "FILENAME" itself) command tells DOS to take the information you're typing at the console (the keyboard and screen) and copy it into a file with the name you entered after the word CON. Pressing the F6 function key when you're all done puts a special character at the end of your file called (surprise) an *end-of-file-marker*. This special character has an ASCII value of 26, and there are several other ways you could put this character there. The easiest is to hold down the Ctrl key and press the Z key while you're holding it down. The ^Z that shows up on the screen when you do either is shorthand for Ctrl-Z.

DOS generally stops in its tracks when it sees an end-of-file marker, as do many commercial software products. So, when creating text files, be careful not to let a stray ^Z wander into your file or DOS will ignore everything that follows.

The only real problem with using the COPY CON technique is that you can't back up and correct a line above the one you're working on. You can fix problems only in the current line. If you make a mistake and don't catch it in time, you have to start over, or go in and edit the file later with EDLIN or a real word processor. And if you have one of those handy, you might as well create the whole file on it.

Anyway, once you've created the SHOWCHAR.SCR script file, locate your supplemental DOS disk and look for DEBUG.COM on that disk.

Copy DEBUG.COM onto the disk that has SHOWCHAR.SCR on it. If you're way ahead of this discussion and have a hard disk with DEBUG in a subdirectory that you've included in your path, fine. If you don't understand a word of that last sentence, go back to the Hard Disk chapter to review the PATH command.

Finally, to create the final program, make sure both SHOWCHAR.SCR and DEBUG.COM are on the disk you're currently using, and at the DOS prompt type:

```
DEBUG < SHOWCHAR.SCR
```

You'll see the SHOWCHAR.SCR scroll down your screen. You don't want to see anything that says "error." If you do see any error messages, use the DOS TYPE command (as mentioned above) to make sure you actually did create a pure ASCII file. If the file goes by too quickly, you can stop and start it from scrolling by holding down the Ctrl key and pressing the S key. Also, be sure you left a blank line above RCX; if you didn't you'll see a string of error warnings.

If your whole system locks up, it's because you forgot to press the Enter key after the final Q. Reboot, then go back and retype the SHOWCHAR.SCR file and press the Enter key twice for good measure at the end. What the "DEBUG < SHOWCHAR.SCR" command does is take the script file you just created and redirect it into the DEBUG.COM program. Essentially, it takes the keystrokes that you typed in earlier when you created the file and feeds them into DEBUG. Those keystrokes contain data and DEBUG commands to assemble the data into a file called a COM file or command file (one that you can run in DOS and that ends in .COM). Script files like this are handy, especially when you create them with a real word processor, because they let you correct previous mistakes and it's easy to modify them slightly and create improved versions of the COM files.

When you're all done, just be sure you're looking at a DOS prompt, and type:

```
SHOWCHAR
```

and you'll see every ASCII character.

Chip Logic

Dealing with all the binary 1s and 0s is a nuisance. But they really come in handy when you have to do *logical operations*.

Why is the ASCII value for *A* 65 and for *a* 97? Look at the binary representations of the first few letters of the alphabet:

A 65 1000001	B 66 1000010	C 67 1000011
a 97 1100001	b 98 1100010	c 99 1100011
↑	↑	↑
sixth	sixth	sixth
bit	bit	bit
(2^5)	(2^5)	(2^5)
=32	=32	=32

The lowercase version of each is identical to the uppercase version, except that in all cases the sixth binary digit over from the right is a 1 in the lowercase version and a 0 in the uppercase one.

The easy way to find out the decimal value of a binary bit is to count over from the right "1, 2, 4, 8, 16, 32, 64...." Do this and you'll reach 32 when you get to the sixth binary digit. You could also try to remember that the sixth bit over is 2^5, since computer numbering systems generally start with 0 rather than 1 and since the rightmost bit is 2^0. But some users forget, and make the sixth bit 2^6, which is wrong.

Subtract 65 (the value of uppercase A) from 97 (the value of lowercase A) and you'll get 32. So you can instantly calculate the value of any capital letter by subtracting decimal 32 from the value of the lowercase letter. And, of course, you could add 32 to the value of the uppercase letter to obtain the ASCII value of the lowercase letter.

If you wanted to convert every lowercase character in a typical text file to uppercase you couldn't just subtract 32 from the ASCII value of every letter, since files contain mixtures of uppercase and lowercase letters. Subtracting 32 from all the lowercase letters would indeed yield uppercase ones. But if you did this blindly, you'd also end up subtracting 32 from the letters that were already uppercase, which would turn them into something unrecognizable.

Here's a short sentence, with the decimal ASCII value of each character shown beneath it:

I	L o v e	N Y
73	76 111 118 101	78 89

Subtract 32 from each and you get:

)	, O V E	. 9
41	44 79 86 69	46 57

As you can see from the "ABC" and "abc" examples above, subtracting 32 from the value of a number is the same as turning the sixth bit (2^5) from a 1 to a 0. So what you really want to do is find a way to look at the sixth bit and turn it into a 0 only if it's currently a 1.

Your computer can do this instantly, by using logical operations. In this case, you would use the logical AND operation to make letters uppercase, and the logical OR operation to make them lowercase.

The most useful logical operations are AND, OR, NOT, and XOR. They're fairly intuitive, but as with binary numbers, they take some getting used to. Think of them as miniature legal contracts.

If a contract says you will be paid if you:

write a novel
AND
write greeting cards

obviously you'll get paid only if you write both. If a contract says you will be paid if you:

write a novel
OR
write greeting cards

you have to write only one of these to get paid (what a choice). If a contract says you will be paid if you:

do NOT grow crops this year

you'll fatten your bank account only if your back 40 sit idle.

We all deal with AND, OR, and NOT operations regularly. XOR, which stands for *eXclusive OR*, simply flips one binary state to another, but can also add binary numbers together (see "Chomping at the Bit"). Flipping twice brings you back to the original state.

Computers use XOR operations for all sorts of things. If you XOR a value with itself, you cancel it out and end up with 0. And if you want to produce graphic animations, you first XOR one image onto the screen to draw something at a certain location, and then XOR the same image at the same location again to restore the screen to the way it was originally. Since the second XOR effectively erases the image (by canceling out the changes), you can move an image across your screen by having XOR repeatedly draw it and then erase it.

Bit Masks

ANDing any ASCII value with decimal 223 will capitalize lowercase letters and leave uppercase letters alone. AND works by comparing two values (the example below will compare one bit at a time) and returning a 1 only when both values are nonzero.

	AND Table			
1	AND	1	=	1
1	AND	0	=	0
0	AND	1	=	0
0	AND	0	=	0

In binary notation, 223 is 11011111, and this number works as a *bit mask*. ANDing any binary number of eight digits or less with it will leave things the way they were in every position except the sixth over from the right, where it will leave 0s alone and change 1s to 0s. This forces the digit in that position to become a 0, which is the same as subtracting 32. But it does this only when there's a 1 in that position. In other words, it subtracts 32 only when there's a 32 there to subtract. It's called a mask because it masks out any changes except in the one place where we want the change to happen — the 0 in the 2^5 position.

Since A (decimal 65) is binary 01000001, while a (decimal 97) is binary 01100001, ANDing these numbers with 11011111 could be represented as:

```
        01000001   (65)
AND     11011111   (223)
        01000001   (65)
```

```
        01100001   (97)
AND     11011111   (223)
        01000001   (65)
```

ANDing either a 0 or a 1 with 1 in effect leaves the value alone, and ANDing both a 0 and a 1 with 0 in effect turns the value into a 0. The binary number 11011111 forces the 2^5 bit — the sixth one from the right — to become a 0 and leaves all the other bits the way they were.

Changing a bit from 0 to 1 is often referred to as *setting* the bit, and changing it from a 1 to a 0 as *unsetting* the bit. The only difference between a lowercase letter and its capital counterpart is that the 2^5 bit is *set* (=1) in the lowercase version. ANDing it with 11011111 *unsets* the bit, changing it to a 0 and lowering the ASCII value by 32.

To reverse the process and turn capital letters into lowercase ones, use the logical OR operation to OR a value with 32.

	OR Table			
1	OR	1	=	1
1	OR	0	=	1
0	OR	1	=	1
0	OR	0	=	0

32 equals binary 00100000. Since ORing either a 1 or a 0 with 0 in effect leaves the value alone, and ORing either a 1 or a 0 with 1 in effect turns the value into a 1, the binary

number 00100000 forces the 2^5 bit to become a 1 and leaves all the other bits the way they were.

This sets the unset 2^5 bit in an uppercase letter, changing it to a 1 and raising the ASCII value by 32. But it leaves already set bits just the way they were.

```
        01000001   (65)
OR      00100000   (32)
        01100001   (97)


        01100001   (97)
OR      00100000   (32)
        01100001   (97)
```

Hex Marks the Spot

Nobody likes dealing in cumbersome eight-bit binary numbers. But our more comfortable decimal (base-ten) system doesn't really lend itself to the base-two world of computers. A base-16 number system does, since every eight-bit binary number can be expressed as two single-digit base-16, or *hexadecimal*, numbers strung together. In fact, it's easier to translate binary numbers into hexadecimal and back than to translate binary into decimal and back.

Hexadecimal (hex for short) numbering works just like decimal numbering except that it provides six additional digits. The first ten digits are the same as the ten decimal ones you use every day. But you run out of digits after you get to 9. Hex then tacks on the first six letters of the alphabet. So, you count to 10 in hex like this (decimal values are shown in parentheses):

0 (0)
1 (1)
2 (2)
3 (3)
4 (4)
5 (5)
6 (6)
7 (7)
8 (8)
9 (9)
A (10)
B (11)
C (12)
D (13)
E (14)
F (15)
10 (16)

How do you tell a hexadecimal 10 (which is really equal to decimal 16) from a garden-variety decimal 10? Hex numbers usually end with an H (or an h), or have a &H (or &h) prefix attached. So,

```
10h
10H
&H10
&h10
```

are all the same number.

Programmers often like working with two-digit hex numbers, so they'll stick zeros onto the left side. 0D is the same as D; 0A the same as A. Scripts often use ",0D,0A" at the end of the messages to tell the program to insert a carriage return (an 0D character) and a linefeed (an 0A character) at the end of the text.

Hex is handy because you can squeeze lots of values into a compact amount of space. Using decimal numbers takes three digits to write 156 of the ASCII characters (all the ones greater than 99). But every ASCII character can fit into two hex digits (decimal 255 is the same as hex FF).

Your system comes from the factory containing certain important gut-level tools and programs already loaded on ROM chips (which will be discussed in the next chapter), and each generation of these chips has important changes from previous versions. You can figure out which set of chips is in your system by peeking at a specific memory location, or address. The address that tells you the date your system ROM was released is 61440:65525 in decimal, but is F000:FFF5 in hex.

To see this date yourself, get into DOS, make sure DEBUG.COM is on your disk, and type:

```
DEBUG
```

You'll see a (-) at the left edge of your screen; this is DEBUG's prompt the same way that "OK" is BASIC's prompt and A> or C> is DOS's default prompt. Type:

```
D F000:FFF5 L8
```

and press the Enter key. The date will appear at the right edge of your screen. Then press Q and then Enter to quit DEBUG and return to DOS.

You could also retrieve the date by plugging the numbers into a short BASIC program:

```
100 DEF SEG=61440!
110 FOR A=0 TO 7
120 PRINT CHR$(PEEK(65525!+A));
130 NEXT
```

The hex version of this program doesn't save much typing, though:

```
100 DEF SEG=&HF000
110 FOR A=0 TO 7
120 PRINT CHR$(PEEK(&HFFF5+A));
130 NEXT
```

Hex also makes binary translations a dream. For instance, what is the binary equivalent of FF? Well, that one's too easy, since it's equal to 255, and 255 is the highest number you can make out of 1s and 0s, which means it must be made up of all 1s:

11111111

But pick any other hex number: &H3D (61 in decimal notation). Each hex digit stands for half of an eight-digit binary number. Remember that one binary digit is a bit and that eight bits make a byte. And that half a byte is called a nibble. (Get it? Byte? Nibble?)

In &H3D, the 3 stands for the lefthand (or *high*) nibble, and the D for the righthand (or *low*) nibble. In binary notation, decimal 3 is 0011, while decimal 13 — which is what hex D is equal to — is 1101. We figured that out above.

So hex 3D is equal to 00111101. This is easier to see if you put a space in the middle: 0011 1101.

Going from binary to hex is also easy. What's 10100101? First break it in half: 1010 0101. The left half (or high nibble) is 1010:

1	x	2^3	=	8	
0	x	2^2	=	0	
1	x	2^1	=	2	
0	x	2^0	=	0	
		Total	=	10	decimal, or A in hex

The right half (low nibble) is 0101:

0	x	2^3	=	0	
1	x	2^2	=	4	
0	x	2^1	=	0	
1	x	2^0	=	1	
		Total	=	5	decimal, or 5 in hex

Therefore, 10100101 is A5 in hex, or 165 in decimal. Note that the numbers 1 through 9 are the same in decimal and hex. Most new users get the hang of it pretty quickly, but they all make a common mistake of putting 10 after 9 in hex, when everyone knows hex 9 is followed by hex A. Don't worry, you'll get used to it. It's not really all that hard to convert two-digit hex numbers into decimal. First, convert each digit into decimal. From the above example, A is equal to 10, and 5 is equal to 5. Multiply the value of the left-hand digit by 16 and add the righthand digit to it:

(10 x 16) + 5 = 165.

Converting a decimal number 256 or less to hex is only a little harder. First divide the number by 16. You'll probably end up with a whole number quotient and a remainder. Convert them each to single digit hex numbers. Put the whole number on the left and the remainder on the right:

165 / 16 = 10 with a remainder of 5
              10 = A
               5 = 5

So the hex representation is A5.

Hex is the language of DEBUG. And DEBUG is an incredible power tool. It lets you rip open the DOS covers and repair, examine, or customize anything. And it makes it easy to create and customize short assembly language programs like SHOWCHAR.COM above.

Multiplying and Dividing Hex Numbers

Translating numbers into and out of hex is hard enough, and adding or subtracting them is no picnic, but multiplying and dividing is out of the question. Lots of books show you how; we'll spare you the grief. Actually, we will tell you how: just install a copy of Borland's classic *SideKick* on your system. Even the older version of the software comes with an ASCII chart, a powerful notepad/clipboard that can lift text off your screen and move it to another program or store it in a file, and a terrific decimal/hex/binary calculator. Some programmers even use the *WordStar*-like notepad as their main program editor.

BASIC makes it a snap to translate most integer values in and out of hex. And it can simplify working with ASCII values. Type either BASICA or GWBASIC to get the ball rolling. To have it figure out the decimal value of the hex number 7ABC, just type:

```
PRINT &H7ABC
```

and press the Enter key. BASIC will print out:

```
31420
```

Unfortunately, since BASIC has to work with both positive and negative integers, the largest positive integer it can deal with is 32,767 (7FFFH). Tell it to PRINT &H7FFF and you'll indeed get 32767 (without the comma). But since BASIC can handle only 65,536 possible integers, it has to rope off the half starting with 32,768 and pretend they're negative numbers. So entering:

```
PRINT &H8000
```

will get you

```
-32768
```

Note that while you may use either &H or &h as a prefix, BASIC won't understand H or h suffixes on hex numbers. If you tried to type PRINT 7FFFH you'd get:

```
7 0
```

since BASIC would think you were asking it to print the value of 7 (which is 7) and then print the value of the variable FFFH, which would be zero unless you had by chance assigned it another value previously.

However, if you treat this operation as a calculation, BASIC will oblige with higher numbers. Enter:

```
PRINT &H7FFF+1
```

and BASIC will return:

```
32768
```

Try:

```
PRINT &H7FFF+&H7FFF
```

and you'll get:

```
65534
```

You can go the other way, from decimal to hex, without such headaches. Type in:

```
PRINT HEX$(64206)
```

and BASIC will respond with:

```
FACE
```

(&HFACE is a valid hex number). You can go all the way up to:

```
PRINT HEX$(65535)
```

which will produce:

```
FFFF
```

Try anything higher, such as:

```
PRINT HEX$(65535+1)
```

and BASIC will simply print the error message "Overflow."

To figure out the ASCII value of any character, nestle it inside parentheses and quotes, and preface it with ASC. Type:

```
PRINT ASC("A")
```

and you'll get its decimal ASCII value:

```
65
```

To convert numbers from 0 to 255 into their respective ASCII characters, put the decimal ASCII value inside parentheses and preface it with CHR$. Enter:

```
PRINT CHR$(65)
```

and you'll see:

```
A
```

You can also use hex notation when producing ASCII characters. You could have typed:

```
PRINT CHR$(&H41)
```

to produce the same:

```
A
```

since hex 41 is equal to decimal 65.

But if all you have to do is add or subtract hex numbers, which is usually the case, you can do it for free by using DEBUG. Just get into DOS, type DEBUG, and at the DEBUG hyphen (-) prompt, type in the letter H followed by any two hex numbers of four digits or less, and press the Enter key. DEBUG will print out the sum of your numbers and the difference.

It might look something like this:

```
-H FFFF 0001
0000 FFFE
```

DEBUG reports sums in four digits only, as you can see from the example above, since FFFFH + 1 equals 10000H, not 0000H. But that doesn't matter much, because four digits is plenty for what you'll have to do with hex.

The Keys to the Kingdom

Sure, sure. You're an old hand at the keyboard, and your fingers automatically reach for the home row when you climb out of bed in the morning. But you may not know all the PC keyboard's basic tricks.

First, a quick history: the earliest PC sported an 83-key keyboard that divided the user community into two camps. Most of us loved it, since it had the best "feel" of any keyboard ever made. IBM spends a lot of time sticking people in chairs and watching them work, and all this ergonomic research paid off handsomely.

The few ragtag complainers and malcontents who hated it did have one valid point — the placement of some of the keys was nonstandard. The Enter key was somewhat small and too far to the right. The left Shift key was a little far to the left. The whole right side of it was a bit crowded. And you couldn't tell what state the Shift keys happened to be in.

The original 84-key PC-AT keyboard fixed all these woes, and bcame an instant and absolute classic. However, IBM didn't know when to stop, and ended up moving the function keys from the left side to the top, doing random damage to the Ctrl and Alt keys, and using a slightly cheaper mechanism to pop the keys up after you press them down.

The subsequent generation of 101/102-key keyboards featured separate number and cursor pads, stuck on a handful of new keys, and were as wide as your desk. They also made it difficult to use some software products. For example, millions of *WordStar* users depended on having the Ctrl key beside the A key.

But all the IBM keyboards shared the same glorious feel. Each had exactly the right amount of "overstrike" so that you had to build up a certain amount of pressure to reach a trigger point before the key sprang into action. Each clicked on the way down and on the way up, giving users unparalleled tactile feedback and boosting their morale by subconsciously making them think they were typing twice as fast. Every key was bounce-free; pallid plastic clone keyboards commonly stuttered extra characters onto the screen, but not IBM's. IBM's was angled perfectly, and expertly scooped and dished so that your fingers fit precisely onto the wide keytops. It was also heavy, so that muscular typing wouldn't chase it around the desktop.

Some users liked competitors' keyboards because they were silent. That's like preferring beer to vintage champagne because the bottles are easier to open. The IBM keyboard is so good that it's almost reason enough to stick with IBM (unless you can't resist increased power from a company like Compaq or low price from a mail order vendor). Using anything else is like kneading gummy marshmallows or typing on a pocket calculator.

Users switching from typewriters to computers are often stymied by the welter of extra PC keys. After all, four separate ones have left arrows on them. Function keys are intimidating to new users, as are such foreign-looking characters as:

```
^ { } | \ ~ ' < >
```

And labels like SysReq, PgDn, and PrtSc can initially confound anyone. However, until someone comes up with a flawless voice recognition device, IBM's crisp, solid, elegant keyboards will remain the best ways to digitize your thoughts and data.

The keys to the kingdom come in four families:

1. The normal typewriter keys (and their less familiar cousins such as <, >, and |).
2. The shift and special purpose keys.
3. The cursor-movement and number-pad keys.
4. The grey function keys (F1 through F10 on older models, F1 through F12 on newer ones).

Typewriter Keys

Nothing is really different about these on the PC keyboard except that you get a few extras thrown in — and some common keys, such as the cents sign, are missing.

This is because computer keyboards are designed to work with the ASCII character set. As mentioned earlier, IBM adopted (and enhanced) a character-numbering system called ASCII (American Standard Code for Information Interchange). Deep down, computers don't know anything about letters. But they're terrific at juggling numbers. So when it has to move an A from one place to another, your computer actually uses the number 65 to represent the A. Programs in your ROM chips translate these values into the dot patterns that draw the actual characters on your screen. But to the computer, an A is always a 65 (unless it's a lowercase a, in which case it's a 97).

You can type in 95 of the ASCII characters shown in Figure 6.1 from your keyboard. In the chart, the number in each lefthand column is the ASCII value of the character beside it.

ASC	CHR	ASC	CHR	ASC	CHR	ASC	CHR	ASC	CHR	ASC	CHR
32*	(SPC)	48	0	64	@	80	P	96	`	112	p
33	!	49	1	65	A	81	Q	97	a	113	q
34	"	50	2	66	B	82	R	98	b	114	r
35	#	51	3	67	C	83	S	99	c	115	s
36	$	52	4	68	D	84	T	100	d	116	t
37	%	53	5	69	E	85	U	101	e	117	u
38	&	54	6	70	F	86	V	102	f	118	v
39	`	55	7	71	G	87	W	103	g	119	w
40	(	56	8	72	H	88	X	104	h	120	x
41	)	57	9	73	I	89	Y	105	i	121	y
42	*	58	:	74	J	90	Z	106	j	122	z
43	+	59	;	75	K	91	[	107	k	123	{
44	,	60	<	76	L	92	\	108	l	124		
45	-	61	=	77	M	93	]	109	m	125	}
46	.	62	>	78	N	94	^	110	n	126	~
47	/	63	?	79	O	95	_	111	o	127**	Δ

*Character 32 is a space, and is generated when you tap the spacebar.
**IBM calls character 127 a *delta* but it's actually shaped like a small house.

Figure 6.1. ASCII Typewriter Keys

The characters you see onscreen will differ slightly from system to system. Characters on IBM monochrome screens are made up of lots of dots. Those on EGA displays are nearly as sharp and clear as monochrome characters. But CGA character sets are crude. The dot patterns for each monitor are contained on special ROM chips attached to the respective display adapters. But IBM keeps a set of these CGA patterns in the main system ROM so it can draw characters when you're in BASIC graphics screens 1 and 2. The characters are crude because they're drawn in a grid eight dots wide and eight dots high — not very conducive to graceful curves and tricky angles.

You can't easily look inside your main system ROM but the BASIC ROMPRINT.BAS program below can (starting at address F000:FA6E). It reads the values stored there and interprets them as light and dark blocks on your screen. The main ROM stores the patterns for each character as a sequence of eight binary numbers, one per row. ROMPRINT retrieves the decimal value of each number and translates it into the binary pattern for each row. It lets you strike actual keys from the keyboard, or enter ASCII values between 0 and 127 from the chart shown in Figure 6.1. If you want to see the dot patterns for the digits 0-9, enter their ASCII values (0 = 48, 1 = 49 ... 9 = 57). If you do type in ASCII numbers, press the Enter key after entering any values with fewer than three digits. When you're all done, press the F10 function key to end the program.

```
100 'ROMPRINT - displays ROM ASCII dot patterns
110 SCREEN 0:COLOR 2,0,0:LOCATE ,,0:KEY OFF:DEFINT A-Z:CLS
120 DEF SEG=0:POKE 1047,PEEK(1047) OR 32:KEY 10,""
130 ' --- points to ROM; sets up print characters ---
140 DEF SEG=&HF000:A$=STRING$(2,219):B$=STRING$(2,176)
150 ' --- gets ASCII value ---
160 PRINT "Type a key, or enter any number between"
170 PRINT "000 and 127 (press the <F10> key to end): ";
180 I$=INKEY$:IF I$="" THEN 180 ELSE IF I$=CHR$(0)+"D" THEN END
190 IF I$=CHR$(13) THEN IF C$="" THEN D=13:GOTO 240 ELSE 220
200 IF I$>CHR$(57) OR I$<CHR$(48) THEN D=ASC(I$):GOTO 240
210 C$=C$+I$:PRINT I$;:IF LEN(C$)<3 THEN 180
220 IF VAL(C$)>127 THEN C$="":CLS:GOTO 160 ELSE D=VAL(C$)
230 ' --- draws dot pattern row by row ---
240 CLS:FOR E=1 TO 8
250 F=PEEK(&HFA6D+(8*D)+E)
260 IF F=0 THEN PRINT STRING$(16,176):GOTO 300
270 FOR G=7 TO 0 STEP -1
280 IF F<2^G THEN PRINT B$; ELSE PRINT A$;:F=F-2^G
290 NEXT:PRINT
300 NEXT:PRINT:IF D<>11 AND D<>12 THEN PRINT TAB(8);CHR$(D)
310 PRINT:C$="":GOTO 160
```

The program also displays the actual life-size character beneath the enlarged dot pattern. It won't display the whole character set, since the system uses some with values like 7, 10, 12, and 13 to control the position of the cursor, clear the screen, beep, and manage other display chores. But ROMPRINT will show you the actual patterns stored in ROM for every single one.

High-Bit Characters

Display adapters are designed to zap the appropriate character dot patterns onto the screen very rapidly. BASIC's graphics modes have to go in and draw text characters a dot at a time. And in all 1.x and 2.x versions of DOS, users couldn't put any of the *high-bit* foreign language, math, and border-drawing characters (with ASCII values over 127) onto BASIC graphics screens, since the patterns for these weren't stored on the system ROM chips.

But DOS version 3.0 offered a new utility called GRAFTABL.COM that made it possible to display the high-bit characters. All you had to do was type in GRAFTABL before loading BASIC and DOS would create a memory-resident lookup table containing the proper values. GRAFTABL.COM remained the same in versions 3.1 and 3.2, but when IBM introduced its confounding foreign language features in version 3.3 it made

GRAFTABL.COM five times larger to accommodate slight differences in foreign character sets.

The GRAFPRNT.BAS program below looks inside GRAFTABL.COM, reads the character patterns into an array, and uses ROMPRINT's binary pattern printer to display an enlarged version of any ASCII character from 128 through 255. It checks to make sure you have a proper version handy, and automatically sniffs out whether it's dealing with an older GRAFTABL.COM or a fat new one, since the internal structures are different.

```
100 ' GRAFPRNT - prints GRAFTABL.COM hi-bit ASCII patterns
110 SCREEN 0,0:KEY OFF:COLOR 2,0,0:CLS:DEFINT A-Z
120 DEF SEG=0:POKE 1047,PEEK(1047) OR 32:DEF SEG:KEY 10,""
130 DIM H(128,8):M$=STRING$(2,176):N$=STRING$(2,219)
140 ' --- open GRAFTABL, get version, validate, fill array ---
150 OPEN "GRAFTABL.COM" AS #1 LEN=1:FIELD #1,1 AS A$
160 IF LOF(1)=1169 THEN S=4 ELSE S=48
170 GET #1,1+S:IF ASC(A$)<>120 THEN CLOSE:GOTO 360
180 FOR B=1 TO 128:LOCATE 1,1,0:PRINT 128-B:FOR C=1 TO 8
190 GET #1,(B-1)*8+C+S:H(B,C)=ASC(A$):NEXT:NEXT:CLOSE:CLS
200 ' --- gets ASCII value ---
210 PRINT "Enter any number between 128 and 255"
220 PRINT "or (press the <F10> key to end): ";
230 I$=INKEY$:IF I$="" THEN 230 ELSE IF I$=CHR$(0)+"D" THEN END
240 IF I$>CHR$(57) OR I$<CHR$(48) THEN BEEP:GOTO 230
250 C$=C$+I$:PRINT I$;:IF LEN(C$)<3 THEN 230
260 IF VAL(C$)<128 OR VAL(C$)>255 THEN C$="":CLS:GOTO 210
270 ' --- draws dot pattern row by row ---
280 CLS:FOR E=1 TO 8
290 F=H(VAL(C$)-127,E)
300 IF F=0 THEN PRINT STRING$(16,176):GOTO 340
310 FOR G=7 TO 0 STEP -1
320 IF F<2^G THEN PRINT M$; ELSE PRINT N$;:F=F-2^G
330 NEXT:PRINT
340 NEXT:PRINT:PRINT TAB(8);CHR$(VAL(C$)):PRINT:C$="":GOTO 210
350 ' --- if correct file is not found ---
360 PRINT "Put DOS 3.0 or later GRAFTABL.COM on disk and restart"
```

If you want to see the cents sign that's missing from the IBM keyboard, just run GRAFPRINT and type in 155. (If your printer can handle it, you can insert this character into your documents where needed, by using the Alt-key method described below.)

The nonalphanumeric typewriter keys have their own ASCII codes:

- Backspace   8
- Tab   9
- Enter   13

You can see the characters produced by these three by pressing the actual keys. Or you could press Ctrl-H to print a backspace, Ctrl-I to print a tab, and Ctrl-M to print a backspace. (Pressing Ctrl-H means holding down the Ctrl key and pressing the H key.) In fact, you could also see the lower 26 ASCII characters by running ROMPRINT, and holding down the Ctrl key while you type the letters of the alphabet.

Why?

Shift and Special Purpose Keys

A typewriter contains just one set of Shift keys, in which both keys do the exact same thing and are duplicated just to make two-handed typing easier. The PC keyboard contains three different sets of Shift keys, not just one. Each changes the meaning of an alphanumeric key just as pressing the A key by itself produces an "a" but pressing it while holding the Shift key down produces a capital A. To your computer, a and A are totally different characters with different ASCII codes (although certain programs, such as DOS and BASIC, automatically translate most lowercase keys to their uppercase versions).

When you type an A, the keyboard sends two special codes to the CPU — the first a hardware interrupt telling it to wake up because a key has been struck, and the second a *scan code* telling it that this particular key happened to be a capital A. Then, when you lift your finger off the A, the keyboard actually sends a third *release code* telling the CPU you're all done, which comes in handy when you're holding down a key to repeat a whole row of the same character, such as an underline.

But your PC needs to keep track of more than just letters, numbers, and punctuation. It has to know when you want to go to the next line, or the next page, or tab over to the right — or when to beep to get your attention, or to stop when you press the panic button because something is going wrong. And the programs you run have to know lots more, such as when text should be underlined or boldfaced.

To make it easy for you to generate these additional codes, your PC gives you two extra Shift keys, Ctrl and Alt. All these extra Shift keys really do is change the codes generated by your normal alphanumeric typewriter keys. It's up to the program you're running to interpret the special codes that you type into meaningful commands. Unfortunately, there's virtually no standardization of codes today; just about every program uses its own completely unique set. The code that tells one word processor to shift into boldfaced text might tell another word processor to change the right margin.

When you type any letter, your computer looks at a special pair of *status bytes* at locations 417 and 418 in the very bottom (0000) segment of memory to see if any of the Shift keys are engaged. Whenever you hold down a Shift key or toggle one on, your computer "sets" (turns from 0 to 1) an individual bit in one of these two bytes to keep track of every shift state in the system. It then resets (turns back to 0) the relevant bits when you lift your finger or toggle a Shift key off. Later we'll provide tools that give you control over these bytes and let you set them in any state you want.

If the status bytes show that no Shift keys are active, your computer translates the scan code sent by the letters on your keyboard into ASCII values somewhere between 97 (an a) and 122 (a z).

If you're holding down the normal Shift key, your computer knows you want a capital letter, and translates the keystroke into an ASCII value between 65 (A) and 90 (Z). The ASCII value for each uppercase letter is the same as the value for the lowercase letter minus 32, and your computer can instantly turn a lowercase letter into its uppercase version simply by turning the sixth bit from a 1 to a 0. In the binary representation of the ASCII code for every lowercase letter, the sixth bit over from the right is always on (set to 1). In every uppercase letter, this bit is turned off (set to 0). When this bit is on, it adds a value of 2^6 (or 32) to the ASCII code. Turning the bit on adds 32 and lowercases any letter; turning it off subtracts 32 and uppercases the letter.

You can verify this by looking at Figure 6.1, which is conveniently arranged in columns 16 entries long. The uppercase letters in columns 3 and 4 are in the same relative positions as the lowercase versions in columns 5 and 6. Each is just shifted 32 table entries (or exactly two columns) over.

When you type in letters while holding down the Ctrl key, your computer generates codes between 1 (for both A and a) and 26 (for both Z and z). The ASCII value for these is the same as the value for the corresponding uppercase letter minus 64.

Typing Ctrl-A is the same to your computer as typing Ctrl-a; the Ctrl key takes precedence over the normal Shift key. (When manuals refer to Ctrl-shifted keys they always use capital letters, so you'll see Ctrl-A and Ctrl-B but never Ctrl-a and Ctrl-b.)

If you're in DOS, typing Ctrl-A will put a ^A onscreen. The caret (^) as a prefix is shorthand for Ctrl. As mentioned earlier, some of the Ctrl-shifted keys trigger DOS or BASIC operations. You can tell DOS you're done creating a file by typing Ctrl-Z. You can make DOS beep by telling it to ECHO a ^G. To see this in action, get into DOS, type the following line, and press the Enter key. To generate the ^G, hold down the Ctrl key and type G while the Ctrl key is down:

```
ECHO ^G
```

You could also have typed:

```
COPY CON BEEP
^G^Z
```

which would have created a file called BEEP. (To create the ^G and the ^Z, hold down the Ctrl key and press GZ.) Then type:

```
TYPE BEEP
```

and you'd hear the familiar tone. If you try this, erase the BEEP file you just created by typing ERASE BEEP, or else you'll clutter up your disk.

The important DOS Ctrl and alphabetic key combinations are:

| Ctrl | C | Generally breaks out of whatever you happen to be doing at the time. Interchangeable most of the time (not in BASIC) with Ctrl-Break. |

| Ctrl | G | Beep (only when used in certain ways). |

| Ctrl | H | Same as backspace. |

| Ctrl | I | Same as Tab. |

| Ctrl | M | Same as Enter. |

| Ctrl | P | Acts as a "toggle" to turn a feature on and off that sends whatever is appearing onscreen simultaneously to your printer. Be sure your printer is on before trying this. If your system "hangs" and all you get is an error message, press Ctrl-P again to toggle it off. Typing in Ctrl-PrtSc is usually the same as typing Ctrl-P, although Ctrl-PrtSc works in BASIC while Ctrl-P doesn't. This shouldn't be confused with Shift-PrtSc, which dumps an image of whatever is onscreen to your printer one whole screen at a time. |

| Ctrl | S | Freezes and restarts some DOS operations (like scrolling DIR listings); similar to Ctrl-NumLock except that Ctrl-Numlock will only suspend things while Ctrl-S will pause and restart them |

| Ctrl | Z | DOS end-of-file marker. |

You can see the characters IBM uses to represent all the ASCII codes below 32 by running ROMPRINT and typing in Ctrl-A for ASCII character 1, Ctrl-B for character 2, etc. Figure 6.2 shows the ASCII Ctrl characters. To extend the ASCII chart, shown in Figure 6.1, attach these two columns to the left side:

ASCII	Crtl	CHR	ASCII	Ctrl	CHR
0	^@		16	^P	►
1	^A	☺	17	^Q	◄
2	^B	☻	18	^R	↕
3	^C	♥	19	^S	‼
4	^D	♦	20	^T	¶
5	^E	♣	21	^U	§
6	^F	♠	22	^V	▬
7	^G	•	23	^W	↨
8	^H	◘	24	^X	↑
9	^I	○	25	^Y	↓
10	^J	◙	26	^Z	→
11	^K	♂	27	^[	←
12	^L	♀	28	^\	∟
13	^M	♪	29	^]	↔
14	^N	♫	30	^^	▲
15	^O	☼	31	^_	▼

Figure 6.2.   ASCII Ctrl Characters

Some of the characters in Figure 6.2 may look a little strange. The ^^ means Ctrl-caret and the ^_ means Ctrl-underline, which look odd, but don't worry, since you'll never really have to use them. The ^[represents ASCII character 27, or Esc, and you definitely will have lots of reasons to use this one. It plays a critical role in issuing *escape codes* or *escape sequences* that can put your printer through its paces or help send DOS commands to set screen colors or redefine keys using ANSI.SYS.

The ^@ (ASCII character 0) is a *null* that your system uses to identify plain old function keys, function keys you press while holding down Shift keys (Shift, Ctrl, Alt), or various keys you press while holding down the Alt key (such as Alt-A, Alt-5, or Alt-=). Some programs, especially communications software, insert nulls as placeholders in data files, which can play havoc with noncomprehending applications like old-fashioned word processors.

As mentioned above, the Ctrl key has a special role when used with some of the nonalphabetic keys:

Ctrl **PtrSc** *	Same as Ctrl-P; toggles simultaneous printing to screen and printer.
Ctrl **Num Lock**	Nearly the same as Ctrl-S; suspends some DOS operations (but another key has to restart them).

| Ctrl | Scroll Lock | Nearly the same as Ctrl-C; breaks or stops many DOS operations. Stops BASIC operations while Ctrl-C won't. |

| Ctrl | Alt | Del | Performs "warm" reboot that restarts system but bypasses time-consuming diagnostic tests. Hold Ctrl and Alt down first and then press Del. |

interchangeable in DOS, but only Ctrl-PrtSc will echo what's on the screen to the printer; Ctrl-NumLock will pause the display but Ctrl-S won't, and Ctrl-Break will stop BASIC in its tracks but Ctrl-C won't.

However, BASIC throws in a few Ctrl-key gifts of its own. Ctrl-Home clears the screen, Ctrl-left arrow (or Ctrl-B) moves the cursor to the previous word, Ctrl-right arrow (or Ctrl-F) moves the cursor to the next word, and Ctrl-End (or Ctrl-E) erases to the end of the current line. Ctrl-K moves the cursor to the home position at the screen's upper left corner, Ctrl-L clears the screen (just like Ctrl-Home), Ctrl-N moves the cursor to the end of the current line (like the End key), Ctrl-G really does beep, Ctrl-R toggles between insert and overwrite modes, and Ctrl-[simulates an Esc. The odd quartet of Ctrl-\, Ctrl-], Ctrl-caret, and Ctrl-underline move the cursor right, left, up, and down, respectively.

Both Shift keys work exactly alike, although your computer can tell whether you've pressed the left or right one. Game designers often use the different Shift keys to perform different tasks, such as triggering left or right flippers in pinball games. Each Shift key doesn't do much more than flip the case of letters. It turns lowercase letters into uppercase ones, just like the Shift on a typewriter. It also works backwards when the CapsLock key is toggled on, so that uppercase keys turn into their lowercase cousins.

The Shift key also temporarily reverses the state of the cursor/number pad. The NumLock toggle is normally off so the pad works in cursor mode when you first boot up (although IBM turned it back on when it delivered the 101-key wide-load keyboard, since it assumed everyone would use the number pad for numbers and the independent cursor pad to move the cursor). Pressing the Shift key switches the state of the cursor/number pad for as long as you hold it down, so that if NumLock is toggled on, pressing Shift-8 will move the cursor up a line rather than putting an 8 onscreen. Dedicated spreadsheet users can take advantage of this so they don't have to keep toggling the NumLock back and forth to move the cursor between numeric entries.

And of course, the reverse is also true — holding down the Shift key while the cursor pad is in cursor mode will let you type in numbers without having to change the state of the pad. This is especially handy on machines that don't have shift indicator lights, since it lets users stay in one mode all the time and use the Shift key only when they have to switch temporarily to the other mode and back.

Shift does have one special trick up its sleeve. You can use it to make *hard copies* on your printer of whatever text happens to be on your screen, simply by pressing Shift-PrtSc. This is referred to as a *screen dump*. The dump will show only the current screen;

if you want to take every single line on your screen and "echo" it simultaneously to your printer, use Ctrl-PrtSc or Ctrl-P instead. (While Ctrl-P will toggle simultaneous printing, all Shift-P will do is print a capital S on your screen.)

The problem with Shift-PrtSc is that if you trigger it inadvertently it will either waste a sheet of paper if your printer is currently turned on and *online* (connected to your PC and ready to receive characters), or freeze your system if the printer is either turned off or *offline*. If this happens, the easiest thing to do is turn the printer on, let it print the screen dump, and then turn it off. If you don't have a printer connected, you may have to wait for the system to *time out* since it will give up and unfreeze the system after a good long wait.

It's fairly simple to deactivate the screen dump feature, since a screen dump is an interrupt (INT 5). The first thing such an interrupt does when triggered is look in the Interrupt Vector Table to find the address of the actual dumping program. You could poke around in the table and change the address to something harmless, but this would disable the feature the whole time your system was running, unless you went back and restored it. A better way is to use the utility we provide, which puts a message on your screen after you press Shift-PrtSc and asks if you really want to go ahead or if you just pressed the keys by mistake. If you did press them accidentally, the utility will go away and give you back control of your system before it has a chance to lock up.

Screen dumps don't always work. Text screens often contain high-bit ASCII border and box-drawing characters that many printers don't understand. While your screen may display a very fancy menu box with shadows on two sides giving it a classy 3-D effect, dumping the image to your printer may produce an ugly mess. And true graphics images often send printers into fits. If you want to dump unusual characters or fancy graphics images to your IBM-compatible printer, load the memory-resident DOS GRAPHICS utility first (simply by typing GRAPHICS at the DOS prompt). Then type Shift-PrtSc. If you don't have an official IBM printer, this may not work. Some printer manufacturers who persist in using nonstandard codes may supply their own graphics screen dump programs. And just about every non-IBM Shift-PrtSc graphics dump will have little white horizontal stripes on it, since IBM's official graphics resolution is — surprise — different from most other manufacturers'.

Shift	Temporarily reverses whatever shift state the keyboard is in. Normally, all this does is turn lowercase letters into capital letters. But if CapsLock is on and everything you're typing is capitalized, holding either Shift key down lets you type a few lowercase letters. Even better, it flips the state of the cursor/number pad, to let you move the cursor while in numeric mode or enter numbers while in cursor mode.

Shift	PrtSc *	Prints a screen dump — a copy of whatever is currently on the screen. If you want a graphics image printed, you have to execute the external DOS GRAPHICS command first, and hope when your salesman sold you that "IBM compatible" printer he wasn't just blowing smoke.

The Alt key doesn't really do much on its own, but team it up with the number pad and you get a powerful tool. About the only thing the Alt key does, in fact, is provide a shorthand way of writing and editing BASIC programs. When you're using the BASIC editor, instead of having to type SCREEN, you can just press Alt-S and the word SCREEN will pop onto the screen. BASIC supplies Alt-key shortcuts for every letter of the alphabet except J, Q, Y, and Z. But not too many programmers really use these. Figure 6.3 shows the Alt-key combinations that can be used in BASIC.

Alt-A	AUTO	Alt-M	MOTOR
Alt-B	BSAVE	Alt-N	NEXT
Alt-C	COLOR	Alt-O	OPEN
Alt-D	DELETE	Alt-P	PRINT
Alt-E	ELSE	Alt-R	RUN
Alt-F	FOR	Alt-S	SCREEN
Alt-G	GOTO	Alt-T	THEN
Alt-H	HEX$	Alt-U	USING
Alt-I	INPUT	Alt-V	VAL
Alt-K	KEY	Alt-W	WIDTH
Alt-L	LOCATE	Alt-X	XOR

Note: No Alt-key combinations for J,Q,Y,Z

Figure 6.3.   BASIC Alt-Key Shortcuts

Although these shortcuts are currently built into IBM hardware, they're really out of date. The MOTOR command, for instance, is used only to start and stop tape cassette operation, and the mechanism for this was discontinued years ago. But the command remains. (Actually, early BASIC programmers found a legitimate use for this command. All it really did was turn a mechanical switch called a solenoid on or off, and programmers found that by repeatedly and rapidly turning it on and then off, they could generate a motorboat sound.)

The Alt key's real magic is in generating ASCII characters. By holding down the Alt key, typing in a decimal ASCII value on the number pad, and then releasing the Alt key, you can make any character appear at the cursor except one — a null, or ASCII character 0. Null identifies shifted key combinations or nonalphanumeric keys such as Home, End, or F1. (IBM claims you can generate this null character by typing in Alt-2, but that doesn't work. However, pressing the F7 function key in DOS will generate an ASCII 0 and put a ^@ onscreen; if you're using the DOS COPY CON technique to create a small file, just tap F7 to insert a null.) This technique works only with the number pad. Holding down the Alt key and typing the numbers on the top-row typewriter keys just won't do it.

The Alt-number pad technique is extremely useful for creating fancy borders, boxes, math formulas, foreign language characters, and anything else you can construct out of the high-bit ASCII characters — those with values greater than 127. It's also handy for exercising the ASCII characters with very low values — less than 32.

Want to see a smiling face in DOS? Just type ECHO and a space, hold down the Alt key, type 1 (or 2), release the Alt key, and press the Enter key. Then have a nice day. You could have also typed Ctrl-A in place of Alt-1, or Ctrl-B instead of Alt-2, to generate the face character. It's easy to remember that A is the first letter of the alphabet, B the second, C the third, and Z the 26th. But quick — which letter do you hold down for V? It's far easier to type Alt-22.

And while you can use the Ctrl-key combinations as well as the Alt- key ones for very low characters, once you get past Z, you're strictly in Alt territory.

To generate little boxes in DOS, type the two sets of keystrokes that follow. An instruction like ALT-201 means:

1. Hold down the Alt key.
2. Type 201 on the number pad, not the top row.
3. Release the Alt key.

An "Enter" means press the Enter key, "space" means tap the spacebar, and "F6" means lean on the grey F6 function key.

For a small single-line box

For a small double-line box:

```
COPY CON SINGLE          COPY CON DOUBLE
Enter                    Enter
ALT-218                  ALT-201
ALT-196                  ALT-205
ALT-196                  ALT-205
ALT 191                  ALT 187
Enter                    Enter
ALT-179                  ALT-186
space                    space
space                    space
ALT-179                  ALT-186
Enter                    Enter
ALT-192                  ALT-200
ALT-196                  ALT-205
ALT-196                  ALT-205
ALT-217                  ALT-188
Enter                    Enter
F6                       F6
Enter                    Enter
```

When you're done, type:

```
TYPE SINGLE
```

for a single-line box, and

    TYPE DOUBLE

for a double-line box.
The boxes look like this:

Once you have the basic box parts — the four corners, the horizontal line, and the vertical line — created, you can work on the files with your word processor and use the block copy feature to expand it and change its shape. Some word processors may be confused by the high ASCII values, however.

You can combine single and double-line boxes in four possible ways. The ASCII values you need to know to draw these are as follows:

Single horizontal, single vertical:

```
    218    196    194    191
     ┌      ─      ┬      ┐
179  │                   │ 179
195  ├            197─ ┼  ┤ 180
     └      ─      ┴      ┘
    192    196    193    217
```

Double horizontal, double vertical:

```
    201    205    203    187
     ╔      ═      ╦      ╗
186  ║                   ║ 186
204  ╠            206─ ╬  ╣ 185
     ╚      ═      ╩      ╝
    200    205    202    188
```

Single horizontal, double vertical:

```
    214    196    210    183
     ╓      ─      ╥      ╖
186  ║                   ║ 186
199  ╟            215─ ╫  ╢ 182
     ╙      ─      ╨      ╜
    211    196    208    189
```

Double horizontal, single vertical:

```
     213     205     209     184
      ╒       ═       ╤       ╕
 179  │                       │  179
 198  ╞             216- ╪    ╡  181
      ╘       ═       ╧       ╛
     212     205     207     190
```

You can also use the high-bit solid and shaded characters to draw pictures onscreen. You may want to use the GRAFPRNT.BAS program to look at these in more detail. IBM provides a kit of eight:

219	solid box
178	75% grey
177	50% grey
176	25% grey
220	bottom half
223	top half
221	left half
222	right half

These may not seem like a flexible enough arsenal, but with a little ingenuity you can use these and other high-bit characters to draw charts, tables, graphs, and even animated pictures.

You use the Alt key in BASIC instead of the usual CHR$(n) notation. If you wanted to print a capital A you could tell BASIC:

```
PRINT CHR$(65)
```

Or you could say:

```
PRINT "A"
```

The same is true with high-bit characters. Just type in PRINT and the left quotation mark, use the Alt-number pad technique to generate the character you want, and then type a closing quotation mark. It's all the same to BASIC. But even if you never want to touch a line of BASIC, the Alt key can be very useful, especially if you keep sensitive files on your disks.

One of the very best uses of the Alt key is in adding a special kind of blank character in your filenames that can prevent casual users who don't know the trick from gaining access to your sensitive files.

If you keep a file on your disk that you don't want anyone to see, you can do several things to keep it out of harm's way:

1. Lock your system whenever you walk away from it for even a few seconds.
2. Hide the file from normal directory searches.
3. Hide the subdirectory in which the file is stored.
4. Give the file an incomprehensible name such as LVX_1TQY or an innocent one like DIAGNOST.PRG.
5. If your applications software can handle it (some can't), put a Ctrl-Z DOS end-of-file marker as the first character in the file, to prevent casual snoops from using the DOS TYPE command to view the contents.
6. Slap (mostly) invisible character on the end of it that most users won't figure out.

Actually, there's only one way to keep your data safe, and that's to maintain it on removable media such as floppy disks or Bernoulli cartridges, and keep these locked up. (To edit or consult such secret files, security-conscious users frequently copy them from floppies to their hard disks and then put them back on floppies when they're done. Then they erase the sensitive files from their hard disk. Programs like the *Norton Utilities* make it easy for someone to come along and "unerase" these files. But Norton also provides a utility called WIPEFILE that can totally obliterate any traces of your secret data. If you do use a program like WIPEFILE, be sure to check your hard disk for all erased files, since many applications create temporary work files without your knowledge that remain hidden on your disk. These can be just as dangerous in the wrong hands as the originals.)

Trick #6 above is easy. To try it, create a dummy file called DUMMY.BAT by typing the program below and pressing the Enter key at the end of each line. Press the F6 function key where it says <F6>, and then press the Enter key again at the very end. Note — don't actually enter the @ sign shown in the filename. In place of the @ after the word DUMMY, enter Alt-255 by holding down the Alt key, typing 255 on your number pad, and then releasing the Alt key. What looks like a space will appear above the cursor. Then continue typing the letters .BAT that follow this character.

```
COPY CON DUMMY@.BAT
ECHO OFF
ECHO Most users couldn't get this far
<F6>
```

Verify that the file is on your disk by typing:

```
DIR DUM*.*
```

and you'll see something like:

```
DUMMY BAT 49 9-08-90 10:59p
```

Since this is a batch file, you should be able to execute it simply by typing the part of the filename before the BAT extension. But if you type just:

```
DUMMY
```

all you'll get is an error message that says:

```
Bad command or filename
```

This is because the name of the file isn't DUMMY.BAT; it's DUMMY@.BAT, where the @ represents the ASCII 255 blank character. Now press the F3 key, which will dredge up the last command you typed, and put the letters DUMMY at the DOS prompt — but don't press the Enter key yet. Instead, use the Alt-key trick to type in the Alt-255 character, and then press the Enter key. You should see:

```
ECHO OFF
Most users couldn't get this far
```

Remember, this filename has six characters before the BAT extension, not five. The sixth is ASCII character 255, which is a blank. It may be annoying to have to use the Alt-255 technique every time you want to do anything with the file, but it will keep the honest people from snooping into it.

Unscrupulous users will always find a way. They may know the Alt-key trick. If they don't, they'll realize something is fishy when they try the DOS TYPE command:

```
TYPE DUMMY.BAT
```

and nothing happens. If they're smart, they'll know another way to display the contents of files. All they have to do is type:

```
COPY DUM*.* CON /B
```

This command tells DOS to display the full contents every file beginning with the letters DUM. Adding a /B at the end gets around the trick of putting a Ctrl-Z as the first character of the file.

This trick works fairly well with directory listings, since DOS puts spaces between the left half of the filename and its extension rather than a period. But if you copied a file that had an Alt-255 character in its filename, DOS would tip its hand. If this file were the only one on your disk that started with the letters DUM, and you typed:

```
COPY DUM*.* ZUM*.*
```

DOS would print:

```
DUMMY  .BAT
         1 File(s) copied
```

which would reveal the extra blank character before the period. Still, it will keep casual users from causing problems.

If you already know what subdirectories are, you might want to use this Alt-255 trick the next time you create one. (If you don't, refer to Chapter 3, and then come back here and try this.) When you type MD (or MKDIR) to create a subdirectory, add an Alt-255 to the end of the subdirectory name just as you did with the DUMMY filename above. Once you've created it, you won't be able to log into it, or remove it, or do anything to it unless you tack on the Alt-255. The only problem with this is that if you change your DOS prompt (with a command like $P:) the blank space will look odd. If you created a subdirectory called C:\DOS* (again, where the * represents an Alt-255), and your prompt was indeed $P:, when you logged into it you'd see:

```
C:\DOS  :
```

Still, casual users would think the blank was a space, and wouldn't be able to log into the subdirectory unless they knew how to generate an ALT-255.

Holding down the Alt key and typing an ASCII code on the number pad, and then releasing the Alt key produces an ASCII character for that code, here an upside down ¡ for ASCII character 173.

```
 ┌──────┐
 │ Alt  │
 └──────┘

 ┌────┐ ┌──────┐ ┌──────┐
 │ 1  │ │  7   │ │  3   │
 │End │ │Home  │ │ PgDn │
 └────┘ └──────┘ └──────┘
```

You don't have to type in all three numbers; Alt-1 works just like Alt-001. And if you type more than three numbers, the PC first does a mod 256 operation on the it (converts it to an integer between 0 and 255). One interesting note about the Alt key — if you press it and the Ctrl key and either Shift key at the same time, the PC gives the Alt key priority, and then Ctrl. It works alphabetically.

While you can't use the top row numbers to generate Alt-key ASCII codes, they'll work just as well as the number pad when it comes to entering numbers in most applications. But numbers aren't the only characters that you can enter in different ways.

Cursor Movement and Number Pad Keys

Your keyboard sports two pluses and two minuses, as well as two periods and two asterisks. This redundancy makes sense, since IBM had to keep users happy who were accustomed to typewriter layouts, while appealing to green eyeshade types who use adding machine keypads all day long. IBM's wide-body keyboard goes even further in this direction.

One thing that confuses legions of new users are the four keys with arrows on them pointing left. These do four very different things:

Backspace — moves the cursor left one character at a time, erasing characters as it plows through them.

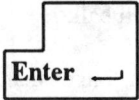

Enter — tells DOS (and most applications) to process the line you just typed.

Tab — moves the cursor a preset number of spaces. DOS tabs only to the right, but some applications let you use Shift-Tab to move to previous tab stops.

Left Arrow (or Cursor Left) — moves the cursor left, like the backspace, but nondestructively, sliding under characters without erasing.

But these aren't the only potentially troublesome pairs or trios of keys.

New users have to learn that they can't type a lowercase L when they want to enter the digit 1. Some typewriter keyboards don't have 1s on them, since "ell" and l are so similiar. But to a computer, these are totally different classes of characters that it treats in two distinct ways. And the PC even provides two keys to enter the digit 1.

Similarly, the digit 0 is not a capital O. Since these are often hard to distinguish on some systems, experienced users put a slash through zeros whether entered from the top row or the number pad.

Everybody uses slashes, in fractions, in dates, or in constructions like either/or. But unless you've spent much time with integer division or with DOS subdirectories, you probably haven't had to use a backslash much. Don't worry, you will.

In school, we learned to use an x as a multiplication operator. Your computer prefers an asterisk (*). In fact, it insists on it. Either * key will do.

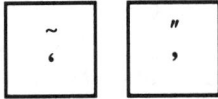

Many computer operations let you substitute a single quote (') for a double quote (") and vice versa (although there are times when this won't work). The ' is a grave accent, and is definitely not a quotation mark. Although you may get away with using it in a word processor as a single left quote, if your computer is expecting a quotation mark of some sort and sees an accent, it will balk.

The underline isn't actually much longer than the hyphen or minus sign, unless you look at it very carefully. Of course, it's down at the bottom of the line, so you can't miss it. But is its lowercase version a hyphen or a minus? It doesn't really matter, since it's usually interchangeable with the grey minus key.

Similarly, is a period different from a decimal point? Not when you type it in using either of these two keys.

Isn't there a song about these two? "You must remember thus, a plus is just a plus..." Here, that's very true.

The funny thing is that when most new users first get their hands on a PC keyboard, they complain about all the extra keys. Once they master the new keyboards, if they ever have to use a typewriter again they end up echoing Ronald Reagan's line "where's the rest of me?"

The NumLock key — which toggles the cursor pad between its numeric and cursor-moving states — is the source of much user consternation. Somehow it always seems to wriggle itself into the opposite state from the one you want. If you're trying to move your cursor up the screen, for instance, you may end up with a row of 888888s instead, since Up Arrow and 8 share the same key.

It's possible to set the state of a Shift Lock key more or less permanently, and then run a short program that disables it for as long as you want. A second program is for users who don't ever enter numbers on the cursor pad and causes the PC to beep if NumLock is set wrong. A third program can change any shift state with a single command. But most

Bit:	7	6	5	4	3	2	1	0
	0	0	0	0	0	0	0	0

Right Shift
Left Shift
Ctrl
Alt
ScrollLock
NumLock
CapsLock
Insert

PC Shift Key	Bit	If bit is set to 1	If bit is set to 0	6th Line Replacement for ShiftKey Script turns on	turns off
Insert	7	on	off	OR AL,80	AND AL,7F
CapsLock	6	on	off	OR AL,40	AND AL,BF
NumLock	5	on	off	OR AL,20	AND AL,DF
ScrollLock	4	on	off	OR AL,10	AND AL,EF
Alt	3	down	up	OR AL,08	AND AL,F7
Ctrl	2	down	up	OR AL,04	AND AL,FB
Left Shift	1	down	up	OR AL,02	AND AL,FD
Right Shift	0	down	up	OR AL,01	AND AL,FE

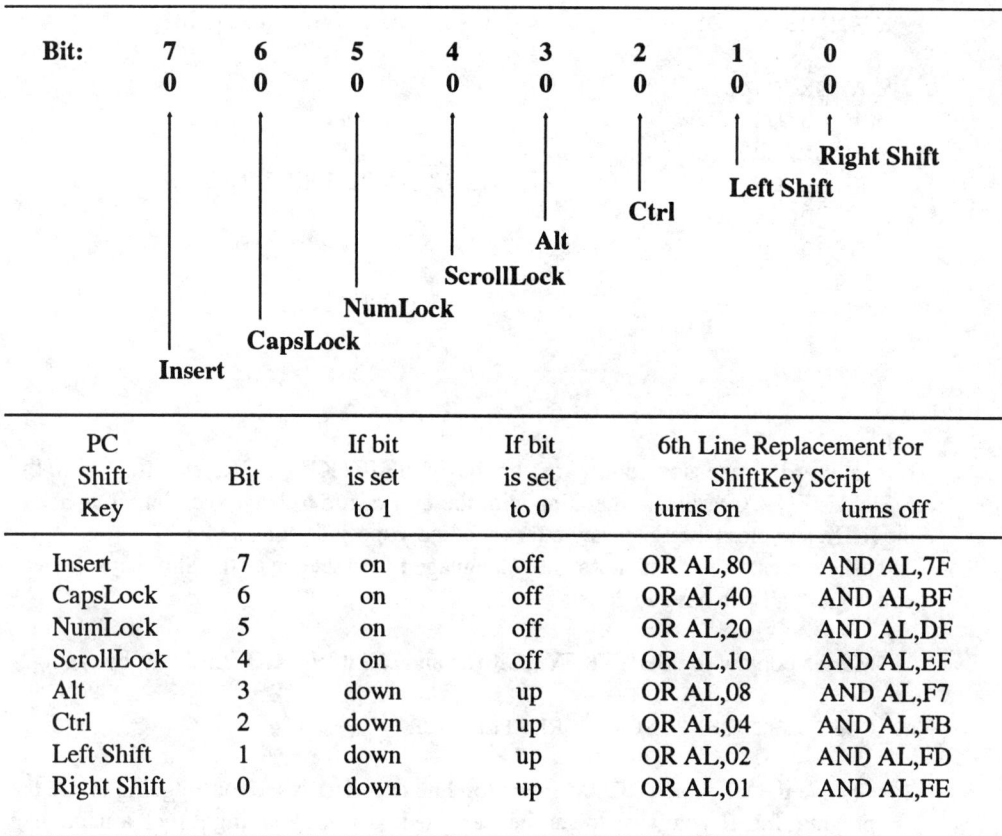

Figure 6.4.   Keyboard Status Control Bytes at Address 0000:0417

users want the flexibility to shift it back and forth, and they don't need any extra beeps. If you want to take our word for this, and skip the slightly technical explanation that follows, jump ahead in this chapter right now to the section on freezing your display.

Since IBM's 101/102-key keyboard provides a number pad and a separate cursor pad, it designed the keyboard to start operating with the number pad already in numeric mode. Some users hate this. If you're among them, you can create a tiny program that will reset the NumLock state for you. You can add the name of this tiny file to your AUTO-EXEC.BAT program to do the resetting right after you boot up. Figure 6.4 shows you how.

The PC keeps track of the state of each Shift key by setting (turning to 1) and unsetting (turning to 0) individual bits in the Keyboard Status Control Byte at address 0000:0417 in RAM. It's easy to adapt an all-purpose assembly language program to set or unset any of these Shift keys. The basic framework is a file called SHIFTKEY.SCR:

```
N UNAMEIT.COM              <— 1. REPLACE THE FILENAME.
A
MOV DX,0040
MOV DS,DX
MOV AL,[0017]
AND AL,DF                  <— 2. CHANGE THIS LINE.
MOV [0017],AL
INT 20

RCX
F
W
Q
```

Use a word processor to create the basic SHIFTKEY.SCR, starting with the N UNAMEIT.COM line and ending with the Q. Be sure to leave the blank line above the RCX, and press the Enter key after each line, especially the last line.

Then, to create a particular assembly language file to set one of the Shift keys the way you want it, all you have to do is:

1. Make a copy of the SHIFTKEY.SCR file and call it WORKFILE.SCR, by typing:

    ```
    COPY SHIFTKEY.SCR WORKFILE.SCR
    ```

2. Change the UNAMEIT.COM in the top line to reflect what you're going to use the program for. If you want to set the CapsLock key on, you might pick a name like CAPSON.COM. If you want to set the NumLock key off, choose a name like NUMOFF.COM.

3. Here's the only slightly tricky part. Replace the entire sixth line — the one that now says

    ```
    AND AL,DF
    ```

    with a line from Figure 6.4. If you look at the two righthand columns in the chart, you'll see that the AND AL,DF turns NumLock off (if this is what you want, leave it alone). If you want to do something like turn the CapsLock on, however, you'd change it to

    ```
    OR AL,40
    ```

4. Then save this WORKFILE.SCR file with the changes you just made, and put it on the same disk as DEBUG.COM version 2.0 or later. To create the file, type:

    ```
    DEBUG < WORKFILE.SCR
    ```

Obviously, this isn't much use in changing the status of a key like Alt or Ctrl. But these individual files are very useful for toggling the shift locks on your keyboard the exact way you want just as if you manually leaned on them yourself. You can put these in batch files that first set the appropriate shift state and then load your favorite commercial software, so the program comes up with all the shifts properly set and ready to go.

The assembly language utilities that you create this way all use the same technique. First they load the segment (0040) and the offset (0017) addresses. As mentioned earlier, you can express just about every address in many different ways. The address 0040:0017 is the same as 0000:0417, which is the same as absolute address 417. IBM calls the byte at this address the Keyboard Status Control Byte, or the Status Byte, and you'll often hear this important location referred to as the byte at address 417.

The utility then looks up the value at this address, and puts it into a workspace called a register. It performs a logical bit-mask operation on this value, forcing one particular bit to turn on or off, and then moves the newly changed value back to its old 417 address.

All a bit mask does is turn a single specified bit on (so it's a 1) or off (so it's a 0) while making sure the other seven bits in the byte aren't disturbed. The logical operation process itself is interesting since it has to be smart enough to switch the state of a bit when the bit is set incorrectly, but leave the state of the bit alone if it's already set properly. (Bit masks are explained in detail in the previous chapter.)

Remember that either Shift key will temporarily switch the state of the cursor/number pad. So if you're entering a series of numbers with NumLock set on, and you see a mistake and want to move the cursor up a few rows, just hold down either the left or right Shift and tap the Up Arrow key a few times. When you're done, release the Shift and you're back in numeric mode. And this works just as well the other way around.

But be careful. If NumLock is on and you're entering figures into the number pad, and you decide to hold down the Shift key to move the cursor, don't type in a period, since a shifted period is the same as a tap of the Delete key and something will vanish.

Incidentally, you can perform several bit mask operations at once. If you want to turn CapsLock and NumLock on at the same time, just add the two hex numbers in the OR column.

CapsLock	OR AL,40
+ NumLock	OR AL,20
Both	OR AL,60

(Remember that these are hex numbers. Adding 40 + 20 equals 60 both in decimal and hexadecimal notation. But adding 80 + 20 equals A0 in hex.)

Figuring out the combination AND numbers to turn shift states off isn't really all that hard. If you'll notice, the numbers in the AND column are just hex FF minus the numbers in the OR column. If OR AL,60 turns both the CapsLock and NumLock on, you can figure out which values will turn them off when used with a logical AND:

```
    FF
  - 60
  ----
    9F
```

So to turn CapsLock and NumLock off with the same command, use:

```
AND AL,9F
```

Crtl	Num Lock

And of course you freeze DOS displays in mid-scroll by pressing Ctrl-NumLock. But to restart things you have to press a letter or number key. Ctrl-S is a better bet because the two keys are close together and because you can unfreeze the paused display just by pressing Ctrl-S again.

Freezing the Display

"Now hold on a minute," you might say, "let me get this straight. If I want to freeze my display while it's scrolling I have to hold down the Ctrl key and press NumLock? The key right next to NumLock on most systems is ScrollLock, but it doesn't seem to have anything to do with scrolling. You mean IBM named one key ScrollLock but didn't give it any connection with scrolling, and then went ahead and assigned a key the power to stop scrolling, but called it NumLock? Does IBM make up this stuff as it goes along?"

Well, you said it, we didn't.

To make matters worse, written below the ScrollLock label almost as an afterthought, and invisible in poor light, is the word "Break." Now ask yourself this: If you're new at this, and someone's just spent a pile of money on a system that's taken you and an installer a week to get working, and you already have a deadline staring you in the face, are you going to let any of your fingers even close to a key named Break? Especially a key that's somehow supposed to lock scrolling but doesn't do anything of the sort?

If you think about it for a second or two you'll realize that a panic button key isn't such a bad idea, since it's so easy for a computer to start running madly off in the opposite direction, and you need a device to get its attention again. But when your system is cranking madly away processing something you don't want it to, or scrolling through a long list that suddenly reveals the items you were searching for, the last thing you want to have to do is grope for two different keys. Imagine if a huge stamping press had a two-part red emergency stop button. If OSHA ever bought a PC they'd have the guy who designed the Break feature making little rocks out of big ones.

But remember, IBM provides an easier way to hit the brakes, with Ctrl-C, even through Ctrl-C and Ctrl-ScrollLock aren't exactly the same. The one thing they both may do is put a ^C on the screen if they manage to bring a process to its knees. Why didn't IBM use the far more mnemonic Ctrl-B to trigger this? They thought Ctrl-C was easy to remember, since by the time you find the two proper keys to press you're screaming "Come on already, break!"

The worst thing about having to grope blindly for Ctrl-ScrollLock or Ctrl-NumLock is that if your fingers slip a bit you may end up pressing Ctrl-PrtSc, which may indeed stop everything in its tracks as your system tries to send output to a printer that's turned off.

Break isn't just for emergencies. Some programs, like the current versions of EDLIN distributed along with DOS, are so primitive that they make you use Ctrl-ScrollLock to stop normal editing commands. Give us a break.

Pawing at Ctrl-ScrollLock or Ctrl-break won't always stop what you're doing. Some programs use these key combinations to trigger their own commands. Typing Ctrl-C in *WordStar* is the same as pressing the PgDn key. And if you press Ctrl-ScrollLock all *WordStar 3.3* will do is put a

```
(Vp6w6n?
```

on your screen.

Programmers can write software using a variety of keyboard-reading techniques that explicitly check or refrain from checking to see whether the user pressed Ctrl-C. DOS checks to see whether a user typed Ctrl-C only during standard input/output such as accepting keystrokes or displaying a file using the TYPE command, and when it's in control of printing or communications. But version 2.0 let users add the command:

```
SET BREAK=ON
```

to their CONFIG.SYS system configuration file, which forces DOS to check for this combination of keystrokes more frequently. However, forcing DOS to do anything usually slows it down a bit, and increased break-checking is no exception.

You can turn the extra break-checking on and off at the DOS prompt. Just type BREAK ON to enable the additional checks and (surprise) BREAK OFF to disable them. Typing just BREAK by itself will report the current ON or OFF status.

| Ctrl | Scroll Lock | Mostly interchangeable with Ctrl-C, and both stop or "break out" of DOS operations most of the time. |

| Scroll Lock | Used alone, this key exercises the finger muscles only. |

CapsLock

New users often gripe that the CapsLock key doesn't work properly. On typewriters it usually hunkers down a quarter inch or so and stays there to let you know it's set. Early PCs offered a feature to let you know as well. It was called looking at the screen to see whether everything you were typing was iN tHE wRONG sTATE.

The AT and subsequent systems changed all this, by providing status lights to display the current state of the CapsLock, NumLock, and ScrollLock shifts. For some inexplicable reason, IBM left these off some of its later keyboards, even though the spaces for them were clearly visible. And with enough fancy fingerwork, you can knock these status lights out of synch, so they blink on when they should be off and vice versa. We'll explain how to reset them later.

The other complaint most often voiced by novices is that CapsLock doesn't shift "uppercase" punctuation marks properly. Toggle the CapsLock on and press the comma key expecting to see its upstairs < sign, or type the top row 1 when you want a ! and all you get is the unshifted version of each. Presumably IBM either felt the downstairs keys were more important, or thought that the only keys the CapsLock should adjust were the ones with just one character stamped on them — the alphabetic keys. Any key with two characters on it needs a tap on the Shift key to produce its upper version.

Esc

The Esc key is another (smaller scale) panic-button. In DOS, it stops what you're typing, prints a backslash, drops the cursor down to the next line, and gives you a chance to start over. It won't give you back your DOS prompt though, because it figured if you wanted to do that you'd pound on Ctrl-C. Instead, it assumes you interrupted your earlier command and want to try entering it again.

In most commercial applications, Esc steps you backwards through a succession of hierarchical menus or commands, or cancels operations. It's one of the few conventions adopted by a large number of program designers; the only other one is that F1 will summon some sort of help screen. If you're ever using a new application and the manual isn't handy or isn't indexed (hard to believe but true) or was written by the programmer and not a professional manual writer, and you're stuck, try drumming on the Esc key until you land in a familiar place.

ASCII character 27, generated by the Esc key, wakes up certain printers and screens. When you print a page all you're really doing is sending a stream of characters out the back of your system and down a cable to another set of processors in another hardware box. These other processors watch the data go by and convert it into printed characters by moving the printer's motors, gears, or mirrors. But they also watch for special *control* or *escape* codes that trigger the printer's processor to change the current configuration.

Commands like these can tell your printer to use larger or smaller characters, change paper trays or ribbon colors, adjust spacing measurements, shift to different type fonts, even print sideways (in *landscape* mode rather than *portrait* — these terms were borrowed from the art world where portraits are generally taller than they are wide and landscapes the other way around).

Escape sequences can also tell DOS you're trying to send it a special ANSI.SYS command. Few users take advantage of ANSI (which stands for the American National Standards Institute and is pronounced ANN-see), since its commands are nasty to deal with and don't work all the time. When everything is properly set, they can turn drabs screens into lush, colorful ones. But if you're not expecting an ANSI file brimming with escape characters and left brackets, and you try to do anything with it, you end up with a mess.

DOS screens are usually a dull grey on black, and work only one line at a time. And even if you've set your screen colors using a small utility like any of the ones we provide later, as soon as you type CLS to clear the screen, DOS jumps back to grey on black. The ANSI screen commands can position your DOS cursor anywhere you want it and set any character to any color. And the colors stick, so that CLS simply erases characters but doesn't meddle with any colors you've chosen.

You can also use the ANSI codes to redefine and add primitive macro features to your keyboard. And you can get at much of its magic through the underused DOS PROMPT command.

Function Keys

Function keys (F1 through F10 on older systems, F1 through F12 on newer ones) fall neatly into two categories — underused and overused. Some software, like *WordPerfect*, makes such extensive use of the these keys that it can be hard to remember whether to press F8, Ctrl-F8, Shift-F8, or Alt-F8 to get something done. Other software, like DOS, makes such feeble use of function keys that a few keys remain unassigned and most that are assigned remain unpopular with users.

Actually, function keys can be helpful in two ways. They can compress lots of hard-to-remember or tricky-to-type keystrokes onto one single key. And they can act as dedicated command keys so that pressing F1 brings up a help screen, or striking F9 jumps you to the beginning of a file and F10 to the end.

DOS uses the first seven function keys, F1 through F7, to make life a little easier at the keyboard. One key, F3, is indeed a terrific tool. The others are occasionally handy. (BASIC gives function keys far more intrinsic power.) You can harness ANSI's redefinition abilities to make function keys more useful, but few users bother. Most either don't use function keys much, or else purchase a full-fledged keyboard macro package like *ProKey* or *SuperKey* to redefine keys.

The majority of DOS's built-in function keys let you re-execute the previous DOS command you just entered, either exactly as you entered it earlier, or with changes. DOS puts all the keystrokes you type for each command into a *template*. If you typed in:

```
DIR
```

the template would contain just the letters D, I, and R. If you typed:

```
COPY C:\DOS\UTILITY\*.PRG B:\BACKUP\DOS\PROGS *.PBK /V
```

that whole long string of characters from the intial COPY to the final /V would be in the template. The ability to re-execute commands isn't such a big deal when all you're doing is typing DIR repeatedly. But even then, it's easier to press one key than three, and when you're dealing with long and thorny commands this can be an absolute blessing.

Some of the examples below use the same sample template, and assume you are logged onto drive C:

```
COPY A:ABCD B:WXYZ
```

F1	or	6 →

Both of these take one key at a time from the previous command and copy it to the current command. So if you had finished executing the sample COPY command shown here, and were back again at the DOS prompt, the first time you press either of these keys, you'd see:

```
C
```

Press either key once again and the screen would look like:

```
CO
```

Press either one of these seven more times and you'd see:

```
COPY A:AB
```

So if you wanted to repeat the previous command, you could simply hold down the F1 or right-arrow key until DOS displayed the entire previous template. If you then press the Enter key, DOS would execute this command just as if you had typed it in. But there's a far easier way than dredging up all the keystrokes one at a time.

F3	One tap on F3 zaps the last command entered back onscreen. This is one of the best things the designers of DOS ever did. Since users frequently find themselves repeating DOS commands, and since many commands involve hard-to-type combinations of slashes, backslashes, colons, and hierglyphic filenames, F3 is a genuine boon.

Even better, you can use these keys to "fill out" the rest of a command. Here's a good example: Once you copy critical files, you may want to check the validity of the copies by using the COMP command to compare them to the originals. Both COPY and COMP are four letters long, and both share the same basic syntax. So once you type in:

```
COPY A:ABCD B:WXYZ
```

and press the Enter key to make the copies, you can simply type in:

```
COMP
```

and then press the F3 key. DOS will fill in the rest of the template for you, supplying drives and filenames of both the original files and the copies:

```
COMP A:ABCD B:WXYZ
```

You may have to edit the command slightly. If you used a /V suffix, or *switch*, at the end of the original COPY command to verify the accuracy of your copies, you'll have to delete it from the COMP command. But this is simple; just backspace it away. (Incidentally, adding a /V to verify the copying process — which is the same as giving DOS a VERIFY ON command — doesn't compare the two files byte by byte. Instead, it simply makes sure that DOS can read the appropriate sectors that contain the copy of your file, and then does a CRC check — a crude test for errors that catches flagrant mistakes but can be fooled. To compare two files more precisely, use the limited PC-DOS COMP or the better MS-DOS FC commands.)

Pressing F3 to COMP a file after you COPY it isn't really necessary unless your drives are acting up and generating error messages. But it doesn't hurt, especially when you're copying a vitally important file from a RAMdisk or hard disk to a single backup floppy. We've had lots of trouble with IBM's awful 1.2 megabyte floppy drives, where COPY /V bubbles blithely along without reporting any errors but COMP catches them by the fistful.

F1/right arrow and F3 can also turn a:

```
DISKCOPY A: B:
```

command into a:

```
DISKCOMP A: B:
```

with a few simple keystrokes. Just tap F1 six times, type in MP to replace the final two PY characters of DISKCOPY, and then press F3. (You really shouldn't use DISKCOPY to back up your files, for reasons we'll get to later.) But again, DOS provides an easier way.

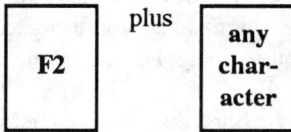

F2	plus	any char-acter

The first six letters of DISKCOPY and DISKCOMP are identical. You can have DOS copy those six letters from the old template into the new one by entering F2 and the seventh letter (in this case, the P in DISKCOPY). Typing F2 and the P would produce:

```
C>DISKCO
```

You could then type MP and then press F3 to finish changing the DISKCOPY A: B: into a DISKCOMP A: B:.

Typing F2 and then a character will look inside the template created by the previous command and copy everything up to (but not including) that character onto the screen. In the unlikely event that you want to do the reverse — copy everything after a specific character — DOS will happily oblige.

SWEEP.COM, a program on one of the accompanying disks, lets you execute commands in all the subdirectories on your disk. You can see all the backup files that end with a .BAK in all of your subdirectories, by typing:

```
SWEEP DIR *.BAK
```

While this will display the backup files in every subdirectory, you might want to focus on the ones in the subdirectory you're currently working in (you can be in only one subdirectory at a time). You could re-enter the command:

```
DIR *.BAK
```

but DOS provides a slightly easier way.

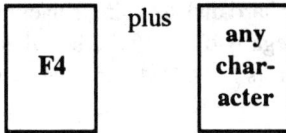

| F4 | plus | any char- acter |

Just type F4 and then D, and DOS will skip over all the characters up to the D in the word DIR. However, you won't see anything onscreen. But then press F3 and DOS will put the rest of the previous command onscreen, from the D onward. The F4 key works like the F2 key in reverse.

So, if the previous command was:

```
SWEEP DIR *.BAK
```

and you typed F4, then D, then F3, you'd see:

```
DIR *.BAK
```

The F2 and F4 keys will always jump over or to the first occurrence of the character you specify. If you want to jump over or to a second or third occurrence of that character you can repeat the command a second or third time. But this gets confusing, especially when you're working with F4 and can't see what you're doing. Few users rely on the F2 key, and virtually nobody uses F4.

If you're trying any of the above tricks and you get hopelessly lost or confused, you can always press Ctrl-ScrollLock or Ctrl-C to abort, and start again on the next line. However, if you want to make some corrections in the current line, and keep working on it, you can do so.

| F5 |

Pressing F5 replaces the old template from the previous command with the new one you're working on. You can then continue to edit this new one, using the F1, F2, F3, and F4 keys. This is another fairly useless and unpopular function key.

While DOS provides the F1 through F5 keys to edit the command line template, it tosses in two more simple tools.

When you create files in DOS you have to tell it when you're done. You do this by adding an *end-of-file marker* as the very last character. This special character is a Ctrl-Z, with an ASCII value of 26 — easy to remember since Z is the 26th letter of the alphabet. You can generate this character using three different techniques. First, you could hold down the Ctrl key and press Z. Second, you could hold down the Alt key, type 26 on the number pad (not the top row number keys), and then release the Alt key. Or third, you could simply press F6. Each will put a ^Z onscreen and an end-of-file marker (which may show up under certain circumstances as a small right-pointing arrow) in your file.

Pressing F6 isn't much more efficient than typing Ctrl-Z. But it's there, and lots of users are accustomed to ending files by pressing F6 and then the Enter key.

F6	Puts an ASCII character 26 (Ctrl-Z end-of-file marker) onto the screen at the current cursor position.

The only other function key that does anything at all is F7, which sticks a null — with an ASCII value of 0 — onto the screen at the current cursor position. Pressing F7 prints a ^@ and can generate a CHR$(0) if you need one. You probably won't. But if you do, be glad F7 is there, since this null character is the only one you can't create using the Alt-key-plus-number-pad technique.

F7	Puts an ASCII character 0 (null) onto the screen at the current cursor position.

Several other keys can help you edit in DOS:

Esc	Pressing the Esc key cancels whatever you're doing, prints a backslash (\), and drops the cursor down one line without disturbing the contents of the old template. You can often get a similar interrupted result by pounding on Ctrl-ScrollLock or Ctrl-C.

Ins	Pressing the Ins key lets you insert characters at the cursor position without wiping out any characters in the template. DOS is normally in *overstrike* or *overwrite* mode, which means that if you put the cursor in the middle of a word and start typing, DOS will obliterate the old characters with any new ones you type. The Ins key will tell DOS to go into *insert* mode, which pushes existing text to the right as you type in new characters.

You'll find yourself using the Ins key often. If you were currently logged into drive C: and you tried to execute the example mentioned earlier:

```
COPY A:ABCD B:WXYZ
```

but you forgot the A: before ABCD, you'd end up with:

```
COPY ABCD B:WXYZ
```

This would tell DOS to copy the file ABCD from your current drive (which in this case would be C:) to drive B: and rename it WXYZ. What you really wanted to do however was copy the ABCD file on drive A:, but you forgot to specify the A:. If DOS found a file on drive C: called ABCD it would copy C:ABCD to B: and rename it during the process. But if DOS couldn't find it (which was probably the case) it would print an error message. To fix the command, you'd either lean on the F1 or the right arrow key to read the:

```
COPY
```

out of the old template, or you'd press F2 A, which would do the same thing a little faster. Then, press Ins to put DOS into insert mode and type A:

```
COPY A:
```

and finally, press F3 to put the rest of the old template onscreen:

```
COPY A:ABCD B:WXYZ
```

> **Del**   Del simply deletes keys from the template one by one. If you spelled COPY COPPY, you'd just position the cursor on one of the Ps and press Del to erase it. You need to use the Del key when dealing with characters inside words. (COP Y isn't the same thing as COPY.) The Del key lets you close up the word and get rid of the extra space.

However, if the letter you have to erase happens to be at the beginning or end of a word, you can usually just press the space bar to get rid of it, since DOS interprets one space the same way it treats many continuous spaces. So:

```
C> COPY A:ABCD B:WXYZ
```

will do the same thing as the original example. If you spelled COPY mistakenly as COPYY, you could simply position the cursor on the second Y and press the spacebar.

If you realize you've made a typing mistake while you're working on the same line, you could either press F5 to replace the old template with the new one, and then move to the offending character and write over it, or you could backspace to the mistake, correct it, and then re-enter the rest of the command. The left arrow key will do the same thing. Both backspace "destructively" since they erase everything as they move.

> ◻   or   ◻ **4**   Erases characters and moves the cursor to the left.

Of all the DOS function keys, the best is clearly F3. You'll find yourself using it all day long. One of the handiest F3 tricks lets you verify wildcard deletions. If you're working on a corporate contest, and have a lot of old files on your disk like CON-TEST.RUL, CONTEST.TXT, CORP.LOG, and CORP.TXT, and you want to delete them all with the command:

```
DEL CO*.*
```

you'd better be careful, since this command would also erase files such as COM-MAND.COM and COMP.COM. To see what files you would erase with such a wildcard command, first type:

```
DIR CO*.*
```

If all you see is something like:

```
CONTEST  RUL    1920    8-17-90    8:00p
CONTEST  TXT   26624    9-08-90    3:07p
CORP     LOG    3968    9-12-90    9:03p
CORP     TXT    7552    8-21-90    1:02p
```

Then just type:

```
DEL
```

and press the F3 key, which will add the remaining characters from the previous template:

```
DEL CO*.*
```

However, if you see files like COMMAND.COM in the directory listing, you can avoid potential trouble by making the DEL command more specific. In this case you might want to try it in two stages, first:

```
DEL CON*.*
```

and then:

```
DEL COR*.*
```

But even then it doesn't hurt to try DIR CON*.* and DIR COR*.* first and then use F3 when you're satisfied you won't erase any unexpected files.

F2 can be a real lifesaver as well. Whenever you tell DOS about a disk drive you have to use a colon. Unfortunately, the colon is a shifted character, and it's common when typing rapidly or working late to press the lowercase semicolon instead. If you end up with a command such as:

```
COPY A;ABCD B:WXYZ
```

DOS will become confused, since it treats a semicolon like a space (tabs, equals signs, and commas are also turned into *delimiters* that work like spaces). It will think that you're trying to copy a file called A on your current drive and rename it to ABCD in the process.

But it won't understand the B:WXYZ and will print an "Invalid number of parameters" message.

To fix this, simply press F2 and then a semicolon, which will put a:

```
COPY A
```

onscreen. Then type a colon and press F3 and the command will be ready to go.

Figure 6.5 summarizes the keys that will execute certain DOS functions.

Key	DOS Function
F1 *	Copies characters one by one from old template to new
F2	Copies up to specified character from old template
F3	Copies all remaining characters from old template
F4	Skips up to specified character from old template
F5	Replaces old template with existing one
F6 **	Generates ASCII 26 end-of-file marker (^Z)
F7	Generates ASCII 0 null (^@)
Esc	Interrupts and cancels changes in current line
Ins	Switches DOS from overwrite mode into Insert mode
Del	Erases character at cursor and skips over it in template
Bksp ***	Erases one character to the left

* Same as right arrow key
** Same as Ctrl-Z
*** Same as left arrow key

Figure 6.5.   Keys that Produce Selected DOS Functions.

Assuming that you're logged onto drive C: and that the previous command was COPY A:ABCD B:WXYZ, here's what you can do with function keys:

Pressing	Produces
F1	C
F2 + W	COPY A:ABCD B:
F3	COPY A:ABCD B:WXYZ
F4 + W + F3	WXYZ

If you then press F5, DOS would replace the old COPY A:ABCD B:WXYZ template with these.

New Keyboard Tricks

IBM started letting users program their keyboards with the first AT. By issuing a few simple BASIC commands you can experiment with IBM's programmable keyboards to see how they work, or to customize the key action.

To change the keyboard's LED shift-lock indicators, just issue an OUT &H60,&HED (the SET/RESET LEDS command), and follow this immediately with an OUT &H60,nn (where nn is a binary value indicating which LEDs to turn on). Bit 0 is for the ScrollLock indicator, bit 1 is for NumLock and bit 2 is for CapsLock.

The KBD program on the accompanying disk allows you to toggle the key values.

It's simple to change both the typeamatic repeat rate and delay, using the KBD, QKRP, or EQKRP programs on the accompanying disks, or the MODE command in DOS 4.0 and 5.0. If you are forever frustrated by the slowness of the keyboard,

```
MODE CON RATE=32 DELAY=1
```

will speed things up to the maximum directly allowed by DOS, while

```
MODE CON RATE=1 DELAY=4
```

will give you lots of time to reflect on the meaning of life between keystrokes.

You can also create two assembly language files, FAST.COM and SLOW.COM, that will also set the rates. Just make sure DEBUG.COM is handy and type in the following ten lines, pressing Enter at the end of each one.

```
DEBUG
E 100 B0 F3 E6 60 B9 00 10 90 E2 FD B0 00 E6 60 C3
N FAST.COM
RCX
F
W
E 10B 7F
N SLOW.COM
W
Q
```

When you're done, you'll have two new files on your disk. For a laugh, type:

```
SLOW
```

and press Enter. See what your typematic rate is like. You won't believe it. Then, to speed things up considerably, type:

```
FAST
```

and press Enter. If you've never speeded up your keyboard before, you won't believe this either. To change the rates, patch the byte in either SLOW.COM or FAST.COM at address 10B.

Keyboard Magic with DOS 5.0's DOSKEY

Beyond the simple line-editing capabilities of the function keys, DOS 5.0's DOSKEY provides an entirely new set of features for dealing with the command line. DOSKEY lets you recall, modify, and execute previously issued DOS commands, using the arrow keys and the PageUp/PageDn keys to go back and forth through the DOS-maintained stack of recent commands. Unlike the STACK utility on the accompanying disks, DOSKEY only displays one previous command line at a time — although you can display all the previous commands in the buffer with F7, you can't cursor to them directly and execute them as you can in STACK.

You can either make DOSKEY a permanent part of your system utilities, by including it in your AUTOEXEC.BAT, or just invoke it from the command line when you know you're going to have a lot of repetitive command sequences or keystrokes to wade through. There are two basic approaches to using DOSKEY, and deciding which one is best for you is a simple matter of taste. If you're most comfortable finding solutions by trial and error, DOSKEY's ability to recall previous commands lets you experiment with a variety of commands, and then only reuse those you like. If, on the other hand, you find it hard to go on a picnic without making a list first, DOSKEY's macro capability lets you create your own custom commands based on the exact sequences of keystrokes you'll need to accomplish the task at hand. Let's suppose you want to find a very important snippet of information about Windows you saw while glancing through one of the many READ.ME files you know are scattered throughout your hard disk. Of course, you no longer have a clue as to which particular READ.ME it was in, or even if it was called READ.ME or README.1ST, so the task is to locate and search each of the possible files. You could start by typing

```
ATTRIB \READ*.* /S
```

which produces a response like

```
A          C:\SYS\DOS\README.DOC
A          C:\SYS\DOS\README.TXT
A          C:\SYS\SIDEKICK\READ.ME
A          C:\SYS\WIN\README.TXT
A          C:\SYS\DEVS\READ.ME
A          C:\SYS\INSET\README.DOC
```

```
A            C:\SYS\HIJAAK\READ.ME
A            C:\WP\WS4\README.COM
A            C:\WP\WS4\README.TXT
A            C:\LANGS\PASCAL\DOC\READ.ME
A            C:\LANGS\MSPASCAL\README.DOC
A            C:\APPS\Q2\README.COM
A            C:\APPS\Q2\README
```

To look through the files, you'd normally summon up your favorite word processor or file browser with the first file name, as in

```
EDIT C:\SYS\DOS\README.DOC
```

Then after perusing the file, use F2 and F3 to change the filename to

```
EDIT C:\SYS\DOS\README.TXT
```

and so on down the list. Of course, at some point, the file names will start scrolling off the top of the screen, and you'll need to stop, reissue the ATTRIB command, and then pick up where you left off with EDIT and the pathname for the next file. With DOSKEY installed, a few simple up-arrow keystrokes will get you to the ATTRIB command, and after you've gotten the file names back on the screen, a few more keystrokes will get you to the last EDIT command you issued.

If you're even more organized, you can start the whole process by using DOSKEY to define the first step, issuing the ATTRIB command, as a single keystroke:

```
DOSKEY 1=ATTRIB \READ*.* /S
```

so when the file names scroll off the screen, you need only type 1 to refresh the list, and up-arrow only twice to get back to the last EDIT command. Once you get started with DOSKEY, it's easy to get carried away. Have fun!

The following figures summarize the ASCII hex and decimal values, and the scan code values in both hex and decimal for the various keys and key combinations.

Character	Decimal	Hex	Character	Decimal	Hex
^@	0	00	@	64	40
^A	1	01	A	65	41
^B	2	02	B	66	42
^C	3	03	C	67	43
^D	4	04	D	68	44
^E	5	05	E	69	45
^F	6	06	F	70	46
^G	7	07	G	71	47
^H	8	08	H	72	48
^I	9	09	I	73	49
^J	10	0A	J	74	4A
^K	11	0B	K	75	4B
^L	12	0C	L	76	4C
^M	13	0D	M	77	4D
^N	14	0E	N	78	4E
^O	15	0F	O	79	4F
^P	16	10	P	80	50
^Q	17	11	Q	81	51
^R	18	12	R	82	52
^S	19	13	S	83	53
^T	20	14	T	84	54
^U	21	15	U	85	55
^V	22	16	V	86	56
^W	23	17	W	87	57
^X	24	18	X	88	58
^Y	25	19	Y	89	59
^Z	26	1A	Z	90	5A
^[	27	1B	[	91	5B
^\	28	1C	\	92	5C
^]	29	1D	]	93	5D
^^	30	1E	^	94	5E
^_	31	1F	_	95	5F
SP	32	20	`	96	60
!	33	21	a	97	61
"	34	22	b	98	62
#	35	23	c	99	63
$	36	24	d	100	64
%	37	25	e	101	65
&	38	26	f	102	66
'	39	27	g	103	67
(	40	28	h	104	68
)	41	29	i	105	69
*	42	2A	j	106	6A
	43	2B	k	107	6B

Figure 6.6.   ASCII Characters with Decimal and Hex Values

Character	Decimal	Hex	Character	Decimal	Hex
,	44	2C	l	108	6C
-	45	2D	m	109	6D
.	46	2E	n	110	6E
/	47	2F	o	111	6F
0	48	30	p	112	70
1	49	31	q	113	71
2	50	32	r	114	72
3	51	33	s	115	73
4	52	34	t	116	74
5	53	35	u	117	75
6	54	36	v	118	76
7	55	37	w	119	77
8	56	38	x	120	78
9	57	39	y	121	79
:	58	3A	z	122	7A
;	59	3B	{	123	7B
<	60	3C	|	124	7C
=	61	3D	}	125	7D
>	62	3E	~	126	7E
?	63	3F	⌂	127	7F

Figure 6.6. ASCII Characters with Decimal and Hex Values *(continued)*

Key	Hex Scan Code	Decimal Scan Code
Escape	01	01
! 1	02	02
@ 2	03	03
# 3	04	04
$ 4	05	05
% 5	06	06
^ 6	07	07
& 7	08	08
* 8	09	09
(9	0A	10
) 0	0B	11
_ -	0C	12
+ =	0D	13
Backspace	0E	14
Tab	0F	15
Q q	10	16
W w	11	17

Figure 6.7. Key Scan Codes

Key	Hex Scan Code	Decimal Scan Code
E e	12	18
R r	13	19
T t	14	20
Y y	15	21
U u	16	22
I i	17	23
O o	18	24
P p	19	25
{ [	1A	26
}]	1B	27
Enter	1C	28
Ctrl	1D	29
A a	1E	30
S s	1F	31
D d	20	32
F f	21	33
G g	22	34
H h	23	35
J j	24	36
K k	25	37
L l	26	38
: ;	27	39
" '	28	40
~ `	29	41
Left Shift	2A	42
| \	2B	43
Z z	2C	44
X x	2D	45
C c	2E	46
V v	2F	47
B b	30	48
N n	31	49
M m	32	50
< ,	33	51
> .	34	52
? /	35	53
Right Shift	36	54
PrtSc *	37	55
Alt	38	56
Space Bar	39	57
Caps Lock	3A	58
F1	3B	59
F2	3C	60
F3	3D	61

Figure 6.7. Key Scan Codes *(continued)*

Key	Hex Scan Code	Decimal Scan Code
F4	3E	62
F5	3F	63
F6	40	64
F7	41	65
F8	42	66
F9	43	67
F10	44	68
Num Lock	45	69
Scroll Lock	46	70
7 Home	47	71
8 Cursor Up	48	72
9 Pg Up	49	73
- (gray key)	4A	74
4 Cursor Left	4B	75
5	4C	76
6 Cursor Right	4D	77
+ (gray key)	4E	78
1 End	4F	79
2 Cursor Down	50	80
3 Pg Dn	51	81
0 Insert	52	82
. Del	53	83
Sys Req(84 Key)	54	84

101 Key Board Extended Keys

	Key	Hex Scan Code	Decimal Scan Code
	Pause	E1	225
Gray Keys	Cursor Left	E0 4B	
	Cursor Right	E0 4D	
	Cursor Down	E0 50	
	Cursor Up	E0 48	
	Delete	E0 53	
	End	E0 4F	
	Home	E0 47	
	Insert	E0 52	
	Page Down	E0 51	
	Page Up	E0 49	
	Pause	E1 1D 45 E1 9D C5	
	Print Screen	E0 2A E0 37	
Keypad Area	Enter	E0 1C	
	/	E0 35	
Other Keys	Right Alt	E0 38	
	Right Ctrl	E0 1D	

Figure 6.7. Key Scan Codes *(continued)*

Key Combination	Decimal Code	Hex Code	Key Combination	Decimal Code	Hex Code
NUL	3	03	Shift-F1	84	54
Shift-Tab	15	0F	Shift-F2	85	55
Alt-Q	16	10	Shift-F3	86	56
Alt-W	17	11	Shift-F4	87	57
Alt-E	18	12	Shift-F5	88	58
Alt-R	19	13	Shift-F6	89	59
Alt-T	20	14	Shift-F7	90	5A
Alt-Y	21	15	Shift-F8	91	5B
Alt-U	22	16	Shift-F9	92	5C
Alt-I	23	17	Shift-F10	93	5D
Alt-O	24	18	Ctrl-F1	94	5E
Alt-P	25	19	Ctrl-F2	95	5F
Alt-A	30	1E	Ctrl-F3	96	60
Alt-S	31	1F	Ctrl-F4	97	61
Alt-D	32	20	Ctrl-F5	98	62
Alt-F	33	21	Ctrl-F6	99	63
Alt-G	34	22	Ctrl-F7	100	64
Alt-H	35	23	Ctrl-F8	101	65
Alt-J	36	24	Ctrl-F9	102	66
Alt-K	37	25	Ctrl-F10	103	67
Alt-L	38	26	Alt-F1	104	68
Alt-Z	44	2C	Alt-F2	105	69
Alt-X	45	2D	Alt-F3	106	6A
Alt-C	46	2E	Alt-F4	107	6B
Alt-V	47	2F	Alt-F5	108	6C
Alt-B	48	30	Alt-F6	109	6D
Alt-N	49	31	Alt-F7	110	6E
Alt-M	50	32	Alt-F8	111	6F
F1	59	3B	Alt-F9	112	70
F2	60	3C	Alt-F10	113	71
F3	61	3D	Ctrl-PrtSc	114	72
F4	62	3E	Ctrl-Cursor Left	115	73
F5	63	3F	Ctrl-Cursor Right	116	74
F6	64	40	Ctrl-End	117	75
F7	65	41	Ctrl-PgDn	118	76
F8	66	42	Ctrl-Home	119	77
F9	67	43	Alt-1	120	78
F10	68	44	Alt-2	121	79
Home	71	47	Alt-3	122	7A

Figure 6.8. Key Combination Codes

Key Combination	Decimal Code	Hex Code		Key Combination	Decimal Code	Hex Code
Cursor Up	72	48		Alt-4	123	7B
PgUp	73	49		Alt-5	124	7C
Cursor Left	75	4B		Alt-6	125	7D
Cursor Right	77	4D		Alt-7	126	7E
End	79	4F		Alt-8	127	7F
Cursor Down	80	50		Alt-9	128	80
PgDn	81	51		Alt-0	129	81
Ins	82	52		Alt--	130	82
Del	83	53		Alt-=	131	83
Shift-F1	84	54		Ctrl-PgUp	132	84

Figure 6.8.   Key Combination Codes *(continued)*

Value	Alt	Ctrl	L-Shft	R-Shft
00				
01				X
02			X	
03			X	X
04		X		
05		X		X
06		X	X	
07		X	X	X
08	X			
09	X			X
0A	X		X	
0B	X		X	X
0C	X	X		
0D	X	X		X
0E	X	X	X	
0F	X	X	X	X

Note: X means key is pressed

Figure 6.9.   Shift-Mask Value Table

Chips and Memory

Deep down, all people are pretty much alike. True, some have blue eyes and some have brown, some are well over six feet tall and others short and stumpy, and one may pick up the Unified Field Theory where Einstein left off while another becomes the nation's latest celebrity thrill killer. But their internal parts are basically similar. The same is true with PCs.

The CPU — The Brains of the PC

At the heart of every microcomputer is a microprocessor, a skinny sliver of purified crystaline silicon that has been *doped* — coated with impurities that give it electronic switching abilities — etched with a witch's brew of poisonous gasses, and then entombed in a small ceramic block. When people talk about "the chip" inside a PC they mean this one. It's often referred to as a CPU or *central processing unit*, although you never hear anyone say "hey, nice unit in that computer."

The two most popular microcomputer CPUs these days are made by Intel and Motorola in "clean rooms" straight out of science fiction movies, where workers pad the halls wearing sneeze masks and special dust-free booties. (Chips are fast because they're so small and densely packed that signals can move from one place on them to another a few millionths of an inch away in a few billionths of a second. The scale is so infinitesimal that a dust speck on a chip would be like an aircraft carrier in your bathtub.) The two biggest microcomputer companies are Apple and IBM. Apple switched from chips made by MOS Technology to the Motorola 68000 family of CPUs. IBM has stuck with the Intel 8088/8086/80x86 line of chips from the beginning.

What distinguishes a CPU from humbler chips is its ability to do arithmetic and logical operations, decode special instructions, and issue appropriate controlling signals to other chips in the system. One typical instruction might store a character in the computer's main memory, while another instruction will fetch the character back when needed. The CPU can communicate with the rest of the system through numbered *ports*. And it comes from the chip foundry with a tiny amount of memory aboard, located in places called *registers*. An 8088 CPU has a scant 14 registers, each capable of storing two bytes. A byte can hold any eight-bit binary address or a single character like an A or a 4. When two bytes are strung together, as they are in registers, they're called a *word*. Virtually everything your computer does is in one form or other shuttled in and out of those registers at incredible speeds.

For their tiny size, registers are power-packed. They do things like store memory addresses (the PC's 8088 registers can handle up to a million different ones), hold data, keep track of which instructions to execute next, and maintain status and control indicators called *flags* that report on the success or failure of previous instructions and can control how the CPU executes current and future ones.

The CPU sits astride the computer's *bus*, a multilane highway of wires that carries data, controlling signals, and electrical power to all the major parts under the hood. The wider the bus the greater the amount of data a computer can move in a single operation. A PC or PC-XT has eight data lines, an AT-class machine 16, and an 80386/486 system 32.

The original PC is classed as a 16-bit machine, since its 8088 CPU does indeed manipulate information in 16-bit chunks — but only inside the CPU itself. When its CPU needs raw data to work on, or when it finishes processing some information and wants to store it back in memory, it has to break the data into eight-bit pieces so it can squeeze through the narrow eight-bit bus. A timer circuit commonly called the *clock* sends pulses down one of the bus lines several million times each second to keep everything synchronized. In a PC the timer ticks at 4.77 megahertz (MHz). Since *mega-* means million and *Hertz* means cycles-per-second, that may seem pretty fast. Well, compared to a postal worker maybe, but these days 4.77 MHz is a real crawl. Current hardware runs at up to ten times the original PC's clock speed.

A clock is like the big sweaty guy on a galley slave ship in a gladiator movie beating out the rowing tempo on a drum. The more energetic his drumming the faster the ship moves. However, no microcomputer actually performs calculations at anywhere near the clock rate. The PC, like virtually every other computer, is a *Von Neumann* machine (named after mathematician John Von Neumann who contributed to the design of early room-sized computers such as ENIAC). Von Neumann machines execute all instructions one at a time. Some state-of-the-art supercomputers, like those made by Cray, can process similar groups of instructions concurrently in what is called *parallel processing*. Every Von Neumann CPU wastes lots of time waiting for the current instruction to finish so it can trigger the next one. And instructions can hog lots of timer cycles. Even the PC's NOP (pronounced no-opp) instruction, a placeholder that is expressly there to do nothing except wait, takes three clock cycles to execute.

(The clock in the original PC is actually a special Intel chip that oscillates at 14.31818 MHz, or three times as fast as the often-quoted 4.77 MHz clock speed. This is too fast for most circuits, so other timer chips inside the PC use every third or fourth or fifth of these ticks to slow down the pace for their own needs.)

Most CPUs are pretty capable at doing basic integer arithmetic (remember, they were first designed as calculator chips) but stumble over *floating point* operations, which require juggling of decimal points and so take longer and demand more precision than working with whole numbers. Normally, when software has to work with decimal numbers it uses relatively slow brute-force tricks, and can end up dragging its feet and rounding off calculations crudely.

When IBM first introduced the PC it left a large empty socket next to the CPU that it eventually filled with a *numeric coprocessor* chip called an 8087. This number-crunching chip was designed to perform the complex calculations Intel's main 8088 and 8086 CPUs couldn't handle efficiently. And it included special built-in circuitry to zip through things like trigonometric operations in the blink of an electronic eye. As Intel re-engineered its 8088/8086 into an 80286 and then an 80386 and later an 80486, it made sure the companion math coprocessors kept pace.

However, just sticking a math chip in the empty socket doesn't make every software application run faster. Some applications, such as word processors or data base managers, don't do much tricky math. And while some applications, such as CAD (computer aided design) packages, engineering programs, and spreadsheets, could run far faster by using such a number cruncher, unless the software includes special instructions to wake up the math chip and send data to it, the chip will just sit idly by.

Computers can get things done one of two ways. They can actively and repeatedly go out and check whether something has happened yet, or they can lie back and wait for events to announce themselves. Continuously *polling* the hardware to see whether the user has hit a key, a disk drive has stopped spinning, or a printer is turned on is incredibly wasteful. Today's CPUs are *interrupt-driven*, somewhat like a hospital emergency room staff that's normally in low gear doing routine record keeping but can spring into action when necessary. And as in an emergency room, certain interrupts have priority over others. If a physician is adjusting one patient's bandage and the local rescue crew wheels in a sword swallower who tried shoplifting a chain saw, the focus of attention changes instantly. If your computer is leisurely printing out a document and you happen to start typing, its attention has to shift quickly or the keystrokes will be lost forever.

When a computer detects an incoming interrupt, it parks or "pushes" critical information about what it was originally doing into a section of memory called a *stack* and attends to the interrupt. Then when the CPU is finished handling the interrupt, it retrieves or *pops* the critical information it temporarily stored so it can get back to what it was originally working on. And it can stack such information many levels deep, so that if a second, more urgent interrupt barges in, the CPU parks information about the first interrupt while it works on the second, and so on.

This temporary storage device is called a stack because it resembles a box-shaped device in a cafeteria with a hole in the top for dishes and a spring at the bottom to push the dishes upward. Both the cafeteria and the computer stacks are designed so that only the top item on the stack is accessible; as you push each new item onto it, it presses all the items beneath it down one level each time. And when you remove an item from either stack, the one directly under it pops up and rises to the top. It's like a union seniority system when times are hard: LIFO — last in, first out.

If you were very methodical and had just finished washing a pile of dishes with the letters of the alphabet painted on them, and you wanted to store them in the right order, you'd put dish labeled Z in the cafeteria storage device first.

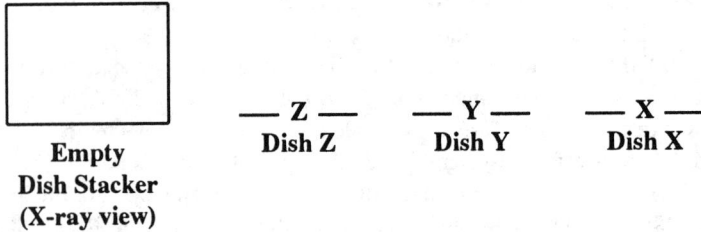

```
┌─────────┐
│         │      — Z —      — Y —      — X —
│         │      Dish Z     Dish Y     Dish X
└─────────┘
  Empty
Dish Stacker
(X-ray view)
```

Dish Z would then be at the very top of the stack, since it was the only one in the stack.

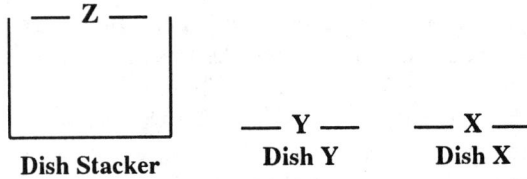

```
┌─────────┐
│ — Z —   │
│         │
│         │      — Y —      — X —
└─────────┘      Dish Y     Dish X
Dish Stacker
```

Then, you'd put dish Y on top of dish Z. Dish Y would push dish Z down inside the storage box and then would become the top dish.

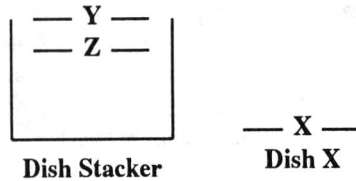

```
│ — Y — │
│ — Z — │
│       │
│       │      — X —
└───────┘      Dish X
Dish Stacker
```

Continue by putting dish X on top of dish Y, which then disappears down the stack along with dish Z. Only dish X is visible.

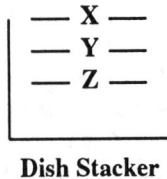

```
│ — X — │
│ — Y — │
│ — Z — │
│       │
└───────┘
Dish Stacker
```

To get to dish Z at this point, you'd have to first pop dish X off, and then pop off dish Y.

As any harried office worker knows, processing interrupts is a tricky business. You have to be able to respond quickly to genuine crises, ignore persistent but trivial ones, put all such interruptions in proper priority order, and make sure that everything is eventually dispatched. To take pressure off the main CPU, IBM routed all interrupt requests through a chip cleverly named an *Interrupt Controller.* In the PC and PC-XT this chip can juggle as many as eight interrupts at once; by daisy-chaining two of these chips together, the PC-AT's designers were able to have it handle up to 15 simultaneously.

Other semi-intelligent chips control other important aspects of operation, leaving the CPU free to chew its way through programs and data while leaving the actual dirty work to specialists. Instead of filtering every last byte of your data through its registers, the CPU knows how to delegate. Handling data on disks is painfully slow since the system has to make sure the disks are spinning at the proper rate, move a magnetic head to a directory table to figure out where the data is, wait for that area of the disk to come spinning around, move the heads to read it, and maybe even go back and repeat the process if the data is scattered over several locations (as it often is). Shuffling data around in memory is fast; there are no moving parts.

One common CPU chore is to move large amounts of information from slow disks to fast memory and back. Passing it all through the CPU's skimpy registers would be ridiculously inefficient (as it was on the PC*jr*). The PC's DMA (direct memory access) controller can bypass this potential bottleneck; it's like an interstate beltway that skirts a city while the main highway chugs its way downtown.

Other controller chips manage the disk drives, the keyboard, the video output, and some of the input and output. Fortunately, DOS — with the help of some gut-level BIOS (basic input/output software) programs built into the PC — takes care of all the messy details so you don't have to.

RAM

Some chips, like the CPU and the DMA controller, contain small amounts of onboard memory for temporary storage. But all the garden-variety day-to-day storage and retrieval activities take place in the main system RAM.

Every microcomputer comes with two kinds of memory, RAM and ROM. RAM originally stood for *random access memory,* but it really should be called RWM for read/write memory. ROM stands for *read only memory,* which is correct. RAM, ROM, and disks are all random-access storage devices since they let you jump directly to any point on them to store or look up information. You don't have to slog through storage areas 1 and 2 to get to storage area 3. But RAM and ROM chips have several important differences. ROM chips contain vital, permanently stored information put there by your computer manufacturer. Turn the power off and this information remains intact. You can't change, or "write" over this information directly (although IBM provided a clever way to update it). But you can retrieve, or "read" it. That's why it's called read-only.

When you turn your system on, programs stored on a ROM chip tell the hardware how to begin operating. After sniffing around to figure out what hardware happens to be hooked up to your system, a special program on a ROM chip tests your RAM to make sure it's working properly. In all but the earliest PCs, as it checks memory, this POST (Power On Self Test) diagnostic program displays the amount of RAM it has tested and approved. This is the slowly changing number you see in the upper lefthand corner of your screen when you start. The POST tests memory by writing information into RAM and then reading it back and comparing it with the original information to make sure RAM hasn't mangled it. You can read from both ROM and RAM. But you can write only to RAM.

ROM never changes. The information on it always stays the same, whether the power is on or off. The only way to fix serious bugs on them is to yank them out and replace them with newer models. IBM's early PC ROM chips had several annoying deficiencies. One chip couldn't divide properly by 10, but that was corrected in a hurry. And the early PC ROMs made it hard for users to stuff the maximum 640K of RAM into their systems, or to boot up from hard disks.

We'll get to where all this memory is located a little later in this chapter. For now, think about memory as a concert hall, with several sections, and numbered seats in each section. ROM is all the way in the back of the hall. RAM hogs all the good seats, from the first row to about two-thirds of the way toward the rear.

Each new version of DOS contains patches to some of the gut-level programs and tables delivered on ROM chips. These patches can't alter the ROM chips themselves. But when the PC starts up each day, it takes some of the permanent ROM information and copies it into "low" RAM memory — the first rows of theatre seats — and then goes to the copy of the information rather than the original ROM chip when it needs to look something up. (The million or so characters of memory in a PC are arranged in regions called *segments* that will be discussed soon; ROM data is stored in a distant Siberia far from the "lower" 640K of RAM where most of the computer's action takes place.) The patches provided with each new DOS version can and regularly do overwrite the older ROM information that's been copied into low memory.

As you use your system, you write information into RAM. When RAM fills up, you have to erase unwanted information to make room for new data. And, when you turn your system off, all the information stored in RAM vanishes forever. Sometimes your local power company or a fellow employee turning on an air conditioner or heater that's plugged into the same outlet accidentally does this for you while you're working, so you have to be fanatical about taking the data stored in memory and copying it onto a more or less permanent storage medium like a disk frequently.

RAM and ROM are both memory chips that store information. The important similarities and differences in storage devices are shown in Figure 7.1.

Storage Devices	RAM	ROM	Disks
Data already on it when you turn computer on	No	Yes	Maybe
Data remains on it when you turn computer off	No	Yes	Yes
Can read information from it	Yes	Yes	Yes
Can write information to it	Yes	No	Yes
Can change the information on it	Yes	No	Yes
Can handle information very quickly	Yes	Yes	No

Figure 7.1. Characteristics of Storage Devices

Here's an easy way to remember the difference between memory chips. Let's say you walk into a classroom, and see an empty blackboard at one end of the room (RAM), and a bulletin board inside a glass display case at the other (ROM).

The bulletin board may contain schedules, fire drill codes, and lists of telephone numbers. The blackboard has nothing on it. You can write on the blackboard. But you can't write on the glass-covered bulletin board. You can read information from both. When you fill the blackboard, you have to erase some older information so you have room to write down the newer data. When class is over, you erase the blackboard, turn out the lights, and leave. The blackboard is again empty. But the bulletin board at the other end of the room still contains the information that was on it when you entered. And it will be there tomorrow.

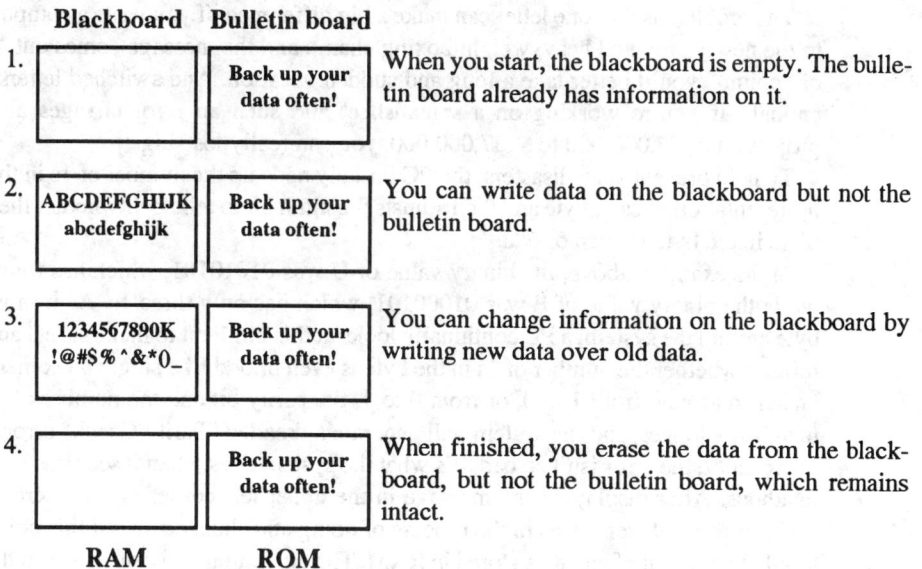

Blackboard   Bulletin board

1.
| | Back up your data often! |

When you start, the blackboard is empty. The bulletin board already has information on it.

2.
| ABCDEFGHIJK abcdefghijk | Back up your data often! |

You can write data on the blackboard but not the bulletin board.

3.
| 1234567890K !@#$%^&*()_ | Back up your data often! |

You can change information on the blackboard by writing new data over old data.

4.
| | Back up your data often! |

When finished, you erase the data from the blackboard, but not the bulletin board, which remains intact.

RAM   ROM

All data stored in RAM vanishes when you turn the power off; such storage is *volatile*. Information on ROM chips remains intact when the power snaps off; this kind of storage is *non-volatile*.

Parity Problems

While there are eight bits in a byte, the PC's RAM normally handles small packages of information nine bits at a time rather than eight. The extra bit is called a *parity* bit and it's a crude way to insure the integrity of your data. One bit can make a whale of difference. Here's why:

To your CPU, the letter U is a just the decimal number 85. The binary representation of 85 is:

01010101

(If you skipped ahead to here, and you're mystified by all those 1s and 0s, go back two chapters and read how binary numbers work. It's actually pretty simple.)

Change just a single bit from one state to the other — say the fourth one over from the left — and the binary number becomes:

01000101

which translates to decimal 69, or the value of E.

The problem is that one letter can make a big difference. If you write a computer letter to the newly crowned heavyweight boxing champ and the message comes out "chump" or "chimp" you'd better take a long and sudden vacation. And switched letters are bad enough. If you're working on a spreadsheet and such an error changes an income projection of $7,000,000 to $237,000,000, you can really lose big.

To help prevent such disasters, the PC initially adds up the number of 1s in the binary representation of each byte and then adjusts the ninth bit to tell itself whether the number of 1s in the byte is even or odd.

In the example above, the binary value of U was 01010101, which has four 1s in it, while the binary value of E was 01000101, which has only three 1s. As it moves each byte around the system, a PC continually looks at this ninth bit to make sure it accurately reflects whether the number of 1s in the byte is even or odd. If a single bit somehow gets switched around from 1 to 0, or from 0 to 1, the parity bit and the number of 1s won't match any longer, and the system will generate a dreaded "Parity Check" error.

Actually, the error isn't so bad, it's what the system does when it sees this error that's insidious. After displaying the message in the upper left corner of your screen, it just plain stops whatever it was in the process of doing and shuts down. At this point you're totally locked out of any data stored in RAM. The only thing you can do is turn the power off and start everything all over again. If you've been careful about saving your work to a disk every few minutes, all you lose are the few changes you made since the last disk save. If you haven't saved anything, you say "darn" and learn to save next time.

The parity error may have occurred because a RAM chip failed — they do mysteriously break from time to time. Or a stray cosmic ray may have zapped the chip as it passed through you and the earth on its way to Neptune. Or a balky generator at your local power company may have burped out some fluctuation in the line voltage that got past your computer's power supply. If it was a bad chip you'll get the same message again after you reboot, and you either have to figure out which chip went south, yank it out, and replace it, or pay your dealer to do it. If a chip on your main system board — the one that the CPU is attached to — fails, the system will display PARITY CHECK 1. If it senses a broken chip on an add-in board it will display PARITY CHECK 2. While the PC-AT is a little less terse, if this happens to you, a cheerier message is not what you want or need.

You'll know you have a bad chip if you reboot and see an error message beginning with a string of numbers followed by 201. The four hexadecimal digits that precede the 201 can pinpoint the exact chip that failed. On a PC, the machine will boot and you'll get an instant PARITY CHECK message that overwrites the 201 numbers, so you have to look quickly. On an XT, the message is not overwritten. On PS/2 systems, IBM replaced the PARITY message with two numerical error codes:

- 110 for PARITY CHECK 1
- 111 for PARITY CHECK 2

These are two numbers you won't want to see.

What the PC really should do when it detects such an error is put the offending data onscreen (if it's still able to) with the message: "Error detected in this data. Should I continue (Y/N)?" If the error was in the programming code that puts your software through its paces, or in a long list of numbers, you may want to quit and restart. But if all you see is the message:

The bank robber's holdup note said "I have a gub."

you can fix the error and continue without losing any work.

What is particularly irritating about parity errors is every one out of nine (11.11%) times such errors occur it's the result of the error-detecting mechanism and not incorrect data. All a parity error detector does is compare eight bits to one bit. If the chip with the one parity bit on it fails, your data — the other eight bits — may be perfectly fine, but the comparison test will indicate a problem and shut down your system.

Parity-checking can prevent data integrity problems. But only some of them. If one bit gets changed in a byte, the system will ferret out the problem. But if two bits in a single byte change, the parity detection bit will accurately reflect the oddness or evenness of the number of 1s. If the original byte was U or 01010101, the number of 1s is four, which is even. If you flip any two bits from 1 to 0 or from 0 to 1, you'll still have an even number of bits, although the new number won't represent a U anymore.

ROM is not parity checked. Some clone makers let you flick a switch to disable RAM parity checking. And some portable computers don't check parity, since that lets the manufacturers put in fewer chips that consume less power, and power sipping is the name of the game with laptops. If you have the option of turning parity checking on or off, you should probably leave it on anyway. But in any case you should save your work to disk often.

Larger computers that can't afford to stop dead in their tracks use a more sophisticated system called error correction. But this takes even more space, and incorporating error corrections into the PC would mean changing the underlying system architecture. And it's not perfect. The common error correcting scheme used today can fix one-bit errors, but it can only detect — not fix — errors of two or more bits in a single byte. All PCs will have error correction abilities someday, but they don't yet.

Future microcomputers may also have *static* RAM. All but a few of today's PCs use *dynamic* RAM that needs to be recharged or "refreshed" hundreds of times each second, which limits memory speeds. Static RAM doesn't need to be continually recharged, and is faster than dynamic RAM, but far more expensive. However, it's great for memory caches.

ROM — Free Programs

When you buy a PC you get two sets of free programs. One set, called microcode, is permanently *hard-wired* into the circuitry of the CPU and tells it (in the tersest, most inscrutable *machine code* possible) how to operate. The other set comes on a few ROM chips and provides software routines that help the system function. Programs that are delivered on chips are in a netherworld somewhere between hardware and software. Hardware is the machinery itself. Software is the list of instructions that tell the hardware what to do.

Your home phonograph, tape deck, or CD player is hardware. The records, disks, and tapes contain software. The general rule is if it has a wire coming out of it, it's hardware. If it doesn't do anything until you memorize a manual that sounds as if it was translated from a foreign language by a bored high school student, it's software.

Programs (software) that come delivered on ROM chips (hardware) are called *firmware*. Firmware includes copyright information, tests, tables, error messages, and a toolkit of useful routines that display characters on the screen in the colors of your choice, read information from a disk or keyboard, or send a copy of what's on your screen to your printer. ROM chips on IBM computers also include a stripped down version of the BASIC language.

Every piece of commercial software on the market uses at least some of these routines, by issuing what are called *software interrupts*. Software interrupts are different from the hardware interrupts mentioned earlier, which let the computer know you're pressing a key or that the printer just ran out of paper. And they're also different from the panicky interrupts triggered inside the CPU when something truly bizarre or unexpected happens like when something tries to divide by zero.

All programs have to perform the same basic operations such as interpreting key-strokes, displaying characters on a screen, or reading information from disks. The routines on ROM chips handle the hard part. Some programs, in a mad quest for extra speed or control, bypass these routines and control the hardware directly. But most programs are content to use the toolkit IBM (and its copycat clone makers) provided.

To see one of these routines in action, walk over to any IBM computer and turn the power on without putting a disk in the drive. If the computer doesn't have a hard disk, BASIC will appear onscreen. If it does have a hard disk, load BASIC by typing:

```
BASIC
```

and then pressing the Enter key. Then type the following line exactly as it appears:

```
DEF SEG=61440:R=57435:CALL R
```

Press the Enter key and your system will reboot. What this command does is use the BASIC language that comes on one IBM ROM chip to run a little firmware program on another ROM chip that restarts your system.

The PC's 8088 CPU can keep track of, or *address*, slightly more than a million memory locations. Just about everything the CPU does use addresses in one form or another. It's either looking in one location to see what's there, parking data temporarily in another location so it can process other data, or running short programs that are kept at certain addresses.

But a million is a big number, and it's sometimes easier to work with smaller numbers. If you're in New York City, which has a telephone area code of 212, and you have to call someone nearby, you want to be able to dial just the seven-digit phone number and not have to punch in a 1 and the extra three digits of the area code each time you make a local call. If most of your calls are indeed local, this saves time as well as wear and tear on the dialing finger. When you dial any seven digits (that don't start with a 1), the phone company assumes you're calling a number in the immediate vicinity.

If you want to talk to someone in Seattle, you can add the extra area code numbers, and the phone company knows you're not placing a local call.

The 8088 CPU addresses memory locations in a similar way. It divides the whole one-megabyte range of possible addresses into 16 regional sections called segments that are each 64K bytes long. (Newer systems can address more memory, and do it directly.)

The DEF SEG in the example that appeared earlier switches BASIC to one of these segments (in this case the very topmost one), which happens to be where IBM keeps track of the ROM chip routines that make up its main BIOS input/output toolkit.

This kind of memory segmentation can be useful, since it can let programs use smaller numbers to keep track of important local addresses. Working with most smaller numbers is faster than struggling with bigger ones. But they can also be the bane of programmers, since the advantage in using smaller, local numbers applies only to whatever 64K segment the programmer happens to be using at that time. Most programs these days are considerably larger than 64K, which means jumping repeatedly from one 64K segment to another.

Remember, computers are built around chips that have a really limited perspective. The fundamental piece of information in any chip is a bit. And a bit can be in only one of two states, on or off. So a one-bit chip (if one existed) could theoretically keep track of only two possible locations, at address 0 or address 1. Not very useful.

A two-bit chip — one with room for twice as many binary digits as a one-bit chip — could theoretically keep track of 2^2 (2 x 2, or four) locations, at binary addresses:

00 (decimal 0)
01 (decimal 1)
10 (decimal 2)
11 (decimal 3)
| |
two
bits

If you kept on adding bits to the addressing mechanism, you would double the number of locations each time. A three-bit system could handle 2^3 (2 x 2 x 2, or eight) locations:

000 (decimal 0)
001 (decimal 1)
010 (decimal 2)
011 (decimal 3)
100 (decimal 4)
101 (decimal 5)
110 (decimal 6)
111 (decimal 7)
|||
three
bits

A 16-bit chip like the 8088 can address only 2^16 (65,536) bytes directly. So 17 bits could address 2 x 65,536 (131,072) bytes; 18 bits 2 x 131,072 (262,144) bytes; 19 bits 2 x 262,144 (524,288) bytes; and 20 bits 2 x 524,288 (1,048,576) bytes — the "megabyte" used as the standard measure of memory.

Now hold on . . . . It says here that the PC can address one megabyte of memory. But the calculations above show that it would take 20 bits to address a full 1,048,576 bytes. The CPU inside the PC is a 16-bit 8088, and with 16 bits all you can address is 65,536 bytes. How does a 16-bit CPU handle 20-bit addresses?

Easy. Well, not exactly. It uses two addresses for each memory location, one for the segment itself and one for the *offset* into that segment. If you use the concert hall metaphor mentioned earlier, the segment is the section and the offset is the seat. So you could have two seats numbered 27 — one in the orchestra and one in the balcony. Just as the full number of the seats might be something like O27 and B27, you can express the address of any byte in your PC as SEGMENT:OFFSET.

In the DEF SEG statement, the number 61440 was the segment address. The other number, 57435, was the offset. So:

```
DEF SEG=61440:R=57435:CALL R
```

was the same as saying "look at the 57,435th byte in from the beginning of the segment that begins at address 61440 and run the program that starts there."

If you think this sounds confusing, you're right. Instead of having to wrestle with segmented addresses, programmers would much rather have had a chip that could do direct *linear* addressing, where each byte had an address from 0 to 1,048,576. If the PC had a linear addressing system, the BASIC program could have said "run the program at address 1,040,475."

You may be scratching your head now and wondering two things. First, how did 61440 and 57435 become 1,040,475? Second, do you really have to know all this?

The answer to the second question is a qualified no. PC users should really never have to take the tops off their computers and fiddle with the boards inside. Their systems should figure out what equipment is attached and then configure all the important settings automatically. DOS should be smart enough to anticipate what the user wants to do next, and deal with the user in a far friendlier and more intelligent way. Software should be infinitely flexible and understanding, and continually customize itself to the user's changing needs and abilities.

But we're still in the frontier of this business. We're pioneers (although at least we don't have to load programs from paper tape and read blinking lights to get our work done like the computer scouts who blazed the early trails in the 70s.) It's still the Wild West out there. Each new software company gallops onto the scene yelling "My standard is better than your standard." The ensuing Darwinian gunfights weed out the real losers but wound a lot of bystanders like us in the process.

You can have someone else set up and repair your system, and can struggle through your favorite software without ever knowing about memory segments. But the more you know about your system the better off you'll be. Most users discover that the longer they spend at their systems the more proficient they get and the more they want to be able to do. If you know the basics you'll be able to adapt your system and get it to do far more things far faster and far more easily. And prevent disasters.

Here's a specific example: Once a week like clockwork our support line gets a panicky phone call from someone who inadvertently exited a word processor without ever having saved the file to disk. If the caller was using mainstream word processing software, and didn't touch the computer after realizing what happened, it's usually fairly simple to look inside the user's RAM, find the file, and copy it from memory to a disk.

A rescue job like this starts by having the DOS DEBUG.COM program search through memory for the first few words of the user's file. DEBUG is very good at this, but can search only one segment at a time. If you know how segments work, finding unsaved files is a snap.

As mentioned earlier, the 14 registers inside the CPU are each two bytes long. A two-byte register can hold 16 bits, so the biggest number any of its registers can manipulate is 2^16, or 65,536. (If you want to use *signed* numbers that could be either positive or negative, the largest value would be 32,767 and the smallest -32,768. But take it from us, for the purposes of this book you don't want to.)

"Since there are 16 64K memory segments," you might argue, "the CPU could have used a kind of shorthand and called the first segment 0, the second segment 1, the third 2, and the last one 15. Then our BASIC reboot program could have been written DEF SEG=15:R=57435:CALL R." But that won't work.

The reason is that while the addressable memory in a PC is indeed split into 16 segments each 64K long for certain purposes, programmers need to divide available RAM into much finer slices than in such whopping chunks.

Just about all programs use memory in several standard ways. Some RAM has to store the actual program instruction code itself — the part that "runs." Some is needed to store the data that the program creates or changes. A little is needed for the stack, a storage area that holds addresses and miscellaneous amounts of temporary information. And sometimes programs have to work with so much data that they need a little extra room for it.

The 8088 CPU has four different segment registers to keep track of these four kinds of segments:

- Code segment (CS)
- Data segment (DS)
- Stack segment (SS)
- Extra segment (ES)

Since registers control segment addresses, the maximum number of addresses can't be greater than the largest number a 16-bit register can hold — 65,536, or 64K. In dealing with PCs you keep coming across that 64K number. 64K is the:

- number of possible segment addresses
- maximum number of bytes in a segment
- number of port addresses the CPU can use for I/O
- maximum size of a COM program
- maximum size of a BAS (BASIC) program

all because:

- the 8088 is a 16-bit chip
- each bit can be in two states (0 or 1)
- so 2^{16} = 65,536 (64K)

But while the maximum size of each segment is 64K, the segments can (and do) overlap each other. And they can be far smaller than 64K.

A stack segment can be fairly tiny. Unless you change it with a CLEAR command, for instance, the default size of the stack in BASIC is either 512 bytes or one-eighth of the available memory, whichever is smaller. If you're not nesting lots of short routines, or trying to fill in or "paint" complex pictures (both of which need more than the usual amount of stack space so BASIC can interrupt operations and jump to other operations repeatedly and then get back to what it was doing) this 512 bytes will do just fine. If programmers had to lop off 64K for each segment, they'd end up wasting tons of space.

If each segment had to be 64K, it could start at only one of 16 fixed places in memory. So to make things more flexible, the CPU lets programmers deals with any one of 65,536 different segment addresses. The only restriction is that each segment has to start at the beginning of a *paragraph*.

Paragraph?

In computer parlance, a paragraph is simply a number that is evenly divisible by 16. The reason for this is that while the 8088 CPU can address 1,048,576 total bytes, its segment registers can handle only 65,536 possible segment starting addresses. Divide 1,048,576 by 65,536 and you get 16. You can have a segment start at the very first paragraph (0), or at paragraph 1, or at paragraph 65,535. But it can't start at paragraph 1.5.

It's sort of like talking about fingers. You like to deal with whole hands, not fractions like 1.5 hands. And just as each set of hands is made up of ten smaller parts (fingers), each paragraph is made up of hexadecimal 10 smaller parts (bytes). What is written as 10 in hex notation is equal to 16 in our more familiar decimal system.

The idea of paragraphs is familiar to anyone who has used DEBUG. If the lower 128 ASCII characters were loaded into the very bottom part of your system's memory (and there's a good reason why they aren't, since other important things are kept there), and you used the DEBUG D command to display them, you'd see something like:

```
0000:0000   00 01 02 03 04 05 06 07-08 09 0A 0B 0C 0D 0E 0F    ................
0000:0010   10 11 12 13 14 15 16 17-18 19 1A 1B 1C 1D 1E 1F    ................
0000:0020   20 21 22 23 24 25 26 27-28 29 2A 2B 2C 2D 2E 2F     !"#$%&'()*+,-./
0000:0030   30 31 32 33 34 35 36 37-38 39 3A 3B 3C 3D 3E 3F    0123456789:;<=>?
0000:0040   40 41 42 43 44 45 46 47-48 49 4A 4B 4C 4D 4E 4F    @ABCDEFGHIJKLMNO
0000:0050   50 51 52 53 54 55 56 57-58 59 5A 5B 5C 5D 5E 5F    PQRSTUVWXYZ[\]'_
0000:0060   60 61 62 63 64 65 66 67-68 69 6A 6B 6C 6D 6E 6F    'abcdefghijklmno
0000:0070   70 71 72 73 74 75 76 77-78 79 7A 7B 7C 7D 7E 7F    pqrstuvwxyz{|}~.
```

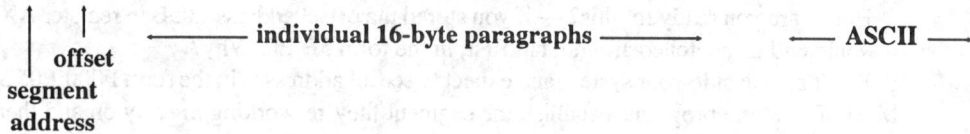

|
| offset ——— individual 16-byte paragraphs ———→ —— ASCII ——
segment
address

Each horizontal line is one paragraph, and contains 16 bytes. The two groups of four-digit numbers on the left, separated by the colon, are the segment and offset addresses. (Each is only four digits long because DEBUG works exclusively in hexadecimal notation and can cram any number from 0 to 65,536 into four hex digits.) The numbers in the middle are the hexadecimal representations of the bytes in each paragraph. DEBUG will display the actual characters each byte represents at the right side of its display, if the characters have ASCII values greater than 31 (1F in hex) and less than 127 (7F in hex). Otherwise it prints dots.

The decimal number for the segment 61440 is actually F000 in hex. And the decimal 57435 offset is hex E05B. The conventional notation for memory addresses is SEGMENT:OFFSET, so this address is really F000:E05B.

To translate a two-part address like F000:E05B into a single linear or *absolute* address that actually points to the precise one byte in the PC's megabyte of memory that you want, just shift and add.

In this case, shifting means bumping the number up by one decimal place, or order of magnitude. The decimal orders of magnitude start with 1, 10, 100, 1000, 10000; each time you add a zero. What you're really doing is multiplying the previous number by 10, since we use a base-10 number system.

Shifting over a digit in hex means multiplying by 16. The decimal equivalents of the first few hex orders of magnitude are 1, 16, 256, 4096, 65536. In hex, these are 1H, 10H, 100H, 1000H, 10000H; multiplying by 16 is really multiplying by 10H. So first, multiply the segment address by 16 to shift it up a notch. This is simple; stick a 0 on the end of F000 and you get F0000. Then add the offset to it:

```
    F0000
 +   E05B
    FE05B
```

Hex FE05B is indeed equal to decimal 1,040,475. To check it, multiply decimal 61440 by 16 and add 57435 to it.

While only the four segment registers mentioned earlier can keep track of the segment, your system can calculate and juggle offsets in lots of different ways. Segment and offset registers deal with two-byte addresses. General purpose registers (called AX, BX, CX, and DX), which can be pressed into action to hold two-byte offsets, can also store single byte values. Because of this, the four general purpose registers are often divided in halves. If you looked inside AX and found it holding the value E05B, the "low" half of that two-byte pair (5B) would be in register AL (L = Low) and the "high" half (E0) in register AH (H = High).

But — are you ready for this? — if you stored the offset address E05B in register AX, it would end up switched around, tail first, in the form 5B E0. Why?

Don't peek inside your system and expect to see all addresses in the form F000:E05B. Most of the time programs establish the segment they're working in early on and then just specify offsets inside that segment — like dialing local phone numbers without the area codes.

But if the segment you're using is F000, you'll never see it written that way. F000 is really two bytes, F0 and 00. A pair of bytes joined like this is called a word. Your PC uses a backwards (or "backwords") method for storing each of these, so F000 is actually stored 00F0.

In the word F000 (or any hex number bigger than a single byte), the *most significant* byte is the larger one (F0) and the *least significant* byte is the smaller one (00). The PC stores such two-byte addresses with the least significant byte first. It stores *strings* of letters such as error messages in the normal non-backwards way, however.

That's because the PC puts the upper half of the number higher in memory and the lower half lower in memory, which makes perfect sense. When you scan through memory, you generally start from near the bottom and move upward, which also makes sense, so you hit the low byte first. When you refer to the address of a word, you always mean where the word starts, and it starts at the lower half.

To simplify things, say you're storing the word F000 at absolute memory address 1. The normal way to map out on paper how memory works is to put the very bottom part at the top of the page and work downward:

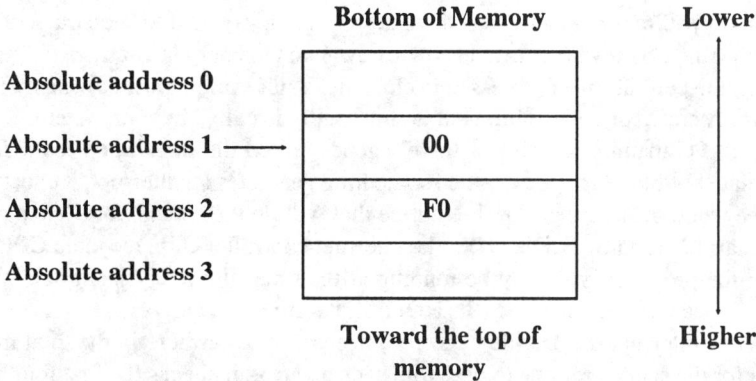

<table>
<tr><td></td><td>**Bottom of Memory**</td><td>**Lower**</td></tr>
<tr><td>**Absolute address 0**</td><td></td><td></td></tr>
<tr><td>**Absolute address 1** ———</td><td>**00**</td><td></td></tr>
<tr><td>**Absolute address 2**</td><td>**F0**</td><td></td></tr>
<tr><td>**Absolute address 3**</td><td></td><td></td></tr>
<tr><td></td><td>**Toward the top of
memory**</td><td>**Higher**</td></tr>
</table>

Confusing? At first. It's especially diabolical when dealing with the 12-bit addresses that the PC-XT File Allocation Table (FAT) used to keep track of clusters. But for now, just remember that if you're using DEBUG to search for segment F000, you'll have to tell it to hunt for 00 F0.

One more note about addresses — the same absolute address can be expressed in many different ways. This is sort of like saying you could express the decimal number 10 as (5 + 5) or (8 + 2).

The very bottom of memory is at relative address 0000:0000, and absolute address 00000. (The very top is F000:FFFF or FFFFF.) The absolute hex address one paragraph up from the bottom of memory (10H bytes up in hex; 16 bytes up from the bottom in decimal) would be 00010. You could express this as 0000:0010. But you could just as easily write it as 0001:0000. All three refer to the same location in memory.

To test this, use the shift-and-add technique mentioned earlier:

```
for 0000:0010 ┐              for 0001:0000 ┐
       |      |                     |      |
     00000    |                   00010    |
   + 0010 ────┘                 + 0000 ────┘
     00010                        00010
```

Obviously, the higher up you go into memory the more ways you have of referring to paragraph addresses (sometimes called paragraph *boundaries*) using relative SEGMENT:OFFSET notation. One is just as good as another in telling your CPU how to behave.

Mapping the Meg

But you can't get your hands on the whole megabyte of memory. IBM originally divided the available megabyte into 16 blocks, each one 64K long, and reserved some for ROM, and some for the displays, some for expansion room, which was used eventually by gut-level BIOS *extension* programs to handle things like hard disks that weren't offered originally. It left the remaining ten blocks, or 640K, for your programs.

Well, almost 640K. DOS takes up a good chunk, and the amount grew with each release prior to DOS 5.0. BIOS needs a little, to store keystrokes when you type so fast the program you're using can't soak them all up right away, and to keep track of things like whether the Ctrl key is being held down, how much memory is installed, the current video mode, the current time (expressed in clock ticks since midnight), how many lines can fit on your screen, or what equipment is supposedly installed in your system.

Each PC maintains a sort of travel agency called the *Interrupt Vector Table* at the absolute bottom of memory. When something generates an interrupt, it checks this table to see where it should go for the routine that will do the actual work. This table is very popular; it's used by BIOS, DOS, the interrupt controller chip, the main CPU itself, and even the programs you may be running at the time. It's really just a list of up to 256 four-byte addresses, in SEGMENT:OFFSET form.

When interrupt 0 ("Divide by Zero") needs to know where in the total megabyte to look for the special routine to deal with such an error, it checks the first four bytes (table entry #0) for the address or *vector*. When interrupt 1 (used by DEBUG) drops in, it checks the next four byte address (table entry #1). When INT 2 (which is usually how interrupts are abbreviated) is involved, you have problems, because odds are that's a parity error lurching toward its fatal nonmaskable interrupt goodnight kiss. If you poke around in this table and replace an existing entry with the address of your own program, the table will send the respective interrupt to your program rather than the old one.

The top segment of the megabyte is taken up by your system ROM, which needs this space to store the tests that are performed during the initial power-on diagnostic check to make sure things are working properly, and the gut-level BIOS routines that take care of the nitty-gritty details in controlling your drives, keyboard, clock, displays, printer, serial port, and memory.

The middle B000 segment was originally allocated for video. PC displays are *memory-mapped*, which means that each video memory address corresponds with a small but specific area of the screen. If you have a color system, running this program:

```
100 DEF SEG=&HB800
120 POKE 1,78
130 POKE 0,1
140 POKE 3999,100
150 POKE 3998,2
```

will put four values into memory at segment B800H that your CRT controller will turn instantly into characters and colors onscreen. This particular program will put a small yellow-on-red face in the upper lefthand corner of your screen and a red-on-yellow one in the lower righthand corner. (If you're using a monochrome screen, omit lines 120 and 140, and change the &HB800 in line 100 to &HB000.)

A rough map of the entire megabyte would look something like:

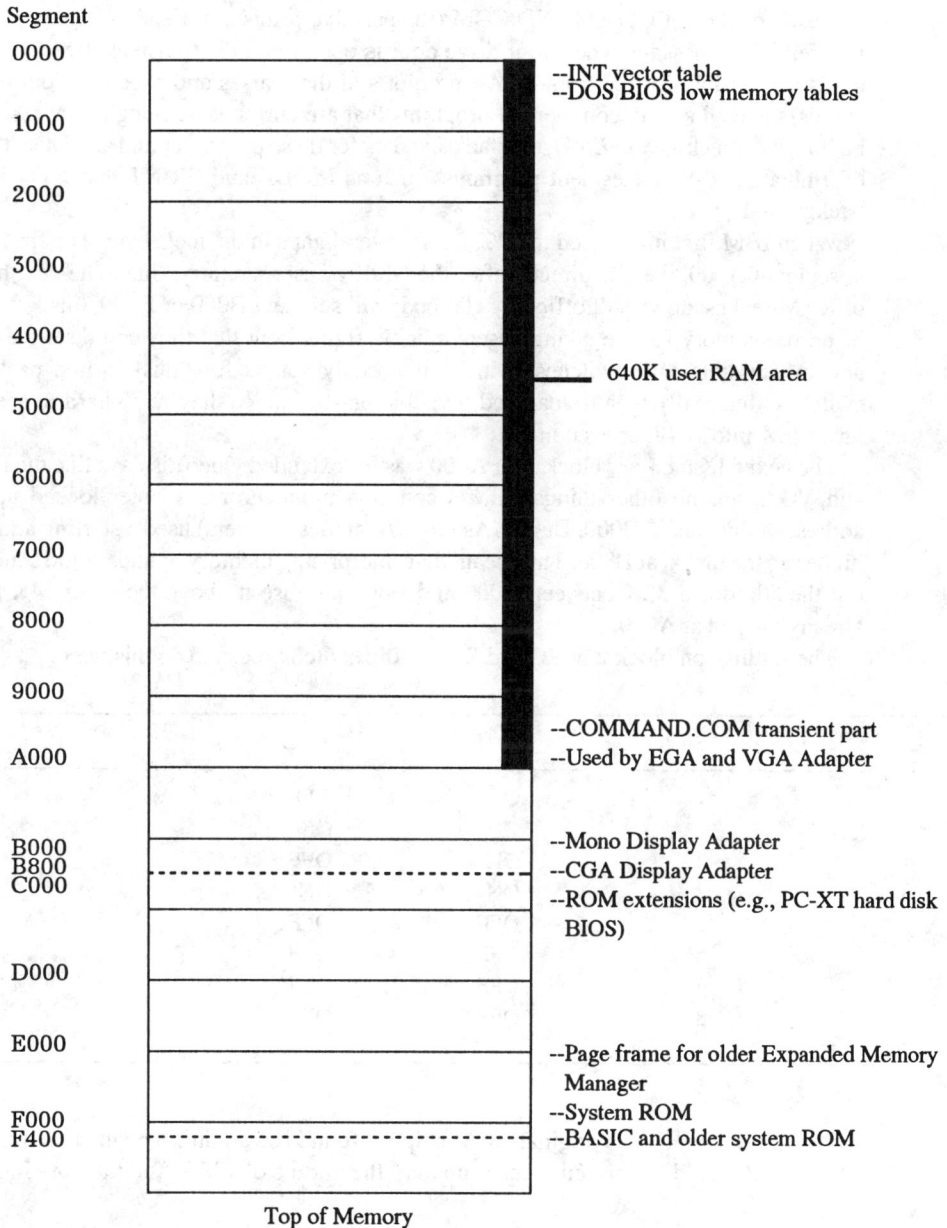

Segment

```
0000  ┌──────────────────────────┐ --INT vector table
      │                          │ --DOS BIOS low memory tables
1000  ├──────────────────────────┤
      │                          │
2000  ├──────────────────────────┤
      │                          │
3000  ├──────────────────────────┤
      │                          │
4000  ├──────────────────────────┤
      │                          │──── 640K user RAM area
5000  ├──────────────────────────┤
      │                          │
6000  ├──────────────────────────┤
      │                          │
7000  ├──────────────────────────┤
      │                          │
8000  ├──────────────────────────┤
      │                          │
9000  ├──────────────────────────┤
      │                          │ --COMMAND.COM transient part
A000  ├──────────────────────────┤ --Used by EGA and VGA Adapter
      │                          │
B000  ├──────────────────────────┤ --Mono Display Adapter
B800  │- - - - - - - - - - - - - │ --CGA Display Adapter
C000  ├──────────────────────────┤ --ROM extensions (e.g., PC-XT hard disk
      │                          │    BIOS)
D000  ├──────────────────────────┤
      │                          │
E000  ├──────────────────────────┤ --Page frame for older Expanded Memory
      │                          │    Manager
F000  ├──────────────────────────┤ --System ROM
F400  │- - - - - - - - - - - - - │ --BASIC and older system ROM
      └──────────────────────────┘
```

Top of Memory

The lower 640K (segments 0000 through 9000) can get pretty crowded. Users commonly wedge in the Interrupt Vector Table, the low-memory BIOS control area, the updated IBMBIO.COM and IBMDOS.COM system file patches and services (or their generic Microsoft equivalents), the guts-level DOS *kernel* (which manages system functions such as file and memory management), any device drivers (such as MOUSE.SYS or ANSI.SYS), disk buffers, stacks, environment and file control blocks, the resident slice of COMMAND.COM (the part that prints the friendly "Abort, Retry, Ignore, Fail?" message when your drive door is open), and the transient slice (the part that's responsible for the friendly A> prompt and that parses and executes your commands), as well as any commercial programs that are currently running or are resident but inactive (such as *SideKick*), the stack and data for these programs, and any DOS TSRs (Terminate-and-Stay-Resident programs) such as MODE and PRINT that lurk in the background.

When IBM first introduced the PC, it left several gaps in the megabyte. The first was at segment A000, the one directly after the 640K of user memory. Since the next hunk of RAM real estate wasn't officially claimed until segment B000 or B800, this left 64K of prime memory for the taking. Users quickly figured out that they could set the tiny and inaccessible DIP switches (which supposedly stands for "dual in-line package switches" but really means "damned invisible plastic" since they're so hard to see) to turn 640K into 704K or even more.

The next 64K memory block after A000 was for extended video displays like the EGA and VGA, among other things. IBM's common monochrome adapter locked up an address in this block, B000. But CGAs (color/graphics adapters) used a starting address higher up the block, at B800. This meant that enterprising memory hounds could squeeze out the additional 32K between B000 and B800 and use it above the extra 64K they already swiped at A000.

The settings on block 2 of PC and PC-XT dip switch blocks to do this were:

Switch	704K	736K
1	ON	OFF
2	ON	ON
3	OFF	OFF
4	ON	ON
5	OFF	OFF
6	OFF	OFF
7	OFF	OFF
8	OFF	OFF

Users who had IBM's original ROM chip set found it wouldn't recognize more than 544, but IBM sold a replacement part up until the middle of 1987. And memory hungry users had to purchase expansion RAM boards sophisticated enough to let them set the addresses of such additional RAM to A000 and B000, so it wouldn't conflict with existing memory, and so that DOS could find it. This undocumented memory enlarger worked fine for a few years. The POST memory diagnostic routine would examine this additional user memory, and the DOS CHKDSK.COM utility would report it.

But a new generation of IBM displays created a new problem. IBM's outdated CGA was, in a word, pathetic. It produced an image so grainy you thought you were looking at it through a screen door.

Display adapters draw letters and numbers out of dot patterns in a grid called a character box. The monochrome adapter's relatively detailed character box measures 9 dots x 14 dots. However, this really works out to 7 x 11 since the leftmost and rightmost columns and the top two rows and bottom row are blank, and serve as *character separators* to keep nearby letters from touching. And the bottom two rows are reserved for descenders on characters such as q, y, j, g, and p.

The CGA character box is a crude 8 x 8. The only character separators are the rightmost column and the bottom row, so this produces 7 x 7 dot characters. However, the bottom row also doubles as space for descenders, so the lower parts of letters such as q and y actually touch the tops of tall letters below them.

Worse, the CGA adapter didn't have enough memory on it, so that each time it scrolled up one line the entire display would go dead and turn black for a fraction of a second and then flash back into life. Repeated scrolling meant an extremely disturbing flicker. And to top it off, while the memory on the monochrome adapter was *dual ported* so you could write data to it at the same time you were reading other data from it without disturbing the onscreen image, trying this on a monitor attached to a CGA card produced a jarring burst of visible static called "snow." The monochrome adapter put a total of 720 x 350 dots onscreen (and came with a long-persistence phosphor that removed any hint of flicker, and blurred the last traces of dots into what looked like solid lines), while all the CGA could muster was 640 x 200. And the mono adapter could form characters faster and pump data onto the screen faster. IBM really seemed to have designed the CGA to hook up to television sets. As proof, its CGA characters were all constructed of double-dot patterns to overcome the inherent fuzziness and imprecision of home TVs. Users could change jumper J3 on the CGA itself so that it would produce slightly sharper single-dot characters in a 5 x 7 grid. But to do this you had to rip open your system, pull out the board, and solder in a wire! Would you?

IBM wasn't interested in color back then, and still makes life hard for users of color systems. The CLS clear screen command still resets any existing colors to grey on black, unless the user happens to have ANSI.SYS loaded and properly configured, and ANSI can be a pain in the neck, since not all software can handle it.

However, IBM wised up and realized it had to upgrade the color display, and eventually introduced the EGA and VGA (and the 8514/A).

The EGA and VGA devoured memory, and claimed the block at A000 for the start of their high-resolution graphics modes, which conflicted with users who had reset their system switches to push RAM past 640K.

The Original Way to Expand Memory

IBM's very first PC came standard with a tiny 16K of RAM, on 16K memory chips. One reason DOS was so scrawny back then is that it had to squeeze inside this small scrap of RAM. If you were really adventurous you could expand it all the way up to 64K, but all that extra memory wasn't cheap back then.

Several years later IBM started putting 64K RAM chips on its system board, and just about everyone bought multifunction/memory expansion cards and shoved the full complement of 640K into their machines. Eventually IBM would move to 256K and one megabyte chips and let users play with eight megs or more.

But users quickly found 640K wasn't enough.

First, programmers who had written very tight, compact assembly language applications software soon found that they could crank out programs faster, and maintain them more easily, if they wrote them in a compiled language that ended up taking more disk space. And programs began getting feature-crazy, so that software vendors could crow about how their packages offered fancy but useless chrome strips and tailfins that competitor's products didn't.

Second, users began creating larger data files. Instead of keeping separate yearly spreadsheets on company performance, for instance, they found they could combine the last five years into one massive whopper.

Finally, users discovered memory-resident, or TSR, programs. You'd load these into memory and they'd sit idly in the background waiting to spring into the foreground. TSR (Terminate-and-Stay-Resident) programs like these turned out to be so useful and popular that many users couldn't get any work done unless three or four of them were stuffed into RAM.

SideKick, the granddaddy of them all, provided a pop-up calculator, ASCII table, clipboard/notepad, dialer, and calendar. Others let you create keyboard macros, so that one or two keystrokes could trigger hundreds more and pare repetitive tasks down to size; or would kick your modem into action periodically to download your electronic mail; or back up your hard disk onto a tape drive every night at 5:00.

All PCs shared three space problems. You couldn't run programs that were larger than 640K, and even that figure was low, since you also had to take into account the overhead required by DOS and BIOS. You couldn't put more than 640K of data into memory, and again, you had to leave space for DOS, BIOS, and at least part of your program. And you couldn't have DOS handle individual hard disks that were larger than 32 megabytes.

Lotus Development Corporation, the makers of *1-2-3*, finally got tired of listening to their customers scream that they couldn't create enormous spreadsheets. So together with chip-maker Intel, they developed a variation of an old "bank switching" technique and named it the Expanded Memory Specification 3.0. Later, they twisted Microsoft's arm to endorse a 3.2 mutation of it and called the result the Lotus/Intel/Microsoft (LIM) Expanded Memory Specification 3.2, or "LIM spec memory" for short.

Shortly afterward, board manufacturer AST enlisted two other industry heavyweights, Quadram and Ashton-Tate, and published a much more flexible EMS version they called

EEMS (Enhanced EMS). EEMS was a superset of EMS, which caused problems since software designed for EMS boards would run on EEMS hardware but it wouldn't always work the other way around. Both gave users up to eight megabytes of additional memory, although various headaches with drivers and multiple memory boards prevented the spec from being exploited fully.

The Lotus/Intel/Microsoft trio then enhanced some of AST's ideas and added a few of their own and announced an improved version called LIM 4.0. This new LIM spec quadrupled the potential amount of expanded memory in a system from eight megs to 32, gave developers a whole new set of programming tools, and added better support for multitasking and program execution in high memory. This solved the "large data" problem temporarily. It didn't solve the "large program" problem. Recent operating systems such as OS/2 and hot chips like the 80386 make short work out of memory problems. And both Microsoft and IBM have tricks up their sleeves as larger hard disks become common. Compaq was first to smash the 32 meg hard disk barrier with DOS 3.31, although other vendors had done it in a wasteful way by increasing sector size past 512 bytes.

The original LIM bank switcher used expanded memory that wasn't a part of the PC's addressable one megabyte. Just add a bank-switching memory expansion board to your system, tell your CONFIG.SYS bootup configuration file about a program called an Expanded Memory Manager (EMM), and any LIM-aware software could toss enormous data files around in RAM with abandon.

The trick was to grab (or *map*) one unused 64K segment near the top of the PC's addressable megabyte of RAM and use it as a narrow doorway into the far greater amount of memory on the bank switching card itself. This doorway was called a *page frame* and contained four smaller 16K sections called *windows*.

While the original spec demanded one contiguous 64K chunk of RAM, later enhancements eased the requirements slightly, and made the mapping process far more accommodating.

When a program like *1-2-3* needed more space in RAM for a growing spreadsheet, it could put information into expanded memory, and retrieve it later, by shuttling it up and back 16K at a time through one of the windows. The EMM had to be smart enough to know when *1-2-3* needed something that wasn't currently in one of these little windows, and shuffle things around to snag it and bring it down to the page frame.

Expanded memory is like a research department in a small office using a bank of four elevators connected to a vast warehouse of archives. Whenever they need a single document from the warehouse, they can send the elevator up to retrieve it. But if they want several hundred volumes, they're going to have to use all the elevators and make several trips. The elevators are all one size, which makes it wasteful to get just one scrap of paper, and slow to retrieve large amounts of data. Since the warehouse manager doesn't want his precious data to get lost, and since there isn't much room to spare in the research department office, when the researchers want something new they have to send some of the older stuff back.

Unofficial Ways to Expand Memory for DOS (Pre-5.0)

Even though your application software could get around the 640K barrier, DOS versions before 5.0 couldn't — at least not officially. As you collect TSRs, begin experimenting with DOS device drivers and resources like IBMCACHE, FASTOPEN, and VDISK, and/or upgrade to newer (and larger) releases of DOS, what's left of that original 640K grows smaller and smaller. If you want to see exactly how your system uses memory, the RAMMAP and MAPMEM utility programs on the accompanying disks or DOS 5.0's MEM /C will really open your eyes to how much memory is used by the typical array of startup devices and programs in your CONFIG.SYS and AUTOEXEC.BAT files. To paraphrase Everett Dirksen, "A couple of Kb here, a couple of Kb there, pretty soon it adds up to real memory."

Before EGA came along, several brave souls had tried poaching over the 640K boundary to use the then-vacant 64K block starting at A000. When IBM began using this block for the EGA adapter card, many of these same memory-hungry power users cast covetous eyes on the other gaps in the 640K-1Mb address space — if you're using an EGA, then the memory dedicated to an MDA or CGA adapter should be free to use for other purposes, shouldn't it? Even though these gaps are not contiguous to the original 640K (and thus of limited use to regular applications), a lot of high-powered thought has gone into finding some use for this memory space.

From these efforts, a number of products are now available to allow you to free up space in the 640K area of conventional memory by mapping any available expanded memory into the unused memory areas between 640K and 1 MB, to create *high RAM*. Programs like *386-to-the-Max* from Qualitas and QEMM86, QEMM 50/60, and QRAM from Quarterdeck Systems install as device drivers in your CONFIG.SYS file. Once installed, they allow you to load your TSRs and other device drivers up in high RAM using special loader programs, leaving free the space these TSRs and devices would otherwise occupy in regular RAM. However, not all these products work with all PCs. Basically, there are three levels of hardware-dependent functionality available:

1. 386 and 486-specific products, such as QEMM-386 from Quarterdeck and 386-to-the-Max from Qualitas. On some high-speed 286 and 386 machines, the contents of the ROM BIOS is copied to RAM during bootup, to take advantage of the faster access time of high-speed RAM relative to ROM. This RAM is then mapped to the normal ROM address space, and is known as *shadow RAM*. On machines where this technique is supported (using the Chips and Technology NEAT or LEAP chip sets), these 386 and 486 memory managers can map RAM directly to the gaps between physical devices in the address space between 640K and 1024K. On other 386 or 486 machines, the memory managers can convert some of the extended memory present above 1024K to expanded RAM in the 640–1024K region. Once converted, TSRs, device drivers, and even DOS resources like FILES and BUFFERS (in the 5.0 version of QEMM386) can be moved to high RAM.

2. products for older 8088-8086, or 80286 machines machines with either add-in expanded memory boards or with shadow ram. Unless you have an AT compatible

with shadow RAM, you must have an expanded RAM card to be able to make use of high RAM without disabling your graphics capabilities. Even though the PS/2s and many AT compatibles come with 1024K of memory standard, the additional 384K above 640K is configured as extended memory, and the various software EMS simulators such as EMS40.SYS can't provide the hardware support needed to allow the expanded memory manager to remap the converted memory to useful high RAM.

3. on machines with extended memory but no expanded memory, you can get an additional 96K of room for DOS or for high memory, but at the cost of limiting yourself to character-only graphics. Quarterdeck's VIDRAM will allow you to expand the memory available to DOS to 736Kb by temporarily disabling your CGA, EGA, and VGA graphics capabilities, taking over the address spaces used by the video RAM and filling them with any available extended memory it finds in your system. If you absolutely must use three or four large TSRs and a memory-hungry program like *dBASE IV* or *Paradox* on your XT simultaneously, this approach is worth a look, but most folks won't want to give up the graphics.

When all else failed, a simpler, slightly more labor intensive approach to managing memory was via the CONFIG.CTL utility for controlling which device drivers were loaded in CONFIG.SYS at bootup, and the INSTALL/REMOVE utilities for loading and unloading TSRs. With DOS 5.0, of course, HIMEM.SYS and EMM386.SYS manage the Upper Memory Block (UMB), and expanded or extended memory.

DOS 5.0 Memory Management

New with DOS 5.0 are several tools that help solve the perennial memory problem inherent in IBM's original decision to allocate only 640K for user applications. On systems with extended memory, DOS 5.0 can load much of its code into the High Memory Area (HMA) which is the first 64K block above 1 Megabyte, leaving only a small kernel in the 640K application area to grab commands and service requests and then vector them to the appropriate routines in the HMA. HIMEM.SYS and EMM386.SYS are two device drivers that provide extended and expanded memory management on machine capable of supporting these features, typically 80386 or later machines with more than 1 megabyte of RAM.

HIMEM.SYS manages extended memory, using the XMS (eXtended Memory Specification) standard, and the High Memory Area (HMA), the first 64K block above 1 Megabyte. It must be the *first* device driver that manages or uses extended memory in your CONFIG.SYS file, as it controls other drivers' access to both the HMA and extended memory areas. If you're already using the version of HIMEM.SYS that came with Windows 3.0, you should replace the older HIMEM.SYS with the one that comes with DOS 5.0.

EMM386 is both an expanded memory manager, taking extended memory from HIMEM and converting it to simulate expanded memory for applications that need it, and the manager of the Upper Memory Blocks (UMBs) between 640K and 1 Meg. On 386 or better systems with more than 1 megabyte of memory, the CONFIG.SYS sequence

```
DEVICE=drive:\path\HIMEM.SYS
DEVICE=drive:\path\EMM386.EXE NOEMS
DOS=HIGH,UMB
```

will give you the ability to free up as much of the 640K memory area as possible, by loading DOS into high memory and allowing you to load your other device drivers and TSRs into the UMB area using the new DEVICEHIGH and LOADHIGH (or LH) commands. If you absolutely need expanded memory for your applications, put RAM instead of NOEMS on the DEVICE=EMM386.EXE line — this will give you expanded memory capability, but will significantly reduce the amount of UMB space you can use.

With the UMB area properly set up, you can now load subsequent device drivers in your CONFIG.SYS file into high memory using the syntax DEVICEHIGH=*drive:\path*\devicename. Unfortunately, HIMEM.SYS and EMM386.EXE can't themselves be loaded high (at least in this release), but almost anything else is fair game. Obvious candidates are ANSI.SYS, MOUSE.COM or MOUSE.SYS, network drivers and SHARE.EXE (which, by the way, you only need load if you're using a network or multitasking software that really might need SHARE's file locking capability — it's no longer needed just because your disk partitions are greater than 32Mb, as it was for DOS 4.0.)

To get the most efficient use of the UMB, it's best to load the larger devices first — you can experiment with different sequences and check the results using MEM /C. The same holds true for TSRs in your AUTOEXEC.BAT, which are loaded with the comparable LOADHIGH *drive:\path*\filename syntax.

With HIMEM.SYS and EMM386.EXE installed on a 80386 or i486 and the rest of the normal assortment of device drivers and simple TSRs loaded high, CHKDSK should show about 630K free. On a stock IBM 80286-based machine, DOS itself will load high but the UMB space won't be available for device drivers or TSRs, so the best you can reasonably hope for is about 600K. And on an 8088/8086 machine, don't expect to see any real benefit at all — just consider DOS 5.0 as yet another reason to upgrade your hardware.

Expanded vs. Extended

Who names these things? Few enough users really understand what's going on under their hoods anyway, and you'd think the folks who invent all this stuff would go out of their way to make it clear and unconfusing. Then again, these are the same people who created a multibillion dollar industry based around a computer system so hostile to novices that if brand new users somehow manage to get their systems hooked up properly and figure out which one of eight possible ways to insert their DOS floppy disks is right, their reward is a black screen with nothing on it but an A> in the corner.

Some rascals decided to call bank-switched RAM *expanded memory*, while calling the special kind of RAM available in 80286 and 80386 machines (like the PC-AT and most PS/2s) *extended memory*. These even sound the same if you say them both fast enough.

Working on one of today's hot chips in a normal everyday one-megabyte configuration with 640K or less of usable RAM is called running in *real mode*. However, you can tweak chips like the 80286 to run in a special, enhanced state called *protected mode*. A protected mode system lets users directly address more than one megabyte of memory, and lets them *multitask*, or run several programs simultaneously.

Previous attempts at multitasking ran into lots of trouble. The usual bugaboo was that if three programs were churning through their paces at the same time and one crashed, the whole house of cards would tumble down. That's bad enough in real mode when one program with one set of data crashes and burns; it's downright evil when a crashed multitasking system does two or three times the normal damage. Protected mode protects the user from this nightmare — when one program crashes, the others keeping humming blithely away.

When people mention the bit-size of a computer, they're really talking about the microprocessor register size used for storing data within the CPU. (However, if they mention two numbers, the second one is the width of the bus.) The register size was eight bits (one byte) for the ancient generation of 8080 and Z-80 chips popular before the PC was introduced; 16 bits (one word) for the 8088, 8086 chips, and 80286, which are used in the PC, AT, and some of the PS/2 systems; and 32 bits (a *long word* or *double word*) for the 80386 and i486. These chips can often divide larger registers into several smaller ones.

The CPU includes an *arithmetic logic unit* (ALU) that can do addition and subtraction, logical ANDs and ORs, bit shifts, and negation on the data in the registers. To be efficient, the ALU has to operate on whole registers at once. Microprocessors also generate addresses to access data from memory, and perform arithmetic operations on these addresses. Ideally, the microprocessor should use the same ALU to operate on both data and addresses.

The early eight-bit 8080 chip would have been simpler if it had used only eight bits for addressing. But this would have limited its addressing abilities to just 256 bytes (2^8). Instead, the 8080 forms addresses by sticking two bytes together. This chip has minimal 16-bit arithmetic capabilities.

Both the 8086 and 8088 CPUs handle data internally in 16-bit chunks, although the 8088 used in the PC and XT accesses memory externally only eight bits at a time. The easiest way for the designers of the PC to handle memory addresses would have been to limit the machine to 64K (2^{16}) so the CPU could address everything directly. But 64K is just too small. Instead, they had the CPU in the PC and XT calculate physical addresses by adding a 16-bit offset register to a 16-bit segment register that has been shifted to the left four bits. The result is a 20-bit address that can access one megabyte. But the chip is really only working with 16 its for both data and address.

With the advent of the 80286 chip things got even more complex. In real mode, the 80286 works the same as the 8086 and 8088. In protected mode, however, the segment registers are *selectors* for accessing a 24-bit *base address* from memory. The chip then adds this to the 16-bit offset address. This yields a 24-bit address that can handle 16 megabytes of memory.

The 80386 and i486 are full-fledged 32-bit microprocessors. They store data in 32-bit registers and can do full 32-bit arithmetic. They use a 32-bit address that can directly access four gigabytes (four billion bytes) of memory. Like the 80286 in protected mode, the 80386 and i486 use a selector to reference a base address that it adds to an offset address, but the base address and offset address are both 32 bits. The only time they use 64 bits is when doing double word multiplication and division.

The 80286 chip at the heart of the PC-AT can theoretically address 16 megabytes of RAM directly. The 80386 or i486 can go to 4GB. Anything past the normal one megabyte is extended. The PC-AT's designers figured that three megabytes would be enough, but recent developments have given power users several times that amount. Still, there really aren't very many programs that can take advantage of this extended RAM. The most common is the DOS 3.x and later RAMDRIVE RAMdisk.

Because of significant differences between real mode and protected mode, current versions of DOS and most application programs cannot use this additional 15 megabytes of extended memory. Getting access to it requires OS/2 or one of the many protected mode operating systems trying to compete with it. DOS 4.0 can do few measly tricks with extended and expanded memory, while DOS 5.0 gives you many more options.

Lots of clones these days brag about how they come straight from the factory with a megabyte of RAM while IBM's machines sport a relatively meager 512K or 640K. What they don't explain is that this additional 384K can't be addressed directly. In fact, about all you can do with the excess RAM is make a large RAMdisk out of it, which isn't such a bad idea.

RAMdisks are nothing more than areas of memory that your system treats just like physical disk drives. You don't have to format them, and at least with the VDISK version supplied by IBM, you can't use the DISKCOPY or DISKCOMP utilities with them (although you can do this with RAMdisk software supplied by other manufacturers such as AST). RAMdisks are extremely fast, since they have none of the arms and motors and other moving parts that slow down mechanical disk drives. But they're volatile, so that you have to take any information temporarily stored on a RAMdisk and copy it to a floppy or hard disk before you turn your system off or you'll lose it all.

You can use this kind of extra clone memory for a RAMdisk by making sure the DOS 3.x and later VDISK.SYS or RAMDRIVE.SYS device driver is on your disk in a subdirectory called \DOS. Then put this line in your CONFIG.SYS file:

```
DEVICE=\DOS\RAMDRIVE.SYS 384 /E
```

The VDISK driver uses a BIOS call that temporarily switches to protected mode, access-es the extended memory, and then switches back to real mode.

To make things even more confusing, vendors eventually introduced products to use extended memory that emulated LIM expanded memory. Clear?

Memory and the Bus

One last note about chips and memory: The PC used a 16-bit chip but an eight-bit bus. The PC-AT came with an interim 16-bit chip that used 16-bit bus. (Intel later revealed that it was sort of a mistake and that the 80386 was really the chip the 80286 should have been. Now they're saying the 80486 is really it, not the 80386.) The new top-level generation of PS/2s use a 32-bit chip and a 32-bit bus.

One of the big speed advantages of the PC-AT was that it could move memory around on the bus twice as efficiently as the PC. New 16-bit memory boards came with a small stub that fits into a special plug on the system board to handle the extra data lines. And users who upgraded from PCs to PC-ATs thought that they'd have to throw their old memory boards away when they switched. Well, it turns out that they didn't have to. But maybe they should have.

The PC and XT expansion board bus connectors carry 62 signals including the 20 address lines (which allow the 8088 microprocessor to access one megabyte of memory) and eight bidirectional data lines. The PC-AT has eight expansion board slots. Six of these have a second bus connector with 36 signals, including four additional address lines (for the total 16-megabyte memory space) and eight more bidirectional data lines, because the 80286 accesses data in words rather than bytes.

The 62-signal connector on the PC-AT is highly compatible with that on the PC and XT. The two PC-AT expansion board slots that have only the old 62-signal connector are designed for older boards with byte-accessible memory and I/O. Existing video cards work in these slots, for instance. However, the 62-signal connectors on the other six slots are wired exactly the same as these two. Here's the catch: The 36-signal bus connector on the PC-AT has two signals called "MEM CS16" and "I/O CS16." These signals must be generated by any AT board that can handle 16-bit memory or I/O transfers. If these signals are not present — and they won't be if the board doesn't use this second connector — the AT will access memory (or I/O) with eight bit transfers.

This means the PC-AT can indeed handle old memory boards. But users will notice a significant speed penalty for programs that run in this memory space or use data in it. It's just not worthwhile to spend the money for a PC-AT and then slow it down by inhibiting 16-bit memory transfers, which is one of the major speed advantages of the 80286 over the 8088. The AT bus is a defacto standard — it's commonly known as the Industry Standard Architecture, or ISA, bus.

Most PS/2 systems use a 32-bit bus called Micro Channel Architecture (MCA). A consortium of competitors is pushing a different 32-bit bus standard called EISA. The battle is on, but for the moment, the ISA bus is the market leader.

Part II

The DOS Tools

C H A P T E R 8

EDIT and EDLIN

The single most popular microcomputer application is word processing. Nearly every serious user has one handy, and the people who don't own one use text entry functions of programs such as *1-2-3* to create memos and batch files.

Longtime DOS users are probably familiar with the EDLIN line editor and know its limitations. However, EDLIN is a useful tool for creating and making changes to the CONFIG.SYS and AUTOEXEC.BAT startup files, as well as batch files in general. In fact, as a line editor, it's perfect for creating batch files which usually consist of one-line commands. EDLIN is still part of our tool kit because it loads quickly and provides a simple, easy-to-remember command set. It is also useful for creating files that send ANSI escape codes to the screen and keyboard.

Before DOS 5.0, if you needed a better editing tool than EDLIN, you had to buy a third-party editor or use a word processor like Microsoft Word. DOS didn't include a full-screen editor with scrolling features, only the line-oriented EDLIN editor. With the introduction of DOS 5.0, however, users now have EDIT. It fits in a niche just above EDLIN, but is not meant to be used to write professional documents. It doesn't offer character formatting, style sheets, spell checking or other features. EDIT can be useful, however, to users who need to write program code, batch files, lists and notes.

EDIT's main advantage over EDLIN is that you can scroll between lines using the arrow keys; in EDLIN you must type the number of each line you want to edit. EDIT also offers a user interface that makes cutting and pasting, as well as search and replace operations, much simpler. One thing it still doesn't have, though, is word-wrap. You can type a line up to 256 characters long, which is fine for program coding, but to write a letter to a friend, you'll have to press Enter every time you get near the right margin.

Because of EDIT's line-oriented approach, it is clear that it was designed as a programmer's tool. In fact, EDIT is a product of the BASIC language development environment called QBASIC now included with DOS 5.0. QBASIC comes with a debugger and a full-screen editor to provide a self-contained programming environment. When you run EDIT, you're actually running a version of QBASIC's full-screen editor.

EDIT looks a lot like its cousins, Windows Notepad and Windows Write. Those familiar with Windows will already know how to use the EDIT menu options and keystroke commands. But why would you use EDIT if you already have Windows Notepad and Windows Write? If you're like many users, you don't start Windows every time you turn on your computer. Users who are comfortable and familiar with DOS continue to work at the DOS level when interacting with the operating system and manipulating files. EDIT provides a quick and easy tool to use from the DOS level, and while it doesn't load as quickly as EDLIN, it provides many more features.

How to Start EDIT

EDIT can be started from the DOS 5.0 command prompt, or from within the DOSSHELL program. Both startup methods are described here. Note that EDIT will *not* start if the file QBASIC.EXE is not in the current directory or on the current path.

Starting EDIT from the DOS Prompt

From the DOS prompt, simply type EDIT, but before doing so, you may want to view startup information. This can be done by typing the following at the DOS prompt:

```
EDIT /?
```

You'll see a list of options similar to those listed here:

```
Starts the MS-DOS Editor, which creates and changes ASCII files.

EDIT [[drive:] [path] filename] [/b] [/g] [/h] [/nohi]

   [drive:] [path] filename  Specifies the ASCII file to edit.
   /b    Allows use of a monochrome monitor with a color graphics card.
   /g    Provides the fastest update of a CGA screen.
   /h    Displays the maximum number of lines possible for your hardware.
   /nohi Allows the use of a monitor without high-intensity support.
```

To start EDIT and load an existing file, type EDIT followed by the filename. If the file is not in the current directory, specify its path. You can also type the name of a file you want to create. For example, to create a new file called MYFILE.TXT, type the following:

```
EDIT MYFILE.TXT
```

You may also need to type one of the command line switches when you start EDIT. Switches are always typed last on the command line. The switches are shown in the help information listed above. If you have a monochrome monitor, you may need to use the

/b switch as shown below. This will start EDIT in black-and-white mode and allow you to see all of its menu options.

```
EDIT /b
```

If you have a color monitor, EDIT will load with color background and borders. Normally, EDIT displays up to 16 colors, but some monitors show only eight colors, which means that some high-intensity menu options may not show up. First, check to make sure EDIT is loaded in the proper color mode. This can be done by opening one of the pull-down menus to see if high-intensity characters are displayed. Press the Alt key, then press F to view the File menu. If your monitor does not support 16 colors, high-intensity characters on the File menu will be invisible. You'll see options like "ew" instead of "New" or "pen" instead of "Open." To correct this, exit EDIT by pressing the X key, assuming the File drop-down menu is still open, then type the following command at the DOS prompt to restart EDIT:

```
EDIT /nohi
```

This starts EDIT in the "no high-intensity" mode. The menu options will then display the previously missing characters in a color that is visible on your monitor. If you have this problem with a CGA monitor, start EDIT by typing:

```
EDIT /b
```

Some graphics monitors have the capability to display more than 25 lines of text. You can try loading EDIT with the /h switch as shown below to see if your monitor supports this mode and if you can work with the smaller character size.

```
EDIT /h
```

The /h switch displays the maximum number of lines possible on your monitor. If you don't see any change, or you don't like the smaller text size presented by this mode, exit EDIT by pressing the Alt key first, then pressing the F and X keys. Start EDIT again without using a switch.

If you have a CGA (Color Graphics Adapter) monitor, which was the original graphics standard for IBM PCs, you should start EDIT using the /g switch, which provides faster screen updating.

Starting the Editor from DOSSHELL

If the DOSSHELL program is loaded, press the Tab key until the highlight is in the Main section at the lower portion of the screen. Use the arrow keys to highlight "Editor," then press the Enter key. If you have a mouse, just double-click on the Editor icon.

EDIT asks for the name of the file you want to edit or create. You can type in a filename and press Enter, or click on the OK button. If the file is on another drive or directory, or

```
  File  Edit  Search  Options                              Help
                        Untitled



            Welcome to the MS-DOS Editor

      Copyright (C) Microsoft Corporation, 1987-1991.
                 All rights reserved.

        ◄ Press Enter to see the Survival Guide ►

          < Press ESC to clear this dialog box >







  F1=Help   Enter=Execute   Esc=Cancel   Tab=Next Field   Arrow=Next Item
```

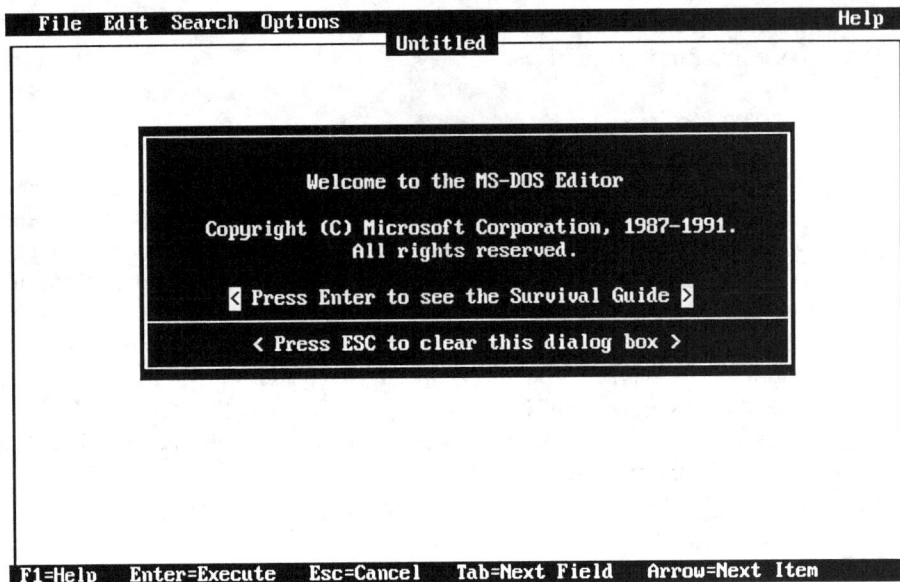

Figure 8.1.   EDIT's Welcome Message

you want to create a file in a location other than the current directory, type the drive letter
and path with the filename.

The first thing you see when EDIT starts is the welcome message and copyright screen
shown in Figure 8.1. Press the Enter key to view the Survival Guide, which is an on-line
help system. On-line help will provide assistance when working with the various EDIT
options, but in this chapter, we'll do a step-by-step tutorial of the tool. So, continue
reading this chapter if you are learning EDIT for the first time, then use the Survival
Guide as a reference when using EDIT in your day-to-day work. Press the Escape key
now to bypass the Survival Guide.

Accessing EDIT's Menu Options

Edit presents a window with pull-down menu options at the top and messages at the
bottom. All typing and editing is done in the workspace between. Notice that the name
of the document may appear in the second line of text at the top. In Figure 8.1, this bar
displays *Untitled,* which means that an existing document has not been loaded or that a
new document name has not been specified yet.

To quickly learn some of EDIT's features, start by loading the README.TXT file in
the \DOS directory. To open a new file, you need to access the Open option on the File
pull-down menu. Select an option by scrolling to it with the arrow keys and pressing the
Enter key, or by typing the capitalized (or highlighted) letter in the option. Or, if you have

```
File   Edit   Search   Options                                    Help
```

Figure 8.2.   EDIT'S Menu Bar

a mouse, point and click on the option. All pull-down menus originate from the menu bar at the top of the screen, as shown in Figure 8.2. Press the Alt key to access this menu bar now.

The highlight jumps to the menu bar. If you have a monitor that displays high-intensity colors, one letter in each option will be highlighted. These keys are referred to as the shortcut keys and are designed to make menu options easier to access. There are four available main menu options and a Help option further to the right. To select one of the options, do one of the following:

- Type the highlighted or capitalized letter.
- Click on the menu option with the mouse.
- Use the left or right arrow keys to move the highlight to the target option, then press the Enter key.

Choose the File option by pressing the F key. The pull-down menu shown in Figure 8.3 appears. You can now select a menu item using one of the selection techniques described above. For this example, just press the letter O key to select the Open option.

All menu options are selected in the same way. If you have a mouse, you can just point and click, but sometimes it's easier to use the keyboard method rather than reaching for the mouse. After a while, you'll become familiar with the keyboard shortcut keys and be able to use them without looking at the menus. We'll review each of them in this section.

```
Alt+F,O
```

This key sequence displays the Open dialog box. First press the Alt key, then the F key and finally the O key. Note that the letters used for selections are capitalized, and on some monitors, highlighted, to remind you of the keys to press.

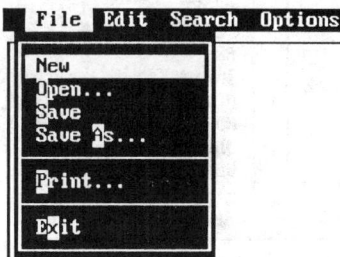

```
File   Edit   Search   Options
┌──────────┐
│ New      │
│ Open...  │
│ Save     │
│ Save As...│
├──────────┤
│ Print... │
├──────────┤
│ Exit     │
└──────────┘
```

Figure 8.3.   EDIT's File Option

Using Dialog Boxes

When you press Alt+F,O, the Open dialog box will appear (see Figure 8.4). Dialog boxes are used to set options for EDIT commands before actually executing the command. The methods used to access options in dialog boxes are discussed below. Because the Open dialog box has features that are common to other EDIT dialog boxes, such as Save and Find, it is used here as an example.

The dialog box has five sections. The top line is the File Name field. Under that is the current directory, which, in this case, is the root directory of drive C. The Files box is in the middle left portion, and the Dirs/Drives box is in the middle, right portion. At the bottom of the screen are the OK, Cancel or Help options. You can press the Tab key to move to a section, or you can press Shift+Tab to move back to a section. Mouse users can simply point and click on an option in a section.

The wild card characters * and ? can be typed in the File Name field to display a list of files in the Files box. EDIT always displays *.TXT in the File Name field, but you can type over this with your own file specification. In Figure 8.4, no files are listed in the Files field because there are no TXT files in the root directory of drive C. You can display files for a different directory by selecting the DOS directory in the Dirs/Drives box. To do so, press the Tab key until the cursor is in the Dirs/Drives box, then press the down arrow key to highlight DOS. Notice that the File Name field is updated with the new directory. Press the Enter key to display the list of TXT files in the DOS directory. If you have a mouse, just click on the directory you want to view.

README.TXT is now listed in the Files box. Press the Tab key until the cursor is in the Files box, then press the down arrow until the file is selected. Press Enter to load the file. To cancel the operation, press the Tab key until you get to the Cancel option at the bottom of the dialog box and press Enter, or better yet, just press the Escape key.

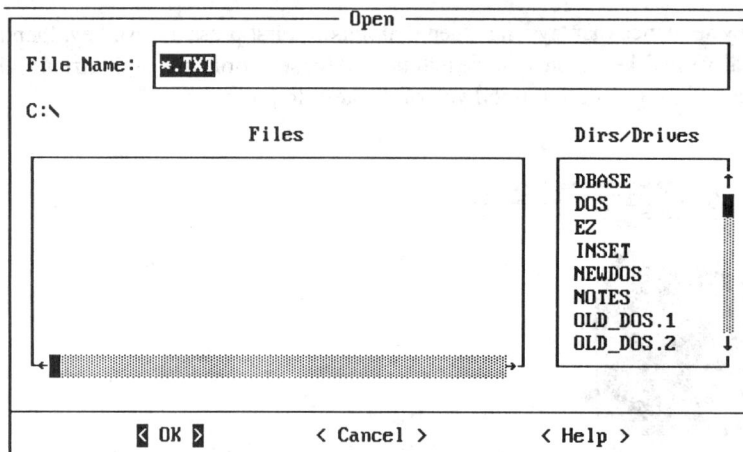

```
┌─────────────────────── Open ───────────────────────┐
│                                                     │
│  File Name: ┌─────────────────────────────────────┐ │
│             │ *.TXT                               │ │
│             └─────────────────────────────────────┘ │
│  C:\                                                │
│              Files                    Dirs/Drives   │
│  ┌───────────────────────────┐  ┌────────────────┐  │
│  │                           │  │ DBASE        ↑ │  │
│  │                           │  │ DOS          ▓ │  │
│  │                           │  │ EZ           ▒ │  │
│  │                           │  │ INSET        ▒ │  │
│  │                           │  │ NEWDOS       ▒ │  │
│  │                           │  │ NOTES        ▒ │  │
│  │                           │  │ OLD_DOS.1    ▒ │  │
│  │                           │  │ OLD_DOS.2    ↓ │  │
│  └█░░░░░░░░░░░░░░░░░░░░░░░░░░─┘  └────────────────┘  │
│                                                     │
│      █ OK ▌         < Cancel >        < Help >      │
└─────────────────────────────────────────────────────┘
```

Figure 8.4. Open Dialog Box

There are of course other methods for using the Open dialog box. If you have a mouse, you can point and click on each of the different drives, directories or files listed. Another method is to simply type the drive, path and filename of the file you want to open in the File Name field, assuming you know the name and location of the file. In this example, you could have typed the following in the File Name field:

```
C:\DOS\README.TXT
```

In the future, when working with other dialog boxes, keep the following in mind:

- You can jump to some dialog box sections by pressing the Alt key and the highlighted letter above the section.
- When you first open a dialog box, some fields will already be filled in. You can Tab to these fields and type over them with new text, or press the spacebar to clear the current text.
- Some options will be in groups, with the currently selected option indicated with a dot. You can move the dot with the arrow keys, or click on a different selection with the mouse.
- To execute the changes you have made in a dialog box, press the Enter key if the OK button is highlighted, otherwise, Tab to it and press Enter. To cancel a dialog box, press the Escape key or choose the Cancel option.

To leave the Editor at any time, press Alt+F,X.

Customizing the Editor

One of the first things you might want to do before you continue is to customize the way EDIT appears on the screen. If you use a mouse, this section will be of particular interest since it shows you how to turn the mouse scroll bars on. Press the Alt+O key sequence now to open the Options pull-down menu, then type D to open the Display dialog box, which is shown in Figure 8.5.

In the Display dialog box, you can change the foreground and background colors of the EDIT screen by choosing options in the top boxes. The options in the Display Options box are used to turn the scroll bars on, if you have a mouse, and to set the size of tabs.

To change screen colors, use the Tab key to move to either the Foreground or Background box, or press Alt+F or Alt+B. When the cursor is in the correct box, use the up or down arrow keys to select a new color. As you select colors, the sample foreground and background colors on the left change.

With a mouse, you can point and click directly on a color you want to select. Mouse users also can use the scroll bars on the right of each color selector box. Simply click on the top or bottom of the slider bar to adjust the list of colors. You can also click on the slider button and drag it into the slider bar while holding down the mouse.

Before closing the Display dialog box, you can change the size of tabs from the default 8-characters width to another width. Press the Tab key until you get to the Tab Stops box,

```
┌─────────────── Display ───────────────────────────────┐
│  ┌──────────── Colors ─────────────────────────────┐  │
│  │                   Foreground    Background       │  │
│  │                  ┌─────────┐   ┌─────────┐       │  │
│  │                  │ Black  ↑│   │ Black  ↑│       │  │
│  │                  │ Blue   ▓│   │ Blue   ▓│       │  │
│  │  ┌────────────┐  │ Green  ▒│   │ Green  ▒│       │  │
│  │  │Set colors for the │ Cyan   ▒│   │ Cyan   ▒│       │  │
│  │  │text editor window:│ Red    ▒│   │ Red    ▒│       │  │
│  │                  │ Magenta▒│   │ Magenta▒│       │  │
│  │                  │ Brown  ▒│   │ Brown  ▒│       │  │
│  │                  │ White  ↓│   │ White  ↓│       │  │
│  │                  └─────────┘   └─────────┘       │  │
│  └─────────────────────────────────────────────────┘  │
│                                                        │
│  ┌──────────── Display Options ────────────────────┐  │
│  │  [X] Scroll Bars            Tab Stops: 8         │  │
│  └─────────────────────────────────────────────────┘  │
│  ┌──────────────────────────────────────────────────┐ │
│    ◄ OK ►        < Cancel >        < Help >           │
└────────────────────────────────────────────────────────┘
```

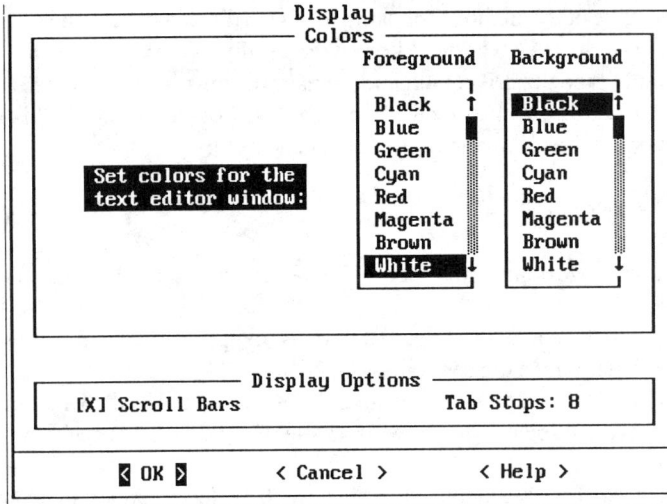

Figure 8.5.   Display Dialog Box

then enter a new value. Mouse users should click on Scroll Bars in the Display Options box. An X will appear in the field to indicate that scroll bars will be activated. Once the colors and other options are adjusted to your liking, you can press Enter, or click on OK, to make the changes permanent. When the Display dialog box disappears, the new changes take effect.

Using the Mouse Scroll Bars

Mouse users should experiment with the scroll bar on the right and bottom of the display. They consist of arrow buttons, a slider and a slider bar. To scroll up and down through text, click on the right slider and drag it while holding the mouse button, then release the button. Think of the right slider bar as a ruler that represents the entire length of your document. Moving the slider to any position on the slider bar scrolls you to that relative position in the document. If you drag the slider to the middle of the slider bar, you will be in the middle of the document.

If you click in the slider bar immediately above or below the slider itself, text will scroll one screen at a time either up or down. You can also click in the up or down arrow at the top or bottom of the slider bar to scroll text one line at a time in either direction. If you click and hold the mouse button on the arrows, the text will scroll continuously.

The bottom scroll bar is used to move left or right in a document when working with wide text. This is often the case when writing program code. The operation of the lower scroll bar is similar to the right scroll bar, except that text scrolls left and right.

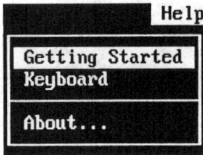

Figure 8.6. EDIT's Help

Getting Help

If you need help while using EDIT, press Alt+H at any time to open the Help pull-down menu as shown in Figure 8.6. For general help instructions, choose the Getting Started option. For a list of keyboard commands, select Keyboard. The About option is used to display the version number of Edit, which you may need to provide if you ever call Microsoft for technical support.

You can get immediate help by pressing the F1 key at any time. If you are in the editing area, this key opens the general Help menu. If you have a menu option highlighted, help information for that menu option will be displayed. For example, if you press Alt+F and press the F1 key, you will see help information for the New command since the highlight is currently on that menu option.

Also notice that help information for each menu option is displayed at the bottom of the screen as you scroll through a pull-down menu. Use the arrow keys now to scroll through the File menu as you watch the status bar at the bottom of the screen.

The following keys can be used while working with the help system:

View Help information	F1
	(or click the right mouse button)
Exit Help:	Esc
View Getting Started	Shift+F1
Display the Help menu	Alt+H
Move cursor to next Help topic	Tab
Move cursor to previous Help topic	Shift+Tab
Jump to topic:	1st letter of topic
Jump to previous topic	Shift+topic letter.
View next topic in Help	Ctrl+F1
View previous topic in Help	Shift+Ctrl+F1

Viewing Help Text While Editing

You can keep a help window open while you work with the text of a document. In this way, you can display keystrokes or procedures you don't remember. The following keys are used to resize a help window. You can then jump between text and help windows by pressing the F6 key. Some help windows are already small enough that you won't need to resize them, but others may need to be reduced so you can see the document window. Press F6 to move the cursor to the help window, then press Alt+Minus until the window is the correct size. When a help window is reduced, you may need to jump to it periodically with the F6 key to scroll through the help text.

Increase size of current window	Alt+Plus
Decrease size of current window	Alt+Minus
Move to next window	F6

Printing Help Information

The help information displayed on the screen can be printed for quick reference. Printing the keystrokes information for the keyboard is especially useful. To do so, first open the Help menu by pressing Alt+H, then press K to choose the Keyboard option. When the keyboard options appear, press Tab until the cursor is in the "Text-Scrolling Keys" field, then press Enter. When the list appears, press Alt+F,P to display the Print dialog box. Make sure the dot is in the Current Window option by moving it with the up or down arrow keys, then press Enter to print the list.

The next few sections will discuss the techniques for scrolling through text, selecting text, and editing documents. You may want to print all of the keystroke commands before continuing.

Browsing Through a Document

Assuming that README.TXT is still loaded in EDIT's workspace, you can experiment with some of the edit and jump keys, or if you have a mouse, with the mouse techniques. By the way, README.TXT offers important information about DOS 5.0 you may want to read now while you have it on the screen. If you want to make changes to this file for practice, go ahead. You can always exit EDIT later without saving your changes.

If you use a mouse, refer to the scroll bar techniques described earlier for methods used to move through the text of a document. In some cases, keyboard techniques may be faster, as described next.

To move through the text using the keyboard, press the PgDn or PgUp keys to move one window at a time. You can also press Ctrl+R to page up and Ctrl+C to page down. Another method is to use the up and down arrow keys. This causes the cursor to jump through lines until you reach the top or bottom border, then the text starts scrolling. To scroll the text one line at a time no matter where the cursor is, hold the Ctrl key while pressing the up or down arrow. You can also press Ctrl+W to move up one line or Ctrl+Z to move down one line. When working with wide documents, you can scroll left one window by pressing Ctrl+PgUp and right one window by pressing Ctrl+PgDn.

As you scroll through the text of the document, notice the numbers in the lower-right corner. The left number indicates the current line and the right number indicates the character position of the cursor in the line.

The Text scrolling keys are listed below.

Line up	Ctrl+Up Arrow or Ctrl+W
Line down	Ctrl+Down Arrow or Ctrl+Z
Page up	PgUp or Ctrl+R
Page down	PgDn or Ctrl+C
Left one window	Ctrl+PgUp
Right one window	Ctrl+PgDn

Setting Bookmarks

Bookmarks can be used to mark parts of a document you want to refer back to later. By pressing a keystroke, you can then quickly jump to the marked position in the text. Up to four bookmarks can be set, numbered 0 through 3.

To set a bookmark, first move the cursor to the position in the text you want to mark, then press Ctrl+K,0, to set the 0 bookmark, or substitute another number to set bookmarks 1 through 3. After scrolling away from the bookmark, you can return to it at any time by pressing Ctrl+Q,0 or the number that corresponds to the marker you set.

Moving the Cursor for Editing

There are a whole set of keystrokes you can use to move the cursor to a location in your document when you need to make changes, or when you need to select a block of text for an operation. To delete a block of text, first select it by moving the cursor to the beginning of the text and then hold down the shift key while moving through the text you want to delete. The selected text is highlighted and you can press the delete key to remove it.

The keystrokes described here are used to move the cursor to positions where you want to insert new text or delete a character. When selecting a block of text, you can also use these keys while holding down the Shift key to extend a selection, as discussed later.

Character left	Left Arrow or Ctrl+S
Character right	Right Arrow or Ctrl+D
Word left	Ctrl+Left Arrow or Ctrl+A
Word right	Ctrl+Right Arrow or Ctrl+F
Line up	Up Arrow or Ctrl+E
Line down	Down Arrow or Ctrl+X
First indent of line	Home

End of current line	End
Beginning of current line	Ctrl+Q,S
Beginning of next line	Ctrl+Enter or Ctrl+J
Top of window	Ctrl+Q,E
Bottom of window	Ctrl+Q,X

As an example, to remove a paragraph, you would first move to the beginning of the paragraph using the arrow keys or other methods listed above. Then hold down the Shift key while pressing Ctrl+Right Arrow to extend the selection one word at a time through the paragraph. Since EDIT is a line-oriented editor, you'll often need to jump to the beginning or end of the current line or next line. This can be accomplished by pressing the Home or End keys.

Editing Text

Once the cursor has been moved to the position in the text where you want to make changes, you can add or remove text or begin marking a block of text you want to copy, move or delete. Many text operations are done with the Clipboard. You can delete a block of text to the Clipboard, then move to another location in the document and paste the Clipboard contents.

The following keys can be used to insert new text or lines, and to delete characters. Note that you can delete the character you're on by pressing the Delete key, and delete the character to the left by pressing the Backspace key. If overstrike is on, you can type over characters. Or, you can toggle between the insert and overstrike modes by pressing the Ins or Ctrl+V keys. In most cases you'll want to have the insert mode on, but overstrike is often used when replacing an existing set of characters with a new set of characters. For example, if you create a menu with borders using the high ASCII graphics characters, you'll need to align these characters in several different lines. It is easier to make editing changes with overstrike mode on to prevent the characters from moving out of alignment.

Toggle insert or overstrike modes	Ins or Ctrl+V
Insert a blank line below the cursor	End+Enter
Insert a blank line above the cursor	Home,Ctrl+N
Insert special characters	Ctrl+P,Ctrl+key
Delete character to left of cursor	Backspace or Ctrl+H
Delete character at cursor	Del or Ctrl+G
Delete remainder of current word	Ctrl+T
Delete selected text	Del or Ctrl+G
Delete leading spaces to left	Shift+Tab

Inserting Special Characters

EDIT users who want to reassign keys or change the colors of their screen using the ANSI.SYS keyboard and screen driver can create special files with EDIT that contain the codes to do so. Press Ctrl+P, then press the Escape key to introduce an escape sequence into the file. Follow this with the ANSI codes required to change the keyboard or screen as discussed in Chapter 10.

You can also insert high ASCII characters into your documents by holding down the Alt key while you type the characters ASCII value on the numeric keypad. After typing the number, let up on the Alt key to display the character in the document. For example, to create a menu with borders, you could enter the following ASCII codes.

Alt+201	╔	Alt+203	╦	Alt+187	╗
Alt+204	╠	Alt+206	╬	Alt+185	╣
Alt+200	╚	Alt+202	╩	Alt+188	╝
Alt+205	═	Alt+186	║		

Copying, Cutting, and Pasting with the Clipboard

As already mentioned, text can be placed on the Clipboard, then pasted elsewhere in your document. Think of the Clipboard as a holding area. It lets you remove text in one location, then scroll to another location and paste it. Text placed on the Clipboard can be copied or cut from anywhere in your document, so you'll first need to select a block of text using the selection keys described in the next section.

Be aware, however, of the difference between copied text and cut text. When the text you highlight is *copied* to the Clipboard, it remains in the document. When highlighted text is *cut* to the Clipboard, it is removed from the document. Cutting text in the document is the same as deleting it, but since the text is placed on the Clipboard, you can paste it elsewhere. Keep in mind that text currently on the Clipboard is lost when you copy or cut new information to it, so you must paste Clipboard contents you want to save before using the copy or cut commands. To delete a block of text and not overwrite the Clipboard, press the Delete key after selecting text.

Selecting Text to Copy, Cut or Delete

Text is easy to select if you have a mouse. Simply point to the beginning of the text to select, then click and hold the mouse button while you drag through the text you want to copy, cut or delete. When done, let up on the mouse.

To select text with the keyboard, first move the cursor to the beginning of the block of text you want to copy or cut. Then use one of the following keystokes to select text — a character, word, line or screen at a time. The last two keystokes in the list are used to select all text from the current cursor position to the top or bottom of the document.

Character left	Shift+Left Arrow
Character right	Shift+Right Arrow
Word left	Shift+Ctrl+Left Arrow
Word right	Shift+Ctrl+Right Arrow
Current line	Shift+Down Arrow
Line above	Shift+Up Arrow
Screen up	Shift+PgUp
Screen down	Shift+PgDn
To beginning of file	Shift+Ctrl+Home
To end of file	Shift+Ctrl+End

Using the Clipboard

Once you've selected text, use one of the keystokes listed here to copy or cut it to the Clipboard. Or, you can select the Cut or Copy option on the Edit pull-down menu using the mouse or keyboard methods. If you just want to delete text and not place a copy of it on the Clipboard, press the Delete key.

Copy selected text to the Clipboard	Ctrl+Ins
Delete selected text to the Clipboard	Shift+Del

Alternate methods for cutting a single line or part of a line to the Clipboard are listed below and do not require that you select the text ahead of time. You must place the cursor on the line you wish to cut, then press one of the keystrokes. These options are useful when writing programs to remove a line of code and place it elsewhere. Note that both commands delete the text at the current position. If you just want a copy of the text using these keystrokes, first cut the text, then paste it back immediately before moving the cursor. This places a copy on the Clipboard so you can paste it elsewhere in the document.

Delete current line to the Clipboard	Ctrl+Y
Delete up to end of line to the Clipboard	Ctrl+Q,Y

To paste the contents of the Clipboard, first position the cursor in the appropriate document location, then press Shift+Ins, or select Paste from the Edit menu.

Paste the contents of the Clipboard	Shift+Ins

Using the Search Options

The options on EDIT's Search pull-down menu are used to find text or change text within a document. All searches start at the current cursor position, but when the end of the document is reached, searching continues at the top of the document. To limit the search to a specific area of your document, first highlight that part of the document using the text selection keys.

The Find option on the Search menu is used to locate text within a document you want to edit, or to reposition the cursor to a specific location. For example, if you need to temporarily jump back to the beginning of a document to review it or copy some text to the Clipboard, you can mark your current position by typing "***" or another suitable marker. To quickly return to the section, you would type "***" as the search text in the Find command. When Edit returns you to the position, the marker will be highlighted and you can press Delete to remove it. If you have text on the Clipboard, don't press delete until you've pasted the text, however. The Change option is used to change the text found in a search with the text you specify. You could search for all occurrences of "Tom" in a document and replace it with "Joe."

Using the Find Option

To find text, select the Find option on the Search menu, or press Ctrl+Q,F. The dialog box shown in Figure 8.7 appears.

In the Find What field, type the text you want to find, including any spaces or other punctuation that might appear in it. You can type whole words or parts of words in the field. Alternatively, you can limit the search to only whole words by tabbing to the Whole Word field and pressing the space bar to mark it. When the Whole Word field is marked, the text you type is treated as a whole word so that occurrences within other words are not found. For example, a search for "son" would not display "person" when the Whole Word field is marked.

You can also mark the Match Upper/Lowercase field to limit the search to text that specifically matches the case of the text in the Find What box. For example, a search for "Uppercase" would not find "uppercase."

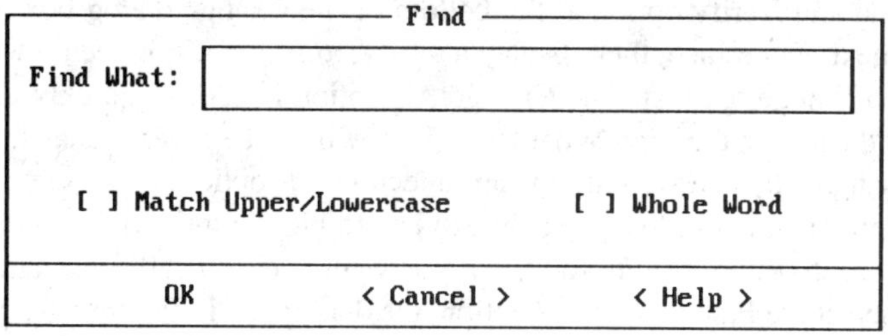

```
┌──────────────────────── Find ────────────────────────┐
│                        ┌──────────────────────────────┐ │
│ Find What:             │                              │ │
│                        └──────────────────────────────┘ │
│                                                         │
│   [ ] Match Upper/Lowercase        [ ] Whole Word       │
│ ├─────────────────────────────────────────────────────┤ │
│        OK          < Cancel >         < Help >          │
└─────────────────────────────────────────────────────────┘
```

Figure 8.7.   Find Dialog Box

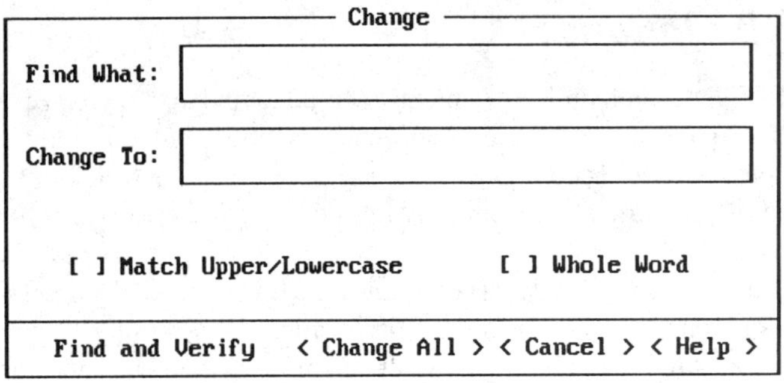

```
┌───────────────────── Change ──────────────────────┐
│                                                     │
│  Find What:  ┌──────────────────────────────────┐ │
│              └──────────────────────────────────┘ │
│                                                     │
│  Change To:  ┌──────────────────────────────────┐ │
│              └──────────────────────────────────┘ │
│                                                     │
│                                                     │
│     [ ] Match Upper/Lowercase      [ ] Whole Word  │
│                                                     │
├─────────────────────────────────────────────────────┤
│   Find and Verify    < Change All > < Cancel > < Help >│
└─────────────────────────────────────────────────────┘
```

Figure 8.8.   Change Dialog Box

When the fields of the dialog box have been set to the criteria for the search, press the Enter key. The first occurrence of the search text is highlighted. You can then make changes to the document at that location. To continue the search, press the F3 key. The criteria used in the last search is used again. To start a new search, choose the Find option from the Search menu and enter a new set of search criteria.

Finding and Changing Text

The Change option on the Search menu is used to search and replace text within a document or selected block of text. As with the Find command, the search starts at the cursor location and wraps back to the beginning of the document when the end of the document is encountered. The Change dialog box is shown in Figure 8.8.

As with the Find command, you specify the text you want to search for in the Find What field. Type the text replacement text in the Change To field. You can also mark the Match Upper/Lowercase and Whole Word fields to limit the search as discussed in the previous section.

In most cases, you won't want to change every occurrence of text found during the search. The Find and Verify option at the bottom of the Change dialog box is used to search for the next occurrence, then display a verify box so you can decide whether or not you want to change the text. The Change All option is used to quickly change all occurrences of the text in the Find What field. You will not be given a chance to verify when using Change All, so use caution when selecting this option.

After filling in the upper fields, press the Alt key to highlight the field options. Press Alt+V to verify each occurrence; if you know you want to change all occurrences, press Alt+C. If you select the Find and Verify option, the dialog box in Figure 8.9 appears for each find. You can press C to change the text, or S to skip over it and jump to the next occurrence. To stop the search, tab to Cancel and press Enter, or just press Escape.

```
┌──────────────── Change ────────────────────┐
│                                             │
│  < Change >   < Skip >    < Cancel >   < Help >  │
└─────────────────────────────────────────────┘
```

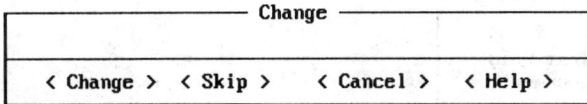

Figure 8.9.   Find and Verify Dialog Box

Using the File Options

You've already learned how to open a new file using the Open option. However, there are several options on the File menu that we haven't investigated yet. If you've made changes to a file, you can save those changes using the Save and Save As options, or you can discard the changes and clear the workspace using the New option. You can also open another file using the Open option.

The Save option is used to save a file that already has a filename. A dialog box does not appear when you select this option; instead the file is quickly saved under the name that appears in the second line on the EDIT window. If a document has not yet been named, you'll see "Untitled" in the second line. If you select Save when an untitled document is in the workspace, the Save As dialog box appears to request a filename.

The Save As option is used to save a file for the first time, or to save an existing file under a new name. To do either, choose the Save As option on the File menu, or press Alt+F,A to access the dialog box, which is shown in Figure 8.10.

Type the new filename, or type over an existing filename. To save the file on a different drive or directory, type the drive and directory path in the File Name field, or tab to the Dirs/Drives box and use the arrow keys to select a new drive or directory. When the File Name field is filled out correctly, press Enter or click on the OK option with the mouse.

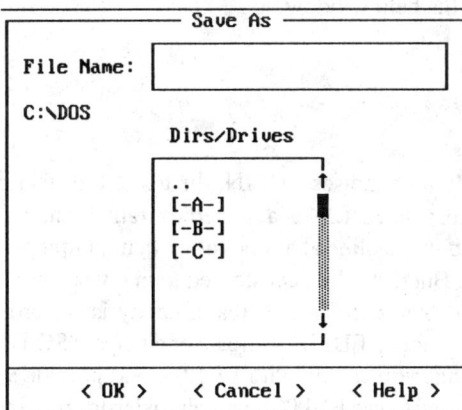

```
┌──────────────── Save As ────────────────────┐
│                                              │
│  File Name:  ┌──────────────────────────┐    │
│              │                          │    │
│              └──────────────────────────┘    │
│  C:\DOS                                      │
│                Dirs/Drives                   │
│              ┌──────────────────┐ ↑          │
│              │  ..              │ ▓          │
│              │  [-A-]           │ ▓          │
│              │  [-B-]           │ ▓          │
│              │  [-C-]           │ ▓          │
│              │                  │ ▓          │
│              │                  │ ▓          │
│              │                  │ ↓          │
│              └──────────────────┘            │
│                                              │
│   < OK >      < Cancel >     < Help >        │
└──────────────────────────────────────────────┘
```

Figure 8.10.   Save As Dialog Box

```
┌──────────── Print ────────────┐
│                               │
│   ( ) Selected Text Only      │
│   (•) Complete Document        │
│                               │
├───────────────────────────────┤
│   OK      < Cancel >  < Help > │
└───────────────────────────────┘
```

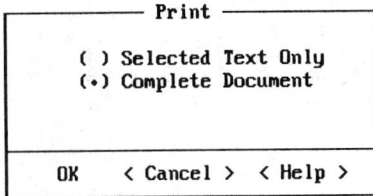

Figure 8.11.   Print Dialog Box

To clear the EDIT workspace and start a new untitled document, choose the New option on the File menu. If the current document has not been saved, a warning message appears to ask if you want to save it now. If you answer Yes and the file has already been named, the changes will be saved under that filename. If you answer Yes and the file has not been named, the Save As dialog box appears so you can enter a new name for the file as described above.

Printing the Document

In EDIT, you can choose to print your entire document, or you can select a portion and just print what is highlighted. When you're ready to print, choose the Print option on the File menu. The dialog box shown in Figure 8.11 will appear.

To print the entire document, press Enter or click on the OK button with the mouse. To print just the selected text, press the up arrow key to move the dot to the Selected Text Only field.

If you have the help window open and the cursor is in the help window, an option called Current Window will appear on the Print dialog box. Choose this option if you want to print only the contents of the help window.

EDLIN

As a matter of preference virtually no one uses EDLIN, the text editor that came with DOS prior to 5.0, and with good reason. EDLIN is a line editor rather than a full-screen editor, which means you can edit only one line at a time rather than jumping all over the screen. And it's far from friendly. But if you're accustomed to one word processor, and you find yourself on someone else's system and all that's handy is a word processor you've never used, you can always boot up EDLIN to create or change ASCII files. We'll let you in on some interesting things you can do with EDLIN, and provide an armload of shortcuts. We'll also show you how to use EDIT, the much easier-to-grasp edition that comes with DOS 5.0.

Don't get us wrong, however. EDLIN won't do any fancy text formatting. It doesn't have an adjustable right margin that will automatically wrap your text down to the next line the way every word processor does. You can't use it to create double-spaced documents. It makes you use truly awful DOS brute-force commands such as Ctrl-Z and Ctrl-Break to get serious work done. It can't handle any lines longer than 254 characters (the manual says 253 but 254 works on our systems), or any file with more than 65,529 lines in it. It can't back up to the previous screen line once you've wrapped the cursor around from the right edge of your screen to the next line. And you have to switch constantly back and forth from command mode to editing mode. But you can copy or move groups of lines, search for particular strings of characters, or even replace one chunk of text with another. And the price is right.

You need to specify a filename when starting EDLIN from DOS. EDLIN has two modes, command mode and edit/insert mode. When you're in command mode the EDLIN prompt — an asterisk (*) — hugs the lefthand screen margin; when you're in edit/insert mode this prompt is indented eight spaces. To switch from command mode to edit/insert mode, enter a command such as I, to add new text, or a valid line number, to edit the line with the number you specified. The easiest way to switch from edit/insert mode to command mode is to hit Ctrl-Break or Ctrl-C.

Every example below starts with an asterisk to show you what the screen should look like. However you don't ever have to type an asterisk; EDLIN will take of that for you.

EDLIN numbers all lines only for your and its own convenience; the line numbers that appear before each line aren't put into the actual file. Since EDLIN is a line editor rather than a full-screen editor it can really edit only one line at a time. It refers to the line it's working on as the *current* line, and puts an asterisk on this single line, after the line number and before the text. This current-line asterisk is different from the asterisk EDLIN uses as a prompt.

In virtually all cases you may enter EDLIN commands in uppercase or lowercase (or a combination of the two), and you can usually insert spaces inside the command. These three commands will all do the same thing:

```
*1,2P
*1,2p
* 1 , 2 P
```

However, EDLIN's Search (S) and Replace (R) commands are pickier about extra spaces, since they let you search for spaces and replace them. And when using these commands you have to make sure that you specify the exact strings you want to search for — if you ask EDLIN to find "HELLO" it will catch every HELLO but ignore variations such as "Hello" and "hello."

With commands that can work with ranges of lines, EDLIN lets you omit the actual line numbers and accept default settings.

However, with operations such as Move or Copy, you still have to include the comma separating the beginning and end of the range, even if you omit the line numbers themselves. Other EDLIN commands such as List, Page, Delete, Search, and Replace, are less fussy, and don't require either line numbers or commas. You can specify lines one at a time or in ranges, or you can refer to them in relative terms. To edit line 3, just type:

```
*3
```

To list just line 3 you could type:

```
*3,3P
```

(which tells EDLIN to start and stop with just line 3). Once you issue either of these commands, EDLIN makes line 3 the current line. If you then wanted to edit line 5, you could type either:

```
*5
```

or:

```
*+2
```

as the +2 tells EDLIN to edit the line with a line number two higher than the current line. Or if you had just listed line 3, and wanted to broaden the display one line on either side, you could either type:

```
*2,4P
```

or:

```
*-1,+1P
```

To exit prematurely from a long process (such as a Replace Text command) hit Ctrl-Break or Ctrl-C. To quit and save your changes, type E. To quit without saving your changes, type Q and then tell EDLIN you're sure you want to abort your file, by typing Y. Be careful when using Ctrl-Break or Ctrl-C when inserting or editing text, since this tells EDLIN to cancel any changes made in the line. To register a change, you have to press the Enter key. If you want to insert a special control character, preface it with a ^V. Normally you can't enter an Escape character in your file, since DOS interprets this as a signal to interrupt what you're doing. But if you're trying to create an ANSI file that needs a CHR$(27) Esc prefix, simply type:

```
^V[
```

If you need to put any other control character (such as ^A or ^B) into your file to trigger a special effect on your printer, just enter the uppercase version of the letter after ^V (or the Ctrl- shifted version). Be sure not to enter the lowercase version. To put a ^A in your file, you could type either:

```
^VA
```

or:

```
^V^A
```

If you want to put high-bit ASCII math, border, or foreign language characters into your file, use the Alt-plus-number-pad technique: Just hold down the Alt key, type the ASCII value on the number pad (not the top row number keys), and release the Alt key. If you wanted to put the pi symbol in your text, you'd simply hold down Alt, type 227 on the number pad while holding it down, and then release the Alt key. A pi sign would then appear at the cursor. Unfortunately, not all printers can reproduce such high-bit characters accurately. Nor will this Alt key technique let you put a CHR$(0) null in your text. If you need to do this, just press the F7 key. A ^@ will appear at the cursor, and an ASCII character 0 will be inserted into your text.

It's possible to put more than one command on a single line by separating the commands with a semicolon. If you wanted to display lines 7-8 and lines 12-14 together, you could do it with the single command:

```
7,8L;12,14L
```

If you want to add a second command to the same line as a search, you have to separate the commands with a Ctrl-Z or else EDLIN will think that the second command, semicolon and all, is part of the string involved in the search.

While EDLIN can help you put your files into shape, it's not designed to print anything. You could use your word processor to print the file, or you could use the DOS PRINT or COPY commands. To use the PRINT command, make sure the DOS PRINT.COM file is on the disk you're using, or is in a drive or subdirectory that your PATH command knows about. Then just type PRINT FILENAME (substitute the name of your own file for FILENAME). Or just type COPY FILENAME PRN.

Finally, one simple tip that can save lots of keystrokes — make a copy of EDLIN.COM and call it E.COM. You could simply rename EDLIN.COM to E.COM, but it's a good idea to keep all the files on your \DOS subdirectory intact if someone else has to use your system, and doing so makes it easier to upgrade from one version of DOS to the next. You may decide EDLIN is so clanky and unintuitive that you'd rather use your word processor or a vastly better quick editor like *SideKick*'s notepad instead. But if you do plan to use EDLIN, it's a lot easier and faster to type:

```
E CONFIG.SYS
```

than:

```
EDLIN CONFIG.SYS
```

especially if you use it all day long. If you try this, either keep E.COM on your main floppy disk (the file is so small you should be able to squeeze it on), or put it in your hard disk \BIN subdirectory along with the rest of your important utilities.

All examples below assume the file you started out with consists of the following five lines. The current line is always line 1, unless otherwise specified:

```
1:*line 1
2: line 2
3: line 3
4: line 4
5: line 5
```

Starting EDLIN

Format: **EDLIN FILENAME**

You can't start EDLIN without specifying a filename. If you enter the name of an existing file, EDLIN will try to load the whole file into memory. However, EDLIN will stop loading a file if it determines that RAM is filling up so fast that only 25 percent of available memory is free. If this happens, you'll have to edit the file in pieces, then use the Write Lines (W) and Append Lines (A) commands to write the beginning of the edited file to disk and load the unedited part of the file into memory. You really shouldn't have to worry about this, since you shouldn't be editing long files with EDLIN. It's really best for batch files, short memos, and other miscellaneous DOS tasks, like changing your CONFIG.SYS system configuration file or creating an ANSI string to change colors. For longer files, use your word processor instead.

EDLIN is actually an *external* DOS program called EDLIN.COM. Some commands such as DIR or TYPE are *internal*, which means they're part of COMMAND.COM and are always available to you whenever you see the DOS prompt. But you have to tell DOS where the EDLIN.COM program is on your disk, so DOS can find and load it if you are currently in a subdirectory that doesn't contain a copy of EDLIN.COM. If you're using a hard disk, the best way to handle this is to have a dedicated \DOS subdirectory that contains all your DOS files, including EDLIN.COM, and nothing else. To make sure DOS knows where all its important files are kept, include the \DOS subdirectory in your PATH command. By setting your disk up this way, you'll be able to use EDLIN no matter what subdirectory you happen to be using. Either issue this PATH command at the DOS prompt, or include a variation of it in your AUTOEXEC.BAT bootup file.

If you start EDLIN by specifying the name of a file that's not on your disk, EDLIN will create a new one, and tell you so, with a "New file" message. This means that if you're trying to edit an existing file and you see the "New file" message you either made a typing mistake when you entered the filename, or you're in the wrong subdirectory. Quit (by typing Q and then Y) and when you're back at the DOS prompt, type DIR FILENAME and press the Enter key (but of course substitute the actual name of your file). If you see the file, restart EDLIN and watch your typing. If you don't see the file, you're probably in the wrong subdirectory. Use the CD (Change Directory) command to log into the correct one.

Even if there's plenty of free memory in your system, EDLIN will stop loading any existing file when it sees a special character (with an ASCII value of 26) called a Ctrl-Z end-of-file-marker. EDLIN makes sure this special character is at the end of each file it edits, and puts one there if none exists, along with an extra carriage return and line feed. It doesn't expect to stumble over this character in the middle of a file.

But EDLIN can remove such nasty Ctrl-Z end-of-file characters that have somehow crept into your files by mistake. If you know you have a file that's 100 lines long, but EDLIN will display only the first three lines, odds are that an ASCII character 26 mysteriously found its way into the beginning of line 4. Other DOS commands such as TYPE will also screech to a halt when they see this end-of-file character, as will some commercial products such as *WordStar*.

If you think this has happened, add a /B to the end of the EDLIN FILENAME command. So if you have a file called PHONE.LST and EDLIN seems to be loading only the beginning of it, type Q and then Y to quit, and then reload the file with the command:

```
EDLIN PHONE.LST /B
```

(DOS almost always lets you enter switches such as /B either in uppercase or lowercase. But version 3.3 contains a bug that doesn't recognize /b, so it's always safe to use /B. In fact, version 3.3 has a hard time with uppercase and lowercase commands in general. Normally, if you try to edit a backup file that ends in BAK, EDLIN will refuse to load it and will just print a "Cannot edit .BAK file — rename file" message. If you try this with version 3.3 and enter a filename that ends in BAK you'll indeed get such an error message, and EDLIN will drop you back into DOS. But enter the extension using lowercase characters (bak) and EDLIN will blithely edit and save the file.)

You can either page through your document using the Page (P) command to see if any lines contain a stray ^Z, or you can have EDLIN's Search (S) hunt for it. To have EDLIN do the work, as soon as you load the file type:

```
*S^V^Z
```

When you first load a file, EDLIN makes line 1 the current line. Using the S command without line numbers will search from the line immediately following the current one (since the current line is 1, the search would start with line 2), and continue all the way to the last line loaded in memory. This won't catch any Ctrl-Z characters in line 1, but there probably wasn't an end-of-file marker there since in the above example EDLIN managed to display the first few lines. If you wanted to broaden the search to include the first line, just add a 1, prefix to the command right before the S.

You couldn't just enter the command as *S^Z since EDLIN uses ^Z in search commands to mark the end of the command, and not as a literal keystroke to hunt for. Fortunately, EDLIN lets you enter control characters by prefacing them with a ^V. So when you tell it to search for ^V^Z you're really saying "try to find a ^Z character."

If you do find a Ctrl-Z character in your file you can edit the line to remove it, and then continue searching for others. Or you can simply use the Replace (R) command to delete every Ctrl-Z in your file. The command:

```
*R^V^Z^Z
```

will do just that. (Again, to include line 1 in the search, add a 1, at the beginning of the command.) Then save and exit the file with the E command.

Let's get right into EDLIN's commands. Then, at the end of the chapter you'll find more advice on using EDLIN.

The EDLIN Commands

Append Lines

Format: **[n] A**

This command loads additional lines from disk to memory. You need to do this only when EDLIN wasn't able to load your entire file into memory when you started. EDLIN will stop loading your file if it figures out that 3/4 of your available memory is full. If this happens, and you want to edit the rest of your file, first use the Write Lines command (W) to write the beginning of your file from memory to a disk. Then use Append to read in [n] additional lines from your disk to the end of the file in memory. You probably won't have to use this, since you should edit large files with your word processor rather than EDLIN. (See Write Lines.)

Copy Lines

Format: **[line],[line],line[,count]C**

This command copies one line or a block of lines from one place in your file to another. Copying lines leaves the original lines alone and simply duplicates them elsewhere. If you want to copy lines from one place to another and delete the originals, use the Move command instead. The optional [,count] lets you make multiple copies of the block of lines you specified — if you omit this number EDLIN will make only one copy. If you omit either of the first two [line] numbers, EDLIN will assume you want to copy the current line (but you have to type in the commas even if you omit the numbers). And you have to specify where you want the copied block to go. The line number you want the block copied to has to be outside the range of the block you want copied, so you can't tell EDLIN to take lines 3 through 5 and copy them to line 4.

For example:

```
*3,4,5c
```

makes one copy of lines 3 and 4 and puts these two lines before line 5. It will then make the second line 3 the current line and renumber all the lines:

```
1: line 1
2: line 2
3: line 3
4: line 4
5:*line 3
6: line 4
7: line 5
```

```
*,,6,3c
```

makes three copies of the current line (here it's line 1) and adds these after line 5. It will then make the first of these three copied lines the current line, and renumber all your lines:

```
1: line 1
2: line 2
3: line 3
4: line 4
5: line 5
6:*line 1
7: line 1
8: line 1
```

Delete Lines

Format: **[line][,line]D**

This command deletes the current line and moves all following lines up a notch, when used without any line numbers. Specifying just one line number deletes that particular line. Omitting the first parameter (but leaving in the initial comma) deletes all lines from the current one to the one specified. Specifying two numbers deletes everything between them, including the specified lines themselves. EDLIN then makes the line immediately following the deletion the current one.

If you want to get rid of several lines in a row, it's best to specify the beginning and end of the range you want deleted rather than erasing them one at a time. Users often forget that EDLIN renumbers their documents each time a line is deleted. So if you use the P or L command to view your text, and see that you want to erase lines 10 and 11, issuing the commands:

```
*10D
*11D
```

won't do it. After the first command (10D) gets rid of line 10 it will then move the old line 11 down a notch and turn it into the new line 10, move the old line 12 down and make it the new line 11, etc. The second command (11D) would mistakenly end up erasing what used to be line 12, since everything moved down a notch after the first deletion. If you did want to erase lines 10 and 11 one at a time you could type:

```
*10D
*10D
```

An easy way to do this is to type in the command the first time and press Enter, then press F3 to repeat the previous command, and then press Enter.

For example:

```
*,3D
```

deletes everything from the current line (in this case line 1) up to and including line 3:

```
1:*line 4
2: line 5
```

```
*2,4D
```

deletes everything from lines 2 through 4, including lines 2 and 4:

```
1: line 1
2:*line 5
```

```
*2D
```

deletes line 2:

```
1: line 1
2:*line 3
3: line 4
4: line 5
```

```
*D
```

deletes the current line only (in this case line 1):

```
1:*line 2
2: line 3
3: line 4
4: line 5
```

Edit Line

Format: **[line]** *or* **[special symbol]** *or* **[Enter key alone]**

This command lets you edit any existing line. If you're in the command mode (with the asterisk hugging the left margin) and you simply press the Enter key without specifying a number, EDLIN will assume you want to edit the line *following* the current one. If you're not at the end of the file, it will take the line following the current one and display it in edit mode (indented eight spaces), and treat this new line as the current one. So if the current line happens to be line 2, and you simply press the Enter key in command mode, EDLIN will display line 3 in edit mode and turn line 3 into the current line. Typing a question mark (?) and then pressing the Enter key is the same as pressing the Enter key by itself.

If you're in command mode and you want to edit the current line, just type a period (.), a minus sign (-), or a plus sign (+) and then press the Enter key. If you want to edit a specific line, just enter the number of that line and press Enter. Although it's not documented, if you want to edit the next two lines, just type a semicolon (;) and press Enter. Typing a pound sign (#) and then pressing Enter will take you past the last line of your file; if you then type I and press the Enter key to go into insert mode, EDLIN will let you append text to the end of your file.

Once you've edited a line, pressing the Enter key replaces the original version of the line with the edited version. Once you've switched from command mode to edit mode, if you want to abort the process and leave the original line intact, either press the Enter key before making any changes, or press either Ctrl-Break or Ctrl-C. You can also press Esc and then the Enter key to avoid making any changes.

When you're in edit mode you can use all the familiar DOS editing keys, such as F2 plus a character to display everything from the beginning of the original version of that line to the first occurrence of the specified character in the line.

If you're not comfortable with the F2-plus-a-character technique, you can edit an existing line simply by pressing F3 to have DOS type in the previous version of the line automatically for you, and then use the backspace or left arrow keys to erase the part of the line you want to change. Or instead of hitting F3 to reproduce the entire line, you can hold down the F1 or right arrow keys to retype the previous version of the line one character at a time. If you're careful about it, you can use the Insert and Delete keys to add and remove individual characters in the middle of the line, and then press F3 when you're done, to type in the rest of the line for you.

For example:

```
*.
```

or:

```
*+
```

or:

```
*-
```

brings the current line (in this case line 1) into edit mode:

```
1:*line 1

*
```

Just pressing the Enter key by itself when in command mode brings the following line into edit mode. In this case the current line is line 1, so the following line is line 2:

```
2:*line 2

*3
```

Specifying any valid line number brings that line (in this case line 3) into edit mode:

```
3:*line 3

*;
```

Typing a semicolon and then pressing the Enter key brings the two following lines into edit mode. In this case the current line is line 1 so the two following lines are 2 and 3. This example assumes you then press the Enter key twice and didn't make any changes:

```
2:*line 3
2:*
3:*line 3
3:*
```

End Edit

Format: **E**

This command saves the file to disk and exits. (If you want to exit without saving any changes you made, type Q to quit.) If you're editing an existing file called OLDFILE.TXT and exit EDLIN with an E command, EDLIN will save the newly edited version as OLDFILE.TXT and tack a BAK extension onto the old, unchanged version, renaming the old version to OLDFILE.BAK. If you're just starting a file, EDLIN won't create such a backup file. Each subsequent time you edit the file, EDLIN will get rid of the previous BAK version of it and create a new BAK version. EDLIN makes sure there is a carriage return/line-feed/end-of-file marker trio of characters (ASCII characters 13, 10, and 26) at the end of any file it saves.

If your disk doesn't have enough room to save all the changes you made, EDLIN will save as much as it can onto your disk, and discard the rest. If this happens, EDLIN will give the partially saved version a $$$ extension, and it won't give the original version of your file a BAK entension.

(See Quit Edit.)

Import Files

See Transfer Lines.

Insert Lines

Format: **[line]I**

This command lets you start adding text to a new file, or insert new text in an existing file directly before the line you specified. When you type I, EDLIN assumes you want to insert multiple lines, and will keep displaying the next higher line number each time you press the Enter key. If you want to stop inserting lines, you have to press Enter to lock in the last line you inserted, and then press either the Ctrl-Break or Ctrl-C keys to abort the insertion process. If you don't press the Enter key at the end of your last line of inserted text before aborting, EDLIN will think you want to abort this last line, and discard it.

If you type I by itself and then press Enter, or type a period (.), and then I, and then press Enter, EDLIN will start inserting text directly before the current line. If you type a valid line number, then I, and then Enter, EDLIN will insert any text you type directly before the line number you specified. If you type a pound sign (#) and then I and press Enter, or a ridiculously high number such as 65000 and then I and Enter, EDLIN will move to the end of your file and start appending text there.

If you type a semicolon (;), then I, and then press Enter, strange things will happen depending on what you do next. In all cases, EDLIN will increase the number of the current line by 1. If you press the Enter key without entering any text, EDLIN will give you a second chance to insert text on that same line. Type in a line of text at that point and EDLIN will accept it and move on to the next line. But if you enter text at the first opportunity, EDLIN will accept it, make it look as if you have a second chance to enter text on that same line, accept that as well, and put the second line before the first.

In fact, the insert function gets confused and will do all sorts of odd things if you follow I with a plus (+) or minus (-) sign before pressing Enter, or type several IIIIs in a row before you press Enter. None really helps you very much.

The following examples assume the new single line you insert is always "This is a new line" and ignore the curious but useless variations such as I+ and ;I:

```
*.I
```

or:

```
*I
```

lets you insert new lines before the current line. In this case the current line is line 1:

```
1:*This is a new line
2:*^C
```

produces:

```
1: This is a new line
2:*line 1
3: line 2
4: line 3
5: line 4
6: line 5
```

```
*3I
```

lets you insert new lines directly before line 3:

```
3:*This is a new line
4:*^C
```

produces:

```
1: line 1
2: line 2
3: This is a new line
4:*line 3
5: line 4
6: line 5
```

```
*65000I
```

or:

```
*#I
```

lets you append new lines at the very end of your file, assuming your file is smaller than 65000 lines:

```
6:*This is a new line
7:*^C
```

produces:

```
1: line 1
2: line 2
3: line 3
4: line 4
5: line 5
6: This is a new line
```

List Lines

Format: **[line][,line]L**

This command lists, or displays, one or more lines without changing which line EDLIN thinks is the current one. If you type L by itself and then press Enter, EDLIN will try to display a screenful (23) of lines, with the current line in the middle of the screen. The 11 lines preceding the current line will appear above the current line, and the 11 lines following the current line will appear below it. If EDLIN can't find 11 lines that precede the current line, it will try to add extra lines at the end until it can display a total of 23.

If you type one valid line number followed by L, and then press Enter, EDLIN will try to display 23 lines beginning with the line you specified. Type a single line number, and then a comma, and then L and press Enter, and EDLIN will do the same thing. Both variations of this command tell EDLIN to display the specified line and up to 22 lines that follow it.

If you type a comma, and then a valid line number, and then press Enter, EDLIN will try to display the 11 lines preceding the current one, and all the lines following the current one up to and including the specified line. However, if you try this and the specified line is very far after the current line, EDLIN will end up displaying too many lines and will scroll the display off the screen. Worse, if the specified line is more than 11 lines before the current line, EDLIN will ignore your numbers and treat the command as if you had simply typed in a naked L.

If you type two valid line numbers separated by a comma and followed by an L, and then press Enter, EDLIN will display the lines starting with the first line number and going up to and including the second line number. Since EDLIN uses a pound sign (#) to mean "the last line in the file," you can view a 60-line file in one big continuous gulp by typing:

```
*1,#L
```

to produce:

```
1:*line 1
       .
       .                      60 lines total
       .
60: line 60
```

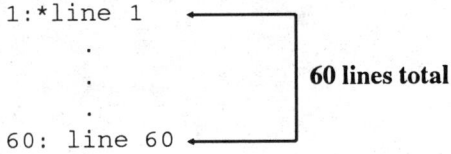

The following examples assume a 60-line file in which each line is simply the word "line" followed by the appropriate line number, and where line 30 is the current line:

```
*L
```

lists the 11 lines before the current line (30), plus the current one itself, and then the 11 lines after the current line. If EDLIN finds fewer than 11 lines before the current line it will try to display more than 11 lines after the current line. However, if you had just started to edit, and hadn't yet identified a current line, typing L would list the first 23 lines of your file.

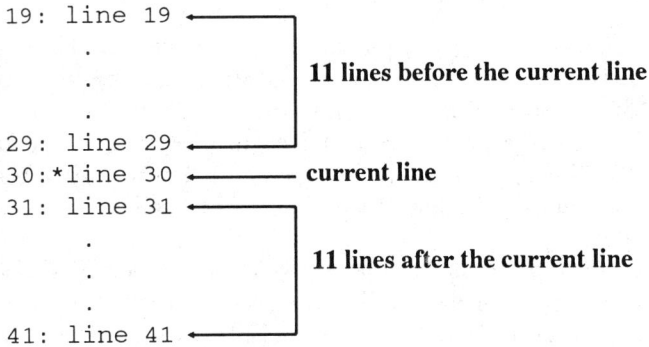

```
19: line 19
       .
       .               11 lines before the current line
       .
29: line 29
30:*line 30    current line
31: line 31
       .
       .               11 lines after the current line
       .
41: line 41
```

```
*25L
```

displays the line specified (25) plus the 22 lines that follow it.

```
25: line 25
       .

       .

       .
29: line 29
30:*line 30
31: line 31
       .

       .

       .
47: line 47
```

```
*,25L
```

displays lines starting 11 lines before the current one, and ending at the line specified (25). Since the current line in this case is line 30, the display begins 11 lines earlier (line 19). If you had just started to edit, and hadn't yet identified a current line, typing ,25L would list the first 25 lines of your file (scrolling the first few off the top of your screen):

```
19: line 19
20: line 20
21: line 21
22: line 22
23: line 23
24: line 24
25: line 25


*25,28L
```

lists everything from the first specified line to the second specified line, inclusive:

```
25: line 25
26: line 26
27: line 27
28: line 28
```

See Page.

Merge Files

See Transfer Lines.

Move Lines

Format: **[line],[line],lineM**

This command moves a line or lines, in the range defined by the first two numbers, to a position in your text directly before the third line number. The new location (the third number) must be outside the range defined by the first two numbers, so you can't move lines 3 through 5 to a position directly before line 4. If you omit either of the first two numbers, EDLIN will assume you want to move the current line — but you'll still need to type in the commas, and you must specify a third (destination) line number.

For example:

```
*3,5,1M
```

moves all the lines from 3 through 5 to a new location directly before line 1:

```
1:*line 3
2: line 4
3: line 5
4: line 1
5: line 2
```

```
*5,5,1M
```

moves the single line 5 directly before line 1:

```
1:*line 5
2: line 1
3: line 2
4: line 3
5: line 4
```

```
*1,1,5M
```

or:

```
*,,5M
```

moves the single line 1 directly before line 5. Omitting the first two numbers tells EDLIN to assume that you want to move the current line, which in this case is line 1:

```
1: line 2
2: line 3
3: line 4
4:*line 1
5: line 5
```

```
*1,1,6M
```

or:

```
*1,1,#M
```

or:

```
,,#M
```

moves line 1 to the end of the file, since in this case line 1 is the current line and line 5 is the last line:

```
1: line 2
2: line 3
3: line 4
4: line 5
5:*line 1
```

Page

Format: **[line][,line]P**

This command displays lines, and changes the number of the current line. The similar List Line (L) command also displays lines — though according to slightly different rules — but doesn't alter the number of the current line. When you use the P command without any line numbers, EDLIN will display the 23 lines following the current line (but won't show the current line itself), and will change the current line in the process. This is very handy for examining your file a screen at a time; when you start EDLIN if you just keep tapping P and Enter you'll page all the way through from beginning to end. You can't do this with repeated L commands, since L won't change the number of the current line and will keep displaying the same screen over and over. (See List.)

The following examples assume a 60-line file where each line is simply the word "line" followed by the appropriate line number, and where line 30 is the current line. The examples are identical to those presented for the List command, to make it easy for you to compare the Page and List commands:

```
*1,#P
```

displays the entire file just as List (L) does, except that P will turn the last line in the file into the current one, while L will leave the current line alone.

```
1: line 1
        .
        .                       60 lines total
        .
60:*line 60                     this becomes the new current line

*P
```

displays the line immediately after the original current line plus the 22 lines following it, and will then turn the last line displayed into the new current line. While List (L) will also display 23 lines, it will try to show the 11 lines before and after the current line, and will not change the current line.

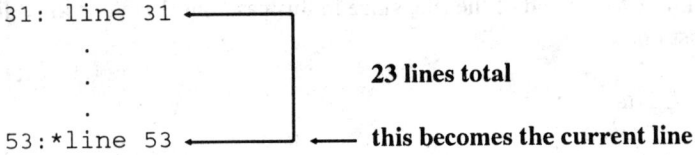

```
31: line 31
         .
         .
         .
53:*line 53
```
                                  23 lines total

                                  this becomes the current line

```
*25P
```

displays the line specified (in this case it's line 25) and the 22 lines following it, and will make the very last line displayed (in this case 25 + 22, or line 47) the current one. Here, Page (P) works about the same as List (L) except that L doesn't change the current line.

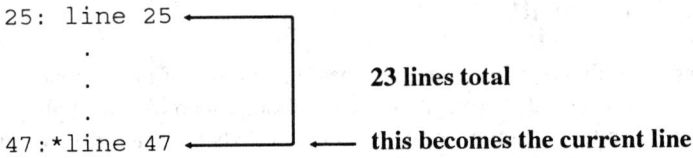

```
25: line 25
         .
         .
         .
47:*line 47
```
                                  23 lines total

                                  this becomes the current line

```
*,25L
```

produces only an "Entry error" message if the current line is 30, since in effect you're asking it to display from lines 30-25, and EDLIN can't page backwards. However, the List (L) command can indeed handle such a command, since it tries to start displaying text starting 11 lines before the current one, and ending at the line specified. So if the current line is 30, the command ,25L will display from line 19 (30 - 11) through 25. If the current line was line 1, both the ,25L and ,25P commands would display the first 25 lines of your file, and would end up scrolling the first few off the top of your screen. The only difference would be that the P version would make line 25 the current line, while the L version would leave the current line as line 1.

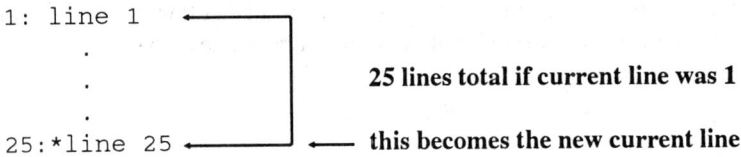

```
1: line 1
         .
         .
         .
25:*line 25
```
                                  25 lines total if current line was 1

                                  this becomes the new current line

```
*25,28P
```

lists everything from the first specified line to the second specified line, inclusive. In this case P works just like L except that P will turn the last displayed line into the current one.

```
25: line 25
26: line 26
27: line 27
28:*line 28
```

Note: The EDLIN P (Page) command displays just 23 lines when arguments are not specified. By changing the line count byte it's possible to have EDLIN display any number of lines from 1 to 128. For instance, since 43-line screens are becoming more popular, you may want to patch EDLIN so the P command displays 41 lines rather than just 23.

The hex offset address of the line count byte varies according to the DOS version:

Version	Offset
2.0	700
2.1	700
3.0	102B
3.1	105C
3.2	105C
3.3	105C

(DOS 4.0 handles this differently.)

The default value at this address is 16, since this is part of the instruction:

```
ADD DX,+16 .
```

The value of this byte cannot exceed 7F hex, unless you want your whole document to streak past. Values lower than hex 16 will cause the P command to display fewer than 23 lines. Note that the actual number of lines EDLIN will display is one greater than the value at this byte.

Screen Size	Hex Value at Offset
25	16
35	20
43	28

To patch EDLIN so the P command lists 41 lines, be sure DEBUG.COM is handy. Make a copy of EDLIN.COM called EDLIN41.COM. Then use the E command to make the change at the address appropriate for the DOS version you're using.

For versions 3.1 through 3.3 the process would look like:

```
C>COPY EDLIN.COM EDLIN41.COM
          1 File(s) copied
C>DEBUG EDLIN41.COM
-E 105C
30F9:105C 16.28
-W
Writing 1D66 bytes
-Q
```

Once you've copied EDLIN.COM to EDLIN41.COM, DEBUG prints the hyphens, this line (the 30F9 right before the colon is a hex number that will vary from system to system and doesn't matter here):

```
30F9:105C 16.
```

and the "Writing 1D66 bytes" message. You type everything else.

See List.

Quit Edit

Format: **Q**

This command lets you abort a file — quit EDLIN without saving any changes you may have made — and return to DOS. To make sure you don't lose your work inadvertently by typing Q when you don't mean it, EDLIN displays an "Abort edit (Y/N)?" message to allow you to confirm the action. If you type Y, EDLIN will quit and all your changes will be lost. Type N (or any character other than Y or y) and EDLIN returns you to command mode with your file intact.

Read In Files

See Transfer Lines.

Replace Text

Format: **[line][,line][?]R[oldstring][<F6>newstring]**

This command replaces one string of characters with another. EDLIN can replace strings in just one line or throughout your entire document, with confirming prompts or without, and can handle multiple occurrences of a string in the same line. (Each time it replaces a string it will print the entire revised line, so if it's making multiple changes in the same line you'll see that line onscreen several times.) EDLIN identifies the last line that it changes as the current line.

The R command can replace one single character or a whole series of words, but as with the Search Text (S) command, the matches have to be exact. If you tell EDLIN to find every "the" it will skip over "THE" and "The" — but it will find imbedded strings such as the letters t-h-e inside "them" and "whether" and "Goethe." If you want to find whole words only, you can try putting a space on either side of the word when you specify it in the R command. This will work most of the time with a word like "the" which is almost never followed by punctuation. But many words could be followed by commas, periods, or question marks, so this technique is far from foolproof. And since EDLIN can't ignore cases, you may have to search through once for each "the" and repeat the command to catch any "The" that happens to start a sentence. If you do try putting a space on either side of the old string, remember to put spaces on either side of the replacement string as well. Note that quotes are used here to make the examples clearer — don't use quotation marks in the actual EDLIN commands unless a quote mark is indeed part of the string you're replacing.

You can ask to preview each potential replacement, with the change already in place, by putting a question mark (?) before the R. If you do this, EDLIN will show you what the replacement would look like and then print a very terse "O.K.?" prompt. If you type either Y or y or press the Enter key, EDLIN will make the change. If you type any other character EDLIN will leave that particular string alone. In either event it will then continue searching. If you use this prompt feature, make sure you put the ? before the R, not after it, since EDLIN interprets anything after the R as part of the old string you want to replace, and will end up hunting for a string beginning with a question mark.

EDLIN uses a Ctrl-Z to separate the old string from the new one. You can generate a Ctrl-Z either by tapping once on the F6 function key; by holding down the Ctrl key and typing Z; or by holding down the Alt key, typing 26 on the number pad (not the top row keys), and then releasing the Alt key. Be sure not to put any extra spaces on either side of the Ctrl-Z or EDLIN will interpret them as part of the string to replace.

You may use this feature to delete strings of text. After the R in the command, simply enter the old string you want deleted, press the F6 function key, and then press Enter instead of specifying a new string. In effect you're telling EDLIN to replace something (the old string) with nothing. If you try this, be sure to consider any leading or trailing spaces around the string you're deleting.

If you omit the first line number, EDLIN will start trying to replace strings in the line immediately following the current line. Omit the second line number and EDLIN will scan through to the end of the document, or at least as much of it as is currently in memory. Omit both line numbers and EDLIN will start the replacement process with the line following the current one and stop only when it reaches the final line in memory.

Each time you specify a Search string or a Replace string, EDLIN stores it in a special buffer. If you omit either string the next time you issue the command, EDLIN will use the strings from the previous command. If you wanted to find every occurrence of the word "flower" and replace it with "Zantedeschia aethiopica" between lines 1 and 50 of your document, you would type:

```
*1,50Rflower^ZZantedeschia aethiopica
```

(where ^Z represents a Ctrl-Z character, not a ^ and a Z). If you then wanted to replace the same old string with the same new one in lines 51 through 100, all you'd have to type is:

```
*51,100R
```

If you omit the first string (the old text that you want to replace), EDLIN will look in its buffers and try to dredge up either the previous initial R (Replace Text) string, or the previous S (Search Text) string, whichever is more recent. But if you omit the second string (the new text that replaces the old), EDLIN will try to hunt down the last R string.

Since EDLIN can't work with lines longer than 254 characters, it won't be able to handle such lengthy lines when you're replacing a short string with a longer one.

The following examples assume the file is the simple five-line file used above, and that the current line is line 1. And don't forget that the ^Z represents a Ctrl-Z character, not a ^ and a Z. See the text above for the three ways to generate this character:

```
*Rline^ZLINE
```

starts the replacement process on the line following the current one (line 2 in this case, since the current line is line 1), and replaces each "line" it finds with a new "LINE" string.

```
2: LINE 2
3: LINE 3
4: LINE 4
5: LINE 5
```

```
*1,3Rline^ZLINE
```

limits the replacement process to all lines between 1 and 3, and changes each "line" it finds there to "LINE."

```
1: LINE 1
2: LINE 2
3:*LINE 3
4: line 4
5: line 5
```

```
*,3Rline^ZLINE
```

since no beginning line is specified, EDLIN starts the replacement process with the line following the current one. The current line is line 1, so this starts at line 2 and ends with line 3, changing each "line" it finds to "LINE."

```
1: line 1
2: LINE 2
3:*LINE 3
4: line 4
5: line 5
```

```
*1,#Rline^Z
```

searches through the entire document from line 1 to the final line loaded in memory and replaces every "line" string with a null string, effectively deleting the word "line" throughout the document.

```
1:* 1
2:  2
3:  3
4:  4
5:  5
```

```
*1,#?Rline^ZLINE
```

searches through the entire document from line 1 to the final line loaded in memory and asks whether or not to replace every occurrence of "line" that it finds with "LINE." When EDLIN prompts the user in this way it displays what the replacement would look like if the user answered the prompt with Y or y or Enter. It interprets any other character keypress as a No. In the example below, the user responded to the five prompts with: Y N y A Enter. EDLIN replaced strings in the first, third, and fifth lines, but not the second and fourth, since only Y or y or Enter tells EDLIN to go ahead with the change.

```
            1:*LINE 1
O.K.? Y
            2: LINE 2
O.K.? N
            3: LINE 3
O.K.? y
            4: LINE 4
O.K.? A
            5: LINE 5
O.K.?

            1: LINE 1
            2: line 2
            3: LINE 3
            4: line 4
            5:*LINE 5
```

Search Text

Format: **[line][,line][?]S[string]**

This command scans through the file for occurrences of a specified string. Just about all the tricks and caveats that apply to the Replace Text command also apply here. Since searches are case-sensitive you have to specify search strings exactly. You can often isolate words by specifying spaces before and after. If you omit line numbers EDLIN starts with the line immediately following the current one and searches until it finds the last line in memory. Once you've specified a search string using the S or R commands, you can repeat the search without having to type in that string.

And, as with the Replace command, you can insert a question mark (?) in the command to have EDLIN prompt you by asking "O.K.?" when it finds a match. At that point if you do anything other than type Y or y or just press Enter, EDLIN will search for the next occurrence of the string. If you don't use a question mark, EDLIN will stop the first time it finds the string and make the line with the string the current one. If you do use a prompt EDLIN will turn the first line you accept into the current one.

EDLIN will print a "Not found" message if it can't locate the string you specified, or if you ask it to prompt you and it finishes searching through a range without having you accept any of the matches it uncovered.

It's possible to add a second command to Search Text, by tacking a Ctrl-Z and then the new command (with no intervening spaces) onto the end. For instance, if you knew you had used the word "banana" only once in your document and wanted to see the line it was in along with the 23 lines following it, you could issue the command:

```
1,#Sbanana^ZP
```

and EDLIN would execute a P (Page) command as soon as it found the word banana.

The following examples assume the file is the simple five-line file used above, and that the current line is line 1:

```
*S3
```

searches from the line after the current one to the last file in memory for the first occurrence of the string "3." Here the current line is line 1, so the search begins at line 2:

```
3: line 3
```

```
*Sline
```

searches from the line after the current one to the last file in memory for the first occurrence of the string "line." Here the current line is line 1, so the search begins at line 2:

```
2: line 2
```

```
*1Sline
```

or:

```
*1,Sline
```

or:

```
*1,#Sline
```

searches from line 1 to the last file in memory for the first occurrence of the string "line."

```
1:*line 1
```

```
*,3Sline
```

since no beginning line is specified, EDLIN starts the replacement process with the line following the current one. In this case the current line is line 1, so this starts at line 2. As specified, EDLIN would continue searching until line 3, but it stumbled over the string it was looking for in line 2.

```
2: line 2
```

```
*1?Sline
```

searches through the entire document from line 1 to the final line in memory for occurrences of the string "line" and asks whether each is the one the user wants. In the example below, the user responded to the four prompts with: N n A Enter. EDLIN will stop searching only when it reaches the end of the range specified, or when the user types a Y or y or presses Enter in response to the "O.K.?" prompt. In this case, the user didn't respond positively until the fourth request:

```
          1:*line 1
O.K.? N
          2: line 2
O.K.? n
          3: line 3
O.K.? A
          4: line 4
O.K.?
```

See Search Text.

Transfer Lines

Format: **[line]T[d:]filename**

This command merges an existing file from disk into memory directly before the specified line, or before the current line if no line number is specified.

The following examples assume that the current line is line 1 and that you have a file on drive A: called ONELINE.TXT that contains the single line "IBM keyboards are the best:"

```
*3TA:ONELINE.TXT
```

merges the file ONELINE.TXT from drive A: into the current file directly before line 3.

```
1: line 1
2: line 2
3:*IBM keyboards are the best
4: line 3
5: line 4
6: line 5
```

```
*TA:ONELINE.TXT
```

merges the file ONELINE.TXT from drive A: into the current file directly before the current line. In this case the current line is line 1, so EDLIN reads the new file in at the very beginning of the existing one.

```
1:*IBM keyboards are the best
2: line 1
3: line 2
4: line 3
5: line 4
6: line 5
```

```
*#TA:ONELINE.TXT
```

merges the file ONELINE.TXT from drive A: into the current file at the very end of the current file.

```
1: line 1
2: line 2
3: line 3
4: line 4
5: line 5
6:*IBM keyboards are the best
```

Write Lines

Format: **[n]W**

This command writes lines to disk to provide space for EDLIN to load an additional part of a file that was originally too large to fit into memory. If you tried to edit a file that EDLIN couldn't load in one gulp, you have to edit the part that it could load, use this command to write the beginning of the file to disk and automatically renumber the remaining part of the file, and then read in more of the file from disk using the Append (A) command. This command won't work if more than 25 percent of memory is available.

If needed, EDLIN will write lines to disk starting with line 1 and continue until 25 percent of memory is free. (See Append Lines.)

Using EDLIN

Be careful when mixing EDLIN output with redirected DOS output. For instance, if you redirect the output of ECHO to create a sample TEST.TXT file:

```
ECHO Line 1 > TEST.TXT
ECHO Line 2 >> TEST.TXT
ECHO Line 3 >> TEST.TXT
```

and then enter:

```
TYPE TEST.TXT
```

to see what's in the new file, DOS will display:

```
Line 1
Line 2
Line 3
```

Load TEST.TXT into EDLIN and save it with the E command. Now append another line onto the file:

```
ECHO Line 4 >>TEST.TXT
```

and do another TYPE command:

```
TYPE TEST.TXT
```

and all you'll see is the first three lines:

```
Line 1
Line 2
Line 3
```

What happened here was that EDLIN added an end-of-file marker to the file, and the next redirection command appended the line after that end-of-file marker. Line 4 was still in the file, but was located after the end-of-file marker. When the DOS TYPE command hit the end-of-file marker it quit before it reached the new line. DOS lets you get around this by using a /B switch (the /B stands for *binary* since binary, or nontext, files treat ASCII character 26 as just another character and not a signal to quit).

Programs written for DOS should not really need an end-of-file marker because the exact size of the file is contained in the directory entry. This was not always the case. Before DOS, the most popular eight-bit microcomputer operating system was CP/M, which stored files in blocks of 128 bytes. The CP/M directory entries indicated only the number of 128-byte blocks and not the exact size of the file. ASCII text editors needed an end-of-file marker to determine what was actually part of the file and what was junk. When you redirect standard output to a file, DOS does not append an end-of-file marker to the file it writes. And if the file already contains an end-of-file marker, DOS does not remove it. However, EDLIN always adds an end-of-file mark to files it saves. And the DOS TYPE command always stops at the first end-of-file marker it finds.

To see what's going on, add a /B when you load the file into EDLIN:

```
EDLIN TEST.TXT /B
```

(Some versions of EDLIN contain a bug that won't let EDLIN recognize a lowercase /b switch. To be safe, make sure any /B you enter is a capital letter.) This tells EDLIN to load in the entire file regardless of imbedded end-of-file marks. You'll see the whole file with the fourth line if you do an L (list) in EDLIN. You can also see the whole file by entering:

```
COPY /B TEST.TXT CON
```

or:

```
COPY TEST.TXT CON /B
```

both of which do a *binary mode* copy of the file to CON (the screen, or *console*). The end-of-file markers show up as little right arrows.

But even if you use EDLIN in binary mode, it will still append an end-of-file marker to the end of the file. To get rid of it you could execute the following commands right after you exited EDLIN:

```
TYPE TEST.TXT >TEMPFILE
DEL TEST.TXT
REN TEMPFILE TEST.TXT
```

The TYPE command normally displays the file TEST.TXT up to (but not including) the end-of-file marker. Redirecting the output of this TYPE process into a temporary file like TEMPFILE will copy everything in the TEST.TXT file except the end-of-file marker. Then just delete the original TEST.TXT file, rename the new TEMPFILE to TEST.TXT, and then delete TEMPFILE. You could automate the whole process with a batch file:

```
ECHO OFF
IF %1!==! GOTO OOPS
EDLIN %1
```

```
TYPE %1 >TEMPFILE
DEL %1
REN TEMPFILE %1
GOTO END
:OOPS
ECHO Enter a filename after %0
:END
```

You can try using EDLIN to remove end-of-file characters one at a time. If there aren't too many in your file you may be able to get away with a global replacement operation. Since you can't specify a Ctrl-Z directly, you have to enter it as Ctrl-V Ctrl-Z, which looks like ^V^Z.

However, EDLIN will choke if you try a R (Replace) command and the end-of-file markers are too thick. If this happens, use DEBUG to ferret out the offending ASCII 26 characters. (The process described here is for files less than 64K in length; for longer ones you'll have to work with the CX and BX registers. See Chapter 9 on DEBUG for details.) DEBUG works exclusively in hex, so use the hex 1A notation for decimal ASCII 26. First, make a copy of the file, and work with the copy of the file rather than the original. If you make a mistake you can start the whole process again.

Load the file into DEBUG. See how large it is by typing RCX and pressing Enter twice. Then take the hex number that DEBUG prints out in response, and plug it into a S (Search) command. The whole process will look something like:

```
C>DEBUG TESTFILE  ──────  This uses a file called TESTFILE.
-RCX              ──────  You type RCX and press Enter twice.
CX 00AC           ──────  DEBUG responds with a file length in
:                              hex; here it's 00AC.
-S 100 L00AC 1A   ──────  Plug the length into this S command.
30DD:0102         ──────┐
30DD:0105
30DD:0108
30DD:010B                 These are all addresses of hex 1A end-of-
30DD:010E                 file markers DEBUG found.
30DD:0111
30DD:0114
30DD:0117
30DD:011A
30DD:01AB         ──────┘
-E 0102 20        ──────  This replaces the first 1A with a space
-W                        (hex 20); W writes it to disk.
-Q                ──────  And Q quits.
```

The example used only one E command to fix just the first occurrence of the hex 1A. To get rid of all the end-of-file markers you'd have to repeat the E command with every address DEBUG reported.

Note: If you're good at hex, and you see that all the addresses of the 1A characters are in one continuous block, you can use a single DEBUG F (Fill) command to repair the damage. So if you see something like:

```
30DD:10C9
30DD:10CA
30DD:10CB
30DD:10CC
30DD:10CD
30DD:10CE
30DD:10CF
```

You can issue the command:

```
F 10C9 10CF 20
```

which will fill the range of addresses from 10C9 (the first one on the list) to 10CF (the last one on the list) with hex 20 characters — spaces. Then type W (and press Enter) and Q (and press Enter) to save the changes. However, in the main example above, the addresses aren't in one continuous block.

Ignore the four digits to the left of the colon in the long list of addresses DEBUG prints out (here it's 30DD). This will vary from system to system and doesn't matter here. The four hex numbers to the right of each colon are the DEBUG offsets of each hex 1A character (remember, DEBUG works in hex — a hex 1A is the same as a decimal 26).

Then, use the E command with each address to replace the 1A with a 20 (a hex 20 is a space):

```
E 0102 20
```

and work your way through. When you're done, enter W to write the changes to disk and Q to quit. Again, work only on a copy of your file, not the original. And note that the above procedure is for files 64K or less in length only.

ECHO Version Madness

If you created batch files before DOS version 3.1 and used the trick of printing a blank line by following the ECHO command with two spaces, when you upgrade to a newer DOS version these ECHO commands will simply print "Echo is off" messages rather than blank lines. A batch file and EDLIN can fix the problem. ECHO will print a blank line if you follow it with a space and then an ASCII 255 character rather than with two spaces. ASCII 255 shows up as a blank on the PC screen, but to DOS, it's nonblank, so you won't get the "Echo is off" message. You can enter an ASCII 255 by holding down the Alt key, typing 255 on the number pad (not the top row number keys), and then releasing the Alt key.

Some text editors and word processors will have trouble with this ASCII 255, but the DOS EDLIN editor can handle it without any problems.

To fix the double space problem with EDLIN, use the R command to replace the final space with the a character 255,by entering this line:

1. Type: 1,RECHO (with two spaces after the ECHO).
2. Press the F6 function key.
3. Type just: ECHO.
4. Generate a character 255 by holding down the Alt key, typing 255 on the number pad, then releasing Alt.

The line looks like this:

```
*1,RECHO   ^ZECHO
```

The first number tells EDLIN to start at line 1. Since you didn't enter a second number after the comma, this tells EDLIN to repeat the operation on every line loaded in memory. The R is EDLIN's Replace command, and here it's followed immediately by the old string — ECHO and two blanks. When you press the F6 key after entering the old string, you'll see a ^Z. Then type the new string — ECHO followed by a blank followed by the ASCII code 255. Character 255 will appear as a blank on your display. EDLIN's search and replace is case-sensitive, so you'll have to repeat the command for occurrences ECHO, echo, and Echo.

Since EDLIN gets keyboard input through DOS (unlike most word processors and text editors), you can use it with redirection of standard input. Begin by creating a small script file (in EDLIN, of course) called REPLACE that looks like:

```
1,RECHO  <F6>ECHO<255>
1,REcho  <F6>Echo<255>
1,Recho  <F6>echo<255>
E
```

To enter the above four lines, first enter:

```
I
```

to put EDLIN into Insert mode. Then type each line, but press the F6 key where each one has an <F6> and generate a character 255 where each has a <255>. Be sure to observe the capitalizations carefully.

If you ever have to edit REPLACE after you create it, use the /B option with EDLIN. Since F6 is the same as a Ctrl-Z, which normally means "end of file," EDLIN will stop reading the file at the first Ctrl-Z unless it has the /B flag.

After typing the fourth line (with the solitary E), press Ctrl-C to get back to command mode and then enter E to save the file and quit.

To change a particular batch file (here called OLDFILE.BAT), all you have to do is enter the command:

```
EDLIN OLDFILE.BAT < REPLACE
```

DOS will take its input from **REPLACE** to do the search-and-replace operations automatically for you.

If you have lots of batch files with two spaces after ECHO, you can change them all with a pair of one-line batch files. First, create a one-line batch file called CHGBAT.BAT:

```
EDLIN %1 < REPLACE
```

Then create another one-line batch file call CHGALL.BAT that looks like:

```
FOR %%X IN (*.BAT) DO COMMAND /C CHGBAT %%X
```

If you run CHGALL.BAT, it will execute CHGBAT.BAT for every batch file on the disk (or subdirectory). Each time CHGBAT runs, it loads another batch file into EDLIN and uses REPLACE for the keystrokes to do the search-and-replace.

One interesting side effect of this process is that some batch files get edited twice. EDLIN renames the old version of an edited file with an extension .BAK, and creates a new directory entry to save the new version. Because of this, the FOR command in CHGALL.BAT stumbles over the file a second time. Note that CHGALL.BAT and CHGBAT.BAT will themselves be edited by EDLIN during this process. Neither of these peculiarities should cause a problem.

DEBUG

Don't be put off by the name or the formidable set of commands: DEBUG is a serious computer user's best friend. Those of you who are already familiar with DEBUG may wish to go directly to the summary of commands in the second part of this chapter.

IBM and Microsoft need some real help when it comes to being friendly. They shouldn't have called this wonderful program DEBUG, which sounds as if it's for programmers only and that it involves something that's broken. Instead, they should have named it something like POWERUSR, or SLIKTOOL, or DOITALL. Well, maybe not.

It's almost as if these two companies tried to scare users away. Okay, DEBUG can be used as a high-level tool for fixing broken programs. But most real programmers have moved on to more powerful debugging aids produced by Microsoft and others. IBM would like us to believe that DEBUG is there mostly to "provide a controlled testing environment so you can monitor and control the execution of a program to be debugged" and "execute object files." Lost in the shuffle is a fragment admitting that it can "load, alter, or display any file." Totally ignored is its crude but useful ability to assemble and unassemble code — to translate assembly language instructions used by programmers into the *machine language* your CPU speaks, and back again.

Actually, DEBUG is for two sets of users. It's true that a handful of its commands are only for hard-core programmers who really need to trace though the underlying chip instructions one step at a time, or set *breakpoints* so that a program will screech to a halt and display the contents of the main CPU registers, or suck in data from a computer port.

But to the average power user, DEBUG is the ultimate program generator, analyzer, and customizer. Once you learn its few simple rules you can create short, powerful new programs and add flash to existing ones.

Unfortunately, because DEBUG is so incredibly powerful, it's also incredibly dangerous. (And, like every other part of DOS, it's frequently counterintuitive.) It's sort of like a carpenter's shop — filled with sharp tools you can use to build or fix just about anything safely, so long as you wear goggles and watch out for your fingers.

Most users are smart enough to work with copies of their programs rather than the originals when trying any sort of customization, so they won't end up ruining a $500 program with an errant keystroke. But certain madcap copy protection schemes can cause trouble because the programs they "protect" often don't play by the rules even if you and DEBUG do. Worse, because DEBUG lets you write information to absolute addresses on your disk rather than forcing you to have DOS take care of this safely for you, you can wipe out an entire hard disk with one simple erroneous command.

The general DEBUG safety rules are:

1. Always work with copies of your programs, *never* the originals.
2. Don't fool around with copy protected programs unless you're positive you know exactly what you're doing.
3. Whenever you are about to write sector information (with the W command) stop and triple-check your typing and your intentions. If you had read information from drive B:, had changed it slightly, and are about to write it back to the same drive, be sure your drive specification is correct. DEBUG uses a 0 to represent drive A:, a 1 to represent drive B:, and a 2 to represent drive C:. If you're trying to alter the disk directory, or (heaven forbid) the File Allocation Table (FAT) on drive B:, and it's late at night, and you inadvertently write the new information to drive 2, well, that's what backups and four-letter words (like "oops") are for.
4. If you have any doubt whatsoever about what you're doing, get back to the DEBUG prompt (by hitting Ctrl-Break or Ctrl-C), type Q on a line by itself to quit, and then press the Enter key to return to the main DOS prompt. You can always go back later and try your DEBUG work again. If you're at all hesitant about a change you made or a value you entered, make absolutely sure that you *don't* enter the W (Write) command. And avoid using the DEBUG G (Go) command to execute the program you're fiddling with, since unpredictable things can happen if you haven't reset all the registers properly, or if you've entered some but not all the changes you're working on.
5. While it may be tempting to change real gut-level aspects of the program, such as timing settings, again, don't, unless you're an expert. It's true that you can goose up the performance of your system by altering table settings that control such things as floppy disk head movement. It's also true that putting the wrong value in the wrong part of a table can send a disk head mechanism careening into someplace noisy and destructive.
6. There's a saying that "software can't destroy hardware." Unfortunately, it's not true. Apart from sending sensitive disk drive mechanisms into never-neverland, it's possible to blow out monitors or transformers. Again, if you simply follow reliable instructions to the letter and heed all of the warnings, you should be safe.

If you're in doubt about a particular DEBUG trick, *don't try it*. We hear lots of horror stories where users say "I know the instructions said 'for IBM hardware only' but my salesman told me this Yamagazi AT was virtually identical to an IBM." Or where the user says "I know it said 'for color monitors only' but my monochrome was a color — green. Now it's black."

Every DEBUG technique discussed in this book has been tested extensively on IBM equipment. However it is impossible to test every technique presented here on every single nonstandard system, given all the combinations and permutations on the market. Again, if you're not using an IBM system and you have any doubts whatsoever, *don't even think of trying these*!

Now that that's out of the way, we have to mention one more nasty thing — DEBUG works exclusively in hex. Hexadecimal notation is pretty basic stuff, and it's not hard to master. If you're uncomfortable with it, see the earlier chapter on hex and binary.

Addresses

The smallest four-digit hex number is 0000 (same as decimal 0). The largest is FFFF (same as decimal 65,535). This means that four hex digits can represent 65,536 different decimal values (1 through 65,535, plus 0). Decimal 65,536 is often abbreviated as 64K. 1K is equal to 2^{10}, or 1024 (not 1000, as some users think). $64 * 1024 = 2^{16}$, or 65,536.

The PC can address one megabyte of memory. One megabyte is equal to 2^{20}, or decimal 1,048,576. $16 * 65,536$ is also equal to 1,048,576. The lowest address is address 0. The highest is 1,048,576.

For many common tasks it's easier and quicker to work with smaller numbers rather than larger ones. Anyway, the original PC came with a 16-bit chip, and the biggest number this chip could address "directly" was 2^{16}, or 65,536.

But since 65,536 is 1/16th of 1,048,576, being able to handle only 65,536 addresses directly meant working with only 1/16th of the available memory at any one time. To give users access to the rest, IBM designers employed relative addressing. They chopped the one megabyte into 16 chunks called segments, each 64K long. Once you specified which of the 16 segments you wanted to work with, you could address any of the 65,536 bytes in that segment directly.

If you have to know what's at address 5, you can tell DEBUG simply to report the value at address 5. Because you didn't mention any particular segment, it will tell you the value at address 5 of whatever segment you're in at the time. If you want to look at address 5 in another segment, you have to specify both the address and the segment you want.

Manuals sometimes provide maps that show the one meg of memory divided neatly into 16 even chunks 64K apart from each other, starting out:

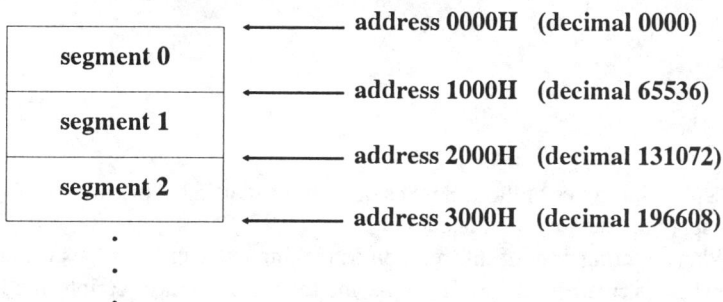

	◄─────── address 0000H (decimal 0000)
segment 0	
	◄─────── address 1000H (decimal 65536)
segment 1	
	◄─────── address 2000H (decimal 131072)
segment 2	
	◄─────── address 3000H (decimal 196608)

It doesn't really work like that. Segments can have any starting absolute address from 0 to 1048560, so long as the address is evenly divisible by 16. So 16 and 32 and 524288 are all valid absolute addresses, but 1 and 17 are not. And segments can overlap, either partially or totally.

Relative, or segmented, addresses are usually expressed as a pair of two four-digit hex numbers separated by a colon:

```
XXXX:YYYY
```

The XXXX represents the segment. The YYYY stands for the *offset* into that segment.

Once you've mastered hex, start putting it into action. DEBUG.COM is usually on the DOS Supplemental or Operating disk, depending on the version. If you have a hard disk, be sure to copy it into your main DOS subdirectory, and be sure you're using a PATH command that includes this DOS subdirectory. This will let you use DEBUG anywhere on your hard disk. If you don't have a hard disk, you should put DEBUG.COM on your main bootup or utilities disk and keep it handy at all times.

The DEBUG prompt is simply a hyphen hugging the left edge of your screen:

All of DEBUG's commands are single letters. You may enter them in upper- or lowercase, or a mixture of both. The examples here will use uppercase text to avoid confusing 1 with "ell." And you don't have to separate the single-letter commands from the parameters that follow them. Typing:

```
RCX
```

to see what's in the CX register (this will be covered shortly) is the same as typing:

```
R CX
```

Similarly, you can use either:

```
D120
```

or:

```
D 120
```

to display the values of the 128 bytes of memory starting at offset 120H (again, we'll get to displaying memory a bit later).

When entering a lot of information or making extensive changes using DEBUG, it's often best to create pure-ASCII *scripts* and then redirect these scripts into DEBUG. DOS versions 2.0 and later treat such redirected files as if they were actual keystrokes.

Scripts are handy because they make it easy for you to proofread your typing before executing actual DEBUG commands. If you find a typo in your script it's a whole lot easier to correct it with a word processor or EDLIN than to end up with a real mess that you created while in DEBUG because you typed something incorrectly.

Scripts are also valuable because in some cases you can add nonexecutable comments that DEBUG ignores but that can remind you much later of what you did. And if you store your scripts on disk, you can cannibalize them and use them to create other slightly different scripts. They're also handy for transmitting via modem. Many telecommunications services work with text files only, and won't let you send programs. But you can send scripts, since they're just ASCII files, and have the recipient redirect these scripts into DEBUG to create the program you wanted to send.

Redirectable scripts have to be pure-ASCII files, without any extra word processing formatting commands imbedded in them. The easiest way to create them is with a pure-ASCII editor like *SideKick*'s notepad, or with a word processor that can export DOS files (such as *WordPerfect* or *Word*), or with a word processor that has a built-in ASCII mode (such as *WordStar* in nondocument mode). EDLIN isn't bad for shorter scripts, and you could even use the DOS COPY CON command.

DEBUG doesn't execute a command until you press the Enter key. So any script you create has to have a carriage return at the end of every line — especially the last one, which is always Q on a line by itself to quit. If you don't end every script file with a Q that has a carriage return after it, redirecting it will hang your system. *So be sure you press the Enter key at the very end of any DEBUG script, or you'll have to reboot.*

Most DEBUG commands perform just one task and then return you to the DEBUG prompt. If the task takes too long to execute (displaying the contents of a huge chunk of memory, for instance), you can hit Ctrl-Break or Ctrl-C to interrupt it and return to the DEBUG prompt. If you're using the DEBUG mini-assembler to turn assembly language statements into machine readable code, press the Enter key twice after you enter your final statement, to return to the DEBUG prompt.

Since many DEBUG scripts contain assembly language commands and statements, you can simulate pressing the Enter key at the end of the final statement by leaving a blank line after that statement. If you don't do this, DEBUG will try to interpret everything that follows as additional assembly language statements. If you try typing in the example scripts that follow, be sure to copy them exactly as they appear, blank lines and all.

Here's an example of a DEBUG script file, called BEEP.SCR:

```
N BEEP.COM      ; gives the file a name
A
MOV DL,7        ; ASCII 7 is the beep character
MOV AH,2        ; the DOS "display output" function
INT 21          ; kicks DOS into action
RET             ; return to DOS — next line is blank!

RCX
7
W
Q
```

DEBUG ignores any text following semicolons, and the semicolons themselves. They're included just to remind you later what the program is doing. You have to be careful when you use them, since DEBUG may interpret such comments as part of a command to execute, and get thoroughly confused. It's pretty safe to use them with assembly language instructions like the ones above, and very unsafe when you're entering single letter commands.

You can type this script in using any of the tools mentioned above. If by some crazy circumstance you don't have a word processor handy and refuse to learn EDLIN, you could create the script by adding a COPY CON BEEP.SCR line before the first "N BEEP.COM" line, and pressing Enter, then the F6 function key, and then Enter when you're done.

In any case, be sure to leave the blank line above RCX. You can do this by pressing the Enter key twice after RET. And double check that you press the Enter key at the very end, after the Q. If you did, the cursor will be on the line below the Q. Call the file BEEP.SCR. When you're all done, get back to your main DOS prompt and type:

```
DEBUG < BEEP.SCR
```

DOS will feed the BEEP.SCR commands into DEBUG a line at a time, and you'll be able to see DEBUG processing them one by one. If everything goes the way it should, near the bottom of the screen you'll see the message:

```
Writing 0007 bytes
```

If you make a typing mistake, DEBUG will show you where the trouble is by pointing to it and printing the word Error. If you had typed "MOV LD,7" instead of "MOV DL,7," you'd see:

```
33DB:0100 MOV LD,7
                 ^ Error
```

If DEBUG detects such a syntax error, it may or may not continue and create the file, depending on the severity of the problem. Watch the screen closely as DOS redirects the script file into DEBUG. If you see any error messages do not try to execute the program you were trying to create! Instead, erase any erroneous file it may have created, check your typing, and try again.

If you type the BEEP.SCR file correctly and redirect it properly into DEBUG, you'll end up with a seven-byte program on your disk called BEEP.COM. Type BEEP to run it and DOS will beep. Here's how it works:

The first "N BEEP.COM" line tells DEBUG to give the file a name. DEBUG can't create a file unless you specify a filename. Since you want to create an executable file, you have to give the file a COM or EXE extension. When creating any kind of files with DEBUG, use COM extensions only.

The "A" command turns on DEBUG's mini-assembler, which will convert any assembly language statement(s) that follow into a machine-level form your CPU can readily understand. If you haven't used the Assemble command previously and you enter an A without specifying an address after it, DEBUG will start assembling these machine-level instructions at address 100. If you're using the A command more than once in a particular DEBUG session, or you want to have DEBUG put the assembled code at an offset higher than 100, be sure to include the proper addresses.

The next four lines are the actual assembly language statements. "MOV DL,7" moves, or puts, the value 7 into the register DL. "MOV AH,2" moves, or puts, the value 2 into the register AH. INT 21 is the main interrupt that kicks DOS into action. When your program invokes INT 21, DOS looks at the value in the AH register to figure out which of its dozens of function calls it's supposed to execute. Other values in other registers provide the raw material for the specific DOS function call to process, or narrow how some of the more flexible function calls should act. In this example, the value of 2 in register AH tells DOS to use function call 2 to print one character onto the screen. When you trigger DOS with an INT 21 and it sees a 2 in AH, it looks in the DL register for a number and displays onscreen the ASCII character represented by that number. Printing an ASCII 7 character beeps. As it's used here, the final "RET" will jump control of the system back to COMMAND.COM when the program finishes executing.

Registers are tiny storage areas inside the main CPU chip, and virtually every instruction or slice of data in your computer either passes through these registers or is in some way controlled by what's temporarily stored there. Chips in the Intel 8088 family contain 14 registers, each of which is 16 bits (two bytes) long. Four of these are general purpose, or *scratch-pad* registers: AX, BX, CX, and DX. Each of these four two-byte scratch-pad registers can be divided into high and low bytes. Remember, one byte contains eight bits. Two bytes together form what's called a *word*, so each of these 16-bit registers is actually a word. And each word has high and low halves, the way the decimal number 27 does — in this case the 2 would be the high half since it's actually 2 x 10 (or 20), while the 7 is the low half, since it's actually 7 x 1 (or 7). The number on the left, in the tens column, is always higher, or worth more than, the lower number on the right, in the ones column.

The high bytes are referred to as AH, BH, CH, and DH, and the low bytes as AL, BL, CL, and DL. Each of these high and low registers can store a single byte; the full AX, BX, CX, and CX registers can store two bytes (one word) in a single gulp. If you need to manipulate just one byte, you generally use the high or low registers. If you have to handle two bytes together, you use the full-size registers. The above example used AH to tell DOS which function call you wanted, and DL to store the value of the character you wanted to display.

Four additional segment registers tell the CPU the starting address of four important 64K memory segments: the code segment (CS), data segment (DS), stack segment (SS), and extra segment (ES). Another five registers provide the necessary offsets: the instruction pointer (IP), stack pointer (SP), base pointer (BP), source index (SI) and destination index (DI). The final one, called the *flags* register, maintains the on-off status of 16 individual bits. Processes can change individual bit settings to keep track of events, or refer to the settings changed by other processes or events and act accordingly.

When you initially load DEBUG, it sets the addresses of the CS, DS, ES, and SS segments so they're all located in memory directly after the space taken up by the DEBUG

program itself. It also normally sets the values of the main registers you'll be using —
AX, BX, CX, and DX (as well as some of the others) to zero. If you loaded a file shorter
than 64K bytes from the DOS command line at the same time that you started DEBUG,
DEBUG will set the CX register to reflect the length of this file. If the file is larger than
64K, DEBUG will use both the CX and BX registers to maintain the file length. If you
later load a file using the N (Name) and L (Load) commands, DEBUG will then put the
file's length into the CX register (and the register BX if necessary).

The last four lines of the example above reset the CX register to 7 (since CX is a
two-byte register, this actually set CX to 0007 — the high byte is 00 and the low one 07),
write the file to disk (W), and then quit (Q). When you ask DEBUG to write a file, you
have to specify a filename and a file length. You tell it the filename either by using the
N (Name) command, or by including the name on the command line when you first start
DEBUG (as in C>DEBUG BEEP.COM). You specify the file length by putting a value
in the CX register.

At times you may want DEBUG to process strings of characters. When entering such
strings, you can use pairs of either single quotes (') or double quotes ("). This lets you
include the opposite kind of quote in the string you're entering. So if you entered "The
word 'gub' will appear in quotes" or 'The word "gub" will appear in quotes,' sure enough
both statements will be true. It gets tricky, but you can also use the same type of quotation
marks inside and outside the string, if you double them inside: "This uses the ""double
quote"" mark twice."

The purpose of the DEBUG examples in this chapter is not to teach you every last
thing you have to know about assembly language, but to familiarize you with the kinds
of things DEBUG can do. If you really want to learn about assembly language, purchase
the IBM or Microsoft MASM programs and read the manuals. The programs you'll learn
to create here are all very short and single-minded, and they use a lot of shortcuts and
defaults.

Also, unless you're a serious assembly language programmer, you don't really have
to know every last command in DEBUG. All you need to learn are the basic commands
to create and modify programs. For the purpose of working more productively you don't
have to learn how to use DEBUG as a "controlled testing environment." Commands that
execute programs from within DEBUG, or trace through them one instruction at a time
are extremely helpful to professional programmers, but they're not necessary here. And
virtually all the following examples will concentrate on creating and customizing files
rather than tearing into your disk sectors and fooling around with underlying system
structures.

You can make a permanent record of any DEBUG activity either by redirecting your
efforts to a file, or by *echoing* them simultaneously to your printer. To get a printed copy
of your DEBUG session, turn your printer on, then type Ctrl-P or Ctrl-PrtSc. Anything
that appears onscreen will also be sent to your printer a line at a time, although your
printer may have a hard time trying to reproduce some of the nontext characters that your
screen can handle with ease. To turn this printer echo feature off when you're done, just
type Ctrl-P or Ctrl-PrtSc one more time.

While it's often useful to redirect a DEBUG output to a file, this can be a bit tricky
since you won't be able to see what you're doing. Redirecting output to a file is the

opposite of the script file process mentioned earlier. When you redirect input (such as a script file) into DEBUG, DOS feeds characters from the script file into DEBUG just as if you were typing at the keyboard. When you redirect the output from DEBUG into a file, DOS takes all the characters that would normally show up on your screen and instead reroutes them into a file on your disk. Because DOS will intercept each character before it gets to your monitor, you won't see be able to see what's going on until you finally type Q to quit, press Enter, and return to the main DOS prompt. So if you try redirecting the DEBUG output with the simple command:

```
DEBUG > OUTPUT.FIL
```

you have to know exactly what you want to type, because you'll be flying blind.

A better way to end up with a DEBUG output file on disk is to first step through the exact DEBUG process you want — without worrying about redirection. Write down every keystroke you use, or have a screen-capture utility like *SideKick*'s notepad record your keystrokes for you. Then type all these keystrokes into a script file called DEBUG.SCR (or edit the file *SideKick* created). Remember to insert blank lines in the script file if necessary, and be absolutely sure to press the Enter key at the very end after the final Q.

Then review the DEBUG.SCR file carefully. It should contain all the keystrokes you would normally enter in the particular DEBUG session you want to capture on disk, and nothing else. Put this script file on the same disk as DEBUG and type:

```
DEBUG < DEBUG.SCR > DEBUG.OUT
```

Your disk will churn for a second or two as DOS feeds the DEBUG.SCR keystrokes into DEBUG and then creates a file on your disk called DEBUG.OUT that contains everything DEBUG would have displayed on your screen.

For example, let's say you wanted to see the text parts of the main DOS command processor, COMMAND.COM. These include internal commands, error messages, prompts, etc.

As we've seen, DOS commands come in two flavors — internal and external. External commands are individual programs (with COM or EXE extensions) delivered on your DOS disks. Commands like CHKDSK and SORT are external commands, since you execute them by running programs called CHKDSK.COM and SORT.EXE. However, the instructions for executing commands like DIR and TYPE are internal, since they're actually imbedded inside COMMAND.COM.

When you enter something at the DOS prompt, DOS first looks inside COM-MAND.COM to see if what you typed is an internal command. If not, it tries to find a file with the name you specified ending with COM, then EXE, or finally BAT in the current subdirectory. If it doesn't locate one, it will scan through all the other subdirectories listed in your PATH statement for COM, EXE, or BAT files, in that order. As soon as it finds one it will stop looking and execute it. If it doesn't, it will issue a "Bad command or filename" error message.

So, let's look inside COMMAND.COM. The following example uses DOS version 5.0, but any version 2.0 or later will work the same way. If you are using a DOS version other than 5.0, some of the numbers shown below will be different. And while it assumes you're on drive C:, the process is the same on any drive so long as COMMAND.COM and DEBUG.COM are on a disk in that drive.

First, at the main DOS prompt, start DEBUG and tell it you want to load the COMMAND.COM program into memory:

```
DEBUG COMMAND.COM
```

Then, when you see the DEBUG hyphen prompt, find out how long the program is by typing:

```
RCX
```

DEBUG will respond by printing:

```
CX BAE5
:
```

(The hex number after CX will be different if you're trying this on a version other than DOS 5.0. Note this number, since you'll have to use it shortly.)

Typing RCX (or R CX, or r cx, or rcx) tells DEBUG to display the value currently in register CX and then pause and wait to see if you want to change this value. If you do want to enter a new value, type a hex number immediately after the colon and then press the Enter key. If you don't want to change the value, but just wanted to see what the value was, just press the Enter key without entering a new value.

You could also type just an R by itself, and then press the Enter key. Doing this right after you typed DEBUG COMMAND.COM would print:

```
AX=0000  BX=0000  CX=BAE5  DX=0000  SP=FFFE  BP=0000  SI=0000  DI=0000
DS=1297  ES=1297  SS=1297  CS=1297  IP=0100    NV UP EI PL NZ NA PO NC
33F7:0100 E95D14        JMP      1560
```

Entering R without anything after it will display the contents of all your system's registers, the state of all its flags, and the actual instruction that will be executed next. In the above display, the registers are the 13 blocks of characters with equals signs in the middle, the flags are the eight pairs of letters, and the bottom line indicates that the JMP 0E30 instruction at address 100 is the next one to execute. For the purpose of this example, all you need is the value in register CX. The third number in the top row tells you this value is BAE5.

Once you learn the file's length, have DEBUG search all the way through the COMMAND.COM file that's currently loaded in memory for the string "Batch." COMMAND.COM stores its main messages, commands, and prompts in a lump near the very end of the file. The first bit of text stored there is a "Batch file missing" error message, so if you find the address of this particular message you can jump to this address and browse through all the text that follows.

DEBUG needs to know where it should start and stop searching for something (in this case the "Batch" string). You can specify the search parameters one of two ways. Either give DEBUG explicit starting and stopping addresses, or tell it the starting address and then provide a number representing how many bytes after this address DEBUG should scan through.

The starting address is simple; DEBUG always loads COM files so they start at memory offset 100 (remember, all these numbers are in hex, not decimal). Since you want to search a file from beginning to end that is BAE5 bytes long, starting at 0100, the ending address is BBE5. So you would specify explicit starting and stopping addresses by typing:

```
-S 100 BBE5 "Batch"
```

In the procedure above, you snooped inside the R register to learn how long the COMMAND.COM file was. DOS version 5.0 DEBUG will report BAE5; this number will be different if you're using a different version of DOS. But notice that while the length of the file is BAE5 bytes, you have to enter BBE5 as the explicit ending address. Why?

The number BBE5 is 100 higher than the actual file length BAE5. DEBUG normally loads files at address 100, not at address 0 (unless they're EXE files), and this moves all the addresses in the file up by 100. If you want to look at the first two bytes in a file — bytes 0 and 1 — you actually have to tell DEBUG to look at the contents of addresses 100 and 101.

The first byte in the file is loaded into address 100, the second byte at address 101, and the BAE5th byte at BBE5. So you have to add 100 to the length of the file if you want DEBUG to search all the way through to the last byte loaded in memory. To do this, just add 1 to the third hex digit over from the right. The third digit from the right in this example is 2, so you add 1 to it and it becomes 3.

The process of adding 100 like this is trivial unless the third digit over is hex F. In the decimal number system, if you add:

```
  1
+ 9
```

you end up with a 0 in the column that has the 9 in it, and you carry a 1 over to the column immediately to its left. In the hexadecimal number system, if you add:

```
  1
+ F
```

you end up with a 0 in the column that has the F in it, and you carry a 1 over to the column immediately to its left. If DEBUG had reported a file length of 1111, adding 100 to it would give you 1211. But if the file length were 1F11, adding 100 to it would produce

2011. And if the file length were 9F11, adding 100 would yield A011. Don't mix hex and decimal numbers when in DEBUG; be careful to work exclusively in hex.

If you feel squeamish about adding hex numbers, let DEBUG do it for you. If you wanted to add 100 to BAE5, all you have to do is make sure you see the DEBUG hyphen prompt and then type:

```
H BAE5 100
```

DEBUG will respond by printing:

```
BBE5   B9E5
```

The first number (BBE5, the one you're looking for) is the sum of BAE5 + 100. The second number (B9E5) is the difference of BAE5 - 100. You don't need to use the subtraction feature of this H (hex math) command here, but if you ever do, make sure you enter the numbers in the proper order. Adding numbers in either order will produce the same result (3 + 5 and 5 + 3 will both yield 8). But this even-handedness doesn't apply to subtraction; 3 - 5 is definitely not the same as 5 - 3.

DEBUG makes it even easier to specify a search range. All you really have to do is enter the starting address and the number of bytes to search. Since you want to scan through the entire COMMAND.COM file, the number of bytes to search is equal to the length of the file. So instead of entering explicit starting and stopping addresses, you could issue a variation of the search command used earlier:

```
-S 100 L BAE5 "Batch"
```

This command tells DEBUG to start a search for the string "Batch" at address 100 and continue searching for a length of BAE5 bytes. You'll get the same results whether you use an "L" like this to specify the search length, or instead specify the explicit starting and stopping addresses. But this way you don't have to do any hex math.

DEBUG will search through the file and report all occurrences of the "Batch" string. Since searches are case sensitive, DEBUG will ignore any "batch" or "BATCH" strings it may find. It's important in this example to specify all lowercase letters except for the initial capital B, since COMMAND.COM does indeed contain other "batch" strings that you don't want to examine.

If you had wanted DEBUG to locate every occurrence of this word including all-lowercase versions ("batch") as well as lowercase versions with initial capital letters ("Batch") you could have changed the search command to:

```
-S 100 L BAE5 "atch"
```

or:

```
-S 100 BBE5 "atch"
```

Of course, this would also find words like patch, or snatch, or potlatch if any existed in the file you were scanning.

But since you really wanted DEBUG to look for just the string "Batch" it will find just one occurrence:

```
1359:8191
```

The number to the left (in this case 1359) is the segment address, and it will vary from system to system depending on how much memory your computer has and what else you currently have loaded in memory. Manuals sometimes replace the varying segment addresses with a row of "xxxx" characters, so if you see something that looks like:

```
xxxx:0A51
xxxx:4DCA
xxxx:4DF4
```

all it really means it that any four-digit hex number can appear where the xxxx characters are.

Jot down the offset address — the rightmost four bytes, or 8191 — because you'll need it for the next process.

To make sure you've found the proper string, use the DEBUG Display (D) command. You can use the same basic syntax rules for the Display command that you used with the search command. The display range can either be an explicit starting and stopping address, or a starting address and a length of bytes for DEBUG to display. Since the word "Batch" is five characters long, both of the following commands will display the string at the offset address the above search command located:

```
D 8191 8195
```

or:

```
D 8191 L 5
```

The top command first lists the starting address and then the stopping address. Note that the stopping address is the starting address + 4, not the starting address + 5. This is because you want DEBUG to display the value of the byte at address 8191 (the "B" in "Batch") plus the next four characters ("atch"). Again, if you're a little shaky on hex math, you can use the DEBUG H command to add the two numbers together for you.

The bottom command first lists the starting address and then tells DEBUG to display five bytes starting with that address. In this case you specify five rather than four, since you're asking DEBUG to display a total of five bytes.

Either way, you'll see something like:

```
1359:8190          42 61 74 63 68          Batch
```

Every DEBUG D display has three parts. The first part, at the lefthand edge of your screen, is the address of the memory that DEBUG is displaying, in SSSS:OOOO segment:offset format. The second, in the middle of your screen, are the individual values of the chunk of memory DEBUG is displaying, in hexadecimal notation. The third, at the righthand edge of your screen, is the ASCII representation of what's in memory at the addresses you specified. To avoid cluttering up this part of the display with things like happy faces, musical notes, or Greek and math characters, DEBUG will print a period (.) when it sees any value below hex 20 (decimal 32) or above hex 7E (decimal 126).

DEBUG will often display what looks like random letters, numbers, and punctuation in the rightmost third of the screen. These are just artifacts, and don't mean anything. DEBUG isn't smart enough to know what parts of a program are text that should be displayed and what parts are actually meachine-level instructions that shouldn't be displayed. Whenever it sees a hex value of 50 (decimal 80), for instance, DEBUG will display a "P." If this value of 50 happens to be in a message such as "Path not found" you'll be glad it did. But the 50 could just as easily have been part of an address or value in a gut-level instruction.

For instance, if the internal code of a program moved a value of 5000 into register AX (with the command MOV AX,5000), the actual machine-level version of this instruction would be:

```
B80050
```

DEBUG would display the B8 and the 00 as periods, since B8 is above hex 7E and 00 is below hex 20. But it would display the 50 in the righthand third of the screen as a P. In fact, one particular assembly language command (PUSH AX) is represented in machine-level code as the single value:

```
50
```

which would show up in a DEBUG display as a solitary P.

Artifacts like these occur because your system has a small, 256-unit vocabulary. Every message, prompt, command, instruction, and address has to be made up of single-byte values between 0 and 255. Your CPU is smart enough to sort it all out when it processes the stream of bytes, but DEBUG isn't. So ignore these random characters in DEBUG displays.

You can't use the Search (S) command without specifying an address range and something to search for. So typing S by itself at the DEBUG prompt would be meaningless, and would only generate an error message. But you can (and will frequently want to) issue a Display (D) command on a line by itself.

If you start DEBUG, load COMMAND.COM into it, then type D by itself and press Enter, DEBUG will display the first 128 bytes of the file, from address 100 through address 17F. Each subsequent time you type D without any parameters after it and press Enter, DEBUG will display the next 128 bytes in memory immediately following the previous block. If you keep pressing just D and then Enter enough times — 512 to be exact — you'll work all the way to the end of the current segment and start over again at the beginning of the segment.

DEBUG displays such blocks of memory information in a grid 16 bytes wide, and either eight or nine rows tall. (If you specify a starting address at the beginning of a paragraph — one that ends in a 0 such as 100 or 3D0 — you'll see a tidy block of bytes eight rows high. But if you specify any other address DEBUG will stagger the display into a ninth row.) So if you type the following two lines to display the beginning of COMMAND.COM version 5.0:

```
C>DEBUG COMMAND.COM
-D
```

(don't type the DOS C prompt or the DEBUG — prompt; these are just included to illustrate what your screen should look like) you'll see:

```
1359:0100  E9 5D 14 00 78 14 00 00-B7 0E 00 00 75 0D 00 00   .]..x.......u...
1359:0110  85 11 00 00 00 00 00 00-00 00 00 00 00 00 00 00   ................
1359:0120  00 00 00 00 00 00 00 00-00 00 00 00 00 00 00 00   ................
1359:0130  00 00 00 00 00 FB E8 64-00 1E 0E 2E FF 2E 04 01   .......d........
1359:0140  FB E8 59 00 1E 0E 2E FF-2E 08 01 FB E8 4E 00 1E   ..Y..........N..
1359:0150  0E 2E FF 2E 0C 01 FB E8-43 00 1E 0E 2E FF 2E 10   ........C.......
1359:0160  01 E8 39 00 1E 0E 2E FF-2E 14 01 E8 2F 00 1E 0E   ..9........./...
1359:0170  2E FF 2E 18 01 E8 25 00-1E 0E 2E FF 2E 1C 01 E8   ......%.........
```

Again, if you try this on your own DOS 5.0 version of COMMAND.COM the only difference will be the 1359 segment at the left edge of the display.

Each row of 16 bytes is called a paragraph. DEBUG doesn't label the individual columns, but if it did, you'd see something like:

```
1359:0100  E9 5D 14 00 78 14 00 00-B7 0E 00 00 75 0D 00 00   .]..x.......u...
1359:0110  85 11 00 00 00 00 00 00-00 00 00 00 00 00 00 00   ................
```

It's simple to find a value at a particular address. First, locate the paragraph (the row) with the offset address at or just below the precise address you're seeking. Then count over from left to right one byte at a time. As you can see from the column labels above, the address of the first byte in each paragraph ends with 0, the second byte with 1, the third with 2, and the last (16th) byte with F. (Remember, these labels don't actually appear in DEBUG displays. Neither do the pairs of xx characters below; they simply mean that here you should ignore everything marked xx.) In the above example the value at address 100 is E9 since this is the number at the intersection of the row starting with 0100 and the column with the label of 0:

```
1359:0100  E9 xx xx xx xx xx xx xx-xx xx xx xx xx xx xx xx   .]..x.......u...
1359:0110  xx xx xx xx xx xx xx xx-xx xx xx xx xx xx xx xx   ................
```

The value at address 112 is 00, since this number appears at the intersection of the row beginning 110 and the column with the label 2:

```
1359:0100  xx xx xx xx xx xx xx xx-xx xx xx xx xx xx xx xx   .]..x.......u...
1359:0110  xx xx 00 xx xx xx xx xx-xx xx xx xx xx xx xx xx   ................
```

While DEBUG doesn't show column labels, it does make the process of counting over somewhat easier by putting a hyphen halfway across the display, between columns 7 and 8. So if you want to see the value at an address ending with a 7, find the appropriate row and look at the number directly to the left of the hyphen. The value at 107 is 00:

```
1359:0100  xx xx xx xx xx xx xx 00-xx xx xx xx xx xx xx xx   .]..x.......u...
1359:0110  xx xx xx xx xx xx xx xx-xx xx xx xx xx xx xx xx   ................
```

Once you've used the D command to verify that the "Batch" search address is correct, start displaying the next few 128-byte blocks of memory following that address. Your displays will be neater if you round the address down to an even paragraph address. To do this just replace the rightmost digit with a 0.

Since the Search command found the "Batch" string at address 8191, replace the rightmost 1 with a 0 and enter the command:

```
D 8190
```

You should see a chunk of memory that contains DOS error messages:

```
1359:8190  14 42 61 74 63 68 20 66-69 6C 65 20 6D 69 73 73   .Batch file miss
1359:81A0  69 6E 67 0D 0A 1F 0D 0A-49 6E 73 65 72 74 20 64   ing.....Insert d
1359:81B0  69 73 6B 20 77 69 74 68-20 62 61 74 63 68 20 66   isk with batch f
1359:81C0  69 6C 65 0D 0A 1A 42 61-64 20 63 6F 6D 6D 61 6E   ile...Bad comman
1359:81D0  64 20 6F 72 20 66 69 6C-65 20 6E 61 6D 65 0D 0A   d or file name..
1359:81E0  10 41 63 63 65 73 73 20-64 65 6E 69 65 64 20 0D   .Access denied .
1359:81F0  0A 29 43 6F 6E 74 65 6E-74 20 6F 66 20 64 65 73   .)Content of des
1359:8200  74 69 6E 61 74 69 6F 6E-20 6C 6F 73 74 20 62 65   tination lost be
```

Ignore the segment addresses, which will be different on your system. Keeping pressing just D and the Enter key a few times and you'll see more error messages:

```
1359:8210  66 6F 72 65 20 63 6F 70-79 0D 0A 24 49 6E 76 61   fore copy..$Inva
1359:8220  6C 69 64 20 66 69 6C 65-6E 61 6D 65 20 6F 72 20   lid filename or
1359:8230  66 69 6C 65 20 6E 6F 74-20 66 6F 75 6E 64 0D 0A   file not found..
1359:8240  13 25 31 20 66 69 6C 65-28 73 29 20 63 6F 70 69   .%1 file(s) copi
1359:8250  65 64 0D 0A 0B 25 31 20-66 69 6C 65 28 73 29 20   ed...%1 file(s)
1359:8260  1D 49 6E 76 61 6C 69 64-20 64 72 69 76 65 20 73   .Invalid drive s
1359:8270  70 65 63 69 66 69 63 61-74 69 6F 6E 0D 0A 26 43   pecification..&C
1359:8280  6F 64 65 20 70 61 67 65-20 25 31 20 6E 6F 74 20   ode page %1 not
```

and then, later, some prompts, and finally a list of internal DOS commands:

```
1359:A8C0  26 24 9D 1E 00 03 4E 4F-54 EF 0A 0A 45 52 52 4F   &$....NOT...ERRO
1359:A8D0  52 4C 45 56 45 4C B2 0B-05 45 58 49 53 54 46 0B   RLEVEL...EXISTF.
1359:A8E0  00 03 44 49 52 03 8D 10-D2 84 04 43 41 4C 4C 02   ..DIR......CALL.
1359:A8F0  27 0C 34 85 04 43 48 43-50 02 0F 21 A2 84 06 52   '.4..CHCP..!...R
1359:A900  45 4E 41 4D 45 03 DF 1A-0E 85 03 52 45 4E 03 DF   ENAME......REN..
1359:A910  1A 0E 85 05 45 52 41 53-45 03 57 1A CA 84 03 44   ....ERASE.W....D
1359:A920  45 4C 03 57 1A CA 84 04-54 59 50 45 03 8D 1B 24   EL.W....TYPE...$
1359:A930  85 03 52 45 4D 06 04 01-3A 85 04 43 4F 50 59 03   ..REM...:..COPY.

1359:A940  C3 38 B4 84 05 50 41 55-53 45 06 4A 1A 3E 85 04   .8...PAUSE.J...
1359:A950  44 41 54 45 02 C4 2F C4-84 04 54 49 4D 45 02 2D   DATE../...TIME.-
1359:A960  30 1E 85 03 56 45 52 02-B7 1D 28 85 03 56 4F 4C   0...VER...(..VOL
1359:A970  03 BB 1C 30 85 02 43 44-03 77 25 A8 84 05 43 48   ...0.CD.w%...CH
1359:A980  44 49 52 03 77 25 A8 84-02 4D 44 03 E2 25 EA 84   DIR.w%...MD..%..
1359:A990  05 4D 4B 44 49 52 03 E2-25 EA 84 02 52 44 03 56   .MKDIR..%...RD.V
1359:A9A0  26 0A 85 05 52 4D 44 49-52 03 56 26 0A 85 05 42   &...RMDIR.V&...B
1359:A9B0  52 45 41 4B 02 BC 37 9E-84 06 56 45 52 49 46 59   REAK..7...VERIFY

1359:A9C0  02 FF 37 2C 85 03 53 45-54 06 D7 22 16 85 06 50   ..7,..SET..".."..P
1359:A9D0  52 4F 4D 50 54 06 BD 22-F6 84 04 50 41 54 48 02   ROMPT..".."..PATH.
1359:A9E0  1F 1F EE 84 04 45 58 49-54 00 19 22 E6 84 04 43   .....EXIT..".."..C
1359:A9F0  54 54 59 03 6B 20 C0 84-04 45 43 48 4F 06 82 37   TTY.k ...ECHO..7
1359:AA00  42 85 04 47 4F 54 4F 06-5B 0C 48 85 05 53 48 49   B..GOTO.[.H..SHI
1359:AA10  46 54 02 E0 0B 4E 85 02-49 46 06 8F 0A 52 85 03   FT...N..IF...R..
1359:AA20  46 4F 52 06 24 0F 62 85-03 43 4C 53 00 CB 1F B0   FOR.$.b..CLS....
1359:AA30  84 08 54 52 55 45 4E 41-4D 45 03 97 21 6C 85 08   ..TRUENAME..!l..

1359:AA40  4C 4F 41 44 48 49 47 48-02 27 59 70 85 02 4C 48   LOADHIGH.'Yp..LH
1359:AA50  02 27 59 70 85 00 2E 43-4F 4D 2E 45 58 45 2E 42   .'Yp...COM.EXE.B
1359:AA60  41 54 3F 56 42 41 50 57-52 48 53 76 44 41 4E 45   AT?VBAPWRHSvDANE
1359:AA70  44 53 47 00 20 00 00 00-00 00 02 01 00 A5 98 56   DSG. .........V
1359:AA80  87 00 01 03 01 00 A5 98-56 87 00 01 02 01 00 A5   .......V.......
1359:AA90  98 56 87 00 00 00 02 00-A5 98 56 87 01 2F 50 00   .V........V../P.
1359:AAA0  83 87 00 00 01 89 87 00-00 01 20 02 00 A5 98 92   .......... .....
1359:AAB0  87 00 03 00 00 02 00 9C-87 66 9F 87 4F 4E 00 4F   .........f..ON.O
```

As you can see, the interesting text parts of DOS 5.0 COMMAND.COM start at the even paragraph address 8190 and end at address AA4F. Now you can create a script file called DEBUG.SCR that contains the commands:

```
D 8190 AA4F
Q
```

Be sure to press the Enter key after the final Q. Put this DEBUG.SCR script file on the same disk as DEBUG.COM and type:

```
DEBUG COMMAND.COM < DEBUG.SCR > DEBUG.OUT
```

Since this process creates a file, make sure you have room on your disk for a new file and that if you're using a floppy disk the write-protect notch isn't covered. When DOS finishes redirecting the files in and out of DEBUG it will simply print a new DOS prompt onscreen. It won't tell you that it created a new file, but you can verify that it did by typing:

```
DIR DEBUG.OUT
```

You'll see something like:

```
DEBUG     OUT      9733  10-14-90   4:52p
```

You can examine this file with your word processor, or with the EDLIN text editor on your DOS disk. Or you could simply type:

```
MORE < DEBUG.OUT
```

This command will redirect the DEBUG.OUT output file into MORE.COM, which will display a screenful of the file at a time. You can either type any character key to see each additional screenful, or press Ctrl-Break or Ctrl-C to abort the display and return to the DOS prompt.

Notice that the command:

```
DEBUG COMMAND.COM < DEBUG.SCR > DEBUG.OUT
  (1)        (2)         (3)        (4)
```

had four parts. The first part started running DEBUG. The second had DEBUG load COMMAND.COM into memory. The third provided the necessary DEBUG Display and Quit commands, and the fourth told DOS to send the output to a file rather than to the screen.

You could remove the second step and shorten the process a bit, by changing the DEBUG.SCR file. Add two lines to the beginning and call this new file DEBUGNEW.SCR:

```
N COMMAND.COM
L
D 8190 AA4F
Q
```

Then then issue the shorter command:

```
DEBUG < DEBUGNEW.SCR > DEBUG.OUT
```

The N (Name) command in the first line of DEBUGNEW.SCR tells DEBUG that a future Write or Load command will apply to the file whose name follows. The L (Load) command on the second line loads that file into memory just as if you had typed it in after the word DEBUG at the DOS prompt.

Be careful when dealing with files that end in EXE. Both DOS and DEBUG have to shuffle things around a bit in memory when working with EXE files. You'll notice a difference right away if you load one (try the DOS SORT.EXE file, for instance) into DEBUG and type D. Instead of starting the display at address 100, DEBUG will begin at address 0. And if you try to change the file and write it back to disk, DEBUG won't let you.

It is possible to change the contents of an EXE file with DEBUG. If you read about an interesting patch for an EXE file, copy the file and give the copy an extension other than EXE, such as XXX. (Put the original safely away on another disk or in another subdirectory so you don't accidentally write over it later.) Then load this copy into DEBUG, and treat it like any other file. After you make the changes in the file with the XXX extension, write them to disk and quit. When you're back at the main DOS prompt, make sure you put the original EXE file on another disk or in another subdirectory, and use the RENAME (or REN) command to change the extension from XXX to EXE. Then run it to check your changes. Finally, decide whether you want to use the newer version or the older version of the program — don't keep two similarly named versions of a file on any hard disk. If you prefer the older version, erase the newly changed one. If you like the new, patched version better, rename the old one by giving it an OLD suffix, or copy it to an archive floppy disk and make sure it's gone from your hard disk.

As was shown earlier with the BEEP.COM program, DEBUG makes it a snap to create small programs. All BEEP.COM really does is use DOS function call 2 to display a single character onscreen. It just so happens that printing this ASCII 7 character onscreen makes your system beep.

But printing one character isn't very dramatic. Fortunately, it's nearly as easy to print a whole screenful. You wouldn't actually want to fill the entire screen, since the DOS prompt that appears after such a program finishes running will scroll some of the lines off the top. So we'll settle for 23 lines. And we'll fill these lines with hearts.

One of the hallmarks of topnotch programming these days is the ability to make screens "pop." It's much more dramatic to have a screenful of information flash instantaneously onto your screen than to watch it flicker slowly down the glass a line at a time. However, speedy displays and DOS don't mix. Virtually all the fast screen techniques involve low-level BIOS or memory-shuffling routines. The HEART.COM program below is designed to extend the DOS-based BEEP.COM example, not break any speed limits. Type in the following HEART.SCR script file:

```
N HEART.COM
A
MOV CX,730     ; repeat 1,840 times (23 lines x 80 chars)
MOV DL,3       ; ASCII 3 is a heart character
MOV AH,2       ; DOS "display output" function
INT 21         ; gets DOS rolling
LOOP 107       ; jumps back a line 1,839 times
RET

RCX
C
W
Q
```

(If you don't have a word processor or EDLIN available, you can create this file in DOS by adding a line at the very top that says:

```
COPY CON HEART.SCR
```

Then type the above script, omitting the comments after the semicolons and the semicolons themselves. When you're all done, press the Enter key an extra time, then press the F6 function key, then Enter again.)

Once you've created the script file, put it on the same disk as DEBUG and type:

```
DEBUG < HEART.SCR
```

This will create a slightly enhanced version of the BEEP.COM file called HEART.COM. It prints a heart-shaped character instead of a character that beeps, and does it 1,840 times (23 rows x 80 characters per row). Run it and 92 percent of your screen will fill up with hearts. Put it in someone's AUTOEXEC.BAT file on Valentine's Day.

(Okay, nobody likes slow programs. If you really want to see how must faster it can be to use BIOS services than DOS routines, type in the following script:

```
N FILLFAST.COM
E 100 B4 02 BA 00 00 B7 00 CD 10 B4 08 CD 10 88 E7 B8
E 110 00 06 B9 00 00 BA 4F 18 CD 10 B4 02 BA 00 00 B7
E 120 00 CD 10 B9 30 07 B8 03 0A B7 00 CD 10 B4 02 BA
E 130 00 17 B7 00 CD 10 C3
RCX
37
W
Q
```

This program, FILLFAST, reads the attribute in the upper lefthand corner of the screen and fills most of the screen instantly with hearts in that color.)

Let's look at the original HEART.COM program closely to see what's going on. To do this, use DEBUG's U (Unassemble) command. Get the ball rolling by typing:

```
DEBUG HEART.COM
```

When you see the familiar DEBUG prompt, find out how long the file is by typing:

```
RCX
```

and pressing the Enter key twice. Or, cheat by looking at the line in the HEART.SCR script between RCX and W. Either way, you'll figure out that it's 0C bytes (decimal 12) in length.

As with most of DEBUG, you could issue an Unassemble command using one of two syntaxes. The easy way is entering the starting address and the length:

```
U 100 L C
```

This looks cryptic, but it simply means "try to convert the 12 (hex C) bytes of machine-level code starting at memory offset 100 into recognizable assembly language commands." Finally, type Q to quit and press Enter. The whole process look like:

```
C>DEBUG HEART.COM
-RCX
CX 000C
:
-U 100 L C
33F7:0100 B93007        MOV     CX,0730
33F7:0103 B203          MOV     DL,03
33F7:0105 B402          MOV     AH,02
33F7:0107 CD21          INT     21
33F7:0109 E2FC          LOOP    0107
33F7:010B C3            RET
-Q
```

(Ignore the 33F7 segment address, as always.) The harder way to issue the Unassemble command is to enter explicit starting and stopping addresses. The starting address is easy since DEBUG loads all COM files at offset 100. And since the file is 0C bytes long, the ending address is starting address + length - 1, or:

```
100 + C - 1 = 10B
```

Technically you don't have to subtract the 1, since all leaving it in will do is stretch out the display one extra line. But the file starts at address 100, not address 101. The first byte of the file is at address 100, the second at 101, the third at 102, and the last (12th) at address 10B. So the command:

```
U 100 10B
```

would have produced the same display as U 100 L C.

You may have noticed that the display produced by the U command is almost identical to the HEART.SCR script file that created it. The Unassemble command usually produces a reasonable facsimile of the original, although since certain assembler programs turn slightly different assembly language instructions into the same machine-level code, DEBUG may not be able to turn things back exactly the way they were. But it'll almost always be close enough.

DEBUG's U display does provide something very useful that wasn't in the script — the addresses of each instruction. In this case you really need to have the addresses handy to see what's going on.

The middle of both the BEEP.COM and HEART.COM programs are pretty much the same:

```
BEEP.COM              HEART.COM
     .                    .
     .                    .
     .                    .
MOV DL,7              MOV DL,3
MOV AH,2              MOV AH,2
INT 21               INT 21
     .                    .
     .                    .
     .                    .
```

Both programs use the DOS "display output" function call 2, which looks at the value in the DL register and prints the ASCII character with that value onscreen. With BEEP.COM the value here is 7; with HEART.COM it's 3. And both programs use the RET instruction to jump control back to COMMAND.COM when they're finishing executing.

But HEART.COM adds two additional lines that work hand in hand:

```
MOV CX,730
     .
     .
     .
LOOP 107
```

If you're handy with BASIC, the MOV CX and LOOP instructions are similar to BASIC's FOR...NEXT commands. Both tell your program to repeat a process a certain number of times. The BASIC version of HEART.COM would look something like:

```
100 FOR A=1 TO 1840
110 PRINT CHR$(3);
120 NEXT A
130 SYSTEM
```

In assembly language you can specify how many times you want something to repeat by moving that number into the CX register. Filling 23 lines, each 80 characters long, means printing the heart character 1,840 times (730 in hex). The first time the HEART.COM program executes, it stuffs this hex 730 value into CX, displays the ASCII 3 character, and then executes the LOOP 107 instruction. At this point LOOP does two things. First, it subtracts 1 from the number in the CX register, turning the original 730 into 72F (since hex 730 - 1 = 72F). Then it checks to see if this number is equal to 0 (after subtracting 1 from the current value enough times it will be). Since 72F is greater than 0, LOOP tells the program to loop back to the address specified after the word LOOP — offset 107.

As you can see from the unassembled listing, address 107 contains the instruction INT 21, which tells DOS to execute a function call again. Nothing has changed in any of the registers, so DOS looks in register AH, sees the 2 that was there earlier, and starts executing the same "display output" function call 2. It looks in register DL to see which character to display, finds the 3 that was there before, and prints a character 3 heart. Then it reaches the LOOP instruction once more, reduces the value in the CX register by 1 from 72F to 72E, sees that this number is not yet equal to 0, and loops back to address 107.

After 1,839 loops the value in the CX register will be 1. This time (after printing the 1,840th heart), when the program hits the LOOP instruction, LOOP will subtract 1, check and see that the value in the CX register is finally 0, and end the looping process. The program will have its first opportunity to execute the instruction on the line following the LOOP 107; each previous time LOOP jumped it back to address 107. Since this instruction is RET, the program finishes running and hands control back to COM-MAND.COM.

But this program gets boring after you run it a few times. So to spice it up, change the character it prints. If you like music, you might want to see a screen full of notes. All you have to do is change the value in the DL register from 3 to E (decimal 14). You can change this value one of two ways. But first you have to figure out where in memory the value is. By looking at the Unassemble listing you can spot it in a second:

```
33F7:0103 B203          MOV     DL,03
```

The Unassemble listing is made up of three parts. The lefthand column contains the address of the instruction in memory, in segment:offset form. (Yes, ignore the 33F7 segment address. But jot down the 103 offset address.) Immediately after the address is the second part of the listing — a hexadecimal representation of the actual machine-level code that puts the CPU through its paces. In this case it's B203. B2 is shorthand that tells the CPU to move a value into the DL register. The 03 is the value it moves. At the right edge of the listing is DEBUG's best guess at what the programmer's original assembly language instruction was.

Each address in memory contains a single byte that DEBUG displays as a two-digit hex number (it pads a single digit value like A with a 0, turning it into 0A). The B203 machine-level code actually represents two bytes, B2 and 03. Since the two-byte B203 code begins at offset 103, the actual hex value at address 103 is B2. The address of the 03 value is 104.

So to change the HEART.COM program so it displays musical notes instead of hearts, all you really have to do is put a value of 0E at address 104, and then use the Write command to make the change stick. You'll probably also want to give the file a new name like MUSIC.COM or NOTE.COM.

The easiest way to do this is to use the E (Enter) command (although you could also manage with the somewhat similar F (Fill) command). You can use the Enter command in expert or nervous mode. In expert mode you enter the address and the new value blindly at the same time and then write the changed file to disk. In nervous mode you first enter just the address and have DEBUG report what's there before you make the change. If you see a value there that tells you you're at the wrong address, you just press the Enter key to cancel the command and return to the DEBUG prompt.

Here's what the process would look like in expert mode, assuming you're absolutely sure the value you want changed is at address 104, and assuming you want to save the new file as MUSIC.COM:

```
C>DEBUG HEART.COM
-E 104 0E
-N MUSIC.COM
-W
Writing 000C bytes
-Q
```

You would type everything shown except the C and - prompts and the "Writing 000C bytes" message. And you could enter the new value after the 104 as E instead of 0E if you liked.

Because you specified a new name with the N command, DEBUG will create a brand new file called MUSIC.COM the same length as the HEART.COM program you started out with, and otherwise identical except for the one change at address 104. It won't alter the original HEART.COM program; all it did was borrow HEART.COM's code. You'll end up with two programs on your disk, HEART.COM and MUSIC.COM.

If you're the cautious type, you'll probably want to use the nervous mode. Type DEBUG HEART.COM to get the ball rolling, and when you see the DEBUG - prompt, just type:

```
E 104
```

and press the Enter key. When you specify an address after the E command but not a new value, DEBUG displays the address and the value that's currently there and then prints a period (.). It parks the cursor directly to the right of the period, ready for you to enter a new value that will replace the existing one:

```
33F7:0104   03._
```

If you're satisfied that this is where you want to make the change, just type in the new value and press Enter. If you realize you're at the wrong address, you can press Enter without putting in a new value, to abort the process.

If you do type in a new value at this point and then lock it in by pressing the Enter key, you can check to make sure you entered the correct number at the correct address by pressing F3. DEBUG uses the same function key tricks as DOS and EDLIN. So whenever you hit the F3 key, DEBUG will type in the previous command for you automatically. If you did enter a new value, pressing the F3 key will display the address and the new value, and a period, and sit there waiting to see if you want to change it again. Since you probably don't, just tap the Enter key and you'll be right back at the DEBUG prompt.

If you entered the new value in nervous mode, and then pressed F3 to check on your handiwork, the screen would look like this:

```
C>DEBUG HEART.COM
-E 104
33F7:0104   03.0E
-E 104
33F7:0104   0E.
-N MUSIC.COM
-W
Writing 000C bytes
-Q
```

The E command is actually far more flexible than these simple changes indicate. The following few examples are just dummies; don't try typing them in since they won't do anything except illustrate the proper E command syntax.

You can use E to enter a new string of characters:

```
E 4D3 "This is a test"
```

Or you can enter a series of bytes in hex notation:

```
E A27 41 7C 3C 3E 24 28 29 29
```

Or you can mix strings and bytes:

```
E 2F0 41 7C "A test" 3C 3E 24 28 29 29
```

If you use the E command in nervous mode (okay, it's not actually called nervous mode) instead of working a single byte at a time, you can move forward and backward through your entire file by pressing the space bar or the minus key. Each time you tap on the space bar DEBUG will print the value of the next higher address onscreen and skip to it. When it has printed eight values onscreen it will jump down to the next line and start to print another eight. If you hit either of the minus keys, DEBUG will start marching in the other direction and print the next lower address onscreen, one to a line. (If you lean on the space bar or minus key long enough, you'll reach the top or bottom of the segment and DEBUG will cycle through the entire segment again.)

To try scanning forward and then backward through the NOTE.COM file, load it into DEBUG with the command:

```
DEBUG NOTE.COM
```

and then type:

```
E 100
```

to get the ball rolling. Then start tapping on the space bar and minus keys to navigate your way through. The following example steps all the way through the 12-byte file from front to back (by pressing the space bar 11 times) and then from back to front (by hitting the minus key 11 times):

```
-E 100
33F7:0100  B9.    30.    07.    B2.    0E.    B4.
02.    CD.
33F7:0108  21.    E2.    FC.    C3.-
33F7:010A  FC.-
33F7:0109  E2.-
33F7:0108  21.-
33F7:0107  CD.-
33F7:0106  02.-
etc.
```

When you're all done, press the Enter key by itself, or Ctrl-Break or Ctrl-C to return to the DEBUG prompt.

DEBUG's Fill (F) command is especially handy for replacing a large chunk of memory with one repeating character. If you wanted to put a 0 in every memory address from offset 100 to offset D000 — nearly 53,000 (decimal) zeros — you could do it instantly with the command:

```
F 100 D000 0
```

You could also use the Fill command to change the one value at address 104 so the program displays a musical note rather than a heart. The command:

```
F 104 L 1 0E
```

would do it. This tells DEBUG to start at address 104 and fill a range of memory 1 byte long with the value 0E.

DEBUG provides another way to change BEEP.COM. When you originally created the file you used a script file that turned on DEBUG's mini-assembler with an A command and then fed assembly language instructions (such as MOV AH,2 and INT 21) into it. You can use the A command to make selective patches as well. The assembly language instruction that tells the DOS "display output" function call 2 which character to display is:

```
33F7:0103 B203              MOV      DL,03
```

As you can see from the Unassemble (U) listing, this instruction is located at address 103 in memory. To insert one or more new assembly language instructions in memory, enter the A command followed by the address where the new instructions will start, and then enter the new lines. When you're done, just press the Enter key by itself to exit the mini-assembler and return to the DEBUG prompt. Finally, use the Unassemble command to check your work. To turn HEART.COM into MUSIC.COM using this technique, first Unassemble the code to see which address to alter, then enter the A command along with this address to make the change, then use Unassemble again to check your typing. Enter the new name (with N), write the new file to disk (with W), and quit (Q). The whole process would look like:

```
C>DEBUG HEART.COM
-U 100 L C
33F7:0100 B93007            MOV      CX,0730
33F7:0103 B203              MOV      DL,03
33F7:0105 B402              MOV      AH,02
33F7:0107 CD21              INT      21
33F7:0109 E2FC              LOOP     0107
33F7:010B C3                RET
-A 103
33F7:0103 MOV DL,0E
33F7:0105
-U 100 L C
33F7:0100 B93007            MOV      CX,0730
33F7:0103 B20E              MOV      DL,0E
33F7:0105 B402              MOV      AH,02
33F7:0107 CD21              INT      21
33F7:0109 E2FC              LOOP     0107
33F7:010B C3                RET
-N MUSIC.COM
-W
 Writing 000C bytes
-Q
```

If you're not crazy about hearts or notes, you can substitute just about any character at address 104. For an interesting effect, try values B0, B1, or B2 (which produce interesting textures), or F8, F9, or FA, which will fill your screen with dot patterns. The IBM character set has some other interesting possibilities as well. Once you've created HEART.COM, type in the following PICTURE.SCR script file to see some of the possibilities:

```
N HEART.COM
L
E 104 B0
N PATTERN1.COM
W
E 104 B1
N PATTERN2.COM
W
E 104 B2
N PATTERN3.COM
W
E 104 F8
N DOT1.COM
W
E 104 F9
N DOT2.COM
W
E 104 FA
N DOT3.COM
W
E 104 0B
N MAN.COM
W
E 104 0C
N WOMAN.COM
W
E 104 01
N FACE1.COM
W
E 104 02
N FACE2.COM
W
Q
```

To create the files, make sure HEART.COM, PICTURE.SCR, and DEBUG.COM are on your disk, that your disk has room on it for a few files, and that if you're using a floppy disk, that the write-protect notch isn't covered. Then type:

```
DEBUG < PICTURE.SCR
```

When it finishes, run PATTERN1, PATTERN2, PATTERN3, DOT1, DOT2, DOT3, MAN, WOMAN, FACE1, and FACE2 to see what these look like.

While DEBUG offers a handful of additional commands, the only other one serious power users probably need to know about is Move (M). Microsoft and IBM misnamed this command since it really copies memory values instead of moving them. The term "move" incorrectly suggests that DEBUG gets rid of the original after relocating it to a new place. In fact, DEBUG leaves the original alone, unless the new place you move it to overlaps itself.

If your file contains the message "This is a test" at address 100 and you move (copy) this block of 14 characters to a new location 15 bytes later (at address 10E), you'll end up with:

```
"This is a testThis is a test"
```

at address 100. But if you take the same block of text and instead move it up just five bytes (to address 104), you'll get:

```
"ThisThis is a test"
```

since the new address overlaps most of the old one.

Moves can be a bit tricky, because you have to make sure you don't accidentally obliterate any existing parts of your program, and because you have to remember to adjust the value in the CX register to compensate for any change in length.

To see Move in action, first create a small file called MOVETEST.COM, by typing in the following MOVE1.SCR:

```
N MOVETEST.COM
A
MOV AH,09
MOV DX,0108
INT 21
RET

E 108 "DEBUG is",D,A
E 112 "very",D,A
E 118 "powerful.",D,A,24
RCX
24
W
Q
```

Be sure to leave the blank line after RET, and to press the Enter key after the final Q. Then redirect this script file into DEBUG with the command:

```
DEBUG < MOVE1.SCR
```

When you run MOVETEST.COM (by typing MOVETEST at the DOS prompt), all it will do is print:

```
DEBUG is
very
powerful.
```

MOVETEST.COM takes advantage of the DOS "display string(s)" function call 9. When DOS sees a value of 9 in the AH register, it looks in the CX register for an address that tells it where the text strings are located. Then it displays any ASCII strings it finds starting at that address and continuing until a character 24 ($) tells it to stop. (If you try this yourself, remember that you need to put an:

```
,0D,0A
```

or simply:

```
,D,A
```

at the end of each string when you want a carriage return and line feed.)

When you use the Move command you have to give DEBUG two pieces of information — what you want copied, and where you want it copied to. You can tell DEBUG what part of memory you want copied either by specifying explicit starting and stopping addresses, or by listing the starting address and telling it how many bytes to copy. In either case you then have to specify the new destination address (where you want this copied chunk of memory to go).

All of the examples below use starting addresses and lengths rather than explicit starting and stopping addresses, but either technique will work. The number immediately following each M is the starting address. The number following each L is the length — the number of bytes to move. The final number in each line is the new destination address.

Let's say that after looking at everything DEBUG can do, you want to change the MOVETEST.COM message to be more emphatic. To do this, create the following MOVE2.SCR script file:

```
N MOVETEST.COM
L
M 118 L C 130
M 112 L 6 118
M 112 L 6 11E
M 112 L 6 124
M 112 L 6 12A
RCX
3C
W
Q
```

Then redirect the file into DEBUG with the command:

```
DEBUG < MOVE2.SCR
```

Finally, run the changed version MOVETEST and you'll see the new message:

```
DEBUG is
very
very
very
very
very
powerful.
```

The MOVE2.SCR script file contains five Move instructions that copy small blocks of information from one place to another in memory. First it summons the old MOVE-TEST.COM file by using the N command to tell DEBUG which file you want to work on, and then the L command to load this file into memory. Then it uses the Move command to insert an additional copy of the line:

```
"powerful.",D,A,24
```

18 hex (24 decimal) bytes higher (later) in memory. Here's a step-by-step scorecard of what happens:

Original arrangement of MOVETEST.COM text:		After the first Move instruction:	
Address	Text starting at this address	Address	Text starting at this address
108	"DEBUG is",D,A	108	"DEBUG is",D,A
112	"very",D,A	112	"very",D,A
118	"powerful.",D,A,24	118	"powerful.",D,A,24
		.	
		.	
		.	
		130	"powerful.",D,A,24

MOVE2.SCR has to copy the line containing "powerful" before it makes any other moves, to get it safely out of the way. The second Move instruction copies the word "very" (plus the 0D and 0A carriage return and line feed characters) on top of it. This obliterates the first six letters of the original "powerful" at address 118:

After the second Move instruction:

Address	Text starting at this address
108	"DEBUG is",D,A
112	"very",D,A
118	"very",D,A,"ul.",D,A ,24
	.
	.
	.
130	"powerful.",D,A,24

The third Move instruction finishes wiping out the tail end of the original "powerful" at address 118:

After the third Move instruction:

Address	Text starting at this address
108	"DEBUG is",D,A
112	"very",D,A
118	"very",D,A,
11E	"very",D,A,
	.
	.
130	"powerful.",D,A,24

The final two Move instructions fill in the gap:

After the fifth Move instruction:

Address	Text starting at this address
108	"DEBUG is",D,A
112	"very",D,A
118	"very",D,A,
11E	"very",D,A,
124	"very",D,A,
12A	"very",D,A,
130	"powerful.",D,A,24

All these five Move commands really do is push the word "powerful" up to a higher address in memory, and then fill in the gap by making four additional copies of the word "very" (plus the 0D and 0A carriage return and line feed characters that follow it). Each of the four new occurrences of "very" (and its 0D,0A) takes up six characters. So the file has to be 4 x 6 = 24 bytes longer (decimal 24 = 18 in hex notation). The old MOVE-TEST.COM file was 24 (hex) bytes long. MOVE2.SCR reset the CX register to 3C to reflect the increased length (hex 24 + 18 = 3C).

Now that you lengthened the file, what about making it smaller? Shortening a file with the Move command is even easier than stretching it out. Let's say you want to change the display so it says simply:

```
DEBUG is
powerful.
```

All you have to do is move the "powerful" line down from its 130 address so it overwrites the first "very" at address 112. Actually, since the string "powerful" (along with the 0D,0A,24 characters that follow it) is twice as long as each "very" string (and its 0D,0A characters), this will overwrite the first two occurrences of "very."

This short MOVE3.SCR script file will do it:

```
N MOVETEST.COM
L
M 130 L C 112
RCX
1E
W
Q
```

Once you've created MOVE3.SCR, redirect it into DEBUG with the command:

```
DEBUG < MOVE3.SCR
```

Moving the line "powerful" (and its 0D,0A,24 suffix) from address 130 down to address 112 actually leaves a lot of unneeded text still in memory — three orphaned occurrences of "very" at addresses 11E, 124, and 12A as well as the original "powerful" at address 130. The DOS display string function call won't even get to all this extra text, because it will stop printing when it hits the first character 24 ($). When you moved the "powerful" line down from address 130 to address 112, you brought the $ with it. DOS will stop dead in its tracks when it reaches this $, even though more text is in memory beyond it.

In order to get rid of all this unneeded MOVETEST.COM text, the MOVE3.SCR script file adjusted the value in the CX register from 3C (decimal 60) bytes down to 1E (decimal 30) bytes. Technically it really didn't have to make the file any smaller. Because of the way DOS allocates disk space, even a one-byte file takes up a minimum of 2,048 (2K) bytes, and can hog as much as 8,192 bytes (8K) on an XT. So making the file 30 bytes shorter isn't going to save any disk space. And since the DOS display text function call will stop working as soon as it reaches the first $, it will ignore the unneeded text that follows. But why be sloppy?

Here's what your system's memory looked like after MOVE3.SCR shortened the MOVETEST.COM file:

After the single MOVE3.SCR
Move instruction:

Address	Text starting at this address
108	"DEBUG is",D,A
112	"powerful.",D,A,24
11E	"very",D,A,
124	"very",D,A,
12A	"very",D,A,
130	"powerful.",D,A,24

— **All of this is unused.**

Starting Up DEBUG

Format: **DEBUG *or* DEBUG d:[path]FILENAME**

To start DEBUG, type either:

```
DEBUG
```

or:

```
DEBUG [d:] [path] filename [.ext]
```

substituting the name of the file you want to examine or change in place of [d:][path]filename[.ext].

If you type just DEBUG and press Enter all you'll see is the DEBUG - hyphen prompt. If you type DEBUG and then the name of a file DOS can locate, you'll still see nothing but the DEBUG hyphen prompt. However, when you specify a filename on the DOS command line (e.g., DEBUG COMMAND.COM), DEBUG will load that file into memory. You can then display or modify any part of that file. If you do make any changes you can then write the modified file back to disk. You can start DEBUG without including a filename on the command line, and then later use the N (Name) and L (Load) commands to load a file for DEBUG to examine or change.

Most of the time you'll want to start DEBUG by specifying a filename on the DOS command line. The only times you wouldn't want to are when you need to examine what's already loaded in memory or create a brand new file. But even then you still may want to include a filename on the command line.

If you specify a file DEBUG can't locate, such as a brand new file you're trying to create, you'll see a "File not found" message, followed on the next line by the normal hyphen prompt. If you're trying to load an existing file and you see this message, you either typed in the filename incorrectly or you were trying to load a file in another subdirectory or on another disk that DOS couldn't locate. If this happens, type Q and hit Enter to quit, then make sure that file is handy and restart.

If you are trying to create a brand new file, you have to tell DEBUG what to name it. While you can do this with the N (Name) command, specifying the new name on the DOS command line will have the same effect. You'll still see the "File not found" message, but this will let you Write (W) the new file to disk later without having to re-enter it with the DEBUG N command.

For example, if you were on drive C: and you wanted to look inside your system ROM to see the copyright date, or if you wanted to examine any other part of memory, you'd start by typing simply DEBUG. All you'd see is the DEBUG prompt:

```
C>DEBUG
-
```

If you then entered D to display the contents of memory, DEBUG would show you whatever happened to be loaded at offset 100 (hex) of DEBUG's data segment.

If you wanted to examine the copy of COMMAND.COM in your \DOS subdirectory, you'd type DEBUG and the path and filename:

```
C>DEBUG \DOS\COMMAND.COM
-
```

Type D and then press Enter at this point and you'd see the first 128 bytes of COMMAND.COM.

If you wanted to create a brand new file called NEWHEART.COM, you could either specify it on the command line:

```
C>DEBUG NEWHEART.COM
File not found
-
```

or you could use the N (Name) command:

```
C>DEBUG
-N NEWHEART.COM
-
```

Naming a File for Loading or Writing

Format: **N [d:][path]filename[.ext]**

You can't load or write a file unless you first specify a filename one of two ways. You can either enter a filename on the DOS command line (e.g., DEBUG COMMAND.COM), or you can use the N command to do it later. For example,

```
DEBUG GREEN.COM
```

or

```
-N GREEN.COM
```

If you try to use the W command to write a file without having first specified a name, DEBUG won't oblige, and will simply print the error message "(W)rite error, no destination defined."

If you start DEBUG without specifying a filename, and want to load an existing file (like YELLOW.COM) later, you have to use the N command to give DEBUG the filename you want it to load:

```
C>DEBUG
-N YELLOW.COM
-L
```

The N command comes in very handy when you're modifying a file and you want to save the modified version without destroying the original. Let's say you had a file on your disk called RED.COM that cleared your screen, set the colors (on a CGA, VGA, or EGA only) to red text on a white background, and even set the border to red if you were using a CGA (and did nothing if you weren't). Don't have such a file handy? Then make sure DEBUG is on your disk, and at the DOS prompt type:

```
DEBUG RED.COM
E 100 B8 00 06 B9 00 00 BA 4F 18 B7 74 CD 10 B4 02
E 10F BA 00 00 B7 00 CD 10 B0 04 BA D9 03 EE C3
RCX
1D
W
Q
```

Ignore the "File not found" message DEBUG prints when you start. If you wanted to change the file slightly so it set the text and border colors to blue instead of red, you could patch the program at locations 10A for the text color and 117 for the border. To do this, you'd use the E command and type the following:

```
DEBUG RED.COM
E 10A 71
E 117 01
N BLUE.COM
W
Q
```

Notice that after entering the patches with the E command, you used the N command to give the modified file a new name. By doing this you created a second file called BLUE.COM and left the first RED.COM file alone. If you hadn't done this you would have saved the changed file as RED.COM — and RED.COM would have set your colors to blue.

You could also have created a file called PURPLE.COM at the same time you created RED.COM, by adding two new E instructions and another N and W command. If you had typed:

```
DEBUG RED.COM
E 10A 71
E 117 01
N BLUE.COM
W
E 10A 75
E 117 05
N PURPLE.COM
W
Q
```

the first W would have written the changes to a file called BLUE.COM that set your colors to blue on white. The second W would have written the second set of changes to a file that the second N named PURPLE.COM.

Displaying Memory Contents

Format: **D [address][address]** *or* **D address length**

Microsoft and IBM call the D command "Dump" but you may want to think of it as "Display." Use it to examine from 1 to 65,536 bytes of memory at a time.

Issuing a D command on a typical 80-column screen will display three things:

1. *At the left edge of your screen,* the segment and offset addresses of the memory you want to examine, in even-paragraph chunks. A paragraph is a slice of memory 10 hex (decimal 16) bytes long that is evenly divisible by hex 10; in other words a chunk of memory that starts at an offset address ending in a 0. 100 and 110 and FE0 and CC0 are all paragraph addresses. 101 and 112 and FE9 and CCF are not.

2. *In the middle part of your screen*, the hex values of the bytes in that paragraph. If you ask DEBUG to display the whole paragraph, you'll see decimal 16 bytes. If you ask it to start displaying memory at an address that's not a paragraph boundary, you'll see fewer than decimal 16. DEBUG will insert a hyphen between bytes 7 and 8. (Since the first byte in each paragraph is byte 0, the hyphen is smack in the middle, between the 8th and 9th byte in each row.)

3. *At the right edge of your screen*, the ASCII representation of any values between hex 20 and 7E (decimal 32 and 126). DEBUG displays a period (.) for any value below hex 20 or greater than hex 7E.

If you issued the command:

```
-D F000:0 L 30
```

to display the hex 30 (decimal 48) bytes starting at offset 0 of segment F000 on an IBM AT (this address happens to be the beginning of the AT's BIOS), you'd see:

```
F000:0000   36 36 31 31 38 38 31 31-30 30 32 32 38 39 20 20   66118811002289
F000:0010   43 43 4F 4F 50 50 52 52-2E 2E 20 20 49 49 42 42   CCOOPPRR.. IIBB
F000:0020   4D 4D 20 20 31 31 39 39-38 38 34 34 FA B4 DD E8   MM  11998844....
```

    ↑   ↑ ↑   ↑

               Offset Value at address F000:0020   **ASCII representation**

Segment   **of 4D value at address**

                                                         F000:0020

Note that in this case DEBUG displayed periods after 11998844 because the values there (FA B4 DD E8) are higher than 7E. But it displayed periods after CCOOPPRR because the values there (2E 2E) are the hex representation of actual periods.

The double letters in the message are there because of the way display memory is arranged, in odd- and even-address chunks. To see what this really says, you can copy this message from the part of memory where it normally sits — the very beginning of segment F000 — to the part of memory that controls your video display. On a color system the beginning of video memory is located at address B800:0. On a monochrome system it's B000:0. (If you have a mono system, substitute B000 for B800 in the statement below.) Load DEBUG and type:

```
-M F000:0 L 2C B800:0
```

The M command (Move) copies the first 2C (decimal 44) bytes of memory from offset 0 of segment F000 — the beginning of the AT ROM BIOS — to offset 0 of segment B800 (the beginning of color video memory, and the upper lefthand corner of a color screen). On the upper lefthand corner of either screen you'll see a crazy-quilt of attributes and the letters:

```
6181028 COPR. IBM 1984
```

The long number is the part number for the ROM chip that contains the message. The rest is IBM's copyright notice. The unusual colors (or mono attributes on a mono system) are artifacts.

Video memory is arranged so that the even-numbered bytes contain the values of the characters you want to display, and the odd-numbered ones hold the attributes. Since each value appears twice, the system will display the even-numbered ones as the characters these represent, and then translate the odd-numbered versions of each into the attributes for these characters. You may enter D commands in four slightly different ways:

1. If you enter D by itself, DEBUG will display 128 bytes of memory. If you begin the display on an even paragraph boundary, as you would if you had just loaded DEBUG and issued no other commands, DEBUG will display these 128 bytes in eight even rows (paragraphs). If you had previously displayed a part of memory that didn't start on a paragraph boundary (an offset that ends in a 0), DEBUG would stagger the 128 bytes over nine rows.

   Once you enter D and see 128 bytes of memory, entering D by itself will display the next 128 bytes. If the display reaches the top of a 64K segment, DEBUG will cycle back to the bottom; if it reaches the bottom DEBUG will begin again at the top.

   If you start DEBUG and do not specify an address, DEBUG will generally start displaying memory at offset 100 of the current data segment.

   However, if you enter a D without any address after it, and display a few successive memory blocks by entering just D a few more times, and then later load a COM file (by entering an N and a filename that ends with .COM and then an L), and then enter a D all by itself, DEBUG will start displaying bytes at 100 again, instead of remembering the last address it displayed.

2. If you enter a D with a single address after it, DEBUG will display the 128 bytes beginning with that address. If you follow this immediately by entering just a D with no address after it DEBUG will show you the very next 128 bytes after the first 128 that you specified.

   If you enter an address in segment:offset form, DEBUG will show you the contents of memory in the segment you specified. If you omit the segment and simply enter the offset, DEBUG will assume you want it to look inside its default data segment — the one it will load your programs into if you ask it to.

   You can also enter segment:offset addresses by using the alphabetical shorthand form of the segment (such as DS:100 when you want to specify offset 100 of the data segment), but this is really just for serious programmers.

3. If you enter a D followed by an address, then an L and a hex number range from 1 to 0000 (0000 is shorthand for 10000), DEBUG will display the number of bytes in the range specified, starting at the address specified. This will let you examine just one single byte (if the range number is 1), or an entire 64K segment (if the range number is 0000 and you're starting at offset 0) in one continuous scrolling list. If you want to break out of an overly long display, just type Ctrl-Break or Ctrl-C.

4. If you enter a D followed by two addresses, DEBUG will display the contents of memory starting at the first and continuing to the second. You may specify a segment and offset for the first address, but only an offset for the second.

For example, to display the single byte of memory starting at offset 0 of segment F000, you could enter either:

```
-D F000:0 0
```

which tells DEBUG to display memory starting and stopping at offset 0 of segment F000, or:

```
-D F000:0 L 1
```

which tells DEBUG to display one byte of memory starting at offset 0 of segment F000. To display the entire F000 64K segment of memory, you could enter either:

```
-D F000:0 FFFF
```

or:

```
-D F000:0 L 0000
```

Or you could type:

```
-D F000:0
```

and press the Enter key 512 times. The first two examples will scroll the display in one continuous gulp. The third will do it in 128-byte slices.

All of the following examples assume you loaded COMMAND.COM version 5.0 into memory either by typing DEBUG COMMAND.COM at the DOS command line, or by entering DEBUG, then using successive N COMMAND.COM and L commands to take care of it.

To view COMMAND.COM from the beginning of the file in even eight-paragraph chunks, you'd simply keep typing D and pressing the Enter key:

```
1359:0100  E9 5D 14 00 78 14 00 00-B7 0E 00 00 75 0D 00 00   .]..x.......u...
1359:0110  85 11 00 00 00 00 00 00-00 00 00 00 00 00 00 00   ................
1359:0120  00 00 00 00 00 00 00 00-00 00 00 00 00 00 00 00   ................
1359:0130  00 00 00 00 00 FB E8 64-00 1E 0E 2E FF 2E 04 01   .......d........
1359:0140  FB E8 59 00 1E 0E 2E FF-2E 08 01 FB E8 4E 00 1E   ..Y..........N..
1359:0150  0E 2E FF 2E 0C 01 FB E8-43 00 1E 0E 2E FF 2E 10   ........C.......
1359:0160  01 E8 39 00 1E 0E 2E FF-2E 14 01 E8 2F 00 1E 0E   ..9........./...
1359:0170  2E FF 2E 18 01 E8 25 00-1E 0E 2E FF 2E 1C 01 E8   ......%.........

-D
1359:0180  1B 00 1E 0E 2E FF 2E 20-01 E8 11 00 1E 0E 2E FF   ....... ........
1359:0190  2E 24 01 E8 07 00 1E 0E-2E FF 2E 28 01 9C 2E 80   .$.........(....
1359:01A0  3E 34 01 00 74 08 E8 0C-00 73 03 E8 1A 00 9D C3   4..t....s.......
```

```
1359:01B0   EA 35 01 00 00 53 50 B4-07 2E FF 1E 30 01 0B C0    .5...SP.....0...
1359:01C0   58 5B 75 02 F9 C3 F8 C3-53 50 B4 05 2E FF 1E 30    X[u.....SP.....0
1359:01D0   01 0B C0 74 03 58 5B C3-EB FE CD 21 FA 0E 17 BC    ...t.X[....!....
1359:01E0   3E 05 FB 0E 1F 9C 2E A0-40 05 A8 80 74 07 24 7F    .......@...t.$.
1359:01F0   2E FF 1E 2C 01 2E 80 26-40 05 7F 9D E9 62 FF 02    ...,...&@....b..
```

and so on. Not really much to look at here.

To view a continuous list of internal DOS commands, you would enter:

```
-D A8C6 AA4F
```

which tells DEBUG to display everything from offsets A8C6 through AA4F:

```
1359:A8C0                4E 4F-54 EF 0A 0A 45 52 52 4F         NOT...ERRO
1359:A8D0   52 4C 45 56 45 4C B2 0B-05 45 58 49 53 54 46 0B    RLEVEL...EXISTF.
1359:A8E0   00 03 44 49 52 03 8D 10-D2 84 04 43 41 4C 4C 02    ..DIR......CALL.
1359:A8F0   27 0C 34 85 04 43 48 43-50 02 0F 21 A2 84 06 52    '.4..CHCP..!...R
1359:A900   45 4E 41 4D 45 03 DF 1A-0E 85 03 52 45 4E 03 DF    ENAME......REN..
1359:A910   1A 0E 85 05 45 52 41 53-45 03 57 1A CA 84 03 44    ....ERASE.W....D
1359:A920   45 4C 03 57 1A CA 84 04-54 59 50 45 03 8D 1B 24    EL.W....TYPE...$
1359:A930   85 03 52 45 4D 06 04 01-3A 85 04 43 4F 50 59 03    ..REM..:..COPY.
1359:A940   C3 38 B4 84 05 50 41 55-53 45 06 4A 1A 3E 85 04    .8...PAUSE.J...
1359:A950   44 41 54 45 02 C4 2F C4-84 04 54 49 4D 45 02 2D    DATE../...TIME.-
1359:A960   30 1E 85 03 56 45 52 02-B7 1D 28 85 03 56 4F 4C    0...VER...(..VOL
1359:A970   03 BB 1C 30 85 02 43 44-03 77 25 A8 84 05 43 48    ...0..CD.w%...CH
1359:A980   44 49 52 03 77 25 A8 84-02 4D 44 03 E2 25 EA 84    DIR.w%...MD..%..
1359:A990   05 4D 4B 44 49 52 03 E2-25 EA 84 02 52 44 03 56    .MKDIR..%...RD.V
1359:A9A0   26 0A 85 05 52 4D 44 49-52 03 56 26 0A 85 05 42    &...RMDIR.V&...B
1359:A9B0   52 45 41 4B 02 BC 37 9E-84 06 56 45 52 49 46 59    REAK..7...VERIFY
1359:A9C0   02 FF 37 2C 85 03 53 45-54 06 D7 22 16 85 06 50    ..7,..SET..".. P
1359:A9D0   52 4F 4D 50 54 06 BD 22-F6 84 04 50 41 54 48 02    ROMPT..".. .PATH.
1359:A9E0   1F 1F EE 84 04 45 58 49-54 00 19 22 E6 84 04 43    .....EXIT..".. .C
1359:A9F0   54 54 59 03 6B 20 C0 84-04 45 43 48 4F 06 82 37    TTY.k ...ECHO..7
1359:AA00   42 85 04 47 4F 54 4F 06-5B 0C 48 85 05 53 48 49    B..GOTO.[.H..SHI
1359:AA10   46 54 02 E0 0B 4E 85 02-49 46 06 8F 0A 52 85 03    FT...N..IF...R..
1359:AA20   46 4F 52 06 24 0F 62 85-03 43 4C 53 00 CB 1F B0    FOR.$.b..CLS....
1359:AA30   84 08 54 52 55 45 4E 41-4D 45 03 97 21 6C 85 08    ..TRUENAME..!l..
1359:AA40   4C 4F 41 44 48 49 47 48-02 27 59 70 85 02 4C 48    LOADHIGH.'Yp..LH
```

Remember that since DEBUG loads COM files at address 100, these offsets are hex 100 bytes higher than they actually appear in the file.

You could have viewed the same list of version 5.0 internal commands by typing:

```
-D A8C6 L 18A
```

This would display hex 18A bytes of memory starting at offset A8C6.

Or, you could examine these commands simply by typing:

```
-D A8C6
```

and pressing Enter, and then typing just D and pressing Enter twice. Entering D and a single address will display 128 bytes starting at that address. Typing D by itself after that will keep displaying consecutive 128-byte chunks following the one you specified.

Note that while you can enter a range (using the L command to specify a length of bytes to display) after you enter an address, you can't just enter a range by itself. The command:

```
-D L18A
```

will produce an error message.

DEBUG remembers which addresses you specified most recently when using the D command. If you use D to view memory between offsets 100 and 200, then use the U command to unassemble the code between offsets 600 and 700, and then enter D by itself, DEBUG will display memory starting at 201 rather than 701, because the last byte the D command displayed was at offset 200.

Entering New Memory Contents

Format: **E address [list]**

The versatile Enter command lets you insert new memory values and modify existing ones. You can use it in one of two modes:

1. You may specify an address and a value and have DEBUG blindly enter that value at that address.
2. Or you may enter an address, have DEBUG display the value currently stored at that address, and change the value only if you want to.

The first brute-force technique lets you enter a block of new information at one time. This comes in handy when you're entering strings of characters, or when you're following a script.

The second technique lets you confirm your modifications by verifying the current values before you make any changes. And it lets you jump forward or backward through the file a byte at a time. For example, many users rely on the E command to enter small COM programs. Try typing in the following REMINDER.SCR file using a pure ASCII word processor:

```
N REMINDER.COM
E 100 B4 09 BA 08 01 CD 21 C3 42 61 63 6B 20 75 70 20
E 110 79 6F 75 72 20 77 6F 72 6B 20 64 61 69 6C 79 21
E 120 0D 0A 24
RCX
23
W
Q
```

Of course, since all this program does is print a message that says:

```
Back up your work daily!
```

it's actually easier to use the E command to enter the message directly than to type in the individual hex values of the letters in the string:

```
N REMINDER.COM
E 100 B4 09 BA 08 01 CD 21 C3
E 108 "Back up your work daily!"
E 120 0D 0A 24
RCX
23
W
Q
```

In both cases you're creating a new file, so you really don't care what memory values your brand new program is overwriting. And since you're following a published script you can pretty much enter the values without worrying about damaging anything.

But when you're changing values inside an existing file you really should verify that you're modifying the proper bytes.

Let's make a simple change in the REMINDER.COM file so it beeps at you to drive the "Back up..." message home. One easy way is to replace the exclamation point (character 21 hex) with an ASCII character 7. Printing a character 7 onscreen causes a beep.

To do this you have to find the memory address that currently stores a value of 21, and enter a 7 at that address. You can see from looking at the script file you typed previously that the file is hex 23 bytes long (this is the value entered below the RCX command that sets the file length), and that the exclamation point is very near the end of the file.

To figure out the exact address, look at the middle of the second script file:

```
E 108 "Back up your work daily!"
E 120 0D 0A 24
```

Notice that the actual message starts at address 108, and that the three characters that follow the message begin at address 120. Since the exclamation point is the last character in the string, its location is right before the three characters that start at offset 120.

(You could, of course, zero in on the exact address by counting from the "B" in "Back" — at address 108 — and working your way one byte at a time across to the "!" at the end. Each character represents one byte, so you'd simply count 108...109...10A etc. But it's easier to assume that the exclamation point is at the address directly before the three characters starting at 120.)

Here's where the the interactive mode of the E command comes in handy: New DEBUG users sometimes forget that in hex the number right before 20 is 1F, not 19. So if you used the interactive E mode to change 21 to 7 and you thought the right address was 119, when you entered the 119 address you'd see:

```
-E 119
30F9:0119  20.
-Q
```

(If you try this yourself, remember that you'll see another number in place of the 30F9 to the left of the colon, because this is the segment address, which will vary depending on your system configuration.)

Notice that the E 119 command reported that the value at address 119 was 20. Since you wanted to replace an existing value of 21, not 20, offset 119 is the wrong address.

Fortunately, the interactive E mode lets you scan ahead in the file byte by byte until you reach the proper value. To scan ahead, just tap the space bar until you see the value you're looking for. This would look like:

```
-E 119
30F9:0119  20.    64.    61.    69.    6C.    79.    21.
```

The value of 21 is actually located six bytes later, at address 11F. Once you found it by leaning on the space bar, you could enter a new value of 7 to the right of the period DEBUG displays, then use the W and Q commands to write the changed file to disk and quit:

```
-E 119
30F9:0119  20.    64.    61.    69.    6C.    79.
21.7
-W
Writing 0023 bytes
-Q
```

If you wanted to keep the original REMINDER.COM file (with the exclamation point) intact and create an additional file that beeped, you could add a line to give the modified file a new name like REMINDR2.COM:

```
-E 119
30F9:0119  20.    64.    61.    69.    6C.    79.
21.7
-REMINDR2.COM
-W
Writing 0023 bytes
-Q
```

It's easy to get too far ahead in the file when jumping byte by byte by tapping the space bar. If this happens you can move backward by hitting the minus (hyphen) key. You'll know you went too far if you see the three final characters — the 0D, 0A, and 24. If this happens, hit the minus key several times to back up to the 21, enter the new value, then execute the same closing commands as above.

```
-E 119
30F9:0119  20.    64.    61.    69.    6C.    79.    21.
30F9:0120  0D.    0A.    24.-
30F9:0121  0A.-
30F9:0120  0D.-
30F9:011F  21.7
-REMINDR2.COM
-W
Writing 0023 bytes
-Q
```

The interactive E command also comes in handy when you have to replace several characters in a row.

Some commercial word processing programs stick hex 1A (decimal 26) end-of-file markers onto the back of text files to pad out their lengths. If you combine two such files into one, it's possible to end up with end-of-file markers in the middle of the file — which will confuse these programs (and DOS as well) into thinking the files end prematurely. If this happens, you can use DEBUG to scan through the file byte by byte. Whenever you see a value of 1A in the middle of your text, you can replace it with a space (a hex 20). Whenever you see any other value you can press the space bar to skip over it and leave it untouched.

If you know that you combined two files, but when you try to load them into your word processor or examine them with the DOS TYPE command, the file seems to end with:

```
This is the end of the first little file.
```

Examine the file with DEBUG. Figure out the hex file length by typing RCX, and then use the Search (S) command to look for any 1A characters that aren't right at the end. You may see something like:

```
-RCX
CX 0780
:
-S 100 L 780 1A
30DD:062B
30DD:062C
30DD:062D
30DD:062E
30DD:062F
30DD:087C
30DD:087D
30DD:087E
30DD:087F
```

The four addresses at the end (087C, 087D, 087E, and 087F) are where they belong — at the end. Remember, if RCX tells you the file is hex 780 bytes long, the file will actually end 100 hex bytes highter, since DEBUG loads files at address 100, not address 0. So these are the last four addresses in the file.

The other five occurrences of 1A that DEBUG's Search command uncovered — 062B, 062C, 062D, 062E, 062F — shouldn't be there, since 1A characters don't belong anywhere in a text file except at the very end. You can see them by using the D command. Here these 1A characters are at the end of the third paragraph (row):

```
-D 600
30DD:0600  54 68 69 73 20 69 73 20-74 68 65 20 65 6E 64 20   This is the end
30DD:0610  6F 66 20 74 68 65 20 66-69 72 73 74 20 6C 69 74   of the first lit
30DD:0620  74 6C 65 20 66 69 6C 65-2E 0D 0A 1A 1A 1A 1A 1A   tle file........
30DD:0630  41 6E 64 20 74 68 69 73-20 69 73 20 74 68 65 20   And this is the
30DD:0640  62 65 67 69 6E 6E 69 6E-67 20 6F 66 20 74 68 65   beginning of the
30DD:0650  20 73 65 63 6F 6E 64 20-6C 69 74 74 6C 65 20 6F    second little o
```

It's easy to get rid of them. You could use the E or Fill (F) commands to do it without confirmation, but if you're the cautious type you might want to make sure you're making changes at the proper addresses. To do so, type:

```
-E 620
30DD:0620  74.    6C.    65.    20.    66.    69.
6C.    65.
30DD:0628  2E.    0D.    0A.    1A.20  1A.20  1A.20
1A.20   1A.20
30DD:0630  41.
-W
Writing 0780 bytes
-Q
```

When DEBUG displayed any character other than 1A, simply press the Enter key to leave it unchanged and skip to the next one. When you do finally see the string of 1A characters, change them by entering hex 20 values (spaces) beside the periods DEBUG prints. Then write the modified file to disk and quit, using the W and Q commands.

If you used the DOS TYPE command now, you'd see something like:

```
This is the end of the first little file.
     And this is the beginning of the second little one.
```

The second line is pushed over several spaces to the right because you changed the end-of-file characters separating the two lines into space characters. You can use your word processor to remove these extra spaces, or you could have used the DEBUG Move (M) command to wipe them out by moving everything five addresses lower from the word "And" on up.

Filling a Block of Memory

Format: **F range list**

The Fill command can double as a brute-force, noninteractive Enter command.

Here are two similar ways to create a program called FOOTBALL.COM. The first uses the Enter (E) command:

```
N FOOTBALL.COM
E 100 B4 09 BA 08 01 CD 21 C3 "Hi Mom!" 0D 0A 24
RCX
12
W
Q
```

The second uses the Fill (F) command:

```
N FOOTBALL.COM
F 100 L 12 B4 09 BA 08 01 CD 21 C3 "Hi Mom!" 0D 0A 24
RCX
12
W
Q
```

You can see that these two programs are almost identical.

The Fill command is useful for converting data files to text files. Many database managers produce ASCII files that contain nontext information in a "header" at the beginning of the file. If you try to read this file into your own database program, word processor, or spreadsheet, you'll end up with a mess. Sometimes database programs even put end-of-file markers at the beginning of such files to prevent nonauthorized users from peeking at the contents of the file. But you can have DEBUG examine the beginning of the file to see where the ASCII data actually starts, then cover over any nontext information. Just use the Fill command to put spaces (hex 20 characters) over anything before your data. Then use your word processor to remove the spaces. (An even better way is to use the DEBUG Move command to move the part of the file with your data over the nondata part, obliterating anything non-ASCII.)

You can also use the Fill command to wipe out a whole block of troublesome repeating characters in a file. Some word processors insert large numbers of end-of-file markers into text files. And some communications programs stick nulls — character 0s — into files. Both can confound certain commercial programs.

To get rid of these, browse through the file with the Display (D) command or scan through with the Search (S) command to find out where the block of 00 or 1A characters is located. Then use the Fill command to change these characters into something harmless like spaces. (Again, the Move command does this even better.)

If nulls creep into a text file, you might load a file and see nothing but:

^@^

signs. Worse, once your cursor hits these null signs your word processor may choke to a halt and force you to reboot. To get rid of these, figure out where they start and stop:

```
C>DEBUG EXPAND.RPT
-D
3482:0100  00 00 00 00 00 00 00 00-00 00 00 00 00 00 00 00   ................
3482:0110  00 00 00 00 00 00 00 00-00 00 00 00 00 00 00 00   ................
3482:0120  00 00 00 00 00 00 00 00-00 00 00 00 00 00 00 00   ................
3482:0130  00 00 00 00 00 00 00 00-00 00 00 00 00 00 00 00   ................
3482:0140  00 00 00 00 00 00 00 00-00 00 00 00 00 00 00 00   ................
3482:0150  00 00 00 00 00 00 00 00-00 00 00 00 00 00 00 00   ................
3482:0160  00 00 00 00 00 00 00 00-00 00 00 00 00 00 00 00   ................
3482:0170  00 00 00 00 00 00 00 00-00 00 00 00 00 00 00 00   ................
-D
3482:0180  00 00 00 00 00 00 00 00-00 00 00 00 00 00 00 00   ................
3482:0190  00 00 00 00 00 00 00 00-00 00 00 00 00 00 00 00   ................
3482:01A0  00 00 00 00 00 00 00 00-00 00 00 00 00 00 00 00   ................
3482:01B0  00 00 00 00 00 00 00 49-74 20 73 65 65 6D 73 20   .......It seems
3482:01C0  74 68 65 20 66 69 67 75-72 65 73 20 77 65 27 76   the figures we'v
3482:01D0  65 20 62 65 65 6E 20 75-73 69 6E 67 20 74 6F 20   e been using to
3482:01E0  70 6C 61 6E 20 6F 75 72-20 77 65 73 74 65 72 6E   plan our western
3482:01F0  20 65 78 70 61 6E 73 69-6F 6E 20 61 72 65 20 6F   expansion are o
```

When you tell DEBUG to fill an area of memory you can specify explicit starting and stopping addresses. Or you can enter a starting address and then tell DEBUG how many bytes it should fill beginning with that address.

The 00 null characters start at address 100 and continue to address 1B6. You could change these to asterisks (hex 2A) with either of the following Fill commands:

```
-F 100 1B6 2A
```

or:

```
-F 100 L B7 2A
```

In either case, if you used the:

```
-D 100
```

command to examine the changes, you'd see:

```
-D 100
3482:0100  2A 2A 2A 2A 2A 2A 2A 2A-2A 2A 2A 2A 2A 2A 2A 2A   ****************
3482:0110  2A 2A 2A 2A 2A 2A 2A 2A-2A 2A 2A 2A 2A 2A 2A 2A   ****************
3482:0120  2A 2A 2A 2A 2A 2A 2A 2A-2A 2A 2A 2A 2A 2A 2A 2A   ****************
3482:0130  2A 2A 2A 2A 2A 2A 2A 2A-2A 2A 2A 2A 2A 2A 2A 2A   ****************
3482:0140  2A 2A 2A 2A 2A 2A 2A 2A-2A 2A 2A 2A 2A 2A 2A 2A   ****************
3482:0150  2A 2A 2A 2A 2A 2A 2A 2A-2A 2A 2A 2A 2A 2A 2A 2A   ****************
3482:0160  2A 2A 2A 2A 2A 2A 2A 2A-2A 2A 2A 2A 2A 2A 2A 2A   ****************
3482:0170  2A 2A 2A 2A 2A 2A 2A-2A 2A 2A 2A 2A 2A 2A         ****************
-D
3482:0180  2A 2A 2A 2A 2A 2A 2A 2A-2A 2A 2A 2A 2A 2A 2A 2A   ****************
3482:0190  2A 2A 2A 2A 2A 2A 2A 2A-2A 2A 2A 2A 2A 2A 2A 2A   ****************
3482:01A0  2A 2A 2A 2A 2A 2A 2A 2A-2A 2A 2A 2A 2A 2A 2A 2A   ****************
.3482:01B0  2A 2A 2A 2A 2A 2A 2A 49-74 20 73 65 65 6D 73 20   *******It seems
3482:01C0  74 68 65 20 66 69 67 75-72 65 73 20 77 65 27 76   the figures we'v
3482:01D0  65 20 62 65 65 6E 20 75-73 69 6E 67 20 74 6F 20   e been using to
3482:01E0  70 6C 61 6E 20 6F 75 72-20 77 65 73 74 65 72 6E   plan our western
3482:01F0  20 65 78 70 61 6E 73 69-6F 6E 20 61 72 65 20 6F   expansion are o
```

Later you can use your word processor to get rid of these extra asterisks.

You can also use Fill to clean out a block of memory. If you want to do some serious DEBUG string moving on a file called FIXIT.TXT, it's hard enough to figure out where all the important strings start and stop. If you load a file into a part of memory that already contained similar strings you can get hopelessly lost. To prevent this, you can wipe out any existing values by filling the whole bottom of DEBUG's data segment with uniform background characters. If you wanted to fill the entire workspace with 00 characters, you'd load DEBUG without specifying a filename, fill a large chunk of memory with 00 characters, then Name and Load the file:

```
C>DEBUG
-F 100 7000 00
-N FIXIT.TXT
-L
```

Since IBM and IBM-compatible video displays are memory-mapped, you can see how fast DEBUG fills memory. If you stick decimal 4000 (hex FA0) characters into the right part of memory (address B800:0 for color systems; B000:0 for mono), your screen will instantly fill with the characters you entered. If you have a color system, type:

```
C>DEBUG
-F B800:0 L FA0 "q"
```

and 2,000 blue lowercase "q" characters will appear in a flash. Or substitute a lowercase "t" to end up with 2,000 red lowercase "t" characters. (Use B000:0 instead of B800:0 on mono systems, and forget about colors. Using "q" will underline the entire screen, however.)

A typical 80-column screen holds 2,000 characters. But hex FA0 is equal to decimal 4,000, not 2,000. Why? Standard PC video memory is divided into even and odd halves. Putting a value at an even address (B800:0, B800:2, etc.) will display the ASCII representation of that character onscreen. Putting a value at an odd address (B800:1, B800:3, etc.) provides the attribute for the character at the next lower address. The hex value for "q" is 71, which produces blue text (blue = 1) on a white background (7 = white). The hex value for "t" is 74, which produces red text (red = 4) on a white background. On mono screens, blue text ends up as underlined text.

Moving a Block of Memory

Format: **M range address**

The Move command is misnamed. It really should be called the Copy command, since it copies data from one place in memory to another rather than moving it. The term "Move" suggests that DOS deletes the original. It doesn't, unless you intentionally overlap the areas involved so the new location overwrites the old one.

You can end up with some strange effects by moving strings into video memory. If you try this, remember that to be recognizable, text has to load at even bytes and attributes for the text at odd bytes.

To see this in action, create the following three short files. First SCRNTST.BAT:

```
ECHO OFF
DIR
PAUSE
DEBUG < SHIFT1
PAUSE
DEBUG < SHIFT2
```

Then SHIFT1:

```
M B800:0 L FA0 B800:52
Q
```

And finally, SHIFT2:

```
M B800:52 L FA0 B800:0
Q
```

Remember to press the Enter key after typing the Q in SHIFT1 and SHIFT2, or your system will hang and you'll have to reboot. Also, these files are written to work on color systems. For mono screens, change the each of the four B800s to B000.

All this will do is fill your screen with a directory listing, then move one 80 x 25 screenful — 4,000 bytes (hex FA0) — of video memory to a slightly higher address and then back. The DIR display will shift over to the right side of the screen and then return to its normal position. If you change the 52 in both SHIFT1 and SHIFT2 to an odd number like 51 or 53, DEBUG will move the even numbered part of memory, your text, into the odd part, turning it into attributes. Then it will move it back to text.

Move is very useful when it comes to eliminating headers on data files. Many database managers create pure ASCII fixed-length files that you can import into a word processor or spreadsheet, except that these files begin with coded information that tells the database the record structure, number of entries, and so on. You can get rid of this header with a few simple DEBUG instructions. Here's a simplified example, using a very small file:

Let's say someone gives you a file called ADRSBOOK containing names and addresses that you need. If you don't have the database program that created the file, and your own database program won't import it, you can't really do much with it. Unless you fix the problem with DEBUG.

First, load the file into DEBUG. Use the RCX command to see how long it is, then plug this length into the Search (S) command to see if it contains a hex 1A end-of-file marker:

```
C>DEBUG ADRSBOOK
-RCX
CX 0400
:
-S 100 L 400 1A
30DD:03B4
```

Now you know that the file is 400 bytes long and that it may end at offset 3B4. (Obviously, not all database file formats will be this easy. But this example uses a genuine database file.) Type D and press the Enter key a few times until you see where the actual data begins:

```
-D
30DD:0100  02 03 00 06 06 58 39 00-4C 41 53 54 00 00 00 00   .....X9.LAST....
30DD:0110  00 00 00 43 0F D9 AA 00-46 49 52 53 54 00 00 00   ...C....FIRST...
30DD:0120  00 00 00 43 08 E8 AA 00-53 54 52 54 41 44 52 53   ...C....STRTADRS
30DD:0130  00 00 00 43 12 F0 AA 00-43 49 54 59 00 00 00 00   ...C....CITY....
30DD:0140  00 00 00 43 08 02 AB 00-53 54 00 00 00 00 00 00   ...C....ST......
30DD:0150  00 00 00 43 02 0A AB 00-5A 49 50 00 00 00 00 00   ...C....ZIP.....
30DD:0160  00 00 00 4E 05 0C AB 00-0D 00 00 00 00 00 00 00   ...N............
30DD:0170  00 00 00 00 00 00 00 00-00 00 00 00 00 00 00 00   ................
-D
30DD:0180  00 00 00 00 00 00 00 00-00 00 00 00 00 00 00 00   ................
30DD:0190  00 00 00 00 00 00 00 00-00 00 00 00 00 00 00 00   ................
30DD:01A0  00 00 00 00 00 00 00 00-00 00 00 00 00 00 00 00   ................
30DD:01B0  00 00 00 00 00 00 00 00-00 00 00 00 00 00 00 00   ................
30DD:01C0  00 00 00 00 00 00 00 00-00 00 00 00 00 00 00 00   ................
30DD:01D0  00 00 00 00 00 00 00 00-00 00 00 00 00 00 00 00   ................
30DD:01E0  00 00 00 00 00 00 00 00-00 00 00 00 00 00 00 00   ................
30DD:01F0  00 00 00 00 00 00 00 00-00 00 00 00 00 00 00 00   ................
-D
30DD:0200  00 00 00 00 00 00 00 00-00 00 00 00 00 00 00 00   ................
30DD:0210  00 00 00 00 00 00 00 00-00 00 00 00 00 00 00 00   ................
30DD:0220  00 00 00 00 00 00 00 00-00 00 00 00 00 00 00 00   ................
30DD:0230  00 00 00 00 00 00 00 00-00 00 00 00 00 00 00 00   ................
30DD:0240  00 00 00 00 00 00 00 00-00 00 00 00 00 00 00 00   ................
30DD:0250  00 00 00 00 00 00 00 00-00 00 00 00 00 00 00 00   ................
30DD:0260  00 00 00 00 00 00 00 00-00 00 00 00 00 00 00 00   ................
30DD:0270  00 00 00 00 00 00 00 00-00 00 00 00 00 00 00 00   ................
-D
30DD:0280  00 00 00 00 00 00 00 00-00 00 00 00 00 00 00 00   ................
30DD:0290  00 00 00 00 00 00 00 00-00 00 00 00 00 00 00 00   ................
30DD:02A0  00 00 00 00 00 00 00 00-00 00 00 00 00 00 00 00   ................
30DD:02B0  00 00 00 00 00 00 00 00-00 00 00 00 00 00 00 00   ................
30DD:02C0  00 00 00 00 00 00 00 00-00 00 00 00 00 00 00 00   ................
30DD:02D0  00 00 00 00 00 00 00 00-00 00 00 00 00 00 00 00   ................
30DD:02E0  00 00 00 00 00 00 00 00-00 00 00 00 00 00 00 00   ................
30DD:02F0  00 00 00 00 00 00 00 00-00 00 00 00 00 00 00 00   ................
-D
30DD:0300  00 00 00 00 00 00 00 00-00 20 54 65 6E 6E 79 73   ......... Tennys
30DD:0310  6F 6E 20 20 20 20 20 20-20 41 6C 20 20 20 20 20   on       Al
30DD:0320  20 31 38 20 48 6F 67 62-6F 6E 65 20 4C 61 6E 65    18 Hogbone Lane
30DD:0330  20 20 20 54 68 75 64 77-65 6C 6C 47 41 33 30 32      ThudwellGA302
30DD:0340  37 33 20 41 72 6E 6F 6C-64 20 20 20 20 20 20 20   73 Arnold
30DD:0350  20 20 4D 61 74 74 20 20-20 20 31 31 31 20 57 69     Matt    111 Wi
30DD:0360  6E 65 64 61 72 6B 20 53-74 2E 20 20 54 68 69 72   nedark St.  Thir
30DD:0370  73 74 79 20 54 58 37 37-36 31 39 20 44 75 6E 6E   sty TX77619 Dunn
```

The data starts at address 30A. And it presumably stops at the end-of-file marker at address 3B4. (Remember, it's a short file.) What you then have to do is move this block of data down into memory to the beginning of the file so the data overwrites the header:

```
-M 30A 3B4 100
```

You can use the D command to display the new memory contents at address 100:

```
-D 100
30DD:0100  54 65 6E 6E 79 73 6F 6E-20 20 20 20 20 20 20 41   Tennyson        A
30DD:0110  6C 20 20 20 20 20 20 31-38 20 48 6F 67 62 6F 6E   l       18 Hogbon
30DD:0120  65 20 4C 61 6E 65 20 20-20 54 68 75 64 77 65 6C   e Lane    Thudwel
30DD:0130  6C 47 41 33 30 32 37 33-20 41 72 6E 6F 6C 64 20   lGA30273 Arnold
30DD:0140  20 20 20 20 20 20 20 20-4D 61 74 74 20 20 20 20          Matt
30DD:0150  31 31 31 20 57 69 6E 65-64 61 72 6B 20 53 74 2E   111 Winedark St.
30DD:0160  20 20 54 68 69 72 73 74-79 20 54 58 37 37 36 31     Thirsty TX7761
30DD:0170  39 20 44 75 6E 6E 65 20-20 20 20 20 20 20 20 20   9 Dunne
```

Now you want to write this new file to disk. You don't want to destroy the old one, in case you made a mistake, so give the new file a name like NEWDB.FIL:

```
-N NEWDB.FIL
```

If you want, you can adjust the length. The data used to start at address 30A, but you moved it down to address 100. So you can now make the file 30A minus 100, or 20A bytes shorter. The old file length was 400. If you subtract 20A from 400, you get a new length of 1F6. Use the DEBUG H (Hex math) command if you're shaky about hex calculations:

```
-H 30A 100
040A  020A
-H 400 20A
060A  01F6
```

(After you type in the numbers after the H, DEBUG prints first the sum of the two numbers and then the difference.)

If you've been paying close attention, you might think this file length of 1F6 is too long. After all, if the data started at address 30A and stopped at the end-of-file marker at address 3B4, 3B4 minus 30A is 0AA bytes. Actually, the data in this example is just about this short. What happened was that the database manager padded out the end of the file.

Finally, use the W command to write the new NEWDB.FIL file to disk and the Q file to quit. In this case you were fortunate — the process got rid of the header and left you with a perfectly readable ASCII file. You won't always be so lucky. Sadly, the structure of every database file is different. Some don't even contain ASCII text. But in most cases you can use DEBUG to extract the important data. The critical thing here is to give any files you write to disk a new name so you don't wipe out the old. (Instead of using the N command, you could copy the file before you started working with DEBUG, then load, modify, and write the copy to disk.)

While you can use the Move command to copy text, you may have a harder time moving program instructions. Unless you're really sure you know what you're doing, don't start slicing and dicing your programs by moving blocks of instructions around. For example, if you're starting out with a file that looks like this when displayed with the D command:

```
30DD:0100  41 42 43 44 45 46 47 48-49 4A 4B 4C 4D 4E 4F 50   ABCDEFGHIJKLMNOP
30DD:0110  51 52 53 54 55 56 57 58-59 5A 31 32 33 34 35 36   QRSTUVWXYZ123456
30DD:0120  00 00 00 00 00 00 00 00-00 00 00 00 00 00 00 00   ................
30DD:0130  00 00 00 00 00 00 00 00-00 00 00 00 00 00 00 00   ................
30DD:0140  00 00 00 00 00 00 00 00-00 00 00 00 00 00 00 00   ................
30DD:0150  00 00 00 00 00 00 00 00-00 00 00 00 00 00 00 00   ................
30DD:0160  00 00 00 00 00 00 00 00-00 00 00 00 00 00 00 00   ................
30DD:0170  00 00 00 00 00 00 00 00-00 00 00 00 00 00 00 00   ................
```

you could copy this text by specifying explicit starting and stopping addresses (100 and 11F respectively) and then telling DEBUG where to put the copy (120). After issuing this command, check your work by using the Display command (but tell it to start displaying at address 100):

```
-M 100 11F 120
-D 100
30DD:0100  41 42 43 44 45 46 47 48-49 4A 4B 4C 4D 4E 4F 50   ABCDEFGHIJKLMNOP
30DD:0110  51 52 53 54 55 56 57 58-59 5A 31 32 33 34 35 36   QRSTUVWXYZ123456
30DD:0120  41 42 43 44 45 46 47 48-49 4A 4B 4C 4D 4E 4F 50   ABCDEFGHIJKLMNOP
30DD:0130  51 52 53 54 55 56 57 58-59 5A 31 32 33 34 35 36   QRSTUVWXYZ123456
30DD:0140  00 00 00 00 00 00 00 00-00 00 00 00 00 00 00 00   ................
30DD:0150  00 00 00 00 00 00 00 00-00 00 00 00 00 00 00 00   ................
30DD:0160  00 00 00 00 00 00 00 00-00 00 00 00 00 00 00 00   ................
30DD:0170  00 00 00 00 00 00 00 00-00 00 00 00 00 00 00 00   ................
```

You can also give DEBUG a starting address and a range of bytes to copy. The first M command took 20 (hex) bytes and copied them without any overlap, yielding 40 bytes. To copy these 40 bytes (again without any overlap) by using an address and a range length, specify the starting address (100), the range length (40), and the destination address (140). The use the D 100 command to view your work:

```
-M 100 L 40 140
-D 100
30DD:0100  41 42 43 44 45 46 47 48-49 4A 4B 4C 4D 4E 4F 50   ABCDEFGHIJKLMNOP
30DD:0110  51 52 53 54 55 56 57 58-59 5A 31 32 33 34 35 36   QRSTUVWXYZ123456
```

```
30DD:0120   41 42 43 44 45 46 47 48-49 4A 4B 4C 4D 4E 4F 50    ABCDEFGHIJKLMNOP
30DD:0130   51 52 53 54 55 56 57 58-59 5A 31 32 33 34 35 36    QRSTUVWXYZ123456
30DD:0140   41 42 43 44 45 46 47 48-49 4A 4B 4C 4D 4E 4F 50    ABCDEFGHIJKLMNOP
30DD:0150   51 52 53 54 55 56 57 58-59 5A 31 32 33 34 35 36    QRSTUVWXYZ123456
30DD:0160   41 42 43 44 45 46 47 48-49 4A 4B 4C 4D 4E 4F 50    ABCDEFGHIJKLMNOP
30DD:0170   51 52 53 54 55 56 57 58-59 5A 31 32 33 34 35 36    QRSTUVWXYZ123456
```

Both of the examples above assumed you wanted to move text without overlapping anything. Let's assume you wanted to copy just the first line (ABCDEFGHIJKLMNOP) and get rid of the second (QRSTUVWXYZ123456). The Move command makes it easy. First, start with the original file again:

```
30DD:0100   41 42 43 44 45 46 47 48-49 4A 4B 4C 4D 4E 4F 50    ABCDEFGHIJKLMNOP
30DD:0110   51 52 53 54 55 56 57 58-59 5A 31 32 33 34 35 36    QRSTUVWXYZ123456
30DD:0120   00 00 00 00 00 00 00 00-00 00 00 00 00 00 00 00    ................
30DD:0130   00 00 00 00 00 00 00 00-00 00 00 00 00 00 00 00    ................
30DD:0140   00 00 00 00 00 00 00 00-00 00 00 00 00 00 00 00    ................
30DD:0150   00 00 00 00 00 00 00 00-00 00 00 00 00 00 00 00    ................
30DD:0160   00 00 00 00 00 00 00 00-00 00 00 00 00 00 00 00    ................
30DD:0170   00 00 00 00 00 00 00 00-00 00 00 00 00 00 00 00    ................
```

Then move just the first line down so it overwrites the second one. Both of the following commands would do it:

```
-M 100 10F 110
```

or:

```
-M 100 L 10 110
```

The first tells it to take everything from addresses 100 through 10F and copy it to address 110. The second says to take the hex 10 bytes starting at address 100 and copy them down to address 110. In either case, use the D 100 command afterward and you'd see:

```
30DD:0100   41 42 43 44 45 46 47 48-49 4A 4B 4C 4D 4E 4F 50    ABCDEFGHIJKLMNOP
30DD:0110   41 42 43 44 45 46 47 48-49 4A 4B 4C 4D 4E 4F 50    ABCDEFGHIJKLMNOP
30DD:0120   00 00 00 00 00 00 00 00-00 00 00 00 00 00 00 00    ................
30DD:0130   00 00 00 00 00 00 00 00-00 00 00 00 00 00 00 00    ................
30DD:0140   00 00 00 00 00 00 00 00-00 00 00 00 00 00 00 00    ................
30DD:0150   00 00 00 00 00 00 00 00-00 00 00 00 00 00 00 00    ................
30DD:0160   00 00 00 00 00 00 00 00-00 00 00 00 00 00 00 00    ................
30DD:0170   00 00 00 00 00 00 00 00-00 00 00 00 00 00 00 0A    ................
```

Searching for Characters

Format: **S range list**

The Search command will scan through up to 64K of memory at a time for a list of specified characters and report the starting addresses of any it finds. If DEBUG stumbles over lots of occurrences, it will scroll the addresses off the screen. If it doesn't find any matches it will simply print another DEBUG - prompt.

You can search for individual hex values such as 49 42 4D or for text strings "IBM" or for combinations of both such as "IBM" 41 54. Make sure you specify the precise characters you want DEBUG to find. Looking for "IBM" won't find "I.B.M." and "DIR" won't find "Dir" or "dir" or any other inexact match. To look for such variations, execute multiple searches.

What you see onscreen is not necessarily what you get. *WordStar*, for instance, adds decimal 128 to the ASCII value of the last character in most words. If you search for the word "bullnose" in a *WordStar* file, you may never find it. But if you lop off the last letter, and search for "bullnos" you probably will.

If you're searching all the way through your main 640K of memory, you'll end up seeing reports of phantom matches. When you type in the Search command, DOS enters the command itself in memory, and DEBUG will find occurrences like these as it scans through. So if you make an extensive all-sector search and then go back and use the D command to verify the occurrence, you may not see why DEBUG reported it in the first place. For example, to search through the top segment of memory (ROM BIOS segment F000) for the string "/84" — the copyright date of an early AT — you could use explicit starting and stopping addresses:

```
-S F000:0 FFFF "/84"
```

This tells DEBUG to start searching at address F000:0000 for the string "/84" and continue the search until offset FFFF in that same segment. You could also use a starting address and a range to perform the same search:

```
-S F000:0 L 0000 "/84"
```

This has DEBUG scan 10,000 bytes for the same string, starting at address F000:0000. When searching for text, it's easiest to wrap it in quotes. But you could have specified the actual hex representation for the characters / and 8 and 4 ("/" = 2F; "8" = 38; and "4" = 34):

```
-S F000:0 L 0000 2F 38 34
```

And, obviously, you don't have to scan through an entire segment each time. To search for this string in the first hex 100 bytes of segment F000, you could enter:

```
-S F000:0 FF "/84"
```

or:

```
-S F000:0 L 100 "/84"
```

DEBUG searches through memory very quickly. If it finds lots of occurrences of the string you're looking for, it will scroll the addresses rapidly off the top of the screen. You can get around this problem by echoing everything to your printer, or by redirecting the output to a file.

To send the output to both your screen and printer, turn on your printer and type Ctrl-P or Ctrl-PrtSc. To stop this echoing process, type Ctrl-P or Ctrl-PrtSc again.

To redirect the output to a file, type:

```
DEBUG > OUTPUT.FIL
```

then type in the command that produced the overly large output and press Enter. (Be careful; since DOS is redirecting all of DEBUG's output, you won't be able to see what you type.) Then type Q and press Enter. You should see the DOS prompt again. To view the list of addresses, load the OUTPUT.FIL into your word processor, or use the DOS TYPE command (TYPE OUTPUT.FIL). If the file is long, make sure the DOS MORE.COM utility is handy and type:

```
MORE < OUTPUT.FIL
```

You could also create a tiny file with the single DEBUG command and a Q (to quit) and call the file INPUT.FIL. It might look like:

```
S F000:0 L 100 "/84"
Q
```

(Be sure to include the Q and to press the Enter key after typing the Q or your system will freeze and you'll have to reboot.) Then get into DOS and type:

```
DEBUG < INPUT.FIL > OUTPUT.FIL
```

To search through version 3.3 COMMAND.COM for the DIR command, load COMMAND.COM into DEBUG, use the RCX command to find out how long the file is, then specify this length in the Search command:

```
C>DEBUG COMMAND.COM
-RCX
CX 62DB
:
-S 100 L 62DB "DIR"
30FB:5170
30FB:5464
```

```
30FB:54E2
30FB:54F1
30FB:5500
```

You can check to see exactly what the Search command found by using the D command. To make the screen tidy, replace the very last digit in the addresses DEBUG reported with a 0. So if DEBUG reported a match at 30FB:5464, ask it to look for the hex 10 bytes starting with 5460. (When you're searching through a file and then using the D command to verify the matches, you don't have to specify the segment — the offset address will do fine by itself.)

```
-D 5170 L 10
30FB:5170  44 49 52 3E 20 20 20 00-0E 3B 49 42 4D 20 50 65   DIR>   ..;IBM Pe
-D 5460 L 10
30FB:5460  DB 09 00 03 44 49 52 03-CB 0E 04 43 41 4C 4C 02   ....DIR....CALL.
-D 54E0 L 10
30FB:54E0  43 48 44 49 52 01 C2 18-02 4D 44 01 05 19 05 4D   CHDIR....MD....M
-D 54F0 L 10
30FB:54F0  4B 44 49 52 01 05 19 02-52 44 01 49 19 05 52 4D   KDIR....RD.I..RM
-D 5500 L 10
30FB:5500  44 49 52 01 49 19 05 42-52 45 41 4B 00 F5 28 06   DIR.I..BREAK..(.
```

If you want to scan all the way through a segment such as 3000 for a string like "IBM" you can issue the command:

```
-S 3000:0 0000 "IBM"
```

If you want to scan through every one of the ten segments in main memory (the main 640K is made up of ten individual 64K segments), you can use the DOS function keys to streamline the process of entering so many similar commands. First look through the lowest segment (0000):

```
-S 0000:0 0000 "IBM"
```

Then tap either the right arrow key or the F1 key twice, which repeats the S and the space that follows it from the previous command. Assuming DEBUG didn't find any matches in segment 0000, the screen will look like:

```
-S 0000:0 0000 "IBM"
-S
```

Type in a 1 and press F3, which fills in the rest of the previous command. The screen will look like:

```
-S 0000:0 0000 "IBM"
-S 1000:0 0000 "IBM"
```

You can also use the DOS F2 key plus a character, which repeats the previous command up to the specified character. Pressing F2 and the 1 at this point would print the previous S and space and stop before the 1. You could then enter a 2 and press F3 to complete the command.

An easier way to search through all 16 of your system's segments (including things like ROM BIOS and video areas) is to use a SCAN.BAT batch file:

```
ECHO OFF
IF %1!==! GOTO OOPS
ECHO S 0000:0 L0000 %1 %2 %3 %4 %5 %6 %7 %8 %9 >  RAWFILE
ECHO S 1000:0 L0000 %1 %2 %3 %4 %5 %6 %7 %8 %9 >> RAWFILE
ECHO S 2000:0 L0000 %1 %2 %3 %4 %5 %6 %7 %8 %9 >> RAWFILE
ECHO S 3000:0 L0000 %1 %2 %3 %4 %5 %6 %7 %8 %9 >> RAWFILE
ECHO S 4000:0 L0000 %1 %2 %3 %4 %5 %6 %7 %8 %9 >> RAWFILE
ECHO S 5000:0 L0000 %1 %2 %3 %4 %5 %6 %7 %8 %9 >> RAWFILE
ECHO S 6000:0 L0000 %1 %2 %3 %4 %5 %6 %7 %8 %9 >> RAWFILE
ECHO S 7000:0 L0000 %1 %2 %3 %4 %5 %6 %7 %8 %9 >> RAWFILE
ECHO S 8000:0 L0000 %1 %2 %3 %4 %5 %6 %7 %8 %9 >> RAWFILE
ECHO S 9000:0 L0000 %1 %2 %3 %4 %5 %6 %7 %8 %9 >> RAWFILE
ECHO S A000:0 L0000 %1 %2 %3 %4 %5 %6 %7 %8 %9 >> RAWFILE
ECHO S B000:0 L0000 %1 %2 %3 %4 %5 %6 %7 %8 %9 >> RAWFILE
ECHO S C000:0 L0000 %1 %2 %3 %4 %5 %6 %7 %8 %9 >> RAWFILE
ECHO S D000:0 L0000 %1 %2 %3 %4 %5 %6 %7 %8 %9 >> RAWFILE
ECHO S E000:0 L0000 %1 %2 %3 %4 %5 %6 %7 %8 %9 >> RAWFILE
ECHO S F000:0 L0000 %1 %2 %3 %4 %5 %6 %7 %8 %9 >> RAWFILE
ECHO Q >> RAWFILE
DEBUG < RAWFILE | FIND /V "-" > HITLIST
DEL RAWFILE
ECHO The results are in a file called HITLIST
GOTO END
:OOPS
ECHO Specify something for %0 to search
ECHO such as hex bytes, eg :  %0 45 3B 61 FF
ECHO or text in quotes, eg:   %0 "qwerty"
ECHO or both, eg:             %0 "qwerty" 45 61
END
```

Be sure to include the line:

```
ECHO Q >> RAWFILE
```

If you omit this, the script won't execute the proper instruction to quit DEBUG, and your system will freeze, forcing you to reboot.

The SCAN.BAT batch file starts out by using the line:

```
IF !%1==! GOTO OOPS
```

to make sure you entered a string to search for. DOS substitutes the first thing that you typed on the command line after the name of the batch file, in place of each %1 replaceable parameter that it sees inside the batch file. If you typed:

```
SCAN "IBM"
```

DOS will replace every occurrence of %1 in the batch file with the string "IBM". If you typed:

```
SCAN "IBM" 20 31
```

DOS would still replace every %1 with "IBM". But it would also replace any %2 it finds with the hex value 20, since 20 is the second thing you typed after the name of the batch file, and any %3 with 31. It replaces any %0 in the batch file with the name of the batch file itself. So in:

```
SCAN "IBM" 20 31
```

DOS would replace any occurrences of %0, %1, %2, and %3 as follows:

```
SCAN    = %0
"IBM"   = %1
20      = %2
31      = %3
```

If you entered just:

```
SCAN
```

the %1 replaceable parameter would be equal to (nothing), since you didn't type anything in after SCAN. The test:

```
IF !%1==! GOTO OOPS
```

means that if you did type something in after SCAN (such as SCAN "IBM"), the %1 would be replaced by "IBM" and the test would become:

```
IF !"IBM"==! GOTO OOPS
```

Now since ! "IBM" is clearly not equal to ! the test fails. (Remember, you have to use a double equal sign in batch file tests.) If you didn't enter anything, the test becomes:

```
IF !==! GOTO OOPS
```

This test is true since ! does equal ! and the batch file then executes the rest of the command, jumping to a label named OOPS. Labels are short words starting with colons. When the batch file jumps to the OOPS label it executes the three lines following it, printing a message onscreen that tells the user to enter a parameter next time.

You don't have to specify the colon before the label in a GOTO command (although it won't hurt), but you do have to include it at the point in the batch file where it actually serves as a label. Labels and conditional GOTO commands let you jump around, or *branch*, inside a batch file, adding tremendous power and flexibility.

If you entered just a single parameter, such as "IBM", the batch file would replace every %1 it finds with it, turning a line such as:

```
ECHO S 0000:0 L0000 %1 %2 %3 %4 %5 %6 %7 %8 %9 >   RAWFILE
```

into:

```
ECHO S 0000:0 L0000 "IBM" >   RAWFILE
```

(If your batch file included a line such as:

```
ECHO %1 %1 %1
```

DOS would translate this to:

```
ECHO "IBM" "IBM" "IBM"
```

since it would replace all three instances of %1.)

If you entered only one parameter on the command line after the name of the batch file, DOS would make the rest of the replaceable parameters — %2 through %9 — equal to (nothing) and would effectively discard them.

The single > redirection sign followed by a filename (RAWFILE) tells DOS to send the characters following the ECHO command into the file specified instead of printing them on the screen. A single > command will wipe out an existing file with the name specified; a double >> sign will append the new information without destroying the old one. By starting out with a single > sign you erase any old RAWFILE file that happens to be on your disk. And by following this with a succession of double >> signs, you build up the new RAWFILE file one line at a time.

The SCAN.BAT batch file creates a new script file called RAWFILE. RAWFILE contains instructions to search through all 16 memory segments one by one for the string or hex characters that you entered. In this particular case the file will look like:

```
S 0000:0 L0000 "IBM" 20 31
S 1000:0 L0000 "IBM" 20 31
S 2000:0 L0000 "IBM" 20 31
S 3000:0 L0000 "IBM" 20 31
S 4000:0 L0000 "IBM" 20 31
```

```
S 5000:0 L0000 "IBM" 20 31
S 6000:0 L0000 "IBM" 20 31
S 7000:0 L0000 "IBM" 20 31
S 8000:0 L0000 "IBM" 20 31
S 9000:0 L0000 "IBM" 20 31
S A000:0 L0000 "IBM" 20 31
S B000:0 L0000 "IBM" 20 31
S C000:0 L0000 "IBM" 20 31
S D000:0 L0000 "IBM" 20 31
S E000:0 L0000 "IBM" 20 31
S F000:0 L0000 "IBM" 20 31
Q
```

(You'll never see RAWFILE, since the batch file erases it before it exits.)

SCAN.BAT uses two kinds of redirection — sending a file into DEBUG and capturing the output from DEBUG. First, it redirects the contents of RAWFILE into DEBUG just as if you had typed in all the search instructions yourself. Then, it redirects the DEBUG output to a file called HITLIST. When it's all done, all you have to do to see the address of each occurrence of the information you were hunting for is look at HITLIST. The best way to do this is to load HITLIST into your word processor or, use the DOS TYPE command. If HITLIST is long, use the MORE command; make sure the DOS MORE.COM program is handy and type:

```
MORE < HITLIST
```

The SCAN.BAT batch file also pipes the DEBUG output through a FIND filter with the line:

```
DEBUG < RAWFILE | FIND /V "-" > HITLIST
```

As DOS sends each line of output through its FIND.EXE filter utility, it checks to see if the line contains a specified character or string of characters. In this case the specified character it looks for is a hyphen (-). The /V switch after the FIND tells DOS to discard any line it finds that happens to have a hyphen anywhere in it. The FIND utility can either screen out lines that do contain the specified string, or those that don't contain it. (As it's used here the command excludes anything with a hyphen. All DEBUG commands have a hyphen as the first character in each line and you don't want your file cluttered with these commands — you want just the results.) However, filtering the text this way takes a bit more execution time and means you have to have the DOS FIND.EXE program handy. If you don't mind seeing the actual commands in the output, and you want to speed things up slightly, change the line to:

```
DEBUG < RAWFILE > HITLIST
```

This means that once you put the SCAN.BAT file and DEBUG.COM in the same directory you can search all the way through memory for any string, or (up to 9) hex values, or combinations of both simply by typing the word SCAN and the information you're looking for. Make sure that you enclose any text you're hunting for inside quotation marks, and that any values you enter on the command line are in hex notation rather than decimal.

As mentioned earlier, DEBUG will report some phantom addresses where it or DOS temporarily puts copies of the string you specified.

Assembling ASM Instructions

Format: **A [address]**

DEBUG's mini-assembler is an extremely powerful tool. As with all power tools, however, you have to be careful how you use it. If you're carefully copying a program out of a book or magazine, or you're an old hand at assembly language, this DEBUG feature can be incredibly useful. Otherwise, don't experiment, unless you're absolutely sure every last file on your system is backed up — and be especially wary about fooling around with anything that deals with disks, and especially anything that writes.

Serious assembly language programmers will use the IBM/Microsoft full-fledged assembler, which is far more powerful and sophisticated. The mini-assembler is for creating and fixing short programs like the ones in this book.

You can use most of the standard 8086/8088 assembly language syntax in DEBUG. But DEBUG's mini-assembler is not built to handle complex programs. For instance when you want the program flow to jump from one place to another you have to furnish precise addresses of where to go; with full-fledged assemblers you can use "labels" instead of addresses. And DEBUG isn't as flexible or understanding about certain kinds of instructions. But for quick-and-dirty programs it's just what the doctor ordered.

To figure out what to do with it, you'll have to get your hands on a book specially written for serious users who want to pick up the fundamentals of programming. One of the best for beginners is Peter Norton's *Programmer's Guide to the IBM PC & PS/2* from Microsoft Press.

To use the mini-assembler for the first time, just get into DEBUG and type A at the main DEBUG - prompt. DEBUG will print an address in segment:offset form starting with offset 0100:

```
C>DEBUG
-A
30DD:0100
```

(Ignore the four hex digits to the left of the colon. This will vary from system to system and won't affect what you're doing.)

At this point DEBUG expects you to enter an assembly language instruction. If you don't want to, just press the Enter key and you'll return to the DEBUG prompt. If you do want to, go ahead and enter it. Type MOV AH,05 and press the Enter key:

```
C>DEBUG
-A
30DD:0100  MOV AH,05
30DD:0102
```

DEBUG will accept what you typed, assemble the instruction into machine-readable code at that address, and skip ahead the proper number of bytes to the next free space in memory waiting for you to enter another instruction. Here it translated the MOV AH,05 instruction into something two bytes long, since the next address it displayed was 0102. If you type something DEBUG doesn't understand, it prints an error message and lets you try again at the same address. For instance, if you had accidentally typed:

```
C>DEBUG
-A
30DD:0100  MOV HA,05
                  ^ Error
30DD:0100
```

DEBUG would have caught the mistake and indicated where it was by pointing to it. Then it would put the same 0100 address onscreen a second time to let you enter the corrected version of this instruction.

But since DEBUG liked the MOV AH,05 (you could have just as easily typed MOV AH,5 by the way), it asked you to enter another instruction at address 102. So type in MOV DL,0C:

```
C>DEBUG
-A
30DD:0100  MOV AH,05
30DD:0102  MOV DL,0C
30DD:0104
```

Again, you can tell it liked what you typed, since it dropped down a line and offered you the chance to enter another instruction at an address two bytes higher, 0104.

(DEBUG is smart enough to know what's legal and what isn't. But it obviously can't tell what's ridiculous. So long as you enter the proper syntax, it will blithely let you create a program to wipe out all the files on your hard disk, or spin into an endless loop that will crash your system. Be extremely careful about all this; one mistyped digit can have catastrophic results. For instance, BIOS interrupt 13 lets you read disk sectors by putting a value of 2 in the AH register. But it lets you write disk sectors by putting a value of 3 in AH. If you accidentally type a 3 instead of a 2, you can kiss your data goodbye.)

To finish the sample program, enter INT 21 to launch DOS into action, and then RET to return to the DOS prompt. You could use INT 20 instead of RET to end short COM programs, but they'll both have the same effect, and RET is easier to type:

```
C>DEBUG
-A
30DD:0100 MOV AH,05
30DD:0102 MOV DL,0C
30DD:0104 INT 21
30DD:0106 RET
30DD:0107
```

When you've entered the last assembly language instruction, you'll see the next address — 0107. Just press the Enter key and you'll return to the main DEBUG prompt. Note the 0107 address, however, since you'll need it for the next step.

You can check your typing by using the Unassemble (U) command. DEBUG will look at the machine-readable code it just assembled, and try to take it apart and reproduce the assembly language instructions you typed in. Since you just started entering instructions at address 0100 and stopped right before 0107, you could type either:

```
-U 100 106
```

or:

```
-U 100 L 7
```

Since you stopped entering instructions right before address 0107, the assembled code occupies seven bytes of memory, not six. Remember that the first byte is at address 100, not 101. And the last byte is at address 106. The first version of the Unassemble command above tells DEBUG to unassemble everything from addresses 100 through 106. The second tells it to unassemble the seven bytes starting at address 100. Both will generate the same display:

```
30F9:0100 B405        MOV  AH,05
30F9:0102 B20C        MOV  DL,0C
30F9:0104 CD21        INT  21
30F9:0106 C3          RET
```

The leftmost column contains the segment:offset memory addresses that you wanted to examine. The next column shows the hexadecimal representations of the actual machine-level code that DEBUG translated the assembly language instructions into. Sending the two bytes B4 and 05, here stuck together as B405, to the CPU tells it to put a value of (MOV) 05 into register AH. The rightmost column is DEBUG's best guess about which instructions you originally typed.

If you saw at this point that you had made a mistake, you could use the A command to correct it. The program you're in the process of creating will send an ASCII decimal character 12 to the printer, which should generate a form feed. Since DEBUG works exclusively in hex, you have to enter the character in its hex form, 0C (or just plain C). If you forgot this, and entered a decimal 12 instead of a hex C, you'd be telling the program to send a hex 12 (decimal 18) to the printer. If you unassembled your typing, you'd see something like:

```
30F9:0100 B405        MOV  AH,05
30F9:0102 B212        MOV  DL,12
30F9:0104 CD21        INT  21
30F9:0106 C3          RET
```

To fix this, tell DEBUG you want to reassemble the instruction beginning at address 102, since you'll have to re-enter the entire MOV DL,0C and this starts at offset 0102:

```
-A 102
```

DEBUG will respond with:

```
30F9:0102
```

Just type in the correct instruction:

```
30F9:0102 MOV DL,0C
```

and press the Enter key. DEBUG doesn't know if you wanted to fix just one instruction or enter several new ones, so it will print the next memory address and offer you the chance to change it as well:

```
30F9:0102 MOV DL,0C
30F9:0104
```

Since all you wanted to re-enter was the single instruction at address 102, press the Enter key to exit the mini-assembler and return to the main DEBUG prompt. Then repeat the unassemble command to verify the correction.

(You could have also used the Enter (E) command to make the change. By looking at the unassembled code you could see that the erroneous value of 12 was at address 103:

```
30F9:0102 B212        MOV  DL,12
```

         /   \
    address   address
      102   103

You could then have typed:

```
-E 103
```

and pressed the Enter key. DEBUG would have responded with:

```
30F9:0103  12.
```

Then enter the correct value of 0C by typing it in and hitting Enter. Use either the Unassemble or Enter commands to verify the change.)

To create the program you just entered, you have to name it, using N FF.COM. First tell DEBUG how long it is, by typing RCX and pressing Enter, then enter 7 when DEBUG displays the colon, and write it to disk (with W), and quit (Q):

```
-N FF.COM
-RCX
CX 0000
:7
-W
Writing 0007 bytes
-Q
```

This program will send a form-feed character (decimal 12, hex 0C) to LPT1:, unless you rerouted printer output somewhere else.

If you go back later to work with the mini-assembler again in the same DEBUG session, DEBUG will remember the last address you used. If you type A without specifying an address after it, DEBUG will assume you want to continue entering new instructions where you left off. Since you left off at address 107 in the above example, you can do some other DEBUG chores and then type:

```
-A
```

to have DEBUG would respond with:

```
30DD:0107
```

Keeping track of the last memory address is handy if you want to continue working on a program in progress. But if you want to create a brand new, unrelated program, you'll have to tell the mini-assembler to start again at address 100:

```
-A 100
```

The mini-assembler is terrific at handling text. To do so, just prefix the text with a DB opcode:

```
C>DEBUG
-A
30DD:0100 MOV AH,09
30DD:0102 MOV DX,108
```

```
30DD:0105 INT 21
30DD:0107 RET
30DD:0108 DB "Common sense is not so common.",0D,0A
30DD:0128 DB "                  - Voltaire",0D,0A,24
30DD:0149
-RCX
CX 0000
:49
-N HOWTRUE.COM
-W
Writing 0049 bytes
-Q
```

DEBUG will calculate how long each string is and automatically start the next instruction (or string) at the next available location. So after you entered:

```
30DD:0108 DB "Common sense is not so common.",0D,0A
```

DEBUG figured out that the next string would begin at address 128, and printed:

```
30DD:0128
```

Each line of text is followed by an 0D,0A (or D,A) carriage-return and line-feed combination. The commas separating these from the text are optional; spaces will work just as well. Note also that when you use function 9 of interrupt 21 you have to put a final "$" after the end of the last string. You could have just as easily entered:

```
30DD:0108 DB "Common sense is not so common." D A
30DD:0128 DB "                  - Voltaire" D A "$"
```

If you put your strings at the end of the program, DEBUG makes it a snap to figure out how many bytes to tell the CX register to write. Just look at the address the mini-assembler prints after you enter the last string. In this case it's 149. Since DEBUG began assembling instructions at offset 100, subtract 100 from 149 and tell the CX register to write 49 bytes.

Unassembling Instructions

Format: **U [address]** *or* **U [range]**

Just as DEBUG lets you translate assembly language instructions into machine-readable code (with the Assemble (A) command), it will reverse the process and turn a stream of hex bytes only a CPU can understand back into recognizable assembly language statements. Or at least it will try to.

One of the main problems is that the Unassemble command can't distinguish program instructions from data, and will try to translate the data back into assembly language statements instead of roping it off and indentifying it as something other than program instructions. Another problem is that different assembler programs can turn different variations of assembly language instructions into the same basic code. The DEBUG Unassembly command has no idea which one of the original variations the programmer used, and may not translate every byte back to the exact source code used to create the program. A third problem is that if you give the Unassemble command the wrong starting address, it will start translating things in mid-instruction, and end up with gibberish. And finally, it's best at translating the kinds of short and sweet COM programs DEBUG can create. Long complex programs, and code created by compilers jump around so much and use so many intertwined libraries of subroutines that you really won't be able to make much sense of most Unassembled output.

But this command can be extremely useful in fixing short programs you or someone else created with DEBUG's mini-assembler. Let's say that someone put a program called WARNING.COM on your disk that was supposed to print the message "DO NOT ERASE YOUR FILES NOW!" Unfortunately, the programmer goofed. When you run it, the program prints "ERASE YOUR FILES NOW!"

The first thing to do is load WARNING.COM into DEBUG, see how long it is (by typing RCX and hitting Enter twice), and display the program using the D command:

```
-RCX
CX 0027
:
-D 100 L 27
30F9:0100  B4 09 BA 0F 01 CD 21 C3-44 4F 20 4E 4F 54 20 45    ......!.DO NOT E
30F9:0110  52 41 53 45 20 59 4F 55-52 20 46 49 4C 45 53 20    RASE YOUR FILES
30F9:0120  4D 4F 57 21 0D 0D 24                                NOW!..$
```

What this tells you is that the actual message inside WARNING.COM is accurate, but that something is wrong with the program portion. You can see by looking at the ASCII display and counting over that the text begins at address 108. But the machine-readable program code from addresses 100 to 107 is inscrutable. Until you use the Unassemble command:

```
-U 100 107
30F9:0100  B409       MOV  AH,09
30F9:0102  BA0F01     MOV  DX,010F
30F9:0105  CD21       INT  21
30F9:0107  C3         RET
```

Now you have to do a little detective work. How does the program work? The first thing to do is look for the workhorses of the programming world — interrupts. In this case the program contains just one instruction that begins with INT. The 21 after the INT tells you the program uses the main DOS interrupt.

By consulting a book such as Norton's *Programmer's Guide to the IBM PC* or IBM's *DOS Technical Reference Manual,* you can look at the description of INT 21 and see that this key interrupt executes dozens of individual function calls and identifies which one to execute by putting the hex value of that function call into the AH register. Sure enough, the very first instruction puts a value of 09 there.

If you then jump to the section detailing function call 09H, you'll see all the important facts that govern its operation. DOS refers to this function call as "Print String" while Norton cautions that it really should be called "Display String." Both sources provide the following information:

1. The string must end in a $ (hex character 24).
2. DOS will send the string to the standard output device (Norton adds that the default is the screen).
3. The value in the data segment's DX register "points" to the beginning of the string.

The second line of the unassembled code shows that the value in DX is 010F. But when you used the D command to display the contents of the program you saw that the text actually started at address 108. So in the erroneous WARNING.COM program, the DX register is pointing somewhere inside the text string rather than at the very beginning of it:

```
DO NOT ERASE YOUR FILES NOW!

    ↑           ↑
address    address
  108         10F
```

To fix the problem, change the value in the DX register from 10F to 108. You can do this by using the Assemble (A) command to create a whole new MOV DX,010F instruction at address 102:

```
-A 102
30F9:0102 MOV DX,0108
30F9:0104
```

and then pressing the Enter key when DEBUG prints the following 104 address. Or you can look at the actual machine-level hex byte code, figure out which bytes store the incorrect 010F value, and use the Enter (E) key to replace the old incorrect number with the correct one.

Using the E command on two-byte addresses is a bit tricky. If you look carefully at the unassembled line beginning at address 102:

```
30F9:0102 BA0F01          MOV DX,010F
```

you'll notice that the BA0F01 machine-level code seems to have scrambled the 010F address into 0F01. This happens because of the seemingly backwards (or "backwords") way your computer stores two-byte numbers, *words*.

Each offset address is two bytes long. Two bytes together make up what is called a word. In any word, one byte is higher, or worth more than, the other, just as in the decimal number 39, the 3 is worth more than the 9, since the 3 digit actually stands for 30, not 3. The byte that is worth more is called the *most-significant byte* and the one that's worth less is the *least-significant byte*. These are sometimes abbreviated as MSB and LSB. Grammarians might quibble that these should really be called "more-significant" and "less-significant" but engineers designed this system, not grammarians.

Here's the important part: It takes two bytes in memory to store a word. One byte has a higher address than the other. Your computer stores the most-significant byte of any word at the higher address of the two (and, obviously, the least-significant byte at the lower address).

The word 010F is actually made up of two individual bytes, 01 and 0F. The 01 byte is the most significant, and the 0F the least significant. So the higher 01 byte is at the higher address and the lower 0F at the lower address.

By looking at the output of the D command you issued earlier:

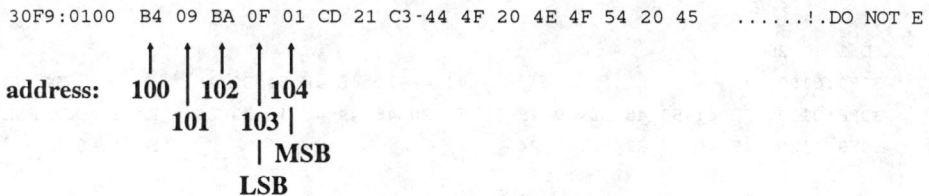

```
30F9:0100   B4 09 BA 0F 01 CD 21 C3-44 4F 20 4E 4F 54 20 45      ......!.DO NOT E

               ↑   ↑   ↑
address:     100 | 102 |104
               101   103 |
                   | MSB
               LSB
```

you can count over from the left and see that the lower 0F byte is indeed at the lower address (103) and that the higher 01 byte is at the higher (104) address.

To replace the old incorrect 010F value with the proper 0108 value, first divide the 0108 word in half. Then enter the least-significant byte (the 08 part) at the lower address (103) and the most-significant byte (the 01 part) at the higher address (104). Since the value at address 104 is already 01, you can just replace the 0F at address 103 with 08.

It doesn't matter whether you use the Assemble (A) or Enter (E) command to change the MOV DX,010F instruction to MOV DX,0108. Each has its advantages. In any case, go back and unassemble the beginning part of WARNING.COM again. This time you should see:

```
-U 100 107
30F9:0100 B409              MOV  AH,09
30F9:0102 BA0801            MOV  DX,0108
30F9:0105 CD21              INT  21
30F9:0107 C3                RET
```

Use the W command to write the changed program to disk and the Q command to quit. If you're nervous about all this, you may want to add another line:

```
-N WARN.COM
```

before you write the modified version. This will create a new file called WARN.COM that won't overwrite the existing WARNING.COM program. If you goofed when modifying the original program, you can erase WARN.COM and try again on the undamaged original. Another way to safeguard the original is to make a copy of WARNING.COM called WARN.COM (or whatever) before making any changes, and then load the WARN.COM copy into DEBUG rather than the WARNING.COM original.

If you had used the Unassemble command on the text part of WARNING.COM (the part that started at address 108), DEBUG would have ended up displaying a meaningless series of instructions. First figure out how long the program is, by typing RCX and pressing Enter twice. Then use the D command to display everything from address 108 (where you know the text starts) to the end:

```
-RCX
CX 0027
:
-D 108 126
30F9:0100                          44 4F 20 4E 4F 54 20 45          DO NOT E
30F9:0110 52 41 53 45 20 59 4F 55-52 20 46 49 4C 45 53 20   RASE YOUR FILES
30F9:0120 4E 4F 57 21 0D 0D 24                              NOW!..$
```

Then Unassemble the same range of addresses:

```
-U 108 126
30F9:0108 44            INC  SP
30F9:0109 4F            DEC  DI
30F9:010A 204E4F        AND  [BP+4F],CL
30F9:010D 54            PUSH SP
30F9:010E 204552        AND  [DI+52],AL
30F9:0111 41            INC  CX
30F9:0112 53            PUSH BX
30F9:0113 45            INC  BP
30F9:0114 20594F        AND  [BX+DI+4F],BL
30F9:0117 55            PUSH BP
30F9:0118 52            PUSH DX
30F9:0119 204649        AND  [BP+49],AL
30F9:011C 4C            DEC  SP
30F9:011D 45            INC  BP
30F9:011E 53            PUSH BX
30F9:011F 204E4F        AND  [BP+4F],CL
```

```
30F9:0122 57              PUSH DI
30F9:0123 210D            AND  [DI],CX
30F9:0125 0D2461          OR   AX,6124
```

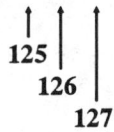

125

126

127

Junk. That's why when you're trying to fix a program you have to use the D and U commands together. In many cases neither the U or D will help, since programs often insert (or *hard-wire*) important data into the program code. Programmers use such data to set defaults, provide lookup tables, etc.

Incidentally, you may have noticed that in the above example even though you asked DEBUG to unassemble memory between addresses 108 and 126, DEBUG went all the way to address 127. If you didn't notice, look at three bytes in the unassembled listing at address 125. (They're all lumped together here, but the first is 0D, the second 24, and the third 61. The second value — 24 — is the actual end of the program. Hex 24 is the code for the final "$" you used to mark the end of the string.")

So why did DEBUG display more memory than you specified? It interpreted the 0D2461 clump of bytes that started at address 125 as one big instruction, and displayed the entire instruction rather than lopping the end of it off prematurely. In fact, the Unassemble listing would have been the same if you had used any of the three following ranges:

```
-U 108 125
```

or:

```
-U 108 126
```

or:

```
-U 108 127
```

In each case, once the Unassemble command sniffs out what it thinks is even a single byte of an instruction it will print the entire instruction.

The Unassemble command can interpret the same stream of hex codes in different ways depending on where you tell it to start. Begin at the beginning, and DEBUG will get it right:

```
-U 100 L8
30F9:0100 B409            MOV  AH,09
30F9:0102 BA0801          MOV  DX,0108
30F9:0105 CD21            INT  21
30F9:0107 C3              RET
```

But start at an address one byte too high and DEBUG will turn the first two instructions into mush:

```
-U 101 L8
30F9:0101 09BA0801      OR   [BP+SI+0108],DI
30F9:0105 CD21          INT  21
30F9:0107 C3            RET
30F9:0108 44            INC  SP
```

Start even farther up and you get equally meaningless results:

```
-U 104 L8
30F9:0104 01CD          ADD  BP,CX
30F9:0106 21C3          AND  BX,AX
30F9:0108 44            INC  SP
30F9:0109 4F            DEC  DI
30F9:010A 204E4F        AND  [BP+4F],CL
```

If you're trying to unassemble something and you just know the program is in there somewhere, try a few different starting addresses until you see a display that contains recognizable instructions. It can be especially confusing when you're just a byte or two off. If you're looking for a specific address, start a dozen or so bytes earlier so the Unassemble command has a chance to get properly on track.

When you first start DEBUG, if you enter the U command without any address or range after it, DEBUG will unassemble the first 32 bytes starting at offset 100 (and possibly a few more than 32, if the 32nd byte is in the middle of a single instruction it's trying to display). Each successive time you then hit U without any parameters after it, DEBUG will unassemble the next 32 or so bytes. DEBUG will always remember the last byte it unassembled. If you enter another command, such as D, between two U commands, the second U command will start displaying code right after the address where the first U command stopped — ignoring whatever you happened to do with D. For example, if you want to unassemble the first 32 bytes of COMMAND.COM (version 5.0):

```
-u
1359:0100 E95D14        JMP   1560
1359:0103 007814        ADD   [BX+SI+14],BH
1359:0106 0000          ADD   [BX+SI],AL
1359:0108 B70E          MOV   BH,0E
1359:010A 0000          ADD   [BX+SI],AL
1359:010C 750D          JNZ   011B
1359:010E 0000          ADD   [BX+SI],AL
1359:0110 8511          TEST  DX,[BX+DI]
1359:0112 0000          ADD   [BX+SI],AL
1359:0114 0000          ADD   [BX+SI],AL
```

```
1359:0116 0000              ADD    [BX+SI],AL
1359:0118 0000              ADD    [BX+SI],AL
1359:011A 0000              ADD    [BX+SI],AL
1359:011C 0000              ADD    [BX+SI],AL
1359:011E 0000              ADD    [BX+SI],AL
```

DEBUG will actually display the first 33. If you then entered U again without any parameters after it, DEBUG would continue the unassembly process with address 121.

You don't ever have to specify a stopping address. And you can tell DEBUG to start anywhere. If you entered:

```
-U 121
```

DEBUG would display the 32 bytes (and actually end up showing you 33) starting at address 121 and stopping at address 141. If for some perverse reason you wanted to unassemble all of COMMAND.COM version 5.0 you would first find out how long the program is by typing RCX and pressing Enter twice. DEBUG would report a length of BAE5 bytes. Then you'd enter the command:

```
-U 100 BAE5
```

and sit back and watch for a long while. To stop the display, just hit Ctrl-Break or Ctrl-C.

If you wanted to see the assembly language code for the first two instructions, you could type either:

```
-U 100 105
```

or:

```
-U 100 L 6
```

Both would display the same unassembled code:

```
30F9:0100 E92D0D           JMP   1560
30F9:0103 BADA0A           MOV   DX,0ADA
```

Fine, fine, you may be saying. But what can you really do with this command that's useful?

Here's something:

It's really incredible that DOS is still back in the dark ages (well, maybe the black and white ages) when it comes to color. Even after half a decade of changes, DOS still clears the screen to grey on black. But it doesn't have to. In fact, the code to set the foreground and background colors to anything you want is already in COMMAND.COM. It's just that the folks who maintain the code have decided they want you to see everything in attribute 07 — and that translates to whitish-grey (the 7) on a black (0) background.

Some programmers feel that you should never patch COMMAND.COM. They say that if you start getting patch-happy you may change something that will have unexpectedly awful results later. But the truth is that if you keep your patches to the barest minimum, it's not so terrible. The only thing you do have to guard against, however, is mixing versions of COMMAND.COM on the same disk, which confuses DOS.

DOS and most other programs do video tasks such as clearing the screen by using BIOS interrupt 10 (hex). Some fancy programs come with their own proprietary screen utilities. But not DOS. When you type CLS, COMMAND.COM scans its list of internal commands, sees that CLS is indeed an internal command, then executes the screen-clearing routine inside itself.

BIOS interrupt 10 provides two similar services called Scroll Window Up (Service 6) and Scroll Window Down (Service 7). These will both open just about any size window onscreen and insert blank lines at the top or bottom to scroll the existing text away. You can tell it exactly how big a window to scroll and what color to make the blank lines by using the following registers:

- AH = the service itself (6 means up, 7 means down)
- AL = how many lines to scroll (a 0 here clears the window)
- BH = the color of the blank lines
- CH = upper lefthand window row
- CL = upper lefthand window column
- DH = lower righthand window row
- DL = lower righthand window column

To clear an entire 25 x 80 screen to blue text on a white background using Service 6, you could create the following code fragment:

```
MOV AX,0600   ; AH=6 means up; AL=0 means clear screen
MOV BH,71     ; color (7=white bkgnd; 1=blue frgrnd)
MOV CX,0000 ; start at row 0, column 0 (top left corner)
MOV DX,184F ; stop at row 18 (dec 24; col 4F (decimal 79)
INT 10
```

(The reason this fragment tells interrupt 10 to stop the window on the 79th column of the 24th row is that since the screen actually begins on column 0 of row 0, the lower righthand corner is indeed column 79 of row 24. In wouldn't hurt anything to specify row 25 and column 80 unless you're doing something fancy such as using more than one screen "page." You're probably not.)

This code fragment uses a sort of shorthand in filling the appropriate registers. Instead of putting two separate byte values into the AH and AL registers, it combined the single-byte values (06 and 00) into one double-byte word (0600) and moved this word into the AX register. In this example:

```
MOV AX,0600
        ↑ ↑
       AH AL
```

the 06 fills the AH register and the 00 fills the AL register. This is the same as saying:

```
MOV AH,06
MOV AL,00
```

except that the first way is shorter. The example fills the CX and DX registers using the same kind of shorthand.

You can even assemble this if you want. If you do, be sure to stick a RET command onto it below the INT 10. Tell DEBUG it will be 0E bytes long (with the RCX command). Name it BLUE.COM. Then write it and quit, and when you're back at the DOS prompt type BLUE. To make this really effective you'd have to add some cursor positioning code too, but that's not the point of this exercise.

COMMAND.COM uses a variation of this code fragment to do its screen clearing. To find this COMMAND.COM screen clearing mechanism, use DEBUG's Search (S) command to look for interrupt 10. Load COMMAND.COM into DEBUG. Find out how long your version is by typing RCX and pressing Enter twice (this example uses version 5.0). Then search the whole file for all occurrences of CD 10, the machine-readable code for interrupt 10:

```
C>DEBUG COMMAND.COM
-RCX
CX BAE5
:
-S 100 L BAE5 CD 10
1359:432B
1359:4337
1359:435F
1359:436C
1359:4370
1359:4376
```

Fortunately these addresses are clumped closely together, which makes it easy to display them all with the Unassemble command in one gulp. Start a few bytes before the first match that the Search command found, and continue a bit past the last one:

```
-u 4322 437f
1359:4322 7505          JNZ       4329
1359:4324 E85200        CALL      4379
1359:4327 EB2C          JMP       4355
1359:4329 B40F          MOV       AH,0F
1359:432B CD10          INT       10
1359:432D 3C03          CMP       AL,03
1359:432F 760A          JBE       433B
1359:4331 3C07          CMP       AL,07
1359:4333 7406          JZ        433B
1359:4335 B400          MOV       AH,00
```

```
1359:4337  CD10        INT    10
1359:4339  EB1A        JMP    4355
1359:433B  1E          PUSH   DS
1359:433C  B84000      MOV    AX,0040
1359:433F  8ED8        MOV    DS,AX
1359:4341  8B164A00    MOV    DX,[004A]
1359:4345  8A368400    MOV    DH,[0084]
1359:4349  1F          POP    DS
1359:434A  0AF6        OR     DH,DH
1359:434C  7502        JNZ    4350
1359:434E  B619        MOV    DH,19
1359:4350  FEC6        INC    DH
1359:4352  E80100      CALL   4356
1359:4355  C3          RET
1359:4356  FECE        DEC    DH
1359:4358  FECA        DEC    DL
1359:435A  52          PUSH   DX
1359:435B  B40B        MOV    AH,0B
1359:435D  33DB        XOR    BX,BX
1359:435F  CD10        INT    10
1359:4361  5A          POP    DX
1359:4362  33C0        XOR    AX,AX
1359:4364  8BC8        MOV    CX,AX
1359:4366  B406        MOV    AH,06
1359:4368  B707        MOV    BH,07
1359:436A  32DB        XOR    BL,BL
1359:436C  CD10        INT    10
1359:436E  B40F        MOV    AH,0F
1359:4370  CD10        INT    10
1359:4372  B402        MOV    AH,02
1359:4374  33D2        XOR    DX,DX
1359:4376  CD10        INT    10
1359:4378  C3          RET
1359:4379  BE7885      MOV    SI,8578
1359:437C  AC          LODSB
1359:437D  8AC8        MOV    CL,AL
```

This display may look a bit daunting, but you'll see how easy it is to map it out. Incidentally, this whole process is easier when you do it on paper. To get a printout of it, turn your printer on and type either Ctrl-P or Ctrl-PrtSc before you issue the U 2B80 2BC0 command. DOS will print each line both on the screen and on the printer. Then type Ctrl-P or Ctrl-PrtSc one more time to turn this printer "echoing" feature off.

The first thing to do is to figure out what each of the six INT 10s does. Get out your copy of Norton's *Programmer's Guide to the PC & PS/2* or any other reference book that lists the various BIOS services. Scan through the instructions right before each INT

10 until you see a MOV AH. In some programs you may have to look for a MOV AX, since it may use the same kind of "shorthand" mentioned earlier. When the program gets to an INT 10 it looks at the value in the AH register to figure out which interrupt 10 service to execute. Here's an annotated version of the unassembled listing, trimmed on the top and bottom:

```
1359:4329 B40F          MOV     AH,0F    ; Service 0F =
1359:432B CD10          INT     10       ; get video mode
===================================================================
1359:432D 3C03          CMP     AL,03
1359:432F 760A          JBE     433B
1359:4331 3C07          CMP     AL,07
1359:4333 7406          JZ      433B
1359:4335 B400          MOV     AH,00    ; Service 00 =
1359:4337 CD10          INT     10       ; set video mode
===================================================================
1359:4339 EB1A          JMP     4355
1359:433B 1E            PUSH    DS
1359:433C B84000        MOV     AX,0040
1359:433F 8ED8          MOV     DS,AX
1359:4341 8B164A00      MOV     DX,[004A]
1359:4345 8A368400      MOV     DH,[0084]
1359:4349 1F            POP     DS
1359:434A 0AF6          OR      DH,DH
1359:434C 7502          JNZ     4350
1359:434E B619          MOV     DH,19
1359:4350 FEC6          INC     DH
1359:4352 E80100        CALL    4356
1359:4355 C3            RET
1359:4356 FECE          DEC     DH
1359:4358 FECA          DEC     DL
1359:435A 52            PUSH    DX
1359:435B B40B          MOV     AH,0B    ; Service 0B =
1359:435D 33DB          XOR     BX,BX    ; set palette
1359:435F CD10          INT     10
===================================================================
1359:4361 5A            POP     DX
1359:4362 33C0          XOR     AX,AX
1359:4364 8BC8          MOV     CX,AX
1359:4366 B406          MOV     AH,06    ; Service 06 =
1359:4368 B707          MOV     BH,07    ; scroll window up
1359:436A 32DB          XOR     BL,BL
1359:436C CD10          INT     10
===================================================================
1359:436E B40F          MOV     AH,0F    ; Service 0F =
```

```
1359:4370 CD10          INT     10      ; get video mode
===================================================================
1359:4372 B402          MOV     AH,02   ; Service 02 =
1359:4374 33D2          XOR     DX,DX   ; set cursor position
1359:4376 CD10          INT     10
```

The one we're hunting for is the large Service 06 near the bottom. This doesn't look exactly like the BLUE.COM example mentioned above, but all the necessary values and settings are there, even if COMMAND.COM does things differently. For instance, when BLUE.COM put a 00 in register AL to tell interrupt 10 to clear the window it did it with the instruction:

```
MOV AX,0600
```

(The 00 at the end of 0600 filled AL.) COMMAND.COM does it with the command:

```
XOR AX,AX
```

since using a XOR operation on any value cancels out that value and turns it into 0. It followed this with a MOV AH,06 instruction to put the 6 into AH.

The register that controls color settings for Service 06 is BH. BLUE.COM put a 71 there:

```
MOV BH,71
```

The left digit of the value in BH (here it's 71) controls the background. The right digit controls the foreground (text). The basic IBM color scheme is:

0 Black	8 Dark grey
1 Blue	9 Bright blue
2 Green	A Bright green
3 Cyan (light blue)	B Bright cyan
4 Red	C Bright red
5 Magenta (purple)	D Bright magenta
6 Brown (dark yellow)	E Yellow
7 White (light grey)	F Bright white

So 71 will produce blue text on a white background.

COMMAND.COM puts a value of 07 into this register, which means grey-white text on a black background. All you have to do to patch this permanently is to change the value to something more colorful. A value of 4E will clear your screen to bright yellow text on a red background, so try it. Once you know the technique you can always change it to something else.

Look at the annotated listing again. The 07 byte is at address 4369. So to patch COMMAND.COM so that it will clear the screen and print bright yellow text on a red background in version 5.0, type:

```
C>DEBUG COMMAND.COM
-E 4369
```

and press the Enter key. Make sure you see something like:

```
1279:4369   07.
```

(Remember, ignore the first four hex digits to the left of the colon; they'll vary from system to system and don't affect anything here.) If you don't see an 07, press Enter to return to the DEBUG prompt, then type Q and Enter to quit and make sure you're using version 5.0. Then start again. If you do see an 07, type in the new value (4E) next to the period and press Enter.

Then, give the file a new name. Use the N command to name it COMMAND1.COM. Then type W and Enter to write the file and then Q and Enter to quit:

```
-N COMMAND1.COM
-W
Writing BAE5 bytes
-Q
```

With older versions of DOS and ANSI.SYS, you could test your work to this point by running COMMAND1 (as a secondary processor), then typing CLS to see the colors take effect. Later versions, including DOS 5.0 will let you run COMMAND1, but ANSI.SYS won't surrender screen control, so CLS gives you the same colors you started with.

To test the color change, format a floppy with the /s option, then copy COMMAND1.COM to the floppy as COMMAND.COM. (For example, COPY COMMAND1.COM A:COMMAND.COM, which replaces the original COMMAND.COM on the A: drive with the modified COMMAND1.COM.)

Now if you boot from the floppy, CLS will clear the screen to the color combination you've chosen. Once you're convinced you like the new colors, you can rename the patched COMMAND1.COM to COMMAND.COM and put it on your start-up disk to replace the older version. Boot up with the patched version and type CLS to set the colors properly. You can also set colors by using ANSI.SYS (see the chapter on ANSI.SYS).

The instructions above are for DOS 5.0 only. For other versions of DOS use these addresses to patch COMMAND.COM to add color to CLS:

DOS Version	Address
2.0	2346
2.1	2359
3.0	2428
3.1	2642
3.2	282E
3.3	2BAD
4.01	3EC7 (IBM)
4.01	3E97 (Generic MSDOS)

If you have a CGA system these patches won't set the border color. EGA and VGA screens don't have borders that can be set, and, anyway, adding code to set CGA borders is far more complex than just changing a byte value.

Displaying Register and Flag Contents

Format: **R [registername]**

This command is primarily for hard-core programmers, but all users need to understand one very important aspect of it: it shows the current state of the CPU registers and flags and lets you change them.

The R command can work three different ways:

1. Typing R by itself will print the hex values in all 14 of the system registers, show all eight flag settings, and display the next instruction DEBUG is poised to execute.
2. Typing R with an F after it will display just the flag settings.
3. Following R with the name of a specific register will display the contents of that single register and let the user either enter a new value or just press the Enter key to keep the old one.

If you're not a serious programmer you never really have to see the state of your system flags. And while you do need to examine and change one or two system registers, you really don't need to see them all at once. So you can pretty much ignore modes 1 and 2 above. But here's what they look like, if you're curious:

```
C>DEBUG COMMAND.COM
-R
AX=0000  BX=0000  CX=62DB  DX=0000  SP=FFFE  BP=0000  SI=0000  DI=0000
DS=30F9  ES=30F9  SS=30F9  CS=30F9  IP=0100     NV UP EI PL NZ NA PO NC
30F9:0100 E92D0D        JMP 0E30
-R F
NV UP EI PL NZ NA PO NC
```

DEBUG initially sets the value of the four general-purpose or scratch-pad registers (AX, BX, CX, and DX) to zero. However, when you tell DEBUG to load a typical (short) program into memory it moves the program's length into register CX. COM-MAND.COM version 3.3 is decimal 25307 bytes long, or 62DB in hex, so these four registers would look like:

*   AX = 0000
*   BX = 0000
*   CX = 62DB
*   DX = 0000

Each register can hold two-byte values from hex 0000 (0 decimal) to FFFF (65535 decimal — or 64K). If a program is larger than 64K, DEBUG uses both the CX and BX registers to store the length.

Remember, a pair of bytes together is word. You can manipulate each of these registers one word (two bytes) at a time by referring to them as AX, BX, CX, and DX. Or you can chop each in half and manipulate just a single byte at a time: the high half and the low half. The high halves are called AH, BH, CH, and DH. The low halves are AL, BL, CL, and DL.

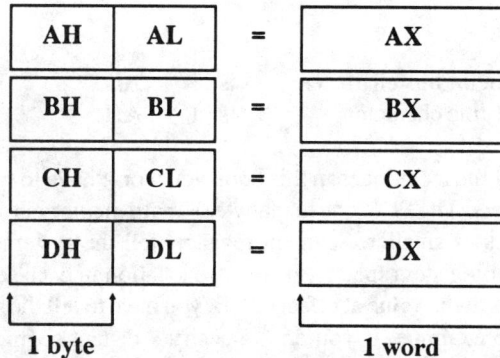

AH	AL	=	AX
BH	BL	=	BX
CH	CL	=	CX
DH	DL	=	DX

1 byte   **1 word**

If the two-byte value in CX is 62DB, then CH holds the high 62 byte and CL the low DB byte. Used by itself, DEBUG's R command will show you all the two-byte registers. And it will let you examine, and change, any single two-byte register. But you can't use it to see just the high or low halves; you have to look at the value of the whole word.

Virtually all the examples in this book use the CX register to set or change program lengths. Many of the programs use one or more of these general-purpose registers to feed parameters into interrupts. For instance, if you're using Service 6 of BIOS interrupt 10 to clear the screen (or scroll a window of any size upward) you put the following values into the following registers:

- The number of the service itself   into   AH
- The number of lines to scroll   into   AL
- The color of the new blank lines   into   BH
- The upper lefthand row number   into   CH
- The upper lefthand column number   into   CL
- The lower righthand row number   into   DH
- The lower righthand column number   into   DL

In this case you simply put the appropriate values' inputs into the proper registers and execute the interrupt without having to worry about the state of the registers afterward. In other cases, interrupts perform operations for you and leave the results in certain registers.

390 DOS Power Tools, 2nd Edition, Revised for DOS 5.0

For instance, to find out what character and color are at the current cursor position (with Service 8 of BIOS interrupt 10) you put the following numbers into the following registers:

- The number of the service itself   into   AH
- The video page number   into   BH

(In most cases, the *page* — the slice of video memory that displays the image — is 0.) After you execute this interrupt you can look into two registers to get the information you need:

- The ASCII value of this character   is in   AL
- The attribute of this character   is in   AH

To master most of the techniques in this book you won't have to work much (or at all) with the other registers. The PC's one megabyte of main memory is segmented (divided) into slices 64K bytes or smaller. Segment registers tell the system which slice you're working with. Offset registers specify the precise location in each segment slice.

If you want to look at the value at offset 62DB, you have to tell the system which 62DB address you want to examine. If you don't specify a distant segment, the system will assume you're talking about the one you've been using, the one you're currently in, or the one it normally checks for similar requests.

Each of the four segment registers (CS, DS, SS, and ES) has a special role. CS tells the system where to find the *code* segment, the slice of memory where your program is loaded. DS contains the address of the *data* segment, the place your program stores its data. SS points to the *stack* segment, a special storage area where the program can temporarily park information it needs to function properly. And ES lets the system know where to find an *extra* segment it can use to squirrel away working data.

These CS, DS, SS, and ES segments may be at different parts of memory, or they may overlap. When DEBUG loads a program like COMMAND.COM, all four of these segments share the same exact area of memory, starting at the first unused memory space — in this case right after where DEBUG itself is loaded:

- DS=30F9
- ES=30F9
- SS=30F9
- CS=30F9

While you'll use the four general-purpose registers frequently, and the four segment registers on occasion, you probably won't need to worry about the other five — the segment registers. One special offset register, the *instruction pointer* (IP), specifies where inside the code segment to find the very next executable instruction. The other offset registers are divided into *pointer* and *index* registers.

The *stack pointer* (SP) and *base pointer* (BP) help programs manage the flow of information onto and off of the stack. A computer like the PC can handle only one tightly focused task at a time. A seemingly simple task such as printing one character onscreen can actually be made up of lots of smaller, discrete ones such as moving values around in memory, checking modes, looking up dot patterns, setting attributes, deciding whether or not to scroll the screen, advancing the cursor, and doing other miscellaneous house-keeping. As your computer executes one main task it frequently has to pause and execute others, and then return to the original task at hand. When it puts one thing on hold so it can do another, it stores the values, addresses, and other settings needed by the first task temporarily in the chunk of memory called the stack. Then when it's done with the second task, it can retrieve all this needed information from the stack and resume working on the first task. Pointer registers keep track of offsets in the stack segment.

The *source index* (SI) and *destination index* (DI) registers work somewhat like the pointer registers, except that index registers normally maintain offsets into the current data segment rather than the stack segment. They're used for things like moving strings from one place in memory (the source) to another (the destination).

DEBUG initially sets the index registers and base pointers to zero. Unless it's working with an EXE file, DEBUG sets the stack pointer to FFFE, or as high as the available memory allows. And it usually puts a value of 100 in IP, since the instruction pointer initially stores the address of the first executable instruction at the very beginning of the program. After DEBUG loaded COMMAND.COM (at offset 100), these looked like:

- SP=FFFE
- BP=0000
- SI=0000
- DI=0000
- IP=0100

Apart from the four general-purpose registers, four segment registers, and five offset registers, the PC maintains a special two-byte storehouse of data called the *flags* register. A flag is an individual bit (a 1 or a 0) that can show the status of — or control — gut-level operations. Six of these are *status* flags that act as a scoreboard to report what happened during recent arithmetic and logical operations. Three are *control* flags that influence the behavior of certain processes. (In Intel's early CPUs, the other seven bits in the flag register remain unused; more advanced chips take advantage of a few other flags.)

The status flags report on the outcome of events. Programs constantly test to see whether two numbers have the same value, or whether numbers are equal to zero. If they are, the system sets the zero flag bit; turns it "on" by giving it a value of 1. If they're not, the system clears the zero flag, turns it off by giving it a value of 0. Flags can also tell whether the result of an arithmetic process was so big that the system had to *carry* a digit out of a register. And they can specify whether a number is negative, or so huge that it totally overflows the system's working range. The system also monitors *parity* by setting a flag if the binary number representing a value has an even number of 1s in it. And it maintains a special *auxiliary carry* flag to help straighten out the messy conversions required when dealing with *binary-coded decimal* (BCD) calculations. (Take our word for it — you don't want to know.)

Control flags can send certain repeated operations in one direction or another, or tell the system whether or not it may use external interrupts, or let programmers step through (*trap*) executable code one instruction at a time.

Packing all these flags into a single register lets you treat them as a single unit. This makes it easier to save, examine, or change the state of your system with special flag instructions. When you first load a program such as COMMAND.COM into DEBUG and enter R all by itself, or R followed by F, all you'll see is:

```
NV UP EI PL NZ NA PO NC
```

The abbreviations are vaguely mnemonic. NV, the least obvious abbreviation, stands for "No oVerflow" (the reverse OV would spell trouble). UP reveals that the direction is UP (the opposite is DN for DowN). EI stands for "Enable Interrupts" (DI would indicate that external interrupts were temporarily DIsabled). PL is used when the sign of a number is a PLus; if the number were NeGative the abbreviation would be NG. NZ obviously says "Not Zero" (and ZR would mean a number was equal to ZeRo or that two numbers were equal to each other). NA tells us "No Auxiliary" carry correction is necessary (AC would let us know one was needed). PO spells out "Odd Parity;" even would trigger a PE. And NC informs us "No Carry" was involved; a CY would tell us a CarrY did occur. The codes are summarized in the following chart:

Flag	Set (=1)	Clear (=0)
Overflow (yes/no)	OV	NV
Direction (down/up)	DN	UP
Interrupt (enabled/disabled)	EI	DI
Sign (negative/positive)	NG	PL
Zero (equal/not equal)	ZR	NZ
Auxiliary carry (yes/no)	AC	NA
Parity (even/odd)	PE	PO
Carry (yes/no)	CY	NC

DEBUG's R command will display the state of all six status flags, and two of the three control flags (direction and interrupt). If you want to single-step your way through a program, you have to turn the trap flag on by invoking DEBUG's Trace command.

At any point you can examine the state of all the registers and flags by typing R and pressing Enter:

```
-R
AX=0000  BX=0000  CX=62DB  DX=0000  SP=FFFE  BP=0000  SI=0000  DI=0000
DS=30F9  ES=30F9  SS=30F9  CS=30F9  IP=0100   NV UP EI PL NZ NA PO NC
30F9:0100 E92D0D        JMP 0E30
```

If you want to display just the flags, add an F:

```
-R F
NV UP EI PL NZ NA PO NC   -
```

(The spaces between the R command and any register after it are optional. R F is the same as RF. RCX and R CX will both work.) If you issue an R F command, DEBUG will wait for you to change one or more flag settings. If you want to leave things exactly as they were (and most of the time you probably should), just press the Enter key. If not, enter the opposite code(s), shown in the table above.

For example, if you wanted to disable external interrupts and switch parity from odd to even, you could type:

```
NV UP EI PL NZ NA PO NC   -  DI PE
```

or:

```
NV UP EI PL NZ NA PO NC   -  PE DI
```

or:

```
NV UP EI PL NZ NA PO NC   -  PEDI
```

or:

```
NV UP EI PL NZ NA PO NC   -  DIPE
```

and then press Enter. The order, spacing, and uppercasing are optional. To check your typing, enter R F again and you should see:

```
-R F
NV UP DI PL NZ NA PE NC   -
```

The only time you'll probably ever have to use the R command is when you create or modify a program. If you used the Assemble (A) command to create a tiny program called AMERICA.COM:

```
C>DEBUG
-A
30DD:0100 MOV AH,9
30DD:0102 MOV DX,108
30DD:0105 INT 21
30DD:0107 RET
30DD:0108 DB "Back in the US" 0D 0A 24
30DD:0119
-N AMERICA.COM
-W
```

and tried to write the file to disk without specifying a length, DEBUG would create a file zero bytes long:

```
Writing 0000 bytes
```

To have DEBUG create the file you wanted, you have to tell it how many bytes to write. Whenever you use its mini-assembler to assemble a program, DEBUG figures out how many bytes the machine-level version of the previous command would fill in memory and prints the very next address onscreen as a prompt. In this case the last line of the program was:

```
30DD:0108 DB "Back in the US" 0D 0A 24
```

so DEBUG assembled that line and then printed:

```
30DD:0119
```

To exit the mini-assembler and return to the main DEBUG prompt, you would note this address (119) and press the Enter key. Then, since the file starts at offset 100, tell DEBUG how long the file is by subtracting 100 from 119 and entering the result, 19, in the CX register:

```
-RCX
CX 0000
:19
```

Now use the W command to write the file to disk (and then Q to quit). You should see:

```
-W
Writing 0019 bytes
-Q
```

New users sometimes forget to subtract the 100. It usually won't hurt a program to make it a bit longer, since programs stop when they reach instructions like INT 20 or RET, and anything past that is ignored. The AMERICA.COM program uses the DOS "Display String" function call 9, which stops when it sees a $ (here this is entered as a hex 24). So DOS would ignore anything after the equals sign.

However, it can be dangerous to make programs too short. If the final instruction were INT 20 or RET (to quit the program and return to the main COMMAND.COM prompt), and you entered a length in the CX register that was one byte too short, DOS wouldn't be able to execute this last instruction, and would never be able to exit the program. You'd then have to reboot.

You also may have to use the RCX command when you modify a program. If you run the AMERICA.COM program, it will simply print:

```
Back in the US
```

To add a few characters to the string this program displays, load AMERICA.COM into DEBUG, type RCX and press the Enter key twice to find out how long the program is, then use the Display (D) command to show you the contents:

```
C>DEBUG AMERICA.COM
-RCX
CX 0019
:
-D 100 L 19
30F9:0100  B4 09 BA 08 01 CD 21 C3-42 61 63 6B 20 69 6E 20    ......!.Back in
30F9:0110  74 68 65 20 55 53 0D 0A-24                         the US..$
```

The actual string that AMERICA.COM displays ends at address 115, and is followed at addresses 116 through 118 by an 0D 0A 24 — a carriage return, a line feed, and a $ string terminator. So add two more letters to the existing string, starting at address 116, and then slap on the required 0D 0A 24:

```
-E 116 "SR" 0D 0A 24
```

If you tried to write the program to disk at this point, you'd end up with a mess, since DEBUG still thinks the program is 19 hex bytes long and will truncate it prematurely, omitting the final two characters from the file. The final few characters of the original and new programs would look like:

	Address 114	Address 115	Address 116	Address 117	Address 118	Address 119	Address 11A
Original	U	S	(CR)	(LF)	$		
New	U	S	S	R	(CR)	(LF)	$

(CR) = carriage return
(LF) = line feed

end of program

(Remember, the program starts at address 100, not address 101. So the last — hex 19th — byte is at address 118, not 119.)

In the original program, the final character was a $ that DOS needed to terminate the string. But in the modified version, the two new bytes of text pushed the final two characters — the line feed and the $ — into addresses 119 and 11A. The new program is 1B bytes long (hex 19 + 2 = 1B), but since you didn't tell DEBUG the program was larger, it wrote only the first 19 bytes to the new file. So when DOS executes the new one, it won't find a $ to tell it to stop, and will keep printing whatever garbage is in memory until it inevitably stumbles onto a random value of 24 that just happens to be in memory.

To prevent this from happening, tell DEBUG the program is now 1B bytes long instead of 19. And since you're modifying an existing file, give the new one a new name so you don't wipe out the old one. Then write the file and quit:

```
-RCX
CX 0019
:1B
-N BEATLES.COM
-W
Writing 001B bytes
-Q
```

This time when you run BEATLES.COM you'll see:

```
Back in the USSR
```

If all you want to do is examine the contents of a register like CX, you can type RCX and press the Enter key twice, or you can just type R and press Enter once. The second way involves a bit less typing, but it clutters up your screen by showing you the contents of all the registers and flags. Either way will work.

Performing Hexadecimal Arithmetic

Format: **H value value**

Counting in hex is daunting for beginners, who commonly forget that the number after 19 is 1A, not 20, and that the number right before 20 is 1F, not 19. Doing even simple math, especially with hex numbers several digits long, can be hair-raising.

But the only real math you have to do is add and subtract hex numbers. To help, DEBUG gives you a free hex calculator. Just get to the DEBUG prompt, type H and two numbers, and DEBUG will print first the sum and then the difference.

You can't enter numbers larger than FFFF (about 65,000 decimal). And DEBUG can't handle sums larger than FFFF, or negative numbers. If you ask it to add FFFF and 1 it will print 0000:

```
-H FFFF 1
0000  FFFE
```

Tell it to subtract 1 from 0 and you'll get FFFF:

```
-H 0 1
0001  FFFF
```

While these examples are trivial, this command really comes in handy when you're fumbling with two thorny numbers such as:

```
-H C79B E8AF
B04A  DEEC
```

Note that the order in which you specify the raw hex numbers is critical. Entering:

```
-H 2 3
```

will produce:

```
0005  FFFF
```

while switching the numbers around:

```
-H 3 2
```

will print:

```
0005  0001
```

The additions will always be the same, but subtracting 3 - 2 is far different from subtracting 2 - 3.

If you keep DEBUG.COM and the DOS FIND.EXE filter on your disk, you can write a small batch file to do hex addition and subtraction for you automatically. Create the following batch file using a pure ASCII word processor, or EDLIN:

```
ECHO OFF
IF !%2==! GOTO OOPS
ECHO H %1 %2 > DEBUG.SCR
ECHO Q >> DEBUG.SCR
ECHO The sum and difference of %1 and %2 are:
DEBUG < DEBUG.SCR | FIND /V "-"
DEL DEBUG.SCR
GOTO END
```

```
:OOPS
ECHO You have to enter %0 followed by
ECHO 2 hex numbers each FFFF or less
ECHO (e.g. %0 4D7F 5A4)
:END
```

(You can also create this file by using the DOS COPY CON command. To do so, add a line at the top that says:

```
COPY CON HEX.BAT
```

When you're done typing the last line, press the Enter key, then press the F6 function key, and then press the Enter key a final time.)

To use it at the main DOS prompt, make sure you have DEBUG.COM, FIND.EXE, and this HEX.BAT batch file handy. Then type the word HEX followed by the two hex numbers (hex FFFF or smaller) that you want to add or subtract.

After issuing the ECHO OFF command to suppress screen clutter, the batch file first makes sure you entered two hex numbers. When you execute a batch file, DOS looks for any delimiters such as spaces or commas that separate what you typed into groups of characters. It then takes these groups and uses them to set the values of up to ten replaceable parameters.

The first replaceable parameter is always the name of the batch file itself, and DOS refers to this as %0. DOS calls the second discrete thing you type %1, the third one %2, etc. If you put a %0 or %1 in your batch file, DOS will replace these with what you typed on the command line. So if you execute the batch file HEX.BAT by typing:

```
HEX 1A 3B
```

DOS will make the following substitutions:

%0	HEX
%1	1A
%2	3B

To make sure you entered two hex numbers after the word HEX on the command line, the batch file checks to see if parameter %2 contains something or not. If you entered just one hex number on the command line after the word HEX, or didn't enter any hex numbers at all after the word HEX, %2 would be equal to nothing. The test:

```
IF !%2==! GOTO OOPS
```

would replace the %2 with nothing, leaving:

```
IF !==! GOTO OOPS
```

Since ! is indeed equal to ! (you could have used another symbol such as @ if you don't like exclamation points), the test is true, and the batch file executes the command following the test (GOTO OOPS). The batch file will look for a label called :OOPS and jump directly there without executing any intervening instructions. In this batch file, the commands following the :OOPS label will provide a reminder about the proper syntax.

If you did enter two hex numbers, such as 1A and 3B, DOS will replace the %2 with 3B and make the test:

```
IF !3B==! GOTO OOPS
```

Since !3B is clearly not the same as !, the test will fail (which is what you want), and the batch file will grind into action.

The lines:

```
ECHO H %1 %2 > DEBUG.SCR
ECHO Q >> DEBUG.SCR
```

will first redirect the letter H, plus the two hex numbers you entered on the DOS command line after the word HEX, into a file called DEBUG.SCR. (The double >> symbol appends the redirected characters to an existing file rather than creating a new one.)

What this will end up doing is creating a temporary file called DEBUG.SCR that contains two DEBUG commands and the hex numbers you entered. If these hex numbers were 1A and 3B, the contents of the DEBUG.SCR file would be:

```
H 1A 3B
Q
```

The batch file will then display a message onscreen to clarify what's happening. DEBUG will replace the %1 and %2 here as well, and end up printing:

```
The sum and difference of 1A and 3B are:
```

It then takes the DEBUG.SCR file it just created and redirects the characters in this file into DEBUG just as if you had typed them at the keyboard. These characters issue the DEBUG commands to perform hex arithmetic on the numbers you entered. The same batch file line then sends the resulting DEBUG output through a FIND filter to get rid of the actual DEBUG commands. If you didn't use this filter, you'd see

```
The sum and difference of 1A and 3B are:
-H 1A 3B
0055  FFDF
Q
```

However, the:

```
/V "-"
```

at the end of the FIND command tells DOS to display only those lines that do *not* contain a "-." Since all DEBUG commands contain a hyphen, this filters out the actual commands and cleans up the display. All you see is:

```
The sum and difference of 1A and 3B are:
0055  FFDF
```

Finally, the batch file deletes the temporary DEBUG.SCR file and exits. While HEX.BAT can check to make sure you entered two hex numbers, it can't check to see if these numbers are valid. So if you enter something DEBUG can't handle, you'll see an error message.

Comparing Two Blocks of Memory

Format: **C range address**

This command is useful in isolating file differences, though you probably won't use it much (if at all). The pathetic PC-DOS COMP command (Microsoft's MS-DOS FC is far superior) will refuse to work if you ask it to examine two things of unequal length. And, the DOS COMP utility will stop in its tracks after ten mismatches, while the DEBUG C command will grind merrily away reporting them by the screenful.

To use the C command, type in C, then a first range of memory, and then a second starting address. When entering the first range you can use explicit starting and stopping addresses, or you can specify a starting address and a length of bytes to check. When specifying the second block of memory you want to check, all you have to enter is the starting address. DEBUG will calculate the length of the first block and apply that length to both comparisons.

The two commands below will each direct DEBUG to compare two blocks of memory each 10 hex (16 decimal) bytes long — one starting at address 100 and the other at address 110:

```
-C 100 L 10 110
```

and:

```
-C 100 10F 110
```

If you had used the E command to enter the following values into addresses 100 and 110:

```
-E 100 0 1 2 3 4 5 6 7 8 9 A B C D E F
-E 110 0 1 2 3 4 5 6 8 7 9 A B C D E F
```

you could then view these values by using the D command:

```
-D 100 L 20
30DD:0100 00 01 02 03 04 05 06 07-08 09 0A 0B 0C 0D 0E 0F
30DD:0110 00 01 02 03 04 05 06 08-07 09 0A 0B 0C 0D 0E 0F
```

Notice that the seventh and eighth bytes are switched. The C command tells DEBUG to look at every byte in the first range you specified and compare it to the corresponding byte in the second chunk. If it finds mismatches, it will sandwich them between the two addresses of the differing bytes, so the two Compare commands above would each yield the report:

```
30DD:0107   07   08   30DD:0117
30DD:0108   08   07   30DD:0118
```

If DEBUG doesn't find any mismatches it will simply print another hyphen prompt.

If you had two programs on your disk of the same length called REDWHITE.COM and WHITERED.COM that cleared the screen to different colors (red on white vs. white on red), to find the differences in the files; you could use the DOS COMP utility

```
C>COMP REDWHITE.COM C:WHITERED.COM
C:REDWHITE.COM and C:WHITERED.COM
Compare error at OFFSET A
File 1 = 74
File 2 = 47
```

Or you could use the DEBUG C command. But since DEBUG will load any file with a COM extension at address 100, you'd have to rename one of the files. Then get into DEBUG, Name (with N) and Load (with L) the file that still had the COM extension, and find out its length by entering RCX and pressing the Enter key twice. DEBUG will load this COM file at address 100. Then load the other file (without the COM extension) at address 200. Issue a Compare command that tells DEBUG to check two blocks of memory 1D bytes long, starting at addresses 100 and 200. Then enter Q to quit:

```
C>RENAME WHITERED.COM WHITERED
DEBUG
-N REDWHITE.COM
-L
-RCX
CX 001D
:
-N WHITERED
```

```
-L 200
-C 100 L 1D 200
30F9:010A   74   47   30F9:020A
-Q
```

The COMP command reported that the files were the same except for the bytes at off-set A. Since DEBUG loaded the files at offsets 100 and 200, it found the same mismatches at addresses 10A and 20A.

(If you want to try this, you can create the two color setting files with the following DEBUG script. Type it in using a pure-ASCII word processor or the DOS EDLIN utility. Name the script COLOR.SCR:

```
N REDWHITE.COM
E 100 B8 00 06 B9 00 00 BA 4F 18 B7 74 CD 10 B4 02
E 10F BA 00 00 B7 00 CD 10 B0 04 BA D9 03 EE C3
RCX
1D
W
E 10A 47
N WHITERED.COM
W
Q
```

Be sure to press the Enter key at the end of each line, especially the last one, with the Q. Then put COLOR.SCR and DEBUG on the same disk and type:

```
DEBUG < COLOR.SCR
```

(If you don't have a pure-ASCII word processor handy, use the DOS COPY CON command. Add a line to the very beginning of the program that says:

```
COPY CON COLOR.SCR
```

When you're all done, press the Enter key after the final Q, then press the F6 function key, and then press Enter again.)

Loading Disk Information into Memory

Format: **L [address [drive sector sector]]**

This powerful command lets you take just about any information from any part of a disk and put a copy of it in memory. You can then use DEBUG's editing commands to modify it and very carefully write the new information back to the disk.

DEBUG lets you load information in two forms — files and disk sectors.

Loading files is safe and easy. Loading sectors is trickier. Users often load something so they can change it and then write the changes back to disk, so working with sectors is *playing with fire*:

WARNING!
Unless you know exactly what you're doing, are sure your disks are completely backed up, take every possible prudent measure to safeguard your system, and triple-check every command before you execute it, be extraordinarily careful when loading and working with sectors, and utterly paranoid and overcautious when writing them. Be sure you always work on copies of your files, *never* the originals. If you're the least bit nervous or uncertain about this kind of activity, *don't do it*. Just type Q and press the Enter key to Quit.

Loading Files

The easiest way to load a file is to specify it on the DOS command line after the word DEBUG. To load a copy of the DOS MODE.COM utility that's in your \DOS subdirectory on drive C: you could do it from any subdirectory on any disk by typing:

```
DEBUG C:\DOS\MODE.COM
```

(This of course assumes that DEBUG.COM is itself in the current subdirectory or is in a directory that your PATH command knows about.)

If you're loading a copy of MODE.COM that's in the subdirectory you're currently logged into, just type:

```
DEBUG MODE.COM
```

If DEBUG can locate the file it will usually load it into memory at offset 100 and then just print the DEBUG hyphen prompt to tell you it's ready for a command. If DEBUG can't find the file it will print the "File not found" error message to let you know it had trouble, and then display the hyphen prompt. It won't be able to find files in other directories unless you specify the precise subdirectory the file is in, even if it's in a subdirectory you've included in your system's path. While you can run any executable file in any subdirectory that your path knows about, DEBUG won't let you load a file in another directory unless you explicitly include the file's path on the DOS command line.

So if your normal PATH command is:

```
PATH C:\BIN;C:\DOS;C:\;D:\
```

and you're currently in a subdirectory called C:\WORK and you want to load C:\DOS\MODE.COM into DEBUG, just typing:

```
DEBUG MODE.COM
```

won't do it. But:

```
DEBUG \DOS\MODE.COM
```

would.

Incidentally, when you want to write a file to disk, you have to make sure DEBUG knows the file's name beforehand. You can load a file from the DOS command line (by putting the filename after DEBUG), or you can use the N and L commands together:

```
DEBUG
-N \DOS\MODE.COM
-L
```

If DEBUG can't find the file you specified using this Name and Load technique, it will tell you so by printing a "File not found" message. But be careful — even if DEBUG prints this message, it will use the name of this file that it couldn't find the next time you issue a Write (W) command, unless you enter a new name later.

So if you type:

```
DEBUG PI.FIL
```

and it comes back and tells you:

```
File not found
```

it will still register the name "PI.FIL." If you forget to enter a different name later, and you use the W command to Write some information to disk, DEBUG will use the filename PI.FIL for the file it creates.

So if you originally loaded DEBUG by typing DEBUG PI.FIL, and had DEBUG tell you it couldn't find a file with that name, but you went ahead anyway and entered some information and then told the CX register how many bytes to write, and used the W command to write it:

```
-E 100 "PI=3.14159265"
-RCX
CX 0000
:D
-W
Writing 000D bytes
-Q
```

DEBUG will create a brand new file called PI.FIL. If you later issue the DOS command:

```
TYPE PI.FIL
```

you'll see:

```
PI=3.14159265
```

Loading any file is easy. Just type an N and then the filename (and its path, if the file is located in another subdirectory) and then an L. You can see if DEBUG knows the filename by peeking at the address where DEBUG stores it — offset 82 of the code segment. To check, just type:

```
D CS:81
```

DOS uses the area at this offset in its Program Segment Prefix control block to store the characters you entered on the command line after the main program name — often called the command tail. When you type CHKDSK /F, for instance, everything after the final K in CHKDSK — the space, the slash, and the F — goes here. When you load a file into DEBUG by specifying it after the DEBUG name on the command line, DOS puts this filename at offset 81, and it uses the single byte at offset 80 to tell it how many characters you typed after the main program name. Using the DEBUG Name (N) command also puts the name you entered at this offset.

If you load one file and then later load a different one, DEBUG will load them both at offset 100, and the second one will overwrite the first. DEBUG normally loads files at offset 100, so if you want to load two files at different addresses, you can do so by including the addresses after the L command.

If you also have a file on your disk called E.FIL that contains the text E=2.71828, you could load both PI.FIL and E.FIL into memory at the same time with the commands:

```
C>DEBUG
-N PI.FIL
-L 100
-N E.FIL
-L 110
```

Then, typing:

```
D 100 L 20
```

would display something like:

```
30DD:0100   50 49 3D 33 2E 31 34 31-35 39 32 36 35 00 00 00   PI=3.14159265...
30DD:0110   45 3D 32 2E 37 31 38 32-38 00 00 00 00 00 00 00   E=2.71828.......
```

You really didn't have to specify the address of 100 when you loaded the first PI.FIL file, since DEBUG normally loads files at offset 100. But you did have to tell DEBUG to load the second E.FIL file at offset 110. If you loaded these two files one after the other but forgot to specify addresses, DEBUG would put the second one over the first one. It would look like:

```
C>DEBUG
-N PI.FIL
-L
-D 100 L 20
30DD:0100  50 49 3D 33 2E 31 34 31-35 39 32 36 35 00 00 00    PI=3.14159265...
30DD:0110  00 00 00 00 00 00 00 00-00 00 00 00 00 00 00 00    ................
-N E.FIL
-L
-D 100 L 20
30DD:0100  45 3D 32 2E 37 31 38 32-38 39 32 36 35 00 00 00    E=2.718289265...
30DD:0110  00 00 00 00 00 00 00 00-00 00 00 00 00 00 00 00    ................
```

Note that since the PI.FIL file is longer than the E.FIL file, the contents of the E.FIL file overwrite just the beginning of the PI.FIL file; the end of the PI.FIL string is still visible after DEBUG plunks the E.FIL file on top of it.

In addition, you have to be careful when loading COM files, since DEBUG always loads files ending with COM at offset 100. So if you try to load a COM file at an address other than 100, DEBUG won't let you:

```
C>DEBUG
-N MODE.COM
-L 110
      ^ Error
-L 101
      ^ Error
-L 100
```

If you do need to load two COM files at the same time, you'll have to rename one of them before starting DEBUG, and then load the renamed COM file at an address higher than 100. If you wanted to load two short color-setting COM files called RED.COM and BLUE.COM, you would first rename BLUE.COM to BLUE.TMP. Then you'd load RED.COM into memory without specifying an address (DEBUG will load it at offset 100), and then load BLUE.TMP at a higher address. You can use the RCX command to find out how long the RED.COM file is so you don't overwrite it with the BLUE.TMP file:

```
REN BLUE.COM BLUE.TMP
DEBUG
-N RED.COM
-L
-RCX
```

```
CX 001D
:
-N BLUE.TMP
-L 120
```

The RCX command reported that the RED.COM file was 1D bytes long, which means the last byte in the file was at address 10E. You could have loaded BLUE.TMP directly after it — at address 10E — but it's often easier to work with files that are loaded at even paragraph boundaries, with offsets that end in 0, such as 100, or 120, or FD0.

COM vs. EXE

DEBUG loads different kinds of files in different ways. First, some background.

DOS can execute only three kinds of files, those with BAT, COM, or EXE extensions. Two of these, COM and EXE files, are generally called programs, although frustrated users sometimes call them far more colorful things. (Originally, "COM" stood for "command" and "EXE" stood for "executable" but these names don't mean much these days.) Files that end in BAT are called batch files.

Program files contain long sequences of machine-level commands in binary format that put your CPU through its paces. If you peeked inside one (with the DOS TYPE command) you'd see lots of seemingly meaningless strings of odd-looking characters. Batch files are ASCII files that contain recognizable English-language commands to load and run programs or perform certain DOS functions.

An executable program is simply a collection of instructions (and the data for these instructions) kept in a language your system can readily process. Some programs can be short and simple; others need to span several different 64K segments and do fancy footwork with memory.

Programs that end in COM are exact images of the instructions in memory that make the programs do their magic. And they're relatively short; COM files, their internal data, and their temporary stack storage areas, must all squeeze into 64K. Actually, the largest size of a COM file is 65,278 bytes, rather than the full 64K (65,536), since each COM file must reserve a minumum of two bytes for its stack, and 256 bytes (100 hex bytes) for a Program Segment Prefix that contains certain important addresses and data needed by DOS. (This is why DEBUG loads most files at offset 100.) Since no translation is required when reading them off a disk and putting them into memory, COM files load and start quickly. DOS just copies the block of instructions that constitutes the file to a certain memory address and presses the start button.

Programs that end in EXE, (pronounced "ex-ee"), are not exact duplicates of what ends up in memory. EXE files aren't limited to 64K, and in fact can take up all available memory. Each EXE file is prefaced by a block of information called a *header* that tells DOS how to allocate the proper amount of memory space it needs and then load the various parts of the file into the proper memory areas.

DEBUG is more than just a file editor; as mentioned earlier, it's a programming development and debugging environment. Programmers can work on a file and then run it from inside DEBUG without having to exit to DOS. Because of this, if you load an EXE file directly into DEBUG, DEBUG looks at the header and performs all the necessary memory allocation, segment juggling, and other fancy DOS tricks.

When you load a COM file into DEBUG the first byte of the file is at offset 100, the second at offset 101, etc. When you load a file with an EXE extension into DEBUG, the first few bytes of the actual file are discarded; these tell DOS that it's working with an EXE file, and specify how many sectors long the file is, how big the header is, etc.

If you want to examine or modify an EXE file with DEBUG, you'll have to first make a copy of the file that has an extension other than EXE (or no extension at all). Then when you load this renamed version of the file, the first byte will indeed be at offset 100, and the second at offset 101. (These bytes should be 4D and 5A, which are the EXE "file signature" that tells DOS to give them special treatment.) Working with the non-EXE version of the file will make it easier to modify, but you won't be able to run it while inside DEBUG (no great loss). You can see how differently DEBUG treats the versions by looking at the shortest DOS file that has an EXE extension — SORT.EXE. Copy SORT.EXE to a file named SORT.XXX. Load each into DEBUG and use the RCX command to see how long DEBUG thinks the file is. Then look at the first hex 10 (16 decimal) bytes at offset 0 — the very beginning of each file, and the hex 10 bytes at offset 100 — where DEBUG normally loads all files:

```
C>DEBUG SORT.EXE
-RCX
CX 05B9
:
-D 0 L 10
30F9:0000  CD 20 6A 31 00 9A 10 06-AB FF F4 02 2E 2D 2F 03   . j1.........-/.
-D 100 L 10
30F9:0100  00 00 2F 00 00 00 00 00-B4 30 CD 21 3D 03 1E 74   ../......0.!=..t
-Q


C>DEBUG SORT.XXX
-RCX
CX 07B9
:
-D 0 L 10
30DD:0000  CD 20 00 A0 00 9A EE FE-1D F0 F4 02 2E 2D 2F 03   . ...........-/.
-D 100 L 10
30DD:0100  4D 5A 9D 01 04 00 01 00-20 00 01 00 01 00 3D 00   MZ...... .....=.
-Q
```

Remember, here you're looking at the exact same file with two slightly different names.

If you do have to modify an EXE file, be sure to make a copy of it with a non-EXE extension. Then, when you're done making the changes, rename the changed file back to an EXE file again so DOS will run it. DOS will refuse to execute a file called SORT.XXX, even though it may be a perfectly executable file.

Loading Sectors

Data is data. Whether it's in memory or on your disk, it's just magnetically coded information. But storing this data is very tricky. You could keep it permanently in memory, but you'd need a huge amount of memory to maintain all your programs and data as well as a surefire way to prevent it from disappearing when you turned the power off. (You could actually do it, if you used very expensive *static* or battery backed-up CMOS RAM chips rather than the cheaper but power-hungry *dynamic* RAM chips in most systems.) And while such a storage system would be blazingly quick, it wouldn't let you transport your data easily from machine to machine.

Disks are a far better way to store data; they're vastly cheaper, more transportable, and secure. But you can't just throw data onto the surface of a disk. You have to organize it so storage and retrieval are fast and reliable. You have to know exactly what's on each disk, and which of the different versions of your data is the most recent. And you have to allow frequent modification; users are constantly changing their files — making them bigger, smaller, editing them, and moving the information in them around.

The best way to store data is in chunks. But the chunks have to be a workable size. If the chunks are too small you'll spend all your time figuring out where each is located. Storing just one byte at a time would be a logistical nightmare; the map needed to record where each byte is would take up more space than the data itself. Make the chunks too large, however, and you'll end up with utter inefficiency. If each chunk is 10,000 bytes long and you're storing five 200-byte programs, you'll waste 49,000 bytes of space.

The standard chunk on a PC disk is called a sector, and the standard sector is 512 bytes long. Sectors are actually parts of tracks. Tracks are concentric rings like circles on bull's-eye targets. Each track is divided into wedges shaped like slices of pie. These wedges form the disk sectors.

But your system doesn't always store data in individual sectors. Instead, it uses something called an *allocation unit*, more commonly referred to as a *cluster*. A cluster can be a single sector (as is it on single-sided 5-1/4 inch diskettes, or the godawful AT 1.2 megabyte floppies). Or it can be two sectors long (as with the common 360K diskette), or four (on the original AT 20-megabyte drive), or even eight (on some mammoth hard disk partitions under DOS 4.0).

Manipulating these sectors directly is an elaborate and tedious process, but DOS does all the dirty work for you, organizing and keeping track of your files. And it also knows where all the little pieces of the file are scattered across your disk.

When you first create a file on a brand new disk, all the sectors that contain the information in that file are in the same contiguous area. But as you add and delete files on the disk, and make existing files bigger and smaller, DOS ends up storing pieces of your files in clusters scattered over the entire disk surface. This kind of fragmentation slows everything down, since DOS has to churn through numerous read and write operations each time you load or save a file. One of the best ways to improve performance of your hard disk is to back up all your files (very assiduously) to floppies, reformat the hard disk, and then copy them back. Doing this will make your files contiguous and do away with fragmentation — until you start chomping away at them again.

DOS uses two tables to keep track of where all the individual clusters in every file are located. The first one is the disk directory itself, which maintains the name, size, creation date and time, and attribute (which is a label that lets you hide files or prevent them from being changed or erased). It also tells DOS where the very first cluster of the file is located. The second one, called a file allocation table (or FAT), takes over after the initial directory entry and keeps track of where all the remaining clusters are stashed.

As we've seen, it's relatively safe and easy to load whole files into DEBUG and then write them back to disk, since DOS takes care of the tricky loading and writing processes for you. However, it's extraordinarily risky to load specific sectors into DEBUG, then modify and write these back to disk, since one little slip could corrupt your directory or FAT. Scramble those two tables (especially the FAT) and you'll make it impossible for DOS to figure out where all the little pieces of your files are located.

The FAT is so important, in fact, that your disks contain two identical versions of it. Actually this is a bit short-sighted. Mariners know to take either one compass or three to sea, but never two. If two don't agree, which one is wrong? DOS should have allocated space for three FATs, on the theory that it's unlikely two will fail spontaneously. Of course, with DEBUG, nothing's impossible.

It's bad enough that you could destroy all the data on a floppy disk with an errant DEBUG command. But the same thick-fingered command could eradicate the key FAT and directory information on your hard disk, leaving you with a funny expression on your face and your foot through the screen.

So while you can load and write disk sectors, don't experiment unless you're totally backed up, and are the kind of belt-and-suspenders type who checks every action five times before he does anything. And be absolutely sure to keep DEBUG away from your hard disk sectors — one little slip and goodbye.

The following examples all apply to floppy disks only. In fact, they all illustrate how to work with the floppy disk in drive A:, for two reasons:

1. Some users with hard disks don't have a floppy disk that's strictly called drive B: (although they can simulate it by temporarily renaming drive A:).

2. Worse, one of the biggest pitfalls in working with sectors is that DEBUG refers to drive A: as drive 0, drive B: as drive 1, drive C: as drive 2, etc. It's easy to forget this late at night and put something on drive 2 when you really wanted to write to drive B:. Accidentally writing a floppy disk FAT sector onto the hard disk FAT will zap your data to dust. Your files will still be on your disk, in lots of little scattered pieces, but with the FAT gone you won't have any way to find where the pieces are located. If you use drive A: exclusively (which DEBUG refers to as drive 0) and you

accidentally write something to drive 1 thinking that 1 is A:, you may wreak havoc on the floppy in drive B: but at least your hard disk will still be intact.

So remember:

Drive Letter	*What DEBUG Calls It*
A:	0
B:	1
C:	2
D:	3

You won't really need to load and write absolute disk sectors very often. But this ability can come in handy. If you do somehow bomb your FATs, you can put the broken disk in drive A: and laboriously go through it sector by sector, loading the information from each sector to figure out where your text and data files are located. Then, once you've mapped out the contents of each sector, you can load the sectors from the bombed-out disk in the proper order and write them sequentially to a blank, formatted disk in drive B:. When you're done, you can load all the sequential sectors from drive B: into higher and higher addresses in memory, then use the N and W commands to name and write a new file containing all these pieces. It's nasty work, but it beats losing all your files. Barely.

This technique won't work with binary files (programs), since you won't be able to tell where all the pieces are, and even if you could, if you're off by even one byte when you put everything together you'll end up with garbage. With text or most data files you can always go into the file with your editor or word processor when you're done and clean things up. Better yet, use a program like the Norton or Mace Utilities to handle all the drudgery for you.

A real problem with this kind of rescue operation is that you may end up hopelessly confused because of all the slightly different versions of your file scattered over the disk. When you create a text file, your word processor generally saves the previous version as a backup (BAK) file. Some programs also create working files with extensions like TMP or $$$ while they're operating; they usually erase these or give them BAK extensions when you save or quit. When you look at your disk with DEBUG you may find several sectors that seem to have nearly identical contents, since they stored temporary or backup versions of your file. Sorting them all out can give you a big headache. The real answer is to back up all your work carefully and often, assuming the worst, since the computer definition of "the worst" is "just a matter of time."

One place where you really can use DEBUG's sector reading and writing abilities is with directories. Remember, however, don't try meddling with absolute sectors on your hard disk!

DOS disks are arranged as follows:

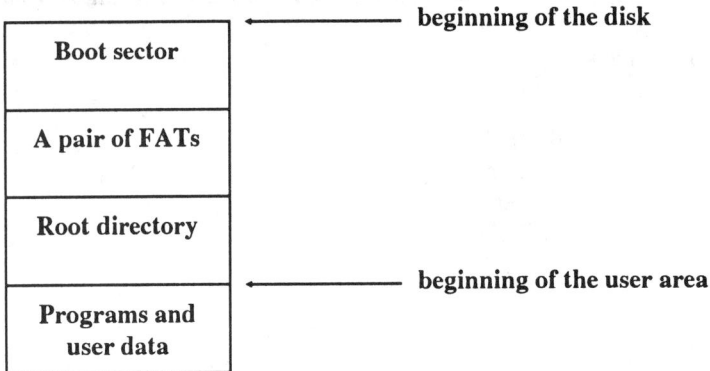

```
                          ←——————————— beginning of the disk
   ┌─────────────────┐
   │   Boot sector   │
   │                 │
   ├─────────────────┤
   │  A pair of FATs │
   │                 │
   ├─────────────────┤
   │ Root directory  │
   │                 │
   ├─────────────────┤    ←——————————— beginning of the user area
   │ Programs and    │
   │   user data     │
   └─────────────────┘
```

The boot sector does three things: It lets DOS know that the disk is indeed an MS-DOS or PC DOS-formatted disk, and not a disk for an Apple, DEC, or other system. It provides a table (called the BIOS Parameter Block, or BPB) of important values that DOS needs to know, such as the size of the disk's sectors, clusters, and directory. And it runs a bootstrap program that looks for the main operating system files and launches them into action.

The two FATs keep tabs on every cluster on your disk. When DOS needs to store a chunk of information, it looks at the FAT to see where the first available unused cluster is on your disk, and puts the data there. When it later has to retrieve the data it consults the FAT to see which cluster holds the information.

The main directory is called the root directory because it's at the beginning of a "tree-structured" (or hierarchical) system with subdirectories branching off it.

The root directory maintains the name, size, creation (or last modification) time and date, and the initial cluster location for a specified number of files — the number varies depending on the type of system you're using. (DOS limits the number of root directory entries, but lets subdirectories hold as many files as disk space permits.) Finally, the directory maintains a key piece of information about each file called an *attribute*.

A file attribute tells DOS what kind of file it's dealing with. Some files contain such important gut-level utilities and information that erasing them would bring your system to its knees, and DOS prevents you from altering or deleting these. Some files perform special services; the volume label and every subdirectory on your disk are just special kinds of files that can't be copied or deleted using normal DOS file management commands. And DOS lets you "hide" sensitive files from normal directory searches, or stamp them as "read only" so users can examine them but not change or erase them.

Each directory listing takes up 32 (or hex 20) bytes. The file attribute information is kept in the 12th byte (byte number 11, or hex 0B, since the first byte is byte number 0). You can look at the first few directory entries on a 360K floppy disk in drive A: with the command:

```
C>DEBUG
-L 100 0 5 1
-D 100 L C0
```

The first command told DEBUG to load the one sector starting at sector 5 on drive A: (which DEBUG calls drive 0) into memory at offset 100. The second command had DEBUG display the first hex C0 bytes starting at offset 100. DEBUG will display something like:

```
30DD:0100  49 42 4D 42 49 4F 20 20-43 4F 4D 27 00 00 00 00   IBMBIO  COM'....
30DD:0110  00 00 00 00 00 00 00 60-72 0E 02 00 54 56 00 00   .......'r...TV..
30DD:0120  49 42 4D 44 4F 53 20 20-43 4F 4D 27 00 00 00 00   IBMDOS  COM'....
30DD:0130  00 00 00 00 00 00 00 60-71 0E 18 00 CF 75 00 00   .......'q....u..
30DD:0140  43 4F 4D 4D 41 4E 44 20-43 4F 4D 20 00 00 00 00   COMMAND COM ....
30DD:0150  00 00 00 00 00 00 00 60-71 0E 36 00 DB 62 00 00   .......'q.6..b..
30DD:0160  50 43 20 4D 41 47 41 5A-49 4E 45 28 00 00 00 00   POWER_TOOLS(....
30DD:0170  00 00 00 00 00 00 45 6E-5B 0F 00 00 00 00 00 00   ......En[.......
30DD:0180  48 49 44 44 45 4E 20 20-46 49 4C 22 00 00 00 00   HIDDEN  FIL"....
30DD:0190  00 00 00 00 00 00 51 6E-5B 0F 4F 00 29 00 00 00   ......Qn[.O.)...
30DD:01A0  53 55 42 44 49 52 31 20-20 20 20 10 00 00 00 00   SUBDIR1    .....
30DD:01B0  00 00 00 00 00 00 6A 6E-5B 0F 50 00 00 00 00 00   ......jn[.P.....
```

(Obviously the contents will be different on your own system, but the structure will be similar.)

The first 32-byte entry, for IBMBIO.COM, is made up of the following parts:

Time   Date
(in coded form)

Byte:	00	01	02	03	04	05	06	07	08	09	0A	0B	0C	0D	0E	0F
0100	..	..	..	..	..	..	..	..	..	..	..	..	..	..	..	..
0110	..	..	..	..	..	..	..	..	..	..	02	00	..	..	..	..

First cluster in FAT

Byte:	00	01	02	03	04	05	06	07	08	09	0A	0B	0C	0D	0E	0F
0100	..	..	..	..	..	..	..	..	..	..	..	..	..	..	..	..
0110	..	..	..	..	..	..	..	..	..	..	..	..	54	56	00	00

File size

(The area from offset 0C through 15 is "reserved" for future use; all bytes in this part of the entry have a value of zero.)

By looking at the DEBUG display, you can tell this floppy disk is probably bootable, since the first two files in the directory are IBMBIO.COM and IBMDOS.COM. These two files have an attribute value of hex 27, which means that the following bits are "set" to 1 rather than 0:

- Read-Only
- Hidden
- System
- Archive

Most bytes in the directory entry are values that tell DOS what ASCII characters to display, or how big something is, or where in a table to look up something. Some are *coded* values — the date and time words (remember, a word is two bytes) compress a lot of information into a short space.

But the attribute byte is just a collection of bits. Its value depends on which bits happen to be set to 1 and which aren't. If the first (0th), second (1st), third (2nd), and sixth (5th) bits are set:

Bit:	7	6	5	4	3	2	1	0
	0	0	1	0	0	1	1	1
			↑			↑	↑	↑
			set			set	set	set

the value of the byte would be $2^0 + 2^1 + 2^2 + 2^5$, or $1 + 2 + 4 + 32$, or decimal 39 (hex 27). The value of hex 27 itself means nothing — it just happens to be a convenient way to store a lot of information, the above bit pattern, in one compressed chunk.

But how can you tell which bits represent which attributes? Just look them up in Figure 9.1:

Bit:	7	6	5	4	3	2	1	0
Dec:	128	64	32	16	8	4	2	1
Hex:	80	40	20	10	8	4	2	1

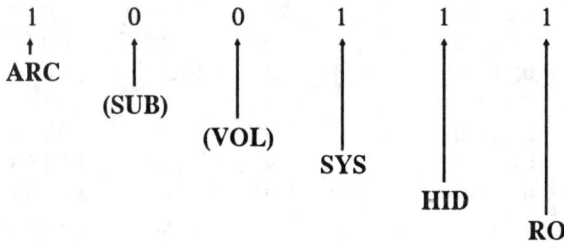

*	*						
(reserved)		↑	↑	↑	↑	↑	↑
		archive					
			subdir				
				volume			
					system		
						hidden	
							read-only

Figure 9.1   Interpretation of Directory Attribute Byte

Bit = number of bit
Dec = decimal value of bit
Hex = hexadecimal value of bit

To use this, you obviously have to be able to know the binary representation of the byte. Hex 27 in binary is:

```
1        0        0        1        1        1
↑
ARC      |
        (SUB)    |
                (VOL)    |
                        SYS      |
                                HID      |
                                         RO
```

Translating bytes from hex to binary isn't all that hard, if you know how to count from 0 to F (0 to 16 decimal) in binary:

```
0000 = 0      1000 = 8
0001 = 1      1001 = 9
0010 = 2      1010 = A
0011 = 3      1011 = B
0100 = 4      1100 = C
0101 = 5      1101 = D
0110 = 6      1110 = E
0111 = 7      1111 = F
```

Notice that the first column (0-7) has the same bit pattern as the second column (8-F), except that on binary numbers lower than 8 the leftmost digit is a 0 and on those from 8 through F this digit is a 1.

Now take the hex digit 27, and divide it in half. Translate each half into binary and then put the two halves together, to see that hex 27 equals binary 00100111:

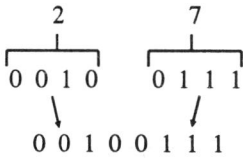

```
      2            7
  ┌───┴───┐    ┌───┴───┐
  0 0 1 0      0 1 1 1
     \            /
      0 0 1 0 0 1 1 1
```

Here's a decimal/hex/binary table for all hex values from 0 to 3F (decimal 0 through 63), if you'd rather look things up than puzzle them out:

Dec Val	Hex Val	Six-Bit Binary Representation	Dec Val	Hex Val	Six-Bit Binary Representation
0	0	0 0 0 0 0 0	32	20	1 0 0 0 0 0
1	1	0 0 0 0 0 1	33	21	1 0 0 0 0 1
2	2	0 0 0 0 1 0	34	22	1 0 0 0 1 0
3	3	0 0 0 0 1 1	35	23	1 0 0 0 1 1
4	4	0 0 0 1 0 0	36	24	1 0 0 1 0 0
5	5	0 0 0 1 0 1	37	25	1 0 0 1 0 1
6	6	0 0 0 1 1 0	38	26	1 0 0 1 1 0
7	7	0 0 0 1 1 1	39	27	1 0 0 1 1 1
8	8	0 0 1 0 0 0	40	28	1 0 1 0 0 0
9	9	0 0 1 0 0 1	41	29	1 0 1 0 0 1
10	A	0 0 1 0 1 0	42	2A	1 0 1 0 1 0
11	B	0 0 1 0 1 1	43	2B	1 0 1 0 1 1
12	C	0 0 1 1 0 0	44	2C	1 0 1 1 0 0
13	D	0 0 1 1 0 1	45	2D	1 0 1 1 0 1
14	E	0 0 1 1 1 0	46	2E	1 0 1 1 1 0
15	F	0 0 1 1 1 1	47	2F	1 0 1 1 1 1
16	10	0 1 0 0 0 0	48	30	1 1 0 0 0 0
17	11	0 1 0 0 0 1	49	31	1 1 0 0 0 1
18	12	0 1 0 0 1 0	50	32	1 1 0 0 1 0
19	13	0 1 0 0 1 1	51	33	1 1 0 0 1 1
20	14	0 1 0 1 0 0	52	34	1 1 0 1 0 0
21	15	0 1 0 1 0 1	53	35	1 1 0 1 0 1
22	16	0 1 0 1 1 0	54	36	1 1 0 1 1 0
23	17	0 1 0 1 1 1	55	37	1 1 0 1 1 1
24	18	0 1 1 0 0 0	56	38	1 1 1 0 0 0
25	19	0 1 1 0 0 1	57	39	1 1 1 0 0 1
26	1A	0 1 1 0 1 0	58	3A	1 1 1 0 1 0
27	1B	0 1 1 0 1 1	59	3B	1 1 1 0 1 1

(continued)

Dec Val	Hex Val	Six-Bit Binary Representation	Dec Val	Hex Val	Six-Bit Binary Representation
28	1C	0 1 1 1 0 0	60	3C	1 1 1 1 0 0
29	1D	0 1 1 1 0 1	61	3D	1 1 1 1 0 1
30	1E	0 1 1 1 1 0	62	3E	1 1 1 1 1 0
31	1F	0 1 1 1 1 1	63	3F	1 1 1 1 1 1

The following BASIC ATTRBUTE.BAS program will do all the work for you by looking at which bits are set to 1 in any attribute value you enter, and reporting the appropriate attributes.

```
100 ' ATTRBUTE.BAS
110 SCREEN 0:COLOR 3,0:KEY OFF:CLS
120 S$=STRING$(5,32):PRINT STRING$(56,61)
130 PRINT "Enter hex attribute value ";
140 INPUT "(or just hit Enter to end): ",N$
150 N=VAL("&H"+N$)
160 IF N>63 THEN BEEP:GOTO 130
170 IF N=0 THEN END
180 PRINT "File Attributes are:"
190 IF N AND  1 THEN PRINT S$;"Read-Only"
200 IF N AND  2 THEN PRINT S$;"Hidden"
210 IF N AND  4 THEN PRINT S$;"System"
220 IF N  =  8 THEN PRINT S$;"Volume"
230 IF N AND 16 THEN PRINT S$;"Subdirectory"
240 IF N AND 32 THEN PRINT S$;"Archive"
250 GOTO 120
```

If you examine the attribute byte values for the other files in the above DEBUG display:

Byte:	00	01	02	03	04	05	06	07	08	09	0A	0B	0C	0D	0E	0F			
0100	..	..	..	..	..	..	..	..	..	..	27	..	..	..	..	..	IBMBIO	COM'....
0120	..	..	..	..	..	..	..	..	..	..	27	..	..	..	..	..	IBMDOS	COM'....
0140	..	..	..	..	..	..	..	..	..	..	20	..	..	..	..	..	COMMAND	COM ....
0160	..	..	..	..	..	..	..	..	..	..	28	..	..	..	..	..	POWER_TOOLS(....
0180	..	..	..	..	..	..	..	..	..	..	22	..	..	..	..	..	HIDDEN	FIL"....
01A0	..	..	..	..	..	..	..	..	..	..	10	..	..	..	..	..	SUBDIR1	.....

you can look at Figure 9.1 to figure out which attribute bits are set:

Filename	Hex value	Binary value	Attributes
IBMDOS.COM	27	1 0 0 1 1 1	ARC, SYS, HID, RO
COMMAND.COM	20	1 0 0 0 0 0	ARC
POWER_TOOLS	28	1 0 1 0 0 0	ARC, VOL
HIDDEN.FIL	22	1 0 0 0 1 0	ARC, HID
SUBDIR1	10	0 1 0 0 0 0	SUB

This tells you that IBMDOS.COM, like IBMBIO.COM, has its archive bit set, and is a hidden, system, read-only file. The only bit set in the COMMAND.COM entry is the archive bit. POWER_TOOLS is the disk's volume label (which appears in DIR listings, CHKDSK output, etc.) since its 2^3 bit is set. The archive bit is also set in HIDDEN.FIL, and since the 2^1 bit is set, this is also hidden from normal directory searches. And SUBDIR1, with its 2^4 bit set, is a subdirectory.

Don't start meddling with volume labels or subdirectory entries. And if any file is marked as a system file, keep your hands off that as well. But the other attributes are fair game. For example:

- DOS sets the directory archive bit on (to 1) whenever it creates or modifies a file. When you use the DOS BACKUP or XCOPY commands with a /M switch, DOS unsets (turns off, or sets to 0) this bit after it makes the copy. This lets subsequent backup operations skip over any files that you haven't changed since you last backed up your disk. By setting the read-only bit on (to 1) you can prevent anyone from changing or erasing any file. You'll still be able to read or copy it, but DOS won't let you alter its contents.
- By setting the hidden bit on (to 1) you can keep a file from showing up in DIR searches. Actually, setting the system bit on will exclude it from DIR searches as well. (Since a subdirectory is just a special kind of file, you can even hide whole subdirectories from DIR listings. You'll still be able to change (CHDIR or CD) and remove (RMDIR or RD) and they'll show up if your PROMPT contains a $P.)

Here's where DEBUG's sector-handling ability can be very useful. DOS maintains file attributes in your disk's directory. You can't use the L FILENAME command to load your directory into DEBUG as if it were a file. Instead, you have to tell DEBUG to read specific sectors off your disk and put them into memory.

The problem is that directories aren't all the same length, and they don't start at the same sector on every disk. DOS supports 160K, 180K, 320K, 360K, 720K, 1.2M and 1.44M diskettes. The number of possible listings in the root directories of these diskettes varies from 64 to 224. And since the directories occupy space on the disks after the two FATs of varying sizes, the starting directory sectors vary widely.

To figure out where each directory starts, and how long it is, you can examine the BIOS Parameter Block (BPB) in the boot sector (sector 0 — the first one on the disk). *Note:*

DOS 4.0 changed things slightly by allowing 32-bit addresses and altering the BPB on some hard disks. For the diskette examples here you can ignore this fact.

The root directory is located right after the single boot sector and the two redundant FATs. So if you figure out how many sectors each FAT takes up, multiply this number by 2 (since FATs come in pairs), and then add 1 (for the boot sector), the directory will start at the sector with the very next number.

The BPB uses the single byte at offset 10 (hex) of the boot record to keep track of how many FATs are on the disk — one or two. And it uses the two bytes at offset 16 (hex) to keep track of how many sectors each FAT contains.

To examine the boot sector (sector 0) on a 360K diskette in drive A: load DEBUG without specifying a filename. Then issue a Load command with four parameters:

1. The address in memory where you want DEBUG to load the information (any address will do, but use 100 hex).
2. The drive number. Remember that drive A: is drive number 0, drive B: is drive number 1, drive C: is drive number 2, etc. To avoid disaster, always think twice when specifying DEBUG drive numbers!
3. The first sector you want loaded.
4. How many sectors you want to load — starting with the first sector specified in the previous step. You can't load more than hex 80 sectors (64K) at once, but this shouldn't be a problem.

To load the single sector 0 on drive A: (drive number 0) into address 100, issue the command:

```
-L 100 0 0 1
```

Then display the first hex 20 bytes. To make life easier, display the one byte at BPB off-set 10 (which is at offset 110 in memory, since you loaded the file at address 100 rather than address 0), and the two bytes starting at offset 16 (DEBUG offset 116):

```
C>DEBUG
-L 100 0 0 1
-D 100 L 20
30DD:0100   EB 34 90 49 42 4D 20 20-33 2E 33 00 02 02 01 00   .4.IBM  3.3.....
30DD:0110   02 70 00 D0 02 FD 02 00-09 00 02 00 00 00 00 00   .p..............
-D 110 L 1
30DD:0110   02
-D 116 L 2
30DD:0110                       02 00
```

The value of 2 at offset 110 specifies that this disk contains two FATs (all DOS disks do). And the value of 2 at offset 16 tells you that each FAT sprawls over two sectors.

Armed with this information, you can figure out that the directory on a 360K floppy begins on sector 5:

- The boot sector starts at sector 0 and stops at sector 1
- The pair of FATs start at sector 1 and stop at sector 4
- The directory begins at sector 5

So the formula for figuring out the starting directory sector is:

(number of sectors in FAT x 2) + 1

Since all FATs on floppy disks use fewer than 256 sectors, you can figure out the number of sectors per FAT with the simple DEBUG commands:

```
C>DEBUG
-L 100 0 0 1
-D 116 L 1
```

This would look on drive A:. To look on drive B: change the first line to:

```
-L 100 1 0 1
```

Fine. Now you know where the directory starts; but where does it end? The two-byte value at offset hex 11 gives you the maximum number of entries in the root directory; you can see by looking at the DEBUG display above that the value here is hex 70 (decimal 112).

(Two-byte values can be tricky, since they're stored in "backwords" format. Users gave IBM's storage system this informal name because two eight-bit bytes combine into one 16-bit word and because the low-order byte — the half that's worth less — is at the lower address, which sometimes seems backward. You'll see why in a second.)

This book contains many warnings that caution you against fooling around with hard disk sectors. To make sure you don't try to fiddle with the real thing yourself, here's what one looks like on a typical hard disk system:

```
30DD:0100 EB 34 90 49 42 4D 20 20-33 2E 33 00 02 04 01 00
30DD:0110 02 00 02 07 A3 F8 29 00-11 00 04 00 11 00 80 00
```
                                    bytes 11 and 12

The number of root directory entries is obviously more than 2. Since the bytes are stored in backwards order, flip 00 02 around and you get 02 00, or hex 200 (decimal 512).

The floppy disk directory used in these examples can hold hex 70 (decimal 112) entries, and because each entry is 20 hex (decimal 32) bytes long, this particular directory will take up E00 hex bytes. Sectors are always 200 hex bytes long, so E00 / 200 = 7, which means that the directory will span seven sectors, starting at sector 5.

The formula for figuring out how many sectors the whole root directory takes up is:

Number of root directory entries * hex 20 / hex 200

which translates to:

Number of root directory entries / hex 10

And while you're at it, you can figure out the total number of bytes taken up by the root directory either with:

Number of root directory entries * hex 20

or:

Number of sectors taken up by the root directory * 200

Since the number of root directory entries on a floppy disk is less than 256, you can figure out the number (on drive A:) with the simple DEBUG commands:

```
C>DEBUG
-L 100 0 0 1
-D 111 L 1
```

You could load the entire directory on a 360K floppy disk in drive A: and then display it with the command:

offset where DEBUG loads it

    drive (A:)

      starting sector

        how many sectors you want loaded

```
-L 100 0 5 7
-D 100 L E00
```

number of bytes to display

starting display offset

Dumping E00 (3,584 decimal) bytes will scroll the listing quickly off the screen, but you can stop and restart the display by alternately pressing Ctrl-S. You could also press Ctrl-NumLock to halt the display, but you'd then have to press an alphanumeric key to restart it. Or, to end up with a printed copy of the listing, you could turn your printer on and type Ctrl-P or Ctrl-PrtSc before you start. When you're finished, press Ctrl-P or Ctrl-PrtSc again to toggle this printer echoing feature off. And if you want a copy of it on your disk, you could always create a file called DEBUG.SCR that contained the three lines:

```
L 100 0 5 7
D 100 L E00
Q
```

Make sure you press the Enter key after each line, especially the last one with the Q! Then, at the DOS prompt, type:

```
DEBUG < DEBUG.SCR >DIRLIST
```

and DOS will redirect the DEBUG listing into a file called DIRLIST.

To make things easier, Figure 9.2 presents all the necessary DEBUG loading and display addresses:

	Sectors in boot record	Sectors in FATs	Sectors in root DIR	Entries in root DIR	DEBUG commands to see root directory in A
5-1/2 160K	1	2	4	64	L 100 0 3 4 D 100 L 800
5-1/2 180K	1	4	4	64	L 100 0 5 4 D 100 L 800
5-1/2 320K	1	2	7	112	L 100 0 3 7 D 100 L E00
5-1/2 360K	1	4	7	112	L 100 0 5 7 D 100 L E00
5-1/2 1.2M	1	14	14	224	L 100 0 F E D 100 L 1C00
3-1/2 720K	1	6	7	112	L 100 0 B E D 100 L E00
3-1/2 1.44M	1	18	14	224	L 100 0 13 E D 100 L 1C00

Note: All values in decimal format; DEBUG command parameters in hexadecimal

Figure 9.2.   DEBUG Loading and Display Addresses

Writing Information from Memory to Disk

Format: **W [address [drive sector sector]]**

Write is potentially the most dangerous tool in DEBUG's arsenal. It lets you write information to any part of any disk in your system. If you're not extremely careful, you can destroy good data on your disk by writing bad data over it. Worse, if you accidentally write the wrong data over the two key tables that DOS uses to organize every disk — the pair of FATs and the directory — you can pretty much just kiss your data goodbye.

DEBUG lets you load and write information in two forms — as files and as absolute disk sectors.

Working with files is relatively safe and easy, so long as you always work with *copies* of your important files rather than the originals. This way you can start over again if the DEBUG changes you made weren't exactly right. But working with sectors is *playing with fire.* Once again, a warning:

WARNING!

Unless you know exactly what you're doing, and are sure your disks are completely backed up, and take every possible prudent measure to safeguard your system, and triple-check every command before you execute it, be extraordinarily careful when loading and working with sectors, and utterly paranoid and overcautious when writing them. And be sure you always work on *copies* of all your files, *never* the originals. If you're the least bit nervous or uncertain about this kind of activity, *don't do it.* Just type Q and press the Enter key to Quit.

The easiest way to use the Write command is to load an existing file (either with the N and L commands or by specifying it at the end of the DOS command line), then change it and write the modified file back to the same disk with the simple command:

```
-W
```

You can't write a file to disk unless DEBUG knows the name and size of the file. When you load an existing file 64K or smaller, DEBUG keeps track of the filename at offset hex 82 of the code segment and puts the number of bytes (the file size) into the CX register. If the file is larger than 64K, DEBUG uses the CX and BX registers to store the file size.

To patch version 5.0 of COMMAND.COM so CLS clears the screen to red text on a white background, you could issue just three commands:

```
C>DEBUG COMMAND.COM
-E 4369 74
-W
```

```
Writing BAE5 bytes
-Q
```

Since you specified the name of a file at the end of the DOS command line, after the word DEBUG, DEBUG knows the name of the file and how many bytes to write.

But if you tried to create a file from scratch, you'd have to make sure you gave DEBUG a proper name and size. If you simply typed:

```
C>DEBUG
-E 4369 74
-W
```

DEBUG wouldn't know what you wanted to name the file, and would respond with a "(W)rite error, no destination defined" message. And if you specified a brand new filename like XYZ.COM without telling DEBUG how long the file was, either by typing:

```
C>DEBUG XYZ.COM
File not found
-E 4369 74
-W
-Q
```

or:

```
C>DEBUG
-E 4369 74
-N XYZ.COM
-W
-Q
```

DEBUG would create a directory entry, but wouldn't write anything to the file. You'd see the message "Writing 0000 bytes." A subsequent DIR listing would display the XYZ.COM filename, the correct creation time and date, but a file size of 0.

So when creating a new file, specify both the name (either at the end of the DOS command line after the word DEBUG, or by using the N command), and the size (with the RCX command — and the RBX command if you're creating a real monster). Here's a sample script file:

```
N DRIVE.COM
E 100 B4 09 BA 14 01 CD 21 B4 19 CD
E 10A 21 04 41 88 C2 B4 02 CD 21 C3
E 114 "Current drive is $"
RCX
26
W
Q
```

Type this in using a pure-ASCII word processor or EDLIN, and call the file DRIVE.SCR. Or, if you don't have either of those tools handy, make sure you're at the DOS prompt and insert the line:

```
COPY CON DRIVE.SCR
```

at the very top, and when you're all done, press the F6 function key and then the Enter key at the very end. In either case, be sure to press the Enter key after each line, especially the final one (with the Q). Then put this DRIVE.SCR file in the same directory as DEBUG (unless DEBUG.COM is in a subdirectory that your path knows about) and type:

```
DEBUG < DRIVE.SCR
```

This will create a simple program that reports the current drive. Nothing special. In fact, you could do the same thing with the DOS PROMPT command:

```
PROMPT Current drive is $n$_
```

Note that the script file starts off by naming the file that DEBUG will create. You can put this N command just about anywhere before the W command (except in the middle of a set of continuous Assemble (A) instructions). The RCX command near the end sets the value in the CX register to hex 26 — the length of the file. You always need to specify the length. But you could also have named the file by omitting the:

```
N DRIVE.COM
```

line and instead issuing a:

```
DEBUG DRIVE.COM < DRIVE.SCR
```

command at the DOS prompt. In either case a simple, unadorned W will write the file to disk.

Using a naked W without anything after it tells DEBUG to write the information starting at offset 100 of the code segment. If the information you plan to write starts elsewhere, you can tell DEBUG where to start looking by specifying W and then the appropriate address. So if DRIVE.SCR used the E command to Enter information 100 hex bytes higher than normal, at offset 200, you would type:

```
N DRIVE.COM
E 200 B4 09 BA 14 01 CD 21 B4 19 CD
E 20A 21 04 41 88 C2 B4 02 CD 21 C3
E 214 "Current drive is $"
RCX
26
W 200
Q
```

You'd have to use the W 200 command to tell DEBUG where to look in memory for the information you want it to write to disk. You might want to do this if you have two programs loaded into different places in memory and you wanted to write the one to disk that didn't start at offset 100. Or you might want to write a module of a larger program to disk.

If you do plan to change the contents of an existing file, always make sure you're working on a copy of the file, never the original. Mistakes do happen. Or you might decide you liked the older version better. This is especially necessary when patching files that end in EXE. DEBUG loads EXE files differently from other files. DEBUG doesn't load the first byte of an EXE file at offset 100 the way it does with COM files or virtually every other kind of file. When customizing an EXE file, change the extension to something other than EXE at the same time you're copying it. So if you wanted to patch off-set 1A5 of ABCD.EXE, do it this way:

```
C>COPY ABCD.EXE ABCD.XXX
          1 File(s) copied
C>DEBUG ABCD.XXX
-E 1A5 41
-W
Writing 2BC0 bytes
-Q
C>REN ABCD.XXX ABCDNEW.EXE
```

Then experiment with the ABCDNEW.EXE program to make sure you like it before you replace the older ABCD.EXE with it. In any case, save the original ABCD.EXE safely on a floppy disk somewhere. Or name it ABCDOLD.EXE. But don't patch originals. And don't try to write EXE files in DEBUG — it won't let you.

While we're at it, unless you're a programming ace, refrain from using commands like Trace (T), Proceed (P), or Go (G) to run programs from inside DEBUG. Doing this can alter the values in the CX and BX registers. If you're not careful about resetting these registers later so they contain the proper file sizes, DEBUG can end up writing the wrong number of bytes to disk. And it can do very strange things with EXE files, even if you've renamed them. These commands are really for serious programmers only.

If you forget to make a copy of your COM or text file before you start slashing away at it from inside DEBUG, you can prevent DEBUG from overwriting the original. Just use the N command to give a new name to the program currently loaded in memory. So if you're modifying a series of bytes in XYZ.COM and you don't want to obliterate the original version of the program by writing the patched version over it, you could rename the program before you wrote it. Or you could write it to another disk:

```
DEBUG XYZ.COM
-E 111 34
-E 12D C0
-E 20A 4F
-N XYZNEW.COM
```

```
-W
Writing 302 bytes
-Q
```

or:

```
DEBUG XYZ.COM
-E 111 34
-E 12D C0
-E 20A 4F
-N A:XYZ.COM
-W
Writing 302 bytes
-Q
```

The first example gives the file a new name before it writes the file to disk. The second example writes a file with the same name but to a different disk.

Always be sure you're writing the proper number of bytes. If you use the Move (M) command to make a file larger, add instructions to a program, or increase the size of messages that are stuck at the end, be sure to specify the new length with the RCX command. You may have to use the Unassemble (U) and Dump (D) commands to see exactly where the new file ends. Even if you're a single byte too short you can cause problems, especially since the last bytes of a program often jump control of the program back to DOS with code like CD 20 or C3. Truncate those and the program will hang, and you'll have to reboot. It usually doesn't hurt to make programs a bit longer than necessary. And remember when calculating lengths that files generally start at address 100 rather than 101 — so to be on the safe side, add 1 to the length you specify with RCX.

You can't really do much harm when writing entire files, so long as you're working with copies rather than originals. But you can cause devastating heartache if you're not careful when using DEBUG to write absolute sectors.

If you want to create or patch a file, DEBUG will take care of all the dirty DOS work for you. But if you want to alter a directory listing, or work with other fundamental disk underpinnings, you have to manipulate specific sectors directly. And while DEBUG is superb at doing delicate sector surgery, it won't stop you from destroying your disk if you issue a bone-headed or thick-fingered command at the wrong time.

The problem with writing sectors is that it's easy to wipe out or corrupt two key disk structures. DOS relies on two tables — the directory and the duplicate pair of FATs — to tell it where all the little pieces of your file are located. All programs and data are stored in small chunks called clusters, which are in turn made up of disk sectors. On just about all systems where users are constantly making changes to their data, and adding and deleting files, these clusters end up scattered in various places all over the disk surface.

The directory tells DOS where the initial cluster is on your disk, and the FAT maps out where all the remaining clusters (containing the rest of the file) are located. Without these, DOS won't know where to find the pieces of your programs and files. When you ask DOS to load a file, it consults these tables, figures out where the pieces are, and jumps around the disk gathering them all in the correct order and stringing them together properly in memory.

What makes writing sectors especially tricky is that all the parameters have to be in hexadecimal notation, and that DEBUG refers to the first number in any series as 0 rather than 1.

Here's where the trouble happens:

Users sometimes forget what they're doing and mix hex and decimal numbers. Or worse, they forget that DEBUG calls drive A: drive 0 rather than drive 1. If you're trying to write to drive A: and you accidentally specify a 1 when you meant to type a 0, you may damage the disk in drive B:, since DEBUG treats drive 1 as drive B: and will write the sectors to drive B: when you really wanted them to go to drive A:. That's bad, but presumably you have up-to-date backup copies of all your floppy disks, so you won't really lose anything.

However, if you're trying to write sectors to drive B: and you accidentally specify drive 2 when you really meant drive 1, DEBUG will happily oblige and write the sectors to drive C:, since it thinks of drive 2 as drive C:. Unfortunately, drive C: is usually a hard disk. If you're working with sectors from a floppy disk directory, and you inadvertently write these to a hard disk, that one errant keystroke will cost you days or weeks of reconstruction anguish. The data and program pieces will still be on your disk but you won't have any way to find out where they are or be able to assemble them into useful units. To be absolutely safe make sure every last byte of every important file is totally backed up before you start using DEBUG to fiddle with sectors.

Above all, etch into your consciousness how DEBUG refers to drives.

Then, pause whenever you're about to write absolute sectors, and then triple-check your typing and your intentions. Be especially careful if you decide to write to drive B: or your hard disk. If you're at all nervous about it — *don't*. Just erase your Write command (with the backspace or left arrow keys) or press Esc, Ctrl-C, or Ctrl-ScrollLock, then type Q and press Enter to quit.

The following examples all apply to floppy disks *only*. To keep things as safe as possible, they all illustrate how to work with the floppy disk in drive A:.

You don't often need to manipulate absolute disk sectors. One time you do is when you've stupidly destroyed your FATs and are scanning through all your disk sectors one by one looking for the pieces to pick up. This kind of emergency reconstruction is tedious, nasty work, and you'll barely be able to use it to put your text files back together in reasonable form. Splicing your programs or any other binary files together is pretty much out of the question. In fact, doing any work like this is such an arduous undertaking that you're probably better off using commercial utility programs such as Peter Norton's or Paul Mace's to rescue your files.

But if you're adventurous and extraordinarily careful, you can do things like alter your disk directory by patching the relevant sectors. See the Load (L) section for details.

To reduce the risk when working with sectors, use the exact same syntax for loading and writing. So to load an entire directory on a 360K floppy disk in drive A:, you would specify the seven directory sectors starting with sector 5 with the command:

```
L 100 0 5 7
```

You can later write these back to the same disk by changing the initial L to a W:

```
W 100 0 5 7
```

Here's what this particular Write command tells DEBUG:

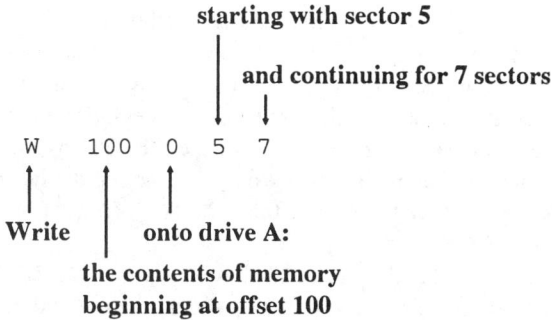

starting with sector 5

and continuing for 7 sectors

```
W    100   0   5   7
```

Write   **onto drive A:**

**the contents of memory
beginning at offset 100**

A sector is 512 (hex 200) bytes. When you use the D command without any parameters after it, DEBUG normally displays eight paragraphs, or 128 (hex 80) bytes at a time. So each four times you type D and press the Enter key, you display one sector.

It's a good idea when you're working with sectors to jot down on a notepad the parameters you used to load the sectors, and then refer to your notes and very carefully type the same exact parameters when you're ready to write them back to disk. Then, when you're ready to issue any Write command, always stop and check your typing — and be sure to verify that the disk you've specified is the one you want DEBUG to write to.

You can't write more than hex 80 sectors (64K) at once or write any sectors when using a network drive. And if DEBUG senses a problem when it's trying to write (if a drive door is open, for instance), it will print an error message and halt. If this happens, fix the problem, then press F3 to repeat the previous command and try again to write the file. But the single most important thing to remember is to pause and check all Write commands several times before actually writing any sectors to disk. It may take an extra few seconds. But it sure beats trying to piece together a bombed hard disk.

Quitting DEBUG

Format: **Q**

You can't exit DEBUG and return to DOS unless you issue this simple Quit command. DEBUG doesn't process any commands until you press the Enter key. So if you're using ASCII script files to redirect keystrokes into DEBUG, make sure you press the Enter key after typing in the Q. When you do press Enter after the final Q, the cursor will drop down a line and hover directly below the Q. If you don't do this, your system will freeze and you'll have to reboot.

Quitting does not automatically save your work. If you use the Q command before issuing any W commands, all the work you did in the DEBUG session will be lost. If this happens you may be able to load DEBUG again and hope everything is intact in memory and then use the W command to save — but you can't rely on this technique.

If you realize that you've made a mistake or are afraid you're about to write bad information over good information, you can abandon your work by quitting DEBUG. Or you can use the N command to give the file in memory a different name or write it to a different drive. It's better to redo things than to end up with a mess on your disk.

To wriggle out of a command you're typing, either backspace the command away with the backspace or left arrow keys and press the Esc key to cancel the line, or press Ctrl-C or Ctrl-ScrollLock to cancel everything and return to the DEBUG hyphen prompt. If you're using the Assemble (A) command, once you've cancelled the current line you may have to press the Enter key once to return to this prompt. Then just type Q and press the Enter key to get back to DOS.

It's entirely possible that you'll end up using all 14 of the above DEBUG commands to examine and modify files and parts of your disk — and create brand new files. But unless you're a serious programmer, you probably won't ever need the following bare-metal commands. So they're included here in abbreviated form just so you know that they exist.

Advanced Commands

Input/Display a Single Byte from a Port

Format: **I portaddress**

and

Output/Send a Single Byte to a Port

Format: **O portaddress byte**

PCs use ports to control and determine the status of various timers, controllers, coprocessors, printer and communications gateways to the outside world, expansion units, and the keyboard. Each port has a unique number. You can read the current values at some (but not all) ports, and can send, or write, new values to some (but not all) ports. In many cases, consecutive ports work together as pairs. First you send a value to the port with the lower address to tell it which function you want to read or write, then you send a value to or read a value from the port with the higher address.

The various AT models (and many newer systems) use a battery-backed-up slice of CMOS memory to store your system's configuration. To see the stored CMOS values you first use the DEBUG O command to tell port hex 70 which function you want to examine, and then use the DEBUG I command to read the specified value from port hex 71.

Type in the following CMOS.SCR script using a pure-ASCII word processor, or EDLIN:

```
E 0 "Century is:"
O 70,32
I 71
E 0 "Year is:"
O 70,9
I 71
E 0 "Month is:"
O 70,8
I 71
E 0 "Day is:"
O 70,7
I 71
Q
```

Note that the first character in the lines with 70s in them is a capital O (although a lowercase one will work just fine) and not a zero. Be sure to press the Enter key after the final Q. You can also create the file at the DOS prompt by adding a line at the very beginning:

```
COPY CON CMOS.SCR
```

Then enter each line as shown — making sure you press the Enter key after the final Q. When you're done, after you typed the last Q and press Enter, press the F6 key, and then Enter one more time.

The E 0 commands are just dummy labels to let you know what's going on. You should see something like:

```
-E 0 "Century is:"
-O 70,32
-I 71
19
-E 0 "Year is:"
-O 70,9
-I 71
88
-E 0 "Month is:"
-O 70,8
-I 71
11
-E 0 "Day is:"
```

```
-O 70,7
-I 71
08
-Q
```

This tells you that the date stored in CMOS is 08-11-1988. You can read lots of important information this way, but you'll have to interpret some of it by turning it into binary and looking at which bits are 1 and which are 0.

For instance, the fixed disk type is maintained at CMOS port hex 12. (*Be very careful if you have to examine anything having to do with your fixed disk!* Follow instructions to the letter. And don't experiment unless you truly know what you're doing.) So if you wanted to see your hard disk type you could enter:

```
DEBUG
-O 70,12
-I 71
20
-Q
```

In this case the value stored at this address is hex 20, which doesn't tell you much. To make sense out of it you have to translate the hex 20 into high and low binary *nibbles* (a nibble is four bits, or half a byte):

```
HEX 20 = 0 0 1 0   0 0 0 0
                ↑           ↑
           drive C:    drive D:
```

The high nibble on the left represents the first hard disk (drive C:). The low nibble on the right represents the second hard disk (drive D:). If the value of a nibble is 0000 you don't have the appropriate hard disk installed, or at least your CMOS RAM doesn't know about it.

In this case, a hex 20 means the system contains only one hard disk (since the low nibble is 0000) and that the drive C: hard disk type is type 2 (because binary 0010 = decimal 2).

You could similarly examine the equipment byte at port hex 14 with the commands:

```
DEBUG
-O 70,14
-I 71
43
-Q
```

Again, translate the 43 that DEBUG reported in this case into its binary representation:

43 = 01000011

but split up the binary number as follows:

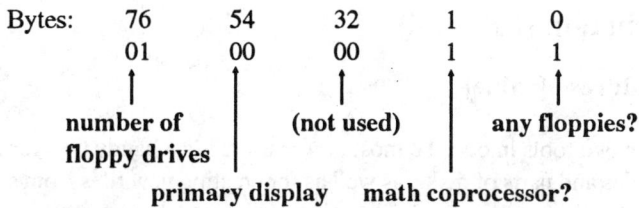

Bytes: 76   54   32   1   0
         01   00   00   1   1
          ↑   ↑   ↑   ↑   ↑
    number of   **(not used)**   **any floppies?**
    floppy drives
              primary display   **math coprocessor?**

Then consult a table that explains what's going on (like the one in the *Technical Reference* manual):

- Bits 6,7:   A 00 means 1 floppy drive
               A 01 means 2 floppy drives

- Bits 5,4:   A 00 means no monitor or an EGA or better
               A 01 means primary display is 40-column color
               A 10 means primary display is 80-column color
               A 11 means primary display is monochrome

- Bit 1:   A 0 means math coprocessor is not installed
               A 1 means math coprocessor is installed

- Bit 0:   A 0 means no floppy drives installed
               A 1 means floppy drives are installed

So a value of hex 43 means:

- 2 floppy drives are installed.
- Either no monitor or something fancier than a CGA.
- A math coprocessor is installed.

Execute Program in Memory (Go)

Format: **G [=address][address[address...]]**

and

Execute and Show Registers/Flags (Trace)

Format: **T [=address][value]**

and

Execute One Instruction (Proceed)

Format: **P [=address][value]**

DEBUG is really two tools in one. To most power users it's a handy tool for examining and modifying files and parts of disks, as well as for creating new files from scratch. But to programmers it's also a testing and debugging environment. You can load a program into DEBUG and watch it run step by step, which lets you trace the flow of execution from one instruction to the next, and look at the values of all the registers and flags in the process.

Once you've loaded a program (by specifying it at the end of the DOS command line after the word DEBUG, or by using the N and L commands), issuing a Go (G) instruction will execute it. If the program doesn't have any serious programming problems, and is designed to exit gracefully to DOS, DEBUG will print a "Program terminated normally" message onscreen. Don't issue another G at this point, or your system may hang. If you want to execute it a second time, reload the program first by typing:

```
L
```

Then re-enter the G command to run it again.

You may set breakpoints by specifying one, or as many as ten, addresses after the G. If the program execution flow reaches any of these breakpoint addresses while it's running, the program slams on its brakes and DEBUG displays the register and flag settings in force at that instant. You may also tell DEBUG to start the program execution at an address other than the default offset 100 of the code segment. To do so, you would add an equal sign (=) and an address right after the G.

Here's a script for the tiny program BEEP.COM we saw at the beginning of the chapter. (It beeps the speaker by printing a character 7.) Type in the script using any pure-ASCII word processor or EDLIN and call it BEEP.SCR:

```
A
MOV AH,02
MOV DL,07
INT 21
RET

RCX
7
```

```
N BEEP.COM
W
Q
```

Make sure you leave the blank line above RCX, and that you press the Enter key after each line (especially the last one with the Q). You could also create the file at the DOS prompt by inserting one line at the very beginning:

```
COPY CON BEEP.SCR
```

Then type in all the lines indicated, and be sure you press the Enter key after each one. When you're done, press the F6 function key, and then tap the Enter key one final time.

Either way, put BEEP.SCR on the same disk as DEBUG (or make sure DEBUG is in a subdirectory that your PATH knows about) and then type:

```
DEBUG < BEEP.SCR
```

To execute BEEP, just type BEEP at the DOS prompt. Then try running it from inside DEBUG. Load BEEP.COM either by typing:

```
DEBUG BEEP.COM
```

or:

```
DEBUG
-N BEEP.COM
-L
```

and then type G and press the Enter key. The program will run and you'll hear a beep. DEBUG will then display the message "Program terminated normally."

At this point if you want to run it again, first type L and press the Enter key to reload it. Then type G and press Enter to re-execute it.

DEBUG lets you trace through a program one or more steps at a time, displaying the state of the registers and flags after each instruction. You can single-step your way through by repeatedly pressing T and then Enter, or can specify a number directly after the T (without an equal sign) that tells DEBUG how many consecutive instructions to execute in a row. If you don't specify a starting address (with an equal sign and an address, just like G) DEBUG will begin tracing through the program at offset 100 of the code segment or at whatever offset address the Instruction Pointer (IP register) is pointing to.

The T command will trace through every single instruction — including those in each interrupt, loop, subroutine, call, etc. If you want to execute these separate processes but not step your way through them one instruction at a time, you can jump to the end of each process with the P command. T will slog through every last step of your program, while P will jump over the repetitive and tangential steps. Some programmers even refer to P as the jumP command.

Using T can get very complicated even in tiny programs, since when it reaches an interrupt, DEBUG will start tracing through the complex code that makes up the actual interrupt instead simply executing it and jumping to the next step in your program. It's useful if you need to see how a particular subroutine or interrupt changes your system's registers. But for nonprogrammers, P is definitely the one to use.

If you took a trip from New York to Portland, Oregon, the P equivalent description of the trip might be:

1. Took cab from home to JFK airport.
2. Took flight to Chicago.
3. Changed planes and took flight to Portland.
4. Took cab from PDX airport to Intel office.

The T instruction would look like:

1. Went out door to hail cab.
2. Located cab.
3. Got in.
4. Told driver to go to JFK.
5. Driver muttered softly and made U-turn.
6. Driver ran first red light.
7. Driver made illegal left turn onto CPW.
8. Driver ran second red light.
9. Driver swerved and narrowly avoided oncoming bus.

and so on. If you need to know the details of each operation, you would use T. If you want just the main points, use P.

Proceed will display the same registers and flags as the Trace command, and let you run the command multiple times by specifying a value after the P (but without an equal sign). Again, if you don't specify a starting address (with an equal sign followed by an address), DEBUG will begin at offset 100 of the code segment. If you try this with BEEP.COM you'll see something like:

```
-P 5

AX=0200  BX=0000  CX=0007  DX=0007  SP=FFFE  BP=0000  SI=0000  DI=0000
DS=3131  ES=3131  SS=3131  CS=3131  IP=0102   NV UP EI PL NZ NA PO NC
3131:0102 B207          MOV     DL,07
AX=0200  BX=0000  CX=0007  DX=0007  SP=FFFE  BP=0000  SI=0000  DI=0000
DS=3131  ES=3131  SS=3131  CS=3131  IP=0104   NV UP EI PL NZ NA PO NC
3131:0104 CD21          INT     21

AX=0207  BX=0000  CX=0007  DX=0007  SP=FFFE  BP=0000  SI=0000  DI=0000
```

```
DS=3131  ES=3131  SS=3131  CS=3131  IP=0106   NV UP EI PL NZ NA PO NC
3131:0106 C3              RET


AX=0207  BX=0000  CX=0007  DX=0007  SP=0000  BP=0000  SI=0000  DI=0000
DS=3131  ES=3131  SS=3131  CS=3131  IP=0000   NV UP EI PL NZ NA PO NC
3131:0106 CD20            INT    20

Program terminated normally
```

Note that the original BEEP.COM program consisted of the four lines:

```
MOV AH,02
MOV DL,07
INT 21
RET
```

The first line is missing in the P display, and DEBUG added a final INT 20 line.

The first line isn't there because the tracing process didn't kick in until after the first instruction. You can see the first instruction, and the state of things at the very beginning of the process, by typing R. The last INT 20 line is listed because a coded version of this instruction makes up the first two bytes — offset 0 — of the Program Segment Prefix that DOS uses to keep track of important information it needs to run the program properly. Under certain circumstances, such as ending a program with RET, execution jumps to offset 0, which executes INT 20. INT 20 shuts things down and returns to DOS.

If you do find yourself creating short assembly language programs to set colors, change file attributes, handle odd inputs for IF ERRORLEVEL batch tests and the like, you'll invariably end up making mistakes. By loading your ailing (or developing) program into DEBUG — complete with command line parameters — you can use P to step through the code and diagnose the trouble. The P command will usually pause at the right places and ask for input, print any of the executing program's built-in messages onscreen, and execute chores like changing colors.

A program like the screen-clearer mentioned elsewhere in this book accepts color numbers from the user on the command line. If you're writing a program like this, you can watch it read in and process the actual user input. Just enter something like:

```
DEBUG COLOR.COM 4e
```

(with the COM extension) and press P repeated to step through the program, keeping your eyes on the registers that are supposed to be affected. You might have constructed the program to process uppercase letters only and see that the value in a certain register is hex 20 too high, since the hex ASCII value for "e" is 65 while its uppercase version is 45. DEBUG's P command won't fix the problem for you, but it will help you spot it, which is often the hardest part of finishing something.

Expanded Memory Magic

DOS 4.0 introduced four new DEBUG commands that let you fiddle with expanded memory. But seriously, unless you're a high-powered programmer working with a memory-gluttonous application, you can pretty much ignore these.

Neither DOS 4.0 nor DOS 5.0 really provide much in the way of serious expanded memory tools. You can have the MEM /C command tell you how much extended and expanded memory your system is using and how it's being used. And if you really want to experiment, you can play with the four new DEBUG commands, XA, XD, XM, and XS.

XA and XD allocate and deallocate 16K pages. To use XA, specify how many new EMS pages you want. If DEBUG successfully makes the allocation it will return the number of a "handle" it uses as shorthand to refer to this block of pages. To deallocate the block of pages, use XD and specify the handle number DEBUG reported with XA. You can "map" a logical page onto one of the existing physical pages by using XM and specifying the logical page, the physical page, and the appropriate handle.

For the vast majority of users, the only really interesting command of the four is XS, which provides a status report. Just enter XS and DEBUG will give you three pieces of information:

1. The list of handles (starting with 0) and how many pages have been allocated to each. This will look something like:

    ```
    Handle 0000 has 0018 pages allocated
    Handle 0001 has 0003 pages allocated
    ```

2. A long list of individual physical pages and their respective "frame segment" addresses in the form:

    ```
    Physical page 0A = Frame segment 4000
    Physical page 0B = Frame segment 4400
    Physical page 0C = Frame segment 4800
        .
        .
        .
    Physical page 07 = Frame segment E400
    Physical page 08 = Frame segment E800
    Physical page 09 = Frame segment EC00
    ```

3. A report on how many EMS pages and handles DOS has been allocated, in the form:

    ```
    1B of a total   98 EMS pages have been allocated
     2 of a total   FF EMS handles have been allocated
    ```

ANSI and Other DOS Drivers

You can clear your screen on a color system to a color other than the dull default grey on black by running a short program. Likewise, you can redefine your keys with another set of programs that would, for example, put the Ctrl key back where it belongs on IBM's unwieldy 101-key keyboards. And you can switch from one screen width to another with the DOS MODE command, if you happen to have MODE.COM handy.

But DOS provides one direct way to accomplish all these tasks — with ANSI.SYS. And it even tosses in a few special new tricks. ANSI's abilities are a bit cumbersome to work with, and horribly documented, but once you start fiddling with ANSI you may find it hard to stop. We'll present ANSI (and other DOS drivers) in this chapter, and show you how to master all of its commands.

ANSI.SYS is a *device driver*. DOS uses device drivers as bridges between the operating system and the vast array of hardware gadgets on the market. In an ideal world, hardware manufacturers would get together and agree on one set of immutable standards. This way, users would need to learn only one command to set any printer's right margin, or move a cursor on a screen.

But the reverse has occurred. Manufacturers are loathe to tell each other what they're up to. And they often try to widen their markets by producing hardware that can run on dozens of different computers and dozens of operating systems. In addition, many hardware designers simply invent new standards either because they think their way of doing things is better, or because they want to lop off a share of the market and make all other vendors' products incompatible. Even if everyone agreed on one existing set of commands, vendors would undoubtedly slap on brand new features so often that any standard would need frequent and constant upgrading.

DOS couldn't possibly keep up with this perplexing vendor shivaree by maintaining internal tables of codes and instructions. The tables would be huge, and would slow lots of operations down. And they'd be out of date as soon as they were compiled. So the designers of DOS came up with an ingenious solution — they published a specification that all hardware manufacturers could use to develop their own hooks to the operating system. Any vendor who wanted his hardware to plug into DOS would provide a program called a driver that purchasers could copy onto their disks. Then, the user would simply tell DOS which drivers were there, and DOS would attach the driver and sniff out the necessary information.

Device drivers come in two classes — *block drivers* and *character drivers*. Block drivers move data around in relatively large chunks and are used to control random I/O on mass-storage devices such as hard disks, tape drives, and optical disks. Character drivers shuttle data in and out of systems serially (one character at a time), and deal with things like screens, printers, mice, keypads, and modems.

To install such a device all a user has to do is include the name and path of the device's driver in a CONFIG.SYS file. So if you're hooking up a mouse, you need to have a CONFIG.SYS file in the main root directory of your bootup disk that contains a line like (with the correct path for the file, of course):

```
DEVICE=MOUSE.SYS
```

When your computer boots up, your IBMBIO.COM system file (or IO.SYS file in non-IBM systems) checks for a CONFIG.SYS file, and loads the appropriate drivers into memory.

DOS provides several drivers of its own: DRIVER.SYS and VDISK.SYS (aka RAMDRIVE.SYS on some systems), as well as a few to handle its confounding "code page switching" abilities — DISPLAY.SYS, KEYBOARD.SYS, COUNTRY.SYS, and PRINTER.SYS. DOS 4.0 introduced a pair of EMS utilities, XMAEM.SYS and XMAZEMS.SYS.

DOS 5.0 offers a complete set of memory management utilities, HIMEM.SYS and EMM386.EXE, to handle both extended and expanded memory, as well as the High Memory Area (HMA) just above 1 Megabyte and the Upper Memory Blocks (UMBs) between 640K and 1 Meg.

DRIVER.SYS

DRIVER.SYS lets you do for any diskette drive what DOS does automatically for a system with a single floppy. If you need to copy files from one 3-1/2 inch diskette to another, for instance, the best way is to trick your system into thinking you have two logical drives for the same physical drive.

DRIVER.SYS: Format

Here's the form DRIVER.SYS should follow in the CONFIG.SYS file:

```
DEVICEHIGH=[d:] [path]DRIVER.SYS /D:ddd
[/T:ttt] [/S:ss] [/H:hh] [/C] [/N] [/F:f]
```

where:

/D:ddd is the drive number, from 0 to 127 (if you're up to 127 we'd like to see your system). A 0 here refers to the first diskette drive (A:), a 1 to the second diskette drive, and a 2 to the third diskette drive.

/T:ttt is the number of tracks on each side, from 1 to 999. If you omit this switch, DOS uses a default of 80 tracks.

/S:ss is the number of sectors per track, from 1 to 99. Omit this and DOS assumes 9 sectors.

/H:hh is the number of read/write heads per drive, from 1 to 99. Leave this out and DOS will use 2 heads. (In virtually all cases the number of heads is the number of disk surfaces, or sides.)

/C means you need changeline support. This is a special hardware feature of AT-class and above systems that knows when you've changed the disk in a particular drive. You don't really have to worry about this

/F:f tells DOS what type (form factor) of drive you're talking about. Omit this and DOS assumes you want a 720K 3-1/2-inch diskette (type 2). However, you could also specify any one of these values for f, depending on the type of drive:

0	160/180/320/360K 5-1/4″ floppy
1	1.2Mb 5-1/4″ floppy
2	720K 3-1/2″ diskette
7	1.44Mb 3-1/2″ diskette
9	2.88Mb 3-1/2″ diskette

The most common use for this driver is in hooking up an external 3-1/2 inch diskette. You have to tell DOS the drive number. But apart from that, if you don't specify anything to the contrary, the default is:

- 80 tracks per side
- 9 sectors per track
- 2 sides
- no changeline support required
- 3-1/2 inch 720K diskette

If you need to specify another type of diskette, you should consult the documentation furnished with it.

Since the defaults are set for a 3-1/2 inch 720K external diskette, to hook one up to a system with a single hard disk (assuming you stored the DRIVER.SYS file in your \DOS subdirectory), you would use the simple CONFIG.SYS command:

```
DEVICE=C:\DOS\DRIVER.SYS /D:2
```

You could then treat this external device as drive D:. Some of the more popular laptops on the market come with a cable that attaches to the external floppy disk controller port on a PC or XT. By using a command like the one above, and then running a special program on the laptop, you can temporarily turn the laptop diskette drive into a *slave* drive. Your PC or XT will then use this remote laptop drive as an additional floppy drive, which it will refer to as C: on a PC or D: on an XT. This makes it a snap to move information back and forth from your desktop and laptop systems, and transfer files from 5-1/4 to 3-1/2 inch formats and vice versa.

A generation of original XT users learned that they could treat the single floppy drive as both A: and B:, which made it less of a chore to copy diskettes. DRIVER.SYS makes it possible for users to give any internal or external drive an additional drive letter. If you installed one external 3-1/2 inch 720K diskette and want to refer to it both as drive D: and E: just use the above command twice:

```
DEVICE=C:\DOS\DRIVER.SYS /D:2
DEVICE=C:\DOS\DRIVER.SYS /D:2
```

Your system will bump up the drive letter one notch each time it processes this command. You could then copy files from one 3-1/2 inch 720K diskette to another with a command like:

```
COPY D:*.* E:
```

Similarly, if you're using an AT with a 1.2 megabyte 5-1/4 inch diskette in drive A:, and you want to copy files from one of these dead-end disks to another, you can have the DRIVER.SYS command customize your system so you can refer to this drive both as A: and D:

To do this, you have to use a 0 after the /D: switch to tell DOS to work its magic on the first diskette drive in the system. And remember that the default switch settings are designed for 720K diskettes:

```
/T:80  /S:9  /H:2  /F:2
```

while 1.2M floppies require these settings:

```
/T:80  /S:15  /H:2  /F:1
```

The number of tracks and heads is the same on both, but you'll have to redefine the other parameters. So on an AT with a 1.2Mb floppy as drive A:, a second floppy, and a hard disk, and all the DOS files in a subdirectory called C:\DOS, you could treat the 1.2Mb drive both as A: and D: with the command:

```
DEVICE=C:\DOS\DRIVER.SYS /D:0 /S:15 /F:1
```

When DOS assigns drive letters, it always refers to the first diskette drive as A:. If it finds a second internal diskette drive, DOS calls this B:. If it finds only one internal diskette drive it refers to this single drive both as A: and B:. The lowest drive designation for a hard disk is C:, but since you can have such a welter of hard disks, external floppies, RAMdisks, and external block devices of all sorts, once it gets past the floppies, DOS starts checking out your configuration and assigns drive letters in the order in which it finds things. If you're using RAMDRIVE.SYS to set up RAMdisks, put the RAMDRIVE commands after the DRIVER.SYS commands.

RAMDRIVE.SYS

RAMDRIVE.SYS (or VDISK.SYS on some systems) is used to create a RAMdisk, by fooling your system into treating part of RAM like a disk. DOS won't install RAMDRIVE if it determines that you have less than 65K of memory free. And even if you specify a smaller value (for bbb), the smallest virtual drive it will try to set up is 64K. However, if you're short on memory, DOS may reduce the size of the virtual disk that you specified since it will always leave a minimum 64K of memory free after the VDISK is in place. The size specified for the RAMdisk includes space allocated for normal disk structures (the boot sector, file allocation table (FAT), and directory), so you won't be able to use the entire space you specified for data.

If you have a system with one or two floppies and a single hard disk and low memory to spare, and you keep your DOS files in a \DOS subdirectory on drive C:, and you accept all the defaults by including the line:

```
DEVICE=C:\DOS\RAMDRIVE.SYS
```

RAMDRIVE.SYS: Format

Here's the syntax of RAMDRIVE.SYS in the CONFIG.SYS file:

```
DEVICEHIGH=[d:][path]RAMDRIVE.SYS
[bbb] [sss] [ddd] [/E] [/A]
```

where:

bbb is the size of the virtual disk, expressed as the decimal number of kilobytes, ranging from 1 to the maximum amount of free memory in your system. The default is 64K.

sss is the sector size in bytes. The default is 512 bytes, but you can use 128, 256, or 512.

ddd is the number of directory entries, from 2 to 512. The default is 64. Obviously the number of directory entries determines the number of files you can store on this virtual disk (except that one entry is used to store the volume label). If you specify a value for the number of entries, you must also specify the disk and sector size.

Note: You may stick in "comments" (text such as "buffer size=") before the bbb, sss, and ddd parameters, but why bother?

/E installs the virtual disk in extended memory.

/A works just like /E but uses expanded memory rather than extended memory.

in your CONFIG.SYS file, DOS will set up a 64K RAMDRIVE on drive D: with the following specifications:

Total sectors:	512
Bytes per sector:	512
Directory entries:	64
Memory location:	Conventional
Maximum root directory entries:	64

RAMDRIVE is one of the only DOS functions that uses extended memory. Most other applications that go past 640K use expanded rather than extended RAM. Extended memory works only on ATs and later hardware with properly configured memory above the 1 megabyte address space. You can use up to 4 megabytes for each VDISK in extended memory.

You can't use the DOS DISKCOPY command with a virtual disk created by VDISK. You can't format VDISK's virtual disks, but they come already formatted so you don't have to. And if you create multiple virtual disks, DOS will automatically give them increasingly higher drive letters.

HIMEM.SYS

HIMEM.SYS manages extended memory, using the XMS (eXtended Memory Specification) standard, and the High Memory Area (HMA), the first 64K block above 1 Megabyte. It provides a hardware independent way of reading and writing data in the HMA via the A20 handler, which provides physical access to the machine's A20 address line. To get at HMA, the basic trick is to togggle the the A20 line on and shift the contents of a segment register left 4 bits, giving you a 21-bit address. If that means nothing to you, don't worry — you don't have to be able to derive Maxwell's equations to turn on a light switch. The A20 handler is implemented in different ways on different machines — sometimes even on different models from a single manufacturer.

HIMEM.SYS arbitrates other programs' usage of extended memory and the HMA, and thus must be the first device driver that manages or uses extended memory in your CONFIG.SYS file. HIMEM.SYS has several switches which let you control HMA use by other programs, define the number of extended memory block handles that can be used at one time, describe your machine's A20 handler, and set a number of options which are specific to certain applications software and to particular hardware systems. If you're already using the version of HIMEM.SYS that came with Windows 3.0, you should replace the older HIMEM.SYS with the one that comes with DOS 5.0.

EMM386.EXE

On an 80386-class machine, with HIMEM.SYS or an equivalent extended memory manager in place, EMM386.EXE gives you two distinct capabilities — the ability to use

HIMEM.SYS: Format

Here's the syntax for HIMEM.SYS in CONFIG.SYS:

```
DEVICE=[d:][path]HIMEM.SYS [/hmamin=mm] [/numhandles=nnn]
[int15=xxxx] [/machine:yy] [a20control:on|off] [shadowram:on|off]
[cpuclock:on|off]
```

where

/hmamin=mm is the minimum amount of memory (in kilobytes, from 0 to 63) a program must use before HIMEM.SYS will grant it access to the HMA. The default is 0, which means that the HMA is available to any program that requests it on a first-come, first served basis. If necessary, you can deny HMA access to programs by raising this threshold value to just less than that needed by the largest program you want to let use HMA. Application programs rarely use the HMA, anyway (one of Microsoft's key motivations in moving DOS there, or so it would appear), so you're unlikely to have to worry about this switch too often.

/numhandles=nnn is the maximum number of extended-memory-block handles that can be open at one time. The range of allowable values is 1 to 128, and the default is 32. Again, this is something you're unlikely to have to tinker with, unless the installation instructions for a specific piece of software explicitly ask you to change this value.

/int15=xxxx allocates kilobyte-sized chunks of extended memory for programs which use an Interrupt 15 interface for accessing extended memory. You can allocate from 64K through 65535K of extended memory for this purpose, at least according to the DOS 5.0 docs. As a general rule of thumb, you should try to stay away from any program that needs 64Mb for its interface to extended memory. The default is zero.

/machine=yy is a setting you might actually need to use someday. It tells HIMEM.SYS about your machine's hardware and ROM BIOS, to enable HIMEM.SYS to use the HMA via the A20 handler. You can enter either the code or value from the following table:

Value	Code	A20 Handler
1	at	IBM PC/AT
2	ps2	IBM PS/2
3	pt1cascade	Phoenix Cascade BIOS

4	hpvectra	HP Vectra (A and A+)
5	att6300plus	AT&T 6300 Plus
6	acer1100	Acer 1100
7	toshiba	Toshiba 1600 and 1200XE
8	wyse	Wyse 12.5 MHz 286
9	tulip	Tulip SX
10	zenith	Zenith ZBIOS
11	at1	IBM PC/AT
12	at2	IBM PC/AT (alternative delay)
12	css	CSS Labs
13	at3	IBM PC/AT (alternative delay)
13	philips	Philips
14	fasthp	HP Vectra

If your machine isn't listed, check the README.TXT for additional values or suggestions as to which existing value to use. The default value is 1.

/a20control:on|off tells HIMEM.SYS whether or not to take control of the A20 address line if it's already in use. If you follow Microsoft's advice about loading HIMEM.SYS first, this shouldn't be a problem unless you're trying to do something seriously masochistic like attempting to run DOS 5.0 in extended memory as a task under OS/2. The setting /a20control:off means that HIMEM.SYS will not grab the A20 line if it's already in use; the default is on.

/shadowram:on|off allows you to specify whether shadow RAM — memory used to hold a copy of information normally read from ROM — should be disabled and used by HIMEM.SYS as extended memory. Not all machines support shadow RAM in the first place, but using shadow RAM will speed up most machines that have this feature. For systems with less than 2 megabytes of RAM, the default HIMEM.SYS setting is /shadowram:off. If you turn it on, you're making a decision to go for speed at the expense of memory.

cpuclock:on|off doesn't literally turn your CPU's clock on or off — it can be used to try to correct a problem on some systems, where loading HIMEM.SYS lowers the CPU clock speed. Unfortunately, setting /cpuclock:on to fix this problem slows HIMEM.SYS down.

EMM386.EXE: Format

The syntax for the EMM386.EXE device driver is:

```
device=[d:] [path]EMM386.EXE [on|off|auto] [eeee] [w=on|w=off]
[mx|frame=mmmm|/pmmmm] [pn=mmmm] [x=mmmm-nnnn]
[i=mmmm-nnnn] [b=mmmm] [L=xxx] [a=aaa] [h=hhh] [d=ddd] [RAM]
[NOEMS}
```

where

on|off|auto turns the device driver on or off, or puts it in auto mode, where expanded memory support is enabled only if a program requests it. The default is on.

eeee is the amount of expanded memory (in kilobytes) to be provided by EMM386.EXE. The default value is 256, from a range of 16 to 32768.

w=on|w=off enables or disables Weitek coprocessor support. The default is off.

The next three switches provide three different but equivalent ways of doing the exact same thing — telling EMM386.EXE where to put the page frame area for expanded memory.

mx specifies the page frame address from the following table:

Value	Address	Value	Address
1	C000	8	DC00
2	C400	9	E000
3	C800	10	8000
4	CC00	11	8400
5	D000	12	8800
6	D400	13	8C00
7	D800	14	9000

FRAME=*mmmm* lets you specify the starting address of the page frame directly. Any of the values above are valid.

/p*mmmm* does the same thing with even less typing.

p*n*=*mmmm* lets you do something slightly different — specify the starting address of page n from the same range of values. Since the LIMS 3.2 standard requires that all 4 pages be contiguous, this option is only useful if you have a rather contorted memory arrangement and are using LIMS 4.0 compatible software. You can't use this option if you've used any of the three previous ones.

x=*mmmm-nnnn* tells EMM386.EXE to exclude a range of memory addresses from possible use by an EMS page. Rather than specifying a particular page address, this options tells the device driver, "Anywhere but here." Valid values range from A000 to FFFF — from 640Kb to 1Mb.

i=*mmmm-nnnn* tells EMM386.EXE to use a particular memory range for either EMS pages or UMB RAM. Valid values are also from A000 to FFFF; if x= and i= values overlap, the x= values take precedence.

b=*mmmm* specifies the lowest address to be used for swapping EMS pages into conventional memory (EMS "banking"). Values range from 1000 to 4000, with a default of 4000.

L=*xxx* provides a minimum value for available extended memory after EMM386.EXE loads. The default is 0, so if you're using both expanded and extended memory, you may need to plug in a number here to keep some extended memory in play.

a=*aaa* sets the number of alternate high-speed register sets to be allocated to EMM386.EXE. These are useful for multitasking, but incur a cost of about 200 bytes per set. Values can range from 0 to 254, with a default of 7.

h=*hhh* sets the number of handles available to EMM386.EXE. Valid values range from 2 to 255, with a default of 64.

d=*ddd* reserves memory to be used for buffering direct memory access (DMA) transfers, such as might occur with high-speed I/O devides or networks. This should be set to the size of the largest anticpated DMA transfer that might occur while EMM386.EXE is active. The range of possible values for this option is 16 to 256, with a default of 16.

RAM tells EMM386.EXE to provide both expanded memory and UMB support.

NOEMS tells EMM386.EXE to provide UMB support but not expanded memory.

existing extended memory to emulate expanded memory for applications that need it, and the ability to make use of Upper Memory Blocks (UMBs) between 640Kb and 1 Mb to load device drivers and TSRs up out of the 640Kb application area. EMM386.EXE is unusual, as compared to most other DOS device drivers, in that it's an .EXE file rather than a .SYS file, which means you can also use it from the command line after booting to examine the status of EMM386.EXE's memory services and to reset parameters.

There are a number of EMM386.EXE switches that control the creation and allocation of expanded memory. What EMM386.EXE is really doing is taking extended memory and simulating expanded memory with it — convincingly enough to fool any application that conforms to the LIMS 3.2 and 4.0 standards. Expanded memory is inherently inefficient in its need to shuffle blocks of memory into and out of the page frame area, but large applications that need to keep compatibility with AT-type machines don't have any other real choice. The 80286 processor can't access any extended memory besides the HMA, and that's only through some programming sleight of hand. So while expanded memory, like the 80286, is heading for the status of historical footnote, it's not going to disappear overnight — anymore than the legions of PC/XTs still out there performing faithfully.

The two switches that provide access to the UMBs, and allow DOS 5.0 to work its memory magic, are the RAM and NOEMS options. RAM enables the UMBs in addition to the expanded memory services, while NOEMS enables the UMBs while suppressing the expanded memory services. Since the page frame for expanded memory takes up a 64K block from a typical UMB area of 96K, you won't get a lot of mileage from the UMBs with expanded memory in action.

From the command line in DOS, EMM386.EXE provides a status report on memory services provided by the driver, and allows you to turn expanded memory on or off, as well as toggling on or off support for Weitek co-processors.

EMM386.EXE won't work on machines prior to the 80386 series, returning the message "".

SMARTDRV.SYS

SMARTDRV.SYS is a logical successor to earlier caching software that came with prior DOS versions, such as IBMCACHE.SYS. It will greatly speed up your disk I/O, and its use, where available memory permits, is strongly encouraged by Microsoft. The cache can be located in either extended or expanded memory, and the device driver itself loaded into high memory, so there's no real memory cost to running SMARTDRV.SYS on a system with available UMB memory and extended or expanded memory. You can control both the initial cache size and the minimum cache size (some application programs reduce the cache to free up memory for themselves), as well as where the cache is located, using the SMARTDRV switch options. At present Windows 3.0 is the only program you need worry about trying to reduce your cache; if you're running Windows, putting in a nominal value here may help keep things moving along. If you experiment, you'll find that there is a definite law of diminishing returns in increasing the cache size — doubling the cache size will bring a smaller and smaller improvement in speed once you get past a certain size.

SMARTDRV.SYS: Format

The syntax for running this device driver is:

```
DEVICE|DEVICEHIGH=[d:] [path] SMARTDRV.SYS [mmmm] [nnn] [/a]
```

where

mmmm is the initial size of the cache in kilobytes. Valid values range from 128 through 8192; the default is 256.

nnn is the minimum cache size; the default is zero. Obviously, the minimum value should not be larger than the initial value.

/a tells SMARTDRV.SYS to install the cache in expanded memory; the default is to install it in extended memory.

DISPLAY.SYS, EGA.SYS, PRINTER.SYS, and SETVER.EXE

Both DISPLAY.SYS and PRINTER.SYS are for specialized font loading, which IBM perversely calls *code page switching*. You can wrestle with this pair of drivers to add multilingual, Portugese, French-Canadian, or Norwegian touches to your work. As IBM sheepishly points out, "The U.S. user normally does not need" this aggravation. Skip it.

EGA.SYS is needed if you're going to use the Task Swapper with an EGA display. SETVER.EXE is used to fool applications that look at the DOS version number to run anyway.

ANSI.SYS

While RAMDRIVE.SYS can help you by speeding up disk-intensive operations, and DRIVER.SYS is useful in certain hardware configurations, the one real gem of a DOS device driver is ANSI.SYS. But although users of all types could benefit from the extended screen and keyboard control that ANSI offers, this feature is documented poorly and hard to implement with the meager tools DOS provides. Worse, IBM took its turgid but factual descriptions of how to use this driver out of the DOS manual and put them instead in the *DOS Technical Reference* manual, which few users own.

In some respects DOS hasn't changed much since its early days on tiny 16K single-sided floppy hardware. Even on today's capable color systems the default DOS display

---

EGA.SYS

To solve a problem encountered when using the Task Swapper in the DOS Shell with EGA monitors, this device driver is included with DOS 5.0. If you have an EGA monitor and plan on using the Task Swapper, this one is mandatory. If you're also using a mouse, you can save a bit of memory by loading EGA.SYS first.

The syntax for EGA.SYS is:

```
DEVICE|DEVICEHIGH=[d:][path]EGA.SYS
```

No switches, no decisions to make.

---

is a dingy grey text against a black background. DOS normally doesn't make it easy to use foreign language alphabets, symbols like cents signs, or common characters like 1/2. And its macro abilities are limited to repeating and editing previous commands.

DOS treats screens as TTY (teletype) devices, displaying just one line at a time. It can't handle graphics (apart from clumsy ASCII border characters), or put characters anywhere other than the line the cursor is currently on, and it can't back up past the left margin. In fact, DOS behaves as if it were driving a printer instead of a full-sized screen.

SETVER.EXE

Like EMM386.EXE, SETVER.EXE is both a device driver and a command. As a device driver, it installs a MS-DOS version table into memory. Some applications check for DOS version numbers on startup; if they were written to check for valid numbers in the range of, say, 2.1 to 3.3, they'll come to a rapid halt when they see 5.0. To allow these applications to run, DOS will compare the application's filename against a user-modifiable entry in the table, and return the table entry value. Table entries for some commonly encountered programs are predefined; you can use SETVER.EXE from the command line to add others.

The syntax for the SETVER.EXE device driver is simply:

```
DEVICE|DEVICEHIGH=[d:][path]SETVER.EXE
```

DISPLAY.SYS and PRINTER.SYS: Format

Here's the syntax of DISPLAY.SYS and PRINTER.SYS in CONFIG.SYS.

```
DEVICEHIGH=[d:][path]DISPLAY.SYS CON[:]=(type[,[hwcp][,n]])
```

or

```
DEVICEHIGH=[d:][path]DISPLAY.SYS CON[:]=(type[,[hwcp][,(n,m)]])
```

where:

type is the display (MONO, CGA, EGA, or LCD). Under DOS 4.0 and 5.0, use either LCD for the PC convertible, or EGA for all other types including VGA or 8514/A.

hwcp is the hardware code page (437, 850, 860, 863, or 865).

n tells how many additional "prepared" code pages you want, from 0 to 6, although on MONO or CGA systems this number has to be 0. The default is 0 for MONO and CGA, and 1 for everything else. Under DOS 4.0 and 5.0, use 1 for code page 437, and 2 for anything else.

m defines the number of "sub-fonts" per code page. The default is 1 for the LCD screen on IBM's Convertible laptop, and 2 on EGA and VGA screens. You can skip this parameter for DOS 4.0 and 5.0.

```
DEVICEHIGH=[d:][path]PRINTER.SYS LPT#[:]=(type[,[hwcp][,n]])
```

or

```
DEVICEHIGH=[d:][path]PRINTER.SYS LPT#[:]=(type[,[(hwcp1,hwcp2,...)][,n]])
```

where:

LPT# is the printer, from LPT1 to LPT3 (you may use PRN instead of LPT1).

type is either 4201 (for the IBM Proprinter) or 5202 (for the IBM Quietwriter III) or 4208 for the Proprinter X24 or XL24.

hwcp is the hardware code page (437, 850, 860, 863, or 865).

n is the number of additional code pages, from 1 through 6.

You can also use COUNTRY.SYS and KEYBOARD.SYS to help in code page switching. COUNTRY.SYS contains the specific idiosyncratic country-dependent information, and is specified as a NLSFUNC parameter. KEYBOARD.SYS is a KEYB parameter that specifies which of several possible country-specific keyboard layouts you want to use.

ANSI fixes all that (well, most of it). By installing the ANSI driver, and coming up with an automated method for issuing its thorny commands, you can dress your color screen in a rainbow of attributes, put text anywhere you like, redefine any alphanumeric key on the keyboard (sorry, it won't alter keys like Alt or CapsLock), and even give your system primitive macro powers.

CONFIG.SYS is the place to tell your system that you want to use ANSI.SYS. (You should already have a CONFIG.SYS configuration file on your bootup disk to specify how many disk buffers you want, increase the number of files you can open at one time if you're using a large database, expand the number of drive designations, specify a much larger environment size than the wimpy 160 bytes DOS normally allots, and load drivers for devices like mice or fancy hard disks.) Just include this line in CONFIG.SYS:

```
DEVICE=ANSI.SYS
```

or

```
DEVICEHIGH=ANSI.SYS
```

If you're using a hard disk, you should keep all your DOS files — including the DOS device drivers — in their own subdirectory called \DOS. If ANSI.SYS is properly in your \DOS subdirectory on drive C:, the CONFIG.SYS command to load it would actually look like:

```
DEVICE=C:\DOS\ANSI.SYS
```

or

```
DEVICEHIGH=ANSI.SYS
```

Be sure to include the SYS extension in this command. If you haven't ever used ANSI, copy the ANSI.SYS file from your DOS diskettes into your \DOS subdirectory. If you're using a floppy disk system (and these days there's little reason to do so), copy ANSI.SYS onto your main system disk — once DOS loads ANSI it will keep it in memory so you can replace your bootup disk with an applications disk if you need to. Either way, if you're changing your CONFIG.SYS file or creating one for the first time, reboot your system when you're done since it has to read the CONFIG.SYS file at bootup to load and set everything properly. If you're using a 2.x version of DOS, and this line is the last (or only) one in your CONFIG.SYS file, be sure to press the Enter key at the end of the line or else DOS may become hopelessly confused, refuse to load ANSI.SYS, and print a garbled message onscreen. DOS 3.x fixed this problem.

You can add optional /X, /K, or /L parameters at the end of the command. The first two, /X and /K enable and disable ANSI's ability to handle extended keyboards. The last, /L, tells it to retain screen size after MODE changes.

When you load ANSI.SYS, DOS will grab the module containing the ANSI code, and grow slightly in size — by about 4K — if you haven't loaded it into high memory using DEVICEHIGH.

Once ANSI is hooked up and ready to go, every DOS command will filter through it. The ANSI driver will assiduously look for two special "signature" characters and execute whatever legal ANSI instructions follow.

All ANSI commands must begin with the same two characters:

1. The ESC character — decimal 27, hex 1B
2. The left bracket ("[") — decimal 91, hex 5B

If it doesn't see these two characters it will pass everything on to be processed normally.

Because every ANSI command begins with an ESC, the ANSI commands are sometimes referred to as *escape sequences*. If you don't have ANSI loaded, and you display these escape sequences, you'll see a small arrow pointing left followed by a left bracket and a tangle of other characters. If you do have ANSI loaded, you'll never see these characters since the ANSI driver will intercept them and act on the commands they contain.

The rest of the commands are combinations of upper- and lowercase letters, decimal numbers, text, and punctuation. DOS usually doesn't care whether you type commands in uppercase or lowercase, since it generally turns everything into capital letters. However, ANSI is case-sensitive. If the command calls for a small "u" and a capital "K" you have to type these in exactly as specified or they won't work. Its syntax is precise and a bit jarring, so be careful to type everything in exactly as it appears here.

Since every ANSI command starts off with an ESC character, you can't just type in the appropriate escape sequence at the DOS prompt. This is because DOS interprets any tap on the Esc key as an instruction to abort whatever you happened to be doing. Regardless of what you were typing, as soon as you press the Esc key, DOS will print a backslash (\), cancel the command you were trying to execute, and drop down a line waiting for a new one.

DOS does let you issue an ESC by following its PROMPT command with the *meta-string* $E or $e. (A meta-string is just a fancy name for a sequence of characters beginning with a dollar sign.) But using this technique makes your existing system prompt disappear, leaving you with a blank, promptless screen. And it forces you to work with raw, unfriendly ANSI codes.

It's fairly easy to create COM or BAT files that execute ANSI strings. All the major word processors, including *WordPerfect*, Microsoft *Word*, and *WordStar*, let you insert an ASCII 27 in your text. (To do it in *WordStar*, for instance, type ^P^Esc — hold down the Ctrl key and while you're holding it down, press the P key and then the Esc key. Then release the Ctrl key.) In some cases you'll see a ^[onscreen if you're successful.

Don't be confused by the left bracket following the caret if you do see ^[— this just happens to be one way to display the single ASCII 27 ESC character (another way is a little arrow pointing left). This has nothing to do with the real left bracket character that follows ESC in every ANSI command. If your word processor uses ^[to signify an ESC, it will make the beginning of every ANSI command look like:

```
^ [ [
```

So on some word processors, an ANSI command to clear the screen, ESC[2J, would actually look like:

```
^ [ [2J
```

(Remember, the ESC in ESC[2J and all the other examples shown here actually stands for the ASCII 27 escape character, not the letters "ESC.")

With many other word processors, you can insert an ESC character by holding down the Alt key, typing 27 on the number pad while you're holding it down, and then releasing the Alt key. (This technique works only with the numbers on the cursor/number pad, not with the top row number keys.)

You can also use EDLIN or DEBUG to create files that contain ANSI commands, with all the required ESC characters. With EDLIN, type Ctrl-V and then type a left bracket to enter the ESC character. EDLIN will display ^V[if you do this properly. Again, this left bracket is part of the representation of the ESC character; you'll have to type an additional left bracket (without the Ctrl-V this time) to enter the second character of each ANSI command. EDLIN will show the pair of characters as ^V[[. Note that some 3.x versions of EDLIN have trouble displaying this pair.

To execute an ANSI command, you first have to make sure you booted your system with a CONFIG.SYS file that included a line that loaded ANSI.SYS. Then you have to check that the ANSI command you want to issue begins with an ESC character and a left bracket, and that you typed the rest of the command precisely. If you're following instructions that say 2J and you type 2j instead, all that will happen when you execute the command is that DOS will display the erroneous "j."

You then have to print the correct ANSI instruction onscreen for it to take effect. You can use a DOS command like TYPE or COPY or MORE to do this. Or you can put the ANSI command in a batch file and use the ECHO batch command. Or issue a PROMPT command either at the DOS command line or inside a batch file. But doing so will wipe out your normal C> or other customized DOS prompt, so you'll have to follow it with another PROMPT command to reset it.

NOTE

All examples presented use the abbreviation "ESC" to represent the decimal ASCII 27 (or hexadecimal 1B) escape character. Don't type in the letters "E-S-C" since this won't do anything except exercise your fingers. Use the techniques mentioned above to insert this ESC character in each command. And remember that each ESC character is always followed by a left bracket ([) character, so every ANSI string begins with the two characters ESC[.

If you're looking at an ANSI string in DEBUG, you'll see that every one begins with 1B 5B, since 1B is the hex value for the ESC character, and 5B the hex value of the left bracket character.

Creating ANSI Commands with EDLIN and DEBUG

Using the DOS EDLIN.COM utility to create ANSI files is a bit tricky. First, make sure EDLIN.COM is on your disk. If not, copy it from the DOS disk into your \DOS subdirectory. To have EDLIN create a new file, type EDLIN and then the name of the file you want to create. (You can't start EDLIN unless you enter a filename after it on the command line.) This example will produce a small file called CLEAR that clears the screen. So you start off by typing:

```
C>EDLIN CLEAR
```

EDLIN will then respond with a message indicating that it can't find an existing file with the name CLEAR, and then print an asterisk on the next line:

```
New file
*
```

An asterisk hugging the lefthand edge of your screen is EDLIN's prompt, just as A> or C> is DOS's prompt and a hyphen ("-") is DEBUG's prompt. The prompt tells you EDLIN is waiting for a command.

If you don't see the "New file" message, or see something like "End of input file" this means you do have a file called CLEAR on your disk. Abort the process by typing Q (then Enter) and then Y (and Enter). Then pick another filename and start over.

To start entering characters in this file, just type I and press the Enter key. You'll see.

```
*I
        1:*
```

The "1:" tells you that you're working on line 1. EDLIN is a line editor that can work only one line at a time. The asterisk following the 1: is EDLIN's way of indicating the current line — the one it's working on at the moment. (For details, see the chapter on EDLIN.)

Now you start entering characters. The ANSI command to clear the screen is only four characters long:

1. The first character has to be: ESC
2. The second character has to be: [
3. The third character is: 2
4. The fourth character is: J

So the entire command looks like:

```
ESC[2J
```

To enter the ESC character, type `^V` and then a left bracket ("["). This combination of `^V[` inserts an ESC character into your file. Note however that the left bracket that follows the `^V` is different from the actual left bracket character required by ANSI. It just so happens that you create an ESC character by typing `^V` and then [. But all that typing `^V[` does is put an ESC character in your text. It has nothing to do with the [that DOS requires in all ANSI commands. So you'll have to type a SECOND [character. Then type the remaining 2 and J characters. Be careful to type a capital J rather than a lowercase one, since ANSI is case-sensitive. Line 1 would now look like:

```
1:*^V[[2J
```

This tells you that line 1 contains four characters:

1.   `^V[` (ESC character)
2.   [([character)
3.   2 (2 character)
4.   J (J character)

Press the Enter key to enter the four characters. EDLIN won't accept anything you typed on a particular line until you press Enter at the end of that line. Once you press Enter, it will offer you the chance to type in something on line 2:

```
2:*
```

You don't want to, so type Ctrl-C or Ctrl-Break to tell EDLIN both that you're done entering characters and that you want it to go back to command mode. This will look like:

```
2:*^C

    *
```

To save the text you just created, type E and press Enter:

```
*E

C>
```

Then, assuming you had previously loaded ANSI.SYS by including a line in your CONFIG.SYS file that said something like:

```
DEVICE=ANSI.SYS
```

or:

```
DEVICE=C:\DOS\ANSI.SYS
```

you can test the file you just created by typing:

```
TYPE CLEAR
```

If you did everything properly the screen should clear. If DOS simply prints a 2J on the screen, you probably forgot to type the second left bracket character.

If you didn't originally have a DEVICE=ANSI.SYS line in your CON-FIG.SYS file, and you just added it, you'll have to reboot for it to take effect. DOS has to see this line in your CONFIG.SYS file when it boots up, or else it won't load ANSI or process ANSI commands.

The whole process looks like:

```
C>EDLIN CLEAR
New file
*I
         1:*^V[[2J
         2:*^C

*E

C>
```

The only problem with using EDLIN is that it automatically puts a carriage return and line feed (as well as ^Z end-of-file marker) at the end of the files it creates. So when you execute an ANSI command created with EDLIN it may bounce the DOS prompt down an extra line. You could fix this by using DEBUG to subtract the last three bytes from the file.

First, make sure the DEBUG.COM file is in the current directory or is in a subdirectory that your PATH knows about. If it's not, copy it from your DOS diskette into your \DOS subdirectory.

Load the CLEAR file into DEBUG with the command:

```
C>DEBUG CLEAR
```

You should see just the DEBUG hyphen prompt. If DEBUG prints a "File not found" message above the hyphen, abort the process by typing Q and then pressing Enter. Make sure CLEAR is in the subdirectory you're currently logged into, and try again.

To have DEBUG report the length of the file in hexadecimal representation, just type RCX and press the Enter key. In this case you should see:

```
-RCX
CX 0007
:
```

Typing RCX instructs DEBUG to display the contents of the CX register. When you load a typically short file like CLEAR into DEBUG, DEBUG looks at the directory entry for this file, figures out how many bytes the file contains, and then puts this number of bytes into the CX register. So typing RCX right after you load the file will display this number (in hex notation).

The 0007 following the CX tells you that the value in CX is hex 7, or that the file is seven bytes long.

The colon on the next line is a special DEBUG prompt that offers you the opportunity to change the value of a register, which is exactly what you want to do.

If you had used the DEBUG Display (D) command to view the seven bytes of the file, you would have seen something like:

```
-D 100 L7
34E5:0100   1B 5B 32 4A 0D 0A 1A                        .[2J...
```

The D 100 L7 command tells DEBUG to display seven bytes starting at memory offset 100. Ignore the 34E5; this number is the segment address and varies from system to system. The 0100 is the starting address of the memory contents DEBUG is displaying. And:

```
1B 5B 32 4A 0D 0A 1A
```

is the hexadecimal representation of all seven bytes in the file, as follows:

1B — ESC character
5B — [character
32 — 2 character
4A — J character
0D — carriage return
0A — linefeed
1A — ^Z end-of-file marker

EDLIN added three extra characters (a carriage return, a linefeed, and an end-of-file marker), so if you subtract 3 from the length of the file, DEBUG will make the file three characters shorter, chopping those extra meddlesome characters off. DEBUG reported that the length of the file (the value in register CX) is 7, and 7 - 3 = 4. So type a 4 to the right of the colon and press the Enter key:

```
CX 0007
:4
-
```

You might want to check your work by examining the new value in the CX register. Just type RCX again and press the Enter key:

```
CX 0004
:
```

Since this is the value you wanted, just press the Enter key again without entering a new number, and you'll return to the DEBUG hyphen prompt. Then, save the truncated file and quit DEBUG by typing W (then Enter) and then Q (and then Enter). The whole process looks like:

```
C>DEBUG CLEAR
-RCX
CX 0007
:4
-W
Writing 0004 bytes
-Q

C>
```

However, if you're going to use DEBUG to trim the extra characters off, you might as well use it to create the whole file.

Remember that DEBUG works exclusively in hex. But once you get the hang of it, you can bang out ANSI commands in seconds. To create the ESC[2J clear-screen instruction in DEBUG you would type everything following the DEBUG hyphen prompts:

```
C>DEBUG
-E 100 1B "[2J"
-N CLEAR
-RCX
```

```
CX 0000
:4
-W
Writing 0004 bytes
-Q
```

The line:

```
E 100 1B "[2J"
```

tells DEBUG to enter a group of characters starting at memory offset 100. The characters it enters are 1B (the hexadecimal represention of the ESC character itself), then a left bracket, a 2, and a capital J. Normally you make DEBUG entries in hex as you did with the 1B. But when entering normal letters and numbers, you can put them in quotes and have DEBUG translate them into hex for you.

You specify a filename with the DEBUG N command. The line:

```
N CLEAR
```

tells DEBUG to name the file that you'll eventually save as CLEAR. You also have to tell DOS how long to make the file. The 1B ESC counts as one character, and the [2J add up to three more, for a total of four. You specify the length by typing:

```
RCX
```

and then entering:

```
4
```

when you see the cursor blinking beside a colon. Then, write the CLEAR file to disk and quit DEBUG by typing W and pressing Enter and then typing Q and pressing Enter.

With DOS 5.0's EDIT utility, life is a bit simpler. You can use its Wordstar emulation to create the Esc character by typing ^P^Esc — hold down the Ctrl key and while you're holding it, press the P key and then press the Esc key. What you'll see is a left arrow, but what you've created is an ASCII 1B — the Esc character.

The methods DOS provides are all relatively primitive and cumbersome:

1. Putting the commands in a file (called something like ANSI.FIL, although you can give it any legal filename) and then using any DOS command that displays text, such as one of these:

    ```
    TYPE ANSI.FIL
    MORE < ANSI.FIL
    COPY ANSI.FIL CON
    ```

2. Putting the commands after the word ECHO in a batch file, e.g. ECHO ESC[2J (to clear the screen). This ECHOANSI.BAT batch file will make setting colors a bit less painful (remember to substitute the actual escape character for the ESC below):

    ```
    ECHO OFF
    IF %1!==! GOTO OOPS
    :TOP
    ECHO ESC[%1m
    SHIFT
    IF %1!==! GOTO END
    GOTO TOP
    GOTO END
    :OOPS
    ECHO You have to specify at least
    ECHO one parameter, eg:
    ECHO %0 0 to reset all attributes, or
    ECHO %0 34 47 for blue text on white
    :END
    ```

3. Using a $E or $e meta-string with the DOS PROMPT command, in the form $c (where c = meta-string). Remember that meta-strings are not case-sensitive, and you can combine them, so that a sample sequence like:

    ```
    PROMPT $P (Time is $T$H$H$H$H$H$H) :
    ```

    at 3:20 PM in directory \DOS on drive C: yields:

    ```
    C:\DOS (Time is 15:20):
    ```

Here are the meta-strings and their purposes:

Meta-String	DOS Functions
t	Time
d	Date
p	Current directory on default drive
v	DOS version number
n	Default drive letter
	Drawing Characters
$	$ character
g	> character
l	< character
b	| character
q	= character
	Special Characters
h	Backspace (erases previous character)
e	Escape character (ASCII 27 decimal, 1B hex)
_	Carriage return/line feed (drops down one (line and moves to left edge of screen)

As an example, you could reset any previous screen attributes (with ESC[0m), then set the colors to bright (with ESC[1m) cyan text (with ESC[36m) on a blue background (with ESC[44m), then clear the screen (ESC[2J) and reset your prompt to show the current subdirectory, by using:

```
PROMPT $E[0;36;1;44m
PROMPT $E[2J
PROMPT $P:
```

An even better way to use the PROMPT meta-strings is to create and run the following ANSIPROM.BAT batch file:

```
ECHO OFF
IF %1!==! GOTO OOPS
SET OLDPROM=%PROMPT%
ECHO ON
PROMPT $E[%1
ECHO OFF
SET PROMPT=%OLDPROM%
SET OLDPROM=
GOTO END
```

```
:OOPS
ECHO You forgot to specify an ANSI string, eg:
ECHO %0 34;47m   (for blue text on white)  :END
```

The ANSIPROM.BAT batch file will let you enter ANSI codes without having to worry about the ESC or left bracket characters. And it will reset the PROMPT automatically for you. If does this by using environment variables (%PROMPT% and %OLDPROM%), so be sure your environment can handle the few extra bytes this process requires. You can expand your environment in later versions of DOS with the CONFIG.SYS SHELL command, which will look something like:

```
SHELL=C:\COMMAND.COM /E:512 /P
```

(This particular example expands the default 160-byte environment to 512 bytes.)

To use ANSIPROM.BAT, enter the part of the ANSI command that follows the ESC and left bracket. To clear the screen, just type:

```
ANSIPROM 2J
```

Note: You can't use PROMPT to generate ANSI sequences when ECHO happens to be off. If you remove the:

```
ECHO ON
```

line from the ANSIPROM.BAT batch file above, DOS won't set any colors. Most users routinely set ECHO OFF at the beginning of their batch files so commands in the batch file don't clutter up the screen as they execute. But if one of the commands is a PROMPT that is supposed to set attributes, and ECHO is off, nothing will happen. To set colors with PROMPT when ECHO is off, include an ECHO ON line directly above the PROMPT color-setting line, and an ECHO OFF line right below it.

If you do want to keep ECHO off for the duration of your batch file, have ECHO issue your ANSI commands (just as ECHOANSI.BAT does) instead of using PROMPT.

But it's fairly simple to learn a few simple techniques that can really tame ANSI.

Working with Color

One of the easiest ways to use ANSI is to create a small COM file that writes ANSI escape sequences to standard output (as IBM suggests half-heartedly). Here's a COLOR1.SCR DEBUG script that creates such a file:

```
A
MOV BX,1
MOV CX,E
```

```
MOV AH,40
MOV DX,10E
INT 21
RET
DB 1B,"[0;34;47m",1B,"[2J"

N ANSCOLOR.COM
RCX
1C
W
Q
```

Every attribute-setting ANSI command ends with a lowercase "m." You can issue just one color-changing command at a time, or you can stack several together. But you need only one "m" per line. So the command:

```
ESC[34m
```

by itself will change the foreground to blue, while the longer:

```
ESC[0;34;47m
```

will also undo any existing attributes, and set the background to white at the same time.

The COLOR1.SCR DEBUG script will create a file called ANSCOLOR.COM that will set your screen colors to blue text on a white background and then clear the screen. You can substitute other colors by replacing the 34 with the foreground color of your choice, and 47 with the background color of your choice. The line:

```
DB 1B,"[0;31;43m",1B,"[2J"
```

would yield red text (31) on a yellow background (43).

The first 0 in either color version resets all the existing attributes. This is necessary because ANSI adds attributes in layers. If your text is red and blinking, changing the color to green will yield green blinking text; it won't do away with the blink. The 0 will first reset everything before it changes the colors the way you want them. So the string that this program sends to your screen contains three parts:

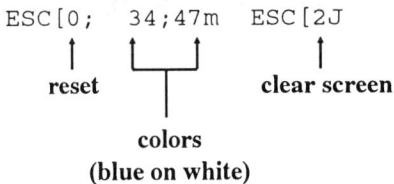

ESC[0;   34;47m   ESC[2J

  ↑   ↑ ↑   ↑

reset   **clear screen**

colors

(blue on white)

You can create both a blue-on-white ANSCOLOR.COM and a special black-on-black INVIS.COM with the following COLOR2.SCR DEBUG SCRIPT:

```
E 100 BB 01 00 B9 0E 00 B4 40 BA 0E 01 CD 21 C3
E 10E 1B 5B 30 3B 33 34 3B 34 37 6D 1B 5B 32 4A
N ANSCOLOR.COM
RCX
1C
W
E 104 8
E 110 38
M 117 L5 111
N INVIS.COM
RCX
16
W
Q
```

Type in either of these DEBUG script files with a pure-ASCII word processor, or EDLIN. If you don't have one handy, add a line at the very top of each that says:

```
COPY CON COLOR1.SCR
```

or:

```
COPY CON COLOR2.SCR
```

and then carefully enter the lines at the DOS prompt. When you're all done typing, press the Enter key after the final Q (very important!), then press the F6 function key, then press the Enter key one final time. You should see the message "1 File(s) copied." If you're creating the COLOR1.SCR script, be sure to leave the blank line directly above N ANSCOLOR.COM.

Then put either script file in the same directory as DEBUG.COM (or make sure you have DEBUG in a subdirectory your path knows about) and type:

```
DEBUG < COLOR1.SCR
```

or:

```
DEBUG < COLOR2.SCR
```

If you later want to use DEBUG to substitute your own colors in ANSCOLOR.COM, put the hex ASCII value of the last digit of the foreground color of your choice at address 113 and the hex ASCII value of the last digit of the background color of your choice at address 116. You can figure out the values to patch ANSCOLOR.COM from this table:

| | *Hex ASCII Value to Use at* |
| *Color* | *DEBUG Addresses 113 and 116* |

Black	of "0" is 30
Red	of "1" is 31
Green	of "2" is 32
Yellow	of "3" is 33
Blue	of "4" is 34
Magenta	of "5" is 35
Cyan	of "6" is 36
White	of "7" is 37

So if the ANSCOLOR.COM you originally created set the colors to blue on white, and you wanted yellow text on a red background instead, you would use DEBUG to put a value of 33 at address 113 and a value of 31 at address 116. Then you'd give the file a new name like REDYEL.COM (so you don't wipe out the existing ANSCOLOR.COM file):

```
C>DEBUG ANSCOLOR.COM
-E 113 33
-E 116 31
-N REDYEL.COM
-W
-Q
```

Or you could do the same thing with:

```
C>DEBUG ANSCOLOR.COM
-E 113 "3"
-E 116 "1"
-N REDYEL.COM
-W
-Q
```

This may seem confusing at first, because you're entering the hex representation of the last digit of the color numbers, and not the value of the numbers themselves. The hex representations of the digits 0 through 7 happen to be 30 through 37 ("0" is ASCII 30, "1" is ASCII 31, etc.). When you patch the original ANSCOLOR.COM file to set new colors, what you're really doing is replacing just the second digit of the foreground and the second digit of the background. The first digits of each remain the same.

Languages like BASIC use the same color numbers for foreground and background, but ANSI has a different set for each. All ANSI color numbers have two digits. The first digit of all foregrounds is "3" and the first digit of all backgrounds is "4" in the ANSI color system. In each case the second numbers specify the color (0=black, 1=red, 2=green, etc.). So a green foreground is 32, and a green background would be 42, for example. These ANSI numbers are slightly different from IBM's standard color values, as is shown here:

Color	IBM	ANSI
Black	0	0
Red	4	1
Green	2	2
Yellow	6	3
Blue	1	4
Magenta	5	5
Cyan	3	6
White	7	7

For high-intensity IBM colors, add 8 to the value of the color. So high-intensity yellow is 6 + 8, or 14 decimal; E hex. For high-intensity ANSI colors the command ESC[1m will do it.

The special INVIS.COM program will turn your colors to black on black and then clear the screen. This is useful when you have to leave your system unattended and you don't want anyone else to look through your directories. When you get up to take a break, just type:

```
INVIS
```

Unauthorized users will still be able to meddle by typing DEL *.* or COPY *.* A: for instance, but they'll have to do it on a totally blank screen. If they're smart, and they know you have a program such as *WordStar* that isn't affected by ANSI color settings, they can use the directory-reporting and file manipulation abilities of the program to poke around.

When you return, type ANSCOLOR (or REDYEL or whatever you've named your real color-setting program to) to unblank the screen. You can use a variation of this technique to keep nosy co-workers from using the TYPE command to examine things like your CONFIG.SYS or AUTOEXEC.BAT files. Just put the INVISIBLE ANSI string itself at the beginning of the file. When your system tries to execute it you'll get either a "Unrecognized command in CONFIG.SYS" message or a "Bad command or filename" message, which won't hurt anything. But if someone tries to use the TYPE command to see what's in your text files, ANSI will intercept the string and turn the display off.

You can create this invisible string with the DEBUG INVIS.SCR script:

```
E 100 1B 5B 38 6D 1B 5B 32 4A
N LINEONE
RCX
8
W
Q
```

(Or just get into DEBUG and type each of the six lines.) This will create a tiny file called LINEONE. You can then blank out your screen with the command:

```
TYPE LINEONE
```

But the trick here is to use your word processor to read the LINEONE file into the beginning of your CONFIG.SYS or AUTOEXEC.BAT or related files. If you do this and you see a string of ^@^@^@^@^@ characters, erase these.

One final variation of this technique will make it very easy to prevent anyone from getting into your hard disk when you're not there. Rename both the color-setting file (ANSCOLOR.COM, REDYEL.COM or whatever you call it) to something innocuous like WRDCOUNT.COM. Put this file in a directory that your PATH knows about (such as \DOS). And rename the INVIS.COM program to an equally uninteresting name like SETMODEM.COM.

Then add a line to your AUTOEXEC.BAT that says something like:

```
SETMODEM /1 /12 /N81
```

When DOS reaches this line of the batch file it will execute SETMODEM (and ignore the innocent-looking parameters after it), which will blank the screen. The only way to unblank it is to type WRDCOUNT, or whatever you named ANSCOLOR.COM to. Remember, WRDCOUNT.COM either has to be in the root directory or a subdirectory that's included in your PATH setting for this to work properly.

This isn't foolproof, since another user could boot off a diskette in the floppy drive and circumvent your AUTOEXEC.BAT file. But, as they say in the locksmith business, it will keep the honest people out.

Okay, okay. Just one more. But you have to promise that you'll check your typing very, very carefully and that you won't try this on your hard disk. And if you haven't read about DEBUG in the chapter dedicated to it, you might want to give it a quick scan. The following instructions are designed for a floppy disk in drive A: only.

If you have a hard disk system that loads ANSI.SYS, you can keep prying eyes from seeing what's on your floppies. All you have to do is put the INVIS code into your floppy disk directory. A good place is in the directory entry that holds the disk's volume label.

This example will use a 360K 5-1/4 inch floppy and add the system files to it. This way you can put ANSI.SYS on your diskette along with a CONFIG.SYS file that contains the line:

```
DEVICE=ANSI.SYS
```

Then you can copy your DOS files to the disk and label it "DOS 3.3" (or whatever version you happen to be using). If you've locked intruders out of your hard disk, the first thing they'll probably try to do is boot off a floppy disk with the DOS system files on it. If you leave this disk around they'll find it, try to boot off of it, and end up temporarily stymied. First, format a blank disk, using the:

```
FORMAT A: /S /V
```

syntax, which will copy the system files onto it and then prompt you to enter a volume label. If you're using an AT high-density drive you can either add a /4 switch to the end of the above command, or format the disk in drive B:. IBM admits that the /4 option is unreliable, so format the floppy in drive B: and then switch it into drive A:.

After DOS finishes, it will tell you the format was successful and then ask for a volume label:

```
Format complete
System transferred

Volume label (11 characters, ENTER for none)? POWER
TOOLS
```

As the example illustrates, type in:

```
POWER TOOLS
```

or any other 11-letter name.

Make sure this formatted disk is in drive A:, and that DEBUG.COM is in a directory that your PATH knows about (if it's not, put it there). Load it by typing:

```
DEBUG
```

Now very carefully load the first four directory entries from drive A: by typing:

```
-L 100 0 5 1
```

(Note: The 0 in this command refers to drive A:. Be very careful not to have anything other than a 0 in this position!)

Tell DEBUG to display these four directory entries by typing:

```
-D
```

You should see something like:

```
3140:0100  49 42 4D 42 49 4F 20 20-43 4F 4D 27 00 00 00 00    IBMBIO  COM'....
3140:0110  00 00 00 00 00 00 00 60-72 0E 02 00 54 56 00 00    .......'r...TV..
3140:0120  49 42 4D 44 4F 53 20 20-43 4F 4D 27 00 00 00 00    IBMDOS  COM'....
3140:0130  00 00 00 00 00 00 00 60-71 0E 18 00 CF 75 00 00    .......'q....u..
3140:0140  43 4F 4D 4D 41 4E 44 20-43 4F 4D 20 00 00 00 00    COMMAND COM ....
```

```
3140:0150  00 00 00 00 00 00 00 60-71 0E 36 00 DB 62 00 00   ........'q.6..b..
3140:0160  50 43 20 4D 41 47 41 5A-49 4E 45 28 00 00 00 00   POWER TOOLS(....
3140:0170  00 00 00 00 00 00 09 B3-74 0F 00 00 00 00 00 00   ........t.......
```

Ignore the first four characters in each row (here they're 3140); these will vary from system to system and don't affect this. Note that the fourth entry is POWER TOOLS. The 28 in the same row tells you that this entry is the disk's volume label. Use DEBUG's E command to replace all 11 characters in "POWER TOOLS" with the INVIS string plus three ASCII 7 beep characters. Type this very carefully:

```
-E 160 1B,"[8m",1B,"[2J",7,7,7
```

This will overwrite all the letters in "POWER TOOLS." Use a variation of the D command to check your work:

```
-D 160 L 10
```

Apart from the 3140 at the beginning of the line, your screen should look exactly like this:

```
3140:0160  1B 5B 38 6D 1B 5B 32 4A-07 07 07 28 00 00 00 00   .[8m.[2J...(....
```

If it doesn't, type Q and press Enter to quit. Then start again.

If it does, write the file to disk. *Be extraordinarily careful and type this exactly as it appears!* Type this in wrong on a hard disk and you could lose everything, so check your typing several times before finally pressing the Enter key. Above all, make sure that the number between the 100 and the 5 is a 0:

```
-W 100 0 5 1
```

Then type Q to quit and press Enter. Make sure you included the line:

```
DEVICE=ANSI.SYS
```

(or a variation with your particular system's path to ANSI.SYS in it) in your CONFIG.SYS file. Also, be certain you have your ANSI color-setting program (ANSCOLOR.COM or REDYEL.COM) handy. And type DIR A:.

As soon as DOS tries to display the directory and prints the volume label onscreen, ANSI.SYS will intercept the code and blank the screen. Then DOS will beep three times. This should deter any unauthorized user, who's probably wondering if he or she just broke your system. Again, you can get around this by booting up from a factory-fresh DOS disk.

If you want to see the files on drive A:, just be sure the DOS FIND.EXE utility is in a subdirectory your PATH knows about, and type:

```
:DIR A:  |  FIND  "-"
```

This will filter out everything that doesn't have a hyphen in it, which means the volume label won't print onscreen but all the filenames will.

The entire FORMAT and DEBUG process looks like this, for DOS version 3.3:

```
FORMAT A:  /S /V

Format complete
System transferred

Volume label (11 characters, ENTER for none)? POWER
TOOLS

     362496 bytes total disk space
      78848 bytes used by system
     283648 bytes available on disk

Format another (Y/N)?n
```

```
C>DEBUG
-L 100 0 5 1
-D
3140:0100  49 42 4D 42 49 4F 20 20-43 4F 4D 27 00 00 00 00    IBMBIO  COM'....
3140:0110  00 00 00 00 00 00 00 60-72 0E 02 00 54 56 00 00    .......'r...TV..
3140:0120  49 42 4D 44 4F 53 20 20-43 4F 4D 27 00 00 00 00    IBMDOS  COM'....
3140:0130  00 00 00 00 00 00 00 60-71 0E 18 00 CF 75 00 00    .......'q....u..
3140:0140  43 4F 4D 4D 41 4E 44 20-43 4F 4D 20 00 00 00 00    COMMAND COM ....
3140:0150  00 00 00 00 00 00 00 60-71 0E 36 00 DB 62 00 00    .......'q.6..b..
3140:0160  50 43 20 4D 41 47 41 5A-49 4E 45 28 00 00 00 00    POWER TOOLS(....
3140:0170  00 00 00 00 00 00 09 B3-74 0F 00 00 00 00 00 00    ........t......
-E 160 1B,"[8m",1B,"[2J",7,7,7
-D 160 L 10
3140:0160  1B 5B 38 6D 1B 5B 32 4A-07 07 07 28 00 00 00 00    .[8m.[2J...(....
-W 100 0 5 1
-Q
```

If you want to do something particularly sensitive in DOS, and you don't want to have it appear on your screen, ANSI can turn off the display if you set the colors to ESC[8m (where ESC represents a decimal 27 or hex 1B character), clear the screen with ESC[2J, and then reset the screen to your default colors when you're done. If you like blue text on a white background, you'd reset them to ESC[34;47m, so the batch file would look like:

```
ECHO ESC[8m;ESC[2J
REM (sensitive things happen here)
ECHO ESC[34;47m
```

Obviously, replace the "REM (sensitive things happen here)" line with the actual sensitive command(s).

If you're not using ANSI, you could get the same basic effect with two small COM programs, BLANK.COM and UNBLANK.COM. Create them both by typing in the following BLANK.SCR with a pure ASCII word processor or EDLIN:

```
A 100
MOV DX,184F        ;80 x 25
MOV CX,0000        ;Top left corner
MOV AX,0600        ;Scroll window up
MOV BH,00          ;00 = black on black
INT 10             ;Do it
MOV AH,02          ;Set cursor position
MOV BH,00          ;Main page
MOV DX,0000        ;Top left corner
INT 10             ;Do it
RET                ;Back to DOS

RCX
17
N BLANK.COM
W
E 10A 71
N UNBLANK.COM
W
Q
```

Omit the semicolons and the text following them. Be sure to leave a blank line above RCX, and to press the Enter key at the end of each line, especially the last one with the Q. Be certain DEBUG.COM is handy and type:

```
DEBUG < BLANK.SCR
```

Then put lines in your batch file that look like:

```
BLANK
REM (sensitive things happen here)
UNBLANK
```

Both of these techniques use the same color settings. BLANK will clear your screen to black on black, and UNBLANK will restore it to blue on white. You may change either of these as follows:

To change the BLANK.COM program, make sure you set the foreground and background to the same color. If you use the BLANK.SCR script, change:

```
MOV BH,00          ;00 = black on black
```

by replacing the 00 with any other pair of digits. Using 11 would give you a solid blue screen, 22 a solid green screen, 33 solid cyan, 44 solid red, 55 solid magenta, 66 solid brown, and 77 solid white.

To change the color of the UNBLANK.COM program, replace the 71 in the BLANK.SCR script line:

```
E 10A 71
```

with any other color you like. The lefthand digit is the background color, and must be in the range 0 to 7. The righthand digit is the text (foreground) color and must be a hex number between 0 and F. Once again, here are the available colors:

Value	Color		Value	Color
0	Black		8	Grey
1	Blue		9	Bright blue
2	Green		A	Bright green
3	Cyan (Lt Blue)		B	Bright Cyan
4	Red		C	Bright red
5	Magenta		D	Bright magenta
6	Brown		E	Yellow
7	White		F	Bright white

←—— **background only** ——→

←——————————— **foreground** ———————————→

Changing the hex number from 71 to 74 would give you red text on a white background. Changing it to 4E would give you yellow text on a red background. The advantage to using the ANSI method is that typing CLS when the black on black setting is in effect would keep things black on black. However, typing CLS when BLANK.COM had temporarily made things black on black would reset your attributes to the default DOS grey on black, so you'd be able to see what you were doing. If you use BLANK.COM in a batch file, you won't have to worry about this.

A completely different (and more flexible) way to master ANSI is to enter commands via the ESCAPE.COM program below. You can create this program either of two ways. You could type in the following DEBUG ESCAPE.SCR script:

```
A 100
MOV DX,0120          ;point to device name CON at offset 120
MOV AX,3D01          ;open the standard input device
INT 21               ;do it
MOV BX,AX            ;save file handle in BX
MOV SI,0080          ;point to buffer containing inputed string
MOV CL,[SI]          ;get count of characters in string
INC CL               ;adjust count for prefix
XOR CH,CH            ;zero out high byte of count
MOV WORD PTR [SI],5B1B
                     ;put ANSI ESC[ sequence at beginning
MOV DX,SI            ;point to start of string
MOV AH,40            ;output string to the standard input device
INT 21               ;do it
MOV AH,3E            ;close handle
INT 21               ;do it
RET                  ;back to DOS
DB "CON",20,20,20,20,20,0


RCX
N ESCAPE.COM
2B
W
Q
```

While this lets you enter ANSI escape sequences from the command line, it uses a slow and slightly cumbersome trick (writing to standard output). A faster way is simply to have DOS display the string. Here's an adaptation of the above program that uses an undocumented DOS interrupt 29 "Quick TTL" display:

```
A
MOV SI,0080          ;point to buffer containing inputed string
MOV CL,[SI]          ;get count of characters in string
INC CL               ;adjust count for prefix
XOR CH,CH            ;zero out high byte of count
MOV WORD PTR [SI],5B1B
                     ;put ANSI ESC[ sequence at beginning
MOV AL,[SI]          ;put character from string into AL
INT 29               ;undocumented "quick TTL" interrupt
INC SI               ;point to next character in string
LOOP 010D            ;go back and put next character into AL
RET                  ;return to DOS


RCX
15
```

```
N ESCAPE.COM
W
Q
```

But since running undocumented commands can be potentially troublesome, try this slightly longer, legal version that's nearly as fast:

```
A
MOV SI,0080              ;point to buffer containing inputed string
MOV CL,[SI]             ;get count of characters in string
INC CL                  ;adjust count for prefix
XOR CH,CH               ;zero out high byte of count
MOV WORD PTR [SI],5B1B
                        ;put ANSI ESC[ sequence at beginning
MOV AH,02               ;DOS "display output" function
MOV DL,[SI]             ;put character from string into DL
INT 21                  ;execute main DOS interrupt
INC SI                  ;point to next character in string
LOOP 010D               ;go back and put next character into AL
RET
RCX
17
N ESCAPE.COM
W
Q
```

If you try any of these ESCAPE.SCR methods, use a pure ASCII word processor or EDLIN, call the file ESCAPE.SCR, and be sure that you leave a blank line above RCX, and that you press the Enter key after each line — especially the last one with the solitary Q. You may omit the comments following the semicolons and the semicolons themselves. Then put the ESCAPE.SCR script file in the same directory as DEBUG.COM (or be sure DEBUG is in a directory that your path knows about) and type:

```
DEBUG < ESCAPE.SCR
```

The ESCAPE.COM program that these techniques creates will let you enter ANSI commands without having to worry about the ESC character or the left bracket that follows it. So to clear the screen, just type:

```
ESCAPE 2J
```

or:

```
ESCAPE J
```

To reset all attributes to grey on black:

```
ESCAPE 0m
```

or:

```
ESCAPE m
```

To set the foreground to bright red, type:

```
ESCAPE 31;1m
```

Or to redefine Alt-1 so it prints the Spanish upside-down exclamation point, type:

```
ESCAPE 0;120;173p
```

(To save wear and tear on your typing fingers, you might want to rename ESCAPE.COM to E.COM. Then you could simply type:

```
E 0;120;173p
```

to redefine Alt-1, or:

```
E J
```

to clear the screen, etc.

And if you don't want to deal with ANSI numbers (such as 34 for a blue foreground, or 1 for highlighting) you can use the following FORE.BAT, BACK.BAT, and SPE-CIAL.BAT batch files:

First, FORE.BAT, to change foreground colors. Just type FORE and then a color — black, red, green, yellow, blue, magenta, cyan, or white. You may enter the colors in uppercase, lowercase, or a combination of both:

```
ECHO OFF
REM This is FORE.BAT
IF %1!==! GOTO OOPS
GOTO %1
ECHO ON
:BLACK
ECHO ESC[30m
GOTO END
:RED
ECHO ESC[31m
GOTO END
```

```
:GREEN
ECHO ESC[32m
GOTO END
:YELLOW
ECHO ESC[33m
GOTO END
:BLUE
ECHO ESC[34m
GOTO END
:MAGENTA
ECHO ESC[35m
GOTO END
:CYAN
ECHO ESC[36m
GOTO END
:WHITE
ECHO ESC[37m
GOTO END
:OOPS
ECHO You must enter a new text color, eg:
ECHO %0 WHITE  or  %0 red
:END
```

Next, BACK.BAT. This works exactly the same as FORE.BAT except that it lets you set the background color. Again, enter the color you want on the command line after the name BACK:

```
ECHO OFF
REM This is BACK.BAT
IF %1!==! GOTO OOPS
GOTO %1
ECHO ON
:BLACK
ECHO ESC[40m
GOTO END
:RED
ECHO ESC[41m
GOTO END
:GREEN
ECHO ESC[42m
GOTO END
:YELLOW
ECHO ESC[43m
GOTO END
```

```
:BLUE
ECHO ESC[44m
GOTO END
:MAGENTA
ECHO ESC[45m
GOTO END
:CYAN
ECHO ESC[46m
GOTO END
:WHITE
ECHO ESC[47m
GOTO END
:OOPS
ECHO You must enter a new background color, eg:
ECHO %0 WHITE  or  %0 red
:END
```

Finally, SPECIAL.BAT, to give you control over ANSI's other attributes (blinking, underlining on mono systems, high-intensity, etc.). You can also use it reset all your existing attributes back to plain white on black. You'll need to do this if you want to turn off blinking, or high-intensity, or any of the other special features:

```
ECHO OFF
REM This is SPECIAL.BAT
IF %1!==! GOTO OOPS
GOTO %1
ECHO ON
:RESET
:NORMAL
ECHO ESC[0m
GOTO END
:BOLD
:BRIGHT
:HIGHLIGHT
ECHO ESC[1m
GOTO END
:UNDERLINE
ECHO ESC[4m
GOTO END
:BLINK
ECHO ESC[5m
GOTO END
:REVERSE
  ECHO ESC[7m
GOTO END
```

```
:CANCEL
:BLANK
ECHO ESC[8m
GOTO END
:CLS
ECHO ESC[2J
GOTO END
:OOPS
ECHO You must enter a special attribute from this list:
ECHO RESET, NORMAL, BOLD, BRIGHT, HIGHLIGHT, CLS
ECHO UNDERLINE, BLINK, REVERSE, CANCEL, BLANK
ECHO eg:    %0 RESET    or    %0 CLS
:END
```

This trio lets you set attributes by typing in words rather than codes. So to set the foreground to blue, you'd type:

```
FORE blue
```

or:

```
FORE BLUE
```

or even something like:

```
FORE bLuE
```

To set the background to white, type:

```
BACK white
```

or:

```
BACK WHITE
```

And you can use the SPECIAL.BAT batch file to reset everything back to the default grey on black, or make the foreground blink or become bold. To reset everything to normal, just type:

```
SPECIAL reset
```

or:

```
SPECIAL RESET
```

or:

```
SPECIAL normal
```

or:

```
SPECIAL NORMAL
```

The choices are listed at the end of the SPECIAL.BAT file — and they appear onscreen if you simply type SPECIAL with nothing following it. Some definitions are duplicates. Here's the full slate of special ANSI attributes:

Action	Code
Normal grey-on-black (cancels any attributes currently in effect)	0
Bold (bright, or high-intensity; works on foreground only)	1
Underline (on IBM-compatible mono screens only; blue foreground on color systems)	4
Blink (foreground only)	5
Reverse video (white on black)	7
Canceled (black on black; invisible)	8

Most non-ANSI color-setting programs simply invoke one of the two BIOS INT 10 Scroll Window video services (Scroll Up or Scroll Down). But the colors these set aren't "sticky." If you run a program to give yourself bright magenta text on a cyan background, and then type CLS, DOS will reset your colors to grey on black, although you can patch the Scroll Window BIOS routine buried inside COMMAND.COM so that CLS will clear the screen to a predefined set of colors. But when you set colors and then clear the screen with ANSI, any subsequent CLS commands will wipe away existing text while maintaining the attributes you specified.

In fact, when you type a normal CLS command, DOS sends an ESC[2J to your BIOS to clear the screen. You can see this in action by redirecting the output of the CLS command into a file called CLRSCRN:

```
A>CLS > CLRSCRN
```

Then use the DOS TYPE command to display the contents of the file:

```
A>TYPE CLRSCRN
```

and the screen will clear.

Actually, this gives you one more way to create ANSI files that contain the elusive ESC character. Once you've redirected the CLS command into a file, you can edit that file with your word processor or EDLIN and change the command following the ESC[to execute whatever ANSI sequences you like. You can even add an ECHO to the beginning of the line and then rename the file by adding a BAT extension, which will turn it into a batch file that can set your colors or redefine your keys.

You could also have the following ANSICOLR.BAT batch file create individual files called COL.COM that you can run whenever you need to set your screen attributes to the predefined colors that you like. For this to work, your DEBUG.COM utility has to be in the same directory or in a directory that your path knows about:

```
ECHO OFF
IF %1!==! GOTO OOPS
IF EXIST COL.COM GOTO RENAME
ECHO N COL.COM                                      > COL.SCR
ECHO E 100 B4 9 BA 8 1 CD 21 C3 1B "["             >> COL.SCR
IF %4!==! GOTO THREE
ECHO E 10A "%1;%2;%3;%4m$"                         >> COL.SCR
GOTO FINISH
:THREE
IF %3!==! GOTO TWO
ECHO E 10A "%1;%2;%3m$"                            >> COL.SCR
GOTO FINISH
:TWO
IF %2!==! GOTO ONE
ECHO E 10A "%1;%2m$"                               >> COL.SCR
GOTO FINISH
:ONE
ECHO E 10A "%1m$"                                  >> COL.SCR
:FINISH
ECHO RCX                                           >> COL.SCR
ECHO 16                                            >> COL.SCR
ECHO W                                             >> COL.SCR
ECHO Q                                             >> COL.SCR
DEBUG < COL.SCR
DEL COL.SCR
ECHO Now run COL to set your color(s) to %1 %2 %3 %4
GOTO END
:OOPS
ECHO Enter from one to four ANSI color values after %0
ECHO eg: %0 34    for a blue foreground
ECHO or: %0 34 47 for blue text on a white background
ECHO or: %0 0 1 37 44 to reset the existing attributes
ECHO         then set your colors to bright white on blue
ECHO (And you must have ANSI loaded)
GOTO END
:RENAME
```

```
ECHO First rename your existing COL.COM so this
ECHO doesn't write over it, then restart %0
:END
```

Once you've typed in ANSICOLR.BAT, you could create a small program called COL.COM that would set your text color to blue, by typing:

```
ANSICOLR 34
```

The ANSICOLR batch file would redirect a customized script into DEBUG and create the appropriate COL.COM file. Typing:

```
COL
```

at the DOS prompt would set the foreground to blue. The:

```
IF EXIST COL.COM GOTO RENAME
```

in this batch file prevents it from overwriting any COL.COM you may have created previously. If ANSICOLR.BAT finds an existing COL.COM it will print a message telling you to rename the one you already have and then restart.

You may enter from one to four attributes on the command line after the name of the batch file itself. So:

```
ANSICOLR 5 35 42
```

would create a version of COL.COM that sets your colors to blinking magenta on green — a combination so horrid you would immediately erase COL.COM and type something like:

```
ANSICOLR 0 1 37 44
```

to create a COL.COM that would cancel any existing attributes and set the colors to bright white on a blue background.

One nice thing about having a program like COL.COM around is that you can stick it in your AUTOEXEC.BAT startup file and have DOS set your colors automatically. And if something accidentally resets your colors, you can run the COL.COM version you've created to put them back the way you like.

Full Screen Displays

While DOS ordinarily keeps you confined to the single line your cursor is on, ANSI gives you full control over the screen. You can move anywhere you want by issuing either of the commands:

```
ESC[row;columnH
```

or:

```
ESC[row;columnf
```

substituting the row you want for "row" and the desired column for "column." So ESC[13;35f and ESC[13;35H will both position the cursor on row 13, column 35, roughly in the center of the display. This doesn't do much good unless you display something at that location. So you could print a centered "WARNING!" either with:

```
ESC[13;35fWARNING!
```

or:

```
ESC[13;35HWARNING!
```

You can make this even more dramatic by adding:

```
ESC[5m
```

on the previous line to make the message blink. If you do this, you'll later have to get rid of the blink (with ESC[0m) and then reset your colors (with something like ESC[34;47m) on the line following it. Or you could combine the reset and color-setting operations into one line. The whole process would look like:

```
ESC[34;47m
ESC[5m
ESC[13;35fWARNING!
ESC[0;34;47m
```

The first line sets the colors; in this case to blue on white. The second makes the foreground blink. The third positions the message and prints it. The fourth gets rid of the blink by resetting everything back to white on black (with ESC[0), and then resets the colors to blue on white.

Actually, you could put all of these on the same line. The following short batch file would do it:

```
ECHO ESC[34;47mESC[5mESC[13;35fWARNING!ESC[0;34;47m
```

You don't have to put spaces between ANSI commands when you concatenate them like this. In fact, ANSI will print any leading and trailing spaces you specify, and these will show up if you print the message in a color that contrasts with the background. The following variation of the above command would put two spaces on either side of the WARNING message, and print the message in magenta on green:

```
ECHO ESC[34;47mESC[5;35;42mESC[13;35f  WARNING!  ESC[0;34;47m
```

ANSI uses decimal numbers only. If you omit both parameters when using the ESC[row;columnH positioning command, DOS will move the cursor to the home position, in the upper lefthand corner. Include just a single parameter and ANSI will use a default of 1 for either missing value. So:

```
ESC[fWARNING!
```

will print the word WARNING! in the upper lefthand corner, since both the row and column parameters are missing. ANSI treats this as if you entered the command:

```
ESC[1;1fWARNING!
```

If you type:

```
ESC[10;fWARNING!
```

ANSI will fill in a 1 for the missing column and print the message on column 1 of row 10. If you issue the command:

```
ESC[;10fWARNING!
```

ANSI will insert a default value of 1 for the row, and print the message on column 10 of row 1.

The following ANYWHERE.BAT batch file will let you position one word of text anywhere on your screen:

```
ECHO OFF
IF %3!==! GOTO OOPS
IF %4!==! GOTO START
ECHO ESC[2J
:START
ECHO ESC[s
ECHO ESC[%1;%2f%3
ECHO ESC[u
GOTO END
:OOPS
ECHO You must specify three parameters
ECHO (row, column, word) after %0, eg:
ECHO %0 10 15 Hello
ECHO (Adding any 4th parameter clears screen)
:END
```

If you enter:

```
ANYWHERE 10,20,Hello
```

or:

```
ANYWHERE 10   20   Hello
```

it will print the word "Hello" on column 20 of row 10. Include any dummy fourth parameter, to clear the screen first. So:

```
ANYWHERE 10,20,Hello,1
```

or:

```
ANYWHERE 10 20 Hello Sports Fans
```

will print the word "Hello" on row 10, column 20 of a blank screen. This works because DOS scans across the command line when you enter any batch file command and assigns replaceable parameter values to each successive chunk of text separated by a space, comma, colon, or other delimiter. All replaceable parameters begin with percent signs. DOS would assign five of these to the command:

```
C>ANYWHERE   10  20   Hello   Sports   Fans
      |        |   |     |       |       |
     %0       %1  %2    %3      %4      %5
```

The very first chunk of text DOS sees after the C> or A> prompt is always a command or the name of an executable file, and it gives this special string of characters the parameter %0. The next chunk becomes %1, the one following that %2, etc. If your batch file doesn't use replaceable parameters, DOS ignores this special feature. But whenever it does see a % sign followed by a number from 0 to 9 it will try to replace it with the respective chunk of text from the command line. So if you execute the ANYWHERE batch file using the above command syntax, whenever DOS sees a %0 in the batch file it will replace the %0 and print out "ANYWHERE" instead.

If the batch file included the line:

```
ECHO The password is %0
```

DOS would print:

```
The password is ANYWHERE
```

If the line said:

```
ECHO The password is %1
```

DOS would display:

```
The password is 10
```

since 10 is the second discrete lump of text on the command line, and DOS assigns the second chunk of text on the command line a parameter of %1.

The ANYWHERE.BAT batch file uses a %0 at the bottom to print out the name of the batch file itself. This way if you rename it to something like POSITION.BAT, it will print out the new batch file name. This batch file also uses replaceable parameters %1 through %4. It will replace %1 with the first thing it found after the name of the batch file itself (here this is 10), %2 with the second thing (here it's 20), and %3 with the third thing (Hello). It doesn't really care what %4 is, since it uses this simply to test whether or not you specified any additional parameters after %3. If you did enter a word there like "Sports," DOS will turn the:

```
IF %4!==! GOTO START
```

test into:

```
IF Sports!==! GOTO START
```

The characters "Sports!" are clearly not equal to the single character "!" so the test fails (note that batch file tests like this use double equals signs). Since the test failed, DOS won't execute the command that follows at the end of the line (in this example the conditional command is GOTO START). If you hadn't entered anything on the command line after Hello, %4 would be equal to (nothing), and DOS would have translated the test into:

```
IF !==! GOTO START
```

Sure enough, "!" does equal "!" so DOS will jump to the label named START. (A label is a short word preceded by a colon). So if you didn't enter a parameter for %4, DOS will jump around the line that follows the test and go directly to :START. As illustrated here, this will skip the following clear-screen command.

Before it does anything else, the ANYWHERE.BAT batch file checks to see if the user entered any third parameter. The first two parameters are the row and column, but these won't do much if the user didn't enter anything on the command line to display. So DOS checks to make sure %3 isn't equal to (nothing) with the test:

```
IF %3!==! GOTO OOPS
```

If it finds nothing there, it will jump to the OOPS label and print a message displaying the proper syntax and reminding the user to enter a row, a column, a message, and an optional fourth parameter to clear the screen.

While ANSI's ESC[row;columnH and ESC[row;columnf positioning commands let you print messages at a precise location, there are times when you want to print text at relative locations. For example, if you want to display a message below the prompt, you could position the prompt at a certain predefined place on the screen and then print the message. However, if you didn't want to disturb what was on the screen, you could tell ANSI to figure out where the prompt happened to be at the time, and print the message directly below wherever that location was.

To make such relative positioning commands easy, ANSI lets you move the cursor up, down, left, or right one or more characters at a time with the following commands:

Up	ESC[#A
Down	ESC[#B
Left	ESC[#C
Right	ESC[#D

The # in each command equals the number of rows or columns to move; the default is 1. ANSI will ignore these commands if further movement in the specified direction is impossible. So if the cursor is already at the left edge of the screen, issuing an ESC[2C command won't do anything. If you leave out a number, ANSI will move just one row or column, so ESC[B will move down one row. When ANSI moves the cursor left or right it maintains the original row; when it moves up or down it keeps the original column position.

It's possible to blank a line by moving up and then printing spaces over it. You can use the ECHO command to do this in a batch file if you want to obliterate the initial commands. But you can't just put spaces after ECHO or DOS will think you're asking it whether ECHO currently happens to be set on or off.

The following CLEARSLF.BAT batch file will erase both the command line and the ECHO OFF message it prints. The line of xxxx's represents spaces; if you try this be sure to type a space in place of each x (you may have to vary the number of spaces to suit your screen). You have to use a character like a colon or period directly after the the ECHO for this to work.

```
ECHO OFF
ECHO ESC[2A
ECHO:xxxxxxxxxxxxxxxxxxxxxxxxxxx
ECHO ESC[4A
ECHO:xxxxxxxxxxxxxxxxxxxxxxxxxxx
```

Wiping out text with spaces isn't very efficient. ANSI provides two erasing commands to make it far easier. Many of the above examples above use one of these commands, ESC[2J, to clear the entire screen. (Incidentally, the DOS manuals say to use ESC[2J, but ESC[J works just as well; both will clear the screen to the foreground and background colors currently in effect. It doesn't really matter what reasonably sized number precedes the J.) But ANSI gives you finer erasing control than that. It lets you erase any line from and including the cursor position and extending to the right edge of the screen. Just issue the command:

```
ESC[K
```

You might want to position the cursor first and then erase to the end of the line. To get rid of everything to the right of column 40 on row 5, type:

```
ESC[5;41fESC[K
```

or:

```
ESC[5;41HESC[K
```

A better CLEARSLF.BAT batch file that incorporated this technique looks like:

```
ECHO OFF
ECHO ESC[2A
ECHO ESC[K
ECHO ESC[4A
ECHO ESC[K
```

While you're jumping all around the screen printing messages in various places it's handy to return to your original position when you finish. ANSI makes this a snap. Just issue this command:

```
ESC[s
```

to store the current cursor position, and then a:

```
ESC[u
```

command to put it back where it originally was when you stored it.

ANSI provides a set of commands called CPR (Cursor Position Report) and DSR (Device Status Report) that you almost certainly won't ever need. Issuing a DSR:

```
ESC[6n
```

will trigger a CPR in the form:

```
ESC[row,columnR
```

where row and column represent the current cursor position.

Mode-Setting Commands

You probably won't use ANSI's mode-setting commands either, since most users do all their DOS work exclusively in their system's 80 x 25 default text mode. However, ANSI provides one of the only ways to set the more recent EGA and VGA screen modes, but with DOS later than 4.0 only. It also lets you disable and enable line wrapping, something most users just don't have a burning desire to do.

To set screen widths and modes, use the similar commands ESC[=#l or ESC[=#h, substituting a number from 0 to 19 in place of the #. Note that the l in the first version is a lowercase L, not a 1.

#	Screen Mode
0	40 x 25 black and white
1	40 x 25 color
2	80 x 25 black and white
3	80 x 25 color
4	320 x 200 color
5	320 x 200 black and white
6	640 x 200 black and white
13	320 x 200 color
14	640 x 200 color
15	640 x 350 mono
16	640 x 350 color
17	640 x 480 color
18	640 x 480 color
19	320 x 200 color

While the l and h suffixes work exactly the same with values from 0 through 6, they behave very differently when used with a value of 7. To set line wrap off, issue the command:

```
ESC[?7l
```

or:

```
ESC[=7l
```

To turn it back on, type:

```
ESC[?7h
```

or:

```
ESC[=7h
```

If you're typing something long and you reach the right edge of your screen, DOS normally wraps the text down one line and over to the left edge of the screen. Turning line wrap off means that once you reach the right edge of a typical 80-column screen, instead of bouncing down a line, DOS will print each character on the 80th column. Every letter will overlap the previous letter. You won't lose any keystrokes, but you won't really be able to see what you've typed. Turning line wrap off may have made sense once, but it's an anachronism today.

Redefining Keys

ANSI's attribute-handling abilities are extremely welcome on today's increasingly common color screens. But equally handy is its talent for redefining keys.

You can harness ANSI's formidable key definition abilities to:

- create duplicate keys
- switch keys around on the keyboard
- configure or redefine function keys to execute commands and cut down on typing

For example, some people need to type quotation marks far more often than they need the apostrophe that's on the same physical key as the quote mark. Or they may use question marks frequently but never have to type slashes. Normally you have to hold down the shift to have your keyboard generate quotation and question marks. But it's simple for ANSI to swap the uppercase and lowercase versions of these keys.

And some new users keep pressing the forward slash / key when they really mean to type the backslash \ key. ANSI can turn the slash key into a duplicate backslash. Then whenever the user pressed either key his system would think he typed a backslash. The only problem is that this would prevent him from using a normal slash, unless the slash function was moved somewhere else.

Finally, if you're tired of having to issue repetitive, long-winded DOS commands full of tricky syntaxes, you can assign these commands to single keys. This makes it easier to handle daily DOS chores — and far more accurate.

Redefining keystrokes can be dangerous, so be very careful, and think about what you're doing. Users often give their files shorthand names to save typing. If you're writing a massive report on the 1990 plans for the Atlanta regional office, you may temporarily call the file just A rather than ATLOFC90.RPT. This makes it easier to work with, since it's faster to load the file into your word processor by typing:

```
WS A
```

(for *WordStar*) than:

```
WS ATLOFC90.RPT
```

When you're all done with the report, you can rename the file to give it its properly inscrutable but far more descriptive name. These same time-pressured users may also use ANSI to switch the semicolon (which they don't use in DOS) with the colon (which they do use frequently). This way they don't have to hold down the shift key when referring to a drive like C:.

If you have a long file on your C: drive that you've temporarily named A, and you've switched the colon and semicolon keys, and it's late at night, and you're tired, you could wipe out the whole file with an innocent command. How? If you want to copy a small file called C:MEMO to drive A: and you accidentally hold down the shift key, you'll end up with:

```
C>COPY MEMO A;
```

DOS will interpret the semicolon as a space, and copy the short MEMO file on top of the long file you've named A. Okay, maybe it's not a good idea to use single-letter names (especially names you could confuse with disk drive letters), and of course you should have backed up your work, and anyway DOS should alert you when you're about to copy one file onto another one (but it doesn't). These things happen. Back up often and be careful.

ANSI isn't perfect when it comes to redefining keys. It limits the number of keys you can redefine and the amount of information you can assign to them. Most programs come with their own keyboard handlers that bypass DOS, so your macros won't work in all cases. But you can use them at the DOS prompt, in DEBUG, EDLIN, or in certain editors such as IBM's *Personal Editor.*

You also have to make sure you don't reset a key such as Enter or space, or replace a letter of the alphabet that would prevent you from issuing normal DOS commands. You can reassign uppercase letters while leaving the lowercase ones intact (or vice versa), which lets you type practically anything. But if you reassign both the uppercase "I" and lowercase "i" you won't be able to execute commands like PRINT or DIR. And if you fool around with character 13 — the Enter key — you're dead in the water.

Finally, while DOS does let you reset any ANSI key redefinitions back to normal, it doesn't provide any method for listing the current key reassignments or clearing them out of memory to make room for others. Fortunately, you can do it yourself, if you're extremely careful and you follow the directions below.

First, however, move some keys around to see what ANSI can do.

If you never ever use square brackets — the "[" and "]" characters — but you rely heavily on normal parentheses and you hate having to hold the Shift key down to type them, just have ANSI turn the brackets into a duplicate set of parentheses.

You'll still be able to type them the old way, by leaning on Shift and pressing the 9 and 0 keys. But once you've executed a short ANSI script you'll also be able to generate parentheses by tapping the lowercase bracket keys. However, this will temporarily prevent you from putting brackets into your text — a minor drawback if you have to create any new ANSI sequences, since the second character of every ANSI command is a left bracket. Any key redefinitions you make using this technique will stay in effect until you reboot, unless you know the trick below for doing an ANSI lobotomy.

The decimal ASCII codes for the characters involved in this particular redefinition process are:

```
[ = 91
] = 93
( = 40
) = 41
```

To redefine any key, issue the usual ANSI ESC[prefix, follow it with two ASCII codes separated by a semicolon, and tack a lowercase p onto the end. The first ASCII code is the key you want to press and the second is the character you want that key to produce. To redefine the [and] keys so they'll generate parentheses rather than brackets, for example, run the following two-line batch file:

```
ECHO ESC[91;40p
ECHO ESC[93;41p
```

Remember, this ANSI command has five parts:

ESC[	93	;	41	p
↑	↑	↑	↑	↑
normal	key you want	semicolon	character you	ANSI
ANSI prefix	to hit		want key to	reassignment
			generate	suffix

You can enter the characters themselves in quotes rather than the ASCII codes if you like, but this can look confusing, especially when you're assigning lots of characters to a single key as you will a bit later. The following two lines will do the exact same redefinition as the ones above:

```
ECHO ESC["[";"("p
ECHO ESC["]";")"p
```

If you redefine these keys, and you discover that you do need to type brackets, you can reset the keys back to normal by putting the same ASCII code on both sides of the semicolon. This will do the trick:

```
ECHO ESC[91;91p
ECHO ESC[93;93p
```

You could also reset things by running a batch file that you created previously containing the two lines:

```
ECHO ESC["[";"["p
ECHO ESC["]";"]"p
```

However, you can't create these lines in DOS while the old redefinitions are in effect, because reassigning parentheses to the bracket keys temporarily did away with the brackets. (If you really had to do it, you could run a word processor such as *WordStar* that disregarded any ANSI changes.)

Redefining keys often ends up preventing you from typing certain characters, as it did above with brackets. However, ANSI makes it just as easy to swap one set of characters for another. If you use quotation marks more often than apostrophes, both of which share the same physical key, you can switch them so a tap on the unshifted key generates a quotation mark, while holding down the Shift and pressing the key yields an apostrophe. The ASCII values of these two keys are:

```
" = 34
' = 39
```

So you could run the following two-line batch file:

```
ECHO ESC[34;39p
ECHO ESC[39;34p
```

To switch both characters you have to execute both lines. Running just the first one by itself:

```
ECHO ESC[34;39p
```

would assign the apostrophe character to the shifted version of the key — the one that normally produces a quotation mark. This would cause the key to produce an apostrophe regardless of whether you were holding the Shift key down, which isn't what you want.

Again, you could also use the actual characters themselves in the ANSI command rather than the ASCII codes. But this gets tricky when one of the keys you're trying to redefine is a quotation mark, since you have to use quotation marks to identify the characters you want to change.

DOS can treat pairs of single quotation marks (which are really just apostrophes) the same way it handles pairs of double quotation marks. So you can run the following, two-line batch file to make the swap:

```
ECHO ESC['"';"'"p
ECHO ESC["'";'"'p
```

and then either:

```
ECHO ESC[34;34p
ECHO ESC[39;39p
```

or:

```
ECHO ESC['"';'"'p
ECHO ESC["'";"'"p
```

to reset things to their original state.

Swapping or duplicating alphanumeric keys is straightforward and easy. But ANSI can also assign characters to dozens of special key combinations that generate what IBM calls *extended* codes.

ANSI deals with normal "typewriter" keys like A, a, 1, or $ by manipulating single ASCII values between 32 (a space) and 126 (a Spanish tilde). A capital "A" has an ASCII value of 65, and a lowercase "a" an ASCII value of 97. Refer back to the chart of ASCII values for the typewriter keys in Chapter 6. Any of these values can be plugged into the examples above to move the keys around the keyboard.

ANSI can also handle nonalphanumeric keys such as the F1 function key, the Home key, and the Ins key. And it can work with less common shifted key combinations such as Ctrl-End, Alt-E, or Shift-F1. All of the special key combinations generate a pair of ASCII values rather than just a single value. The first value in the pair is always an ASCII 0, or NUL character. Figure 10.1 is an index of all key combinations and their values.

Key Combination	Code[*]	Key Combination	Code[*]
NUL	0;3	Shift-F1	0;84
Shift-Tab	0;15	Shift-F2	0;85
Alt-Q	0;16	Shift-F3	0;86
Alt-W	0;17	Shift-F4	0;87
Alt-E	0;18	Shift-F5	0;88
Alt-R	0;19	Shift-F6	0;89
Alt-T	0;20	Shift-F7	0;90
Alt-Y	0;21	Shift-F8	0;91
Alt-U	0;22	Shift-F9	0;92
Alt-I	0;23	Shift-F10	0;93
Alt-O	0;24	Ctrl-F1	0;94
Alt-P	0;25	Ctrl-F2	0;95
Alt-A	0;30	Ctrl-F3	0;96
Alt-S	0;31	Ctrl-F4	0;97
Alt-D	0;32	Ctrl-F5	0;98
Alt-F	0;33	Ctrl-F6	0;99
Alt-G	0;34	Ctrl-F7	0;100
Alt-H	0;35	Ctrl-F8	0;101

Figure 10.1. Index of Extended ASCII Codes

Key Combination	Code[*]	Key Combination	Code[*]
Alt-J	0;36	Ctrl-F9	0;102
Alt-K	0;37	Ctrl-F10	0;103
Alt-L	0;38	Alt-F1	0;104
Alt-Z	0;44	Alt-F2	0;105
Alt-X	0;45	Alt-F3	0;106
Alt-C	0;46	Alt-F4	0;107
Alt-V	0;47	Alt-F5	0;108
Alt-B	0;48	Alt-F6	0;109
Alt-N	0;49	Alt-F7	0;110
Alt-M	0;50	Alt-F8	0;111
F1	0;59	Alt-F9	0;112
F2	0;60	Alt-F10	0;113
F3	0;61	Ctrl-PrtSc	0;114
F4	0;62	Ctrl-Cursor Left	0;115
F5	0;63	Ctrl-Cursor Right	0;116
F6	0;64	Ctrl-End	0;117
F7	0;65	Ctrl-PgDn	0;118
F8	0;66	Ctrl-Home	0;119
F9	0;67	Alt-1	0;120
F10	0;68	Alt-2	0;121
Home	0;71	Alt-3	0;122
Cursor Up	0;72	Alt-4	0;123
PgUp	0;73	Alt-5	0;124
Cursor Left	0;75	Alt-6	0;125
Cursor Right	0;77	Alt-7	0;126
End	0;79	Alt-8	0;127
Cursor Down	0;80	Alt-9	0;128
PgDn	0;81	Alt-0	0;129
Ins	0;82	Alt--	0;130
Del	0;83	Alt-=	0;131
Shift-F1	0;84	Ctrl-PgUp	0;132

[*]In the form ASCII 0;code.

Figure 10.1. Index of Extended ASCII Codes *(continued)*

When IBM designed the BIOS support for the enhanced keyboard, it added over 30 new extended keyboard codes starting at 133. However, it did not make these keyboard codes available to programs through the normal BIOS keyboard interface. To do so would have created incompatibilities with some existing programs. For instance, some keyboard macro programs define their own extended keys and these may conflict with the new IBM codes. DOS (and most programs) get keyboard information from the BIOS through interrupt 16H, function calls 0, 1, and 2. For the enhanced keyboard, IBM defined new function calls numbered 10H, 11H, and 12H that duplicated 0, 1, and 2 except that the new calls also return the new extended keyboard codes in addition to the old ones.

Under DOS 4.0 and 5.0, ANSI can handle these if you specify a /X parameter when loading it. Or just issue a ESC[1q to do so. The program below lets you do this with earlier DOS versions.

Here's a DEBUG script for a NEWKEYS.COM program you can create that allows DOS access to the new codes and lets you use these new keys with ANSI.SYS:

```
N NEWKEYS.COM
A
JMP     013A            ; Jmp Initialize
DW      0,0
CMP     AH,00           ; NewInt16:
JZ      0115            ; Jmp GetKey
CMP     AH,01
JZ      0121            ; Jmp GetStatus
CS:
JMP     FAR [0102]      ; Jmp OldInt16
MOV     AH,10           ; GetKey:
PUSHF
CS:
CALL    FAR [0102]      ; Call OldInt16
CALL    0131            ; Call FixUp
IRET
MOV     AH,11           ; GetStatus:
PUSHF
CS:
CALL    FAR [0102]      ; Call OldInt16
JZ      012E
CALL    0131            ; Call FixUp
RETF    0002
CMP     AL,E0           ; FixUp:
JNZ     0139
SUB     AL,AL
CMP     AL,01
RET
MOV     AX,3516         ; Initialize:
INT     21              ; Get OldInt16
MOV     [0102],BX       ; Save it
MOV     [0104],ES
MOV     DX,0106
MOV     AX,2516
```

```
INT    21             ; Set NewInt16
MOV    DX,013A
INT    27             ; Stay Resident

RCX
54
W
Q
```

Create NEWKEYS.COM by typing the lines shown into a file called NEWKEYS.SCR. (Don't type the semicolons or the comments that follow them.) Then type:

```
DEBUG < NEWKEYS.SCR
```

to creates the program.

NEWKEYS.COM is a *Terminate and Stay Resident* (TSR) program so you need to load it only once during your PC session. Like most TSRs, it may have some compatibility problems with other programs. If everything seems to work OK once you load it, then you're probably in good shape.

When NEWKEYS is loaded, you can use the extra keyboard codes for ANSI.SYS redefinitions. The new codes are shown in Figure 10.2.

Miscellaneous Key Combination	Code [*]
F11	0;133
F12	0;134
Shift-F11	0;135
Shift-F12	0;136
Ctrl-F11	0;137
Ctrl-F12	0;138
Alt-F11	0;139
Alt-F12	0;140
Ctrl-Up-Arrow	0;141
Ctrl -	0;142
Ctrl-5	0;143
Ctrl-+	0;144
Ctrl-Down-Arrow	0;145
Ctrl-Insert	0;146
Ctrl-Delete	0;147
Ctrl-Tab	0;148
Ctrl-/	0;149
Ctrl-*	0;150

Figure 10.2. IBM 101/102-Key Keyboard Extended Codes

Miscellaneous Key Combination	Code[*]
Alt-Home	0;151
Alt-Up-Arrow	0;152
Alt-Page-Up	0;153
Alt-Left-Arrow	0;155
Alt-Right-Arrow	0;157
Alt-End	0;159
Alt-Down-Arrow	0;160
Alt-Page-Down	0;161
Alt-Insert	0;162
Alt-Delete	0;163
Alt-/	0;164
Alt-Tab	0;165
Alt-Enter	0;166

[*] In the form ASCII 0;code.

Figure 10.2. IBM 101/102-Key Keyboard Extended Codes *(continued)*

Note: Under DOS 4.0 and 5.0, you can enable ANSI's use of extended keys by loading it with a /X parameter or entering ESC[1q. To disable this, use a /K parameter, or enter ESC[0q.

As an example, if you have ANSI.SYS loaded and want to redefine the F11 key to do a DIR command, just issue the command:

```
ESC[0;133;"DIR";13p
```

(where ESC is a hex 1B or decimal 27 Esc character, not the letters ESC).

You can examine the ASCII values of all the keys on the keyboard — except for the Ctrl, Alt, CapsLock, NumLock, ScrollLock, Sys Req, and Shifts — by running this BASIC KEYCODE.BAS program:

```
100 ' KEYCODE.BAS
110 DEF SEG=0:POKE 1047,PEEK(1047) AND 223      ' turns cursor pad on
120 DEF SEG:KEY OFF:COLOR 2,0:CLS               ' sets screen
130 FOR A=1 TO 10:KEY A,"":NEXT                 ' disables function keys
140 PRINT "Press a key (or Enter to end):",     ' instructions
150 I$=INKEY$:IF I$="" THEN 150                 ' waits for key to be hit
160 IF I$=CHR$(13) THEN END                     ' ** hit Enter to end **
170 IF LEN(I$)>1 THEN PRINT "ext",:GOTO 190     ' is it extended code?
180 PRINT I$,                                   ' print character
190 IF LEN(I$)>1 THEN PRINT "0 +";              ' again, is it extended?
```

```
200 PRINT ASC(RIGHT$(I$,1))            ' print ASCII code
210 GOTO 140                           ' loop back for new key
```

BASIC has trouble displaying certain characters such as ASCII 7, 10, 11, and 12, since it interprets these as commands to beep, clear the screen, and so on. But you'll be able to see the ASCII values for all the alphanumeric and extended keys.

The ASCII code method for swapping or duplicating extended keys is exactly the same as for normal alphanumeric keys except that you have to include an extra "0;" prefix. To to swap F1 and F3, run the following two-line batch file:

```
ECHO ESC[0;59;0;61p
ECHO ESC[0;61;0;59p
```

In notation that ANSI can understand, the extended ASCII codes for F1 and F3 are 0;59 and 0;61. At the DOS prompt, pressing the F1 key normally repeats the previous DOS command one character at a time, while F3 reproduces the entire previous command with a single tap. But after you run the two-line ANSI command above, the functions will reverse.

You can restore the original functions of these two keys with the two lines:

```
ECHO ESC[0;59;0;59p
ECHO ESC[0;61;0;61p
```

When dealing with extended keys you have to use ASCII codes exclusively since DOS doesn't provide any method for referring to these keys in quotes. You can't make F1 duplicate the function of F3 with a command like:

```
ECHO ESC["F1";"F3"p
```

All this will do is assign the character string "1F3" to the uppercase F key.

You could also have the following ANSICHAR.BAT batch file (similar to the attribute-setting ANSICLOR.BAT file above) create a series of individual files called CHAR.COM that you can run whenever you need to redefine a key. Again, for this to work, your DEBUG.COM utility has to be in the same directory or in a directory that your PATH knows about:

```
ECHO OFF
IF %2!==! GOTO OOPS
IF EXIST CHAR.COM GOTO RENAME
ECHO N CHAR.COM                              > CHR.SCR
ECHO E 100 B4 9 BA 8 1 CD 21 C3 1B "[" >> CHR.SCR
IF %4!==! GOTO THREE
ECHO E 10A "%1;%2;%3;%4p$"               >> CHR.SCR
GOTO FINISH
:THREE
```

```
    IF %3!==! GOTO TWO
    ECHO E 10A "%1;%2;%3p$"                        >> CHR.SCR
    GOTO FINISH
    :TWO
    ECHO E 10A "%1;%2p$"                           >> CHR.SCR
    :FINISH
    ECHO RCX                                       >> CHR.SCR
    ECHO 7F                                        >> CHR.SCR
    ECHO W                                         >> CHR.SCR
    ECHO Q                                         >> CHR.SCR
    DEBUG < CHR.SCR
    DEL CHR.SCR
    ECHO Now run CHAR whenever you want to reset this key
    GOTO END
    :OOPS
    ECHO Enter two ANSI key codes after %0
    ECHO eg: %0 126 155   to have the ~ key print a
    ECHO cent-sign (And you must have ANSI loaded)
    ECHO Remember to use a 0 for extended characters
    ECHO eg: %0 0 68 0 61 to make F10 work like F3, or
    ECHO     %0 0 67 ""DIR/W"" 13 to make F9 do a wide DIR
    ECHO (Note the double quotes around character strings!
    ECHO - and note you CAN'T have spaces in strings, so
    ECHO you cannot enter: %0 0 67 ""DIR /W"" 13)
    GOTO END
    :RENAME
    ECHO First rename your existing CHAR.COM so this
    ECHO doesn't write over it, then restart %0
    :END
```

Once you've typed in ANSICHAR.BAT, you could create a small program called CHAR.COM that would turn your dollar sign into an English pound sterling sign, by typing:

```
ANSICHAR 36 156
```

The ANSICHAR batch file would redirect a customized script into DEBUG and create the appropriate CHAR.COM file. Typing:

```
CHAR
```

at the DOS prompt would redefine your dollar sign key so it printed a pound symbol instead.

As with ANSICOLR.BAT, the:

```
IF EXIST CHAR.COM GOTO RENAME
```

line in this batch file prevents it from overwriting any CHAR.COM you may have created previously. If ANSICHAR.BAT finds an existing CHAR.COM it will print a message telling you to rename the one you already have and then restart. If you're redefining extended keys such as function keys, cursor-pad keys, or Alt-key combinations, be sure to include the 0 prefix that ANSI requires.

So, to turn F8 into an additional Insert key, you'd type:

```
ANSICHAR 0 66 0 82
```

Then you'd run the CHAR program it created to do the actual redefining. Or if you wanted to have DOS print a pi symbol whenever you typed Alt-P, you'd enter:

```
ANSICHAR 0 25 227
```

and then type CHAR to finish the process. If you want to define a function key like F10 so it executes a command such as DIR/W, you'd type:

```
ANSICHAR 0 67 ""DIR/W"" 13
```

(The double quote marks are necessary only because of the way the batch file interacts with DEBUG; if you attach this definition to this key using a technique other than ANSICHAR.BAT you'd use only one set. And if you enter a string, be sure not to insert any spaces in it, so:

```
""DIR/W""
```

will work just fine, while:

```
""DIR /W""
```

won't work at all.)

The 13 at the end of the line represents the Enter key (which has an ASCII value of decimal 13). If you include this at the end of a redefined key command, DOS will print the command out when you press the appropriate key and then execute it. If you leave the 13 off, DOS will simply print out the command without running it.

As with COL.COM, it's handy to have versions of CHAR.COM around to put in your AUTOEXEC.BAT startup file so DOS will redefine your keys automatically each time you boot up. Be sure to rename previous versions of CHAR.BAT each time you create new ones. It's helpful to give them descriptive names like CHARPI.COM if it types a pi symbol, or CHARDIRW if it executes a DIR/W.

Macro Magic

If you want to assign a text string or a command to any key, ANSI will let you if there's room left. DOS maintains an area inside the ANSI.SYS code itself as a table of redefinitions. This table is absurdly small. DOS 2.x provides only 196 bytes of space for this purpose, DOS 3.x a mere 204 and DOS 4.0 and 5.0 just 404 — and some of this space at the end of the table can't be used.

In fact, even in the later versions, you can cram in a maximum of 131 redefinitions — assuming you're not using any extended keys (which take up slightly more space) and that each redefinition is only a single key long. Wedging in more can create problems.

Worse, if you try using ANSI to attach text messages to your keys you'll run out of space almost before you begin. If you try hard under DOS 4.0 or 5.0 you can define a maximum of 387 characters — by creating four macros, three of 127 characters, and the fourth just six characters. For instance, you could define one that turned "a" into 127 capital As:

```
ESC[97;"AAAAAAAAAAAAAAAAAAAAAAAAAAAAAAAAAAAAAAAAAAAAAAAAAAAAA
       AAAAAAAAAAAAAAAAAAAAAAAAAAAAAAAAAAAAAAAAAAAAAAAAAAAAA
       AAAAAAAAAAAAAAAAAAAAAAAAAA"p
```

and the same with B(ESC[98;"BBB...) and C(ESC[99;"CCC...).

Then just six Ds:

```
ESC[100;"DDDDDD"p
```

However, if you want a true macro processor, get your hands on a powerful commercial package like *SuperKey*, *ProKey*, *SmartKey*, *KeyWorks*, or any of the other similar products crowding the market. For quick and dirty macro work, ANSI does just fine. If you miss having a cent sign at your fingertips, ANSI can put one there. To define Alt-C so that it prints a cent sign (which is ASCII character 155), run this one-line batch file:

```
ECHO ESC[0;46;155p
```

Or you could define a group of keys at once. The following CHARS.BAT batch file will give you direct keyboard access to the ten characters shown. It's sometimes handy to add text as this batch file does to keep you (or other users you give the file to) informed. ANSI won't start processing commands in a line until it sees an ESC[, so the initial descriptive labels won't affect the definition process:

```
ECHO OFF
ECHO Defining keys as follows:
ECHO ALT+1=square-root radical sign   ESC[0;120;251p
ECHO ALT+2=degree sign                ESC[0;121;248p
ECHO ALT+3=old-fashioned division sign ESC[0;122;246p
ECHO ALT+4=pi                         ESC[0;123;227p
ECHO ALT+5=infinity                   ESC[0;124;236p
```

```
ECHO ALT+6=(squared)^2                    ESC[0;125;253p
ECHO ALT+7=1/2                            ESC[0;126;171p
ECHO ALT+8=1/4                            ESC[0;127;172p
ECHO ALT+9=pound sterling                 ESC[0;128;156p
ECHO ALT+0=yen                            ESC[0;129;157p
```

You can, of course, attach more than one character to a key. So after running EIN-STEIN.BAT:

```
ECHO ESC[0;18;"E=MC";253p
```

typing Alt-E will display the familiar formula.

A more practical application would give you one-key execution of a complex command that you perform all day long, such as:

```
DIR C: | SORT /R /+14 | FIND "-" | MORE
```

This displays the contents of the current directory on drive C: with the largest files at the top of the list. It also screens out extraneous information about volume labels and bytes free by filtering the output through FIND.EXE, and pauses a screenful at a time. The NEWDIR.BAT batch file:

```
ECHO ESC[0;46;"DIR C: | SORT /R /+14 | FIND ";34;"-";34;" | MORE";13p
```

lets you run this command simply by typing ALT-C.

The pair of 34s on the above line provide the two quotation marks that you need to surround the "-" in the FIND command, since 34 is the decimal ASCII value of ". The 13 at the end is the ASCII representation of a carriage return, which executes the command. If you omitted the 13, ANSI would print the command but not execute it.

What makes this especially handy is that you can add two more lines to the batch file so the three keys Alt-A, Alt-B, and Alt-C, will execute this command on the three drives A:, B:, and C:

```
ECHO ESC[0;30;"DIR A: | SORT /R /+14 | FIND ";34;"-";34;" | MORE";13p
ECHO ESC[0;48;"DIR B: | SORT /R /+14 | FIND ";34;"-";34;" | MORE";13p
ECHO ESC[0;46;"DIR C: | SORT /R /+14 | FIND ";34;"-";34;" | MORE";13p
```

You can attach any text to any key, if there's room. The following ADDRESS.BAT batch file would print a three-line return address each time you typed Alt-P:

```
ECHO ESC[0;25;"Bantam Books";13;"666 Fifth Avenue";13;"New York, NY 10103";13p
```

You won't be able to use this with any word processor that has its own internal keyboard handling routine. But if you create a letter using the DOS COPY CON command, or EDLIN, or a commercial product like IBM *Personal Editor*, tapping Alt-P once will put:

```
Bantam Books
666 Fifth Avenue
New York, NY 10103
```

at the cursor position.

The only real problems with having ANSI assign text and commands to specific keys are that you normally can't see what key assignments you've previously made, and that you run out of space for new commands very quickly. And, while ANSI lets you reset keys to their original values, it doesn't provide a way to clear everything out of memory and start afresh. Fortunately, we do.

Part III

Power User's Secrets

Batch Techniques

A batch file is simply a file with a BAT extension that contains a list of DOS instructions you want to execute and programs you want to run. When you execute the batch file, DOS looks at each line and executes the instruction or runs the program specified on that line just as if you had typed it in directly.

Once you master its dozen or so batch commands, you can have DOS automate all your daily chores and chop tedious file management tasks down to size. You can even use these commands to dial your phone, look up names and addresses, or keep track of your appointments. All at the touch of a key or two.

Batch files are really just computer programs, written in DOS. All programming languages share certain basic features. One is the *conditional* ability to execute commands only when the proper conditions are met. Other features are the ability to loop repeatedly, or use variables with changeable values, or divide jobs into small subroutines. Microsoft's batch file language isn't elegant, and it needs a little help. But it packs a wallop into its few commands and gives you astonishing control over your system.

Batch File Basics

To illustrate how a batch file works, you need a program for it to run. The examples that follow will use the DOS CHKDSK.EXE program.

Batch file creation and operation are complex and exacting. It's a little like trying to write a novel in a language with only a handful of words — or commands. To give you a feel for how the commands work and what you have to do whip them into shape, this section will start out by providing a brief overview of the most important commands. Then it will explore each command in painstaking detail, fleshing out the fundamentals where necessary. Finally, it will provide a slate of useful samples.

Once you have CHKDSK.EXE handy, run it by typing:

```
C>CHKDSK
```

The program simply checks your current disk drive and memory usage. You might find that, in working with large files or experimenting with TSRs, you may need to check both the disk space and available memory quite often, and having to type CHKDSK each time gets tedious. You could rename CHKDSK.EXE to something shorter, like K.EXE (on the somewhat arbitrary basis that you're measuring kilobytes, and besides, there are more Ks than anything else in the original file name.) Then all you'd have to do to run the program is type:

```
K
```

However, the program would then show up in your DIR listings simply as K.EXE, and if you didn't use it for a long time and then happened to see the not-very-descriptive K.EXE filename several months later, you might forget what the program did.

You could run it to find out, but some programs don't do anything immediately apparent when you execute them. For instance, try running the DOS GRAPHICS.COM program. Your disk will spin for a second or two and nothing will appear onscreen to tell you what just happened. All programs should at least put a message onscreen to keep you informed, but many don't. In this case the message should have been something like "Graphics print screen function (Shift-PrtSc) now properly configured for IBM compatible printers."

Even worse, a program could have potentially destructive results. That K.EXE program could have once been named KILL.EXE and you may have used it long ago to erase all the files on your disk for security purposes.

Easy Batch File Creation

But you can execute the CHKDSK.EXE program with a single keystroke without having to rename it. Just create a one-line batch file called K.BAT that will do all the typing for you. You could use your word processor to create this file, but DOS provides three quicker, easier ways — the COPY CON command, EDIT, and EDLIN.

To use the COPY CON technique, type:

```
COPY CON K.BAT
```

and press Enter. The cursor will simply drop down a line. Then type:

```
CHKDSK
```

and press the F6 function key, then the Enter key. When you press F6 you'll see a ^Z appear, and when you press Enter you should see a message that says "1 File(s) copied."

If you make a mistake while using COPY CON, hold down the Ctrl key, and press either C or ScrollLock to abort the process. Then press the F3 key and then Enter to restart.

EDIT makes it easy to correct typing mistakes without having to start the process over again. Start by typing:

```
EDIT K.BAT
```

which will bring you into a blank edit screen. Now just type:

```
CHKDSK
```

then issue an Alt-F-S and an Alt-F-X key sequence to save and exit. If you make a mistake in typing CHKDSK, you can either cursor back to the mistake and correct it before saving, or re-open the file and use the cursor to fix the error.

To use the EDLIN technique, type:

```
EDLIN K.BAT
```

You should see a message that says:

```
New file
*
```

When EDLIN displays an asterisk hugging the left margin, it means it's waiting for you to enter a command. An asterisk in column 1 like this is the EDLIN "prompt" just as A> or C> is the default DOS prompt.

If you don't see this "New file" message, or you see something that says:

```
End of input file
*
```

this tells you that you're editing an existing file rather than creating a new one, which is definitely not what you want to do. If this happens, type Q to quit, and when you see the message:

```
Abort edit (Y/N)?
```

type Y to confirm that you do indeed want to quit. Then restart the process, but pick a different name, such as A.BAT (which is short for Answer).

However, if you did see the:

```
New file
*
```

message, type an I (or an i) to start Inserting text. EDLIN will indent itself and print:

```
   1:*
```

Here EDLIN uses the asterisk to tell you that line 1 is the "current" line. EDLIN can work on only one line at a time (which it refers to as the current line) and it signifies which line is the current one by putting an asterisk beside its line number.

Type in:

```
   1:*CHKDSK
```

either in uppercase or lowercase; DOS isn't picky when it comes to ordinary batch file commands. Press the Enter key and you should see:

```
   1:*CHKDSK
   2:*
```

Now EDLIN is telling you that line 2 is the current line. But all you wanted to do was create a one-line batch file, so to tell EDLIN you're done inserting text, just hold down the Ctrl key and press either C or ScrollLock while you're holding it down. You should see:

```
   1:*CHKDSK
        2:*^C
   *
```

Then End the EDLIN file creation process by typing:

```
   *E
```

(or e).

Whether you used EDLIN, EDIT, or the COPY CON approach, after you get back to the familiar DOS prompt, type K to execute the batch file. DOS executes a batch file one line at a time. The first (and only) line in K.BAT is:

```
   CHKDSK
```

DOS tries to execute this line by first seeing if CHKDSK is an internal DOS command. The instructions to execute common DOS commands such as DIR, TYPE, or COPY are buried inside the DOS COMMAND.COM program, and Microsoft refers to these as internal commands. External commands, like SORT.EXE or CHKDSK.EXE, are separate programs, and are not a part of COMMAND.COM at all. You can always execute an internal command like TYPE or DIR, since they're built into COMMAND.COM. But you won't be able to run an external command such as FORMAT unless the FORMAT.COM program happens to be on your disk.

DOS maintains a list of all the internal commands inside COMMAND.COM, and it won't find one called CHKDSK.EXE there. So it then looks for a program called CHKDSK.EXE in the current directory. Since you just put this file there, DOS will run it.

Incidentally, if you created the K.BAT file and you happen to have a file in the same directory called K.COM or K.EXE, you'll never be able to run K.BAT. Whenever you enter a command or the name of a file you want to run, COMMAND.COM first checks to see if you entered an internal DOS command. If it doesn't find an internal command that matches what you typed, it next checks for a file with the same name but with a COM extension. If it doesn't find a COM file with the same name, it looks for a similarly named file with an EXE extension. It will run a batch file with the name you typed only if it can't find an internal command, a COM file, and an EXE file with the same filename.

Similarly, don't ever try giving any executable file a name that duplicates an internal command. If you tried to create a file called TYPE.COM or DIR.BAT you'd have a hard time trying to run it, since DOS would see that you wanted to execute something called TYPE or DIR and think you were referring to the internal command with the same name.

Well, okay, DOS provides a tricky way to run a file with a name similar to an internal command, by letting you put a drive letter or pathname in front of it. When you add a drive or path, DOS knows you can't be talking about an internal command. To try it, make a copy of K.BAT called DIR.BAT. Then enter:

```
.\DIR
```

(The ".\" prefix tells DOS that the filename after the prefix is in the current directory.) But spare yourself the trouble and avoid such names.

Turning ECHO Off

Running a batch file like K.BAT really clutters up your screen. You type:

```
K
```

You should see:

```
C>CHKDSK

Volume PARTITION_1 created 11-10-1987 10:40a
Volume Serial Number is 16A5-B482

 22167552 bytes total disk space
    81920 bytes in 32 directories
 19324928 bytes in 1144 user files
     2048 bytes in bad sectors
  2758656 bytes available on disk
```

```
   2048 bytes in each allocation unit
  10824 total allocation units on disk
   1347 available allocation units on disk

 655360 total bytes memory
 629952 bytes free
```

This is a bit better than the original version, because it suppresses the name of the program the batch file executes when you run it. But you do have to look at the initial ECHO OFF command.

However, if you're using DOS version 3.3 or later, you can prevent any batch file command from appearing onscreen by putting a @ sign at the beginning of the line. So if you're using a later DOS version and you changed K.BAT to read:

```
@ECHO OFF
CHKDSK
```

when you ran this version all you'd see is:

```
C>K

Volume PARTITION_1 created 11-10-1987 10:40a
Volume Serial Number is 16A5-B482

 22167552 bytes total disk space
    81920 bytes in 32 directories
 19324928 bytes in 1144 user files
     2048 bytes in bad sectors
  2758656 bytes available on disk

     2048 bytes in each allocation unit
    10824 total allocation units on disk
     1347 available allocation units on disk

   655360 total bytes memory
   629952 bytes free
```

Still, while this prevents the DECIDE filename from appearing onscreen, and suppresses the ECHO OFF command, it makes you stare at the name of the batch file itself, D.BAT. You can get rid of this by clearing the screen with a CLS command. So adding a third line to D.BAT:

```
ECHO OFF
CLS
DECIDE
```

will clear the screen and print in the upper lefthand corner.

You can tell whether or not ECHO is off or on by typing ECHO on a line by itself and pressing Enter. If your batch file ever displays a line that says:

```
ECHO is off
```

or:

```
ECHO is on
```

it means that the batch file either had the command ECHO on a line by itself with nothing following it, or thought it did. Since DOS treats equal signs, tabs, semicolons, and commas as spaces, it will interpret lines such as:

- ECHO =
- ECHO ;
- ECHO ,

simply as ECHO commands with nothing after them other than meaningless spaces, and think you're asking it to report whether ECHO happens to be toggled off or on.

REMinding Yourself

Running the CHKDSK.EXE program from the K.BAT batch file rather than renaming CHKDSK.EXE to K.EXE does help prevent your disk from filling up with mysterious-sounding programs like A.COM, BB.EXE, and Z.COM that don't really tell you what they do.

However, months from now if you stumble across K.BAT you may forget what it does. It sounds harmless enough, but if you have a few dozen megabytes of critical information on your hard disk, and, well, one of these days you're definitely going to back up every last file, don't take chances.

To make life easier, use the DOS REM (Remark) batch command to add a nonexecuting comment to D.BAT:

```
ECHO OFF
REM K.BAT runs CHKDSK.EXE
CLS
CHKDSK
```

Lines beginning with REM can contain up to 123 characters of text. If you turn ECHO off earlier in the batch file they won't appear onscreen. If you don't turn ECHO off, or if you turn ECHO back on before the REM line, DOS will display it onscreen, REM and all. So a batch file such as:

```
REM K.BAT runs CHKDSK.EXE
CHKDSK
```

or:

```
ECHO OFF
CLS
ECHO ON
REM K.BAT runs CHKDSK
CHKDSK
```

would display:

```
C>REM K.BAT runs CHKDSK

CHKDSK
Volume PARTITION_1 created 11-10-1987 10:40a
Volume Serial Number is 16A5-B482

 22167552 bytes total disk space
    81920 bytes in 32 directories
 19324928 bytes in 1144 user files
     2048 bytes in bad sectors
  2758656 bytes available on disk

     2048 bytes in each allocation unit
    10824 total allocation units on disk
     1347 available allocation units on disk

   655360 total bytes memory
   629952 bytes free
```

The second example above would, of course, clear the screen first. If you don't turn ECHO off, and you indent the lines in your batch file, DOS will maintain the indentation when it displays them. So a batch file that contained the lines:

```
REM Be very
    REM very
        REM very
            REM very
                REM careful
REM when you use the FORMAT command
```

would show up onscreen as:

```
C>      REM Be very

C>            REM very

C>                  REM very

C>                        REM very

C>                              REM careful

C>      REM when you use the FORMAT command
```

Since DOS won't display any lines beginning with REM if ECHO is off, adding an ECHO OFF at the beginning of the above batch file would end up spinning your disk but displaying nothing except a blank line or two.

If you wanted to print a warning message like the one above, and you didn't want it cluttered with REMs and DOS prompts and extra spaces, you could use the ECHO command to display it.

Putting the word ECHO at the beginning of a line tells DOS to print onscreen everything that follows it on the same line.

If you included the line:

```
ECHO Hello there
```

in a batch file, DOS would print:

```
Hello there
```

When using ECHO command to display messages, be sure to turn ECHO off before you print the first one. Otherwise you'll end up printing both the words you want displayed and the command to display them. If you didn't first turn ECHO off, the "ECHO Hello there" line would appear as:

```
C>ECHO Hello there
Hello there
```

So a better version of the FORMAT-cautioning batch file would be:

```
ECHO OFF
ECHO Be very
ECHO       very
ECHO             very
ECHO                   very
ECHO                         careful
ECHO when you use the FORMAT command
```

DOS will display:

```
Be very
     very
          very
               very
                    careful
when you use the FORMAT command
```

The indentation trick that staggered REM statements across the screen won't work with ECHO commands. To indent text that ECHO displays you'll have to add spaces between the word ECHO and the text that it prints.

ECHO can print boxes and borders onscreen as well as text. The BOXMAKER.BAS program on the accompanying disk will create a BOX.BAT batch file that displays a single-line or double-line box any size you want, and indented wherever you want it. You can use your word processor or EDLIN to add text inside the box.

DOS executes batch files one line at a time. If you have a system with a fast hard disk or RAMdisk, you can get away with using the ECHO command to print a large block of text onscreen. But on a floppy disk system all you'll get is a lot of disk grinding and a painfully slow display as DOS churns the floppy line by line to see what it should ECHO next.

If you don't have a hard disk, set up a RAMdisk and copy your batch files onto it. The DOS VDISK.SYS or RAMDISK.SYS virtual disk driver supplied with versions 3.0 and later works well, or you can use the program furnished with your system's memory expansion card.

An alternative method is to use the TYPE command to display any really large text blocks. If you want your batch file to print a long involved set of instructions, you could type these into a separate file called INSTRUCS and then insert a line into your batch file at the appropriate place that said:

```
TYPE INSTRUCS
```

While using the TYPE command to display text in a separate file is far faster than ECHOing it to the screen a line at a time, you'll have to remember to keep both the batch file with the TYPE command and the file to be typed together. If you want to give your batch file to a co-worker, you may forget to pass along the text file. Or the co-worker may see the file, not know what it is, and unwittingly erase it. And if your batch file uses TYPE to display the contents of multiple message files, you complicate things even more.

One final problem is that small files take up more space than you think. On an old PC-XT, even a two-line file took up 4K of disk space.

The best solution in this case (and in just about every other one) is to get yourself a jet-propelled hard disk, and a speedy CPU. Speed is addictive. One of the reasons you started using a computer in the first place was to do more chores in less time, and a neck-snapping system makes this easier. The highly competitive hardware market ensures that hot, muscular new systems are always coming down in price. Or you can purchase an accelerator board. And in any event, stuff your system with memory, then have your start-up AUTOEXEC.BAT file copy your important batch files to a RAMdisk and run them directly out of memory.

Jumping, Skipping, Looping, and Branching

Say you wanted to print a whole bunch of identical banners for a party, using the BANNER.EXE program on the accompanying disks. You could type

```
BANNER "Happy Birthday, Terry!"
```

umpteen times, or you could also write a short NONSTOP.BAT batch file to rerun the program automatically until you tell it to stop:

```
@ECHO OFF
:TOP
BANNER "Happy Birthday, Terry!"
GOTO TOP
```

(Be sure to put a carriage return at the end of the last line, or the batch file will print one banner and then quit.) Run the NONSTOP.BAT file, and your printer will start spewing forth banners. The only way to stop it, other than rebooting your computer, is to press Ctrl-C or Ctrl-Break, at which point DOS will print a message that says "Terminate batch job (Y/N)?"

If you type Y or y the batch file will abort and you'll return to the DOS prompt. If you type N or n the batch file will continue doing whatever it was doing. Type anything else and DOS will stubbornly keep printing the same (Y/N) request.

The mechanism that repeated the NONSTOP.BAT batch file output — a loop — is one of the fundamental computer tools. Remember, computers aren't smart, they're just fast. They're especially good at executing the same basic instruction over and over. This comes in handy more often than you might think, since computer programs are loaded with loops. Even something as simple as figuring out what you typed on the DOS command line is a loop, since what DOS really does is examine and interpret the first character and then move on to examine the next character, and the next, until it's reached the end of the line and processed each one.

Loops are terrific tools. But endless loops that force you to break out of them by typing Ctrl-C or Ctrl-ScrollLock aren't so terrific.

ERRORLEVEL — Best Command, Worst Name

Knowing how to use ERRORLEVEL is vital if you want to turn ordinary batch files into screaming power tools. Don't be thrown off by its rotten name; it's the only real method

DOS provides for making batch files dynamically interactive. But while the framework is there, it needs a little help. DOS does let you use replaceable parameters to pass information from the command line into a batch file when you first execute it, but this won't let you or your system talk to a batch file while it's running.

The only problem is that while ERRORLEVEL provides the raw muscle, DOS doesn't give you any convenient way to harness it. So you have to create your own tiny assembly language programs to help. It's easy once you get the hang of it. And you'll be amazed at the increased power and flexibility of DOS when you grab the assembly language front-end reins.

We'll explore every aspect of the IF ERRORLEVEL command later on in this chapter. For now, just type in the examples that follow to get a sense of what DOS can do in the right hands. They'll show you how to really make DOS purr when you're trying to create your own menu systems or run a complex series of tasks with lots of options.

Many times you want the user to be able to stop a program at the appropriate time by pressing a key. But you don't want the stopping mechanism to interfere with the loop, and you don't want to force the user to press something as awkward as Ctrl-ScrollLock.

To solve this problem, create a tiny KEYSTROK.COM program by typing in the following seven lines:

```
DEBUG
E 100 B8 00 06 B2 FF CD 21 74 04 B4 4C CD 21 C3
N KEYSTROK.COM
RCX
E
W
Q
```

The program it creates looks like this:

```
MOV AX,0600    ;Direct-console I/O function
MOV DL,FF      ;Select input request
INT 21         ;Do it
JZ  010D       ;If no key pressed, exit
MOV AH,4C      ;Otherwise, terminate with code in AL
INT 21         ;Do it
RET            ;Back to DOS
```

Then, create a brand new version of NONSTOP.BAT:

```
ECHO OFF
ECHO Press any key to stop
:TOP
BANNER "My message is . . ."
KEYSTROK
IF NOT ERRORLEVEL 1 GOTO TOP
```

Now NONSTOP.BAT will loop continuously until you press any key (other than a shift key such as Ctrl or NumLock). If you don't press a key it will keep looping. If you're familiar with BASIC, this is similar to:

```
100 PRINT "Press any key to stop"
110 REM (The repeating command goes here)
120 IF INKEY$="" GOTO 110
```

You can fine-tune the KEYSTROK.COM program to work only if the user presses a specific key. If you want to limit this process so the user has to press the Esc key to stop, you could create a file called TEST4ESC.COM by typing in the following eight lines:

```
DEBUG
E 100 B8 00 06 B2 FF CD 21 74 0A 3C
E 10A 1B 75 06 B0 FF B4 4C CD 21 C3
N TEST4ESC.COM
RCX
14
W
Q
```

This jazzes up the KEYSTROK.COM program slightly:

```
MOV AX,0600      ;Direct-console I/O function
MOV DL,FF        ;Select input request
INT 21           ;Do it
JZ  0113         ;No key pressed, so exit
CMP AL,1B        ;Key was pressed; was it Esc?
JNZ 0113         ;No, so exit
MOV AL,FF        ;Yes, so put FF in AL for ERRORLEVEL
MOV AH,4C        ;Terminate with code
INT 21           ;Do it
RET              ;Back to DOS
```

Then change the NONSTOP.BAT batch file to read:

```
ECHO OFF
ECHO Press the Esc key to stop
:TOP
BANNER "My message is . . ."
TEST4ESC
IF NOT ERRORLEVEL 255 GOTO TOP
```

The version of NONSTOP.BAT that used KEYSTROK.COM let you quit by pressing any key, and required a value of 1 after the word ERRORLEVEL. The new NON-

STOP.BAT that uses TEST4ESC won't quit unless you press the Esc key, and needs a value of 255 after the word ERRORLEVEL.

You can change the trigger key from Esc to Enter, space, or tab, or any other single-purpose key that doesn't have different uppercase and lowercase versions, simply by changing one byte. Notice that the TEST4ESC.SCR script contained a line:

```
CMP AL,1B
```

The 1B is the hexadecimal representation of decimal 27, which is the ASCII value of Esc. To change this so a user would have to press the Enter key to stop, substitute an 0D (the hex version of decimal 13) in place of the 1B. To change the trigger to the spacebar, substitute a 20 (the hex representation of decimal 32) in place of the 1B.

If you're typing in the lines that begin with E 100, replace the 1B directly after the E 10A.

The process becomes a bit trickier if you want the user to type a letter, such as Q (for Quit), A (for Abort), X (for eXit), or S (for Stop), since the uppercase and lowercase versions of these letters have different ASCII values. However, by adding an additional logical OR instruction, you can create a program that will recognize both the uppercase and lowercase versions of any alphabetic character.

Type in the following eight lines:

```
DEBUG
E 100 B8 00 06 B2 FF CD 21 74 0C 0C 20 3C
E 10C 61 75 06 B0 FF B4 4C CD 21 C3
RCX
16
N TEST4A.COM
W
Q
```

This produces a TEST4A.COM program that looks like:

```
MOV AX,0600      ;Direct-console I/O function
MOV DL,FF        ;Select input request
INT 21           ;Do it
JZ  0115         ;No key pressed, so exit
OR  AL,20        ;Make sure the letter is lowercase
CMP AL,61        ;Was it an 'a' ?
JNZ 0115         ;No, so exit
MOV AL,FF        ;Yes, so put FF in AL for ERRORLEVEL
MOV AH,4C        ;Terminate with code
INT 21           ;Do it
RET              ;Back to DOS
```

Again, change NONSTOP.BAT to read:

```
ECHO OFF
ECHO Press A to Abort
:TOP
BANNER "My message is . . ."
TEST4A
IF NOT ERRORLEVEL 255 GOTO TOP
```

To change the trigger key from **A** to any other letter key, replace the hex 61 in the TEST4A.SCR script line:

```
CMP AL,61
```

or if you're typing the eight lines directly into DEBUG, replace it in the second line directly after E 10C. To figure out the new values, consult the chart below, which contains the hexadecimal ASCII representation of the lowercase version of each letter. The program converts uppercase values to lowercase ones, and leaves lowercase ones alone.

Hex Lowercase ASCII Values

a - 61	j - 6A	s - 73
b - 62	k - 6B	t - 74
c - 63	l - 6C	u - 75
d - 64	m - 6D	v - 76
e - 65	n - 6E	w - 77
f - 66	o - 6F	x - 78
g - 67	p - 70	y - 79
h - 68	q - 71	z - 7A
i - 69	r - 72	

You may take this even one step further, and allow the user to enter any letter of the alphabet. Type:

```
DEBUG
E 100 B8 00 06 B2 FF CD 21 74 0E 0C 20 3C
E 10C 61 72 08 3C 7A 77 04 B4 4C CD 21 C3
N ANYLETR.COM
RCX
18
W
Q
```

to produce the ANYLETR.COM program:

```
MOV AX,0600        ;Direct-console I/O function
MOV DL,FF          ;Select input request
```

```
INT 21              ;Do it
JZ  117             ;No key pressed, so exit
OR  AL,20           ;Make sure letter is lowercase
CMP AL,61           ;Is letter lower than 'a' ?
JB 117              ;Yes, so exit
CMP AL,7A           ;Is letter higher than 'z' ?
JA 117              ;Yes, so exit
MOV AH,4C           ;Terminate with code
INT 21              ;Do it
RET                 ;Back to DOS
```

Once you've created ANYLETR.COM, type in the following LETTER1.BAT batch file:

```
ECHO OFF
ECHO Type Z to quit
:TOP
ANYLETR
IF ERRORLEVEL 122 GOTO END
IF ERRORLEVEL 0   IF NOT ERRORLEVEL 1 BANNER "My message is . . ."
IF ERRORLEVEL 97  IF NOT ERRORLEVEL 98  ECHO You typed A
IF ERRORLEVEL 98  IF NOT ERRORLEVEL 99  ECHO You typed B
IF ERRORLEVEL 99  IF NOT ERRORLEVEL 100 ECHO You typed C
IF ERRORLEVEL 100 IF NOT ERRORLEVEL 101 ECHO You typed D
IF ERRORLEVEL 101 IF NOT ERRORLEVEL 121 ECHO You typed E-Y
GOTO TOP
:END
ECHO Ok, you typed Z; quitting...
```

This will repeat the same old BANNER.EXE program, but will also quit if the user types in a Z (or a z), and will report any other letter he or she types. Each letter requires a separate test on a separate line, so to keep things short, LETTER1.BAT explicitly echoes back A, B, C, or D (or a, b, c, or d) but will lump together E through Y. Otherwise it would have to contain 21 additional lines of tests.

While reporting which letter the user typed may be interesting, it's not really all that practical. But if you want to include a menu in your batch file that gives a user several choices, this technique comes in very handy, as the following LETTER2.BAT batch files suggests:

```
ECHO OFF
:MENU
ECHO Type Q to quit, M for this menu
:TOP
ANYLETR
IF ERRORLEVEL 113 IF NOT ERRORLEVEL 114 GOTO END
```

```
IF ERRORLEVEL 109 IF NOT ERRORLEVEL 110 GOTO MENU
BANNER "My message is . . ."
GOTO TOP
:END
ECHO Ok, you typed Q; quitting...
```

LETTER2.BAT will also run BANNER.EXE repeatedly. But it will quit if the user enters Q, or print the menu if the user enters M. Okay, it's a short menu, but you could make it much longer.

All of the above keystroke-sniffing programs — KEYSTROK.COM, TEST4ESC.COM, TEST4A.COM, and ANYLETR.COM — will sit back and let a batch file loop, acting only if the user types a key. This is definitely a plus if you have to run a program continuously and you don't want your batch file stopping at frequent intervals to ask users if they want to continue.

But if you want to create a simple menu system that waits patiently for the user to enter a menu choice, and screens out invalid choices, you'll need a keystroke-sniffer such as WAIT4A-Z.COM that's a bit more sophisticated. Type in these ten lines:

```
DEBUG
E 100 BA 2A 01 B4 09 CD 21 B8 07 0C CD 21 0C 20
E 10E 3C 61 72 F5 3C 7A 77 F1 50 88 C2 B4 02 CD
E 11C 21 B2 0D CD 21 B2 0A CD 21 58 B4 4C CD 21
E 12A 'Enter a letter from A to Z: $'
N WAIT4A-Z.COM
RCX
47
W
Q
```

Since you may want to modify this program later, you could create WAIT4A-Z.COM by turning the assembly language instructions below into a DEBUG script file called WAIT4A-Z.SCR. Type it in exactly as shown (although you may omit the semicolons and the comments following them), being careful to leave a blank line above RCX and to press the Enter key at the end of each line — especially the last one.

```
A
MOV DX,12A      ;Address of 'Enter a letter...'
MOV AH,09       ;Ready to print message
INT 21          ;Do it
MOV AX,0C07     ;Flush buffer then input char
INT 21          ;Do it
OR  AL,20       ;Make sure letter is lowercase
CMP AL,61       ;Is letter lower than 'a' ?
JB 107          ;Yes, so exit
CMP AL,7A       ;Is letter higher than 'z' ?
```

```
JA 107              ;Yes, so exit
PUSH AX             ;Save keystroke
MOV DL,AL           ;Then get ready to
MOV AH,02           ;Print it
INT 21              ;Do it
MOV DL,0D           ;Now print carriage return
INT 21              ;Do it
MOV DL,0A           ;And line feed
INT 21              ;Do it
POP AX              ;Retrieve keystroke
MOV AH,4C           ;Terminate with code
INT 21              ;Do it
DB 'Enter a letter from A to Z: $'

RCX
47
N WAIT4A-Z.COM
W
Q
```

When you're done, put the WAIT4A-Z.SCR file in the same directory as DEBUG.COM, or make sure DEBUG.COM is in a directory your PATH knows about, and at the DOS prompt type:

```
DEBUG < WAIT4A-Z.SCR
```

Then you'll need a batch file like MENU.BAT that handles all the other menu details:

```
ECHO OFF
:TOP
PAUSE
CLS ECHO    ************************
ECHO        A -- Run dBase
ECHO        B -- Run WordStar
ECHO        C -- Run 123
ECHO        Z - Quit
ECHO        ************************
WAIT4A-Z
IF ERRORLEVEL 122 GOTO END
IF NOT ERRORLEVEL 100 GOTO OPTION3
ECHO You typed D - Y; no options here
GOTO TOP
:OPTION3
IF NOT ERRORLEVEL 99 GOTO OPTION2
```

```
ECHO This would run 123
GOTO TOP
:OPTION2
IF NOT ERRORLEVEL 98 GOTO OPTION1
ECHO This would run WordStar
GOTO TOP
:OPTION1
ECHO This would run dBase
GOTO TOP
:END
ECHO Ok, you typed Z; quitting...
```

You could change this to ask the user to type a number between 1 and 9 rather than a letter between A and Z. To do this, replace four lines in the WAIT4A-Z.COM program:

1. Change: `CMP AL,61 ;Is letter lower than 'a'?`
   to: `CMP AL,31 ;Is number lower than '1'?`

2. Change: `CMP AL,7A ;Is letter higher than 'z'?`
   to: `CMP AL,39 ;Is number higher than '9'?`

3. Change: `DB 'Enter a letter from A to Z: $'`
   to: `DB 'Enter a number from 1 to 9: $'`

4. Change: `N WAIT4A-Z.COM`
   to: `N WAIT41-9.COM`

To make the patches, type everything below:

```
DEBUG WAIT4A-Z.COM
E 10F 31
E 113 39
E 132 "numb"
E 13E 31
E 143 39
N WAIT41-9.COM
W
Q
```

If you prefer the WAIT41-9.COM number version to the WAIT4A- Z.COM letter version, you'll have to change the MENU.BAT batch file as well:

```
ECHO OFF              ECHO OFF
:TOP                  :TOP
PAUSE                 PAUSE
```

```
CLS                                        CLS
ECHO  ************************             ECHO  ************************
ECHO      A -- Run dBase                   ECHO      1 -- Run dBase
ECHO      B -- Run WordStar                ECHO      2 -- Run WordStar
ECHO      C -- Run 123                     ECHO      3 -- Run 123
ECHO      Z - Quit                         ECHO      9 - Quit
ECHO  ************************             ECHO  ************************
WAIT4A-Z                                   WAIT41-9
IF ERRORLEVEL 122 GOTO END                 IF ERRORLEVEL 57 GOTO END
IF NOT ERRORLEVEL 100 GOTO OPTION3         IF NOT ERRORLEVEL 52 GOTO OPTION3
ECHO You typed D - Y; no options here      ECHO You typed 4 - 8; no options here
GOTO TOP                                   GOTO TOP
:OPTION3                                   :OPTION3
IF NOT ERRORLEVEL 99 GOTO OPTION2          IF NOT ERRORLEVEL 51 GOTO OPTION2
ECHO This would run 123                    ECHO This would run 123
GOTO TOP                                   GOTO TOP
:OPTION2                                   :OPTION2
IF NOT ERRORLEVEL 98 GOTO OPTION1          IF NOT ERRORLEVEL 50 GOTO OPTION1
ECHO This would run WordStar               ECHO This would run WordStar
GOTO TOP                                   GOTO TOP
:OPTION1                                   :OPTION1
ECHO This would run dBase                  ECHO This would run dBase
GOTO TOP                                   GOTO TOP
:END                                       :END
ECHO Ok, you typed Z; quitting...          ECHO Ok, you typed 9; quitting...
```

This example will assume you're using the A-Z letter version. Note that in both cases, the MENU.BAT batch file only simulates running programs. To make the batch file useful, substitute the actual commands that execute your programs instead of the messages telling the programs would have run. So where the batch file says something like:

```
ECHO This would run WordStar
```

replace the line with the actual command that runs *WordStar*. Here you'd replace this line with:

```
WS
```

The WAIT4A-Z.COM program works by printing a message on the screen, waiting for the user to enter a keystroke, testing the keystroke to make sure it's in an acceptable range, and then putting the keystroke in a special place when it exits so the DOS IF ERRORLEVEL command can handle it.

The message it prints is "Enter a letter from A to Z:". If you wanted, you could limit the range to something like "Enter a letter from A to H:".

WAIT4A-Z.COM rejects all keystrokes that aren't letters of the alphabet. To modify the range of acceptable inputs, you'll have to change the actual values that the program tests. WAIT4A-Z.COM automatically turns uppercase letters into lowercase ones (and leaves lowercase letters alone) to reduce the number of tests it has to make. The test for the lower limit is the line:

```
CMP AL,61        ;Is letter lower than 'a' ?
```

You probably don't want to change this. If you do, the 61 is the hexadecimal number of a lowercase 'a.' To change this to 'b' you'd replace the 61 with a 62. But again, you probably shouldn't.

The test for the upper limit is:

```
CMP AL,7A        ;Is letter higher than 'z' ?
```

The 7A is the hexadecimal representation of a lowercase 'z.' If you do want to limit the range, and change the program so it rejects anything other than the letters A through H, substitute the hex value of lowercase 'h' (which the chart in Chapter 6—Figure 6.6—tells you is hex 68):

```
CMP AL,68        ;Is letter higher than 'h' ?
```

You don't have to modify the comments, but it doesn't hurt, and it makes it far easier later to see what you did.

Obviously if you chop the top off the range, you won't be able to have the user type Z to quit. You'll probably want to make the highest letter H the exit key. MENU.BAT tests for a 'z' with the line:

```
IF ERRORLEVEL 122 GOTO END
```

To change this so H quits, replace the 122 (the decimal value of lowercase 'z') with the decimal value for lowercase 'h' — 104. Unfortunately, DEBUG requires hex notation but the DOS IF ERRORLEVEL command works exclusively with decimal numbers. One more thing — if you do limit the range to something like A-H, make sure you modify all references to it. This means changing:

1. The CMP AL,hexvalue test(s) for upper/lower limits in the WAIT4A-Z.SCR script.
2. The DB 'Enter a letter from A to Z: $' message at the bottom of the WAIT4A-Z.SCR script.
3. The decimal number in the MENU.BAT exit test that normally reads ":IF ERRORLEVEL 122 GOTO END."
4. The "You typed D - Y; no options here" MENU.BAT error message two lines below the test in #3 above.
5. The "ECHO Z - Quit" menu choice itself.

6. And the "ECHO Ok, you typed Z; quitting..." message it triggers at the very end of MENU.BAT

You don't have to patch the program to limit the choices, since the WAIT4A-Z.COM program filters out anything that isn't a letter, and the MENU.BAT batch file "traps" any keystrokes that aren't currently menu choices. Here's how to add another menu option: First, make the little menu larger by adding a D option:

```
ECHO     * * * * * * * * * * * * * * * * * * * * * * * *
ECHO        A - - Run dBase
ECHO        B - - Run WordStar
ECHO        C - - Run 123
ECHO        D - - Run ProComm
ECHO        Z -  Quit
ECHO     * * * * * * * * * * * * * * * * * * * * * * * *
```

Then, change the message that said D was out of range from:

```
ECHO You typed D - Y; no options here
```

to:

```
ECHO You typed E - Y; no options here
```

Finally, (and this is the only tricky part), add a module near the top of the batch file to accommodate D entries. The top of the batch file currently looks like:

```
       .
       .
       .
IF ERRORLEVEL 122 GOTO END
IF NOT ERRORLEVEL 100 GOTO OPTION3
ECHO You typed D - Y; no options here
GOTO TOP
:OPTION3
IF NOT ERRORLEVEL 99 GOTO OPTION2
ECHO This would run 123
GOTO TOP
:OPTION2
       .
       .
       .
```

Since D (with a lowercase decimal value of 100) is now the highest legal value, you'll have to change the test for invalid entries so it starts at 101 (the decimal value of the lowest new invalid entry — E) rather than 100. And you'll also have to insert the D module directly after the test that executes the menu choice. The code that replaces the above section will look like:

```
        .
        .
        .

IF ERRORLEVEL 122 GOTO END
IF NOT ERRORLEVEL 101 GOTO OPTION4
ECHO You typed E - Y; no options here
GOTO TOP
:OPTION4
IF NOT ERRORLEVEL 100 GOTO OPTION3
ECHO This would run ProComm
GOTO TOP
:OPTION3
IF NOT ERRORLEVEL 99 GOTO OPTION2
ECHO This would run 123
GOTO TOP
:OPTION2
        .
        .
        .
```

Two final cosmetic notes — the MENU.BAT file echoes a very small menu onscreen. You may prefer to use the DOS TYPE command to display a separate, fancier menu file. A tiny program such as MAKESCRN.BAS can create a template called MENU with a little 3-D shadow behind it; you can use your pure-ASCII word processor to add text to it. Actually, EDLIN is terrific at this, once you know how to use the F3 and arrow keys.

```
100 ' MAKESCRN.BAS -- makes MENU
110 ' screen you can TYPE in DOS
120 CLS
130 OPEN "MENU" FOR OUTPUT AS #1
140 S$=STRING$(26,219)
150 T$=S$+STRING$(2,177)
160 U$=STRING$(26,177)
170 FOR A=1 TO 5:PRINT #1,:NEXT
180 PRINT #1,TAB(27);S$
190 FOR A=10 TO 20
200 PRINT #1,TAB(27);T$
210 NEXT
220 PRINT #1,TAB(29);U$
230 FOR A=1 TO 3:PRINT #1,:NEXT
```

```
240 PRINT "Now type TYPE MENU"
250 CLOSE:SYSTEM
```

When you've created the MENU with MAKESCRN.BAS and entered text with EDLIN, EDIT, or your word processor, replace the lines:

```
ECHO    * * * * * * * * * * * * * * * * * * * * * * * *
ECHO        A -- Run dBase
ECHO        B -- Run WordStar
ECHO        C -- Run 123
ECHO        Z -  Quit
ECHO    * * * * * * * * * * * * * * * * * * * * * * * *
```

in MENU.BAT with a single line:

```
TYPE MENU
```

Create a fancy menu or text screen and call it something like SCREEN1 — but make sure it's no larger than 24 rows by 79 columns. Then run the MAKECOM program and when prompted for a filename, enter SCREEN1. MAKECOM will attach an assembly language program to your text screen that makes it leap instantly onto your display. And it retains the existing screen colors.

You could create several text screens, with fancy boxes and borders, and call them HELP1.COM, HELP2.COM, HELP3.COM. Put a centered message at the bottom of each one that says "Press any key for the next screen...." Then add a section to a batch file that looks like:

```
ECHO Instructions follow
PAUSE
HELP1
PAUSE > NUL
HELP2
PAUSE > NUL
HELP3
```

The fancy text screens will flash onto the display one by one. When the user presses a key he'll instantly get the next one. You can also use this to display menus, introductory sign-on screens, etc. Redirecting the output of PAUSE to NUL with the command:

```
PAUSE > NUL
```

will suppress the normal DOS "Strike a key when ready . . ." message in version 3.x. However, version 2.x will display this message even if you try to get rid of it, so if you try this on a 2.x system, allow for this intrusive message.

The MENU.BAT batch file clears the screen each time it displays a menu. If you don't have ANSI.SYS loaded, this will cancel any attribute settings you may have in effect, and turn the screen to a drab grey on black. Issuing the CLS command with ANSI loaded will clear the screen but retain the preset colors.

To avoid this, either load and use ANSI.SYS (see the chapter on ANSI techniques), or replace the CLS line with a line such as BLUWHITE or WHITEBLU and then make sure you have a short COM program handy to clear the screen to the colors you like. The following COLOR.SCR DEBUG script will create both BLUWHITE.COM (blue text on a white background) and WHITEBLU.COM (the reverse):

```
N BLUWHITE.COM
E 100 B8 00 06 B9 00 00 BA 4F 18 B7
E 10A 71 CD 10 B4 02 BA 00 00 B7 00
E 114 CD 10 B0 04 BA D9 03 EE C3
RCX
1D
W
E 10A 17
N WHITEBLU.COM
W
Q
```

Type this in using a pure-ASCII word processor, or EDLIN, or else insert a COPY CON COLOR.SCR script at the very top, then after typing the final line with the Q, press Enter, then the F6 function key, then Enter again.

In any event, make sure you press Enter at the end of each line, especially the last one. Then get into DOS, make sure DEBUG.COM is handy, and type:

```
DEBUG < COLOR.SCR
```

The byte that actually sets the color is at DEBUG offset 10A — the first entry on the second line, directly after E 10A. In the above script this value is 71.

This byte is a two-digit hex number where the first digit is the background color and the second digit is the foreground color. The choices for each are: 0 = black, 1 = blue, 2 = green, 3 = cyan (light blue), 4 = red, 5 = magenta (purple), 6 = brown or yellow, and 7 = white. You can make the foreground number (but not the background) high intensity by using: 8 = grey, 9 = bright blue, A = bright green, B = bright cyan, C = bright red, D = bright purple, E = yellow, or F = bright white as the second digit.

To change the color, either replace the 71 directly after the E 10A on the second line with a different color value, and then change the name in the first line from BLU-WHITE.COM to something that reflects your new colors, Or, once you've created the above files, you can change the color by using DEBUG directly. This series of commands would produce a program called YELRED.COM with bright yellow text on a red background:

```
DEBUG BLUWHITE.COM
E 10A 4E
N YELRED.COM
W
Q
```

Breaking Out of a Batch Job

We started the discussion of looping and branching with an example that printed out lots of banners for a party by looping back to a label. DOS provides another way to set up a continuous loop by making use of the filename and a concept called recursion. Just create a batch file called REPEAT.BAT by typing:

```
COPY CON REPEAT.BAT
ECHO OFF
BANNER "Happy Birthday, Terry!"
REPEAT
```

Then press F6 and then the Enter key. Run this new batch file by typing:

```
REPEAT
```

and your printer should start cranking out banners.

DOS executes each batch file one line at a time. The first line turns off the ECHO feature to prevent screen clutter. The second line runs the BANNER program. And the third line starts the whole process all over again by executing its own name. A program which calls itself is *recursive*.

Once you start REPEAT it will loop endlessly until you turn your system off or "break" out of it. To break out, hold down the Ctrl key and press either the C key or the ScrollLock key. DOS will temporarily halt the scrolling, display a ^C onscreen, and then print the message: "Terminate batch job (Y/N)?" If you answer No by typing an N or n, DOS will resume where it left off and continue scrolling. If you tell it Yes by typing a Y or y, DOS will break out of the loop and return to what you were doing previously. (Usually this returns you to the DOS prompt, but since batch files can in turn run other batch files, as you'll see soon, breaking out of the second one will return you to the first one.)

If you type anything other than a Y, y, N, or n, DOS will stubbornly keep repeating the "Terminate batch job (Y/N)?" message.

As it's written above, the REPEAT batch file will keep invoking itself and looping only if you keep its name REPEAT.BAT. If you renamed it to AGAIN.BAT, it would execute normally the first time through until it reached the third line. Then it would try to run a command or file called REPEAT. But since you renamed it, it wouldn't find such a command, and would simply print a "Bad command or file name" error message and crash to a halt.

DOS provides an easy way to solve this problem. Create a new file called ONCEMORE.BAT containing the three lines:

```
ECHO OFF
BANNER "Happy Birthday, Terry!"
%0
```

The %0 is a replaceable parameter. When DOS starts running any batch file, it looks at what you entered on the command line and parses it into as many as ten separate parts separated by the standard DOS delimiters.

A command line delimiter is a character that DOS uses to separate entries that you type at the DOS prompt. You may use spaces, commas, tabs, semicolons, or equals signs as delimiters.

DOS scans through whatever you typed at the DOS prompt and assigns replaceable parameters %0 through %9 to the first ten things it identifies as separate, discrete entries. The first entry on the command line is always the name of a command or file, and DOS assigns a %0 to this. So if you type:

```
A>ONCEMORE
```

DOS will make %0 equal to ONCEMORE. It will execute the first line by turning ECHO off, then will run the BANNER program specified on the second line, and finally will replace the %0 on the third line with the ONCEMORE that you typed directly after the DOS prompt. Since this is the name of the batch file itself, it will re-execute itself and continue looping until you press Ctrl-C or Ctrl-Break.

If you typed:

```
ONCEMORE INTO THE BREACH G-G-GUYS SAID PFC A121763
```

DOS would assign the following parameters:

```
ONCEMORE INTO THE BREACH G-G-GUYS SAID PFC A121763
   ↑       ↑    ↑    ↑        ↑       ↑    ↑     ↑
  %0      %1   %2   %3       %4      %5   %6    %7
```

You actually could have typed:

```
ONCEMORE INTO;THE=BREACH,G-G-
GUYS,SAID;;;PFC==;;,,A121763
```

and DOS would have assigned the same parameters, since it treats all the delimiters shown above as spaces. And it treats repeating delimiters just the same as single ones.

(If you renamed ONCEMORE.BAT to DOITAGIN.BAT or XYZ.BAT and ran either of those files, they too would repeat endlessly, since DOS would substitute the new DOITAGIN or XYZ names for the %0 on the third line.)

DOS will replace every single occurrence of %0 with the name of the batch file itself, so if you modified ONCEMORE.BAT to contain the lines:

```
ECHO OFF
ECHO This is a batch file called %0.BAT.
ECHO You typed %0 to start it.
ECHO Now %0 is going to run the BANNER program.
BANNER "Happy Birthday, Terry!"
ECHO And %0 will now start over again
%0
```

running it would produce something like:

```
C>ONCEMORE
This is a batch file called ONCEMORE.BAT.
You typed ONCEMORE to start it.
Now ONCEMORE is going to run the BANNER program.

And ONCEMORE will now start over again
This is a batch file called ONCEMORE.BAT.
You typed ONCEMORE to start it.
Now ONCEMORE is going to run the BANNER program.
```

etc.

If DOS sees a replaceable parameter on any line beginning with an ECHO, it will try to substitute the appropriate parameter that you typed on the command line. If the replaceable parameter following ECHO is %0, something will definitely appear in place of the %0 since you had to enter some filename to run the batch file in the first place, and since %0 always represents that filename.

So the command:

```
ECHO You typed %0
```

will always print something after the word "typed." But it you changed the line to:

```
ECHO You typed %8
```

DOS would replace the %8 with the ninth thing you typed on the command line (remember, the first thing on the command line is %0 rather than %1, so %8 prints the ninth command line entry). If you didn't type nine separate things (and you probably wouldn't have), DOS would print a blank after the word "typed:"

```
You typed
```

Note that DOS replaces the %0 with the actual command you typed, not the whole filename. Since you typed ONCEMORE at the DOS prompt, it makes %0 = ONCEMORE, not ONCEMORE.BAT.

You can tell your batch file to add the BAT extension to an ECHO display by tacking it on after the %0:

```
ECHO This is a batch file called %0.BAT.
```

Technically you could execute the batchfile by typing either:

```
ONCEMORE
```

or:

```
ONCEMORE.BAT
```

However, virtually no one adds the BAT extension when they run a batch file, and there's really no reason to. But if you did enter ONCEMORE.BAT rather than just plain ONCEMORE, and your batch file included the line:

```
ECHO This is a batch file called %0.BAT.
```

DOS would print:

```
This is a batch file called ONCEMORE.BAT.BAT.
```

The %0 parameter will duplicate exactly what you typed. So it you start the ball rolling by typing:

```
OnCeMoRe
```

You'll end up with:

```
This is a batch file called OnCeMoRe.BAT.
You typed OnCeMoRe to start it.
Now OnCeMoRe is going to run the DECIDE program.
```

If you want to experiment with replaceable parameters, run the following SHOWPARM.BAT batch file:

```
ECHO OFF
ECHO Parameter 0 is %0
IF NOT %1!==! ECHO Parameter 1 is %1
IF NOT %2!==! ECHO Parameter 2 is %2
IF NOT %3!==! ECHO Parameter 3 is %3
IF NOT %4!==! ECHO Parameter 4 is %4
```

```
IF NOT %5!==! ECHO Parameter 5 is %5
IF NOT %6!==! ECHO Parameter 6 is %6
IF NOT %7!==! ECHO Parameter 7 is %7
IF NOT %8!==! ECHO Parameter 8 is %8
IF NOT %9!==! ECHO Parameter 9 is %9
```

EDLIN makes it easy to create a batch file like this one with so many similar lines. To start the process, type:

```
EDLIN SHOWPARM.BAT
```

When you see the EDLIN "New file" message and asterisk prompt, type:

```
I
```

to start inserting lines, then enter the first three lines. This should look like:

```
New file
*I
        1:*ECHO OFF
        2:*ECHO Parameter 0 is %0
        3:*IF NOT %1!==! ECHO Parameter 1 is %1
```

Then hold down the Ctrl key and press either the C or ScrollLock keys while you're holding it down. You'll see a:

```
4:*^C
```

and you'll return to EDLIN's command mode, where the asterisk is in column 1. Then, make nine more copies of the:

```
3:*IF NOT %1!==! ECHO Parameter 1 is %1
```

line you just typed by issuing the EDLIN command:

```
*3,3,4,8C
```

If you wanted to make sure you had copied line 3 the correct number of times, you could type:

```
*L
```

which would list:

```
1: ECHO OFF
2: ECHO Parameter 0 is %0
```

```
 3:  IF  NOT  %1!==!  ECHO  Parameter  1  is  %1
 4:*IF  NOT  %1!==!  ECHO  Parameter  1  is  %1
 5:  IF  NOT  %1!==!  ECHO  Parameter  1  is  %1
 6:  IF  NOT  %1!==!  ECHO  Parameter  1  is  %1
 7:  IF  NOT  %1!==!  ECHO  Parameter  1  is  %1
 8:  IF  NOT  %1!==!  ECHO  Parameter  1  is  %1
 9:  IF  NOT  %1!==!  ECHO  Parameter  1  is  %1
10:  IF  NOT  %1!==!  ECHO  Parameter  1  is  %1
11:  IF  NOT  %1!==!  ECHO  Parameter  1  is  %1
```

Now all you have to do is increase the number references in each of the lines you just copied, so that all the 1s become 2s in line 4, 3s in line 5, and so on. Again, EDLIN makes this surprisingly easy. Actually, the DOS function keys make it easy, and EDLIN is one of the few programs that knows how to use them.

While the arsenal of DOS editing tricks is not exactly overwhelming, its function keys can really cut down on repetitive keystrokes. Most users know that tapping the F3 key once will repeat the previous DOS command. But they rarely use the powers of the F2 key, probably because they'd rather just press F3 and backspace the errant characters away.

While the F3 key will repeat the entire command that you typed previously at the DOS prompt, entering the F2 key followed by a character will repeat just part of the previous command — up to but not including the character you entered. So if the previous command was:

```
A>ONCEMORE abcdefghijklmnopqrstuvwxyz
```

and you pressed the F3 key, you'd end up again with:

```
A>ONCEMORE abcdefghijklmnopqrstuvwxyz
```

But if you pressed the F2 key and then typed a lowercase e you would see:

```
A>ONCEMORE abcd
```

since this tells DOS to display the part of the previous command starting from where the cursor currently is and ending right before the first occurrence of the letter you entered. When you're staring at a bare DOS prompt, the cursor is at column 1, so tapping the F2 key and then typing e at that point will display everything from column 1 right up to (but not including) where the first lowercase e is located.

If you had pressed the F2 key and typed an uppercase E, DOS would have displayed:

```
A>ONC
```

since the F2 key is case-sensitive and will stop right before the first uppercase E it finds.

This technique makes it a snap to replace all the 1s with 2s and 3s and 4s when you're using EDLIN.

Tell EDLIN you want to edit the first line that needs changing — line 4 — by typing:

```
*4
```

EDLIN will respond by printing the current contents of line 4 and then dropping down a line to let you edit it:

```
4:*IF NOT %1!==! ECHO Parameter 1 is %1
4:*
```

If you were to type F3, DOS would fill the lower line with an exact duplicate of the upper one:

```
4:*IF NOT %1!==! ECHO Parameter 1 is %1
4:*IF NOT %1!==! ECHO Parameter 1 is %1
```

But this isn't what you want. Instead, press the F2 key and type a 1. EDLIN will display the beginning of the upper line right up to but not including the first occurrence of a 1:

```
4:*IF NOT %1!==! ECHO Parameter 1 is %1
4:*IF NOT %
```

Now, type in a 2 to replace the 1:

```
4:*IF NOT %1!==! ECHO Parameter 1 is %1
4:*IF NOT %2
```

But don't press the Enter key yet. Instead, repeat the same process to get to the next 1 — press F2 and type a 1. You should see:

```
4:*IF NOT %1!==! ECHO Parameter 1 is %1
4:*IF NOT %2!==! ECHO Parameter
```

Type another 2 and press F2 one more time, so your screen looks like:

```
4:*IF NOT %1!==! ECHO Parameter 1 is %1
4:*IF NOT %2!==! ECHO Parameter 2 is %
```

Add a final 2 and press the Enter key:

```
4:*IF NOT %1!==! ECHO Parameter 1 is %1
4:*IF NOT %2!==! ECHO Parameter 2 is %2
```

Then try this with line 5, this time replacing the 1s with 3s. It looks more complicated than it actually is. All you have to do to fix line 5 is:

1. Type 5 (and press Enter).
2. Press F2 and type 1 then type 3 (do this three times).

It really goes quickly once you get the hang of it. Be sure to press Enter when you're all done and you reach the very end of each line, since EDLIN won't register any changes until you do.

After editing the last line (line 11), type:

```
*E
```

to save and exit. Then type SHOWPARM at the DOS prompt and try following it with different kinds of parameters. First enter SHOWPARM with nothing after it:

```
C>SHOWPARM
Parameter 0 is SHOWPARM
```

Try it with nine other entries on the command line:

```
C>SHOWPARM a b c d e f g h i j
Parameter 0 is SHOWPARM
Parameter 1 is a
Parameter 2 is b
Parameter 3 is c
Parameter 4 is d
Parameter 5 is e
Parameter 6 is f
Parameter 7 is g
Parameter 8 is h
Parameter 9 is i
```

Since SHOWPARM.BAT displays only ten parameters, you'll see the same result as the one directly above if you try:

```
C>SHOWPARM a b c d e f g h i j k l m n o p q r s t u v w x y z
Parameter 0 is SHOWPARM
Parameter 1 is a
Parameter 2 is b
Parameter 3 is c
Parameter 4 is d
Parameter 5 is e
Parameter 6 is f
```

```
Parameter 7 is g
Parameter 8 is h
Parameter 9 is i
```

Various collections of delimiters will have predictable results:

```
C>SHOWPARM a=bb=ccc
Parameter 0 is SHOWPARM
Parameter 1 is a
Parameter 2 is bb
Parameter 3 is ccc

C>SHOWPARM a,,,b====c;;;;;;d        e,=; ;=,f
Parameter 0 is SHOWPARM
Parameter 1 is a
Parameter 2 is b
Parameter 3 is c
Parameter 4 is d
Parameter 5 is e
Parameter 6 is f
```

You may have noticed that SHOWPARM displayed a message like "Parameter 6 is" only when you typed a seventh entry on the command line that required it. The batch file was smart enough to know how many entries you had typed so it could print the appropriate number of "Parameter N is..." messages.

If DOS weren't able to do this, and you had entered just one parameter, the display would have looked something like:

```
C>SHOWPARM a
Parameter 0 is SHOWPARM
Parameter 1 is a
Parameter 2 is
Parameter 3 is
Parameter 4 is
Parameter 5 is
Parameter 6 is
Parameter 7 is
Parameter 8 is
Parameter 9 is
```

The mechanism that prevented this was an IF STRING1==STRING2 test. Each line contains one. The first line with a test is:

```
IF NOT %1!==! ECHO Parameter 1 is %1
```

If you entered:

```
SHOWPARM XXX
```

DOS would make %0 equal to SHOWPARM, and %1 equal to XXX. So when it executed the test it would substitute XXX for %1 and end up with:

```
IF NOT XXX!==! ECHO Parameter 1 is XXX
```

Since XXX! is not equal to !, the test fails. However, it's a negative test, so you want it to fail. Note that you have to use double equal signs in IF tests like these.

If you had entered just:

```
SHOWPARM
```

without anything after it, DOS would have made %0 equal to SHOWPARM, and %1 equal to nothing. So the test would have turned into:

```
IF NOT !==! ECHO Parameter 1 is XXX
```

Here the single ! on the left side of the == is equal to the single ! on the right side. The test passes. The "NOT" in the test means that DOS won't execute the ECHO command that follows the test at the end of the line.

Putting It All Together

By combining environment variables, replaceable parameters, FOR commands, ECHO statements, fancy branching, nested batch file calling, and IF ERRORLEVEL tests you can do something that will make cleaning up cluttered disks a joy.

This CLEANUP process will queue up selected groups of files and present them to you one file at a time with a simple menu that makes it a snap to examine them, delete them, or leave them intact.

For this to work you need four files:

1. A small assembly language program called GETANS.COM that makes your batch files interactive. (You'll create GETANS.COM below.)
2. A main CLEANUP.BAT batch file that screens unwanted files from the cleanup process. (You'll also create CLEANUP.BAT.)
3. A secondary DOIT.BAT batch file loaded by CLEANUP.BAT that does most of the work and is the part the user ends up interacting with.
4. The custom version of the MORE.EXE file that DOIT.BAT uses to display the beginnings of files. (This version of MORE.EXE is on one of the accompanying disks.)

You also should make sure the DOS FIND.EXE program is in the same directory as these four files, or is in a directory that your path knows about. If you're using a floppy disk system, copy the FIND.EXE file onto your floppy and make sure COMMAND.COM is also on the diskette if you're running a version of DOS earlier than 3.3.

GETANS.COM is an example of a customized keystroke-sniffing program that returns exit codes that the DOS IF ERRORLEVEL command can process. Power users often end up writing their own variations of programs like this, or customizing similar ones.

To create GETANS.COM, type in the following eight lines:

```
DEBUG
E 100 B8 00 08 CD 21 0C 20 3C 79 74 0C 3C 63 74
E 10E 08 3C 64 74 04 3C 65 75 04 B4 4C CD 21 C3
N GETANS.COM
RCX
1C
W
Q
```

The actual GETANS.COM program looks like:

```
MOV AX,0800       ;Get keystroke
INT 21            ;Do it
OR  AL,20         ;Make sure it's lowercase
CMP AL,79         ;See if it's a 'y'
JZ  0117          ;Yes, so goto exit with code
CMP AL,63         ;See if it's a 'c'
JZ  0117          ;Yes, so goto exit with code
CMP AL,64         ;See if it's a 'd'
JZ  0117          ;Yes, so goto exit with code
CMP AL,65         ;See if it's an 'e'
JNZ 011B          ;No, so go to exit no code
MOV AH,4C         ;Exit with code
INT 21            ;Do it
RET               ;Exit without code
```

You could save typing by using the DOS MORE.COM utility in place of our MORE.EXE. However, MORE.COM will display the entire file one screenful at a time rather than just showing you the beginning of the file and then letting you quit, the way MORE.EXE does.

In any event, create CLEANUP.BAT next:

```
ECHO OFF
SET VAR=%1
IF %1!==! SET VAR=*.*
```

```
FOR %%I IN (%VAR%) DO COMMAND /C DOIT %%I
SET VAR=
:END
```

If you're using DOS version 3.3 or later, you may want to substitute the line:

```
FOR %%I IN (%VAR%) DO CALL DOIT %%I
```

in place of:

```
FOR %%I IN (%VAR%) DO COMMAND /C DOIT %%I
```

shown above. If you do use CALL instead of COMMAND /C the process will run a bit more smoothly. However, CALL won't work in any version of DOS older than 3.3. And finally, DOIT.BAT:

```
ECHO OFF
IF %1!==! GOTO WRONG
:TOP
ECHO [Alt-255 or Character 0]
ECHO Examine/Delete/CheckDIR/Skip %1 (E/D/C/S)?
GETANS
IF ERRORLEVEL 102 GOTO SKIP
IF ERRORLEVEL 101 GOTO EXAMINE
IF ERRORLEVEL 100 GOTO DELETE
IF ERRORLEVEL  99 GOTO DIRLIST
:SKIP
ECHO %1 NOT deleted...
GOTO END
:DELETE
ECHO Are you sure you want to delete %1 (Y/N)?
GETANS
IF ERRORLEVEL 121 IF NOT ERRORLEVEL 122 GOTO DOIT
GOTO SKIP
:DIRLIST
DIR %1 | FIND "-"
GOTO TOP
:DOIT
DEL %1
ECHO %1 deleted...
GOTO END
:EXAMINE
ECHO The beginning of %1 looks like:
TYPE %1 MORE.EXE
ECHO [Alt-255 or Character 0]
```

```
GOTO TOP
:WRONG
ECHO Run the accompanying CLEANUP.BAT first
:END
```

The fourth line from the top and the fifth line from the bottom in DOIT.BAT look like:

```
ECHO [Alt-255 or Character 0]
```

Don't actually type "[Alt-255 or Character 0]" after the ECHO and the space. This simply tells you to put either an ASCII 255 blank character or ASCII 0 null character here; both are impossible to display. By following the word ECHO with a space and then either an ASCII 255 character or an ASCII 0 character you can have DOS print a blank line when the batch file executes.

If you're entering these batch files with a word processor, you're probably better off trying to create a character 255. Most good word processors let you enter ASCII characters by holding down the Alt key, typing the ASCII value (in this case 255) on the number pad — not the top row number keys — and then releasing the Alt key. So type in:

```
ECHO
```

then press the spacebar once, then hold down Alt, tap 255 on the number pad, and then let the Alt key up.

If you're entering the batch files using EDLIN or the DOS COPY CON command, you may use the same technique to insert an ASCII 255, or you may use a simpler trick to put an ASCII 0 in your file. To enter an ASCII 0 in DOS (or EDLIN) just press the F7 function key. Again, remember first to type in the word ECHO, then press the spacebar once, then press F7.

Now that you've got all the files you need, you can clean up any disk. Make sure CLEANUP.BAT, DOIT.BAT, GETANS.COM, MORE.EXE, and FIND.EXE — and COMMAND.COM if you're using a version of DOS older than 3.3 — are handy, and type:

```
CLEANUP [filespec]
```

Omitting filespec and typing simply:

```
CLEANUP
```

has the same effect as typing:

```
CLEANUP *.*
```

If you wanted to clean up all your TXT files, for example, you could type:

```
CLEANUP *.TXT
```

Or if you wanted to clean up all files that began with the letter T you could type:

```
CLEANUP T*.*
```

Once you've entered your choice, the batch files will click into action and start displaying one by one the names of all files that match the filespec you specified. So if you have three BAK files on your disk:

- REPORT90.BAK
- MEMOPC.BAK
- INCOME90.BAK

and you enter:

```
CLEANUP *.BAK
```

DOS will begin by printing:

```
Examine/Delete/CheckDIR/Skip REPORT90.BAK (E/D/C/S)?
```

At this point you have four choices. Press E and DOS will display the first 22 (or fewer) lines of REPORT90.BAK and then print the:

```
Examine/Delete/CheckDIR/Skip REPORT90.BAK (E/D/C/S)?
```

prompt again.

If you want to delete it, type D. You'll get a confirmation message "Are you sure you want to delete REPORT90.BAK (Y/N)?" Here you'll have to type Y or y to erase the file. Typing any other key will abort the deletion process, print a "REPORT90.BAK NOT deleted..." message to keep you posted, and move on to the next file:

```
Examine/Delete/CheckDIR/Skip MEMOPC.BAK (E/D/C/S)?
```

If you have no idea what MEMOPC.BAK was, and you want to see the size of the file or the date you created it, type C to Check the DIR listing:

```
MEMOPC    BAK      6253  12-18-90    2:57a
```

You'll then again see the familiar:

```
Examine/Delete/CheckDIR/Skip MEMOPC.BAK (E/D/C/S)?
```

This process uses environment variables, which won't work in DOS 3.0, and can work erratically in earlier versions. The main CLEANUP.BAT file does only two jobs:

1. It uses a FOR command to execute the DOIT command repeatedly, once for each element in the filespec. If you wanted to look at all the *.BAK files and you had four of these on your disk, the FOR command would execute DOIT four times.
2. It also looks at the filespec you entered, and substitutes *.* if you didn't enter anything. It does this by setting an environment variable — here called VAR — to the filespec you enter, and then testing to make sure you entered something. If you forgot to enter something it sets the variable to "*.*" and assumes you want to look at all the files on your disk.
3. The DEL and ERASE commands in DOS 4.0 let you erase files selectively.

If you haven't increased the size of your environment, and you have a long PATH and some other space-eaters, setting a new variable may fill up the environment. It's easy to run out of space, since the default is a paltry ten 16-byte paragraphs, or 160 bytes.

To increase the environment size under DOS 3.0 and 3.1, just put this command in your CONFIG.SYS file:

```
SHELL [d:][path]COMMAND.COM /E:n /P
```

where n represents the number of 16-byte paragraphs. For versions 3.2 and later, use the same SHELL command but specify the actual number of bytes rather than paragraphs. The default in all cases is 160 bytes (ten paragraphs). You can increase it all the way to 32K in DOS 3.2 and 3.3, but are limited to 62 paragraphs (992 bytes) in earlier versions.

If you're using DOS 2.0 or 2.1 these techniques won't work. You'll have to patch COMMAND.COM at hex address ECF to represent the number of 16-byte memory paragraphs that will make up your new environment. (For DOS 2.11 the address is hex DF3.)

Now that you have a taste of what batch files can do, read the list of guidelines below, and then roll up your sleeves and plunge in by learning the nuances of each command. Then when you're done, try the very useful examples provided.

The Batch Commands

This section describes each batch command in detail, with lots of sample programs to show you just how the commands work. The commands are presented roughly in the order in which they are usually crop up in a file.

First, some rules and advice:

- The general format for executing a batch file is:

  `[d:] [path] filename [.BAT] [parameters]`

- Each line in a batch file must be shorter than 128 characters.
- Generally, all lines must end with carriage returns. However, a carriage return may be omitted from the very last line in cases when including it would print a double DOS prompt upon exiting.
- Since DOS processes batch files one line at a time, it's best to run them from fast hard disks or RAMdisks for optimal performance.
- When branching conditionally, batch files will always start searching for labels at the beginning of the file, so duplicate labels are ignored.
- Labels are not case sensitive, but all other aspects of batch file operations are.
- Batch filenames must end in BAT. Make sure that no COM or EXE file shares the same filename as your batch file. If you have a file on your disk called RUN.COM or RUN.EXE, and you create a batch file called RUN.BAT, DOS will always execute the RUN.COM or RUN.EXE file first, and never get around to running the RUN.BAT file.
- DOS processes batch files differently in versions 2.x from the way it does in later versions. Earlier versions cannot use IF EXIST tests outside the current subdirectory or redirect PAUSE messages, insist that labels begin in column 1, and become confused if label names are longer than eight characters.
- Versions 3.x and later offer the ability to CALL other batch files without having to run an additional copy of COMMAND.COM, can suppress line displays by prefacing them with @ signs, and in recent editions document the use of environment variables (although these won't work in 3.0).
- Finally, each version of DOS uses slightly different (but overlapping) techniques for generating blank lines with the ECHO command.

ECHO

Format: **ECHO [ON|OFF|message]**

Controls display of onscreen messages and can create files or append data to existing files by redirecting ECHO output.

ECHO ON displays all commands as they execute. This is the normal default.

ECHO OFF suppresses commands (including REM remark statements) from displaying as DOS executes them. But messages and errors will still appear. To prevent screen clutter and suppress as many messages as possible, make ECHO OFF the first line in your batch file.

If you nest batch files by using COMMAND /C to jump back and forth from one to the other, you'll have to put an ECHO OFF at the beginning of each. When COMMAND /C loads a secondary command processor, the new command processor turns ECHO on again, forcing you to turn it off manually. The CALL command introduced in version 3.3 maintains the ECHO state when jumping from one batch file to another.

In versions 3.3 or later, prefacing any command with an @ sign tells DOS not to display the command, as if ECHO were turned off. By starting all your batch files with @ECHO OFF you not only prevent subsequent commands from displaying, but you also keep the ECHO OFF command itself from showing up onscreen.

You probably don't use any programs that begin with a @ character. But if you do, and you want to execute one in a version 3.3 or later batch file, add an extra @ sign to the beginning of the filename, when you refer to it in the batch file.

Following ECHO with up to 122 characters of text displays this text, so that:

```
ECHO Back Up Your Disks Often
```

would print:

```
Back Up Your Disks Often
```

regardless of whether ECHO is currently on or off. If ECHO is off, just the text will appear. If ECHO is on, the actual ECHO command will appear first, followed on a separate line by the message it's printing, so you'll see something like:

```
C>ECHO Back Up Your Disks Often
Back Up Your Disks Often
```

Actually, ECHO can display any printable ASCII character. This lets you print fancy borders and boxes around your text, or display foreign language characters or math symbols. However, DOS doesn't make it easy to generate these characters except by using the Alt-keypad technique or by letting you harness ANSI.SYS to redefine certain shifted keys so they print characters with ASCII values greater than 127.

To ECHO a message with a DOS operator symbol (such as |, <, or >) in it, wrap the symbol between quotation marks, as in:

```
ECHO "|" is the Piping Symbol
```

You may dress up your screen by using ECHO to display fancy box and border high-bit ASCII characters (with values over 127). Some of the accompanying utilities will make it easy to work with such characters, or you can use the Alt + numeric keypad technique or redefine your keyboard using ANSI.SYS or a commercial keyboard macro program.

To create or append data to a file, use:

```
ECHO data > filename
```

which creates a brand new file called filename, or:

```
ECHO data >> filename
```

which appends data to an existing file.

Entering ECHO on a line by itself, or with nothing after it other than spaces, tells DOS to report whether ECHO currently happens to be set ON or OFF.

Be careful when using ECHO to display characters that DOS treats as delimiters (commas, semicolons, or equals signs) to separate parameters and commands. DOS will treat these as blanks and, if nothing else is on the same line other than the word ECHO, will think you're asking for a report on the current ON/OFF state.

Also, since batch files use percent signs to indicate environment variables or replaceable parameters, DOS will display every other one if you try to ECHO a string of them. So a batch file like:

```
ECHO OFF
ECHO ,,,,,,,,,,
ECHO ==========
ECHO ;;;;;;;;;;
ECHO %%%%%%%%%%
```

will produce:

```
ECHO is off
ECHO is off
ECHO is off
%%%%%
```

The addition of the message-suppressing @ symbol is welcome, but still won't prevent DOS from printing messages such as "1 File(s) copied." The way to suppress these is to add a NUL after any DOS command that would normally generate a message onscreen:

```
COPY C:\DOS\*.COM D: > NUL
```

The following UPDATE.BAT batch file will change the date and time in the directory listing for any file you specify:

```
ECHO OFF
IF %1!==! GOTO OOPS1
IF NOT EXIST %1 GOTO OOPS2
COPY /B %1 +,,
ECHO %1's date and time now updated.
GOTO END
:OOPS1
ECHO You must specify a filename to update.
```

```
GOTO END
:OOPS2
ECHO There is no file called %1 in this directory.
:END
```

If COMMAND.COM is in the current directory and you enter:

```
UPDATE COMMAND.COM
```

you'll see:

```
C>ECHO OFF
COMMAND.COM
        1 File(s) copied
COMMAND.COM's date and time now updated.
```

To clean this up, change the:

```
COPY /B %1 +,,
```

line to read:

```
COPY /B %1 +,, > NUL
```

Then when you enter UPDATE COMMAND.COM, all you'll see is:

```
C>ECHO OFF
COMMAND.COM's date and time now updated.
```

(And in versions 3.3 or later, you can change the first line in the batch file to @ECHO OFF to suppress the initial ECHO OFF message.)

If you try this yourself, be sure to include the /B in the COPY line. The COPY +,, process actually copies the file onto itself, and updates the directory listing in the process. By adding a /B switch, you tell DOS to copy the entire length of the file specified by the number of bytes in the directory listing. If you don't include this, DOS will stop copying if it sees an ASCII character 26, since it interprets this as an end-of-file marker. Many text files slap on such an end-of-file indicator, but program files treat occurrences of these ASCII 26 characters differently. If you forget to add the /B parameter you'll end up truncating your program files, which makes them utterly worthless — so be careful.

If you really want to shut things down, you can sandwich any potential screen-clutterers between the lines:

```
CTTY NUL
```

and:

```
CTTY CON
```

But if you try this, be very careful, since CTTY NUL effectively disconnects your keyboard and screen from what's going on, and unless you're absolutely certain that the batch file is going to make it back to the restorative CTTY CON line, you're playing with fire.

Assuming you don't have a file in your current directory called !@#$, running the following ERROR.BAT batch file:

```
ECHO OFF
DIRR
DIR !@#$
```

will display two error messages — "Bad command or file name" since DIR is misspelled, and "File not found" since the !@#$ file isn't on your disk. But if you add CTTY NUL and CTTY CON commands:

```
ECHO OFF
CTTY NUL
DIRR
DIR !@#$
CTTY CON
```

nothing will display except ECHO OFF.

The normal DOS default setting is ECHO ON. You can turn ECHO off directly at the command line if you want, which makes the prompt disappear. Executing a subsequent CLS wipes everything off your screen.

Some users patch COMMAND.COM to flip the default to ECHO on. If you aren't comfortable doing this (and there are valid reasons for being squeamish about it), you can suppress initial ECHO OFF commands in batch files several ways. The obvious one is to prefix the command with an @ sign, but this won't work in versions prior to 3.3.

If you have ANSI.SYS loaded, you can follow ECHO off with the ANSI sequence:

```
ESC[1A ESC[K ESC[B
```

on the line below (being sure to substitute an actual ASCII character 27 — hex 1B — in place of the three ESCs in the example). ESC[1A moves up a line, ESC[K erases that line, and ESC[B moves down a line when done.

However, most users don't load ANSI. The alternative is to use the NOECHO.COM program on the accompanying disk, which does essentially the same thing without forcing the user to deal with ANSI codes.

NOECHO.COM moves cursor up one line on the current video page, then erases that line. To use this, make the first line in your batch file ECHO OFF and make the second NOECHO.

Adding blank lines to your batch files is a bit trickier. Under later versions of DOS, you can print blank lines in your batch files by typing any of 35 different characters (ASCII values 0, 1, 2, 3, 4, 5, 6, 7, 8, 11, 12, 14, 15, 16, 17, 18, 19, 20, 21, 22, 23, 24, 25, 27, 28, 29, 30, 31, 34, 43, 46, 47, 58, 91, or 93) right after the word ECHO, without any intervening space (as in ECHO: or ECHO[).

Many of these ASCII values represent *control characters* that you can enter in DOS by using the Alt-keypad method. Just hold down the Alt key, type in the ASCII value on the number pad (not the top row number keys), then release the Alt key. You won't be able to do this with all of them, however. DOS will interpret entries like ASCII 3 as Ctrl-Break, 8 as a backspace, and 27 as Esc. You can enter a character 0 in DOS by pressing the F7 key.

To enter such difficult characters, you could use a BASIC program such as ECHOMAKR.BAS:

```
100 ' ECHOMAKR.BAS -- for blank lines
110 OPEN "ECHOBLNK.BAT" FOR OUTPUT AS #1
120 PRINT #1,"ECHO OFF"
130 FOR A=1 TO 3:READ B
140 PRINT #1,"ECHO USING CHARACTER";B;"--"
150 PRINT #1,"ECHO";CHR$(B)
160 NEXT:CLOSE
170 DATA 0,8,27
```

Or you could type in dummy characters and use DEBUG to patch them. If you created a file called DUMMY.BAT that looked like:

```
ECHO OFF
ECHO USING CHARACTER 0 --
ECHOa
ECHO USING CHARACTER 8 --
ECHOb
ECHO USING CHARACTER 27 --
ECHOc
```

You could then go into DEBUG and replace the a, b, and c with 0, 9, and 1B (1B is the hexadecimal representation of decimal 27 and DEBUG works exclusively in hex):

```
C>DEBUG DUMMY.BAT
-RCX
CX 0071
:
-D 100 L 71
30DD:0100  45 43 48 4F 20 4F 46 46-0D 0A 45 43 48 4F 20 55  ECHO OFF..ECHO U
30DD:0110  53 49 4E 47 20 43 48 41-52 41 43 54 45 52 20 30  SING CHARACTER 0
```

```
30DD:0120   20 2D 2D 0D 0A 45 43 48-4F 61 0D 0A 45 43 48 4F    --..ECHOa..ECHO
30DD:0130   20 55 53 49 4E 47 20 43-48 41 52 41 43 54 45 52     USING CHARACTER
30DD:0140   20 38 20 2D 2D 0D 0A 45-43 48 4F 62 0D 0A 45 43    8 --..ECHOb..EC
30DD:0150   48 4F 20 55 53 49 4E 47-20 43 48 41 52 41 43 54    HO USING CHARACT
30DD:0160   45 52 20 32 37 20 2D 2D-0D 0A 45 43 48 4F 63 0D    ER 27 --..ECHOc.
30DD:0170   0A                                                  .
-S 100 L 71 "a"
30DD:0129
-E 129 0
-S 100 L 71 "b"
30DD:014B
-E 14B 8
-S 100 L 71 "c"
30DD:016E
-E 16E 1B
-W
Writing 0071 bytes
-Q
```

You type everything following the DEBUG hyphen (-) prompts; DEBUG prints out all the rest. Typing RCX and pressing the Enter key twice reports how long the file is. The D 100 L 71 command tells DEBUG to display (D) the contents of the file starting at address 100 and continuing for a length (L) of 71 bytes (you have to start at address 100 because DEBUG loads just about all files at that address rather than at address 0).

One way to figure out where the a, b, and c are located is just to eyeball the display, but DEBUG's search (S) command can do it for you automatically. A command like S 100 L 71 "a" tells DEBUG to Search for the character "a" starting at address 100 and continue searching for 71 bytes. In the example above, DEBUG found an "a" at address 30DD:0129. When you're dealing with virtually any batch file you can ignore the four hex digits to the left of the colon; these will vary from system to system and don't matter here. The 0129 number does matter — it's the address of the "a."

To replace the "a" with a character 0, use the Enter command in the form E 129 0. This tells DEBUG to Enter (E) a value of 0 at address 0129.

Remember to use hex notation exclusively. Consult a decimal-to-hex chart if you need to. So when entering decimal ASCII character 27, you have to first convert it to its hex form, 1B. If you tried to enter a 27 rather than a 1B, DEBUG would think you meant a hex 27, which is equal to decimal 39.

When you're all done, use the W and Q commands to write the file to disk and then quit. If you're not an experienced DEBUG user, work on a copy of DUMMY.BAT called DUMMY2.BAT (or whatever). That way if you make a mistake you can always make another copy of the original and try again.

You can type some version 3.x and later blank-producing characters directly:

```
ECHO"
ECHO+
```

```
ECHO.
ECHO/
ECHO:
ECHO[
ECHO]
```

Again, this will work only in 3.x and later versions. (Under DOS 3.x you can also follow ECHO with a space and then one of the ASCII characters 0, 8, or 255.)

Unfortunately, earlier versions of DOS behave very differently.

Under version 2.x you can print a blank line by following ECHO directly with any of the ASCII characters 0, 1, 2, 3, 4, 5, 6, 7, 8, 9, 10, 11, 12, 14, 15, 16, 17, 18, 19, 20, 21, 22, 23, 24, 25, 27, 28, 29, 30, 31, 32, 34, 43, 44, 47, 58, 59, 61, 91, 92, and 93 — and then adding an extra space. If you forget the extra space at the end this technique won't work at all.

Note that this list is different from the 3.x and later list above. You can generate a blank line in version 3.x and later by putting a period (character 46) directly after ECHO, but this won't work with 2.x. However, under version 2.x, putting characters 9, 10, 32, 44, 59, and 61 (tab, line feed, space, comma, semicolon, or equals sign) and then a space after ECHO will display a blank line while these won't do the trick in version 3.x and later . And recent versions don't really care whether you have an extra space at the end of the line, while 2.x won't budge unless you include this final space. DOS is consistently inconsistent.

You can also generate blank lines by following ECHO with a space, and then one of a short list of characters. In DOS 2.x you can use this method with characters 0, 8, 9, 32, and 255. Under DOS 3.x and later, characters 9 and 32 won't work. In both cases you don't need to slap on an additional space at the end of the line.

However, the safest way in just about every version is to use ASCII character 0 and a space, in either order. Type:

```
ECHO
(then press the space bar)
(then press the F7 function key)
```

or type:

```
ECHO
(then press the F7 function key)
(then press the space bar)
```

Following ECHO with just a character 0 will work under DOS 3.x but not 2.x, 4.0, or 5.0.

When you press F7 at the DOS prompt, DOS will display a @ sign. Don't confuse this with the @ character itself, and don't try entering a @ by typing the shifted 2 key.

Some versions of DOS also insist that every line that begins with an ECHO end with a carriage return. Recent editions have gotten around this problem, but if you're using an older version and DOS prints the ECHO command itself as well as the message it's supposed to ECHO, try inserting a carriage return at the end of the offending line.

This is especially true if an ECHO command is the last line of a batch file. If you use the ECHO + space + ASCII 0 technique (which will appear as ECHO @):

```
ECHO OFF
ECHO First line
ECHO @
ECHO Last line
```

If you omit the carriage return after:

```
ECHO Last line
```

DOS 3.x and later won't mind, but DOS 2.x will become confused and print the "Echo Last line" command onscreen along with the "Last line" message that it's supposed to ECHO. So be sure to include a carriage return at the end of any ECHO command that happens to be on the final line of a batch file.

Automated ECHO Entry

ECHO can come in very handy when you have to simulate user response in a batch file, or when you want to combine commands. You can delete all your files, for instance, by using ECHO to send DOS a Y as if you had typed it in response to the "Are you sure (Y/N)?" prompt:

```
ECHO Y | DEL *.*
```

Use this command sparingly, since it will wipe out all your files.

A similar trick will print the time or date without any user intervention. Just type:

```
ECHO | MORE | TIME
```

Normally you'd have to press Enter when you just want to print the time or date onscreen, since DOS always asks you if you want to change the current settings. ECHO helps do this for you.

ECHO will trigger the MORE command, which sends a carriage return into the TIME command. Sounds complicated, but it's actually very simple, and it lets you harness TIME and DATE without having to be there to bang on the Enter key. You can use this to redirect the output of TIME and DATE into a log file:

```
ECHO | MORE | DATE | FIND "C" > LOGFILE
ECHO | MORE | TIME | FIND "C" >> LOGFILE
```

The extra FIND command screens out the DOS update requests and cleans up LOGFILE by looking only for the lines with the word "Current" in them and tossing anything else. Without them you'd end up with a file that looked like:

```
Current date is Sun 1-14-1990
Enter new date (mm-dd-yy):
Current time is 2:47:36.80
Enter new time:
```

REM

Format: **REM [message]**

REM lets you add comments and titles to your batch files.

It will display up to 123 characters of text following the word REM — but only when ECHO is on. When ECHO is off, DOS won't display anything. Under version 2.x, you could put a period in the first column and follow it with a text message to add remarks to your batch files, but Microsoft removed this from version 3.x.

To include a DOS operator symbol (such as |, <, or >) in the remark, enclose the symbol in quotes, e.g.:

```
REM "|" is the Piping Symbol
```

The text following REM may actually be longer than 123 characters, but DOS will display only the first 123 when ECHO is turned ON.

You can also add comments to your batch files by prefacing them with a colon and treating them as unreferenced labels — labels for which there is no corresponding GOTO command (see GOTO). DOS treats any line beginning with a colon as a label, and won't display it or process it regardless of whether ECHO happens to be ON or OFF. (This means you don't have to wrap operators such as | or < inside quotation marks when using them as label-type comments.) Comments can be far longer if you treat them as labels than if you preface them with REMs.

If you do use labels to insert comments, be sure that the first word of the comment is not the same as any of the real labels paired with a GOTO statement. DOS always starts searching for labels at the beginning of a batch file, and will stop as soon as it finds a match. If you have two identical labels in the same batch file, DOS will always jump to the first one and will never get around to any others with the same spelling.

DOS 2.x was fussy about having labels begin at the left edge of the screen, and it insisted that colons be in column 1. DOS 3.x, 4.0, and 5.0 are far more liberal.

Some users include a REM and the name of the batch file in each batch file:

```
ECHO OFF
REM This is DIRSORT.BAT
DIR | SORT
```

Not too many people ever want their REM statements to display, and most generally use colons instead to fool DOS into treating remarks like labels, which never print onscreen.

If you do want to print a message, it's probably better to use ECHO. But if you insist on sticking with REM, you can eliminate the actual word REM from the display. Just add a string of backspaces after the word REM. You can't do this when using COPY CON to create your batch files, since DOS uses the backspace key for making corrections. But any word processor that allows embedded control codes (such as *WordStar*) makes the process a snap. With *WordStar* you can enter a backspace by typing Ctrl-P then Ctrl-H.

If your word processor can't imbed ASCII character 8 backspaces in your file, try running the following BASIC program, which will create a REMLESS.BAT demonstration file:

```
100 ' REMLESS.BAS — creates REMLESS.BAT test batchfile
110 OPEN "REMLESS.BAT" FOR OUTPUT AS #1
120 PRINT #1,"CLS"
130 PRINT #1,"REM this is a remark"
140 PRINT #1,"REM";STRING$(3,8);"this is a REMless remark"
150 CLOSE:END
```

GOTO

Format: **GOTO [:]LABEL**

This is a powerful command that sends control of a batch file (or *branches*) to another location in the batch file identified by a unique *label.*

A batch file label is simply a string of characters with a colon prefix in the leftmost column. (DOS 2.x is fussier than later versions about what constitutes the leftmost column; under 2.x the colon has to be at the very left edge of the screen. Version 3.x simply wants a colon as the first character, and can handle leading spaces and indentations.) The rules for naming labels are virtually the same as for naming files, except that for some reason, DOS version 3.x accepts question marks as labels. If you ran the following QUESTION.BAT batch file using version 3.x:

```
ECHO OFF
ECHO This is the first line
GOTO ???
ECHO This middle line won't appear
:???
ECHO This is the bottom line
```

The middle line won't ever appear, since the GOTO ??? command skips around it and jumps execution directly to the :??? label. However, other illegal filename characters such as < >[ ]|;,*=." won't work.

Run QUESTION.BAT under version 2.x, however, and DOS would display the first line onscreen but stumble over the ??? and print a "Label not found" error message. If DOS scans all the way through a batch file and can't locate a label specified by a GOTO command, it prints this message and stops the batch file in its tracks.

If you hadn't exactly matched the NONSTOP.BAT label with the reference in the GOTO command:

ECHO OFF		ECHO OFF		ECHO	
:TOPP	*or*	:TOP	*or*	OFF	
DECIDE		DECIDE		:TOP	
GOTO TOP		GOTO		DECIDE	

each example would run the DECIDE program once then grind to a halt.

It's smart to give your labels names that help you debug, enlarge, or otherwise adapt them later. So you'd be better off changing QUESTION.BAT to read:

```
ECHO OFF
ECHO This is the first line
GOTO CONTINUE
ECHO This middle line won't appear
:CONTINUE
ECHO This is the bottom line
```

DOS is fussy about not allowing reserved devices names (such as CON and NUL) in filenames, so it won't let you create a file such as NUL.BAT or PRN.TXT. But you can use these as batch labels. So the RESERVED.BAT file:

```
ECHO OFF
GOTO CON
:NUL
ECHO This is NUL
GOTO PRN
:AUX
ECHO This is AUX
GOTO END
:CON
ECHO This is CON
GOTO NUL
ECHO This is the right place
:PRN
ECHO This is PRN
GOTO AUX
:END
```

would print out:

```
This is CON
This is NUL
This is PRN
This is AUX
```

When DOS hunts for labels it starts at the top of the batch file and works down toward the end. So if you try the following NEVER.BAT batch file with duplicate labels:

```
ECHO OFF
GOTO LABEL1
REM Dummy line
:LABEL1
ECHO It will print this
GOTO END
:LABEL1
ECHO It will never print this
:END
```

when DOS sees the GOTO LABEL1 label it will jump to the first instance of it and never get to the second one. Even if you moved the GOTO command below the first occurrence of the label it specifies:

```
ECHO OFF
REM Dummy line
:LABEL1
ECHO It will keep printing this
GOTO LABEL1
:LABEL1
ECHO It will never print this
:END
```

DOS will still circle back to the beginning of the file and jump to the first :LABEL1 label. In this particular case it would display the "It will keep printing this" line and then loop back endlessly — or at least until you type Ctrl-C or Ctrl- ScrollLock and then Y to stop it.

While you can use very long label names in your batch files, such as:

```
:THIS_IS_WHERE_THE_PROGRAM_WILL_GO_NEXT
```

all that DOS really cares about is the first eight letters, not including the colon, which isn't actually part of the label.

So under version 3.x, 4.0, and 5.0, running the LONG.BAT batch file:

```
ECHO OFF
GOTO THIS_IS_
GOTO END
:THIS_IS_WHERE_THE_PROGRAM_WILL_GO_NEXT
ECHO Yes, the program did get here.
:END
```

will print out:

```
Yes, the program did get here.
```

since DOS whittles the THIS_IS_WHERE_THE_PROGRAM_WILL_GO_NEXT label down to THIS_IS_.

Unfortunately, different versions of DOS handle long label names differently. While DOS 3.x truncates extra long labels, DOS 2.x doesn't. Under version 2.x, the long

```
:THIS_IS_WHERE_THE_PROGRAM_WILL_GO_NEXT
```

label is totally different from:

```
:THIS_IS_
```

So under 2.x, running the above batch file would simply display "Label not found."

If you tried using long, similar label names, in the following variation of the above NEVER.BAT batch file under 3.x, 4.0, or 5.0:

```
ECHO OFF
GOTO LONGLABEL1
REM Dummy line
:LONGLABEL2
ECHO This is the wrong place.
GOTO END
:LONGLABEL1
ECHO This is the right place.
:END
```

DOS would print out:

```
This is the wrong place.
```

because it would interpret the GOTO LONGLABEL1 command simply as GOTO LONGLABE, and truncate the :LONGLABEL2 label (which is ten characters long) to simply LONGLABE. So to this version of DOS, the NEVER.BAT batch file really looks like:

```
ECHO OFF
GOTO LONGLABE
REM Dummy line
:LONGLABE
ECHO This is the wrong place.
GOTO END
:LONGLABE
ECHO This is the right place.
:END
```

But try to run this new NEVER.BAT batch file under DOS 2.x and all you'll get is a nasty "Label not found" error, since DOS will chop off the end of the instruction "GOTO LONGLABEL1" and turn it into "GOTO LONGLABE." It will then scan through the batch file looking for a ":LONGLABE" label but will find only ":LONGLABEL1" and ":LONGLABEL2" and it will consider these to be different from plain old ":LONGLABE."

If you shortened the labels in NEVER.BAT down to the maximum eight characters long:

```
ECHO OFF
GOTO LONGLBL1
REM Dummy line
:LONGLBL2
ECHO This is the wrong place.
GOTO END
:LONGLBL1
ECHO This is the right place.
:END
```

and then ran it under any version of DOS, you'd see:

```
This is the right place.
```

Be sure to put a colon in the leftmost column when you actually use a label on a line by itself to tell the batch file where to jump. You don't have to attach the colon to the label name in the GOTO command, but it won't hurt. The original NONSTOP.BAT batch file could would work either way:

```
ECHO OFF              ECHO OFF
:TOP                  :TOP
          or
DECIDE                DECIDE
GOTO TOP              GOTO :TOP
   │                     │
   │                     │
(no colon)            (colon)
```

Batch files often boast multiple GOTO commands that share the same label destination. It's common practice to end complex batch files with an ":END" label and include lots of different GOTO END commands that will jump execution there when appropriate.

DOS doesn't mind if you include labels in your batch files that aren't matched with GOTO commands. Such unreferenced labels are treated as REM statements, except that DOS will never display them. (It will display REM statements if ECHO is turned on.)

Labels are not case sensitive, so a batch file such as:

```
:tOp
ECHO This line will keep printing.
GOTO ToP
```

will loop until you press Ctrl-C or Ctrl-ScrollLock. Later you'll see how useful this can be in branching user input to the right label without having to do all sorts of repetitive tests for TOP, top, Top, ToP, TOp, toP, etc.

If your batch file does contain an error such as a missing label, DOS won't detect the mistake unless it tries unsuccessfully to execute it. So a batch file like:

```
ECHO OFF
GOTO END
GOTO ABCD
:END
ECHO This is the end
```

will execute flawlessly, since DOS will never have the chance to see that the :ABCD label is missing.

You may mix GOTO commands with conditional IF commands:

```
IF %1==RED GOTO COLOR
```

or:

```
IF NOT ERRORLEVEL 255 GOTO END
```

This lets you include provisions for many different potential user responses or system configurations in one large batch file, and branch to the one that's appropriate.

You can easily exploit the case-insensitivity of labels. It's common to ask a user to enter information from the command line and then have your batch file process this information so it can branch properly. This is usually done by handling the user input as a replaceable parameter (such as %1 or %2) and then passing it through a series of IF %1==STRING tests. If the user entered a parameter n characters long, you would normally have to set up 2^n tests to trap every possible combination of uppercase and lowercase letters.

Even if the user entered a three-letter parameter from the command line, you'd have to examine eight potential variations. If you were testing for JFK to jump to the :AIRPORT label, this would mean a cascade of tests:

```
IF %1==JFK GOTO AIRPORT
IF %1==JFk GOTO AIRPORT
IF %1==JfK GOTO AIRPORT
IF %1==jFK GOTO AIRPORT
IF %1==jFk GOTO AIRPORT
IF %1==jfK GOTO AIRPORT
IF %1==jfk GOTO AIRPORT
```

And all these tests are for just one possible user parameter. If you had to test for other airports the batch file would quickly grow long and ponderous.

Because labels are case-insensitive, you could eliminate all these tests by having one "dispatcher" line at the beginning of your batch file:

```
GOTO %1
```

You'd then make the label names the same as the parameters that the user might enter. So if you had a :JFK label (or one spelled :jfk or :Jfk, etc.) in a batch file called FLIGHT.BAT, and the user entered:

```
FLIGHT JFK
```

or:

```
FLIGHT jfk
```

or even something like:

```
FLIGHT jFk
```

the GOTO %1 dispatcher would branch immediately to the :JFK label without having to wade through dozens of tests.

However, while the IF %1==STRING method lets you screen out every possible right or wrong entry, a GOTO %1 command won't test for invalid entries or errant keystrokes. If a label exists that exactly matches the letters in the parameter the user entered, the batch file will jump execution to it. But if the user entered a parameter for which there was no matching label, DOS would panic, print a "Label not found" error message, and abort the batch file.

CALL

Format: **CALL [d:][path]filename**

Starting with version 3.3, this lets you execute one batch file from inside another and return execution to the original batch file when the second one finishes. When DOS returns command to the original batch file it will jump to the line immediately following the CALL. Beginning with version 2.x, users had been able to nest batch files by using COMMAND /C to load additional command processors, but this had environment drawbacks, and ate up unnecessary space.

Each time you load another command processor, it makes the default ECHO ON. This means that if you turn ECHO OFF in the first line of a batch file, and then use COMMAND /C to load a second batch file, you'll have to include a second ECHO OFF in the second batch file to keep DOS from cluttering up your display. But when you use CALL the ECHO state is maintained in any nested batch files so you don't have to keep resetting it.

However, COMMAND /C has its uses. While DOS claims you can't nest FOR commands, you can do it by inserting a COMMAND /C at the right place. This technique won't work with CALL.

Both COMMAND /C and CALL let you nest batch files several levels deep. You may have a batch file CALL itself, so long as you're certain you'll be able to exit properly and avoid an endless loop.

If you have a file on your disk called BATCH1.BAT:

```
ECHO OFF
ECHO This is BATCH1.BAT
COMMAND /C BATCH2
ECHO Now you're back to BATCH1
```

and another one called BATCH2.BAT:

```
ECHO OFF
ECHO Now you're in BATCH2.BAT
```

and you run BATCH1.BAT in any version of DOS 2.0 or later, DOS will:

1. Start executing BATCH1.BAT by turning ECHO OFF and printing just the "This is BATCH1.BAT" message.
2. Load a second copy of COMMAND.COM.
3. Have this additional copy of COMMAND.COM start running BATCH2.BAT.
4. Turn ECHO OFF and print just the "Now you're in BATCH2.BAT" message.
5. Exit both BATCH2.BAT and the second copy of COMMAND.COM.
6. Return to BATCH1.BAT.
7. Print the final "Now you're back to BATCH1" message.

This will take a few seconds, since DOS has to find a copy of COMMAND.COM to load, read it off the disk into memory, and then load and run the second batch file. The whole process will look like:

```
C>ECHO OFF
This is BATCH1.BAT

C>ECHO OFF
Now you're in BATCH2.BAT
Now you're back to BATCH1
```

If you're using a DOS version 3.3 or later, you can change BATCH1.BAT to read:

```
ECHO OFF
ECHO This is BATCH1.BAT
CALL BATCH2
ECHO Now you're back to BATCH1
```

This time DOS doesn't have to hunt for a version of COMMAND.COM to load. And it doesn't need the additional ECHO OFF at the beginning of BATCH2.BAT. The process takes far less time and will look like:

```
C>ECHO OFF
This is BATCH1.BAT
Now you're in BATCH2.BAT
Now you're back to BATCH1
```

If you try the COMMAND /C version, be sure you have a copy of COMMAND.COM handy for the batch file to load. And also note that when you load a secondary command processor you have to turn ECHO OFF again in the second batch file.

DOS is very liberal about handling different COMMAND /C syntaxes. All of the following versions will work identically:

- COMMAND   /C   BATCH2
- COMMAND/C   BATCH2
- COMMAND   /CBATCH2
- COMMAND/CBATCH2

Don't assume that DOS will be so cavalier about spacing with most other commands. It's not.

Fast Exits

Users often want to have DOS treat direct calls to batch programs the same way it handles other executable commands from within batch files — as subroutines. You can call another batch file by loading a secondary command processor that runs the second batch file and then returns to the first, or you can use CALL to turn batch branches into subroutines (in versions 3.3 or above).

However, calls to executable programs and system commands *always* act as subroutine calls, returning processing to the next line in the batch file. Many times it's necessary for a batch file to branch to one other command after an IF test and then exit. This is usually done with a cumbersome and clutter-producing GOTO command that branches to another part of the batch program, runs the desired command, and then branches again to a common exit point, such as a final line called :END.

All this branching, especially in long batch programs, can be time-consuming and confusing to edit. An quick alternative is to capitalize on DOS's absolute branching feature by calling a batch file that simply runs a program or an internal DOS command and then quits. A tiny DO.BAT batch file can accomplish this for you with just one line:

```
@%1 %2 %3 %4
```

(The initial @ will prevent the line from displaying, and works only in versions 3.3 or later. Omit it if you're using an older version of DOS.)

This technique works very quickly. Just have an IF test (or an IF ERRORLEVEL check) branch to an executable DOS command or COM or EXE program and then quit.

As an example, you could use DO.BAT in a program called #.BAT that displays either a selected phone number or your entire phone list, depending on whether you specify a parameter when you run it. So:

```
# Nixon
```

or:

```
# (212)
```

would find all listings with Nixon or (212) in them, while:

```
#
```

by itself would display the entire list. The batch file looks like:

```
ECHO OFF
REM #.BAT
IF %1!==! DO TYPE C:\DATA\PHONE.DAT
FIND "%1" C:\DATA\PHONE.DAT
```

Of course, #.BAT is short and doesn't really need such a trick. But DO.BAT does save time and space. Without it, the original batch file would have been written:

```
ECHO OFF
REM #.BAT
IF !%1==! GOTO SEELIST
FIND "%1" C:\DATA\PHONE.DAT
GOTO END
:SEELIST
TYPE C:\DATA\PHONE.DAT
:END
```

You can adapt this technique with two other speedy batch files — ABORT.BAT and COMPLETE.BAT — that can branch absolutely. These will quickly quit any batch file after an IF check, with the option of including a message:

```
REM ABORT.BAT
IF NOT %1!==! ECHO %1 %2 %3 %4 %5 %6 %7 %8 %9
ECHO Operation aborted.
```

```
REM COMPLETE.BAT
IF NOT %1!==! ECHO %1 %2 %3 %4 %5 %6 %7 %8 %9
ECHO Operation completed.
```

So you can have a line in your program like:

```
IF NOT EXIST ABC ABORT ABC not found.
```

If DOS doesn't find ABC, the batch file will quit without executing any GOTO statements and display:

```
ABC not found.
Operation aborted.
```

If the words after ABORT had been omitted, then the only closing message would be "Operation aborted."

You can combine the two techniques into one big #.BAT batch file:

```
ECHO OFF
REM #.BAT
IF NOT EXIST ABC ABORT ABC not found.
IF %1!==! DO TYPE C:\DATA\PHONE.DAT
FIND "%1" C:\DATA\PHONE.DAT
```

In this case, whether or not you type anything after the #, the program simply won't proceed if ABC isn't on your disk. If you create a dummy ABC file (that contains just the word REM), the program will bypass this test and look up numbers with aplomb. If you erase ABC, all you'll get is the:

```
ABC not found.
Operation aborted.
```

message and the #.BAT file will grind to a halt.

These examples assume that you have a list of your phone numbers called PHONE.DAT in your C:\DATA directory, and that this file is in a form, with each entry on one line with a carriage return at the end of it, that FIND can handle.

Passing Parameters

You may pass parameters from one batch file to another. Just include a parameter after the filename on the line with the CALL or the COMMAND /C.

If you had a file on your disk called TEST1.BAT:

```
@ECHO OFF
ECHO this is TEST1
CALL TEST2 TESTPARM
ECHO Back to TEST1
```

and another called TEST2.BAT that was called by TEST1.BAT:

```
ECHO This is TEST2
ECHO %1
```

if you ran TEST1, you'd see:

```
This is TEST1
This is TEST2
TESTPARM
Back to TEST1
```

The first batch file passed the parameter TESTPARM to the second by including it after the name of the file it called. The second batch file picked up the parameter with %1.

If you're using a version of DOS earlier than 3.3, substitute COMMAND /C in place of CALL, and add an additional ECHO OFF line at the very beginning of TEST2.BAT.

You can make this process more useful by blitzing out parameters repeatedly with a FOR command.

If you run the following FIL1.BAT batch file:

```
@ECHO OFF
Echo Starting out in FIL1.BAT
FOR %%A in (*.BAK) DO CALL FIL2 %%A
ECHO Back to batch file #1
```

the third line will CALL the next FIL2.BAT batch file:

```
ECHO OFF
ECHO **********************
ECHO Now you're in FIL2.BAT
ECHO The contents of %1 are:
TYPE %1
ECHO **********************
PAUSE
```

and pass parameters from FIL1.BAT to FIL2.BAT using the %%A in FIL1.BAT and the %1 in FIL2.BAT.

FIL1.BAT will seek out all the files that have BAK extensions and FIL2.BAT will ECHO the name of each one and then use TYPE to display the contents of each one. After FIL2.BAT has displayed the last *.BAK file, it will stop running and DOS will return command to the line in FIL1.BAT following the line with the CALL. If you try this yourself and you're using an older version of DOS, substitute COMMAND /C for CALL.

Later you'll see how you can construct some very useful disk management utilities by combining FOR commands with CALL or COMMAND /C.

You can also pass values to other batch files without having to first load them with COMMAND /C or CALL. Just use SET to store the value as an environment variable.

You can have your batch files detect whether any specified settings are currently in force with a test like:

```
IF %MONITOR%!==! GOTO NOSETTNG
```

You could test to see if you had previously set any variables, check the validity of the setting, and act on it with a batch file like this:

```
ECHO OFF
IF %MONITOR%!==! GOTO SETMON
IF %MONITOR%==MONO GOTO GREENCOL
IF %MONITOR%==mono GOTO GREENCOL
IF %MONITOR%==COLOR GOTO NORMLCOL
IF %MONITOR%==color GOTO NORMLCOL
ECHO %MONITOR% monitor setting invalid
GOTO END
```

```
:SETMON
ECHO No monitor variable in use
GOTO END
:GREENCOL
ECHO Mono attribute setter would go here
GOTO END
:NORMLCOL
ECHO Color setter would go here
:END
```

FOR...IN...DO

This integrated trio allows repeated execution of a command on a specified set of files. The format is :

```
FOR %%variable IN (set) DO command [%%variable]
```

inside batch files, and:

```
FOR %variable IN (set) DO command [%variable]
```

outside of batch files. (Note that you use double %% signs inside batch files and single % signs outside batch files.)

%%variable and %variable are variable names, generally single letters such as %%a or %Z. You can't use the digits 0-9 for variable names, since DOS reserves these for replaceable parameters.

(set) is the filespec or collection of filespecs that DOS will act on, and can be a wildcard such as:

```
(*.*)
```

or:

```
(*.BAK)
```

or a group of files such as:

```
(MORE.ASM MORE.OBJ MORE.COM)
```

So a batch file command such as:

```
FOR %%A IN (*.*) DO DEL %%A
```

would erase all the files in your directory one by one without asking for a confirming:

```
Are you sure (Y/N)?
```

the way DEL *.* does.

However, a batch file that used a FOR command to delete all your files would end up erasing itself, and you'd get a "Batch file missing" error message. To avoid this, put a drive letter or path in front of the *.* and run it from another directory or drive.

To see a directory listing of all you COM and EXE files, you'd type:

```
FOR %%A in (*.COM *.EXE) DO DIR %%A
```

Be sure to add the final %%A. If you leave it off, DOS won't do a DIR *.COM and a DIR *.EXE. Instead it will just do a plain old DIR, since there wouldn't be any parameters after it. When you don't enter any parameters after DIR, DOS assumes you mean:

```
DIR *.*
```

The command:

```
FOR %%A in (*.COM *.EXE) DO DIR
```

would sniff out all the files that ended in COM and EXE, but would end up doing the same repeated DIR *.* listing for each occurrence of a COM or EXE file. So if there are two COM files and three EXE files, DOS will do a DIR *.* command five times. You must add the %%variable command onto the end for the FOR command to act on what you've specified in the (set).

Be sure that the %%variable matches in case at the beginning and end of the line.

```
FOR %%A IN (*.BAK) DO DEL %%A
```

and:

```
FOR %%a IN (*.BAK) DO DEL %%a
```

will erase all your BAK files, but:

```
FOR %%a IN (*.BAK) DO DEL %%A
```

and:

```
FOR %%A IN (*.BAK) DO DEL %%a
```

won't.

If you had a lot of quarterly expense reports on your disk, with names like 88Q1EXP.RPT, 88Q2EXP.RPT, 88Q3EXP.RPT, 88Q4EXP.RPT, 87Q4EXP.RPT, 87Q3EXP.RPT, 87Q2EXP.RPT, and 87Q1EXP.RPT, and you wanted to print out just the ones from the first and second quarters, you could run a batch file with the single line:

```
FOR %%A IN (1 2) DO COPY 8?Q%%AEXP.RPT PRN
```

DOS would replace the ? with the last digit of the year (7 or 8) and replace the %%A with 1 or 2.

One of the simplest and most useful FOR applications can check to see whether you've backed up your files, and will make backup copies only when you haven't. Just create a one-line batch file, called BACKCHEK.BAT:

```
FOR %%A IN (*.*) DO IF NOT EXIST B:%%A COPY %%A B:
```

This is far from the perfect backup tool, since it won't copy newer versions of files over older ones, or pause when your B: diskette is full and prompt you to insert another floppy. And it works within one directory only. But it can come in handy for quick brute-force backups and puts a lot of DOS intelligence into one line.

By adding replaceable parameters you can enhance this one-line backup command to accept filespecs from the command line and copy files to another disk or subdirectory only if they're not already there. The following COPYFAST.BAT batch file will do it:

```
ECHO OFF
IF %2!==! GOTO HELP
ECHO Copying files from %1 that are not already on %2
CTTY NUL
FOR %%A IN (%1) DO IF NOT EXIST %2%%A COPY %%A %2
CTTY CON
GOTO END
:HELP
ECHO %0 copies files from a source disk or directory to a
ECHO destination if they're NOT already on the destination.
ECHO Syntax: %0 *.* c:
ECHO %0 *.DOC \subdir
ECHO You must be in the directory you want to copy from.
:END
```

This batch file uses CTTY NUL to disconnect the keyboard and screen temporarily so you don't see a long line of "1 File(s) copied" messages. The CTTY CON command puts things back the way they were. Unfortunately, if something goes wrong after the CTTY NUL but before the CTTY CON has a chance to return control to you, you'll be locked out of your system. If you want to avoid this potential problem, without having to concoct a scheme where this batch file loads another batch file, just remove the two lines that begin with CTTY.

You can adapt this technique to help make various directory chores a whole lot easier. For instance, if you want to compare the contents of two disks or a disk with a subdirectory to see which files are in one and not in the other, you can use the UNIQ.BAT batch file:

```
ECHO OFF
IF %2!==! GOTO HELP
ECHO Files on %1 but not on %2
FOR %%A IN (%1*.*) DO IF NOT EXIST %2%%A ECHO %%A
ECHO Files on %2 but not on %1
FOR %%A IN (%2*.*) DO IF NOT EXIST %1%%A ECHO %%A
GOTO END
:HELP
ECHO %0 lists files that are not on both disks
ECHO Syntax: %0 A: C: where C: is the default drive
:END
```

To have UNIQ.BAT tell you what files are on drive C: but not drive B: and vice versa, just type:

```
UNIQ C: B:
```

This won't work with DOS versions earlier than 3.0, since these can't handle IF EXIST searches with paths in them.

If you want to log the list of files reported by UNIQ.BAT to disk rather than just displaying them on the screen, create a small file called LOG.BAT:

```
ECHO OFF
IF !%2==! GOTO OOPS
COMMAND /C UNIQ %1 %2 > LOGFILE
GOTO END
:OOPS
ECHO Syntax: %0 A: C: where C: is the default drive
:END
```

Combining the FOR command with both replaceable parameters and environment variables gives it real power. If your path included the root directory (which is why the NOT test is required) and it specified subdirectories on one disk only, a batch file called PATHDIR.BAT containing the command:

```
FOR %%A IN (%PATH%) DO IF NOT %%A==C:\ DIR %%A\%1
```

would let you find all your COM files in all the subdirectories in your PATH by typing:

```
PATHDIR *.COM
```

DOS would replace the %PATH% variable with the actual list of subdirectories specified by your PATH command, and the FOR command would perform a DIR search through each for any *.COM files. Elements in the set must be separated by delimiters such as spaces, but the semicolons used in path specifications will work admirably.

To use the FOR command directly at the DOS prompt, replace the twin %% signs with single % signs. However, double %% signs are required for use in batch files.

DOS won't normally let one FOR command execute another FOR command. Try it and DOS will print a "FOR cannot be nested" error message. However, you can make an end run around this restriction by having the first FOR load a secondary command processor right before the second FOR.

If you try nesting these without COMMAND /C in a batch file called FOR-NEST1.BAT:

```
FOR %%A IN (1 2) DO FOR %%B IN (A B) DO ECHO %%A %%B
```

you'll just get a "FOR cannot be nested" error message. But create a file called FORNEST2.BAT that adds a COMMAND /C to invoke a secondary command processor:

```
FOR %%A IN (1 2) DO COMMAND/C FOR %%B IN (A B) DO ECHO %%A %%B
```

and sure enough DOS will execute it, nest the two commands, and print:

```
C>FOR %A IN (1 2) DO COMMAND/C FOR %B IN (A B) DO ECHO %A %B

C>COMMAND/C FOR %B IN (A B) DO ECHO 1 %B
C>ECHO 1 A
1 A

C>ECHO 1 B
1 B

C>COMMAND/C FOR %B IN (A B) DO ECHO 2 %B
C>ECHO 2 A
2 A

C>ECHO 2 B
2 B
```

You could reduce the clutter a bit by adding an initial ECHO OFF, but this won't suppress the bulk of the display since DOS turns ECHO back on when it loads the second copy of COMMAND.COM. This nesting technique works only with COMMAND /C, so if you're using a DOS version 3.3 or later, don't try replacing the COMMAND /C with CALL.

Commands like COPY and DIR don't take multiple arguments. A way around this is to have DOS execute the command multiple times, each with a different argument. For example, to copy all COM and EXE files to a floppy disk, you could type directly at the DOS prompt:

```
FOR %F IN (*.COM *.EXE) DO COPY %F A:
```

While this works, DOS will grind through the process one file at a time rather than ganging things up as it does with wildcards.

Using a FOR loop on the command line isn't limited to just filenames. Commands can also be used as FOR loop variables as in:

```
FOR %C IN (COPY ERASE) DO %C A:*.EXE
```

to copy .EXE files from a floppy disk, then erase them from the disk.

Another way to do multiple copies on the same command line is to use piping. The following command will copy all your COM and EXE files to drive A:

```
COPY *.COM A: | COPY *.EXE A:
```

PAUSE

Format: **PAUSE [message]**

This momentarily halts execution. Nothing more.

PAUSE is helpful if you have to change disks, turn on a printer, or perform some other time-consuming task, since it puts the batch file on hold until you press a key to continue:

```
ECHO Put a blank formatted
ECHO diskette in drive A:
PAUSE
```

Used on a line by itself, this command temporarily halts the batch file execution, then prints a "Strike a key when ready . . ." message, and waits for the user to press any nonshift key other than Ctrl-C or Ctrl-ScrollLock. If the user presses either of those "break" key combinations the process aborts and DOS displays the usual interruption message "Terminate batch job (Y/N)?".

If you type Y or y DOS will abort the batch file and return you to whatever you were doing before. If you type N or n, DOS will continue running the batch file as if nothing had happened. Press any other key and DOS will stubbornly repeat the "Terminate..." message.

It's possible to put a message after the word PAUSE, but this message displays only when ECHO is off, which means that the user also sees the DOS prompt and the word PAUSE. Very unsightly.

Users of version 3.x and later can replace the normal "Strike a key when ready" message with an ECHO command and then redirect the normal PAUSE output to NUL with a trio of lines like:

```
ECHO OFF
ECHO Make sure your printer is on, then press any key
PAUSE > NUL
```

but this won't suppress the "Strike" message on older versions. If users of DOS 2.x want to display a message, they can at least prevent the word PAUSE from showing up onscreen by putting five backspaces directly after it. They can add backspace characters using most good word processors (with *WordStar*, for example, they'd simply type Ctrl-P Ctrl-H five times).

Replaceable Parameters

%0 %1 %2 %3 %4 %5 %6 %7 %8 %9

These handy tools let batch files use text entered on the DOS command line to control how the batch files work or display custom messages and prompts.

When you execute a batch file, DOS scans the command line, looks for delimiters such as spaces, equals signs, semicolons, commas, and tabs that separate what you entered into discrete chunks, and then assigns the text that makes up these chunks to ten variables — %0 through %9.

DOS can handle up to 127 characters typed on the command line. If you enter more than nine separate clumps of text after the name of a batch file, DOS can't immediately assign replaceable parameters to anything past the ninth one. But by using the SHIFT command, you can have DOS gradually work its way through them all.

If you enter fewer than nine discrete parameters after the name of the batch file, DOS assigns *null strings* that are zero characters long to any variables for which there isn't any text.

The first discrete chunk of text is assigned to %0. This is always the name of the batch file itself. The next is assigned to %1, and the one after that to %2, etc.

If you run the simple ENDLESS.BAT batch file, the sole contents of which are the two characters:

```
%0
```

DOS will substitute the name of the batch file itself — ENDLESS — for the %0, and then execute it, which will rerun itself until you press Ctrl-C or Ctrl-ScrollLock and then type Y to stop.

When DOS replaces the variables with the actual text from the command line, it's sensitive about spacing. So if you created a batch file called OVER.BAT:

```
%1%2%3%4 %1 %2 %3 %4
```

and then ran it by typing:

```
OVER O V E R
```

DOS would keep repeating the batch file endlessly since it would concatenate the O, the V, the, E, and the R that you entered after the batch file name itself, and lump them together into OVER.

You can display all the replaceable parameters you entered with the following short SEEALL.BAT batch file:

```
ECHO OFF
FOR %%A IN (%0 %1 %2 %3 %4 %5 %6 %7 %8 %9) DO IF NOT
%%A!==! ECHO %%A
```

If you type in just SEEALL, all you'll get is:

```
SEEALL
```

But enter something like:

```
C>SEEALL 12345 abc LMNOP !!!!!!!
```

and the batch file will print out:

```
SEALL
12345
abc
LMNOP
!!!!!!!
```

If you have ANSI.SYS loaded, and you use a color monitor and like white backgrounds, but you sometimes want black text, red text, or blue text, you could create a file called TEXT.BAT:

```
ECHO OFF
IF %1!==! GOTO OOPS
GOTO %1
:OOPS
ECHO Enter %0 BLUE or %0 RED or %0 BLACK
GOTO END
:BLUE
ECHO ESC[0;47;34m
GOTO END
:BLACK
ECHO ESC[0;47;30m
GOTO END
```

```
: RED
ECHO ESC[0;47;31m
: END
```

Note: Don't type this in exactly as shown — instead, substitute the actual Esc character, decimal ASCII 27 (or hex 1B) in place of the three occurrences of "ESC." Also, be sure your CONFIG.SYS file includes a line like:

```
DEVICE=ANSI.SYS
```

If you've loaded ANSI.SYS and have inserted actual Esc characters in place of each ESC, you can change your foreground color to red simply by typing:

```
TEXT RED
```

just as shown, or in mixed case or lowercase — it doesn't matter.

Typing TEXT BLACK will give you black text on a white background, and TEXT BLUE will yield blue letters against white. However, if you typed simply:

```
TEXT
```

without any color after it, TEXT.BAT would print out instructions on how to use this file, and quit. You'd see something like:

```
Enter TEXT BLUE or TEXT RED or TEXT BLACK
```

The line that prints the instructions:

```
ECHO Enter %0 BLUE or %0 RED or %0 BLACK
```

uses %0 rather than the name TEXT.BAT, so if you rename TEXT.BAT to something like FOREGRND.BAT or COLORSET.BAT the instructions will always print out the correct new batch filename.

This batch file uses labels that are the same as the replaceable parameters entered by the user. Labels are not case-sensitive, so this technique eliminates the long list of tests normally required to see whether a user entered Red, RED, or ReD, for example.

To see whether you did enter a color on the command line, TEXT.BAT uses the line:

```
IF %1!==! GOTO OOPS
```

If you entered something like:

```
TEXT RED
```

DOS would assign replaceable parameter %1 the value RED. It would then replace each occurrence of %1 in the batch file with RED, so the test would become:

```
IF RED!==! GOTO OOPS
```

Since the characters "RED!" obviously do not equal the single character "!" the test fails and the batch file does not jump execution to the :OOPS label.

However, if the user didn't enter any color, and simply typed:

```
TEXT
```

on the DOS command line, %1 would be equal to (nothing) and the test would become:

```
IF !==! GOTO OOPS
```

Clearly, "!" is equal to "!" so the batch file will execute the command at the end of the line, which jumps execution to the :OOPS label. The commands at this label will print instructions on how to use the program and then quit.

You don't have to use exclamation points; any pair of characters will do. The test could just as easily have been:

```
IF %1@==@ GOTO OOPS
```

If you didn't mind slogging through a cascade of case-sensitive tests, and you were willing to forego tests for unusual capitalizations such as bLuE, you could change the top of the batch file so that TEXT.BAT looked like:

```
ECHO OFF
IF %1!==! GOTO OOPS
IF %1==BLUE GOTO COL1
IF %1==blue GOTO COL1
IF %1==BLACK GOTO COL2
IF %1==black GOTO COL2
IF %1==RED GOTO COL3
IF %1==red GOTO COL3
:OOPS
ECHO Enter %0 BLUE or %0 RED or %0 BLACK
GOTO END
:COL1
ECHO ESC[0;47;34m
GOTO END
:COL2
ECHO ESC[0;47;30m
```

```
GOTO END
:COL3
ECHO ESC[0;47;31m
:END
```

In this case if the user entered a color that TEXT.BAT wasn't able to handle, such as:

```
TEXT MAUVE
```

the batch file would pass the first IF %1!==! test, but fail all six IF %1==COLOR tests. Execution would "fall through" this sieve of tests and end up at the :OOPS label, where the batch file would display the message about which colors were allowed, and then exit.

Unfortunately, if the user entered:

```
TEXT Blue
```

the batch file would think this was a disallowed color, since the only versions of color entries that TEXT.BAT is prepared to accept are all uppercase and all lowercase. It would be easy to add an additional test for each color that accepted variations where the first letter was uppercase and all the remaining ones were lowercase. But then if the user entered:

```
TEXT BLue
```

(which is a common typing mistake), the batch file wouldn't recognize this variant.

There is a way to get around this (DOS is nothing if not flexible), but it's preposterous. Add a few lines so the TEXT.BAT file looks like:

```
ECHO OFF
IF %1!==! GOTO OOPS
ECHO :%1 > TEMPFILE
ECHO COPY %0.BAK %0.BAT >> TEMPFILE
ECHO DEL %0.BAK >> TEMPFILE
COPY %0.BAT %0.BAK > NUL
COPY %0.BAT+TEMPFILE > NUL
DEL TEMPFILE
GOTO %1
:OOPS
ECHO Enter %0 BLUE or %0 RED or %0 BLACK
GOTO END
:BLUE
ECHO ESC[0;47;34m
GOTO END
:BLACK
ECHO ESC[0;47;30m
GOTO END
```

```
:RED
ECHO ESC[0;47;31m
:END
```

This uses the ECHO command and DOS redirection to create a temporary file called TEMPFILE containing a brand new label that matches whatever you typed in, as well as some commands to copy and delete backup versions of the main file. TEXT.BAT then appends this new file to the end of itself. Since the new file contains a valid label, you won't get a "Label not found" message.

If you typed in an invalid color such as PUCE, you'll end up with a meaningless :PUCE label at the very end that won't change any colors and is there simply to guard against error messages. If you typed in a valid color such as RED, you'll end up with two :RED labels. However, since (1) this process appends the phony label at the end, (2) DOS starts looking for labels at the beginning of the file, and (3) DOS will execute the first occurrence of a label if a batch file contains more than one, TEXT.BAT will jump to the first :RED label and execute the proper command to set the foreground to red.

This enhancement will clean up after itself by making a backup copy of the original file, copying this unblemished backup copy onto the changed one, and then erasing the extra backup. But it's not really worth it. For one thing, DOS 2.x can become confused if you enter a label name that's longer than eight characters. And this won't work with any version of DOS if you enter an invalid label, such as one with a period in it. But it shows what you can do to get around a DOS bottleneck.

If you had a batch file on your disk called READBACK.BAT:

```
ECHO OFF
ECHO %0.BAT is the name of the batch file
ECHO %1
ECHO %2
ECHO %3
ECHO %4
ECHO %5
```

and you entered at the DOS prompt:

```
READBACK This message
```

you'd end up with:

```
C>ECHO OFF
READBACK.BAT is the name of the batch file
This
message
ECHO is off
ECHO is off
ECHO is off
```

DOS would substitute "READBACK" for %0, "This" for %1, and "message" for %2. But since you didn't enter any other text, DOS would make the parameters %3, %4, and %5 equal to nothing. When it got around to executing the lines:

```
ECHO %3
ECHO %4
ECHO %5
```

DOS would turn them into:

```
ECHO
ECHO
ECHO
```

and report the current ON/OFF ECHO state.

To prevent this from happening, you can put an ASCII character 0 at the end of each of the bottom five lines (by using EDLIN to create READBACK.BAT and pressing the F7 key and the end of each line).

Adding a character 0, which will appear onscreen as a blank, to each line will make sure that DOS will ECHO something and not interpret a missing parameter as just an ECHO command on a line by itself.

DOS can handle up to nine replaceable parameters %1 through %9 in one gulp, and will always replace %0 with the name of the batch file itself (just as it was entered at the DOS prompt). If you want to use more than nine replaceable parameters you have to use the SHIFT command.

SHIFT Parameters

Each time DOS executes the SHIFT command it moves each replaceable parameter down in value one notch. So the value that was stored as %3 moves down and becomes %2, and the value stored at %2 becomes %1, and %1 becomes %0 (which originally held the name of the batch file). Each time you execute SHIFT the old %0 value disappears.

If you had a batch file called SHIFTIT.BAT:

```
ECHO OFF
ECHO %0 %1 %2 %3
SHIFT
ECHO %0 %1 %2 %3
SHIFT
ECHO %0 %1 %2 %3
SHIFT
```

and you typed:

```
SHIFTIT A B C D
```

DOS would print:

```
C>ECHO OFF
SHIFTIT A B C
A B C D
B C D
```

as it shifted all the parameters down one by one.

In the first line DOS replaced %0 with the name of the batch file and printed three of the four letters entered on the command line. After the first shift, the name of the batch file disappears as DOS moves everything down a notch, but this time the batch file prints the fourth parameter entered on the command line (the D) even though the fourth parameter didn't appear the first time.

If you want to preserve the name of the batch file itself when using the SHIFT command, you have to set an environment variable as this new SHIFTIT2.BAT batch file does:

```
ECHO OFF
SET NAME=%0
ECHO %0 %1 %2 %3
SHIFT
ECHO %NAME% %0 %1 %2 %3
SHIFT
ECHO %NAME% %0 %1 %2 %3
SHIFT
SET NAME=
```

DOS will still wipe out the name of the batch file originally stored as %0 the first time it executes the SHIFT command, but it will still be able to remember and display it since you stored it as an environment variable called NAME with the:

```
SET NAME=%0
```

command, and then dredged it back up when you used the:

```
ECHO %NAME%
```

command. This time, using the same four parameters after SHIFTIT2.BAT:

```
SHIFTIT2 A B C D
```

would yield:

```
C>ECHO OFF
SHIFTIT2 A B C
```

```
SHIFTIT2 A B C D
SHIFTIT2 B C D
```

retaining the name of the batch file each time even though the SHIFT command wrote over it. Unfortunately, because of a DOS bug, environment variables won't work in version 3.0.

The SHIFT command can read as many parameters off the command line as you entered, and you can type in only 127 characters including the name of the batch file itself. If your batch file had a name that was just one letter long and you entered only single-character parameters, with spaces between them, you could have SHIFT squeeze out 63 of them. The MAXSHIFT.BAT batch file below:

```
ECHO OFF
:TOP
IF %1!==! GOTO END
ECHO %1
SHIFT
GOTO TOP
:END
```

will keep reading all the parameters off the command line and ECHOing them one by one until they've all been processed. You could enter:

```
MAXSHIFT A B C D E F G H I J K L M N O P Q R S T U V
```

and continue all the way through the uppercase and lowercase alphabets and MAXSHIFT would display every letter. It knows when to stop because it runs a:

```
IF %1!==! GOTO END
```

test each time it shifts. This test will be true (and it will stop displaying characters) only when %1 is finally equal to nothing because all the parameters have been used up. When this happens the test will become:

```
IF !==! GOTO END
```

Until then, %1! will always be equal to A! or B! or z! or whatever variable just shifted over. And something like:

```
IF A!==! GOTO END
```

will not be true, because "A!" is not equal to just "!" by itself.

Environment Variables

Format: **SET ENVVAR=VALUE** (*to create an environment variable*)
ECHO %ENVVAR% *or* **IF %ENVVAR%==PRESET GOTO LABEL**
(*to use it*)

Although it wasn't documented until PC-DOS version 3.3, doesn't always work properly with earlier versions, and doesn't work at all under 3.0, you may use a special section of memory called the environment as a storage area for variables.

You can see what DOS currently stores in your environment by typing SET at the DOS prompt. You'll always see a line beginning COMSPEC= which tells your system where to look for the COMMAND.COM command processor. And you'll probably also see your path, your PROMPT, and possibly an APPEND path and a few variables set by some commercial software (such as *WordPerfect*).

Entering the word SET followed by a variable name of your choice, then an equal sign, then a character string:

```
SET SCREEN=EGA
```

will add:

```
SCREEN=EGA
```

to your environment.

Once you've added a variable to your environment, you can change it simply by using another SET command:

```
SET SCREEN=VGA
```

You can remove the variable from the environment by entering the variable name and an equals sign with nothing after it:

```
SET SCREEN=
```

If you have two screens and you're changing to a monochrome display, the batch file that does the changing can also reset the SCREEN variable:

```
SET SCREEN=MONO
```

Then any other programs and batch files can tell which screen is active by looking at the %SCREEN% variable.

The ability to keep track of a state and pass the information to a batch file can help you debug batch files. When you're creating and testing a batch file you often want ECHO to be ON so you can see where any potential problems are. But when you run the batch file you want ECHO to be off so it doesn't clutter your screen with commands. To solve this, make the first line in your batch file:

```
ECHO %ECHO%
```

Then, at the DOS prompt, type:

```
SET ECHO=ON
```

when you want to see all the commands execute, and:

```
SET ECHO=OFF
```

when you want to suppress them.

Be careful when setting environment variables since they're case-sensitive and space-sensitive. If you set ECHO=ON you'll have to test for:

```
IF %ECHO%==ON GOTO OKAY
IF %ECHO%==on GOTO OKAY
IF %ECHO%==On GOTO OKAY
```

In addition, you should first test to see whether you've given the %ECHO% variable any setting at all, with a test like:

```
IF %ECHO%!==! GOTO NOTSET
```

And watch your typing if you reset environment variables. If you initially set ECHO=ON and you tried to reset the value to OFF by typing:

```
SET ECHO =OFF
```

DOS would think you were trying to establish an additional environment variable with a space as the fifth character, and you'd end up with two variables:

```
ECHO=ON
ECHO =OFF
```

The first one would be %ECHO% and the second would be %ECHO %.

However, while extra spaces are always a concern, you don't have to worry about case on the left side of the equals sign when setting a variable. The three commands:

- SET ECHO=OFF
- SET echo=OFF
- SET eChO=OFF

will all set an environment variable ECHO to OFF.

You can put all these tests into a batch file that would look like:

```
ECHO OFF
IF %ECHO%!==! GOTO NOTSET
IF %ECHO%==ON GOTO OKAY
IF %ECHO%==on GOTO OKAY
IF %ECHO%==On GOTO OKAY
IF %ECHO%==OFF GOTO OKAY
IF %ECHO%==off GOTO OKAY
IF %ECHO%==Off GOTO OKAY
ECHO %ECHO% is an invalid ECHO setting
GOTO END
:NOTSET
ECHO Set your ECHO variable
GOTO END
:OKAY
ECHO ECHO is current set to %ECHO%
:END
```

Note: If you insert too many strings into your environment you can run out of environment space. The default is a paltry ten 16-byte paragraphs, or 160 bytes.

Under DOS 2.0 and 2.1 you can patch COMMAND.COM at hex address ECF to represent the number of 16-byte memory paragraphs that will make up your new environment. (For DOS 2.11 the address is hex DF3.)

For DOS 3.0 and 3.1, there's a much better way. Just put a:

```
SHELL [d:][path]COMMAND.COM /E:n /P
```

command in your CONFIG.SYS file, where n represents the number of 16-byte paragraphs. For versions 3.2 and later, use the same SHELL command but specify the actual number of bytes rather than paragraphs. The default in all cases is 160 bytes (ten paragraphs). You can increase it all the way to 32K in DOS 3.2 and later, but you're limited to 62 paragraphs (992 bytes) in earlier versions.

IF

Format:

```
IF EXIST [d:][path]filename[.ext] command
IF NOT EXIST [d:][path]filename[.ext] command

IF string1==string2 command
IF NOT string1==string2 command
```

```
IF ERRORLEVEL number command
IF NOT ERRORLEVEL number command
```

IF allows conditional command execution. It is invaluable for finding files, string hand-ling, and other uses including IF ERRORLEVEL, DOS's undocumented gem.

File Finding

One of DOS's most powerful tools, IF allows batch files to execute specific commands or branch to specific batch routines depending on external conditions. This lets you make your batch files smarter and interactive, with the addition of a tiny utility to process user input (which DOS neglected to provide).

The simplest IF command tests whether a file is present. Under DOS 2.x, you couldn't specify a path, so all tests had to be within the current directory. However, DOS 3.x and later versions remedied this glaring oversight. The command:

```
IF EXIST HELP.TXT TYPE HELP.TXT
```

will display a HELP.TXT file only if one exists in the current directory. This can come in handy if you want to create a log file and check that the header in the file says what you want.

A section of a batch file like:

```
IF EXIST LOGFILE GOTO FOUNDIT
ECHO This is a new file > LOGFILE
:FOUNDIT
```

will create a new file and put a line of text in it only if no file with the specified name existed previously. Or, if you've kept a blank LOGFILE file in a subdirectory called C:\MISC, you could copy it to the current directory, if none existed, with the command:

```
IF NOT EXIST LOGFILE COPY C:\MISC\LOGFILE
```

Batch files often use DOS filters like MORE.COM, FIND.EXE, and SORT.EXE. It's simple to have a batch file check whether these happen to be in the current directory. But you can also tell it to see whether these files happen to be in a directory that your path knows about. If these executable files are either in the current directory or one specified by your path, a batch file that needs them will be able to do its job. If they're not in either of those places the batch file will stumble. You can test whether a file is in a directory your path can handle with a CHEKPATH.BAT batch file like:

```
ECHO OFF
IF %1!==! GOTO OOPS
FOR %%A IN (%PATH%) DO IF EXIST %%A\%1 GOTO YES
FOR %%A IN (%PATH%) DO IF EXIST %%A%1 GOTO YES
```

```
GOTO END
:YES
ECHO %1 is in a directory your PATH knows about
GOTO END
:OOPS
ECHO Enter a file (with extension) to search for
:END
```

DOS replaces the %PATH% in the FOR commands with your actual path, then has each FOR command execute an IF EXIST check in every directory your path specifies. All elements in a set specified by a FOR command have to be separated by normal DOS delimiters. Usually this delimiter is a space, and you end up with a set like:

```
(*.COM *.EXE *.BAT)
```

space   space

However, a semicolon works just as well as a space, and path directories happened to be separated by semicolons. So DOS translates a (%PATH%) set to something like:

```
(C:\;C:\DOS;C:\DOS\BIN)
```

which is the same as:

```
(C:\ C:\DOS C:\DOS\BIN)
```

You need both versions of the FOR test since your path can include directories that end in a backslash (such as C:\) as well as those that don't (such as C:\DOS). Fortunately, DOS won't choke on the inevitable syntax errors that result from some of the tests. Unfortunately, DOS versions earlier than 3.0 won't do an IF EXIST test outside the current directory. And 3.0 has trouble with environment variables such as %PATH%.

You'd obviously have to adapt this demonstration CHEKPATH.BAT batch file to look for the specific files your particular batch file needs.

If you're writing this for someone else you may want to include a test to make sure that a path does in fact exist. You could do this with a line:

```
IF %PATH%!==! GOTO NOPATH
.
.
.
:NOPATH
ECHO Set up a proper path!
GOTO END
```

The following DIRSORT.BAT batch file will check to make sure that the DOS SORT.EXE utility is either in the current directory or a directory that your path knows about, that you have a path, and that you entered a parameter after the name of the batch file to tell it how to sort. If everything is okay it will then sort your directory by name, size, or extension. If it finds something wrong it will print the appropriate error message:

```
ECHO OFF
IF %1!==! GOTO OOPS1
IF %PATH%!==! GOTO OOPS2
IF EXIST SORT.EXE GOTO YES
FOR %%A IN (%PATH%) DO IF EXIST %%A\SORT.EXE GOTO YES
FOR %%A IN (%PATH%) DO IF EXIST %%ASORT.EXE GOTO YES
ECHO Put SORT.EXE on your disk for this to work
GOTO END
:YES
IF %1==S GOTO SIZE
IF %1==s GOTO SIZE
IF %1==F GOTO FILEN
IF %1==f GOTO FILEN
IF %1==E GOTO EXTEN
IF %1==e GOTO EXTEN
GOTO OOPS1
:SIZE
DIR | SORT /+14
GOTO END
:FILEN
DIR | SORT
GOTO END
:EXTEN
DIR | SORT /+10
GOTO END
:OOPS1
ECHO Enter %0 S to sort by size, %0 F to sort by
ECHO filename, or %0 E to sort by extension
GOTO END
:OOPS2
ECHO Set up a proper PATH
:END
```

String Handling

You can also use the IF command to compare two sets of character strings. For the comparison to be valid, the strings must be identical in length, content, and case.

One of the most important uses for this type of IF test is in processing replaceable parameters. If you want to protect your hard disk against accidental formatting, you can rename your FORMAT.COM command to something like FMT.COM, and run it out of a batch file called FORMAT.BAT:

```
ECHO OFF
IF %1!==! GOTO OOPS
IF %1==A: GOTO OKAY
IF %1==a: GOTO OKAY
IF %1==B: GOTO OKAY
IF %1==b: GOTO OKAY
ECHO You can't format drive %1 !!
GOTO END
:OKAY
FMT %1
GOTO END
:OOPS
ECHO Enter FORMAT then a drive letter A: or B: only
:END
```

Note that you have to use a double equal sign in a string comparison test.

Since users can enter text in uppercase or lowercase, you need two IF tests (IF %1==A: GOTO OKAY and IF %1==a: GOTO OKAY) to catch both variations of each drive letter.

If the user enters FORMAT B:, DOS will make replaceable parameter %1 equal to B: and then plug this into the IF tests. The test:

```
IF %1==B: GOTO OKAY
```

will become:

```
IF B:==B: GOTO OKAY
```

Since the replaceable parameter string B: is indeed equal to the preset string B:, the batch file will jump to the :OKAY label and run the real FORMAT.COM program — which you've named to FMT.COM — and pass the B: drive letter to it.

FORMAT.BAT will accept only four parameters — A:, a:, B:, and b:. If the user enters anything other than one of these, all four tests will fail and the batch file will eventually reach the error message "ECHO You can't format drive %1 !!". Again, it will replace the %1 with whatever the user entered. If he or she entered FORMAT C:, the batch file will take the C: and replace the %1 with it, producing the message "ECHO You can't format drive C: !!". Then it will exit by jumping to the :END label.

FORMAT.BAT contains an initial IF %1!==! GOTO OOPS test to make sure that the user entered something on the command line after the name of the batch file. If the user didn't enter anything at all after the name of the batch file, the test becomes:

```
IF !==! GOTO OOPS
```

Since ! clearly does equal ! the batch file jumps to a message at the :OOPS label that gives the user instructions. You may use any character on both sides of the double == sign, but make sure it's something unusual such as !, #, or $. So:

```
IF $%1==$ GOTO OOPS
```

is just as valid a test.

DOS offers considerable flexibility in writing batch files like these. For example, you could rephrase the tests to make them negative and nest them all on one line in NEST.BAT if you wanted:

```
ECHO OFF
IF %1!==! GOTO OOPS
IF NOT %1==A: IF NOT %1==a: IF NOT %1==B: IF NOT %1==b:
GOTO NOPE
FMT %1
GOTO END
:NOPE
ECHO You can't format drive %1 !!
GOTO END
:OOPS
ECHO Enter FORMAT then a drive letter A: or B: only
:END
```

Another clever way to allow multiple inputs but screen out invalid keystrokes is to use the FOR command. The FORTEST.BAT batch file will accept A, B, or C, or the lowercase version of each, while rejecting everything else. And it does this all on one line:

```
ECHO OFF
FOR %%A in (A B C a b c) DO IF !%1 == !%%A GOTO OKAY
ECHO No, Enter: %0 A or %0 B or %0 C
ECHO (or the lowercase versions of these).
GOTO END
:OKAY
ECHO Entering %1 is okay
:END
```

It's often necessary to avoid long strings of IF commands, especially on slower systems. EASYAS.BAT tests three conditions in a single line:

```
ECHO OFF
IF NOT %2!==! IF %1==123 IF %2==456 GOTO YES
ECHO Sorry, you entered the numbers wrong
GOTO END
```

```
:YES
ECHO Yes, you entered both numbers correctly
:END
```

If you enter just the name of the batch file, the first test, for a missing second parameter (if not %2!==!) will jump execution down to the "Sorry..." line. The same is true if you enter just one number, or any two numbers other than the correct ones, after the name of the batch file. However, if you enter:

```
EASYAS 123 456
```

the file will print the correct "Yes, you entered..." message.

One of the best places to use string tests is in dealing with environment variables. If you have two color-setting routines on your disk, one that uses direct BIOS calls (like the programs on the accompanying disks) and one that uses ANSI.SYS commands, you can have your batch file figure out which color system is active and execute the appropriate setting program.

To do this, make sure you issue a batch file command SET ANSI=OFF (or BIOS=ON) when you configure your system to run without ANSI.SYS. Here it's easier to test for the absence rather than the presence of ANSI.SYS, since you load ANSI through your CONFIG.SYS file and not through a batch file. If you happened to have a batch file that loaded ANSI, it could set ANSI=ON at the same time.

Some users have complex batch file schemes to rename various versions of their CONFIG.SYS and AUTOEXEC.BAT files and then reboot, in an effort to load ANSI or start their systems without it, and it's possible to have the batch file that triggers the whole process create a file called YESANSI when it does this. Then you could use an IF EXIST YESANSI command to detect whether ANSI is loaded. If you did try this, you'd have to make sure you erased YESANSI when you weren't starting your system with ANSI active. A lot of bother.

Once your AUTOEXEC.BAT file executed a line like:

```
SET ANSI=OFF
```

or:

```
SET BIOS=ON
```

or:

```
SET ANSI=ON
```

later batch files could include a line like IF ANSI==ON GOTO ANSISET or IF BIOS==ON GOTO BIOSSET. If ANSI was loaded, you could then jump to the ANSI color setter rather than the BIOS color setter. When you weren't using ANSI, the test would look at the environment and see that ANSI was not equal to ON, and branch to the BIOS setter rather than the ANSI one.

Being able to phrase tests using negative conditions adds flexibility. The ANSI TEST.BAT batch file could be written:

```
ECHO OFF
IF NOT !%ANSI%==!ON GOTO BIOSSET
:ANSISET
ECHO ANSI color setter goes here
GOTO END
:BIOSSET
ECHO BIOS color setter goes here
:END
```

The exclamation points are needed to prevent a syntax error if no ANSI variable exists in the environment. Without something there (you could use any two other identical symbols such as IF NOT @%ANSI%==@ON) you would end up with a line that translated to

```
IF NOT ==ON
```

which would trigger a syntax error.

Case Insensitivity

DOS is flexible about combinations of uppercase and lowercase text when it processes labels, but it's rigid and inflexible when comparing strings.

This means that if you want to test all the possible ways to enter something as short as a three-letter word you'd have to make eight tests ($2^$ number of letters). And longer words mean dramatically longer tests.

To speed things up, you can use the COMPARE.COM utility on the accompanying disk. COMPARE.COM compares two strings and ignores the case of the alphabetic characters. On return, it sets ERRORLEVEL 255 if both strings are equal and ERRORLEVEL 0 if they are not equal or if a syntax error has occurred. After executing COMPARE.COM, your batch file may take appropriate action with the statement:

```
IF ERRORLEVEL 255 action
```

You can try this out by creating a sample batch file called COMPTEST.BAT:

```
ECHO OFF
IF %2!==! GOTO OOPS
COMPARE %1==%2
IF ERRORLEVEL 255 GOTO MATCH
ECHO The strings are not equal
```

```
GOTO END
:MATCH
ECHO The strings are equal
GOTO END
:OOPS
ECHO The format required is:
ECHO COMPTEST STRING1 STRING2
:END
```

Then, at the DOS prompt, type:

```
COMPTEST hello HELLO
```

and it will respond with the message:

```
The strings are equal.
```

But type something like "COMPTEST hello HELLOE" and the batch file will let you know the strings don't match.

IF ERRORLEVEL

One of the single most powerful DOS batch file tools is also one of the most poorly documented — IF ERRORLEVEL.

ERRORLEVEL makes your batch files truly interactive, and lets you create slick, friendly, foolproof menus that can run your whole system — or help a beginner through a complex task.

Before users knew about IF ERRORLEVEL techniques, they'd slap together primitive menu systems that involved lots of little batch files. The main batch file would do nothing other than use the DOS TYPE command to display the contents of a text file like:

```
─────────────── Menu ───────────────

          1 - Spreadsheet
          2 - Wordprocessor
          3 - Database

     Pick a number (1–3) then press Enter
```

Then they'd write short batch files called 1.BAT, 2.BAT, and 3.BAT. Each would contain just the name of the software they wanted to load, and perhaps a CD\ command to jump into the proper subdirectory.

While this worked, it had many drawbacks. After the batch file used TYPE to display the menu, it dropped back to DOS. The user saw a DOS prompt, and wasn't sure whether to type in a number or enter a command. You could get around this by using the PROMPT command to change the DOS prompt itself from C> or A> to:

```
Type a number from 1 to 3 then press Enter ==>
```

But when you were done running a particular program, the prompt would still ask you to pick a number. Then again, you could have the individual 1.BAT, 2.BAT, 3.BAT batch files reset the prompt back to normal, but you might want to make another menu selection.

Worse, if the user entered the wrong kind of response, the menu would scroll up off the screen. In addition, the user had to press the Enter key after typing in the proper response, and some couldn't figure that out. And when the user was finished running the program he or she had chosen, the menu had long since vanished, leaving a bare screen. Again, the individual batch files could redisplay the menu when they finished, but that might be confusing to users who wanted to do something other than what was listed.

Finally, dozens of little menu batch files, each with its own array of program-loading files, can waste a tremendous amount of space, especially on a system like an XT with its greedy 4K clusters.

ERRORLEVEL avoids every one of these problems, and lets you create menus that are smart, easy, and compact.

An ideal menu system would display the options and wait for the user to enter a (preferably) single-digit choice, then execute that choice, without forcing him or her to hit the Enter key.

It would be single-minded, preventing the user from stumbling into some other command. This defect alone makes the primitive 1.BAT, 2.BAT system worthless, since it returns to the DOS command line after displaying its choices. If the user enters a command like DIR, DOS will scroll the menu choices off the screen.

And it would retain control by looping back to the beginning every time a program finished running. One of the menu options would be to exit gracefully, and the menu system would restore the screen back to normal.

IF ERRORLEVEL is one of the worst-named and most powerful of all DOS commands. According to IBM, all it really does is let your batch files know whether DOS successfully completed commands such as BACKUP, KEYB, REPLACE, RESTORE, or FORMAT. These programs set *exit codes* (also called *return codes*) depending on whether the programs were able to work completely or partially. And they can tell if the user or some system error interrupted the program in midstream.

The IF ERRORLEVEL command can read these exit codes and act accordingly. So you could create a batch file to execute BACKUP or FORMAT and have provisions in the batch file to print customized messages onscreen if something goes wrong. IBM spends a lot of space in its manuals on this, and nobody uses it.

On the other hand, IBM doesn't talk at all about how to send user input into batch files, which is something that DOS desperately needs. And DOS doesn't provide any direct utilities for putting IF ERRORLEVEL to work this way.

But it's simple to harness IF ERRORLEVEL and make your batch files truly interactive. All you need is a version of a short assembly language program that reads keystrokes and translates them into exit codes that IF ERRORLEVEL can process. Then you just include the name of the program in your batch file and follow it with tests for the appropriate exit codes. These tests can jump to different labels inside the batch file, or they can execute programs or commands directly if the codes match.

The basic test is in the format:

```
IF ERRORLEVEL number action
```

or:

```
IF NOT ERRORLEVEL number action
```

where number is the decimal value of the exit code, and action is the command to execute.

Note: The tricky part of this is that IF ERRORLEVEL will execute the action if the exit code is equal to — or greater than — the number after the word ERRORLEVEL.

DOS allows 256 possible exit codes from 0 to 255, so the command:

```
IF ERRORLEVEL 0 ECHO True
```

will always work, since all 256 possible exit codes are equal to or greater than 0. So this test will always print the message "True." You don't even need a batch file to test this. Just type it in at the DOS prompt.

At the other end of the spectrum:

```
IF ERRORLEVEL 255 ECHO True
```

will work in only one case — when the exit code happens to be 255.

If you want to isolate a character like a space (which has an ASCII value of decimal 32), you have to first screen out any higher exit codes:

```
IF ERRORLEVEL 33 ECHO Nonspace
IF ERRORLEVEL 32 ECHO Space
```

You can combine such tests into one long line:

```
IF ERRORLEVEL 32 IF NOT ERRORLEVEL 33 ECHO Space
```

The most primitive example of a keystroke processing program is GETKEY.COM, which you can create by making sure DEBUG.COM is handy and then typing these seven lines:

```
DEBUG
E 100 B4 00 CD 16 B4 4C CD 21
N GETKEY.COM
RCX
8
W
Q
```

Here's the assembly language program that this creates:

```
MOV AH,00    ; BIOS read a character and
INT 16       ; puts its ASCII code into AL
MOV AH,4C    ; ready to exit with code
INT 21       ; do it
```

(Both DOS and your system's BIOS can process keystrokes for you. This particular example uses BIOS, but you could just as easily have substituted a DOS function call. In fact, DOS is better for certain applications because it offers several options. It can display the character you entered, or discard it. It can wait for a keystroke — which you usually want to do in menu systems — or process one only if it's there waiting. And it can handle attempts to break out of the operation, or ignore them.)

Then create a batch file called ERRTEST.BAT:

```
ECHO OFF
:TOP
ECHO You may break out of this loop
ECHO by pressing Enter. Or press
ECHO any other key to continue . . .
GETKEY
IF ERRORLEVEL 13 IF NOT ERRORLEVEL 14 GOTO END
GOTO TOP
:END
```

This batch file simply tests to see whether the user pressed the Enter key, which has an ASCII value of decimal 13.

When ERRTEST executes, it will print the three-line message and then run GETKEY.COM. GETKEY.COM waits for the user to press a single alphanumeric key, and sets the return code to the ASCII value of that key. The single line:

```
IF ERRORLEVEL 13 IF NOT ERRORLEVEL 14 GOTO END
```

in the batch file tests whether the return code was 13, and at the same time screens out any higher values. You could just as easily change the batch file to:

```
ECHO OFF
:TOP
ECHO You may break out of this loop
ECHO by pressing Enter. Or press
ECHO any other key to continue . . .
GETKEY
IF ERRORLEVEL 14 GOTO TOP
IF ERRORLEVEL 13 GOTO END
GOTO TOP
:END
```

The following CASETEST.BAT batch file uses GETKEY.COM to fetch keystrokes and pass the ASCII value for each one to a "cascade" of IF ERRORLEVEL tests:

```
ECHO OFF
:ERR
ECHO Enter a lowercase or
ECHO an uppercase letter
ECHO (Or spacebar to quit)
:TOP
GETKEY
IF ERRORLEVEL 123 GOTO ERR
IF ERRORLEVEL 97 GOTO LOWER
IF ERRORLEVEL 91 GOTO ERR
IF ERRORLEVEL 65 GOTO UPPER
IF ERRORLEVEL 33 GOTO ERR
IF ERRORLEVEL 32 GOTO END
IF ERRORLEVEL 0 GOTO ERR
:LOWER
ECHO Lowercase
GOTO TOP
:UPPER
ECHO Uppercase
GOTO TOP
:END
```

All lowercase letters have decimal ASCII values from 97 through 122. All uppercase letters have decimal ASCII values from 65 through 90. The chart below shows all the IF ERRORLEVEL ASCII Characters.

Characters	255–224:	math, Greek letters, symbols
Characters	223–219:	blocks
Characters	218–179:	box and border elements
Characters	178–176:	shaded blocks
Characters	175–169:	miscellaneous symbols
Characters	168–155:	miscellaneous currency signs and symbols
Characters	154–128:	various diacritical marks and symbols
Characters	127–123:	miscellaneous exotic punctuation
Characters	122–97:	lowercase alphabet (z=122; a=97)
Characters	96–91:	more miscellaneous exotic punctuation
Characters	90–65:	uppercase alphabet (Z=90; A=65)
Characters	64–58:	punctuation
Characters	57–48:	digits (9=57; 0=48)
Characters	47–33:	punctuation and symbols
Character	32:	space
Character	27:	escape
Character	26:	end-of-file marker (^Z)
Character	13:	enter (^M)
Character	10:	line feed (^J)
Character	9:	tab (^I)
Character	8:	backspace (^H)
Character	7:	beep (^G)
Character	0:	null

CASETEST.BAT first uses a test for 123 to screen out anything higher than the top range of lowercase values. The second test will detect anything from 97 through 122 and jump to the label that identifies this as a lowercase letter. The next test screens out the few odd characters with values from 91 through 96. It's followed by a test that detects anything from 65 through 90 and jumps to a label identifying these as uppercase letters.

Finally, a test for 33 screens out any key with a value greater than a space (remember, a space is 32) but lower than the bottom range of uppercase letters. Then a test for 32 isolates spaces, and a last test for 0 traps any other keystrokes.

Most single keys on your keyboard generate single ASCII codes. But key combinations like Ctrl-End, Ins, or F7 generate two-character values called extended codes, where the first value is always a 0. Key-sniffing programs more sophisticated than GETKEY.COM can detect these; GETKEY thinks all such keys are returning codes of 0. Later you'll see how you can soup up GETKEY to handle such keys.

More sophisticated key-processing programs, like GET.EXE on the accompanying disks, let you print customized onscreen prompts telling the user which of several keys to press. If the program doesn't do this, you have to have an ECHO command display a message prompting the user.

The following PROGMAKR.BAT batch file will actually create a version of GETKEY.COM that displays its own customized message:

```
ECHO OFF
REM PROGMAKR.BAT
IF %2!==! GOTO ERROR
CTTY NUL
ECHO E 100 B4 09 BA 0F 01 CD 21          > DBG.ZZZ
ECHO E 107 B4 00 CD 16 B4 4C CD 21      >> DBG.ZZZ
ECHO E 10F '%2 %3 %4 %5 %6 %7 %8 %9$'   >> DBG.ZZZ
ECHO N %1.COM                           >> DBG.ZZZ
ECHO RCX                                >> DBG.ZZZ
ECHO 100                                >> DBG.ZZZ
ECHO W                                  >> DBG.ZZZ
ECHO Q                                  >> DBG.ZZZ
DEBUG < DBG.ZZZ
DEL DBG.ZZZ
GOTO END
:ERROR
ECHO The correct syntax is:
ECHO %0 PROGNAME WORD1 [WORD2] . . . [WORD8]
ECHO Where: PROGNAME is the name of the .COM file and
ECHO WORD1 to WORD8 are words the program will print.
ECHO eg: %0 BATCHKEY Enter a number from 1 to 5:
ECHO Notes: 1) DON'T use single quotes (') or dollar signs.
ECHO 2) DON'T put a .COM extension on PROGNAME!
ECHO (%0 will do it for you automatically.)
:END
CTTY CON
IF NOT %1!==! ECHO Now type %1
```

To use PROGMAKR.BAT, you need to have DEBUG.COM in the current directory or in one your path knows about. It lets you enter a program name (such as GETKEY or BATCHKEY) and then a prompt of up to eight words after it. So if you entered:

```
PROGMAKR BATCHKEY Enter a number from 1 to 5:
```

it will automatically create a small file called BATCHKEY.COM that displays the prompt:

```
Enter a number from 1 to 5:
```

and waits for a key. When you press any normal (nonextended) key, BATCHKEY will turn its ASCII value into an exit code that IF ERRORLEVEL can process.

This is a very powerful little batch file. But if you use it, note:

1. Be sure you have DEBUG.COM handy.
2. It uses a CTTY NUL command to shut off the display temporarily while it's working. If something unexpected happens before the batch file gets to the restorative CTTY CON command at the end, you'll be frozen out of your keyboard. Check your typing carefully and make sure you don't have any unsaved files lurking around when you try this for the first time.
3. You can enter up to eight discrete words or clumps of characters, but don't enter any single quotes or dollar signs, since DOS treats these specially.
4. Type in everything exactly as it appears, and watch for small but important characters like the single quote marks in the ECHO E 10F '%2 %3 %4 %5 %6 %7 %8 %9$' line.
5. Remember that directly below the CTTY NUL the first ECHO line ends with a single > DBG.ZZZ while the others have double >> DBG.ZZZ signs. A single > sign creates a file and a double >> sign appends data to an existing file.
6. Remember to type in the name of the program you want to create before you start entering the message. And be sure to leave off the .COM extension; the batch file will add it for you automatically.

PROGMAKR.BAT will create a file that looks (at least for the sample prompt above) like:

```
MOV AH,09     ; DOS message printer
MOV DX,010F   ; address of the message
INT 21        ; print it
MOV AH,00     ; BIOS read a character and
INT 16        ; puts its ASCII code into AL
MOV AH,4C     ; ready to exit with code
INT 21        ; do it
DB 'Enter a number from 1 to 5: $'
```

Narrowing the Search

In any IF ERRORLEVEL process something has to screen out erroneous keystrokes. You can have the batch file do it by including a series of IF ERRORLEVEL tests. Or you can have the assembly language program do it, either by refusing to budge unless the user presses certain keys, or by setting one kind of exit code for correct responses and another kind for incorrect keypresses. You can adapt GETKEY.COM to do either.

This version will set a code of 13 if the user presses Enter, and a code of 0 otherwise:

```
DEBUG
E 100 B4 00 CD 16 3C 0D 74 02 30 C0 B4 4C CD 21
N GETKEY2.COM
```

```
RCX
E
W
Q
```

You can run this with a shorter version of ERRTEST.BAT called ERRTEST2.BAT:

```
ECHO OFF
:TOP
ECHO You may break out of this loop
ECHO by pressing Enter. Or press
ECHO any other key to continue . . .
GETKEY2
IF ERRORLEVEL 13 GOTO END
GOTO TOP
:END
```

Here you don't need to test for any exit code other than 13, since GETKEY2.COM does all the keystroke screening by making sure that the exit code for every key other than Enter is 0. The assembly language program for this looks like:

```
MOV AH,00     ; BIOS read a character
INT 16        ; puts ASCII code into AL
CMP AL,0D     ; is character an Enter?
JZ 010A       ; yes; skip next step
XOR AL,AL     ; make the exit code a 0
MOV AH,4C     ; ready to exit with code
INT 21        ; do it
```

The exit code that the program sets doesn't have to be the same as the ASCII code of the key that the user pressed. GETKEY3.COM sets a code of 255 if the user pressed Enter. Create it by typing:

```
DEBUG
E 100 B4 00 CD 16 3C 0D 75 02 B0 FF B4 4C CD 21
N GETKEY3.COM
RCX
E
W
Q
```

This is almost identical to GETKEY2.COM:

```
MOV AH,00     ; BIOS read a character
INT 16        ; puts ASCII code into AL
```

```
CMP AL,0D       ; is character an Enter?
JNZ 010A        ; no; skip next step
MOV AL,FF       ; make the exit code a 255
MOV AH,4C       ; ready to exit with code
INT 21          ; do it
```

The ERRTEST3.BAT batch file to use this program might look like:

```
ECHO OFF
:TOP
ECHO You may break out of this loop
ECHO by pressing Enter. Or press
ECHO any other key to continue . . .
GETKEY3
IF ERRORLEVEL 255 GOTO END
GOTO TOP
:END
```

or even simpler:

```
ECHO OFF
:TOP
ECHO You may break out of this loop
ECHO by pressing Enter. Or press
ECHO any other key to continue . . .
GETKEY3
IF NOT ERRORLEVEL 255 GOTO TOP
```

GETKEY3.COM sets the exit code to 255 if the user presses the Enter key. It leaves all other values intact, so that if the user happened to press the space bar, which has an ASCII value of 32, the exit code would be 32. But testing for an ERRORLEVEL of 255 heads all other lower exit codes off at the pass.

The only problem with this is that if the user happened to enter character 255 (by holding down the Alt key, typing 255 on the number pad, and then releasing the Alt key), ERRTEST3.BAT would treat it as if the user had pressed the Enter key. Both would end up with an exit code of 255. Screening this out would be trivial, but seriously, how many users are going to enter character 255?

You could have the assembly language program do even more work by rejecting any keystrokes other than the ones your batch file is designed to handle. GETKEY4.COM will sit and wait for the user to press a key, and will discard all keypresses other than Enter (with a code of decimal 13, or hex 0D) and Escape (with an exit code of decimal 27, or hex 1B):

```
DEBUG
E 100 B4 00 CD 16 3C 0D 74 04 3C 1B 75 F4 B4 4C CD 21
N GETKEY4.COM
RCX
10
W
Q
```

If you ran the ERRTEST4.BAT batch file:

```
ECHO OFF
:TOP
ECHO Press Esc to loop again
ECHO or Enter to quit . . .
GETKEY4
IF ERRORLEVEL 27 GOTO TOP
```

pressing Esc would loop through the batch file and repeat the message, pressing Enter would quit, and pressing any other key would do nothing. GETKEY4.COM looks like:

```
MOV AH,00      ; BIOS read a character
INT 16         ; puts ASCII code into AL
CMP AL,0D      ; is character an Enter?
JZ 10C         ; yes; goto exit code
CMP AL,1B      ; is character an Esc?
JNZ 100        ; no; go back and get another
MOV AH,4C      ; exit code
INT 21         ; do it
```

These tiny exit-code setters can really enhance the operation of your system. Earlier a program called FORMAT.BAT used string tests to screen out attempts to format any drive higher than B:. You could adapt a batch file like that to use a small drive-sensing program called DRIVE.COM together with a few IF ERRORLEVEL tests to exit automatically if it found that you were on drive C: or D:. To create DRIVE.COM, just type:

```
DEBUG
E 100 B4 19 CD 21 B4 4C CD 21
N DRIVE.COM
RCX
8
W
Q
```

DRIVE.COM is somewhat similar to GETKEY.COM:

```
MOV AH,19    ; get current drive
INT 21       ; do it (A=0, B=1, etc)
MOV AH,4C    ; put drive in exit code
INT 21       ; do it
```

A DRIVER.BAT batch file to show how this worked might look like:

```
ECHO OFF
DRIVE
IF ERRORLEVEL 0 IF NOT ERRORLEVEL 1 ECHO Drive A
IF ERRORLEVEL 1 IF NOT ERRORLEVEL 2 ECHO Drive B
IF ERRORLEVEL 2 IF NOT ERRORLEVEL 3 ECHO Drive C
IF ERRORLEVEL 3 IF NOT ERRORLEVEL 4 ECHO Drive D
IF ERRORLEVEL 4 ECHO Higher than Drive D
```

You could add a DRIVE command at the beginning of your FORMAT batch file, and if the following IF ERRORLEVEL test detected a value of 2 or more, just have it GOTO END.

The easiest way to create IF ERRORLEVEL-based menus is probably to limit yourself to ten choices — the digits 0 through 9. Or you could use letters rather than numbers, since letters offer 26 single-digit choices rather than ten. But you'd have to test for both uppercase and lowercase entries, and all the ASCII characters in between, which means lots of IF tests or a clever assembly language program to do all the work.

You could expand the GETKEY.COM program slightly to handle function keys, which don't have uppercase and lowercase versions. Or, you could limit all your ERRORLEVEL decisions to Yes/No questions. This second method works very well in some cases, but not in menus.

Typing in the following few lines will create a GETFKEY.COM program designed to work with extended key combinations:

```
DEBUG
E 100 B4 00 CD 16 3C 00 74 04 B0
E 109 FF EB 02 88 E0 B4 4C CD 21
N GETFKEY.COM
RCX
12
W
Q
```

The GETFKEY program looks like:

```
MOV AH,00    ; BIOS read a character
INT 16       ; puts ASCII code into AL
CMP AL,00    ; is character extended?
```

```
JZ 010C          ; yes; go to register mover
MOV AL,FF        ; no; so make exit code 255
JMP 010E         ; and skip next step
MOV AL,AH        ; make extended code the exit code
MOV AH,4C        ; exit with code
INT 21           ; do it
```

It works just like GETKEY.COM, except that it can handle function keys and shifted key combinations as well as normal alphanumeric keys. When you press an alphanumeric key, BIOS puts the ASCII value of the key in the AL register and the scan code in the AH register. When you trigger an extended key combination, BIOS puts the ASCII code in the AH register and a NUL, or character 0, in the AL register.

GETFKEY.COM waits until the user presses a key, then checks to see if the AL register is set to 0. If not, GETFKEY assumes the key was a normal garden-variety letter or number, makes the exit code 255, and quits. If it does see a 0 in AL it moves the ASCII code down from AH to AL and makes it the exit code. At this point any normal key has an exit code of 255; anything less means the user pressed an extended key combination.

On IBM's old reliable keyboards you actually have a lot of possible extended keys from which to choose (the newer IBM Chinese typesetting version offers even more):

Function Keys				*Keypad Keys*		
F1...F10	unshifted =	59...68			Unshifted	Ctrl
F1...F10	+ Shift	=	84...93	Home	71	119
F1...F10	+ Ctrl	=	94...103	Up	72	-
F1...F10	+ Alt	=	104...113	PgUp	73	132
				Left	75	115
				Right	77	116
Alt / Regular Key				End	79	117
QWERTYUIOP	16...25			Down	80	-
ASDFGHJKL	30...38			PgDn	81	118
ZXCVBNM	44...50			Ins	82	-
1234567890-=	120...131			Del	83	-

A typical batch EXTENKEY.BAT file that used extended keys would look something like this:

```
ECHO OFF
:START
ECHO INS - See a sorted DIR
ECHO DEL - Return to DOS
ECHO *** Hit Ins or Del ***
GETFKEY
IF ERRORLEVEL 84 GOTO START
IF ERRORLEVEL 83 GOTO 2
IF ERRORLEVEL 82 GOTO 1
```

610 *DOS Power Tools, 2nd Edition, Revised for DOS 5.0*

```
GOTO START
:1
DIR | SORT
PAUSE
GOTO START
:2
```

This uses the Ins (82) and Del (83) keys, and rejects anything else.

While the previous examples demonstrate how ERRORLEVEL can manage menus, IF ERRORLEVEL can also come in handy when a batch file gives a user a two-way choice — continue or not, load a program or not, echo something to the printer or not, and so on.

In all these cases, the batch file pauses and asks a Yes or No question, and then proceeds with the option only if the user answers with Y or y.

The GETYES.COM program below checks for Y or y and puts an ASCII 255 value into the AL register if it finds one. Batch files that use this technique can get away with just a single IF ERRORLEVEL test — for a value of 255 only.

You can create GETYES.COM by typing:

```
DEBUG
E 100 B4 00 CD 16 3C 59 74 04 3C
E 109 79 75 02 B0 FF B4 4C CD 21
RCX
12
N GETYES.COM
W
Q
```

The program it creates looks like:

```
MOV AH,00      ; BIOS read a character
INT 16         ; puts ASCII code into AL
CMP AL,59      ; is character a 'Y' ?
JZ 010C        ; yes; go to 255 stuffer
CMP AL,79      ; is character a 'y' ?
JNZ 010E       ; if not, skip next step
MOV AL,FF      ; make exit code 255
MOV AH,4C      ; exit with code
INT 21         ; do it
```

You can see this in action by running the following YESNO.BAT batch file:

```
ECHO OFF
:TOP
ECHO Hit y or Y or another key:
```

```
GETYES
IF ERRORLEVEL 255 GOTO YES
GOTO NO
:YES
ECHO You said yes.
GOTO CONTINUE
:NO
ECHO You didn't hit y or Y.
:CONTINUE
ECHO Now, want to quit (Y/N)?
GETYES
IF ERRORLEVEL 255 GOTO END
GOTO TOP
:END
```

GETYES.COM checks for Y (hex 59) and y (hex 79). You could substitute 4E (the hex code for N) and 6E (the hex code for n) for 59 and 79 and create GETNO.COM.

Just use DEBUG to patch GETYES.COM and make a new copy of it called GETNO.COM:

```
DEBUG GETYES.COM
E 105 4E
E 109 6E
N GETNO.COM
W
Q
```

Then adapt the above batch file and turn it into NOYES.BAT:

```
ECHO OFF
:TOP
ECHO Hit n or N or another key:
GETNO
IF ERRORLEVEL 255 GOTO NO
GOTO YES
:NO
ECHO You said no.
GOTO CONTINUE
:YES
ECHO You didn't hit n or N.
:CONTINUE
ECHO Now, want to quit (Y/N)?
GETNO
IF ERRORLEVEL 255 GOTO TOP
:END
```

GETYES.COM and GETNO.COM behave quite differently, as you can see from experimenting with the YESNO.BAT and NOYES.BAT batch files. These batch files are designed to do one task if the user presses one specific letter, and another task if he or she presses any other key. If you're asking whether a user is sure he or she wants to FORMAT a hard disk, you'd better be sure you accept only a Y or y answer. Having programs handy that operate only on Y (or y) and only on N (or n) gives you flexibility in phrasing such potentially dangerous questions.

It's simple to turn a handful of IF ERRORLEVEL tests into a menu system. If you want to write your own keyboard processor, one of the easiest ways is to use numeric entries, since you don't have to worry about uppercase and lowercase variations. Of course you're limited to ten entries.

A very simple MENU1.BAT menu system might look like:

```
ECHO OFF
:TOP
ECHO +----------------------+
ECHO |  1 - Run 123         |
ECHO |  2 - Run WordStar    |
ECHO |  3 - Return to DOS   |
ECHO +----------------------+
:MENU
ECHO Select 1, 2 or 3
GETNUM
IF ERRORLEVEL 52 GOTO MENU
IF ERRORLEVEL 51 GOTO END
IF ERRORLEVEL 50 GOTO STAR
IF ERRORLEVEL 49 GOTO LOTUS
GOTO MENU
:LOTUS
123
GOTO TOP
:STAR
WS
GOTO TOP
:END
```

You could just run a program like GETKEY.BAT that returns an exit code for any key on the keyboard. But it's not much more difficult to create a small program called GETNUM.COM that rejects all keystrokes other than 0 through 9:

```
DEBUG
E 100 B4 00 CD 16 3C 30 72 F8 3C 39 77 F4 B4 4C CD 21
N GETNUM.COM
RCX
10
W
Q
```

This program looks like:

```
MOV AH,00      ; BIOS read a character
INT 16         ; puts ASCII code into AL
CMP AL,30      ; is character < 0 ?
JB 100         ; yes; get another key
CMP AL,39      ; is character > 9 ?
JA 100         ; yes; get another key
MOV AH,4C      ; exit code
INT 21         ; do it
```

While IF ERRORLEVEL works exclusively in decimal notation, DEBUG handles only hex. The ASCII value for character 0 is 30, and for 9 is 39.

Digit	Decimal	Hex
0	48	30
1	49	31
2	50	32
3	51	33
4	52	34
5	53	35
6	54	36
7	55	37
8	56	38
9	57	39

If you press any number key between 0 and 9, GETNUM.COM transfers its ASCII value to the exit code. If you press any other key GETNUM simply rejects it and goes back for another.

The MENU1.BAT program accepts only the choices 1, 2, or 3. The topmost:

```
IF ERRORLEVEL 52 GOTO MENU
```

bounces any exit code of 52 or higher, screening out any digit from 4 through 9.

You could narrow the test by going into DEBUG and changing the:

```
CMP AL,30    ; is character < 0 ?
```

and:

```
CMP AL,39    ; is character > 9 ?
```

lines so they were more restrictive, but it's really not necessary.

Many users prefer working with letters rather than numbers.

But if you want to create a menu with options A, B, and C you have to worry about uppercase and lowercase entries.

Actually this isn't much of a problem. All you have to do is perform a logical OR operation on the key, which turns uppercase letters into lowercase ones and leaves lowercase ones alone.

The lowercase letters have ASCII values 20 hex (32 decimal) higher than their uppercase counterparts:

Letter	Dec	Hex	Letter	Dec	Hex
A	65	41	a	97	61
B	66	42	b	98	62
C	67	43	c	99	63
D	68	44	d	100	64
E	69	45	e	101	65
F	70	46	f	102	66
G	71	47	g	103	67
H	72	48	h	104	68
I	73	49	i	105	69
J	74	4A	j	106	6A
K	75	4B	k	107	6B
L	76	4C	l	108	6C
M	77	4D	m	109	6D
N	78	4E	n	110	6E
O	79	4F	o	111	6F
P	80	50	p	112	70
Q	81	51	q	113	71
R	82	52	r	114	72
S	83	53	s	115	73
T	84	54	t	116	74
U	85	55	u	117	75
V	86	56	v	118	76
W	87	57	w	119	77
X	88	58	x	120	78
Y	89	59	y	121	79
Z	90	5A	z	122	7A

So to make all letters lowercase, just add the line:

```
OR AL,20
```

to the GETKEY.COM program:

```
MOV AH,0
INT 16
```

```
OR AL,20
MOV AH,4C
INT 21
```

You could create the small LOWERIT.COM program by typing:

```
DEBUG
E 100 B4 00 CD 16 0C 20 B4 4C CD 21
N LOWERIT.COM
RCX
A
W
Q
```

Then run the following sample HALFTEST.BAT demonstration batch file:

```
ECHO OFF
ECHO Press any letter key
ECHO Or press spacebar to quit
:TOP
LOWERIT
IF ERRORLEVEL 123 GOTO TOP
IF ERRORLEVEL 110 GOTO BACK
IF ERRORLEVEL 97 GOTO FRONT
IF ERRORLEVEL 33 GOTO TOP
IF ERRORLEVEL 32 GOTO END
:BACK
ECHO N-Z
GOTO TOP
:FRONT
ECHO A-M
GOTO TOP
:END
```

Type in any uppercase or lowercase letter and the batch file will tell you which half of the alphabet it's in.

You could, of course, go the other way and make all letters uppercase. Instead of the line:

```
OR AL,20
```

substitute:

```
AND AL,DF
```

Create UPPERIT.COM by typing:

```
DEBUG
E 100 B4 00 CD 16 24 DF B4 4C CD 21
N UPPERIT.COM
RCX
A
W
Q
```

The program looks like:

```
MOV AH,0      ; BIOS read a character and
INT 16        ; puts its ASCII code into AL
AND AL,DF     ; uppercase all letters
MOV AH,4C     ; ready to exit with code
INT 21        ; do it
```

And you'll have to change the HALFTEST.BAT demonstration batch file slightly:

```
ECHO OFF
ECHO Press any letter key
ECHO Or press Enter to quit
:TOP
UPPERIT
IF ERRORLEVEL 91 GOTO TOP
IF ERRORLEVEL 78 GOTO BACK
IF ERRORLEVEL 65 GOTO FRONT
IF ERRORLEVEL 14 GOTO TOP
IF ERRORLEVEL 13 GOTO END
:BACK
ECHO N-Z
GOTO TOP
:FRONT
ECHO A-M
GOTO TOP
:END
```

ANDing any ASCII value with 223 (hex DF) will capitalize lowercase letters and leave uppercase letters alone. The logical AND operation works by comparing two values (the example below will compare one bit at a time) and returning a "1" only when both values are nonzero.

- 1 AND 1 = 1
- 1 AND 0 = 0

- 0 AND 1 = 0
- 0 AND 0 = 0

223 equals binary 11011111. Capital A (decimal 65) is binary 01000001, while lowercase a (decimal 97) is binary 01100001. The AND operation on these numbers could be represented as

```
        01000001 (65)
AND     11011111 (223)
        01000001 (65)
```

```
        01100001 (97)
AND     11011111 (223)
        01000001 (65)
```

ANDing either a 0 or a 1 with 1 in effect leaves the value alone, and ANDing both a 0 and a 1 with 0 in effect turns the value into a 0. The binary number 11011111 forces the 2^5 bit — the sixth one from the right — to become a 0 and leaves all the other bits the way they were. (The rightmost bit is 2^0; the leftmost is 2^7.)

The only difference between a lowercase letter and its capital counterpart is that the 2^5 bit is set (equals 1) in the lowercase version. ANDing it with 11011111 unsets the bit, changing it to a 0 and lowering the ASCII value by 32.

To reverse the process and turn capital letters into lowercase ones, use the logical OR operation to OR a value with 32:

- 1 OR 1 = 1
- 1 OR 0 = 1
- 0 OR 1 = 1
- 0 OR 0 = 0

32 equals binary 00100000. Since ORing either a 1 or a 0 with 0 in effect leaves the value alone, and ORing either a 1 or a 0 with 1 in effect turns the value into a 1, the binary number 00100000 forces the 2^5 bit to become a 1 and leaves all the other bits the way they were.

This sets the unset 2^5 bit in an uppercase letter, changing it to a 1 and raising the ASCII value by 32.

```
        01000001 (65)
OR      00100000 (32)
        01100001 (97)
```

```
        01100001 (97)
OR      00100000 (32)
        01100001 (97)
```

618 *DOS Power Tools, 2nd Edition, Revised for DOS 5.0*

One problem with blanket logical operations like the OR AL,20 and the AND AL,DF is that they switch uppercase to lowercase and vice versa, but end up changing the values of many of the nonletter keys as well.

The solution is to test each letter to make sure it's in the right range before performing the logical operation on it. GETLETR.ASM does just that:

```
MOV AH,08      ; get a keystroke
INT 21         ; do it
CMP AL,1B      ; is it escape?
JE 11E         ; bye
CMP AL,7A      ; higher than 'z' ?
JA 0102        ; get another one
CMP AL,60      ; lower than 'a' ?
JBE 0114       ; then try next test
AND AL,DF      ; otherwise uppercase it
JMP 011C       ; and jump to subtract
CMP AL,5A      ; higher than 'Z' ?
JA 0102        ; get another one
CMP AL,41      ; lower than 'A' ?
JB 0102        ; get another one
AND AL,3F      ; subtract 64
MOV AH,4C      ; exit with code
INT 21         ; do it
```

But you could create an executable version, GETLETR.COM, easily by adding an:

A

on a line by itself at the very beginning of GETLETR.ASM, a blank line, and then the following five lines at the end:

```
RCX
22
N GETLETR.COM
W
Q
```

at the end (don't forget the blank line above RCX).

This won't accept nonletter entries, and is case insensitive. It will generate a code of 1 for A, 2 for B, and 26 for Z. It will also generate a 27 for Esc, which lets you use Esc as an exit.

It takes advantage of a DOS keyboard-reading routine rather than the BIOS interrupt 16H used in the GETKEY.COM series. Either will do.

Then create a sample batch file like MENU2.BAT:

```
ECHO OFF
:TOP
ECHO Enter a letter from A to E (or type Esc to quit):
:START
GETLETR
IF ERRORLEVEL 27 GOTO END
IF ERRORLEVEL 6 GOTO START
IF ERRORLEVEL 5 GOTO LABELE
IF ERRORLEVEL 4 GOTO LABELD
IF ERRORLEVEL 3 GOTO LABELC
IF ERRORLEVEL 2 GOTO LABELB
:LABELA
ECHO (this simulates menu choice A)
PAUSE
GOTO TOP
:LABELB
ECHO (this simulates menu choice B)
PAUSE
GOTO TOP
:LABELC
ECHO (this simulates menu choice C)
PAUSE
GOTO TOP
:LABELD
ECHO (this simulates menu choice D)
PAUSE
GOTO TOP
:LABELE
ECHO (this simulates menu choice E)
PAUSE
GOTO TOP
:END
```

This example uses only five choices. When you start adding lots more, the tests can become cumbersome.

As mentioned above, it's possible to shorten long cascades of IF ERRORLEVEL tests by using a FOR command to dispatch the branching operation correctly.

The demonstration LEVEL.BAT batch file uses seven programs called ERR-TEST0.COM through ERRTEST6.COM that simulate the errors in their filenames. It's a little complicated, but the batch file crams a ton of performance into a relatively small space:

```
ECHO OFF
IF %1!==! GOTO OOPS
```

```
FOR %%A IN (0 1 2 3 4 5 6) DO IF %1==%%A GOTO NEXT
GOTO OOPS
:NEXT
ERRTEST%1
FOR %%E IN (1 2 3 4 5 6) DO IF ERRORLEVEL %%E GOTO
LABEL%%E
ECHO Everything is okay
GOTO END
:LABEL1
ECHO ERROR #1
GOTO END
:LABEL2
ECHO ERROR #2
GOTO END
:LABEL3
ECHO ERROR #3
GOTO END
:LABEL4
ECHO ERROR #4
GOTO END
:LABEL5
ECHO ERROR #5
GOTO END
:LABEL6
ECHO ERRORLEVEL GREATER THAN 5
GOTO END
:OOPS
ECHO Enter %0 and then a number from 0 to 6
:END
```

The line:

```
IF %1!==! GOTO OOPS
```

tests to make sure you entered something after the name of the batch file, and the:

```
FOR %%A IN (0 1 2 3 4 5 6) DO IF %1==%%A GOTO NEXT
```

screens out any entries that aren't the digits 0 through 6.
    When you enter a valid digit, the line:

```
ERRTEST%1
```

tacks on (concatenates) the appropriate number in place of the %1 replaceable parameter, turning the ERRTEST string into something like ERRTEST2 or ERRTEST4. DOS then executes one of the seven error-simulating files on the disk, and the line:

```
FOR %%E IN (1 2 3 4 5 6) DO IF ERRORLEVEL %%E GOTO LABEL%%E
```

reads the error the small program generated and branches to the appropriate comment
line in the batch file.

While LEVEL.BAT simply prints a message and exits, you could easily modify it to
include specific actions to be taken for each error type. Also, note that if ERRORLEVEL
is some value larger than any in the list, control will transfer based on the last value in
the list.

To test this out, make sure DEBUG is handy and type in the following 24 lines. Or use
a pure ASCII word processor to type them into a script file called ERR.SCR, and when
you're done, get back to the DOS prompt and type:

```
DEBUG < ERR.SCR
```

This creates seven small files, ERRTEST0.COM through ERRTEST6.COM. Substitute them one at a time for the ERRTEST line in the LEVEL.BAT batch file. Each will
set an ERRORLEVEL equivalent to the number in its name.

```
E 100 B8 00 4C CD 21
RCX
5
N ERRTEST0.COM
W
E 101 1
N ERRTEST1.COM
W
E 101 2
N ERRTEST2.COM
W
E 101 3
N ERRTEST3.COM
W
E 101 4
N ERRTEST4.COM
W
E 101 5
N ERRTEST5.COM
W
E 101 6
N ERRTEST6.COM
W
Q
```

All of the key-processing programs above discard the keystroke after reading it and
setting an exit code. Since batch files execute painfully slowly on a slow system, an
impatient user may repeatedly press the key several times until he or she sees something

happen. The computer stores these extra keystrokes in the keyboard buffer, and they may cause problems.

You could adapt the basic GETKEY.COM program to display the key entered by changing it to:

```
MOV AH,0       ; BIOS read a character and
INT 16         ; puts its ASCII code into AL
MOV DL,AL      ; ready to display character
MOV AH,02      ; DOS display output
INT 21         ; do it
MOV AH,4C      ; ready to exit with code
INT 21         ; do it
```

Type the following to create it:

```
DEBUG
E 100 B4 00 CD 16 88 C2 B4 02 CD 21 B4 4C CD 21
N GETNEW1.COM
RCX
E
W
Q
```

If you wanted to adapt this to display uppercase letters for any uppercase or lowercase letters you entered, type:

```
E 100 B4 00 CD 16 24 DF 88 C2 B4 02 CD 21 B4 4C CD 21
N GETNEW2.COM
RCX
10
W
Q
```

This creates a program called GETNEW2.COM that will automatically uppercase any lowercase letter you enter while leaving uppercase entries alone. However, it works by performing a logical AND operation on the value in register AL:

```
AND AL,DF
```

If you entered a lowercase "a" (with a hex value of 61), ANDing this value with DF will turn it into 41, which is the hex value of uppercase "A." Enter an uppercase "A" and the AND DF operation will leave it alone.

Since this process forces the 2^5 bit to become unset (turning it into a 0), it will subtract a value of 32 from any number that has its 2^5 bit set, and leave any number that already has a 0 in that bit position alone.

- From 0 to 31 — values remain the same
- From 32 to 63 — it subtracts 32 from the value
- From 64 to 95 — values remain the same
- From 96 to 127 — it subtracts 32 from the value
- From 128 to 159 — values remain the same
- From 160 to 191 — it subtracts 32 from the value
- From 192 to 223 — values remain the same
- From 224 to 255 — it subtracts 32 from the value

So use a program like GETNEW2.COM with care.

Incidentally, as mentioned earlier, DOS offers a variety of key-processing functions, some of which display the key you press and some of which don't. Function 1 of interrupt 21 does. So you could just as easily have used:

```
MOV AH,1      ; DOS read a character and
INT 21        ; displays it
MOV AH,4C     ; ready to exit with code
INT 21        ; do it
```

to echo the keystroke to the screen.

Speeding Things Up

You may notice a lag when running batch files containing long strings of IF ERRORLEVEL tests on a slow system. The first rule of batch files is to execute them from RAMdisks or fast hard disks.

But you can also streamline the operation by designing your batch files properly. One method for speeding things up is to limit the number of choices. But this isn't really practical for many applications.

The second rule of batch files is that it's always better to do processing outside of the batch file. DOS executes batch files one slow line at a time. But an assembly language program can process keyboard information virtually instantly. You'll be able to take out almost all the potential delays by putting the tests you want in the key-processing program rather than in the batch file. That's why this section included so many examples and provided the assembly language code for each. You should be able to adapt one of the above programs to do all the testing you need.

But if you do have to put a cascade of IF ERRORLEVEL tests in your batch files, you'll find one method is indeed faster than the other. Tests generally work in one of two ways. You either put the muscle on each line or spread it over a dispatching cascade:

To put it on each line, test for a value, and make sure the next higher value isn't valid:

```
ECHO OFF
:TOP
ECHO Type a letter key (A-Z) or Esc to quit:
```

```
GETLETR
IF ERRORLEVEL 27 GOTO END
IF ERRORLEVEL 26 IF NOT ERRORLEVEL 27 ECHO Z
IF ERRORLEVEL 25 IF NOT ERRORLEVEL 26 ECHO Y
IF ERRORLEVEL 24 IF NOT ERRORLEVEL 25 ECHO X
```

and so on. To dispatch the command execution, try something like:

```
ECHO OFF
:TOP
ECHO Type a letter key (A-Z) or Esc to quit:
GETLETR
IF ERRORLEVEL 27 GOTO END
IF ERRORLEVEL 26 GOTO Z
IF ERRORLEVEL 25 GOTO Y
IF ERRORLEVEL 24 GOTO X
     .

     .

     .

:Z
ECHO Z
GOTO TOP
:Y
ECHO Y
GOTO TOP
:X
ECHO X
GOTO TOP
:W
```

etc. The second way is faster.

Batch File Applications

The small demonstration programs above were designed to exercise the various batch commands and show you how they operate. But if you really want to put these commands to work, try some of the following batch file applications.

DOS Notepads

Batch files make it easy to harness the DOS COPY CON command and turn it into a quick notepad. One method for doing this is to type in the BUILD.BAT batch file below, and then enter:

```
BUILD filename
```

when you're in DOS (substituting the name of your own file). BUILD.BAT will clear the screen, display a ruler line, and save all your input in an ASCII file called filename. When you're finished entering text, simply hit the Z key while holding down the Ctrl key and then press the Enter key — or just press the F6 function key, which does the same thing. If a file with the same name as filename already exists, BUILD.BAT will rename it to have a BAK extension. By specifying PRN as the filename, all text entered is dumped to your default printer. This is useful for short memos or notes.

Since BUILD.BAT allows only the current line to be edited, it won't replace your word processor. In fact, even EDLIN leaves it in its dust. But it does allow you to create tiny batch files or memos quickly and painlessly in DOS. And it's forgiving enough not to write over an existing file.

```
ECHO OFF
IF %1!==! GOTO OOPS
IF %1==PRN GOTO START
IF EXIST %1.BAK GOTO OOPS2
IF NOT EXIST %1 GOTO START
REN %1 *.BAK
:START
CLS
ECHO ** Press F6 and then the Enter key when you're all done to save %1 **
ECHO    5   10   15   20   25   30   35   40   45   50   55   60   65   70   75
ECHO ----!----!----!----!----!----!----!----!----!----!----!----!----!----!----
COPY CON %1
GOTO END
:OOPS
ECHO Enter a filename after %0
GOTO END
:OOPS2
ECHO You already have a file called %1.BAK
ECHO Rename or erase it so this can proceed
:END
```

Another memo maker, QUIKNOTE.BAT, creates a small memo file and lets you update it automatically without having to use a word processor.

After you've entered any information, typing QUIKNOTE will display it. To update the information, just type QUIKNOTE followed by up to nine words of text. The next time you type QUIKNOTE the new text will appear, appended to the old.

QUIKNOTE.BAT also prints instructions even if you don't enter anything after the filename:

```
ECHO OFF
IF %1!==! GOTO DISPLAY
ECHO %1 %2 %3 %4 %5 %6 %7 %8 %9 >> %0.DOC
```

```
:DISPLAY
CLS
IF NOT EXIST %0.DOC GOTO OOPS
TYPE %0.DOC
GOTO END
:OOPS
ECHO You haven't entered anything yet . . .
ECHO To enter data, type %0 and then type
ECHO up to 9 words on each line
ECHO (You can enter up to 23 lines.)
ECHO ----
ECHO To see what you've typed, just type %0
:END
```

A Date with DOS

You can adapt the above techniques to create a small appointment book that lets you add and delete entries, sorts your appointments for you automatically, and can show you in just a few seconds what you have lined up on any day:

```
ECHO OFF
IF %1!==! GOTO LIST
IF %2!==! GOTO TODAY
ECHO %1 %2 %3 %4 %5 %6 %7 %8 %9 >> NEW.DAT
SORT < NEW.DAT > TODO
ECHO (%1 %2 %3 %4 %5 %6 %7 %8 %9 ADDED)
GOTO DONE
:LIST
IF NOT EXIST TODO GOTO FIRSTIME
ECHO ****** APPOINTMENTS ********
MORE < TODO
:FIRSTIME
ECHO ***************************
ECHO To enter appointments, type:
ECHO ---------------------------
ECHO %0 DATE TIME MEMO
ECHO ---------------------------
ECHO WHERE DATE = MM/DD
ECHO TIME = HH/MM
ECHO MEMO = 7 OR FEWER WORDS
GOTO DONE
:TODAY
ECHO *** TODAY'S APPOINTMENTS ***
```

```
IF NOT EXIST TODO GOTO FIRSTIME
FIND "%1" TODO
:DONE
```

To use APPT.BAT just type:

```
APPT APPTDATE APPTTIME APPTMEMO
```

where APPTDATE is in MM/DD format (and you pad out single digit months and days with zeros), APPTTIME is in HH:MM format (and you pad out single digit hours and minutes with zeros here also), and APPTMEMO is text from one to seven words long.

If you simply type:

```
APPT
```

the batch file will type all your appointments. And if you type:

```
APPT MM/DD
```

(substituting a real date, such as 01/05 for MM/DD), the batch file will display all the appointments for that particular date.

For APPT.BAT to work, you must either have the DOS SORT.EXE, MORE.COM, and FIND.EXE files on your disk or have them properly pathed to. Still, it's not perfect. If you ask it to find 2/1 it will also show any line with a 2/11 or 12/11 date at the beginning, as well as any line with a 2/1 in the memo part of a listing that starts with a totally unrelated date.

However, you can also use it to display all your appointments on all dates with Mr. Jones, by typing APPT Jones (it's case sensitive, so it won't find JONES if you ask for Jones), or all your meetings with different people on the subject of taxes if the word taxes appears in the memo area of several different appointments with those different people. If you try searching for key words rather than dates, remember these have to be single words — you can search for "Jones" but not "John Jones."

You can indeed have DOS remove names as well as add them. APPT.BAT keeps track of things with the files NEW.BAT and TODO. REMOVE.BAT uses the FIND /V command to expunge any date you don't want from these two files:

```
ECHO OFF
IF %1!==! GOTO OOPS
FIND /V "%1" NEW.DAT | FIND /V "-" | FIND " " > TEMP
DEL NEW.DAT
DEL TODO
REN TEMP NEW.DAT
COPY NEW.DAT TODO > NUL
GOTO END
:OOPS
```

```
ECHO Enter the date you want removed after
ECHO the word %0
:END
```

To remove everything on 6/12, type:

```
REMOVE 6/12
```

Or to remove all references to Mrs. Smith, type:

```
REMOVE Smith
```

(observing case sensitivity and remembering that this will also remove any references to Mr. Smith if one exists).

Free Dialer

Now that you have a memo pad and an appointment book, you'll need a telephone dialer. By using features of the Hayes Smartmodem and the output redirection capabilities of DOS, you can turn a simple batch file into your own telephone dialer with its own built-in directory,

DIAL.BAT will automatically dial the phone (with a 1200 baud modem), disconnect the modem, and allow you to continue the call. In addition, it lets you set up an extensive dialing directory by expanding the conditional tests for names within the program. You'll need to have the DOS MODE.COM and FIND.EXE programs in the same directory as the dialer program or in a directory your PATH command knows about.

```
ECHO OFF
MODE COM1:1200 >NUL
IF %1!==! GOTO OOPS
IF %1 == # GOTO LIST
IF %1 == TOM GOTO TOM#
IF %1 == Tom GOTO TOM#
IF %1 == tom GOTO TOM#
IF %1 == DICK GOTO DICK#
IF %1 == Dick GOTO DICK#
IF %1 == dick GOTO DICK#
IF %1 == HARRY GOTO HARRY#
IF %1 == Harry GOTO HARRY#
IF %1 == harry GOTO HARRY#
ECHO ATDT%1; >COM1:
GOTO END
:TOM#
```

```
ECHO ATDT111-1111; >COM1:
GOTO END
:DICK#
ECHO ATDT222-2222; >COM1:
GOTO END
:HARRY#
ECHO ATDT9-333-3333; >COM1:
GOTO END
:LIST
ECHO The %0 batch file currently
ECHO contains numbers for:
FIND "#" %0.BAT | FIND /V "%%"
GOTO BYE
:OOPS
ECHO You have to enter a number or a name that
ECHO you've put in the batch file after %0
ECHO eg %0 555-1212 or %0 TOM
ECHO OR - Type %0 # to see a list of names
ECHO currently in the %0.BAT directory
GOTO BYE
:END
ECHO -------------------------------
ECHO When the dialing is done, press
ECHO any key to disconnect the modem.
ECHO -------------------------------
PAUSE
ECHO ATH >COM1:
:BYE
```

To use DIAL.BAT, just type:

```
DIAL number
```

or:

```
DIAL name
```

where number is the telephone number you wish to dial, and name is the name of someone in the batch file's directory. Listen to the speaker in the modem to determine when the dialing is done, lift the handset, and then press any key to disconnect the modem and reconnect the handset. Complete your call as usual.

So if you want to call your friend Tom, and you've put his name in the directory, you can enter:

```
DIAL TOM
```

(or DIAL Tom or DIAL tom). If you haven't put his name in the directory, but you know his number is 123-4567, enter:

```
DIAL 123-4567
```

You can see which names are currently included in your DIAL.BAT batch file by typing:

```
DIAL #
```

The names TOM, DICK, and HARRY in the sample DIAL.BAT batch file and the phone numbers that follow are obvious dummies. Replace them with your own entries. Note the following rules, however:

1. You should add three tests for each name, so you can type them in in uppercase, lowercase, or with an initial capital letter.
2. Make sure you put a # at the end of each label, as shown by :TOM# or :DICK#, as well as in the GOTO TOM# or GOTO DICK# commands. This lets the FIND command isolate the names if you enter DIAL # to see which names are currently listed in the batch file.

MODE insures that the right COM port is set to the proper baud rate. If you're using COM2 or a different baud rate, change the values in the program accordingly. MODE usually prints a message to the screen; DIAL.BAT gets rid of this by redirecting it to the NUL device.

When using modems by manufacturers other than Hayes, be sure the RS-232-C lines CTS (clear to send) and DSR (data set ready) from the modem are on, or else you'll get a DOS error. And although some non-Hayes modem options can be set for DSR and CTS on, the lines may be disabled until the "wake up" signal is sent to the modem. DOS, however, aborts the transmission to the modem before it sends any characters at all since the modem does not appear to be ready.

Free Telephone Directory

Hate to look up numbers in your telephone book or Rolodex? You don't ever have to again; DOS can do all the work for you.

The trick is to whip together three batch files — ADD.BAT, REMOVE.BAT, and LOOKUP.BAT. Then create a subdirectory called \PHONES that contains these batch files and room for the NAME.LST list of names.

ADD.BAT is very straightforward:

```
ECHO OFF
IF %1!==! GOTO OOPS
IF %1==# GOTO SEELIST
```

```
ECHO %1 %2 %3 %4 %5 %6 %7 %8 %9 >> NAME.LST
SORT < NAME.LST > TEMP
DEL NAME.LST
REN TEMP NAME.LST
GOTO END
:OOPS
ECHO To add data, enter up to 9 words after %0:
ECHO -------------------------------------------------
ECHO LASTNAME FIRSTNAME PHONENUMBER ADDRESS MEMO
ECHO -------------------------------------------------
ECHO (Try to avoid spaces, so use 212-555-1212
ECHO rather than (212) 555 1212)
ECHO -------------------------------------------------
ECHO ** Or enter %0 # to see the whole list **
GOTO END
:SEELIST
IF NOT EXIST NAME.LST GOTO OOPS
MORE < NAME.LST
:END
```

You either type ADD followed by up to nine words:

```
ADD Cleaver Theodore 312-555-1111 34 Elm, Chicago, IL 34567
```

or:

```
ADD #
```

to see the whole list.
   REMOVE.BAT is also simple:

```
ECHO OFF
IF %1!==! GOTO OOPS
FIND /V "%1" NAME.LST | FIND /V "NAME.LST" | FIND " " > TEMP
COPY NAME.LST NAME.OLD > NUL
DEL NAME.LST
REN TEMP NAME.LST
GOTO END
:OOPS
ECHO Enter a key word from the line you want
ECHO removed after the word %0
:END
```

To delete a name, just type:

```
REMOVE Cleaver
```

But be careful, since this will remove any line that has the character string Cleaver in it. However, if you find you've made a mistake, you won't lose anything since RE-MOVE.BAT creates a backup file each time called NAME.OLD.

LOOKUP.BAT is the simplest of all:

```
ECHO OFF
IF %1!==! GOTO OOPS
IF %1==# GOTO SEELIST
FIND "%1" NAME.LST | MORE
GOTO END
:OOPS
ECHO To look up data, enter %0 then a single key word
ECHO ** Or enter %0 # to see the whole list **
GOTO END
:SEELIST
IF NOT EXIST NAME.LST GOTO OOPS2
MORE < NAME.LST
GOTO END
:OOPS2
ECHO First use ADD.BAT to create your NAME.LST
:END
```

You can retrieve information in all sorts of useful ways. You could, of course, hunt for a name by typing something like:

```
LOOKUP Benway
```

But you could also get a list of all the names and numbers in NY by typing:

```
LOOKUP NY
```

Or if you remember that someone has a telephone number containing a 98 in it, but you can't remember the name or anything else, you could type:

```
LOOKUP 98
```

You can also add "keys" like BB to indicate business, or HH to tell you the listing is a home address.

Obviously this isn't perfect. It's case sensitive, so it wouldn't report Dr. Benway if you typed the lowercase:

```
LOOKUP benway
```

But it would find him if you entered an abbreviated form, like:

```
LOOKUP enwa
```

since it looks for occurrences of character strings. In any event, it's fast and handy, and it can retrieve names and numbers when all you have to go on is a scrap of information such as part of a phone number or a recollection that the person was on the west coast (with a 90xxx Zip code).

Again, to make this work, you have to have FIND.EXE, SORT.EXE, and MORE.COM in the same subdirectory, or in one your path knows about.

Daily Chores

If you need a way to run your systems unattended overnight to reindex data base files, print reports, and get your electronic mail, or if you want to run certain programs on certain days only, you can have batch files do all the dirty work for you.

You need a few small utilities to help. GETDATE.COM returns an ERRORLEVEL of 1 to 31 equal to the current date-of-month. GETMONTH returns an ERRORCODE of 1 to 12, equal to the current month. DOW.COM returns an error code related to the day of the week, where Sunday equals 0 and Saturday equals 6.

To create the three programs, type in the following 15 lines:

```
DEBUG
E 100 B4 2A CD 21 88 F0 B4 4C CD 21 CD 20
N GETMONTH.COM
RCX
C
W
E 105 D0
N GETDATE.COM
W
E 104 B4 4C CD 21 CD 20
N DOW.COM
RCX
A
W
Q
```

Then create the three batch files below: SHOWMON.BAT, SHOWDATE.BAT, and WEEKDAY.BAT. Substitute your own commands in place of the dummy ECHO statements to execute your programs at specified times. First, SHOWMON.BAT:

```
ECHO OFF
REM This is SHOWMON.BAT
GETMONTH
```

```
IF ERRORLEVEL 1 IF NOT ERRORLEVEL 2 ECHO Month = Jan
IF ERRORLEVEL 2 IF NOT ERRORLEVEL 3 ECHO Month = Feb
IF ERRORLEVEL 3 IF NOT ERRORLEVEL 4 ECHO Month = Mar
IF ERRORLEVEL 4 IF NOT ERRORLEVEL 5 ECHO Month = Apr
IF ERRORLEVEL 5 IF NOT ERRORLEVEL 6 ECHO Month = May
IF ERRORLEVEL 6 IF NOT ERRORLEVEL 7 ECHO Month = Jun
IF ERRORLEVEL 7 IF NOT ERRORLEVEL 8 ECHO Month = Jul
IF ERRORLEVEL 8 IF NOT ERRORLEVEL 9 ECHO Month = Aug
IF ERRORLEVEL 9 IF NOT ERRORLEVEL 10 ECHO Month = Sep
IF ERRORLEVEL 10 IF NOT ERRORLEVEL 11 ECHO Month = Oct
IF ERRORLEVEL 11 IF NOT ERRORLEVEL 12 ECHO Month = Nov
IF ERRORLEVEL 12 ECHO Month = Dec
```

Next, SHOWDATE.BAT:

```
ECHO OFF
REM This is SHOWDATE.BAT
GETDATE
IF ERRORLEVEL 1 IF NOT ERRORLEVEL 2 ECHO Date = 1st
IF ERRORLEVEL 2 IF NOT ERRORLEVEL 3 ECHO Date = 2nd
IF ERRORLEVEL 3 IF NOT ERRORLEVEL 4 ECHO Date = 3rd
IF ERRORLEVEL 4 IF NOT ERRORLEVEL 5 ECHO Date = 4th
IF ERRORLEVEL 5 IF NOT ERRORLEVEL 6 ECHO Date = 5th
IF ERRORLEVEL 6 IF NOT ERRORLEVEL 7 ECHO Date = 6th
IF ERRORLEVEL 7 IF NOT ERRORLEVEL 8 ECHO Date = 7th
IF ERRORLEVEL 8 IF NOT ERRORLEVEL 9 ECHO Date = 8th
IF ERRORLEVEL 9 IF NOT ERRORLEVEL 10 ECHO Date = 9th
IF ERRORLEVEL 10 IF NOT ERRORLEVEL 11 ECHO Date = 10th
IF ERRORLEVEL 11 IF NOT ERRORLEVEL 12 ECHO Date = 11th
IF ERRORLEVEL 12 IF NOT ERRORLEVEL 13 ECHO Date = 12th
IF ERRORLEVEL 13 IF NOT ERRORLEVEL 14 ECHO Date = 13th
IF ERRORLEVEL 14 IF NOT ERRORLEVEL 15 ECHO Date = 14th
IF ERRORLEVEL 15 IF NOT ERRORLEVEL 16 ECHO Date = 15th
IF ERRORLEVEL 16 IF NOT ERRORLEVEL 17 ECHO Date = 16th
IF ERRORLEVEL 17 IF NOT ERRORLEVEL 18 ECHO Date = 17th
IF ERRORLEVEL 18 IF NOT ERRORLEVEL 19 ECHO Date = 18th
IF ERRORLEVEL 19 IF NOT ERRORLEVEL 20 ECHO Date = 19th
IF ERRORLEVEL 20 IF NOT ERRORLEVEL 21 ECHO Date = 20th
IF ERRORLEVEL 21 IF NOT ERRORLEVEL 22 ECHO Date = 21st
IF ERRORLEVEL 22 IF NOT ERRORLEVEL 23 ECHO Date = 22nd
IF ERRORLEVEL 23 IF NOT ERRORLEVEL 24 ECHO Date = 23rd
IF ERRORLEVEL 24 IF NOT ERRORLEVEL 25 ECHO Date = 24th
IF ERRORLEVEL 25 IF NOT ERRORLEVEL 26 ECHO Date = 25th
IF ERRORLEVEL 26 IF NOT ERRORLEVEL 27 ECHO Date = 26th
IF ERRORLEVEL 27 IF NOT ERRORLEVEL 28 ECHO Date = 27th
```

```
IF ERRORLEVEL 28 IF NOT ERRORLEVEL 29 ECHO Date = 28th
IF ERRORLEVEL 29 IF NOT ERRORLEVEL 30 ECHO Date = 29th
IF ERRORLEVEL 30 IF NOT ERRORLEVEL 31 ECHO Date = 30th
IF ERRORLEVEL 31 ECHO Date = 31st
```

(This long batch file is actually easy to create using the copy commands of your word processor or EDLIN.) And finally WEEKDAY.BAT:

```
ECHO OFF
REM This is WEEKDAY.BAT
DOW
IF ERRORLEVEL 0 IF NOT ERRORLEVEL 1 ECHO Sun
IF ERRORLEVEL 1 IF NOT ERRORLEVEL 2 ECHO Mon
IF ERRORLEVEL 2 IF NOT ERRORLEVEL 3 ECHO Tue
IF ERRORLEVEL 3 IF NOT ERRORLEVEL 4 ECHO Wed
IF ERRORLEVEL 4 IF NOT ERRORLEVEL 5 ECHO Thu
IF ERRORLEVEL 5 IF NOT ERRORLEVEL 6 ECHO Fri
IF ERRORLEVEL 6 ECHO Sat
```

The sample batch files are based on pairs of IF ERRORLEVEL tests on each line. Since IF ERRORLEVEL tests are true if the exit codes they test are equal to — or greater than — the value after IF ERRORLEVEL, you have to screen out the next higher one to isolate any exit code.

You could put just one test on each line, interspersed with GOTO statements. The following WEEK2.BAT would yield the same results as WEEKDAY.BAT, but it's far longer:

```
ECHO OFF
REM This is WEEK2.BAT
DOW
IF ERRORLEVEL 1 GOTO 1
ECHO It's Sunday
GOTO END
:1
IF ERRORLEVEL 2 GOTO 2
ECHO It's Monday
GOTO END
:2
IF ERRORLEVEL 3 GOTO 3
ECHO It's Tuesday
GOTO END
:3
IF ERRORLEVEL 4 GOTO 4
ECHO It's Wednesday
GOTO END
```

```
:4
IF ERRORLEVEL 5 GOTO 5
ECHO It's Thursday
GOTO END
:5
IF ERRORLEVEL 6 GOTO 6
ECHO It's Friday
GOTO END
:6
ECHO It's Saturday
:END
```

You could also try setting environment variables rather than ECHOing directly. The following WEEKDAY2.BAT batch file will cycle through the choices, resetting the environment variable DAY until the IF test is no longer true, and then retrieve the current setting and ECHO it to the screen.

```
ECHO OFF
REM This is WEEKDAY2.BAT
DOW
IF ERRORLEVEL 0 SET DAY=Sun
IF ERRORLEVEL 1 SET DAY=Mon
IF ERRORLEVEL 2 SET DAY=Tue
IF ERRORLEVEL 3 SET DAY=Wed
IF ERRORLEVEL 4 SET DAY=Thu
IF ERRORLEVEL 5 SET DAY=Fri
IF ERRORLEVEL 6 SET DAY=Sat
ECHO Day is %DAY%
```

The advantage here is that once you've run WEEKDAY2.BAT, other programs and batch files can grab the DAY variable directly from the environment without having to rerun the WEEKDAY2.BAT and DOW.COM. The DAY variable and its value don't take up much environment space, but you should consider expanding your environment just to make sure you don't run out. Or insert a placeholder:

```
SET DAY=XXX
```

command in your AUTOEXEC.BAT file to reserve the few bytes needed.

It's simple to adapt this process to report on anything DOS can sniff out. For instance, create the ID.COM and MODEREAD.COM programs by typing in this MODEID.SCR file:

```
A
MOV AX,F000      ; top segment
MOV DS,AX        ; ready to use it
MOV BX,FFFE      ; ID offset
MOV AX,[BX]      ; ready to read it
MOV AH,4C        ; exit with code
INT 21           ; do it


RCX
E
N ID.COM
W
A 100
MOV AH,0F        ; get video mode
INT 10           ; do it
MOV AH,4C        ; exit with code
INT 21 ; do it


RCX
8
N MODEREAD.COM
W
Q
```

Be careful to leave the two blank lines above each **RCX**, and to press the Enter key at the end of each line — especially the last one. Then, at the DOS prompt, type:

```
DEBUG < MODEID.SCR
```

Or, just type the following 12 lines:

```
DEBUG
E 100 B8 00 F0 8E D8 BB FE FF 8B 07 B4 4C CD 21
N ID.COM
RCX
E
W
E 100 B4 0F CD 10 B4 4C CD 21
N MODEREAD.COM
RCX
8
W
Q
```

Then run HARDWARE.BAT:

```
ECHO OFF
REM This is HARDWARE.BAT
ID
IF ERRORLEVEL 255 ECHO System = PC
IF ERRORLEVEL 254 IF NOT ERRORLEVEL 255 ECHO System = XT or Portable
IF ERRORLEVEL 253 IF NOT ERRORLEVEL 254 ECHO System = PCjr
IF ERRORLEVEL 252 IF NOT ERRORLEVEL 253 ECHO System = AT or Model 50 or 60 or XT/286
IF ERRORLEVEL 251 IF NOT ERRORLEVEL 252 ECHO System = XT
IF ERRORLEVEL 250 IF NOT ERRORLEVEL 251 ECHO System = Model 30 or 25
IF ERRORLEVEL 249 IF NOT ERRORLEVEL 250 ECHO System = Convertible
IF ERRORLEVEL 248 IF NOT ERRORLEVEL 249 ECHO System = Model 80
```

Obviously these are demonstration programs and not workhorse batch files. To put them to use, you'd have to jump to different system-handling and screen-handling routines instead of just printing messages as these do here.

Time of the Month

Or, you may want to execute a specific program at boot-up on a specific day, perhaps to run CHKDSK once each week and Peter Norton's DISKTEST once each month to monitor the condition of a fixed drive. Batch files make it easy.

First, create the DATECHEK.COM program by typing in the DATECHEK.SCR script:

```
A
MOV AH,2A     ; get date
INT 21        ; do it
CMP AL,02     ; is it Tues?
JNZ 0113      ; no, AL=2
MOV AL,00     ; yes, AL=0
CMP DL,08     ; first week?
JNB 0115      ; no, AL=0
MOV AL,01     ; yes, AL=1
JMP 0115      ; skip next line
MOV AL,02     ; set level
MOV AH,4C     ; exit with code
INT 21        ; do it

RCX
19
```

```
N DATECHEK.COM
W
Q
```

Again, be careful to leave the blank line above RCX and to press Enter after each line, especially the last one. Then get back into DOS and type:

```
DEBUG < DATECHEK.SCR
```

Or just type the following eight lines:

```
DEBUG
E 100 B4 2A CD 21 3C 02 75 0B B0 00 80 FA 08
E 10D 73 06 B0 01 EB 02 B0 02 B4 4C CD 21
N DATECHEK.COM
RCX
19
W
Q
```

Then create a CHKDATE.BAT batch file:

```
ECHO OFF
DATECHEK
IF ERRORLEVEL 2 GOTO 2
IF ERRORLEVEL 1 GOTO 1
ECHO It's Tues (not the 1st)
GOTO END
:2
ECHO It's not Tuesday
GOTO END
:1
ECHO It's the first Tuedsay
:END
```

DATECHEK program requests the system date via function 2AH, looks for the day of the week and, if it is Tuesday, then checks to see if it is the first Tuesday of the month. The program terminates with function 4CH, which returns a value in AL that the IF ERRORLEVEL command can test in a batch file.

You can alter the day of the week to be tested by changing the line:

```
CMP AL,02
```

in the listing (00 = Sun, 02 = Tues, 06 = Sat). If you wanted to patch an existing DATECHEK.COM program with DEBUG, change the value at offset 105. So to change it to Wednesday, which has a value of 3, type:

```
DEBUG DATECHEK.COM
E 105 3
W
Q
```

The day of the month is reported in DL. Tuesday was chosen to avoid missing the monthly test due to a holiday (July 1 and January 1 present problems only infrequently).

The CHKDATE.BAT uses the ERRORLEVEL returned by DATECHEK.COM to branch to the appropriate test. It's a dummy file for demonstration purposes; substitute your own commands for the ECHO messages shown.

Current Events

It's usually difficult to give DOS access to the date or time when running batch files. But there's a way to get around this problem.

Assume you want to run a program called ONCEONLY.COM only once a day. Add the following line to your AUTOEXEC.BAT:

```
ECHO | MORE | DATE > READDATE.BAT
```

and make:

```
READDATE
```

the last line in your AUTOEXEC.BAT. Then create a batch file called CURRENT.BAT:

```
ECHO OFF
IF !%TODAY%==!%4 GOTO END
SET TODAY=%4
REM ONCEONLY program goes here
:END
```

You can even arrange that it runs only once a week, say every Friday, by adding a line:

```
IF NOT %3==Fri GOTO END
```

after the line SET TODAY=%4. And as a bonus, you wind up with today's date in the environment.

This works by creating a file READDATE.BAT, containing the output of DATE:

```
Current date is Sun 9-30-1990
Enter new date (mm-dd-yy):
```

DOS tries to run the line beginning with "Current date is" by looking for an executable file (with an extension COM, EXE, or BAT) called CURRENT — and finds the one we created called CURRENT.BAT. DOS then interprets the groups of words and numbers following the word "Current" as parameters for CURRENT.BAT. So it reads "date" as %1, "is" as %2, the day of the week as %3, and the actual numeric date as %4.

One special trick that's worth noting is the use of the MORE command in the middle of the ECHO | MORE | DATE > READDATE.BAT line. All this does is supply the extra carriage return that the DATE command needs to execute properly. (To make this work, MORE.COM has to be in the same directory or be in one your path knows about.) Note also that adding READDATE as the final line in your AUTOEXEC.BAT means that as soon as AUTOEXEC.BAT finishes, DOS will load and execute READDATE.BAT.

You could adapt this process slightly if you didn't have an internal clock but needed to reboot frequently. First, put these lines near the top of your AUTOEXEC.BAT file:

```
ECHO OFF
IF NOT EXIST D.BAT GOTO SETIT
COMMAND /C D
:SETIT
DATE
DATEMAKE
```

and then a final AUTOEXEC.BAT line:

```
DATEMAKE
```

The COMMAND /C allows one batch file to run another batch file and then jump execution back to the first when the second is done. Users of DOS 3.3 or later could substitute CALL for COMMAND /C. D.BAT is a short batch file created by DATEMAKE.BAT, containing the lines

```
Current date is Sun 9-30-1990
Enter new date (mm-dd-yy):
```

(or whatever the last set date was).

The DATE command below COMMAND /C D lets you correct the date the first time you run AUTOEXEC.BAT each day. DATEMAKE.BAT contains the single line:

```
ECHO | MORE | DATE > D.BAT
```

Again, MORE.COM has to be in the current subdirectory or in one your PATH knows about. The only other file you need for this to work is a tiny one called, you guessed it, CURRENT.BAT:

```
DATE %4
```

Real-Time Batch File Entries

If you could send a command from the keyboard to a batch file while it was executing, you could enter a switch or a command as needed during execution. To do this, include a line:

```
COPY CON TEST.BAT
```

in your batch file. As soon as DOS reaches this line it will pause and let you enter anything you want. Then when you type Ctrl-Z and press Enter, DOS will resume processing the batch file.

To see this in action, type in the SAMPLE.BAT batch file below:

```
ECHO OFF
REM SAMPLE.BAT
ECHO    To edit or create a file
ECHO    using WordStar, type:
ECHO    WS followed by a filename
ECHO    Then Enter, Ctrl-Z, then Enter
ECHO       example: WS MYFILE.LET
ECHO (then Enter, Ctrl-Z, Enter)
COPY CON TEST.BAT
COMMAND /C TEST
ECHO end of demo
```

The COMMAND /C command (you may substitute CALL if you're using DOS 3.3 or later) executes the new TEST.BAT file that you just created. Then, when TEST.BAT finishes running, DOS returns control to the main SAMPLE.BAT batch file.

This is handy for giving instructions to new users and then executing the commands they type.

You can adapt this technique to create a real-time log that will keep track of who's using your system. Just create the following LOGIT.BAT batch file:

```
ECHO OFF
IF EXIST LOG GOTO NEXT
ECHO === Logfile === > LOG
:NEXT
ECHO This will add your name to the logfile
ECHO Instructions:
ECHO    1. Enter your name
ECHO    2. Hit the Enter key
ECHO    3. Hit the F6 key
ECHO    4. Hit the Enter key again
CTTY NUL
COPY CON ADD
```

```
COPY LOG+ADD /B
ECHO | MORE | TIME | FIND "Current" >> LOG
ECHO ------------------------- >> LOG
CTTY CON
MORE < LOG
```

Run it by typing LOGIT. When prompted, enter your name, then press Enter, then press F6, then Enter. Your name and the current time will be added to the log. You may also add comments below your name, on separate lines — just be sure to press Enter, then F6, then Enter when you're done.

More Efficient Copies

DOS doesn't make it easy to copy groups of files from the current directory to another directory or disk with a single command — unless you do it with a batch file. The COPYEASY.BAT batch file lets you use as many as eight shorthand filespecs on a single command line:

```
ECHO OFF
IF "%2" == "" GOTO HELP
ECHO This will copy %2 %3 %4 %5 %6 %7 %8 %9
ECHO from
CD
ECHO to %1
ECHO Hit Ctrl-Break to abort, or
PAUSE
SET MYVAR=%1
SHIFT
:AGAIN
ECHO Copying %1 to %MYVAR%
FOR %%A IN (%1) DO COPY %%A %MYVAR% > NUL
SHIFT
IF NOT "%1" == "" GOTO AGAIN
SET MYVAR=
GOTO END
:HELP
ECHO To use this %0 utility, enter:
ECHO %0, DESTINATION, and up to 8 filespecs
ECHO in current directory. For example:
ECHO ----------------------------------
ECHO %0 B: *.BAT *.D?? MYFILE.TXT TEST.*
ECHO ----------------------------------
:END
```

This batch utility provides help if it's needed and specific feedback on what to type on the command line; it also requests confirmation before proceeding. This version uses only DOS commands, but you can streamline it by adding IF ERRORLEVEL branching.

COPYEASY really takes advantage of DOS variables. It starts out by using replaceable parameters to read everything off the command line, and then has the DOS SHIFT command process them one by one. Each time the SHIFT command executes it moves all the replaceable parameters up a notch, so %3 becomes %2 and %2 becomes %1 and the old value for %1 is discarded.

So if you entered:

```
COPYEASY D: *.BAT C*.COM ??.EXE
```

- %1 would = D:
- %2 would = *.BAT
- %3 would = C*.COM
- %4 would = ??.EXE

Execute SHIFT once and:

- %1 would = *.BAT
- %2 would = C*.COM
- %3 would = ??.EXE

The old D: value of %1 would vanish, and %4 wouldn't have any value. Remember, the %0 parameter is a special case — it represents the name of the batch file itself.

The %1 parameter originally represents the destination for all the copies, and this is used the whole time the batch file runs. But the first time SHIFT executes, it wipes out the old value of %1 and replaces it with what used to be %2. COPYEASY gets around this by taking the original value of %1 and setting it to an environment variable, with the command:

```
SET MYVAR=%1
```

It can then use this destination at any subsequent time in the batch file by referring to it as %MYVAR% rather than %1. And it cleans up when finished by removing the variable from the environment with the command:

```
SET MYVAR=
```

If you do try this, make sure your environment is large enough to hold the extra variable. Under DOS 2.0 and 2.1 you can patch COMMAND.COM at address ECF to represent the number of 16-byte memory paragraphs that will make up your new environment. (For DOS 2.11 the address is DF3.) For DOS 3.0 and 3.1, use a SHELL [d:][path]COMMAND.COM /E:n /P command in your CONFIG.SYS file, where n represents the number of 16-byte paragraphs. For versions 3.2 and later, use the same SHELL command but specify the actual number of bytes rather than paragraphs. The default in all cases is 160 bytes (ten paragraphs). You can boost it all the way up to 32K in DOS 3.2 and later, but are limited to 62 paragraphs in earlier versions.

AUTOEXEC.BAT

Virtually all users start their systems with AUTOEXEC.BAT files. But there are times when you want to start without all of the various programs your AUTOEXEC.BAT normally loads.

A combination of resident programs loaded by your AUTOEXEC.BAT might cause your machine to hang. Or, you might not want to run a product your AUTOEXEC.BAT installs (for example, you might not want to bring up your network before doing backups).

You could simply begin the file with a PAUSE command, but this means you'd have to sit by and watch the disks grind until you reached the PAUSE. And you'd end up just banging the space bar to proceed 99 percent of the time.

Or, you could boot off a floppy disk in your A: drive, or do what most users do — continually press Ctrl-Break while your machine is booting, hoping your AU-TOEXEC.BAT will be aborted before the critical instructions occur. Either solution is fine if you only run into the problem once in a while, but neither solution is ideal.

A far better method is to use a small program called KBFLAG.COM to monitor your keyboard as you boot up, and send a code to your AUTOEXEC.BAT file that an IF ERRORLEVEL instruction can trap. Once you install this program, you can press one single key while your machine is booting to avoid running your AUTOEXEC.BAT.

To create KBFLAG.COM, type in the following KBFLAG.SCR script:

```
A
MOV AX,40      ; segment 0040
MOV DS,AX      ; get it ready
MOV AL,[17]    ; get value at offset 17
MOV AH,4C      ; exit with code
INT 21         ; do it

RCX
C
N KBFLAG.COM
W
Q
```

Be sure to leave a blank space above RCX, and press the Enter key at the end of each line, especially the last one. Then get into DOS and type:

```
DEBUG < KBFLAG.SCR
```

Or just type in the following seven lines:

```
DEBUG
E 100 B8 40 00 8E D8 A0 17 00 B4 4C CD 21
N KBFLAG.COM
RCX
C
W
Q
```

Then, add these two lines at the very beginning of your AUTOEXEC.BAT:

```
KBFLAG
IF ERRORLEVEL number GOTO END
```

(replacing "number" with one from the chart below).

You'll also need a label at the end of your batch file that says simply:

```
:END
```

KBFLAG sets the DOS ERRORLEVEL to the value of the KBFLAG in the ROM BIOS area. You can use different keys to trigger KBFLAG. These keys, and the codes read by IF ERRORLEVEL, are:

1	=	Right shift
2	=	Left shift
4	=	Ctrl key
8	=	Alt key
16	=	ScrollLock
32	=	NumLock
64	=	CapsLock
128	=	Insert

For example, you can avoid running AUTOEXEC.BAT if you press and hold a Shift key while your machine boots, or if you simply press NumLock while your CONFIG.SYS is running.

You can add the above key values together. If you wanted the trigger to be the Right and Left Shift keys plus the Ins key (toggled on), you would use an ERRORLEVEL trap of 131 (1 + 2 + 128 = 131).

You could make your batch file test for several ERRORLEVELs, and act differently when different keys are pressed. For example, CapsLock could mean abort the AUTOEXEC.BAT, while NumLock could do everything but load a couple of resident programs. KBFLAG can be used in any BAT file, not just AUTOEXEC.BAT.

A handy way to do this is to use a value of 128. Then you can avoid running your AUTOEXEC.BAT file by toggling the Ins key when you boot up. KBFLAG will send a 128 to the IF ERRORLEVEL trap, which will branch to the :END label.

This is a far more elegant solution to avoiding AUTOEXEC.BAT than pounding on the keyboard, which can generate bootup errors and force you to press the F1 key and then restart the whole operation. Using the Ins (or NumLock, ScrollLock, or CapsLock) toggle means that you can branch out of the program with one simple key press, or start running normally by keeping your fingers off the keyboard.

The DOS Environment

The term "DOS Environment" is a little misleading. Novice users might think this is a discussion of the DOS interface and how users interact with it. The DOS environment could more appropriately be called the "DOS Cubbyhole," because it's a block of memory that has been set aside for the storage of variables used by DOS, batch files and some programs.

Typically, the environment is referred to as the *environment space*. This space is a block of memory set at a default size, depending on the version of DOS you are using. It is also resizable, which may be necessary when you start creating environment variables of your own. Casual DOS users are usually not aware of the environment and its contents until one day, the message "Out of environment space" appears on the screen. This message may appear if the environment space is not large enough for a program that uses it. More likely, it appears after you've been experimenting with the PATH, PROMPT, and SET commands. All of these commands insert variables into the environment, and if you like to set long paths or interesting DOS prompts, as discussed later in this chapter, you can rapidly use the memory allocated in the environment. Gaining more environment space is a simple matter of making a change in the CONFIG.SYS file and rebooting the system, unless you're using version 2.x or version 3.0 of DOS, in which case you'll need to patch COMMAND.COM, as described later.

The SET command can be used to see what's in the environment and to understand the way it works. If DOS has been installed and configured on your system already, or if you've previously set a system PATH and PROMPT, type SET now to see a listing of your environment. It may look similar to the following:

```
COMSPEC=C:\DOS\COMMAND.COM
PROMPT=$P$G
PATH=C:\DOS;\BATCH
TEMP=C:\WINDOWS\TEMP
```

Note: DOS 5.0 users may also see the DIRCMD variable, which specifies the default switches to be used with the DIR command when listing files.

From this listing, you can tell that the DOS environment space is the place where DOS stores information that it needs to refer to at a later time. Notice that variables are "equal" to values. For example, the COMSPEC variable is equal to the drive and path of the COMMAND.COM file. This variable is used to specify where DOS can find COM-MAND.COM if it needs to reload it into memory at a later time. Some programs remove parts of COMMAND.COM to free memory for their own use. When you exit the program, DOS looks in the environment for the COMSPEC variable to find out where COMMAND.COM is located.

Another variable is the line that reads TEMP=C:\WINDOWS\TEMP, which may or may not be in your listing. The TEMP variable is created by some programs to specify the directory where temporary files can be stored. Temporary files are created as a place to store information or the contents of memory while a program runs. The files are usually unnecessary after the program ends. In most cases, you can safely delete all the files in a temporary directory as long as the programs are not still running, but check the programs documentation before doing so. Microsoft Windows, for example, created the TEMP variable shown above. During installation, it inserted a SET commands in the AU-TOEXEC.BAT file to create the variable in the environment whenever the system is started.

DOS commands related to the environment are PATH, PROMPT, COMSPEC and SET, as listed below. The variables set by these commands are stored as strings in the environment. They can be referenced later by DOS, batch files or programs.

- PATH: Sets the path of directories that DOS will search when an executable file is called.
- PROMPT: Sets the format of the DOS prompt.
- COMSPEC: Specifies the location of COMMAND.COM.
- SET: Used to create custom environment variable for use by batch files or programs.

In addition, COMMAND.COM and the SHELL command (in CONFIG.SYS) will also be discussed in this chapter since they can be used to work with or change the environment size. For example, invoking COMMAND.COM at any time after DOS has already been loaded will install a second copy of COMMAND.COM. While this second command processor inherits the environment variable set in the original command processor, you can change them to suit your needs. When you exit to the first command processor, the original environment variable will be intact. You may want to load a second command processor so you can temporarily change the environment, then return to the way it was.

After the PATH, PROMPT, and COMSPEC commands have been executed and their variable have been placed in the environment, any remaining environment space can be used to store custom variables. A popular technique for overcoming some of the limitations of batch files has been to create environment variables that can be passed to other batch files. (Several interesting methods for doing so are discussed at the end of this chapter.)

Setting Environment Variables

To assign a value to a variable and place it in the environment, the SET command is used in the following form:

```
SET variable=value
```

where *variable* is the name of the new variable you want to define and *value* is the text string it will represent. For example, you could set a variable called MYDIR to the value C:\USERS\TOM with the following command:

```
SET MYDIR=C:\USERS\TOM
```

To see how this command affects the environment, type the SET command. The new entry will look similar to the following:

```
MYDIR=C:\USERS\TOM
```

You could then create a set of batch files that use the variable to copy, move or delete files in the directory specified by the variable value. In DOS batch files, the variable is used by surrounding it with percent (%) signs. For example, a batch file to move files from the directory specified by the MYDIR variable might have the following commands:

```
COPY %MYDIR%\*.DOC C:\ARCHIVE
DEL %MYDIR%\*.DOC
```

The first command copies all files with the DOC extension from the source directory specified by the MYDIR variable to the ARCHIVE destination directory. When the batch file is executed, this command would take the form:

```
COPY C:\USERS\TOM\*.DOC C:\ARCHIVE
```

The second command then clears the DOC files from the directory. It would take the form:

```
DEL C:\USERS\TOM\*.DOC
```

The environment variable name is always capitalized while the value maintains its lowercase format if you typed it that way. So, for example, if you typed:

```
SET homedir=c:\docfiles
```

a listing of the environment with the SET command would reveal the following:

```
HOMEDIR=c:\docfiles
```

Be careful not to include spaces on either side of the equal sign. If you do, those spaces become part of the variable name or its value. If you typed "HOMEDIR " you'd get

```
HOMEDIR =c:\docfiles
```

in the environment. You can copy over an existing environment variable by assigning it a new value, or you can clear an environment variable by issuing a new SET command without a value. To clear the HOMEDIR variable created above, you would type:

```
SET HOMEDIR =
```

Notice that the extra space was put in to remove the correct variable. Type SET and view the environment if you're not sure a variable has been removed.

Another thing to keep in mind is the 127-character limit for commands typed at the DOS prompt. And, when using the SET command, you are limited to a 123-character string since four characters are required to type "SET" at the beginning of the command. This is sometimes a problem when using the PATH command to set a long search path, but we'll give you ways to get around the problem in a moment.

You don't really need to include the SET command when using the PATH or PROMPT commands. It is an option that can be included for clarity. For example, the following commands accomplish the same thing, although you must use SET when creating your own environment variables.

```
SET PATH=C:\DOS
PATH=C:\DOS
```

Once you start adding your own variables to the environment, you run the risk of running out of environment space. However, expanding the environment space is a simple matter of including the SHELL command in the CONFIG.SYS file with an appropriate parameter to specify the new environment size.

In some cases, you may want to know how many bytes are being used in the environment. For instance, when running some batch files that set environment variables, you may need to know in advance if there will be enough room in the environment space for the new variables. To determine the amount of space used by the existing variables and their values, type the SET command, then count each character, including the equal sign. Because an ASCII 0 terminates each string in the environment, you'll need to add 1 for each line plus 1 for an additional ASCII 0 used to terminate the entire set of strings.

The remainder of this chapter descibes each of the commands, features and techniques you can use to affect the environment or work with environment variables. It may be important for you to expand the size of your environment, so the steps for doing so are covered first. Discussion of the COMSPEC, PATH, PROMPT and SET commands and the use of environment variables in batch files follows.

Expanding Environment Size

With the introduction of DOS 3.1, expansion of environment space became easy to accomplish by inserting a SHELL command to specify the new environment size in the CONFIG.SYS file, followed by a restart of your system. But keep in mind that you should not increase the environment space unless absolutely necessary since doing so reduces the amount of memory available to applications.

SHELL can also be used to specify the location of COMMAND.COM in a directory other than the root directory. Removing COMMAND.COM from the root makes sense for several reasons. First, you probably already have a duplicate copy in the \DOS directory anyway so you should remove the one in the root directory not only to free disk space but also to reduce clutter. Second, the copy of COMMAND.COM in the root directory is more likely to be copied over or accidentally deleted than the copy in the DOS directory. Third, a virus attack on COMMAND.COM is less likely if it is not located in the root directory, although this is no guarantee that a virus will not attack it.

SHELL also can take the place of the COMSPEC command. An additional parameter can be used to specify where COMMAND.COM is located in case it needs to be reloaded. As mentioned earlier, some utilities and programs temporarily remove COM-MAND.COM from memory to gain more room. When the program ends, COM-MAND.COM is reloaded from the location specified by either the COMSPEC variable or the directory specified in the SHELL command as shown below. The SHELL command takes a form similar to the following:

```
SHELL=C:\DOS\COMMAND.COM C:\DOS /P /E:512
```

where C:\DOS\COMMAND.COM is the location at which COMMAND.COM can be found when your system first boots. The second parameter, C:\DOS, can take the place of the COMSPEC variable by pointing to the directory where COMMAND.COM is located. To increase performance, you can specify the drive letter of a RAM disk in this parameter, then include a command in AUTOEXEC.BAT that copies COM-MAND.COM to the RAM disk. The /P option should always be included since it specifies that the command processor remain permanently in memory. The last parameter is used to expand the environment, as discussed next.

Altering the Environment Size

The default size of the environment in DOS versions 2.x, 3.x and 4.x is 160 bytes. With DOS version 5.0, the default environment size has been increased to 256 bytes. If you want to change the size, you can use the SHELL command with the /E parameter as described here. After placing the command in the CONFIG.SYS file, remember to reboot your system to initialize the new settings.

If you are still using DOS 3.1, the new environment size is specified in blocks of 16 bytes each with a range of 11 to 62 blocks. So, to increase to a new environment size of

256 bytes, you would specify 16 blocks. The SHELL command in the CONFIG.SYS file would look like:

```
SHELL=C:\DOS\COMMAND.COM /P /E:16
```

If you have DOS 3.2 or later, all you have to do is specify the new environment size in bytes, with a range of 160 bytes to 32,767 bytes. The following command specifies a new environment size of 320 bytes:

```
SHELL=C:\DOS\COMMAND.COM /P /E:320
```

Remember, the first parameter, C:\DOS\COMMAND.COM, specifies where COM-MAND.COM can be found during boot up. The second parameter (C:\DOS\) specifies where COMMAND.COM is located in case it needs to be reloaded. The /P option makes this copy of COMMAND.COM permanent.

Besides using SHELL to expand the environment space, it is often used when booting a hard drive system from a floppy disk for security reasons. For example, if you remove COMMAND.COM from the root directory, and remove the SHELL command from the CONFIG.SYS file, a system will not boot. However, you *can* start the system from a bootable diskette with a SHELL command in its CONFIG.SYS file that looks like:

```
SHELL=C:\DOS\COMMAND.COM C:\DOS\ /P
```

This command points to the copy of COMMAND.COM on the hard disk. From then on, the system will use the hard disk as its default drive. In this way you can hide the boot disk and prevent would-be snoopers from starting your system. While this method won't stop experienced DOS users, it might prevent your kids from logging on and using up all your disk space for games.

Patching DOS 2.x and DOS 3.0

Since the SHELL command cannot be used to expand the environment in DOS 2.x and 3.0, you'll need to use the brute force method of patching the COMMAND.COM file. This should always be done to a copy of COMMAND.COM, preferably on a diskette. Then you can boot from the diskette to test the altered version before copying it to your main boot disk.

To fix PC DOS 2.0 or 2.1, first format a floppy disk using the /S option, then issue the following commands to set the environment at a size of 256 bytes. Note that if you have MS DOS version 2.1, replace ECF in the second line with DF3.

```
DEBUG A:COMMAND.COM
E ECF 10
W
Q
```

To increase the size of the environment further, change the 10 in the second line to one of the following:

```
14    320 bytes
1E    480 bytes
28    640 bytes
32    800 bytes
3C    960 bytes
```

To patch DOS 3.0, format a floppy disk using the /S parameter, then type the following commands to increase the environment size to 256 bytes:

```
DEBUG A:COMMAND.COM
E F2C 10
W
Q
```

To increase the environment size further, replace the 10 in the second line with one of the other values listed above.

Using COMMAND to Load a Temporary Environment

A temporary command processor can be loaded by executing the COMMAND.COM command at the DOS prompt. Doing so installs a secondary command processor (or "child" process), complete with its own environment. The important point is that the environment of the second processor can be changed without affecting the environment of the first or "parent" command processor. To return to the parent, the EXIT command is typed. This clears the second command processor and restores the first, along with its original environment. In reality, the original environment was never removed or changed but continued to occupy space in memory while the second processor ran.

This feature offers several advantages for DOS users. Say, for instance, you need an expanded environment space, but only temporarily. You could load a secondary command processor. When you exit, the smaller environment and its variables are restored. In another case, you might want to temporarily change your environment variables. You could do so in the secondary environment, then return to your original environment variables by exiting the secondary processor. This is also useful if another person wants to use your system. Assume a coworker needs to run a program on your system that requires a change in the path and some environment variables, but you want to save your current settings. Just load a secondary processor and let the coworker make any changes he wants. When done, just type EXIT to return to your original environment.

Loading a secondary command processor takes about 5K of memory in DOS version 3.x and 4.x. If you use DOS 5.0 and DOS is loaded in the High Memory Area (HMA), only about 2K of memory is used by the secondary processor. If you are running short on memory, the amount used by the a secondary processor may be of consideration, but in most cases, the amount is too small to cause a problem.

To install a second command processor, type a command similar to that shown below. In this example, the /E parameter is used to specify an environment size of 512 bytes for the secondary processor.

```
COMMAND /E:512
```

If you don't specify an environment size, don't think that DOS will create a new environment space that matches the existing environment space in size. Instead, DOS makes the environment only as large as the existing number of characters in your current environment. This could be a problem if additional environment variables need to be added, or a new path setting has more characters than the existing path setting. To be on the safe side, always use the /E parameter to specify the exact environment size you need in the secondary environment. Remember to type EXIT to free up the memory used by the secondary environment when done.

The COMSPEC Command

As mentioned already, the SET COMSPEC command can be included in the AU-TOEXEC.BAT file to specify the location of COMMAND.COM. This command string is inserted into the environment space where it serves as a pointer to the COM-MAND.COM file. In this way, COMMAND.COM can be reloaded in memory if parts of it were discarded by a running program. The parts of COMMAND.COM that are normally discarded are those in the high memory area such as the DOS internal commands. Since most programs don't need to use these portions of COMMAND.COM while they run, the designers of DOS allowed them to be temporarily discarded to free up memory. An alternative method for specifying the location of COMMAND.COM is to include its directory location as the second parameter in the SHELL command, which was discussed earlier.

If DOS cannot find COMMAND.COM when it needs to reload it in memory, you will see the following message and the system will have to be rebooted, probably from a floppy disk until COMSPEC or SHELL are set correctly.

```
Cannot load COMMAND, system halted
```

COMSPEC is an acronym for COMmand SPECification. The string should include the drive and path to the file COMMAND.COM. Normally, COMSPEC can be inserted into the AUTOEXEC.BAT file using the form shown below. In this example, the DOS directory on drive C is specified as the location of COMMAND.COM.

```
SET COMSPEC=C:\DOS\COMMAND.COM
```

You may need to substitute a different drive or path, depending on the location of your COMMAND.COM, but if you don't set a command specifier using either COMSPEC or SHELL, the default COMSPEC will be as follows:

```
COMSPEC=C:\COMMAND.COM
```

To see what the current command specification is, type the SET command by itself at the DOS prompt.

On systems with fast hard drives and clock speeds, DOS reloads the discarded portions of COMMAND.COM very quickly and you probably won't notice a delay. On slower systems and those where COMMAND.COM needs to be reloaded from floppy disk, a noticeable delay may occur. This can be resolved by creating a RAM drive and copying COMMAND.COM to it. Then you can specify the RAM drive as the location of COMMAND.COM in the COMSPEC or SHELL command. The commands below can be inserted in the AUTOEXEC.BAT file to copy COMMAND.COM to RAM drive D and to set the new command specification.

```
COPY COMMAND.COM D:
SET COMSPEC=D:\COMMAND.COM
```

The PATH Command

The PATH command was introduced to DOS when hard disk filing systems began to appear. In fact, IBM announced DOS 2.0 and the IBM PC XT at the same time (March of 1983). The XT was IBM's first personal computer to include a hard drive, all 10MB of it! Before hard drive systems, users simply organized their files by separating them onto different floppy disks. With the large storage space available on hard drives, personal computer users could now keep many files available at once on one hard disk volume. Directories and subdirectories came into use in the DOS world as a method to separate and organize files. The PATH command allowed the user to specify which of these directories contained executable program files so those files could be run from outside the directory. In other words, the user could switch to a "data" directory, then start programs stored in a "program" directory. In this way, data files could be kept separate from program files.

Later versions of DOS included the APPEND command, which allows you to specify the location of directories where data files are located, so that you can request the use of a data file stored in a directory other than the one you are currently working in.

The PATH command lets you specify a set of directories on one or more drives that DOS will look through when you type an executable file name at the DOS prompt. However, DOS always looks in your current directory for the requested file before it starts looking down the path. The PATH command takes the following form:

```
SET PATH=d:\directory;\directory
```

where *d* is an optional drive letter and *directory* is the path of the directory to search. You can include many different directories by separating them with a semicolon. Also note that the SET portion of the command is optional. For example, the following PATH command sets the search path to the DOS directory on C, the BATCH directory on C, and the LOTUS directory on D.

```
PATH=C:\DOS;C:\BATCH;D:\LOTUS
```

Because DOS searches each directory in the list one after the other, you could optimize the search by placing directories most likely to contain the programs and batch files you use most at the beginning of the path. If, for instance, you always execute batch files to start other programs on your system, you might want to change the previous path to that shown below:

```
PATH=C:\BATCH;C:\DOS;D:\LOTUS
```

With such a small search path, this change is not likely to give you a big gain in performance. However, if your path is long, be sure to specify the most important or the most used directories first. If you have a RAM drive, you can copy your most used programs and batch files to the RAM drive, then include its drive letter at the beginning of the path. For example, the following command assumes that the RAM drive is E:

```
SET PATH=E:\;C:\BATCH;C:\DOS;D:\LOTUS
```

While you may be tempted to include as many directories as possible in a path, that may not be beneficial. First, long paths use environment space that may be needed for other variables. Second, typing an incorrect command will send DOS searching through every directory on the path before it displays an error message stating that the command could not be found. Methods for reducing the path are discussed later in this section.

If you have only one hard drive, you can eliminate the drive letters in the path, thus saving environment space for other variables. So, if drive C is the only drive you need to search, the previous path example could be changed to the following:

```
SET PATH=\DOS;\BATCH;\LOTUS
```

Additional methods for reducing the size of the path string and for optimizing the path search will be covered in a moment. But first, there are a few other features you need to know about PATH.

One school of thought on DOS directory organization maintains that data directories should branch from the directory of the application that creates them. Thus, you might have a directory called C:\LOTUS and, branching from it, a subdirectory called C:\LOTUS\DATA. When the directory structure is set up this way, you can include the parent directory symbol (..) in your path to make DOS search back one directory level, no matter what the current directory is. An example of the PATH command is shown below:

```
PATH=..;C:\DOS;C:\BATCH
```

Now, no matter what directory you are in, DOS will always search its parent directory first. If you were in the \LOTUS\DATA directory, you could start programs stored in the \LOTUS directory, even though it is not specifically named in the path.

To display the current path settings, type PATH at the DOS prompt without parameters, or type the SET command to display the PATH setting as it appears in the environment. To remove the path settings and have DOS search only the current directory, type either of the following commands:

```
PATH ;
PATH=
```

If a PATH command is not specified, only the current directory is searched. In fact, the current directory is automatically searched before DOS begins searching down the path. That means you don't need to include a . (the current directory specifier) in the path to search the current directory. Use this advantage when running batch files. Assume you have a set of batch files in a directory called C:\BATCH. Because this directory is on the path, you can run any batch file in it from any directory. But assume you have a directory where the batch file in the BATCH directory should not be used. Then, a slightly altered version must be run. If you create the altered version in this directory, DOS will always run it before running the one in the BATCH directory because the current directory is always searched first.

One more point about the lineup: DOS runs COM files before EXE files and EXE files before BAT files. So, if you had three files, STARTUP.COM, STARTUP.EXE and STARTUP.BAT in the same directory, STARTUP.COM would be executed when you typed STARTUP at the DOS prompt. If only STARTUP.EXE and STARTUP.BAT were in the directory, STARTUP.EXE would be executed.

Methods for Reducing the PATH String

When saving space in the environment becomes important, you may want to reduce the size of the path as touched on earlier. One method is to use the SUBST (Substitute) command to assign drive letters to the directory names you intend to put on the path. The three directories below are assigned to drive letters E through G.

```
SUBST E: C:\DOS
SUBST F: C:\BATCH
SUBST G: C:\LOTUS
```

Then the PATH command below could be issued to place the three directories in the path, thereby saving 16 bytes of environment space.

```
PATH=E:;F:;G:
```

When using the SUBST command on a drive letter higher than E, you must include the LASTDRIVE command in the CONFIG.SYS file. Therefore, to substitute paths for drive letters up to drive S, you would include the following command in the CONFIG.SYS file.

```
LASTDRIVE=S
```

Keep in mind that each additional drive letter takes up 81 bytes in RAM, so only set as many drive letters with LASTDRIVE as you really need. Also remember, when using SUBST you cannot or should not use the following commands with substituted drives:

```
BACKUP
CHKDSK
DISKCOMP
DISKCOPY
FDISK
FORMAT
LABEL
MIRROR (DOS 5 only)
RECOVER
RESTORE
SYS
```

Another way to shorten the path is to create batch files in a directory called BATCH that starts all of your applications. Then, the only directories you need to have on the path are DOS and BATCH as shown below.

```
PATH=C:\DOS;C:\BATCH
```

Using substituted drive letters, this can become as short as:

```
PATH=E:;F:
```

If you use batch files to start your applications, you can include commands in them to temporarily change the path if necessary. The following batch file, called WORD.BAT, can be created and stored in the \BATCH directory. It places the user in a directory where documents are stored, then runs Microsoft Word.

```
CD \DOCS
PATH=\WORD
```

```
WORD
CD %HOMEDIR%
PATH=%DEFAULT%
```

The first line changes directories to the \DOCS directory where documents are stored. The second command changes the path so WORD can be run from the \DOCS directory and the third command starts Word. The last two commands execute when the user exits from Word. They rely on previously set environment variables to return the user to his or her home directory and restore the path. These variables are initially set in the AUTOEXEC.BAT file with commands similar to the following.

```
SET HOMEDIR=C:\USERS\TOM
SET DEFAULT=C:\DOS;C:\BATCH
```

Because they remain in the environment, they can be used in batch files to restore paths and directories as shown above. This will be covered further at the end of this chapter.

Editing and Saving the PATH

Any time you enter a new PATH statement, the old path is removed. In some cases, you may want to keep part of your existing path or add a new directory to it. One method is to execute a second command processor as discussed previously. Another method is to simply save the old path in a batch file using the following redirection technique,

```
SET > OLDPATH.BAT
```

then issue a new path. This command copies the listing produced by PATH to the batch file OLDPATH.BAT. You can then create a new path, and when done, restore the original path simply by typing OLDPATH.

In some cases, you might want to temporarily add a directory to the path, then restore the original path. This can be done using the following two batch files. The first batch file is called NEWPATH.BAT and is listed here:

```
ECHO OFF
SET OLD=%PATH%
PATH=%OLD%;%1
```

After creating this file in the \BATCH directory or another directory on the path, you can add a new directory to the path by typing the following command:

```
NEWPATH \DBASE
```

The second line of the NEWPATH.BAT batch file saves the existing path to an environment variable called OLD. Type SET to see this new variable in the environment.

Note that percent signs surround the variable PATH; this is how environment variables are used in batch files. The third line appends parameter %1 which is \DBASE in the command above to the OLD environment variable. The last command looks like the following when it executes, assuming \DOS and \BATCH were already on the path:

```
PATH=\DOS;\BATCH;\DBASE
```

To change the search priority of the directory you are adding, change line 3 in the batch file as shown to make \DBASE appear first in the path.

```
PATH=%1%;OLD%
```

The following batch file must be created to restore the old path which is stored in the OLD environment variable. This must be done in a batch file to restore the value that the OLD variable represents. Type the commands shown below in a file called OLDPATH.BAT.

```
ECHO OFF
PATH=%OLD%
SET OLD=
```

To restore the old path, type OLDPATH. Note that the last command clears the OLD variable from the environment. As mentioned earlier, you could set a default path in the environment by including a SET command similar to the following in your AUTOEXEC.BAT file.

```
SET DEFAULT=C:\DOS;C:\BATCH
```

Then the OLDPATH.BAT file could be changed as follows:

```
ECHO OFF
PATH=%DEFAULT%
```

Another method for changing the PATH settings is to create a batch file that executes a new PATH command for each path setting you need. For example, if you are working on a newsletter, you might set paths to a directory for a graphics program and a directory for a page layout program using a batch file called NEWS.BAT. Other batch files could set different paths depending on the programs you need to use. However, creating a lot of batch files may not be a good idea if you have limited disk space. The batch file below illustrates how you can combine them all into one batch file used to select different paths. The filename is PATHSET.BAT.

```
ECHO OFF
IF "%1"=="" ECHO Options are DEFAULT, NEWSLETTER, REPORTS
IF "%1"=="DEFAULT" PATH=C:\DOS;C:\BATCH
```

```
IF "%1"=="NEWSLETTER" PATH=C:\PAGEMAKER;C:\DESIGNER
IF "%1"=="REPORTS" PATH=C:\LOTUS;C:\DBASE
```

You can, of course, create this file using path settings appropriate to your own system. The second line displays help if PATHSET is typed on the command line without parameters. The last three lines set a path based on the value of parameter %1. For example, if PATHSET DEFAULT is typed, the path returns to its default setting of C:\DOS;C:\BATCH as shown in line 3. The batch file can be expanded to include startup commands for programs associated with the new paths. An example is shown below.

```
REM ECHO OFF
IF "%1"=="" GOTO HELP
GOTO %1
:DEFAULT
PATH=C:\DOS;C:\BATCH
GOTO END
:NEWSLETTER
PATH=C:\PAGEMAKER;C:\DESIGNER
WIN /S
GOTO END
:REPORTS
PATH=C:\LOTUS;C:\DBASE
123
GOTO END
:HELP
ECHO Options are DEFAULT, NEWSLETTER, REPORTS
:END
```

Because this batch file has become more of a startup routine for your programs, it might be more appropriately named START.BAT. Note that the third line jumps to a label that matches the %1 parameter entered by the user on the command line. You can include any commands between the jump label and the GOTO END statement in each section. More information on these types of batch files can be found in the batch file chapter of this book.

The PROMPT Command

The PROMPT command is used to change the DOS prompt. It takes the form

```
SET PROMPT string
```

The string option can include text characters or special characters called *meta-strings*. The SET command is optional; in most cases, simply type PROMPT and the string. As a quick example, type the following at the DOS prompt and press Enter:

```
PROMPT Sir, yes sir!
```

The DOS prompt changes to display "Sir, yes sir!" Now change the prompt again using one of the prompt meta-strings. These are codes used to display the date, time or other value in the prompt. Type the command below to display the date in the prompt, as well as the greater than sign (>).

```
PROMPT $d$g
```

The $d meta-string displays the date, and the $g meta-string adds the greater than sign at the end of the prompt. The all-time classic DOS prompt is shown below. It displays the current directory and helps you keep track of where you are in the filing system. Your system may have already been set to this prompt before you started experimenting with the PROMPT command, so type the command now to restore the prompt.

```
PROMPT $p$g
```

You can type SET at any time to view the environment settings and the command used to set the current prompt. There are a number of interesting prompts you can set, some quite useful while others are just fun. A complete list of meta-strings is shown below. If you have DOS 5.0, you can get a listing at any time by typing PROMPT /?.

$$	Displays the dollar sign in the prompt
$t	Displays the time
$d	Displays the date
$p	Displays the current directory
$v	Displays the DOS version number
$n	Displays the default drive
$g	Displays the > character
$l	Displays the < character
$b	Displays the | character (vertical bar)
$q	Displays the = character
$h	Backspaces over the previous character
$e	The Escape code
$_	Starts a new line

To display the date and time on separate lines, followed by the normal system prompt, type the following:

```
PROMPT $t$_$d$_$p$g
```

There's one prompt that demonstrates the use of the $h backspace character and creates an animated effect that looks like a spinning wheel by first displaying the \, /, and -

characters. If you create this string, do so in a batch file called WHEEL.BAT so you can use or edit it later. Each character is displayed three times to prolong its time on the screen. The $h backspace meta-string is used to backspace over it and display the next character. There are four sequences, so the "wheel" spins four times. If your system has a fast processor, the sequence may run too fast to see, so if you're a real computer nerd, you'll slow the processor down to see it. Note that the first and last character meta-strings in the sequence display the normal DOS prompt.

```
prompt=$p\$h\$h\$h/$h/$h/$h-$h-$h-$h\$h\$h\$h/$h/$h/$h-$h-$h-
$h\$h\$h\$h/$h/$h/$h-$h-$h-$h\$h\$h\$h/$h/$h/$h-$h-$h-$h$g
```

When you find a prompt you like, add the command to the AUTOEXEC.BAT file so it appears every time you boot your system. Or, if you're experimenting with PROMPT and you create an interesting one that you'd like to show your friends later, save it, then return to the more generic pg prompt until they are ready to see it. To save any prompt, type a command similar to the following:

```
SET > PROMPT$.BAT
```

This sends the display of environment variables to the file PROMPT$.BAT. You can then edit this file to remove all lines except the PROMPT command. To redisplay your unique prompt, run the PROMPT$.BAT batch file. If you create several interesting prompts, be sure to save each in its own batch file.

The $e meta-string lets you send ANSI Escape sequences to DOS so you can reassign the keyboard or make changes to the display. You could assign your company name to the F1 key, or change the color of text that appears on the screen. To make these changes, you must first install the ANSI.SYS device driver by including the following command in your CONFIG.SYS file. To load the driver, you must then reboot your system.

```
DEVICE=C:\DOS\ANSI.SYS
```

Once your system reboots, you can use the PROMPT command to reassign keys. To assign the DIR /P command to the F10 key, type the following:

```
PROMPT $e[0;68;"DIR /P"13p
```

Because this removes the existing prompt, you'll need to type another prompt command to restore the DOS prompt to its original setting, but the key assignments will remain. For example, the following command restores the generic directory prompt:

```
PROMPT $p$g
```

For a complete discussion of screen and keyboard controls using the ANSI.SYS device driver, refer to Chapter 10.

The SET Command

The SET command is used to display a copy of the current environment to the screen. It is also used to add or remove custom environment variables. You might want to refer to these custom variables as *global variables* because they can be used by any program or batch file once they are set. To set a global variable, use the SET command in the following form:

```
SET variable=value
```

where *variable* is the variable name you want to create and *value* is the string you want to assign to it. So, to assign the string TOM to the variable USER, you would type the following command:

```
SET USER=TOM
```

Notice that there are no spaces on either side of the equal sign. If you include a space, it becomes part of the variable or value.

Type SET to view the environment and its new variable. To clear an environment variable, type the SET command, the variable and an equal sign, but *not* a value. The following command would remove the USER variable from the environment:

```
SET USER=
```

Variables cannot be used on the command line but can be used in batch files when surrounded by percent signs. Here's an example of a command you could place in a batch file to use the USER variable. It would copy all files in the directory represented by the USER variable to drive A. When USER is set to TOM, it would copy all files in the TOM directory.

```
XCOPY \%USER%\*.* A:
```

Environment variables are important tools in batch file design. You can set variables when the system boots, when a user logs in or when a batch file is executed. The variables can then be used by batch files or programs later in the session. Batch files using the variables can be created to work in a wide variety of situations and with more than one user. If several people are using a computer, you could create a startup batch file that assigns their startup name to a variable called USER. You can then create batch files that execute commands based on the USER variable. The next section will present a few more examples of this.

Using Environment Variables in Batch Files

Once you know how to get variables into the environment, you can begin to build batch files that use them. You've already seen how a command in the AUTOEXEC.BAT file might set the default directory path, such as:

```
SET DEFAULT=C:\DOS;C:\BATCH
```

If you ever change the path, you can easily return to the default by running a batch file with the following command:

```
SET PATH=%DEFAULT%
```

A more elaborate example of environment variables can be demonstrated by capturing the current day and date in the environment. This is done by first combining the ECHO, MORE and DATE commands in a way that was never intended by the designers of DOS. The combination, however, directs the screen output of the DATE command to a file where it can be used later to add the current day and date to the environment. Type the command shown below, keeping in mind that you can place this command in your AUTOEXEC.BAT file if you want to capture this information every time you start your system.

```
ECHO | MORE | DATE > DATE$.BAT
```

Next create a batch file called CURRENT.BAT and add the following lines to it:

```
SET DAY=%3
SET TODAY=%4
```

Then, execute the DATE$.BAT batch file that was created with the ECHO command above, and type SET to display your environment variables, which will now appear similar to those listed here:

```
DAY=Sat
TODAY=04-20-1991
```

You can now use these variables in other batch files with commands that rely on the day or date. If you're wondering how the above commands managed to capture the day and date as environment variables, look inside the DATE$.BAT file, which will look something like this:

```
Current date is Sat 04-20-1991
Enter new Date (mm-dd-yy)
```

The messages that normally appear on the screen when you type the DATE command are now lines in a batch file. When you run the batch file, DOS executes the first line as if it were a command. In this case, you've created a batch file called CURRENT.BAT, so DOS runs the batch file and uses the remaining words on the line as if they were command line parameters. So Sat becomes parameter %3 and 04-20-1991 becomes parameter %4. CURRENT.BAT assigns these parameters to the DAY and TODAY variables respectively.

Now for an example of how you might use these variables. Assume you create a memo or appointment file for each day of the week. These files have names like MON.DOC, TUE.DOC, and so on. The following commands, placed in the AUTOEXEC.BAT file, would automatically display the memo file that matches the DAY setting in the environment.

```
ECHO | MORE | DATE > DATE$.BAT
DATE$
MORE < %DAY%.DOC
```

If DAY were Sat, the third line of the batch file would execute the following command, which would display any messages or reminders for Saturday.

```
MORE < Sat.DOC
```

You could also include commands similar to the following to remind yourself of birthdays or other important dates.

```
IF %TODAY%==01-03-92 ECHO **** Today is Alex's birthday!!!!!
IF %TODAY%==04-10-92 ECHO **** Tax deadline in 5 days!!!!!
```

One thing to keep in mind is that these types of commands in batch files tend to slow your system down. You can create a RAM drive, then copy a batch file containing all your startup commands and other batch files to the RAM drive for faster execution. Here's an example of a modified AUTOEXEC.BAT file that accomplishes this task.

```
ECHO OFF
COPY C:\DOS\STARTUP.BAT E:
E:STARTUP
```

All of the commands normally in AUTOEXEC.BAT file should be included in the STARTUP.BAT file, which is then copied to the RAM drive in the second command. It is then executed from the RAM drive.

The next example demonstrates how to create a password system that determines who is logging onto a system shared by several users. This allows you to set environment variables specific to each user. The main task of the AUTOEXEC.BAT file in this routine is to ask the user for their password, then temporarily blank the screen using ANSI.SYS screen control codes. You'll need to ensure that ANSI.SYS is loaded before proceeding. The password typed by the user is the name of a batch file that contains the startup commands you would normally put in AUTOEXEC.BAT. In addition, it sets variables like USER to the name of the user and HOMEDIR to the path of the users home directory. These variables can then be used in batch files. This routine is not a fullproof security system, but it does serve to capture environment variables specific to each user logging onto the shared system. In addition, it demonstrates how you might capture and use environment variables during startup.

First, determine the password you'll use for each user, then copy the current AUTOEXEC.BAT file to a file with their password names. If John will use the password FROGGY, you would issue the command shown below.

```
COPY AUTOEXEC.BAT FROGGY.BAT
```

Next, create a new AUTOEXEC.BAT file with the following commands. Note that the last command is an ANSI command that blanks the screen to keep users from going astray during the login procedure.

```
ECHO OFF
CLS
ECHO Enter your password
PROMPT $e[8m
```

You should then edit the password file for each user to include commands relevant to their login session, making sure to insert the following line at the beginning of each password batch file. This command is important because it restores the screen to visible mode.

```
PROMPT $e[0m
```

Other relevant commands you might enter in the users' password file are shown below. These commands are for John's password file.

```
SET USER=JOHN
SET DEFAULT=C:\DOS;C:\BATCH
SET HOMEDIR=C:\HOME\JOHN
SET DATA=\HOME\JOHN\DATA
```

You can now create generic batch files that use these variables. The USER variable could be used in a batch file to display message files from other users. The command below, placed in a batch file called MAIL.BAT, would display the mail file for the current user.

```
MORE < C:\MAIL\%USER%.DOC
```

When John is logged in and USER is set to John, the batch file would display his message file in the MAIL directory. This routine assumes that other users are creating and editing mail files to their coworkers in the MAIL directory.

Another batch file called HOME.BAT uses the HOMEDIR variable to quickly return the current user to their home directory.

```
CD %HOMEDIR%
```

The DATA variable can be included in batch files to move users to their data directories, then start applications. A batch file to start LOTUS might include the following commands:

```
CD %DATA%
LOTUS
```

Obviously, environment variables enable you to create versatile batch files. And because the environment variables have different values for each user that logs on, you won't need to create specific batch files for each user and you can store the batch files in a single directory. In addition, fewer batch files mean it is easier to manage and make changes to your batch files.

Screens and Color

Okay, you've worn the letters off your keytops, and you've ground the heads on your disk drives down to the bare metal, but the one part of your system you probably know better than any other is your screen. If you're like most avid users, you're glued to it hypnotically each day for hours on end. So you might as well make staring at it as pleasant as possible.

The first important thing to learn is that color is a true productivity tool. You can cram 2,000 characters onto a typical 80-column, 25-line screen (and twice as much text on newer 50-line displays). With information this dense, you need a way to highlight important information without making it blink or drawing little boxes around it.

The only method DOS provides for setting screen colors is through ANSI.SYS. However, ANSI is cumbersome because it makes you deal with escape characters that DOS normally treats as abort commands, and its color numbering scheme is different from the standard one used by BIOS and BASIC. But without ANSI, DOS consigns users of color systems to a drab grey-on-black existence.

According to insiders, IBM designers considered color frivolous, and were reluctant to produce a color system for the original PC. Colors were for games, they reasoned, and adding color meant handling lots more information — you not only had to put a character at a certain location on the screen, but had to worry about setting its display attribute at the same time.

Anyway, the PC's high-resolution monochrome adapter produced crisp, detailed characters on IBM's rock-solid mono monitor. The cool green persistent phosphor was touted as ergonomic perfection. To sweeten the monochrome deal, IBM threw in a parallel printer port for free.

(Way back then IBM didn't even offer a color display; you had to spend close to a thousand dollars to buy a third-party monitor. And when IBM did eventually advertise one, serious business users dismissed it as a toy. Besides which, coaxing color out of existing software was next to impossible. For users accustomed to the razor-sharp monochrome output, IBM's gritty, flickery color hardware made work on it nearly impossible. It was like reading text through a twitching screen door.)

But the IBM design team caved in at the last minute and offered a board called the CGA (Color Graphics Adapter) that offered several low-resolution color text and graphics modes, and a small selection of available colors. If you knew the right tricks, you could run a few applications in color, and you could use the system's built-in BASIC language to write graphics routines that addressed 320 x 200 pixels (short for "picture elements" — really just dots) in two palettes of three colors each, or 640 x 200 pixels in grey on black.

Trouble is, whether you bought an early CGA card and a grainy color monitor, or one of the newest high-tech color systems on the market, you'll still end up with a grey-on-black DOS. If you set colors with ANSI.SYS, typing CLS will clear the screen to those colors. But without ANSI, COMMAND.COM is hard-wired to use the color attribute number 07 when clearing the screen. The 0 yields a black background, and 7 is IBM's number for grey.

You can use DEBUG to patch COMMAND.COM so that typing CLS will clear the screen to any color you choose. Just pick the background and foreground colors you want, look up their single-digit hex values on the charts below, and combine the individual digits into a two-digit hex number. The background goes on the left and the foreground on the right. If you wanted bright yellow (hex E) text on a red (hex 4) background, for instance, you'd use the number 4E. Bright white text on a dark blue background would be 17. Then pick the appropriate patching address:

DOS Version	DEBUG Address
2.0	2346
2.1	2359
3.0	2428
3.1	2642
3.2	282E
3.3	2BAD
4.01 (IBM)	3EC7
4.01 (MS)	3E97
5.0	4369

To patch IBM's version 5.0 so CLS will change your colors to bright yellow text on a red background, just type:

```
DEBUG COMMAND.COM
E 4369 4E
W
Q
```

If you're not using version 5.0, substitute the proper addresses in place of the 3EC7. Then either reboot, or load the patched version of COMMAND.COM by typing COM-MAND. When you type CLS, DOS should clear your screen and print the prompt in bright yellow on red. Don't pick a background color (lefthand digit) higher than 7 unless you want your screen to blink.

This procedure won't set the border color, however. It's possible to move things around inside COMMAND.COM and add a routine to set the color of the border, but it's really not worth it these days, since the EGA and VGA screens don't really support borders. And while patching one attribute byte in COMMAND.COM is really not all that dangerous, moving chunks of instructions around can cause problems. (Remember, if you do try patching COMMAND.COM, don't mix patched and unpatched versions on the same disk, and work only with copies of COMMAND.COM, never your original.)

If you're using a CGA system and you're desperate to set the border color, type in the following 12 lines. Omit the semicolons and the comments that follow them. Be certain to leave a blank line after the RET (just press Enter twice after typing RET), and make sure you press the Enter key at the end of each line, especially the last one with the Q:

```
DEBUG
A
MOV AH,0B          ; set color palette on CGA
MOV BL,4           ; to produce a red (4) border
INT 10             ; have BIOS do it
RET                ; back to DOS

RCX
7
N REDBORDR.COM
W
Q
```

This will create a tiny program called REDBORDR.COM that sets CGA borders to red. To have it use a different color, substitute the hex value of the color you want in place of 4 in the fourth line. So to have a bright cyan border (with a value of hex B), change the fourth line to:

```
MOV BL,B
```

Or you could type in the following 14 lines:

```
DEBUG
A
SUB BH,BH          ; color ID=0
MOV BL,[5D]        ; get paramter from FCB
AND BL,0F          ; keep 4 low bits
MOV AH,0B          ; BIOS palette setter
INT 10             ; do it
INT 20             ; back to DOS
```

```
RCX
F
N BORDRSET.COM
W
Q
```

to create a program called BORDRSET.COM. Again, omit the semicolons and the comments that follow them. Be certain to leave a blank line after the INT 20 (just press Enter twice after typing INT 20), and make sure you press the Enter key at the end of each line, especially the last one.

You can enter the border color you want on the DOS command line directly after the name of the program. So:

```
BORDRSET 1
```

will give you a dark blue border, and:

```
BORDRSET E
```

will produce a bright yellow one.

Even better is to use the program on one of the accompanying disks, which lets you reset border colors on the fly. For more behind-the-scene details, see the chapter on DEBUG. And for advanced techniques involving the EGA and VGA systems and beyond, see the chapter that follows.

One last note about ANSI and the CLS command. If you type CLS, DOS will generate the ANSI command to clear the screen — ESC2J (where ESC stands for the decimal 27 or hex 1B escape character and not the letters E-S-C). To see this, type:

```
CLS > SEEIT
```

which redirects the output of the CLS command into a file called SEEIT. If you then examine the SEEIT file by typing:

```
TYPE SEEIT
```

you'll see a little arrow pointing left (the escape character) followed by a 2 and a J. If you have ANSI loaded, using TYPE to display the file will end up clearing the screen instead, since ANSI will see its CLS command onscreen, and process it. If you need to work with ANSI or printer escape sequences, you can use EDLIN or your word processor to customize this SEEIT file, since the hard-to-type ESC character will already be in the file and you can simply add any other non-ESC commands after it.

The first thing most decent programs do these days when they start up is figure out whether or not a color adapter (CGA, EGA, or VGA) is active, and set the screen colors accordingly. Other programs simply use one set of colors that works on both monochrome and color systems.

Basic CGA text screens can use only eight possible colors (including black). IBM assigned the following numbers to these:

Color	Dec	Hex	Binary
Black	0	0	000
Blue	1	1	001
Green	2	2	010
Cyan	3	3	011
Red	4	4	100
Magenta	5	5	101
Brown	6	6	110
White	7	7	111

Cyan is otherwise known as light blue; magenta as purple. Brown is the hardest color to produce on many monitors, and may end up appearing as dingy yellow or purplish orange.

All of these numbers can be expressed in three binary digits (bits) as varying combinations of 0s and 1s. Three of these — red, green, and blue — have just a single 1 in them:

- Red   100
- Green   010
- Blue   001

Early IBM color displays were often referred to as "RGB" monitors since they had three electron guns behind the CRT that handled individual red, green, and blue signals. A binary color 100 meant that only the red gun was active; 001 turned on just the blue gun. By mixing and matching IBM came up with the other five. Black (000) meant that all guns were off, and white (111) that all were on.

Turn the rightmost bit (001) on by itself and you get blue. Turn the middle bit (010) on and you end up with green. Set the leftmost bit to 1 (100) and the screen displays red. Turn both the red and blue bits on (101) and your monitor activates the red and blue guns and ends up with purple (which IBM calls magenta).

By slapping one additional bit of information onto the three other color bits, IBM increased the number of color choices to 16. It named the leftmost bit the "intensity" bit, and when this bit was turned on, the screen displayed a brighter version of the color determined by the other three bits.

Turning this fourth bit on (setting it to 1) is the same as adding 8 to the value of the other three bits. So if the value of a normal color happened to be 5 (binary 101), turning on the intensity bit would add 8 to the color value, yielding 13:

```
   101      (magenta = decimal 5)
+ 1000      setting the intensity bit (adding 8)
  1101      (bright magenta = decimal 13 or hex D)
```

This chart shows the decimal, hex, and binary values for the high-intensity colors:

High-Intensity
Color	Dec	Hex	Binary
Bright black	8	8	1000
Bright blue	9	9	1001
Bright green	10	A	1010
Bright cyan	11	B	1011
Bright red	12	C	1100
Bright magenta	13	D	1101
Bright brown	14	E	1110
Bright white	15	F	1111

Bright black turned into grey. Bright red became a sort of salmony pink color, and bright brown emerged as yellow.

Displays that could handle the intensity bit were called "IRGB" monitors. Some displays were blind to this intensity bit and made a color like bright magenta (color 13) look exactly like normal magenta (color 5). Others had trouble with the intensity circuitry and made bright colors too bright or too close to normal colors.

However, by limiting the color information to four bits — half of a byte, or a nibble — IBM could put the color information for both the foreground and background into one byte. It specified that the text or foreground data would be in the rightmost ("low") nibble and the background data in the leftmost ("high") nibble. So bright blue text (1001) on a cyan background (0011) would be coded as:

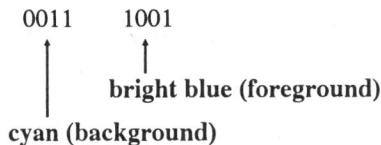

0011   1001

bright blue (foreground)

cyan (background)

The value of this byte would be 00111001, or decimal 57 (hex 39). This is one case where hex numbering is clearly easier to work with than decimal. The binary number for bright blue text on cyan is 0011 1001. Again, the high nibble is the four bits on the left, while the low nibble is the four bits on the right. (The left half is called high because it's worth more than the right half, just as in the decimal number 57, the 5 is the high half because it's really equal to 5 x 10, or 50, and the 7 is the low half because it's equal to 7 x 1, or 7.)

The high nibble — cyan — is equal to 3. The low nibble — bright blue — is equal to 9. Together the hex value for this byte is 39:

0011 1001
 (3)   (9)

Each nibble can be one of 16 values, from 0 (0000) to 15 (1111). So a color byte can have 256 possible values, from a low of 0 (0000 0000) to a high of 255 (1111 1111).

Incidentally, these examples insert a space between the high and low nibbles for clarity; but your system doesn't. To it, 255 is just 11111111.

But IBM wanted this one byte to store all the attributes, not just the color. By turning on the leftmost bit in the low (foreground) nibble it could highlight text the same way boldface type stands out on a page. And by rotating the foreground and background around, it could produce the reverse of a normal display so that text appeared black against white (or black on green in monochrome).

IBM felt that two other attributes — blinking and underlining — were important. But virtually no room was left in the byte, since three bits in each nibble were taken up by red/green/blue color information, and the remaining bit in the low nibble served as a high-intensity on/off switch.

After puzzling over underlines, IBM's designers gave up and cheated. They realized that the resolution of the original CGA color screen was truly rotten. Every one of the 255 possible displayable characters had to be made up out of a crude box or grid eight dots wide and eight dots high. That's eight rows and eight columns (actually one of the eight columns was left blank in most cases so adjacent letters wouldn't touch, and one of the eight rows was reserved for descenders on lowercase letters, yielding a 7 x 7 box). Try making characters like @, &, and % on such a small grid yourself and see how hard it is.

Worse, the bottom of one 8 x 8 CGA character box touched the top of the one below it. This meant that descenders, like the tails on the letters y or j or p, actually touched the tops of capital letters and ascenders on lowercase letters like l, d, or b. The only way to add an underline would have been to sacrifice one of the eight rows that made up the characters. Things were so tight already that the engineers decided to allow underlining on monochrome screens only, where the character box measured 9 x 14. They assigned the first nonzero value — 0001 — as a switch to turn on underlining. This value of 1 happens to be the setting for blue on a color monitor. So anything designed to appear in blue text on a color monitor ends up underlined on a mono display and vice versa.

Probably after staring at a high-intensity purple background for too long, IBM engineers realized they could sacrifice the high-intensity bit in the background (high) color nibble and use it instead to control blinking. Nobody would want to look at a glaring bright green or pulsing purple background anyway. So the leftmost bit in the low nibble controls intensity, while the leftmost bit in the high nibble controls blinking.

Actually, you can disable blinking and use high-intensity backgrounds. The easiest way to see this is in BASIC. Load BASIC by typing either QBASIC (for DOS 5.0), BASIC (for IBM systems) or GWBASIC (for generic systems). Then type:

```
COLOR F,B
```

substituting a foreground color from 0 to 15 in place of the F, and a background color from 0 to 7 in place of the B. Entering COLOR 15,1 will produce bright white text on a dark blue background. If you add 16 to the foreground color, it will blink. Entering COLOR 31,1 will yield blinking bright white text on a blue background. Now, assuming you're using an 80-character screen, type:

```
OUT &H3D8,9
```

The text should stop blinking, and the background will turn high-intensity blue.

This technique won't work on all color systems or on all color monitors; the older your system the more likely this command will disable blinking and brighten your background. And note that BASIC actually lets you enter three color numbers (COLOR F,G,B) where the B sets the border color — the area between the 80 x 25 screen and the bezel of your monitor. IBM stopped using border colors with the EGA and made them only slightly better on the VGA, so borders are pretty much passé by now.

Since the background nibble is on the left, and the text nibble on the right, this meant that the very leftmost bit — the eighth one — would determine whether or not blinking was turned on. The eighth bit is equal to 128 (2^7 or 1000 0000). So if this bit is on, or set to 1, the text color blinks. Turning this bit on is the same as adding 128 to the existing combination of color and intensity attributes. So the bright-blue-on-cyan hex 39 example above:

```
0011 1001
```

doesn't blink. But adding 128, or binary 1000 0000 to it:

```
  0011 1001
+ 1000 0000
  1011 1001
```

would produce a blinking bright blue on cyan display. The decimal value of 1011 1001 is 185. The nonblinking version of this was 57.   57 + 128 = 185.

But again, it's easier to work with hex. 1011 is equal to hex B. 1001 is equal to hex 9. So the hex notation for this is B9. Any hex number with a lefthand digit higher than 7 will blink.

In summary, an attribute byte looks like this:

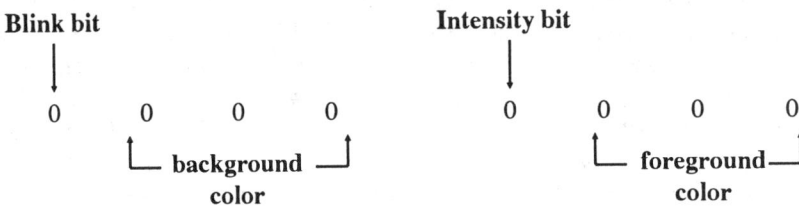

Blink bit   **Intensity bit**

0   0   0   0   0   0   0   0

└─ background ─┘   └─ foreground ─┘
      color   color

If the value of this byte is over 7F hex (127 decimal), the blink bit will be set and the text color will blink. If the blink bit is 0, it won't. In both cases the lefthand hex digit is the background color and the righthand digit is the foreground (text) color.

Most programs that set colors or clear the screen use BIOS interrupt 10. (Some programs bypass BIOS and go straight to the hardware, but such ill-behaved software won't be discussed here.) DOS doesn't offer any underlying color facilities other than ANSI, and uses the BIOS functions itself. It can write individual characters, or strings of characters, but these will appear in whatever attribute happens to be set at the time.

BIOS INT 10 offers a fat toolkit of character-based functions to handle just about everything you'll need to add sparkle to your display. While IBM enhanced INT 10 when it released the AT, and then jazzed it up even more when it brought the PS/2 series to market, the original services are still very capable. Figure 13.1 summarizes the standard text arsenal available (though it doesn't include pixel-oriented services, and ones that deal with things like light pens).

Since BIOS is your system's hardware specialist, just about all video tools use BIOS interrupt 10. However, DOS gets into the act a bit with a scant few teletype-oriented interrupt 21 routines (Figure 13.2).

Name of Service	What You Specify	What You Get Back	Notes

Set mode (text)	AH=0
	AL=mode
	(On EGA and later
	  systems, add 80H
	  to mode number
	  to prevent screen
	  from clearing)
			Modes:
			0 = 40x25 16-color
			1 = 40x25 16-color
			2 = 80x25 16-color
			3 = 80x25 16-color
			4 = 320x200 4-color
			5 = 320x200 4-color
			6 = 640x200 2-color
			7 = 80x25 monochrome
			0D = 320x200 16-color
			0E = 640x200 16-color
			0F = 640x350 monochrome
			10 = 640x350 16-color
			11 = 640x480 16-color
			12 = 640x480 16-color
			13 = 320x200 256-color

Set cursor type and size	AH=1
	CL=starting line
	CH=ending line
			Largest mono cursor is:
			  0 starting line
			  D ending line
			Largest CGA cursor is:
			  0 starting line
			  7 ending line
			Default mono is:
			  CH=0B CL=0C
			Default CGA is:
			  CH=06 CL=07
			Default EGA/MDA is:
			  CH=11 CL=12
			Default VGA/MCGA is:
			  CH=13 CL=14
			Setting CH=20 may make
			  the cursor vanish
			A start line larger than its
			  ending line will produce
			  a 2-part cursor.

(continued)

Name of Service	What You Specify	What You Get Back	Notes

Set cursor position	AH=2
	DH=row
	DL=column
	BH=page (0)
			Upper lefthand corner is
			  0,0, so DX=0000
			Unless you're really tricky,
			  page is always 0

Read cursor position	AH=3
	BH=page (0)
		DH=screen row
		DL=screen column
		CH=starting line
		CL=ending line
			Again, assume the page
			  is 0, although BIOS
			  maintains positions
			  for each page

Set active page	AH=5
	AL=page
			AL=0–3 for 80-column
			  screens (modes 2,3)
			AL=0–7 for 40-column
			  screens (modes 0,1)
			EGA and later systems can
			  handle pages in 16-color
			  graphics modes

Scroll up window	AH=6
	AL=number of lines
	  to scroll
	CH=upper lefthand
	  window row
	CL=upper lefthand
	  window column
	DH=lower righthand
	  window row
	DL=lower righthand
	  window column
	BH=attribute to
	  fill window
			To clear 80x25 screen use:
			  AL=0
			  CH=0
			  CL=0
			  DH=18
			  DL=4F
			  BH=color
			DH and DL are 1 less
			  than 80x25 (hex 4F and
			  18 since these start
			  at 0, not 1)
			Use AL=0 to clear screen

Scroll down window	AH=7
	AL=number of lines
	  to scroll
	CH=upper lefthand
	  window row
	CL=upperlefthand
	  window column
	DH=lower righthand
	  window row
	DL=lower righthand
	  window column
	BH=attribute to
	  fill window
			To clear 80x25 screen use:
			  AL=0
			  CH=0
			  CL=0
			  DH=18
			  DL=4F
			  BH=color
			DH and DL are 1 less
			  than 80x25 (hex 4F and
			  18 since these start
			  at 0, not 1)
			Use AL=0 to clear screen

Name of Service	What You Specify	What You Get Back	Notes
Read attribute, character at cursor	AH=8 BH=page (0)	AL=ASCII value of character AH=attribute	Use 0 for page. This comes in handy for clearing screen to existing color.
Write attribute, character at cursor	AH=9 BH=page (0) CX=number of characters to write AL=ASCII value of character to write BL=attribute of character		Use 0 for page. This can fill an 80x25 screen instantly by putting a hex 7D0 (same as decimal 2000) in RCX. Have to worry about moving the cursor yourself.
Write character at cursor	AH=0A BH=page (0) CX=number of characters to write AL=ASCII value of character to write		Use 0 for page. You can use this without having to worry about getting the existing color or coming up with a new one.
Set color palette (border in text mode)	AH=0B BH=0 BL=border color		Works on CGAs only Border may be 0-16. (Function 0B has other graphics abilities.)
Write character as TTY (teletype)	AH=0E AL=ASCII value of character to write		Advances cursor automatically but can't handle colors and treats ASCII 7, 8, 10, and 13 characters specially
Get current video state	AH=0F	AL=mode AH=number of columns BH=active page	

Figure 13.1. Original INT 10 Tools

Name of Service	What You Specify	What You Get Back	Notes
Set Palette Register	AH=10 AL=0 BH=palette 　register value BL=palette 　register value		EGA, VGA, only
Set Border Register	AH=10 AL=1 BH=border color		EGA, VGA only
Set Palette Registers and Border	AH=10 AL=2 ES:DX=17-byte 　table of palette 　and border values		EGA, VGA only
Select Blink or Background Colors	AH=10 AL=3 BL=choice: 　0=16 background 　　colors and no blink 　1=8 background 　　colors and blink		EGA, VGA only
Read Palette Register	AH=10 AL=7 BL=palette register 　number	BH=palette 　register value	VGA only
Read Border Register	AH=10 AL=8	BH=border color	VGA only
Read Palette/ Border Register	AH=10 AL=9	ES:DX=17-byte 　table of palette 　and border values	VGA only
Set DAC (digital=to=analog converter) Color	AH=10 AL=10 BX=register DH=6-bit red value CH=6-bit green value CL=6-bit blue value		VGA, MCGA only

Name of Service	What You Specify	What You Get Back	Notes

Set Multiple DAC colors	AH=10
	AL=12
	BX=initial register
	CX=number of
	  registers
	ES:DX=table of RGB
	  values
			VGA, MCGA only

Set DAC Page Configuration	AH=10
	AL=13
	BL=0
	BH=choice:
	  0=4 pages,
	    64 registers
	  1=16 pages,
	    16 registers
			VGA only

Set DAC Page	AH=10
	AL=13
	BL=1
	BH=page
			VGA only;
			4 pages 0–3 if 64
			  registers
			16 pages 0–F if 16
			  registers

Read DAC Color	AH=10 AL=15 BX=register	DH=6-bit red value CH=6-bit green value CL=6-bit blue value	VGA, MCGA only

Read Multiple DAC Colors	AH=10
	AL=17
	BX=initial register
	CX=number of
	  registers
	ES:DX=location of
	  table
		ES:DX 17-byte table
		  filled in
			VGA, MCGA only

Get DAC Page Configuration	AH=10
	AL=1A
		BH=current page
		BL=current page
		mode:
		  0=4 pages,
		    64 registers
		  1=16 pages,
		    16 registers
			VGA only

(continued)

Name of Service	What You Specify	What You Get Back	Notes
Convert DAC Colors to Greys	AH=10 AL=1B BX=initial register CX=numbers of registers		VGA, MCGA only

Load Custom Text Character Set	AH=11
	AL=0
	BH=bytes/character
	BL=table
	CX=number of
	   characters
	DX=ASCII code of
	   initial character
	ES:BP=table of bit
	   patterns
			EGA, VGA, MCGA only

Load 8 x 14 Text Character Set	AH=11 AL=1 BL=table		EGA, VGA only
Load 8 x 8 Text Character Set	AH=11 AL=2 BL=table		EGA, VGA, MCGA only
Select Loaded Text Character Set	AH=11 AL=3 BL=table		EGA and MCGA allow 4 tables VGA allows 8 tables
Load 8 x 16 Text Character Set	AH=11 AL=4 BL=table		VGA, MCGA only

Load Custom Text Character Set and Adjust Height	AH=11
	AL=10
	BH=bytes/character
	BL=table
	CX=number of
	   characters
	DX=ASCII code of
	   initial character
	ES:BP=table of bit
	   patterns
			EGA, VGA, MCGA only

Name of Service	What You Specify	What You Get Back	Notes
Load 8 x 14 Text Character Set and Adjust Height	AH=11 AL=11 BL=table		EGA, VGA only
Load 8 x 8 Text Character Set and Adjust Height	AH=11 AL=12 BL=table		EGA, VGA only
Load 8 x 16 Text Character Set and Adjust Height	AH=11 AL=14 BL=table		VGA only
Load 8 x 8 Graphics Custom Character Set	AH=11 AL=20 ES:BP=table of bit patterns		EGA, VGA, MCGA only (For high-bit characters only)

Load Custom Graphics Character Set	AH=11
	AL=21
	CX=bytes/character
	ES:BP=table of bit
	    patterns
	BL=0 (and DL=
	    number of rows)
	BL=1 (for 14 rows)
	BL=2 (for 25 rows)
	BL=3 (for 43 rows)
			EGA, VGA, MCGA only

Load 8 x 14 Graphics Character Set	AH=11 AL=22 BL=0 (and DL= number of rows) BL=1 (for 14 rows) BL=2 (for 25 rows) BL=3 (for 43 rows)		EGA, VGA only

(continued)

Name of Service	What You Specify	What You Get Back	Notes
Load 8 x 8 Graphics Character Set	AH=11 AL=23 BL=0 (and DL= number of rows) BL=1 (for 14 rows) BL=2 (for 25 rows) BL=3 (for 43 rows)		EGA, VGA, MCGA only
Load 8 x 16 Graphics Character Set	AH=11 AL=24 BL=0 (and DL= number of rows) BL=1 (for 14 rows) BL=2 (for 25 rows) BL=3 (for 43 rows)		VGA, MCGA only
Get Character Set Parameter Sizes	AH=11 AL=30	CX=height of characters DL=number of rows (-1)	EGA, VGA, MCGA only
Get Character Set Table Information	AH=11 AL=30 BH=0 (for 8x8 CGA high-bit characters pointed to by INT IF) BH=1 (for current characters) BH=2 (for 8x14 characters) BH=3 (for 8x8 characters) BH=4 (for top of 8x8 character table) BH=5 (for 9x14 characters) BH=6 (for 8x16 characters) BH=7 (for 9x16 characters)	ES:BP=location of bit-pattern tables CX=character height DL=number of on-screen rows (-1)	EGA, VGA, MCGA only

Name of Service	What You Specify	What You Get Back	Notes

Get Video Configuration	AH=12
	BL=10
		BH=current video
		  mode
		    (0=color)
		    (1=mono)
		BL=Blocks of EGA
		  RAM
		    (0=64K)
		    (1=128K)
		    (2=192K)
		    (3=256K)
		CH=EGA feature
		  connector input status
		CL=EGA switch
		  settings
			EGA, VGA only

Alternate Print Screen Select	AH=12 BL=20		EGA, VGA, MCGA, only (for rows > 25)
Select Text Scan Line Number	AH=12 BL=30 AL=0 (for 200 lines) AL=1 (for 350 lines) AL=2 (for 400 lines)		VGA only 200=CGA emulation 350=EGA emulation 400=VGA default

Enable/Disable Palette Loading on Mode Change	AH=12
	BL=31
	AL=0 (enables default
	  palette)
	AL=1 (disables palette
	  loading; keeps
	  current values)
			VGA, MCGA only

Enable/Disable Buffer/Port Addressing	AH=12
	BL=32
	AL=0 (enables
	  addressing)
	AL=1 (disables
	  addressing)
			VGA, MCGA only;
			  See AL=35 (for use
			  together in same
			  system)

Enable/Disable Grey Scale	AH=12
	BL=33
	AL=0 (to enable grey
	  scale)
	AL=1 (to disable grey
	  scale)
			VGA, MCGA only
			  (can force grey
			  scale display on
			  color system with
			  AL=0)

(continued)

Name of Service	What You Specify	What You Get Back	Notes
Enable/Disable Cursor Emulation	AH=12 BL=34 AL=0 (to enable CGA- type cursor) AL=1(to disable it)		VGA only

Switch Display	AH=12
	BL=35
	AL=0 (initial adaptor
	   off)
	AL=1 (inital adaptor
	   on)
	AL=2 (turn active
	   video off)
	AL=3 (turn inactive
	   video on)
	ES:DX=128-byte
	   buffer address
			VGA, MCGA only;
			See AL=32 (lets
			you switch between
			PS/2 video adaptors)

Enable/Disable Refresh	AH=12
	BL=36
	AL=0 (enables refresh)
	AL=1 (disables
	   refresh for faster
	   screen updates
			VGA only

Write Text String Without Moving Cursor	AH=13 AL=0 BL=attribute BH=page DX=cursor start CX=string length ES:BP=string address		AT, New XT, PS/2, EGA only
Write Text String and Move Cursor	AH=13 AL=1 BL=attribute BH=page DX=cursor start CX=string length ES:BP=string address		AT, New XT, PS/2, EGA only

Name of Service	What You Specify	What You Get Back	Notes
Write Text/Attribute String Without Moving Cursor	AH=13 AL=2 BH=page DX=Cursor Start CX=string length ES:BP=string address		AT, New XT, PS/2, EGA only (Form: character1, attribute1, character2, attribute2,... etc.)
Write Text/Attribute String and Move Cursor	AH=13 AL=3 BH=page DX=cursor start CX=string length ES:BP=string address		AT, New XT, PS/2, EGA only (Form: character1, attribute1, character2, attribute2,... etc.)
Get Video Combination Code	AH=1A Al=0	AL=1A BL=active display code BH=inactive display code	VGA, MCGA only Codes for BL/BH: 0=no display 1=MDA 2=CGA 4=color EGA 5=mono EGA 6=PGC 7=mono VGA 8=color VGA B=mono MCGA C=color MCGA FF=unknown
Set Video Combination Code	AH=1A AL=1 BL=active display BH=inactive display	AL=1A	VGA, MCGA only Codes for BL/BH: 0=no display 1=MDA 2=CGA 4=color EGA 5=mono EGA 6=PGC 7=mono VGA 8=color VGA B=mono MCGA C=color MCGA FF=unknown

(continued)

Name of Service	What You Specify	What You Get Back	Notes
Get BIOS Functionality Information	AH=1B BX=0 ES:DI=64-byte buffer	AL=1B ES:DI=video mode and configuration table	VGA, MCGA only

Get VGA State Store/Restore Buffer Size	AH=1C
	AL=0
	CX=state to store
	    (0=DAC)
	    (1=BIOS)
	    (2=registers)
		AL=1C
		BX=number of 64-byte buffer blocks required
			VGA only; use this before AL=1 save

VGA State Store	AH=1C
	AL=1
	CX=state to store
	    (0=DAC)
	    (1=BIOS)
	    (2=registers)
	ES:BX=buffer address
			VGA only; use AL=0 first

VGA State Restore	AH=1C
	AL=2
	CX=state to restore
	    (0=DAC)
	    (1=BIOS)
	    (2=registers)
	ES:BX=buffer address
			VGA only; use after AL=0 and AL=1

Figure 13.2. Enhanced INT 10 Tools

Name of Service	What You Specify	What You Get Back	Notes
Display output	AH=2 DL=character		One character at a time
Display String	AH=9 DS:DX=pointer to output string		Must end string with a $ which means you can't display a $

Figure 13.3. INT 21 Tools

DOS's INT 21 tools are far more feeble than INT 10's. While DOS lets you display single characters, or strings of characters, it doesn't let you set or change the colors. It just displays them in whatever colors happen to be active. And since its Display Output function 9 uses a dollar sign to indicate the end of the string, you can't have function 9 *display* a dollar sign.

You could also use some of the other slightly more exotic DOS services such as the output half of Direct Console I/O function 6, or Write to File or Device function 40, or you could even use Open File 3D and write to the CON (console) device rather than a file. (The discussion of ANSI in an earlier chapter showed how to use the undocumented INT 29 "Fast TTY" function.) But the Display Output (function 2) and Display String (function 9) services, or the speedier BIOS services, can handle just about anything you'll need.

To create a short program that will display the letters "PC" you could try several different approaches. Each of the examples below uses the DEBUG (2.0 or later) mini-assembler. DEBUG works exclusively in hex, so be careful not to mix hex and decimal notation. If you're confused about registers, read the chapters on memory and DEBUG first.

After starting DEBUG (by typing DEBUG) you turn on the assembler by typing A at the DEBUG hyphen (-) prompt. You'll be creating COM files that start at hex offset 100. If you're creating several COM files in succession without leaving DEBUG, use the command:

```
A 100
```

to start each new one at offset 100. After you've created the first one, don't just use A without adding a 100 after it or else you'll end up telling DEBUG to begin the next program at the wrong starting address.

When you're done entering the interrupt 10 BIOS or interrupt 21 DOS instructions, be sure to include an instruction to exit your small program and return to DOS. If you don't, the program will freeze, or "hang" your system. There are all sorts of ways to exit. Most experts tell you that you should use function 4C of interrupt 21, the code for which looks like:

```
MOV AH,4C
INT 21
```

This approach is handy when you have to set an *exit* code (or *return* code) that a batch file can process. Adding a line before the INT 21:

```
MOV AH,4C
MOV AL,FF
INT 21
```

will set an exit code of hex FF (decimal 255). Your batch file can then include a line that says:

```
IF ERRORLEVEL 255 GOTO LABEL1
```

so the batch file jumps, or *branches* to :LABEL1 if your display program worked properly. See the batch techniques chapter for more information.

However, you can also exit a program and return to DOS with a simple:

```
INT 20
```

And with short programs like the ones below, you can use a still simpler:

```
RET
```

After you enter the final instruction to return your program to DOS, you'll have to press the Enter key twice to exit DEBUG's mini-assembler. Then just give DEBUG a name that ends with a COM extension (by using the N command), tell DEBUG how long the program is (by using the RCX command), write the program to disk (with a W), and quit (by typing Q).

To use DOS service 2 of Interrupt 21, the process would look like:

`C>DEBUG`	**You type DEBUG to start.**
`-A`	**Then type A at the hyphen prompt.**
`30DD:0100 MOV AH,2`	
`30DD:0102 MOV DL,50`	**Here DEBUG prints the AAAA:BBBB**
`30DD:0104 INT 21`	**addresses; you type in the instructions**
`30DD:0106 MOV DL,43`	**like MOV AH,2 or INT 21 and press**
`30DD:0108 INT 21`	**Enter after each.**
`30DD:010A RET`	
`30DD:010B`	**Just press Enter here.**
`-N SERVICE2.COM`	**You type N and the filename.**
`-RCX`	**You enter RCX.**
`CX 0000`	**DEBUG responds with this.**
`:B`	**And you enter the length (B bytes) here.**
`-W`	**Then you enter W to write the file.**
`Writing 000B bytes`	**DEBUG prints this message.**
`-Q`	**And you type Q to quit.**

The 30DD before the colon on seven of the lines is the segment address, and will probably be different on your system. It doesn't matter here.

Each time you enter an instruction, DEBUG figures out how many bytes it took and offers you a chance to enter an additional instruction at the next available address. When you're all done entering instructions, just press Enter. In the above example, you'd do this when you see the line:

```
30DD:010B
```

To figure out how long your program is, just look at the offset address of this line (the one following your last instruction). Ignore the leftmost four digits. Since DEBUG starts all files at address 100, subtract 100 from the rightmost four digits:

```
30DD:010B
```

↑   ↑
          subtract 100 from this
ignore this

With small programs, hex subtraction is easy:

```
   010B
−  100
    B
```

If even this scares you, use the free hex calculator supplied with DEBUG. Just enter H (for "H math") then the rightmost four digits (here these are 010B) and finally the 100 you want to subtract. The whole command looks like:

```
-H 010B 100          You type everything after the hyphen.
020B 000B            DEBUG responds with this.
```

The first number DEBUG prints is the sum of the two numbers. The second number is the difference. You want the difference (000B). You can skip the leading zeros; 000B is the same as just plain B. Hex numbers are often expressed as pairs of digits, so you'll often see hex B written as 0B.

If you enter everything as it appears above, you'll end up with a small program on your disk called SERVICE2.COM that uses DOS service 2 to display a P and then a C and then exit. Once you've created it, just type SERVICE2 at the DOS prompt.

This program uses service 2 twice — once to print the P (which has a hex value of 50), and once to display the C (with has a hex value of 43). You tell the program you want to use service 2 of interrupt 21 by putting a 2 into the AH register with the MOV AH,2 instruction. Then you put the hex values of the characters you want to display into the DL register one at a time, with the MOV DL,50 and MOV DL,43 instructions. Then you issue an INT 21 to put DOS to work. DOS will look in the AH register to see what you want it to do, figure out that you'd like it to display a character, then get the value in register DL and display the character with that value.

This example used only one:

```
MOV AH,2
```

instruction, but two:

```
MOV DL,50
MOV DL,43
```

instructions. This is a shortcut; the first MOV AH,2 instruction lasts for both of the MOV DL,50 and MOV DL,43 instructions since the program doesn't meddle with the AH register at all after putting the 2 into it. Sometimes this won't work and you'll have to specify the MOV AH,2 twice:

```
MOV AH,2
MOV DL,50
INT 21
MOV AH,2
MOV DL,43
INT 21
RET
```

You could modify this SERVICE2.COM program and turn it into SERVICE6.COM, by repeating the process but changing the line:

```
30DD:0100 MOV AH,2
```

to:

```
30DD:0100 MOV AH,6
```

and then changing the line:

```
-N SERVICE2.COM
```

to:

```
-N SERVICE6.COM
```

Both will work almost identically. About the only difference is that while you can break out of the SERVICE2.COM program by pressing Ctrl-C (very quickly), you can't do this to the SERVICE6.COM program. However, these programs are both so short this doesn't really make any difference.

If you then wanted to see what the actual assembly language instructions looked like, you could use DEBUG's U (Unassemble) command:

```
C>DEBUG SERVICE2.COM
-U 100 LB
30F9:0100 B402      MOV      AH,02
30F9:0102 B250      MOV      DL,50
```

```
30F9:0104  CD21      INT      21
30F9:0106  B243      MOV      DL,43
30F9:0108  CD21      INT      21
30F9:010A  C3        RET
```

To use the U command, specify the starting address (on programs like these it will always be 100), then the letter L, then the hex length. If you don't know the hex length of a file you just loaded into DEBUG (with a command like DEBUG SERVICE2.COM), you can have DEBUG tell you — just type RCX and press Enter twice. The number DEBUG prints after the CX is the length. The process will look something like:

```
-RCX
CX 000B
:
-
```

Both SERVICE2.COM and SERVICE6.COM printed one character at a time. If you wanted to print both at once, you could use service 9, which prints a string of characters. Just type:

`C>DEBUG`	**You type DEBUG to start.**
`A`	**Then type A at the hyphen prompt.**
`30DD:0100  MOV AH,9`	**Here DEBUG prints the AAAA:BBBB addresses; you type in the instructions like MOV AH,9 and INT 21 and press Enter after each.**
`30DD:0102  MOV DX,108`	
`30DD:0105  INT 21`	
`30DD:0107  RET`	
`30DD:0108  DB 'PC$'`	
`30DD:010B`	**Just press Enter here.**
`-N SERVICE9.COM`	**You type N and the filename.**
`-RCX`	**You enter RCX.**
`CX 0000`	**DEBUG responds with this.**
`:B`	**And you enter the length (B bytes) here.**
`-W`	**Then you enter W to write the file.**
`Writing 000B bytes`	**DEBUG prints this message.**
`-Q`	**And you type Q to quit.**

When you use service 9 of DOS interrupt 21, all you have to do is:

1. Put a 9 in register AH (with MOV AH,9).
2. Use register DX to point to the address in memory of the string that you want to print (with MOV DX,108 for instance, if the string starts at offset address 108).
3. Make sure the string you want to print starts at the address you specified in step 2, and ends with a $ (a hex 24 character).

4. Issue an INT 21 to have DOS do it for you.
5. Use one of the exit commands (such as RET or INT 20) to return to the DOS prompt once you're done.

When entering a string with the DEBUG A (Assemble) command, put it inside a pair of single or double quotation marks, and precede it with a DB. And be sure you end the string with a dollar sign, which won't appear onscreen when DOS displays the rest of the string.

You could have used the hex value of the dollar sign (24) instead of putting the $ between the quotes. Both:

```
30DD:0108 DB 'PC$'
```

and:

```
30DD:0108 DB 'PC' 24
```

will work the same.

With simple programs like this the dollar sign is often the last character in the file. If you forget to add the dollar sign, or if you specify a file length that's a byte too short so DEBUG doesn't include the final dollar sign when it writes the file to disk, you can run into problems. When you run the file DOS will print the string (in this case, PC), but since there's no dollar sign to tell it to stop it will keep printing whatever characters happen to be loaded in memory after the string until it hits a character 24 by chance. DOS may stumble over a character 24 right away, or it may print a screen or two of beeping, flashing garbage before it finally stops.

Technically, the MOV DX,108 instruction that points to the string skips a step. If you were writing a longer program, you'd have to specify an additional value, for DS, since the address of the string is pointed to by DS:DX, where DS is the segment address and DX is the offset address. (See Chapter 7 for details.) With tiny programs like these you don't have to worry about the DS segment address.

However, this time, if you try to use the DEBUG Unassemble command, you'll see:

```
C>DEBUG SERVICE9.COM
-U 100 LB
30DD:0100 B409         MOV     AH,09
30DD:0102 BA0801       MOV     DX,0108
30DD:0105 CD21         INT     21
30DD:0107 C3           RET
30DD:0108 50           PUSH    AX
30DD:0109 43           INC     BX
30DD:010A 2426         AND     AL,26
```

The first four lines are correct, but the:

```
30DD:0108 DB 'PC$'
```

instruction that specifies the string disappeared and was replaced by three other assembly language instructions:

```
30DD:0108 50            PUSH    AX
30DD:0109 43            INC     BX
30DD:010A 2426          AND     AL,26
```

DEBUG's U command tries to turn everything into instructions. It isn't smart enough to see that you're using a Display String instruction and that you're telling it that the string begins at address 108. So it looks at the bytes that make up the string (and the final dollar sign) and translates these into meaningless instructions rather than identifying them as data.

If you used the DEBUG D (for Dump or Display) command instead of the U command, you'd see your string:

```
-D 100 LB
30DD:0100 B4 09 BA 08 01 CD 21 C3-50 43 24   ......!.PC$
```

The SERVICE2.COM, SERVICE6.COM, and SERVICE9.COM programs all use display services of DOS interrupt 21. They don't meddle with the color settings, and will display the characters you specified in whatever colors happen to be active at the time. They essentially treat your screen like a teletype device (abbreviated as TTY).

In this respect, they're similar to the BIOS Write Character as Teletype service E of interrupt 10. You could adapt the SERVICE2.COM program above very easily to use this BIOS function:

```
C>DEBUG
-A
30DD:0100 MOV AH,E
30DD:0102 MOV AL,50
30DD:0104 INT 10
30DD:0106 MOV AL,43
30DD:0108 INT 10
30DD:010A RET
30DD:010B
-N SERVICEE.COM
-RCX
CX 0000
:B
-W
Writing 000B bytes
-Q
```

Service E of BIOS interrupt 10 lets you use screen *pages* on a color system. In fact, you could add a line before the first INT 10 that says:

```
MOV BH,0
```

This tells your system to write the characters to screen page 0 — the one you normally work with. If you did this you'd have to increase the length of the program that you specified with the RCX command. Fortunately, you shouldn't have to worry about this, since just about nothing takes advantage of screen pages other than page 0.

What's a page?

It's far easier to display a screenful of characters than a screenful of dots. A 25-row, 80-column screen can hold 2,000 characters (25 x 80 = 2,000). It takes one byte to store the value of each character, and one additional byte to store the color of each character. So displaying one complete 25 by 80 screenful of text requires 2,000 bytes of memory to store the characters, plus another 2,000 bytes to store the colors of each character.

However, IBM's original four-color 320 by 200 medium-resolution graphics screen required 16,000 bytes of memory. The system has to keep track of 64,000 dots (320 x 200) and the colors of these dots. It does this by using two bits — a quarter of a byte — to represent the color of each dot (pixel). Two bits yields four possible colors (actually three colors plus color 00, which is the same as the background color):

Bits	Decimal	Result
00	0	no color
01	1	first color
10	2	second color
11	3	third color

These four values (0-3) will produce different colors depending on which "palette" of possible colors is active. You can see this palette by typing in the following PALS-HOW.BAS BASIC program, using a pure ASCII word processor, EDIT, or EDLIN. Omit the single quotation (') marks and the comments following them

```
100 'PALSHOW.BAS — shows different graphics palettes
110 SCREEN 1                      ' 320 x 200 graphics
120 COLOR 1,0                     ' blue background, palette 0
130 CLS                           ' clear screen
140 FOR A=1 TO 3
150 CIRCLE (60+A*50,50),25,A      ' draw three circles
160 PAINT (60+A*50,50),A,A        ' color them with colors 1, 2, and 3
170 NEXT
180 LOCATE 20,4
190 PRINT "Press any key to switch palettes"
200 LOCATE 21,9
210 PRINT "(or press Esc to end)"
```

```
220 I$=INKEY$:IF I$="" THEN 220
230 IF I$=CHR$(27) THEN END ELSE K=K+1
240 COLOR 1,K                    ' switch to the other palette
250 GOTO 220
```

Once you've created the program, run it on any color system by typing QBASIC PALSHOW, BASICA PALSHOW (or GWBASIC PALSHOW if you're not using IBM hardware). Press any key and you'll see the three circles change from palette 0 (where they're green, red, and brown/yellow) to palette 1 (where they're cyan, magenta, and white). Press the Esc key to quit.

The location of the dot onscreen is simply its relative position in the 16,000 possible bytes of memory. The very first of the 16,000 bytes of display memory represents the first four dots on the screen (since each byte contains eight bits and each dot takes up two bits), starting in the upper lefthand corner. The second byte represents the next four dots, and so on. It actually gets fairly complicated, since the odd-numbered rows and even-numbered rows are maintained separately. More on that later.

Originally, IBM also offered a "high resolution" graphics screen measuring 640 by 200. This meant keeping track of 128,000 dots (640 x 200). Each bit of each of the 16,000 bytes stood for one dot. A dot was either on (white) or off (black), and no color was allowed unless you knew how to program the graphics controller directly.

The total 16,000 bytes x 8 bits per byte = 128,000 bits. In high resolution, all the bits were used up just telling your system whether each of the 128,000 dots was on or off. In medium resolution, you could use two bits to specify one of four colors (with binary values 00, 01, 10, or 11) so 64,000 dots x 2 bits = 128,000. And if you knew how to tweak your system, you could even experiment with a low-resolution screen that displayed 160 x 200 dots in 16 colors.

Each CGA system came with 16K of display memory on the display adapter. Graphics used it all. But a full 80-column screen of text used only 4,000 of the 16,000 bytes. IBM let you use the rest by dividing the 16,000 total bytes into four screen pages each 4,000 bytes long. The default was always page 0. But you could write on any of the four pages and then switch instantly to any of them.

With 40-column screens you could use eight pages. Nobody really ever uses 40-column text screens, which were developed originally so that users could hook up their systems to home television sets. Home TVs didn't have decent enough resolution to display 80-character text, but they could handle 40-character text decently. You can't ordinarily mix 40-character text and 80-character text on the same screen. The following BASIC SIZEMIX.BAS program will do it, however, on most color systems:

```
100 ' SIZEMIX.BAS
110 SCREEN 2:OUT 985,2:CLS
120 LOCATE 5,30:PRINT "This is small type"
130 DEF SEG=0:POKE 1097,4:POKE 1098,40:DEF SEG
140 LOCATE 7,12:PRINT "This is large type"
150 DEF SEG=0:POKE 1097,6:POKE 1098,80:DEF SEG
160 LOCATE 9,30:PRINT "And back to small type"
```

Screen pages are potentially very useful, since you could put things like menus and help screens on pages 1, 2, and 3, and then flip to these instantly without disturbing the contents of your main page 0. Unfortunately, few (if any) programs ever use this. Why? Because users with monochrome screens don't have any extra screen memory, so they don't have any extra pages. And software vendors don't like to create programs that owners of some systems can't use properly.

Also, by putting slightly different images on different screen pages and then switching rapidly from one page to another you can create the illusion of movement or animation.

You could also see how pages work by running the small PAGEDEMO.BAS program below:

```
100 ' PAGEDEMO.BAS — shows color screen pages
110 ' --- set up array of 200 screen positions ---
120 DIM R(200),C(200)
130 FOR A=1 TO 200
140 R(A)=INT(RND*23+1)
150 C(A)=INT(RND*79+1)
160 NEXT
170 CLS
180 LOCATE 12,30
190 PRINT "Building screens . . . "
200 ' --- fill array with arrows ---
210 FOR C=3 TO 0 STEP -1
220 IF C>1 THEN E=C+2 ELSE E=C
230 SCREEN ,,C,0
240 COLOR E,7:CLS
250 FOR D=1 TO 200
260 LOCATE R(D),C(D)
270 PRINT CHR$(24+C)
280 NEXT
290 LOCATE 25,13
300 PRINT "Press any key to switch to ";
310 PRINT "another page (or Esc to end)";
320 NEXT
330 ' --- switch from one page to next ---
340 I$=INKEY$:IF I$="" THEN 340
350 IF I$=CHR$(27) THEN 380 ELSE K=(K+1) MOD 4
360 SCREEN ,,,K
370 GOTO 340
380 SCREEN 0,1,0,0:SYSTEM
```

PAGEDEMO first figures out 200 random screen coordinates, then puts four different sets of arrows in four different colors on the four 80 x 25 video pages. It lets you flip from one to the next by pressing any key. Pressing Esc sets things back to normal and quits.

In the Cards

When the PC was first introduced, just about everyone purchased IBM's monochrome display adapter (MDA), which could be hooked up only to IBM's monochrome display. A handful of pioneers purchased IBM's color graphics adapter (CGA), which they used to drive either an RGB monitor (which cost over $1,000 way back then), or a home television set.

Hooking up a PC to a TV set meant having to purchase a separate RF modulator, or trying to run the signal through the RF circuitry of a video tape recorder. The results were totally unsatisfactory, since the definition was crude. If you were lucky you could just about make out text in 40-column modes. When the CGA was attached to an RGB monitor it used separate outputs for the red, green, and blue (and intensity) signals. When it was attached to a TV, it used a *composite* output that blurred all the information into one signal. The *burst* parameter that turns color on and off with things like BASIC's SCREEN command applies to composite output only.

Composite screens often have trouble displaying colors other than black (0) and white (7 or F). However, if you know what you're doing, you can produce interesting *artifact color* displays by experimenting with different black-and-white line patterns.

PCs use *memory-mapped* displays. The system builds an image of the screen in memory, which the video circuitry reads and turns into recognizable text or graphics. The adapter card translates the information in video memory into signals that control one or more electron guns. These scan beams of electrons onto chemical phosphors painted on the monitor glass that glow when energized.

The CGA had several nasty habits. It occasionally produced a random pattern of interference called "snow" when programs tried to write directly to this video memory memory at the same time that the display electronics was putting the image onscreen. (The MDA and most recent video adapters have *dual-ported* video RAM that lets the CPU update memory without interfering with the reading process.) Relatively sophisticated programs write data to CGA video memory only during the 1.25 millisecond *vertical retrace interval.*

The electron beam sweeps from left to right and from top to bottom as it zigzags its way across the entire surface of the screen. Each time it reaches the right edge it has to scurry down a line and over to the left edge again. This is the *horizontal retrace.* And each time it reaches the very bottom righthand corner of the screen it has to jump all the way back to the upper lefthand corner and start over. This is the *vertical retrace.* In addition, the beam always overscans each line a hair past the edge, which wastes a tiny bit of time.

CGA screens also flickered when they scrolled up a line, which produced a disturbing strobe effect if you were reading through a long document. The display circuitry was supposed to paint images onto the screen 60 times each second, but the CGA put just 30 images onto the screen and alternated these with all-black screens. This wasn't that noticeable when the image didn't change much, or when the background was black. But if you used a light-colored background and scrolled lines repeatedly, you ended up goggle-eyed.

The CGA was also slower and fuzzier than the MDA. The MDA could handle more dots (720 across and 350 up and down compared to the CGA's maximum 640 x 200 resolution). And it boasted a *long-persistence* phosphor that blurred the individual dots together into solid-looking characters and did away with just about all flicker. The MDA also had a higher *bandwidth* than the CGA, which let the mono adapter pump more information per second to a mono screen than the CGA could send to a color screen.

But while the MDA and CGA could both juggle 2,000 characters on each screen, the CGA could manipulate discrete dots, which let users draw lines, circles, and other graphic images.

One year after the PC hit the market, an independent hardware manufacturer developed a display adapter called the Hercules Graphics Card (HGC) that handled monochrome text on mono monitors just like the MDA but added dot-addressable graphics abilities like those on the CGA. This was followed four years later by an upgraded Hercules Graphics Card Plus (HGC+) that could work with different customized onscreen fonts, and a year after that with a proprietary Hercules InColor Card that could display 16 colors out of a palette of 64 in graphics mode, in 720 x 348 resolution.

In 1985 IBM introduced a display card called the Enhanced Graphics Adapter (EGA) that produced text and dot-addressable graphics on both color and IBM monochrome screens. It could drive a higher resolution color screen than the CGA, could juggle more colors, didn't flicker when it scrolled, and didn't have problems with snow. It could use customizable fonts, and could display a very readable 43 lines of text onscreen, 72 percent more than the CGA or MDA. IBM's original EGA card was expensive, and didn't come with the full complement of memory required. But manufacturers soon began stamping out inexpensive clones with the full 256K of video RAM, and the EGA became an instant standard. See the following chapter for more details.

These early adapters had *digital* outputs. When IBM brought out its PS/2 computer series, it stunned the monitor industry by using *analog* graphics systems. Analog outputs can handle color gradations more adroitly than digital ones. But all of the monitors sold by IBM were digital. Some of the popular *multisynching* monitors sold by companies like NEC and Sony could handle both digital and analog inputs.

IBM's integrated a new standard called Multi-Color Graphics Array (MCGA) — a sort of beefed-up CGA — into the main circuit board of the bottom-of-the-line PS/2 Models 25 and 30. Maximum MCGA resolution was decent (640 by 480 dots) and it could put 256 colors onscreen at once, out of a palette 256K colors wide, in 320 by 200 resolution. And it could produce 64 shades of grey on IBM's newer monochrome displays.

But the MCGA was overshadowed by a more capable system named after a chip called the Video Graphics Array, or VGA. The VGA handled all MDA, CDA, and EGA modes, and tossed in a few new ones of its own. It also worked with an IBM enhancement add-in card with the euphonious name 8514/A that boosted performance even more.

Figure 13.4 compares the various types of displays.

System	Bandwidth (MHz)	Horizontal Scan Rate (KHz)	Vertical Scan Rate (Hz)	Dot Box (width x height)
MDA	16.257	18.432	50	9x14
HGC	16.257	18.432	50	9x14
CGA	14.318	15.75	60	8x8
EGA color	14.318-16.257	15.75-21.85	60	8x8,8x14
EGA mono	16.257	18.432	50	9x14
MCGA	25.175	31.47	60–70	8x16
VGA	25.175-28.322	31.47	60–70	8x8,8x14, 9x14,9x16
8514/A	44.9	35.52	43.48 (interlaced)[*]	Superset of VGA

[*] *Note:* Only the 8514 is interlaced; its effective scan rate looks like 87 Hz.

Figure 13.4. Video Hardware Specifications

The *bandwidth* determines the maximum number of dots each system can handle per second. The relatively slow CGA can push just 14,318,000 dots down the line each second, while the sprintier VGA can shuttle nearly twice than number in the same amount of time. The *horizontal scan rate* tells how many lines each system can display per second. Again, the PS/2 displays can handle double the number of lines (31,500 per second) compared to the older CGA. The *vertical scan rate* is the number of fully refreshed screens each system produces per second. The *dot box* is the dimensions of the box in which a character is formed.

The horizontal scan rate divided by the vertical scan rate yields the maximum displayable lines per screen. (Some of these are used for other things, however, such as vertical retrace intervals and overscan margins.) The bandwidth divided by the horizontal scan rate yields the number of dots per line (although some of these are used for the horizontal retrace and overscan). You can then divide these by the various dot widths and heights to see how many characters each could handle.

You can put combinations of these display adapters into the same system. IBM originally assigned different memory and port addresses to the MDA and CGA cards:

System	Video Memory Address	Port Addresses
MDA	B000	3B0 - 3BF
CGA	B800	3D0 - 3DF

Since an EGA can drive either a color or mono display, you can add it to a system that already has an MDA or CGA attached. You can also mix an MDA with a VGA or MCGA.

Hercules monochrome cards will work with just about everything (other than an IBM MDA). However, since Hercules cards use 64K of video RAM starting at address B000:0, 32K of this overlaps memory allotted to the CGA that begins at address B800:0. You can use the two together if you configure the Hercules video memory to avoid conflicts with the CGA.

The EGA (and VGA) can use 32K of video RAM beginning either at the normal mono address of B000:0, or the normal color address of B800:0. Or it can start at A000:0 and use just the 64K A000 segment, or take 128K by spanning both the A000 and B000 segments. The MCGA uses the 64K A000 segment.

Or you could combine VGA and MCGA, using subservices 32H and 35H of BIOS INT 10 Service 12H. But you wouldn't really want to.

Storage Schemes

PCs store text in character/attribute pairs of ASCII values. The position of each character onscreen depends on its position in video memory. Since each 80-column, 25-line screen can display 2,000 characters, it takes 4,000 bytes of memory to hold the characters and attributes for a full screen. The first of the 4,000 bytes in video memory stores the ASCII value of the text character in the upper lefthand corner. The second byte stores the attribute of that character. The third byte stores the ASCII value of the second character on the top line. The fifth byte stores the value of the third character on the top line.

So if you're using a color system with blue text on a white background, and you have the letters ABC in the upper lefthand corner of your screen, the hex representation of the contents of memory starting at address B800 would look like:

Address	Value	Contents
B800:0000	41	the letter A
B800:0001	71	the color for A
B800:0002	42	the letter B
B800:0003	71	the color for B
B800:0004	43	the letter C
B800:0005	71	the color for C

The hex value for "A" is 41, so this is the first value in video memory. This is followed at the very next address by the color in which the "A" appears (71 is blue on white). The third memory address contains a value of 42 ("B") which is again followed by the color (71), and so on.

You can see this better by using DEBUG. If you're using a color system, just clear your screen, make sure DEBUG.COM is handy, and at the DOS prompt, type:

```
DEBUG
D B800:0 LB0
```

Depending on what your prompt looks like, you should see something like:

```
B800:0000 20 07 20 07 20 07 20 07-20 07 20 07 20 07 20 07  . . . . . . . .
B800:0010 20 07 20 07 20 07 20 07-20 07 20 07 20 07 20 07  . . . . . . . .
B800:0020 20 07 20 07 20 07 20 07-20 07 20 07 20 07 20 07  . . . . . . . .
B800:0030 20 07 20 07 20 07 20 07-20 07 20 07 20 07 20 07  . . . . . . . .
B800:0040 20 07 20 07 20 07 20 07-20 07 20 07 20 07 20 07  . . . . . . . .
B800:0050 20 07 20 07 20 07 20 07-20 07 20 07 20 07 20 07  . . . . . . . .
B800:0060 20 07 20 07 20 07 20 07-20 07 20 07 20 07 20 07  . . . . . . . .
B800:0070 20 07 20 07 20 07 20 07-20 07 20 07 20 07 20 07  . . . . . . . .
B800:0080 20 07 20 07 20 07 20 07-20 07 20 07 20 07 20 07  . . . . . . . .
B800:0090 20 07 20 07 20 07 20 07-20 07 20 07 20 07 20 07  . . . . . . . .
B800:00A0 43 07 3E 07 44 07 45 07-42 07 55 07 47 07 20 07  C.>.D.E.B.U.G. .
```

Then type Q and press the Enter key to quit. (If you're trying this on a mono system, substitute B000 for B800 in the example.) Clearing the screen with CLS on many systems actually puts the DOS prompt on the second line, as is the case here, so the first line is blank. A blank line is made up of 80 spaces, which takes 160 bytes of storage — 80 for the space characters themselves and another 80 for the color of the spaces. The ASCII character for a space is hex 20. The first, third, fifth, etc. characters above are all hex 20 spaces.

When you type CLS, COMMAND.COM normally clears the screen to white (color 7) on black (color 0). The second, fourth, sixth, etc. characters above are all 07 white-on-black attributes.

The command you typed:

```
DEBUG
```

appears hex A0 (decimal 160) characters into the DEBUG display.

Again, each character is followed by its attribute. These show up as dots in the right-hand column of the DEBUG display, since DEBUG uses dots to represent anything with ASCII values lower than hex 20 (decimal 32) or higher than hex 7E (decimal 126).

You can use DEBUG to write information to video memory, which is a lot more interesting than just reading from RAM.

If you're using a color system, type:

```
DEBUG
F B800:0 LA0 41
```

This will put the value hex 41 into the first A0 (decimal 160) bytes of video memory. Each 80-column screen line uses 80 spaces in RAM to store the character values and another 80 addresses to maintain the attributes for these characters, for a total of decimal 160 bytes. So this command will fill the top line of your screen with the hex character 41 — uppercase A. And since the attribute 41 happens to be blue (color 1) on red (color 4), the line of AAAAAAAs will appear in blue on red.

If you enter:

```
F B800:0 LA0 61
```

you'll get a top row of lowercase "a" characters in blue (color 1) on a yellow (color 6) background. If you enter:

```
F B800:0 LA0 FE
```

the top row will fill with blinking bright yellow boxes (character hex FE) on a white background, since the E produces a high-intensity yellow foreground and the F makes the background white and blinks the foreground. Or try:

```
F B800:0 LA0 DD
```

which produces a top line of blinking alternate light and dark purple horizontal stripes. The LA0 in each of these tells DEBUG to fill just hex A0 (decimal 160) bytes, or one line. By expanding this to hex FA0 (decimal 4,000), you can fill the entire screen. The command:

```
F B800:0 LFA0 DD
```

will blanket your entire screen with these blinking purple stripes.
If you type:

```
E B800:0 "aabbccddeeffgghhiijjkkllmmnnooppqqrrssttuuvvwwxxyyzz"
```

you'll end up with a lowercase alphabet in various foreground colors on brown and white backgrounds. The hex ASCII values of the letters "a" through "z" are all between 61 and 7A. The color for brown is 6 and for white is 7, which happens to be the lefthand digits of the character values.
If you tried:

```
E B800:0 "AABBCCDDEEFFGGHHIIJJKKLLMMNNOOPPQQRRSSTTUUVVWWXXYYZZ"
```

you'd see an uppercase alphabet in assorted text colors on a red and purple background, since the hex ASCII values of the letters "A" through "Z" are all between 41 and 5A. The color for red is 4, and the color for purple (magenta) is 5.
Since the position in memory dictates the position onscreen, you could put a string anywhere you want by varying its address. The following three DEBUG commands will put three messages in three colors in three places on screen:

```
E B800:0 "TGOGPG"
E B800:7CA "MVIVDVDVLVEV"
E B800:F94 "BaOaTaTaOaMa"
```

The top command will put the letters "TOP" in white text on a red background in the upper lefthand corner of the screen. The first, third, and fifth characters of "TGOGPG" are the ones that show up onscreen. The second, fourth, and sixth "G" characters don't actually appear; instead, these set the color to white (7) on red (4), since the hex ASCII value of "G" is 47. The 0 address after B800: tells DEBUG to put the "TGOGPG" string at the very beginning of color video memory.

```
    "TGOGPG"              "TGOGPG"
     ↑  ↑ ↑                ↑  ↑ ↑
     T  O  P               G  G  G
    characters            attributes
```

The second command will put the word "MIDDLE" in the middle of your screen. The alternate "V" characters will make the word appear in brown (6) text on a purple (5) background, since the value of "V" is hex 56. And the 7CA offset address after the B800: told DEBUG to insert the "MVIVDVDVLVEV" string hex a little less than halfway through the 4,000 bytes of video memory. Hex 7CA is equal to decimal 1994.

Similarly, the third command will put the word "BOTTOM" in the lower righthand corner of a 25-line, 80-column screen. The lowercase "a" characters in the "BaOaTaTaOaMa" string set the color to blue (1) on brown (6), since the hex ASCII value of "a" is 61. The F94 offset address following the B800: starts the string near the very end of the 4,000 bytes of video memory, since F94 is equal to 3,988.

The attribute value for blue text on a white background is 71, which is also the hex value of the "q" character. To print "THIS IS A TEST" in the upper lefthand corner of your color screen, just type:

```
DEBUG
E B800:0 "TqHqIqSq qIqSq qAq qTqEqSqT"
```

DEBUG will put the values for all these characters into the beginning of color video memory, which will interpret the hex 71 "q" characters as blue-on-white attributes. Remember that your system stores characters first and then attributes. If you accidentally started the string off with a "q" rather than a text character:

```
DEBUG
E B800:0 "qTqHqIqSq qIqSq qAq qTqEqSqT"
```

all you'd end up with is a multicolored string of qqqqqqs. Memory numbering systems start with 0. Even-numbered addresses contain ASCII values of characters. Odd-numbered addresses store the attribute values for these characters.

This technique provides a quick and dirty way to set the screen attributes while using DEBUG. If you normally prefer blue text on a white background, and you're using DEBUG to trace through a program, you can run into color trouble. Programs often contain routines to clear the screen, and if you stumble over one of these your screen may suddenly turn a dismal grey on black (unless you have ANSI.SYS loaded). To fix it, just issue a command like:

```
F B800:0 LFA0 "q"
```

and your screen will instantly be filled with blue-on-white lowercase "q" characters. Lean on the Enter key until the "q" characters disappear off the top, and you'll be left with a cleared blue-on-white screen. Substitute "t" for "q" if you want a red-on-white screen, since the hex ASCII value for "t" is 74.

If you want to clear your screen to a color such as cyan (3) on dark blue (1), you won't be able to enter a character such as "t" or "q." So just enter the hex number directly:

```
F B800:0 LFA0 13
```

As an added bonus, when you're all done working with DEBUG and you enter Q to return to DOS, the colors this trick set will remain in effect until something else changes them.

Note that you can put a red-on-white "$" character at the very bottom righthand corner of a 25-line, 80-column screen, by typing:

```
E B800:F9E "$t"
```

Since video memory starts at page 0, this will display a red dollar sign character on the default 0 page. And, as mentioned earlier, page 1 follows page 0. You might think that since F9E (the address of the $) and F9F (the address of the red-on-white attribute value) were the last two memory addresses of page 0, you could print a blue-on-white dollar sign at the top of the following video page — page 1 — by using an address two bytes higher:

```
E B800:FA0 "$q"
```

Try this and nothing visible will happen. Page 1 does indeed follow page 0 — but not directly. The second video page starts at the even hex address 1000, which is equal to decimal 4096, not 4000. The:

```
E B800:FA0 "$q"
```

command put the blue dollar sign in an unused area between page 0 and page 1. To put this blue dollar sign at the top of page 1, type:

```
E B800:1000 "$q"
```

To see that the blue dollar sign actually appeared at the top of page 1, create a tiny program called PAGE1.COM by typing:

```
E 100 B4 05 B0 01 CD 10 C3
N PAGE1.COM
RCX
7
W
Q
```

The PAGE1.COM program looks like:

```
MOV AH,5    ; set video page
MOV AL,1    ; to page 1
INT 10      ; have BIOS do it
RET         ; back to DOS
```

You can return to the default page 0 by using the PAGE.COM program or, if you're using a color system, by making sure the DOS MODE.COM utility is handy and typing:

```
MODE CO80
```

The video page map for an 80 x 25 display would look like:

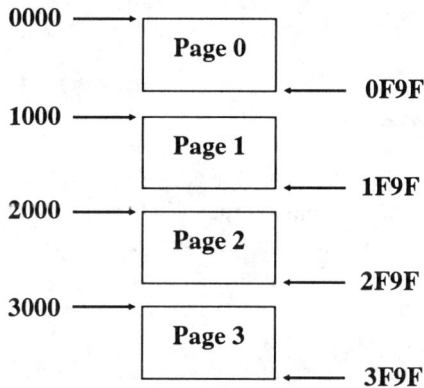

Your system wastes the hex 60 (decimal 96) bytes of memory between each of the pages.

While the focus of this book is on text rather than graphics, it's interesting to note that IBM uses odd-even distinctions in graphics areas as well.

If you run the following BASIC HIRES.BAS program:

```
100 ' HIRES.BAS
110 KEY OFF:SCREEN 2:CLS
120 FOR A=200 TO 1 STEP -2
130 LINE (0,A)-(639,A):NEXT
140 FOR E=1 TO 150
```

```
150 A=RND*600+1:B=RND*180+1:C=RND*20+5
160 LINE (A,B)-(A+C,B+C),0,BF
170 LINE (A+4,B+1)-(A+C+4,B+C+1),,BF
180 NEXT
190 DEF SEG=&HB800
200 BSAVE "IMAGE,"0,&H4000
```

BASIC will create a 640 x 200 graphics image, and store it on disk as a 16K file containing a bank of even-numbered lines and a bank of odd-numbered lines.

Once you've run HIRES.BAS, run the short RELOAD.BAS program to load the disk file onto the screen:

```
100 SCREEN 2
110 BLOAD "IMAGE"
```

You'll see BASIC recreate the image in two passes. You can have the HIRES.BAS program store only one bank by changing line 200 to:

```
200 BSAVE "IMAGE,"0,&H2000
```

RELOAD.BAS will then only restore every other line.

Blanking Out the Screen

Of course, black is a color too. And it's very useful. If you're using a CGA, for instance, you can reduce (but not eliminate) the effects of scroll-flicker by using a black background. A black background also makes foreground colors look brighter. But one of the best uses for black is in blanking screens.

It's possible to "burn" a permanent image into the long-persistence phosphor on an IBM monochrome display. If you use one program all day long on a mono system, and the software has certain screen elements in the same place all the time — such as the *1-2-3* grid or the *WordStar* function keys — you can actually etch this element into the screen so you see it even when the monitor is turned off.

Lots of utilities can shut off monochrome displays attached to monochrome adapters if a certain period has elapsed when nothing has been typed on the keyboard. These utilities usually won't work on other video boards such as the EGA. Screen blanking programs for the mono adapter shut off the display by writing a 0 to bit 3 of output port 3B8H, which disables the video signal. Port 3B8H does not exist on boards like the EGA. And although these screen-blanking utilities have no effect on the EGA, some of them have very serious effects when used with a Hercules Monochrome Graphics Adapter.

You can turn an IBM or compatible CGA display off by using the BASIC statement:

```
OUT 984,1
```

To turn it back on, type:

```
OUT 984,41
```

While this works on a CGA, it will run into problems on something like a Hercules Graphics Card, or a regular IBM mono system. This OUT command manipulates the "Mode Control Port Register," which has a different address on color adapters and monochrome adapters (including the Hercules Graphics Card). The control port for monochrome displays is at address 952 rather than 984. (In hexadecimal, these addresses are 3B8 and 3D8.)

You can blank an IBM Monochrome Adapter or Hercules Graphics Card with the statement:

```
OUT 952,1
```

and unblank it with:

```
OUT 952,41
```

but that's not the best way to do it.

The control port address is always four higher than the I/O address of the 6845 video chip. That port address is a word (two bytes) stored at hexadecimal address 0040:0063 in the BIOS data area. So, you can define a variable for the control port with the BASIC commands:

```
DEF SEG=&H40
CTRLPORT = 4 + 256 * PEEK(&H64) + PEEK(&H63)
```

Now you can simply use the variable CTRLPORT instead of 984 or 952.

Or, you can simply clear the screen to black on black. The BLANK-IT.COM program on one of the accompanying disks will:

1. Figure out the existing screen colors and store them.
2. Blank the screen by clearing the display to black on black.
3. Sit there waiting for you to press a certain key (in this case the spacebar).
4. Clear the screen back to the existing colors as soon as the spacebar is pressed.

Cursor Words

The blinking onscreen cursor is controlled by hardware. Some users would prefer that the cursor be a different size, or refrain from blinking. Changing the size is easy. Turning off the blinking isn't. It's possible to write a routine that continuously figures out where the cursor is, makes the cursor invisible, temporarily stores the value and attribute of the character at the cursor position, writes a solid unblinking block ASCII 219 character over that character, and then restores the old character and attribute when you move the cursor to another position. It's not worth it.

Monochrome display adapters use a 9 x 14 dot box to form all characters. Uppercase letters actually take up a maximum of nine rows and seven columns. The two outside columns provide interletter spacing. Descenders on letters such as y and g use the 10th and 11th lines. The 12th and 13th lines (hex 0C and 0D, since the first line is 00) are used by the cursor. The 14th (bottom) line keeps the lines of text separated from each other.

CGA display adapters use an 8 x 8 dot grid. Default EGA is 8 x 14 and VGA 9 x 16. Uppercase letters take up a maximum of seven rows and seven columns. The rightmost column keeps letters separated. The bottom two lines do double duty — they display descenders on lowercase letters, and also display the cursor.

You can change the size of the cursor by using service 1 of BIOS interrupt 10. And you can read the size of the cursor by using service 3 of interrupt 10. But there's a serious catch with the EGA that's explained in detail in Chapter 14.

When dealing with cursors you have to keep track of two values — the starting line and the ending line. On monochrome systems, the default starting line is hex 0C (decimal 12) and the default ending line is hex 0D (decimal 13). On CGA systems, the default starting line is 6 and the default ending line is 7.

You can make the cursor larger by widening the distance between the starting and ending lines. Using values of 0 (start) and 0D (end) will produce a full-size cursor on mono systems. Settings of 0 (start) and 7 (end) will do the same on CGA systems. You can experiment with different settings by using the BASIC LOCATE statement:

```
LOCATE  , , ,S,E
```

where S represents the starting line and E represents the ending line.

Some settings will produce bizarre effects, such as two-part wraparound cursors, or no cursor at all.

IBM's newer hardware is a little trickier. The MCGA doubles the CGA starting line and ending line, then adds 1 to the ending line in an effort to map 8 x 8 settings onto an 8 x 16 box. The EGA and VGA try to scale monochrome and CGA values into settings appropriate to the dot box that happens to be in use — but with slight differences.

The EGA cursor starts at the starting line but ends one line sooner than the specified value of the ending line. This means that you have to specify an ending line that's actually 1 greater than the one you really want. If the ending line is less than the starting line, the cursor wraps around from the bottom to the top and splits into two parts. If the values of the starting and ending lines are the same, the cursor takes up just one line instead of the usual two. And if the ending line is larger than the total number of rows in the dot box, the EGA displays a full-block cursor.

The VGA extends from the specified starting line to the ending line. You don't have to worry about adding 1 to the value of the ending line as you do with the EGA. And if you specify a starting line that's larger than the ending line, the cursor won't wrap.

(The newer PS/2 hardware offers many more options than earlier systems, and the PS/2 BIOS provides a far richer assortment of interrupt 10 tools to handle it all.)

You can run the CURSOR.COM program on one of the accompanying disks to experiment with cursors of different sizes. CURSOR.COM lets you modify the cursor either from the command line or interactively.

In its interactive mode, CURSOR.COM lets you use the arrow keys interactively to adjust the start line and the end line. The up-arrow and down-arrow keys will adjust the start line, and the left-arrow and right-arrow keys will change the end line. You'll be able to see the size of the new cursor as you press the keys. When you see a cursor that you like, you can press the Enter key to lock it in. Or, if you press the Esc key, you can exit the program without making any changes.

These programs all assume you're using page 0. BIOS actually keeps track of the different cursor positions on each video page, although it will use the same cursor shape for all pages. But these demonstration programs are busy enough without having to worry about other pages.

Clear Colors

Several of the programs on the accompanying disks make it easy to fiddle with your screen's colors, cursor shape and appearance, and line heights. COLSET.COM and SA.EXE give you lots of flexibility in setting your basic screen colors. 0x10.EXE lets you use additional colors (like dark grey or bright white) as background colors, or lets you emulate a monochrome display (which can be real handy for previewing screen shots that will be printed in black and white later). BC3.COM, CURSOR.EXE, and CUR-LOCK.COM let you adjust and lock the appearance of your cursor, while you can use FONTHT.COM and SETV.EXE to set the number of lines per screen and video modes, and then use MODSAV.COM to save your video mode when you go into most applications. To find out what video display adapter is installed on an unfamiliar machine, try WHATVID.EXE. Cutting and pasting from text screens is a snap with NAB.COM. SETUP.EXE lets you determine whether your monitor is in shape, while BLANK-IT.COM, SS.COM, and QUIXX.COM help you keep it that way through a variety of ways to blank the screen when you step away for a few minutes. And if you've got a VGA display, you're going to be blown away by the color palette setting capabilities of PRISM.EXE. The next chapter provides more details about EGA and VGA displays.

EGA, VGA, and Beyond

Adapters

Most computers on the market today come with display adapters which are VGA (Virtual Graphics Array) compatible. Many of these adapters are called Super VGAs, and the latest IBM entry is called the XGA (eXtended Graphics Array). The VGA and its progenitors were derivations and extensions of the EGA hardware introduced by IBM in 1984. The EGA marked IBM's first attempt to market an affordable graphics system with enough quality (in terms of resolution and available colors) to use in day-to-day work. The 640 x 350 resolution essentially matched the fairly crisp character definition of the monochrome monitor, while adding graphics support and 16 simultaneous colors (selectable from a palette of 64).

EGA had its problems, though. For programmers, many of the critical hardware settings could be changed, but it was difficult (or impossible) to read the current values. This was especially problematic to programmers who wrote memory-resident programs — if you can't read the settings, you can't be sure the screen will restore properly when the memory resident application ends. As the PC world moved toward multitasking systems and GUIs (Graphical User Interfaces), it became clear that further improvement was necessary.

With the advent of the PS/2 line and an eye toward multitasking systems using OS/2, IBM improved the graphics interface by making the adapter hardware completely readable, and thus completely restorable, when the system switched from one program to another. As an added benefit, the new VGA improved resolution slightly to 640 x 480 and increased the size of the color palette to over 260,000 colors. However, in most modes only 16 colors could be displayed simultaneously (the VGA has one 320 x 200 mode which can use 256 colors at once).

One often overlooked attribute of the improved VGA resolutions was their use of a square pixel. In earlier IBM adapters, the pixels were slightly elongated. Thus, drawing a box of 100 x 100 pixels would produce a rectangle rather than a square, and circles would look like ellipses. With a square pixel, everything comes out "right" — a development particularly important to the then fairly new field of desktop publishing.

When IBM designed the highest resolution EGA and VGA modes, they did not use all of the graphics memory available to the adapter. Thus, the EGA could use the extra memory to store an extra screen full of information. But, the increased resolution of the VGA used only part of this second "page" and a large portion of memory went totally unused. Other manufacturers had already been creating new modes with the EGA which required all memory for a single page (most programs did not use the second page), and the Super EGA was born. With the full 256K memory of the EGA/VGA, there was enough room to increase 16-color resolution to 800x600 while maintaining a square pixel.

To a programmer, 800 x 600 mode is nearly identical to 640 x 480 mode — it requires recalculations for line length and the number of lines available. But, in terms of setting colors and accessing memory, the instructions remain the same, and there were a few problems. One was detecting a Super VGA and setting the new mode. IBM set the standards for numbering other VGA modes, but the question was how to extend that without risking incompatibilities? If the manufacturers simply used the next available number (14h), IBM might later design an adapter which used that number for a different resolution.

Monitor timing was another problem. For each supported resolution, the video adapter and monitor must be synchronized. IBM used unique signal voltage combinations on the adapter output pins to set the monitor to particular modes and IBM monitors will work at fixed (pre-programmed) frequencies. But, some monitor manufacturers, such as NEC, designed "smart" monitors which could analyze the signal frequencies and set the mode accordingly. Since color monitors are one of the more expensive pieces of hardware, these multifrequency monitors were designed to outlast the adapter — hopefully, working with the higher resolutions of the next graphics standard.

Although a multifrequency monitor can adapt to differing frequencies well enough to form a displayable picture, it cannot always get the picture aligned quite right. The image may seem shifted to one side or compressed along one axis. Depending on the monitor/adapter combination, manual adjustments are sometimes required when switching to new modes. Many of the newer multifrequency monitors can be programmed to shift and size the image automatically when a particular frequency is detected.

To solve some of the problems in programming and synchronizing the Super VGA's, several manufacturers started a new organization — the Video Electronic Standards Association (VESA). One of their first goals was to set a common number for 800 x 600 mode (6Ah was selected). But already, manufacturers were adding memory to increase the number of colors (800 x 600 with 256 colors), and the resolution (1024 x 768 with 16 colors). This could be done by doubling the memory from 256K to 512K and adding bank switching techniques to address the greater range. The next set of VESA Super VGA standards added a new set of function calls. These calls could return information about the adapter and its supported modes, set modes and switch banks.

Monitors

The display quality of a graphics system depends as much (or more) on the quality of the monitor as on the resolution of the adapter driving it. There are several factors involved in display quality in addition to the already-mentioned synchronization problem. Therfore, when buying a monitor, or even setting the adjustments on newer models, it helps if you understand some of the basic concepts behind the monitor's design.

The front of a color display is coated with three phosphors which make up the primary colors: red, green, and blue. The phosphors are arranged either as stripes or dots in a triangular pattern (if you look at the display very closely, you may be able to see the pattern). There are three electron guns in the back of the monitor — one assigned to each color of phosphor. The electron beams produced by the guns sweep across the display and the strength of the beam at any one point determines the brightness with which the phosphors glow.

Just behind the screen (before the electrons strike the phosphors) is a mask. The mask has one hole or slit for each phosphor trio. The spacing is called the dot pitch — generally, the smaller the dot pitch, the better the image (see Figure 14.1). (There are other factors, such as alignment, that can affect the quality of the display and the best way to determine image quality is to view it yourself. Look for sharply defined, white characters with minimal artifacts, such as noticeably colored edges, in the center and corners of the screen.) After scanning across the face of the display, the beam is turned off and returns to the other side. This interval is called the horizontal retrace, during which the beam is moved down to the next line (or, in the case of an interlaced display, down two lines). When the beam reaches the bottom, the beams are disabled again and returned to the top — this is known as the vertical retrace (See Figure 14.2). The beam must be able to scan the entire face of the display quickly enough to prevent flicker. Normally, this requires updating the entire display 60–70 times per second (60–70 Hz). This figure, called the vertical scanning rate, can sometimes be reduced slightly by using phosphors which glow a bit longer (long persistence phosphors).

During each scan, the horizontal lines must be drawn. As the horizontal scanning rate increases, so does the vertical resolution. The highest resolution standard VGA modes require a horizontal scanning rate of about 31.5kHz, or 31,500 lines per second (480 lines per scan x 60 scans per second plus some overhead for the retrace intervals and borders). Once a basic rate has been set, the vertical resolution may be adjusted by slightly increasing the vertical scanning rate and/or the border sizes (fewer lines), or decreasing the vertical scanning rate and/or border size (more lines).

The border areas are called the overscan or blanking intervals. The vertical overscan forms the top and bottom borders, and the horizontal overscan the left and right borders. To some degree, the position and size of the displayable area may be changed by adjusting the synchronization between the retrace signals and the blanking intervals. Indeed, the reason that Super VGA modes sometimes require screen adjustments is that the timing has not been standardized.

Some of the more expensive multifrequency monitors will analyze the timing information and then store the current position and size settings. After setting the monitor for

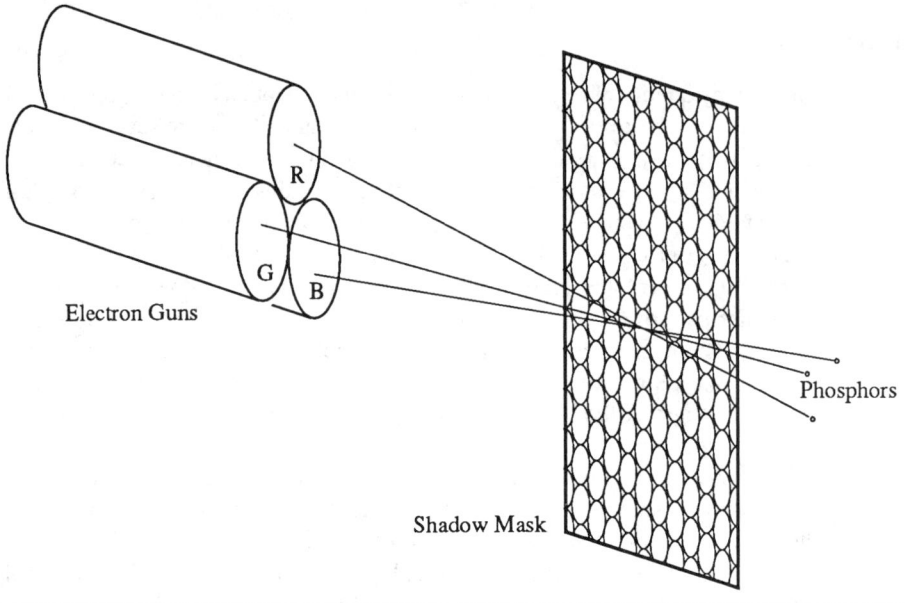

Figure 14.1.   Dot-Pitch Geometry

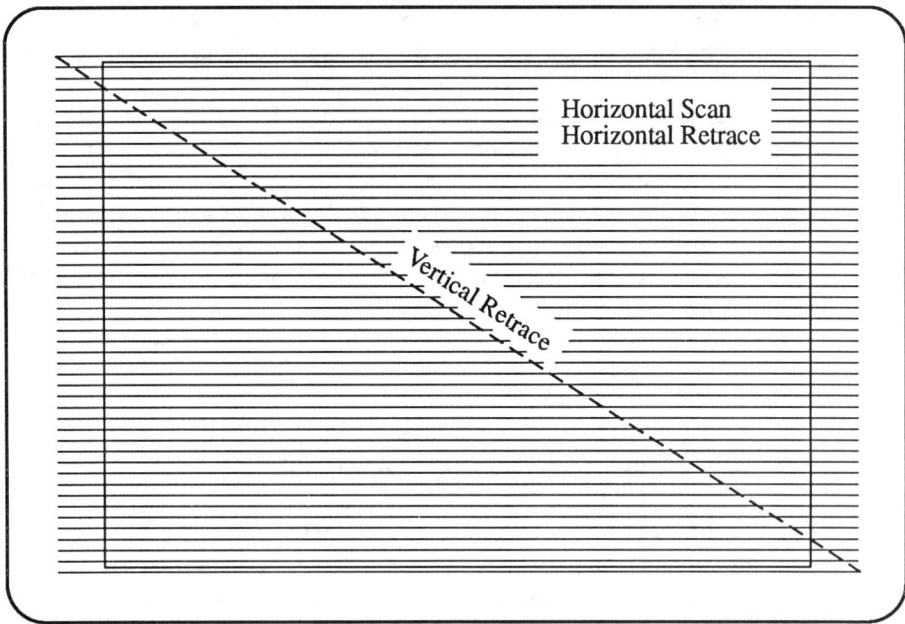

Figure 14.2.   Scan Intervals

each mode, you needn't set the controls every time the display switches between a standard and Super VGA mode. If you work with graphical applications such as CAD or desktop publishing, you should fine-tune the adjustments to get square squares and circular circles.

As scanning rates go up, the electronics become more expensive. To hold down costs (especially at resolutions beyond 800 x 600), some monitors run in interlaced mode. Interlaced monitors scan every other line during the first vertical scan and then fill in the skipped lines during the second vertical pass. Thus, the horizontal scan rate can be dropped by a factor of two, although many people find the resulting flicker annoying. Manufacturers sometimes use longer persistence monitors to reduce the flicker, but it is often still noticeable — especially on horizontal lines that are one pixel wide.

Increasing horizontal resolution is perhaps the simplest operation of a monitor. The adapter simply toggles the signal faster during the horizontal scan. In essence, the horizontal resolution is more a function of the adapter than the monitor. Of course, the monitor's electronics must respond quickly enough, otherwise, the pixels may fade at the edges as the guns respond (called "roping" because of the rope-like lines that result). Also, the dot pitch and alignment must be fine enough so that the pixels are distinguishable. Some Super VGAs extend the horizontal resolution in text mode to create displays that have 132 characters per line.

VGA Internals

Now that we've covered some of the background, it's time to look at the details of the VGA architecture. The VGA supports several different text and graphics modes. Many of these modes are backwards compatible to the earlier CGA and EGA adapters. A summary of the modes appears in Table 14.1. Super VGAs can support higher resolution text and graphics modes. VESA has brought some standardization to these extended modes, though there is still quite a bit of variation. The VESA-defined modes are listed in Table 14.2. Note that a particular VESA monitor may support any (or none) of the VESA-defined modes — VESA also provides a method whereby a manufacturer may include mode descriptions for proprietary modes.

VGA graphics work in one of two mapping modes (we'll ignore the CGA compatibility modes which are seldom used). The simplest is the 256-color mode. Each byte stores the color for one pixel. The lowest memory location is the upper left corner of the screen. As the memory addresses increase, the mapping moves to the right and then down. Calculating the address of a pixel is simple: multiply the pixel's row number by the total number columns, and add the pixel's column number (numbering always starts with 0). Then, add the result to the base address of the display memory.

The more common 16-color modes are a bit more complicated — primarily because of the limited memory space available to the PC. IBM originally reserved 128K for graphics adapter memory. And, due to other considerations, such as dual monitor configurations and the 80 x 86 segmentation scheme, it's desirable to limit the address space to 64K whenever possible. But, if each pixel of a 640 x 480 display required one byte, 300K would be required. Even at half a byte per pixel it would exceed the graphics address area.

Number	Type	Colors	Resolution	Segment
00	Text	16	40 x 25	B800h
01	Text	16	40 x 25	B800h
02	Text	16	80 x 25	B800h
03	Text	16	80 x 25	B800h
04	Graphics	4	320 x 200	B800h
05	Graphics	4	320 x 200	B800h
06	Graphics	2	640 x 200	B800h
07	Text	2	80 x 25	B000h
0dh	Graphics	16	320 x 200	A000h
0eh	Graphics	16	640 x 200	A000h
0fh	Graphics	2	640 x 350	A000h
10h	Graphics	16	640 x 350	A000h
11h	Graphics	2	640 x 480	A000h
12h	Graphics	16	640 x 480	A000h
13h	Graphics	256	320 x 200	A000h

Table 14.1.   VGA Modes

Modes under 100h are vendor proprietary modes, except for 6Ah which is the same as 102h (for backwards compatibility to the earliest VESA standard).

Number	Type	Colors	Resolution
100h	Graphics	256	640 x 400
101h	Graphics	256	640 x 480
102h	Graphics	16	800 x 600
103h	Graphics	256	800 x 600
104h	Graphics	16	1024 x 768
105h	Graphics	256	1024 x 768
106h	Graphics	16	1280 x 1024
107h	Graphics	256	1280 x 1024
108h	Text	16	80 x 60
109h	Text	16	132 x 25
10ah	Text	16	132 x 43
10bh	Text	16	132 x 50
10ch	Text	16	132 x 60

Table 14.2.   VESA Modes

To reduce the footprint, the VGA uses a bit-plane architecture. In essence, the VGA stacks four layers of memory at every address. Every linear bit represents a pixel, just as in the 256-color mode every linear byte represents a pixel. However, the stack of four bits at one location allows 16 (2^4) combinations for 16 colors. This architecture presents three complications. First, the address (as compared to 256-color mode) must be multiplied by the number of bytes in a row rather than the number of pixels in a row, or divided by eight to get the byte offset. Then, the remainder (from the division) must be used to select a pixel offset and the unmodified pixels must be masked so that they will not be overwritten.

The second complication is that the planes must be masked. If all four planes were modified with every write, then you still would get only two colors. So, the program must first inform the VGA which color is about to be written. These masking operations, the bit mask for pixel selection and map mask for color selection, are performed through the I/O channel (the 80 x 86 In and Out instructions). While the bit plane architecture reduces the size of the memory map, it comes at a cost: more overhead, which translates to slower programs.

Finally, as a third complication, there probably will be pixels within the byte which must be saved. Although the mask registers tell the VGA which pixel and planes should be changed, it isn't smart enough to change only the selected bits. You must first tell the VGA to read the old values (even though you won't be able to see all four planes). This is done by first reading the memory that's about to be written — the process is called loading the latch registers (each bit plane has a register which can *latch*, or temporarily save, the contents of a single byte within the plane). When the program then writes to the VGA, the new pixel data is combined with the latch registers. Note that if a program is writing pure colors by masking planes, it must first write 0 to all four planes to clear current values. Figure 14.3 shows a graphical representation of the plotting process.

There are, however, ways to reduce the overhead. The VGA allows several write modes. Each mode is more efficient for particular types of operations, such as transfers from VGA memory to VGA memory, writing several pixels of the same color, or writing individual pixels of fairly random colors. A talented programmer can switch the write modes as the needs of the application change, and thus improve the performance of the program. Thus, instead of setting a color by clearing all four planes and then setting the selected planes, you can use a mode which writes a color number which the VGA translates into plane data. This is one of the many reasons that programmers bypass the BIOS calls for writing pixels and write directly to video registers and memory.

Let's look at a simple 256-color program. The LINE256 color program draws a vertical line in column 7 from row 24 down to the bottom of the screen. The color changes with each pixel.

```
debug
a
mov ax,13          ;256 color mode
int 10             ;set mode
mov ax,a000        ;video memory segment
mov es,ax
```

```
mov ax,18          ;start at row 24
mov bx,140         ;screen is 200 pels wide
mul bx             ;byte offset of row 24
add ax,7           ;add col 7 to byte offset
mov bx,ax          ;put pel address in BX
mov cx,b0          ;start with color/row 176
es: mov [bx],cx    ;write color to adapter
add bx,140         ;next row (add 200)
loop 11b           ;color number-1
                   ;stop at color 0
int 20             ;end program
rcx
126
n line256.com
w
q
```

The same program in a 16-color mode requires more work. LINE16.COM has essentially the same effect, but draws a longer line in column 38. Note that the pixel is selected with a binary mask. In this case, position 6 (value of 4, or 00000100b) within the byte is selected. Each byte addresses 8 columns. Since we will use byte 4, the eight columns start at pixel 32.

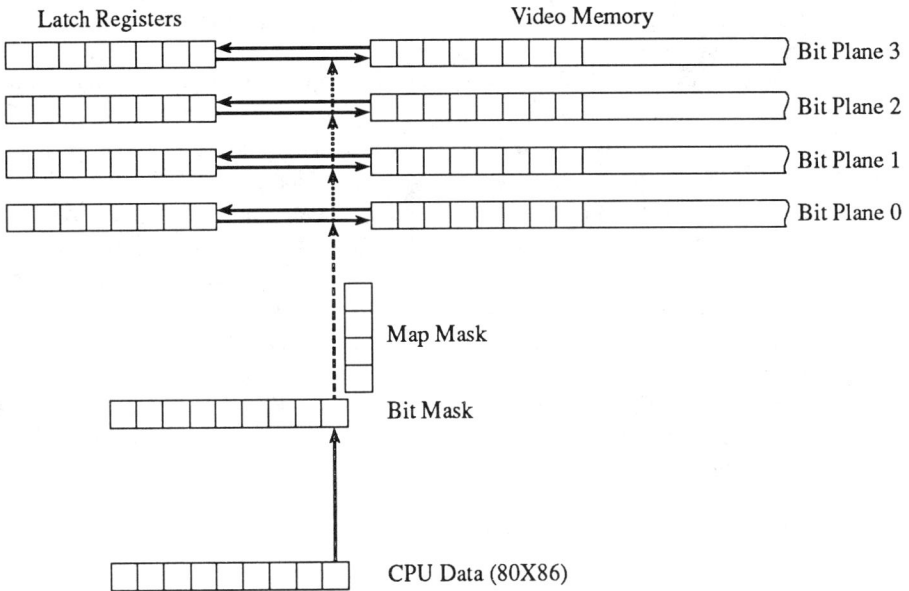

Figure 14.3.   The Screen Plotting Process

```
debug
a
mov ax,10            ;640x480, 16 color
int 10               ;set mode
mov ax,a000          ;video memory segment
mov es,ax
mov ax,18            ;start at row 24
mov bx,50            ;screen is 80 bytes wide
mul bx               ;byte offset of row 24
add ax,4             ;add cols 32-39 to byte offset
mov bx,ax            ;put pel address in BX
mov al,8             ;bit mask index
mov dx,3ce           ;Graphics Control Register
out dx,al            ;Select bit mask function
mov al,4             ;pixel 00000100b
inc dx               ;Graphics Control Data
out dx,al            ;set bit mask
dec dx               ;Graphic Control again
mov al,5             ;Mode Register Index
out dx,al            ;Select mode register function
inc dx               ;Graphics Control Data
in al,dx             ;get old mode
and al,fc            ;Clear bits 0 and 1
or al,2              ;Write mode 2 (write
out dx,al            ;color value to memory)
mov cx,1c8           ;set row count to 456
mov ax,cx            ;put count in AX
and ax,f             ;reduce to 4-bit color
es: mov dx,[bx]      ;latch current data
es: mov [bx],ax      ;write color to adapter
add bx,50            ;next row (add 80 bytes)
loop 12f             ;count (cx) - 1, stop at 0
mov dx,3ce           ;Graphics controller
mov al,5             ;Mode register
out dx,al            ;select mode register
inc dx               ;point to mode register
in al,dx             ;get current mode
and al,fc            ;clear bits 0-1 back to 0
out dx,al            ;set write mode
dec dx               ;Graphics controller
mov ax,ff08          ;Shortcut: bit mask (8)
out dx,ax            ;value ff (unmask all)
int 20               ;end program
rcx
```

```
151
n line16.com
w
q
```

That's a lot of work to draw a simple line! The final resetting of the mode register and bit mask (after the LOOP instruction) is necessary for the BIOS. The BIOS assumes that the VGA is always in write mode 0 with all bits accessible — if it were not, the characters would not display properly after the program runs. When these sample programs run, the display ends up in graphics mode. You can return to normal text mode with MODE CO80, MODE MONO, or by using the mode set utility.

Note that the LINE16 program reads the mode register. This is the type of operation that was impossible on the EGA. Because the mode register stores several pieces of information in the different bits, the program cannot blindly write a new value to the register. On the EGA, the program was responsible for tracking all of the changes to the registers and restoring them accordingly. And, the program had to calculate the initial value based on the current hardware configuration — a method that's not always reliable under a multitasking system or memory-resident program.

Other Features

The VGA has about 70 registers. Many of these registers provide low-level hardware control such as timing information for the display. But, several provide support for functions that are seldom incorporated into commercial programs. These include screen disabling, smooth scrolling support, dual windows, data rotation, and alternate character fonts. A few programs alter the timing information and memory mapping to create non-standard video modes. Other functions are widely used, such as setting the color palette, cursor size and underlining characters.

As you can see, the VGA has support for a fairly broad family of features. However, some of these features (particularly those that are rarely used), can be rather difficult to program. And sometimes, incompatible hardware will create an undesired side effect. For example, a few VGAs will jitter when attempting smooth horizontal scrolling.

Vertical Interrupt

IBM is responsible for some of the confusion regarding the minor features. For example, the EGA's hardware could signal a program when the adapter started a vertical retrace (through the vertical interrupt). When IBM introduced the VGA on the PS/2 motherboard, the vertical interrupt remained as part of the new standard. But, when IBM created an adapter for ISA computers, the interrupt was dropped. So, how should a compatible manufacturer respond? Since all Micro Channel machines included a VGA, the marketing opportunities were for the ISA bus. Should a compatible adapter follow the PS/2 VGA convention, or keep strict compatibility with the ISA standard?

This was a rather unfortunate situation. The VGA must share memory access time between the microprocessor (CPU) and the display. If both are allowed to access standard memory at the same time, snow will appear on the display, a common problem on the older CGA standard. On the CGA, a program could check whether the adapter was in a vertical retrace (when the display is not reading adapter memory), and write data at that time to avoid snow. The EGA inserted wait states to temporarily block memory access, so that no checking was required. However, there are still reasons for checking the retrace status. First, there are adapter registers which should be changed only during a retrace interval. Second, some operations will seem more "polished" if done during a retrace.

Imagine you're writing a video game. One of your fanciful creations, a greebidger, comes flying across the screen. Just after the top half of the greebidger's been drawn, the program determines that it's time to move the greebidger. The program restores the background scenery over the bottom half of the greebidger just before the electron beam draws that portion of the screen. For a brief instant (about 1/60th of a second) you only have half a greebidger. This really isn't enough time for most people to realize that only half a greebidger's hanging around, but it does cause a noticeable flickering of the image. You could make your program sit and wait to draw the greebidger until the next retrace, but this may cause it to run too slowly. The most elegant (but very difficult to program) option is to have the VGA inform the program when an interrupt occurs. In essence, the program is written in two parts. The main portion runs continuously — it calculates the position of objects on the screen, but doesn't draw. The other portion, which draws objects, sits idle most of the time. But, when a retrace occurs, the drawing portion "wakes up," reads the positions (as calculated by the main program) and redraws those portions of the screen that have changed. However, there are many complications with this method. Most VGA modes have very short retrace intervals, so very little drawing can take place during that time. But, most importantly, the IBM ISA VGA does not have a vertical interrupt, and several VGA compatibles have no interrupt support, either.

Alternate fonts

The VGA fonts are completely programmable in both text and graphics modes. The process is rather convoluted (it is a C programmer's delight, relying upon pointers to pointers to pointers), but fairly simple once the technique is mastered. Internally, the VGA handles text and graphics mapping a bit differently. In both modes the program must keep a bit image of the characters in memory (each byte of the character table contains one row from a character — 8 bits = 8 character dots). In the graphics modes, the VGA reads this table directly, transferring the appropriate character to video memory as it is written. Character drawing in graphics mode is a programming function — the BIOS simply builds characters pixel by pixel.

In text modes, the VGA moves all of the character data into a bit plane reserved for character definitions. Then, the VGA hardware constructs the pixels based on the ASCII and attribute codes. The adapter can load eight 256-character sets. However, only one or two sets may be displayed simultaneously for a total of either 256 or 512 characters. If a

512-character set is activated, the VGA uses the bold attribute to select the second set of 256 characters.

Obviously, such programmability is important for supporting special character sets such as international letters and symbols or scientific/mathematical symbols. However, the tables which define the character sets have entries which define the height of the character and the number of rows on the display. By decreasing the height of the character, you can increase the number of rows. Many programs, such as PICK.COM and FONTHT.COM wlong with VFONT.COM and VFONT4.COM, can extend the number of rows displayed from 25 to 43 or 50.

Palettes

A standard VGA can display only 16 or 256 colors, but can select those colors from a palette of over 256,000. In most color modes, the color information stored in the attribute bytes or bit planes is converted into a color on the display in several stages. First, the four-bit (16-color) color value selects an entry from the corresponding palette register (16 palette registers, total). The palette registers encode the color in six bits for a total of 64 color combinations, the older EGA total. The VGA then uses a select register to add two more bits for a total of eight bits, or 256 colors.

The eight-bit color value selects a DAC (Digital to Analog Converter) register that translates the digital color value into an analog color signal for the display. Each register of the DAC can be programmed with an 18-bit color value (six bits each for the red, green and blue signal), giving the final color selection of 262,144 colors. Although the colors cannot be displayed simultaneously, the various stages of the color selection process make some interesting effects possible.

The color selection index, which adds the final two bits to the DAC register selection, acts much like the Segment:Offset architecture of the 80 x 86 family of microprocessors. The total set of DAC registers can thus be grouped into smaller sets of 16 or 64 colors, just as the total memory of the PC is grouped into 64K pieces. A program can cycle through these sets to change the colors across the entire display — sometimes subtly, sometimes dramatically. For example, a screen could start with a greyscale palette at the top 16 DAC registers, and fade in colors by cycling down through the DAC maps. Each step down would brighten the colors until reaching the brightest set at the bottom of the DAC registers.

VGA Extensions

Manufacturers of compatible VGA adapters are constantly seeking ways to improve the design: extended palettes, anti-aliasing, extended resolution, and faster memory access are some of the more popular features added to their products. A few extensions, such as a 24-bit DAC can be done rather naturally, but require knowledge that the feature exists. One company, Edsun Laboratories Inc., has created a modified DAC which performs anti-aliasing. This process softens the transitions between edges with subtle shadings —

in effect, calculates a softer color that will make the edge appear smoother, hence raising the apparent resolution. The anti-aliasing mode must be activated by a program, but the procedure is fairly simple.

Other enhancements, such as faster memory access, don't require special programming. There are a number of ways the speed of a VGA can be improved. As mentioned earlier, the VGA must block programs from accessing memory during the display intervals. During the vertical retrace an adapter can grant more frequent access. Further improvements can be made during the horizontal retrace — this interval is extremely short, but occurs more often than the vertical retrace.

The retrace interval can be used for other improvements, too. For example, ATI implements two clocks on some of their VGA models. During the display interval, the dot clock (which determines the horizontal resolution) works as the memory clock, as in a normal VGA. But, during the retrace intervals, ATI switches the memory to a faster clock, improving memory access time.

Buffering is another common technique for improving access time. Rather than writing directly to memory, the CPU can immediately write to a buffer and move on to the next instruction. When the VGA is ready for the next CPU memory access, it uses the value stored in the buffer. A few vendors use VRAM (Video RAM) in some of their models. VRAM lets two devices access memory at the same time. However, VRAM is much more expensive than the DRAMs normally installed in a VGA. So, most manufacturers continue to use DRAMs and squeeze cycles wherever they can.

Sometimes performance can be improved through special register access. For example, Headland Technology provides a direct masking register that completely masks access to the video bits. If a program uses this direct mask, it can skip instructions such as the memory read that loads the latch registers. While additional hardware features can make dramatic performance improvements, it's very difficult for programmers to support the features. There are so many varieties of VGAs (and no hardware standards beyond the IBM specifications) that large video driver libraries would become necessary, a time consuming, and thus expensive, proposition for programmers.

On the other hand, programmers can use commercial libraries or systems that take care of this overhead. *Windows 3.0* has become a very popular program on IBM compatibles. Because of its popularity, VGA vendors place a high priority on *Windows* display driver development. Programs written under *Windows* do not access hardware directly. Rather, they make graphics calls that provide higher-level functions, such as line drawing. *Windows* then takes care of details like register and memory access mechanisms. The VGA manufacturer can then write a *Windows* driver that takes advantage of their own unique VGA features. And, the scftware programmer can write *Windows* programs and leave the messy details of programming hardware to someone else.

VESA

Programming for a GUI (Graphical User Interface) such as *Windows* or OS/2 has its own advantages and disadvantages. DOS-based programs are still a long way from breathing their last breath. So, standards for some of the shared extensions are very useful to both hardware vendors and programmers. The programmers can write routines that will work on many varieties of VGA (thus pleasing their clients). And, the vendors can list more programs that run on their VGAs. As already noted, several companies interested in creating a Super VGA compatibility started an organization called VESA to standardize the high resolution modes.

The extended resolution modes of the Super VGAs comprise one of their most attractive features. Higher resolution and more colors grab attention! The 800 x 600 modes are an easy extension — add a few bytes to the row multiplier (for the wider columns) and increase the address range (for the additional rows). But, at 1024 x 768, or 256 colors in resolutions above 320 x 200 the address space exceeds the 64K segment limit. Super VGA vendors worked around this limit using several different techniques.

First, even a standard VGA can be custom programmed to use a 128K address space from segment A000h to Bfffh. That's enough room to accommodate 1024 x 768, 16-color mode, or 320 x 400, 256-color mode. But this method is incompatible with dual monitor systems (which have a monochrome adapter at B000h), and it doesn't allow high-resolution, 256-color modes.

Second, the VGA can be programmed to present only a portion of the video memory in the 64K segment from A000h to Afffh. Then, by using a special register, the portion of video memory filling this space can be changed. This technique is called bank switching, and is the same type of process used to access LIM EMS memory. However, VESA calls the banks "windows" (a rather confusing term given the context of a video environment). There are three different implementations of VESA windows: Single Window, Non-overlapping (dual) Windows, and Overlapping (dual) Windows.

The single-window technique uses one 64K bank that is both readable and writeable. Of the three methods it is the simplest to use. Consider, for example, a 1024 x 768, 16-color mode. It requires about 96K of address space and four bit planes. The first 64K is mapped to the 64K segment at A000h and can be read and written. To access the remaining 32K, the program requests a bank switch, and the 64-96K portion is mapped into the 64K segment.

Super VGAs which use Overlapping Windows may set the adapter to read and write different areas in video memory. Thus, the processor could request that CPU writes to segment A000h go to the first 64K of video memory, and that reads from segment A000h come from the bank 1 of video memory (64K–96K). This may seem like an odd feature — it's designed to make transfers from one section of video memory to another run faster. Video-to-video transfers can execute more quickly than conventional memory-to-video transfers.

Like Overlapping Windows, Non-overlapping Windows use two banks. Both banks are readable and writeable. However, each is only 32K — one starts at segment A000h and the other at A800h. With either type of dual window method, a single window may be emulated by setting the banks appropriately (most standard plotting applications will use such a setup).

You may notice that in 1024 x 768 mode, the area from 96-128K is unused. This area is accessible, but not displayable. Fonts or frequently drawn objects such as icons can be

AX	Purpose
4F00h	Return Super VGA Information
4F01h	Return Mode Information
4F02h	Set Super VGA Mode
4F03h	Return Super VGA Mode
4F04h	Save/Restore Super VGA State
4F05h	CPU Video Memory Window Control (bank switching)
4f06h	Set/Get Logical Scan Line Length
4f07h	Set/Get Start of Display Memory (video pages)

Table 14.3.   VESA Calls

stored in the additional memory for fast access. However, to perform the transfer, the adapter must be able to read this area while writing to any portion of the display. Dual windows make this possible.

The VESA standards emphasize software rather than hardware. For example, the standards do not specify the design or address of the bank-switching hardware. Rather, the standards provide a BIOS call (and the address of a function that may be called directly) to set the bank. Likewise, there are no standards for modes which must be supported. Why so much variation, both in terms of supported modes and memory access techniques? Because VESA standards were written after Super VGA hardware was on the market. The standards were designed in such a way that vendors could write memory-resident programs to add VESA to their existing products.

Indeed, the VESA standards were written in such a way that a program can "learn" how to access proprietary modes. Proprietary modes may use unusual resolutions or memory structures (such as CGA four-color bit maps in a high-resolution mode). VESA includes several functions to return detailed information about the Super VGA, and set the extended attributes. The functions are called through the video BIOS (INT 10h) as call 4Fh, set through register AH. The VESA call consists of several sub-functions designated in register AL. A list of these functions appears in Table 14.3.

Each function requires several parameters, and detailing the operation is beyond the scope of this chapter. But, it is interesting to see how the VESA call returns adapter information: it should give you a feel for the flexibility of the standard. The two critical information calls are 4f00h and 4F01h. Both calls require the program to reserve at least 256 bytes for the information. The ES:DI registers must point to this area before making the call. The 4F01h call requires a Super VGA mode number in register CX. If a VESA-compatible adapter is installed, call 4F00h will return 004Fh in register AX.

The Super VGA information is organized as follows:

Offset	Description
0	The letters 'VESA'
4	Version number
6	Address of vendor ID
Eh	Address of mode list
12h	Amount of memory on VGA

The Mode information includes:

Offset	Description
0	Mode Attributes
2	Window A Attributes (i.e., is the bank readable and/or writeable?)
3	Window B Attributes
4	Window Granularity (offset of each bank in Kb)
6	Window size (bank size in granularity units)
8	Address of Window A
Ah	Address of Window B
Ch	Address of window (bank switching) function
10h	Length of one scan line in bytes

This is followed by a section of optional information. For the VESA-defined modes, the information would be identical for every card, and would waste ROM space. However, the information is very useful, so many vendors include it for all modes.

Offset	Description
12h	Horizontal resolution
14h	Vertical resolution
16h	Character width in pixels
17h	Character height in pixels
18h	Number of bit planes
19h	Bits per pixel (includes bits in planes)
1Ah	Banks (interleaved memory segments, *not* bank switching)
1Bh	Memory model
1Ch	Bank size (interleaved memory segment size)
1Dh	Number of pages available for multiple screens
1Eh	Reserved

Some items, such as the bank size, which gives the number of interleaved memory banks (like the CGA's four-color mode), are of little interest except for unusual vendor proprietary modes. An example will highlight some of the more important features. The following debug session was run on on an ATI VGA Wonder+:

```
271A:0100 mov ax,4f00
271A:0103 mov di,200
271A:0106 int 10
271A:0108 mov ax,4f01
271A:010B mov di,300
271A:010E mov cx,103
271A:0111 int 10
271A:0113 int 20
271A:0115

-g

Program terminated normally

d 200 l 20

271A:0200  56 45 53 41 01 01 46 01-98 22 00 00 00 00 50 01
271A:0210  98 22 00 00 00 00 00 00-00 00 00 00 00 00 00 00

d 2298:146 l 20

2298:0140                    37 36-31 32 39 35 35 32 30 00
2298:0150  08 01 09 01 0A 01 00 01-6A 00 02 01 01 01 03 01
2298:0160  FF FF FF FF FF FF

d 300 l 20

271A:0300  1B 00 07 00 40 00 40 00-00 A0 00 00 70 0A 98 22
271A:0310  20 03 20 03 58 02 08 0E-01 08 01 04 00 C7 02 8A
```

I cheated a bit in the program. I already knew this Super VGA supported mode 103h. To save space, the program doesn't read the mode table. But, if you look at the hex dump at address 271A:0200, you will see the values 50 01 at the end of the first line, and 98 22 at the beginning of the second. This is the address (2298:0150) of the mode table. In the next instruction, I also dumped the Vendor ID bytes at address 2298:0146 (this address also appears in the 271A:0200 dump).

The vendor ID is a C-style string, ending in a Null (00). The ATI string is rather uninteresting: it is simply the numbers '761295520'. The manufacturer decides what to place in this area — some include the vendor name and/or product name. This is followed by the mode list (though other VESA adapters may locate it elsewhere), which ends with FFh. The list, which conveniently fills the second line, shows that modes 108h, 109h, 10Ah, 100h, 6Ah, 102h, 101h, and 103h are available.

Finally, there is the mode information — hex dump 271A:0300 in the example. The first two bytes are the mode attributes. The next byte is the attribute of Window A (07) followed by the attribute of Window B (00). The attributes are assigned to bit fields. Bit

0 is set if the window exists, bit 1 is set if the window is readable, and bit 2 is set if the window is writeable. This is a single window mode — Window B has no attributes. Window A exists, and is both readable and writeable.

The window granularity (the next word) is 64K. This means each bank maps to a distinct area within video memory. Sometimes, the granularity is smaller and there will be some overlap in the mapping scheme (much like the 80 x 86 can map 64K segments on any 16-byte boundary). This is different than overlapping windows, which use a smaller window size, the next word in the information section. In this case, the window size is also 64K. And, Window A is located at segment A000h (no surprise there). Window B does not exist. The bank switch can be performed through a far call to address 2298:0A70, the next double word.

The scan line is 320h, or 800 bytes long. Since this is an 800 x 600 mode, there is one byte per pixel (the standard method for 256-color mode). The remaining section is redundant since this is a VESA standard mode, but ATI chose to include it anyway (which makes the programmer's task a bit simpler). You can confirm that the resolution is 800 x 600 (320h and 258h). At 318h and 319h, we can see that there is one bit plane and eight bits per pixel (256 colors). Had this been a 16-color mode the parameters would show four bit planes and four bits per pixel. To get the number of linear bits per pixel, you must divide the total bits per pixel by the number of bit planes.

The descriptions are set up in such a way that a vendor could use a proprietary combination like two linear bits per pixel (following the CGA mapping) in four bit planes (with a VGA-like feature). Even and odd scan lines could appear at different addresses (what VESA calls the *banks*). Fortunately, the VESA compliant modes (those that are numbered 100h and higher), must follow the VGA format: eight linear bytes per pixel for 256 colors or one linear bit with four planes for 16 colors.

VESA programming can be rather complicated. There are many different implementations of the bank switching scheme. And, if you want to support proprietary modes, many possible memory mapping schemes. It's not even unusual to see an adapter mixing several techniques. It may support several proprietary modes and include multiple bank switching techniques depending on the video mode selected.

Because of the complexity, a sample plotting algorithm would be too long for this chapter. Further details about VESA programming can be obtained through VESA at 1330 South Bascom Avenue, Suite D; San Jose, CA 95128, or found in recent books on VGA programming such as the second edition of *EGA/VGA: A Programmer's Reference Guide*, McGraw-Hill, 1990.

Coprocessors

Graphics on the VGA require extensive support from the CPU. The program must calculate and plot every pixel on the screen. On a 640 x 480 screen, that's up to 307,200 pixels. At 1024 x 768, the number of pixels more than double to 786,432. Many of the plotting operations include common tasks: draw a character, plot a line, fill a boundary, copy a portion of the screen from one area to another (called BITBLT, for Bit Block Transfer), etc.

A graphics coprocessor can accept instructions from a program. These instructions can be sent to an I/O port (I/O-mapped) or a reserved memory area (memory-mapped). The coprocessor reads the instructions, performs the required calculations and displays the appropriate results. While the coprocessor is processing, the program can move on to other tasks such as accepting user input. The coprocessor can usually process graphics related tasks much faster than the program. So, even if the program is sending long streams of graphics instructions and must wait on the coprocessor, execution is usually much faster than with a bit-mapped graphics adapter such as the VGA.

Consider a line drawing example. This is usually implemented as a *polyline* where several lines can be drawn — each new line starting at the end of the last. The coprocessor may assign a code to the polyline command, say 1. Then it might accept the number of lines to draw. We'll say 3. Finally, it might accept the coordinates in x,y pairs: start of line 1, end of line 1, end of line 2, end of line 3. The instruction stream might look like:

```
01  03  06  06  6A  6A  06  6A  06  06
```

which would draw a right triangle from (6,6) to (106,106), then to (6,106), and back to (6,6). Since the shape is closed, another instruction might tell the coprocessor to fill the shape. Compared to VGA plotting, the number of bytes sent from the program to the adapter has been reduced from hundreds (or thousands with a fill) to a handful. And, the program needn't calculate the position of every intermediate point — a fairly simple, but time consuming, task.

There are many coprocessors on the market. Some, such as the IBM 8514/A and XGA, have a fixed set of operations (mostly line drawing, area fills and area moves). Others, like those based on the Texas Instruments 34010 and 34020, are programmable. Each vendor who produces a 34010-based product can implement advanced shape drawing routines or give the user access to the programming features to define their own. A coprocessor may limit its operations to the more common tasks such as lines and fills, or implement more complex tasks such as drawing ellipses and Bezier curves. Usually, straight lines and fills are sufficient. Most CAD packages, the prime market for graphics coprocessors, have an adapter interface which works strictly at a line drawing level — even if the coprocessor supports ellipses, for example, the CAD package will translate an on-screen circle into line segments for screen display.

As GUIs such as *Windows* and *OS/2 Presentation Manager* become more common and the price of coprocessors drop, we will probably see graphics coprocessors as standard equipment on many machines. Such environments benefit from line drawing, area fills and BITBLT. A character drawing and scaling function would also help most GUI applications, but this is a capability which is still fairly primitive (or non-existent) in most coprocessors.

8514/A

The 8514/A was hailed as the next standard up from VGA. When IBM released the 8514/A it had several factors working against it as a standard. First, the price was much higher than VGA. Second, IBM did not release details for the hardware interface. The only official programming method was to use a graphics library called the AI (Adapter Interface). The AI consisted of several C functions which translated function calls and parameters into hardware instructions. Third, the 8514/A supported 1024 x 768 resolution on an interlaced display, and many users objected to the resulting flicker. Fourth, the 8514/A did not have a native support mode and has always been an accessory rather than standard equipment. A computer cannot boot directly into 8514/A modes complete with DOS and BIOS support. Rather, a separate VGA handles the initial functions, and the 8514/A is later activated by programs which specifically request the advanced modes.

Although other vendors could develop AI-based products on hardware which was not 8514/A-compatible, a few products were released or announced which wrote directly to hardware. It was clear that AI compatibility was not sufficient for every 8514/A application. Since the hardware specifications were not readily available, vendors began reverse engineering the 8514/A and developing standards for 8514/A compatibility through VESA. The ensuing delays have kept 8514/A from developing as quickly as the EGA/VGA market. However, 8514/A still shows signs of life.

The 8514/A is I/O-mapped. Although IBM has never documented the hardware, details can be found in Jake Richter's and Bud Smith's, *Graphics Programming for the 8514/A*, M&T Books, 1990. With the availability of detailed programming information and reverse engineering, the compatible market is growing. And, the compatibles add features that make the 8514/A an attractive alternative. With lower prices, non-interlaced displays, bus support for both ISA and Micro Channel, and other features available on some of the compatibles, the 8514/A remains a viable platform.

XGA

XGA is IBM's latest attempt at a graphics standard. Like the 8514/A, the advanced functions of the XGA are programmed through the AI, but the XGA is memory-mapped rather than I/O-mapped. Additionally, the XGA is much faster and addresses some of the deficiencies of the 8514/A: IBM has documented the XGA hardware, the adapter is standard equipment in the PS/2 Models 90 and 95, and it is backwards compatible with the VGA. There are still a few drawbacks: the XGA uses interlaced 1024 x 768 modes, and the current design requires the bus-mastering support of Micro Channel machines. Moreover, the current interface specifically requires some of the features of the 80386 and 80486 processors.

The VGA compatibility modes have a few enhancements. Most importantly, IBM has widened the data path and improved the performance using the same techniques employed by many of the VGA compatible vendors. A new 132-column character mode is also available. In its higher-resolution, extended modes, the memory-mapping can be manipulated in several ways, including a bank switching and bit-mapped mode that is accessed in the same address range as VGA. It is possible, for example, that a VESA driver could be developed for the high-resolution XGA modes. For more advanced operating systems that have better access to the memory above the first megabyte, the XGA can be mapped into a flat 1Mb address space near the top of the system's addressable memory.

Favorite Tips

Over the years many friends and readers have sent us basketfuls of their favorite tips, and we've assembled (and enhanced) the most popular ones below. You'll find tips here on the DOS commands, filters, printers, security, communications, and more.

DOS Commands

RECOVER

Just about everyone knows that the FORMAT command can be dangerous if it's used indiscriminately or carelessly. However, few users know about another potentially destructive DOS command — RECOVER.COM.

The DOS manual says RECOVER.COM is supposed to "recover files." Novice users who have lost or corrupted files may try this command in desperation without fully understanding what it does, and accidentally type RECOVER C: at the DOS prompt. Even though DOS prints a warning message most users will probably type Y to proceed with the recovery.

RECOVER then does the following:

1. Removes the subdirectory structure from the disk.
2. Places all the files into the root directory.
3. Renames all files FILE0001.REC, FILE0002.REC, etc.

You're then forced to back up all of these similarly named REC files, reformat the disk, and then filter through the files to try and discover which file is which. It's nearly impossible to recover from RECOVER.

The description in the DOS manual is truly inadequate, and doesn't provide nearly enough warning about how potentially dangerous the command is is. It's another case of the moronic names in DOS. DEBUG really ought to be called something friendlier like PATCHER or TOOLBOX. The IF ERRORLEVEL command should be called something like TEST. It's no wonder that a panicky and inexperienced user might think a command named RECOVER will fix his disk right up.

RECOVER isn't so bad if you ask it to dig out the pieces of just one file that had a sector go south somewhere. And if you've somehow wiped out your whole directory, laboriously sorting out the puzzle pieces of your text files is better than losing everything. But it's far too easy to wipe out a whole disk with it. Back up often, plod through the manual before trying anything you're not familiar with, and take RECOVER.COM off your hard disk.

CHKDSK

When used with a /V parameter, CHKDSK churns out a long list of all the directories and files on the specified or default disk. This can come in very handy when you have to locate a file or group of files. To see every file with MAC in it, for instance, you could type:

```
CHKDSK /V | FIND "MAC"
```

However, if you start experimenting with this feature, you'll notice that the filenames are sometimes not listed under the directory where they are actually located.

The problem results from the confusing and downright deceptive manner in which CHKDSK lists directories and files. To illustrate this, start with a formatted blank disk in drive A: and run the following four commands:

```
COPY   CHKDSK.COM A:
MD     A:\SUBDIR
COPY   TREE.COM A:\SUBDIR
COPY   BACKUP.COM A:
```

Now execute a CHKDSK A:/V command. You'll probably see the listing shown below:

```
Directory A:\
      A:\CHKDSK.COM
Directory A:\SUBDIR
      A:\SUBDIR\TREE.COM
      A:\BACKUP.COM
```

It sure seems like BACKUP.COM is in the SUBDIR directory, doesn't it? But look closer. The files are listed with the full path name. So A:\BACKUP.COM means that BACKUP.COM is in the root directory, which is absolutely correct. CHKDSK lists the files and directories in the order that it finds them in the directory. Since SUBDIR is the second entry of the root directory, CHKDSK lists all files in the SUBDIR directory and then finishes listing the files of the root directory.

Whenever you do a DIR command and see files listed below directory entries, be aware that CHKDSK /V will list those files after it lists the files in the directory.

On a disk where a lot of deletion and creation of directories and files has taken place, the CHKDSK /F listing may be almost unreadable. Use the TREE /F command instead for seeing what files are in what directories.

CHKDSK can also let you know about potential disk problems. Almost nothing is as terrifying as seeing a list of unfamiliar messages from CHKDSK (except perhaps a zinger such as "General Failure Error Reading Drive C:"). Sometimes CHKDSK messages indicate very serious problems with the data on the disk. Sometimes they don't.

Among other things, CHKDSK checks for consistency between a disk's directory listing and its file allocation tables (FATs) — the critical maps that tell DOS how a disk's clusters are chained together. Files are stored in separate chunks, and the redundant FATs keep track of where these individual pieces are located on the disk.

When you get a message from CHKDSK indicating "lost clusters," it's usually not much to worry about. It simply means that an area on the disk had been allocated for a file, but the file was never properly closed. The lost clusters are "orphaned" — the FAT says they've been allocated, but they don't belong to any file. This sometimes happens if the program creating the file terminates abnormally, or runs out of disk space and doesn't clean up afterwards.

If you run CHKDSK with a /F parameter, it will convert the lost clusters to files with the extension CHK in the root directory. If your normal files are missing something, the data could be in one of the CHK files. You can take a look at the CHK files with the TYPE command, but unless they're in ASCII format and came out of a word processing document, you probably won't be able to do much with them.

If you're missing entire files from your directory, these CHK files may correspond to the missing files. This could result from a damaged directory. The FAT still allocates chained clusters as if they belonged to a file, but the directory doesn't indicate where the chains begin.

Messages from CHKDSK indicating "cross-linked files" are cause for concern. Cross-linking means that the FAT's cluster chain for two or more files intersects at some point, so that some clusters seem to belong to multiple files. In other words, your FAT or directory has probably been badly mangled. Although cross-linking is relatively rare, it could be caused by gremlins (i.e., a power surge or line drop during a disk write operation).

You can easily create a cross-linked FAT and a mangled directory yourself by replacing a diskette before typing an answer to an "Abort, Retry, Ignore, Fail?" message.

For instance, if you're running a program and you try to save something to a diskette that has a write-protect tab, DOS will try to write to the disk and will end up displaying a "Write Protect Error" message followed by "Abort, Retry, Ignore, Fail?" If instead of removing the write-protect tab from the disk you insert another disk in the drive and press R for Retry, you can kiss that data goodbye. This often happens when you realize you're trying to save a file on the wrong disk.

The problem is that DOS keeps FAT and directory information in memory, but doesn't check to make sure that it's writing data back to the original disk it thinks is still in the drive. If you switch disks without telling it, it will write the FAT and directory map (or part of it) from the first disk onto the second disk, and you'll end up with an unusable mess.

Sometimes you can salvage chunks of mangled files by using disk surgery programs like the *Norton Utilities* to piece them back together, but it's hard work and you need to know what you're looking for.

To prevent this, don't switch disks in the middle of a program unless you're very careful about it. And if you're about to write data to a floppy and you get an "Abort, Retry" message, choose abort, then make sure the disk you originally read from is in the drive you want to write to. If it's not, try to execute a DIR command to read the new directory information into memory.

COPY

COPY will usually detect when you are trying to copy a file to itself. For instance, if you have a file called MYFILE and you enter:

```
COPY MYFILE MYFILE
```

it will tell you it can't do it. But COPY can be fooled. If MYFILE is located in the root directory and you enter:

```
COPY MYFILE \MYFILE
```

COPY gets confused and doesn't realize you're referring to the same file two different ways. This can be a serious problem if the file is larger than 64K.

Here's what will happen in that second case: COPY will open the first file for reading. It will read 64K of the file into memory (or less if the full 64K is not available). It will then tell DOS to create the second file. If the second file already exists (as it does in this case), the file gets truncated to zero bytes and the space in the FAT is freed up. Then COPY writes the 64K buffer to the second file. Now COPY goes back to read the next chunk of the first file. DOS takes a look at the FAT for the first file and finds out all the clusters have been freed up. It says "Hey, what happened?" and generates an error message.

You can also run into trouble if you try a command like:

```
COPY FILE1 FILE2
```

If FILE2 already exists, but FILE1 is much larger than available disk space, DOS aborts the COPY with an "Insufficient disk space" message, but also deletes FILE2. It may seem like a "Shoot first, ask questions later" approach.

To determine whether enough disk space exists to copy FILE1 to FILE2, COM-MAND.COM would have to check if the space available on the disk plus the size of FILE2 is less than or equal to the size of FILE1. Instead, the COPY command creates the destination file FILE2 (erasing the old one in the process) and then tries to copy the contents of FILE1 to it. If this fails, FILE2 is gone. Usually this won't create a serious problem, since you were intending to get rid of the existing FILE2 anyway.

But one other COPY problem can cause heartache. Let's say you're trying to copy all your programs to a subdirectory called SUBDIR, and you issue the two commands:

```
COPY A:*.COM SUBDIR
DEL A:*.COM
```

If you make a mistake and type something like SUBDIT (rather than SUBDIR), which is not an existing directory name, COPY will create a file called SUBDIT and copy all the COM files into it. Since this is an ASCII copy, because the syntax implies you're concatenating the files, it stops copying after the first ASCII end-of-file marker in each on the COM files. Result: garbage.

Here's another COPY quirk — you can display an ASCII file to the screen with:

```
COPY filename CON
```

because the output device CON is the display. This command does basically the same thing as:

```
TYPE filename
```

Likewise, you can copy a file to the printer with:

```
COPY filename PRN
```

The file goes to the printer and a "1 file(s) copied" message appears on the screen. Using redirection of standard output, you can also copy a file to the printer with the command:

```
TYPE filename >PRN
```

So far, so good. Based on this, you might think that the command:

```
COPY filename CON >PRN
```

would copy the file to the printer, because the COPY command is copying it to the screen, and the screen is redirected to the printer. But it doesn't. Instead, it just copies the file to the screen and puts the "file(s) copied" message on the printer.

While the results look a little peculiar, DOS is actually working consistently. To see why, you have to understand the distinction between devices (CON and PRN) and the handles that programs use to refer to these files and devices.

Beginning with version 2.0, DOS adopted a *handle* approach to working with files and devices. When a program such as COMMAND.COM opens a file or device for the COPY or TYPE commands, it tells DOS the filename and DOS returns a handle (which is simply a number) that refers to the file.

DOS maintains two tables that correlate the handles and the files or devices they refer to. The first table is located in the program's Program Segment Prefix starting at offset 18H. The number at address [18H + handle] refers to a second table internal to DOS that contains the file or device name and other information that DOS needs to read from or write to the file. (This is not documented, by the way.)

The restriction of 20 file handles per program derives from the length of this table in the Program Segment Prefix. The maximum number of open files that DOS can maintain depends upon the space allocated for the internal DOS tables and is governed by the FILES statement in a CONFIG.SYS file.

When a program begins execution, five file handles are already defined. Normally, handle 1 (which is defined as standard output) is mapped to the output device CON, which is the display.

The internal workings of the TYPE command are simple. It reads a file and writes it with function call 40H using a handle of 1, so output normally goes to the CON device. However, when you specify on the command line that standard output should be redirected to PRN with the command:

```
TYPE filename >PRN
```

COMMAND.COM opens the PRN device to get a handle for it, and then uses the FORCDUP function call (46H) to make handle 1 refer to the PRN device. So, TYPE is still writing the file using handle 1, but the handle refers to a device other than CON.

When you specify CON or PRN as the destination in a COPY command, COMMAND.COM opens that device through DOS, gets back a handle for it (which will *not* be one of the predefined handles), and uses that handle for writing the file. So, the two commands:

```
COPY filename PRN
```

and:

```
TYPE filename > PRN
```

are not really the same thing. In the first case, the COPY command uses a handle that refers to the device PRN. In the second case, the TYPE command uses handle 1, but this handle has been redirected to the device PRN. Because of this, when COMMAND.COM executes the command:

```
COPY filename CON >PRN
```

it first redirects handle 1 to the PRN device. But then COPY opens the device called CON for the destination and DOS returns a new handle that refers to this device. The file appears on the screen because the COPY command is writing it using this new handle. It then writes the "file(s) copied" message to standard output (the handle 1), but this message goes out to the printer because the handle has been redirected.

Copying files to devices can come in handy when you want to scan through several files one after the other, or peek inside executable files.

If you use the TYPE command on a binary, nontext file like COMMAND.COM, DOS will stop when it reaches the first ASCII character 26, since it will erroneously think this is an end-of-file marker and grind to a halt.

But you can see the whole COMMAND.COM file by typing:

```
COPY /B COMMAND.COM CON
```

The /B (for "Binary" file) tells DOS to look up the length of the file in the disk directory and copy that number of bytes. Using CON as a destination tells DOS to copy these bytes to the console (screen) rather than a file.

Get to know the /B switch. It can prevent lots of COPY problems. For instance, you can use the COPY command to update (or backdate) the time and date in the directory listing of any file. But be extremely careful when using this update feature. If you have a short text file on your disk called OLDFILE that you created a long time ago, you can make the date and time in its directory listing current by typing:

```
COPY OLDFILE +,,
```

However, DOS thinks all files it copies this way are ASCII files unless you tell it otherwise, and will stop copying the contents if it sees an ASCII character 26, which it interprets as an end-of-file marker. If you're not careful, you can end up with a copy of just the beginning of a non-ASCII file.

Most text files don't contain any ASCII 26 characters (except at the very end), but just about every COM or EXE file contains several. You can tell DOS to bypass this problem by making copies based on the file's true length, as reported by the directory listing.

While adding a /B after the word COPY tells DOS to make copies based on file length rather than the detection of an ASCII 26, adding a /A (for "ASCII" file) does the reverse. When you tack on a /B or /A switch, DOS will handle all files listed after the switch in that particular COPY command with these rules in mind.

You can mix-and-match /A and /B switches, file by file, if you are concatenating several smaller ASCII and binary files into one big one. When you don't specify any switches, DOS assumes all concatenations are for ASCII files, while all non concatenating (normal) copies are for binary files.

The "+" sign in the "COPY filename +,," updating command makes DOS treat the process like a concatenation, even though it is really dealing with only one file at a time. Because of this, it is important to add a /B switch to the command.

So the final command to update the directory listing for both ASCII and binary files is:

```
COPY /B filename +,,
```

You can create a one-line batch file called UPDATE.BAT that uses a replaceable parameter:

```
COPY /B %1 +,,
```

Then, you can make the date of any file current by typing:

```
UPDATE filename
```

You can also use this technique to change the date backwards or forwards. Before you run UPDATE.BAT, just reset the DATE (and TIME, if you want) commands.

You can't update all your files using wildcards. The command:

```
COPY /B *.* +,,
```

won't work. But you can bring all your files up to date using FOR...IN...DO. To enter the command directly in DOS, type:

```
FOR %F IN (*.*) DO COPY /B %F +,,
```

To put this into a batch file called REDATE.BAT, substitute a %%F for each %F, and redirect the output to NUL to suppress the one-by-one executions and "1 File(s) copied" messages produced by the FOR...IN...DO command. The contents of REDATE.BAT would be:

```
FOR %%F IN (*.*) DO COPY /B %%F +,, > NUL
```

An even better way is to use the TOUCH.COM program on the accompanying disk.

If you're nervous about making copies, and you want to verify that the backup is indeed valid, don't bother with the /V COPY option. All this does is make sure that DOS can read the copied file; it doesn't check the copy against the original to make sure that every byte is the same. And it slows the whole process down.

A better way is to use the COMP command immediately after you make any copies. Since the actual commands COPY and COMP are the same length and use the same syntax, once you've copied the files you can check the accuracy of the copies by pressing F1 or the right cursor arrow key twice, typing "MP" to replace the "PY" in the word COPY, and then pressing F3 to finish repeating the command. So:

```
COPY *.* B:
```

with just a few keystrokes becomes:

```
COMP *.* B:
```

If you're using XCOPY, just insert an extra space at the beginning, so the process would look like:

```
C>XCOPY *.* B:
C> COMP *.* B:
```

DOS will ignore the space directly after the prompt.

If you want to look at lots of files — such as a collection of your small batch files — in succession, you can adapt this technique with:

```
COPY *.BAT CON
```

Another good way to do this is to create two short batch files called SCANBATS.BAT and READ.BAT. First, SCANBATS.BAT cycles through all the BAT files on your disk:

```
ECHO OFF
FOR %%F IN (*.BAT) DO COMMAND /C READ %%F
```

Then, READ.BAT, which is called by SCANBATS.BAT, does the actual displaying:

```
ECHO OFF
CLS
ECHO %1
MORE < %1
PAUSE
```

If you create these files using EDLIN or the DOS COPY CON command, you may want to add a line before the final PAUSE in READ.BAT that says:

```
ECHO <F7>
```

But instead of actually typing <F7>, press the F7 key. If you're in DOS, this will generate an ASCII 0 null character (unless you've redefined the F7 key). Following ECHO with a null will put a blank line onscreen. You may need this if the files you're trying to display don't end with carriage returns. If they don't, the "Strike a key when ready . . ." message generated by the PAUSE command will appear at the end of the last line of the batch file rather than on a line by itself.

To try SCANBATS and READ, create both batch files, then enter:

```
SCANBATS
```

If you're using a 3.3 or later version of DOS you can make the process slightly more efficient by changing the second line of SCANBATS.BAT to:

```
FOR %%F IN (*.BAT) DO CALL READ %%F
```

If you are using a more recent DOS version, you can also omit the ECHO OFF at the top of READ.BAT. And you'll find that using CALL instead of COMMAND /C makes it easier to break out of the process prematurely if you want.

Users often ask about turning their computers into typewriters. It's hard to have each letter appear on your printer as you type it, but you can harness the COPY command and end up with something halfway close. At the DOS prompt, try typing:

```
COPY CON PRN
```

CON refers to both the keyboard and screen, although here DOS will use the keyboard half of the device. PRN refers to your printer. After you enter this command, start typing. Press the Enter key at the end of each line. If you make a mistake on a screen line, you can use the backspace or left arrow key to correct it, but after you've pressed Enter, or wrapped down to the next screen line, you're stuck with it (which is why it's better to use a word processor or EDLIN). And don't try any lines longer than 127 characters.

The text won't appear on the printer until you're done. To finish, press the F6 key (or Ctrl-Z) and then press Enter one final time. The text will then be printed.

You may have to add a Ctrl-L before the Ctrl-Z to issue a form feed after the text is printed.

One final note — be careful about the order of filenames or devices when making copies. Users of non-DOS systems may be accustomed to listing these in reverse order. If you wanted to send a small file's output to your printer, and typed:

```
COPY LPT1 filename
```

instead of the correct:

```
COPY filename LPT1
```

you'll end up with a "0 file(s) copied" message and a deleted file.

VERIFY

The DOS VERIFY option often confuses users, who wonder whether running their systems with VERIFY on actually does anything. They also want to know if their word processor, data base, and spreadsheet programs take advantage of whatever protection VERIFY provides.

The good news is that because most applications do their file handling by calling DOS functions, the VERIFY option is invoked whenever data is written to the disk. The bad news is that turning the VERIFY option on in DOS actually does little more than slow down your disk operations.

The syntax of the VERIFY switch is easy to understand. You turn it on with the command VERIFY ON, and off with VERIFY OFF. Entering VERIFY with no argument displays the current status. But while the syntax is fairly obvious, the effect of the command isn't.

Common sense would lead you to expect that VERIFY makes sure the correct data had been written to the disk. A logical procedure for the operation might be: write the data to the disk, read it back from the disk, and compare the returned data to the original. If it isn't the same, retry the operation a specified number of times. If the process continues to be unsuccessful, signal an error. Logical as this may seem, in reality, it doesn't happen that way.

One of the reasons for creating DOS was to free applications from the burden of having to include code for handling disk I/O directly. Consequently, most programs interact with the disk by going through DOS. DOS, in turn, accesses the disk hardware through your system's hardware-specific BIOS routines.

Consider what happens when you save a file from inside an application program. The program first calls DOS with the request to save the file. DOS must then move the data, which is stored in a buffer in memory, to the disk. This is accomplished by providing the correct parameters to the BIOS disk write routine. BIOS, in turn, then sends the correct commands to the disk controller. Before the data is written onto the disk, however, some additional information is appended. This extra information is used to detect errors, and it is written to the disk at the same time as the data. The most common addition is called a Cyclical Redundancy Check (CRC), which is a halfway sophisticated type of checksum. The same data will always generate the same CRC value. So, by calculating the CRC and writing it to the disk along with the data, two independent representations of the same data are recorded.

The read function is simply the reverse of the write function. It causes data to be transferred from the disk to a memory buffer. Each time the data is read, however, the CRC is again calculated and compared with the CRC that was recorded when the data was originally written. If the two CRCs match exactly, the data is assumed to be correct, and is copied to the buffer. If not, the operation may be retried several times, but if the old CRC and the new CRC still don't match, the BIOS reports an error and does not return the data. (This discussion uses a little legerdemain by lumping BIOS and the disk controller together. In fact, the disk controller itself can actually detect and correct certain errors, which provides one more level of defense.)

The verify function operates nearly identically to the disk read operation, except that no data is moved to a buffer, even if the read is successful. VERIFY causes the data to be read from the disk and the CRC to be recalculated. The new CRC is compared to the old CRC to ensure that they match. Again, typically, if they don't match, the operation is retried a specified number of times, and then an error is returned. The important thing to note is that at no time is the data itself on the disk compared to anything. Thus, the verify function serves simply to check the continued readability and integrity of the disk, not of the data.

When you turn on the DOS VERIFY switch, a flag is set inside DOS. From then on, each disk write operation that DOS is requested to perform is immediately followed by a similar call to the verify operation. In other words, DOS simply checks to see that the area of the disk it just wrote your data to is readable — not that it wrote the correct data! Excluding bad sections, each normal area of a disk always has a valid CRC. If the data your program tried to write was somehow sidetracked into the Twilight Zone, and never made it to the disk, the verify call would still return a good value, and DOS would never know.

VERIFY has one other effect. The disk drive hardware must always wait for the correct area of the disk to rotate under the head, read the data, and calculate the CRC. The new CRC must then be compared to the recorded CRC. All this takes a certain amount of time. In the case of disk access, an operation that might normally have been accomplished in a single rotation might take three or more to complete. So, VERIFY's most obvious effect is to slow down disk I/O.

DISKCOPY

Many new users make backups of their files by using the DISKCOPY command. This isn't smart. The only times you should use DISKCOPY are when you want to back up a commercial software disk or when you have a data-integrity problem with a diskette. Ironically, what could have caused the problem is DISKCOPY itself.

New users like DISKCOPY because it's faster than COPY *.* and because it formats on the fly. Experienced users know that COPY *.* and the even better XCOPY handle two problems better — fragmentation and bad tracks.

The more you use a disk the more fragmented the files on it become. Ideally your files should be contiguous. Having pieces of your files scattered over the disk results in time-consuming head "churning," or "thrashing" as your system retrieves all the far-flung chunks of each file. This also causes unnecessary wear and tear on the disk and the drive heads and motor.

You should periodically back up any disk you've used for a while onto a freshly formatted one using the COPY *.* or XCOPY *.* commands.

The second, and more troublesome, reason not to use DISKCOPY is that it puts a mirror image of the original disk's contents onto the new one. If the blank disk has internal defects such as bad sectors, especially bad sectors that have bitten the dust after the FORMAT command originally roped off defective areas, DISKCOPY can write a copy of the original disk's data onto these bad areas, rendering such information unusable on the copy.

You should use DISKCOPY when you discover that you're having a data-integrity problem with a floppy, or when you accidentally erase a file on a disk and realize you're going to have to perform surgery with something like the *Norton Utilities* to recover the data. If this happens, you can use DISKCOPY to make a perfect copy of the affected disk, and first try the surgery on the copy. If you make a mistake in the recovery process and end up ruining it, you can make another DISKCOPY of the original and try again.

When you open a fresh package of floppy disks, format them all, without the system files (you can always add these later with SYS). It's always a good idea to have a box of blank formatted disks around, since you somtimes need one when you're in the middle of a program and can't quit to format one then or you'd lose data.

Then use XCOPY (or COPY if you're using an older version of DOS) to make backups onto these blank, formatted disks.

ASSIGN

Sometimes users expect DOS to be a whole lot smarter than it actually is, especially when they try to outfox it. So beware of dangerous collisions when using "alias" commands such as ASSIGN that trick DOS into treating one drive as another.

The ASSIGN program included with PC-DOS is potentially bad news. ASSIGN is a remain-resident program that intercepts most DOS file calls and simply swaps disk drive letters. It was included with DOS 2.0 and later to deal with pre-XT programs that assumed every PC had only drives A: and B: and nothing more. All of the PC-DOS manuals include warnings about using ASSIGN.

If you must use ASSIGN with certain programs, don't issue the ASSIGN commands manually. Put them in a batch file like this:

```
ASSIGN A=C B=C
```

[then execute the program that can't use drive C:]

```
ASSIGN
```

The second ASSIGN undoes all the ASSIGNments so you don't accidently do something dangerous with a command such as COPY. For instance, if you had typed:

```
ASSIGN A=C
```

and then later had tried to copy a hard disk file to a floppy disk with the command:

```
COPY C:filename A:
```

DOS would have attempted to copy the file on top of itself. If the file was larger than 64K you could end up with a "File Allocation Table Error" and a truncated version of the original.

APPEND

Since version 2.0, you've been able to tell the DOS PATH command which subdirectories to check for executable files (ending in COM, EXE, or BAT). But nonexecutable files remained immune to even the most comprehensive search.

DOS executes internal commands such as DIR, VER, or TYPE directly, since the instructions for these are imbedded inside COMMAND.COM. If DOS doesn't recognize the command you typed, it first checks the current directory (if you entered something like CHKDSK), or any directory you may have specified (if you typed something like

D:\BIN\CHKDSK). It then looks in each of the subdirectories that you included in your path. So if you added a line to your AUTOEXEC.BAT file that read:

```
PATH C:\;C:\DOS;D:\
```

if DOS didn't immediately find the file you specified it would hunt for one by that name with a COM, EXE, or BAT extension in the root and \DOS subdirectories on drive C:, and on the root directory of drive D:.

However, if you or your program needed to find a file that had an extension other than COM, EXE, or BAT, you had to purchase a path extender program. Or, if you were working with DOS 3.1 or 3.2, you could use the SUBST command to trick DOS into thinking a subdirectory was actually a logical drive with its own drive letter.

For example, the main classic *WordStar* 3.3 WS.COM file always needed to know where you'd stored its two .OVR overlay files. If these files were kept in C:\PROGS you could use DEBUG to patch WS.COM so that it looked on drive E:

```
DEBUG WS.COM
E 2DC 5
W
Q
```

and then tell DOS about it with the command:

```
SUBST E: C:\PROGS
```

(For anything higher than drive E: you also had to add a LASTDRIVE command to your CONFIG.SYS.) If your MEMO file was stored in C:\STAR\WORK and you had used SUBST to turn that subdirectory into F: you could then type WS F:MEMO.

APPEND makes the process relatively easy — and a lot cleaner. Just follow the PATH command in your AUTOEXEC.BAT file with an APPEND command using similar syntax and telling DOS where your important nonexecutable files are located. If you keep overlays in the subdirectory mentioned above, and correspondence with royalty in \KING\LTRS, your APPEND command could be:

```
APPEND C:\PROGS;C:\KING\LTRS
```

DOS gives you two ways to keep tabs on your APPEND list. You can start off with an extra APPEND /E command, which loads APPEND strings into your environment and lets you change them with the SET command, just as with PATH. But, if you or your programs switch command processors (by exiting the one you're currently using) such strings become inaccessible. With long PATH and APPEND strings, you may have to expand your environment size by using the SHELL command. In fact, these days the default 160 byte environment is straining at the seams.

You can also add an additional APPEND /X command to spiff up the way DOS looks for files. Or you can add both /E and /X, but you then have to run APPEND twice — first with any switches, and then with the actual list of subdirectories DOS will search.

The DOS manual contains all sorts of dire warnings on using APPEND with BACKUP and RESTORE, running it with ASSIGN, or having it anywhere near IBM LAN commands of the same name (hard to believe IBM didn't change the name, but true). And as with any path extender, you have to be careful that you're not accidentally pulling in a long-forgotten file from a distant subdirectory that APPEND knows about but that you don't.

EXE2BIN

When IBM first delivered DOS 2.0 it included some very valuable programs and documentation. But it gradually did away with some key tools. First, it removed all mention of ANSI.SYS from the DOS manual. Then in version 3.3 it got rid of the manual section on DEBUG and replaced it with some turgid prose about using foreign character sets.

And, for some incomprehensible reason, IBM removed the EXE2BIN.EXE program from the DOS program diskettes; to obtain a copy of this program, you have to buy the DOS 3.3 *Technical Reference* manual. If you try using the old 3.2 version under 3.3, you'll just get an "Incorrect DOS Version" message.

EXE2BIN version 3.2 checks the DOS version number right after it's loaded, and exits if it finds itself running under any version of DOS greater than 3.2. Changing the byte at offset 30D converts a JZ instruction to a JMP, causing the program to jump to the right place regardless of what the version test found.

To patch the 3.2 version of EXE2BIN.EXE so it runs under other versions, copy and rename your 3.2 version of EXE2BIN.EXE to EXE2BIN.XXX. Then patch the byte at address 30D from 71 to EB. Finally, rename the EXE2BIN.XXX file EXE2BIN.EXE. The whole process looks like:

```
COPY EXE2BIN.EXE EXE2BIN.XXX

DEBUG EXE2BIN.XXX
E 30D EB
W
Q
REN EXE2BIN.XXX EXE2BIN.EXE
```

KEYBxx

DOS 3.0 to 3.2 came in five international flavors. By executing the appropriate KEYBxx command you could tweak the keyboard into British, German, French, Italian, or Spanish modes. Actually, since you could toggle back and forth between the standard keyboard and the foreign variants, you could adapt the KEYBxx command to print just about anything onscreen.

For instance, you could patch KEYBUK.COM (the smallest of the five KEYBxx files) so that the:

```
QWE
ASD
ZXC
```

block of keys would produce either a single line box (with lowercase letters) or a double-line box (with capital letters). To try this (with DOS 3.2 on an old AT keyboard), type in the following SCRIPT.KBD file:

```
N KEYBUK.COM
L
E 9AB DA C2 BF
E 9B9 C3 C5 B4
E 9C7 C0 C1 D9
E 9E5 C9 CB BB
E 9F3 CC CE B9
E A01 C8 CA BC
N KEYBOX.COM
W
Q
```

For other 3.x versions of DOS, replace the address column directly after the initial Es as follows:

DOS Version

3.0	*3.1*	*3.2*
592	662	9AB
5A0	670	9B9
5AE	67E	9C7
5CC	69C	9E5
5DA	6AA	9F3
5E8	6B8	A01

Once you've created the appropriate KEYBOX.COM file, run it. You can toggle back and forth between the normal keyboard and the new one by hitting Ctrl-Alt-F1 and Ctrl-Alt-F2.

With version 3.3, IBM totally revamped the way DOS handles foreign alphabets. But it did so in the most confusing way possible. First, instead of calling the process something clear and simple like "font loading," IBM referred to it as "code page switching." Then, it forced the user to digest three different and seemingly contradictory chunks of the manual — a whole chapter relegated to the rear between Error Messages and EDLIN, an abstruse few pages under "DEVICE" in the CONFIG.SYS section, and several other dense dollops under MODE, NLSFUNC, and CHCP. Manual writers everywhere should be forced to plod their way through these sections to see the ultimate example of how not to explain things.

Code page switching will show new fonts only with DOS 3.3 or later and only on EGA/VGA monitors and IBM Convertible LCD screens. (You can print the new character fonts only on IBM Model 4201 Proprinters and Model 5202 Quietwriter IIIs.) If you want to see all the new characters, assuming both that the 3.3 or later DIS-PLAY.SYS file is in your C:\DOS subdirectory and that you're using an EGA, first include a line in your CONFIG.SYS file:

```
DEVICE=C:\DOS\DISPLAY.SYS CON=(EGA,437,5)
```

Then create a small SHOWFONT.COM file that will display the high-bit ASCII characters DOS tinkers with, by loading DEBUG.COM and typing in:

```
E100 B4 0E B0 84 CD 10 FE
E107 C0 3C FC 75 F8 B0 0D
E10E CD 10 B0 0A CD 10 C3
N SHOWFONT.COM
RCX
15
W
Q
```

Finally, type in the following CODEPAGE.BAT batch file (assuming COUN-TRY.SYS is in your C:\DOS subdirectory and that MODE, NLSFUNC, and the SHOW-FONT.COM file you just created are in a directory you've included in your path):

```
C:\DOS\COUNTRY.SYS
MODE CON CP PREP=((850,860,863,865) EGA.CPI)
ECHO Hit any key 4 times
MODE CON CP SEL=865 >NUL
SHOWFONT
PAUSE>NUL
MODE CON SP SEL=850 >NUL
PAUSE>NUL
MODE CON SP SEL=860 >NUL
PAUSE>NUL
MODE CON SP SEL=863 >NUL
PAUSE>NUL
MODE CON SP SEL=437 >NUL
```

While code pages 865, 863, and 860 will be interesting only to residents of Norway, French-speaking Canada, and Portugal, Multilingual CP 850 can display some long needed characters, such as ®, ©, ¶, ×, ¢, 3/4, and [1] and [3].

GRAPHICS and GRAFTABL

If you're working with text and you want a permanent copy of what's on the screen, you can just turn your printer on and press Shift-PrtSc.

But if you're working with a language like BASIC or Pascal and you have a fancy graphics image on your screen and want to send a copy of this image to your printer, you can't just use the Shift-PrtSc technique unless you first run the DOS GRAPHICS utility.

The print screen routine coded in ROM BIOS works only with characters. If the display is in a graphics mode, the routine will print only the ASCII characters that it can recognize, but won't translate the graphics. This is a reasonable restriction, since graphics protocols for printers vary a great deal and the ROM BIOS can't support them all.

The GRAPHICS.COM program (or GRAPHICS.EXE in some versions) supplements the ROM BIOS print screen routines. It remains resident in memory, so you need load it only once during your PC session. Once it's loaded, your system can print 320 x 200 four-color graphics (video modes 4 and 5), and 640 x 200 black and white graphics (video mode 6) on an IBM Graphics Printer or compatible. Under DOS 4.0 and 5.0 you can dump newer graphics screens.

GRAPHICS uses different dot densities for the four colors of the 320 x 200 mode to simulate color. More recent DOS versions of GRAPHICS also support various IBM printers that can actually reproduce the colors.

Older versions of GRAPHICS.COM don't support the additional video modes of the IBM Enhanced Graphics Adapter (EGA).

If you're using a graphics screen on a CGA system and you try to generate ASCII characters with values above 127, you'll end up with a mess unless you first load the DOS GRAFTABL utility.

The PC ROM stores the bit patterns for ASCII characters with values from 0 through 127 starting at address F000:FA6E. Each character is represented by eight successive bytes. Interrupt 1F at the very bottom of memory (address 0000:007C) stores the address of an optional table of bit patterns for the high-bit ASCII characters with values from 128 to 255. GRAFTABL loads such a table into RAM and adjusts the address at 0000:007C to point to this table.

If GRAFTABL isn't loaded, the address at 0000:007C will be 0. If you then try to print an ASCII value over 127 in graphics mode, your system will assume the table of high-bit character patterns is stored at address 0, or 0000:0000. This happens to be where your system stores interrupt vectors, not character patterns, so your system will end up trying to make characters out of vector addresses. The result is junk.

Each new hardware release changes the rules. EGA and later video adapter BIOS provide bit patterns for all 255 characters. In the most recent versions of DOS, GRAFTABL can also load the hodgepodge of foreign language code page data into memory.

Starting with the EGA, IBM made it easy to use alternate character sets. The CGA and monochrome adapter ROMs contained character dot patterns that only the adapter could use. But the EGA and all subsequent adapters put copies of the dot patterns into the normal megabyte of the PC's address space, where they're fairly easy to reach.

(Actually, the CGA contains two sets of dot patterns. The normal one draws characters out of lines that are two pixels wide. If you yank out your CGA adapter, find jumper P3, and connect the jumper's two pins, you can see the alternate single-pixel character set. It's not worth the trouble.)

STACKS

If you're stuck using DOS version 3.2, watch out for a nasty but easily correctible bug — an "Internal Stack Error" message. Simply pressing the Pause key on the new IBM keyboard rapidly ten times will produce this message and lock your system, forcing a power-down restart.

The DOS manual states that this error is caused by a "rapid succession of recursive hardware interrupts," and suggests adding the command "STACKS=N,S" to your CON-FIG.SYS file. N represents the number of stack frames, where the default is 9 and the range is 8 to 64. S is the size in bytes of each frame, where the default size of each stack frame is 128 bytes and the range is 32 to 512. Using this STACKS statement reduces available memory.

While most users don't pound on the Pause key, a fast typist entering data into a Lotus *1-2-3* spreadsheet can easily trigger the error, halting your system and resulting in lost data, time, and effort.

You can eliminate the problem by adding a line like:

```
STACKS=32,256
```

to your CONFIG.SYS file, which lets you pound on the Pause key about 25 times before causing an error.

If you're using DOS 4.0 or 5.0, the line STACKS=0,0 will free up a bit more memory for you to use.

XCOPY

Sometimes a new DOS version isn't much of an improvement over the previous one. At other times, however, the new DOS version contains a real gem. One of the most dazzling is the XCOPY command introduced with version DOS 3.2. It's an extended COPY command that includes some of the features of BACKUP, as well.

XCOPY is fast. It reads as many files as will fit into memory from the source disk, then writes the files to the destination disk in one speedy gulp. COPY, on the other hand, reads and writes each file individually, continually switching back and forth between the drives.

When used with its optional /S switch, XCOPY will also copy files from nested subdirectories, creating new subdirectories on the target disk as needed. While subdirectories are more common on hard disks than diskettes, some floppies contain

subdirectories to organize the data on them better or to store more than the maximum
112 or 224 files that a diskette root directory can hold. To copy such a diskette type:

```
XCOPY A:*.* B: /S
```

To copy all the diskette files to a subdirectory of your hard disk while maintaining the
same directory structure, try:

```
XCOPY A:*.* C:\SUBDIR /S
```

where SUBDIR is a subdirectory of your hard disk.

Similarly, if you need to copy a directory of your hard disk (including subdirectories
within just that directory) to a diskette, XCOPY also comes to the rescue:

```
XCOPY C:\SUBDIR\*.* A: /S
```

Sometimes you may want to copy selected files from one disk to another. You could
COPY each of these files individually, or you could use the /P (prompt) switch with
XCOPY:

```
XCOPY C:\SUBDIR\*.* A: /P
```

In this case, XCOPY will ask file by file whether you want to copy each. You simply
type Y or N. And, you can use the /S and /P switches together.

XCOPY is extremely useful for making backups. The /D switch followed by a date
copies just those files created or changed on that date or later. So:

```
XCOPY C:\SUBDIR\*.* A: /D:04-15-91
```

copies to A: only those files created or changed on or after April 15, 1991.

Another aid in backing up files is the file archive bit, which is set to 1 when the file is
first created and every subsequent time you change it. When you tack on a /M parameter,
XCOPY will copy only those files whose archives bit are set to 1. After it copies each
file, XCOPY resets the archive bit to 0. The next time you use XCOPY with a /M
parameter, XCOPY will skip over any file with an archive bit value of 0, which avoids
cluttering up your backup disks with duplicate copies of files that you haven't changed.

You can use XCOPY to back up your C: hard disk with the command:

```
XCOPY C:\*.* A: /S /M
```

When drive A: runs out of space, simply put in a new diskette and rerun the command.
Those files already copied will not be recopied to the next diskette.

The advantage of using XCOPY instead of BACKUP for this chore is that the copies
on the diskette remain normal useable files. While BACKUP can also copy files
selectively, you have to use the RESTORE command on copies made with BACKUP

before you can use them. The one advantage of BACKUP is that it can split huge files over several floppy disks. But until version 3.3, BACKUP and RESTORE could create havoc on your hard disk by copying older versions of your DOS system files over newer versions.

COMMAND

If you're like most users, you know that COMMAND.COM is a part of DOS needed to operate your system properly. Erase it from your root directory and you won't be able to boot your system. You may also know that one of COMMAND.COM's roles is to process the commands you type, like DIR, CHKDSK, or 123. But you may not know that COMMAND.COM itself is also a useful command.

To understand how this works, you have to know what the various parts of DOS do. When you make a disk bootable (by formatting it with a /S parameter, or later using SYS and COPY COMMAND.COM), you're adding three files to it:

- IBMBIO.COM
- IBMDOS.COM
- COMMAND.COM

The first two files (which are called IO.SYS and MSDOS.SYS on DOS 5.0 and on earlier non-IBM systems) are "hidden" since they won't show up in normal directory searches, although you can see them by typing CHKDSK /V or running a program on one of the accompanying disks like DR.COM.

In DOS 2.0 and above, IBMBIO is essentially a series of device drivers that let DOS communicate with the hardware of the PC, including the display, the keyboard, the disk drives, and the printer. In many cases, these IBMBIO.COM device drivers use the ROM BIOS interrupts.

IBMDOS.COM contains the code needed to execute the DOS function calls that actually do the behind-the-scenes file, disk, and basic system work. If a particular function call needs to use a hardware device, it calls a device driver routine in IBMBIO.COM. This is why the chapter on screens deals almost exclusively with BIOS calls rather than DOS calls, since video is hardware-based.

In most cases, programs issue DOS calls to IBMDOS.COM, then IBMDOS.COM issues device driver calls to IBMBIO.COM, then the device drivers issue interrupts to the ROM BIOS, and the ROM BIOS talks to the hardware.

COMMAND.COM is the program that is running when no other program is running. It asks for the date and time when you boot up, displays the DOS prompt, reads in what you type at the DOS prompt, and searches to see if what you typed in is an internal command (DIR, COPY, ERASE, etc.). If so, it will execute that command, often using lots of interrupt 21H DOS function calls. If the command you typed is not an internal command, then COMMAND.COM will search the current directory for a COM, EXE, or BAT file of that name, and then use directory paths set by path to do further searches. COMMAND.COM then loads the program, and takes over when the program is done.

COMMAND.COM also executes batch file programs, including AUTOEXEC.BAT when DOS is first loaded. And it assumes control during critical hardware errors and issues the much-loved "Abort, Retry, Ignore, Fail?" message.

To further complicate matters, COMMAND.COM divides itself into two pieces when it is first loaded into memory. The "resident" part of COMMAND.COM, about 3K bytes, sits in the lower end of memory above the other two DOS files. The "transient" part of COMMAND.COM — the bulk of the program — resides up at the very top of user memory.

The transient part of COMMAND.COM interprets and executes the DOS internal commands and does batch file processing. These facilities are not needed when other programs are running. By sitting at the top of memory, the transient COMMAND.COM does not take up valuable memory space. It can be overwritten by other programs if they need the space.

When a program exits, it returns control to the resident part of COMMAND.COM, which performs a simple checksum calculation of the memory area normally occupied by the transient COMMAND.COM. This way it can tell whether the information loaded in that area of memory is indeed its own transient part or whether the transient part was overwritten. If it was overwritten, the resident part then reloads the transient part of COMMAND.COM back into memory.

That's why exiting from a large program can cause a disk access while COMMAND.COM is reloaded into memory. Some programs — like *1-2-3* and many compilers — always use that top area, so this may happen often.

You can execute any DOS internal command (or any COM, EXE, or BAT program for that matter) from within an assembly language program by loading a *secondary* copy of COMMAND.COM and passing to it a parameter containing the command or program name. COMMAND.COM will then handle all the complicated details and return control back to your program.

If you want, you can load a secondary version of COMMAND.COM directly from the DOS command level. First, figure out how much memory is available by typing:

```
CHKDSK
```

Then type:

```
COMMAND /C CHKDSK
```

and you'll see that a smaller amount of memory is available.

Under DOS 5.0 the memory-reporting part of the listing will look something like:

```
C>CHKDSK

    655360 bytes total memory
    629728 bytes free
```

```
C>COMMAND /C CHKDSK

    655360 bytes total memory
    626912 bytes free
```

The 3000-byte difference is the amount of memory used by the second resident portion of COMMAND.COM. When you add a /C and the name of an executable file (such as CHKDSK), COMMAND.COM will execute the file and then terminate just like any other program by returning control to the previously executing program, which in this case is the primary copy of COMMAND.COM.

This can come in very handy with batch files. Normally if a line in one batch file executes a second batch file, control won't return to the first batch file. But if the first batch file contains a line like:

```
COMMAND /C BATFILE2
```

then the second BATFILE2.BAT batch file will be executed by the secondary command processor. When BATFILE2 finishes, DOS returns control to the original copy of COMMAND.COM, which continues processing the initial batch file at a point directly following the COMMAND /C BATFILE2 line.

(The CALL batch command, introduced with version 3.3, handles this task somewhat more efficiently.)

However, if BATFILE2 contains a PROMPT, PATH, or SET command, then this will affect the environment of the secondary COMMAND.COM which will be lost when BATFILE2 completes execution and control is returned to the primary COM-MAND.COM.

If you load a secondary copy of COMMAND.COM without the /C you can see how this works, by having the two versions juggle different prompts. Try typing in these four commands, one after the other:

```
PROMPT [LEVEL1]
COMMAND
PROMPT [LEVEL2]
EXIT
```

The first command changes your normal prompt to [LEVEL1]. The second command loads a secondary version of COMMAND.COM. The third command changes the prompt to [LEVEL2]. This [LEVEL2] prompt is effective only for the second copy of COM-MAND.COM. Typing EXIT at that point returns you to your original version of COMMAND.COM, so the prompt returns to [LEVEL 1].

Programs often load secondary versions of COMMAND.COM themselves. First, they make sure that enough memory is available for DOS to load another version of COM-MAND.COM. When a program first begins executing, all available memory is allocated to it. So, some of this memory must be freed up. Before the memory is freed up, the stack pointer may have to be moved from the area of memory being freed, so the stack isn't destroyed in some way.

Then, the program has to figure out where you've stored COMMAND.COM on your disk. In DOS 2.0 and above, programs have access to your system's environment, which is designed to keep track of things like the current DOS prompt, any path you may have set with the PATH command, and the drive, directory, and filename of your current command processor.

You can see the current environment setting by typing SET. One of the lines displayed will begin with "COMSPEC=" and will show the drive, directory, and filename of the command processor COMMAND.COM. Any program can get at its environment by accessing the memory beginning at the segment address stored in offset 002CH of the Program Segment Prefix.

Once the program that needs to load COMMAND.COM figures out where it's stored, it can perform a PC-DOS EXEC function call 4BH of interrupt 21H, which loads any COM or EXE file, executes it, and then passes control back when finished.

COMMAND.COM can generate slightly confusing errors based on which parts of it are handy and which are not. If you run programs that use disks without DOS on them, you may see one of the following three messages on the screen:

```
Non-system disk or disk error.
Replace and strike any key when ready.
```

or

```
Insert disk with COMMAND.COM
and strike any key when ready.
```

or

```
Insert disk with batch file
and press any key when ready.
```

The first message occurs when the PC is booting and the disk in drive A: does not have a copy of all the required operating system files on it. If you get the first message after you run a program, it means the program is terminating by rebooting your system. That's not very polite, but some primitive programs do it that way.

The transient section of COMMAND.COM that includes all the internal commands is not needed while another program is running. But once a program terminates, your system does need this section, so the resident part of COMMAND.COM performs the checksum calculation mentioned above. If it can't find COMMAND.COM on the disk, it prints the message:

```
Insert disk with COMMAND.COM
and strike any key when ready.
```

Usually, the transient part of COMMAND.COM looks for COMMAND.COM on the disk it was originally loaded from. For a floppy system, this will be drive A:. You can change this, however, if it will later be more convenient to keep COMMAND.COM somewhere else. With DOS 3.x versions you can tell DOS to look for COMMAND.COM elsewhere by changing the COMSPEC variable in the environment string. If you're using a RAMdisk as drive C:, for instance, you can enter:

```
COPY COMMAND.COM C:
SET COMSPEC=C:\COMMAND.COM
```

Under DOS 2.x, this won't work. You have to load a secondary copy of COMMAND and specify the search path as a parameter:

```
COPY COMMAND.COM C:
COMMAND C:\COMMAND.COM
```

Copying COMMAND.COM onto a RAMdisk and then telling your system you've done so can speed up operation significantly after memory-hungry programs have finished.

The third error message from the above list:

```
Insert disk with batch file
and press any key when ready.
```

means that the program was invoked from a batch file and COMMAND.COM needs the rest of the batch file to continue. What's annoying is that you'll get the third message even if the batch file has just executed its last line. But this message is the easiest to get rid of. Just press Ctrl-Break. You'll be asked if you want to terminate the batch file. Answer with a Y.

If you have a batch file called SAMPLE.BAT and you want a permanent record of its execution, you can't get one by redirecting the output with a command like:

```
SAMPLE.BAT > LOGFILE
```

However, 2.x versions of DOS let you use COMMAND.COM to do it. First, add a final line to your batch file that says:

```
EXIT
```

Then type:

```
COMMAND > LOGFILE
```

This will load a second version of COMMAND.COM and redirect all activity into it. You won't be able to see anything on your screen at this point. Type in the name of your batch file very carefully. The batch file will run normally, then execute the EXIT command when it's done and return to the first version of COMMAND.COM. To see what went on, just inspect the LOGFILE file.

With later versions of DOS, you can try:

```
COMMAND /C SAMPLE.BAT > LOGFILE
```

(replacing SAMPLE.BAT with the actual name of the batch file you want to execute and any parameters you want to pass to it).

You can also record batch activity by typing Ctrl-PrtSc or Ctrl-P to toggle on your system's printer echo feature. Press Ctrl-PrtSc or Ctrl-P when you're done to turn this feature off. While it's on, everything that appears onscreen will also be sent to your printer (unless you're doing something tricky that your printer can't figure out).

SYS

These days there's no excuse for doing anything with floppy disks other than using them to back up your data or move information to another system.

However, some diehards still work on floppy-based systems, and some pesky copy-protected software still forces users to boot from floppies. Booting from a diskette means that the floppy has to have the three DOS system files on it. However, each new, improved version of DOS is even more bloated than the one before it. And sometimes there's almost no room left on your floppies for the fat new system files.

To upgrade the DOS version on a bootable disk, you'd normally use SYS to transfer the new IBMBIO.COM and IBMDOS.COM files (or their generic equivalents) to the old disk, then use COPY to install the new version of COMMAND.COM.

But this may not always be so easy.

Each disk contains a tiny single-sector 512-byte boot record that reads IBMBIO and IBMDOS from the disk and loads them into memory. It's handicapped greatly because IBMBIO and IBMDOS know all about using files and the disk, but the boot record can't use them because the files aren't in memory yet.

Because of this handicap, the boot record requires that IBMBIO.COM and IBMDOS.COM be the first two directory entries and that IBMBIO.COM be at the beginning of the disk data area in *contiguous sectors*. (The IBMDOS.COM can be anywhere on the disk.)

The problem is that DOS has grown so much that diskettes prepared for earlier DOS versions do not have enough room for the later IBMBIO files. A floppy containing a once-popular version of *1-2-3* (1A) allocated 1,920 bytes for IBMBIO.COM and 6,400 bytes for IBMDOS.COM. Under DOS version 3.1 IBMBIO.COM grew to 9,564 bytes. For PC-DOS 3.2, it ballooned to 16,368 bytes. The 4.01 version was 32,816 and DOS 5.0's MSDOS.SYS needs 37,394 bytes of space.

To fix a situation like this, you have to get rid of the file temporarily that prevents IBMBIO.COM from being stored in contiguous sectors. In the case of the *1-2-3* (1A) system disk, this file is the first one you see when you do a DIR command, or run 123.EXE.

So you would first use the COPY command to transfer 123.EXE to another diskette. Next (assuming you have the DOS disk in the default drive A: and the *1-2-3* system disk in drive B:) you'd execute the following commands:

```
DEL B:123.EXE
SYS B:
COPY COMMAND.COM B:
```

Finally, you would copy the 123.EXE file back to its old floppy.

The copy protection used in *1-2-3* (1A) was innocuous so you can safely copy files to other diskettes and then copy them back. Other copy-protected software may require that all the files be in certain sectors, and the above technique won't work with those disks.

FDISK

Fooling around with your hard disk can be very dangerous. Don't even think of doing it if you're not totally backed up or if you're the least bit nervous about it. But because you may have a strange hardware configuration, a funny version of DOS, or some other bizarre and potentially troublesome system quirk, don't try these tricks unless you follow every instruction to the letter and take full responsibility for anything that happens.

When you first turn on your PC or reboot with Ctrl-Alt-Del, ROM BIOS first checks out and initializes your system. BIOS then attempts to load into memory the first sector of the first surface of the first track of the diskette in drive A. The first sector on a diskette contains a single-sector *bootstrap loader* program. If the diskette is bootable, the bootstrap loader loads the rest of the operating system into memory. The operating system is effectively pulling itself up by its own bootstraps, which is why a system reset is called a boot.

On a hard disk system, the BIOS will first attempt to boot from drive A:. If drive A: does not contain a diskette or the drive door is open, the BIOS then attempts to boot from the hard disk. Again, it reads into memory the first sector of the first surface of the first cylinder of the hard disk. If this sector contained a bootstrap loader like the one on a disk-ette, the hard disk could accommodate only one operating system.

Instead, the first sector on a hard disk contains another small *partition loader* program and some partition information. The format of this partition information is documented in IBM's *DOS Technical Reference* manual. Only 16 bytes are required for each partition. These 16 bytes contain a code to identify the operating system, the starting and ending sectors of each partition on the hard disk, and which partition is bootable.

The partition loader searches through the partition information to determine which partition is marked as bootable. Each partition contains its own bootstrap loader in the first sector of the partition. So, all the partition loader need do is load the bootstrap loader for the bootable partition and then let the bootstrap loader take over.

In summary, for a diskette, the BIOS loads the bootstrap loader and the bootstrap loader loads the operating system. For a hard disk, the BIOS loads the partition loader, the partition loader loads the bootstrap loader for the bootable partition, and the bootstrap loader loads the operating system.

The program that lets you juggle hard disk partitions is FDISK, which can divide a hard disk into one, two, three, or four separate partitions. Each of these partitions can accommodate a different operating system. Most people use the whole hard disk for DOS and thus have only one partition on the hard disk. When you first set up a system with a hard disk, you have to use FDISK to define a DOS partition even before you use FORMAT. (Often this is done by the computer store, so if you're using a hard disk and have never used FDISK, don't worry about it.)

If you use FDISK to define more than one partition on your hard disk, FDISK lets you mark one (and only one) of these partitions as "active," which means that it's bootable. If you boot from the hard disk, the operating system in that partition will be the one that comes up.

For a partitioned hard disk, you have several ways to choose one operating system over another when you boot up your machine:

Even if the DOS partition is not marked as bootable, you can still access the DOS partition if you boot DOS from a diskette. So, if you had two partitions on your hard disk — DOS and something else — you could use the DOS partition if you boot DOS from a diskette and the "something else" partition if you boot from the hard disk. The choice between the two partitions simply depends upon the drive A: door being open or not.

Or, you could boot up DOS from a diskette, use FDISK to change the partition, then reboot from hard disk. This is fairly fast and if you do it a lot, you may want to set up a special disk that calls FDISK from an AUTOEXEC.BAT file.

Be very careful — experimenting with hard disk partitions is best done with a clean hard disk or a hard disk with disposable data. Changing the size of the DOS partition with FDISK wipes out the DOS partition (or at least the FAT and directory information). FDISK will warn you about this. Heed the warning.

If you're using a hard disk that seems to devour more than its share of space, you might be able to make things more efficient by reducing the cluster size. Might. And again, you have to very careful about this.

The entire data area of a hard disk is divided into smaller areas called clusters. Files on a disk are always stored in one or more clusters. If the file does not fill up the last cluster it occupies, then the rest of the space in that cluster is lost. The number of bytes in each file reported by the DIR command is the size of the file when it was created or last modified. The amount of space that file actually requires on the disk is the size of the file rounded up to the next multiple of the cluster size.

On average, you would probably lose about half a cluster for each file on the disk. It might be more if you have a lot of small files less than half the cluster size.

You can easily determine the cluster size for a particular disk. First, do a DIR and note the "bytes free" value. Then create a very small file. The easiest method is with the command:

```
ECHO > SMALLFIL
```

Do another DIR and see how much space you've lost. That's your cluster size. DOS 4.0 and 5.0 report the size of the cluster, which are called "allocation units."

The cluster size is always a power of 2 and for most normal disks, a multiple of 512. Some RAMdisks may have cluster sizes of 128 or 256, but real disks have cluster sizes of 512, 1,024, 2,048, 4,096, and 8,192 bytes. For a single-sided floppy diskette, the cluster size is 512 bytes. For a double-sided diskette, it's 512 or 1,024 bytes. For a ten-megabyte hard disk, the cluster size can be 4,096 bytes.

For hard disks larger than ten megabytes, the cluster size is dependent upon the DOS version used when originally configuring the disk using FDISK and FORMAT. A 20-megabyte hard disk originally configured under DOS 2.x has a cluster size of 8,192 bytes.

A cluster size of 8,192 bytes is absurdly large, and is the result of the method introduced way back in DOS 1.0 for storing files on a disk. This method limited the total number of clusters on a disk to 4,078 (4,096 minus a handful of cluster numbers used for special purposes).

With DOS 3.0, the total number of clusters possible on a hard disk was increased to 65,518, which let users make the cluster size on a hard disk smaller. A 20- or 30-megabyte hard disk that has been FDISKed and formatted under DOS 3.x has a cluster size of 2,048 bytes, because DOS 3.x allows cluster sizes on a hard disk to be represented by 16-bit values instead of 12-bit values. However, DOS 2.x can work only with the old 12-bit FAT.

It's a good thing that DOS 2.x doesn't even recognize the 20-megabyte hard disk formatted under DOS 3.x. If it assumed that the FAT contained 12-bit values, it could easily scramble up the FAT beyond recognition. Since the FAT is the most critical part of a disk, this would be a very serious problem.

How does DOS 2.x know enough to leave the disk alone? It's all in the partition table. A hard disk can be divided into one to four partitions, each of which may contain a different operating system. A table with the partition information is stored on the first sector of the disk. Each partition has a *system indicator*, which is a one-byte value that denotes the operating system of the partition. DOS 2.x uses a 01 to indicate a DOS partition. DOS 3.x uses a value of 01 for a DOS partition with a 12-bit FAT and 04 for a DOS partition with a 16-bit FAT. A value of 5 means an extended partition, while 6 means it's a DOS 4.0 or later monster drive. So, when DOS 2.x looks at the hard disk partition table and sees only that 04 system indicator, it thinks the partition is non-DOS even though it really is a DOS partition.

You'll experience this DOS 2.x incompatibility only with hard disks greater than ten megabytes formatted under DOS 3.x. A normal PC-XT ten-megabyte disk can be used by either DOS 2.x or DOS 3.x or later regardless of the formatting.

With 65,518 clusters available, it's theoretically possible to have a cluster size of 512 bytes for a 20- or 30-megabyte disk, but you really don't want a cluster size that small. Since files are stored in noncontiguous areas of a disk, a small cluster size would mean that files could become overly fragmented, which could slow down file access time.

Prior to DOS 3.0 (which was introduced at the same time as the IBM PC-AT) IBM did not sell a hard disk over ten megabytes. The original PC-AT had IBM's first 20-megabyte hard disk. Although it's possible to install a 20- or 30-megabyte drive on a

PC or XT running DOS 2.x, nobody working with strict IBM parts ever had a cluster size over 4,096 bytes. The problem of these excessively large cluster sizes was fixed only when IBM introduced a 20-megabyte hard disk. In one sense, it's not even IBM's problem if you have a 8,192 byte cluster size.

So, what can you do about this? If you have a hard disk over ten megabytes originally configured under DOS 2.x, you can usually reconfigure it under DOS 3.x to get a smaller cluster size.

Warning: don't even think of trying the techniques mentioned in this section unless every single one of your files is absolutely currently backed up, and you're working with a brand new blank hard disk, and you know what you're doing, and you take all the responsibility for any bizarre effects. Otherwise, just read along.

This assumes that your C: hard disk is connected to a hard disk controller card that has its own ROM BIOS, that you don't need anything special in a CONFIG.SYS file to use the hard disk, and that you (or somebody at your computer store) originally configured the hard disk by running the normal FDISK and FORMAT command included in IBM's PC-DOS. It also assumes you're using a version of PC-DOS 3.2 or later.

First, you must back up your entire hard disk. Do it twice to play it safe. For your 12 megabytes of files, you'll need about six boxes of diskettes for two backups. Buy high quality diskettes for this. Format them all before you begin. Don't use any that have bad sectors.

The BACKUP command you want is:

```
BACKUP C:\*.* A: /S
```

which backs up everything on drive C: in all subdirectories. BACKUP will prompt you to put in new diskettes. Label them in sequence.

When you're done with the backup, boot up PC-DOS from drive A:, and run FDISK by typing:

```
FDISK
```

One of the FDISK menu options is to delete the existing DOS partition. Do this first. Then create a DOS partition, which is another menu option. You probably want to use the entire hard disk for DOS, so answer yes to that question. Your system will now reboot. Make sure the DOS diskette is still in drive A:.

When you get back to the DOS prompt, format the hard disk with:

```
FORMAT C:/S/V
```

After this is done, you can verify that everything is running smoothly by doing a DIR and a CHKDSK on drive C:. You can try rebooting with the drive A: door open. Your machine should boot from the hard disk. At this point, you can create a small file to see if your cluster size is indeed smaller. It should be 2,048 bytes.

Boot up again from the floppy. Now you can proceed to RESTORE the backed-up files onto your hard disk with the RESTORE command:

```
RESTORE A: C:\*.* /S /P
```

This whole process can be very scary and you may encounter some "gotchas" along the way. Here are some of them:

First, some copy-protected programs installed on a hard disk may not work after a BACKUP and RESTORE. Others will. Some of the problem programs (Lotus *1-2-3 Release 2*, for instance) can be deinstalled. If you have any of these programs, deinstall them from the hard disk before you begin and reinstall them when you're all done. When in doubt, contact the manufacturer. (After they give you the information you need, tell them what you think about copy protection. Use whatever language you feel appropriate.)

Second, people have sometimes had problems with BACKUP and RESTORE. Sometimes RESTORE chokes in the middle of restoring from a bunch of diskettes. That's why you should do two backups. You may want to take other precautions: your hard disk probably has a number of purchased programs on it and a number of your own data files in various subdirectories. You can probably recreate those purchased programs from the original diskettes. For your own data files, particularly the ones most valuable to you, use the regular COPY or XCOPY command to copy them to diskettes.

Third, if you're using a version of DOS older than 3.3, BACKUP will back up hidden and read-only files, including the DOS files called IBMBIO.COM and IBMDOS.COM. When you run RESTORE, you want to use the /P switch as shown above, which prompts you when it is about to backup over existing read-only files. When you get the prompt for IBMBIO.COM and IBMDOS.COM, answer NO. DOS 4.0 and 5.0 do this automatically.

Older versions of RESTORE will copy the old version of COMMAND.COM from the backed up floppies to your hard disk. When you are done with the RESTORE, copy COMMAND.COM from your newest DOS floppy diskette to the root directory of the hard disk with the command:

```
COPY COMMAND.COM C:\
```

If you booted from the newly formatted hard disk before running RESTORE, DOS will try to load the COMMAND.COM from the hard disk after RESTORE is completed. But this would be the old COMMAND.COM. This is why you should boot from your latest DOS floppy before beginning RESTORE. When RESTORE ends, you will be prompted to put the DOS disk in drive A:, so it can find the correct version of COMMAND.COM.

DOS 3.3 solved these system-file problems by modifying RESTORE so it won't restore IBMBIO.COM, IBMDOS.COM, or COMMAND.COM. However, because it won't restore these files, you have to use SYS to put these system files back on your hard disk, and then use the COPY command to put COMMAND.COM back. Nobody said it would be easy.

Fourth, after you're done with the RESTORE, your hard disk will still contain copies of all the external DOS programs (such as CHKDSK and MODE) from your old DOS version. You should replace these with the latest DOS versions. More recent copies of DOS have a command called REPLACE that automates this process.

Fifth, sometimes after all this, funny things happen. For instance, you may not be able to boot from drive C:. If this is the case, boot from a new DOS floppy and get into FDISK again. Choose "Change the Active Partition" in the menu. If the status of the DOS partition is marked "N," it means it's nonactive and you can't boot from it. Make it active. Sometimes just entering and leaving FDISK fixes the problem.

If you think that your hard disk still has the old DOS IBMBIO, IBMDOS, or COMMAND files on it, you can boot from your new DOS floppy and execute the commands:

```
SYS C:
```

and:

```
COPY COMMAND.COM C:\
```

This will reinstall the newest version of DOS on your hard disk.

Sixth, if you have a tape backup unit and you would rather use that instead of BACKUP and RESTORE, you should determine whether it does a file-by-file backup or an "image" backup. Many tape backup units give you a choice. You want to do a file-by- file backup. If your tape backup unit can only do an image backup, don't use it. The image stored on the tape will include the hard disk's FAT and this will be a different format under newer DOS versions. When you restore the hard disk from the imaged tape, the old File Allocation Table will be copied back to the disk. No good. If you do a file-by-file backup and restore, it will probably copy over the DOS files. Boot your new version of DOS from drive A: and do the SYS command and COPY of COMMAND.COM before you try booting from the hard disk.

Seventh, after you've used DOS 3.x or later FDISK on a 20-megabyte or bigger disk, you cannot use the hard disk with any DOS version prior to 3.0. If you boot up from a DOS 2.x floppy, DOS simply will not recognize the hard disk. Some people (program developers, mainly) need to test programs under several DOS versions. These people may need to have their hard disks recognizable by DOS 2.x. They shouldn't reconfigure their hard disk.

Finally, this whole discussion is based on the IBM version of MS-DOS (which is called "Personal Computer DOS" by IBM and commonly called "PC-DOS" by the rest of us). Some versions of MS-DOS for other manufacturer's machines may not support the smaller cluster size, so doing this will not have any effect. Again, when in doubt, contact the manufacturer.

If in doubt, don't try any of this.

DOS Filters

One of the most useful features of DOS versions starting with 2.0 is the ability to *pipe* or *redirect* data.

These later versions of DOS provide five standard input and output devices (standard input, output, error, auxiliary, and printer) and let you reshuffle the way these devices handle their input and output. For instance, while programs normally receive input from the keyboard and display output on the screen, you could easily reroute things so that a program receives input from a disk file and sends output to your printer.

To give you added power, DOS provides three special programs called filters that can comb through the data on its way from one part of your system to another: MORE.COM, SORT.EXE, and FIND.EXE. You can use MORE to display text a screenful at a time, SORT to arrange the contents of your files in sorted order, and the multitalented FIND to hunt through files for specific strings of characters, count the number of lines in your files, and even add line numbers to your text.

The accompanying disks contain several other useful filters that do useful things like redirect output to two devices, and improve on the DOS MORE and SORT commands.

DOS uses three command-line operators to handle redirection and piping: <, >, and |. The command:

```
DIR > DIRLIST
```

redirects output by taking the directory information that would normally appear onscreen and sending it instead into a disk file called DIRLIST. Similarly, the command:

```
SORT < DIRLIST
```

would redirect input by using the contents of the DIRLIST file as input for the SORT filter rather than keystrokes from the keyboard. The output of this process would go to the screen, and you'd see a directory listing sorted in alphabetical filename order.

(You could even combine redirected input and output on the same line, by adapting this command to:

```
SORT < DIRLIST > DIRLIST.SRT
```

DOS would then take the raw, unsorted DIRLIST file, redirect it as input into the SORT program, and redirect the output into a new alphabetically sorted file called DIR-LIST.SRT.)

By executing the first two commands one after the other, you could produce a sorted directory listing:

```
DIR > DIRLIST
SORT < DIRLIST
```

However, this would leave a file on your disk called DIRLIST that you'd have to erase later. What you really want to do is combine the two lines into one command. But you can't do it with a command like:

```
DIR > SORT
```

Instead, use the | piping symbol:

```
DIR | SORT
```

When you pipe the output of DIR into SORT, DOS will create its own temporary files in the root directory of your disk to hold the information normally sent to standard output by the DIR command. Then it will redirect standard input so this temporary file feeds into the SORT program. When it's done, DOS will automatically delete the temporary files it created.

If you're in the root directory when you try this, you may see two strange files with names like:

```
0D102A1F       0       6-01-88       1:16p
0D102A25       0       6-01-88       1:16p
```

These zero-length files with eight-digit hexadecimal filenames are the temporary files DOS creates during the redirection process.

Recent DOS versions use the PC's clock to derive names for the temporary files, which is why they look like numbers. DOS 2.x gave the temporary files names with the word PIPE in them, which is at least a hint at what they did:

```
%PIPE1      $$$      0       6-01-88       1:16p
%PIPE2      $$$      0       6-01-88       1:16p
```

All temporary PIPE files have 0 bytes lengths since DOS displays the directory listings after it created the files and opened them for input but before it had a chance to close them.

You can also use piping to execute several programs or commands in sequence. For instance, if you had a \GAMES subdirectory and a program in it called CHESS.COM, you could first change directories and then run CHESS by typing:

```
CD \GAMES  |  CHESS
```

If you had another game called CHECKERS.COM in the same subdirectory, you could do the above and then run CHECKERS immediately after CHESS by typing:

```
CD GAMES  |  CHESS  |  CHECKERS
```

While this doesn't work with all DOS commands, it does let you combine certain operations together into one line. To see how this works, type in the following one-line batch file called THISFILE.BAT that creates a subdirectory called TEMP one level lower than the directory you are currently using, copies itself into this new subdirectory, logs into it, and then does a directory listing:

```
MD TEMP | COPY THISFILE.BAT TEMP | CD TEMP | DIR
```

Actually, DOS provides a fourth redirection operator: >>. When you use the double >> symbol, DOS will create a new file for output if the specified file doesn't already exist, but will append information to an existing file without overwriting any old information already in the file. If you use a single > symbol, DOS will always overwrite any existing information.

So if you don't already have a file called DIRLIST on your disk, both of these commands will work identically:

- DIR | SORT > DIRLIST
- DIR | SORT >> DIRLIST

As will DOS 5.0's DIR /O:N > DIRLIST.

But if your disk already contains a DIRLIST file, the first command will wipe it out and replace it with the sorted directory listing, while the second command will just tack the new sorted directory listing onto the end of the existing DIRLIST file.

When you issue a command like DIR | SORT without any parameters after it, DOS assumes you want to sort alphabetically starting with the first character on each line. If SORT finds lines with the same first character, it will look at the second character to break the tie. If these are the same, it will keep looking at the next column until it finds a difference.

SORT arranges text by looking at the ASCII value of each character. The decimal ASCII value of a lowercase "a" is 97 while the value of an uppercase "A" is 65. However, DOS 2.x and later versions sort characters differently. DOS 2.x was case-sensitive, and would arrange a character string like "AAA" before one like "aaa" since the ASCII value of initial uppercase "A" is lower than its lowercase counterpart. Later versions gave lowercase letters the same value as their uppercase versions and treat high-bit accented foreign-language characters the same as their normal low-bit unaccented cousins.

So if you asked DOS 2.0 or 2.1 to sort a file called DATA.RAW that contained the three lines:

```
banana
AVOCADO
apple
```

with the command:

```
SORT < DATA.RAW
```

you'd end up with:

```
AVOCADO
apple
banana
```

But if you tried the same command under more recent versions, you'd get:

```
apple
AVOCADO
banana
```

You can use two different syntaxes for many identical filter operations. For example, if your disk contains a long text file called LONGTEXT, and you tried to view the contents with the command:

```
TYPE LONGTEXT
```

DOS would scroll the display rapidly off your screen before you had a chance to read it. You could pause and then restart the scrolling process by pressing Ctrl-S repeatedly, but this takes too much concentration and is too imprecise. Instead, just send the output of the TYPE command through the MORE.COM filter with:

```
TYPE LONGFILE | MORE
```

DOS will start displaying information, then pause automatically when the screen fills. If you press just about any key, DOS will then display another screenful, and repeat the process until it reaches what it thinks is the end of the file.

You could do the same thing with the command:

```
MORE < LONGFILE
```

Similarly, if you wanted to sort the above DATA.RAW file, you could do it either with:

```
TYPE DATA.RAW | SORT
```

or:

```
SORT < DATA.RAW
```

But be very careful about which way you point the redirection symbol. While:

```
SORT < DATA.RAW
```

will sort the contents of your DATA.RAW file, turning the symbol around:

```
SORT > DATA.RAW
```

will *wipe out* your DATA.RAW file. This is because DOS thinks you want a new file called DATA.RAW to be the output of the SORT process rather than to serve as the input. So it opens the DATA.RAW file and erases everything already in it.

Similarly, typing:

```
DIR | MORE
```

will display your files a screen at a time (as will DIR /P), but typing:

```
DIR > MORE
```

will create a new file called MORE and redirect your directory listing into it. It won't damage the MORE filter, since its real name is MORE.COM.

When a redirection symbol is pointing *into* a filter, DOS will treat the file on the other side of the symbol as a source of input. When a redirection symbol is pointing *out of*, or away from, a filter, DOS will treat any filename on the other side of the symbol as an output file.

If you're using a redirection symbol rather than a piping symbol, the name of the DOS filter has to be the first thing after the DOS prompt. So:

```
C>SORT < DATA.RAW
```

will work just fine, while:

```
C>DATA.RAW > SORT
```

won't do anything other than generate a "Bad command or filename" error, since DOS will view the period between DATA and RAW as a space, and look for a command or executable file named DATA. If you happened to have a file called DATA.COM, DATA.EXE, or DATA.BAT handy, DOS would run it.

When you have the choice, it's more efficient to use redirection than piping. To see the comparison, try running two slightly different sets of batch files that display the contents of all the batch files in your current subdirectory one at a time. Once you've created all four files, see the difference in speed by first running SCANBAT1 and then running SCANBAT2. The first pair, SCANBAT1.BAT and READ1.BAT, use piping:

```
REM SCANBAT1.BAT
ECHO OFF
FOR %%F IN (*.BAT) DO COMMAND /C READ1 %%F

REM READ1.BAT
```

```
ECHO OFF
CLS
ECHO %1
TYPE %1 | MORE
PAUSE
```

The second pair, SCANBAT2.BAT and READ2.BAT, use redirection:

```
REM SCANBAT2.BAT
ECHO OFF
FOR %%F IN (*.BAT) DO COMMAND /C READ2 %%F
```

```
REM READ2.BAT
ECHO OFF
CLS
ECHO %1
MORE < %1
PAUSE
```

The workhorse line in READ2.BAT:

```
MORE < %1
```

is far faster than its equivalent in READ1.BAT:

```
TYPE %1 | MORE
```

(Again, you can speed things up even more by substituting CALL in place of COM-MAND /C for any DOS version 3.3 or later.)

You can have the SORT command start sorting on a column other than the first one. Just add a /+ and a column number after the SORT command.

A normal directory listing looks something like:

```
FILE      001       11759   10-01-87      5:34p
FILE      002        2176   10-02-88      2:45p
FILE      003    11454457   10-03-86     11:27p
```

col 1	col 10	col 14	col 24	col 30	col 34
name	ext	size	month	year	time

The filename itself starts on column 1. The filename extension begins on column 10, its size on column 14, its date on column 24, and its time on column 34.

To sort this list of files by size using SORT, type:

```
DIR | SORT /+14
```

If you wanted to sort them by size, but in reverse order, just add a /R:

```
DIR | SORT /+14 /R
```

or:

```
DIR | SORT /R /+14
```

These numbers are hard to remember. You can create one big SD.BAT (for Sorted Directory) batch file that makes it easy to see any sort of directory listing you want:

```
ECHO OFF
SET DEV=CON
IF %1!==! GOTO OOPS
FOR %%A IN (N n E e S s D d T t) DO IF %1==%%A GOTO OKAY
GOTO OOPS
:OKAY
IF %3!==! GOTO NOTHIRD
SET DEV=%3
IF %2==/r GOTO CHEKNAME
IF %2==/R GOTO CHEKNAME
GOTO OOPS
:CHEKNAME
ECHO This will create a file called %3
ECHO If this is not what you want, press
ECHO Ctrl-C then answer Y. Otherwise,
PAUSE
GOTO MAIN
:NOTHIRD
IF %2!==! GOTO MAIN
IF %2==/r GOTO MAIN
IF %2==/R GOTO MAIN
ECHO This will create a file called %2
ECHO If this is not what you want, press
ECHO Ctrl-C then answer Y. Otherwise,
PAUSE
SET DEV=%2
:MAIN
GOTO %1
:N
DIR | SORT %2 > %DEV%
GOTO END
:E
DIR | SORT /+10 %2 > %DEV%
GOTO END
:S
```

```
DIR | SORT /+14 %2 > %DEV%
GOTO END
:D
DIR | SORT /+24 %2 > %DEV%
GOTO END
:T
DIR | SORT /+34 %2 > %DEV%
GOTO END
:OOPS
ECHO You can sort by name, extension, size, date or time
ECHO by following %0 with a N or E or S or D or T, eg:
ECHO %0 N or %0 n or %0 E
ECHO To sort in reverse order, add a /R, eg:
ECHO %0 N /R or %0 n /r or %0 E /r
ECHO To put the results into a file, add a filename, eg:
ECHO %0 S /R DIRSORTR.FIL or %0 S DIRSORT.FIL
:END
IF %DEV%==CON GOTO BYE
IF %DEV%!==! GOTO BYE
ECHO Now enter: TYPE %DEV%
:BYE
SET DEV=
```

This is a lot of work to go through to get the equivalent of the new DOS 5.0 DIR options, but it shows how versatile SORT can be.

Early versions of DOS may erroneously turn ECHO back on at the end of the batch file. If this happens, stick an ECHO OFF at the offending point.

This batch file is somewhat complicated because it can accept so many different syntaxes and because it tries hard to screen out invalid entries.

If you enter just SD without any parameters, or with invalid parameters, the batch file will jump to the :OOPS label and print instructions. Here's a summary of what the program will do for you:

Sort in Order Of	*Syntax*
Name	SD N (or) SD n
Extension	SD E (or) SD e
Size	SD S (or) SD s
Date	SD D (or) SD D
Time	SD T (or) SD T
Reverse name	SD N /R (or) SD n /R
Reverse extension	SD E /R (or) SD e /R
Reverse size	SD S /R (or) SD s /R
Reverse date	SD D /R (or) SD D /R
Reverse time	SD T /R (or) SD T /R

(Actually, you could substitute /r in place of /R.)

The %0 variables in the ECHO statements following the :OOPS label will make sure that the instructions accurately reflect the batch file's name if you decide to rename it to something like DIRSORT.BAT.

The long test line:

```
FOR %%A IN (N n E e S s D d T t) DO IF %1==%%A GOTO OKAY
```

screens out any sorting parameters that aren't valid. Then it uses the:

```
GOTO %1
```

command to jump execution to the proper batch label, so if you enter S because you wanted to sort by size, the batch file will jump to the :S label. DOS is normally case-sensitive about everything, but it automatically capitalizes labels, so it will jump to the :S label whether you typed SD S or SD s.

The lines that look like:

```
IF %1!==! GOTO OOPS
```

and:

```
IF %2!==! GOTO MAIN
```

and:

```
IF %3!==! GOTO NOTHIRD
```

test to see how many parameters you entered. When you enter a command at the DOS prompt, DOS sets the value of a replaceable parameter called %0 with the name of the command (or executable file) itself. Then it sees if you typed anything after the name of the command or file and sets additional replaceable parameters values accordingly. So if you entered:

```
SD E /R
```

DOS would set the following parameter values:

```
%0 = SD
%1 = E
%2 = /R
```

SD.BAT gives you two options for handling the results of the various directory sorts. You can either have it display the results onscreen (the default) or redirect the results into a file. If you specify a valid filename as a third parameter, SD.BAT will create a file and redirect the sorted listing into it. You may also skip the /R parameter and add a filename as the second parameter.

To give you the option of sending the sorted results to the screen or to a file, SD.BAT uses an environment variable called %DEV%. It first sets the value of %DEV% to CON. If you didn't enter a filename, DOS will substitute CON for %DEV: and turn the line:

```
DIR | SORT /+14 %2 > %DEV%
```

into:

```
DIR | SORT /+14 %2 > CON
```

Here the CON output device stands for the screen, so redirecting output to CON displays the sorted listing on your monitor.

However, if you stuck a filename onto the end:

```
SD S DIRSORT.FIL
```

or:

```
SD S /R DIRSORT.FIL
```

SD.BAT will redefine %DEV% to the filename you entered. The tricky part is that this filename can either be the second or third thing that you enter on the command like after the SD, since you can add an optional /R as the second parameter.

The %DEV% variable doesn't hog much room in the environment, but if yours is already crammed to the gills you may get an error message telling you you're out of environment space. If so, you'll have to make your environment a bit bigger. See the chapter on environments for details.

You can try the same kind of device switching if you program in BASIC. Many programmers who write routines that send output to the printer first write them to display on the screen. This saves paper and makes debugging a lot easier.

The technique involves using PRINT # instead of the normal PRINT command. Before executing any of these PRINT # statements OPEN the screen (SCRN:) for output (e.g., OPEN "SCRN:" FOR OUTPUT AS #1).

Then, whenever the PRINT # statement executes, the output will go to the screen just as it would if it were using an ordinary PRINT statement. If you want a hardcopy version of the same output, CLOSE the file and OPEN it again using your printer as the output device (e.g., OPEN "LPT1:" FOR OUTPUT AS #1).

If you try this, avoid using commands like LOCATE statements that would confuse your printer. A sample routine might look like:

```
100 ' DEVSHIFT.BAS
110 '
120 PRINT "Where should the output go — "
130 PRINT TAB(10);"1 — Screen"
140 PRINT TAB(10);"2 — Printer
```

```
150 I$=INKEY$:IF I$="" THEN 150
160 ON VAL(I$) GOTO 180,190
170 BEEP:GOTO 150
180 OPEN "SCRN:" FOR OUTPUT AS #1:GOTO 230
190 OPEN "LPT1:" FOR OUTPUT AS #1
200 '
210 '   ** program continues here **
220 '
230 PRINT #1, "This is a test"
```

If you do try sorting your files, make sure that similar entries all begin in the same column. SORT will work well with a fixed-field data base but not with a random access file. Fixed field files look like:

```
Allenovitch   Paul      345 Hilltop Lane
Ballmerski    Steve     10 Maple Avenue
Kingstein     Adrian    98612 Hideaway Heights
```

A random-access or comma-delimited version of this might be:

```
Allenovitch,Paul,345 Hilltop Lane
Ballmerski,Steve,10 Maple Avenue
Kingstein,Adrian,98612 Hideaway Heights
```

If you wanted to sort on first names, you'd be able to do it on the fixed-field version.

SORT also won't work on any file longer than 63K. A pity. And it needs to see carriage returns at the ends of the lines it's sorting. Many applications have their own sorting routines that use faster algorithms, but for quick and dirty DOS tasks, SORT works just fine.

FIND is one of the most versatile DOS commands. When combined with other DOS commands and features, it can track down long-forgotten files, scan across hundreds of files in a subdirectory for matching strings, and even give you a rudimentary address book with an automatic lookup feature.

Most users clutter their root directory with dozens of miscellaneous or temporary files. The ideal root directory, however, should contain only your first level of subdirectories and the critical files COMMAND.COM, CONFIG.SYS, and AUTOEXEC.BAT. This way, typing:

```
DIR \
```

will give you an index to the main subdirectory structure of your hard disk.

While DOS will print out a list of subdirectories if you type:

```
DIR *.
```

the list will also include any filename that lacks an extension. The DOS manual provides a better way, using FIND:

```
DIR | FIND "<DIR>"
```

Actually, to prevent wear and tear on your fingers, all you have to enter is:

```
DIR | FIND "<"
```

However, this will show you only the subdirectories in your root directory. For a quick onscreen list of all your subdirectories, type either:

```
TREE | FIND "Path"
```

or:

```
CHKDSK /V | FIND "Dir"
```

For a permanent copy, redirect the output into a SUBDIR.LST file:

```
TREE | FIND "Path" > SUBDIR.LST
```

or:

```
CHKDSK /V | FIND "Dir" > SUBDIR.LST
```

In fact, since CHKDSK /V reports every file on your disk in every subdirectory, along with the full path, you can use it to locate a file buried in a subdirectory many levels deep. The FINDFILE.BAT batch file mentioned earlier can find any file on your disk. It's built around the single line:

```
CHKDSK / V | FIND "%1" | MORE
```

(The newer ATTRIB /S command works even better.)

FINDFILE.BAT isn't as fast as dedicated assembly language utilities such as WHERE or SEARCH but it's slightly easier to use, since it lets you locate files by entering just a fragment of the filename. FINDFILE will uncover any matches containing the specified fragment, regardless of whether the match is to the left or right of the dot in the filename.

If you normally use FIND to uncover single words or parts of single words, and you hate typing in the required quotation marks, you can create another small batch file called F.BAT:

```
ECHO OFF
IF %2!==! GOTO OOPS
```

```
FIND "%1" %2
GOTO END
:OOPS
ECHO The format is: %0 STRING FILE
ECHO where STRING is the one-word
ECHO string you want, and FILE is
ECHO the file you're searching
:END
```

While this saves typing, it won't let you hunt for any strings with spaces in them, since it will interpret the word after the first space as the name of the file you want to search. Remember, too, that FIND is case-sensitive, so it won't locate "String" if you tell it to find "string" or "STRING."

DOS can't handle wildcards when executing a normal FIND command, although you can tell it to look through several files in one operation. To have it search through the first three chapters of a book for the text "DOS version" you would use a command like:

```
FIND "DOS version" CHAPTER.1 CHAPTER.2 CHAPTER.3
```

You can have FIND snoop through every file on your disk by using a FOR...IN...DO command in a batch file like the following FINDALL.BAT:

```
ECHO OFF
IF %1!==! GOTO OOPS
FOR %%A IN (*.*) DO FIND "%1" %%A
GOTO END
:OOPS
ECHO You must enter a one-word
ECHO string you want to find
:END
```

This batch file will uncover every matching single-word string in every file in the logged subdirectory. Unfortunately, while it will print each match it finds, it will also print the name of every file it checks, along with a "----------" whether or not it locates a match.

You can normally get rid of such unwanted lines by piping text through a FIND command that includes a /V parameter. If you wanted to see a listing of all the files in a particular directory, but didn't want to see any subdirectories, you could type:

```
DIR | FIND /V "<DIR>"
```

or the shorthand version:

```
DIR | FIND /V "<"
```

If you're currently in a subdirectory bursting with files and you want to see all the files with the letters "COM" in them, you can type:

```
DIR | FIND "COM"
```

and you may see something like:

```
COMFILES   <DIR>         6-05-88   7:46p
WELCOME  HOM    21376    8-27-88  11:32a
INCOMING MAL     6925    2-22-88  10:22p
MORE     COM     2166    6-17-88  12:00p
COMMON   LST     1561    5-22-88  12:00p
PRINT    COM    14024     8-3-88  12:00p
PROCOMM    <DIR>         6-05-88   7:46p
```

To remove the subdirectories from this list, add a FIND /V command:

```
DIR | FIND "COM" | FIND /V "<"
```

and you'll get:

```
WELCOME  HOM    21376    8-27-88  11:32a
INCOMING MAL     6925    2-22-88  10:22p
MORE     COM     2166    6-17-88  12:00p
COMMON   LST     1561    5-22-88  12:00p
PRINT    COM    14024     8-3-88  12:00p
```

(If all you wanted was the COM files, you could of course type:

```
DIR *.COM
```

But this FIND command would do it as well:

```
DIR | FIND " COM"
```

You need the extra space between the quotation marks, since DOS sticks a space between the filename and the extension in all directory listings.)

However, you can't combine FIND commands in a FOR...IN...DO batch command. Changing the third line in FINDALL.BAT to:

```
FOR %%A IN (*.*) DO FIND "%" %%A | FIND /V "---"
```

wouldn't remove the extraneous filenames and "----------" bars. You could do it by adapting FINDALL.BAT so it passes parameters to a second batch file called FA.BAT that does the actual work:

First, the revised FINDALL.BAT:

```
ECHO OFF
IF %1!==! GOTO OOPS
FOR %%A IN (*.*) DO COMMAND /C FA %1 %%A
GOTO END
:OOPS
ECHO You must enter a one-word
ECHO string you want to find
:END
```

Next, FA.BAT:

```
ECHO OFF
FIND "%1" %2 | FIND /V "---"
```

If you're using a DOS version 3.3 or later, you could improve performance slightly by substituting CALL for COMMAND /C.

It's important to time- and date-stamp your files so you'll always know which versions are most current. And by doing so, you can have the DOS FIND filter help locate recent files for you.

If you have a crowded archive subdirectory that contains an important file you know you created in January, but you can't remember what you named the file, you can isolate all your January files by typing:

```
DIR | FIND " 1-"
```

DOS is finicky about what's inside the quotation marks. FIND "1-" would display dates like "11-23-87" and " 3-21-86" since the "1-" string is part of each. The leading space (directly after the initial quotation mark and before the 1) in " 1-" is unique to January. However, if your subdirectory contains files created over several years, FIND " 1-" may display files created in 1/85, 1/86, 1/87, 1/88, etc. To toss out all but 1/88 files, use FIND twice:

```
DIR | FIND " 1-" | FIND "-88"
```

This pipes the entire directory through the January filter, and then filters out everything that doesn't have an 88 in it. If you suspect that this process would uncover lots of files, you can pause the display a screenful at a time by sending the output through the MORE filter:

```
DIR | FIND " 1-" | FIND "-88" | MORE
```

Piping output through one or two filters in a row doesn't degrade performance very much, but a long chain of successive FINDs could drag on for quite a while. Copy the files to a RAMdisk if you can. And if you try it on a crowded floppy disk, you may as well just go out for lunch.

Directory output contains more information than just a listing of files and subdirectories. If want to see your files without the volume serial number and directory information at the top:

```
Volume in drive A is POWER TOOLS
Volume Serial Number is 104F-16CD
Directory of  A:\SUBDIR
```

or the "bytes free" data at the bottom:

```
5 File(s)       295936 bytes free
```

you can type:

```
DIR | FIND /V "e"
```

All four lines of text contain lowercase "e" characters but no filenames can, and the /V will suppress anything with an "e" in it.

One of FIND's least used features is its ability to count your lines. If you were sure every line of all your files contained something common like a space, you could have FIND look for spaces (by specifying " ") and count them. Unfortunately, many files contain lines with nothing on them except carriage returns, or single unspaced words at the end of paragraphs.

However, since presumably no line in any of your files has a ridiculous string like "&@#$" you can use the /V to count how many lines don't contain this. This NUMBER.BAT file will use this trick to give you an accurate line count:

```
ECHO OFF
IF %1!==! GOTO OOPS
ECHO Number of lines:
FIND /C /V "&@#$" %1
GOTO END
:OOPS
ECHO Enter a filename after %0
:END
```

Run this batch file on the revised FINDALL.BAT batch file above and you'll see:

```
Number of lines:
---------- FINDALL.BAT: 8
```

The FIND command can also number all your lines. Again, use the trick of having the /V report all lines without an unlikely string:

```
ECHO OFF
IF %1!==! GOTO OOPS
FIND /V /N "&@#$" %1 | FIND /V "-----"
GOTO END
:OOPS
ECHO Enter a filename after %0
:END
```

Run this batch file on the new FINDALL.BAT and you'll see:

```
[1] ECHO OFF
[2] IF %1!==! GOTO OOPS
[3] FOR %%A IN (*.*) DO COMMAND /C FA %1 %%A
[4] GOTO END
[5] :OOPS
[6] ECHO You must enter a one-word
[7] ECHO string you want to find
[8] :END
```

You can create a brand new file where each line is individually numbered, by redirecting the output to a file (here called NMBRFILE):

```
ECHO OFF
IF %1!==! GOTO OOPS
FIND /V /N "&@#$" %1 | FIND /V "-----" > NMBRFILE
GOTO END
:OOPS
ECHO Enter a filename after %0
:END
```

You can use FIND to clean up many displays and reports. For instance, if you want to see how many bad sectors are on your hard disk and type CHKDSK, DOS will bury this bad-sector information in with a report on the volume name, the amount of free memory, the number of hidden files, etc. But if you filter the output through FIND with:

```
CHKDSK | FIND "bad"
```

all you'll see is how many bytes of bad sectors that DOS uncovered. By putting other strings inside the quotes, you could use this same technique to report just the number of subdirectories, the amount of free space on your disk, the number of files on your disk, etc.

One of the more annoying aspects of DOS is that it won't ordinarily report the time and date without asking you whether you want to reset them. By using FIND, however, you can create two files, T.BAT and D.BAT, that will print the current time and date without any fuss.

T.BAT contains the single line:

```
ECHO ONE | MORE | TIME | FIND "Cu"
```

Similarly, D.BAT is:

```
ECHO ONE | MORE | DATE | FIND "Cu"
```

If you're using a version of DOS 3.3 or later, put a @ at the very beginning of the line so it doesn't display onscreen as it executes. Using the ECHO command starts the whole process, but it doesn't actually print the word ONE. The MORE command supplies the carriage return needed to trigger the DATE and TIME. And the FIND command screens out everything other than the line with the word "Current" on it.

Many RAMdisk users reset their COMSPEC so that DOS looks on the correct drive if it needs to reload COMMAND.COM. What's your current COMSPEC? A single-line batch file called COMSPEC.BAT will let you know:

```
SET | FIND "SP"
```

If you've ever used the TYPE command to snoop inside a COM file to see what text messages it contains, you've probably been annoyed by a profusion of beeps. Whenever TYPE stumbles across an ASCII character 7 it tells DOS to beep the speaker. You can avoid this in examining a beep-filled file like COMMAND.COM, by typing:

```
FIND /V "^G" COMMAND.COM
```

(Note: You don't actually enter the ^G in the above example, although one will show up onscreen when you enter the ASCII 7 bell character. To enter it, after typing in the FIND /V and the initial quotation mark, type Ctrl-G, then type the second quotation mark and the COMMAND.COM filename.)

The above techniques assume you're hunting for single strings only. By piping the output of one FIND command through another FIND command, you can limit your search to the few instances where two specified strings occur in the same line.

Suppose you have a file called NAMEFILE with the following contents:

```
Buddy Jones, 3 Main Street, Boneville, OK
Mary Smith, 1 Park Lane, Washington, DC
Sam Jonesbury, 21 M Street, Washington, DC
```

If you wanted to locate just the Jones who lived in Washington, typing:

```
FIND "Jones" NAMEFILE
```

would report both the Jones you were looking for and the Jonesbury you weren't. You could limit the search to lines containing both "Jones" and "DC" with the command:

```
FIND "Jones" NAMEFILE | FIND "DC"
```

While SORT required fixed-field records, FIND isn't picky. But it is fussy about quotation marks. If you're searching for these you have to wrap each one in its own set of quote marks. Assume you're hunting through a MORETEXT file covering the MORE filter that contains the passages:

```
Unfortunately, the MORE command isn't
really very friendly. After it fills a
screen with text, it prints a terse
message at the bottom: "— More —"
What it really means at this point is
"Hit a key to see additional text."
```

If you want to find occurrences of the string "— More —" you'd have to use a command like:

```
FIND """— More —""" MORETEXT
```

FIND also makes it easy to print a list of files that you've either created or changed on a particular day. If you've been toiling away all day on 12/9/90, and you want to check a particular file you updated early in the morning but have forgotten its name, you can simply type:

```
DIR | FIND "12-09-90" | FIND "a"
```

The first FIND will search for everything created on 12/9 (you must remember to pad single-digit dates with zeros), and the "a" will limit the search only to files created before noon. This assumes, of course, that you properly date- and time-stamp your files.

While you can pipe the output of one FIND search through several others, such repeated FIND sieves can take an awfully long time unless you're working on a fast hard disk or RAMdisk.

The classic use of FIND is to give yourself a lightning-fast address book. First, to build up your NAMEFILE file of names and addresses, create an ADDNAME.BAT batch file with the following contents:

```
ECHO OFF
ECHO Enter up to one line of name
ECHO and address info at a time
ECHO ---
ECHO When all done, press Enter, then
ECHO the F6 key, then Enter again
ECHO ---
ECHO Enter names and addresses now:
COPY NAMEFILE + CON NAMEFILE > NUL
```

Then, whenever you want to add a new name to your master NAMEFILE list, just type ADDNAME and follow the directions onscreen. When you're all done entering new names, be sure to hit the Enter key and then the F6 function key and then the Enter key one last time. The > NUL in ADDNAME.BAT prevents unnecessary text from showing up onscreen.

The actual LOOKUP.BAT batch file that searches through your address book looks like:

```
ECHO OFF
IF %1!==! GOTO OOPS
FIND "%1" NAMEFILE | MORE
GOTO END
:OOPS
ECHO Enter the string to look up after the %0
:END
```

Again, putting quotation marks in the batch file saves you from having to type them in yourself each time you want to look something up, but it also limits you to single-word entries. If you don't mind typing quotation marks from the command line, and you want the ability to search for strings with spaces in them, remove the quotation marks that surround the %1.

If you create your master NAMEFILE properly, you can use this technique to print out the listings for those people living in NY, or with Zip Codes that start with 100.., or who have area codes beginning with 212. And if you add discrete codes to the NAMEF-ILE listing, such as XM to indicate that the person should be on your Christmas card list, you can sort such listings out easily.

Remember, though, that FIND is case sensitive, and that if you're hunting for Empire State listings by searching for "NY," LOOKUP.BAT would also print out a listing for the "PONY RIDERS ASSOCIATION."

You could create a DELNAME.BAT batch file that used redirection and the /V FIND option to delete names:

```
COPY NAMEFILE NAMEFILE.BAK
FIND /V "%1" NAMEFILE.BAK | FIND /V "---" > NAMEFILE
```

This DELNAME.BAT procedure is far from foolproof, however, since it's all too easy to delete an inadvertent match (which is why the batch file creates an automatic backup file). And this process can pile up extra carriage returns in your files.

Printers

When ROM-BIOS tries to send something to your printer, it checks whether the printer is ready to receive characters. If the printer isn't ready, BIOS sits there continually rechecking the status. To avoid getting trapped in an endless loop, BIOS will give up after a predetermined "timeout" interval, and report that the printer is busy. If you're printing from DOS, you'll be greeted with the friendly "Abort, Retry, Ignore, Fail?" message.

On early PCs, timeouts sometimes occurred during form feeds on the IBM's slow dot matrix printer, so IBM increased the timeout interval starting with version 1.1 of DOS. These delay values are stored in the BIOS data area beginning at hex address 0040:0078. This area contains four-byte values for the four parallel printers that the BIOS (in theory) supports. The current PC ROM BIOS initializes the time-out values to hex 14 (decimal 20).

You can experiment with different timeout values in DEBUG. To double the LPT1 timeout value to 40 (28 hex), for instance, just load DEBUG and enter the following pair of lines at the DOS prompt:

```
E 0040:0078 28
Q
```

Be careful with memory addresses; if you get them wrong, you can write over some other important settings or instructions and get into trouble.

Once you find a value that works well, you can add a line to your AUTOEXEC.BAT file to change it everytime you boot up. Just adapt the two lines shown above and put them into a file called TIMEOUT.SET. Then add the following line to your AU-TOEXEC.BAT:

```
DEBUG < TIMEOUT.SET
```

When your system boots up, BIOS sniffs through your hardware trying to figure out, among other things, how many parallel printer adapters are attached. It uses three possible I/O port addresses to communicate with up to three adapters — hex 278, 378, and 3BC.

When it finds a valid printer adapter, it inserts the adapter's port number into a table starting at BIOS data area 0000:0408. The table has room for four 16-bit entries. BIOS puts the first port address at offset 408, the second (if it exists) at 40A, and the third (if there is one) at 40C. Then it encodes the number of printers it found into the high two bits of the BIOS Equipment List word at offset 410.

DOS uses four device names to refer to printers — PRN, LPT1, LPT2, and LPT3. PRN is the default, and is the same as LPT1.

Many commercial applications are designed to work with LPT1. If you have two printers — LPT1 and LPT2 — hooked to your system and want to swap them, all you have to do is exchange the port addresses at offsets 408 and 40A of low memory.

Several of the programs on the accompanying disks are designed to tame your printer. Some let you generate form feeds from the keyboard. Others make it easy to send commands to your printer or prevent accidental print-screen attempts.

It's really frustrating to hit Shift-PrtSc accidentally. If your printer is on you have to wait until it finishes typing the contents of the screen, and then readjust the paper to the top of the next page. If it's off, your system will hang until DOS realizes that the printer is not going to respond.

When you type Shift-PrtSc, DOS issues an interrupt 5, which first looks at a location in low memory called STATUS_BYTE to see whether your system is already dumping a screen to the printer. If STATUS_BYTE is equal to 1, DOS thinks a screen dump is taking place, and exits the routine without dumping another screen to the printer. If STATUS_BYTE is equal to 0, the routine sets STATUS_BYTE to 1 so that it cannot interrupt itself, then does the actual dump, and finally resets STATUS_BYTE equal to 0 and exits the routine.

This means you can disable the Shift-PrtSc routine with a simple assembly language routine, DISABLE.COM, that sets STATUS_BYTE to 1. A similar routine, EN-ABLE.COM, can turn it back on by setting STATUS_BYTE to 0. Both are on the accompanying disk.

Most printers are capable of doing fancy tricks with fonts, spacing, and unusual operating modes of one sort or another. But sending codes to your printer isn't always easy.

First, many printer command codes begin with an escape character (hex 1B, decimal 27). But if you try to issue an escape character in DOS, you won't be successful, since DOS interprets this character as a signal to abort whatever you were trying to do. However, you can use DEBUG, or EDLIN, or a good word processor, or even BASIC to generate these escape sequences. See the chapter on ANSI.SYS for tips on how to do it (ANSI codes also begin with Escape characters).

To make creating custom printer control files easy, you can use the PRCODER.BAT below. You'll need to have DEBUG.COM in your current subdirectory, or in a directory that your PATH knows about.

PRCODER.BAT reads parameters from the command line and inserts them into a DEBUG script (to send the hex values 1BH, 49H, and 03H you would type PRCODER 1B 49 3). You can enter several dozen codes on the same command line; the SHIFT command reads them in and substitutes them one by one for the %1 replaceable parameter in the:

```
ECHO MOV DL,%1 >> PR.SCR
```

line. PRCODER.BAT then loops back and uses the:

```
IF %1!==! GOTO FINISH
```

test to see if there are any more command-line parameters to process. If it finds any, it concatenates them to the existing DEBUG script. If it doesn't find any, it jumps to the :FINISH label, adds the necessary DEBUG instructions to write the file, redirects the script into DEBUG by loading a secondary command processor with:

```
COMMAND /C DEBUG < PR.SCR
```

to create a COM file, and then erases the DEBUG script.

If the user doesn't enter any parameters, PRCODER.BAT prints instructions and then quits. DOS substitutes the actual name of the batch file for the %0, so you can rename PRCODER.BAT to whatever you want. The process will make each PRCODE.COM file 284 bytes long, the maximum length this process can handle. Be sure to rename existing

PRCODE.COM files before creating new ones so the older version isn't obliterated by the new.

While some users might argue that it really isn't necessary to rewrite the MOV AH,5 line each time, it's a good idea to do so since you can't always be sure the AX register will remain intact after an INT 21.

Note also that the line:

```
ECHO. >> PR.SCR
```

won't work properly in some versions of DOS. Its purpose in this batch file is to generate a solitary carriage return. If your version of DOS stumbles over this, see the comments on ECHO in the chapter on batch files. If you're creating this batch file in DOS, you can press the F7 key instead of typing the period, which will generate a null.

```
ECHO OFF
IF %1!==! GOTO OOPS
ECHO N PRCODE.COM > PR.SCR
ECHO A >> PR.SCR
:TOP
IF %1!==! GOTO FINISH
ECHO MOV DL,%1 >> PR.SCR
ECHO MOV AH,5 >> PR.SCR
ECHO INT 21 >> PR.SCR
SHIFT
GOTO TOP
:FINISH
ECHO INT 20 >> PR.SCR
ECHO. >> PR.SCR
ECHO RCX >> PR.SCR
ECHO 11C >> PR.SCR
ECHO W >> PR.SCR
ECHO Q >> PR.SCR
COMMAND /C DEBUG < PR.SCR
DEL PR.SCR
ECHO PRCODE.COM created
GOTO END
:OOPS
ECHO Enter %0 and then the HEXADECIMAL
ECHO values (each FF or less) of the
ECHO printer codes you want to send, eg:
ECHO %0 1B 49 3
:END
```

The DOS PRINT utility, introduced with version 2.0, is a resident program that lets you print out disk files while you're running other programs. It's fundamentally different from other *background* (or spooler) printing programs, since most software print buffers lop off a large chunk of user memory as a holding area for text being sent to the printer. The print buffer program intercepts printer output, stores it in this memory buffer, and then later transfers it to the printer. This frees up the system for other activities.

PRINT, however, transfers disk files to the printer and takes up much less memory than a print buffer program. The size of these files is limited only by disk space. Once a regular print buffer becomes full, printing slows down to the speed of the printer.

Although PRINT can be used with a diskette system (if you don't change the diskette containing the print file while printing is in progress), it's best suited for a hard disk system.

The PRINT.COM program in DOS versions 2.0 and 2.1 had some real problems. You couldn't specify directory paths with the filename or optimize operation for particular printers. PRINT version 3.0 corrected these problems and added a slate of new parameters designed to make the process far more efficient and painless.

PRINT's syntax looks mystifying:

```
[d:] [path] PRINT [/D:device] [/B:buffsiz] [/U:busytick]
[/M:maxtick] [/S:timeslice] [/Q:quesiz] [/C] [/T] [/P]
[[d:] [path] filename[.ext]]
```

The /D (device name) and /Q (queue size) parameters are simple enough. Most of the time you'll just specify /D:PRN or /D:LPT1 to send output to the first parallel printer. /Q can be set to the largest number of files you'll want to print at one time.

The /B parameter specifies the buffer size; its default is 512 bytes. This is the amount of memory PRINT sets aside for reading the disk file. The default value means that the print file will be read 512 bytes at a time. If the buffer is too small, you'll see frequent disk accesses, particularly with a fast printer. If the buffer is too large, the disk accesses will be less frequent but slightly longer, and PRINT will occupy more memory.

For a hard disk system with 640K, the best buffer size is probably something like 4096 or 8192, both of which are multiples of 512.

To understand the /S, /M, and /U parameters, you have to understand how PRINT works.

During operation of the PC, the 8253 timer chip invokes a hardware interrupt (08H) 18.2 times per second, or about once every .055 seconds. This interrupt executes a short routine in ROM BIOS that counts the number of times it's called so DOS can know what time it is. The interrupt 08H routine also invokes an interrupt 1CH, often called the "Timer Tick." PRINT intercepts the Timer Tick interrupt to trigger it into operation.

The /S parameter, which IBM calls the timeslice, is the number of timer ticks during which PRINT will do nothing. When PRINT is doing nothing, the rest of the PC system will operate as normal, so the /S parameter should really be called the "System Time Slice."

The /M parameter, which IBM calls the *maxtick*, is the number of timer ticks during which PRINT will attempt to shovel characters out to the printer. This is really the time slice allocated to PRINT. Assuming that the printer is ready for these characters, PRINT will have nearly total control during this period and other programs may do nothing.

The default maxtick and timeslice settings are /M:2 and /S:8, which means that PRINT will be alternately active for 0.11 seconds and inactive for 0.44 seconds (assuming that the printer is always ready to accept characters). Consequently, PRINT will be working 20% of the time; any other program will be working at 80% of normal speed.

The /U parameter, which IBM calls the *busytick*, comes into play only if the printer is busy when PRINT attempts to print a character. The default value is /U:1, which means that PRINT will wait one clock tick (.055 seconds) before giving up its /M time slice. The rest of the system can then work for /S timer ticks before PRINT makes another attempt to print.

PRINT also gives up its time slice if a disk access is in progress. The reason for this is obvious — if PRINT has to get another piece of the file during this time, then real problems could develop if another program is accessing the disk. The time slice is also forfeited if a DOS function call is in progress. If /M is very high in relation to /S, you'll notice a significant degradation of system speed. If /M is too low, printing will not proceed as fast as the printer can manage. If /U is too high, PRINT may spend too much time just checking the printer without actually printing anything if the printer is busy.

However, these parameters may be specified only when PRINT is first loaded. So, unless you like doing little three-finger exercises repeatedly, you would normally have a very difficult time optimizing the parameters for your system.

The IBM Graphics Printer that most print utilities consider to be the standard has an 80-character internal buffer. It will not begin printing until the buffer is full or the printer receives a carriage return or a form feed. When the printer begins printing, it is busy and cannot accept any more characters until the internal buffer is empty.

The optimum parameter settings for this printer are an /M value equal to the number of timer ticks needed for PRINT to fill up the printer's buffer, and a /S value equal to the timer ticks required for the printer to print the contents of the buffer.

For the IBM Graphics Printer printing 80 character lines, the optimal values are /S:20, /M:4, and /U:2. These values caused better performance than the default values, even though for most lines, PRINT is active only 1/6th of total system time. The PRINT command would look like:

```
PRINT /D:PRN /Q:20 /B:8192 /S:20 /M:4 /U:2
```

Unlike the IBM Graphics Printer, many other printers have internal buffers larger than 80 characters. If you attempted to set /M equal to the time it takes for PRINT to fill up a large buffer, you may find it to be something like 20 clock ticks or more. In operation, this would be intolerable, because 20 clock ticks is over one second and the rest of your system would halt during that time.

For printers with large internal buffers, set /U equal to 1, and /M equal to 4 or 5 (about 1/4 second), and experiment with /S. For very fast printers, you may find /S to be low in relation to /M. You may want to deliberately slow down the printing so you can get some work done, or speed up the printing if that's what's important.

You can use PRINT to print any text file, with or without control characters, stored on a disk. It expands tabs and assumes that an ASCII 26 (hex 1A) character represents the end of the file, so you can't use PRINT for graphics. PRINT will be active during any program that does not steal interrupt 1C. (Some compiled BASIC programs do this.)

Programs that let you go to the DOS command level and then return when you're done make this process a lot easier. Be sure, though, to load PRINT before you use it from within another program, because you don't want to make it resident on top of some other application.

Here's the real kicker: On the DOS command level, and during execution of any program using DOS function calls to obtain keyboard input, PRINT operates in a totally different manner, and none of the above information about timer ticks applies.

You could set completely wrong values for PRINT (/S to 255 and /M to 1) and when you jump into DOS, the printer will churn away, printing your text as fast as possible. To understand why this happens, you have to look at the internal guts of PRINT.

PRINT works with disk files, so it must make DOS calls to pull these files into memory. During a DOS function call, DOS switches to an internal stack. DOS actually maintains three stacks — one for function calls 01 through 0C, another for function calls 0D and above (which includes the file accesses), and a third for function calls 01 through 0C when a critical error is in progress.

Because of this internal stack, PRINT (or any other multitasking utility triggered by a hardware interrupt) cannot arbitrarily make DOS function calls to access a disk file. If another program is making a DOS function call, PRINT's function calls may clobber the internal stack and eventually cause the system to crash.

To prevent this, PRINT uses the undocumented DOS interrupt 21 function call 34 when it first loads. This function call returns registers ES:BX pointing to a byte in DOS. Whenever this byte is nonzero, a DOS function call is in progress. When PRINT is triggered by a timer tick, it checks this byte. If it's nonzero, PRINT just returns from the interrupt without attempting to print anything.

This creates a real problem, because on the DOS command level, COMMAND.COM executes a DOS function call 0A for keyboard input, and this DOS call is in progress until the user presses the Enter key at the end of a line. Many other DOS programs, such as DEBUG or EDLIN, also use this function call.

So, PRINT takes advantage of another undocumented feature of DOS — interrupt 28. PC-DOS itself continually executes an interrupt 28 whenever it is in a wait state (i.e., when it is waiting for keyboard input) during a function call of 01 through 0C.

When an interrupt 28 is invoked, PRINT knows that a function call of 01 through 0C is in progress. Because a separate stack is used for function calls of 0D and above, which includes all the file access calls, PRINT knows that it's safe to retrieve a file if necessary.

PRINT will always grind to a halt during any disk access. But you'll also see it stop during a TYPE command after the disk has been accessed. This is because TYPE uses function call 40 to write the file to the display, and PRINT cannot use DOS during that time.

Anyone who believes that multitasking is simple to implement in PC-DOS should try dissassembling PRINT.COM and take a look at the backflips and contortions required for simple background printing from disk files.

Security

The more information you can store on your system, the more vulnerable you are to security problems. Hard disks are a treasure of valuable data — about your company, your job, even your personal activities.

It's not bad enough that someone could make unauthorized copies of your important files. What's worse is that he could change or destroy the data. You would certainly know if someone had erased a critical file. But you might never know if someone altered an important record or two.

Starting with its AT, IBM wised up and wired its systems to a lock and key. You don't think IBM added it for show, did you?

Unfortunately, many users are cavalier about security. They leave floppy disks in drawers or plastic disk caddies, and often wouldn't miss a valuable diskette if it vanished. One of the penalties of such portability is that someone could walk out of your office with several file cabinets' worth of confidential information hidden in a pocket or briefcase.

And while you can catalog your floppies and keep sensitive ones locked in a safe, your hard disk is just a sitting duck for anyone who wants to pry. An unbreachable system is certainly not impossible to put together. Legions of government users have to forego the convenience of conventional hard disks for removable mass storage devices that can be locked up at night.

There's even a government standard for erasing files and then writing over them to obliterate any last magnetic trace. The *Norton Utilities* WIPEDISK and WIPEFILE programs use these.

If you really need grade-A security, DOS can't help. And most power users can break into any system in seconds. Encryption is also a possible solution, but a genuine nuisance. However you can keep casual snoops from getting at your files.

Most tricks involve preventing unauthorized users from booting your hard disk. The only drawback with such techniques is that a snoop can start an otherwise unstartable hard disk system by bringing his own diskette along and booting off it. Still, the following tricks are like locks on desk drawers — they keep the honest people out. If someone wants to get in, he or she will.

When DOS boots, it looks to see whether AUTOEXEC.BAT is in your root directory. If it is, DOS passes control to it. So an easy way to keep the honest people out is to patch COMMAND.COM so it looks for another file, especially one that doesn't have a BAT extension. In fact, if you're the cautious type, it shouldn't.

Once you patch COMMAND.COM to start from a hidden AUTOEXEC.BAT file, the AUTOEXEC.BAT clone can then do the magic you want.

An easy example would be to run an IF ERRORLEVEL program that looked for a strange key combination — such as Shift-Tab — to continue. If you press Shift-Tab (or whatever you set the IF ERRORLEVEL test to detect) the program would forge ahead, and would set things up properly.

But if a user typed any other key, like the Enter key, another IF ERRORLEVEL test in the list of IFs would detect it and jump to a batch file command that would execute a small file that reboots your system.

When a PC boots, its BIOS checks a *flag word* at location 0040:0072. (One word equals two bytes; a flag is a part of memory used to keep track of a condition, such as whether something is set off or on.) If the value of the flag is 1234H, BIOS does a warm boot — the fast Ctrl-Alt-Del type. However, if it finds the value of the flag is not 1234H, BIOS does a cold slow boot, going through its tedious memory and equipment checks.

If you use DEBUG to look at low memory addresses 472 and 473 you'll see 34 12 rather than 12 34, since the PC stores words backwards. The high order byte (12) goes into the higher memory address (473), while the low order byte (34) goes into the lower memory address (472). Despite this, the word takes the lower memory address as its own.

You can use the GET W or GET WE from the accompanying disks for this. The effect is the same. Actually, it's probably more infuriating to a data snooper to make him sit through a long memory diagnostic or two.

To further confound unauthorized users, you can do additional mischief. Make sure you've permanently set your COMMAND.COM to ECHO OFF, or use the ECHO-suppressing techniques mentioned in the chapter on batch techniques. Then, since you no longer have a startup file called AUTOEXEC.BAT, create one with the five lines below and leave only it and COMMAND.COM on your root directory:

```
CLS
ECHO ===== Unauthorized Access =====
ECHO Damage to computer will result if
ECHO it is not turned off immediately.
PROMPT Error
```

If the user tries to run this file, he'll get a warning and a blank screen. If he just TYPEs it, he'll know you mean business. The last line — customizing the PROMPT to say "Error" — is a nice touch, since every time the user tries something, the screen will balk and then just print:

```
Error
```

Even more diabolical is preventing the unauthorized user from trying any of the standard DOS commands. The way to do this is simply to rename the important commands inside COMMAND.COM using DEBUG.

COMMAND.COM maintains a table of internal commands for RENAME, ERASE, etc. Two of these, DIR and TYPE, are the ones a snooper would use in trying to figure out what's going on.

If you rename DIR to something like RID or XYZ, and TYPE to EPYT or QRST, whenever the unauthorized user tries the normal version of these, all he'll get is the irritating message "Bad command or file name" since COMMAND.COM will no longer recognize TYPE or DIR.

You can use DEBUG to change the names of the commands stored inside COMMAND.COM. Load COMMAND.COM into DEBUG and find the file length using RCX. Specify a search from 100 to the length reported by RCX for something like "REN" or "TYPE." Use E to replace them, making sure your new commands are the same size as the old ones. Verify with D, write (W), and quit (Q).

You should keep a real copy of COMMAND.COM somewhere on your disk. Once you've gotten past your IF ERRORLEVEL test and screened out the unauthorized users, you can load a copy of the real COMMAND.COM, as a secondary command processor. (If you ever want to, you can drop down to the phony one by entering EXIT.) Using a secondary command processor like this lets you run all the normal DOS commands. But be careful if you try this since DOS sometimes gets mad if you mix different versions of COMMAND.COM.

But the best simple DOS security tip of all lets you hide all your files — including COMMAND.COM, AUTOEXEC.BAT, CONFIG.SYS, and all your subdirectories — with the improved DOS ATTRIB command that adjusts the directory listing so DIR won't show them. And you can bring them all back just as easily. This means that you can hide *everything* in your root directory, presenting the snooper with a bare disk. The files are still there, and they still work, but DIR won't report any.

Of course, CHKDSK /V will still be able to see them, but not all users know this, and you can rename CHKDSK.COM to something like CH.COM, which is far easier to type anyway. Still, any serious user can bring his own DOS disk up to your system and figure out what you did.

This lets you hide and rename your key files and subdirectories, pretty much locking out anyone who doesn't know how to unhide files using DEBUG.

You can hide all your files at once with the command:

```
FOR %F IN (*.*) DO ATTRIB +H %F
```

Just remember how to unhide them with the ATTRIB -H option.

The *Norton Utilities* (and other similar programs) make it child's play for anyone to "unerase" a file that you've deleted from your disk. With the latest iteration of Norton's software, all you have to do is type QU (for Quick Unerase) and your data is back unless something else has written over it in the interim.

This is because DOS doesn't actually erase the file; it simply changes the first character in the directory listing (to tell itself that the old file's space on the disk is available for new files) and adjusts the disk's internal location tables accordingly.

If you start to overwrite the file before you get a chance to unerase it, you may lose the beginning of the deleted file, and may have to puzzle over the pieces somewhat, but if it was a text file you can usually rescue much of it.

Norton's WIPEFILE and WIPEDISK programs can obliterate any trace of deleted files by writing a new file over their entire length. You can even have these programs write specially designed bit patterns over the old data area, and re-execute themselves multiple times to make sure what's gone is gone.

So once you've used a program like WIPEFILE on your deleted files, you can breathe easy, right? Don't be so sure. Such programs expunge only those files you know about. But what about the secret copies of your files you don't know about?

Many programs, especially word processors, create temporary files during their normal operation. They all erase these files before they shut down in normal use, so you almost never see them.

But if something unexpected happens and you crash out of the program, you may see a file with a similar filename to one you were just working on, but with a $$$ or TMP extension.

The trouble is that your word processor almost certainly isn't going to erase the temp file any better than the DOS ERASE (or DEL) command, which, as we've seen, doesn't do a very thorough job. And unless you know they're there, you can't obliterate them with a WIPEFILE-type program.

The solution is simple. Before using WIPEFILE, try to use an unerase program like QU. You should before someone else does.

This means UNerasing all the little tiny orphan clusters too that end up strewn around your disk. When it's time to use WIPEFILE, do a maximum disk-wide unerase first, and follow it up with a maximum text search (Norton again). Then wipe out all the files you didn't know existed, and all the little leftover pieces.

For maximum hard disk security, periodically copy all your files to floppies or tape, or to a Bernoulli Box, and WIPEDISK the entire disk. Then reformat the hard disk and copy everything back. The added benefits to this time-consuming task make the project worth the effort. First, you end up with current backups, which you obviously should lock in a safe place. Also, you do away with the inevitable disk fragmentation that results when you write pieces of files over each other. Your files will fly on a newly formatted, nonfragmented disk.

Another security technique is to keep a large harmless file around, and copy it over the file you want to erase before you erase it. This way if someone unerases a file with a name like SECRET they'll see the contents of the harmless file that you used to obliterate the actual sensitive one.

To keep the honest people out of your files, hide a Ctrl-Z, or decimal ASCII character 26 end-of-file marker, near the beginning of a file. When a DOS TYPE command trips over one of these, it stops in its tracks, no matter how long the directory listing says the file actually is.

You can try using DEBUG to imbed an end-of-file hex 1A at the beginning of your files; it will always stop the DOS TYPE command, but it also may stop the file from working properly.

A better tip is to give your files bizarre, high-bit names. This will freeze beginners out of your files, since they won't be able to figure out how to enter the characters to TYPE, load, or run the filenames. (You know — just use Alt + the numeric keypad.)

Or you can try something odd like inserting spaces in the middle of your filenames. DOS chokes on these, but you can use BASIC to manipulate them. And in a pinch, you can substitute wildcards for spaces in DOS and rename any spaced-out file.

You can also use DEBUG to substitute high-bit characters for COMMAND.COM internal commands if you really want to confuse snoopers. Carrying this one step further, you can turn your normal DOS messages, like:

```
Volume in drive C is POWER TOOLS
Volume Serial Number is 104F-16CD
Directory of  C:\PROGRAM

 34 File(s)    1677312 bytes free
```

into the same kind of high-bit gibberish. If someone boots up and sees undecipherable messages and filenames, odds are he'll give up pretty quickly, thinking you're using some sort of very exotic operating system he couldn't possible figure out.

High-bit messages and filenames, coupled with selectively hidden subdirectories and files, wild-goose-chase AUTOEXEC files, renamed DOS commands, and totally obliterated disk surfaces, should let you sleep a tiny bit easier at night. But they can end up being a pain in the neck for you too.

PC users in corporations often live by a simple rule: if the file contains confidential information, it must be stored on a diskette and kept in a locked desk. Typically some paranoia accompanies this rule, requiring users to turn off the PCs after using a confidential file so nobody can DEBUG the data out of memory, but this is a little extreme outside the CIA.

Another potential trouble area is a print spooler or buffer. Some spoolers hang onto copies of the most recently printed file. If you're nervous about this, reboot after printing something sensitive, and turn any hardware buffers off and on again.

While you're at it, be careful about communications programs that store your password or other secret information in plain ASCII. These days most "comm" software encrypts such information, but users often take advantage of keyboard macro programs to put things like bank account numbers and access codes onto single keys to avoid having to type them in when doing electronic banking. Make sure any program you use for this doesn't make it easy for others to learn more about you than you want them to know.

If you're using a sensitive data base that's much too big and complex for diskettes, another solution is a removable storage medium like the one on Iomega's popular Bernoulli box.

Another possibility is to use an encryption and decryption program. After using a confidential file, you'd run the encryption program with a password, which scrambles up the file. When you want to use it again, you'd run the decryption program with the same password to unscramble it.

Such encryption schemes are very difficult to break without knowing the password, even if you have access to the decryption program. Moreover, if someone maliciously tries to scramble up the encrypted program, it should be obvious when it's decrypted. For such events you should be keeping diskette backups anyway.

Users often want to know how they can install some sort of password protection on their systems. Infortunately, because of the PC's open architecture, password security is very difficult to implement. Unless you put a special ROM in your system, any smart user can defeat just about any password scheme on a hard disk by booting off a floppy.

It is technically possible to install a password program that cannot be circumvented by a drive A: boot. But this program has to be executed before the PC even attempts to boot. Here's how it works:

When the PC is first turned on, it executes a Power-On Self Test (POST) program coded in the PC's ROM BIOS. This program initializes the system, checks memory, and ultimately boots the operating system from a diskette or hard disk. Before the boot, however, the POST program checks memory locations between hex addresses C8000 and F4000 for the presence of additional ROM programs. Generally these programs must perform some extra system initialization before the PC is booted. In fact, the extra BIOS for the XT hard disk is at hex address C8000. You would have to program a small password routine somewhere in that memory space where it wouldn't conflict with anything else. Moreover, the program must stay in memory when the PC is turned off.

Getting the password program encoded in ROM is a bit extreme. An easier approach is to code it into random access memory on a CMOS RAM memory board with battery backup. CMOS RAM uses very little power — almost none at all while inactive — so a rechargeable battery backup should last for many months.

The board's memory address would be set up to begin at D0000, D8000, E0000 or E8000. The program must be in a special format, explained in the ROM BIOS section of the PC or XT *Technical Reference* manuals under the heading "Adapter Cards with System-Accessible ROM Modules." The code must start off with a hex 55 and AA, to tell the BIOS that it is executable. The third byte is the number of 512 byte blocks in the program (probably 1 for a simple password routine). The program itself begins at the fourth byte. It must return to the BIOS with a far return. You should write the program in assembly language and not use any DOS calls (interrupts 20 and up) because DOS will not be loaded when the program runs. You may use all the BIOS resources for the keyboard and display.

The ROM BIOS does a checksum of the bytes of the program and gives you a terse "ROM" message if they don't add up to zero ignoring overflow above 256. So, you're going to have to add up all the bytes in your program, take the negative, and put that byte somewhere in the file.

One final tip — if you have a security system that disables your keyboard when you walk away from it, be sure to lock up any other input devices, like mice. If you're using *Windows*, for instance, someone could come along and use the mouse to do all sorts of damage. Be careful out there.

When It All Goes Wrong

Funny, isn't it. You get up one perfect morning and the air is crisp and clear, you're full of energy, bubbling with ideas and enthusiasm. You roll up your sleeves and snap on your PC to get some real work done. Along about half a disk later you notice a faint odor of toasting plastic. Nothing to worry about, right? The citizens of Pompeii and Herculaneum probably shrugged it off too, when they caught the first slight whiff of sulphur hissing down the slopes of Vesuvius.

Unlike the ancient Romans, however, you have some control over your fate — at least when it comes to your computer. You can protect yourself from obvious problems simply by exercising some care. The following pages contain some important common sense rules.

Don't erase files blindly. And avoid unnecessary shortcuts. If you want to erase the BAK backup files that are cluttering up your disk, typing:

```
DEL *.B*
```

will take all your BAT batch files and BAS basic files with it. Whenever you're using wildcards to delete files, make it a two-step process. First do a directory listing, with something like:

```
DIR *.B*
```

or whatever the wildcard filespec happens to be. If you see any surprises you can make the filespec more specific (*.BAK for instance) and try again. But if everything is fine, just type:

```
DEL
```

and press the F3 function key. DOS will fill in the wildcard filespec from the previous DIR command. For extra peace of mind, use the /P option for both the DIR and DEL commands. It's a new option for DEL in DOS 5.0.

If you're trying to delete all EXE files with names ending with ABC and you accidentally issue the command:

```
DEL *ABC.EXE
```

DOS will get rid of all your EXE files. This is because DOS stops looking at characters after a wildcard, and interprets the command as:

```
DEL *.EXE
```

If you entered:

```
DEL *ABC.*XE
```

DOS would read this as:

```
DEL *.*
```

You'd know you were in trouble when it prompted you with "Are you sure (Y/N)?" which is the sign it's about to get rid of everything.

Back up every day. There are three kinds of backups: the perfectly organized, meticulously verified kind that nobody does; the adequate "throw it all on a disk and sort it out later" kind that's a lot more common; and the "I'll definitely back up everything tomorrow" lie that freezes you in your seat when you see the inevitable "General failure error reading drive C:" message instead of the DOS prompt.

Remember, even expensive hard disks are just aluminum coated with iron oxide. Would you trust your future to a rusty pie plate? You can purchase lots of fancy commercial backup packages to automate the process. Or you could use the ARCOPY.COM utility on the accompanying disk. And the sensational PC-DOS XCOPY command first introduced with version 3.2 is a real treasure.

XCOPY is speedy and powerful. While the older COPY command reads files from the source disk and then writes them laboriously to the target disk one at a time, XCOPY soaks up as many files as memory can handle, and blasts them onto your backup disk *en masse.*

If you add an /S switch it can copy all the files from all your buried subdirectories, and will duplicate any subdirectory structure on the fly so you don't have to sit there and fumble with MD and CD commands.

Adding a /P will automate the decision-making process by pausing at each file and asking whether you want to copy it. Type a Y and it will make the copy, type a N and it will prompt you for the next file. You can use the /S and /P switches in tandem.

Best of all, by adding a /D switch followed by a date you can have it copy only those files created or changed on the specified date or later. And, of course, it can make backups based on whether the archive bit is set, which lets you skip over files that you haven't changed since the last backup.

DOS has gradually improved the BACKUP and RESTORE commands over the years (so they work faster and won't do idiotic things like write old system files back onto your hard disk over newer ones). And BACKUP is ideal when you're copying files to diskettes that are bigger than the diskette, since it can break them up and have RESTORE put them back together later. But BACKUP stores files in a format that's nonexecutable; you have to run them through RESTORE before you can use them again. XCOPY doesn't change a bit; it keeps files in executable form. The astonishing thing is that XCOPY was written by IBM, which is not noted for producing wonderful PC software. This one is a winner, however. Use it every day.

Don't experiment with original copies of files. If you feel adventurous and want to reformat a data file with unusual margins, or replace carriage returns with something else, or if you decide to see just what DEBUG can do to a program, do it to a copy. Originals are sacred.

Be extremely wary of DOS commands like ASSIGN, FORMAT, and RECOVER. Everyone knows that you have to be careful when using the FORMAT command on a hard disk, and DOS has grown more careful over the years, by asking you to enter volume labels, refusing to proceed unless you enter a drive letter, and printing scary boldface warnings in the manuals.

But if you get fancy and start shuffling your drive letters with ASSIGN, JOIN, and SUBST, and then try to run BACKUP, RESTORE, or PRINT, or if you change the configuration of your system drives frequently by putting RAMdisks in odd places, you're just asking for trouble.

Always stop before you FORMAT and check your intentions, especially late at night or when you've been pounding away at the keyboard for so long you're starting to hear voices from the speaker. And if any beginners ever share your system, use one of the tricks described elsewhere in this book to give yourself added protection. One of the slickest tricks is to patch COMMAND.COM so it thinks FORMAT is an internal command, which will head off any FORMAT requests at the pass unless someone boots your hard disk system off a floppy.

And avoid the RECOVER command entirely. It's nothing but trouble, and can turn every file and subdirectory on your hard disk into an undecipherable puzzle piece that will take you days to reconstruct. If you absolutely must use it, make sure you enter a filename after it. Otherwise, pray your backups are current. To be safe, remove it from your system altogether.

DOS makes it almost too easy to delete files, but there's always the DOS 5.0 UNDELETE and/or the Norton Utilities to bring your files back from the netherworld. If you discover that you've just erased a key file or used too broad a wildcard and expunged a whole slate of files, be absolutely sure you don't create or change any other files. Immediately stop what you're doing and drag out your Norton disk (or equivalent), and "unerase" the temporarily lost files.

An innocent-looking command like COPY can also do real damage if you're not careful. First, you could copy an older version of a file over a newer one. Second, if you're concatenating several small files into one big one, and you try combining binary and ASCII files, you can end up mangling the result. You can also end up wiping out a smaller file you're trying to join with others if you use its filename as the name of the final big file. Third, if you're trying to copy a list of program files into another directory (like \BACKUP) and you make a typing error (like COPY *.COM \BAKUP), you may end up concatenating them into one useless mess of a file. Fourth, if you try copying a file over itself and the process somehow gets interrupted, you can end up with garbage where your file used to be. Fifth, if you've been making backup copies of a file to a floppy disk, and the original grows larger than the amount of available space, and you try to copy the oversized file anyway, DOS will erase the previous copy on the floppy. Sixth, if you've forgotten you have an old file on your disk with the same name as the one you're giving to the copy of a file you're about to make, you'll lose the contents of the old file. Seventh, if you try copying a file to another drive with a command like COPY MYFIL B: and you accidentally type a semicolon rather than a colon after the B, you'll end up with a copy on the same drive as MYFIL called B. Think before you copy.

You may think this one's obvious, but guard against stupid power problems. Don't plug your system into a rat's nest of cubetaps and four-way plugs that are so heavy they're falling out of the wall socket. Don't string your power cord across the room. Don't plug into a circuit shared with power-greedy appliances like air conditioners and heating elements. And don't put a power director or power strip on the floor beneath your desk where your toe is going to tapdance on the on/off switch.

Don't ever change add-in boards with the power on. And be careful about static electricity — touch your stereo, a radiator, or a lamp when you shuffle over to your system after petting the cat in the winter. A spark may not seem like much, but those hundreds of thousands of volts can really do damage when they're hurtling down pathways a micron or two wide.

Don't buy floppy disks that are so cheap you can't believe the price. Your data is worth the extra few cents. If you format them and see "bad sector" messages, throw them out, or use them for emergencies. One of the worst sounds known to mankind is the noise of a cheap sandpaper disk grinding down your drive heads.

Watch out when redirecting commands and files. The command:

```
SORT < DATA.FIL
```

will sort the contents of the DATA.FIL file on column one and display the results onscreen. But:

```
SORT > DATA.FIL
```

will trash your DATA.FIL and give it a length of 0. Be careful when using MORE (which, when used backwards, will wipe out your file and replace it with a two-byte file containing just a solitary carriage return and line feed) or any other filter. Redirection is a powerful tool. But learn the rules first — so you can avoid doing things like using the TYPE command to redirect the contents of a file that contains an ASCII 26 somewhere in it, since this tells TYPE to screech to a halt. Also, don't use >, <, or | signs in batch files. If you put a line in your batch file that says:

```
ECHO ----> Enter a key:
```

DOS will think you are asking it to create a file called Enter and use ECHO to redirect text from that line into the file. Even something as innocent as:

```
REM Now returning to the C> prompt
```

ends up generating a file called PROMPT. In later DOS versions you can include such signs in batch files if you put quotes around them:

```
ECHO The "|" is a pipe sign
```

Caveats are usually given for a reason. When you see a program listed somewhere that says "use this on color monitors only" you might as well place the call to your insurance agent before you try it on your monochrome display. Contrary to popular belief, software can indeed destroy hardware. You can break a hard disk activator arm by slamming it into a place where it wasn't supposed to go, or burn out a monitor in an instant by fiddling with the video controller.

If you ever see the message "Are you sure (Y/N)?" when you don't expect it, the answer is always NO. If you're trying to erase a file and you make a typing mistake you can accidentally be telling your operating system to erase everything in a subdirectory. That's what these warnings are for.

Don't mix hex and decimal. The single easiest mistake to make when working with DEBUG is to slip in a decimal value, or subtract 1 from a number like 100 and think the result is 99 when it's really FF. Work with copies of your files, never originals. Educate your fingers so they type only in hex.

And, whenever you're using DEBUG to work with absolute sectors rather than files, and you're about to use the W command — pause and stare at what you're about to enter before going near the Enter key. Remember too that DEBUG treats drive A: as 0 rather than 1. One little slip here, especially when you're fooling with something like the FAT or directory, and it's time to hunt for the backup disks.

Be extremely careful when trying new memory-resident software, especially when you already have other resident software loaded. These things can be tricky and unpredictable enough by themselves; throwing a few together in memory and watching them fight for the same interrupts is not a pretty sight. It's also a recipe for a power-switch reboot. Don't work with any unsaved data files when you're testing out resident software interactions. And to be really safe, use a TSR manager like the INSTALL/REMOVE duo on the accompanying disk, or any of the similar commercial packages available.

Don't mix utilities from different DOS versions, and avoid having different, patched versions of COMMAND.COM on your disk. One of the most chilling messages you can see is "Cannot load COMMAND, system halted." And you're a lot more likely to see it when you mix and match DOS parts.

If you use a RAMdisk, stop working at least once or twice an hour and copy your work to a more tangible medium. RAMdisks are fast. But they can also lose data in the blink of an eye if you bump the power cord, or if the generator at your local power company burps, or if your software just decides to lock up. RAMdisk software ought to come with a little clock that beeps every 15 minutes to remind you to back up your ephemerall files.

Treat hard disks as if they contained little booby-trapped bottles of nitroglycerine. Don't bang, drop, nudge, tap, stomp, poke, jostle, smack, shove, whack, thump, pound, or otherwise knock into any system with a humming hard disk. One little bump is all it takes to send the drive heads plowing into the disk surface. From then on you can just kiss your data goodbye. Be especially careful with systems that are mounted on the floor, since these tend to attract a disproportionate share of kicks, hammer blows from vacuum-cleaners, and other miscellaneous assaults.

Don't mix high-density and low-density floppies, especially when dealing with 720K and 1.44M diskettes. It shouldn't be a problem, but because of the way these disks are formatted, it is. Label potentially confusing disks after you format them, and don't intermingle high- and low-density formats.

Take care in using the CTTY NUL command in batch files. This disconnects your keyboard until the batch file sees a restorative CTTY CON command. If something unexpected happens in the interim, all you can do is reach for the power switch.

It's a great convenience to redirect keystroke scripts into DEBUG rather than having to type each command. This lets you check your typing before you proceed, and modify long, previous DEBUG instructions just by changing the file. But be sure to include blank lines where indicated (after ending A commands) and to include a carriage return at the end of each line, especially the last one that quits.

If you have sensitive files on your disk, don't leave words like "CONFIDENTIAL" or "SECRET" in them if any other users have access to your system. It's easy to scan across the disk for such text, which lets anyone pinpoint such files. And give any sensitive files or subdirectories innocent-sounding names, not names like SECRET.1 or CONFDNTL.

While you shouldn't make it too easy for someone to get at your confidential files, don't make it too hard. If you encrypt your files, don't use keys like F$J#DV!N&1E@ unless you're sure you can remember them later.

If you erase sensitive files, make sure they're gone. Use a utility like Norton's WIPEFILE, or else someone may use Norton's UNERASE utilities to bring the files back to life. And while you're at it, tell Norton's program to wipe out all erased files. You may get rid of the latest version of a confidential report, but if you're not careful, you can end up leaving previously erased BAK or $$$ copies lurking on the disk. Some word processors create backup or temporary work files without your knowledge, and erase them before you exit the program. A snooping co-worker can revive these just as easily as any other "erased" file.

If you lock your system and you have mouse attached, hide the mouse or lock it up too. A mouse is simply an alternate input device, and a knowledgeable user can use it instead of the locked keyboard to change or examine your files.

If you have to print a sensitive document, turn off the printer when you're done, and reset your system as well. It's possible that parts or all of the file are still buffered in memory when you finish.

Be careful when "unerasing" hidden files left by commercial software. Some benighted software, in an effort to be as greedy and hostile as possible, scrambles your disk sectors and then hides a file in these sectors. If you have software like this installed in a subdirectory, and you want to get rid of it, and you try deleting all the files and then using the RD command to remove the subdirectory, you'll get some version of a:

```
Invalid path, not directory,
or directory not empty
```

message. You can see the file by running CHKDSK /V or by using some of the utilities on the accompanying disks. And you can unhide it and delete it. But the sectors will remain scrambled, which can bring your operating system to its knees later. If commercial software comes with a deinstallation program, use it instead of trying to erase all the files yourself. It will usually repair any damage it's caused during installation.

Assume any software that you download from any source other than one that rigorously tests everything, such as Compuserve, is dangerous until proven otherwise. You can use some of the utilities on the accompanying disks to peek inside any just-downloaded programs and look for messages such as "Gotcha!" Or you can run it on a floppy disk system with a RAMdisk configured as drive C: and watch what it does.

If someone wants to corrupt your system, and you like to experiment with downloaded software, you really can't protect yourself entirely. Most bulletin boards are careful to screen out such potentially dangerous software, and much of the electronically distributed software available today is sensational. But nasty "virus" software and "trojan horse" programs do get around. Unless you trust your source implicitly, watch out for programs that intentionally wipe out the files on your hard disk.

Don't use DISKCOPY except in two cases — when you're making a backup copy of a new commercial software disk, or when you've somehow damaged a disk and want to work on it with DEBUG or Norton Utilities-*type products.* For all other copies, format a blank disk and use the COPY *.* or XCOPY command to make the backups.

Except when copy protection schemes are involved, DISKCOPY will make an exact replica of the original disk. This is bad for two reasons:

When you put a lot of wear and tear on a a diskette — erasing, adding, and changing data frequently — you end up fragmenting your files. DOS ends up chopping them into small pieces and pigeonholes the pieces in lots of different locations. Then when it has to load or write a fragmented file, DOS takes a long time to sort everything out. In fact, if you use floppies extensively, you should periodically format a blank disk and copy the files from the older disk to the newly formatted one to enhance performance. Copying them gets rid of the fragmentation — at least until you start slicing and dicing them again.

Also, while DOS is supposed to protect against it, it's possible when using DISKCOPY to copy good information from one disk onto a magnetically unsound area on another without knowing it. The disk formatting process guards against this, but DISKCOPY won't reformat a disk unless it has to. If a sector has gone bad since the disk was formatted, it's possible to write good information onto a bad sector and lose it.

Using DISKCOPY to make exact replicas of commercial disks is certainly a good idea. And if you somehow mangle a disk and want to dig beneath the surface and try to fix it, you should use DISKCOPY to duplicate the broken disk and try to repair the copy. This way if you make matters worse, you can always create another DISKCOPY and try the process again.

It's not always smart to set BREAK to ON. The default DOS setting is OFF, which means DOS will check to see if you pressed Ctrl-C or Ctrl-ScrollLock only during a handful of routine screen, output, and keyboard operations. If you're running a program that chews data all day long and doesn't do much I/O, and you have to break out of it periodically, you may want to set BREAK to ON so DOS will check for Ctrl-C or Ctrl-ScrollLock presses far more frequently.

But this can have a down side as well, since a break signal can grind certain programs to a halt. If you're running *WordStar*, for instance, and you pound incessantly on Ctrl-C you can crash out of the program without saving the file you were working on. Since Ctrl-C happens to be a *WordStar* command to scroll the screen up (same as a PgDn), this can be dangerous when you're paging through a long file. Worse, this may bypass the program's normal cleanup operations (such as resetting interrupt vectors), which can clobber subsequent programs you try to run.

Don't assume you've copied files correctly just because the VERIFY command is active. DOS lets you add a /V switch to the COPY and XCOPY commands, or issue a VERIFY ON command, that supposedly ensures data integrity by verifying that the original and copy are the same.

Unfortunately, this process uses a CRC check, which can catch gross errors but is not utterly foolproof. The COMP command, on the other hand, compares both files byte-by-byte and is more reliable. Unfortunately, COMP.COM is crude and slow, and will stop working if it stumbles over a scant ten mismatches. The generic DOS FC.EXE File Compare utility is vastly better, and it's a real mystery why IBM gave users the pathetic COMP command instead of the far superior FC.

In any event, if you're validating copies, COMP should work just fine, and will uncover potential problems that can fool /V or VERIFY.

Using your computer in a thunderstorm is a bit risky, since lightning strikes can foul up the power lines. If you're nervous about direct lightning hits and you put a lightning arrester in the power circuit, don't forget to isolate the phone line to your modem. A wire's a wire.

Never switch diskettes in the middle of an aborted operation. If you try to copy files to a floppy and DOS for some reason interrupts the process and pauses, and you realize you put the wrong diskette in the drive, don't just remove the wrong floppy and put in the right one. DOS may still think the old one is there and copy data to the wrong place on the new one, which will damage it. Instead, to be safe, stop what you were doing and issue a nonwriting command for that drive like DIR to let DOS know you've switched disks. The SHARE command helps guard against this, but you can't be too careful.

Part IV

The Utilities
DOS Forgot

Utilities

New to this revised second edition are more than 100 utilities, culled from the best freeware and shareware programs available. We've tried to select programs that offer functionality out of the ordinary, and that complement, rather than duplicate, the utilities from the previous editions of this book.

The freeware programs, as the name implies, may be freely used and distributed without obligation. Please note that there is a distinction between a program being considered freeware and a programs specifically put into the public domain. The copyright for freeware generally resides with the author, and thus commercial use or distribution requires permission, whereas material specifically put into the public domain can be used for any purpose without restriction.

Shareware is an interesting approach to distributing intellectual property that has no real counterpart in many other fields of human endeavor. It's hard to imagine a restaurant operating on the proposition that if you like a meal, you'll pay whatever you felt it was worth — at least, not any restaurant since Alice's.

What is Shareware

Shareware distribution gives users a chance to try software before buying it. If you try a shareware program and continue using it, you are expected to register. Individual programs differ on details — some request registration while others require it, some specify a maximum trial period. With registration, you get anything from the simple right to continue using the software to an updated program with printed manual. Copyright laws apply to both shareware and commercial software, and the copyright holder retains all rights, with a few specific exceptions as stated below. Shareware authors are accomplished programmers, just like commercial authors, and the programs are of comparable quality. (In both cases, there are good programs and bad ones!) The main difference is in the method of distribution. The author specifically grants the right to copy and distribute the software, either to all and sundry or to a specific group. For example, some authors require written permission before a commercial disk vendor may copy their shareware.

Shareware is a distribution method, not a type of software. You should find software that suits your needs and pocketbook, whether it's commercial or shareware. The shareware system makes fitting your needs easier, because you can try before you buy. And because the overhead is low, prices are low also. Shareware has the ultimate money-back guarantee — if you don't use the product, you don't pay for it.

We can't police your conscience in this matter, but we've tried to reduce the hassle of locating the author of a specific piece of shareware and registering the software, should you decide that you want to use it regularly. We think you'll be surprised, pleasantly, at the quality of the software, and urge you to support those authors whose work you find worthwhile.

Summary of Programs and Credits

ADDCOMM.EXE   David Foley   Shareware
Version 1.11   Foley Hi-Tech Systems

Purpose: Allows you to define the address of your COM ports in the DOS lower-memory segment. Useful for machines whose BIOS doesn't support COM3 and COM4 ports by default.

Syntax: `[d:] [path]ADDCOMM [port] [address]`

where:

PORT   =   the COM port to add, and

ADDRESS   =   the address of the COM port.

Remarks: In many older machines including early 80386-based systems, the BIOS would only set up COM1 and COM2 for DOS. Newer serial cards and modems allow you to define COM3 and COM4 on the cards but these machines won't allow DOS to see these additional ports unless you place the corresponding address in low DOS memory. ADDCOMM will place this information in the correct location for you and ADDCOMM will also display the current address values for any COM ports that are installed in your system.

By placing the ADDCOMM statements in your AUTOEXEC.BAT file you can have the machine load the correct values without having to intervene. ADDCOMM is not a TSR and will not require any overhead memory to set up your ports from AUTOEXEC or the DOS prompt.

Example: ADDCOMM COM3 3E8 will tell DOS to address COM3 at address 3E8.

ADDCOM.EXE is Copyright © 1989-1991 by Foley High-Tech Systems
This program is not public domain but is "shareware" and a part of the Foley Hi-Tech Systems ExtraDOS collection. To register send a check or money order for $19.00 to:

Foley Hi-Tech Systems
ExtraDOS Registration
172 Amber Drive
San Francisco, CA 94131
(415) 826-6084

ALARMCLK.COM
Version 2.01

David Foley
Foley Hi-Tech Systems

Shareware

Purpose: Together with its companion program ALARMSET.EXE, provides a simple alarm clock for MS-DOS machines.

Syntax: `[d:] [path]ALARMCLK /U`

where

    /U   -   Removes ALARMCLK.COM from memory

Example: ALARMCLK and ALARMSET allow you to set a time for your system to beep at you to remind you of appointments or meetings. You may install as many alarms as you wish per session. The alarm information does not survive rebooting or turning off the system power.

ALARMCLK.COM is Copyright © 1989-1991 by Foley Hi-Tech Systems
This program is not public domain but is "shareware" and a part of the Foley Hi-Tech Systems ExtraDOS collection. To register send a check or money order for $19.00 to:

    Foley Hi-Tech Systems
    ExtraDOS Registration
    172 Amber Drive
    San Francisco, CA 94131
    (415)826-6084

ALARMSET.EXE   David Foley   Shareware
Version 2.00   Foley Hi-Tech Systems

Purpose: Sets alarms with ALARMCLK.

Syntax: `ALARMSET [time] [PM] [options]`

where:

> TIME = Time in HH:mm format. Twelve-hour or 24-hour clocks are both accepted for the time format.
>
> PM -   ALARMCLK will assume AM with 12-hour format unless PM is defined.
>
> /D -   Deactivates all alarms.
>
> /U -   Removes ALARMCLK.COM from memory.

ALARMSET.EXE is Copyright © 1989-1991 by Foley HiTech Systems
This program is not public domain but is "shareware" and a part of the Foley Hi-Tech Systems ExtraDOS collection. To register send a check or money order for $19.00 to:

> Foley Hi-Tech Systems
> ExtraDOS Registration
> 172 Amber Drive
> San Francisco, CA 94131
> (415)826-6084

ALLSUB.COM
Version 1.20

David Foley
Foley Hi-Tech Systems

Shareware

Purpose: Allows any command or program to be run on the current directory as well as on all subdirectories of the current directory.

Syntax: `[d:] [path] ALLSUB [command]`

where

COMMAND   is any valid DOS command or program with its parameters.

Enter the command just as if you were running it from the DOS prompt.

Example: ALLSUB is useful for deleting groups of files or performing tasks with programs that don't normally allow for subdirectories. As ALLSUB is performed in each subdirectory ALLSUB, it displays the directory of execution.

Example: ALLSUB DEL *.BAK will delete all files with the extension of .BAK from all subdirectories on your default drive.

ALLSUB.COM is Copyright © 1989-1991 by Foley Hi-Tech Systems
This program is not public domain but is "shareware" and a part of the Foley Hi-Tech Systems ExtraDOS collection. To register send a check or money order for $19.00 to:

Foley Hi-Tech Systems
ExtraDOS Registration
172 Amber Drive
San Francisco, CA 94131
(415)826-6084

ARCOPY.COM   Eric Meyer   Freeware
Version 1.6

Purpose: Backs up and maintains multiple copies of files.

Syntax: `[d:][path]ARCOPY source [, source2, . . .] [target]`
`[/switches]`

where

> source, source2, . . . are the names of the files to be backed up.
>
> Target is the drive and path destination for the copied files.

and valid switches are:

> /A = copy only source files with archive bit set, but do not clear source file archive bits.
>
> /Bdate:time = copy only files whose timestamp is earlier than the specified date:time. (Defaults are today:midnight)
>
> /E = copy only files that already exist in target directory.
>
> /H = copy hidden and system files.
>
> /Ldate:time = copy only files whose timestamp is later than the specified date:time. (Defaults are today:midnight)
>
> /M = same as A, except that source file archive bits are cleared.
>
> /N = copy only source files whose names do not already exist in target directory.
>
> /P = display "Y/N?" prompt for each file to be copied.
>
> /R = renames or moves files. If a global target filename is given, every specified file will be renamed. For example, ARCOPY *.COM X*.COM /R changes first letter of every source COM file to "X." If different target directory is specified, files are moved to that directory.
>
> /T = if file already exists in target directory, it will be overwritten only if source file has a more recent date/timestamp.
>
> /W = a read-only target file will be overwritten by a source file with the same name.
>
> /X = all source files will be copied, except for the one whose name is given, thus ARCOPY B:*.EXE /X copies all files except those with an EXE extension.
>
> /Z = the high bit in each byte in the source file will be zeroed in the target copy.

Notes: Unless otherwise specified, the drive and path for any source is the same as that specified for the previous source. If the target is not specified, the current directory is the target.

Typing ARCOPY by itself will give you a hyphen prompt, and a help message giving you valid options at that point. To exit the hyphen prompt, type return.

The first switch must be preceded by a slash; additional slashes, spaces are optional. For B and L switches, date format is MMDDYY (month-day-year) and time format is HHMM (hour-minutes). Complete date/timestamp is therefore MMDDYY:HHMM. Use both L and B switches to copy only source files later than L but before B.

If W switch is omitted, a write error is reported if source file attempts to overwrite a read-only target file. The Z switch is an excellent tool for converting a WordStar document into an ASCII file (or for completely trashing a binary file). To quickly read a WordStar document on screen, just type ARCOPY filename CON /Z. Use CON or PRN as targets to display source file on screen or to send it to the printer.

This program is "freeware" and may be freely used and distributed, but not modified or sold for profit without author consent:

Eric Meyer
3541 Smuggler Way
Boulder, CO 80303

AREA.EXE   David Foley   Shareware
Version 2.13   Foley Hi-Tech Systems

Purpose: Helps to locate the region to which an area code applies or to locate the area code
for a specific region.

Syntax: `[d:] [path]AREA [code] [string] [options]`

    [code]   is any three-digit area code.

    [string]   is any string that might match a state or region that you are
searching for.

Options: /L = Load as a TSR. This makes the AREA code program a pop TSR
that allows you to call up an area code or location while running another
application without exiting to DOS. [CTRL][LSHIFT]A is the hotkey to
activate the program once installed as a TSR.

    /U = Uninstall the AREA code program if it is installed as a TSR, freeing
up the overhead that it required. Uninstall works only if AREA was the last
TSR loaded on the Heap. If the program is unable to uninstall it will inform
you when running the /U parameter.

    /NOH = If it is running AREA from a batch file or from another shell
program and you want it not to display the header information.

    /K$nnnn = Allows you to set the default key for the TSR popup command.
You can alternatively set the hotkey by using the environment variable
AREAKEY, but don't use this option unless you are familiar with your
system's currently defined hotkeys. By changing the hotkey value you may
cause conflict with another TSR in your system.
Examples include a chart that shows you the value to use for either the /K
parameter or the environment variable /K.

Examples: AREA /K$0836 /L would specify [ALT][RSHFT] as a new hotkey

Environment Variable for hotkey definition:

    SET AREAKEY=$0836 as a line in the AUTOEXEC.BAT file would set the
[ALT][RSHFT] as the hotkey

Keyboard Scan Codes for Hotkey Use

    Hotkey = $XXYY

where:

    XX   =   aggregate hex code for the Alt, Ctrl, Lshft, and/or Rshft

    Y   =   One of the hex codes from the scancode tables below

Computing the XX value:

Alt	=	$0800
Ctrl	=	$0400
Lshft	=	$0200
Rshft	=	$0100

so, [Alt][Lshft]   = $0800 + $0200 = $0A00 + YY = $0AYY

or, [Ctrl][Rshft]   = $0400 + $0100 = $0500 + YY = $05YY

or, [Alt][Ctrl][Rshft]   = $0800 + $0400 + $0100 = $0D + YY = $0DYY

Notes: If XX = $0000 then this is a single key hotkey which will be defined by the YY keycode.

Computing the YY value:

To use previous examples,

[Alt][Lshft][G]   = $0A00 + 22 (G = hex 22) = $0A22

[Ctrl][Rshft][F10]   = $0500 + 44 (F10 = hex 44) = $0544

You can also use something like [Alt][Lshft] only. To do this, you would use

$0800	+	2A	=	$082A
[Alt]		[Lshft]	=	[Alt][Lshft]

    The XX portion of the hotkey may not use anything "lower" than Ctrl for the following keys: Esc, BkSp, Space, CapsLock, Tab, ENTER, PrtSc, Ins, Del, and NumLock. This means you can't use Lshft-Tab, or Rshft-Tab, but you can use Ctrl-Tab or Alt-Tab. See Table 6-7 for Scan Codes Note that you can use the Alt, Ctrl, L/Rshft keys by themselves. For example, the following hotkeys/codes are valid:

Alt-Rshft	$0836
Ctrl-Rshft	$0436
Lshft-Rshft	$0236
Ctrl-Alt-Lshft	$0C2A

Since the phone company constantly updates regions and expands with more area codes, the data may become outdated. If you know of a new area code, or one that has been changed, please inform us so that we may keep the AREA utility current.

Please contact us either by BBS, FAX or PHONE.

AREA.EXE is Copyright © 1983-1991 by Foley Hi-Tech Systems
This program is not public domain but is "shareware" and a part of the Foley Hi-Tech Systems ExtraDOS collection. To register send a check or money order for $19.00 to:

Foley Hi-Tech Systems
ExtraDOS Registration
172 Amber Drive
San Francisco, CA 94131
(415)826-6084

BANNER.EXE   **David Foley**   **Shareware**
Version 1.21   **Foley Hi-Tech Systems**

Purpose: Displays an ASCII rendition of the letters you put in a message rotated at 90 degrees. This is based on the BANNER that is available in many UNIX systems.

Syntax: `[d:] [path] BANNER [options] [message]`

Options: /? = Display Help

/w = Set to 132-column width

/wnn = Set to nn-column width

/p = Send output to LPT1 *default setting

/pLPTn = Send output to LPTn

/s = Send output to Screen

/o[fname] = Send output to file [fname]

/noh = suppress the header information

To send the banner to your printer type:

`BANNER  /w80  "Hi there "`

This sends an 80-Column-wide "Hi there" to your printer.

BC3.COM and
BC3-SET.EXE

Bob Hummer   **Freeware**

Purpose: BlockCursor3 (BC3) is a small, fast TSR that maintains a block cursor.

Syntax: `[d:] [path] BC3`

Example: BC3 works even with "cursor crunchers" such as the original SideKick. The best
way to start BC3 is by adding the line:

`[d:] [path] BC3`

to your AUTOEXEC.BAT file. This will automatically load BC3 whenever you
start your computer. Unlike many TSRs, BC3 isn't fussy about the loading order.
Certain video displays may require a different value for the bottom scan line in
order to set a block cursor than the preset value in BC3. The companion program
BC3-SET.EXE can be used to change this value in the BC3.COM file.
Just type:

`BC3-SET`

at the DOS command line and follow the instructions. The top scan line is set to 0.
BC3-SET will search the DOS path for BC3.COM, and can thus be operated
from any directory as long as both BC3-SET.EXE and BC3.COM are on the path.
Note that, if BC3 is loaded in memory when BC3-SET started, it will override
BC3-SET's attempt to show you the new cursor shape, and you won't be able to
see what the new cursor will look like until the computer is restarted.

This program is "freeware" and may be freely used and distributed, but not modified or sold for
profit without author consent.

BIGBUFER.COM   Jonathan Kraidin   Freeware
Version 1.11

Purpose: Extends keyboard buffer between 60 and 76 keystrokes.

Syntax: `[d:] [path] BIGBUFER`

Example: This program enhances your keyboard operations by expanding the type-ahead buffer to 60 keystrokes. There are no options; simply place the program in your autoexec.bat file. If you are also using a type-a-matic rate enhancer, place it before the extender. Incompatibilities may exist when using any other utility that manipulates the BIOS keyboard buffer.

This program is "freeware" and may be freely used and distributed, but not modified or sold for profit without author consent.

| **BL.COM** | **Scott Chaney** | **Shareware** |
| **Version 1.3** | **RSE, Inc.** | |

Purpose: Highlights the cursor line.

Syntax: `[d:] [path] BL [/R] [/C]`

Example: Brightline is a TSR program which reverses the text and background screen colors on the cursor line. Therefore, the cursor line text appears in a highlighted bar running across the width of the screen.

Notes: Once BL is loaded, the hotkey combination Alt+O toggles the highlighted bar on and off. If the bar is toggled off, it will automatically come back on again after two minutes of keyboard inactivity, but goes off when keyboard is used again. The registered version supports your choice of color for the highlight; the shareware version lets you choose red only via the /R switch. The /C switch will minimize flicker and "snow" on older CGA displays.

   BL is not compatible with Windows, and may create video artifacts with some applications (QuickBASIC, for example).

This program is not public domain but is "shareware" and part of the RSE, Inc. collection. For registration and fee information contact:

RSE, Inc.
1157 57 Drive S.E.
Auburn, WA 98002
(206)939-4105

BLANK-IT.COM   **Rhode Island Soft Systems, Inc.**   **Shareware**

Purpose: Blanks the screen if there is no keyboard activity.

Syntax: BLANK-IT [N]

where

N is the waiting time, in minutes, until screen is blanked following the last keystroke. Default is 10 minutes.

Example: Press the spacebar to restore the screen display. The keystroke is discarded, so it does not affect whatever is on the screen.
Unlike some TSR screen-blanking utilities, BLANK-IT works when loaded into an upper memory block via the LOADHIGH command.

Notes: Press Ctrl+Left Shift key to blank the screen immediately.
Press Alt+Left Shift to disable BLANK-IT. To re-enable screen blanking function, press Alt+Left Shift again, or Ctrl+Left Shift.

WARNING: Remember to disable BLANK-IT before starting WINDOWS or any other application that takes over control of the keyboard. Otherwise, if the screen blanks, pressing the spacebar will not restore the screen display, and you'll have to do a warm reboot. This is being addressed in an upcoming version.

This program is not public domain but is "shareware" and a part of the Rhode Island Soft Systems, Inc. collection. To receive the entire BLANK-IT package (13 files) on disk, please send a check or money order for $15 to:

Rhode Island Soft Systems, Inc.
P.O. Box 748
Woonsocket, RI 02895
24-hour BBS: (401) 658-3465

BLANK-IT is copyrighted 1990 and 1991 by, and is a trademark of, Rhode Island Soft Systems, Inc.

BOOTLOCK.COM   David Foley   Shareware
Version 1.10   Foley Hi-Tech Systems

Purpose: Locks out the use of the [CTRL] [ALT] [DEL] soft boot sequence and the
[CTRL] C or [CTRL] [BREAK] break sequence. Once installed, BOOTLOCK requires 624 bytes of memory.

Syntax: `[d:][path]BOOTLOCK [/options]`

Where options include:

/? = display help
/R = disable Ctl-Alt-Del
/B = disable Ctl-Break
/C = disable Ctl-C
/U = remove Bootlock from memory

Example: Bootlock /R/C disables both Ctl-Alt-Del and Ctl-C but leaves Ctl-Break enabled.

BOOTLOCK.COM is Copyright © 1989-1991 by Foley Hi-Tech Systems
This program is not public domain but is "shareware" and a part of the Foley Hi-Tech Systems
ExtraDOS collection. To register send a check or money order for $19.00 to:

Foley Hi-Tech Systems
ExtraDOS Registration
172 Amber Drive
San Francisco, CA 94131
(415)826-6084

BRKBOX.COM	**David Foley**	**Shareware**
Version 1.21	**Foley Hi-Tech Systems**	

Purpose: Displays the status of a COM port inside your PC.

Syntax: `[d:][path]BRKBOX [port] [U]`

where,

[port] is the serial port COMx. Valid numbers are 1 through 4.

[U] tells the program to remove itself from memory. This only works if BRKBOX is the last TSR installed.

Remarks: The status of the DTR, DSR, RTS, CTS, DCD, and RI pins, as well as the data rate, parity, number of data bits, and number of stop bits are displayed on the top right hand corner of the screen. This information is sometimes useful when trying to debug a serial port or some associated communications software.

If no communications port is specified the program defaults to COM1. To toggle the display on and off use ALT-C. The program will start with the display toggled off.

BRKBOX can be uninstalled by entering it with the optional U parameter (if it was the last TSR loaded).

Example: BRKBOX COM1 monitors communications port #1.

BRKBOX.COM is Copyright © 1987-1991 by Foley Hi-Tech Systems
This program is not public domain but is "shareware" and a part of the Foley Hi-Tech Systems ExtraDOS collection. To register send a check or money order for $19.00 to:

Foley Hi-Tech Systems
ExtraDOS Registration
172 Amber Drive
San Francisco, CA 94131
(415)826-6084

| **CAL.EXE** | **David Foley** | **Shareware** |
| **Version 1.20** | **Foley Hi-Tech Systems** | |

Purpose: Displays a calendar from DOS in one of two formats, either one month or 12 months of one year.

Syntax: `[d:] [path] CAL [mm] yyyy`

where:

mm is the month [1..12]

yyyy is the year [100..9999]

If you specify two digits for yyyy then it will assume you mean 19xx.

Remarks: To pause the display of a full year, press [CTRL] S to pause the screen and then any key to continue the display.

CAL.EXE is Copyright © 1989-1990 by Foley Hi-Tech Systems
This program is not public domain but is "shareware" and a part of the Foley Hi-Tech Systems ExtraDOS collection. To register send a check or money order for $19.00 to:

Foley Hi-Tech Systems
ExtraDOS Registration
172 Amber Drive
San Francisco, CA 94131
(415)826-6084

CAT.EXE   **David Foley**   **Shareware**
Version 1.11   **Foley Hi-Tech Systems**

Purpose: A UNIX utility written for the MS-DOS world for displaying, printing, and concatenating files together.

Syntax: `[d:] [path] CAT [fname]`

or

`CAT [file1] [file2] > [file3]`

Remark: CAT handles redirection of both input and output. It can be used like COPY CON to create files as well. With only a single filename as an argument, it will copy from the standard input to the filename. With two or more filenames, it will copy the earlier files to the last file.

CAT.EXE is Copyright © 1989-1990 by Foley Hi-Tech Systems
This program is not public domain but is "shareware" and a part of the Foley Hi-Tech Systems ExtraDOS collection. To register send a check or money order for $19.00 to:

> Foley Hi-Tech Systems
> ExtraDOS Registration
> 172 Amber Drive
> San Francisco, CA 94131
> (415)826-6084

CHIMES.COM	David Foley	Shareware
Version 1.01	Foley Hi-Tech Systems	

Purpose: A terminate-and-stay resident program that attaches itself to the BIOS timer-tick interrupt.

Syntax: `[d:][path]CHIMES /code`

These are the available chimes and their codes:

/M0 = Time Tones

/M1 = Westminster Chimes

/M2 = Saint Michael Chimes

/M3 = Whittington Chimes

Remarks: CHIMES counts the time internally, so that it does not bring any overhead into system throughput by using DOS functions. When the program realizes that the time is nearing the hour, the program starts chiming.

In its default mode, chimes produces "Time Tone" beeps. These consist of three short beeps, starting at three seconds before the hour. Then, at the hour, a longer and higher beep is given.

Many of the dial-up time services provide such a time tone. CHIMES can be given the /M option on the command line to provide the different clock chimes. Using chimes /M1 would setup chimes to use the Westminster chimes.

If you select the M0 option of the program, chimes will only become active at the hour. Otherwise, chimes will faithfully reproduce the chimes for each quarter hour of the clock. The program will also strike the hour by chiming for each hour, or chiming just once for the half hour.

COLSET.COM
Version 2.0

Raymond P. Tackett   Freeware

Purpose: Maintains your preferred color settings in the color text mode (video mode 3).

Syntax: `[d:] [path] COLSET [BT] [min max] [set]`

B = background color (0–F). A–F sets blinking text.

T = text color (0–F)

min max = color settings apply to all modes between min and max (must be used together, or not at all)

set = video adapter switched to mode number specified by set

Remarks: COLSET intercepts and examines BIOS calls which manipulate the video 10H interrupt. All bracketed parameters are hexadecimal numbers. Default (no parameters) is grey text on blue background. See Chapter 13 for details of the color codes, and Chapters 13 and 14 for discussions of the video modes that can be selected via set.

Notes: Do not run COLSET on a system with a monochrome monitor. Monochrome hardware may be damaged if COLSET attempts to switch to a color mode. Some screen-blanking utilities will not function in conjunction with COLSET. COLSET does not work with some replacement ANSI.SYS drivers such as UV-ANSI.SYS.

This program is "freeware" and may be freely used and distributed, but not modified or sold for profit without author consent.

COMPORT.EXE   John Woram
Version 1.0

Purpose: Displays list of installed parallel and serial ports.

Syntax: `[d:] [path] COMPORT`

Remarks: Reports the status of COM1 through COMN and Parallel ports 1 though N as "vacant" or "installed" as appropriate.

Example   Comport yields a report similar to the following:

Asynchronous Adapter Ports:
COM 1 installed
COM 2 vacant
COM 3 vacant
COM 4 vacant

Parallel Adapter Ports:
  1 installed
  2 vacant
  3 vacant

COMPORT.EXE is Copyright © 1990 by John Woram

COPYDISK.EXE   Gordon Harris   Freeware

Purpose: Copies volume label, subdirectory structure and all files regardless of attribute type, from one disk medium to another.

Syntax: `[d:] [path] COPYDISK s: t: [-n] [-x] [-f]`

where "s:" and "t:" are valid DOS drives and the optional parameters are:

-n = (no prompt). Useful when using COPYDISK in batch files. With the "-n" parameter, COPYDISK will not prompt you for permission to delete all data from the target disk.

-x = (relaxed media checking). With this parameter, the target disk may be a hard disk and the source data may be larger than the capacity of the target disk.

-f = (format target automatically if media check failure). With this parameter, the DOS FORMAT.COM command will be spawned without prompting if the target disk fails the media check.

Example: COPYDISK is an XCOPY-like utility which allows you to copy an entire disk to a drive of differing type, e.g. copy the contents of a 1.2 m floppy to a 1.44 m floppy, etc.
    Unlike XCOPY, COPYDISK will copy the volume label from the source disk to the target, as well as copying all subdirectories and files including hidden, system or read-only files and directories. All files on the target disk created by COPYDISK will have identical attributes (dates, times, etc) as the files on the source disk. If the source disk is bootable, so will the resulting target disk.

Notes: Given valid parameters, COPYDISK (1) performs a media check on the indicated drives, (2) prompts the user for permission to delete all existing data from the target drive, (3) copies the volume label from the source drive to the target and then (4) proceeds to copy all files and directories from the source to the target.
    COPYDISK aborts if its check of the media type of the target disk reveals that it is a fixed disk. This protects you from inadvertently deleting the contents of a hard disk either by using an incorrect parameter for the target drive or by using a virtual drive name created by ASSIGN or SUBST which represents a fixed disk drive or subdirectory on a hard disk.
    During the media check, COPYDISK installs its own critical error handler. If an error is detected reading either the source or target drives, COPYDISK will prompt you to retry access to the disk. If you choose not to retry access to the target disk, COPYDISK will prompt you as to whether you wish to format the target.
    COPYDISK also aborts if the data on the source disk is too large to fit on the empty target disk, or if any errors occur reading data from the source or writing data to the target disks.

This program is "freeware" and may be freely used and distributed, but not modified or sold for profit without author consent.

CTRLKEY.COM   **Shane Bergl**   **Shareware**

Purpose: Turns the keypad "5" into a second control key, and also changes the "-" key on the numeric keypad to produce control K when it is pressed. Both functions are disabled if Num Lock or Scroll Lock are engaged.

Syntax: [d:] [path] CTRLKEY

Notes: CTRLKEY will usually clash (non-destructively) with keyboard macro programs such as Smartkey, but if you have such a program loaded then you don't really need CTRLKEY. The effects of CTRLKEY will also be overridden by keyboard accelerators if it is loaded before them.

  While there are a number of keyboard macro programs that can do the same thing, CTRLKEY has the virtue of being small enough (500 bytes) to be loaded all the time whereas sometimes there isn't room for Smartkey.

This program and STACK.EXE are not public domain but are "shareware." If you wish to register as a user please send $A20 to:

P.O. Box 78

Dickson, Australia Capital Territory, 2602, Australia

From outside Australia please add $A4 to cover currency conversion costs.

CURLOCK.COM   David Foley   Shareware
Version 1.10   Foley Hi-Tech Systems

Purpose: Locks the cursor shape so that no matter what software you use, the cursor will not be changed.

Syntax: `[d:] [path] CURLOCK`

Example: CURLOCK intercepts all calls to BIOS interrupt 10h and bypasses any calls to change the cursor shape.
It is a TSR requiring 592 bytes of resident RAM.

CURLOCK.COM is Copyright © 1987-1990 by Foley Hi-Tech Systems
This program is not public domain but is "shareware" and a part of the Foley Hi-Tech Systems ExtraDOS collection. To register send a check or money order for $19.00 to:

> Foley Hi-Tech Systems
> ExtraDOS Registration
> 172 Amber Drive
> San Francisco, CA 94131
> (415)826-6084

CURSOR.EXE	David Foley	Shareware
Version 2.11	Foley Hi-Tech Systems	

Purpose: Controls your cursor from the DOS prompt.

Syntax: `[d:] [path] CURSOR [switches]`

where valid switches are:

/D turns the cursor on to the bootup default underline

/H turns the cursor off (hide cursor)

/B makes the cursor a full block

/M displays the values of the registers for the video call

/? displays the help screen

/V returns version information

/I (Interactive Setup) gives you a full screen editor of your cursor

/T:nn sets the top scan line of your cursor

/B:nn sets the bottom scan line of your cursor

/LOCK locks the cursor shape

/UNLOCK unlocks the cursor shape

Example: You can set the cursor to various shapes as listed above. Some software uses the DOS cursor in which case the cursor will stay the same as what you set it using CURSOR. If the software makes its own cursor then the cursor you create with CURSOR will not function inside this software. Some software resets the DOS cursor to its own shape. Therefore you might want to put CURSOR in a batch file after this software to reset the cursor to what you want it to be at the DOS prompt.

CUT.EXE   David Foley   Shareware
Version 1.10   Foley Hi-Tech Systems

Purpose: A UNIX utility written for the MS-DOS world that displays and prints text files in different formats by eliminating columns and other formatting options.

Syntax:
```
[d:][path]CUT -clist [fname1] [fname2] ...
```

where list is the list of columns to display, in the format firstcolumn-lastcolumn.

Examples:
```
CUT -c1-15 test.txt
```

will display all characters in the file test.txt in columns 1 through 15.

```
CUT -c1-15 test.txt > prn
```

would print all the characters in the file test.txt in columns 1 to 15.

```
CUT -c1-15 test.txt > testedit.txt
```

would copy just the material in columns 1 to 15 of test.txt to the file testedit.txt.

Foley Hi-Tech Systems
ExtraDOS Registration
172 Amber Drive
San Francisco, CA 94131
(415)826-6084

D.EXE	Marc Perkel	Shareware
Version 4.0		

Purpose: A small, fast directory lister driven from the command line.

Syntax: `[d:] [path]D <path\mask, (path\mask ...)> options`

where path\mask is of the form dir*.ext and the following options are valid:

/E Sort by Ext	/D Sort by Date
/S Sort by Size	/U Unsorted
/B Sort Backwards	/I Identify Directory
/R Programs that can Run	/A Files with Archive Set
/L Long Display, no Pause	/W Wait for Keypress at End
/O Use Standard Output Device	/P Output to Printer
/F Filenames Only	
/+DATE Files after Date	/-DATE Files before Date
/1/2/3/4/5/6 Controls Number of Columns and Information Displayed	

Notes: You can list multiple directories or several groups of files with different extensions within a directory by specifying a list of paths and masks. For displaying information from within a batch file, it's useful to have all the switches available from the command line.

D.EXE is Copyright © 1988-1991 by Marc Perkel. All Rights Reserved
These programs are part of the Computer Tyme DOS ToolBox.
To Register, ask for the BANTAM BOOK special price of $25. (Reg Price $60)

Contact:
Computer Tyme
411 North Sherman, Suite 300
Springfield, MO 65802
(800) 548-5353

DAAG.EXE
Version 2.34

Steve Leonard

Shareware

Purpose: DAAG.EXE ((Disk-at-a-Glance) provides an easy-to-use map of your hard disk.

Syntax: `[d:] [path]DAAG [drive:]`

From the opening screen, the following commands are valid:

Up Arrow, Down Arrow, PgUp, PgDown, Home, End move you around the directory tree displayed on the screen.

Enter gives you a summary by file extension of the current highlighted directory, showing the amount of space occupied by files of each extension.

Pressing ENTER a second time displays the individual files of a particular highlighted file extension, and pressing ENTER a third time displays the contents of a specific file. This window is also sortable by

FILENAME or by SIZE, and Del deletes the file currently highlighted.

F1 provides on-line help.

F2 saves the current tree map to a file in your root directory named DDyymmdd.DAG, where yymmdd is the current date.

F3 displays files from the current highlighted directory that duplicate the names of other files on the disk. Pressing F5 at this point will save the list of duplicates to disk as DAAG.DUP.

F4 displays a piechart of the top 16 directories by number of bytes of disk used. If you have more than 16 directories, then the smallest ones are grouped collectively under "Other". This option requires an EGA or VGA monitor it's — great for identifying disk hogs!

Remarks: DAAG initially displays a tree-structured directory map, showing hidden directories and providing useful statistics relating to file and directory size.

Notice that the sum of all directories is not exactly equal to the total disk size minus the space available. This is because DOS allocates file space in CLUSTERS, so that a 20 byte batch file will actually use 4096 bytes (depending on cluster size).

DAAG uses an ancillary program called SHOW.EXE to browse through files — if you have a preferred browser, keep a copy under the name SHOW.EXE in a path DAAG can find.

Duplicates displayed are the full pathnames of files from the current directory that replicate the name of another file on the disk, and the full name (including path) of the duplicate filenames. You won't see files from other directories that duplicate filenames elsewhere on the disk, and you won't be able to delete files from the display window of duplicates.

DAAG requires about 390k of memory. If you plan to use the BROWSE function, then you will need additional memory. The included browse program,

SHOW.EXE, requires approximately 131k of memory, making TOTAL MEM-
ORY REQUIREMENTS about 521k. Luckily it is not a TSR!

DAAG has several tables in memory, that hold directory and file information.
The maximum number of directories DAAG can hold (1st window) ..... 200; maximum different extensions in a directory (2nd window)...... 250; maximum files
with the same extension (3rd window)............ 400; maximum number of files on
disk (for duplicate checking)..... 4000;If these maximums are exceeded, DAAG
should still work, but it will give a warning message that not all files are available
for display.

This program is "shareware"; anyone who finds this program of value is encouraged to make a
voluntary donation to the author; those sending $10 or more will receive a free update, if one is
written:

Steve Leonard
260 Dunbar Road
Hilton, NY 14468

DD.EXE   **Dennis Vallianos**   **Freeware**
Version 1.13   **D & D Software, Inc.**

Purpose: Display file and directory information in various screen formats.

Syntax: `DD [/options] [pathspec(s)]`

Options show

/A	=	all files and directories
/D	=	directories only
/J	=	archive files only
/R	=	regular and read-only files (Default)
/6	=	files only

Sort by

/F	=	filename (Default)
/K	=	file size based on clusters taken
/N	=	no sort (show in DOS order)
/S	=	file size
/SI	=	file size in inverted order
/T	=	time and date
/TI	=	time and date in inverted order
/X	=	extension

Toggles

/C	=	Clear screen before displaying listing.
/L	=	Use lowercase for file names.
/P	=	Disable pause between screens.

Screen display format

/1	=	one column; filenames only
/2	=	two columns; filename, size, attributes, time, date
/4	=	four columns; filename, size in Kbytes (Default)

Other options

/H	=	Show directory help screen.
/M	=	Modify default settings (see Notes).

/O   =   Restore original defaults (see Notes).

Notes: Options and pathspec may be repeated to show multiple listings.
The switch before the first option may be a slash (as illustrated) or a hyphen.
If no pathspec is entered, *.* is assumed. To display the current directory followed by the DOS directory, type

```
DD *.* C:\DOS
```

(other pathspecs, as desired).
Each pathspec may be preceded by its own options.
To customize DD.EXE to your display preference, type

```
DD /optionsM.
```

Subsequent use of DD alone will display listing according to the options you listed. To restore original defaults, type

```
DD /OM.
```

DD.EXE is Copyright © 1990 by D & D Software, Inc. All Rights Reserved
This program is "freeware" and may be freely used and distributed, but not modified or sold for profit without author consent.

D&D Software, Inc.
809 Jackson Avenue
Lindenhurst, NY 11757
(516)957-8356

DEL2.COM   Dennis Vallianos   Freeware
D & D Software, Inc.

Purpose: Displays filename(s) that will be deleted, requests verification before proceeding.

Syntax: `DEL2 filespec [C]`

> filespec name and extension of file to be deleted.
>
> Wildcards may be used for name or extension.
>
> C   Confirm each filename separately before deleting.

Remarks: DEL2 displays the names of all files that will be erased, along with an "OK to erase?" prompt. If you answer "yes," all listed files are erased. If the C parameter is appended, filenames are displayed sequentially, and the prompt is repeated for each listed file.

Notes: Use as is or rename as ERA.COM. To use in place of the regular DOS DEL or ERASE command, find either command name within the COMMAND.COM file and patch to XEL or XRASE (or similar), thereby disabling the DOS command. Then replace the disabled command by renaming DEL2.COM to DEL.COM or ERASE.COM, as appropriate.

This program is "freeware" and may be freely used and distributed, but not modified or sold for profit without author consent.

> D&D Software, Inc.
> 809 Jackson Avenue
> Lindenhurst, NY 11757
> (516)957-8356

DELAY.EXE	David Foley	Shareware
Version 1.60	Foley Hi-Tech Systems	

Purpose: Replaces the PAUSE command within a batch file, or provides a pause within CONFIG.SYS.

Syntax: `[d:] [path] DELAY [time]` or

`DEVICE`

or

`DEVICEHIGH=DELAY.EXE [time]`

where time specifies the number of seconds to wait before continuing.
Time can be a value between 0 and 65000, with a default value of 5.
DELAY returns an ERROR LEVEL of :

2 - [CTRL][BREAK] pressed

1 - A key was pressed

0 - Time ran out

Remarks: PAUSE will never continue until a key is pressed, whereas with DELAY you can set the amount of seconds to pause, and then continue or continue immediately by pressing a key. Pressing [CTRL]C will also cause a break in a batch file that can be monitored with the error level returned by DELAY. This is useful if you are trying to break out of a stream of commands from within a large batch file. DELAY can be used in CONFIG.SYS as well as from within BATCH files. This is helpful when trying to delay the execution of device drivers in order to see what is going by on the screen. Specifying no time on the delay batch line acts the same as PAUSE.

Example: To use DELAY error codes in a batch file: DETEST.BAT

```
echo off
echo Now I will wait 5 seconds for you to decide
echo Press [CTRL]C to skip the network loader
delay 5
if errorlevel=2 goto skip
:load
network
:skip
```

The above batch file will skip over the network program if CTRL C is pressed during the delay period.

DELAY.EXE is Copyright © 1989-1991 by Foley Hi-Tech Systems
This program is not public domain but is "shareware" and a part of the Foley Hi-Tech Systems
ExtraDOS collection. To register send a check or money order for $19.00 to:

Foley Hi-Tech Systems
ExtraDOS Registration
172 Amber Drive
San Francisco, CA 94131
(415)826-6084

DETAB.EXE	David Foley	Shareware
Version 1.30	Foley Hi-Tech Systems	

Purpose: Strips any tab characters from an ASCII text file and converts them into four spaces.

Remarks: This capability is useful when working with old formatted .ASM files that you would like to work with in an editor that treats fixed tabs differently.

Syntax: `[d:] [path]DETAB [input filename] [output filename]`

DETAB.EXE is Copyright © 1985-1991 by Foley Hi-Tech Systems
This program is not public domain but is "shareware" and a part of the Foley Hi-Tech Systems
ExtraDOS collection. To register send a check or money order for $19.00 to:

> Foley Hi-Tech Systems
> ExtraDOS Registration
> 172 Amber Drive
> San Francisco, CA 94131
> (415)826-6084

DEVICE.EXE   Kim Kokkonen
Version 2.9   Turbo Power Software

Purpose: Reports on device drivers installed by the CONFIG.SYS file.

Syntax: `[d:] [path]DEVICE`

DEVICE offers the following command line options:

/R   raw report.
/?   write a help screen.

The raw report shows more information about the device drivers, but in a less convenient format.

Notes: DEVICE shows the memory used by DOS itself, any additional drivers installed in CONFIG.SYS, and the space used for DOS file handles and buffers. Here is a simple example of DEVICE output:

```
Address      Bytes     Name            Hooked vectors
---------    ------    -------------   --------------
0070:0BB3        -      CON
0070:0C68        -      AUX
0070:0C7A        -      COM1
0070:0D17        -      PRN
0070:0D29        -      LPT1
0070:0E15        -      CLOCK$
0070:0EE5        -      3 Block Units
0070:2071        -      LPT2
0070:2083        -      LPT3
0070:2095        -      COM2
0000:2C58     37712     NUL             08 0A 0C 0D 0E 13 25 26 29
                                        73 74 75 76 77
09A5:0000      3488     0 Block Units
0A7F:0000        18     EMMXXXX0
0A7F:0012        46     386MAX$$          20
0A83:0000       768     1 Block Unit     19
0AB3:0000       768     1 Block Unit
0AE3:0000     18256     DOS buffers
```

The devices up to and including NUL are all part of DOS. DEVICE lumps their memory usage into a single value next to the NUL device. The memory usage associated with NUL does not include the interrupt vector table, the BIOS data area, or the low-memory DOS data area. If you wish to add this memory to the total, just take the hexadecimal segment of the first driver you see (in this case CON) and multiply it by 16 decimal. When the segment is 0070 as shown, that adds 1792 bytes to the total space for DOS.

Don't expect the sum of the DEVICE bytes to match the bytes reported by MAPMEM in the row labeled 'config'. MAPMEM's report shows what DOS thinks has been allocated, but that number isn't complete since some of the memory was used before DOS was truly loaded. However, you should find that the sum of the DEVICE bytes, plus all of MAPMEM's memory excluding the 'config' row, equals the total normal RAM in the system.

DEVICE also lumps all of the drivers up to NUL into a single block when it comes to reporting hooked interrupt vectors.

Because WATCH can't be installed prior to these device drivers, DEVICE must use an empirical technique to detect which vectors each driver controls. Therefore, some meaningless vectors may appear in the list. Any vectors that are grabbed by another program after the driver is loaded will not appear. "Block units" typically refer to disk drives. Any drivers that appear after the NUL device are in the order that you've entered them in CONFIG.SYS. Drivers loaded for non-standard hard disks, like SpeedStor, sometimes make odd entries in the DE-VICE report, as shown with "0 Block Units" above. RAM disks appear more logically: each of the "1 Block Unit" entries above is a VDISK with the data stored in extended memory.

Devices like 386MAX may also cause odd-looking entries: 386MAX puts most of its code in extended memory, and leaves just a bit behind in normal memory.

Here's an example of the raw report option, taken on the same system as the previous report.

```
Starting      Next                Strategy   Interrupt  Device
Address       Hdr Addr   Attr     Entry Pnt  Entry Pnt  Name
---------     ---------  ----     ---------  ---------  -------
0000:2C58     0AB3:0000  8004     0000:14C6  0000:14CC  NUL
0AB3:0000     0A83:0000  0800     0000:00A9  0000:00D4  1 Block Unit
0A83:0000     0A7F:0012  0800     0000:00A9  0000:00D4  1 Block Unit
0A7F:0012     0A7F:0000  C000     0000:0036  0000:003B  386MAX$$
0A7F:0000     09A5:0000  8000     0000:0036  0000:003B  EMMXXXX0
09A5:0000     0070:0BB3  2000     0000:0012  0000:001D  0 Block Units
0070:0BB3     0070:0C68  8013     0000:00C6  0000:00D1  CON
0070:0C68     0070:0D17  8000     0000:00C6  0000:00D7  AUX
0070:0D17     0070:0E15  A040     0000:00C6  0000:00E6  PRN
0070:0E15     0070:0EE5  8008     0000:00C6  0000:010C  CLOCK$
0070:0EE5     0070:0C7A  0840     0000:00C6  0000:0112  3 Block Units
0070:0C7A     0070:0D29  8000     0000:00C6  0000:00D7  COM1
0070:0D29     0070:2071  A040     0000:00C6  0000:00EC  LPT1
0070:2071     0070:2083  A040     0000:00C6  0000:00F4  LPT2
0070:2083     0070:2095  A040     0000:00C6  0000:00FC  LPT3
0070:2095     0070:FFFF  8000     0000:00C6  0000:00DD  COM2
```

In this report, the drivers are listed in DOS priority order rather than the order in which they are loaded in memory.

Additional columns describe how DOS treats each driver. Ray Duncan's book "Advanced MS-DOS" is a good place to learn more about these details.

The DEVICE program assumes that all device drivers are loaded in the CONFIG.SYS file. That is not the case with the NetWare shell, which patches itself into the device driver chain. DEVICE will write a warning message and terminate before reporting the first patched-in driver. The raw device report will still show all of the devices even in this case.

The TSR Utilites — DEVICE.EXE, DISABLE.EXE, MAPMEM.EXE, MARK.EXE, RAMFREE.COM, RELEASE.EXE, and WATCH.COM — are Copyright © 1986, 1987, 1989 by Kim Kokkonen of Turbo Power Software.

DIRCMP.COM	Eric Meyer	Freeware
Version 1.2		

Purpose: Reconciles two directories: (1)to detect differing versions of a file, or (2)to see which files are in one directory but not the other.

Syntax: `[d:] [path] C>dircmp dir1 [dir2] [/options]`

Remarks: Two arguments are expected: Each may consist of an MS-DOS directory name and/or an ambiguous filename. If the second is omitted, it is assumed to be the current directory, *.*.
In addition, you can specify the options:

/P   =   pause display every 25 lines

You can also choose one of these options to restrict the display:

/E   =   files EXISTING in both directories only
/N   =   files NOT existing in both directories only
/M   =   files MODIFIED only

Otherwise, by default, the complete set of listings will be produced.

Notes: Nonidentical versions of files (same name, different timestamps) will appear in the lists of DIFFERING files. The newer version will be flagged with a "+" sign before the filename, the older version with a "-".
You can also select a more restricted display: The /E option gives only the first listing (common files). The /N option gives only the second and third (differing files). The /M option gives a single listing, of modified versions of files with the same name only.

Remarks: Error messages are as follows:

<Bad argument> = Missing or invalid argument; think (read?) and try again.

<No memory> = You don't have enough free memory (about 45k required).

<Too many> = Too many files to compare (maximum is 1024 in each dir); try a more restrictive filespec, e.g. *.DOC instead of *.*.

Examples: `C>dircmp a:`
`C>dircmp a:\work /mp`
`C>dircmp \prg\*.asm a: /n`

DIRCMP will normally give three alphabetical file listings:

1. files common to both directories;
2. files present in the first but not the second;
3. files present in the second but not the first.

In each case the number of files, and their total size (to the nearest K), is also reported.

DIRR.COM	**Scott Chaney**	**Shareware**
Version 1.6	**RSE, Inc.**	

A non-TSR version of the FN.COM utility. See FN.COM for instructions.

DIRR.COM is Copyright © 1990 by RSE, Inc.
This program is not public domain but is "shareware" and part of the RSE, Inc. collection. For registration and fee information contact:

RSE, Inc.
1157 57th Drive S.E.
Auburn, WA 98002
(206) 939-4105

DISABLE.EXE   Kim Kokkonen
Turbo Power Software

Purpose: Disables or reactivates TSR's, leaving them in memory.

Syntax: `[d:][path]DISABLE TSRname|$PSPaddress [options]`

where TSRname or $PSPaddress identify the TSR to be disabled or reactivated.

Options: Options may be preceded by either / or -. Valid options are as follows:

    /A   reactivate the specified TSR.

    /C   check for the presence of the specified TSR.

    /?   write a help screen.

If no option is specified, DISABLE will disable the named TSR.

Remarks: In order to use DISABLE, you must install WATCH.COM as the first memory resident program in your system. WATCH keeps the detailed information about each memory resident program that DISABLE uses to later control them.

Like the other TSR utilities on these disks, DISABLE is operated from the command line. You specify a single TSR by its name (if you are running DOS 3.0 or later) or by its address as determined from a MAPMEM report (described below). If you specify an address, immediately precede the address with a dollar sign "$" and specify the address in hexadecimal.

The name specified for a TSR is the one reported by MAPMEM in the "owner" column. If the owner column reports "N/A", then you must instead specify the address from the "PSP" column.

Examples:
`DISABLE SK`	disables SideKick
`DISABLE SK /A`	reenables SideKick
`DISABLE SK /C`	checks for the presence of SideKick
`DISABLE $2F2E`	disables the TSR at address 2F2E (hex)

DISABLE sets the DOS ERRORLEVEL in order to return status information to a batch file. It uses the following values of errorlevel:

    0   success: TSR is present, was disabled, or was reenabled.

    1   TSR is present, but no action was required to enable or disable it.

    2   TSR is not present in memory.

    254 invalid command line.

    255 severe error.

Note: You cannot use DISABLE to deactivate SideKick Plus, whose swapping technique is incompatible with DISABLE.

With DISABLE.EXE, you can disable and reenable specified memory resident programs without removing them from memory. Its function is analogous to that performed by REFEREE from Persoft, although

DISABLE has neither a fancy user interface nor an option to work from within other programs. DISABLE can allow conflicting TSR's to coexist, and it can let you run applications whose keystrokes conflict with those of TSR's already loaded. DISABLE also provides a small bonus in that it can be used to detect the presence of a particular TSR in memory, thus allowing the design of semi-intelligent batch files.

The TSR Utilites — DEVICE.EXE, DISABLE.EXE, MAPMEM.EXE, MARK.EXE, RAMFREE.COM, RELEASE.EXE, and WATCH.COM — are Copyright © 1986, 1987, 1989 by Kim Kokkonen of Turbo Power Software.

DL.EXE
Version 1.03a
Stephen S. Bates
Shareware

Purpose: Displays two files simultaneously on the screen.

Syntax: `[d:] [path] DL [d:] [\path\] file1 [.ext]`
`[d:] [\path\] [file2] [.ext]`

Remarks: The files will be displayed initially as text in two horizontal windows, with the first file in the upper window designated as "active". The active file's name (and path, if there's room) is displayed in reverse video; its window is framed in double lines. From the main display, you can use the following commands.

You must give at least one filename. If you omit the second file, the first file will appear in both windows. Full pathnames are accepted. You may abbreviate the second file:

1. use '*' in place of filename or ext (or both), OR
2. give d: or \path\ (or both) and omit the filename.ext altogether.

In either case, the missing parts will be supplied from the first file.
(Note: fullblown wildcards are not supported.)

Q — to leave the program. Press Esc to leave the program and restore the screen to its original contents.

+ — to make the second file active; - to make the first file active.

L — to enter or leave Lockstep mode. In Lockstep mode, both files are active; i.e., scroll simultaneously. Lockstep is very useful for comparing files that are almost alike. NOTE: on some keyboards, with certain versions of BIOS, you may use the Scroll Lock instead of L.

PgUp, PgDn, Up Arrow or Down Arrow — to scroll the active file up or down.

Home — to go the top of the file.

End — to go to the bottom.

Left Arrow and Right Arrow — to scroll right or left 20 columns at a time.

Ctrl Left Arrow and Ctrl Right Arrow — to scroll one column at a time

Ctrl Home — returns to the left margin. The column number will be displayed near the file name.

Other Options:

These keys affect the entire display:

V — changes to a vertical (side-by-side, columnar) display.

H — changes back to horizontal.

Pressing V repeatedly when the display is already vertical to make the left window wider, narrower, or the same as the right. Pressing H repeatedly when the display is already horizontal to make the upper window taller, shorter, or the same as the lower.

4 — enters or leaves 43-line mode on EGA or VGA displays.

Results are unpredictable on mono or CGA displays.

These key commands affect only the active window(s):

T — changes the tab stop spacing to 1, 2, ... 8 characters. By default, tab stop spacing is eight characters.

B — reverses the background color following each line, so that ends of lines are visible. B also causes tabs to be expanded in shaded spaces so they can be distinguished from normal spaces. Press B again to return to normal display.

7 — enters or leaves 7-bit display mode. In this mode, the high-order bit of each character is set 0, and control characters other than new-line are omitted from the display. Seven-bit mode may be set any time, but is suspended while hexadecimal mode is in effect. This mode is useful for viewing files created by some word processors.

X — enters or leaves hexadecimal display mode. By default, if the display is horizontal, 16 bytes will be shown on each line; if vertical, eight. The hexadecimal address within the file of the first byte shown is displayed next to the filename. Hexadecimal offsets from that starting address are displayed to the left of each line.

Four additional keys (shown in parentheses after "heX" on the help line) are available only in hexadecimal mode; these assist in aligning records or arrays within the file for convenient display:

Tab or Shift-Tab — increments or decrements the file address of the first byte displayed in hexadecimal mode. Use Up/Down Arrows or PgUp/Dn to get close to the desired address, then Tab or Shift-Tab to adjust.

Ins or Del — increments or decrements the number of bytes per line, starting from the default eight or 16. Striking V, H, or Home will reinstate the defaults. The offsets to the left of the line will be changed to reflect the new number. Note that use of Ins may create display lines longer than the window width. As in text mode, you may use Right Arrow or Ctrl Right Arrow to scroll the window to the right. The actions of these keys are modified slightly in hexadecimal mode for a more readable display. End of file is not detected in hexadecimal mode; you are not prevented from scrolling (harmlessly) off the end of the file buffer.

F — finds the next occurrence of a string within a line. You will be prompted for a string. Searching is case-sensitive, so enter the exact desired string. Only ASCII printable characters are permitted in the search string. The search begins with the second line currently displayed. To search again for the same string, strike F again and press Enter when prompted for the string. In Lockstep mode, both files will be scrolled until the string is found in either file. If the string is found, the line containing it will be displayed at the top of its window. If the line is long, or if the display is scrolled left or right, the found string may not appear onscreen. If it does appear, it will be brightened. F has no effect in hexadecimal display mode.

D — locates the next difference between the files. Comparison begins with the second line of each window, and proceeds until a difference is found or the end of either file is reached. The first lines to differ are displayed at the top of the windows. You may then strike D again immediately, or scroll one file to realign the files before striking D again. D has no effect in hexadecimal display mode.

Notes: DL uses direct video memory display and works only with IBM mono, CGA, EGA, VGA or HGC or exact compatible display adapters, in an 80-column text mode only. Appearance may suffer on CGA-composite monitors.

The combined size of both files is limited to available main memory. If the files are larger, only part of them will be displayed, up to a maximum of about 128k each. In that case, the End key travels only to the end of the buffer, not to the true end of file, and the message

"Out of Space" is displayed. The first file has priority on available memory, so if you have a big and a little file, enter the little one first.

Lines longer than 2,048 characters will be wrapped without warning.

In hexadecimal mode, Ins can increment the number of bytes per line to a maximum of 511 bytes.

DoubleLister v. 1.03a written by Stephen S. Bates
DL.EXE Copyright © 1989 by Stephen S. Bates
This program is not public domain but is "shareware." To register, send $15 to:

Stephen S. Bates
3510 Gramercy St.
Houston, TX 77025

DLT.COM   Eric Meyer   Freeware
Version 1.1

Purpose: Deletes lists or groups of files (in different directories) with a single command, displaying the number deleted. In addition, options: (1)display and ask for user confirmation before deletion; (2)delete all except specified files; (3)selection of files by time/date; include hidden, system, or read-only files.

Syntax: `[d:][path]DLT filespec [,filespec2,...] [/options]`

where filespec is the target file(s) to delete, and valid options are:

/P = PROMPT to confirm. You will be shown the files and asked "Delete? (y/n)".

/H = HIDDEN and System files (otherwise not found) will be included as well.

/R = READ-ONLY files may be deleted as well (otherwise an error results).

/E = Only files EARLIER than specified date/time (MMDDYY:HHMM) are deleted.

/L = Only files LATER than specified date/time are deleted.

/X = All files EXCEPT those specified will be deleted. (Be careful!)

The /X option cannot be used with a list of files in more than one directory. Also, /X cannot be used with /E or /L.

With the /E and /L options, you can choose to delete only files dated before or after a given date or time. (You can even use both together, to delete files dated between two date/times.)

With /E or /L, the date/time should follow the option letter. Dates must be given as six digits in the form MMDDYY; the date "000000" may be used for a blank timestamp, otherwise YY must be 80 or above. You may also type a colon, followed by a four-digit (24-hour) time in the form HHMM. Given a date with no time, the time defaults to 0000 hrs; given a time with no date (note the leading colon is necessary), the date defaults to today. If time/date are omitted altogether, the default is today, 0000 hrs.

Examples:

/l	since today 0:00
/e:1300	before today 13:00
/l020190:1300	since 2/1/90 13:00
/l120189 /e010190	since 12/1/89 0:00, and before 1/1/90 0:00

Notes: The target is either a single (ambiguous) filespec or a list of them delimited with spaces and/or commas. Sub-directories are supported. If not specified, drive and directory default to the current values.

If the target is a list, the previous item's drive and directory carry over to the next one, unless the latter itself begins with a drive or root directory.

Options must be preceded by one slash "/"; separating spaces and further slashes, are optional.

Use care when deleting groups of files; recovering accidentally deleted files requires special utilities, and can be difficult. While learning to use DLT and its various options always use the "/P" option: you will be shown the selected files, and can choose NOT to delete them!

Type "DLT" alone for a help message.

Examples:
```
A>dlt *.bak read.me todo
A>dlt *.*
```

(Doesn't give the annoying confirmation prompt that DOS does.)

```
A>dlt b:\wrk\*.doc,apr\*.not
```

Deletes all files B:\WRK*.DOC and B:\WRK\APR*.NOT.

```
A>dlt *.doc *.not /x
```

Deletes all files other than *.DOC and *.NOT.

```
A>dlt \*.sys /p/rh
```

All files *.SYS in the root directory (including hidden files like MSDOS.SYS) will be deleted after you are prompted to confirm this.

```
A>dlt *.bak /e010189
```

Every file *.BAK dated earlier than 1/1/89 is deleted.

```
A>dlt *.* /l/e:1200
```

Every file dated today before noon is deleted.

Remarks: Error messages are as follows:

    \<Bad argument\> = missing or invalid argument; think (read?) and try again

    \<No memory\> = you don't have enough free memory or, too many files

(try a more restrictive filespec)

    \<R/O Error\> = DOS error deleting file (is it read/only?)

    \<Aborted\> = you pressed ^C

DLT.COM is Copyright © 1991, Eric Meyer, All Rights Reserved
This program is "freeware" and may be freely used and distributed, but not modified or sold for profit without author consent: Eric Meyer
                                  3541 Smuggler Way
                                  Boulder, CO 80303

DMLITE.EXE　　　Marc Perkel　　　Shareware
Version 3.12

Purpose:　Directory Master Lite copies, moves, and deletes files quickly and easily.

Syntax:　`[d:] [path]DMLITE`

Once you've invoked DMLITE, you can use the following commands:

ESC - Aborts any command.

Right-Arrow - Selects or marks a file.

Left-Arrow - Unselects or unmarks a file.

CTRL-Right-Arrow - Selects or marks all files.

CTRL-Left-Arrow - Unselects or unmarks all files.

Q - Quit Directory Master Lite. ALT-X also exits.

C - Copies the file you are pointing to. DMLITE asks you where to copy the file. You must then enter a path or drive.

M - Moves the selected file DMLITE asks you for.

D - Deletes the selected file.

R - Renames the selected file.

V- Views the file you are pointing to. This only works with text files; therefore, if you see garbage on the screen, the file you are trying to view is not a text file.

S - Changes the sort order. DMLITE normally shows the files sorted by name. You can sort them by date, size, or extension. You can also sort in reverse order. Sort only changes the way the files are displayed and not the order on the disk.

L - Re-reads the directory. If you use DMLITE on a floppy disk and you change floppies, press the L key to read in the new floppy's file information.

Alt-C - This command copies all marked files instead of the one you are pointing to.

Alt-M - This command moves all marked files instead of the one you are pointing to.

Alt-D - This command deletes all marked files instead of the one you are pointing to.

Alt-P - Prints help information to your printer.

F5 - Changes to a different disk drive.

F6 - Changes path and mask. It also lets you change drives, path, and file mask in one command.

F7 - Selects TREE MODE. In Tree Mode, only directories that are in the current directory are displayed. The main purpose of tree mode is to move around through the directory tree to the directory you want to be in. Then you normally switch back to file mode for a list of the files in that particular directory (press ENTER).

In Tree Mode, you use your right and left arrows to move to different levels of the directory tree. The left arrow moves you towards the root directory, the right moves you down the directory tree. You exit Tree Mode by pressing F7 again or by pointing to a directory and pressing ENTER.

While in Tree Mode you can make, rename, and delete directories with the following commands:

M - Makes a new subdirectory. Directory Master Lite will prompt you for a name. Remember, you can't make a directory that has the same name as a file that is already in that directory.

R - Renames the subdirectory you are pointing to. You can't change a directory name to the same name as a file that already exists in that directory.

D - Deletes the subdirectory you are pointing to. You cannot delete a subdirectory that contains files — you must first delete or move all of the files from within the subdirectory.

Additional Tree Mode Commands:

\ - Places you in the root directory's list of subdirectories. This is your "main" directory list.

ENTER - Exits Tree Mode and lists the files residing in the subdirectory you are pointing to.

DM LITE displays a list of files in the left-hand column. You can move up and down the list by using your cursor control keys. The upper right-hand box displays status information. The lower right-hand box displays a list of commands you can use.

Use your LEFT and RIGHT cursor arrows to select files. Selected (or "marked") files are displayed in high-intensity (bold) on the screen. You can copy, move, or delete the marked files all at once.

The status window (upper right-hand corner of the display) shows you how many files there are, their sizes, and how many you have selected and their total size as well. Also displayed are: total disk space in megabytes (that's what the little "m" stands for); free disk space; the current sort method (Name, Date, Size, or Extension); the current path (that is, the drive and subdirectory); and the size and last update time of the file you are pointing to.

Directory Master Lite has two modes: File Mode and Tree Mode. The program always starts in File Mode, which lets you manage your files. In Tree Mode, the left-hand side of the screen displays the current list of directories.

Tree Mode lets you make or delete directories, and change quickly to different directories to get to the files you need to display (see above under "Commands").

Notes: When copying or moving a file, if you select a directory that does not exist, Directory Master Lite will ask you if you want to create the directory or create a file with that name. In the case of creating the directory, Directory Master Lite saves you the step of having to go into Tree Mode and create the directory first.

You can't delete a directory if it has files in it. You must first go into the directory and delete or move the files. Only empty directories can be deleted. You can't make a directory if a file exists with the same name.

In the status window, the total size of all the files is rounded by the cluster size to show how much space it takes on the disk. Marked files are rounded to 1k cluster size. This is done so that if you are marking files to be copied to a floppy disk, it will indicate more accurately how much will fit. This is why if you mark all files, the two totals do not match.

If you are using a laptop computer with an LCD screen and the screen doesn't look right, run DMLITE /L.

These programs are part of the Computer Tyme DOS ToolBox.id DOS command that produces redirectable output, and target1 and target2 are either file or logical device names that can accept input from a DOS pipe.

Remarks: If you don't use redirection a lot, this may seem a bit obscure at first, but it's worth playing with until the old light bulb goes on. What this does is give you two outputs from a single source like a tee fitting on a physical pipe. Say you need to print a directory using DIR >PRN, but you also want to see the directory on screen, too. You'd simply type:

```
DIR | FORK >CON | >PRN
```

Note that the argument immediately following FORK needs a > if the argument is a device and a / if it's a command, but doesn't need the usual > if it's a file.

Examples: ```
DIR|FORK|SORT
DIR|FORK UNSORT.TXT|SORT >SORT.TXT
DIR|FORK/MORE|SORT|MORE
```

Computer Tyme
411 North Sherman
Suite 300
Springfield, MO 65802
(800)548-5353
```

DTA.EXE	Eric Meyer	Freeware
Version 1.4		

Purpose: A super directory that stands for Directory-Tree-Attributes and replaces the DIR, TREE, and ATTRIB commands of DOS, as well as the WHEREIS utility.

Syntax: `[d:][path]dta [filespec] [/options],`

where "filespec" may include a drive, path, or wildcards; "/" is the delimiter for option letters, including:

/? = help: gives version message, brief summary of usage and options.

/T = tree: show it, starting at specified or current directory.

/G = global: search for specified files throughout the tree.

/F = full: for files, show attributes and time/date also (automatically selected for single file display) for directory tree, show total size of contents.

/W = wide: just like DIR /W, five columns with no file sizes

/N = narrow: use only half the usual number of columns

/P = paginate: pause every 24 lines for a keystroke

/X = except: select only items other than those named

/D = directories: select directories instead of files

/U = universal: select both directories and files

/E = earlier: select files earlier than specified time: MMDDYY:HHMM

/L = later: files later than (or equal to) specified time: MMDDYY:HHMM

/A,H,R,S = select only items with the specified attributes: Archive; Hidden; Read/only; System

/a,h,r,s = select only items WITHOUT these attributes

/@ = set timestamp on items, in format: MMDDYY:HHMM

/C = change items to have the following specified attributes

Remarks: If the drive or path is omitted, the defaults are the active ones. If the filespec is omitted it defaults to "*.*". If it is a directory name, the contents of the directory are displayed.

By default, DTA displays a list of all files specified, along with their sizes, and some disk space information. You can modify this considerably with a variety of options. One / must precede any options; additional slashes may be used or not as desired.

The /@ and /C options actually change the DOS timestamp and attributes for files. Timestamps, in particular, provide valuable information about the age and revision of a file, so change only when necessary. Dates must be given as six digits in the form MMDDYY; the date "000000" may be used for a blank timestamp, otherwise YY must be 80 or above. You may also type a colon, followed by a four-digit (24-hour) time in the form HHMM. Given a date with no time, the time defaults to 0000 hrs; given a time with no date (leading colon is necessary), the date defaults to today. If time/date are omitted altogether, /E and /L default to today, 0000 hrs; /@ defaults to today, now. File attributes are case sensitive (uppercase=set, !lower=clear). Those listed alone, or before the "C" option letter, are used for file selection; those after it, represent changes to be made. The /C option can be used alone, with NO following attributes, to cause attributes to display instead of file sizes (no attributes will be changed).

You can pause or abort during operation of DTA by typing ^S or ^C.

Output can be directed to a file or other device in the standard fashion:

```
DTA FILESPEC /OPTIONS >DEVICE.
```

Examples: DIRECTORY TREE

```
dta \work /tp
```

Show the directory tree starting from C:\WORK, pausing after each screenful.

```
dta *.bak /g
```

Find all directories on drive C: containing files *.BAK.

FILES and DIRECTORIES

```
dta a:\*.sys
```

Show all files *.SYS in the root directory on A:. (System, etc included.)

```
dta a:\*.sys /xf
```

Show all files EXCEPT *.SYS, with "full" display (attributes and time/date).

```
dta /d
```

Show all subdirectories in the current directory.

```
dta \work /u
```

Show all files AND subdirectories in C:\WORK.

TIMESTAMPS

```
dta \work /l
```

Show only files in directory C:\WORK created or modified since... today.

```
dta /e090189
```

Show only files in current directory dated earlier than 9/1/89.

```
dta *.doc /l/e:1700
```

Show only files *.DOC dated today earlier than 5:00pm.

```
dta log /@090189:1320
```

Modify the file LOG to have the time/date 9/1/89, 1:20pm.

ATTRIBUTES

```
dta /c
```

Show all files in current directory with their attributes.

```
dta /A
```

Show all files in current directory marked with the Archive attribute.

```
dta a: /SH
```

Show all files in current directory on A: which are System and Hidden.

```
dta a:*.sys /Hca
```

Select all Hidden files *.SYS on A: and clear their Archive attribute.

Notes: File SIZES are displayed to the nearest kilobyte (or "k"; 1k is 1,024 bytes). The "used/free" space shown by DTA is for the entire drive. The "items use" amount is only for the specific files listed. Because allocation clusters on a disk can vary from 128 bytes (on a RAMdisk) to 4k or more (on a hard disk), the space actually "used" can be several K more or a fraction of a K less than a file's actual size.

File ATTRIBUTES, when displayed, show as a letter ("A,H,R,S") if set, or as "." if clear. The Archive attribute indicates to a backup utility that a file has been changed recently and needs to be backed up; the bit is cleared by the utility when it does so. (Simple backup utilities that work well with DTA include the DOS XCOPY command and ARCOPY.COM.)

The Read-only attribute prevents a file from being changed or deleted, though it can be read and copied. The Hidden and System attributes both exclude a file from normal searches: such files cannot be accessed at all by ordinary MSDOS file commands. Ordinarily only the DOS boot files MSDOS.SYS and IO.SYS have these attributes. (If you do NOT want to see hidden or system files, use "/sh".)

DTA can display up to 1,000 files, 64 MB total size. If any file exceeds 999k, its size won't display properly, but other statistics will be correct.

Error messages are as follows:

"0 items" = No such file (or directory) was found. (If you expected something, check your arguments again...)

"<invalid argument>" = You guessed it. Invalid option, bad path, illegal character in filename, etc. Think and try again. (Note: some arguments conflict: you can't specify /ud, or /Aa.)

EQKRP.COM
Version 1.0
Eric Meyer   Freeware

Purpose: Enhanced Quick Key Repeat lets you shorten the two delays associated with key repeat in order to make the keyboard behave more responsively.

Syntax: `[d:][path]EQKRP /D /R`

where D is the length of time a key must be held down before it begins to repeat, and R, the "repeat delay",is the interval between repeats while the key continues to be held down.

In both cases, a shorter delay gives faster action.

Two arguments must be specified with EQKRP:

1. A choice of initial delay: S = short; M = medium; L= long

2. A choice of repeat delay from 1 (shortest) to 9 (longest)

These arguments can be specified in any order; they may be separated by spaces or slashes "/".

Remarks: To restore the original AT BIOS setting, simply type "EQKRP" with no arguments. (This makes both delays longer than the range described here.)

EQKRP will not work if it does not detect the presence of an enhanced keyboard BIOS, or if you do not specify both arguments correctly.

This program is "freeware" and may be freely distributed, but not modified or sold for profit without author consent:

Eric Meyer
3541 Smuggler Way
Boulder, CO 80303

EVAL.EXE	David Foley	Shareware
Version 1.00	Foley Hi-Tech Systems	

Purpose: Evaluates mathematical expressions input on the command line.

Syntax: `[d:][path]EVAL [expression][function][expression]...`

Remarks: EVAL supports the four basic functions: addition, multiplication, subtraction, and division. The syntax used is very similar to that used by most modern computer languages and by most spreadsheet programs. For example, to add 2 to 8 and multiply that result by 13, one would use:

```
EVAL (2+8)*13
```

The operator precedence used for exponents is similar to most high-level languages, as well. Multiplication and division are "higher" than addition and subtraction. Exponents, represented by the carat (^) are lower than all four operators. You can exponentiate values by using ** in place of the carat. Thus, you can use: EVAL 2**1/2 to find 2^0.5.

This is also a good way to find roots. The program has no sqrt() or curt() functions, however.

EVAL uses the full "double" precision of the C language. Thus, answers will be represented to a maximum of 16 digits to the right of the decimal point. EVAL allows all numbers between 1.7E-308 and 1.7E+308 to exist. Of course, the negatives of these numbers are also available.

EVAL doesn't check for overflows or underflows. It will, however, flag "digital math" nono's, such as division by zero and exponentiations resulting in complex numbers. To use these numbers, just write them as you would specify them in a program like 1-2-3 or in a program:

```
3.1415
0.1
-34
18.01
35e-2
6.2e+23
```

EVAL, as well as complementing the four functions with exponentiation, allows the use of the modulo operator. This operator provides the integral "remainder" of division. Since 5 divided by 2 is 2 remainder 1, the command: EVAL 5%2 results in the answer 1.0.

EVAL supports an extensive list of functions. They may be specified either in upper- or lowercase, and may be abbreviated to as few as three characters. (Of course, if the function's name is one or two characters long, all characters must be specified.)

Functions supported by EVAL:

abs(x)	=	absolute value of x
acos(x)	=	arc cos of the angle x radians
acot(x)	=	arc cotangent of the angle x radians
acsc(x)	=	arc cosecant of the angle x radians
asec(x)	=	arc secant of the angle x radians
asin(x)	=	arc sine of the angle x radians
atan(x)	=	arc tangent of the angle x radians
cos(x)	=	cosine of the angle x radians
cot(x)	=	cotangent of the angle x radians
csc(x)	=	cosecant of the angle x radians
deg(x)	=	convert x radians to degrees
exp(x)	=	e to the power of x
fact(x)	=	factorial of x
ln(x)	=	natural (base e) logarithm of x
log(x)	=	base 10 logarithm of x
pi(x)	=	pi times x
rad(x)	=	converts x degrees to radians
sec(x)	=	secant of the angle x radians
sin(x)	=	sine of the angle x radians
tan(x)	=	tangent of the angle x radians
sinh(x)	=	hyperbolic sine of x
cosh(x)	=	hyperbolic cosine of x
tanh(x)	=	hyperbolic tangent of x
sech(x)	=	hyperbolic secant of x
csch(x)	=	hyperbolic cosecant of x

If any of these functions are passed invalid values, EVAL will abort with an error. The arc-trig functions, for example, cannot accept values outside of the closed interval [0,1].

Using these functions is similar to any other high-level language. The function name and its ending left parenthesis function as an opening parenthesis in the precedence of the evaluation. Thus, sin(.7)^2+cos(.7)^2 would evaluate to 1.0. Certain identities don't evaluate to what you would expect them to, because of the limits of precision in computer math when dealing with irrational numbers. While the sin^2+cos^2 identity almost always works, the sec^2-tan^2 identity usually doesn't work, for example.

Along with this problem comes another. For example, mathematically sec(0.5*pi) is undefined. However, EVAL will evaluate sec(pi(0.5)) to be a very (very) large number. This again is because of the rounding errors in binary math. It is a good approximation, considering

```
lim      (sec(x))    ==  +infinity      x -> 0.5+
```

A "memory" feature is part of EVAL. If you make a computation using EVAL, the result is remembered and may be used as needed in any further invocation of EVAL. For example, using the command:

```
EVAL SIN(1
```

would display the sine of one radian. If you executed the command:

```
EVAL ASIN(@)
```

next, you'd get, effectively,

```
ASIN(SIN(1))...
```

the result would be one.
   Similarly, if you used

```
EVAL  35+15,
```

EVAL would print 50. If you did

```
EVAL  @+100,
```

a result of 150 would be displayed.
   EVAL stores the results in your machine's environment. View the previous result by typing the SET command; DOS will list the environment variables it has stored. EVAL's environment variable is listed on the line "EVAL".

FAKEY.COM   System Enhancement Associates, Inc.   Shareware
Version 2.90

Purpose: Preloads keystroke inputs for use within batch file.

Syntax: FAKEY one or more arguments "string"

The characters in the string are inserted in the keyboard buffer. The string may contain various special sequences, as indicated here:

^N	Ctrl+N	\E	Escape	\"	"
!N	Alt+N	\R	Enter	\\	\
\B	backspace	\T	Tab		

decimal number or hexadecimal number

The character represented by the number is inserted in the keyboard buffer.

mnemonics

The following mnemonics can also be used:

ASCII:

ACK	BEL	BS	CAN	CR	DC1-4	DLE	EM	ENQ
EOT	ESC	ETB	ETX	FF	FS	GS	HT	LF	NAK
NUL	RS	RUB	SI	SO	SOH	SP	SUB	SYN	US	VT

Cursor movement:

DASH	DEL	DOWN	END	HOME	INS	LEFT
PGDN	PGUP	PLUS	RITE	UP		

Function key (N = 1–10):

FN	=	Function key N
AN	=	Alt+Function key N
CN	=	Ctrl+Function key N
SN	=	Shift+Function key N

Special:

BEEP	=	Sound a warbling tone.
BOOT	=	Execute a warm system boot.

CBRK   =   Simulate a Ctrl-Break key press.
COLD   =   Execute a cold system boot.
LOAD N =   Load FAKEY but do not display help screen.
            Reserve room for N keystrokes (default is 200).
PSCR   =   Execute a Print Screen.
TOSS   =   Discard previous pending keystrokes
WAIT N =   Wait N seconds before inserting keystrokes into buffer
            (default is 1 second).

Example: To use FAKEY to erase all files within a directory without pausing for the DOS "Are you sure?" message, create the following ZAP.BAT file

```
FAKEY WAIT "Y\R"
DEL %1
```

FAKEY waits one second, to give the "Are you sure?" message time to show up. Then it "presses" the Y key (yes) followed by the Enter key. To erase all files in a DONTNEED directory, type ZAP DONTNEED and press the Enter key.

This program is not public domain but is "shareware" and a part of the System Enhancement Associates, Inc., collection. Copyright © 1986-1989 System Enhancement Associates, Inc. For information, contact:

System Enhancement Associates, Inc.
Attn: Mr. C. J. Wang
925 Clifton Avenue
Clifton, NJ 07013
(201)473-5153

FF.EXE	David Foley	Shareware
Version 2.00	Foley Hi-Tech Systems	

Purpose: Locates files by searching the entire disk for a specified file; will also search within compressed files to search for filenames as well.

Syntax: `[d:] [path] FF [d:] fname [.ext] [options]`

where

d: designates a valid DOS drive
fname[.ext] specifies the file(s) to search for. Wildcards are accepted.

Options:

/V	=	verbose mode, will show file statistics
/T	=	total mode, will show file totals and not found names
/D	=	progress Display, will show files as searching
/R	=	all Drive mode, will search across all drives found
/N	=	normal files only, do not search inside any compressed files (this is a combination of all of the below options)
/O	=	do not search inside .ZOO files
/Z	=	do not search inside .ZIP files
/A	=	do not search inside .ARC files
/P	=	do not search inside .PAK files
/	=	do not search inside .LZH files
Ctrl-C=		will halt the execution of the program at any time
Ctrl-S =		will pause the display at any time

FF searches across your disk looking for any files that you specify. When it finds a matching file it will display the Directory the file was found in, the complete file name, the file size, creation date and time, and any attributes associated with the file.

FF.EXE is Copyright © 1991 by Foley Hi-Tech Systems
This program is not public domain but is "shareware" and a part of the Foley Hi-Tech Systems ExtraDOS collection. To register send a check or money order for $19.00 to:

Foley Hi-Tech Systems
ExtraDOS Registration
172 Amber Drive
San Francisco, CA 94131
(415)826-6084

FIND.EXE   **Marc Perkel**   Shareware
Version 2.5

Purpose: Offers enhanced functionality in searching for text strings over the DOS command of the same name.

Syntax: `[d:] [path] FIND "String" <File File File> /V/C/N/L/P/I`

where:

/V	Displays all lines that do not contain String.
/C	Counts lines that contain String.
/N	Adds line numbers to output.
/L	List only names of files that contain String.
/I	Ignore Case.
/P	Pauses display every 24 lines.

Remarks: In addition to the standard /v, /c, /n, and /i options that DOS provides, this version of FIND lets you list just the file names where a match occurred, and also lets you page the output.

FIND.EXE is Copyright © 1989-1990 by Marc Perkel, All Rights Reserved.
This program is part of the Computer Tyme DOS ToolBox.
To Register, ask for the BANTAM BOOK special price of $25. (Reg Price $60)

Contact:

Computer Tyme
411 North Sherman, Suite 300
Springfield, MO 65802

FINDMODL.EXE John Woram

Purpose: Reports BIOS date and PC model byte data

Syntax: `[d:] [path] FINDMODL`

Remarks: Displays the BIOS date as mm/dd/yy, plus model byte, submodel and revision numbers for IBM computers and clones that follow the IBM convention.

FINDMODL.EXE is Copyright © 1990 by John Woram

FIXPATH.EXE   **Marc Perkel**   **Shareware**
Version 1.0

Purpose: Reads your path environment variable and checks to verify that all referenced directories actually exist. Any directory that doesn't exist, or is inacessible is removed from the path.

Syntax: `[d:] [path]` FIXPATH

Remarks: This program is particularly handy after logging off a network to avoid DOS errors.
        If more than one command processor is in memory, FixPath will affect only the last one.

FIXPATH.EXE is Copyright © 1990-1991 by Marc Perkel. All Rights Reserved
This program is not public domain but is "shareware" and part of a Computer Tyme collection.
To register contact:

> Computer Tyme
> 411 North Sherman
> Suite 300
> Springfield, MO 65802
> (800)548-5353

FN.COM
Version 1.6

Scott Chaney
RSE, Inc.

Shareware

Purpose: Attaches explanatory notes to a filename, plus other file management utilities.

Syntax: `[d:] [path] FN`

Once FN.COM is loaded into memory, you can use the following commands:

Alt-D — Hot key to bring up FileNotes. A two-column directory listing is seen, with highlighted bar at first entry.

Arrow keys — Arrow keys move highlighted bar to desired listing.

J — A "Jump to?" prompt is displayed. Press the first letter of the desired listing. Then move to desired listing as just described.

Insert key — The bottom two lines are cleared. Type in your file notes about the highlighted directory listing (160 character limit).

Enter key — Your file note is displayed on screen and written into a FILENOTE text file for subsequent viewing.

Q — When you are finished entering file notes, press Q to return to the DOS prompt. The next time FN is activated (by again pressing the Alt+D keys), the file note will be seen if you highlight a file for which you have written a note.

Other file management utilities are described below. Press the Alt+D keys and then one of the following keys, as appropriate.

C — Copy. First, use the T (Tag) command to tag files for copying. Then move to the desired target directory and press C. Answer Yes to the "Perform Copy?" prompt.

D — Drive Change. Enter the letter for the drive you wish to view.

Delete key — Highlight any file and press the Delete key. Then answer the "Delete filename?" prompt. If you answer No, a "Cancelled" message is seen. To remove the message, press the Enter key, which enables the View option (q.v.). Now press V to exit the View screen.

R — Rename the highlighted file. If you include a new path, the file is moved to the specified directory.

S — Sort. A menu displays options to sort the directory listing by name, extension, size or date.

T — Tag a file (or files) for copying. Highlight the desired file and press T. A hyphen is seen to the left of the file name. Press T again to remove the tag. Repeat as required and then use the C (Copy) command to copy the files.

V — View the contents of the highlighted file. Press V again to exit the View screen. To review all the file notes you have written, highlight the FILENOTE file and press V.

Remarks: FN.COM is a TSR utility which occupies 26,320 bytes of memory. To remove it from memory, type FN/U at the DOS prompt and press the Enter key. If you cannot spare that amount of memory, use the equivalent but smaller DIRR.COM utility.

FN.COM is Copyright © 1990 by RSE, Inc.
This program is not public domain but is "shareware" and a part of the RSE, Inc. collection. For registration and information contact:

Scott Chaney
c/o RSE, Inc.
1157 57th Drive S.E.
Auburn, WA 98002

FONTHT.COM
Version 1.0

Eric Meyer

Freeware

Purpose: Adapts the line text screen and is capable of a wide range of font sizes. The table below shows some of the possibilities offered by FONTHT. Character height is given in "points" or scan lines, and the two "standard" combinations are marked with asterisks:

Syntax: `[d:][path]FONTHT arg1,` where

nn	changes to font height nn (7-20)
0 or OFF	reverts to normal for your system
?	displays current font information

FONT HEIGHT	TEXT LINES ON EGA	ON VGA	FONT HEIGHT	TEXT LINES ON EGA	ON VGA
7	50	57	14	25 *	28
8	43 *	50 *	15	23	26
9	38	44	16	21	25 *
10	35	40	17	20	23
11	31	36	18	19	22
12	29	33	19	18	21
13	26	30	20	17	20

Remarks: To see as much text as possible on screen at once use the 7-point font which can display a full page. Use larger size characters, such as the 20-point, for easy viewing.

The usefulness of FONTHT depends on the ability of your favorite software to adapt to nonstandard screen sizes. Some older MS-DOS programs simply assume the screen has the standard 25 lines; they won't work well with fewer lines and will ignore any extra. Programs that (re)set the video mode will wipe out any font selected with FONTHT. Experiment to determine compatibility with other software.

Even DOS itself will show a few quirks; for example, the TYPE and CLS commands will not use any screen lines beyond 25. If you have an ANSI.SYS driver installed, you can fix the CLS problem simply by adding "$e[J" to your PROMPT.

When FONTHT changes fonts, the overlapping portion of the screen is preserved, but some text will have disappeared or been added at the bottom, which may make the display slightly confusing at first.

FORK.EXE
Version 2.5

Marc Perkel   **Shareware**

Purpose: Lets you split the output of a DOS piping command into two separate streams.

Syntax: `command | [d:][path]FORK>device > |target2>`

or

`command [d:][path] FORK Filename| >target2`

or

`command [d:][path] FORK/command2| >target2`

where command is a valid DOS command that produces redirectable output, and target1 and target2 are either file or logical device names that can accept input from a DOS pipe.

Remarks: If you don't use redirection a lot, this may seem a bit obscure at first, but it's worth playing with until the old light bulb goes on. What this does is give you two outputs from a single source like a tee fitting on a physical pipe. Say you need to print a directory using DIR >PRN, but you also want to see the directory on screen, too. You'd simply type:

`DIR | FORK >CON | >PRN`

Note that the argument immediately following FORK needs a > if the argument is a device and a / if it's a command, but doesn't need the usual > if it's a file. Examples:

```
DIR|FORK|SORT
DIR|FORK UNSORT.TXT|SORT >SORT.TXT
DIR|FORK/MORE|SORT|MORE
```

Computer Tyme
411 North Sherman
Suite 300
Springfield, MO 65802
(800)548-5353

FREE.EXE
Version 1.3
Marc Perkel
Shareware

Purpose: Reports on available disk space, DOS memory, EMS memory, and DOS environment memory.

Syntax: `[d:] [path] FREE`

Remarks: Provides a useful collection of vital statistics, especially as your file or application keeps growing in size. Also reports on your disk's cluster and sector size.

FREE.EXE is Copyright © 1989-1991 by Marc Perkel. All Rights Reserved
This program is not public domain but is "shareware" and part of a Computer Tyme collection.
To register contact:

> Computer Tyme
> 411 North Sherman
> Suite 300
> Springfield, MO 65802
> (800)548-5353

| **FS.EXE** | **David Foley** | **Shareware** |
| **Version 1.10** | **Foley Hi-Tech Systems** | |

Purpose: Lists each file in a directory's size, then sums that listing and shows total and free space on that particular disk drive.

Syntax: `[d:][path]FS [filespec]`

Remarks: You may pass FS a specific file, or group of files, to list. If no parameters are passed FS will list all files in the current directory.

FS.EXE is Copyright © 1985-1991 by Foley Hi-Tech Systems
This program is not public domain but is "shareware" and a part of the Foley Hi-Tech Systems ExtraDOS collection. To register send a check or money order for $19.00 to:

> Foley Hi-Tech Systems
> ExtraDOS Registration
> 172 Amber Drive
> San Francisco, CA 94131
> (415)826-6084

FT.EXE	**David Foley**	**Shareware**
Version 1.01	**Foley Hi-Tech Systems**	

Purpose: Scans the directory structure of a disk and gives a top down tree listing of the entire disk's directory structure.

Syntax: `[d:] [path] FT`

Note: FT works only on the currently logged drive.

FT.EXE is Copyright © 1985-1990 by Foley Hi-Tech Systems
This program is not public domain but is "shareware" and a part of the Foley Hi-Tech Systems
ExtraDOS collection. To register send a check or money order for $19.00 to:

Foley Hi-Tech Systems
ExtraDOS Registration
172 Amber Drive
San Francisco, CA 94131
(415)826-6084

GET.EXE
Version 2.1b

Bob Stephan   **Shareware**

Purpose: Provides system information via the ERRORLEVEL code and the GET= environment variable.

Syntax: `[d:] [path] GET arg`

where arg is any letter or pair of letters described below.

`A`

The GET= environment and Error Level are both 1 if ANSI.SYS is installed, both
0 if it is not.

`B [new attribute]`

The screen is cleared and color settings change as defined by decimal value of
new attribute. The former attribute value appears in the GET= environment and as
the Error Level.

`BE [new attribute]`

Same, except that new attribute is hexadecimal, as is the former attribute value in
the GET= environment.

`C ["prompt"] [chars] [#secs]`

"prompt" is an optional instruction to the user.
    If any one of the specified characters (chars) is entered within # seconds, that
character echoes to the screen, appears in the GET= environment, and the Error
Level is the character's ASCII value. Otherwise, ERRORLEVEL=0. If no characters are included, GET accepts any key pressed. If a key other than one of the
specified chars is pressed, and/or if #secs is not included, GET waits forever.

`CE ["prompt"] [chars] [#secs]`

Same, except letter is not echoed to screen.

`D`

DOS major version number appears in the GET= environment. The Error Level
shows 10 x the major version number, plus the minor version number. Thus DOS
3.2 gives an Error Level of 32.

`DE`

Same, except DOS minor version number is given.

```
E
```

The remaining environment space, in bytes, appears in the GET= environment and as the Error Level.

```
EE
```

Same, except Error Level is remaining environment space divided by 10.

```
F filespec
```

The hexadecimal size of the filespec appears in the GET= environment. The Error Level is the file size in kilobytes.

```
FE filespec
```

Same, except Error Level is file size divided by 10.

If Error Level =   0, filespec is a directory
2, filename not found
3, path not found

```
H N
```

Depending on the value of N, the indicated time/date information appears in the GET= environment

1 day of the week   16 hour
2 day of the month   32 minute
4 month   64 second
8 year

If 128 is added, the Error Level is 1 for an odd value, 0 for an even value.

```
HE N
```

Same as H, except that if N is the sum of two or more of the listed numbers, the equivalent time/date data appears in the GET= environment. Thus, for GET HE 14, the environment shows mm-dd-yy.

```
K [drive letter]
```

The free space remaining on the drive appears in the GET= environment, in Kbytes. The Error Level is the free space, in Kbytes divided by 10. Error Level is 0 if disk is unformatted, or if diskette drive does not contain a formatted diskette.

```
KE [drive letter]
```

Same, except Error Level is free space divided by 100.

```
L [drive letter]
```

The volume label appears as the GET= environment. The Error Level is 1 if a label if found, 0 is there is no label.

```
LE ["string"] [drive letter]
```

Same, except Error Level is 1 if volume label matches "string" and 0 if there is no match.

```
M
```

The free memory appears in the GET= environment, and as the Error Level, both in Kbytes.

```
ME
```

Same, except Error Level is Kbytes divided by 10

```
N ["prompt"] [secs]
```

Same as C, except that GET accepts only N, n, Y, or y.

```
NE ["prompt"] [secs]
```

Same, except letter is not echoed to screen.

```
P
```

The GET= environment and the Error Level are both 1 if the printer is ready, and 0 if it is not.

```
PE
```

Same, plus printer initialization signal is sent to printer, and Print-Screen functions are disabled if printer is not ready.

```
Q [drive letter]
```

The total disk space on the drive appears in the GET= environment, in Kbytes. The Error Level is the same, but in Kbytes divided by 10.

```
QE [drive letter]
```

Same, except Error Level is disk space divided by 100.

```
S ["prompt"] [string] [#secs]
```

"prompt" is an optional instruction to the user.

Same as C, except that GET accepts only the character sequence given by string. Other characters entered within the string sequence are ignored.

```
U "characters" [number#number]
```

The characters enclosed in quotes are inserted into the keyboard buffer. Each number is an ASCII code or a scan code plus 255. Thus for FI (scan code 59), enter 59 + 255 = 314. Enter #13 to end the character string with a carriage return.

```
UE #number
```

Enter the indicated number to enable the function listed next to it. Sum the numbers to enable two or more functions, or enter #0 to disable all functions.

16 Scroll Lock
32 Number Lock
64 Caps Lock

```
V N
```

Sets new color mode. The GET= environment and Error Level both give the former value of N.

```
VE N
```

Sets EGA or VGA border to color indicated by N. The GET= environment and Error Level both give the former value of N.

```
W
```

Initiates a warm reboot (same as pressing Ctrl+Alt+Del keys).

```
WE
```

Initiates a cold reboot (same as turning system off and back on again).

```
Y
```

The current directory appears in the GET= environment. The Error Level is the level of the current directory (1 = root, 2 = subdirectory, 3 = sub-subdirectory, etc.).

```
YE
```

Same, except Error Level is drive number (0 = A, 1 = B, 2 = C, etc.).

```
Z "string"
```

The string appears in the GET= environment, and the Error Level is the length of the string.

```
7
```

The GET= environment and Error Level are both 1 if a math coprocessor is installed, 0 if it is not.

```
7 E
```

The PC model byte number appears in the GET= environment (hexadecimal) and as the Error Level (decimal).

Remarks: GET is a powerful tool which requires a bit of forethought to use successfully. See the examples under TOUCH.EXE for some ideas. What it does is interrogate the keyboard or other system device or memory location, and write a result to the DOS environment and to the DOS Error Level code. Thus you can test the results either by testing the environment variable GET, via IF %GET%==value, or use the equivalent IF ERRORLEVEL test. See the chapter on batch file and on the DOS environment for more details on setting up applications which test both error levels and environment variable values.

Notes: To display a summary of GET options, type GET only, and press the Enter key.
   K and Q assume sectors are 512 bytes, and are intended for diskette measurements. Very large hard disk sizes may be reported inaccurately.
   Do not use GET V or GET VE to set color modes or border colors not supported by your monitor.

GET.EXE is Copyright © 1991 by Bob Stephan
This program is not public domain but is "shareware" and a part of the Moby Disk collection. For registration and information, contact:

Bob Stephan
Moby Disk
1021 San Carlos Road
Pebble Beach, CA 93953
(408)646-1899

HEX.EXE	**David Foley**	**Shareware**
Version 1.12	**Foley Hi-Tech Systems**	

Purpose: Provides a quick dump of the contents of any file. The dump is very similar in format to what you get with the Norton Utilities file viewer. An advantage of HEX is that you can quickly dump the contents of any file to the screen without having to load the overhead of a shell program. You can display any type of file ASCII or Binary. The default display is to list the HEX values on the left and the ASCII equivalents on the right hand column.

Syntax: `[d:] [path]HEX [filename]  [options]`

where [filename] can be any valid DOS file including .EXE type files

Remarks: /B = dump the file in binary groups rather than hex.
/O = dump the file in octal groups rather than hex.
/H = display the file in raw hexadecimal format rather than showing the hex and ASCII values side by side
/P = pause mode, will pause each screen full

HEX.EXE is Copyright © 1990-1991 by Foley Hi-Tech Systems
This program is not public domain but is "shareware" and a part of the Foley Hi-Tech Systems ExtraDOS collection. To register send a check or money order for $19.00 to:

Foley Hi-Tech Systems
Extra DOS Registration
172 Amber Drive
San Francisco, CA 94131
(415)826-6084

HITAKEY.SYS   **Raymond P. Tackett**   **Freeware**
Version 3.0

Purpose: A dummy device driver that stops to let you look at the screen before you hit a key to continue booting. The effect occurs exactly once at load time, then the driver aborts its load and disappears.

Syntax: `DEVICE or DEVICEHIGH=[d:] [path]HITAKEY.SYS [optional message]`

When that line of your config.sys file is reached, you will see the prompt, "Hit a key when ready" or the remainder of the command line up to 79 characters. The boot process will stop there until you hit a key. Typeahead is cleared, so it WILL wait. After the keystroke, HITAKEY will disappear from memory.

Remarks: Imagine that you have a boot problem, which you believe to be caused by foo.sys. You think there's an error message, but the screen is cleared immediately by bar.sys when it loads. Your present config.sys file contains:

```
device=foo.sys
device=bar.sys
```

Edit your config.sys file to insert HITAKEY.SYS immediately after the driver in question:

```
device=foo.sys
device=hitakey.sys We just loaded foo.sys
device=bar.sys
```

and copy hitakey.sys to the root of your boot drive. The next time you boot, HITAKEY.SYS will halt and let you see whatever else is on the screen, possibly a message from foo.sys. Hitting any key will let the boot process continue. You can invoke HITAKEY.SYS any number of times in config.sys.

The driver needs less than 200 bytes of free memory to load. After it has accomplished its one keystroke mission, it disappears.

NOTES: HITAKEY.SYS should be used only as a debugging aid and should be removed from config.sys once it has served its purpose and the system rebooted.

HUSH.COM
Version 1.21

David Foley
Foley Hi-Tech Systems

Shareware

Purpose: Eliminates a majority of the sounds generated by the PC's internal speaker.

Syntax: `[d:] [path]HUSH [mode]`

where mode is either:

ON   enables HUSH functions
OFF   disables HUSH functions

Remarks: HUSH cannot eliminate all beeps. Tones that it cannot completely silence, it can reduce to a small click. HUSH is a small TSR which, when loaded, watches for output to the speaker. When activated, HUSH will try and suppress the speaker 18.2 times a second.

Note: If you install other timer monitoring functions such as screen blankers after HUSH, you may not be able to disable HUSH's functions.

HUSH.COM is Copyright © 1985-1990 by Foley Hi-Tech Systems
This program is not public domain but is "shareware" and a part of the Foley Hi-Tech Systems ExtraDOS collection. To register send a check of money order for $19.00 to:

Foley Hi-Tech Systems
ExtraDOS Registration
172 Amber Drive
San Francisco, CA 94131
(415)826-6084

KBD.EXE
Version 1.3

Marc Perkel

Shareware

Purpose: Sets various keyboard functions.

Syntax: `[d:][path]KBD function`

Remarks: Valid function arguments include:

CapsON	set Caps Lock ON
CapsOFF	set Caps Lock OFF
Clear	Clear all characters from keyboard buffer
Lock	Lock the keyboard
NumON	set Number Lock ON
NumOFF	set Number Lock OFF
PrtScrON	set Print-screen ON
PrtScrOFF	set Print-screen OFF
ScrollON	set Scroll-lock ON
ScrollOFF	set Scroll-lock OFF
Show	Display keyboard scan codes
Unlock	Unlock the keyboard
0-31	Set keyboard repeat rate (0 is fastest)
, 0-3	Set keyboard repeat delay (0 is fastest, 1 is default)
"string"	Insert string in keyboard buffer
keyword	Insert keyword in keyboard buffer

Notes: Keywords are F1-F10, SF1-SF10, AF1-AF10, CF1-CF10, Alt-A through Alt-Z, Alt-1 through Alt-0, CR, ESC, TAB, LF, FF. For example KBD "DIR" CR puts the DIRectory command and a Carriage Return into the buffer.

The KBD utility is not compatible with some hotkey combinations used by TSR programs (for example, Alt-O in the BL utility).

KBD.EXE is Copyright © 1990 by Marc Perkel. All Rights Reserved
This program is not public domain but is "shareware" and part of a Computer Tyme collection. To register contact:

Computer Tyme
411 North Sherman
Suite 300
Springfield, MO 65802
(800) 548-5353

KILLDIR.EXE
Version 1.02

David Foley
Foley Hi-Tech Systems

Shareware

Purpose: Makes eliminating a directory and all of its contents a lot easier.

Syntax: `[d:] [path]KILLDIR [dirname]`

Remarks: KILLDIR will display the information about the directory that you wish to remove including the number of files and sizes as well as any subdirectory information. KILLDIR will remove all files and file types including hidden or system
files. It's not a good idea to shorten the name of this utility to something easier to
type like KD, as there's at least a minimum level of error protection in having to
type a name as long and ominous as KILLDIR.

KILLDIR.EXE is Copyright © 1990-1991 by Foley Hi-Tech Systems
This program is not public domain but is "shareware" and a part of the Foley Hi-Tech Systems
ExtraDOS collection. To register send a check or money order for $19.00 to:

> Foley Hi-Tech Systems
> ExtraDOS Registration
> 172 Amber Drive
> San Francisco, CA 94131
> (415)826-6084

LHA.EXE   Haruyasu Yoshizaki   Freeware
Version 2.12

Purpose: Serves as a high-performance file-compression program.

Syntax: `[d:][path]LHA command [/option] archive[.LZH]`
`[path][filenames]`

Valid commands are:

a:	Add files
d:	Delete files
e:	Extract files
f:	Freshen files
l:	List of files (default)
m:	Move files
p:	disPlay files
s:	make a Self-extracting archive
t:	Test the integrity of an archive
u:	Update files
v:	View listing of files with pathnames
x:	eXtract files with pathnames

Valid options are:

/a0 won't archive files with hidden or system Attributes (default)
/a1 allows any file Attributes
/c0 Check timestamp before overwriting files
/c1 don't Check timestamp
/h0 no Header (default)
/h1 standard Header
/h2 extended Header
/i0 Ignore case of filenames (default)
/i1 don't Ignore case of filenames
/l0 don't display Long filenames
/l1 display Long names of files stored or to be stored in archive
/l2 display Long names of all files referenced by LHA
/m0 displays Message before overwriting files orcreating directories
/m1 no Messages—assumes "Y" response to queries
/m2 no Message, but renames de-archived file with numeric extension
/n0 No indicator toggle—default shows progress and compression factor
/n1 No indicator—disables "ooo..." progress indicator
/n2 No indicator—disables filenames and compression rates
/o0 Old version (of LH) compatability—default is off
/o1 Old version (of LH) compatability—produces compatible output
/p0 Precise filenames off—will restore all files of a given name
/p1 Precise files on—will distinguish between files of the same name from
       different directories within an archive
/r0 Recursive mode off (default)

/r1 Recursively selects a given file from any subdirectory
/r2 Recursively collects all files from all subdirectories of the named directory
/t0 Timestamp off—defaults to system clock
/t1 Timestamp on—with a, u, f, m, and d commands, sets archive time and
     date to time and date of newest file in archive
/w0 sets Work directory to current directory (default)
/w1path sets Work directory to path specified
/x0 sets eXtended pathnames off
/x1 sets eXtended pathnames on
/z0 Zero compression is off—files are compressed
/z1 Zero compression on—files are stored but not compressed
/z2[ext] files ending in .ARC, .LZH, .LZS, .PAK, .ZIP, and .ZOO are not
     compressed—optionally, any specfied extensions will also be exempted
/-1 allows the character @ as a character in a file name
/-2 allows either - or @ as characters.

Remarks: LHA lets you store files in a highly-compressed format, using an algorithm developed by Haruhiko Okumura. One or more files can be compressed into a single file, called an archive, which has a default extension of LHZ. The basic A, D and E commands, repsectively add, delete, and extract files to or from the archive. To add BIGFILE.TXT to an archive STORTEXT.LHZ, you'd type

```
LHA A STORTEXT BIGFILE.TXT
```

assuming LHA is in your DOS path and you want to store the archive of BIGFILE.TXT in the same (and current) directory where BIGFILE.TXT resides.

The M command moves the specified files into the archive, erasing the originals. This can be useful for compressing files you only need look at occasionally, as it frees up disk space.

The L and V commands let you examine the contents of an archive, while the F, U, and T commands can be used to update and verify archives. Many other options let you use full pathnames, work with files in subdirectories of the specified directory, work with hidden or system files (by allowing any attributes), toggle an indicator of compression or extraction progress on or off, use special characters in filenames, and more. Of particular note are the /x1 and /r2 options, which let you store and extract complete tree structures. The /x1 option is also needed to create a self-extracting file that can have its output redirected at the command line—if you create an archive with /x1:

LHA A /x1 MYARC *.*

then create a self-extracting archive with: LHA s /x1 MYARC

You can then redirect the output of the MYARC.EXE as follows: MYARC /e path

LHA.EXE is Copyright © 1989-1991 by Haruyasu Yoshizaki. This program is "freeware" and may be freely copied and distributed, but not modified or sold without author consent.

LS.EXE
Version 1.00

David Foley
Foley Hi-Tech Systems

Shareware

Purpose: A utility with most of Unix **ls** command's features built in.

Syntax: `[d:] [path]LS [options] [filespec]`

where options include:

-1   list in single column
-C   list in multiple columns
-F   directories are marked with a trailing '\', system files are marked with a trailing '@' and executable files are marked with a trailing '*'
-P   print the directory name before listing
-R   recursively list subdirectories
-S   sort by file size in bytes (cluster size if option 's' is selected)
-a   list all entries including hidden and system files
-d   list directories as if they were a normal file
-f   do not sort (list in the order files appear in the directory)
-l   list in long format ([size in clusters,] mode, size, date, name)
-r   reverse the order of the selected sort
-s   list the file size in clusters
-t   sort by time

Remarks: Any LS options that you set with the SET command will be loaded automatically when you run the program from the DOS prompt. Set your most used parameters in your AUTOEXEC.BAT file with a SET statement like

`SET LS=-td`

and then a plain LS will run those parameters for you.
     As in the Unix **ls** the switches are case sensitive.

LS.EXE is Copyright © 1990 Foley Hi-Tech Systems
This program is not public domain but is "shareware" and a part of the Foley Hi-Tech Systems ExtraDOS collection. To register send a check or money order for $19.00 to:

> Foley Hi-Tech Systems
> ExtraDOS Registration
> 172 Amber Drive
> San Francisco, CA 94131
> (415)826-6084

MAPMEM.EXE   Kim Kokkonen
Turbo Power Software

Purpose: Shows what memory resident programs are loaded.

Syntax: `[d:][path]MAPMEM [options]`

MAPMEM offers the following command line options:

/V   verbose report.

/? write a help screen.

Remarks: MAPMEM.EXE displays a map of DOS memory. It shows the resident programs, how much memory they use, and what interrupt vectors each one controls. MAPMEM also shows information about expanded and extended memory when available.

MAPMEM writes to the standard output — hence, the output can be printed or stored to a file by using DOS redirection.

Examples: A typical MAPMEM report might look something like:

```
PSP   blks bytes owner    command line           chained vectors
----- ---- ----- -------- -------------------- --------------------
0008   1   34240 config
1228   2    3536 command
1315   2    3888 WATCH    TSR WATCHER            16 21 27
140A   2   22128 CED      N/A                    1B 21 64
1973   1     144 N/A      C:\MARK\PS.MRK
197D   2     736 PSKEY    S3                     09 15
19AD   2   68400 PS       /B:0 /E:1 /R:0 /...    01 03 06 0D
2A62   2    1504 MARK     test                   00 3F
2AC2   2   10384 EATMEM   10
2D4D   2  469808 free


block   bytes   (Expanded Memory)
-----   ------
    1   1048576
 free   1048576
total   2097152
                (Extended Memory)
total    379240
```

"PSP" stands for Program Segment Prefix. This is the physical address, specified in hexadecimal, where the program was loaded. If you're running DOS 2.x, you'll need to use an address from this column to pass to DISABLE.

"Blks" is the number of memory blocks DOS is using to manage the program. This will typically be two: one for the program itself and another for the environment that stores the program name, the DOS path, and other environment variables.

"Bytes" is the number of bytes of memory, specified in decimal, allocated to the program.

The "owner" column shows the name of the program that allocated the block. An "N/A" in this column means either that the program deallocated its environment to reduce memory usage (as shown on the fifth row of the report) or that the system is running DOS 2.x, where the owner names are simply not available.

"Command line" shows the command line entered when the TSR was originally loaded. Some TSR's overwrite their command line with other code or data in order to save memory space. MAPMEM can usually detect this behavior and will display "N/A" in the command line column when it does.

The last column will be titled with either "chained vectors" or "hooked vectors". When WATCH is loaded, "chained" will appear; otherwise, "hooked" will. The numbers in this column indicate what interrupt vectors the TSR has grabbed. Without WATCH, MAPMEM must use a heuristic technique to identify the owner of each vector; don't be surprised if you see some ridiculous looking vector numbers. With WATCH, MAPMEM should report an accurate list for each TSR, and should show the complete chain of control for each interrupt.

MAPMEM indicates disabled TSR's by displaying the word "disabled" in the interrupt vector column of the report. The expanded memory report shows each allocated block of expanded memory, as well as the free and total EMS space. When extended memory is available, MAPMEM shows just the total amount available. The extended memory report is not highly reliable because of the lack of a standardized method for allocating extended memory space. Some applications that use extended memory allocate the space by making it appear that the memory is no longer in the system. MAPMEM shows the various types of marks so that you can examine them prior to releasing them. As shown in the example, MAPMEM reports a call to MARK with the owner name "MARK", and the mark name (if any) in the command line area. The result of a call to FMARK or MARKNET will show "N/A" in the owner column (due to the minimal memory kept by an FMARK), and the name of the mark file in the command line area.

The verbose report shows each individual memory block rather than just one for each program. It also adds two new columns of information. "Mcb" stands for Memory Control Block. This is a physical address, expressed in hexadecimal, of the DOS data structure used for managing each block of memory. The MCB address is typically one less than the address of the program. "Files" reports the number of files kept open by the TSR. In most cases this will be zero. When it is non-zero, the maximum number of files opened by the rest of the programs (including the foreground application) is reduced accordingly.

The TSR Utilites — DEVICE.EXE, DISABLE.EXE, MAPMEM.EXE, MARK.EXE, RAMFREE.COM, RELEASE.EXE, and WATCH.COM — are Copyright © 1986, 1987, 1989 by Kim Kokkonen of Turbo Power Software.

MARK.EXE

Kim Kokkonen
Turbo Power Software

Purpose: Marks a position in memory above which TSR's can be released.

Syntax: `[d:] [path]MARK [!] [TSRname]`

where ! is the optional protection mark (see below) and TSRname is the name of the memory mark (it need not be the name of the actual TSR.)

Remarks: MARK.EXE and RELEASE.EXE are used to manage TSR's in memory, without requiring a system reboot. In their simplest form, MARK and RELEASE are used as follows:

1. Run MARK before installing your TSR(s). This marks the current position in memory and stores information that RELEASE will later need to restore the system. A common place to call MARK is in your AUTOEXEC.BAT file.
2. Install whatever TSR's you want, using the normal method for each TSR.
3. To remove those TSR's from memory, run RELEASE. This will release all of the memory above (and including) the last MARK, and will restore the system to the state at the time the MARK was made.

There are a number of variations of this simple method. First, MARKs can be stacked in memory, as shown in the following hypothetical batch file:

```
MARK
TSR1
MARK
TSR2
MARK
TSR3
```

Each call to RELEASE releases memory above and including the last MARK. In this example, the first call to RELEASE would remove TSR3 and the last MARK from memory, the second call would remove TSR2 and its MARK, and so on.

MARK and RELEASE may be called using a command line parameter. The parameter specifies a "mark name" and allows releasing TSR's to a specific point in memory. Consider the following example:

```
MARK TSR1
TSR1
MARK TSR2
TSR2
MARK TSR3
TSR3
```

This loads the three TSR's just as in the previous example. However, if RELEASE were called like this

```
RELEASE TSR2
```

then both TSR2 and TSR3 would be removed from memory. Note that the use of such a name does not allow just a single layer of TSR's to be removed (just TSR2, for example). RELEASE always removes all TSR's including and beyond the one named. A mark name is any string up to 126 characters long. The name may not include white space (blanks or tabs). Case (upper or lower) is not significant when matching mark names.

When named marks are used as in this example, calling RELEASE without specifying a mark name will still remove the last TSR from memory. Assuming that TSR1, TSR2, and TSR3 are still in memory, typing just RELEASE would remove TSR3 and the last mark.

It is possible to change this behavior by using "protected marks", which can be released only by explicitly specifying their names. A protected mark is placed by giving it a name that starts with an exclamation point, '!'. Consider the following:

```
MARK TSR1
TSR1
MARK TSR2
TSR2
MARK !TSR3
TSR3
```

Here !TSR3 specifies a protected mark. Typing just RELEASE would produce an error message "No matching marker found, or protected marker encountered". The same error would occur after entering the command RELEASE TSR2. When this error occurs, RELEASE does not remove any TSR's from memory.

The only way to remove TSR3 in this case is by entering

```
RELEASE !TSR3
```

The TSR Utilites — DEVICE.EXE, DISABLE.EXE, MAPMEM.EXE, MARK.EXE, RAMFREE.COM, RELEASE.EXE, and WATCH.COM — are copyright © 1986, 1987, 1989 by Kim Kokkonen of Turbo Power Software.

MODSAV.COM   Chris Dunford   Public Domain
Version 1.00   The Cove Software Group

Purpose: Saves video mode, defeating the efforts of most (but not all) applications to reset the mode.

Syntax: `[d:] [path] MODSAV`

Remarks: To install MODSAV, simply type MODSAV at the DOS prompt, or include it in a batch file (such as AUTOEXEC.BAT).

     MODSAV will load and remain resident, using about 250 bytes of memory. After MODSAV is loaded, you can temporarily disable it by executing:

```
MODSAV /D
```

     It can later be re-enabled via

```
MODSAV /E
```

     VGA adapters are designed to permit custom RAM-based screen fonts; they can also use a wide variety of screen sizes: 25, 28, 30, 33, 44, 50, and even more lines.

     Many applications reset the video mode as they start up; this has the effect of restoring the default screen font and the standard screen size. MODSAV suppress mode resets when the video system is already in the requested mode. Once loaded, MODSAV watches all requests for video mode resets and discards requests that duplicate the current mode. For example, if a program requests 80-column color text mode and the VGA is already in that mode, MODSAV simply ignores the request and returns to the calling program (with your RAM font and screen size intact).

This program is in the public domain and may be freely used and distributed without restriction.

MORE.EXE
Version 2.5

Marc Perkel

Shareware

Purpose: Replaces the standard MS-DOS MORE program.

Syntax: `Command | [d:] [path] MORE`

Remarks: This replacement for the standard MORE command offers two very useful functional enhancements — it asks you if you want to continue via a "Y/N" prompt, and it lets you move down the screen a line at a time by hitting ENTER rather than Y or N. If you decide to use this as a full-time replacement for the DOS command, rename the original DOS command to something like XMORE.EXE and copy this utility into your DOS directory.

MORE.EXE is Copyright © 1988-1990 by Marc Perkel. All Rights Reserved
This program is part of the Computer Tyme DOS ToolBox.
To Register, ask for the BANTAM BOOK special price of $25 (Reg Price $60).

Contact:

Computer Tyme
411 North Sherman, Suite 300
Springfield, MO 65802
(800) 548-5353

MOVE.EXE	Marc Perkel	Shareware
Version 2.6		

Purpose: Moves files to other names, subdirectories or drives.

Syntax: `[d:] [path]MOVE [file] [path] /option`

where options include:

/Q   ;Quiet mode, no messages are displayed while moving.
/O   ;OverWrite existing files without asking.
/A   ;Always ask before overwriting existing files.
/R   ;Include Read-Only files.
/H   ;Include Hidden, System, and Read-Only files.
/C   ;Copy instead of move.
/D   ;Delete files.

Remarks: Wildcards are allowed. This MOVE utility first attempts to move by renaming. If this fails, it copies the files and then deletes the originals. MOVE will normally overwrite existing files if the source file is newer than the destination file unless you use the /A or /O switches.

Examples:

```
MOVE XYZ.DOC \SUBDIR      ;Moves XYZ.DOC to subdirectory
SUBDIR
MOVE XYZ.DOC D:           ;Moves XYZ.DOC to D:
MOVE *.DOC \SUBDIR        ;Moves all .DOC files to SUBDIR
MOVE ABC.DOC XYZ.DOC      ;Renames ABC.DOC to XYZ.DOC
MOVE A:*.* /D/H           ;Deletes all files on A: in root
MOVE *.DOC \SUBDIR\*.TXT  ;Moves all .DOC files to SUBDIR
                          ; and changes names to .TXT
```

Pipes and redirection are also allowed:

```
TYPE FILE.LST | MOVE C:\UTIL ;Moves all files in FILE.LST
                          ; to C:\UTIL
```

MOVE.EXE is Copyright © 1988-1990 by Marc Perkel. All Rights Reserved
This program is part of the Computer Tyme DOS ToolBox.
To Register, ask for the BANTAM BOOK special price of $25. (Reg Price $60)
Contact:

Computer Tyme
411 North Sherman, Suite 300
Springfield, MO 65802
(800) 548-5353

NAB.COM and NABCONFG.COM

Scott Chaney
RSE, Inc.

Shareware

Purpose: Prints partial screen dumps with NABBIT utility.

Syntax: `[d:}[path]NAB [/U]`

where /U unloads NAB.COM

Remarks: To capture part of the screen display, do the following:

1. Press Crtl-G to activate NABBIT. Cursor size changes to indicate that NABBIT is active.
2. Move cursor to upper lefthand corner of block to be printed.
3. Press S (Start) key.
4. Move cursor to lower righthand corner of block to be printed.

To print the marked screen block, press one of the following keys:

B   Print address on a large envelope.

E   Print address on a standard size business envelope.

L   Print any other screen information.

To capture the marked screen block in an insert buffer, press one of the following keys:

I   Capture marked text in the Insert buffer.

SpaceBar Same, but strip out carriage returns and multiple spaces.

To insert buffer contents elsewhere in a document, do the following:

1. Move cursor to the spot where you want the buffer contents to be inserted.
2. Press the Ctrl+I keys.

Notes: A companion program (NABCONFG.COM) may be used to reconfigure NABBIT to use keys other than the ones described here.

Scott Chaney
c/o RSE, Inc.
1157 57th Drive SE
Auburn, WA 98002
(206)939-4105

ND.EXE	**David Foley**	**Shareware**
Version 1.20	**Foley Hi-Tech Systems**	

Purpose: Renames directories without emptying or modifying their contents.

Syntax: `[d:] [path] ND [olddir] [newdir]`

ND.EXE is Copyright © 1990 by Foley Hi-Tech Systems
This program is not public domain but is "shareware" and a part of the Foley Hi-Tech Systems
ExtraDOS collection. To register send a check of money order for $19.00 to:

> Foley Hi-Tech Systems
> ExtraDOS Registration
> 172 Amber Drive
> San Francisco, CA 94131
> (415)826-6084

PARK.COM   Marc Perkel   Shareware

Purpose: Parks the read/write heads on your hard drive in an unused "landing zone" to prepare the computer for moving.

Syntax: [d:] [path] PARK

Remarks: While many late model drives have a self-parking feature, it never hurts to be sure
that your drive heads aren't doing a flamenco imitation on the drive media while
you trundle the computer to a new office down the hall. PARK moves the read-
write heads to an area of the drive that's not used for data storage, thus safeguard-
ing your bits from an accidental and deletrious jolting encounter with the heads
while the computer is in transit. Run PARK and then turn off the machine. Power-
ing up restores the read-write heads to their normal position.

PARK.COM is Copyright © by Marc Perkel. All Rights Reserved
This program is part of the Computer Tyme DOS ToolBox.
To Register, ask for the BANTAM BOOK special price of $25. (Reg Price $60)

Contact:

Computer Tyme
411 North Sherman, Suite 300
Springfield, MO 65802
(800) 548-5353

PF.EXE	**David Foley**	**Shareware**
Version 1.30	**Foley Hi-Tech Systems**	

Purpose: Allows you to search the file path for any files.

Syntax: `[d:][path]PF [filespec]`

Remarks: You may use any DOS wildcards in the filespec. This utility handy when you are trying to locate a similar program or file that could exist in multiple places in your path statement. It will display the files that it finds in order of appearance within the path.

Foley Hi-Tech Systems
ExtraDOS Registration
172 Amber Drive
San Francisco, CA 94131
(415)826-6084

PIPEDIR.EXE   **Marc Perkel**   **Shareware**
Version 2.7

Purpose: Pipes filenames and directory names into other applications.

Syntax: `[d:][path]PIPEDIR filespec [filespec] [/option]`

where filespec is a file name or valid path, including wildcard characters, and options include:

/S   include all subdirectories below the path of the given filespec.
/W   WHEREIS mode, assumes /S and root directory.
/H   include hidden and system files.
/T   gives only directory names.
/P   same as /T but adds a \ to the end.
/X   exclude current directory.
/A   files that have been modified since last backup.
/N   names only, no path.
/F   full display, size, date, time, attributes.
/D   deletes files.
/R   remove directory, all files, and all subdirectories.
/Q   ask before delete.
/+DATE   all files after date.
/-DATE   all files before date.

Remarks: PIPEDIR is also handy for finding and cataloging files on a hard disk. Using /F will give you a detailed display. The /D and /R options are useful for deleting files and removing directories, but should always be used with caution, lest you delete more than you intended. The /N option, like the /B option in DOS 5.0's DIR, can be used to pass file names to another command, either by saving to and then reading from a list file, or by piping directly through DOS. Try using PIPEDIR with the /F option to get a feel for what it can generate, then try redirecting its ouput to some scratch files to see how the other options can be used. Once you're comfortable with that, you're reading to start piping to commands — and you can always use FORK as the first destination so that you can send a copy to CON to see what's going on. PIPEDIR is an alternate version of WHEREIS.EXE. For amusement, use FC on the two of them, then run each one separately and see how the help screens differ.

PRISM.EXE   David Gerrold   Shareware
Version 1.21

Purpose: Lets you set the color palette on a VGA system to one of 262,144 color combinations.

Syntax: `[d:] [path] PRISM [palette.pal]`

where palette.pal is a stored palette file.

Remarks: PRISM should only be run on a VGA-equipped system. If you run PRISM without a palette filename, the first thing you'll note is the fade-out/fade-in video special effect which transports you to the main screen of the PRISM palette editor. Here, using either the keyboard or the mouse, you can load a predefined color palette, or go off and create your own. To set or alter a palette, click on one of the 16 color panels at the top of the screen, then change the color mix using the slider bars below. The menu at the bottom of the screen offers you help, useful background information and the ability to toggle or change both the sound and video special effects, as well as the usual load/save/exit options. The program comes with a set of 40 predefined palettes, some of which are quite amusing. Even if you don't want to stare at a screen colored by PRISM's BROCCOLI.PAL or NEON.PAL paletes all day, it's definitely worth browsing through them.
   You can load a saved palette file by simply typing PRISM filename.

PRISM.EXE is Copyright © 1990 by David Gerrold
This program is not public domain but is "shareware." To register send a check or money order for $25.00 to:

    David Gerrold/PRISM REGISTRATION
    9420 Reseda Boulevard
    Northridge, CA 91324-2932

QKRP.COM
Version 1.2
Eric Meyer

Freeware

Purpose: Modifies the way the BIOS handles incoming keystrokes. It accelerates key re-peat action, yet stops instantly when the key is released. Furthermore, the delay before repeat action begins can be adjusted.

Syntax: `[d:] [path]` QKRP `[I]` *n*

to Install.

Remarks: QKRP roughly doubles the key auto-repeat rate on an IBM PC. This makes mov-ing the cursor, as well as typing repeated characters, faster and easier. At the same time, it solves a problem in the PC BIOS: when you hold down a key, repeat key-strokes are stored in the type-ahead buffer, whether or not your software is ready for them yet. Then an annoying "overshoot" effect occurs as, even after you've re-leased the key, your software is still reading these keystrokes from the buffer. QKRP avoids this, by engaging auto-repeat only when the typeahead buffer is empty. QKRP does not interfere with normal keyboard operation, for example the use of the Alt and numeric keys to enter graphic characters. However, it will only work on 100 percent PC-compatible computers, and might conflict with other TSR (memory resident) software. Test it out before installing it in your bootup procedure.

    Once QKRP is installed, you can adjust the repeat delay setting (the time, after pressing a key, before auto repeat begins) at will, simply by typing:

    `QKRP` *n* for delay of *n* ranging from 1 (shortest) to 5 (longest).

A value of "3" is the default for a moderate delay. Different settings will suit different typists; experiment to find out which you like. If you prefer a different value, you can specify this at the time of installation:

    `QKRP I 2` to "I"nstall with moderately short delay.

You may include option slashes if desired, eg: QKRP /I /2.

    QKRP consumes only about 400 bytes of memory. It should not be installed more than once, as this wastes memory and complicates the keyboard interrupts. Consequently, QKRP tries to detect the fact that it is already resident; if so, it will accept a command to change the delay setting, but will refuse to install itself again.

    If you simply type "QKRP", with no arguments, the program will tell you whether it is installed.

Note: QKRP cannot tell that it is already memory resident if another keyboard-intercepting TSR has been loaded since. In this situation you can no longer vary the delay setting. (Also, an installation command would result in a duplicate installation, which should be avoided.)

QKRP.COM is Copyright © 1991 by Eric Meyer. All Rights Reserved
This program is "freeware" and may be freely used and distributed, but not modified or sold without author consent:

> Eric Meyer
> 3541 Smuggler Way
> Boulder, CO 80303

QUIXX.COM
Version 2.03

Jonathan Kraidin

Freeware

Purpose: This TSR screen-saver program for DOS 3.0 and above generates beautiful vapor-like trails after a given idle time period.

Syntax: `[d:][path]QUIXX time mode`

or

`QUIXX option`

where time is the idle time in minutes (1 to 99) and Mode is the video mode from 0 to 19.
    Valid options are:

? — provides help

r — removes Quixx from memory

- — stops the timeout counter

+ — restarts the counter

F — speeds up the display

S — slows down the display

Remarks: Modes 1 through 15 select a constant color display for the QUIXX using a color palette corresponding to the Mode. That is Mode 2 = color 2.
    Mode 0 selects an alternating color display. Every time the Quixx pattern bounces off of a wall the color increments. Mode 16 selects a pattern where the colors vary within each line of the Quixx pattern. This yields a constantly changing image as the vapor trail moves. Mode 17 selects the same pattern-type, but in VGA mode19, allows 256 colors. The resolution is 320 x 200. Mode 18 is also in VGA mode19, but the lines of the vapor trail are solid. As a new lines are drawn they go go through all 256 colors.
    Mode 19 is the Glide mode. Here the Quixx pattern is one color, but as the image moves its color goes through a continuous spectrum of 384 shades.
    The options can be changed at any time by retyping the command. If you type:

`QUIXX 2 15`

selecting a two-minute time-out using mode 15, and you then type

`QUIXX 5`

you change the time-out to five minutes and leave the mode unchanged. If you type

```
QUIXX 5 19
```

the mode changes to mode 19.

Quixx disables the sleep countdown and will never become active. Typing Quixx + re-enables the Quixx sleep countdown. Use this feature in a BATCH file if you want to selectively enable/disable Quixx without changing the programs in active memory.

Notes: It is STRONGLY RECOMMENDED that you have expanded or extended memory to prevent memory conflicts when the TSR saves your video screen. While the program will use higher memory without expanded memory, the program may crash your system depending on what applications are running. This program has worked well using expanded memory with programs like WordPerfect and Harvard Graphics.

Quixx will check first for an expanded memory driver, if not found, it will check for an extended memory driver such as HIMEM.SYS. If none of these are found then high memory is used.

The program also has a speed sensing algorithm to adjust the speed of the program to the speed of the computer.

If only a CGA is present the color white is used. No other modes work. Modes 17, 18, and 19 are meant for the VGA and will not work properly on an EGA monitor.

The mouse is polled at COM1 and COM2

QUIXX.COM is Copyright © 1990 by Jonathan Kraidin
This program is "freeware" and may be freely used and distributed, but not modified or sold for profit without author consent.

RAMFREE.COM   Kim Kokkonen
Turbo Power Software

Purpose: Tells you how many bytes of memory are free for the next application.

Syntax: [d:] [path] RAMFREE

Remarks: The number RAMFREE reports is the same as that reported by the DOS CHKDSK utility. RAMFREE's advantage is that you don't need to wait for your hard disk to be analyzed before you find out how much memory is free.

The TSR Utilites — DEVICE.EXE, DISABLE.EXE, MAPMEM.EXE, MARK.EXE, RAMFREE.COM, RELEASE.EXE, and WATCH.COM — are Copyright © 1986, 1987, 1989 by Kim Kokkonen of Turbo Power Software.

RAMMAP.EXE   Marc Perkel.   Shareware
Version 1.3

Purpose: Displays what's in memory, and is able to free up some wasted memory blocks. It can also return an error level code to a batch file to indicate which TSRs are in memory.

Syntax: `[d:][path] RAMMAP [options]`

where options include:

Free — frees up otherwise wasted memory blocks

InMem filename — tests to see if filename is in memory

Remarks: When loading TSRs, each program has its own environment space. Generally, this is wasted memory. Running **RAMMAP FREE** after each TSR load can recover this memory. It won't gain much, but in some situations, every byte counts.

The command InMem tests to see what TSRs are loaded in memory. If the program is found, it returns errorlevel 1. Otherwise it returns errorlevel 0. Besides finding TSRs, InMem will also find BATCH files that are running.

RAMMAP.EXE is Copyright © by Marc Perkel. All Rights Reserved
This program is not public domain but is "shareware" and part of a ComputerTyme collection.
To register contact:

ComputerTyme
411 North Sherman
Suite 300
Springfield, MO 65802
(800)548-5353

RELEASE.EXE   Kim Kokkonen
Turbo Power Software

Purpose: Removes TSRs from memory.

Syntax: `[d:][path]RELEASE Filename [/option]`

The following options, which must start with a slash,'/'include:

/E   do NOT access EMS memory.

/K   release memory, but keep the mark in place.

/S   chars stuff string (<16 chars) into keyboard buffer on exit.

/?   write this help screen.

Remarks: MARK.EXE and RELEASE.EXE are used to manage TSR's in memory, without requiring a system reboot. In their simplest form, MARK and RELEASE are used as follows:

1. Run MARK before installing your TSR(s). This marks the current position in memory and stores information that RELEASE will later need to restore the system. A common place to call MARK is in your AUTOEXEC.BAT file.
2. Install whatever TSRs you want, using the normal method for each TSR.
3. To remove those TSRs from memory, run RELEASE. This will release all of the memory above (and including) the last MARK, and will restore the system to the state at the time the MARK was made.

There are a number of variations of this simple method. First, MARKs can be stacked in memory, as shown in the following hypothetical batch file:

```
MARK
TSR1
MARK
TSR2
MARK
TSR3
```

Each call to RELEASE releases memory above and including the last MARK. In this example, the first call to RELEASE would remove TSR3 and the last MARK from memory, the second call would remove TSR2 and its MARK, and so on.

MARK and RELEASE may be called using a command line parameter.

The parameter specifies a "mark name" and allows releasing TSR's to a specific point in memory. Consider the following example:

```
MARK TSR1
TSR1
MARK TSR2
TSR2
MARK TSR3
TSR3
```

This loads the three TSRs just as in the previous example.

However, if RELEASE were called like this

```
RELEASE TSR2
```

then both TSR2 and TSR3 would be removed from memory. Note that the use of such a name does not allow just a single layer of TSRs to be removed (just TSR2, for example). RELEASE always removes all TSRs including and beyond the one named.

Notes: RELEASE deletes the mark file when it has finished. RELEASE has several command line options to modify its behavior.

None of the options is required for normal use of RELEASE.

/E is made available for systems running early, buggy EMS (expanded memory) drivers that don't correctly implement all of the EMS 3.2 system calls. Don't use it unless you have an EMS-related problem during or after running RELEASE.

/K is useful when you will be releasing and reloading a TSR repeatedly. With it, you avoid the need to replace the mark each time the TSR is released. Using /K in combination with a file mark also prevents RELEASE from deleting the mark file.

/S followed by at least one space and then a short string (15 characters or fewer) tells RELEASE to stuff this string into the keyboard buffer just before exiting. RELEASE automatically adds a carriage return to the end of the string.

To explain why the /S option is important, we must digress a moment. Let's assume that you normally keep SideKick loaded, but that you must unload it in order to have enough memory free to run Lotus 1-2-3. It would seem reasonable to write a little batch file like this:

```
RELEASE SK
LOTUS
MARK SK
SK
```

which would remove the previously loaded SideKick from memory, run Lotus, and then load SideKick again. Unfortunately, this won't work! The reason is complicated to explain. It must suffice here to say that DOS batch files trap memory, and the memory freed by a call to RELEASE does not truly become available the current batch file ends. Now the need for the /S option becomes clear. We can split the previous batch file into two:

```
batch1:
  RELEASE SK /S BATCH2

batch2:
  LOTUS
  MARK SK
  SK
```

The first batch file releases the memory and stuffs the characters 'BATCH2<Enter>' into the keyboard buffer. When the batch file ends, the released memory becomes available. DOS automatically reads the keystrokes waiting in the buffer and starts up the second batch file, which runs Lotus and later reloads SideKick.

To keep things simple, the /S option pokes the specified keystrokes directly into the system keyboard buffer. As a result, the number of keystrokes is limited to 15 (not counting the <Enter> key, which RELEASE adds automatically). This always allows enough keys to start another batch file, however, and the new batch file can take over from there.

RELEASE detects when it is releasing memory within a batch file. It writes a warning message to that effect, but continues processing anyway under the assumption that the batch file is about to end. You can ignore the warning if you've already taken account of DOS's memory management behavior within batch files.

MARK and RELEASE are capable of removing many, but not all, TSRs from memory. The TSRs that cannot be released fall into two categories: those that cannot be released without specific internal knowledge of the TSR, and those that can be released by storing additional general information about the system.

The TSR Utilites — DEVICE.EXE, DISABLE.EXE, MAPMEM.EXE, MARK.EXE, RAMFREE.COM, RELEASE.EXE, and WATCH.COM — are Copyright © 1986, 1987, 1989 by Kim Kokkonen of Turbo Power Software.

RESPRO.COM   **Eric Gans**   **Freeware**
Version 1.35

Purpose: Disables, enables (reactivates), and clears memory-resident programs.

Syntax: `[d:] [path] RESPRO [/switch]`

when valid switches are:

A   filename.ext
Activate (enable) the previously disabled TSR filename.ext program.

C   Same as above.

K   Use at command line only, to change hotkey assignments.

D   filename.ext
Disable the TSR filename.ext program.

R   Same as above.

U   Use at command line only, to change hotkey assignments for
UnCrash feature.

Remarks: Load RESPRO.COM before any other TSR programs, since it only looks for programs loaded above itself.
To use RESPRO once it's loaded, press the Alt+` (accent grave on tilde) keys. The screen displays a numbered list of the TSR programs, together with their starting address and size.
Press one of the following keys:

AN   Activate (enable) the previously-disabled program number N.
See DN below.

C   Clear all memory-resident programs above RESPRO.

DN   Disable program number N (from the numbered list).
A   "** DISABLED **" message appears on the screen next to that program name.

Escape key   Press to clear RESPRO menu from screen.

R   Remove last program from the list, freeing the memory for use by other applications.

V   Verbose. For each TSR, this mode displays the interrupts used and their addresses.

For command line (or batch file) operation, the switch will let you activate or deactivate programs without having to press keys.

UnCrash Feature   In the event of a system hang-up, press the CapsLock and ScrollLock keys simultaneously to return to the DOS prompt.

Remarks: Most screen-blanking programs are disabled while the RESPRO menu is on screen. When the menu is cleared, normal screen-blanking is restored.

In command-line or batch file operation, the /A and /D switches do not recognize pathspecs. Therefore, the program to be disabled/enabled must be in the same directory as RESPRO.COM.

Notes: To disable a screen-blanking utility prior to loading an application (WINDOWS, for example) that takes control of hotkey combinations, try the following batch file:

```
RESPRO /D (screen-blanking utility name)
[path] WINDOWS\WIN
RESPRO /A (screen-blanking utility name)
```

If the RESPRO menu shows a "clubs" symbol (extended character set symbol 005) instead of a filename, then that program can only be disabled via the menu, by referring to its number. The /A and /D command line switches will not operate.

RESPRO.COM is Copyright © by Eric Gans
This program is "freeware" and may be freely used and distributed, but not modified or sold for profit without author consent.

ROMTABLE.EXE　　　　　John Woram

Purpose: Displays the Hard Drive table embedded in ROM in IBM and compatible computers.

Syntax: `[d:] [path] ROMTABLE`

Remarks: If the table contains a listing for the hard drive type(s) installed in your computer, the drive letter and a blinking ":" appear next to the type number. If pointer data is stored in the reserved type-15 location, that line will display "Pointer: Drive C is Type nn" (where nn is the actual drive type. A similar message appears for Drive D, if appropriate.

Notes: The starting address of the drive-type table varies from one IBM computer type to another. If the table displays garbage, then ROMTABLE does not recognize the computer on which it is running.

ROMTABLE.EXE is Copyright © 1990 by John Woram

RV.EXE   **Raymond T. Kaya**   **Freeware**
Version 2.40

Purpose: Displays contents of archived files. Converts self-extracting archive files to normal archive files. Includes other archive management utilities.

Syntax:

```
[d:][path]RV (archive name) /switches [file specs]
[d:][filename(s)]
```

where archive name is the name of the archive file to be searched.
Valid switches include:

/A   Strip all (same as using /C/U/X switches)

/B   Show filename and extension only. Pathnames within LZH and ZIP files are not displayed.

/C[filename]   Strip/attach ZIP file comments. If a valid filename is included, then comments contained in that file will be attached to any ZIP files that match archive name.

/D   Sort ZIP and LZH files. Local and central directory headers are written back to disk in sorted order.

/I   Ignore the switches specified in an RV.CFG file (see Notes), thus temporarily resetting RV to its factory defaults.

/L   Relax checking. If RV default mode will not list contents of archive file, this option may allow it to do so. Do not use with other options that actually modify the archive file.

/N   List archived files in natural order (as actually stored in archive file).

/P   Pause after each full screen. Press any key to continue.

/R   Reset date and time of archive file to that of the most recent file within the archive.

/S   Subdirectory search through directories below the directory implied by archive name.

/U[path]   Converts a self-extracting (SFX) archive to a normal archive. A new archive file is created with the same name but a new extension, as appropriate (ARC, LZH, etc.). If a path is not specified, the new file is written to the current directory.

/W   Show contents of archived file in five-column wide display format. Show filename and extension only.

/X   Strip extra bytes from end of the archive file. Xmodem file transfer protocols often pad transferred files with extra bytes. The /X switch truncates LZH and ZIP archives to their true sizes.

Notes: Each switch must be preceded by a slash or hyphen. To automatically use any of the switches descibed above, use an ASCII text editor to write the switches to a file named RV.CFG. Write the file as /a/b/c/ . . . where a,b,c are your switch choices. The file may also contain comments. Do not include slashes or hyphens in the comments, which might be interpreted as switch instructions.

This program is "freeware" and may be freely used and distributed, but not modified or sold for profit without author consent.

SA.EXE	**David Foley**	**Shareware**
Version 1.10	**Foley Hi-Tech Systems**	

Purpose: Allows you to set the foreground, background and border colors of your monitor.

Syntax: `[d:][path]SA [options] [foreground] [on background]`

Example: SA bright red on green

Notes: The following are valid colors:

Black	Blue	Green	Cyan
Red	Magenta	Brown	Gray
DarkGray	LightBlue	LightGreen	LightCyan
LightRed	LightMagenta	Yellow	White

SA.EXE is Copyright © 1989-1991 by Foley Hi-Tech Systems
This program is not public domain but is "shareware" and a part of the Foley Hi-Tech Systems
ExtraDOS collection. To register send a check or money order for $19.00 to:

Foley Hi-Tech Systems
ExtraDOS Registration
172 Amber Drive
San Francisco, CA 94131
(415)826-6084

SETUP.EXE	**Nathaniel S. Johnson**	**Freeware**

Purpose: Displays test patterns for monitor alignment.

Syntax: `[d:] [path]` SETUP

Remarks: SETUP displays dots, cross hatches, and color bars for determining monitor alignment. In the hands of a qualified technician, it can be used to align the color guns
and CRT yoke in a monitor. For the rest of us, it's got some attractive screens,
and can be used to determine if a call to a technician is warranted — if, for example, the cross-hatch pattern looks more like a soccer ball than the rectilinear grid
it's supposed to be.

SETV.EXE
Bob Eyer   **Freeware**
Version 2.0

Purpose: Sets VGA to seven text resolutions.

Syntax: `[d:] [path] SETV Mode`

The possible modes may be listed by entering SETV with no parameter.

Remarks: There should be virtually no risk of damaging your video equipment on use of SETV: This program will not permit display of anything but the help screen if the adaptor detected is not VGA.

If you run a display program, such as an editor, which scrambles your video after running SETV, just reboot.

Video scrambling is most likely to occur in some programs, when the screen width is set to 132 rather than 80, and is due to the failure of the display program to take into account large screen widths. A few programs, such Vern Buerg's LIST, will take 132-column modes into account.

SETV supports both 132 x 25 and 132 x 44 132-line modes.

Notes: All of SETV's modes except 40 x 25 and (N)ormal mode require a more sophisticated ANSI driver than DOS's ANSI.SYS. The latter is limited chiefly by failing to account for screens longer than 25 lines. Use VANSI.SYS instead. The syntax to use in your CONFIG.SYS will be the same. And VANSI.SYS provides faster screens and more flexible operation.

SETV.EXE was written by Bob Eyer [CI5:73230,2620]
This program is "freeware" and may be freely used and distributed, but not modified or sold for profit without author consent.

SHOW.EXE   Steve Leonard   Shareware

Purpose: Displays a file for easy browsing.

Syntax: `[d:][path]SHOW filename`

Remarks: The filename is non-optional — but given the intended function, that's not unreasonable. SHOW lets you use the normal assortment of cursor keys — Up Arrow, Down Arrow, Left Arrow, Right Arrow, Home, End, Pg Up and Pg Dn — to move around the file.

In addition, it provides on-line help via F1, and supports toggling between text and hex displays via F2,

It also has a search for, and find next, capability using F3 and F4. Pressing F3 prompts you for a string to search for; once one is found, F4 will repeat the search for the next occurrence.

Its one significant limitation is that it only works with the first 64Kb of files longer than that.

This program is "freeware" and may be freely used and distributed, but not modified or sold for profit without author consent.

Anyone who finds this program of value is encouraged to make a voluntary donation to the author.

Steve Leonard
260 Dunbar Road
Hilton, NY 14468

SORT.EXE
Version 2.5

Marc Perkel.

Shareware

Purpose: Improves on DOS SORT command by providing case sensitivity

Syntax: `[d:][path]SORT [/R] [/I] [+N] [<][source] [>target]`

or

`command |[d:][path]SORT [/R] [/I] [+N] [>target]`

where source and target are valid file specifications, command is any DOS command that generates redirectable output, and valid options for SORT are:

/R reverses the sort order from first-to-last to last-to-first

/I ignores upper and lower case

/+N sorts according to the character in column N

Remarks: As in the standard DOS command, the default value for N is 1.

With the /I option in use, this command performs the same as its cousin from Redmond. Without the /I, you can sort according to the ASCII sequence of upper case and lower case — A to Z preceeds a to z.

If you intend to use this in place of the DOS command, consider renaming the DOS command to XSORT, and placing this utility in your DOS directory.

| **SPEEDRAM.EXE** | **David Foley** | **Shareware** |
| **Version 1.10** | **Foley Hi-Tech Systems** | |

Purpose: Increases the speed of your system CPU by changing the refresh rate of your systems 8253 timer chip.

Syntax: `[d:] [path] SPEEDRAM [parameter]`

where valid parameters are:

+ Enable SpeedRam. Entering a + will enable SpeedRam and set the optimum refresh rate.

- Disable SpeedRam. Entering a - will disable SpeedRam and set the refresh rate to stock values.

r:nn Set refresh rate to nn Us. Entering r:nn will set the refresh rate to nn micro seconds. Only use this if you have a good understanding of the refresh rates.

Setting too high a refresh rate will cause memory parity errors or hang your system. If you find that SpeedRam + causes parity errors or hangs your system than you will want to try this option.

If you do not specify a parameter then SpeedRam will list the available parameters for you.

Remarks: All Personal Computers, including the original IBM PC were designed with a very high refresh rate. The rate used by all personal computers is far beyond the rate required by the RAM chips used in these machines. SpeedRam sets the refresh rate to match closer with RAM manufacturers specifications and in turn frees up CPU cycles. These free cycles can be used by your software rather than going to waste by refreshing the RAM too often. The change in refresh rate matches within specifications of most DRAM manufacturers. Depending on your system SpeedRam should increase your CPU's performance from 2% to 10%. You can measure this in many ways such as LANDMARK's CPU SPEED Test or Norton Utilities SI program.

Notes: The memory in your Personal Computer is called DRAM, or Dynamic Random Access Memory. DRAM chips can not hold a charge of electricity for a very long time. In fact, a new charge of 5 volts must be supplied about every 65 micro seconds or it will loose its data. To supply this charge, or refresh, the memory, the CPU must stop processing data and direct the 8253 chip to send the refresh charge to the bank of memory.

Once the refresh is done the CPU can continue processing. SPEEDRAM speeds up your system by reducing the number of times the CPU has to stop to refresh DRAM .

SpeedRam is not a TSR. It does not require any RAM or take any away from your system. SpeedRam only needs to be loaded once and will perform until the machine is rebooted. Be sure to save any critical data in memory before experimenting with SPEEDRAM, as you may experience system crashes before you get it set up correctly for your system.

TROUBLE SHOOTING

SpeedRam has been thoroughly tested on many systems before being released but due to the complexity and variety of equipment available there can be no guarantee that it will work on every Personal Computer.

If SpeedRam causes any problem, it will cause memory problems. If you notice memory errors, parity errors, or that your machine is hanging after running SpeedRam + then the rate that SpeedRam has chosen for your system is causing the DRAM chips to fail. This is in no way a permanent failure, you will just have to pick a lower rate at which to run SpeedRam. To use a manual refresh rate with SpeedRam enter the following:

```
SpeedRam r:nn
```

where nn is the refresh rate you wish to use. Start with 60 and retest your system. If you continue to have problems keep decrements the amount by 5 until you reach a value that your system works with. If the value is less than 18 then you will most likely not benefit from SpeedRam.

SPEEDRAM.EXE is Copyright© 1987-1991 by Foley Hi-Tech Systems.
This program is not public domain but is "shareware" and a part of the Foley Hi-Tech Systems ExtraDOS collection. To register send a check or money order for $19.00 to:

Foley Hi-Tech Systems
ExtraDOS Registration
172 Amber Drive
San Francisco, CA 94131
(415)826-6084

SS.COM   Kevin Curtis   Shareware
Version 2.10

Purpose: Blanks the screen if there is no keyboard (or mouse) activity.

Syntax: `[d:] [path] SS [N] [/switches]`

> N   waiting time, in minutes, until screen is blanked following the last keystroke. Default is 15 minutes. switches
>
> Alt+Tab   Toggle to alternately disable/enable screen saver mode. System beeps when screen saver mode is enabled.
>
> Alt+5   Restores a Hercules monochrome Graphics Card to its graphics mode.
>
> D   Disable screen saver.
>
> E   Enable screen saver.
>
> H   Help screen.
>
> K   Disable keyboard buffer-clearing option (required on some PC clones is system locks up when a key is pressed to restore screen display.
>
> K+   Re-enable buffer-clearing option, if disabled by /K.
>
> M   Enable mouse support.
>
> S   Display current status of screen saver.
>
> U   Unload screen saver (only valid if SS.COM is the last program loaded into memory.
>
> V   Display the Set Video Type help screen.
>
> VM   Force screen saver to work with the following type of monitor:
>
>   C—CGA or color; E—EGA; H—Hercules; M—monochrome; V—VGA

Remarks: Press any key to restore the screen display. The keystroke is discarded, so it does not affect whatever is on the screen (unless the /K switch has been used).

Notes: Press the same Shift key three times to blank the screen immediately.
    To disable SS.COM prior to loading an application (WINDOWS, for example) that takes control of the keyboard, try the following batch file:

```
[path] SS /D
[path] WINDOWS\WIN
[path] SS /E
```

Failure to disable SS.COM before going into Windows may produce either odd displays or system crashes and should be avoided.

STACK.COM   Shane Bergl   Shareware
Version 3.3

Purpose: Utility for editing current and previous command lines.

Syntax: `[d:]STACK [path]` (to load STACK.COM into memory)

Notes: With STACK loaded into memory, various cursor, Alt and Ctrl key combinations perform the functions described here:

Alt-FN   Copy the current command line to the designated Shift+function key. If insert mode is disabled, command is terminated with a carriage return.

Alt-Ctrl-W   Write the current command stack and function key definitions to a designated file (default is STACK.DFL)

Backspace   Delete the character to the left of the cursor.

Ctrl-A   Toggles stack on, so it can be used within applications.

Ctrl-End   Delete from the command line cursor to the end of the line.

Ctrl-FN   Copy the current command line to the designated function key (1-10). If insert mode is disabled, command is terminated with a carriage return.

Ctrl-Home   Delete the command line to the left of the cursor.

Ctrl-Left or right arrow   Move left or right one word on the current command line.

Ctrl-R   Reads the command stack and function key definitions from the file name listed on the command line.

Ctrl-T   Delete from the command line cursor to the beginning of the next word.

Ctrl-W   Writes the command stack and function key definitions to the file listed on the command line.

Del   Delete the character at the cursor position.

End   Move the cursor to the end of the command line.

Escape   Clear the command line and close the Stack window.

FN and Shift-FN   Copy the command associated with the function key to the command line. Execute the command if it ends with a carriage return.

Home   Move the cursor to the beginning of the command line.

Ins   Toggle Insert mode on and off.

PageDown   Move down a page in the Stack window.

PageUp   Move up a page in the Stack window.

Shift Left-Enter key   Transfer the current command line to the bottom of the Stack window.

Shift Right-Enter key   Transfer the current command line to the current (highlighted) line in the Stack window.

Shift-Del   Delete the highlighted command in the Stack or function key window and on the command line.

Shift-Tab   Toggles between an automatic display of the command and function key windows to disabling the automatic display.

Tab   Displays command window if not automatically displayed; toggles between the command window and the function key window otherwise.

Up and down arrows   Toggle through the command list displayed in the Stack window and display the highlighted command at the DOS prompt.

\#   Characters to the left of the \# are displayed but not executed.

^   Use in command1 ^ command2 format to place two or more commands on the same line.

As opposed to DOSKEY, STACK lets you see the commands, and save a standard set of batch commands and function key definitions.

STACK.COM Version 3.3 is Copyright © 1991 by Shane Bergl.
This program is not public domain but is "shareware." If you wish to register as a user please send $A20 to

P.O. Box 78
Dickson, Australia Capital Territory, 2602, Australia

From outside Australia please add $A4 to cover currency conversion costs.

TI.COM	Scott Chaney	Shareware
Version 1.6	**RSE, Inc.**	

Purpose: Prevents accidental deletion of files.

Syntax: `[d:][path]TI [/U]`

where /U uninstalls TI.COM

Remarks: TI stands for Trash-It, a TSR to give you an additional layer of protection against accidental file deletion. Even though UNDELETE and other programs of that type exist, they won't work if you've cleverly clobbered the disk space where your accidentally-deleted files used to reside, by writing new data to the disk.

Trash-It works with DOS, PC-Directory, PC-FileNotes, MS Windows or any program that uses DOS function calls to delete files. Instead of deleting the file, Trash-It moves the file over a directory called \TRASH, which you must create using MD \TRASH.

In other words, your deleted files remain intact, they just get moved out of the way, to the \TRASH subdir where DOS can't overwrite it.

Of course, since you're not actually deleting these files, eventually your hard disk is going to fill up, requiring that you "dump the trash", i.e., go to the \TRASH subdirectory and delete the files. Trash-It doesn't interfere with deletes done in the \TRASH subdir.

Files deleted in the \TRASH subdir are actually deleted.

Notes:
1. Before you use Trash-It for the first time you need to create a subdirectory called "\TRASH" on your hard disk by entering:

   `"MD \TRASH"`

   at the DOS prompt. If you have your hard drive partitioned than create a "\TRASH" subdir in each partition.

   After you've created the "\TRASH" subdir then all you do to run Trash-It is move to the subdir where TI.COM is located and enter "ti" at the DOS prompt. Once loaded Trash-It automatically intercepts all attempts via DOS function calls to delete files, and instead moves the files to the Trash ("\TRASH subdir"). You don't do anything differently than before. It is totally transparent to the user.

   The best way to make sure Trash-It is loaded is to put "TI.COM" in the root directory, and the phrase "TI" in your "AUTOEXEC.BAT" file, also located in the root directory. This will automatically load Trash-It every time you boot your computer.

2. You can remove Trash-It from memory by entering "ti/u" at the DOS prompt.

3. Programs can delete files using two methods. Most programs use DOS function calls do it. However, a few programs directly modify the disk data

(FAT and Directory info) without using DOS. Trash-It works only if DOS function calls are used to delete the file(s). Trash-It can't protect against programs that go in and modify the FAT and Directory information directly. However, almost all programs let DOS do what it's designed for by using DOS function calls to delete files, thereby allowing Trash-It to do its job.

4. Trash-It only works if it finds a "\TRASH" subdirectory on the disk (or partition) where the deleted files are located.

   For example, let's say you have a Trash subdir on your hard drive, C:. You then attempt to delete files on the A: drive. If the disk in the A: drive doesn't have a \TRASH subdir then the files will be deleted, even tho there is a \TRASH subdir on the C: drive. Files will only be moved to the \TRASH subdir if the \TRASH subdir is located on the same disk as the files being deleted. Of course, you can make \TRASH subdirs on all your disks if you want.

   Warning: You shouldn't take deleting files any less seriously than you always have, because in the situations described above (and possibly a few others) the file will actually be deleted.

5. If Trash-It finds a file in the \TRASH subdir with the same name as the file it's trying to move there, then it will increment the last letter of the filename until it's unique.

   For example, if you're trying to delete "TEMP" and a file named "TEMP" already exists in the "\TRASH" subdir then Trash-It would increment the last letter of the filename being moved, in this case from "TEMP" to "TEMQ", and try again.

TI.COM is Copyright © 1990 by RSE, Inc.
This program is not public domain but is "shareware" and part of the RSE, Inc. collection. For registration and information, contact:

Scott Chaney
c/o RSE, Inc.
1157 57th Drive SE
Auburn, WA 98002
(206)939-4105

TICONFIG.COM

Scott Chaney
RSE, Inc.

Shareware

Purpose: Configures TI.COM (Trash-It) for most efficient operation.

Syntax: `[d:] [path]`TICONFIG

where TICONFIG.COM is in the same directory as TI.COM

Remarks: The key to keeping disk space free is to only trash significant files. TICONFIG.COM lets you do just that. You use the configuration program to exempt files from being trashed. You can set a minimum file size in which files greater than the limit are trashed (moved to the TRASH subdir) and those less than the limit are deleted. This can save a lot of disk space. Even a 1 byte file takes up 4K of hard disk space. By having Trash-It delete small files (instead of trashing them) you can free up a significant amount of disk space, without sacrificing any important files.

The configuration program also lets you specify up to five different filename extensions. All "deleted" files with the extension(s) you define will be deleted instead of trashed. This too can save a significant amount of disk space. For example, some programs create temporary files with "TMP" as the filename extension. These files aren't important once the program ends and are deleted. If you specify "TMP" in the configuration program then Trash-It would delete these files rather than trash them. You may use the global character "?" when defining your extensions.

The last item in the configuration program lets you decide whether you want Trash-It to change the trashed file's date/time to the time it was trashed. If you select "No" then Trash-It leaves the date/time of the trashed file unchanged. This lets Trash-It run a little faster. "Yes" is the default value. However if you're a real speed freak, or for some reason you want the deleted files to retain their original date/time, then select "No". To change an item use the up/down arrow keys to select the item and press C for Change. Then input the new value. To delete an extension: select the extension you want to delete, press C to Change, and then press the Enter or Return key without entering anything. When you've finished making all your changes then press the Escape key to save the changes and exit the configuration program.

Scott Chaney
c/o RSE, Inc.
1157 57th Drive SE
Auburn, WA 98002
(206)939-4105

TIDY.EXE	**David Foley**	**Shareware**
Version 1.04	**Foley Hi-Tech Systems**	

Purpose: Finds all the subdirectories on the current disk and removes all *.BAK files, as well as any files that have a length of zero.

Syntax: `[d:] [path]TIDY [extension] [drive] [/p]`

Remarks: TIDY displays the name of each file as it is deleted. Also displays a summary of files that it has erased, as well as a total showing how much disk space was freed.
     Enter any words on the command line after TIDY, and the program will search for files with those extensions and delete them.

Example: `TIDY MAP`

tells TIDY to delete all *.BAK files, as well as all *.MAP files.
     You cannot specify wildcards in the file extension here, but you can list up to 64 extensions to search for.
     Additionally, you can give TIDY a disk drive specifier so that have the program tidies that drive. For example, to clean up on the A: drive, use TIDY A:
     You can use the extensions and disk drive specifier in any order, but the only restriction is that the specifier must contain the colon and there must only be one specifier on a line. So,

`TIDY A: MAP TMP`

will perform identically to

`TIDY MAP TMP A:`

     The /P option will cause the program to prompt the user if the file should really be deleted or not. If the user enters Q, for quit, the program exits and display a status report.

TIDY.EXE is Copyright © 1987-1991 by Foley Hi-Tech Systems
This program is not public domain but is "shareware" and a part of the Foley Hi-Tech Systems ExtraDOS collection. To register send a check or money order for $19.00 to:

     Foley Hi-Tech Systems
     ExtraDOS Registration
     172 Amber Drive
     San Francisco, CA 94131
     (415)826-6084

TOUCH.EXE	David Foley	Shareware
Version 1.20	Foley Hi-Tech Systems	

Purpose: A Unix-like utility used to stamp a file's attributes with the current system date and time.

Syntax: `[d:][path]TOUCH [filespec [filespec]]`

Remarks: Touch is useful if you want to have a group of files with identical date and timestamps. Multiple filespecs are acceptable, as are wildcards within each filespec. If you need to set the time and date to a different time and date than the system clock, you can write a short batch file, using the GET utility, to save the current date and time to environment variables, reset the clock to the desired time and date, TOUCH the files, and then restore the system time and date, like so:

```
GET HE 112
SET savetime=%GET%
GET HE 14
SET savedate=%GET%
TIME 12:00:00
DATE 5-01-91
TOUCH \myfiles\*.*
TIME %savetime%
DATE %savedate%
```

If you're really compulsive you'll want to readjust the seconds afterward.

TOUCH.EXE is Copyright © 1985-1991 by Foley Hi-Tech Systems
This program is not public domain but is "shareware" and a part of the Foley Hi-Tech Systems ExtraDOS collection. To register send a check or money order for $19.00 to:

Foley Hi-Tech Systems
ExtraDOS Registration
172 Amber Drive
San Francisco, CA 94131
(415)826-6084

TS.EXE	David Foley	Shareware
Version 1.01	Foley Hi-Tech Systems	

Purpose: Searches for all occurrences of a given string inside a specified text file.

Syntax: `[d:][path]TS [filespec] [text]`

Note: TS stops ar each occurence and displays the found string, and then prompts the user to continue or exit.TS is case sensitive and does not work on executable files.

TS.EXE is Copyright © 1985-1990 by Foley Hi-Tech Systems
This program is not public domain but is "shareware" and a part of the Foley Hi-Tech Systems ExtraDOS collection. To register send a check or money order for $19.00 to:

Foley Hi-Tech Systems
ExtraDOS Registration
172 Amber Drive
San Francisco, CA 94131
(415)826-6084

TURBOBAT.COM
Version 1.00

David Foley
Foley Hi-Tech Systems

Shareware

Purpose: Allows you to compile standard DOS batch files into .COM binary programs.

Syntax: `[d:] [path] TURBOBAT filename.ext`

The output will be filename.COM.

Remarks: Turbobat greatly enhance the speed of large batch files by allowing them to run in native code rather than interpreted DOS commands. The resulting .COM files may call nested batch files without losing the parent since the parent calling program is no longer a batch file.

TURBOBAT.COM is Copyright © 1990 by Foley Hi-Tech Systems
This program is not public domain but is "shareware" and a part of the Foley Hi-Tech Systems ExtraDOS collection. To register send a check or money order for $19.00 to:

Foley Hi-Tech Systems
ExtraDOS Registration
172 Amber Drive
San Francisco, CA 94131
(415)826-6084

VANSI.SYS   Chris Dunford   Freeware
The Cove Software Group

Purpose: Enhanced ANSI screen driver.

Syntax: `DEVICE=[d:][path]VANSI.SYS`

or

`DEVICEHIGH=[d:][path]VANSI.SYS`

Remarks: To take advantage of screens larger than 25 lines at the DOS prompt, you need a screen driver that understands what's going on.

VANSI.SYS is a modification of Dan Kegel's excellent NANSI.SYS to accomodate the VGA system. To use it, simply install as you would ANSI.SYS by including the statement

`DEVICE=[d:path]VANSI.SYS`

in your CONFIG.SYS. With VANSI installed, you will find that you have full use of all available lines when you're working at the DOS prompt.

VANSI is a modification of the free NANSI.SYS by Daniel Kegel. Both original and modified source are available from the IBM Systems Forum (IBMSYS) on CompuServe.

VERSION.EXE   Marc Perkel   Shareware

Purpose: Lets you fake any DOS version number to avoid the "Incorrect DOS version" error message.

Syntax: `[d:][path]VERSION M.N command arguments`

where M.N is the DOS version number — e.g., 3.3 or 5.0; command is any command that checks the DOS version; and arguments are the normal arguments expected by the command.

Remarks: There are few things more aggravating than backing up a huge file to floppies, carrying them all the way across town, and then finding that you can't RESTORE the file on the system you're trying to move it to because of a slight difference in DOS versions. When you see that "Incorrect DOS version" message instead of the 10 megabyte file you were expecting, you get to explore new frontiers of frustration. Without VERSION, you'd need to go back to the original system and generate a bootable floppy with the correct RESTORE command for that system's version of DOS, and boot from that floppy before you could get at the file. DOS 5.0 addresses this sort of problem with its SETVER.EXE devce driver and command, but some people are leery of Microsoft's solution to this problem, as SETVER creates and maintains a hidden table which is modified without changing the file date or time. This leads to two equally unpleasant possibilities: your virus-checking program is going to think SETVER has been infected and bring your system to a halt, or someone with more time on their hands than is good for them will figure out a way to use the SETVER table as a tool in propagating a virus.

VERSION offers a benign solution to this problem, as it doesn't modify anything on disk.

Example: `VERSION 3.3 A:\RESTORE A: C:\*.* /S`

will fool the copy of RESTORE. EXE on the A: drive into restoring data onto a system not running DOS 3.3.

VERSION.EXE is Copyright © 1989-1991 by Marc Perkel. All Rights Reserved
This program is part of the Computer Tyme DOS ToolBox.
To Register, ask for the BANTAM BOOK special price of $25. (Reg Price $60)

Contact:
    Computer Tyme
    411 North Sherman, Suite 300
    Springfield, MO 65802
    (800) 548-5353

VFONT.EXE	Chris Dunford	Public Domain
Version 1.00	The Cove Software Group	

Purpose: Loads VGA fonts various sizes providing for 25, 30, 33, 36, 44, and 50-line VGA text displays.

Syntax: `[d:] [path] VFONT [option]`

where options include:

R25 load the 25-line ROM-based font provided by your VGA card
R50 load the 50-line ROM-based font provided by your VGA card
file load a font from one of the supplied font files (*.FNT)
[attrib] set the screen attributes as a two-digit number

Remarks: For file names, the FNT extension is assumed if none is provided. When VFONT loads a new font into the VGA, it must perform a screen clear in order to ensure that the video system is in a stable state. Normally it will clear the screen to white-on-black, but you can specify any color attribute you want by adding the ATTRIB option.

Examples: To load the 33-line font (contained in 33.FNT), type:

`VFONT 33`

To load the 36-line font and clear the screen to light cyan on blue:

`VFONT 36 27`

where 27 is the attribute number for light cyan on blue.

Notes:

1. The following fonts are supplied; all are sans serif unless otherwise specified:

   25.fnt 25-line font
   25s.fnt 25-line serif font (similar to the ROM font, but nicer)
   30.fnt 30-line font
   33.fnt 33-line font
   33q.fnt A 33-line "square" font for fun. Impress your non-computing friends with how computery your display looks.
   36.fnt 36-line font
   44.fnt 44-line font
   50.fnt 50-line font

Note that 25.fnt and 50.fnt differ from the ROM-based fonts in that they are sans serif.

2. Two related programs can help in making these fonts more useful.

You may find that some of your applications programs tend to reload the ROM fonts and/or change the number of lines displayed. MODSAV, also from Cove Software, can be helpful in preventing this. MODSAV is a free program that should be included in this archive (along with its separate documentation).

In order to take advantage of screens larger than 25 lines at the DOS prompt, you will need a screen driver that understands what's going on.

Included on disk is a modified version of Dan Kegel's excellent NANSI.SYS to accomodate the VGA system. The modified version (VANSI.SYS) should also be included with this archive. To use it, simply install as you would ANSI.SYS by including the statement

```
DEVICE=[d:path]VANSI.SYS
```

in your CONFIG.SYS. With VANSI installed, you will find that you have full use of all available lines when you're working at the DOS prompt.

3. The format of the font files is as follows:

Offset	Length	Contents
0	2	File signature: "VF"
2	1	Binary 0
3	1	"Points": number of dot rows per character
4	Var	Character definitions

The character definitions are in the format required by the VGA subsystem. The length is 256 * points.

This program is in the public domain and may be freely used and distributed without restriction. VFONT has been donated to the public domain by the author:

Chris Dunford
The Cove Software Group
PO Box 1072
Columbia, MD 21044
301/992-9371 (voice only)
CompuServe 76703,2002

VGACOLOR.COM   Doug Cox   Freeware
Version 2.1

Purpose: Enables you to change any color to any of the 256k (262,144) colors available on a VGA computer.

Syntax: `[d:] [path]`VGACOLOR

Remarks: VGACOLOR is a TSR; to invoke it once it's installed, press an ALT key and the RIGHT SHIFT key at the same time. The following line will appear (in light blue) where the cursor line was:

```
0   Red  0   Green  0   Blue  0   Use PgUp, PgDn, Home, End, Arrows, Esc
```

Press the Page Up key to change from the current color (which is color number 0 as shown at the left of the line) to color number 1, and so on up to color number 15. The color associated with the color number will be shown at the far left of the line.

Press the Page Down key to go through the 16 colors in the opposite direction. Initially, markers bracket "Red 0".

Press the Right Arrow key to move these markers to the right. Press the Left Arrow key to move these markers to the left.

Press the Up Arrow key to increase the intensity level of Red, Green, or Blue (depending on where the markers are). Press the Down Arrow key to decrease the intensity level.

Press the Home key to restore the selected color to its original default color. The default VGA colors are the same as the 16 colors available on CGA computers in alphanumeric mode.

Press Ctrl-Home to restore all colors to the original default colors, and exit.

Press either the End key or the Esc key to exit. The line will disappear and the original cursor line will re-appear.

There is a subtle difference between exiting with the End key and with the Esc key. Normally, when there is a mode change on your computer (such as when you run a game that's in graphics mode), all colors will return to their default color settings. But you probably don't want this to happen after you change a color with this program. So you have a choice of whether the changes you make will "stick" or not. If you exit with the End key, those changes will "stick". If you exit with the Esc key, a mode change will return all colors to their default color settings (and some programs even make a mode change to simply clear the screen).

Notes: 1. VGACOLOR it only works in normal alphanumeric mode, not in graphic or 40-column mode.
   2. There are three components to any color on an RGB screen: red, green, and blue. VGA computers can divide each of these three color components into 64 different intensities, and 64 x 64 x 64 = 262,144.

This program is "freeware" and may be freely used and distributed, but not modified or sold for profit without author consent.

Thanks to Ralph Smith for writing VPT (Video Graphics Adapter Palette Tool), after which this program is modelled. That program has more features than this one, but it can't be run while in another program.

Written by Doug Cox in 80286, using the ShareWare assembler, A86

> 140 Monroe Dr
> Palo Alto, Ca 94306
> (415) 949-0624
> Feb. 26, 1988 & Oct. 23, 1990

VGAEDIT2.COM   **Doug Cox**   **Public Domain**

Purpose: A graphics editor (a bare-bones paint program) for the VGA 320 x 200 256-color graphic mode that enables you to quickly and easily choose and change colors while drawing a screen.

Syntax: `[d:][path]VGAEDIT2 filename.`

where the non-optional filename is any name you make up, or one which you've already used with VGAEDIT2.

Remarks: After VGAEDIT2 starts, you'll see menus at the top of the screen, 256 color boxes at the bottom, three color bars (red, green, and blue) at the right of the screen, four small boxes above the color bars with a diagonal line in one and a solid rectangle in another, a white dot in the center, (and a previously saved drawing, if there was one). The white dot is the cursor.

Pressing the left button of the mouse will leave a dot on the screen under the cursor in the CURRENT COLOR (a shade of blue, initially). Pressing the right button will erase the dot under the cursor, except when the menus have been cleared from the screen, in which case pressing the right button will re-display the menus. The way to erase under the menus is to make the background color the current color and then draw over the area to be erased.

You can move the cursor anywhere on the screen with the mouse. If the menus are displayed, putting the cursor over one of them and pressing either button will activate that menu.

The menus at the top of the screen are: EXIT, CLEAR MENUS, CLEAR SCREEN, BLOCK, ZOOM, and COLOR COMPONENTS/CURSOR LOCATION.

Pressing a mouse button when the cursor is over the numbers at the right of the top menu will toggle between color components and cursor location Cursor location numbers represent the vertical and horizontal components of the cursor location.

Initially, the numbers at the right of the top menu represent the amount of red, green and blue components of the color under the cursor (unless the cursor is over the vertical color bars at the right of the screen, in which case the numbers represent the components of the current color).

The three vertical color bars at the right indicate (and enable you to change) the amount of red, green, and blue in the current color. Moving the cursor over one of these color bars and pressing a button will move the thick part of the color up or down to the cursor location and change that component of the current color. There are 63 gradations for each of the red, green, and blue components.

The 256 colors at the bottom are the colors that can be used. Each one can be changed to any of the 262,144 possible colors. The current color has a border around it. (The color under the cursor is marked by a small square in the center of that color). Moving the cursor over a color box and pressing a button will make that color the current color.

Of the 256 colors available, seven are used for this program. Black is the first color, at the top left of the color boxes, which is used to erase, and serves as the background color. The last six colors, at the bottom right are used for the white cursor; the light blue is for menus and zoom box outlines; the dark green lines in the big zoom box; and the red, green, and blue colors are for the vertical color bars. Naturally, you can change these, too. For example, you may want to change the cursor color when drawing a bright color so you can continue to see the cursor.

Clicking a mouse button on the diagonal line at the right of the screen allows you to draw a line. Press a button again to anchor one end of the line and move the cursor to where you want the other end to be, and press the left button to anchor that line and stay in line-drawing mode, or press the right button to anchor that line and exit from line-drawing mode.

Clicking on solid rectangle allows you to fill an area on the screen with the current color. Be sure there aren't any openings in the boundary of the area where the color could leak out.

Clicking on the BLOCK menu at the top will clear the menus and leave a cursor. Move the cursor to where you want to begin to draw a box and press a button. Then when you move the mouse a box will be drawn with the initial corner remaining stationary. Pressing a button again will free the cursor from the box and put a menu box in the center of the screen. You can choose from either MOVE, COPY, ERASE, WRITE, or CANCEL by moving the cursor over the appropriate menu and pressing a button.

WRITE will write the contents of the current red, green, and blue contents of each color settings and the contents of the block to a file named 'ICON', in ASCII hexadecimal format (for use as data in a program). The color components will be written first, in the order mentioned (red, green, blue). They will be written 24 bytes to a line, 32 lines, for a total of 768 bytes (3 x 256). Each line of the block contents will be on one line.

Clicking on the ZOOM menu at the top will display a small box that can be moved around the screen with the mouse. When a button is pressed again, what is in the small box will be expanded in a large box at one side of the screen. The mouse cursor can now be moved anywhere. Changes can be made inside the large zoom box that will change whatever is in the small box. Selecting ZOOM again will remove the big and little zoom boxes. The zoom boxes can also be removed by moving the cursor to either the CLRMENU or CLRSCRN box and pressing a mouse button.

Clicking on the EXIT menu box causes a menu to be displayed, asking if you DO or DON'T want to save the screen to the file you named when you started the program. If you select DO and press a button, the screen will be saved to the file as you exit. (If you press the ESC key on the keyboard at any time, you'll exit without the screen being saved to the file).

The first 64,000 bytes in the saved file are the screen pixel colors. The 768 bytes at the end hold the red, green, and blue components of each of the 256 colors used in the file. So, for example, if you've changed color number 0 from the original black (which is all 0s) to solid green (which is 0 red, 63 green, and 0 blue), the first three bytes at address 64,000 in the file would be 0,63,0.

This program is released to the public domain by its author and may be freely used and distributed.

VIEW2.EXE
Version 1.41

Steve Leonard

Shareware

Purpose: Lets you view two text files simultaneously, each in its own window.

Syntax: `[d:] [path]VIEW2 [filename.[ext]]`

Remarks: To view two files, e.g., MYFILE.DOC and MYFILE.BAK, type "VIEW2 MYF-ILE.DOC MYFILE.BAK".

Hit the ENTER key to alternate between the two windows. The "active" window will be marked with the word "ACTIVE" on the top line.

You can resize the windows vertically by using the left and right arrow keys. Additionally, text within each window can be scrolled left and right (using F5 and F6) as well as up and down (using the arrow keys).

While in browse, there is a "find" function (the TAB key) which will search either (or both) windows for a text string.

A compare function (F3) starts with the top line in each window and compares the two files line by line.

Though not an editor, View-Two does have the capability to mark text in one window (F7 marks top line), then insert the marked block into the other window (INS key).

Write the "Active" file to disk with the F10 key. The output file will always be named "VIEW2.OUT".

Type "View2" without entering any filenames, and get a half decent Directory Display.

If the names of the files to be viewed are not supplied on the command line, then View-Two will present a scrolling window of files in the current directory. The directory list may be sorted by Name, Date, Size, or Extension at the press of a function key. To select a file for viewing, just highlight the desired file by using the arrow keys, and hit Enter. Hit Escape without selecting a file, and you will be prompted to enter the filename directly.

On the IBM XT, the smallest file possible still requires 4096 bytes. So even if a file (like a small batch file) shows that it takes up 24 bytes, DOS allocates file space in 4096-byte "chunks." Since running short of room on hard disks seems to be a universal problem, View-Two shows the total amount of space required by all files in the listed directory as two totals: the sum of the number of bytes required by all the files, as well as the true number of bytes required because of the way DOS allocates space in 4K chunks. (For AT and 386 machines, as well as DOS versions 3.0 and above, the second total may not be correct).

Notes: If you are viewing a file or files and hit the Shift and Tab keys simultaneously, the file in the active window will be written out to disk to a file called "View2.out". If there already is a file on disk called VIEW2.OUT, it will be overwritten (Gone forever).

If you are viewing a large file (larger than 64k) and it is written to disk (Shift TAB), the VIEW2.OUT file will never contain more than 64k of data.

Notes:
1. On the Directory Screen, F3 allows you to enter a file mask, such as "*.PAS" or "*.ba?" to restrict the files it displays to those matching the wildcard characters in the "mask".
2. The compare function has "WARP DRIVE" capability. Hit the letter "W" after starting a compare by F3, and it will be much faster.
3. Shift F1-Compare Options allows you to restrict a compare to a range of columns within the two files being VIEWED. Also allows you to enter "equivalent strings." For example, if you are comparing 2 files where you cloned a letter, and one letter was full of "Dear Jane" and the other is full of "Dear Sue," you could make "Jane" equivalent to "Sue" for the purposes of comparison. The program would not stop during the compare if one file contains a "Jane" and the other file contains a "Sue" in the same position.
4. Enter the letter "C" on the command line as a third paramter and start the compare automatically.

This program is "freeware" and may be freely used and distributed, but not modified or sold for profit without author consent.

Anyone who finds this program of value is encouraged to make a voluntary donation to the author:

Steve Leonard
260 Dunbar Road
Hilton, NY 14468

WATCH.COM
Kim Kokkonen
Turbo Power Software
Shareware

Purpose: WATCH.COM is a resident program that keeps track of other memory resident programs.

Syntax: `[d:] [path]WATCH`

Remarks: As a TSR goes resident, WATCH updates a data area in memory that contains information about what interrupt vectors were taken over. This information can later be used by MAPMEM and DISABLE to show more details about interrupts than normally available.

Installation of WATCH.COM is optional. All of the TSR Utilities except DISABLE can be used whether or not WATCH is installed.

The TSR Utilites — DEVICE.EXE, DISABLE.EXE, MAPMEM.EXE, MARK.EXE, RAMFREE.COM, RELEASE.EXE, and WATCH.COM — are Copyright © 1986, 1987, 1989 by Kim Kokkonen of Turbo Power Software.

WHATVID. EXE

Orville Jenkins
Panther Associates

Shareware

Purpose: Determines video adapter type and graphic modes available.

Syntax: `[d:] [path]WHATVID`

Remarks: This program can save a lot of rooting throught the innards of systems and adapter card manuals when you're dealing with unfamiliar computers. It identifies the adapter type, and gives you a list of the video modes available. It can save a lot of swearing when you're trying to install VGA-specific software on a system that seems to have a VGA display but doesn't support the mode you need.

WHATVID.EXE is Copyright © 1989, 1990 by Orville Jenkins, Panther Associates,
This program is not public domain but is "shareware." To register send a check or money order for $5.00 to:

> Panther Associates
> Route 1, 1014 Cimarron Circle
> Roanoke, Texas 76262
> (817) 379-5266

Source code in Turbo C is also available for $15.

WHEREIS.EXE   Marc Perkel   Shareware
Version 2.7

Purpose: Searches for files in all directory on the current drive.

Syntax: `[d:][path]WHEREIS filespec [filespec] [/option]`

where filespec is a file name or valid path, including wildcard characters, and options include:

/S include all subdirectories below the path of the given filespec.

/W PIPEDIR mode, does not assume /S and root directory.

/H include hidden and system files.

/T gives only directory names.

/P same as /T but adds a \ to the end.

/X exclude current directory.

/A files that have been modified since last backup.

/N names only, no path.

/F full display, size, date, time, attributes.

/D deletes files.

/R remove directory, all files, and all subdirectories.

/Q ask before delete.

/+DATE all files after date.

/-DATE all files before date.

Remarks: Whereis is handy for finding and cataloging files on a hard disk. Using /F will give you a detailed display. The /D and /R options are useful for deleting files and removing directories, but should always be used with caution, lest you delete more than you intended. The /N option, like the /B option in DOS 5.0's DIR, can be used to pass file names to another command, either by saving to and then reading from a list file, or by piping directly through DOS. Try using WHEREIS with the /F option to get a feel for what it can generate, then try redirecting its ouput to some scratch files to see how the other options can be used. Once you're comfortable with that, you're reading to start piping to commands — and you can always use FORK as the first destination so that you can send a copy to CON to see what's going on. PIPEDIR.EXE is an alternate version of WHEREIS.EXE.

XARC.EXE   System Enhancement Associates, Inc.   Shareware

Purpose: Extracts .ARC compressed files

Syntax: `[d:] [path]XARC archive [options] [path]`

where archive is the *.ARC file you want to decompress, path is the target directory for the decompressed files, and valid options are:

/O overwrite existing files of the same name without asking

/Gpassword to open a password-protected archive

Remarks: XARC is part of the ARC+Plus package from SEA. XARC cannot be used extract only selected files from an archive. The full package features a menu-driven archive management system.

This program is not public domain but is "shareware" and a part of the System Enhancement Associates, Inc., collection. Copyright © System Enhancement Associates, Inc.

For information, contact:

System Enhancement Associates, Inc.
Attn: Mr. C. J. Wang
925 Clifton Avenue
Clifton, NJ 07013
(201)473-5153

XMNDRVRS.EXE   John Woram

Purpose: Displays information about installed device drivers.

Syntax: XMNDRVRS

Remarks: For each installed device driver, XMNDRVRS.EXE displays the following information:

    Starting address in segment:offset format
    Type (character or block)
    Device name (NUL, CON, AUX, LPTn, etc.)
    Removable media? (Yes or No)
    Drive letter(s), if appropriate
    Last line shows "No more device drivers"

XMNDRVRS.EXE is Copyright © 1990 by John Woram

ZDEL.EXE
Version 2.5

Marc Perkel.   **Shareware**

Purpose: Deletes files according to specified options.

Syntax: `[d:] [path]ZDEL [file [file]] [options]`

where file is either a single file or a list of files and valid options include:

/Q prompt before deleting each file

/R include Read-Only files

/H include System, Hidden and Read-Only files

/N delete files without asking permission (as in "All files in directory will be deleted!")

/S delete files from subdirectories

/D delete directory and all subdirectories

Remarks: It's a good idea to try this out with the /Q option first, as you can get into a fair amount of trouble if you're not careful. Consider (but DON'T ATTEMPT) the effects of ZDEL \ /H/N/D — it's an awfully good argument for getting that tape backup you've been putting off buying.

The /S and /D options need to be able to access PIPEDIR to work.

ZDEL also allows pipes, as in:

`TYPE DEL.LST|ZDEL`

Use with care!

ZDEL.EXE is Copyright © 1989, 1990 by Marc Perkel. All Rights Reserved
These programs are part of the Computer Tyme DOS ToolBox.
To Register, ask for the BANTAM BOOK special price of $25. (Reg Price $60)
Contact:

Computer Tyme
411 North Sherman, Suite 300
Springfield, MO 65802
(800) 548-5353

0X10.EXE	William J. Klos	Freeware
	JRyan Application Systems	

Purpose: Toggles the blink bit or enables/disables grey summing on a VGA monitor.

Syntax: `[d:] [path] 0x10 [-G|-g] [-B|-b]`

where

-G	=	enable grey summing
-g	=	disable grey summing
-B	=	blink bit ON
-b	=	blink bit OFF

Remarks: Toggling the blink bit off allows you to use colors 8–15 (dark grey–bright white) as background colors.

Enabling grey summing puts your display in a sort of monochrome emulation mode, changing all colors to a corresponding shade of grey.

Note: 0x10 is the BIOS interrupt used for video functions.

Developed by William J. Klos, CIS[73077,1601], Copyright © by JRyan Application Systems This program is "freeware" and may be freely used and distributed, but not modified or sold for profit without author consent.

3CT.EXE
Version 5.0

Daniel B. Doman
DarrySoft

Freeware

Purpose: File Space Counter

Syntax: `[d:] [path] 3CT [/V0|/V1|/V2|/V3] [MASK=xxx] [/SKIPEQUAL] [NOPATHEXP]`

where:

/V0 = Just give totals for search, show no subdirectories.

/V1 = List totals for Each parent directory, but do not show children. This is a handy option for network administrators.

/V2 = List count for each directory searched (default).

/V3 = List count for each directory searched and display all files. You might use this option if you want to verify that 3CT is finding all of the files that you think that it should find.

/Mask=xxx = Change the default file mask from *.* to something more specific such as "*.bak ".

/SkipEqual = Do not display empty subdirectories.

/NoPathExp = Do not expand partial pathnames such as ".\" into their full canonical value. Use this switch when scanning Novell Drives which tend to have long server and volume names.

Remarks: 3CT counts files and their sizes to show how much space the files in each sub-directory are taking up. It starts counting from the specified location and works its way through the various subdirectories. It can work on only one drive at a time, but is compatible with most LAN environments, and can return four levels of verbiage. The default level gives the total files and bytes used in each subdirectory.

At most, 3CT will list every file it finds; and at least it will return only the total count for the area checked.

Notes: 3CT counts all hidden files, so you will sometimes see it report more files than the DOS DIR command.

3CT requires DOS version 3.x or greater to run.

Examples:

`3CT .`	<-	Calculate from current directory
`3CT \`	<-	Calculate from Root Directory
`3CT F:\FOO`	<-	Calculate from F:\FOO directory
`3CT F:\FOO /V0`	<-	Calculate from F:\FOO directory Give Search Total Only
`3CT F:\UT /V1`	<-	Give subdirectory totals of F:\UTL directory
`3CT ..\  /V4`	<-	Display all files Too
`3CT /Mask=*.zip /skipEqual .`	<-	Count All .Zip Files

This program is "freeware" and may be freely used and distributed, but not modified or sold for profit without author consent.

Part V

Quick Reference

The DOS 5.0 Commands

This chapter covers all the DOS 5.0 commands, including those used by CONFIG.SYS and batch files. Some of the following ones, such as APPEND or FASTOPEN, don't exist in previous editions of DOS. Many, as ATTRIB, BACKUP, RESTORE, or TIME and DATE, work differently in earlier versions. One, XCOPY, isn't on generic DOS disks since it was written by IBM rather than Microsoft. And some terrific Microsoft commands, such as FC, aren't included here since they're not on the standard IBM DOS disk.

See Figures 1.3 and 1.4 in Chapter 1 for a list of new and modified commands in all PC-DOS versions from 1.0 through 5.0.

For more hints and explanations on some of the most powerful DOS commands, such as PRINT or XCOPY, see Chapter 15.

When part of a command's format is specified in brackets ([d:]) it means the part is optional. When two choices are separated by a vertical bar (ON | OFF) it means you should enter one or the other. An *or* means DOS allows multiple syntaxes.

The label [external command] means that a separate program that starts with the name of the command and ends with an extension like .EXE or .COM must be on the disk in the current directory or one that your PATH command knows about. If this [external command] label does not appear after the name of the command in the listing below, the command is "internal," which means you don't have to have a separate file handy to use it. The mechanisms for internal commands are contained inside the main DOS COM-MAND.COM file.

The number below the line containing the name of the command is the DOS version in which the command was introduced. Many of the commands have gone through extensive revision (for instance, DISKCOPY changed in versions 1.1, 2.0/2.1, 3.0, and 3.2), so the syntaxes and features listed are for version 5.0 only.

Primary DOS 5.0 Commands

APPEND [external command]
3.2

Searches a specified list of drives and directories for nonexecutable files and overlays needed by your programs; the PATH command does the same thing for executable files. Under DOS 5.0, APPEND can handle both executable and
non-executable files.

Format: APPEND [d:] path [;[d:]path...] [/X | /X:ON | /X:OFF]
                [/PATH:ON | PATH:OFF]

          or

          APPEND /E [/X | /X:ON | /X:OFF] [/PATH:ON | PATH:OFF]

          or

          APPEND [;]

[d:] [path] = path to search

/X (same as /X:ON) = lets APPEND search for and run executable files
    (.COM, .EXE, or .BAT) just as the PATH command does.

/X:OFF = turns off the ability to run executable files (this is the default setting)
    so that APPEND won't handle files that end in .COM, .EXE, or .BAT.

/E = store APPEND path in environment, which then lets you use the SET and
    APPEND commands to view and change the parameters. Use this command
    first by itself without specifying the path to search; follow it with a second
    APPEND command that does include the path to search.

/PATH:ON = tells DOS to look through the normal APPEND search path even
    when you've tacked on a specific drive and path to the command you want
    it to search for. Some applications add drive and path information to their
    program names so DOS will look in certain locations. If you're using the
    /PATH:ON feature, DOS will also look in your normal search path if it can't
    find the program in the location specified by the application. So if you want
    it to find C:\BIN\RUNME.EXE and DOS can't find RUNME.EXE in the
    C:\BIN subdirectory, DOS will have APPEND hunt through your normal
    search path to see if RUNME.EXE is located in another subdirectory.

/PATH:OFF = tells DOS not to look in its normal search path if you tacked on
    a drive letter or path prefix to the filename. If you're using this /PATH:OFF
    setting, APPEND will look for files only if you omit drive and path

information and specify just the bare-bones filename (so it will hunt for RUNME.EXE but not C:\BIN\RUNME.EXE).

; = resets the APPEND path to null when used alone (the semicolon is also used to separate subdirectories in the path specification)

Used without any parameters, APPEND will print the current APPEN path string.

ASSIGN [external command]
2.0

Gives a drive a new name.

Format: `ASSIGN [ a[=] b [...]]`

a = drive to get new name

b = new name

ASSIGN without parameters clears all assignments

Notes: Don't use colons after the drive letters. With a single assignment you don't have to use the equal sign.

Never use commands like BACKUP, RESTORE, JOIN, LABEL, SUBST, or PRINT while ASSIGN is active. FORMAT, DISKCOPY, and DISKCOMP commands ignore ASSIGN I/O reroutings.

The best way to use ASSIGN is from inside a batch file where the first batch file line makes the new assignment, the second line runs the program requiring the assignment, and the third resets things the way they originally were. In fact, if you can use SUBST instead of ASSIGN, do it.

ATTRIB [external command]
3.0

Displays or changes file attributes.

Format: `ATTRIB [±A] [±H] [±R] [±S] [path][file name] [/S]`

+   =   set the bit (enable the attribute)

-   =   reset the bit (disable the attribute)

A   =   archive file

H = hidden file

R = read-only file

S = system file

/S = Search current directory and all its subdirectories.

Notes: One of the best-kept DOS secrets is that ATTRIB can find the location of any file on your disk. Simply use the following format:

```
ATTRIB [path]\filename /S
```

You can use wildcards and also redirect output to a disk file. So, to find all backup files and store their names in a new file called BAKFILES, just type

```
ATTRIB [path] \*.BAK /S > \BAKFILES
```

To view the contents of bakfiles, type MORE < BAKFILES or TYPE BAKFILES.

When you enter just a filename or global filename after the ATTRIB command, DOS displays the attributes and name of each such file.

Type ATTRIB with no parameters to display the attributes and names of every file in the current directory. Or add the /S switch to show the same information for all files in the current directory and its subdirectories.

BACKUP [external command]
2.0

Backs up files; can split large files over several floppy disks. Use the RESTORE command to put files back.

Format: BACKUP s: [path] [filename[.ext]] t: [/S] [/M] [/A] [/D:mm-dd-yy] [/T:hh:mm:ss] [/F] [/L[:[d:][path][logname.[ext]]]

s: [path] [filename[.ext]] = source drive and/or file(s) to back up

t: = target drive

/S = do files in subdirectories also

/M = back up files changed since last BACKUP (by checking archive bit)

/A = add files to those already on backup disk (so it doesn't erase what's already there)

/D = back up files changed on or after date specified

/T = back up files changed on or after time on date specified

/F = format backup disk if necessary (DOS 4.0 does this automatically so you don't have to use this switch). DOS has to be able to find its FORMAT.COM program for this to work.

/L = create a log file (Default is BACKUP.LOG.)

[d:] [path] [logname.[ext]] = drive/path and filename for log file

Notes: BACKUP stores files in a special format; you must use the RESTORE command to put them back in their original condition. Starting with version 3.3, BACKUP stores backup files in one large chunk; earlier versions maintained individual backup files for each file.

Since early BACKUP and RESTORE versions erroneously let you write system files from earlier versions onto disks using newer versions, be careful when using older versions to restore files.

Version 3.3 can run the DOS FORMAT command (if it's accessible) when you're backing up files onto unformatted disks. DOS 5.0 does this automatically; with DOS 3.3 you have to add a /F switch to do it. Older versions won't do this at all, which forced you to have a tall stack of formatted disks handy before you began. Be careful when using the /F option, since the source and target drive sizes must be identical. And don't use BACKUP when drive or directory mixing commands such as JOIN are in effect.

BREAK
2.0

Lets you specify more or less frequent Ctrl-Break checking, or display the current BREAK status.

Format: BREAK [ON | OFF]

ON = break on demand (for programs with little I/O)

OFF = check for break only during I/O functions (default)

BREAK without parameters displays BREAK status.

You can use this command either in your CONFIG.SYS file or from the command line (or, of course, in AUTOEXEC.BAT).

BUFFERS [CONFIG.SYS]
2.0

Allocates memory for the number of buffers

Format: BUFFERS=B [,S]

B = number of buffers (1–99)

S = number of buffers in a secondary buffer cache (1–8)

Notes: If the Buffers command is not used, the default buffer allocation is a function of system configuration, as shown here.

Configuration RAM Disk	B	S
<128Kb 360Kb	2	2
<128Kb >360Kb	3	3
128–255Kb	5	1
256–511Kb	10	1
512–650Kb	15	1

Each buffer occupies about 532 bytes of memory. The optimum number of buffers varies with the capacity of the hard drive, as follows:

Hard drive capacity	Buffers	
	B	S
<40Mb	20	8
40-79Mb	30	8
80-119Mb	40	8
120 or greater	50	8

Use the secondary buffer cache if you are not using a disk-caching utility. During a disk read operation, additional file data is stored in the secondary buffer area for faster access.

CALL [internal batch]
3.3

Calls one batch file from within another.

Format: CALL [path][filename.bat] [file parameters, if any]

Notes: At the conclusion of the called batch file, control passes back to the calling file. A batch file may call itself, provided some conditional exit command is provided to avoid an endless loop.

CD [See CHDIR]
2.0

CHCP
3.3

Selects DOS code page.

Format: CHCP [nnn]

nnn = number of desired code page

Note: You must load NLSFUNC before using CHCP. May need to have COUNTRY.SYS handy.

CHDIR (CD)
2.0

Changes or displays current directory (moves you from one subdirectory to another or tells you which one you're currently in).

Format: CHDIR [d:][path]

or

CD [d:][path]

d: = drive with path location to change
path = new path location

CHDIR without parameter displays current directory.

Notes: Specifying a directory name without a backslash (\) in front of it tells DOS to switch into a subdirectory one level lower than the current directory. So if the current directory is \DOS, the command CD UTILS will log into \DOS\UTILS. But if you typed CD \UTILS, DOS would log into a subdirectory called \UTILS one level down from the root directory that had no relation to the \DOS subdirectory.

Entering CD \ will return to the root directory. Entering CD .. will change to the parent directory one level up toward the root from the current subdirectory. Since the double dot (..) is shorthand for the parent directory, if you're logged into \DOS\UTILS\PTOOLS and you want to change to \DOS\UTILS\NORTON you could type CD ..\NORTON.

Nobody uses CHDIR, since the much shorter CD works exactly the same.

While typing CD by itself will display what subdirectory you're currently logged into, you can have DOS always report the current subdirectory by issuing the command:

```
PROMPT $P$G
```

or

```
PROMPT $P:
```

(the second version produced a prompt that looks a bit less cluttered).

Since typing CD by itself will display the current subdirectory, you can have DOS redirect this to a file and perform some useful tasks. For instance, if you have the MORE.COM and FIND.EXE utilities handy (they should be in a \DOS subdirectory that your PATH command knows about), you can create a batch file called CHANGE.BAT:

```
ECHO OFF
REM This is CHANGE.BAT
IF %1!==! GOTO OOPS
IF %1==? GOTO PRINTIT
CD %1
ECHO | MORE | TIME | FIND /V "new" >>\LOGFILE
ECHO | MORE | DATE | FIND /V "new" >>\LOGFILE
CD >>\LOGFILE
GOTO END
:OOPS
ECHO Enter %0 followed by the name of the
ECHO subdirectory you want to change into
ECHO Or Enter %0 ? to see the log of
ECHO subdirectories you've switched into
GOTO END
:PRINTIT
MORE < \LOGFILE
:END
```

(If you're using DOS 3.3 or later, change the first line to @ECHO OFF.)

To use CHANGE.BAT, type:

```
CHANGE
```

by itself for instructions. Or enter a subdirectory after CHANGE, e.g.:

```
CHANGE \123\SMITH
```

and CHANGE will not only move into the \123\SMITH subdirectory but will add the name of the subdirectory you switched into into a master log in the root directory called LOGFILE along with the time and date. To see the log, just type:

```
CHANGE ?
```

If you're in a subdirectory and you want to add its name to the log, just type:

```
CHANGE .
```

This is handy if you want to keep track of how much time you spent in which task (if you're a lawyer or a consultant and you keep your different clients' work in different subdirectories).

If you use this batch it, keep it in a subdirectory (like \DOS\UTILS) that your PATH knows about, so DOS can find it no matter what subdirectory you happen to be in.

CHKDSK [external command]
1.0

Checks and repairs disks, reports on memory use and file fragmentation, and can show names and locations of all files on disk.

Format: `CHKDSK [d:][path][filename.[ext]] [/F] [/V]`

[d:] = drive to check

[path] [filename.[ext]] = file(s) for fragmentation report

/F = fix errors

/V = show all files and paths on disk

CHKDSK *.* will produce a file fragmentation report for all files. To fix fragmented files (which slow DOS down), copy them to another disk, erase the originals, then copy them back.

If you're using the /F switch and CHKDSK finds lost clusters, it will recover the lost data and create files on your root directory in the form FILEnnnn.CHK, starting with FILE0000.CHK, then using FILE0001.CHK.

Notes: Using CHKDSK /V | FIND FILE.TXT will locate all occurrences of a file called FILE.TXT on the specified disk. However, ATTRIB /S can do this with just one step.

When CHKDSK reports that it found hidden files, it usually means the two hidden system files (IBMBIO.COM and IBMDOS.COM or their generic MSDOS.SYS and IO.SYS equivalents) plus the hidden volume label. If it reports other hidden files that you don't know about, these are probably sneaky copy protection devices. Don't try using ATTR or DEBUG to unhide such files hidden as copy-protection devices; instead try to uninstall the program that hid them. This is necessary because some nasty copy-protection schemes scramble the underlying disk structure before hiding a file, and will put things back to normal only when you use the authorized deinstallation program that came with software.

Don't use CHKDSK on a drive involved with an active alias command such as SUBST, JOIN, or ASSIGN.

Under DOS 5.0, CHKDSK will display the volume's serial number (a unique 8-digit hex number that DOS can use to tell if you've accidentally switched drives at the wrong time), as well as the size, number, and available number of clusters ("allocation units") on the disk. A cluster is the smallest amount of storage space on a disk. If CHKDSK reports:

4096 bytes in each allocation unit
39157 total allocation units on disk 27821 available allocation units on disk

this means that the cluster size is 4K, so that even if you create a tiny 1-byte file, DOS will eat up 4,096 bytes to store it.

CLS
2.0

Clears a 25-line screen.

Format: CLS

Notes: This will always clear the screen to grey on black (attribute 07) unless ANSI.SYS is active.

Yes, it's hard to believe, but CLS wasn't a part of DOS until version 2.0.

COMMAND [external]
1.0

Starts a new COMMAND.COM command interpreter.

Format: COMMAND [path][device] [/C string] [E/:size] [/MSG] [/P]

or in a CONFIG.SYS file,

SHELL=[DOSpath] COMMAND.COM [path] [device] [E/:nnnn] [/P]

path = path to the COMMAND.COM file

device = a different device than COMMAND.COM for command input and output

string = the command interpreter performs the *string* command and then stops

size = the environment size, in bytes (160-32768). Default is 256 bytes.

/MSG /P = stores all error messages in memory (use if running DOS from diskettes). Note /P switch must also be used.

/P = makes new command interpreter permanent. Use /P only in conjunction with SHELL command in CONFIG.SYS. If /P is *not* used in this application, your AUTOEXEC.BAT file will not run.

Notes: If running DOS from diskette, error messages are not loaded into memory and must therefore be retrieved from the COMMAND.COM resident on the diskette. If this diskette is not available, DOS displays a terse "PARSE ERROR" or "EX-TENDED ERROR." If desired, use the /MSG and /P switches to force DOS to load error messages into memory.

COMP
1.0

Compares files (only if both are same size; stops after 10 mismatches)

Format: COMP [a:][path][filename[.ext]] [b:][path][filename[.ext]]

[a:] [path] [filename[.ext]] = primary file(s)

[b:] [path] [filename[.ext]] = secondary file(s)

Notes: The generic MS-DOS 2.0 FC command is much better than COMP; unfortunately IBM never included FC in PC-DOS versions.

Fortunately, this command accepts wildcards. And, if you want to refer to the current directory, you can use the single period (.) shorthand.

While COMP lets you specify both files on the command line, you can also use COMP interactively. Just type COMP by itself at the DOS prompt. DOS will ask you:

```
Enter primary filename
```

and then

```
Enter 2nd filename or drive id
```

Just fill in the blanks and it will churn away comparing files for you.

If you're comparing lots of files and the display scrolls rapidly off the screen, you can make the screen alternately pause and then restart by pressing Ctrl-S (holding down the Ctrl key and pressing the S key). If you try redirecting the output to a file so you can examine it later, or using the | MORE filter to slow things down, you'll end up with only part of the COMP report, since DOS bypasses standard output when it prints certain error messages like "File not found" and will display these onscreen in a blur regardless of any other tricks you emply.

COPY
1.0

Copies, updates, and concatentates files, and can copy to devices as well as files.

Format: COPY [/A] [/B] [a:] [path] [filename[.ext]] [/A] [/B]
[b:] [path] [filename[.ext]] [/A] [/B] [/V]

or

COPY [/A] [/B] [a:] [path] [filename[.ext]] [/A] [/B] [+[a:]
[path] [filename[.ext]] [/A] [/B] ...] [b:] [path]
[filename[.ext]] [/A] [/B] [/V]

/A = ASCII; stop at first Ctrl-Z end-of-file marker in source; add Ctrl-Z to target

/B = binary; don't treat any Ctrl-Z as an end-of-file marker; instead use file length specified by directory

[a:] [path] [filename[.ext]] = source file(s)

[b:] [path] [filename[.ext]] = destination

/V = use primitive CRC verification

+,, /B = updates date and time

Notes: You can COPY to devices as well as files, so that COPY TEXT.FIL CON would display the contents of a file called TEXT.FIL onscreen and COPY TEXT.FIL PRN would print it on the first parallel printer attached to your system.

If you switch the order around, and type COPY CON TEXT.FIL, DOS will let you create a file (or overwrite an existing file) called TEXT.FIL and enter text into it. This can be useful for creating small batch files if EDLIN or your word processor isn't handy. Unfortunately, you can't back up to the previous line to make corrections. When you're all done entering text, type Enter, then Ctrl-Z (or press the F6 function key) and then press Enter again to tell DOS you're done.

You can also use COPY's concatenation abilities to add lines to files. If you want to add a line at the end of your batch file that says CLS, just type:

```
COPY AUTOEXEC.BAT+CON
```

DOS will print:

```
AUTOEXEC.BAT
CON
```

Then type:

```
CLS
```

(or whatever other line(s) you want to add), press Enter, type Ctrl-Z (or press F6), and then press Enter again. DOS will add the CLS line to the end of AU-TOEXEC.BAT.

It's almost always a good idea to press Enter at the end of a line. If you didn't do this in your original AUTOEXEC.BAT, the above process may stick the CLS at the end of the existing last line instead of putting it on a line by itself.

You can use the COPY /B filespec CON command to display several files in succession (substituting the particular wildcard construction for filespec in this example).

It's possible to erase or truncate files if you're not careful about using the COPY command, especially when dealing with long pathnames or concatenating files. Unless you specify a /B, DOS will stop copying before the end of the file if it sees a Ctrl-Z (ASCII 26 character).

Be careful when you copy a read-only file, since the copy will NOT be read-only. Some protection.

See the COPY section in the Favorite Tips chapter for more tricks.

COUNTRY [CONFIG.SYS]
3.0

Changes the displayed format of time, date, currency symbol, case conversion and decimal separator to suit style of specified country.

sormat: COUNTRY code [,[page] [,[path] COUNTRY.SYS]

code = country code
page = code page for specified country
path = location of the COUNTRY.SYS file

Country or language	Country code	Code pages default	Other
Belgium	032	850	437
Brazil	055	850	437
Canadian French	002	863	850
Denmark	045	850	865
English (international)	061	437	850
English (United Kingdom)	044	437	850
Finland	358	850	437
France	033	437	850
Italy	039	437	850
Latin America	003	850	437
Netherlands	031	437	850
Portugal	351	850	860
Spain	034	850	437
Sweden	046	437	850
Switzerland	041	850	437
United States	001	437	850

CTTY
2.0

Lets you change the way DOS handles standard I/O.

Format: CTTY device-name

device-name = AUX, COM1, COM2, COM3, COM4 to set a new console; CON to restore to screen and keyboard

CTTY NUL = disconnects keyboard and screen; use with care only in batch files with a subsequent CTTY CON command or you won't be able to regain control.

DATE
1.0 as external command; 1.1 as internal command

Reports and sets the system date.

Format: DATE [mm-dd-yy] | [dd-mm-yy] | [yy-mm-dd]

mm = month (1–12)

dd = day (1–31)

yy = year (80–99 or 1980–1999)

DATE without parameters displays the current date (and day of the week). Pressing the Enter key after typing DATE by itself will leave the date unchanged.

Notes: You can use period, dash, or slash to separate elements; various orders of entry are based on the active COUNTRY selection.

DOS won't let you enter a year earlier than 1980 or later than 2079. You may enter two numbers for the year from (19)80 through (19)99 but you'll need four digits and DOS 3.0 or later to go from 2000 to 2079.

While DOS will display the day of the week, don't enter the name of the day yourself.

Believe it or not, DATE and TIME were external commands in DOS version 1.0. In version 3.3 and later these will permanently set the system CMOS clock.

DEL
1.1

Deletes file(s). [see ERASE]

Format: DEL [d:] [path] filename [.ext] [/P]

[d:][path]filename[.ext] = file(s) to delete

Notes: The new DOS 4.0 /P switch tells DOS to print the name of each file that DEL is
about to erase and asks you (with a Delete (Y/N)? message) whether you do indeed want to delete the file. Type N or n and the file remains. Type Y or y and
DOS erases it. This makes it safer for you to use this command with wildcards (?
and *).

If you specify a global *.* DOS will ask for confirmation with:

```
All files in directory will be deleted!

Are you sure (Y/N)?
```

Type N or n if you don't want to erase everything. Be careful if you specify a
directory after DEL (e.g. DEL \SUBDIR) since DOS will assume you mean DEL
\SUBDIR*.*

Take care when using * wildcards, since DOS stops reading characters on each
side of the period when it sees an asterisk. It will interpret the command:

```
DEL *FIL.*NM
```

as DEL *.* which is probably not what you had in mind. Similarly, the command:

```
DEL .
```

tells DOS to erase all files in the current directory.

Use RD or RMDIR to remove subdirectories after deleting all files in them.

Be careful when using DEL while a directory or drive alias command such as
SUBST, ASSIGN, or JOIN is active. DOS won't let you erase read-only files, so
use the ATTRIB command first to remove the read-only attribute.

Utilities like Peter Norton's or Paul Mace's can usually recover inadvertently
erased files so long as you use these utilities immediately after the erasure.

DEVICEHIGH [CONFIG.SYS]
5.0

Loads a device driver into reserved memory.

Format: `DEVICEHIGH=[path] filename.ext [parameters]`   or

`DEVICEHIGH SIZE=size [drive & path name] filename.ext [parameters]`

filename.ext = name and extension of the device driver

parameters = any parameters required by the device driver

SIZE=size = minimum memory that must be available or DEVICEHIGH will
not load filename into reserved memory. Specify in hexadecimal notation.

Notes: CONFIG.SYS file must also include DOS=UMB command plus HIMEM.SYS and EMM386.EXE (or other UMB provider). Otherwise, DEVICEHIGH is ignored and driver is loaded into conventional memory.

If system locks up, insert the hexadecimal SIZE=size parameter in the DEVICEHIGH line. To determine the value for size, first load the driver into conventional memory. Then type MEM /D and note the displayed driver size (third column). Use that value for size and try again to load the driver with DEVICEHIGH.

DIR [internal]
1.0

Lists filenames and related information.

Format: `DIR [path] [filename] [one or more switches, as listed below]`

/A:attributes (see ATTRIB command for list of switches) (If /A is not followed by a parameter, listing shows all files, including hidden and system files.)

/B = brief listing (directory or filename and extension only)

/L = lowercase display

/O:± = *sort order*

+	=	ascending order
-	=	descending order
d	=	by date
e	=	by extension
g	=	directories before (+) or after (-) files
n	=	by name
s	=	by size

(If /O is not followed by a parameter, directories are sorted first, followed by filenames.)

/P = pause between screen listings

/S = search current directory and all its subdirectories

/W = wide display format

Notes: DOS displays all files with names that begin with S if you type DIR S* only. (However, S*.* format must be used to copy or delete all such files.)

DOS identifies subdirectories by showing <DIR> in the size column, or by enclosing the directory name in brackets [NAME] when the /W (wide) switch is used.

Directory names, including current and parent directory (seen as a single and double dot, respectively) are added to the total file count reported at bottom of listing.

Bytes listing to the right of file count now gives total bytes for all files listed.

DISKCOMP [external command]
1.0

Compares two entire diskettes for content differences.

Format: `DISKCOMP [a: [b:]] [/1] [/8]`

> a: = source drive
>
> b: = target drive
>
> /1 = compare the first side only
>
> /8 = use only 8 sectors per track

Notes: DOS won't let you DISKCOMP a VDISK, and is picky about which physical disks you can DISKCOMP. And don't use DISKCOMP while drive or directory mixing commands such as JOIN, SUBST, or ASSIGN are in effect.

Under DOS 4.0, DOS is smart enough to know that two otherwise identical disks with different serial numbers (unique 8-digit hex numbers that DOS can use to tell if you've accidentally switched drives at the wrong time) are in fact identical.

DISKCOPY [external command]
1.0

Copies an entire diskette and formats the copy if necessary.

Format: `DISKCOPY [a: [b:]] [/1]`

> a: = source drive
>
> b: = target drive
>
> /1 = copy the first side only

Entering DISKCOPY without any parameters tells DOS to use the same drive as the source and target, and prompt you when to remove and insert the appropriate disks into this single drive.

Notes: DOS won't let you DISKCOPY to a VDISK, and is picky about which physical disks you can DISKCOPY from and to. And don't use DISKCOMP while drive or directory mixing commands such as JOIN, SUBST, or ASSIGN are in effect.

DISKCOPY is the fastest way to copy similar-sized disks (and formats on the fly if necessary), but XCOPY is almost as fast and avoids potential fragmentation headaches.

Under DOS 4.0, DOS will give the otherwise identical target disk a different serial number (a unique 8-digit hex number that DOS can use to tell if you've accidentally switched drives at the wrong time).

DOS
5.0

Loads part of DOS into the high-memory area and/or sets up a link between conventional and reserved memory.

Format: `DOS=parameter(s)` as listed below

> LOW =   load DOS into conventional memory
> HIGH =   load DOS into the high-memory area
> UMB =   set up a link between conventional and reserved memory

---

DOSKEY [external]
5.0

Maintains a record of recent DOS commands, which may be recalled by pressing
the arrow and page up/down keys. Creates a macro file containing automated
command line instructions.

Format: `DOSKEY [one or more switches, as listed below] [filename=[text]]`

/BUFSIZE=size

> size = the size of the buffer in which DOSKEY commands and macros are
> stored. Minimum is 256 bytes, default is 512 bytes
>
> /HISTORY = display a list of all commands stored in the buffer
>
> /INSERT or /OVERSTRIKE = enable insert or overstrike mode
>
> /MACROS = display a list of all DOSKEY macros
>
> /REINSTALL = clear the buffer and reinstall DOSKEY
>
> filename=text or filename= filename is a name assigned to a macro file, text is
> a series of instructions written into filename

Notes: The DOSKEY command itself uses the following selected keys.

Press this key   **to go**

Up arrow	to the previous command
Down arrow	to the next command
Page up	to the earliest command
Page down	to the latest command
Left arrow	back one character (nondestructive)
Right arrow	forward one character
Ctrl+Left arrow	back one word (nondestructive)
Ctrl+Right arrow	forward one word
Home	to the beginning of the line
End	to the end of the line
Escape key	clear the present command line

To write a keyboard macro to quick-format a diskette, type

```
DOSKEY QF=FORMAT $1 /Q /U
```

Now, whenever QF (the filename) is typed, the DOS quick format command is executed on the diskette in the drive specified by the $1 parameter. The $ sign is the DOSKEY equivalent of the % parameter used in batch files. Thus, QF A: quick-formats the diskette in drive A.

DOSSHELL [external]
4.0

Loads and starts the DOS Shell.

Format: `DOSSHELL [/B] DOSSHELL /T[:res[n] [/B] DOSSHELL /G[:res[n] [/B]`

    /B = black & white display
    /G = graphics mode
    /T = text mode
    res = screen resolution (default is hardware dependent)
          L   low
          M   medium
          H   high

    n = screen resolution if more than one is available within the specified res category (default is hardware dependent)

Notes: Optional values for res and n are listed here

Graphics modes		Text modes	
/G:L	25 lines	/T:L	25 lines
/G:M1	30	/T:H1	43
/G:M2	34	/T:H2	50
/G:H1	43		
/G:H2	60		

If no parameters follow DOSSHELL, screen resolution is whatever it was the last time Shell was loaded.

DRIVPARM [CONFIG.SYS]
5.0

Modifies the default operating parameters of a mass storage device (disk or tape drive, etc.).

Format: `DRIVPARM=/D:n /F:f /I` [and other switches, as listed below]

D = physical drive number (0 = drive A, 1 = drive B, etc.)

f = desired drive type

0	160–360Kb	5.25″
1	1.2Mb	5.25″
2	720Kb	3.5″
5	hard disk	
6	tape drive	
7	1.44Mb	3.5″
8	read/write optical disk	
9	2.88Mb	3.5″

/I = specify a 3.5″ drive, if not supported by ROM BIOS

Other switches

/C = change-line detection: if supported by drive hardware, detects drive door opened (for protection against diskette swapping during read/write operation)

/H:h = number of Heads (1–99)

/N = Nonremovable block device

/S:s = Sectors-per-track (1–99)

/T:t = Tracks-per-side

ECHO [internal batch]
2.0

Turns command-echo mode on or off. Displays a message written in a batch file.

Format: `ECHO switch`
                    `ECHO message`
                    `@command` (in a batch file only)

                    switch

                        ON = turn command-echo mode on

                        OFF = turn command-echo mode off

                        message = a message to be displayed when the batch file is run

                        @command = suppresses screen display of the command.

Notes: Use @ECHO OFF before an ECHO message line to display the message only, but not the command line on which it was written. Thus, the following batch file lines produce the screen displays shown below each line.

```
ECHO This is a message      @ECHO This is a message

C:\ECHO This is a message  This is a message
This is a message
```

EDIT [external]
5.0

Starts the MS-DOS full-screen ASCII text editor.

Format: `EDIT [path & filename] [/B] [/G] [/H] [/NOHI]`

                    path & filename = the location and name of the ASCIII text file to be edited. If the file does not already exist, the editor opens a new file.

                    /B = use black-and-white mode.

                    /G = (for CGA) use fastest screen updating

                    /H = use highest number of text lines possible

                    /NOHI = 8-color monitor mode (see notes)

Notes: If your monitor does not display EDIT shortcut keys, use /B switch (CGA monitors). Use /NOHI switch for systems that do not support boldface characters.
QBASIC.EXE must be available in order to use EDIT utility.

EMM386 [external]
5.0

Enables/disables expanded memory and/or Weitek coprocessor support for systems with 80386 or better MPU.

Format: EMM386 [switch] [W=w]

switch

ON = enable the EMM386.EXE device driver (default)

OFF = disable the EMM386.EXE device driver

AUTO = enable expanded memory support only if program calls for it.

w

ON = enable Weitek coprocessor support

OFF = disable Weitek coprocessor support (default)

Notes: The EMM386.EXE driver must be listed in your CONFIG.SYS file in order to use this command.
Type EMM386 with no switches or parameter to display the current status of EMM386 expanded memory support.

ERASE
1.0

Deletes file(s). [See DEL]

Format: ERASE [d:] [path]filename[.ext] [/P]

[d:][path]filename[.ext] = file(s) to delete

Notes: The new DOS 4.0 /P switch tells DOS to print the name of each file that ERASE is about to delete and asks you (with a Delete (Y/N)? message) whether you do indeed want to delete the file. Type N or n and the file remains. Type Y or y and

DOS erases it. This makes it safer for you to use this command with wildcards (? and *).

If you specify a global *.* DOS will ask for confirmation with:

```
All files in directory will be deleted!

Are you sure (Y/N)?
```

Type N or n if you don't want to erase everything. Be careful if you specify a directory after ERASE (e.g. ERASE \SUBDIR) since DOS will assume you mean ERASE \SUBDIR*.*

Take care when using * wildcards, since DOS stops reading characters on each side of the period when it sees an asterisk. It will interpret the command:

```
ERASE *FIL.*NM
```

as ERASE *.* which is probably not what you had in mind. Similarly, the command:

```
ERASE .
```

tells DOS to erase all files in the current directory.

Use RD or RMDIR to remove subdirectories after deleting all files in them.

Be careful when using ERASE while a directory or drive alias command such as SUBST, ASSIGN, or JOIN is active. DOS won't let you erase read-only files, so use the ATTRIB command first to remove the read-only attribute.

Utilities like Peter Norton's or Paul Mace's can usually recover inadvertently erased files so long as you use these utilities immediately after the erasure.

EXIT [internal]
3.3

Exits a secondary command interpreter and returns to the program that started it (and to the old command interpreter).

Format: EXIT

Note: If COMMAND.COM was executed with the /P (permanent) switch, EXIT has no effect.

FASTOPEN [external command]
3.3

Remembers location on disk of recently accessed files/directories.

Format: `FASTOPEN c:[=n]... [/X]`

or

`FASTOPEN c:=([n][,m])... [/X]`

c: = disk drive

n = # of directory or file buffers for c: (10 to 999; default is 34)

m = # of continuous buffers for files on for c: (1 to 999; default is 34)

/X = tells DOS 4.0 to use expanded memory. For this to work you have to set things up properly (by using the XMA2EMS.SYS P254 page address, etc.)

Notes: Don't use FASTOPEN while directory or drive alias commands such as SUBST, ASSIGN, or JOIN are active. Use FASTOPEN only once each session and be sure you've defined all your active drives before running it. Each additional entry consumes 35 bytes of system memory. Experiment to find the most efficient value; don't just assume the largest one is best.

DOS 4.0 lets you load FASTOPEN by using the CONFIG.SYS INSTALL command; if you use this technique remember to specify the entire FASTOPEN.EXE filename. Make sure the n value is larger than your deepest nested level (\A\B\C\D\E etc.) of subdirectories.

FC [external]
5.0

Compares two files and displays the differences between them.

Format: `FC [one or more switches] [path1]filename1   [path2]filename2`
`FC /B [path1]filename1   [path2]filename2`

paths and filenames give locations and names of files to be compared.

/A = abbreviated display (first and last line only for each set of differences)

/B = binary comparison mode. Do not use with other switches.

/C = ignore case differences.

/ = line comparison of files in ASCII mode

/LB*n* = line Buffer specifies the number of lines to be compared. Default is 100 lines.

/N = display line numbers during ASCII comparison

/T = tabs not expanded to spaces

/W = white space (tabs and spaces) compressed during comparison. Consecutive spaces and tabs are treated as a single space. White space at line beginning/end is ignored.

/n = number of consecutive lines that must match for files to be considered resynchronized. Default is 2.

Notes: For ASCII comparisons, FC shows the following information for both files: The filename, the first matching line, line(s) that do not match, line(s) that appear in one file only, the next line that does match, and so on.

In a binary comparison, the position and contents of each non-matching byte pair is displayed. Thus, two mismatches might look like this:

```
00000018: 6F 69
0000003F: 45 7B
```

FCBS [CONFIG.SYS]
3.0

Specifies the number of FCBS (File Control BlockS) that can be open at the same time.

Format: FCBS=*x*

x = number of FCBS (1-255). The default is 4.

Notes: If a program tries to open more than x control blocks, file 1 may be closed when file x + 1 is opened, and so on. Use FCBS only if required by program. Most newer programs do not require file control blocks.

FDISK [external command]
2.0

Lets you set up, switch, and otherwise manipulate hard disk partitions.

Format: FDISK

Notes: In version 3.3 and later, FDISK lets you create "extended" logical partitions to handle drives larger than 32 megabytes. DOS 4.0 lets you get around this limit and create huge hard disk partitions. If you do create a partition larger than 32 megabytes, be sure to put the DOS SHARE.EXE file in your root directory (or a directory specified by SHELL).

Version 4.0 of FDISK has a friendlier interface, and allows you to do things like enter the size of partitions either by specifying an explicit number of megabytes or by telling it what percentage of the disk you want to use. It also gives you more information about each partition, and makes overall operation easier.

FIND [external command]
2.0

Locates specific strings of characters in files; can count lines or number them.

Format: FIND [/V] [/C] [/N] "string" [[d:] [path]filename[.ext]...]

/V = select lines not containing string

/C = display count of matching lines; ignores /N if both /C and /N specified

/N = display line number of matching lines

"string" = search string enclosed in double quotation marks; DOS interprets two quotes in a row as a single quote mark.

[[d:] [path]filename[.ext]...] = file(s) to search

Notes: Wildcards are not allowed (so you have to use FOR...IN...DO for global searches). However, you can specify several filenames at once at the end of the command.

To count or number all lines, specify a string after the /V option (such as $#@&) that doesn't occur at all in the file.

Searches are case-sensitive and stop at the first occurrence of a Ctrl-Z end-of-file marker.

FOR [internal batch]
5.0

Executes the specified command for each file in a set of files.

Format: in a batch file,

    FOR %%X IN (file set) DO command [command parameters, if any] at the command prompt,

```
FOR %X IN (file set) DO command [command parameters, if any]
```

%X or %%X = any arbitrary variable, sequentially replaced by each file in the specified file set.

(file set) = one or more file names or text strings, enclosed in a single set of parentheses.

command = the command that is to be executed on each file included in the file set

command parameters = parameters required by the command, if any

Notes: To expand a set of files whose extensions end with an underline, use the line below in a batch file. Or use a single % sign at each location to execute the command at the DOS prompt.

```
FOR %%X IN (*.??_) DO EXPAND %%X C:\DOS
```

FORMAT [external]
1.0

Formats the specified hard disk or diskette.

Format:
```
FORMAT drive: [/V:label] [/Q] [/U] [/F:size] [/B or /S]
FORMAT drive: [/V:label] [/Q] [/U] [T:tracks /N:sectors] [/B
or /S]
FORMAT drive: [/V:label] [/Q] [/U] [/1] [/4] [/B or /S]
FORMAT drive: [/V:label] [/Q] [/U] [/1] [/4] [/8] [/B or /S]
```

drive = the drive to be formatted

/B = reserve space for system files, but do not transfer them to the disk.

/F:size = specifies the size (capacity) of the diskette to be Formatted.

160, 320, 360, 720	K or Kb may be appended to size
1.2, 1.44, 2.88	M or Mb may be appended to size

/N:sectors

sectors = number of sectors-per-track.

/Q = quick format (FAT and root directory deleted, surface not scanned for bad sectors)

/S = transfer system files and COMMAND.COM to the formatted disk

/T:tracks

> tracks = number of tracks on the disk.
>
> /U = unconditional format (FAT and root directory deleted, surface scanned for bad sectors, sector headers rewritten)
>
> /Q /U = FAT and root directory deleted, no bad sector check, sector headers not rewritten
>
> /V:label = volume label specified prior to formatting
>
> /1 = format one side only of a diskette
>
> /4 = format a 360Kb diskette in a 1.2Mb diskette drive.
>
> /8 = format a 5.25″ diskette with 8 sectors-per-track.

GOTO [internal batch]
2.0

> Directs batch file program execution to jump to a line identified by a label.

Format: `GOTO label`

> label = a string found elsewhere in the batch file, preceded by a colon.

Notes: In the following batch file, the second line is ignored

```
GOTO blazes
ECHO This line is ignored.
:blazes
ECHO This line is printed.
```

> The GOTO command is usually used in conjunction with IF (or IF NOT), so that the jump is made IF a certain condition is (or is not) met.

GRAFTABL [external command]
3.0

> Loads high-bit ASCII graphics table (characters with values above decimal 128) into memory for CGA mode only; supports code pages.

Format: `GRAFTABL [437 | 850 | 860 | 863 | 865 ]`

or

```
GRAFTABL ?
```

or

```
GRAFTABL /STATUS
```

437 = United States code page (default)

850 = Multilingual code page

860 = Portugal code page

863 = Canada (French) code page

865 = Norway/Denmark code page

? = show number of code page plus list of code page options

/STATUS (or /STA) = show number of current code page

GRAPHICS [external command]
2.0

Allows Shift-PrtSc screen "dump" of graphics image to IBM-compatible graphics printer.

Format: `GRAPHICS [printer type] [,profile] [/R] [/B] [/LCD] [/PB:id]`

[printer type] =

COLOR1 = IBM Color Printer with black ribbon (for up to 19 grey shades)

COLOR4 = IBM Color Printer with red, green, blue, black

COLOR8 = IBM Color Printer with black, cyan, magenta, yellow

COMPACT = IBM Compact Printer (DOS 3.3)

GRAPHICS = IBM normal carriage Graphics Printer, Proprinter, Quietwriter, Pageprinter

GRAPHICSWIDE = IBM wide carriage Proprinter or Quietwriter

THERMAL = IBM Convertible Printer

/R = don't reverse black and white; without it DOS doesn't print any onscreen blacks, and prints all onscreen whites as black

/B = print background color (COLOR4, COLOR8 only)

/LCD = print from IBM Convertible LCD display

profile = under DOS 4.0, file containing specific printer information. Default name is GRAPHICS.PRO, and this file should be in same dorectory as GRAPHICS.COM utility.

/PB:id = uses id "print box" size, where id can be either STD of LCD. STD is default and will print normal screen aspect ratio. LCD will print flattened LCD aspect.

HELP [external]
5.0

Format:
```
HELP command
command /?
```

Note: The help screen associated with command is displayed on screen, and the command itself is not executed. The command /? format is slightly faster than the HELP command.

IF [internal batch]
5.0

Performs conditional command execution in a batch file.

Format:
```
IF [NOT] ERRORLEVEL N command
IF [NOT] string1==string2 command
IF [NOT] %1==%2 command
IF [NOT] EXIST [path] filename command
```

N = if a previous program run by COMMAND.COM did (did NOT) return an exit code equal to, or greater than, N, the designated command is executed.

string1==string2 or %1==%2 (note double-equal signs) = if the strings or parameters are (are NOT) equal, the designated command is executed.

EXIST = if the designated [path] and filename exists (does NOT exist), the designated command is executed.

Note: The IF [NOT] command can be used to cause a conditional jump to a label line in a batch file. For example, the following batch file looks for GORILLA.BAS in two locations. If the "not in DOS directory" message is seen, then GO-RILLA.BAS is in the root directory, unless the "Oh-Oh" message is seen.

```
@echo OFF
IF EXIST C:\DOS\GORILLA.BAS goto FOUNDIT
echo GORILLA.BAS not in DOS directory
IF NOT EXIST C:\GORILLA.BAS goto TROUBLE
:FOUNDIT
```

```
echo The GORILLA has been found.
GOTO END
:TROUBLE
echo Oh-Oh, I can't find him.
END
```

INSTALL [CONFIG.SYS]
4.0

Loads a TSR program from the CONFIG.SYS file instead of from the AUTOEXEC.BAT file.

Format: `INSTALL=[path] filename [parameters, if any]`

> filename [parameters] = the name of the TSR program to be loaded, and its parameters (if any)

Notes: INSTALL does not create an environment block for the TSR program, and so the program occupies slightly less memory than if it were loaded in a batch file or from the command line.

Do not use INSTALL if the program requires environment variables, shortcut keys, or that COMMAND.COM be present to handle critical errors.

JOIN [external command]
3.1

Joins a disk drive with a directory on other drive.

Format: `JOIN`

or

`JOIN a: c:\directory`

or

`JOIN a: /D`

> a: = drive to join
>
> c:\directory = directory to join to (at root only and only one level deep maximum)

/D = disconnect a JOIN

JOIN without parameters displays JOIN status.

Notes: Be careful when using commands like SUBST or ASSIGN while drive or directory alias commands like this are active. Don't use BACKUP, RESTORE, FORMAT, DISKCOPY, or DISKCOMP while JOIN is active.

KEYB [external command]
3.3

Loads a non-U.S. keyboard template.

Format: KEYB

or

KEYB layout [,codepage] [,filename] [/ID:code]

or

KEYB code

code = keyboard code (120=Belgium, 058=French-speaking Canada, 159=Denmark, 153=Finland, 120/189=France, 129=Germany, 141/142=Italy, 171=Latin America, 143=Netherlands, 155=Norway, 163=Portugal, 172=Spain, 153=Sweened, 150=French-speaking Switzerland, 000=German-speaking Switzerland, 166/168=United Kingdom, 103=USA)

codepage = code page for character set

filename = name of keyboard definition file (default is KEYBOARD.SYS)

layout = keyboard layout (BE=Belgium, CF=French-speaking Canada, DK=Denmark, SU=Finland, FR=France, GR=Germany, IT=Italy, LA=Latin America, NL=Netherlands, NO=Norway, PO=Portugal, SP=Spain, SV=Sweened, SF=French-speaking Switzerland, SG=German-speaking Switzerland, UK=United Kingdom, US=USA)

Notes: This replaces individual commands such as KEYBUK and KEYBIT introduced in DOS version 3.0.

DOS lets you shift back and forth between the standard keyboard and any new one specified by KEYB bu pressing Ctrl-Alt-F1 for the US version and Ctrl-Alt-F2 for the foreign version.

IBM seems to redo this with each new version of DOS. Don't mix versions.

You can use the INSTALL command to load KEYB in CONFIG.SYS.

LABEL [external command]
3.0

Sets, changes, or deletes a disk's volume label

Format: `LABEL [d:] [volume label]`

d: = drive to label

volume label = 1 to 11 characters

Notes: You can also create a volume label when you first format a disk by using the FORMAT /V option. It's important to add a label to hard disks, since this provides an added layer of protection against accidentally formatting the hard disk.

Earlier versions allowed lowercase labels, but DOS now automatically capitalizes them. And it lets you insert spaces in the volume name, although in most other respects it follows the same rules (no *, >, or + charactera etc.) as with filenames.

Don't use LABEL when drive alias commands such as SUBST or ASSIGN are active.

Under DOS 4.0, LABEL also prints the serial number (a unique 8-digit hex number that DOS can use to tell if you've accidentally switched drives at the wrong time).

LASTDRIVE [CONFIG.SYS]
3.0

Specifies the letter of the last accessible drive.

Format: `LASTDRIVE=x`

x = any letter in the range from A to Z. The lowest permissible letter corresponds to the number of installed drives. The default is one letter above the last physical drive in your system.

Note: Increase the LASTDRIVE letter as required to accommodate logical or network drives.

To save memory space, do not specify more drives than are actually required.

LOADHIGH [internal]
5.0

Loads a program into reserved memory.

Format: `LOADHIGH [path] filename [parameters]`
          `LH [path] filename [parameters]`

[path] filename [parameters] = specifications of the file to be loaded into
reserved memory.

Notes: Your CONFIG.SYS file must contain DOS=UMB plus the HIMEM.SYS and
EMM386.EXE drivers. These commands must appear before the LOADHIGH
command.

MD [See MKDIR]
2.0

MEM [external]
4.0

Displays a report of system memory usage.

Format: `MEM [/switch]`

switch

/PROGRAM or /P = reports all programs and environments currently loaded in
memory, their size and absolute starting addresses.
/DEBUG or /D = same as /PROGRAM, plus addresses of low-memory areas,
device drivers, and DOS commands like BUFFERS and LASTDRIVE.
/CLASSIFY or /C = summarizes allocation of low memory, upper memory and
expanded memory.

Notes: MEM with no switches reports the following:

bytes total conventional memory
bytes available to MS-DOS
largest executable program size
bytes total contiguous memory
bytes available contiguous memory
bytes available XMS memory
MS-DOS resident in High Memory area (if it is)

MIRROR [external]
5.0

Saves information about one or more disks for subsequent use by UNDELETE and UNFORMAT commands.

Format: MIRROR [drive(s):] [/1] [/TD[-entries]]
MIRROR [/U]
MIRROR [/PARTN]

drives(s) = the drive(s) for which **MIRROR** is to save recovery information for use by UNFORMAT

/1 = (numeral one). Retain only the lastest disk information.

/TD D = the drive letter for which **MIRROR** is to save recovery information for use by UNDELETE. Repeat as requried for multiple drives.

-entries = the maximum number of entries in the deletion-tracking file. The default value depends on the disk being tracked, as listed here.

Disk size	Entries	Maximum file size
360Kb	25	5Kb
720Kb	50	9Kb
1.2Mb	75	14Kb
1.44Mb	75	14Kb
20Mb	101	18Kb
32Mb	202	36Kb
>32Mb	303	55Kb

/U = unload the deletion-tracking program from memory and disable deletion-tracking.

/PARTN = save hard disk partioning information to a diskette.

MKDIR (MD)
2.0

Creates a subdirectory.

Format: `MKDIR [d:]path`

or

`MD [d:]path`

[d:] = drive for new subdirectory

path = subdirectory to make (total 63-character limit including the backslashes)

Notes: Be careful when creating directories if drive alias commands such as JOIN, AS-SIGN, or SUBST are active.

Specifying a new directory name without a backslash (\) in front of it tells DOS to create a subdirectory one level lower than the current directory. So if the current directory is \DOS, the command MD UTILS will create a subdirectory called \DOS\UTILS. But if you typed MD \UTILS, DOS would create a subdirectory called \UTILS one level down from the root directory that had no relation to the \DOS subdirectory.

MODE [external command]
1.0 (with lots of upgrades)

1.   Sets the printer mode.

Pre-DOS 4.0
Format: `MODE LPT#[:] [n] [,[m] [,P]]`

\# = printer number (1, 2, or 3)

n = characters per line (80 or 132)

m = vertical lines per inch (6 or 8)

P = continuous retry on timeout errors

DOS 4.0
Format: `MODE LPT#[:] COLS=c LINES=l RETRY=r`

c = 80 or 132 columns per line

l = 6 or 8 lines per inch of vertical spacing

r = status request response, indefinite retry, with four choices, B, E, R, none

B = (same as P in older syntax); return "busy" from status check of busy port

E = return error from status check of busy port

R = return "ready" from status check of busy port

none = (default) no retry action

2. Sends parallel printer output to a serial port.

Format: `MODE LPT#[:]=COMx`

\# = printer number (1, 2, or 3)

x = COM port number (1, 2, 3, or 4)

Note: You must first initialize your COM port with the following version of the MODE command, including ,P at the end in pre-DOS 4.0, or a RETRY=B under DOS 4.0.

3. Sets the serial communication mode (protocols).

Pre-DOS 4.0
Format: `MODE COM#[:] baud [,[parity] [,[databits] [,[stopbits]`
`[,P]]]]`

\# = COM port being set (1, 2, 3, or 4)

baud = baud rate (110, 150, 300, 600, 1200, 2400, 4800, 9600, 19200; only first two digits of each rate are required)

parity = N, O, or E (for None, Odd, Even; default is Even)

databits = 7 or 8 (default is 7)

stopbits = 1 or 2 (default is 2 if 110 baud, 1 if not)

P = indicates COM port is being used for printer; continuously retries on timeout errors

Note: You must first initialize your COM port with this version of the MODE command, including ,P at the end, before sending parallel printer output to a serial port.

DOS 4.0
Format: `MODE COM#[:] BAUD=b DATA=d STOP=s PARITY=p RETRY=r`

\# = COM port being set (1, 2, 3, or 4)

b = baud rate (110, 150, 300, 600, 1200, 2400, 4800, 9600, 19200; only first two digits of each rate are required)

p = NONE (no parity), ODD (odd parity), EVEN (even parity), MARK (stick odd parity), SPACE (stick even parity)

d = number of data bits from 5 through 8; default is 7

s = 1, 1.5, or 2 (default is 2 if 110 baud, 1 if not)

r = status request response, indefinite retry, with four choices, B, E, R, none

B = (same as P in older syntax); return "busy" from status check of busy port

E = return error from status check of busy port

R = return "ready" from status check of busy port

none = (default) no retry action

4. Sets the video mode.

Format: `MODE n`

n = video mode (40, 80, BW40, BW80, CO40, CO80, MONO)

Notes: MODE doesn't support any of the newer EGA and VGA video modes.

5. Shifts screen to left or right.

`MODE [n] ,m [,T]`

n = video mode (40, 80, BW40, BW80, CO40, CO80, MONO)

m = R or L; shift display right or left 1 or 2 characters

T = shows test pattern for aligning display

6. Sets screen length and width.

`MODE CON LINES=l COLS=c`

l = 25, 43, or 50 onscreen lines (assuming monitor can handle it)

c = 40 or 80 columns per line

7. Sets video mode and screen length

`MODE n,l`

n = video mode (40, 80, BW40, BW80, CO40, CO80, MONO)

l = 25, 43, or 50 onscreen lines (assuming monitor can handle it)

8. Prepares code pages (foreign fonts)

Format: `MODE device CODEPAGE PREPARE=((cplist) [d:]`
`[path]filename[.ext])`

or

`MODE device CODEPAGE PREPARE=((cp) [d:] [path]filename[.ext])` device = CON, PRN, LPT1, LPT2, or LPT3

cp = a single code page number

cplist = code page number or list of numbers; a list must be surrounded by parentheses

[d:] [path]filename[.ext] = CPI file containing code pages

Note: You may substitute CP for CODEPAGE and PREP for PREPARE.

9.   Selects code pages.

Format: `MODE device CODEPAGE SELECT=cp`

device = CON, PRN, LPT1, LPT2, or LPT3

cp = code page (437, 850, 860, 863, 865)

Note: You may substitute CP for CODEPAGE and SEL for SELECT.

10.   Displays the active code page.

Format: `MODE device CODEPAGE [/STATUS]`

device = CON, PRN, LPT1, LPT2, or LPT3

Note: You may substitute CP for CODEPAGE and STA for STATUS.

11.   Refreshes the code page.

Format: `MODE device CODEPAGE REFRESH`

device = CON, PRN, LPT1, LPT2, or LPT3

Note: You may substitute CP for CODEPAGE and REF for REFRESH.

12.   Requests code page status (DOS 4.0)

Format: `MODE device /STATUS`

Note: You may substitute STA for STATUS; this is not available for COM or keyvoard parameters and is required only for LPT#

13.   Sets keyboard typematic rates (DOS 4.0)

Format: `MODE CON RATE=r DELAY=d`

r = a rate related to how many times per second a key will repeat once it's been held down (1 to 32)

d = the delay before your system figures out that the key is indeed held down (1 to 4; corresponds to 1/4 second, 1/2 second, 3/4 second, 1 second)

R VALUE	REPETITIONS/SEC	R VALUE	REPITITIONS/SEC
1	2.0	17	8.0
2	2.1	18	8.6
3	2.3	19	9.2
4	2.5	20	10.0
5	2.7	21	10.9
6	3.0	22	12.0
7	3.3	23	13.3
8	3.7	24	15.0
9	4.0	25	16.0
10	4.3	26	17.1
11	4.6	27	18.5
12	5.0	28	20.0
13	5.5	29	21.8
14	6.0	30	24.0
15	6.7	31	26.7
16	7.5	32	30.0

MORE [external command]
2.0

Displays files one 25-line screenful at a time.

Format: `MORE < FILE.NAM`

or

`TYPE FILE.NAM | MORE`

where FILE.NAM is the file you want to examine one screenful at a time. If the entire file hasn't yet been displayed, DOS will print the message --More--. Press any key at this point to have it display another screenful.

NLSFUNC [external]
3.3

Loads country-specific data for national language support.

Format: in CONFIG.SYS file,

```
INSTALL=[DOSpath] NLSFUNC.EXE [filename]
```

on command line,

```
NLSFUNC [[path] filename]
```

DOSpath = the location of the NLSFUNC.EXE file.

filename = name of a file other than COUNTRY.SYS that contains country-specific data. Use if CONFIG.SYS does not include a COUNTRY command.

Notes: Use NLSFUNC with no filename to access country-specific data in the COUNTRY.SYS file.

PATH
2.0

Tells DOS to extend its normal search so that it looks in a specified list of drives and directories when it tries to run a program that it can't find in the current directory.

Format: `PATH [[d:]path[[;[d:]path...]]]`

or

`PATH [;]`

[d:]path = drive/path for search list

; = resets the search path to null (so DOS will not include any additional drives or directories in the search) when used as PATH ;

PATH without parameters displays the current PATH list of drives and directories to search for executable files.

Note: PATH works with COM, EXE, or BAT files only; the APPEND command lets DOS search for non-executable files. Recent versions of APPEND can also find executable files just like PATH.

PRINT [external command]
2.0

Prints files; can handle background printing and groups (queues) of files.

Format: `PRINT [/D:device] [/B:buffsiz] [/U:busytick] [/M:maxtick]`
`[/S:timeslice] [/Q:quesiz] [/C] [/T] [/P] [[d:] [path]`
`[filename] [.ext]...]`

/D:device = print device (default is PRN; must be first one specified)
/B:buffsiz = bytes for internal buffer (default is 512)
/U:busytick = ticks to wait for printer to be available (default is 1)
/M:maxtick = ticks to use for printing (1–255, default is 2)
/S:timeslice = time slice value (1–255, default is 8)
/Q:quesiz = number of files in print queue (1–32, default is 10)
/C = lets you cancel file(s) in queue
/T = terminate; cancel entire print queue
/P = print preceding file and add all files to queue until a /C or Enter
    [d:] [path] [filename] [.ext] = file(s) to print; wildcards are okay

PRINT without any parameters displays the list of filenames currently in the queue.

Notes: DOS Disables Shift-PrtSc and Ctrl-PrtSc while PRINT is printing.
    PRINT adds a formfeed command after each print job to start each new file at the top of a page, and expands tabs (by inserting spaces) to 8-column boundaries.
    If you don't use a /D option the first time you execute the command, PRINT will pause and ask which printer you want to use. While you can specify PRN (or LPT1) by pressing Enter at this point, using the /D switch saves a step.
    See the Favorite Tips chapter for an explanation of how this works and what settings are best.

PROMPT
2.0

Sets the DOS prompt; transmits strings to ANSI.SYS.

Format: PROMPT [prompt-text]

PROMPT without parameter resets the default DOS prompt. To see the active PROMPT string, type SET.

prompt-text can contain the following meta-string characters, preceded by a $ sign:

$	$ character
T	time
D	date
P	current directory
V	version number
N	default drive letter
G	> character
L	< character
B	| character
Q	= character
H	backspace (erases previous character)
E	Escape character
_	CR/LF sequence (jumps to next lower line on screen)

DOS treats all other characters not on the above list as nulls.

Notes: Every hard disk user should use PROMPT $P: or PROMPT PG to display the current subdirectory.

You can use the PROMPT command to send otherwise hard-to-type Escape sequences to ANSI.SYS for extended screen and keyboard control. However, doing so will change any custom prompt you may have assigned. To avoid this, first type:

SET | FIND "PROMPT" > RESET.BAT

to store your prompt. Then have PROMPT issue the ANSI escape sequence, enter RESET to restore your original prompt, and finally erase RESET.BAT. You can create a batch file to automate this. Or have a batch file save the prompt as an environment variable (by typing SET OLD=%PROMPT%) and later use SET PROMPT=%OLDP% to restore it.

To use ANSI.SYS you must include a line in the CONFIG.SYS file that was active when you booted that says DEVICE=\DOS\ANSI.SYS (if you store

ANSI.SYS in your \DOS subdirectory). See the ANSI and Other DOS Drivers chapter for an extensive discussion of this.

You may use either the uppercase or lowercase versions of the above meta-strings (so that $P works just as well as $p). However, ANSI is picky about the case of its special commands.

QBASIC [external]
5.0

Loads the Microsoft QBASIC interpreter.

Format: `QBASIC [[path] filename] [one or more switches]`

filename = the name of a BASIC file to be edited with the QBASIC interpreter.

/B = use black-and-white mode on color monitor.

/G = graphics, provides fastest screen update on CGA monitor.

/H = high resolution, displays the maximum number of text lines on screen.

/MBF = convert following functions, as indicated

From	To
CVD	CVDMBF
CVS	CVSMBF
MKD$	MKDMBF$
MKS$	MKSMBF$

/NOHI = use with a monitor that does not support high-intensity video.

/RUN = run filename before displaying it for editing.

Notes: If your CGA monitor does not support shortcut keys, use the /B switch. If your monitor does not support high-intensity (bold) characters, use the NOHI switch.

RECOVER [external command]
2.0

Recovers individual defective files or every file and subdirectory on a disk. But don't use it to recover an entire disk unless as a desperate last resort.

Format: `RECOVER [d:] [path]filename[.ext]`

or

```
RECOVER d:
```

[d:] [path]filename[.ext] = file(s) to recover
d: = recover all files on d: [USE WITH EXTREME CAUTION!]

Notes: BEWARE — Don't use this for a whole disk! Use it on specific files only unless there's no hope left for the disk. If you try it without specifying a single filename, RECOVER will turn your entire disk structure into mush.

In addition, RECOVER puts its recovered files in the root directory. Since a typical 5-1/4 inch 360K floppy disk root directory can hold a maximum of 112 files, you may have to repeat the process several times, delete files from the damaged disk, etc. Use only as an absolute last resort.

REN [See RENAME]
1.1

RENAME (REN)
1.0

Renames files.

Format: ```RENAME [d:] [path]filename[.ext] filename[.ext]```

[d:] [path]filename[.ext] = file(s) to rename
filename[.ext] = new name

Notes: You can use wildcards in the filename. If by chance an application (or a program such as BASIC) has created a filename with a space in it, you can use a wildcard to remove the space. So if your directory contains a file called FILE 1.TXT you can type:

```
REN FILE?1.TXT FILE1.TXT
```

REPLACE [external]
3.2

Replaces files in target directory with files in source directory with the same filename(s). Copies new files into target directory from source directory.

Format: REPLACE [path] source [targetpath] [/A] [/P] [/R] [/W]
REPLACE [path] source [targetpath] [/P] [/R] [/S] [/U] [/W]

source = name of the source file or files

targetpath = desired location for target files. If no targetpath is specified, REPLACE uses the current drive and directory as target.

/A = add new files to the target directory

/P = prompt before replacing an existing target file or adding a new one

/R = replace read-only and all other specified target files.

/S = search all subdirectories within the target directory and replace matching files

/U = replace only those target files that are older than matching files in source

/W = wait for diskette insertion before searching for source files

Notes: REPLACE does not replace or add hidden or system files to the target.

RESTORE [external command]
2.0

Restores files saved by the BACKUP command.

Format: RESTORE a: [c:] [path]filename[.ext] [/S] [/P] [/B:mm-dd-yy]
[/A:mm-dd-yy] [/M] [/N] [/L:time] [/E:time]

a: = drive with BACKUP source

[c:] [path]filename[.ext] = destination

/S = restore all files in subdirectories too

/P = prompt before restoring files changed since last backup or marked read-only; respond with Y or N

/B = restore if changed on or before date specified

/A = restore if changed on or after date specified

/M = restore if changed or deleted since backup

/N = restore if no longer on target

/L = restore if changed at or after time specified

/E = restore if changed at or before time specified

Notes: Don't use /B, /A, and /N at the same time. And the DOS manual warns against using RESTORE when a drive or directory alias command such as SUBST, JOIN, or ASSIGN was active when you ran BACKUP. So what are you supposed to do then?

Since early BACKUP and RESTORE versions erroneously let you write system files from earlier versions onto disks using newer versions, be careful when using older versions to restore files.

BACKUP stores files in a special format; you must use the RESTORE command to put them back in their original condition. Version 3.3 stores backup files in one large chunk; earlier versions maintained individual backup files for each file.

RD [See RMDIR]
2.0

RMDIR (RD)
2.0

Removes a directory.

Format: RMDIR [d:]path

or

RD [d:]path

[d:] = drive to remove from

path = directory to remove

Notes: DOS won't let you remove a directory if it contains any files or lower-level directories.

If DOS tells you that the directory is not empty when you try using RD or RMDIR to remove a subdirectory, and you've already erased all the files in it and used RD to remove any lower-level directories, the culprit is probably a hidden file inside the subdirectory. If the subdirectory contained a program that used a copy-protection scheme, try to uninstall the program. If you're sure that no copy protection scheme was employed, use the ATTR program on the accompanying disk to unhide the file, then erase it. RD or RMDIR should now work.

SELECT [external command]
3.0

Sets up DOS on a new disk or replaces an older DOS version with a newer one.

Pre-DOS 4.0
Format: SELECT [[A: | B:] [d:][path]] xxx yy

A: or B: = source drive (default is A:)

[d:] [path] = target drive and path (default is B: root directory)

xxx = country code

yy = keyboard code

Note: Use this command only on brand new disks (if at all) since it runs the DOS FOR-MAT command as part of its overall operation.

DOS 4.0
Format: SELECT (actually runs automatically from installation disks)

Note: DOS 4.0 version can handle drives larger than 32 megabytes without having to divide them into smaller logical volumes. The DOS 4.0 SELECT command is much friendlier and more capable than previous versions.

SET
2.0

Puts strings into the environment; displays environment strings.

Format: SET [name=[parameter]]

name = environment variable (automatically uppercased)

parameter = value for environment variable

SET with just name (and equals sign) clears name from environment
SET without name or parameters displays environment settings

Note: The environment always contains COMSPEC= and probably PATH= and
PROMPT= variables. Many applications can store and read environment variables. Batch files in later versions of DOS can read them by sandwiching them between single % signs (e.g. %PROMPT%).

DOS uses a paltry 160 bytes (or 127 bytes under certain circumstances) for the
environment size. See COMMAND [/E:xxxxx] for instructions on increasing the
default size.

SETVER [external]
5.0

Sets the DOS version number reported to a program that requests it.

Format:
```
SETVER filename  n.nn
SETVER filename  [/DELETE [/QUIET]]
```

filename = the name of a program file (with COM or EXE extension) to add to
   the version table.

n.nn = the version number to be reported

/DELETE = Deletes the *filename* entry in the version table.

/QUIET = Do not display message during /DELETE operation.

Notes: Type SETVER without any parameters to show contents of the version table. Display shows each filename in table and the DOS version with which the file is set
to run. For example,

```
WIN200.BIN   3.40
EXCEL.EXE    4.10
NET.COM      3.30
ZFMT.SYS     4.01
```

SHARE [external command]
3.0

Supports file sharing. In DOS 4.0, helps DOS keep track of things on hard disk
partitions larger than 32 megabytes.

Format: `SHARE [/F:filespace] [/L:locks]`

/F: = bytes to allocate for sharing info (default is 2048); each open file takes length of filename plus 11 more bytes

/L:locks = locks to allocate (default is 20)

If you're using a massive hard disk under DOS 4.0, DOS needs to have the SHARE.EXE file in the root directory (or the directory specified by SHELL) to keep track of where things are. If you don't do this, DOS may become very confused.

SHARE knows when drive doors have been opened and can warn you if you're about to copy data onto the wrong disk, such as one you've switched in the middle of a disk write.

You can run SHARE by adding an INSTALL=SHARE.EXE to your CONFIG.SYS file.

SORT [external command]
2.0

Sorts lines of text inside files starting at the column specified.

Format: SORT [/R] [/+ n]

/R = sort in reverse order

/+ n = sort starting with column n

Notes: DOS treats lowercase letters the same as uppercase ones in version 3.x; but earlier versions assumed uppercase letters came before lowercase ones. And DOS 3.0 and later versions can treat accented high-bit foreign-language characters the same as their unaccented cousins.

SORT doesn't expand tabs (it treats them as single characters) and can't handle files longer than 63K.

SUBST [external command]
3.1

Assigns a drive letter to a path.

Format: SUBST e: c:path

or

SUBST e: /D

or

```
SUBST
```

e: = drive letter to refer to path

c:path = drive/path referred to (nicknamed)

/D = deletes substitution of e:

Entering SUBST without parameters displays substitutions in effect.

Notes: Since SUBST lets you use short drive letters to refer to long paths, you can use it to extend a PATH or APPEND command past the normal character limit.

The default number of drives is five (A: through E:). To use a SUBST drive letter higher than E: you must first include a LASTDRIVE= command in the CONFIG.SYS file that was active when you booted.

DOS commands such as CHDIR (and CD), MKDIR (and MD), RMDIR (and RD), APPEND, and PATH can work differently when SUBST is active. And all sorts of DOS commands, such as ASSIGN, FORMAT, BACKUP, RESTORE, LABEL, JOIN, DISKCOPY, DISKCOMP, and FDISK have trouble with SUBST, so don't use them while SUBST is in effect.

SYS [external command]
1.0

Puts the two hidden system files onto disk.

Pre-DOS 4.0

Format: `SYS t:`

t: = the disk you want to contain the IBMBIO.COM and IBMDOS.COM system files (or their generic equivalents).

DOS 4.0

Format: `SYS s: t:`

s: = source drive

t: = target drive

Notes: SYS doesn't transfer COMMAND.COM; you must use COPY COM-
MAND.COM t: to do so. On the other hand, FORMAT /S will transfer both the
pair of hidden system files and COMMAND.COM

DOS is picky about where certain system files are located on the disk. Since
software vendors aren't allowed to give away the DOS system files on the diskettes they sell, many vendors leave space on the disk for you to use SYS to copy
these system files to the proper place on the disk.

The DOS 4.0 SYS command can transfer the system files from one different
disk to another different disk; the source doesn't have to be the one SYS is currently on.

TIME
1.0 as external command; 1.1 as internal command

Reports and sets the system time.

Format: `TIME [hh:mm[:ss[.xx]]]`

hh = hours (0–23)

mm = minutes (0–59)

ss = seconds (0–59)

xx = hundredths of a second (0–99)

TIME without parameters displays the current time. Pressing the Enter key
after typing TIME by itself will leave the time unchanged.

Notes: So long as you enter at least the hour after the TIME command, you can skip all
the rest of the settings. So entering TIME 8 will set the time to 8:00:00.00.

Pre-DOS 4.0 versions of TIME use a 24-hour clock, so 8 PM is actually
20:00:00.00. Also, while you can enter hundredths of seconds, your system's
clock is actually not that accurate, since it divides each second into just over 18
slices rather than 100.

Starting with DOS 4.0, TIME let you use a 12-hour clock rather than 24-hour
notation. To take advantage of this, add an a or a p directly after the last digit, e.g.
12:15p (rather than 12:15 p).

You may use a period or colon to separate hours, minutes, and seconds. And
you may use a period or a comma to separate seconds from hundredths, depending on whether you're using US or foreign settings.

Believe it or not, DATE and TIME were external commands in DOS version
1.0. Starting with version 3.3 DOS will permanently set the system CMOS clock.

TREE [external command]
2.0

Displays all the directory paths.

Format: TREE [c:] [/F]

[c:] = drive to display

/F = show file names in all directories

/A = use alternate typewriter-like character set rather than high-bit drawing characters (DOS 4.0 only)

Notes: The MORE command (TREE | MORE) pauses the display a screenful at a time.

A picture is worth a K of words, especially here. If you have a version of DOS older than 4.0, use the VTREE or RN utilities on the accompanying disk instead of TREE, since they'll provide a graphical representation of your disk structure rather than just a long list of names. And use CHKDSK /V (or ATTRIB /S) rather than TREE /F to display all your files, especially if you're redirecting the output of the process to a file.

DOS 4.0 finally draws two versions of a graphical tree. If you omit the /A parameter, DOS will create a tree structure using attractive high-bit drawing characters. Since some printers can't handle these, you can make things easier and faster by adding a /A, which tells DOS to use characters like | and - instead.

To see the whole tree, tell it to start with the root directory (by adding a backslash: TREE \)

TRUENAME [undocumented]
4.0

Helps sort through the confusion generated by some of the DOS "alias" commands (SUBST, ASSIGN, and JOIN) that mix and match drives and subdirectories so that drive letters and subdirectory names are not always what they seem. TRUENAME reports the true name of each drive or subdirectory.

Format: TRUENAME

or

TRUENAME drive

or

TRUENAME subdirectory

Notes: If you enter the command by itself, it tells you the real, honest-to-goodness drive
or directory you're using. If you specify a drive or subdirectory after it it will tell
you what that drive or subdirectory was before you gave it another temporary
name.

Since this was not documented, odds are it doesn't always work exactly right.
So make sure everything is currently backed up (you do anyway, don't you?) and
use it at your own risk.

TYPE
1.0

Displays a file by sending it to standard output (default is the screen)

Format: TYPE [d:] [path] filename [.ext]

[d:] [path]filename[.ext] = file to display

Notes: TYPE wraps long lines after 80 columns and expands tab characters to eight-col-
umn boundaries. It stops when it reaches any Ctrl-Z end-of-file marker.

You can't use wildcard characters in TYPE commands but can type several
files one after the other by using a FOR...IN...DO command. Or you could use the
COPY /B filespec CON command to display several files in succession (substituting the particular wildcard construction for filespec in this example). COPY /B
also lets you display a file past a Ctrl-Z character.

You can redirect the output of TYPE to another file (which is sometimes handy
in batch files) or to a device such as a printer.

UNDELETE [external]
5.0

Restores files previously deleted with the DEL or ERASE command.

Format: UNDELETE [[path] filename] [/ALL or /LIST] [/DOS or /DT]

filename = name of file or set of files to be recovered. Default is all deleted
files in the current directory.

/ALL = recover all deleted files without waiting for prompt

/LIST = list the deleted files, but do not initiate the UNDELETE process

/DOS = ignore deletion-tracking file (if any) and recover only those files that
are internally listed in the directory as deleted (first character of filename
replaced by E5). Prompt for confirmation on each file.

/DT = recover only those files listed in the deletion-tracking file created by the MIRROR command. Prompt for confirmation on each file.

Notes: Recovering files via the deletion-tracking file (/DT) is more reliable than consulting the directory listing (/DOS) of deleted files. UNDELETE can neither restore a removed directory, nor a deleted file that was in a removed directory. However, if a removed subdirectory was listed in the root directory, try to use UNFORMAT to restore it, and then use UNDELETE to restore the file(s) that were in that subdirectory.

UNFORMAT [external]
5.0

Restores a disk erased by the FORMAT command or restructured by the RECOVER command.

Format:
```
UNFORMAT drive: [/J]
UNFORMAT drive: [/L] [/P] [/U] [/TEST]
UNFORMAT /PARTN [/L]
```

drive: = the drive to be unformatted

/J = verify that the file created by the MIRROR comand was saved and that it agrees with the system information on the disk to be unformatted. This switch does not UNFORMAT the disk.

/L = list every file and subdirectory found by UNFORMAT, but do not use the MIRROR file.

/P = send output messages to LPT1 printer

/PARTN = restore a corrupted hard disk partition table, using recovery data previously saved to diskette in a PARTNSAV.FIL file created by the MIRROR /PARTN command.

/PARTN /L = as above, but also display current partition table

/TEST = show how UNFORMAT will recover the disk information, but do not actually perform the UNFORMAT operation. Do not use the MIRROR file.

/U = unformat the disk without using the MIRROR file

Notes: UNFORMAT cannot restore a disk that was unconditionally formatted (FORMAT /U).

UNFORMAT restores the root directory to its condition at the time the MIRROR command was last used. Therefore, root directory files created after the last use of MIRROR are not recovered.

Use UNFORMAT to attempt recovery of deleted root directory files only if UNDELETE was unsuccessful.

VER
2.0

Reports the DOS version.

Format: VER

Note: DOS refers to the single digit to the left of the period as the major version number, and the pair of digits to the right of the period as the minor version number.

VERIFY
2.0

Verifies disk writes (in a primitive way)

Format: VERIFY [ON | OFF]

ON = verify that data was written correctly
OFF = do not verify (default)

VERIFY without parameters displays VERIFY status.

Note: This performs a CRC check only, which indicates whether or not DOS wrote something to the disk. It doesn't perform the byte-by-byte comparison that COMP does. COPY /V performs the same primitive checking process.

VOL
2.0

Display the disk's volume label.

Format: VOL [d:]

[d:] = display label of which drive

Note: Under DOS 4.0, LABEL also prints the serial number (a unique 8-digit hex number that DOS can use to tell if you've accidentally switched drives at the wrong time).

XCOPY [external command]
3.2

Copies and backs up files selectively

Format: XCOPY [a:] [path]filename[.ext] [b:] [path] [filename[.ext]]
[/A] [/D] [/E] [/M] [/P] [/S] [/V] [/W]

or

XCOPY [a:]path[filename[.ext]] [b:] [path] [filename[.ext]]
[/A] [/D] [/E] [/M] [/P] [/S] [/V] [/W]

or

XCOPY a:[path] [filename[.ext]] [b:] [path] [filename[.ext]]
[/A] [/D] [/E] [/M] [/P] [/S] [/V] [/W]

[a:] [path] [filename[.ext]] = source

[b:] [path] [filename[.ext]] = target

/A = copy only if archive bit set

/D:mm-dd-yy = copy if date is same or later

/E = create subdirectories on target even if they end up empty

/M = copy modified files and reset archive bit

/P = prompt before copying each; respond with Y or N

/S = copy files in current directory and all lower subdirectories and create
directories on target only if not empty

/V = verify

/W = wait for source disk

Notes: XCOPY is vastly better than COPY, since it avoids the repetitive disk churning
done by COPY. XCOPY uses all available low memory and reads lots of files in
one gulp before writing them to disk. Even better, it can reproduce the subdirectory
structure of the source disk onto the target disk, and can thread its way down
a long line of subdirectories while it works.

While most DOS utilities were created by Microsoft, this one was written by
IBM, so it's not on some generic DOS disks.

If you want to copy a whole disk, be sure to add a backslash right after the
drive letter, or else XCOPY will start copying fromwhatever subdirectory you
happen to be logged into.

XCOPY won't copy hidden or write-only files. If you want to copy a lot of
files and subdirectories to small diskettes, use the /S and /M parameters together.
When the first target disk fills up, insert a new blank one and repeat the same

XCOPY command (the easiest way is by pressing the F3 function key). XCOPY will know where it left off by examining the archive bit of the original files.

DISKCOPY is the fastest way to copy similar-sized disks (and it formats on the fly if necessary), but XCOPY is nearly as fast and avoids potential fragmentation headaches.

The /M option lets you use XCOPY as superior backup utility.

DOS 5.0 CONFIG.SYS Commands

The following commands are used only in the main CONFIG.SYS system configuration file. They have to be in the CONFIG.SYS file when you boot, so you can't change them after starting up and expect DOS to know about them unless you reboot after the change.

To take advantage of these, use the form:

```
DEVICE[HIGH] [=]number
```

or

```
DEVICE[HIGH] [=]status
```

or

```
DEVICE[HIGH] [=] [d:] [path]filename.ext
```

Under DOS 4.0 or later, you can also use the INSTALL command to do this.

You may substitute a DOS delimiter such as a space or semicolon in place of the equal sign. The CONFIG.SYS file must be a text (or pure-ASCII) file containing nothing other than the letters, numbers, and punctutation that you can type directly from the keyboard. And unless you really know what you're doing, the CONFIG.SYS file must be in the root directory of your startup disk.

As with other DOS commands, the syntax and available features differ for versions earlier than 5.0

BREAK
2.0

Allows extended Ctrl-Break checking.

Format: BREAK = [ON | OFF]

ON = check during any DOS function

OFF = check only during I/O functions

Notes: Use BREAK=ON for processes with little I/O; avoid it when using applications that have their own use for Ctrl-C.

You can use this command either in your CONFIG.SYS file or from the command line (or, of course, in AUTOEXEC.BAT).

BUFFERS
2.0

Sets the number of disk buffers.

Format: `BUFFERS = n [,m] [/X]`

n = number of buffers (1–99 in early versions and in DOS 5.0; 1–10,000 under DOS 4.0 if the /X parameter is also specified)

m = number of "read-ahead" or "look-ahead" buffers. Under DOS 4.0 or 5.0, BUFFERS can now read in from 1 to 8 sectors at a time ahead of the data you asked DOS to read; this is helpful when using sequential files since it means the next information you were probably going to look at is already in this special "look-ahead" memeory area.

/X = told DOS 4.0 to put the buffers in expanded memory. For this to work you had to set things up properly (by using an expanded memory manager).

Notes: Each buffer adds 528 bytes to the size of the resident portion of DOS. Don't use BUFFERS if you're running a disk cache program such as SMARTDRV.SYS.

The default number of buffers is 2 to 15 depending on hardware configuration. You'll have to experiment to see what's best for your own system, but you should try numbers like 20 or 30 for newer, more powerful systems.

COUNTRY
3.0

Specifies country-specific data

Format: `COUNTRY = xxx,[yyy],[d:][path]filename[.ext]`

or

`COUNTRY = xxx,[yyy]`

xxx = international telephone country code

yyy = code page; each country has two

[d:][path]filename[.ext] = name of COUNTRY data file

Notes: The default country code is 001 for U.S. systems (and the default code page is 437). The number of the country is the international telephone dialing prefix (001 to 999 in recent versions).

DEVICE and DEVICE HIGH
3.0   5.0

Installs the seven drivers listed below:

Format: `DEVICE=[d:] [path]filename[.ext]`

or

`DEVICE HIGH = [d] [path]filename[.ext]`

[d:][path]filename[.ext] = file containing device driver

1. ANSI.SYS — Extended keyboard and screen device driver (DOS version 2.0)

Format: `DEVICE=[d:] [path]ANSI.SYS`

2. DISPLAY.SYS — Display code page switching device driver (3.3)

Format: `DEVICE=[d:] [path]DISPLAY.SYS CON[:]=(type[, [hwcp] [,n]])`

or

`DEVICE=[d:] [path]DISPLAY.SYS CON[:]=(type[, [hwcp] [, (n,m)]])`

type = MONO, CGA, LCD, EGA (use EGA for PS/2)

hwcp = hardware code page (437, 850, 860, 863, or 865)

n = number of prepared code pages (0–12) For MONO and CGA types, n must be 0

m = number of sub-fonts per page

(U.S. users don't need this (whew))
DOS 4.0 and later check your hardware configuration to pick the display type for you automatically if you don't use type= to specify one.

3.   DRIVER.SYS — Disk device access-provider device driver (3.2)

Format: `DEVICE= [d:] [path]DRIVER.SYS /D:ddd[/T:ttt] [/S:ss]`
`[/H:hh] [/C] [/N] [/F:f]`

/D:ddd = physical drive number of (diskette 0–127, fixed 128–255); 0 is A:; 2 must be external; first physical hard disk must be 128

/T:ttt = tracks per side (1–999, default is 80)

/S:ss = sectors per track (1–99, default is 9)

/H:hh = number of heads/sides (1–99, default is 2)

/C = changeline support required on AT and later only

/N = nonremovable block device (hard disk)

/F:f = form factor (device type)

(Use SUBST rather than DRIVER.SYS for IBM hard drives.)

4.   EGA.SYS — Allows use of EGA monitors with the DOS Shell Task Swapper

Format   `DEVICE|DEVICEHIGH= [d:] [path]EGA.SYS`

No switches, no decisions to make.

5.   EMM386.EXE — Expanded and UMB memory manager

Format   `DEVICE= [d:] [path]EMM386.EXE[on] [off] [eeee] [w=on|w=off]`
`[mx|frame=mmmm|/pmmmm] [pn=mmmm] [x=mmmm-nnnn]`
`[i=mmmm-nnnn] [b=mmmm] [L=xxx] [a=aaa] [h=hhh] [d=ddd] [RAM] [NOEMS]`

on|off|auto turns the device driver on (default), off, or puts it in auto mode.

eeee is expanded memory (in kilobytes) from a range of 16 to 32768. The default value is 256.

w=on|w=off enables or disables Weitek coprocessor support.

mx specifies the page frame address (see table on page 448).

FRAME=*mmmm* lets you specify the starting address of the page frame directly. Any of the values above are valid.

/pmmmm does the same thing with even less typing

pn=mmmm lets you do something slightly differect — specify the starting address of page n from the same range of values.

x=*mmmm-nnnn* tells EMM386.EXE to exclude a range of memory addresses from possible use by an EMS page.

i=*mmmm-nnnn* tells EMM386.EXE to use a particular emeory range for either EMS pages or UMB RAM.

b=*mmmm* specifies the lowest address to be used for swapping EMS pages into conventional memory.

L=*xxx* provides a minimum value for available extended memory after EMM386.EXE loads.

a=*aaa* sets the number of alternate high-speed register sets to be allocated to EMM386.EXE.

h=*hhh* sets the number of handles available to EMM386.EXE

d=*ddd* reservs memory to be used for buffering direct memory access.

RAM tells EMM386.EXE sto provide both expanded memory and UMB support.

NOEMS tells emm386.exe TO PROVIDE umb support but not expanded memory.

6. HIMEM.SYS — The central memory management facility for DOS 5.0

Format
```
DEVICE=[d:] [path]HIMEM.SYS [/hmamin=mm] [/numhandles=nnn]
[int15=xxxx] [machine:yy] [a20control:on|off]
[shadowram:|off] [cpuclock:on|off]
```

/hmamin=mmm is the minimum amount of memory (in kilobytes, from 0 to 63) a program must use before HIMEM.SYS will grant it access to the HMA. The default is 0, which means that the HMA is available to any program that requests it on a first-come, first-served basis.

/numhandles=nnn is the maximum number of extended-memory-block handles that can be open at one time. The range of allowable values is 1 to 128, and the default is 32.

/int15=xxxx allocates kilobyte-sized chunks of extended memory for programs which use an Interrupt 15 interface for accessing extended memory.

/machine=yy tells HIMEM.SYS about your machine's hardware and ROM BIOS, to enable HIMEM.SYS to use the HMA via the A20 handler. You can enter either the code or value from the table found on pages 446 and 447.

/a20control:on|off tells HIMEM.SYS whether or not to take control of the A20 address line if it's already in use.

/shadowram:on|off allowsyou to specify whether shadow RAM should be disabled and used by HIMEM.SYS as extended memory.

cpuclock:on|off corrects a problem on some systems, where loading HIMEM.SYS lowers the CPU clock speed.

7. PRINTER.SYS — Printer code page switcher device driver (3.3)

Format:
```
DEVICE=[d:] [path]PRINTER.SYS LPT#[:]=(type[, [hwcp] [,n]])
```

or

```
DEVICE=[d:] [path]PRINTER.SYS
LPT#[:]=(type[, [(hwcp1,hwcp2,...)] [,n]])
```

LPT# = printer 1, 2, or 3

type = 4201 or 4208 (IBM Proprinters) or 5202 (IBM Quietwriter III)

hwcp = hardware code page (437, 850, 860, 863, or 865)

n = number of additional prepared code pages (0–12)

   8.   RAMDRIVE — VDISK.SYS (older versions)

Pre-DOS 5.0
Format: `DEVICE=VDISK.SYS [comment] [bbb] [comment] [sss] [comment] [ddd] [/E[:m]]`

comment = string of ASCII characters 32–126 except slash /

bbb = disk size in K bytes (default is 64)

sss = sector size in bytes (128 (default), 256, 512)

ddd = maximum directory entries (2–512, default is 64)

/E:m = use extended memory, where m is the number of sectors from 1 through 8 that VDISK should transfer at once.

(You can't use DISKCOPY on this virtual disk.)

DOS 5.0
Format: `DEVICE=RAMDRIVE.SYS [bbb] [sss] [ddd]  [/E] [/A]`

bbb = disk size in K bytes (default is 64)

sss = sector size in bytes (128, 256, 512(default))

ddd = maximum directory entries (2–1024, default is 64)

/E = use extended memory.

/A = use expanded memory.

   9.   SETVER.EXE — Installs a MS-DOS version table into memory to allow applications that check version number to run normally.

Format   `DEVICE|DEVICEHIGH=[d:] [path] SETVER.EXE`

   10.   SMARTDRV.SYS — Installs a smart cache to increase system throughput.

Format   `DEVICE|DEVICEHIGH=[d:] [path] SMARTDEV.SYS [mmmm] [nnn]] /a]`

mmmm is the initial size of the cache in kilobytes. Valid values range from 128 through 8192; the default is 256.

nnn is the minimum cache size; the default is zero. Obviously, the minimum value should not be larger than the initial value.

/a tells SMARTDRV.SYS to install the cache in expanded memory; the default is to install it in extended memory.

FCBS
3.0

Specifies the number of concurrently open files using file control blocks (FCBs).

Format: `FCBS = m,n`

m = max files opened by FCBs at once (1–255, default is 4)

n = files protected from auto-closing if program tries to open more than m files (0–255, default is 0)

(Used primarily with SHARE or networks.)

FILES
2.0

Specifies the maximum number of file handles open at once.

Format: `FILES = x`

x = 8–255 (default is 8)

Note: DOS uses two methods for file access — file control blocks (FCBs) and file handles. The CONFIG.SYS FCBS command deals with file control blocks (the older system). The FILES command deals with handles (the newer and preferable method).

INSTALL
4.0

Lets you automatically load programs when you start up from CONFIG.SYS rather than AUTOEXEC.BAT.

Format: `INSTALL=filename.ext`

DOS 4.0 lets you load four DOS utilities this way — FASTOPEN.EXE, KEYB.COM, NLSFUNC.EXE, and SHARE.EXE. You can also use this option to load commercial TSRs (terminate-and-stay-resident pop-up programs). Remember to include the extension (.EXE or .COM).

LASTDRIVE
3.0

Specifies the largest usable drive letter.

Format: LASTDRIVE = x

x = letter A–Z (default is E)

Note: Colons aren't required after the drive letter. This command is especially handy when used with SUBST. Each additional drive above E: takes up 81 bytes of system RAM.

REM
4.0

Lets you add comments to a CONFIG.SYS file, or prevent CONFIG.SYS commands from taking effect.

Format: REM comment

or

REM command

Note: While you've been able to use REM in batch files to suppress comments since version 2.0, DOS now lets you use this technique in CONFIG.SYS files. This lets you insert comments that DOS won't try to execute. And it also lets you "park" commands that you sometimes use and sometimes don't. For instance, if you sometimes use ANSI.SYS, but you temporarily want to prevent DOS from loading it, stick a REM at the beginning of the DEVICE=C:\DOS\ANSI.SYS line and DOS will ignore it. Then when you want to use ANSI again, just remove the REM.

SHELL
2.0

Specifies substitute for COMMAND.COM, and allows modification of environment size.

Format: SHELL = [d:] [path] filename [.ext] [parm1] [parm2]

For COMMAND.COM:

/E:xxxxx = number of bytes in environment (160–32768;default is 160 — different syntax in earlier versions)

/P = keeps COMMAND.COM loaded and runs AUTOEXEC.BAT

You can do some very powerful tricks with the environment (see the DOS Environment chapter for details), but DOS allocated too little default space for it. To increase the size, just use the SHELL command in any version of DOS 3.2 or later. Assuming you have a C: hard disk, add a line in your CONFIG.SYS file:

SHELL=C:\COMMAND.COM /E:xxxxx /P

where xxxxx is the new environment size in bytes (from 160 to 32768). Be sure to add the /P at the end of DOS won't run AUTOEXEC.BAT when you boot.

STACKS
3.2

Sets stack resources (allowing multiple interrupts to keep interrupting each other without crashing the system).

Format: STACKS = n,s

n = stack frames (0, 8–64)

s = frame size (0, 32–512)

0 means no dynamic STACK support

defaults are 0,0 for PC, XT, Portable; 9,128 for rest

SWITCHES
4.0

Lets your system treat an extended (101-key) keyboard as if it were a classic AT-style 84-key keyboard.

Format: SWITCHES=/K

Note: Some older programs (and some older users) get confused by the extra keys on the newer keyboards. If this happens, just insert the SWITCHES command in your CONFIG.SYS file.

DOS 5.0 Batch File Commands

The following commands are used primarily in batch files, although some (such as FOR...IN...DO) may also be used in slightly different format directly at the DOS prompt.

Because DOS batch file commands provide the muscle of a small, powerful, and slightly complex programming language, a detailed batch command help section follows.

Replaceable Parameter
2.0

Format: %n

n = 0 to 9 (refers to position of parameter on command line)

%0 is always the DOS command itself; %1 is first parameter after the command. Use SHIFT for more than %9 parameters.

Environment Variable
3.3

Format: %name%

name = environment variable

This lets batch files work with variable values stored in the DOS environment. See the DOS SET command in the main command section for details on inserting such values into the environment.

For example, you may want to store the value of your current PROMPT setting if you're also using PROMPT to generate ANSI Escape sequences. To do this, have a batch file save your PROMPT setting as an environment variable (with the command SET OLD=%PROMPT%) and later use SET PROMPT=%OLDP% to restore it.

@
3.3

Prevents any command or comment that follows from displaying.

Format: @command

batch-line = command to execute without display when ECHO is ON.

The most use common use for this is starting a batch file with @ECHO OFF (in version 3.3 and later) to suppress command displays without having this command itself appear onscreen.

CALL
3.3

Runs another batch file then returns to first batch file.

Format: CALL [d:][path]filename

[d:][path] = drive/path for batch file

This is similar to COMMAND /C but is more efficient in that it retains the ECHO state, is easier to break out of, and executes faster. It also makes it easier to work with environment settings.

It can be very useful to have one batchfile run another and then have control return, especially if the first batch file is feeding filenames or parameters to a second batchfile that processes them. The most common way to do this is to have a FOR...IN...DO in the first batchfile and then pass parameters to the second.

ECHO
2.0

Controls message display.

Format: `ECHO [ON | OFF | message]`

ON = show lines as they execute

OFF = do not show lines

message = message to display

ECHO without any parameters after it displays the current display state.

You use ECHO to can redirect output into new file called FILE.NAM by tacking on a > FILE.NAM

If you're using ECHO to display ANSI Escape sequence strings in batch files, make sure ECHO is on.

FOR
2.0

Lets you execute DOS commands repeatedly.

Format: `FOR %%variable IN (set) DO command`

%%variable = variable name

(set) = list of files; wildcards will work

command = DOS command using %%variable

If you use this command outside of a batch file (directly at the DOS prompt), use single % signs rather than the double %% signs required by the batch processor.

GOTO
2.0

Transfers control of execution to an area of the batch file starting with the label specified.

Format: GOTO [:]label

label — a text string similar to a filename but starting with a colon. You may include the colon here as well but it's not necessary.

See the "label" entry.

IF
2.0

Executes commands conditionally.

Format: IF [NOT] EXIST [d:][path]filename[.ext] command

or

IF [NOT] string1 == string2 command

or

IF [NOT] ERRORLEVEL n command

NOT = reverses logical condition

EXIST = TRUE if the specified file exists

string1 == string2 = TRUE if two strings are identical

ERRORLEVEL n = TRUE if previous program's exit code >= n

command = DOS command line, executed only if TRUE

You can limit ERRORLEVEL tests by combining two into one line with something like:

IF ERRORLEVEL 4 IF NOT ERRORLEVEL 5 GOTO FOUND4

This is one of the most powerful (and complex) batch commands, and one requiring the most explanation and help. For instance, while IF ERRORLEVEL allows user intervention in batch files, DOS doesn't provide any direct method for processing user entries. See the longer batch help section that follows for details.

Note that string comparisons require double == signs.

LABEL
2.0

Place marker for GOTO.

Format: `:string`

string = 8 characters significant

Label names generally follow the same kinds of rules as DOS filenames, except that a period (.) is not allowed. However, different DOS versions have their own peculiarities, so be sure to read the following help section for details.

PAUSE
2.0

Pauses execution and wait for a keypress.

Format: `PAUSE [remark]`

remark = message to display at pause

If you don't enter a new remark, DOS will print its familiar "Strike a key when ready . . . " message. Press any key at this point to proceed.

It's possible under some versions of DOS to get rid of this message by redirecting it to NUL and using ECHO to substitute a message of your own:

```
ECHO Now press a key
PAUSE > NUL
```

REM
2.0

Remark or comment.

Format: `REM [remark]`

remark = text up to 123 characters

Lines beginning with REM don't display when ECHO is OFF.

SHIFT
2.0

Allows over standard ten %-parameters %0 through %9.

Format: `SHIFT`

This also lets you move the value of a replaceable parameter down one step at a time (e.g., from %4 to %3 to %2). When you do this you'll lose the value of the lowest replaceable parameter, %0. If you need to retain a lower value you can use the SET command to store it in the DOS environment before executing SHIFT.

EDLIN, DEBUG, and ANSI Commands

EDLIN

To do the following in EDLIN:	*Use the following commands:*
Load and begin EDLIN	EDLIN filename [/B]
Start entering text	I
Stop entering text	Ctrl-Break or Ctrl-C
Edit an existing line	[line] (See note)
Delete existing line(s)	[line][,line]D
Move line(s) to another location	[line],[line],lineM
Copy line(s) to another location	[line],[line],line[,count]C
Display part of your text	[line][,line]L *or* [line][,line]P
Search for a specified string	[line][,line][?]S[string]
Replace one string with another	[line][,line][?]R[oldstring][<F6>newstring]
Merge disk file into current one	[line]T[d:]filename

Write part to disk and load more	[n]W *then* [n]A
Quit and save any changes	E
Quit without saving any changes	Q *then* Y

Note: Substitute the appropriate line number in place of [line] above. And note that [line][,line] and [line],[line] really mean "enter the beginning and ending line numbers of the range of lines you want to work on."

DEBUG

To do the following in DEBUG:	*Use the following commands:*
Load and begin DEBUG	DEBUG *or* DEBUG FILENAME
Name file for loading/writing	N [d:][path]filename[.ext]
Load disk information into memory	L [address [drive sector sector]]
Display memory contents	D [address][address] *or* D address length
Display register/flag contents	R [registername]
Enter new memory contents	E address [list]
Fill block of memory	F range list
Move block of memory	M range address
Compare two blocks of memory	C range address
Perform hexadecimal arithmetic	H value value
Search for characters	S range list
Assemble ASM instructions	A [address]
Unassemble instructions	U [address] *or* U [range]
Input/display 1 byte from port	I portaddress
Output 1 byte to port	O portaddress byte
Execute program in memory (Go)	G [=address][address[address...]]
Execute one main instruction	P [=address][value]

Execute and show registers/flags	T[=address][value]
Write data to disk	W [address [drive sector sector]]
Quit (without saving)	Q

New DEBUG Commands for DOS 4.0 are:

Allocate expanded memory	XA number of 16K EMS pages
Deallocate expanded memeory	XD handle-number
Map logical to physical EMS page	XM logicalpage physicalpage handle
Display expanded memory status	XS

ANSI.SYS

Note: In all examples, ESC represents decimal ASCII character 27 and not the letters E-S-C.

Cursor Movers

Move the cursor to a specific position:

ESC[#1;#2H *or* ESC[#1;#2f

#1 = row
#2 = column

Default is 1. Omitting all parameters moves the cursor to row 1, column 1 (upper lefthand corner of the screen). All numbers are in decimal format, and the upper lefthand corner is row 1, column 1.

Example: ESC[5;8H moves the cursor to row 5, column 8.

Move the cursor up:

ESC[#A

= number of lines to move

Default is 1. Maintains the current column position. If the cursor is already on the top line, nothing changes.

Example: ESC[3A moves the cursor up three rows.

Move the cursor down:	ESC[#B
	# = number of lines to move
	Default is 1. Maintains the current column position. If the cursor is already on the bottom line, nothing changes.
	Example: ESC[6B moves the cursor down six rows.
Move the cursor right:	ESC[#C
	# = number of columns to move
	Default is 1. Maintains the current row position. If the cursor is already at the right edge of the screen, nothing changes.
	Example: ESC[40C moves the cursor 40 columns to the right.
Move the cursor left:	ESC[#D
	# = number of columns to move
	Default is 1. Maintains the current row position. If the cursor is already at the left edge of the screen, nothing changes.
	Example: ESC[25D moves the cursor 25 columns to the left.
Device Status Report (Report Current Cursor Position)	ESC[6n
	Issuing this command (you can't do it via PROMPT) triggers a Cursor Position Report in the form:
	ESC[#1,#2R
	where #1 is the current row and #2 is the current column.
	Example: ESC[6n (if the cursor is at row 3, column 7) will generate a ESC[3,7R string.

Save current cursor position:	ESC[s

Stores most recent cursor position so you can later restore it with the ESC[u sequence.

Example: ESC[s (if cursor is at row 6, column 7) will save these coordinates to be restored later.

Restore saved cursor position:	ESC[u

Restores the current row and column previously stored by the ESC[s sequence.

Example: ESC[u (if ESC[s had previously stored the cursor position as row 6, column 7) will reposition the cursor at those coordinates.

Erasing and Screen Clearing

Clear the screen:	ESC[2J *or* ESC[J

This erases everything and positions the cursor in the upper lefthand corner of the screen — row 1, column 1.

Actually, you don't need the 2 before the J. Just about any number there will work. So will just a J by itself:

ESC[J

Example: ESC[2J clears the screen to the existing colors.

Erase to end of line:	ESC[K

Erases from the current cursor position to the end of the line — including the current column.

Examples: ESC[K (if you're using an 80-column screen and the cursor is on column 8) will erase from column 8 through to column 80 on that row.

ESC[5;8fESC[K will first move the cursor to column 8 of row 5, and will then erase everything from column 8 through column 80 on that line.

Color and Attribute Setting

Set one or more screen attributes: ESC[#;...;#m

#s are the attributes

Also called Set Graphics Rendition (SGR), the attributes that it establishes remain in place until reset by a subsequent SGR command.

Miscellaneous Attributes:

0   All attributes off (resets everything)
1   High intensity (bright/bold) on
4   Underline on (mono screens only; blue otherwise)
5   Blink on
7   Reverse video on (black on white)
8   "Cancelled" (invisible)

Color Attributes:

Color:	(IBM value)	As background:	As foreground:
Black	(0)	40	30
Red	(4)	41	31
Green	(2)	42	32
Yellow	(6)	43	33
Blue	(1)	44	34
Magenta	(5)	45	35
Cyan	(3)	46	36
White	(7)	47	37

Examples:

ESC[0m resets all attributes to normal (white on black).

ESC[m also resets all attributes to white on black.

ESC[8m blanks the screen (black on black).

ESC[5m blinks the current text color.

ESC[1m makes the current text color bold.

ESC[5;1m blinks current text color and makes it bold.

ESC[44m sets background to blue.

ESC[44;37m sets colors to white text on blue background.

ESC[44;37;1m sets colors to bright white text on blue background.

ESC[44;37;1;5m sets colors to blinking bright white text on blue background.

Mode Controls

Set screen widths/modes:	ESC[=#h *or* ESC[=#l

When used with values from 0 to 6 ESC[=#h (SET MODE) and ESC[=#l (RESET MODE) work identically to change screen modes on appropriate displays. (Note that the l is a lowercase L rather than a 1.)

Mode settings (values for #)   (DOS MODE)

0	40x25 black and white	(BW40)
1	40x25 color	(CO40)
2	80x25 black and white	(BW80)(MONO)
3	80x25 color	(CO80)
4	320x200 color graphics	
5	320x200 black and white graphics	
6	640x200 black and white graphics	
13	320x200 16-color	
14	640x200 16-color	
15	640x350 mono	
16	640x350 16-color	
17	640x480 2-color	
18	640x480 16-color	
19	320x200 256-color	

Examples: ESC[=3h and ESC[=3l will each set the screen mode on a color system to 80x25 color.

Set line wrap on:	ESC[?7h *or* ESC[=7h Anything typed past the rightmost column of the screen will wrap down one line to the leftmost column. Example: ESC[?7h will make text wrap normally around from right to left and down one line.
Set line wrap off:	ESC[?7l *or* ESC[=7l If you reach the right edge of the screen DOS will lock the cursor there and overlap any additional text you type meaninglessly on the one rightmost column. However, it won't discard any keystrokes, even though it has trouble displaying them. (Note that the l character is a lowercase L and not a 1.) Example: ESC[?7l will make text disappear once it reaches the rightmost column of the screen.

Keyboard Controls

Redefine one key as another:	ESC[#1;#2p *or* ESC[0;#1;#2p *or* ESC[#1;0;#2p *or* ESC[0;#1;0;#2p #1 is the ASCII code of the key to be redefined #2 is the ASCII value of the new definition If using an extended key, its ASCII value is two characters long; the first character is 0 ANSI can juggle the definitions of any non-Shift keys. (It can't change keys without ASCII values such as Shift or Ctrl or Alt.) To redefine one alphanumeric key (like A or a or 1), first specify the decimal ASCII value of the key you want to

redefine and follow it with its new ASCII value. If you're using an "extended" key (like F7, Alt-U, or Ins) either as the key you want redefined or as the new definition, specify this extended key by preceding it with a 0.

To reset a key to its original value, redefine it as itself (put its ASCII value on both sides of the semicolon).

Examples:

ESC[65;90p turns an uppercase A (65) into an uppercase Z (90) while leaving the lowercase a, and both the upper- and lowercase Z alone. (You

would be able to type an uppercase Z by holding down the shift key and typing either A or Z.)

ESC[65;90p and ESC[90;65p will switch uppercase Z and A but leave the lowercase versions of each alone.

ESC["A";"Z"p and ESC["Z";"A"p will also switch uppercase A and Z and leave everything else alone.

ESC[65;65p will reset the uppercase A key so it again prints and uppercase A.

ESC[65;65p and ESC[90;90p will put the uppercase A and the uppercase Z back they way they were originally.

ESC[34;39p and ESC[39;34p will swap the " and ' keys.

ESC["";"'"p and ESC["'";""p will also swap the " and ' keys.

ESC[0;46;155p will turn Alt-C (an "extended" key with an ASCII value two characters long —

0 46) into a cent sign (which has an ASCII value of 155).

ESC[0;59;0;60p and ESC[0;60;0;59p will switch function keys F1 (0 59) and F2 (0 60).

ESC[0;59;0;59p and ESC[0;60;0;60p will restore function keys F1 and F2 to their original settings.

Assign multiple characters to keys:

ESC[#1;"text"p
ESC[0;#1;"text"p
ESC[#1;#2;...;#127p
ESC[#1;#2;"text";#100p

#1 is the ASCII code of the key to be redefined.

"text" is the text you want to assign to this key.

If using an extended key, its ASCII value is two characters long; the first character is 0.

#2 through #100 or #127 are the ASCII values of the new definitions.

"text" is ASCII text between quotes.

ANSI lets you turn any alphanumeric (nonshift) key on the keyboard into a "macro" key that can enter commands, print messages, etc. You may enter up to 127 characters as the new definition for each key, by specifying the ASCII value(s) of the key(s) in the new definition, or by specifying text (between quotation marks) for the new definition, or by combining both decimal ASCII values and text into the new definition.

To reset a key to its original value, redefine it as itself (put its ASCII value on both sides of the semicolon).

Examples:

ESC[65;66;67;68;69;70p will assign the letters BCDEF to the capital A, so that typing an A will print out BCDEF. This will leave the lowercase "a" alone.

ESC[65;65;66;67;68;69;70p will assign the letters ABCDEF to capital A.

ESC[65;65p will restore the capital A back to normal.

ESC["A";"A"p will also restore the capital A to normal.

ESC[0;59;"DIR "p will put the letters DIR followed by a space on the command line whenever you press the F1 key. It won't actually execute the command, so you'll be able to add a drive letter and then press the Enter key.

ESC["~";"DIR C:";13p will assign the command DIR C: to the tilde (~). Adding a 13 at the end before the p will make DOS execute the command instead of just printing it out, because 13 is the ASCII value of the Enter key, and this will simulate pressing Enter. This will leave the lowercase character on the tilde key alone.

ESC[126;"DIR C:";13p will assign the same DIR C: and Enter command to the tilde.

ESC[0;25;"Name: ";13;"Rank: ";13;"Serial Number: ";13p will have AH-P trigger:

Name:
Rank:
Serial Number:

with a carriage return and a space after each. At the DOS prompt this will produce error messages since DOS will think you're trying to execute files called Name:, Rank:, and Serial. But you can use this when creating files with EDLIN or the DOS COPY command or certain text editors such as IBM PE.

ESC[0;15;"DIR | FIND ";34;"-88";34;13p will turn the little-used Shift-Tab key combination into a command that will list all the 1988 files in

the current subdirectory (assuming the DOS
FIND.EXE utility is handy). The two 34s are
needed because 34 is the ASCII value of the quotation marks needed for the FIND command.

---

*New ANSI.SYS Commands for
DOS 4.0 are:*

Disable Enhanced Keyboards: `ESC[0q`

This makes newer enhanced (101-key) keyboards behave like older 83- and 84-key keyboards by telling DOS 4 to ignore extended key
values and ANSI reassignments. This is the
same as loading ANSI with a /K parameter.

Enable Enhanced Keyboards: `ESC[1q`

This tells ANSI to take advantage of the additional keys on enhanced (101-key) keyboards.
You can do the same thing by specifying a /X parameter when loading ANSI under DOS 4.

Index